MARKETING

Creating Value for Customers

MARKETING

Creating Value for Customers

Gilbert A. Churchill, Jr.
Arthur C. Nielsen, Jr., Chair of Marketing Research / University of Wisconsin

J. Paul Peter
James R. McManus–Bascom Professor in Marketing / University of Wisconsin

AUSTEN
PRESS

IRWIN
Burr Ridge, Illinois   Boston, Massachusetts   Sydney, Australia

Publisher: William Schoof
Acquisitions Editor: Mary Fischer
Production Manager: Bob Lange

Development, design, and production provided by
Elm Street Publishing Services, Inc.
Text Design: Jeanne Calabrese Design

Compositor: Elm Street Publishing Services, Inc.
Typeface: 10/12 Optima
Printer: Von Hoffmann Press Inc.

Library of Congress Cataloging-in-Publication Data

   Churchill, Gilbert A.
     Marketing: creating value for customers / Gilbert A. Churchill,
  J. Paul Peter.
     p.   cm.
     Includes bibliographic references and index.
     ISBN 0-256-12539-2
     ISBN 0-256-17367-2 (Annotated Instructor's Edition)
     1. Marketing.   I. Peter, J. Paul.   II. Title.
  HF5415.C5275   1994
  658.8—dc20   94–8479

Printed in the United States of America
1 2 3 4 5 6 7 8 9 0 VH 9 8 7 6 5 4

Address editorial correspondence:
Austen Press
18141 Dixie Highway
Suite 105
Homewood, IL 60430

Address orders:
Richard D. Irwin, Inc.
1333 Burr Ridge Parkway
Burr Ridge, IL 60521

Austen Press
Richard D. Irwin, Inc.

About the cover: Like the wave on the cover, marketing is a dynamic
process with global impact. It demands an understanding of shifting
cycles and patterns, and the timing to respond instantly to new
trends. The images in the title give us a glimpse of the myriad of
marketing activities that embrace technology and teamwork while
recognizing our world's diversity.

Cover Sources: Wave image © Jeff Divine/FPG International. Images
in the title courtesy of Johnson & Johnson; Jeanne Calabrese Design;
Trek USA; Bell Helicopter Textron; Star Kist Seafood; Motorola
Cellular; reprinted by permission of Ernst & Young; and Citibank.

*To our wives, Helen and Rose, and our children
for creating so much value in our lives.*

Preface

Today's marketing students are a savvy bunch. They know brand names. They speak the latest buzzwords for technology and communications. They are keenly aware that, whatever career they choose, they will be affected by international events. They will be part of a more diverse working environment, which also focuses on quality and customer value. The companies they work for—large or small—will be attuned to issues of social and environmental responsibility, perhaps engaging in such practices as funding shelters for homeless families or using only organically grown food ingredients in their products. These new marketers will be held to strict ethical standards. And most likely, they'll be working as part of a team.

A Marketing Text for Future Marketers

To prepare for this fast-paced, complex new world of marketing, students need to see the ways in which such developments influence marketers. Concerns such as total quality management (TQM), teamwork, and a focus on delivering value cannot be portrayed as special interests, but as impacting the whole marketing effort. *Marketing: Creating Value for Customers* meets this need by incorporating the most current thinking into the basic principles of marketing. Thus, throughout the book, students will find many examples of real companies—from a large pharmaceutical manufacturer to a small chimney-sweep service—that are engaged in doing business in today's world.

QUALITY AND CUSTOMER VALUE

The quality approach to marketing is so essential to today's marketers that it is introduced in Chapter 1, "Marketing: Creating Value for Customers." Subsequent chapters describe how that approach applies to planning and carrying out the marketing effort. The opening vignette for each chapter shows how an actual company—such as MasterCard, Harley-Davidson, and UPS—puts into practice the quality approach and focuses on creating value for its customers.

DIVERSITY

The changing demographics of the U.S. work force means that organizations are serving increasingly diverse markets and that marketers themselves are becoming a more diverse lot. Chapter 3, "Meeting Social and Ethical Standards in Marketing," discusses the impact of diversity directly. The "Marketing Movers & Shakers" boxes and the in-text examples bring this issue to life by introducing students to a variety of marketers and markets—from Ruth Owades of mail-order florist Calyx & Corolla (page 236) to Sari Abul-Jubein of Casablanca Restaurant (page 375).

GLOBALIZATION

Since American marketing does not take place in a bubble, isolated from global influences, *Marketing: Creating Value for Customers* both highlights and integrates international issues. Chapter 4, "Marketing in a Global Environment," provides an overview of the global marketplace, as well as a broad look at possible global marketing strategies. The other chapters in the book include sections on international implications, as well as real-world examples of global marketing (U.S. businesses that market abroad as well as foreign-based businesses). Thus, Chapter 7 describes how cultural differences affect marketing research, Chapter 16 introduces the gray market, and Chapter 18 discusses issues that arise in managing an international communications mix. For easy reference, the international examples are identified by a globe symbol in the text margin.

Many of the text's opening vignettes, boxes, and cases also focus on international applications. For instance, the opening vignette for Chapter 4, "Marketing in a Global Environment," tells the story of Young & Rubicam/Sovero, the first American-Soviet advertising agency (page 91); the part-opening vignette for Part 5, "Pricing," chronicles the adventures of Toys "R" Us as it opens stores from Japan to Spain (page 407). Also, the review and discussion questions at the end of each chapter include opportunities for students to apply marketing principles on a global level.

TEAMWORK AND EMPLOYEE EMPOWERMENT

The ability to work as part of a team continues to gain importance for members of most organizations. Chapter 1, "Marketing: Creating Value for Customers," introduces the role of teamwork, and Chapter 6, "Implementing and Controlling the Marketing Effort," discusses the use of teams in the organization's structure. Other chapters describe how specific areas of marketing are affected by the use of cross-functional or other types of teams. Real-world examples in the text, boxes, and cases show how teamwork can improve the marketing effort. Some chapter projects also give students opportunities to work in teams.

SMALL BUSINESSES

Much of the growth in the U.S. economy continues to come from small businesses. Traditional marketing textbooks rely heavily on Fortune 500 companies for their examples. In contrast, although *Marketing: Creating Value for Customers* does offer some examples of these companies, the book also draws many of its text and box examples from small enterprises. A couple of these include novelty clothing manufacturer Joe Boxer (page 546) and a one-man boat design and building operation called Caribou Kayaks (page 592). Thus, students can see many instances where marketing succeeds as a result of creativity and the marketer's passion, rather than because of a corporation's enormous financial resources.

ETHICS

Organizations' stakeholders are demanding ever higher standards of ethics. Chapter 3, "Meeting Social and Ethical Standards in Marketing," focuses on this issue. Later chapters integrate the principles of ethics and social responsibility into their text discussion. For example, see Chapter 7 for a discussion on ethical considerations to address when doing marketing research (pages 221–223).

CURRENT DEVELOPMENTS IN MARKETING

The integration of all these topics shows students what successful marketers are thinking about and doing today. Other specific topics in *Marketing: Creating Value for Customers* ensure that the book's focus is up-to-the-minute:

- Relationship marketing (Chapters 13 and 20)
- Direct marketing (Chapters 16, 17, 19, and 20), including home television shopping
- Strategic alliances (Chapter 6 and "Looking Ahead") and strategic channel alliances (Chapter 16)
- Network organizations (Chapter 6)
- Virtual corporations ("Looking Ahead")
- Green marketing (Chapter 3)
- Marketing decision support systems (Chapter 7)
- The agreements concluded under the Uruguay round of the GATT talks and the North American Free Trade Agreement (Chapter 4)
- Nonbusiness marketing (Chapters 1 and 13)
- Marketing of services (Chapter 13 and examples throughout the book)

Organization of the Book

Marketing: Creating Value for Customers begins by building a firm foundation, describing the overall challenges faced by today's marketers. It then moves to the specific ways in which marketers meet these challenges in their marketing strategies.

Part 1, "An Overview of Marketing," introduces students to marketing. Chapter 1 defines marketing and its scope, including marketing in nonprofit organizations. Chapter 2 describes the formal dimensions of the marketing environment. Chapter 3 introduces the basic social and ethical issues that affect marketers, including social responsibility and diversity. Chapter 4 discusses global markets so that students can later learn about the elements of the marketing mix in a global context.

Part 2, "Developing and Implementing Marketing Plans," shows how the marketing basics are put into action. Chapter 5 describes how marketers plan their efforts. Following the chapter is a marketing plan for a small business, Little Learners Parent-Teacher Store (page 152). This marketing plan is also available on disk. Chapter 6 describes the process of implementing and controlling a marketing effort. This chapter takes a closer look at the interrelatedness of marketers' activities, discussing such issues as teamwork, communication, and coordination within and across functional lines.

Part 3, "Customers and Markets," introduces students to the broad categories of potential customers and the ways marketers identify and learn about them. Chapter 7 describes the basics of marketing research as practiced by large and small organizations. Chapter 8 is an introduction to consumer behavior, and Chapter 9 to organizational buying behavior. Chapter 10 covers market segmentation, including the standard ways to segment consumer and organizational markets, the process of segmentation, and the decision to use target marketing.

Beginning a look at the elements of the marketing mix, Part 4, "Product Development and Management," covers issues related to product strategies. Chapter 11 discusses new products (goods and services), including product development in cross-functional teams. Chapter 12 focuses on strategies related to existing products, including such dimensions of the product as quality, features, design, and packaging. This chapter also introduces the product life cycle. Because services are so important to the modern economy, Chapter 13 is devoted to discussing the issues peculiar to marketing them.

Part 5, "Pricing," consists of two chapters introducing the basics of pricing strategy. Chapter 14 teaches the fundamental principles underlying pricing decisions. Chapter 15 focuses on the ways marketers set and adjust prices in the context of their marketing environments.

Part 6, "Channels of Distribution," provides an overview of marketing strategies related to distribution channels. Chapter 16 identifies the basic kinds of distribution channels and the marketer's role in those channels as producer or intermediary. Chapter 17 discusses wholesaling, retailing, and physical distribution, focusing on strategy more than taxonomy.

Part 7, "Marketing Communications," examines the last element of the marketing mix, marketing communications. Chapter 18 introduces the elements of the communications mix and discusses how marketers plan a mix. Chapter 19 takes a more in-depth look at advertising, sales promotion, and publicity. Chapter 20 covers personal selling and sales management, including the use of teams and applications of technology.

Following these chapters are materials that help the student take a longer-range view. "Looking Ahead: Maintaining Competitive Advantage" shares with students the vision of today's business experts about where marketing is headed. "Career Opportunities in Marketing" outlines major categories of marketing jobs and some strategies for landing a job in marketing.

PEDAGOGY

Marketing: Creating Value for Customers offers complete pedagogy that makes the world of marketing come alive for students and gives them a glimpse of how marketing is practiced in a variety of organizations.

LEARNING OBJECTIVES   Each chapter opener includes a list of learning objectives linked to major chapter topics. So that achievement of the objectives can be assessed, the objectives use concrete verbs that refer to observable behaviors.

OPENING VIGNETTES   Each part and chapter opens with the story of a real organization that shows how the organization puts marketing principles into action. Each story is related to the part or chapter topic that follows. The organizations illustrated represent a wide range—in size, location, and type of product or service offered. Some of the organizations included are the NBA (page 533), Trek Bicycle Corporation (page 117), Ben & Jerry's (page 465), the *Tallahassee Democrat* (page 565), and Xerox (page 597).

BOXES   Each chapter contains three boxes that help the student apply chapter principles to the real world:

- "Marketing Movers & Shakers" tells the story of an actual marketer. These boxes cover a diverse group of people working in both large and small organizations, such as Anita Roddick of the Body Shop (page 111) and Gianni Agnelli of Fiat (page 35).
- "You Decide" discusses a current marketing issue and invites students to exercise their critical thinking skills by answering questions about the issue. Most of these issues have ethical implications, such as whether slotting allowances should be allowed (page 491), or whether infomercials belong on the air (page 570).
- "Put It into Practice" provides applications for the students to try out marketing principles discussed in the chapter, such as writing a mission statement (page 125) or observing consumer behavior (page 230).

FIGURES AND TABLES   Throughout each chapter, figures and tables serve several functions. They clarify complex principles, expand on subject matter that could become tedious in a text discussion (such as listing the types of retailers), and show how actual marketers have applied marketing principles. Photos of marketers further highlight the diversity of people practicing in this field.

SUMMARY   Each chapter closes with a summary that recaps the major points covered in the chapter.

KEY TERMS AND GLOSSARIES   As a study aid, key terms are set in boldface type and listed at the end of each chapter with page references. A marginal glossary helps students review the meaning of the key terms. For later reference, the terms are also alphabetized in an end-of-book glossary.

REVIEW AND DISCUSSION QUESTIONS   Following each chapter is a series of review and discussion questions. Many of the questions are suitable for class discussion. Each chapter includes a question related to global marketing.

CHAPTER PROJECT   Each chapter includes a project in which the students apply principles covered in the chapter. Most often, the project involves performing or planning how to perform marketing activities for an imaginary organization. The project for Chapter 9, "Organizational Buying Behavior," is a role-play exercise in team buying and selling. For Chapter 12, "Existing Products," students create a brand name and brand mark. In Chapter 17, "Wholesaling, Retailing, and Physical Distribution," the project involves designing a layout of atmospherics for an imaginary store. As with the project for Chapter 9, many of the projects are suitable for group work; all can be performed individually.

CASE   Each chapter includes a case. Following the description of a real company and its marketing environment are three questions. Students apply the chapter principles to analyze the situation and to extend or modify the marketing strategy. These questions are suitable for class or small-group discussion or can be used as a written assignment. The companies represented are varied—large and small, U.S. and foreign-based, service providers and manufacturers. A sample includes Colgate-Palmolive (page 114), Swatch (page 315), Chemical Bank (page 226), and Hugg-a-Planet (page 379).

MATH APPENDIX   An end-of-book appendix, "Mathematics Used in Marketing," shows the students some ways in which marketers use numbers in planning and controlling. For instructors who wish to teach this topic and for students seeking independent practice, the appendix includes review questions and a project.

ANCILLARIES

A number of ancillaries are available to enhance the use of *Marketing: Creating Value for Customers.*

ANNOTATED INSTRUCTOR'S EDITION   The *Annotated Instructor's Edition* of *Marketing: Creating Value for Customers* features teaching suggestions and summaries prepared by Deb Jansky of Milwaukee Area Technical College. This special annotated version includes all the material in the basic text plus additional examples, questions for generating discussion, and teaching tips.

TEST BANK   Written by Nancy Torrence of Liberty University, Linda Anglin of Mankato State University, and Martin Meyers of University of Wisconsin—Stevens Point, the *Test Bank* includes 150 questions for each chapter in *Marketing: Creating Value for Customers,* as well as answers for each question. The questions are multiple-choice (including mini-case application problems), true-false, fill-in-the-blank, and short essay. They are classified by level of difficulty, by learning objective, and by type (recall, comprehension, calculation, application). For each chapter, there is also a 10-question quiz. The answers include a reference to the relevant text page, as well as the rationale for the answer.

STUDY GUIDE   Juanita Roxas at California State Polytechnic University prepared the *Study Guide,* which is available for students who wish support in studying *Marketing: Creating Value for Customers.* For each chapter, the *Study Guide* begins with a chapter outline and a section briefly summarizing the chapter content. A list of key terms and concepts includes definitions and references to the relevant text pages. Application exercises for each chapter allow the student to apply and test knowledge of the chapter's more challenging areas. A variety of test questions with answers enables the student to check his or her own progress.

INSTRUCTOR'S MANUAL   Authored by Kevin Elliott of Mankato State University, the *Instructor's Manual* provides a brief overview of key topics for each chapter, including the opening vignette. A list of key terms for each chapter includes references to the relevant text pages. An expanded version of the learning objectives and a chapter outline help the instructor organize lectures. Supplemental handouts expand the available learning activities in and out of the classroom. Notes about the boxes ("Marketing Movers & Shakers," "You Decide," and "Put It into Practice") help the instructor apply these in lectures.

The *Instructor's Manual* also provides the information instructors need for grading assignments and leading class discussions. Answers are included for Review and Discussion Questions, as well as suggested answers for the "You Decide" box and the chapter case. Synopses are also provided for the case and chapter projects.

Transparency masters for all figures and tables appear at the end of the *Instructor's Manual.* This section also contains teaching notes to help instructors describe key points of these exhibits.

TRANSPARENCIES   Charles Strang of Western New Mexico University has prepared 10 to 12 transparency acetates for each chapter. (These are different from the figures and tables in text.) Teaching notes that describe each transparency and highlight key points accompany the transparencies. With the guidelines provided in the *Instructor's Manual,* instructors can use the transparencies as desired to customize their lectures.

VIDEOS   To show the principles of the book in action, S.J. Garner of Eastern Kentucky University coordinated videos for each chapter. In addition, an integrative video shows how an organization pulls together many marketing principles. Both are available for fall classes in 1995.

VIDEO DISK   Also available for fall classes in 1995, the *Video Disk* features segments of the videos, transparencies, charts, tables, and graphs from the book.

Acknowledgments

Teamwork is a reality in the modern business world. So too are virtual corporations that attempt to leverage the special capabilities of each person or organization when attempting to produce a desired result. Both of these ideas played a role in the development of this book. While we were involved in each stage of the book's preparation, we also used the special expertise of others, and we wish to thank them for their contributions in making this book a reality.

We would especially like to thank Karen Schenkenfelder and Linda Buchanan Allen for their help in making this book come alive with examples, pedagogy, and an engaging writing style. From start to finish, Karen's participation in the project was invaluable, while Linda contributed immeasurably to the development of the pedagogy. We also thank Ann Noe of Noe and Associates for her help with the focus group and survey research that laid the foundations on which the book is based. Jan Huskisson and Karen Schenkenfelder did an especially good job in selecting photo art for the text. The Elm Street Publishing group—especially Phyllis Crittenden, Kelly Spiller, Ted Murach, Melissa Morgan, and Abby Westapher—were on top of things in taking the project from raw manuscript to bound book. We also thank Bill Schoof and Mary Fischer of Austen Press for their support and for working so closely with us throughout the project.

We extend our gratitude to the team of supplement and ancillary authors beginning with Deb Jansky for preparing the annotations for the special annotated instructor's edition of *Marketing: Creating Value for Customers;* to Kevin Elliott for the *Instructor's Manual;* to Charles Strang for the *Transparency Acetates and accompanying Teaching Notes;* to S.J. Garner for coordinating videos for each chapter; and finally to the team of Nancy Torrence, Linda Anglin, and Martin Meyers for their work on the *Test Bank.*

A number of marketing academics played key roles in the book's development, and we would be remiss not to acknowledge their contributions. First, we wish to thank the following people who participated in focus group sessions designed to determine the level of satisfaction with current textbook offerings and to offer suggestions for what was needed in the next generation of principles of marketing texts:

Phillip Balsmeier
Nicholls State University

Jerry Field
Northeastern Illinois University

Charles Ford
Arkansas State University

Kenneth Heischmidt
Southeast Missouri State University

Lewis Hershey
Northeast Missouri State University

J. Steven Kelly
DePaul University

Dean Lewis
Sam Houston State University

Brad O'Hara
Southeast Louisiana State University

Larry O'Neal
Stephen F. Austin State University

Ben Rudolf
Grand Valley State University

Next, we would like to thank the group of professors who responded to our questionnaire concerning specific book features. We can assure the individuals listed here that their responses strongly influenced the final structure and content of our book.

Roger Abshire
Sam Houston State University

Frank Acito
Indiana University

Tom Ainscough
University of Georgia

Pamela Alreck
Salisbury State College

Rick Ambrose
College of San Mateo

Herbert Amster
Elizabeth Seton School—Iona College

Fred Anderson
Indiana University of Pennsylvania

Shelda Aultman
Caldwell Community College

Gilbert Barcus
North Brunswick, New Jersey

Lysbeth Barnett
Ashland Community College

John Bass
Commonwealth College

Richard Becherer
Wayne State University

Karen Berger
Ossining, New York

Jennifer Berry
Parks Junior College

Angela Bloomfield
Montgomery, Alabama

Joe Boelter
BASF Corporation

Robert Boewadt
Georgia College at Milledgeville

John Boos
Ohio Wesleyan University

George Boulware
David Lipscomb College

Duane Brickner
South Mountain Community College

Burton Brodo
Wharton School

Kent Brooks
Wayland Baptist University

Robert Buckley
North Adams State College

Tom Burns
Long Lake, Minnesota

Jim Butts
American University

Charles Caravello
Tidewater Community College

Bill Carens
Geneseo, New York

Gerri Chaplin
Joliet Junior College

Don Chatman
University of Wisconsin—Stout

Reid Christopherson
Saint Ambrose University

Maurice Clabaugh
University of Montevallo

Kevin Coulson
University of Nebraska

Robert Cox
Salt Lake City Community College

Roger Crowe
Pellissippi State Technical College

James Crowell
University of Colorado—Denver

Richard Cummings
College of Lake County

Nancy D'Albergana
University of Northern Colorado

Pierre David
Baldwin Wallace College

Brian Davis
Weber State University

T. Dieck
Thomas Nelson Community College

Michael Drafke
College of DuPage

Ronald Drozdenko
West Connecticut State University

Gary Ernst
Naperville, Illinois

William Ewald
Concordia University

Roland Eyears
Central Ohio Technical College

Barry Farber
University of Maine—Augusta

John Felt
Northern Virginia Community College—Manassas

Edward Felton
Samford University

Ira Fersch
Long Island University C.W. Post College

Ann Fox
Erie Community College

Karen Fritz
Pellissippi State Technical College

S.J. Garner
Eastern Kentucky University

Herbert Gedicks
Liberty University

Mary Gerlow
Ohio State University

John Geubtner
Tacoma Community College

Michael Geurts
Brigham Young University

William Gittler
Fort Washington, Pennsylvania

John Godfrey
Springfield Technical Community College

Larry Goldstein
Iona College

David Good
Central Missouri State University

Kent Granzin
University of Utah

Barbara Gulley
Royal Oak, Michigan

B. Hamm
Oklahoma City University

Ed Hand
Lamar University

Randall Hansen
Stetson University

Judy Hanson
Las Positas College

Mary Harms
Iowa State University

John Havenek
JJH International

Douglas Hawes
University of Wyoming

Lewis Hershey
Northeast Missouri State University

Robert Hilton
University of the Ozarks

Alfred Holden
Fordham University

Sandra Hortman
Columbus College

Ronald Hoverstad
University of the Pacific

Jane Hudson
Muscatine Community College

Robert Ironside
North Lake College

Irving Jacobs
College at Fredonia

Deb Jansky
Milwaukee Area Technical College

Gregory Johnson
City University

James Johnson
Saint Cloud State University

Ann Jones
Lamar University

Jackie Kacen
University of Illinois

Ira Kalb
University of Southern California

Sue Keaveney
University of Colorado—Denver

George Kelley
Erie Community College

Philip Kelman
Fashion Institute of Technology

Algin King
Towson State University

Wayne Kirklin
Heidelberg College

Pat Kishel
Cypress College

Arno Kleimenhagen
University of Wisconsin—Whitewater

Arthur Knaus
Hartwick College

Quentin Korte
Our Lady of the Lake University

Julie Kothapa
Kennesaw, Georgia

Karl Kotteman
University of Missouri—St. Louis

Peter Kraus
Clark College

Rosemary Lagace
University of South Florida

Fred Langrehr
Valparaiso University

Geoffrey Lantos
Stonehill College

Candace Larson
Rolfe, Iowa

John Lavin
Waukesha County Technical College

William Leahy
St. Joseph's University

Stephen LeMay
Mississippi State University

G. Lincoln
Westchester Community College

Donald Lindgren
San Diego State University

Michael Littman
College of Buffalo

Annie Liu
Transylvania University

Doug Livermore
Morningside College

Alicia Lupinacci
Arlington, Texas

Rick Lytle
Abilene Christian University

Richard Marsh
Greenville Technical College

Pat Marzofka
Loras College

John McDowell
Davenport College Corporate Headquarters

C. McElroy
Bucks County Community College

Joanne McManamy
Middlesex Community College

Ed McQuarrie
Santa Clara University

Michael Metzger
Tiffin University

William Meyer
Trinity College

Rebecca Mihelcic
Howard Community College

Edward Miller
Englishtown, New Jersey

James Miller
Lynn University

Lee Miller
Indiana Business College

Robert Moore
University of Colorado—Denver

Wayne Moorhead
Brown Mackie College

Robert Morgan
Southeast Community College

Tom Moritz
Hardin Simmons University

Reza Motameni
California State University—Fresno

John Mow
Bethel College

Robbie Mullins
Oklahoma Baptist University

Gurramkonda Naidu
University of Wisconsin—Whitewater

Sethuramon Narayandas
Purdue University

Don Norman
Pleasanton, California

Brad O'Hara
Southwestern Louisiana University

Eva O'Keefe
Massachusetts College of Pharmacy and Allied Health Sciences

Al Page
University of Illinois—Chicago

Phillip Peters
Keene State College

Doug Peterson
Southeast Community College—Lincoln

Tim Phillips
College at Cortland

Charles Pinzon
University of Kansas

Eric Pratt
New Mexico State University

Shane Premeaux
McNeese State University

Allan Reddy
Valdosta State College

Delores Reha
Fullerton College

Lynne Richardson
University of Alabama

Donald Rogers
Rollins College

Marilyn Romine
Northeast Missouri State University

Leon Rosenfeld
Little Silver, New Jersey

Daniel Rountree
Midwestern State University

Carol Rowey
Community College of Rhode Island

Juanita Roxas
California State Polytechnic University

William Sannwald
San Diego State University

Regina Schlee
Seattle Pacific University

Darrell Scott
Idaho State University

Harold Sekiguchi
University of Nevada

Henry Shaw
Saint Thomas Aquinas College

Leonard Sheffield
Tri-State University

Sara Shryock
Black Hills State College

Don Simmons
Biola University

Leo Sloan
Daniel Webster College

Madeline Slutsky
Ray College of Design

Lois Smith
University of Wisconsin— Whitewater

Richard Spiller
California State University— Long Beach

David Starr
Shoreline Community College

Sherri Stevens
University of Utah

Jeffrey Stoltman
Wayne State University

Charles Strang
Western New Mexico University

Harry Strickland
La Roche College

Gail Strickler
Michigan Christian College

Lynn Suksdorf
Salt Lake City Community College

R. Sukumar
University of Houston

Rawlie Sullivan
University of Saint Thomas

Albert Taylor
Austin Peay State University

Paul Thistlethwaite
Western Illinois University

B. Thornton
Darton College

Anthony Tiberini
Delaware Technical and Community College

Frank Titlow
Saint Petersburg Junior College

Donna Treadwell
Johnson County Community College

Scott Vitell
University of Mississippi

Ronald Volpe
Capital University

Randall Voorn
Trinity Christian College

Gary Walk
Lima Technical College

Kelly Wason
Texas Tech University

Paul Wellen
Roosevelt University

Jerry Wheat
Indiana University Southeast

Charles White
Edison Community College

Roland Whitehall
Volunteer State Community College

Patti Wilbur
Northwestern Oklahoma State University

Esther Williams
Western Iowa Technical Community College

Terrence Williamson
University of South Dakota

Tim Wilson
Clarion State College

Stephen Winter
Orange County Community College

Linda Withrow
Saint Ambrose University

Gene Wunder
Columbus College

Clyde Wynn
Bellevue College

G. Bernard Yevin
Lindenwood College

Laurie Yale
Fort Lewis College

Mark Young
Winona State University

Donna Yancey
University of Northern Alabama

Murray Young
University of Denver

Jere Yates
Pepperdine University

Sherilyn Zeigler
University of Hawaii—Manoa

This book also benefited from the input of an outstanding teacher's panel. The panel was composed of academics who have been recognized by their institutions as being outstanding teachers. The people below were recruited for the panel because of their teaching credentials:

Roger Blackwell
Ohio State University

Richard Lutz
University of Florida

Barbara Brown
San Jose State University

Deborah Mitchell
Temple University

Lewis Hershey
Hershey Consulting

Janice Taylor
Miami University

Sue Keaveney
University of Colorado—Denver

One can see from their many insightful comments why they have been recognized as outstanding teachers.

Finally, we would like to thank the reviewers who made so many helpful suggestions on the several drafts of the manuscript. While we did not embrace every suggestion, we did change the manuscript to incorporate many of them and seriously discussed the others. The book is certainly better because of the reviewers' helpful comments. The reviewers include:

Larry Anderson
Long Island University

J. Steven Kelly
DePaul University

Linda Anglin
Mankato State University

A.B. King
Towson State University

Duane Brickner
South Mountain Community College

Deborah Mitchell
Temple University

Robert Cox
Salt Lake Community College

Iris Mohr-Jackson
Saint John's University

S.J. Garner
Eastern Kentucky University

Reza Motameni
California State University—Fresno

David Good
Central Missouri State University

Rebecca Mihelcic
Howard Community College

Deb Jansky
Milwaukee Area Technical College

Brad O'Hara
Southeast Louisiana State University

James Johnson
Saint Cloud State University

Lawrence O'Neal
Stephen F. Austin State University

Annamma Joy
Concordia University

Lynne Richardson
University of Alabama

Sue Keaveney
University of Colorado—Denver

Juanita Roxas
California State Polytechnic University

George Kelley
Erie Community College

William Sannwald
San Diego State University

Henry Shaw
Saint Thomas Aquinas College

Paul Thistlethwaite
Western Illinois University

Charles Strang
Western New Mexico University

Nancy Torrence
Liberty University

R. Sukumar
University of Houston

John Vann
Ball State University

Rawlie Sullivan
University of Saint Thomas

Mark Young
Winona State University

While the people mentioned above deserve credit for many of the book's strengths, any errors or omissions remain our responsibility. We would appreciate any comments or criticisms of our text so that it can be improved in the next edition.

Gilbert A. Churchill, Jr.
J. Paul Peter
Madison, Wisconsin
August 1994

About the Authors

Gilbert A. Churchill, Jr., DBA (Indiana University) is the Arthur C. Nielsen, Jr., Chair of Marketing Research at the University of Wisconsin—Madison. He joined the Wisconsin faculty in 1966 and has taught there since, except for one year that he spent as a visiting professor at Bedriftsokonomisk Institutt in Oslo, Norway. Professor Churchill was named Distinguished Marketing Educator by the American Marketing Association in 1986, only the second individual so honored. The award recognizes and honors a living marketing educator for distinguished service and outstanding contributions in the field of marketing education. Professor Churchill was awarded the Outstanding Marketing Educator of the Year for 1993 by the Academy of Marketing Science for his significant scholarly contributions. He is a past recipient of the Lawrence J. Larson Excellence in Teaching Award.

In addition, Professor Churchill is a past recipient of the William O'Dell Award for the outstanding article appearing in the *Journal of Marketing Research* during the year. He has also been a finalist for the award four other times. He was named Marketer of the Year by the South Central Wisconsin Chapter of the American Marketing Association in 1981. He is a member of the American Marketing Association and has served as vice-president of publications and on its board of directors as well as on the association's Advisory Committee to the Bureau of the Census. In addition, he has served as consultant to a number of companies, including Oscar Mayer, Western Publishing Company, and Parker Pen.

Professor Churchill's articles have appeared in such publications as the *Journal of Marketing Research,* the *Journal of Marketing,* the *Journal of Consumer Research,* the *Journal of Retailing,* the *Journal of Business Research, Decision Sciences, Technometrics,* and *Organizational Behavior and Human Performance,* among others. He is the author of two books, *Marketing Research: Methodological Foundations,* Sixth Edition (Fort Worth, TX.: Dryden, 1995); and *Basic Marketing Research,* Second Edition (Fort Worth, TX.: Dryden, 1992) and the co-author of *Sales Force Management: Planning, Implementation, and Control,* Fourth Edition (Homewood, Ill.: Irwin, 1993); and *Salesforce Performance* (Lexington, Mass.: Lexington Books, 1984). He is a former editor of the *Journal of Marketing Research* and has served on the editorial boards of *Journal of Marketing Research, Journal of Marketing, Journal of Business Research, Journal of Health Care Marketing,* and the *Asian Journal of Marketing.*

J. Paul Peter is James R. McManus-Bascom Professor in Marketing at the University of Wisconsin—Madison. He was on the faculty at Indiana State University, Washington University, and Ohio State University before joining the faculty at Wisconsin in 1981. He has taught a variety of undergraduate and graduate courses and in a number of executive programs, and has won several teaching awards. Professor Peter has contributed to the marketing literature in the areas of consumer behavior, marketing theory, and research methodology and is widely cited. His work on construct validity won the prestigious William O'Dell Award from the *Journal of Marketing Research.* He has authored or co-authored nine successful texts in marketing and strategic management. Professor Peter has served as Editor of AMA Professional Publications and as Editor of *JMR's* Measurement Section. He has served on the review boards of the *Journal of Marketing, Journal of Marketing Research,* and *Journal of Consumer Research.* He has been a consultant for several corporations as well as the Federal Trade Commission.

Brief Contents

Contents

*Marketing Movers &
Shakers*
**Anita Roddick of the Body
Shop** *111*

You Decide
**At What Price Can the
Rain Forest Be Saved?** *112*

*Part 2
Developing and Implementing
Marketing Plans* 116

Setting the Stage: **Trek Bicycle Corporation**   *117*

CHAPTER 5   Strategic Marketing Planning   *118*

Creating Customer Value: **King's Medical Company**   *119*

Put It into Practice
**Two Mission
Statements** *125*

You Decide
**Can a Museum Benefit
from Marketing?** *130*

*Marketing Movers &
Shakers*
**Pillsbury's Linda
Keene** *132*

Creating a Marketing Plan   151

Note to the Instructor

Austen Press texts are marketed and distributed by Richard D. Irwin, Inc. For assistance in obtaining supplementary material for this and other Austen Press titles, please contact your Irwin sales representative or the customer service division of Richard D. Irwin at (800) 323–4560.

1

An Overview of Marketing

Setting the Stage

Procter & Gamble

If Procter & Gamble isn't quite *everywhere,* it sure seems to be. Its Oil of Olay moisturizer is the best-selling facial moisturizer in Europe. Homemakers in India and Japan use its Ariel laundry detergent. Young women in the United States and United Kingdom wear its Cover Girl cosmetics. Walk down the aisles of almost any drugstore or supermarket, and you'll see P&G products like Pringles snacks, Pampers diapers, and Pert Plus shampoo. Turn on your TV or open a magazine, and you'll see ads for Crest toothpaste and Tide laundry detergent. No wonder P&G is considered a marketing powerhouse.

P&G didn't gain this reputation by chance. The company has long been noted for investing in new products and advertising them heavily. In fact, it pioneered the use of advertising during soap operas. (It is the only consumer-products company that produces them—"Another World," "As the World Turns," and "Guiding Light.") And P&G has no intention of slowing down. In a recent three-year period, the company introduced 30

percent more new products, and its ad spending remains as high as ever.

The company continues to be innovative. In Florida P&G worked with the Publix Super Markets chain to promote its products through a customized magazine called *Publix Family Magazine.* The magazine, mailed to Publix customers, contains recipes, articles, and coupons for P&G products. Using the store's database of purchases by frequent shoppers, P&G tailored the magazine to each household, inserting coupons for the kinds of products it buys.

P&G has further boosted its reputation by demonstrating a concern for the environment. The company has lessened the impact of its packaging by offering refill packs and eliminating unnecessary packaging. Thus, consumers in the United States and Canada can buy refills of Downy fabric softener, and those in Europe and Latin America can buy refills of Mr. Clean products. The company has begun using more recycled plastic in its plastic detergent bottles. And beginning with Bonus compact liquid detergent in Japan,

P&G has introduced concentrated forms of detergent, which offer more cleaning power in smaller packages.

P&G's concern for the environment is not only ethical, it appeals to consumers. Just two years after P&G introduced Ultra concentrated detergent in the United States, it accounted for over 90 percent of the company's sale of powdered detergent.

As you learn about marketing from this book, you'll read the stories of well-known marketers like Procter & Gamble, as well as many lesser known but successful marketers. You'll see how organizations change but stay focused on their customers in order to succeed.

Sources: Zachary Schiller, "Procter & Gamble Hits Back," Business Week, July 19, 1993, pp. 20–22; Jennifer Lawrence and Gary Levin, "P&G Tries Custom Mag," Advertising Age, October 26, 1992, p. 4; Gabriella Stern, "Hope for Tomorrow: P&G Aims to Salvage Soap Operas," The Wall Street Journal, April 25, 1994, pp. B1, B3; Procter & Gamble 1991 annual report; "P&G's Concentrated Liquid Detergents—A New Generation of Cleaning," Procter & Gamble brochure.

CHAPTER 1

Marketing
Creating Value for Customers

LEARNING OBJECTIVES

After completing this chapter, you should be able to:

1. Define marketing and the quality approach to marketing.

2. Describe the scope of marketing.

3. Define the key elements of marketing strategy.

4. Discuss marketing issues in nonprofit settings.

5. Explain the marketing concept.

6. Describe the role of marketing in developing and carrying out strategy.

Creating Customer Value
The Procter & Gamble Company

In recent years, Procter & Gamble's past successes have been difficult to maintain. Consumers in the United States and Europe have discovered that store-brand merchandise often delivers good quality for a lower price than they would pay for competing P&G brands. In the case of disposable diapers—P&G's biggest business—store brands have increased their share of the market from 21 percent to over 30 percent, with half the increase taken from P&G. Furthermore, frequent deep discounts have conditioned consumers to buy only when a product is on sale. As a result of such trends, P&G's overall sales growth in the United States has been slowing.

Procter & Gamble's response is to make sure its customers are getting good value. A key part of this strategy is what P&G calls "value pricing." Instead of offering stores periodic discounts and allowances for promoting the company's products, P&G now keeps its prices relatively stable and lower than full prices had been. Thus, in the first two years of this strategy, the price of Folgers coffee declined an average of 10 to 15 percent.

P&G's objective is to make consumers loyal to its brands based on high quality and continuous improvement of its products, rather than price deals. An example of an improved product is Cheer with Advanced Color Guard. The company introduced it by describing it as a breakthrough that would extend the life of cotton clothes.

Value pricing is a dramatic departure from the traditional approach, which emphasizes special deals to draw attention to the manufacturer's products: two-for-one specials, packages containing extra ounces for free, ads featuring products the store bought at a discount. This approach is costly to manufacturers, because production levels rise and fall as the special deals come and go. Also, they often have to use special packaging and labels for featured products.

Finally, special deals tend to get consumers thinking about price, rather than about why the product is superior.

At first value pricing upset some of P&G's major customers: the stores that benefited from the rise and fall of the company's prices. As a result, P&G has had to work hard to keep these customers happy. It has done so by replacing the tactic of special deals with a long-range commitment to the stores' well-being. This commitment takes the form of working with stores to reduce the total cost of making P&G products available to consumers, as well as matching stores' product offerings more closely to the needs of the consumers they serve. To do this, P&G has reorganized its sales personnel into teams devoted to serving particular customers (stores). Other teams serve customers in specific geographic areas, handling the stores' needs with regard to a group of products.

To keep a lid on prices, P&G has sought to make the organization lean. The company set up ten teams to study the entire organization and look for ways to operate more efficiently around the world. Besides reducing the work force, cost cutting has trimmed marketing expenses thought to be unproductive. Thus, P&G has slashed spending on certain marketing communications such as coupons. Explains a company spokesperson, "Coupons don't contribute to consumer value day-in and day-out, and those dollars are better used to drive lower shelf prices."

The company has also dropped or consolidated products and brands. P&G renamed White Cloud toilet tissue Charmin Ultra and combined Crisco and Puritan vegetable oils into a single Crisco/Puritan brand. For its 100 U.S. brands, P&G eliminated 15 to 25 percent of the colors, flavors, and sizes. Through such slimming down, the company avoids the costs related to producing each version of the product and maintaining a favorable image for each brand.

P&G's tactics seem to be working. Cost cutting allowed the company to reduce prices on Pampers and Luvs diapers and on Tide and Cheer laundry detergent. After two years of value pricing, a P&G spokesperson reported, "Brands that are value-priced have generally done better than nonvalue-

priced brands." Also, P&G's market share rose in roughly two-thirds of its product categories. At a recent meeting of P&G's shareholders, CEO Edwin L. Artzt was able to say, "I believe that our company is better positioned to deal with the economic realities of the marketplace, whatever they may be, than at any time in our past."

Procter & Gamble has responded to challenging times by devising creative ways to meet the needs of stores and consumers. As you read this chapter, consider how well P&G's efforts reflect the principles of marketing and a concern for customer value.

Sources: Zachary Schiller, "Procter & Gamble Hits Back," *Business Week,* July 19, 1993, pp. 20–22; Laura Klepacki, "P&G Commits Its Heavy Guns," *Supermarket News,* April 12, 1993, pp. 1, 10–11; Zachary Schiller, "A Nervous P&G Picks Up the Cost-Cutting Ax," *Business Week,* April 19, 1993, p. 28; Report by Edwin L. Artzt, Chairman and Chief Executive, to the Annual Meeting of Shareholders, Procter & Gamble, October 13, 1992; Gabriella Stern, "P&G Starting to Cut as Many as 10,000 Jobs," *The Wall Street Journal,* June 24, 1993, p. A3

Chapter Overview

Procter & Gamble has long been noted as a leader in marketing. Today its use of teamwork and its focus on customer value maintain P&G's status as a marketing innovator. Such marketing innovations are described in the "Creating Customer Value" section at the beginning of each chapter. These stories will help you see how marketers apply marketing principles to help organizations excel in today's highly competitive environment.

This chapter introduces the basic concepts and responsibilities of marketing. We begin by defining and describing *marketing.* Next we describe the two levels of marketing activities: macromarketing (the total flow of goods and services within a society) and micromarketing (the way an organization plans and executes its marketing strategies). Then the discussion shifts to the scope of marketing and universal marketing functions within organizations. The chapter also introduces the components of marketing strategy and discusses marketing in nonprofit settings. Finally, we describe the role of marketing in the organization, including the use of cross-functional teams as pioneered by P&G and other organizations.

What Is Marketing?

You click on the TV and a commercial for laundry detergent balloons onto the screen, followed by an ad from a nonprofit organization asking for your contributions to feed hungry children. You stroll down a supermarket aisle and snap a coupon out of a dispenser, allowing you to save money on salad dressing. A representative from an envi-

FIGURE 1.1
**Seeking to Create
an Exchange**

marketing
The process of planning
and executing the
conception, pricing,
promotion, and distribution
of ideas, goods, and
services to create
exchanges that satisfy
individual and
organizational goals.

exchange
A process in which two or
more parties voluntarily
provide something of value
to each other.

market
The individuals and
organizations that have the
desire and the ability to
purchase a particular good
or service.

ronmental group gives a talk at your college, soliciting new members. You receive a phone call asking you to participate in a brief survey about what articles readers like to see in magazines. In your job at the college bookstore, you have to keep track of the supply of notebooks so that the store can order more when the supply is low.

All of these situations involve marketing. According to the American Marketing Association, **marketing** is "the process of planning and executing the conception, pricing, promotion, and distribution of ideas, goods, and services to create exchanges that satisfy individual and organizational goals." This broad definition takes into account all parties involved in the marketing effort: members of the organization that produces goods or services, resellers of the goods and services (such as stores), and customers or clients. Furthermore, marketing activities may be carried out by diverse organizations—an automobile insurer providing drivers with protection from exposure to loss, an art museum providing visitors with a chance to view and learn about works of art, a government agency providing the public with inspections designed to ensure safe workplaces, an accounting firm providing businesses with financial statements that they can use in their annual reports.

The objective of marketing is to create exchanges. An **exchange** is a process in which two or more parties voluntarily provide something of value to each other. For example, when you buy a bag of potato chips, you get a snack you value, and the store gets something it values: money. IIT Hartford, the advertiser in Figure 1.1, hopes consumers with a need for financial security (peace of mind) will exchange some money for an insurance policy from ITT. If consumers buy the insurance and receive financial security, the marketing effort (and the exchange) has succeeded.

Exchanges take place within a market. In this sense, a **market** consists of the individuals and organizations with the desire and ability to purchase a particular good or service. Thus, a given market may consist of organizational buyers, consumers, or both. *Organizational buyers* purchase goods and services in order to pro-

**You Can Dip Your Dog For Fleas And Ticks.
Or You Can Use A Squirt Of New Defend.**

You know how much dogs hate being dipped. That's why we created Defend™ EXspot® insecticide for dogs. You apply it in seconds, and yet it's as effective as the leading dip.
One application of revolutionary new Defend provides your dog with up to four weeks of flea and tick protection. You've never seen a product that's both this easy to use and this effective.
Defend for dogs. Ask your veterinarian about it.

It Works Like Nothing Else.

duce something else to sell. Avis buys cars to provide rental services, Wendy's buys ground beef to sell in its hamburgers, and a hospital buys cleaning services so that it can provide patients a clean place in which to recover from surgery or illness. Consumers are individuals who buy goods and services for themselves or their households to use. For example, a consumer can buy a car to drive, ground beef to include in chili for a party, or cleaning services to free up time to relax.

consumers
People who buy goods and services for themselves or their households to use.

PURPOSE OF MARKETING

Successful marketing is customer driven: it addresses customer needs and desires. Needs are the things customers require to survive as individuals and organizations. Desires or wants are the things that customers would like to have to make their lives more pleasant or their activities easier to carry out.

What are these needs and desires? For a consumer, needs include food, clothing, shelter, and transportation. But as you will see in later chapters, different consumers desire to meet their needs in different ways, according to their tastes and expectations. In fulfilling the need for clothing, some people want to be fashionable, while others are more interested in comfort or cost. The ad in Figure 1.2 seeks to translate an owner's need to keep his or her dog free from fleas and ticks into a desire to purchase Defend™ insecticide.

Organizational buyers, too, have needs and desires. They need supplies, personnel, and other resources to carry out their mission, and different organizations wish to meet those needs in different ways. A law firm needs paper on which to write to its clients; the firm's partners may desire letterhead with a design that conveys dignity and prestige.

Sometimes needs and desires are easy to identify. With continued suburban sprawl, resulting in long commutes over poorly maintained roads, commuters' need for public transportation has grown in recent years. So, in 1992, the Virginia Railway Express was launched, just one of many commuter railroad projects around the country. On the first day, passengers lined up on the Fredericksburg platform more than an hour before the first train was scheduled to depart for Washington, D.C. "People have waited for it for a

Put It Into Practice

CONSUMERS' NEEDS AND DESIRES

We're all customers. Every day, we make decisions that reflect our needs and desires. We need food, clothing, and shelter. We want a certain pair of jeans, we like to eat at a particular Mexican restaurant, we've decided to rent a house with friends. As a marketer, always remember the ways in which you are a customer too. This will help you address your customers' needs and desires.

At one time or another, just about everyone has ordered something from a catalog and then returned it because of dissatisfaction with the product. The sweater might have been too big; the game or puzzle might have been missing pieces; the pillowcases might have been the wrong color. As a customer, you can help marketers address your needs and desires by being specific about your likes and dislikes. Here is an effective letter written by a customer returning a suitcase to a catalog company:

> Dear Customer Service:
>
> Enclosed is the soft-sided suitcase, item #1234 in your catalog, which I am returning for a refund. Although it has several features that I do like, overall it isn't exactly what I wanted.
>
> I like the wide, adjustable carrying strap and the sturdy zipper. I'm sure both would hold up well. I also like the nylon lining, which can be wiped clean with a sponge. And I feel that the bag is priced fairly.
>
> But the suitcase doesn't have any internal pockets for small items; one with a zipper would be ideal. Also, there is no way to lock the suitcase. The light beige color would be very hard to keep clean; in the catalog, the color appeared to be a darker tan. Finally, although your catalog states that the suitcase can easily be stowed under an airline seat, when the bag is stuffed full it won't fit. This is important to me because I take a lot of short business trips by plane and don't want to have to check my luggage.
>
> I hope you find these comments helpful. I'd be happy to answer any other questions you might have about the suitcase. Thank you for your service.
>
> Yours truly,
> Carol Customer

Note that the letter states what item the customer is referring to and tells the customer service department exactly what is good and bad about the suitcase. It appears that the customer is generally satisfied with the quality, service, and price of the item, but its specific features don't meet her requirements. The company's marketers should answer this letter and reexamine their product.

Do you think it is sufficient for a company to react to customer complaints, perhaps by operating a complaint department? Or do you think companies should be more proactive? (Being proactive means making an effort to find out what their customers want to see in the company's goods or services so that customers will have no need to complain.) What are some ways in which a company could avoid complaints and deliver value by finding out what satisfies—and even delights—customers?

long time," commented the rail agency's director, Thomas Waldron. "They're hungry for it. I am somewhat wary that we won't be able to meet the demand."[2]

Sometimes marketers misjudge the needs of the customer, or they address the desires of some customers but not others. When Lands' End, the large mail-order company, redesigned the fit of its men's slacks in the early 1990s in response to comments from customers, the company received many letters from other (previously satisfied) customers complaining about the change and asking for traditional-fit slacks. The company responded by offering both fits in some models of its slacks.[3]

Competition for customers is intense, so addressing customers' needs and desires is essential. (For a look at the consumer's role in this process, see "Put It into Practice.") The marketing environment, ethics, and the use of marketing tools and techniques all come into play in gaining potential customers. Each of these topics will be dealt with in greater detail later in this book.

FIGURE 1.3
**Ford's Commitment
to Total Quality**

THE QUALITY APPROACH TO MARKETING

Marketers have long cared about the quality of the goods and services sold by their organizations. After all, it is harder and less gratifying to sell defective goods or inept services. In recent years, however, many organizations have taken their interest in quality a step or two further by embracing **total quality management (TQM)**. TQM is an organization-wide commitment to satisfying customers by continuously improving every business process involved in delivering goods or services. Instead of merely correcting defects when they are identified, organizations that practice TQM commit employees to continually look for ways to do things better so that problems won't arise in the first place.[4] At Ford this commitment involves randomly selecting vehicles from assembly lines and tearing them apart to check the quality of welds (see Figure 1.3).

total quality management (TQM)
An organization-wide commitment to satisfying customers by continuously improving every business process involved in delivering goods or services.

TQM AND CUSTOMER SATISFACTION   At an organization that practices TQM, marketers and other employees don't just say, "Our products should be good." Rather, *every employee* takes the attitude that the people who receive his or her services should be satisfied with them. Some businesses even say that customer satisfaction is not a high enough objective; they say TQM should aim to *delight* customers.[5]

Satisfying or even delighting customers requires not only doing one's current job well, but individually and jointly looking for ways to improve work processes. In the jargon of TQM, such efforts are called "continuous improvement." The philosophy underlying continuous improvement is the Japanese notion of *kaizen:* if you do the little things right, the total gain will be enormous. One way in which organizations can encourage continuous improvement is to invite—and *use*—employee suggestions. For example, teams at Toyota generate almost three million ideas a year, and management implements 85 percent of them.[6]

The "customer" of a particular employee may not be the ultimate customer of the organization.[7] For example, the marketing research staff typically delivers its results to the organization's product teams, not to buyers of the organization's products. However, thinking of the users of the research as customers can help the marketing researchers focus on the importance of delivering useful information at a reasonable cost. High-quality research, in turn, helps marketers develop the kinds of products that will please the organization's customers. Thus, when all employees strive for high quality, ultimately the organization's customers should be pleased with the results. Put another way, TQM is "a system for integrating quality technologies into various functional departments (engineering, production, sales, service) to achieve customer satisfaction."[8]

Because marketers serve as an important link with the organization's customers—identifying them, learning their wants and needs, communicating how the organization's products can help meet those needs—marketers have an especially important role to play in TQM.[9] For example, they can have an enormous impact on customer satisfaction by seeing that customers' experiences with salespeople are positive and that the specifications developed for the organization's goods and services meet customer demands. When the organization provides services, marketers can see to it that the service providers are well trained in marketing and communications skills that will help them satisfy customers.

TQM AND PERFORMANCE   Total quality management has the potential to improve the performance of the marketing group and the organization as a whole. A study by the U.S. General Accounting Office found that at organizations using TQM, sales per employee increased 8.6 percent, and customer satisfaction rose.[10] Black & Decker credits its TQM effort with improved product performance, more efficient ordering procedures, and major cost savings, among other benefits.[11]

However, other evidence shows that many organizations are disappointed with their attempts at TQM. Florida Power & Light developed an extensive—and costly—quality program, but its customers saw only minor improvements in the quality of its services.[12] To avoid disappointment, organizations that try using TQM need to remember two important points.

First, achieving measurable results from TQM (such as improved sales or profits) takes time. Because TQM is based on continuous improvement, it is an ongoing process, not a quick fix. Organizations that reap benefits from TQM usually do so by advancing gradually, adjusting their strategy as they improve. For example, Fred Wenninger, chief executive of Roy, Utah–based Iomega Corporation, suggests that an organization start its TQM efforts by focusing on ways to reduce cycle time, the total time it takes to complete a process.[13] For a marketer, this might include the time it takes to develop a new product or respond to a customer request for information.

The second important point about TQM is that marketing and management efforts must focus on the *customer,* not on the organization itself. A recent survey of *Fortune* 500 executives by a consulting firm called ODI found that very few of the companies' suppliers consistently involved them in setting objectives for quality improvement. Instead, concluded George H. Labovitz, president of ODI, "Their suppliers choose to guess at what would make customers happy. And much of the time, they're guessing wrong."[14] In contrast, Industrial Devices Inc. (IDI) of Hackensack, New Jersey, maker of indicator lights for dashboards, adopted TQM principles in response to a request from a major customer, Ford Motor Company. According to IDI's president, Bernie Schnoll, IDI is using TQM to shorten design and production times for one big reason: "because my customers need it."[15]

TQM AND EMPLOYEES   Total quality management extends beyond the product and the marketing of the product: it includes an emphasis on quality people and quality processes as well. For employees to be willing and able to continuously improve what they do, they need more than an annual performance appraisal. They need to be

Marketing Movers & Shakers

WAL-MART'S SAM WALTON

In 1950 Sam Walton opened his first store—Walton's 5 & 10—in Bentonville, Arkansas. He expanded the chain to 15 stores by 1962, the year he opened his first discount store, the beginning of his famous Wal-Mart chain. When Sam Walton died in 1992, he was one of the wealthiest people in the United States.

Walton didn't start his business with family money, and he didn't have any other head starts. But in 22 years, he built his national chain of Wal-Mart stores into one of the country's

fastest-growing retailers. By the early 1990s, the company's annual sales of over $50 billion enabled it to dwarf its large suppliers such as Procter & Gamble. How did Walton do it?

According to John Huey, *Fortune* magazine senior editor, "He wanted everything to be right for the customer." There's no mystery in that—a satisfied customer is a repeat customer. People who had a good experience shopping at Wal-Mart would be back. "Loyal, repeat customers are at the heart of Wal-Mart's spectacular profit margins, and those customers are loyal to us because our associates treat them better than salespeople in other stores do," Walton wrote in his autobiography, *Made in America*.

But Walton—or, rather, his wife, Helen—went a step further. Helen once asked her husband about the salaries and benefits Wal-Mart paid its employees, exclusive of the company's officers. "I realized how little the company was doing for them,"

explained Helen, according to Sam's account. "I suggested to him that unless these people were on board, the top people might not last long, either." After thinking over his wife's opinion, Sam Walton came to agree with her. Motivated, satisfied employees would do their jobs better, and better employees meant a better operation and more satisfied customers.

So in 1971 Walton offered profit sharing to all Wal-Mart employees and began calling them "associates." He remained a tough, demanding employer, bent on being the best in the business. But he had discovered one of the great secrets of his success: once he made his employees partners, they became just as motivated as he was. When Walton retired, he left behind many long-term cashiers, truckers, clerks, and other workers whose worth exceeded $1 million. After his death, Wal-Mart associates continued to practice Walton's vision; Wal-Mart's success was their own.

Sources: Robert McGarvey, "Sam's Way," *Entrepreneur,* October 1992, pp. 172, 174, 175; Edward O. Welles, "When Wal-Mart Comes to Town," *Inc.,* July 1993, pp. 76–80+.

empowered. This means involving employees in decisions about their own jobs, workplace, and the organization as a whole. (To learn how Sam Walton did this with Wal-Mart employees, see "Marketing Movers and Shakers.") Employees also need the power to carry out the improvements they see a need for and to take the actions that will satisfy customers.

The Stew Leonard's supermarket chain empowers its employees to deliver customer value. For example, when a woman went into the store to order food for a party, she disregarded the chef's warning that she wasn't buying enough for her 20 guests. The chef was right, and the store's manager received a frantic call from the customer during her party. Rather than blaming the customer for her poor judgment, the manager personally delivered another tray of food at no cost to the customer. An expensive instance of poor judgment on an employee's part? Not at all. The guests turned out to be new real estate agents—people well positioned to steer the community's new residents to the store. And to top it off, they all stopped in after the party and spent hundreds of dollars.[16]

Advocates of employee empowerment believe that to participate fully in a business, employees at all levels need four things: power, information, knowledge, and rewards.[17] For example, AT&T gives its operators daily information about changes in the businesses and the markets it serves so that they can better answer questions or respond to customer requests.[18] When employees are thus empowered, they serve the company's customers better.

The Scope of Marketing

So far we have discussed marketing in general terms. To understand just what it is that marketers do—or should do—consider the scope of the marketing function. Two ways to view the scope of marketing are to look at levels of marketing activity and to identify the different activities involved in marketing.

LEVELS OF ACTIVITY

At times marketers may focus on broad marketing activities. They consider the way an entire marketing system works or should work. At other times marketers are interested in the ways individual organizations carry out marketing and how they can improve these efforts.

macromarketing
The total flow of a nation's goods and services to benefit society.

MACROMARKETING   One level at which marketing activities take place is that of the overall economy. Macromarketing refers to the total flow of a nation's goods and services to benefit society.[19] For example, national measures of new-home sales or retailers' inventory levels describe macromarketing activities. Macromarketing also encompasses such broad issues as overall costs, environmental effects, and social responsibilities of marketing. Table 1.1 summarizes the major macromarketing issues of the for-profit and nonprofit sectors of the economy. As shown in the table, these issues may be either positive (related to how the system works) or normative (related to how the system ought to work).

In the United States the macromarketing system is based on a market-directed economy. Buyers determine which goods and services will be produced simply by purchasing the goods and services that they want. Thus, since a lot of people buy tax preparation services each February through April, such services are widely available during those months. Another outcome of this type of economy is that for most products, U.S. buyers can choose from among many makers and sellers. Rarely are they required to buy from one supplier, such as the federal government.

Buyers and sellers have less freedom of choice in many other countries. Government involvement in other marketing systems often creates inefficiencies because lack of a profit motive leads to little concern for customers. A well-known consequence in Russia has been that consumers have to stand in line for hours, waiting for a chance to buy the scarce goods for sale. Thus, to offer workers at its Russian venture a company-sponsored lunch, Nantucket Corporation pays three employees to spend five hours a day standing in line to buy food.[20]

In reaction to such inefficiency, many nations, such as China and those in the former Soviet Union, have been loosening government control over marketing activities. In China, the Communist Party recently embraced what it called a "socialist market economy." Observers expected this would mean the government would continue to own many enterprises but would permit private businesses to flourish as well. Individual investors would be allowed to hold a minority ownership in the state-run enterprises, which should encourage them to operate profitably.[21]

The U.S. macromarketing system has helped to create an economic climate in which businesses can readily start up and grow and consumers can purchase a wide variety of goods and services. But in some cases, the freedoms of the U.S. marketplace can create conflict. This occurs when the goods produced by some manufacturers sat-

This Wrigley gum display is an example of increased marketing activity in China. Wrigley recently opened a factory in China's relatively prosperous Guangdong province.

TABLE 1.1

Major Macromarketing Issues

POSITIVE ISSUES	NORMATIVE ISSUES
For Businesses	
Problems, issues, theories, and research concerning:	Problems, issues, normative models, and research concerning:
a. Aggregate consumption patterns	a. How marketing can be made more efficient
b. The institutional approach to marketing	b. Whether distribution costs too much
c. The commodity approach to marketing	c. Whether advertising is socially desirable
d. Legal aspects of marketing	d. Whether consumer sovereignty is desirable
e. Comparative marketing	e. Whether stimulating demand is desirable
f. The efficiency of marketing systems	f. Whether the poor should pay more
g. Whether the poor pay more	g. What kinds of laws regulating marketing are optimal
h. Whether marketing spurs or retards economic development	h. Whether vertical marketing systems are socially desirable
i. Power and conflict relationships in channels of distribution	i. Whether marketing should have special social responsibilities
j. Whether marketing functions are universal	
k. Whether the marketing concept is consistent with consumer's interests	
For Nonprofit Organizations	
Problems, issues, theories, and research concerning:	Problems, issues, normative models, and research concerning:
a. The institutional framework for public goods	a. Whether society should allow politicians to be "sold" like toothpaste
b. Whether television advertising influences elections	b. Whether the demand for public goods should be stimulated
c. Whether public service advertising influences behavior (e.g., Smokey the Bear)	c. Whether "low informational content" political advertising is socially desirable (e.g., 10-second "spot" commercials)
d. Whether existing distribution systems for public goods are efficient	d. Whether the U.S. Army should be allowed to advertise for recruits
e. How public goods are recycled	

Source: Reproduced from Shelby D. Hunt, *Modern Marketing Theory: Critical Issues in the Philosophy of Marketing Science* with the permission of South-Western Publishing Co. Copyright 1991 by South-Western Publishing Co. All rights reserved.

isfy their customers but don't necessarily benefit society as a whole. For example, disposable diapers are convenient for consumers to use, but they contribute bulky and human waste–contaminated garbage to landfills. And while many people still demand the freedom to smoke cigarettes and thus support the tobacco industry, society suffers due to the numbers of youngsters starting to smoke, the effects of secondhand smoke on nonsmokers, and the cost of treating smoking-related diseases.

micromarketing
The way an individual organization plans, executes, and allocates its marketing activities to benefit its customers.

MICROMARKETING   Although this book will touch on issues related to macromarketing, its main focus is on micromarketing. **Micromarketing** examines the way an individual organization plans, executes, and allocates its marketing activities to benefit its customers. Thus, Kellogg's choice to make some cereals that appeal to children and others that appeal to health-conscious adults is a micromarketing decision. Other micromarketing decisions at Kellogg include the ways in which the company prices the cereals, the channels through which it distributes them, and the ads and coupons it uses to stimulate sales. The remaining chapters address specific issues related to micromarketing strategy.

TABLE 1.2	
Basic Marketing Functions	
FUNCTION	**DESCRIPTION**
Exchange Functions	
Buying	Ensuring that enough units of product are available to meet consumer demand
Selling	Using advertising, personal selling, and sales promotion to match goods and services to customer needs
Physical Distribution Functions	
Transporting	Moving goods from point of production to a location convenient to customers
Storing	Warehousing products until needed for sale
Facilitating Functions	
Standardization and grading	Ensuring that products meet established quality- and quantity-control standards for size, weight, and other variables
Financing	Providing credit for customers
Risk taking	Assuming the uncertainties that result from developing and distributing goods and services customers may purchase in the future
Information gathering	Collecting information about customers, competitors, and resellers to use in making marketing decisions

UNIVERSAL MARKETING FUNCTIONS

A common error is to assume that marketing activities consist only of sales and advertising. In fact, many more functions are encompassed by the definition of *marketing* stated earlier. Marketing involves eight basic functions: buying, selling, transporting, storing, standardization and grading, financing, risk taking, and securing marketing information. (See Table 1.2.) A single organization need not perform all of these functions; most often, some are handled by manufacturers and others by resellers. For example, a supermarket performs the function of buying a variety of foods to make them available in one place. A wholesaler handles the function of transporting these products to the supermarket.

exchange functions
The marketing functions that ensure that the right products are available to meet customers' needs and that customers are aware the products are available.

physical distribution functions
The marketing functions required to get products to the customers who want them.

facilitating functions
The marketing functions that help marketers know what to provide and customers make purchase decisions and purchases.

The eight marketing functions serve several purposes. Buying and selling are **exchange functions**. These functions ensure that the right products are available to meet customers' needs and that customers are aware the products are available.

Physical distribution functions are the activities required to get products to the customers who want them, including transporting and warehousing goods. Other related activities include controlling inventory levels and processing orders.

The **facilitating functions** help marketers know what to provide and help customers make purchase decisions and purchases. Within this category of functions, standardization and grading ensure that products meet quality- and quantity-control standards. Financing involves providing credit to customers so that they can meet their needs as they arise. Risk taking includes developing and offering for sale products that customers have not yet committed to buying. Information gathering involves collecting information about customers, competitors, and other relevant subjects. These various functions are discussed throughout this text.

Marketing Strategy

marketing plan
A plan that specifies marketing objectives, one or more target markets, and a marketing mix to serve each of those target markets.

The most effective way to carry out the marketing functions is for marketers to start by planning what they want to accomplish and how they will do it. Broadly speaking, they prepare a **marketing plan**, which consists of marketing objectives, identification of one or more target markets, and a marketing mix to serve each of the target markets. The creation of marketing objectives and marketing plans is discussed in Chapter 5.

TARGET MARKETS

As described in Chapter 10, most organizations find that different members of a market have different needs. For example, some renters of housing are looking for luxury apartments with many amenities, others are looking for cheap space near school or work, and still others are primarily interested in a yard for children to play in. Further investigation would uncover still more variety within each of these sub-groups. Obviously, one apartment building is not going to please all renters. Therefore, landlords seek to serve only a portion of the total market for rental housing.

target market
The portion of a market that an organization attempts to serve.

The portion of the market that an organization attempts to serve is called its **target market**. For its chain of Olive Garden restaurants, General Mills targeted "recession-strapped baby boomers who want both inexpensive ethnic food and a high chair for the toddler."[22] The Worth Collection, a line of clothing sold by appointment only, targets upper-middle-class women who want quality clothing, insist on personal service, and can afford to pay the price for both.[23] Chapter 10 provides a more detailed description of how marketers select target markets.

THE MARKETING MIX

To return to the example of rental housing, a landlord who knows his or her target market will know how to provide the right product at the right price. The landlord will also have a sense of where and how much to advertise. A marketer who has selected a target market is able to plan a marketing mix to create successful exchanges with its members. A **marketing mix** is "the mix of controllable marketing variables that the firm uses to pursue the desired level of sales in the target market."[24]

marketing mix
The mix of controllable marketing variables that the firm uses to pursue the desired level of sales in the target market; consists of four elements: product, pricing, channels of distribution (placement), and communication (promotion).

As shown in Figure 1.4, the marketing mix consists of four elements: product, pricing, channels of distribution (placement), and communication (promotion). These elements are often called the "four P's" (for product, pricing, placement, and promotion). However, the terms that more accurately describe these elements amount to "two P's and two C's."

product
The actual good or service that a marketer offers a target market; also, the many ways in which the good or service is enhanced to satisfy the customer.

PRODUCT   In the marketing mix, **product** stands for two things. First, it is the actual goods or services that marketers offer their target market. Second, it refers to the many ways in which those goods or services are enhanced to satisfy customers. Thus, cheese is a common product. Shredding it and putting it in a resealable bag make it convenient. Adding a label about its sodium content is helpful to health-conscious consumers.

Packaging and labeling are two major aspects of enhancing a product. Marketers make additional decisions about such attributes as color, style, and convenience. In this way, they create a *product strategy*—the decisions that involve the development of the product, its packaging, and its positioning in the marketplace. Chapters 11, 12, and 13 discuss product strategy in detail.

PRICING   The price of a good or service is its exchange value—that is, what the buyer would pay in exchange for the product. In most cases, price refers to an amount of

FIGURE 1.4

Elements of the Marketing Mix

pricing
The element of the marketing mix that consists of setting prices that support the organization's marketing strategy.

money. However, in some instances the buyer might exchange time or other goods. **Pricing** is the function of setting prices that support the organization's marketing strategy. Pricing can be a tricky business: sometimes prices are regulated by government or industry standards, and prices are always subject to scrutiny by the general public.

Competition is a major factor affecting pricing, and "price wars" are common in many industries. In April 1992, American Airlines announced that it would simplify its fare structure, reducing its prices. Then in May, Northwest decided to undercut American's fares. American countered by beating Northwest's new rates. Meanwhile, consumers jammed telephone lines and ticket counters to get the best deals while they lasted. Competitors accused American of intentionally taking losses in order to drive weaker airlines out of business. Several considered antitrust suits against the company. Some industry people even began to say that it was time for the government to get involved in order to preserve competition. In the end, prices rose again and a number of airlines were thankful to have survived what was termed a "death struggle."[25] Chapters 14 and 15 address pricing in more detail.

channels of distribution
The element of the marketing mix that consists of getting the product to the target market so that it will be convenient to buy.

CHANNELS OF DISTRIBUTION   Marketers also plan how to get the product to the target market so that it will be convenient to buy. This element of the marketing mix is called **channels of distribution** (or placement). A strategy for channels of distribution includes a variety of activities such as transportation, warehousing, and inventory control. Sometimes the producer of the product handles all of these activities. At other times, the producer works with other organizations called resellers, intermediaries, or middlemen to make goods and services readily available to buyers.

Distribution is critical to a successful marketing strategy. No matter how good a product is, how fair its price, or how effectively it is promoted, members of the target market may not buy it if it isn't readily available to them. Channels of distribution are described more fully in Chapters 16 and 17.

Physical distribution functions are the activities required to get products to the customers who want them. The Fleming Company supplies food and related products to more than 4,800 stores in 36 states, the Caribbean, Mexico, and other Central and South American countries. The company, with 32 computer-supported divisions, supplies stores with virtually every brand-name grocery product as well as store-brand items sold in high volume.

communication
The element of the marketing mix that involves informing target markets about the organization and its products.

COMMUNICATION (PROMOTION) To tell members of the target market how a product meets their needs and how they can buy it, marketers develop a communication or promotion strategy. In this sense, **communication** refers to the element of the marketing mix that involves informing target markets about the organization and its products. The strategy for doing so consists of a communication mix that combines some of these elements:

• Advertising
• Personal selling
• Sales promotions, such as coupons or gift offers
• Publicity, such as the media coverage that results from press releases and news conferences.

The communication strategy has succeeded if members of the target market understand and accept the product message that the marketer is sending.

Sometimes the marketer combines elements of the communication mix in one promotional effort; encouraging consumers to try, sample, and then purchase. Such efforts are often a combination of advertising and sales promotion.

Chapters 18, 19, and 20 cover the various elements of the communication mix.

MARKETING IN NONPROFIT SETTINGS

The ultimate marketing goal in business is obvious: to attract and satisfy customers, generating a profit for the company in the process. But 30 years ago, marketers began to see how marketing could be applied to nontraditional, or nonprofit, settings. Marketing experts Philip Kotler and Sydney Levy published an article arguing that marketing should be viewed as applicable to a broader arena than the traditional profit setting.[26] This broadened concept included both profit and nonprofit organizations.

Nonprofit organizations, which operate in both the public and private sectors, include such diverse entities as public schools and hospitals, churches and synagogues, political campaigns, government agencies, the Sierra Club, Save the Children, the American Civil Liberties Union (ACLU), the National Rifle Association (NRA), the Bronx Zoo, Amnesty International, and Overeaters Anonymous. Nearly 11 million people, including volunteers, work for the 1.2 million nonprofit organizations in the United States, generating about $300 billion per year. These numbers continue to grow rapidly: two-thirds of all nonprofit organizations operating today were established after 1960.[27]

TABLE 1.3 **Categories of Nonprofit Marketing**	CATEGORY	DEFINITION	EXAMPLE
	Person marketing	Marketing designed to elicit a favorable response to a person	Bill Clinton's election campaign
	Place marketing	Marketing designed to elicit a favorable response to a specific location	Advertising describing Puerto Rico's "150 white sand beaches"
	Idea marketing	Marketing designed to promote a cause or issue	"Just Say No" campaign to discourage drug use
	Organization marketing	Marketing designed to attract members, donors, participants, or volunteers to a particular organization	Fund-raising drives on public television

Although some marketers have viewed the expanded definition of marketing as too extreme,[28] many nonprofit organizations have put it to good use. Financial pressures and funding cutbacks, as well as competition with other organizations for "customers" (donors) in an increasingly crowded market, mean that nonprofit organizations must be as imaginative and aggressive in their marketing as profit-centered firms.

TYPES OF NONPROFIT MARKETING   While it employs many of the same techniques and concepts that apply to marketing in profit-centered arenas, nonprofit marketing has its own features as well. Table 1.3 identifies four types of nonprofit marketing: person marketing, place marketing, idea marketing, and organization marketing.

With **person marketing**, nonprofit marketers try to elicit a favorable response to a person. The major example of this is political campaigns. The candidate seeks donations, volunteers, endorsements, and, ultimately, votes.

With **place marketing**, marketers try to elicit a favorable reaction to a location. Typically, the objective is to attract tourism, convention business, or new industries. Tourist bureaus of cities, states, and countries seek to attract visitors or businesses by using advertisements, favorable publicity, and sales promotions such as coupons and discounts. The government of New Zealand hired the New York firm of Siegel & Gale to develop a positive image of that country among U.S. consumers. The result was a national logo depicting a stylized silver fern and the motto "the New Zealand way." The logo is intended to go on New Zealand exports that meet government-set quality standards. The government hopes that the fern labels will create an image that leads to more exports and more tourism.[29]

Idea marketing promotes a cause or issue to a targeted market. For example, the Minnesota Department of Public Health used cigarette tax revenues to prepare two ads designed to reduce smoking among women by ridiculing the tobacco industry and its advertising. One ad shows a billboard with the message "Women Are Making the Rush to Rich Flavor." The wind blows away pieces of the billboard until it reads, "Women Are Making Us Rich." After the ads began appearing on Minnesota TV stations, the proportion of adult smokers in the state dropped from 29 to 21 percent.[30]

Organization marketing attempts to attract members, donors, participants, and volunteers to a particular organization. Figure 1.5 is an example. The American Indian College Fund solicits funds with a public service campaign that emphasizes how traditional Indian values are being preserved at the tribal college.

OBSTACLES IN NONPROFIT MARKETING   Nonprofit marketers have some unique hurdles to clear. One is demands by the donor, the very person the marketer seeks to attract. For example, a large contributor to a college might insist that her donation be

person marketing
Nonprofit marketing designed to elicit a favorable response to a person.

place marketing
Nonprofit marketing designed to elicit a favorable response to a specific location.

idea marketing
Nonprofit marketing designed to promote a cause or an issue.

organization marketing
Nonprofit marketing designed to attract members, donors, participants, or volunteers to a particular organization.

FIGURE 1.5

**Example of
Organization
Marketing**

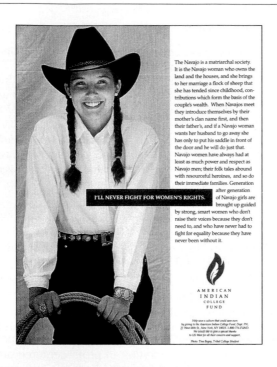

The Navajo is a matriarchal society. It is the Navajo woman who owns the land and the houses, and she brings to her marriage a flock of sheep that she has tended since childhood, contributions which form the basis of the couple's wealth. When Navajos meet they introduce themselves by their mother's clan name first, and then their father's, and if a Navajo woman wants her husband to go away she has only to put his saddle in front of the door and he will do just that. Navajo women have always had at least as much power and respect as Navajo men; their folk tales abound with resourceful heroines, and so do their immediate families. Generation after generation of Navajo girls are brought up guided by strong, smart women who don't raise their voices because they don't need to, and who have never had to fight for equality because they have never been without it.

I'LL NEVER FIGHT FOR WOMEN'S RIGHTS.

AMERICAN INDIAN COLLEGE FUND

Help save a culture that could save ours by giving to the American Indian College Fund, Dept. PN, 21 West 68th St., New York, NY 10023. 1-800-776-FUND. We would like to give a special thanks to US West for all their concern and support.

Photo: Tina Begay, Tribal College Student

used to fund a program that the college is trying to phase out. Another hurdle is lack of a clear hierarchy. Volunteers and paid staff might be working side by side without a structure that dictates accountability. Finally, the lack of a bottom line—the nonnecessity of showing a profit—can hamper marketing efforts. Since the organization's overall goals are not related to profit, marketing objectives may be difficult to quantify. However, a membership drive, fund drive, or capital campaign can be conducted with clear monetary goals.

These hurdles should be viewed merely as challenges to nonprofit marketers. The objective of identifying and addressing the needs and desires of the target market remains the same in profit and nonprofit marketing. Attracting and keeping customers is the "bottom line" in both settings.

The Role of Marketing in the Organization

Virtually all businesses and many nonprofit organizations recognize that effective marketing plays a crucial role in their success. But to appreciate the contemporary approach, as exemplified by marketers like Procter & Gamble, it is important to understand how marketing has evolved throughout most of the twentieth century.

EVOLUTION OF THE MARKETING CONCEPT

Before the Industrial Revolution, a typical example of marketing was a farmer loading a wagon with produce to sell in town on market day. Thus, marketing emphasized the physical distribution function of getting goods to customers. Since then, economic and social changes have required organizations to revise their view of marketing in order to stimulate successful exchanges. Organizations that have prospered throughout the years have been quick to make these changes. However, not all organizations have adopted the same view of marketing at the same time, and some organizations—to their detriment—have been slow to change at all.

PRODUCTION ERA   In the first part of this century, organizations found more and more ways to automate. European and North American companies typically focused on ways to improve the production of goods, because this was how they were able to gain or keep a competitive advantage. The classic example of this *production era* is Ford Motor Company, whose efficient strategy for mass-producing the Model T enabled more consumers than ever to own an automobile. Manufacturers concentrated on producing goods, believing that products would practically sell themselves.

Often, production-era businesses searched for customers *after* having manufactured their goods. Today, such a production orientation seems not only outdated but impossible; the costs of manufacturing are just too high to justify making something without ensuring there will be enough buyers. During the production era, however, producers operated in a **seller's market**—one where demand for products outstrips the supply.

SALES ERA   Thanks to the many production improvements businesses had made, they became able to produce more goods than their regular customers wanted to buy. Businesses began operating in a **buyer's market**—one in which the supply of products exceeds the demand for them. This marketing challenge was intensified by the limitations on spending caused by the Great Depression and World War II. Many businesses responded to the challenge by hiring salespeople and looking for ways to persuade consumers and organizational buyers to purchase more of their products. The period in which this approach to marketing was common is known as the *sales era,* and it prevailed until the 1950s.

MARKETING ERA   As markets continued to grow, many businesses became less satisfied with the principle of selling more and more. They needed a basis for focusing their efforts, and they needed more successful strategies for attracting and keeping customers. This led businesses to enter the *marketing era,* a period during which more and more companies formed marketing (rather than simply sales) departments, sought to identify customer needs and desires, and adopted the marketing concept.

The **marketing concept** states that an organization should seek to meet its customers' needs as it strives to achieve its own goals. To identify and meet customer needs, businesses and other organizations have relied on marketing departments staffed with experts in marketing research, sales, advertising, distribution, and other functions. The process of researching needs and then planning a way to meet them can be time consuming, but it helps ensure that organizations use their resources wisely.[31] At organizations that have adopted the marketing concept, marketing becomes the company's link to the customer.

QUALITY-DRIVEN MARKETING   In the decades that have passed since the beginning of the marketing era, competition has intensified. Technological advances have enabled organizations to serve much larger geographical areas, so that U.S. companies now share the U.S. market with many foreign firms. Government deregulation has increased the level of competition in a number of industries, including banking, trucking, telecommunications, and air travel. In addition, the explosion of information sources has made today's buyers more sophisticated and more demanding. As a result, more and more organizations are finding it necessary to move beyond the marketing era to an emphasis on quality and customer value.

Often the move beyond the marketing concept includes some version of total quality management (TQM), described earlier in this chapter. This quality approach, which became popular during the 1980s, broadens the traditional marketing concept to involve all members of the organization in striving to improve quality in order to satisfy customers. (For an example, see "You Decide," which describes Federal Express's "people-service-profit" philosophy.)

seller's market
A market in which demand outstrips the supply of products.

buyer's market
A market in which the supply of products exceeds the demand for them.

marketing concept
View that an organization should seek to meet its customers' needs as it strives to achieve its own goals.

CAN THE FASTEST SHIPPING COMPANY CONTINUE TO BEAT THE COMPETITION?

Remember the ads? The fastest-talking human on earth talked about the fastest shipping company on earth: Federal Express. In 1990, several years after those commercials had run on television, the Federal Express Corporation won the Malcolm Baldrige National Quality Award, which is intended to "promote quality awareness, recognize quality achievements of U.S. companies, and publicize successful quality strategies." When it won the award, the company was only 17 years old.

Federal Express began operations in 1973 with a fleet of eight small aircraft. Five years later, the company employed 10,000 workers and handled 35,000

You Decide

shipments each day. By the company's most recent count, Federal Express's 90,000 employees now process 1.5 million shipments daily.

With a philosophy of "people-service-profit," Federal Express emphasizes training with interactive videos and a worldwide staff of training professionals. The company has a no-layoff policy and a "guaranteed fair treatment procedure" for handling employee grievances. Federal Express also has a program recognizing team and individual contributions to the company's overall performance. The company is often cited as one of the

best American firms to work for, and in surveys over 90 percent of its employees have said they are "proud to work for Federal Express."

Federal Express faces stiff competition as it attempts to expand its services around the globe. If you were a marketer at Federal Express, what new, specific services might you come up with to satisfy customers and retain your edge over the competition? What incentives would you provide to employees to carry out these new services? If competitors began to "raid" your employees, trying to lure them away, how might you encourage them to stay at Federal Express?

Source: V. Daniel Hunt, *Quality in America* (Homewood, Ill.: Business One Irwin, 1992), pp. 115–122.

Besides competition, another force behind adoption of TQM and quality-driven marketing is the Malcolm Baldrige National Quality Award. The National Institute of Standards and Technology (NIST) gives this award to organizations that have achieved high standards of quality. NIST also publicizes the winners' methods and results. About 200,000 organizations request applications for the Baldrige award each year. Most of them don't actually apply to win but use the criteria for the award as a basis for evaluating their own effort to improve quality.

TQM and the Marketing Concept   The quality approach doesn't toss out the marketing concept but expands on it. For example, Figure 1.6 shows the differences and similarities between the two approaches when the buyer is an organization. In the traditional approach at left, different functions in buying and selling organizations are interested in different aspects of the product. Acting independently, the various functions within the buyer organization spell out which products are of acceptable quality. Members of the selling organization attempt to respond to the buyer's stated needs. All this independent action can be time consuming and disappointing for the customer.

In an organization applying the total quality concept, as shown in the right side of Figure 1.6, the various functions of the buying and selling organizations work together to decide what the buyer needs and how the seller will meet those needs. They act as partners to get their needs met.[32] The goods and services are produced right the first time, the whole process is faster, and the customer and supplier are both satisfied with the results. In effect, practicing total quality management enables the organization truly to put the marketing concept into practice.[33]

Cross-Functional Teams   Whereas traditional marketers view the marketing department as a unilateral decision maker on all issues involving marketing, quality-approach marketers advocate a team effort, including people from research and development, operations, production, and even outside experts such as advertising agencies. These cross-functional teams make decisions designed to improve the orga-

cross-functional team
Team of employees from various functions who make decisions designed to improve the organization's responsiveness to the markets it serves.

FIGURE 1.6

How Total Quality Management Can Affect the Practice of Marketing to Organizational Buyers

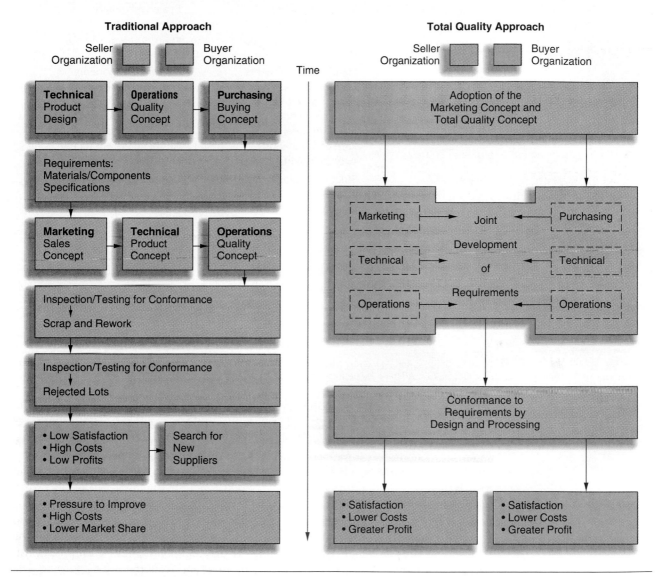

Source: Reprinted by permission of the publisher from "Marketing's Lead Role in Total Quality," *Industrial Marketing Management* 21, p. 135. Copyright 1992 by Elsevier Science, Inc.

nization's responsiveness to the markets it serves.[34] All employees on these teams are thus charged with knowing and attempting to satisfy customers.[35]

Working in cross-functional teams, employees can use a variety of talents and experience to solve marketing problems. For example, to redesign the bottle for Mazola corn oil, CPC International assembled a team of employees from marketing, purchasing, packaging technology, engineering, manufacturing, and logistics management. The team's new design reduced packaging by almost one-third.[36] Also, communication among functions throughout the marketing process helps speed the

TABLE 1.4	FUNCTION	ITS EMPHASIS	MARKETING'S EMPHASIS
Concerns Emphasized by Different Functions in an Organization	Research & Development (R&D)	Basic research Intrinsic quality Functional features	Applied research Perceived quality Sales features
	Production	Long design lead time Few models Standard components Long production lead times Long runs with few models No model changes Standard orders Ease of fabrication Average quality control	Short design lead time Custom components Short production lead time Short runs with many models Frequent model changes Custom orders Aesthetic appearance Tight quality control
	Finance	Strict rationales for spending Hard and fast budgets Pricing to cover costs	Intuitive arguments for spending Flexible budgets to meet changing needs Pricing to further market development
	Accounting	Standard transactions Few reports	Minimum credit examination of customers Medium credit risks Easy credit terms Easy collection procedures

Source: Philip Kotler, *Marketing Management: Analysis, Planning, Implementation and Control,* 8th ed., © 1994, p. 732. Adapted by permission of Prentice-Hall, Englewood Cliffs, New Jersey.

organization's responses to change and keeps employees in all departments close to the customer. The cross-functional approach enables employees to move beyond asking customers what they want to asking them what problems they have, thus anticipating ways to meet needs that customers have yet to expect help with.[37]

Haller M. Moyers, vice president of reliability and quality assurance for San Jose–based VLSI Technology, details how cross-functional teams work at his firm.[38] Each team has a team leader, a facilitator, and a sponsor on the corporate steering committee. The facilitator helps make the team effective by training team members to work as a group and by stepping in when the team needs help to stay on track. The sponsor prepares an initial charter defining the project for which the team is responsible; the team reviews the charter and may revise it and resubmit it for approval. The teams set ground rules—for example, requiring attendance at meetings and forbidding personal attacks. The maximum team size is 15 people, many of whom may be volunteers. Moyers recommends providing for alternate members as well, in case someone leaves. The team may break down a big project into smaller ones to be handled by subgroups. Thanks in part to the commitment of top management, reports Moyers, the teams at VLSI have made improvements that would not have happened if the company used only "business-as-usual approaches."

MARKETING'S ROLE IN DEVELOPING AND IMPLEMENTING STRATEGY

Whatever the organization's approach to marketing, the marketing group is only one part of the total organization. As shown in Table 1.4, employees in other functions

TABLE 1.5

How Marketing and Other Functions Impact One Another

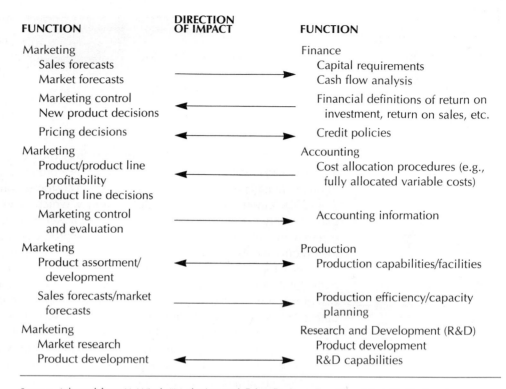

FUNCTION	DIRECTION OF IMPACT	FUNCTION
Marketing		Finance
Sales forecasts	⟶	Capital requirements
Market forecasts		Cash flow analysis
Marketing control	⟵	Financial definitions of return on
New product decisions		investment, return on sales, etc.
Pricing decisions	⟷	Credit policies
Marketing		Accounting
Product/product line	⟵	Cost allocation procedures (e.g.,
profitability		fully allocated variable costs)
Product line decisions		
Marketing control	⟶	Accounting information
and evaluation		
Marketing		Production
Product assortment/	⟷	Production capabilities/facilities
development		
Sales forecasts/market	⟶	Production efficiency/capacity
forecasts		planning
Marketing		Research and Development (R&D)
Market research		Product development
Product development	⟷	R&D capabilities

Source: Adapted from Y. Wind, "Marketing and Other Business Functions," in J. N. Sheth, ed., Research in Marketing, vol. 5 (Greenwich, Conn.: JAI Press, 1981), pp. 237–264.

emphasize different issues in making their contribution to the organization. Marketers must be aware of these differences and consider how their decisions and actions affect other parts of the organization and, ultimately, its customers.[39] Table 1.5 summarizes major ways in which the decisions and actions of marketing and other functions affect one another.

The marketing group ensures that its activities meet organizational needs by participating in the planning process. At the highest level of management, the organization carries out *strategic planning,* whereby it develops long-term strategies for growth and survival. At the product and market levels, the company carries out *strategic marketing planning,* through which it chooses markets in which to participate, decides on marketing programs for those markets, and allocates resources to them.[40] These types of planning are detailed in Chapter 5.

ORGANIZATIONAL STRATEGIC PLANNING In general, strategic planning consists of defining the organization's purpose, setting measurable goals for fulfilling that purpose, and identifying ways to meet those goals. Marketing managers can help to ensure that these activities are carried out in a way that satisfies customer wants and needs.

To see how this works, consider Xerox. In an industry in which its name was synonymous with its products, Xerox was the undisputed front-runner for the first 15 years it was in business. But competitors had reduced the company to an also-ran by the mid-1980s, and Xerox needed to redefine its mission, set new goals, and identify opportunities for growth. The company analyzed data that included monthly surveys of 55,000 equipment owners in order to determine what customers wanted. Then man-

FIGURE 1.7
**Marketing
Management**

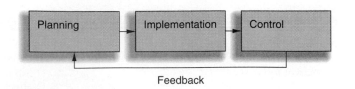

Feedback

agers established business plans with objective, measurable targets for making the improvements customers needed. In 1983, the company established its Leadership through Quality program, whose main aim was customer satisfaction. David T. Kearns, then CEO, announced the Xerox Quality Policy, which states, "Xerox is a quality company. Quality is the basic business principle for Xerox. Quality means providing our external and internal customers with innovative products and services that fully satisfy their requirements. Quality improvement is the job of every Xerox employee."[41]

Xerox looked for opportunities for growth through quality improvement. By the early 1990s, the company had realized a 78 percent improvement in the quality of its machines and a 40 percent improvement in product reliability, while production defects fell by 73 percent. The company continuously sets new standards for quality in copiers. To improve the quality of goods and services it receives from its suppliers, Xerox makes them full partners with the company. Xerox empowers its employees through such means as training opportunities. The company has regained many of its old customers and reversed the decline of its market share against Japanese firms.[42]

MARKETING MANAGEMENT   As shown in Figure 1.7, marketing management consists of three basic activities: planning, implementation, and control. Chapter 5 describes how marketers plan, and Chapter 6 introduces the basics of implementation and control. To carry out strategic marketing planning, marketers analyze the company's position in a market and project where it is headed, then use this information to prepare marketing plans. As explained earlier, a marketing plan contains marketing objectives, identifies target markets, and details the marketing mix to be used to serve each target market.

marketing tactics
Specific, short-term actions for putting a marketing plan into action.

In the implementation phase, marketers put their plans into action by carrying out specific, short-term activities known as **marketing tactics**. These include each of the four elements of the marketing mix. Examples are writing press releases and reducing prices by some percentage. Chapters 11 through 20 describe a variety of marketing tactics.

In the control phase of marketing management, marketers measure the results of carrying out the marketing strategy. Then they strengthen activities that are leading to positive results. When results are disappointing, they look for the underlying problems and make needed corrections.

MARKETING STRATEGY IN THE PIZZA BUSINESS   When Mike and Marian Ilitch entered the pizza business with a $10,000 investment in 1959, their mission wasn't any more complicated than twirling dough for fellow Detroiters. But in 1988, with a successful ad campaign, Little Caesars took off, and it now has more than 4,000 stores nationwide. In the meantime the competition had intensified. Thomas Monaghan, founder of Domino's Pizza, Inc., changed the entire pizza business by promising customers that their pizzas would be delivered hot to their homes within 30 minutes. So Little Caesars had to define itself and its customers in a more concrete way than just as "pizza lovers," and the firm had to find a better way to get pizza to customers.

Mike Ilitch came up with the idea to give customers variety and savings at the same time: they could order two pizzas for one low price. He called this concept "Pizza Pizza," and the idea took off.[43] Little Caesars sliced itself a secure spot in the pizza business by following through with low-cost production. The company has no delivery trucks, and it works with a small staff. The pizzas, while satisfying, aren't loaded with extra ingredients.[44]

In short, Little Caesars conducted strategic marketing planning and carried out that plan. The company analyzed its position in the pizza market and projected where it wanted to be, vis-à-vis Domino's. It identified marketing opportunities in the carryout business and targeted its customers. It executed its "Pizza Pizza" plan while keeping costs to a minimum and continuing to monitor its performance.

Summary

Marketing is the process of planning and executing the conception, pricing, promotion, and distribution of ideas, goods, and services to create exchanges that satisfy individual and organizational goals. These exchanges take place within markets that consist of consumers, organizational buyers, or both. Successful marketing is customer driven; it identifies and addresses customer needs and desires, then seeks to satisfy them with quality goods and services. An increasing number of marketers are adopting a quality approach to marketing based on the principles of total quality management (TQM). Under TQM, all members of the organization are involved in continuously improving business processes to better satisfy the needs and wants of customers. This approach requires empowering employees to make decisions and take actions to improve quality and satisfy customers.

Marketing takes place at two levels: macromarketing and micromarketing. Macromarketing describes the total flow of a nation's goods and services. Micromarketing examines the way an individual organization conducts its marketing activities. In addition, marketing encompasses eight functions: buying and selling (exchange functions); transporting and storing (physical distribution functions); and standardization and grading, financing, risk taking, and information gathering (facilitating functions).

Marketing strategy involves selecting a target market and determining the best marketing mix to reach it. This mix consists of four elements: product, pricing, channels of distribution (placement), and communication (promotion).

Marketing is not limited to businesses; it also occurs in nonprofit settings. Nonprofit marketers may engage in person marketing (seeking a favorable response to a person), place marketing (seeking a favorable response to a location), idea marketing (promoting a cause or an issue), and/or organization marketing (seeking to attract donors and members).

During the past century, marketing has evolved through periods during which different business roles dominated. During the production era, firms typically sought an advantage by producing goods efficiently. During the sales era, many firms saw a need to win more buyers by boosting their selling efforts. During the marketing era, many companies set up marketing departments so that they could focus on meeting customer needs. More recently, organizations have been applying the principles of total quality management. This means that all employees assume a role in satisfying customers. One way organizations are carrying out this approach is by using cross-functional teams, in which employees representing various functions work together to improve the organization's responsiveness to the markets it serves.

The marketing group supports the organization's strategies by participating in strategic planning. At the highest level of the organization, strategic planning defines a mission, sets organizational goals, and determines how to meet those goals. At the level of the marketing group, managers create marketing plans. Marketing managers are also responsible for implementing and controlling the effort to carry out those plans.

KEY TERMS AND CONCEPTS

marketing (p. 7)
exchange (p. 7)
market (p. 7)
consumers (p. 8)
total quality management (TQM) (p. 10)
macromarketing (p. 13)
micromarketing (p. 14)
exchange functions (p. 15)

physical distribution functions (p. 15)
facilitating functions (p. 15)
marketing plan (p. 16)
target market (p. 16)
marketing mix (p. 16)
product (p. 16)
pricing (p. 17)
channels of distribution (p. 17)
communication (p. 18)

person marketing (p. 19)
place marketing (p. 19)
idea marketing (p. 19)
organization marketing (p. 19)
seller's market (p. 21)
buyer's market (p. 21)
marketing concept (p. 21)
cross-functional team (p. 22)
marketing tactics (p. 26)

REVIEW AND DISCUSSION QUESTIONS

1. Name and describe the elements of the marketing mix.
2. What are two possible target markets for a no-calorie, no-sodium, flavored seltzer water? As a marketer, what consumer needs and desires would you seek to address?
3. What two issues important to the quality approach have some companies failed to address?
4. Suppose you wanted to market your company's line of photocopiers in India. What are five questions you would want to answer about the macromarketing system in that country?
5. What would be the role of General Motors in carrying out the universal marketing functions?
6. What variables might go into the pricing of a product?
7. What are the four types of nonprofit marketing? What hurdles unique to nonprofit organizations must marketers in such organizations face?
8. How would you expect a clothing manufacturer to handle marketing during the production era? during the marketing era?
9. How does the quality approach expand on the marketing concept?
10. What are the three activities involved in marketing management? How did Little Caesars carry out those activities as part of its successful marketing strategy?

Chapter Project
Using the Quality Approach

As you've seen in this chapter, the quality approach is an extension of the marketing concept. Imagine that you're the new owner of one of Mike and Marian Ilitch's Little Caesars franchise pizza shops. Place yourself and your shop in a suburban or urban area that you are familiar with. Using the quality approach, begin to develop your marketing strategy for a successful shop. (The instructor might set up this exercise as a group project in which the class organizes into cross-functional teams, with class members representing different functional areas.)

Answer the following questions:

- Who are your customers? What are their needs and wants? How can you best satisfy them?
- Who are your competitors? How can you satisfy customers better than your competitors?
- What types of products would you offer? (Would you offer a wide variety of toppings? Low-calorie or low-fat toppings?) What new products might you offer? (Sandwiches? Desserts?)
- What processes would you use to ensure that you are offering high-quality products and service? (Clean, modern ovens? A clean, well-lit shop?)
- What standards would you set for your staff? How large a staff would you employ, and in which positions? How would you use the team approach with your staff?
- Where would you look for growth in your business? New products? Better service? Special promotional efforts?

Case
Preston Trucking

"Preston People: We Make the Difference," proclaims the slogan painted on the front of the huge cab of an 18-wheeler. Preston Trucking, a 50-year-old trucking company based in Preston, Maryland, lives by its motto. Danny Large, a Teamster shop steward at Preston notes, "Everybody feels the same way. We are a company that works together."

Preston workers *do* make a difference—to themselves, their coworkers, their company, and their customers. By integrating employee empowerment with formal quality objectives and giving the mix plenty of time to work, Preston has managed to stay in business through the energy crises of the mid-1970s, price wars due to deregulation, and recessions of the early 1980s and 1990s. One of the 20 largest trucking firms in the United States, the company increased its payroll from 2,000 to over 4,000 employees during the dozen years leading up to 1990. During the same time period, Preston's total revenues grew 178 percent, or 81 percent per employee.

The company wasn't always so successful, nor was it such a great place to work. Before 1978, management and union members argued daily, creating job dissatisfaction from the top of the company on down. "Every day was a battle," describes Martin Landy, vice president of quality and marketing. "I used to spend my time riding into work wondering who I was going to fight with." The situation reached its flash point when an angry Preston driver, in response to new and unreasonable work goals imposed by management, protested by parking his truck for several hours in a customer's parking lot in Detroit. The customer was Chrysler. Preston got the point.

The company hired Behavioral Systems, Inc. to conduct an employee attitude survey at two of its terminals. The results surprised even Preston management: negative comments about the company outnumbered positive comments by 40 to 1. Something had to be done. The gap between workers and management had to be closed if the company were to survive.

To begin, company management created a purpose statement to guide its own improvement process. The statement opened with a quote from the German philosopher Goethe: "Treat people as though they were what they ought to be and you help them become what they are capable of being." The purpose statement went on with a sentence that is now the company's motto: "The person doing the job knows more about it than anyone else."

Top management then committed to giving employees— now called associates—positive rather than negative feedback. The company turned its focus to solving problems rather than finding scapegoats for them. For nearly five years, management simply concentrated on building trust with union workers. Middle management was streamlined, and those who remained took on the company's new team spirit. "Not one of us alone has the ability to make or break the company," notes Rick Bowen, manager of Preston's Milwaukee terminal, "but all of our efforts combined help."

In 1987, nine years into its turnaround, Preston created its first formal quality teams. By then, an atmosphere of teamwork and camaraderie between management and workers had been established. More than 150 quality teams began examining and correcting various problems at Preston, such as equipment and supply shortages and inaccurate billings. One quality team in the freight bill payment department reduced the time for producing corrected billings from 28 days to 2 days. Sandy Redd, coordinator for that department, says the focus on teamwork and quality improvement has changed the work environment considerably. "Years ago," she explains, "I couldn't go across the hall to, say, the claims department and tell them about an idea I had for them to improve. Now I feel very confident about doing that. When it comes to quality, we're all on the same level."

Preston Trucking hasn't limited its quality imperative to its internal operations; it has involved customers as well, by establishing creative partnerships with them. The basis of the partnerships is communication. Each partnership is made up of teams of union and nonunion workers from Preston and the customer, which meet regularly to exchange data and set goals for improvement in areas such as billing accuracy, timeliness, and safety. Teams have the authority to follow through with their own plans for improvement and measure the results. "There's not much red tape in their way," notes Comber McHugh, manager of customer partnerships for eastern states.

Customers have been enthusiastic about this practice. One of the most successful partnerships has been with chemical manufacturer J.T. Baker, Inc. Employees at Baker and Preston began to communicate about their problems with quality, efficiency, and even communication itself. They discovered that they didn't understand each other's business or processes at all. Baker was unhappy about delays at loading docks and learned that Preston associates hadn't understood the need for extreme attention to safety during transit of the chemicals. The companies decided to track the transport and delivery system in order to see how it could be improved. After six months, they examined the data and immediately involved Preston and Baker employees in the analysis; after all, the employees knew more about their jobs than anyone else.

The effort wasn't easy. "It was awkward to start this whole process," recalls Jack Jones, manager of corporate distribution services at Baker. "Both companies were new at this. But after a time, it's amazing how you start talking. Building trust is tough."

But Preston *has* built trust, among its associates, between associates and management, and between the company and its customers. By emphasizing teamwork and quality, and by giving both the necessary time to have a real impact, the company has managed to keep its trucks rolling.

QUESTIONS

1. How did Preston Trucking's new motto, "The person doing the job knows more about it than anyone else," help change workers' attitudes toward their jobs? What relationship did this new attitude have to the quality of the services the company provides?
2. How does Preston Trucking extend the quality imperative to its relationships with customers?

Source: Nancy A. Karabatsos, "Driving Home Quality," *The Quality Imperative,* September 1992, pp. 49-56.

CHAPTER 2 *The Marketing Environment*

LEARNING OBJECTIVES

After completing this chapter, you should be able to:

1. Explain how marketers scan the marketing environment.

2. Describe the economic environment in terms of business cycles, spending patterns, and consumer income.

3. Describe the political and legal environment, including laws and regulations affecting marketing.

4. Identify major demographic and cultural trends and characteristics of interest to marketers.

5. Identify aspects of the institutional environment that are of interest to marketers.

6. Discuss how technology affects marketers today.

7. Identify aspects of the competitive environment that are of interest to marketers.

Creating Customer Value
Coca-Cola

The external forces that influence the marketing effort of many companies arise not only in the United States, but in many other countries around the world. Coca-Cola has launched itself into this global marketing environment by thinking of itself as a powerful, international business system. Explains Roberto C. Goizueta, chairman of the board and CEO, "At the Coca-Cola Company, we view ourselves today as an international corporation headquartered in the United States, as opposed to a U.S. company with a sizable international business . . . arguably the only truly global business system in existence today." Coca-Cola's management believes that global marketing is a team effort that must include the following elements:

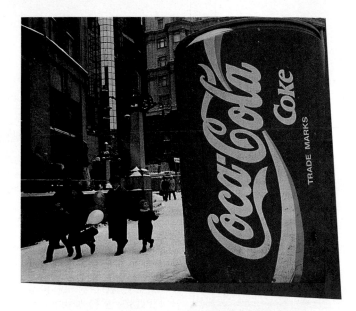

- A strong, recognizable trademark
- A global business system through which to reach consumers (At Coca-Cola, this means the company itself—a worldwide network of employees, bottling partners, vendors, and customers)
- Products and messages tailored to local markets
- A central theme, image, or ideal that binds together the business system, the product, and the customer.

Although Coca-Cola products can be found as far away as Australia and Hong Kong, one of the company's most powerful recent pushes into a new market has been in Eastern Europe, where it has quickly broken PepsiCo Inc.'s hold on the market. Steven Meadows, vice president of A.T. Kearney Inc., a global management consulting firm, notes, "Historically, the first company in a country [in this case, PepsiCo] could stake out the market in terms of suppliers, shelf space, distribution, local partners, and financing. But in a developing country where there's been a significant change in government of economic policy, it can tend to negate the advantage of being first."

Using its global business system, Coca-Cola surveyed the market conditions and launched a campaign to unseat Pepsi. Coke didn't commit itself to Eastern Europe until political conditions favored private enterprise. And it chose Eastern Europe over Russia because Eastern European countries already had experience with private enterprise. Then

Coke worked quickly to privatize its bottlers (Pepsi was unable to) and hired its own sales force to introduce products. This was, perhaps, the most important step in the process, because it gave the company control over marketing and distribution. Coke required that bottlers and distributors drop other products and created a direct-delivery system. In the meantime, Coke executives personally called on stores in Poland, Hungary, and Romania as part of a worldwide customer appreciation week.

Coke marketers also boosted awareness of their product by supplying store owners with neon "Coke" signs. They installed coolers in stores so that consumers could taste the drink cold. In Hungary, for example, soda had been served at room temperature.

The move into Eastern Europe included some challenges resulting from the limitations of less-developed economies. For example, Coke found that the Romanian bottling plant it bought in 1991 for $12.5 million was in bad shape. Recalls a Coke executive, "[The] machinery was antique, the roof was leaking, water was dripping all over the place, some bottles were two-thirds full and some were completely full." The company had to abandon the plant.

Despite such setbacks, Coke's global business system— made up of executives, marketing personnel, distribution workers, bottlers, retailers, and salespeople—has worked to increase the company's presence around the world. Coke is keenly aware of shifting conditions in worldwide markets and is prepared to alter its operations to meet the needs of each market. The company's ability to integrate and aggressively use all its resources to their fullest make it a fierce competitor in the new age of private enterprise in Eastern Europe.

Sources: Janet Guyon and Michael J. McCarthy, "Coke Wins Early Skirmishes in Its Drive to Take Over Eastern Europe from Pepsi," *The Wall Street Journal,* November 11, 1992; 1991 Annual Report, the Coca-Cola Company.

Chapter Overview

marketing environment
The economic, political and legal, social, institutional, technological, and competitive factors—at home and abroad—that affect an organization's marketing effort.

In developing and implementing its global strategy, Coca-Cola's managers have had to plan for and contend with a variety of laws, changing economic conditions, and better-established competition. These and other external forces are important to marketing in all kinds of organizations. Together, they constitute the **marketing environment**: the economic, political and legal, social, institutional, technological, and competitive factors—both here and abroad—that affect an organization's marketing effort.

This chapter introduces the various dimensions of the marketing environment. In the economic environment, business conditions influence patterns of spending and production as well as the amount of money consumers have to spend. In the political and legal environment, laws, regulations, and consumer pressures limit the activities of marketers. The social environment describes the characteristics of groups of buyers—for example, their age and income distributions and their values and beliefs. The institutional environment consists of the organizations such as stores and transportation companies that support the marketing efforts of producers. The technological environment includes opportunities for new products and for new ways to distribute and promote them. (Of course, it also includes limitations on what can be done at present.) The competitive environment consists of other organizations that may be able to satisfy the needs and desires of a market.

Scanning the Environment

environmental scanning
The practice of tracking external changes that can affect markets, including demand for goods and services.

In a recent interview with *Newsweek,* Tom Magliozzi, cohost of National Public Radio's "Car Talk," said about General Motors, "They can make a car if they want to. It's just they don't know what . . . to make. . . . They have lost sight of who Americans are." His cohost and brother, Ray Magliozzi, continued, "They think all Americans live in Michigan. The hierarchy of GM is mostly men." Tom chimed in, "There just aren't that many people who want or can afford a Cadillac. So what are they wasting their time for, making a wonderful Cadillac? Make a wonderful Cavalier."[1]

That's a strong indictment of one of the three major American car manufacturers. But Tom and Ray were making an important point: GM's managers seemed unaware of what customers want; they evidently had failed in their efforts at environmental scanning. **Environmental scanning** is the practice of keeping track of external changes—economic, political and legal, social, institutional, technological, and competitive forces—that can affect markets, including the demand for goods and services. The marketer must monitor the various dimensions of the marketing environment, shown in Figure 2.1.

FIGURE 2.1

Dimensions of the Marketing Environment

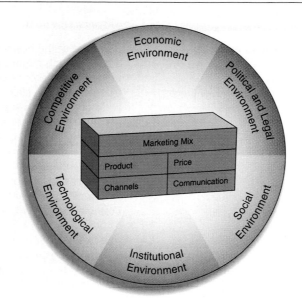

Some organizations have a formal program for environmental scanning. For example, employees of the American Council of Life Insurance regularly review newspapers, magazines, and professional and technical publications, looking for information that may be relevant to future products or strategies in the insurance industry.[2] The scanning effort at other organizations is more informal. Of course, a systematic approach is most likely to spot important trends.

Through environmental scanning, marketers identify ways to act promptly on new opportunities and cope with new challenges. They learn more about their customers' needs and their competitors' strengths and weaknesses. Therefore, before marketers can create a plan, they need to know about the marketing environment. This chapter focuses on the kinds of information marketers need, and Chapter 7 introduces some ways they gather such information.

CONTENTS OF ENVIRONMENTAL SCANNING

Environmental scanning seeks to identify trends that offer previously untapped opportunities or can change the market for goods and services. It answers questions such as: What does the average American family look like? How often does this average family eat out? What laws are likely to affect the firm's choice of packaging? Is the demand for office space likely to increase? Are competitors likely to introduce a fax machine with more features or superior quality? Table 2.1 lists just some of the questions that might be part of the environmental scan for a chain of quick-printing shops.

Few organizations today can afford to limit their view of the marketing environment to the country in which they are based. Many organizations based in the United States have customers in at least a few other parts of the world. In fact, about 70 percent of U.S. economic growth in recent years has come from exports.[3] Even organizations that market only in the United States are likely to have foreign competitors. Thus, modern marketers need to take a global view of the marketing environment.

TABLE 2.1	DIMENSION OF THE ENVIRONMENT	SAMPLE QUESTIONS
Possible Questions in an Environmental Scan by a Chain of Quick-Printing Shops	Economic environment	What stage of the business cycle are we in? What industries with major printing needs are doing well in the current economic climate?
	Political and legal environment	What zoning laws affect our ability to open shops in areas of potentially high growth? Are our advertising claims legal and ethical?
	Social environment	Are buyers willing to go out of their way to choose a printing shop that promotes environmentally friendly choices such as the use of recycled paper and double-sided copies?
	Institutional environment	What firms are available to deliver completed jobs to customers? Can anyone offer same-day service for an attractive price?
	Technological environment	What developments are likely to affect printing and desktop publishing?
	Competitive environment	What other businesses offer printing services within a five-mile radius? What is their rate schedule? Which potential customers handle their own printing needs?

INTERNAL FORCES

Note that while environmental scanning focuses on forces outside the organization, internal forces also affect marketing efforts. For example, limited funding may influence how marketers decide to go about promoting a product. Or a genius on the engineering staff may enable the organization to be a leader in introducing product innovations. The influence of internal forces on marketing decisions is addressed throughout the remaining chapters of this book.

The Economic Environment

To return to an earlier example, when marketers ask about the expected demand for office space, they are asking about the economy. If demand is expected to grow, businesses will be starting up and expanding; they will have money to operate and expect their customers will have money to buy from them. This news is favorable not only for the construction industry; it also tells marketers serving office workers that their target market probably will be expanding.

economic environment
The overall economy, including business cycles, consumer income, and spending patterns.

In general, the **economic environment** for marketing comprises the overall economy, including business cycles, consumer income, and spending patterns. The "Marketing Movers and Shakers" box describes how European economic conditions have affected Fiat.

business cycle
The pattern of the level of business activity; moves from prosperity to recession to recovery.

BUSINESS CYCLES AND SPENDING PATTERNS

Simply put, marketers want to know whether their target markets will be willing and able to spend money. Spending patterns are linked to the **business cycle**, or the pattern in the level of business activity that moves from prosperity to recession to recov-

Marketing Movers & Shakers

GIANNI AGNELLI AND HIS FIAT

Gianni Agnelli said he was ready to retire and spend more time with his grandchildren. At 71, he had reigned over the Italian automaker Fiat for 26 years. During the 1960s he helped organize an unprecedented deal to build cars in the Soviet Union. During the 1970s he managed to keep Fiat running despite strikes and even sabotage by radical political groups. By the late 1980s, Agnelli had established Fiat as a symbol of Italy's rise to a world industrial power: the company had become Europe's largest and most profitable auto manufacturer.

But by the early 1990s, Fiat Auto's sales and profits began to plummet, and the company's European market share slid along with them. Conditions in the European economy were a major contributor to Fiat's problems. A severe recession caused demand for new cars to decline; not only Fiat was affected, but also such giants as Sweden's Volvo and Germany's Daimler Benz. Giorgio Garuzzo, Fiat's chief operating officer, noted, "For the overall European market outlook, we are revising our numbers downward every week." In addition, Italy itself had its own economic woes. High inflation, interest rates, and wages during the late 1980s and early 1990s sent Fiat's overhead manufacturing costs soaring out of sight. For instance, from 1987 to 1992, the cost of Fiat's work force increased at about 8 percent a year. But closer to the French border, labor costs rose only about 4 percent. "For the last four or five years, our competitors have had it easy," said Garuzzo.

So Agnelli couldn't leave. Instead, he had to rev up his engines for another challenge. And he couldn't entirely blame the economy. Fiat had allowed its fleet to age without introducing new models, and political maneuvering within the company had drawn managers' attention away from developing new, high-quality cars. Still, external conditions in the marketing environment were a force to reckon with. Conversely, when Rome decided to devalue the Italian lira in September of 1992, Fiat gained 20 percent in price competitiveness against the French franc and the German mark. In addition, a new agreement with Italian unions ended 40 years of automatic wage indexation, so that labor costs would rise at a more moderate rate.

Agnelli sold off pieces of the company's holdings, approached banks for significant loans, streamlined management, and focused on creating new, desirable car models. He had a lot to do before he retired. Then he could take his grandchildren for a drive.

Source: John Rossant, "Gianni Agnelli's Last Hurrah," *Business Week,* November 30, 1992, pp. 77–79.

 ery. Figure 2.2 shows the basic pattern of a business cycle. In general, the business cycles of the industrialized nations tend to parallel one another.[4] However, major political upheavals such as the recent ones in Germany and the former Soviet Union have sweeping effects on the economies of the countries involved, and thus on their business cycles.

PROSPERITY   During times of *prosperity,* production and employment are high. Consumers demand more goods and services, and they spend freely not only on basics but on luxuries such as vacations, designer clothing, and entertainment. In addition, they may upgrade big-ticket items such as housing and cars. They are also more likely to travel overseas (except in times of foreign political unrest). Consumers in prosperous times often want the "best" of everything and are willing to pay for it, so marketers introduce new products, increase their promotional efforts, and raise prices in order to increase profits.

inflation
A rise in the overall price level.

Inflation—a rise in the overall price level—can occur at any stage in the business cycle, but it is typically most pronounced during periods of prosperity. During inflation, rising prices reduce the amount of goods and services that can be purchased with each dollar. This is a problem for consumers and organizational buyers if their

FIGURE 2.2

Basic Pattern of a Business Cycle

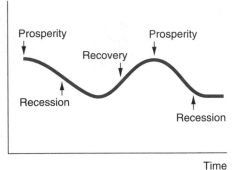

income does not keep pace with the rate of inflation. In addition, inflation can affect marketing strategy. For example, it can make purchasing on credit more appealing because customers will make payments in dollars worth less than they were at the time of purchase. Also, pricing strategies must be developed with care to avoid alienating customers with repeated price hikes to cover rising production costs.

RECESSION   During a *recession*, production decreases and unemployment generally rises; consumers fold their wallets and snap their purses closed. Reduced production and decreased consumer demand lead organizational buyers to reduce their consumption as well. Both types of buyers stick to purchasing the basics and look for the best value for their dollar. In Japan, consumers have kept their vacation travel costs down during the most recent recession by staying close to home and visiting amusement centers such as Ananda Hanayashiki. This three-story building contains food stalls, a game corner, a modern electronics showroom, and a party hall featuring a jet coaster, merry-go-round, haunted house, and sky ship. On the roof is an amusement park where visitors can ride small vehicles. Another Japanese amusement park is shown in Figure 2.3. This park, located 100 miles outside of Tokyo, re-creates in miniature such landmarks as the Eiffel Tower, the Empire State Building, and the Great Pyramids, allowing the Japanese to experience the wonders of foreign countries with minimal travel expense.[5]

Marketers of private-label (store brand) and generic goods may find they have an edge by offering brand-name quality at less than brand-name prices. Some companies even offer "price rollbacks"—price decreases that echo previous, lower prices for individual products. Or they advertise that they haven't *raised* a price in a certain number of years. During the recession of the early 1990s, the mail-order house Lands' End advertised an attaché case at the same price tag it carried in 1985.

Resourceful and creative marketers can prosper during a recession. During the early 1990s, nearly 11 percent of all Americans were carrying their own meals to work instead of eating at restaurants. In response, grocery companies such as Oscar Mayer, Hillshire Farm, and Star Kist offered ready-made, easy-to-carry lunch and dinner foods. Oscar Mayer introduced Lunchables, a tray of cold cuts, cheeses, and crackers that people can mix or eat separately. Hillshire Farm, a unit of Sara Lee Corp., launched a similar product called Lunch 'n Munch, which even has its own "lite" version. Star Kist offers Charlie's Lunch Kit, which includes tuna fish and packets of mayonnaise and relish.[6]

FIGURE 2.3

A Message Well Suited to the Recession in Japan: Consumers See the World with Minimal Travel

RECOVERY   While the economy is in the *recovery* stage, progressing from recession to prosperity, the level of production increases and unemployment decreases. Consumers and organizational buyers have more money to spend but may still be reluctant to increase their purchases. They recall the recent recession and are wary of another slump. Consumers may try harder to save and buy few items on credit. As the economy becomes stronger, buyers begin to relax and spend more freely.

The *perception* of economic recovery can have just as much influence on spending patterns as the reality. During his 1992 reelection campaign, President George Bush continually insisted in interviews that the U.S. economy wasn't "that bad" (and indeed, the first set of economic statistics after the election confirmed Bush's position that the economy was recovering). But American consumers didn't buy it, especially in light of the weakness of the recovery.

RESOURCES   Spending patterns are tied not only to business cycles; they may also be related to the availability of certain resources. Resources may be in short supply because demand for a product exceeds a manufacturer's capacity to produce it. For example, demand for SnackWell's Devil's Food Cookie Cakes outstripped Nabisco's capacity to make the cookies, a four-hour process that includes covering the cake center with marshmallow, chocolate icing, and a chocolate glaze.[7] Or use of certain natural resources may be depleting the supply. An embargo, a war, and political or economic sanctions also can cause shortages. Public pressure to conserve resources for future needs may lead to diminished consumption even when there is enough of those resources to meet present needs.

When the supply is limited in these and other ways, marketers may engage in **demarketing**, an effort to reduce demand for a product. A common use of demarketing is the effort by many electric utilities to provide their customers with tips on how to save energy: insulate their home, use fans instead of air conditioners, install more efficient lighting. Not only do these demarketing efforts help bring demand under

demarketing
An effort to reduce demand for a product.

FIGURE 2.4

Trends in Median Household Income in the United States

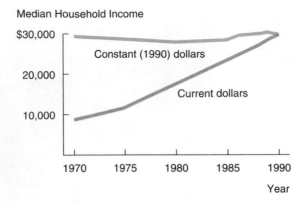

Median Household Income

Source: U.S. Department of Commerce, *Statistical Abstract of the United States,* 112th ed. (Washington, D.C.: U.S. Government Printing Office, 1992), p. 445.

control, they may enhance the utility's public image as an organization concerned about the environment.

CONSUMER INCOME

Although business cycles reflect the overall health of the economy, the income of individual households determines whether or not consumers can—and will—buy products. Marketers are interested in three measures of consumer income: gross income, disposable income, and discretionary income.

gross income
The total amount of money earned in one year by an individual or household.

GROSS INCOME The total amount of money earned in one year by an individual or household is that person's or household's **gross income**. Figure 2.4 shows the median gross income for American households over the two most recent decades. "Current dollars" means the actual dollars the average family earned each year; as the figure shows, this measure of income has steadily risen. In contrast, "1990 dollars" measures the actual purchasing power of family income; in technical terms, it is income adjusted for inflation. This measure has remained rather flat over the period shown in Figure 2.4. In other words, while American households are taking home more dollars now than 20 years ago, their purchasing power has not grown.

Besides showing trends over time, measures of gross income help marketers divide the market into various income groups. Organizations may be interested in targeting consumers at certain income levels. With the slogan "You Know What You're Doing," American Express targets its Optima Card to high-income consumers who can enjoy the attractive interest rate available to those who ring up—and then pay up—big balances.

disposable income
The money an individual or household has left after paying taxes.

DISPOSABLE INCOME As every taxpayer knows, gross income overstates what we can buy. Before we spend a penny, the government takes its cut. **Disposable income** is the money an individual or household has left after paying taxes. This is the money spent on rent or mortgage, groceries, clothing, and any other essentials or luxuries. Obviously, tax rates directly affect disposable income: lower taxes mean more disposable income.

Put It Into Practice

COMPUTE YOUR OWN DISCRETIONARY INCOME

You are a consumer. As a student, you buy the services of your college or university. Most likely, you lease an apartment or other housing from a landlord. You buy groceries at the supermarket or purchase a meal plan. You buy clothing, rent videos, use the telephone, order pizza, send mail. All of these things cost money. You earn or receive a certain income each year (your gross income). Marketers are interested in your disposable income (money left over after taxes) and discretionary income (spending money).

To determine your own discretionary income, first estimate your gross income for *one month* and the taxes you are likely to pay. Subtract your taxes from your gross income; the difference is your disposable income. (If you are a full-time student who does not pay taxes, just use your gross income.) Next write down how much you pay in rent, utilities, groceries, gasoline, and other necessities. Then subtract those expenses from your disposable income to find your monthly discretionary income.

Now write down how you use your spending money: for entertainment? hobbies? sports? extra clothing? When marketers scan the environment, they want to find out not only how much money consumers have to spend, but also how they choose to spend it.

When some expenses rise or fall, people shift the way they spend their remaining disposable income. For example, as energy prices rise, people must spend more of their disposable income on gasoline, heating fuel, electricity, and so forth. This leaves less income for other expenses. Consumers may try to minimize the effect of the higher energy prices by purchasing automobiles that get good gas mileage and other energy-efficient products, from light bulbs to windows.

discretionary income
The money consumers have left to spend after paying taxes and living expenses.

DISCRETIONARY INCOME   The money consumers have left to spend after paying taxes and living expenses is called **discretionary income**. According to the U.S. Census Bureau, 26 million households in the United States have some discretionary income, whereas 57 million do not.[8] The distinction between disposable and discretionary income is somewhat arbitrary because what one person views as a luxury may be a necessity to another. The translation from needs to desires comes into play here: a consumer may need transportation, but the marketer must convince the consumer that he or she wants a car—and a certain make and model at that. But in general, discretionary income pays for vacations, hobbies, entertainment, designer clothing, jewelry, television and music, home decorations and furnishings, gifts, and the like. In other words, discretionary income pays for all the extras. To figure out your own discretionary income, see "Put It into Practice."

The Political and Legal Environment

political-legal environment
The laws, regulations, and social pressure affecting marketers.

Business doesn't function strictly by its own set of rules. It has to answer not only to its customers but also to the federal, state, and local governments, which set the rules in the **political-legal environment**. This dimension of the marketing environment includes laws, regulations, and social pressures affecting marketers. Typically these require organizations to compete fairly and in a manner that doesn't hurt consumers.

Laws and regulations cover many areas relevant to marketers, including packaging, pricing, advertising, and sales to minors. The extensiveness of laws and regulations can make marketing complex. However, laws and regulations can also be a source of opportunity. Efforts of the Environmental Protection Agency to limit the pesticides used

TABLE 2.2
Major Federal Laws Affecting Marketing

LAWS THAT SEEK TO PROMOTE FAIR COMPETITION

Sherman Antitrust Act (1890)	Prohibits monopolies and unreasonable restraint of trade
Clayton Act (1914)	Prohibits actions that substantially limit competition, including exclusive dealing and the tying of a sale to the buyer's promise to buy only from that seller
Federal Trade Commission Act (1914)	Prohibits unfair competition and deceptive trade practices in interstate commerce
Wheeler-Lea Amendent (1938)	Prohibits unfair and deceptive practices, whether or not they damage competitors
Celler-Kefauver Antimerger Act (1950)	Prevents corporate acquisitions that reduce competition
Hart-Scott-Rodino Act (1976)	Requires large companies to notify the government if they intend to merge
Airline Deregulation Act (1978)	Granted commercial airlines greater freedom in setting fares and choosing routes
Motor Carrier Act and Staggers Rail Act (1980)	Permitted trucking and rail firms to negotiate rates and services
Depository Institutions Deregulation and Monetary Control Act (1980)	Permitted all depository insitutions to offer checking accounts; expanded the product offerings available to savings and loan associations; removed ceilings on interest rates paid on customer deposits

LAWS THAT LIMIT PRODUCT STRATEGY

Pure Food and Drug Act (1906)	Controls the quality and labeling of food and drugs in interstate commerce
Wool Products Labeling Act (1939)	Requires labeling of the type and percentage of wool used in products
Fur Products Labeling Act (1951)	Requires that fur products be labeled to indicate from which animal they were made
National Traffic and Safety Act (1958)	Provides for the setting of safety standards for automobiles and tires
Child Protection Act (1966)	Prohibits sale of hazardous toys
Fair Packaging and Labeling Act (1967)	Requires that labels on consumer products identify the product, the supplier's name and address, and (where relevant) the serving size
Consumer Product Safety Act (1972)	Created the Consumer Product Safety Commission to set safety standards for many consumer goods

by farmers have helped persuade many of them to try less toxic alternatives such as ENVIRepel, a garlic solution designed to keep away pests.[9] Thus, the threat to makers of chemical pesticides is an opportunity to suppliers of organic alternatives.

This discussion emphasizes laws and regulations of the U.S. government. State and local laws vary from one location to another. Marketers must be familiar with the foreign, state, and local laws and regulations in effect where they operate. Compliance with laws and regulations is part of the quality approach to marketing. Not only does abiding by them help the organization avoid fines and lawsuits, it promotes confidence among customers and protects the organization's good reputation. Indeed, marketers can use regulations to their advantage. For years, American auto manufacturers resisted putting airbags in their cars, claiming it was too costly. Now that the law requires them to do so, they champion the airbag as an attractive safety feature.

LAWS AFFECTING MARKETING

Although the U.S. government exerts less control over business activities than do other nations, it does set limits in many areas. Its first major effort to regulate business,

Magnuson-Moss Warranty/ FTC Improvement Act (1975)	Authorizes the Federal Trade Commission to make rules for consumer warranties and class-action lawsuits
Nutrition Labeling and Education Act (1990)	Requires that the labels on most food products provide detailed nutrition information

LAWS THAT LIMIT PRICING STRATEGY

Robinson-Patman Act (1936)	Prohibits price discrimination under various circumstances
Miller-Tydings Resale Price Maintenance Act (1937)	Exempts interstate fair-trade (price fixing) agreements from complying with antitrust requirements
Automobile Information Disclosure Act (1958)	Requires manufacturers to post suggested retail prices on cars
Consumer Goods Pricing Act (1975)	Prohibits certain pricing agreements between retailers and manufacturers

LAWS THAT LIMIT CHANNEL STRATEGY

Flammable Fabrics Act (1953)	Prohibits shipment in the United States of any clothing or material that can easily ignite
Fair Credit Reporting Act (1970)	Requires that a consumers' credit reports contain only accurate, relevant, and recent information

LAWS THAT LIMIT COMMUNICATION STRATEGY

Federal Cigarette Labeling and Advertising Act (1967)	Requires cigarette ads and packages to carry a health warning
Truth in Lending Act (1968)	Requires that lenders state the true cost of a loan, including statement of the annual percentage rate in advertisements
Public Health Cigarette Smoking Act (1971)	Prohibits broadcast advertisements of tobacco products
Children's Television Act (1990)	Limits the amount of advertising that may be shown during children's television programs

in the late nineteenth and early twentieth centuries, consisted of laws designed to prevent industry power from being concentrated among a handful of giant firms. These antimonopoly laws included the Sherman Antitrust Act (1890), the Clayton Act (1914), and the Federal Trade Commission Act (1914). During the Great Depression, Congress focused on protecting independent merchants from overwhelming competition by large chain stores. It did so by passing the Robinson-Patman Act (1936) and the Miller-Tydings Resale Price Maintenance Act (1937). Beginning in the 1950s, Congress placed more emphasis on laws designed to protect consumers. These laws included the National Traffic and Safety Act (1958), the Fair Packaging and Labeling Act (1967), and the Consumer Product Safety Act (1972).

The notion that consumers would benefit from industry deregulation became popular in the late 1970s and early 1980s. To lift regulations on specific industries, Congress passed laws such as the Airline Deregulation Act of 1978 and the Depository Institutions Deregulation and Monetary Control Act of 1980. Table 2.2 lists these and other federal laws that govern marketing.

Besides federal laws, marketers must be up-to-date on relevant state and local laws. For example, Maine has banned the sale of individual juice boxes. A

Minneapolis ordinance restricts all packaging to that which is biodegradable or returnable. Consumers can buy fireworks in New Hampshire, *but only if they live elsewhere;* they cannot buy fireworks to use in New Hampshire.

Voters also can pass laws affecting marketers. In state and local elections, they can decide such issues as whether smoking is to be allowed in restaurants; whether liquor can be sold in certain towns, in certain places, or on certain days; whether stores may stay open on holidays or Sundays; by what year all designated hazardous waste sites must be cleaned up; whether special taxes should be levied on cigarettes and gasoline; and where billboards may be placed.

REGULATION OF MARKETING

regulations
Rules that are written by government agencies and have the force of law.

When legislatures pass a law, they may set up an agency to enforce that law. The agency then writes **regulations**, which are rules that have the force of law. Thus, even though regulations are prepared by the executive rather than the legislative branch of government, we are legally bound to abide by them. Regulations can apply to advertising, manufacturing, distribution, pricing, sales, and all other areas of business.

FEDERAL, STATE, AND LOCAL REGULATIONS   At the federal level, many agencies regulate business. For example, the Federal Trade Commission (FTC) seeks to prevent "unfair methods of competition" and "unfair or deceptive acts or practices,"[10] and the Food and Drug Administration (FDA) regulates the distribution and sale of foods and medicines to ensure that they are safe and marketed honestly. Thus, under commissioner David Kessler, the FDA seized 2,400 cases of Citrus Hill "Fresh Choice" orange juice because the word *fresh* was misleading on orange juice made from concentrate. It also sent warnings to marketers of vegetable fats who labeled their 100 percent fat products "no cholesterol," a factual claim that could mislead consumers concerned about heart disease.[11]

Regulation is also conducted at the state and local levels. For instance, local zoning laws limit where a store may open. Sometimes federal and state regulations conflict with each other. The Massachusetts Department of Environmental Protection's definition of wetlands differs from federal guidelines, making it difficult to determine whether a piece of property may be developed. State laws also differ. A national mail-order company must collect the proper sales tax from its customers who live in different states, which have different tax rates.

REGULATION OF INDUSTRIES   Many marketers must comply with regulations aimed specifically at their industry. For example, the Food and Drug Administration has required grocery stores to post nutrition information on the 20 best-selling fruit, vegetable, and raw seafood items.[12] Insurers and others in the health care industry are sure to be affected by health care reform, whatever form it ultimately takes. And the banking industry is still subject to many regulations, despite the deregulation of 1980. For example, commercial banks may make residential mortgage loans and issue credit cards, but they may not engage in real estate development. How much they may lend to one borrower also is limited.[13]

At the state and local levels, banking regulation can become even more complex. In New Jersey, for instance, banks once could conduct business only along county lines. Later the state established three banking districts, then finally allowed banks to operate statewide.[14]

SELF-REGULATION In many industries, organizations have recognized that they have more control over their operations if they regulate themselves well enough that voters and legislators will not step in and set limits. To regulate themselves, organizations use industry groups to set and enforce standards. They may set standards for ethical behavior (discussed in Chapter 3) and for dealing with customer complaints. The Better Business Bureau and the American Medical Association, for example, lack legal authority but are nonetheless powerful regulators.

An industry or single organization may work in conjunction with a number of groups that help establish self-regulation and thus promote a positive, responsible image. Anheuser-Busch, which makes Budweiser beer, works with the National Commission Against Drunk Driving to sponsor ads that promote responsible drinking. Industry groups even at times attempt to influence legislation, as described in the next section.

Some people charge that self-regulation is like asking the fox to guard the chicken coop, and certainly abuses do occur. Ideally, however, self-regulation by those who know the industry intimately can be both intelligent and effective. An industry that monitors itself closely promotes quality in its products, its processes, and its people. For example, when unsubstantiated rumors began to link brain cancer to the use of cellular telephones, the Cellular Telecommunications Industry Association promised to fund research into their safety, thereby sending a message of responsibility and concern for customers' welfare.[15]

INFLUENCES ON LAWS AND REGULATIONS

Of course, the legislators and regulators who develop laws and regulations are influenced by outside forces. For example, public pressure has encouraged legislators to trim defense spending, which in turn has forced defense contractors to adjust their marketing mixes to appeal more to buyers in the private sector. Primary sources of influence in the political/legal sphere include lobbyists and consumer interest groups.

LOBBYISTS Because laws and regulations are so far reaching, individuals and organizations wish to influence government officials. Yet it's not practical to call one's senator every time an important bill comes up for a vote. Rather, organizations use lobbyists to represent their views to government officials. Lobbyists represent big corporations, industry trade groups, and public-interest organizations of all kinds. For example the American Medical Association seeks to influence government leaders and the public about the form healthcare reform should take.

Lobbyists, like the politicians they work with, tend to have a bad name these days. Sometimes they advocate actions that are not in the best interests of the population as a whole. However, most of us belong to, support, or at least sympathize with some of the organizations that lobby public officials. Perhaps some of your family members belong to a large church body that has representatives in Washington, D.C., or the American Association of Retired Persons. The AARP is not only a lobby working for people 50 and older, but it provides services and publishes the *AARP Bulletin* and *Modern Maturity* magazine. And if you want your employer to flourish (and continue paying you), you may be glad that your employer's trade group is lobbying for laws favorable to it.

CONSUMER INTEREST GROUPS One reason that legislators pass laws regulating business practices is that consumers urge them to. Thus, consumers and consumer

FIGURE 2.5

Marketing Influential: Ralph Nader

consumerism
A social force intended to protect the consumer by exerting legal, moral, and economic pressures on the business community.

groups are an important force in the political-legal environment. **Consumerism** is a social force intended to protect the consumer by exerting legal, moral, and economic pressures on the business community.[16] Consumerism took a solid hold in the American consciousness during the 1960s. In 1962, President John F. Kennedy made a statement of four consumer rights:

1. *The right to choose freely.*—Consumers should have the freedom to choose from among a variety of goods and services.
2. *The right to be informed.*—Consumers should be informed about products so that they can be responsible buyers.
3. *The right to be heard.*—Consumers should have the opportunity to express their complaints to sellers as well as to government regulatory agencies.
4. *The right to be safe.*—Consumers should be able to be confident that goods and services they purchase are not harmful (with normal use). Products should be designed so that they can easily be used safely.

U.S. consumers today widely consider these rights to be a minimal standard of acceptable quality.

Perhaps no single person has done more to influence marketing by crusading for consumer rights than Ralph Nader (see Figure 2.5). The founder or supporter of more than 30 separate consumer interest groups, Nader has actively campaigned for legislation regulating auto and highway safety, insurance rates, water safety, pension rights, responsible genetics, and occupational safety, just to name a few. Some of his better-known organizations include the Public Safety Research Institute, Center for Auto Safety, Public Interest Research Groups, Public Citizen, Inc., and Citizens Television System, Inc.[17] Although Nader is extremely popular among the general public, he has not escaped controversy. Lawyers who specialize in personal injury lawsuits are among his best supporters. "We support him overtly, covertly, in every way possible," says one who earned around $6 million in a single year.[18] But there is no doubt that Nader has raised the consciousness of consumers and marketers in the United States.

The North American Free Trade Agreement, passed by the U.S. Congress in November 1993, became effective on January 1, 1994. NAFTA is North America's strategic response to the global economy.

Consumerism dovetails nicely with the quality approach to marketing. It stands to reason that, in their efforts to please customers, marketers will communicate truthfully and do their best to offer products that are safe, nutritious, nonpolluting, and otherwise beneficial. Organizations that adopt a quality focus will also give consumers plenty of opportunity to be heard as they seek to anticipate and meet consumer needs.

COURT ACTIONS

As noted already, the laws and regulations affecting marketing come from the legislative and executive branches of government. The third branch—the judicial branch—also affects marketing through the ways judges interpret these laws and regulations. For example, the U.S. Supreme Court upheld a federal law forbidding advertisers from broadcasting ads for lotteries in states that ban lotteries.[19] If the court had instead affirmed the lower-court ruling against this law, lottery officials would have had more freedom in planning an advertising strategy.

Other court actions lead to opportunities for new goods and services. A recent Supreme Court ruling questioned the constitutionality of affirmative-action programs in which local governments set aside a portion of contracts for minority businesses. The court held that the programs could be challenged unless they meet stringent statistical criteria showing that discrimination exists. Numerous consulting firms have seen the necessary statistical research as an important new service they can offer to local governments.[20]

POLITICAL AND LEGAL FACTORS IN THE GLOBAL ENVIRONMENT

International marketers are affected by agreements between countries and by the laws in every country in which they operate. Perhaps the most vital political and legal factors in the global environment are international trade agreements. For example, the North American Free Trade Agreement is designed to drop trade barriers among Canada, the United States, and Mexico through such means as the elimination of tariffs, or taxes paid on goods imported from the nations participating in the agreement. Similar objectives were behind the establishment of free trade within the 12 European nations that formed the European Community. Other international agreements are important as well. Britain and China signed an agreement for Britain to transfer Hong Kong to Chinese rule in 1997. That agreement has made it politically important for Hong Kong–based Cathay Pacific Airways to shift from being perceived as a British airline to a Chinese one, so it has transferred some of its operations to the People's Republic of China.[21] Finally, marketers also must know and abide by local laws and customs.

Strict licensing and distribution requirements of local and foreign businesses also affect marketers abroad. Consider one California store owner who thought he had a terrific idea when he decided to order 30 tons of Science Diet dog food from his regular distributor to resell to retailers in Japan. Because he was ordering more of the food, he thought he was helping the dog food manufacturer as well as his own business. The makers of Science Diet didn't see it that way. "I was completely astounded that just because my orders increased, [Science Diet officials] wanted to know who I was selling to," the retailer explained. The fact was, the Hills Division of Colgate-Palmolive Co., manufacturers of Science Diet, already had a distributor in Japan, and the California retailer had traveled out of bounds. He was ordered to stop.[22]

The Social Environment

social environment
The current or potential customers of an organization, as measured in terms of demographics and values.

The **social environment** of marketing is made up of potential or existing customers of the organization. Marketers describe this environment in terms of who the people are (their ages, incomes, hometowns, and so forth) and what values they hold. Changes in the social environment, whether subtle or dramatic, can present marketers with new opportunities and challenges.

DEMOGRAPHIC TRENDS

demographics
The study of the characteristics of a human population.

To describe the social environment, marketers begin with basic demographic data. **Demographics** is the study of the characteristics of a human population. These characteristics include age, birth rate, death rate, marital status, education, religious affiliation, ethnic background, immigration, geographical distribution, and so forth. Typically, marketers combine data about several demographic characteristics. Thus, it isn't enough to know how many people moved to San Diego in a given year. Marketers can better identify potential target markets if they know how many of those people are retired, are single parents, or are able to afford restaurant meals.

Marketers use demographic data from a number of sources. Government agencies, including the U.S. Bureau of the Census, the National Center for Health Statistics, the Bureau of Labor Statistics, and the Social Security Administration, are major suppliers of data on the U.S. population. Private organizations such as the Roper Organization and the Gallup Poll provide valuable demographic statistics as well. For example, the Roper Organization reported that "the biggest fans of American cars are aged 50 and older, residents of the South and Midwest, people in nonmetropolitan areas, those with a high-school education or less, and those who earn less than $30,000 a year."[23] Publications such as *American Demographics* also offer useful demographic information. A large organization may employ its own demographers to help analyze its markets.

Marketers use demographics to analyze their markets, learn about customers, and satisfy those customers. Pinpointing changes or trends in the population is vital to marketing strategy. According to "Dr. Demo," the answer columnist for *American Demographics,* the "demographer's real goal is understanding the causes and consequences of population change."[24] Such research told marketers at Oscar Mayer and the other lunch food companies mentioned earlier in this chapter how many Americans were "brown bagging." In 1984, the average American took 42 meals from home, 71 percent of which were sandwiches. By 1992, workers were carrying 53 meals from home, but only 58 percent of those meals were sandwiches.[25] These simple data told marketers that not only were more Americans taking their own meals to work, but the *contents* of those meals were changing.

TRENDS IN THE UNITED STATES   Large shifts in the population, such as the changing American family, are of major interest to marketers. During the 1950s, 70 percent of American families consisted of a stay-at-home mother, a working father, and one or two children. By the late 1980s, only 21 percent of American households fit this mold.[26] Today's families include blended families (the merging of two families through a second marriage or relationship), single-parent families, adoptive or foster parent families, and gay families. Even the composition of single-parent families is changing; although 88 percent of children of divorce still live with their mothers, men are now being awarded custody more often.[27] And although 60 percent of single

FIGURE 2.6

Percent Change in Population Growth: 1990–2010

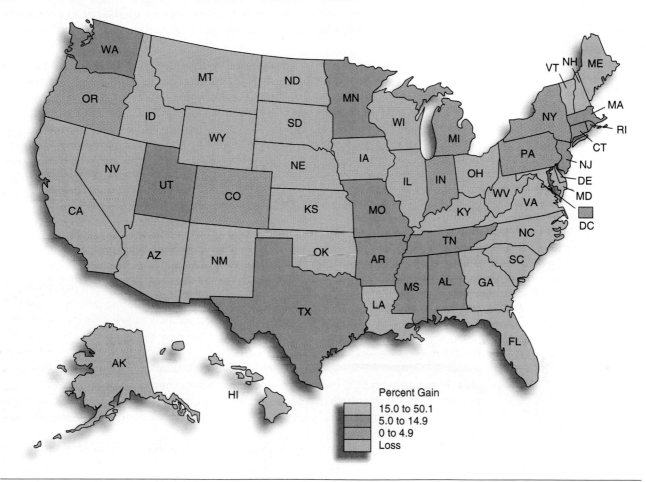

Percent Gain
15.0 to 50.1
5.0 to 14.9
0 to 4.9
Loss

Source: U.S. Bureau of the Census, Current Population Reports, Series P–25, No. 1053, *Projections of the Population of States by Age, Sex, and Race: 1989 to 2010* (Washington, D.C.: U.S. Government Printing Office, 1990), p. 13.

fathers are divorced, 25 percent have never been married, creating still another category of single-parent family.[28]

Another important shift has to do with changes in the age distribution of the U.S. population. The so-called baby boom generation, people born between 1946 and 1964, is so large that roughly half the population was under 28 in 1970, and almost half are expected to be 40 or older in the year 2010.[29] As this group ages, the demand for various products, such as houses, child care, and mutual funds, is likely to change. In addition, many marketers are beginning to focus on the younger generation— sometimes called baby busters or Generation X—because the typical member of this age group has not yet sacrificed discretionary income to house payments and the expenses of raising children.[30] For more details on these trends, see Chapter 10.

As illustrated in Figure 2.6, the geographical distribution of the U.S. population has shifted as well. During the 1980s, the population grew fastest in the western and southwestern states, with the southeastern states close behind. In contrast, the population of a few states actually fell. Some marketers use these data to engage in what has been termed **regional marketing,** which focuses on the specific tastes, needs, and interests of residents of a particular area. Regional marketing can target a broad region such as Thailand or the southern United States, or it can be further focused—say, to encompass only residents of Minneapolis or even of particular neighborhoods.

regional marketing
Marketing that focuses on the specific tastes, needs, and interests of residents of a particular area.

GLOBAL TRENDS   The demographic characteristics of foreign countries are important to marketers who do not limit their vision to serving domestic customers. For instance, the population size of the Pacific Rim—Asia and Australia—makes it an attractive market for many U.S. firms. Nearly 2 billion people live in Asia, and although many live in poverty, it is estimated that by the year 2000, more than 110 million (excluding those in Japan) will have household incomes of more than $10,000.[31] This income may sound low compared to American earnings, but in some Asian countries, such as Nepal, average annual household income is less than $200. In addition, before the year 2000, about one-third of this population will be at the prime purchasing age of 30 to 40 years old.[32]

CULTURE: VALUES AND LANGUAGE

Of course, demographic data alone do not tell marketers enough about potential customers. For example, it is not enough to know how many retirees are in an area. A marketer for a museum would also want information such as what these people like to do with their time and whether they like to learn new things. One way marketers get more information is to study the values of cultures and subcultures. **Cultural values** are the principles, qualities, or beliefs that members of a culture consider desirable. In mainstream U.S. culture, people value achievement, progress, individualism, and freedom. Other values of American culture include efficiency, progress, humanitarianism, and youthfulness (although as the baby boom generation ages, this last value may change somewhat).[33]

cultural values
The principles, qualities, or beliefs that members of a culture consider desirable.

While these values may seem abstract, they have a direct relationship to marketing. The classic example of a promotional strategy appealing to individualism—nonconformity, self-reliance, being true to oneself—is the long-running series of Marlboro Man advertisements for the cigarette of that name.

When serving foreign markets, marketers must be aware that every society has its own values, many different from those held by the majority of Americans.[34] For example, other cultures do not share the U.S. infatuation with change and may instead uphold customs and traditions unless the benefits of changing are obvious. Likewise, while the dominant U.S. culture values individual achievement, most Asian nations and most Hispanic cultures tend to promote group harmony and frown on showing off. Thus, Procter & Gamble stumbled when it ran comparative advertising in Japan, showing how its detergents made clothes brighter than the competing brands. The Japanese considered the ads impolite.[35] As described in the "You Decide" box, value differences are one of the major challenges facing the Euro Disney Resort.

According to Judie Lannon, research and development director for advertising agency J. Walter Thompson–Europe, cultural differences are especially important for marketers of food and drink. For example, in Europe alone, there are several "coffee cultures." In Spain and Italy, people drink tiny amounts of very strong coffee. France offers greater variety; the French drink coffee in larger amounts and link it more to their cuisine. In Britain, coffee is not a part of the culture; tea is.[36]

You Decide

WHAT WENT WRONG AT EURO DISNEY?

In April 1992 the Euro Disney Resort, operated by Euro Disney S.C.A., opened its gates just east of Paris, near a small village called Coupvray. By late summer, *Le Royaume Magique* was dubbed a disaster. The French had spent $1 billion to extend a suburban train line to the park; they designated a separate station for the park on this high-speed train line. They prohibited other theme parks from being built in the area, and they gave Walt Disney Co. (half owner of the project) the opportunity to buy a parcel of land roughly equal to one-fifth the size of Paris to build all the hotels, restaurants, rides, and exhibits it wanted. Marketers determined that 11 million guests would show up during the first year. They were way off. What went wrong?

Although millions of visitors have come to the park, the proportion of French visitors—projected to be the core customers—was far below expectations. "The prices are excessive, unjustifiable," complained Gilles Sultan, one Frenchman who did attend. "I've been here for two days,

and I've spent 9,000 francs [$1,885] . . . They gave discounts to everyone else in Europe," he went on. "But the French got nothing. They figured we would come because it was so close. But they were wrong."

"Nine thousand francs is what a French middle-class family makes in a month and a half," explained his wife. They were able to attend the park because they had obtained discount entrance tickets from Mrs. Sultan's employer, Renault (which sponsored a Euro Disney attraction). The high cost is an especially important problem because the park opened during a long period of recession in Europe.

But price was not the only problem, in the view of the Sultans. So was Disney's failure to account for a long-standing French tradition: the month-long August vacation. "[Disney] complains that nobody came in August. Of course not! August is for vacations, not for coming to Euro Disney," remarked Mr. Sultan.

Another deterrent was fear of traffic jams and big crowds. Euro Disney's own publicity efforts only added to this worry. And the locals, too, complained. Alain Boulet, an official from Coupvray, said Coupvray "is no longer a rural village. We're becoming a suburb of Paris."

Euro Disney's management reacted to the disappointing performance of the resort by postponing expansion plans and closing one of its hotels for the winter. Somewhere, the company failed in its scanning of the marketing environment. What factors do you think it neglected to take into account? In what ways could Disney have scanned the environment more thoroughly? How could the company use such information to improve park attendance?

Sources: Peter Gumbel and David J. Jefferson, "Disney Continues Drive to Expand World-Wide," *The Wall Street Journal,* November 20, 1992, p. B4; Patrick Oster, "The Mouse That Didn't Roar," *Business Week,* October 19, 1992; and "Euro Disneyland Wishes for First Profit Next Year," *Chicago Tribune,* April 18, 1993, sec. 7, p. 11.

RECENT TRENDS   Economic and social forces may cause cultural values to change. For example, in recent years more women have entered the U.S. workplace than in any period since World War II (17 million women were in the work force in 1947, compared to 54 million in 1990). Accompanying this trend, attitudes toward working women have become more positive.[37] But greater time and energy are required to run a single-parent or two-wage-earner household. That fact may underlie the current appeal of "cocooning," or seeking the comforts of life at home rather than going out for entertainment. Table 2.3 summarizes some major shifts that have been observed in common Western values.

Marketers strive to keep up with these changing values. For example, cocooning has led marketers to promote home furnishings,[38] and it is blamed for declining attendance at movie theaters. The workplace has seen a trend away from rigid hierarchies and formality and toward cooperation and teamwork. Reflecting that value shift, businessmen wear suits to work less often, forcing sellers of formal business attire to diversify their product offerings.[39]

Another widely reported trend is that Americans are growing more health conscious. People have always valued being healthy, of course, but modern consumers

TABLE 2.3	TRADITIONAL VALUES	NEW VALUES
Major Shifts in Western Values	Self-denial ethic	Self-fulfillment ethic
	Higher standard of living	Better quality of life
	Traditional sex roles	Blurring of sex roles
	Accepted definition of success	Individualized definition of success
	Traditional family life	Alternative families
	Faith in industry, institutions	Self-reliance
	Live to work	Work to live
	Hero worship	Love of ideas
	Expansionism	Pluralism
	Patriotism	Less nationalistic
	Unparalleled growth	Growing sense of limits
	Industrial growth	Information/service growth
	Receptivity to technology	Technology orientation

Source: Reproduced from "Changing Values: The New Emphasis on Self-Actualization," *The Futurist,* January–February 1989, p. 15, published by the World Future Society, 7910 Woodmont Ave., Ste. 450, Bethesda, MD 20814.

accept the notion that they are responsible for improving their health through diet and exercise. Marketers have responded with a multitude of products: workout equipment and clothing, health clubs and gyms, diet programs, and healthful foods. Whether consumers' health consciousness will translate into longstanding healthful behavior remains to be seen, however. Recent data indicate slow growth in sales of low-fat, low-sodium foods, along with few new introductions in that category. At the same time, consumers are snapping up Häagen-Dazs Triple Brownie Overload ice cream and Wendy Melt sandwiches. Some observers credit this behavior to a search for comfort food during stressful times.[40] Others say a demand for fatty foods and a decline in strenuous exercise reflect aging baby boomers' weariness with the pursuit of fitness.[41]

Since the first Earth Day in 1970, environmentalism has steadily gained value in the United States. As evidence, a recent report showed that the amount of grocery product packaging thrown away by Americans fell by 18 percent over a decade.[42] Whereas environmentalists were once considered extremists, environmentalism is now big business. For example, McDonald's uses paper instead of Styrofoam cups and boxes, and the Shaw's supermarket chain rebates its customers five cents for each paper grocery bag they reuse. The next chapter further examines environmentalism and marketing.

The quality approach to marketing is another response to current values. Today's overburdened buyers don't want the bother of fixing or replacing shoddy merchandise or of contending with poor service.

 LANGUAGE   In communicating across national borders, the language barrier is a cultural factor that poses an added challenge. Mistakes when developing product names or advertisements can be downright embarrassing. A classic example is the marketing in Latin America of GM's Nova, which in Spanish means "doesn't go." In spite of the frequency with which this example is cited, marketers are still making mistakes. For instance, a company marketing tomato paste in the Middle East discovered that in Arabic, "tomato paste" translated to the not-so-appealing "tomato glue,"

and in Spain Chrysler translated the advertising slogan "Dart Is Power" into a phrase that implied buyers were seeking but lacking in sexual vigor.[43]

The Institutional Environment

Typically, the organizations that produce goods and services rely on other organizations to help make those products available to customers. For example, automakers need a network of dealers to sell their cars to consumers, and they need trucks and ships to carry the cars to the dealers. They also may work with a variety of other outside experts who handle such marketing activities as advertising and marketing research.

institutional environment
Marketing intermediaries and their activities.

Organizations that handle these activities are broadly defined as "marketing intermediaries," and they and their activities make up the **institutional environment**. The major players in the institutional environment are resellers, physical distribution firms, marketing services agencies, and financial intermediaries. Chapters 16 and 17 take a more detailed look at most aspects of the institutional environment.

RESELLERS

Imagine you are a marketer at a company that makes greeting cards. How would you make those cards available for sale? Would you hire a multitude of salespeople to carry the cards up and down city streets and quiet suburban neighborhoods, hoping to sell a few? Probably not. It would be an expensive way to find people who are looking for a birthday card. More likely, you would try to persuade stores with greeting-card sections to carry your line. The success of your marketing activities would depend in part on their willingness to do so, as well as on their ability to work closely with you to determine which cards to carry and when to order more.

Stores such as this are one type of resellers. Marketers also use resellers to make goods and services available to organizational buyers, including other resellers. For example, a company that makes nails and screws might sell to a distributor that travels the country selling hardware to stores.

In scanning the environment, marketers seek to learn about the resellers already operating. Marketers are interested in which resellers will distribute their products most effectively, be willing to carry their products, and be able to work with their suppliers.

PHYSICAL DISTRIBUTION FIRMS

Marketers of tangible goods must arrange to have them transported to the customer, be it a reseller, organizational buyer, or consumer. The process of moving tangible goods is called physical distribution. It may involve sending a pair of pants from Lands' End via UPS or shipping an ocean liner full of raisins from California to Russia. UPS and the operator of the ocean liner are physical distribution firms. Such firms may also handle related tasks, such as storing and keeping track of inventory or providing advice on the most efficient way to send a large shipment.

In scanning this portion of the environment, marketers seek to learn what organizations are available to help with the distribution of goods. For example, some marketers would be interested in the ability of modern cargo aircraft to transport a Formula One car across 5,200 miles of ocean in less than 14 hours (see Figure 2.7). Marketers also need to learn about technological developments that may make it possible to ship goods faster or cheaper. For example, emerging high-speed rail lines

FIGURE 2.7

Services Offered by a Physical Distribution Firm

might make railroads an efficient alternative for delivering goods quickly within some range of distances.

MARKETING SERVICES AGENCIES

The organizations that provide marketing services include marketing research firms, advertising agencies, media firms, and marketing consulting firms. These organizations can help the marketer select target markets and implement an effective marketing strategy. The marketer needs to keep track of what services are available and which agencies are best skilled in providing the services needed. Thus, part of environmental scanning includes periodic performance reviews of marketing services agencies.

FINANCIAL INTERMEDIARIES

Carrying out marketing activities requires money. Therefore, the organization's success may depend in part on the availability of funding from such financial intermediaries as banks, credit companies, and insurance companies. For businesses, the major lenders in the United States used to be banks. Today, however, over three-quarters of business loans come from other institutions, including life insurers, brokerage firms, and finance companies.[44]

If the cost of credit goes up or its availability shrinks, the marketer's plans may be in jeopardy. Thus, even if handling financing is not the marketer's direct responsibility, marketers must be aware of financial conditions.

The Technological Environment

Scientific knowledge, research, inventions, and innovations that result in new or improved goods and services all make up the **technological environment** of market-

FIGURE 2.8

Building Demand for a Product That Uses New Technology

technological environment
Scientific knowledge, research, inventions, and innovations that result in new or improved goods and services.

ing. Technological developments provide important opportunities to organizations that can use them to meet customer needs. For example, advances in manufacturing technology have enabled businesses to adopt "flexible manufacturing," meeting precise needs with short production runs. As a result, small manufacturers can now enter markets that were once too expensive to serve.[45]

When the organization fails to keep up with technological change, technology becomes a threat. IBM's dominance of the market for large mainframe computers did not spare the company from posting a huge loss when customers found they could get all the computing power they needed from modern personal computers.[46] To succeed in an industry so volatile, computer makers try to innovate continually.

When their products incorporate new technology, marketers must try to create demand for them. In the mid-1980s, marketers had to convince record buyers to switch over to CDs. The superior quality of the products themselves—better sound, greater longevity—helped bring consumers around. Also, as fewer records were manufactured, consumers had to make a change. Technological developments continued, and manufacturers introduced minidiscs and digital compact cassettes. Again they need to build demand for their new products (see the ad in Figure 2.8).

Keeping up with technological developments is especially important for marketers who serve business customers. These buyers may rely on technological innovations for their very survival in a competitive marketplace. Familiarity with modern technology helps marketers develop products that meet new needs or meet the old needs better. Intergraph Corporation offers computer technology that enables businesses to maintain a competitive edge by using cross-functional teams in the development of new products. Team members can share data and detailed images on their computers, even if they are located in different countries and use different computer hardware.

TECHNOLOGICAL FACTORS IN THE GLOBAL ENVIRONMENT

 The level of technology available in a foreign country affects marketers developing and producing goods and services. In the grocery industry, Spanish consumers of the early 1990s pressured grocery chains for the convenience of fast checkouts through the use of scanners. In 1983, there were only 29 scanning stores in the country; by 1991, there were 4,653.[47] South Korea's Daewoo group turned to Russia for the technology to manufacture a 100-pound, pilotless helicopter. It is used for spraying pesticides in a number of countries, including Thailand, Vietnam, and the United States.[48]

Many U.S. companies that want to operate manufacturing plants, restaurants, and the like abroad must first clear some technological hurdles. When PepsiCo signed an agreement with two Ukrainian partners to allow it to open Pizza Hut units throughout Ukraine, it had to upgrade the existing food-processing standards, especially for the substandard meat and dairy products available there.[49]

TECHNOLOGY AND QUALITY

Organizations use technology to improve the quality of their products, production processes, distribution, communications, pricing techniques, and marketing research. When used appropriately, technological advances can help organizations better serve their customers. For instance, the science of biomimetics studies ways to mimic nature—that is, to imitate biological materials. One British zoologist has created a fiberglass resin composite that closely resembles wood; it is lightweight but tough enough to absorb the impact from a speeding bullet. Other researchers are studying the silk of spiders to find out what makes it water and snow resistant. If they can mimic it, they may be able to create a fabric ideal for protective clothing. Although biomimetics has its critics, its implications for the world of manufacturing are profound.[50]

Pitney Bowes used technology to develop a high-tech postage meter called the Paragon that has helped to transform the company "from a stodgy office equipment supplier into a technologically sophisticated manufacturer with its sights set on growth."[51] The Paragon automatically seals letters, weighs them, prints the appropriate amount of postage on the corner, and shoots them out at the astonishing rate of 240 letters per minute, saving the average mail room as much as three worker-hours of sorting each day.[52]

Technology has been behind many of the quality improvements at Granite Rock, a northern California company that manufactures rock, sand and gravel aggregates, and ready-mix concrete and asphalt. One notable development there is GraniteXpress, a 24-hour automated system for dispensing rock at the company's quarry. The process cut loading time by 70 percent, which reduces costs for Granite's customers, who spend upwards of $1 per minute to operate a truck. In addition, Granite Rock improved its delivery time and achieved an extremely high quality standard for its concrete. "The pursuit of quality is like a stairway," notes Bruce Woolpert, co-president and CEO. "You move up one step at a time and set a new platform so you won't go backward. It's a journey without end."[53]

The Competitive Environment

It is extremely rare for an organization to be the sole supplier of a particular good or service. Therefore, marketers must find out what their competitors are doing and predict what they might do in the future. These activities concern the **competitive environment**—

Technology is behind quality improvements at AT&T. Wireless, small enough to wear on your wrist, yet powerful enough to reach anyone, anywhere in the world, the strap-on telephone represents this type of innovation.

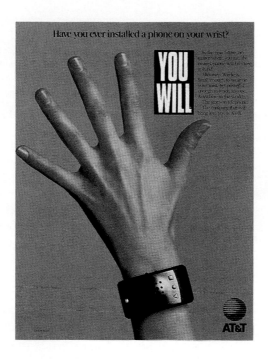

competitive environment
All the organizations that could satisfy the needs and desires of their target markets.

all the organizations that could potentially satisfy the needs and desires of the organization's target markets. In scanning the competitive environment, marketers must remember to consider existing or potential competition from foreign as well as local organizations. Bank of America was able to maintain a strong position by recognizing that its major competitors were not other U.S. banks, but bigger and stronger banks based in Japan and Europe.

TYPES OF COMPETITION

The nature of the competitive environment depends in part on the type of competition that occurs there. Economists describe four main types of competition: pure competition, monopolistic competition, oligopoly, and monopoly.

pure competition
The type of competition that occurs when similar products are offered and buyers and sellers are familiar with and can easily enter the market.

   Pure competition occurs when similar products are offered, buyers and sellers are familiar with the market, and both buyers and sellers can easily enter the market. Examples include the markets for farm goods and forestry products. In this form of competition, marketers compete almost entirely on the basis of price.

monopolistic competition
The type of competition that occurs when there are many sellers of a product and each has a relatively small market share.

   Monopolistic competition occurs when there are many sellers of a product and each has a relatively small market share. For example, banks compete with other banks, credit unions, and savings and loan institutions, to provide financial services to individuals and businesses. Monopolistic competition is the most common form of competition in our economy, and it forces marketers to find ways to distinguish their products. Banks use their locations, personnel, interest rates, and other features to differentiate themselves from their competitors.

oligopoly
The type of competition that occurs when products are similar and a few sellers control most of the market.

   Oligopoly occurs when products are similar and a few sellers control most of the market. Examples are air travel and long-distance telephone service. (Notice that these are industries with high start-up costs; that's a major reason for the small number of competitors.)

FIGURE 2.9

Types of Competitive Forces

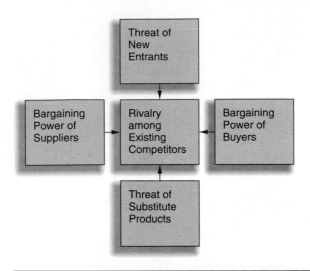

Source: Adapted with permission from Michael E. Porter "Industry Structure and Competitive Strategy: Keys to Profitability," *Financial Analysts Journal,* July–August 1980. Copyright 1980, The Financial Analysts Federation, Charlottesville, VA. All rights reserved.

monopoly
A market in which only one organization sells a good or service.

In some cases, a single entity maintains a **monopoly** on a product—that is, it is the only organization selling the good or service. A monopoly organization has great control over the prices it charges. However, monopolies are rare in our economy. Until the government ordered its breakup into smaller units, AT&T had a monopoly on the telephone communications market in the United States. Likewise, electric utilities once held monopolies in the regions they served, but a recent federal law permits independent power producers to send electricity over the big utilities' transmission lines. This allows the (often cheaper) independents to break the monopolies.[54] Some products enjoy temporary monopolies (as in the case of a drug with patent protection) or most of the market share (as has Gatorade for years, recently holding 90 percent of the market for sports drinks[55]).

COMPETITIVE FORCES

Given that most organizations have at least a few competitors, marketers must consider how these competitors can affect the organization. For example, perhaps a new company will begin marketing a competing product, as in the case of a new maker of IBM-compatible personal computers. Or perhaps an organization will begin marketing new goods or services that take away sales from an existing product, as CD players drove down sales of record turntables. One way to evaluate the competitive forces affecting organizations is to categorize them into five types: rivalry among existing competitors, threat of new entrants, threat of substitute products, bargaining power of suppliers, and bargaining power of buyers.[56] These are illustrated in Figure 2.9.

RIVALRY AMONG EXISTING COMPETITORS To develop a successful marketing strategy for a product, a marketer needs to be aware of existing competitors. Who are the major competitors? What are their annual sales? How much of the market do they control? What are their strengths and weaknesses? What are their marketing strategies? With answers to such questions, a marketer can draw customers away from competitors through superior strategies for pricing, advertising, sales promotion, customer service, and other activities.

THREAT OF NEW ENTRANTS   Unless the government forbids it, there is always a possibility that a new competitor will enter the market for a product. Once the British government gave up control of that nation's telecommunications industry, British Telecom knew that eventually AT&T and others would move in.[57] The threat of new entrants is especially great when an earlier company's success signals a demand for its product. For example, the ability of four young men to sell 65,000 copies each month of *The Source,* a magazine about rap music and hip-hop culture, led media giant Time Warner to test an issue of a competing magazine called *Vibe.* Although Time Warner's staff lacked the insider's view of *The Source,* the company's financial clout enabled it to land major advertisers.

Some markets are easier to enter than others. Barriers to entry might include a need for heavy financial investment or years of experience to reduce the cost of production. For instance, the start-up cost for a new automobile manufacturer would be a lot higher than that for a restaurant. Industries with low entry barriers are more likely to have new entrants and, thus, more competitors.

THREAT OF SUBSTITUTE PRODUCTS   Broadly speaking, all sellers in an industry are competing with sellers who offer substitute products. For instance, officials who operate a suburban bus line into a major city are competing with trains and automobiles for commuter dollars.

The availability of substitutes helps cap the prices of some products. A price that's too high (compared to the competition) may ultimately be unprofitable. Thus, if a business finds that buying accounting software and hiring a part-time bookkeeper is cheaper than paying fees to an accounting firm, the accounting firm will lose sales to the software maker. Likewise, Solar Steam Inc. of Fox Island, Washington, has had trouble finding buyers for its solar energy devices, in part because prices for other sources of energy are relatively low.[58]

BARGAINING POWER OF SUPPLIERS   Suppliers are a key competitive force because they can determine the price or quality of parts or raw materials. When a few suppliers control a large share of the market, as in an oligopoly, buyers may have to accept a price increase or a disappointing level of quality. However, more and more organizations today are looking for suppliers willing to work closely with them, especially to improve quality. An increasingly important type of arrangement is like the one between Harley-Davidson and Parker Hannifin. In supporting Harley-Davidson's drive to improve quality, Parker Hannifin has worked closely with this customer to provide manufacturing technology for its factories and seals for the motorcycles' braking systems.

Sometimes a successful supplier purchases a firm it once supplied. For example, a big printing firm might decide to start publishing as well as printing trade journals. If it bought a publisher of technical magazines, the supplier would become a new competitor in the market.

BARGAINING POWER OF BUYERS   Buyers can force prices down, bargain for higher quality or more services, and set competitors against each other. Whereas a small buyer may have to live with a price increase from a supplier, a large buyer may have the clout to request a lower price. Buyers also can purchase a firm that supplies them or purchase another firm within the supplier's industry.

COMPETITION IN THE GLOBAL ENVIRONMENT

Like Coca-Cola, many U.S. companies have striven to enter the global market. As of 1992, one in three U.S. franchisers had licensed foreign outlets. And according to a survey of 366 franchisers by Arthur Andersen & Co., half of the franchisers without existing foreign outlets planned to establish them within the next five years.[59] One of the reasons for this expansion is an overcrowded U.S. market. "Why take on Chicago when I can go to Brazil and find a virgin market?" commented Gary L. Copp, president of Spee Dee Oil Change Systems.[60]

Just as American firms are aggressively entering foreign markets, so foreign companies provide stiff competition here in the United States. The most notable example is the competition that Japanese cars have given to the American auto industry. Since the 1970s, well-to-do consumers have steered their car purchases toward Japanese makes. And nearly half of Americans interviewed in a 1991 Gallup Poll said Japanese auto manufacturers were "the most likely to come out with technological innovations."[61] However, thanks in part to a quality focus and the efficiencies of cross-functional teams,[62] American cars may be on the road to a comeback. According to a recent Roper Organization poll, 58 percent of college graduates said that American cars are "in," as opposed to 48 percent two years earlier. And 62 percent of baby boomers said they preferred American makes, up from 55 percent in 1990.[63] General Motors' introduction of the Saturn, with its emphasis on quality in product, process, and people, signaled a turnaround for the American auto industry, or at least for GM. In July 1992, Saturn dealers sold 22,305 cars, averaging 115 apiece—twice the rate of sales per dealer for Toyota.[64]

Summary

To recognize and anticipate the opportunities and threats the organization faces, marketers must scan the marketing environment. Environmental scanning includes reviewing the economic, political and legal, social, institutional, technological, and competitive dimensions of the marketing environment.

The economic environment includes the patterns of business activity and consumer income. Business activity follows a cycle of prosperity, recession, and recovery. Consumer income may be measured as gross income (a household's total annual income), disposable income (money left over after taxes), and discretionary income (gross income minus taxes and living expenses).

The political and legal environment includes federal, state, and local laws and regulations relevant to marketing activities, including advertising, pricing, and distribution. Lobbyists and consumers influence which laws are passed. In addition, many court decisions interpreting these laws and regulations affect marketers. On the global level, marketers must also be familiar with any international agreements that affect their activities, as well as the relevant laws of every country in which they operate.

The social environment describes customers in terms of demographic data and culture. Demographics include data on such population characteristics as age, sex, geographic distribution, education, income, and marital status. In addition, cultural values influence customers' needs, wants, and purchase decisions. Marketers operating in foreign countries must also take into account differences in values and languages.

The institutional environment consists of marketing intermediaries and their activities. Marketing intermediaries include resellers, physical distribution firms, marketing services agencies, and financial intermediaries. Their interest in and ability to cooperate with the marketer can determine the success or failure of a marketing strategy.

The technological environment comprises scientific knowledge, research, inventions, and innovations. Technological developments bring both opportunities and threats. Successful organizations use technology to improve the quality of their products and process, including manufacturing, distribution, communications, pricing, and marketing research.

The competitive environment consists of all the organizations that could potentially satisfy the needs and desires of a particular market. Competition in various industries takes the form of pure competition, monopolistic competition, oligopoly, or monopoly. Marketers need to anticipate competition from existing competitors, new entrants, substitute products, suppliers, and buyers.

KEY TERMS AND CONCEPTS

marketing environment (p. 32)

environmental scanning (p. 32)

economic environment (p. 34)

business cycle (p. 34)

inflation (p. 35)

demarketing (p. 37)

gross income (p. 38)

disposable income (p. 38)

discretionary income (p. 39)

political-legal environment (p. 39)

regulations (p. 42)

consumerism (p. 44)

social environment (p. 46)

demographics (p. 46)

regional marketing (p. 48)

cultural values (p. 48)

institutional environment (p. 51)

technological environment (p. 53)

competitive environment (p. 55)

pure competition (p. 55)

monopolistic competition (p. 55)

oligopoly (p. 55)

monopoly (p. 56)

REVIEW AND DISCUSSION QUESTIONS

1. Name and briefly define the six dimensions of the marketing environment.
2. What steps might the owner of a clothing store take to prosper during a recessionary economy?
3. Imagine that you want to open an Italian restaurant that will sell a variety of pasta dishes, bottled water, beer, and wine. What laws and regulations would you expect to have to comply with?
4. Do you think self-regulation by the medical profession is effective? Why or why not?
5. If you were a marketer about to introduce a new line of microwavable party snacks to consumers nationwide, what demographic trends would you first want to research?
6. Based on what you can learn or deduce about the demographics and values of your class members, do you think your class would be a good target market for top-of-the-line CD players? for life insurance? Explain.
7. Suppose you want to begin marketing your line of microwavable party snacks in Great Britain. What would you want to learn about the institutional environment there?
8. How are technology and quality interrelated?
9. a. Name and define the four types of competition.
   b. Which do you think would be faced by a company that markets accounting services to small businesses? Explain.

Chapter Project
Scan Your Marketing Environment

As you've learned in this chapter, marketers must scan the marketing environment for economic, political/legal, social, institutional, technological, and competitive factors that affect their marketing efforts. In this project, you begin scanning these dimensions of the marketing environment.

Imagine that you are involved in the development and launching of a product (a good or service). Choose one of the following or come up with your own:

- a packing and shipping business
- a line of fresh pasta products
- a line of household power tools (drill, power saw, etc.)
- a new magazine
- child-care service for parents who work at night
- a restaurant with a special theme
- a development of new homes.

After you've chosen your product, research at least three facts about each dimension of the marketing environment as it relates to your product. Record them in Table 2.4.

Determine whether these factors are likely to enhance or inhibit your product's success in the marketplace. Then decide how you would use these factors in your marketing strategy for the product. (How would you overcome the challenge of strict legal regulations? How would you use cultural values to support your product?) Report your conclusions in writing and/or to the class.

TABLE 2.4	DIMENSION OF MARKETING ENVIRONMENT	FACTORS
Worksheet for Chapter Project	Economic	1. 2. 3.
	Political and legal	1. 2. 3.
	Social	1. 2. 3.
	Institutional	1. 2. 3.
	Technological	1. 2. 3.
	Competitive	1. 2. 3.

Case
Menu Workshop

If you slid into a restaurant booth one morning, sleepy eyed and hungry, would you like to select your breakfast from a typewritten list on a worn piece of paper, sticky with syrup and stained with butter? Or would you rather receive a slick, clean, full-color menu featuring mouth-watering pictures of Vienna-style French toast and Belgian waffles piled with fresh-fruit toppings? Consultants at Menu Workshop, based in Seattle, think you'd prefer the latter. They showed Friendly's restaurants how to boost profits by shifting around menu items and offering some high-quality new dishes (such as Belgian waffles). Within a month, Friendly's was serving the new offerings to 20 percent of its breakfast clientele.

Menu Workshop uses research to determine how restaurants such as Friendly's can increase their profits and satisfy more customers. For instance, it found that during the recession of the early 1990s, people were more apt to try a lower-priced restaurant and spend less when they were there. Although times were tough for the restaurant industry in general, Americans still spent 43 percent of every food dollar on meals prepared outside the home. Average Americans ate outside the home nearly four times a week in 1991. Men ate an average of 4.3 outside meals a week, while women consumed 3.6. The best demographic indicator of whether people ate in restaurants was their income: people with annual household incomes of $75,000 and up ate an average of 4.9 outside meals; people whose incomes were $15,000 or less ate only 3.1 outside meals.

Leonard Smith, vice president of Menu Workshop, uses geographic and age demographics as well, such as the "3, 5, and 15" rule. Most regular customers of a restaurant live within 3 miles of the establishment. Somewhat less frequent customers live within 5 miles. Nearly all the customers live within 15 miles. Using this rule in conjunction with census reports, Smith pinpoints high-income families that live near a restaurant, then examines the ages of these potential customers. "If most of your customers are 35 or 40, you'll want a different price point than if they were seniors."

Life-style and values also are important to restaurateurs. A dress code might be appropriate downtown in a major city but not at a casual summer resort. A diner that opens for breakfast at 7 a.m. in a fishing town is doomed.

Through his own harsh experience, Leonard Smith of Menu Workshop learned the importance of understanding the marketing environment. He once opened a gourmet seafood restaurant in an affluent neighborhood, figuring the comfortable incomes of residents would make them prime customers. But he had overlooked the fact that most of the local residents had put their money into their boats and expensive homes. They didn't have money left over to spend on a fancy dinner. "Their favorite sauces turned out to be ketchup and mustard," laments Smith. "Had I done a demographic study, I would have saved myself a big mistake."

Menu Workshop has applied such lessons to help a number of restaurants besides Friendly's. Sometimes its consultants have helped by pointing out to clients that they are losing money on certain dishes. The group categorizes each dish a restaurant sells according to its sales and profitability: "stars" (high volume, high profit), "puzzles" (high profit, low sales), "plowhorses" (high volume, low profit), and "dogs" (low sales and profits). After evaluating each dish and the overall quality of the menu, Menu Workshop can revamp the menu in light of the demographic data it has already collected.

The group also helps restaurants find an identity. In one instance, a Menu Workshop client was trying to sell a wide variety of dishes (seafood, chicken, pasta, and sandwiches) with no unifying theme to distinguish the restaurant. When Smith found out that the restaurant was named after someone's dog, he had his theme and the restaurant's identity. He created a teal and pink menu with a poem and illustrations of the dog, including paw prints marked next to the dog's "favorite" dishes (not coincidentally, the restaurant's most profitable offerings).

QUESTIONS

1. Think of a restaurant you have visited recently. If you were a consultant with Menu Workshop, what steps might you take to help increase business at that restaurant?
2. What demographic factors in your local area would be most important to a restaurant?
3. Besides demographic data about potential customers, what other information about the marketing environment would a local restaurant need?

Source: Tibbett Speer, "Something New on the Old Menu," *American Demographics,* October 1992, pp. 27–29.

CHAPTER 3

Meeting Social and Ethical Standards in Marketing

LEARNING OBJECTIVES

After completing this chapter, you should be able to:

1. Discuss the nature of an organization's social responsibility to the community and the environment.

2. Identify and evaluate ethical issues in the marketing mix.

3. Recognize ethical issues surrounding exchange, competition, and technology.

4. Differentiate between personal ethics and organizational ethics.

5. Describe the impact on marketers of diversity among markets and among employees.

Creating Customer Value
Merck AgVet

Merck & Co. isn't just the world's largest pharmaceutical company. The firm has also been voted by *Fortune* magazine's "Corporate Reputations" survey America's Most Admired Corporation several years in a row. According to *Fortune,* the company could be "forecast the winner based on financial performance alone." But Merck's stellar reputation reaches far beyond its shareholders. Why? Because the company takes its position in the community and the environment very seriously.

In addition to its many contributions to and organization of programs that benefit human health, Merck's mission of social responsibility extends to the animal and agricultural world through its AgVet division. "A major emphasis is educating customers about disease control, animal husbandry, improved companion animal care and crop productivity," states a Merck AgVet brochure.

Implementing these lofty goals requires teamwork among many people—Merck employees, customers, and members of the community. One of AgVet's successful, ongoing community projects is the Heartworm Awareness Campaign, which began in 1988 with funding provided by Merck to the American Veterinary Medical Association (AVMA). The campaign is a grassroots consumer education program aimed at increasing awareness among dog owners of the importance of veterinary care in preventing heartworm disease, a serious canine illness. Since the campaign's beginning, Merck marketers, AVMA marketers, veterinarians, and dog owners have participated in a variety of ways:

- Merck AgVet and the AVMA have offered one-day and two-day Spokesperson Training Workshops, which are designed to help veterinarians and state VMA representatives communicate pet health issues (including heartworm awareness) more effectively to the news media.
- In Connecticut, the VMA offered customers at 36 stores the chance to take a Heartworm Challenge quiz. Fifty thousand quiz cards were dropped in dog owners' shopping bags; the first 100 people to return their completed cards received a stuffed toy dog.
- Some states have conducted programs at schools, to educate younger pet owners. The Florida VMA challenged students with heartworm awareness poster contests, and the North Carolina VMA provided youngsters with a coloring book.
- Pet stores, animal shelters, and humane societies have jumped into the campaign with the help of a public relations firm, displaying posters and distributing buttons, as well as offering a toll-free telephone number that dog owners can call for tips on how to prevent canine heartworm disease.
- In a widespread survey conducted in 1991 by 289 veterinary clinics across the United States, 73 percent of 16,000 respondents said that they had recently heard of canine heartworm disease, an increase of 11 percent from a year earlier.
- Public service announcements also have played an important role in the campaign. In 1991 alone, 32 states purchased time on 480 radio stations, and 24 states reserved local TV time for an award-winning infomercial. Merck AgVet supplemented these with advertising in 20 more markets. And celebrities joined the team: Lassie and her trainer Bob Weatherwax, along with the cast from the sitcom "Full House," donated their time for two PSAs in 1992.

Merck AgVet, the AVMA, veterinarians, dog owners—not to mention dogs themselves—have benefited from the

Heartworm Awareness Campaign. According to Merck literature, since the introduction of its *Heartgard-30* (ivermectin), the total market for this heartworm disease preventive has more than doubled. The AVMA and Merck AgVet have received the Mercury Award, an international recognition of outstanding communications programs, for the Heartworm Awareness Campaign.

Notes Dr. Donald Mullen, a Connecticut veterinarian, "This campaign lets veterinarians wear white hats for the public. It's a way of convincing clients that it's cost-effective to provide preventive medical care at a reasonable price. And it offers us the chance to do what's right for the patient, and to expand our practice at the same time."

Dog owners, of course, are happy to have healthy pets. And the dogs? They're wagging their tails in homes all around the country.

Sources: Jennifer Reese, "America's Most Admired Corporations," *Fortune,* February 8, 1993, p. 44; "Creative Approach Succeeds in Spreading Heartworm Awareness," *Journal of the American Veterinary Medical Association* 200, no. 5 (March 1, 1992): p. 594; "'91 Heartworm Awareness Campaigns Were Innovative," *Veterinary Forum,* March 1992, p. 58; "Join the Heartworm Awareness Campaign!" *Veterinary Economics,* May 1992, p. 70; "Lassie Joins Fight Against Heartworm Disease," *Veterinary Forum,* June 1992; "Training Workshops Back by Popular Demand," *Veterinary Forum,* January 1993; *Merck Agvet* brochure, public affairs office, Merck & Co., Inc.; and phone interview with Elizabeth Drbal, product manager, Small Animal Products, Merck AgVet, Merck & Co., Inc.

Chapter Overview

Through its Heartworm Awareness Campaign, Merck AgVet demonstrated a commitment that extended beyond profits and customers to the well-being of pets. At Merck and other organizations, marketers are accepting and even embracing the notion that their organizations are a part of society and therefore must be concerned about societal issues such as ethical, responsible behavior toward people and the environment and sensitivity to the diversity of people in the marketing environment. As Merck has found, such a view of the organization's role can be beneficial to the marketing effort.

This chapter considers marketing's social role. It examines three social issues that can significantly affect a marketing effort: social responsibility, ethics, and diversity. The section on social responsibility describes an organization's accountability to society, especially to the communities in which it operates and to the environment in the ecological sense. The discussion of ethics considers social criticisms of marketing, the distinction between ethics and laws, ethical issues regarding each element of the marketing mix, and ethics in modern organizations. Finally, the chapter addresses diversity—the variations among individuals in the marketplace and within marketing groups.

Social Responsibility in Marketing

social responsibility
An organization's acceptance of accountability to society for its actions.

Who is a business responsible to? Whose needs must it meet? Many economists maintain that the primary responsibility of a business is to earn profits for its owners. The marketing concept adds that a business should do this by meeting the needs of its customers. The prevailing view is that the organization's responsibilities should extend even further, to include **social responsibility**—an organization's acceptance that it is accountable to society for its actions. Thus, a business is responsible to shareholders, customers, employees, others in its marketing channel, society as a whole, and the earth's environment. In the ad in Figure 3.1, Johnson & Johnson makes the point that its responsibility, extends to the health of this nation's children.

One marketer with this perspective is Sidney T. Bowers, founder and president of United Energy of Wisconsin, which installs, upgrades, and maintains lighting products

FIGURE 3.1

A Company That Recognizes Its Social Responsibility

Keep the children well, and you can heal a nation.

America is growing a new generation of healthier children, thanks to programs like Head Start. It does more than just educate low-income kids. It also provides them with important medical, dental and social services. That's important. We support Head Start by funding management training that helps program directors put government allocations to the wisest and most productive use. There is a reason we do this. We are committed to addressing critical issues surrounding our nation's health. And we believe it all begins here. With the children.

Johnson & Johnson

to make facilities' lighting energy efficient. While he readily observes that he is in business to make money, Bowers is pleased to be selling technological innovations that benefit the environment. Furthermore, he makes a point of hiring and training employees from the inner city, where unemployment, especially among African-Americans, is staggering.[1] Similarly, management of Swissair has accepted that concern for the environment is a corporate duty, so the company is seeking to grow without increasing the amount of pollution its operations create. To put a lid on air pollution, Swissair is not only working with aircraft manufacturers to reduce emissions, but provides employees with incentives to use public transportation rather than drive to work.[2]

WHY BE SOCIALLY RESPONSIBLE?

Proponents of social responsibility typically argue that this stance is to the organization's best interests in the long run. Potential customers, so the argument goes, will be in the best position to buy if the organization looks after their welfare as individuals and community members. And in these times of stiff competition, potential customers who have trouble choosing from among competing products may well buy from the company they most respect.

Many businesspeople agree with this view. For example, Telephone Express, a regional long-distance carrier based in Colorado Springs, allows its employees to volunteer at United Way organizations on company time. According to Mary Beazley, one of the company's founders, this raises the company's profile in the area and builds employee morale.[3]

Another company that sees benefits from social responsibility is Gardeners' Supply, a mail-order company based in Burlington, Vermont. Gardeners' Supply started a program to compost yard waste in the Burlington area. The compost is used to fertilize a garden that grows produce for the cafeteria of a local medical center. In addition, many of the company's employees participate in a company-sponsored community garden. Will Raap, president of Gardeners' Supply, believes these products strengthen his employees' knowledge of customers' needs and ways to meet those needs.[4]

RESPONSIBILITY TO THE COMMUNITY

Taking a socially responsible posture with regard to the community is not always easy. Consider the case of Infinity Broadcasting Company, which employs the controversial talk show host Howard Stern. The Federal Communications Commission fined Infinity $600,000 after Stern engaged in a number of offensive jokes and activities on the air. But advertisers pay Infinity more than $3,000 per minute during Stern's show. Thus, the fine was more than paid for by advertising revenues.[5] If Infinity's only responsibility is to make a profit, then it should leave Stern alone and continue to pay the fines. But if the FCC and consumer advocacy groups judge that Stern's behavior is detrimental to listeners, should Infinity require Stern to tone down his crude humor? To be socially responsible, Infinity must consider not only its customers (advertisers), but also the listening community.

Social responsibility to the community can take two forms: ceasing negative activity, such as pollution, or taking a positive action, such as starting an education program that benefits the community. An example of the first approach, in the eyes of many, would be firing Howard Stern.

Positive action may consist of consumer education, partnerships with schools or teachers' organizations, environmental programs, or funding for special projects. McDonald's Corporation sponsors Ronald McDonald Houses, homes located near hospitals that provide housing at little or no cost to families of children who are hospitalized.

community relations
Activities that reinforce a positive image of an organization in the community in which it is located and/or operates.

COMMUNITY RELATIONS Projects undertaken out of social responsibility not only benefit the community, they also enhance **community relations**, reinforcing a positive image of the organization. Anheuser-Busch, Inc., has a Consumer Awareness & Education Program through which it teaches students the consequences of drinking and driving. Other companies underwrite public service announcements designed to educate the public about a number of issues including unsafe behavior (such as drug abuse), illnesses (such as AIDS), and the importance of staying in school (as in the Russell Athletic poster shown in Figure 3.2). As discussed at the beginning of this chapter, Merck & Co. underwrote public service announcements hosted by celebrities as part of the firm's Heartworm Awareness Campaign for animal health.

The organization's efforts are most likely to lead to good community relations when they are related to its strengths and involve the community in some way. Longfellow Clubs, a health and recreation company in Wayland, Massachusetts, donates the use of its health club facilities to local children with disabilities.[6] The Home Depot chain of home improvement stores, based in Atlanta, focuses its corporate giving on community programs to build and renovate low-cost housing. Besides contributing money, the company encourages its employees to volunteer their time on these projects. It decentralizes the decisions about where to get involved by delegating much of the decision making to the district managers who supervise Home Depot stores.[7]

cause-related marketing (CRM)
Marketing that ties charitable donations directly to the sales of a product.

CAUSE-RELATED MARKETING Some organizations undertake **cause-related marketing (CRM)**, a formal version of marketing on behalf of the community. With CRM, charitable donations are tied directly to the sales of a specific product. Virgin Atlantic Airways, which declared itself the "green airline," promised to plant a tree in California for every passenger who flew the airline from Los Angeles to London in 1990.[8] Starbucks, a coffee

FIGURE 3.2

An Ad That Leads to Good Community Relations

The only uniform that outperforms ours.

Even though we make America's best known athletic teamwear, we know that no other uniform can compete with a cap and gown. So we're making posters like this ad available to coaches and teachers to help remind athletes that an education can keep them competitive long after their playing days are over.

STAY IN SCHOOL

For more information about our "Stay In School" campaign, write: Russell Corporation, Dept. M, P.O. Box 373, Alexander City, AL 35010.

retailer, supports the global relief agency CARE. Some of the funds Starbucks donates come from sales of a sampler pack of four packages of coffee. From the $18.95 price, the company sets aside $2.00 for CARE.[9]

CRM is popular among marketers because it sets up a win-win situation. The product or service is promoted, and profits and sales are increased. Customers are satisfied, members of the community benefit from the donations made, and community relations are enhanced.

GLOBAL SOCIAL RESPONSIBILITY   Being a responsible member of the community can be more complex for an organization that operates in more than one country. The organization needs to know what the community expects or wants and must find a way to meet those expectations. In Honduras, for example, thousands of Miskito Indians work as lobster divers. They live in wretched conditions and typically work without safety equipment or training, but they earn a lot of money by local standards. Red Lobster USA, a restaurant chain that buys Honduran lobster, has tried to be socially responsible by financially supporting a conservation program that includes diver training and by specifying that all lobsters it buys be caught in traps, rather than by divers. However, the production manager at a packing plant on the Honduran island of Roatan told reporters that the plant sells Red Lobster both diver- and trap-caught lobsters. Further complicating the situation is the concern among Miskitos that such well-meaning efforts to protect them could curtail their livelihood. In the words of diver Melvin Zelaya, "There is no other way for us to make the money to live."[10]

In spite of the difficulties, the increasing global presence of U.S. companies is leading them to make more of their contributions in other countries. Alcoa worked with local officials in southern Brazil to build a sewage plant. IBM donated computer expertise and equipment to the National Parks Foundation of Costa Rica to develop strategies to preserve rain forests.[11]

FIGURE 3.3
Appealing to Organizational Buyers' Need to Comply with Environmental Laws

RESPONSIBILITY TO THE ENVIRONMENT

green marketing
Marketing efforts to produce and promote environmentally sound products.

With consumers increasingly voicing concern about the environment, marketers have found it necessary, and often profitable, to make environmental consciousness part of their social responsibility efforts. At many organizations, these efforts include **green marketing**, or marketing efforts designed to meet customers' desire to protect the environment. As described later in this section, a green marketing strategy can influence all four elements of the marketing mix.

Green marketing can benefit the marketing organization in various ways. First of all, it appeals to the values of more and more people. Not only do many consumers feel better buying a detergent or air conditioner that is supposed to be environmentally friendly, but they bring that same value to their role as organizational buyers. Organizational customers may "buy green" for other reasons as well. Organizations that are environmentally conscious can see their costs fall. Disposing of waste, mailing catalogs or brochures to uninterested people, and shipping bulky packages are expensive; minimizing such waste saves money. Furthermore, compliance with environmental laws often is a major concern for organizational buyers. The ad in Figure 3.3 appeals to buyers looking for alternatives to cleaning with chlorinated solvents, which are being phased out by environmental laws. Leading off with the headline, "How to get the chlorinated solvent monkey off your back," the ad tells users of chlorinated solvents that Exxon makes alternative cleaning products that meet environmental standards and can even be recycled.

GREEN MARKETING AND THE QUALITY APPROACH   Green marketing is a natural extension of the quality approach to marketing. At 3M Corporation, for example, environmental responsibility is not handled by some "environmental department" but is a part of every employee's job responsibilities along with other aspects of quality improvement.[12] Procter & Gamble has pioneered the application of total quality management to environmental goals. The company uses the same TQM tools to improve its environmental impact that it uses for other areas of business. By seeking continuous improvement, P&G has made a number of changes, such as eliminating outside cartons for Sure and Secret deodorants (saving 80 million cartons or 3.4 million pounds of solid waste per year) and developing concentrated versions of laundry detergents such as Ultra Tide (reducing packaging and the amount of chemicals by 30 percent and reducing the amount of energy needed to transport the product).[13]

In fact, organizations that focus on satisfying their customers are finding that concern for the environment is a necessary part of their drive to improve quality. According to Helen O. Petrauskas, vice president of Environmental and Safety Engineering at Ford Motor Company, customers' demand for "green" products and "green" organizations will eventually surpass the strictest regulatory standards.[14] In other words, marketers who want to satisfy their customers will have to do more than simply meet environmental standards imposed by the government. They will have to find out what environmental "standards" their customers want. When they ask, they are sometimes surprised by the answers. For example, McDonald's Corporation had subscribed to the traditional notion that consumers wanted their food delivered in white bags to convey an image of purity; in fact, consumers were happy to receive their food in recycled, recyclable brown paper.[15]

"GREEN" PRODUCTS   Organizations that practice green marketing try to ensure that their products are helpful to the environment or at least cause little or no harm. AT&T has begun promoting two-sided photocopying by programming its copiers so that two-sided copying is the default mode. The first user of such copiers reported a rise in two-sided copying from 10 percent to 79 percent of all copies—presumably leading to much less use of paper.[16] BMW is developing cars that can be easily taken apart and recycled.[17] The *Real Goods* catalog offers products that use renewable energy sources, such as a solar-powered alarm radio and rechargeable batteries guaranteed to last forever.

Product Development   A "green" product strategy often influences the process of product development. For example, when a product is developed or modified at 3M, a group is assigned to make sure the product is environmentally sound.[18] Similarly, the ability to reuse and recycle parts is part of the design criteria used by Xerox's product development teams.[19]

Levi Strauss recently teamed up with Crane & Company, a Massachusetts-based maker of paper goods, to recycle Levi's denim scraps. Levi Strauss sends the scraps to Crane, which process them into a "denim paper." The paper was first used internally at Levi Strauss for various needs, including all the company's stationery. Eventually, Crane's offered a line of denim paper to the public. According to the paper company's Tim Crane, the new paper "is the first and only closed-loop recycling of textile waste into paper products." And none of the denim scraps at Levi's Albuquerque jeans factory are going into the trash anymore, saving garbage collection fees and about 8,000 trees a year.[20]

Packaging   Green marketers are also seeking to package goods in ways that have less impact on the environment. This may mean using recycled packaging or simply less packaging. For example, 3M has reduced packaging by more than 4 million pounds in a single year.[21]

The High Density Film Products division at Sonoco Products Company was a pioneer in establishing customer-center recycling programs for plastic sacks. There are more than 8,000 plastic bag collection sites set up in supermarkets in the United States.

The choice is not always a simple one, however. For example, containers made of recycled plastic are more likely to break, so the manufacturer has to use more of the material, making the containers heavier and requiring more energy to transport them.[22] Eventually, federal law may help marketers make that particular choice: A bill called the Resource Conservation and Recovery Act would require various packaging materials to meet standards of recyclability. Packaging that didn't meet the standards would have to carry a label listing the environmentally harmful substances used.[23]

According to packaging experts, marketers can also encourage recycling by making recyclable materials look recyclable. To convey this image to consumers, glass and plastic containers should be clear, and labels should be removable.[24] Then there's the next step in environmentally friendly packaging: making packaging that is returnable, so that the manufacturer can reuse it. Of course, to older consumers who remember glass bottles of milk and soda pop, this concept doesn't sound so new.

"GREEN" PRICING   Green marketers have learned that making a product friendly to the environment does not mean they can charge a higher price. According to a study by Syracuse University's School of Public Communications, 93 percent of adults said a product's environmental impact was important to them in making purchase decisions, but two-thirds said environmentally friendly products should not cost more.[25] Fortunately, "green" product development need not be costly. Ford Motor Company met California's 1997 pollution standards with its 1993 Escort and Mercury Tracer at a cost of only $100 per car.[26]

Some marketers have been able to combine an advantageous pricing strategy with green marketing. Superconcentrate laundry detergent, such as Ultra Tide and Ultra Cheer, costs consumers more per wash than standard detergents. For example, an industry analyst determined that the cost per wash of Tide powder with bleach was 37 percent higher using the superconcentrate formula.[27] Producers are able to enjoy this price advantage because differences in the sizes of the packages and the measuring scoops they include make it almost impossible to shop by price. Furthermore, today's consumers tend to run big loads of laundry and pour in generous amounts of detergent; a little scoopful just doesn't look like enough in spite of the manufacturer's recommendations. Thus, making detergents that require less packaging and less energy to ship has also turned out to be more profitable.

"GREEN" CHANNEL STRATEGY   "Green marketing" seeks to ship goods with a minimal amount of energy and to reuse packing materials. Merck AgVet, featured in "Creating Customer Value," is committed to using as little packing and packaging material as possible.[28] Patagonia tries to ship its outdoor clothing in recycled and recyclable plastic.[29] Furniture maker Herman Miller used a waste prevention team to evaluate its shipping practices. The team determined that 80 percent of the products could be shipped in movers' blankets rather than the complete cardboard and plastic packaging that had been used.[30] The Home Depot works cooperatively with suppliers to help them find ways to use single-material packaging, which is easier to recycle than packaging that combines, say, paper and plastic.[31]

Zytec Corporation, a maker of computer supplies and equipment based in Eden Prairie, Minnesota, sends some of its suppliers reusable carts designed to hold specific parts that would normally be shipped in boxes. The carts also come in handy at Zytec's plant, where employees wheel them from the warehouse to the production line as needed. Zytec even sends finished goods to one of its customers in the carts before returning them to the supplier.[32]

"GREEN" COMMUNICATION   Given the desire of consumers to buy "green" products, it is tempting to position products as beneficial to the environment. However, such claims, if exaggerated or vague, can mislead customers. Besides being unethical, such behavior may violate laws and regulations, including guidelines developed by the Federal Trade Commission for green marketing.[33]

Before marketers at 3M can make environmental claims about the company's products, they must obtain approval from the company's environmental claims committee. 3M's standards are conservative. For example, the company will not call a product "environmentally friendly" because, in the words of Thomas Zosel, manager of pollution prevention programs, "It's an ambiguous statement. It's a marketing gimmick." Rather, 3M will make specific statements about the product's contents. Thus, its product labels tell what, if any, percentage of the product is made of recycled materials.[34]

Marketing experts support the notion that it's better to keep claims modest.[35] This approach avoids disappointing customers. It is also less likely to attract one-upmanship from competitors or investigations from the government.

Consumers are concerned about the large amount of paper devoted to mailing catalogs and advertisements. Thus, green marketers who use the mail are looking for ways to limit their mailings without sacrificing sales. Hanna Andersson, mail-order supplier of cotton children's clothing, offers a gift certificate to customers who report that they are receiving duplicate catalogs (see Figure 3.4). Patagonia limits its catalog mailings to two adult and two children's catalogs per year.[36]

SOCIAL RESPONSIBILITY AND THE QUALITY FOCUS

Social responsibility fits well with a quality-driven approach to marketing. Both convey that the organization cares about doing the right thing and doing things right.

Ideally, an organization should carry out its social responsibilities in ways that reinforce the quality image of its products. Mail-order retailer Hanna Andersson does just that. Its catalogs tell customers they may return any of their "hannas" in good condition. When they do, the company credits them with 20 percent of their cost, good for future purchases, then donates the clothes to charities for needy children. Not only does this program, called Hannadowns, help poor children, it reinforces the message that the clothes are so durable that children outgrow them before they wear out.

FIGURE 3.4
Catalog Retailer with a Program to Eliminate Waste in Direct Mail

Ethical Issues in Marketing

The wide acceptance of social responsibility is based in part on the view that it is in the organization's best interests, but consider the following responses to an informal poll of *Inc.* readers:[37] "It's naive to believe anybody can be successful and totally ethical." "Often what we do is not what we would like to do." "Many business questions are more a matter of survival than ethics." "Ethics are defined by the situation. Therefore, good judgment is paramount."

As is evident from these statements, marketers and other businesspeople often struggle with the solutions to ethical problems. **Ethics** are the moral principles and values that govern the way an individual or group conducts its activities.[38] **Marketing ethics** are the principles, values, and standards of conduct followed by marketers.

ethics
Moral principles and values governing the way an individual or group conducts its activities.

marketing ethics
The principles, values, and standards of conduct followed by marketers.

Isn't it obvious that marketers should behave ethically? Why are these issues so difficult? One reason is that ethical standards vary from one person to another. Sometimes the only available courses of action contain a blend of hurtful and helpful actions. Even when people agree on what is the most ethical course of action, that alternative may seem unduly costly—especially to the owner of a start-up company with little cash or to the employee trying to hold onto a job during a recession.

Operating in a global marketplace makes ethical issues even more complicated. Marketers must be attuned to the values not only of mainstream American society, but also of the other cultures in which they hope to market their products. One psychologist and business consultant says, "It's immoral to eat a dog in St. Louis. Is it unethical in Seoul, Korea? It's unethical to pay a bribe in the United States, but is it unethical in Mexico?"[39] These are just two of the myriad questions—large and small—that marketers face as they make ethical judgments.

Yet ethical principles are important for marketers from both a moral and a business standpoint. In the words of Scott Cook, founder of a Menlo Park, California, software company called Intuit, "Being truthful is good business." Cook offers the example of software salespeople who overstate sales forecasts to persuade dealers to buy more than enough of a product. This gets the salesperson a hefty commission for the period, but it destroys dealers' trust in the software company. Intuit's salespeople, by contrast, are honest to the point of telling dealers when they have ordered too much; the dealers often respond with unquestioning willingness to order new products from Intuit.[40]

SOCIAL CRITICISMS OF MARKETING

Public perception of businesspeople is negative. According to public polls, 58 percent of American adults consider the ethical standards of business executives to be "fair" or "poor," 90 percent believe white-collar crime to be "very common" or "somewhat common," and 76 percent feel that these low ethical standards have contributed to falling societal morals.[41] Marketers reinforce this view whenever they bend the rules, favoring a quick sale over a long-term relationship.

Society wants marketers to adhere to its values, beliefs, and principles. As these have become more complicated, criticism of business practices has grown more strident. Add issues of legality to the pot, and the result is a rather spicy stew. By obeying the law, the marketer can avoid actions that have legal penalties. But not all legal behavior is ethical; it would be impossible to write enough laws to require ethics in all business dealings. At the same time, an action that a marketer considers ethical might violate the law. For example, a marketer might think that customers would benefit from an arrangement with several competitors to avoid price increases, but this arrangement likely would violate federal antitrust laws.

To see the complexity facing marketers, consider Genzyme, maker of the drug Ceredase, which treats Gaucher's disease, a genetic illness affecting about 20,000 people worldwide. A federal "orphan drug" law grants to companies that develop medications for rare diseases a seven-year monopoly on their product. Presumably, the freedom from competition allows drug companies to earn enough to offset the high cost of researching and manufacturing drugs for small markets. However, Genzyme, which charges up to $200,000 for a year's worth of Ceredase, has been accused of using the orphan law for profiteering. Genzyme responds that its Ceredase profits are low by industry standards and that it will give away the drug to patients without insurance. Furthermore, the company argues, once patients begin responding to treatment, they require smaller amounts of Ceredase.[42] Are the criticisms of Genzyme valid? Are the company's responses adequate? The answers depend on how you define Genzyme's responsibilities.

As a practical matter, however, most ethical behavior is legal, and many businesspeople have concluded that when an industry behaves ethically, its actions are less apt to be regulated.[43] Even more important, ethical behavior can avoid the pitfall of shifting the organization's focus away from where it should be: on customers. Consider the case of British Airways. To compete with upstart Virgin Atlantic, BA employees approached Virgin's customers in airline terminals, trying to persuade them to switch flights. BA employees also pretended to work for Virgin and allegedly obtained information about that airline's customers by tapping into Virgin's computer. When these and other questionable tactics were revealed, BA not only appeared unethical, it appeared to have little concern for its customers, placing a gain in sales over honest dealings.[44] In contrast, an organization that is sensitive to its customers' concerns will choose tactics that—even when aggressive—are ethical.

TABLE 3.1
Areas of Ethical Concern in Marketing Research

AREA OF CONCERN	EXAMPLE	ETHICAL STANDARDS
Preserving participant's anonymity	Keeping the names of survey respondents anonymous, even though the client would like to use them to create a mailing list	This is a basic standard of ethical research.
Exposing participants to mental stress	Arriving late for a scheduled interview; conducting experiments in which subjects are embarrassed at their lack of knowledge about products	When stress is unavoidable, researcher should debrief subjects afterward.
Asking participants questions against their self-interest	Asking about the acceptability of various prices in order to plan a price increase	Such issues tend to place ethical standards in conflict with technical standards for accurate research.
Using special equipment and techniques	Using equipment to measure physiological responses to a product or promotional message	These must be properly maintained to avoid injury.
Involving participants in research without their knowledge	Secretly observing the behavior of shoppers	Informed consent is a basic ethical standard unless minimal risk to subjects is involved and the research could not be practically carried out with consent.
Using deception	Showing subjects sample advertisements without telling them that they will have to take a recall test afterward	Incompletely informed consent is considered ethical only if there is minimal risk to subjects and research cannot be practically carried out another way.
Using coercion	Harassing consumers by repeatedly requesting telephone interviews	Coercion is unethical and tends to bias results.
Depriving participants of their right to self-determination	Changing participants in ways they could not expect, such as a taste test in which they cannot identify their preferred brand and unexpectedly lose confidence in their ability to judge	Researchers should try to restore participants to their original condition when this occurs.

Source: Adapted from Gilbert A. Churchill, Jr., *Basic Marketing Research,* 2nd ed. (Fort Worth: The Dryden Press, 1992), pp. 62–65.

ETHICS OF MARKETING RESEARCH

In the practice of marketing research, marketers have to run a gauntlet of changing technology, regulations, attitudes, and the threat of lawsuits. One marketing research firm, Atkinson Research, was sued for using a survey questionnaire to solicit viewer response to programs for its client, KARE-TV. The survey asked respondents to watch a certain TV channel as often as possible. This may seem innocent enough, but the suit charged that the survey was deliberately conducted during a Nielsen ratings period in order to rig the ratings in favor of KARE-TV.[45] Also troublesome are so-called telephone surveys that become sales pitches or requests for donations (in the case of nonprofit organizations). As this trend has increased, nearly half the states in the United States are considering legislation that would prohibit different types of unsolicited phone calls—perhaps even genuine research calls.[46]

The relationship between the researcher and the participant must be maintained ethically. Table 3.1 outlines the main areas of ethical concern to marketing researchers

FIGURE 3.5
Maintaining a Quality Image by Promoting a Product's Safety

One Friday morning, an 18-wheeler didn't see Darlene and Tom driving to work until it was too late. Their Saturn sedan was blind-sided. It spun around and rolled, ending up in the highway median.

The hospital stay was short—under two hours. But still, being thrown against shoulder and lap belts at highway speed, no matter how safe your car is, hurts. For Tom, the old college lineman, the aches and pains felt kind of familiar. And he was back at work on Monday. For Darlene, who'd never played football, it took a little longer.

Everyone at work was glad to hear how the car held up in the crash. Many of them own Saturns, too. In fact, there's quite a high percentage of Saturn owners where the Robisons work.

The Saturn SL2

At Saturn, safety is one of our top priorities. So, among other things, we use a reinforced steel spaceframe, offer optional anti-lock brakes on all our models, and our 1995 cars all come with driver-side airbags as a standard feature.

They happen to work for us, in Spring Hill. And, after ordering another Saturn, Tom let everyone know, recent events not-withstanding, that he liked his present job just fine, and had no plans to become a test driver.

A DIFFERENT KIND *of* COMPANY. A DIFFERENT KIND *of* CAR.

DARLENE and TOM ROBISON were run off the highway, rolled their car, and took the rest of the day off.

in their relationships with research participants. Such concerns include preservation of privacy, and avoidance of situations that expose participants to mental stress, questions that are harmful to participants' self-interest, equipment or techniques that may threaten safety or privacy, deception or coercion, and involvement of participants in research without their knowledge. Chapter 7 takes a more detailed look at ethics in marketing research.

ETHICS AND THE MARKETING MIX

Ethical issues arise with regard to all the elements of the marketing mix: the product itself, its price, its channels of distribution, and its marketing communications.

ETHICS AND PRODUCT DEVELOPMENT Perhaps the largest ethical issue related to products is their quality. The House Energy and Commerce subcommittee on telecommunications recently held a hearing critical of the quality of children's television programming. The Children's Television Act of 1990 required stations to air programs designed to service children's "educational and information needs," but many local broadcasters are simply offering old cartoons and situation comedies, billing them as educational. One broadcaster said the cartoon series "The Jetsons" prepares children for the twenty-first century.[47] In contrast, such ethical objectives as seeking to develop safe products enable an organization to become known for its high-quality products, as in the case of the Saturn automobile (see Figure 3.5).

A common complaint about product quality is **planned obsolescence.** Obsolescence refers to products wearing out or becoming obsolete. Planned obsolescence means the producer built the products *not* to last, at least not as long as buyers would like to use them. From the marketer's point of view, if some of these goods were made more durable, they might have to be priced beyond the reach of most buyers.

planned obsolescence
Wearing out or becoming obsolete as a result of the product being designed and made to last only a short time.

Furthermore, today's rapidly changing technology makes it hard to find an enduring product that can meet the demand for state-of-the-art goods.

Computers are a notable example of products that are obsolete by this standard long before they wear out. To satisfy the customer, should the computer marketer offer a computer that wears out in the short time it takes to become obsolete, thereby holding down the cost so customers can afford to replace it? Or should the computer company make an enduring product and try to provide ways to continually upgrade it? These are just two alternatives marketers might consider in trying to avoid criticism for planned obsolescence.

Packaging Further ethical issues arise with regard to packaging. The use of large packages, designed to use more shelf space or to make the consumer believe that the package contains more of the product than that of the competitor, is a common but questionable practice. Odd-shaped bottles or boxes that appear to contain more are common as well. Is misleading packaging unethical or an acceptable way to remain competitive?

Labeling Especially in the areas of food and cosmetics, labeling has become a real battleground for competing marketers. Terms such as "Lite," "Low Fat," "Reduced Calories," and "Natural" do not guarantee nutritious ingredients. Even fresh produce such as apples may be injected or sprayed with chemicals to make it look more appealing. Claims that cosmetics have "anti-aging" effects are dubious at best. Is it the responsibility of the marketer to present accurate information on labels or of the customer to confirm marketers' claims?

According to the statement of consumers' rights discussed in Chapter 2, consumers have the right to honest information about products so that they can be responsible buyers. A company that practices quality marketing can present the product attractively without offering misleading information.

ETHICS AND PRICING In many instances, pricing is regulated by law. For example, **price fixing**, or reaching an agreement with competitors about what price to charge, is illegal. Some states, such as Massachusetts, require retailers to display their return policies (whether they offer cash refunds or store credit). But consider the earlier example of Genzyme. Its pricing policy was legal. Whether it was ethical is open to debate.

price fixing
Reaching an agreement with competitors about what price to charge.

ETHICS AND CHANNELS OF DISTRIBUTION In quality marketing, the relationship between a manufacturer and its resellers is vital. A high standard of ethics is important to this relationship, which at its most successful creates a team. As described in the beginning of this book, Procter & Gamble teams cooperate with resellers to satisfy consumers and thereby improve the bottom lines of both P&G and the resellers.[48] In an ad directed to supermarkets that appeared in *Progressive Grocer,* Smith Dairy promises its resellers that it will give supermarket customers "our best. . . products and services which meet or exceed their expectations." (See Figure 3.6.)

The way the organizations in a marketing channel exercise control over one another can be a matter of ethics. For example, is it ethical for a fast-food franchisor to require that all outlets purchase their food and supplies from the parent company as a condition of the franchise agreement? Is it ethical for a big brand-name manufacturer to refuse to supply its products to a store that doesn't want to display them in a certain way? One tactic the Home Depot chain uses to ensure ethical behavior is to forbid its employees from accepting any gifts from suppliers.[49]

Sometimes ethical issues create conflict between organizations in a marketing channel, ultimately affecting consumers. Sears, Roebuck and Co. recently came under fire when investigators discovered that some of its auto repair shops were jack-

FIGURE 3.6

Communicating a High-Quality Relationship between Manufacturer and Reseller

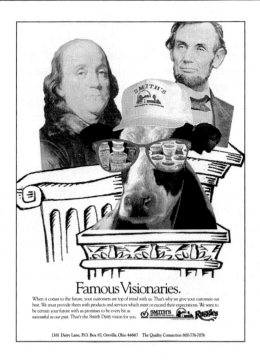

Famous Visionaries.

When it comes to the future, your customers are top of mind with us. That's why we give your customers our best. We must provide them with products and services which meet or exceed their expectations. We want to be certain your future with us promises to be every bit as successful as our past. That's the Smith Dairy vision for you.   SMITH'S   Ruggles

1381 Dairy Lane, P.O. Box 87, Orrville, Ohio 44667   The Quality Connection 800-776-7076

ing up bills for unnecessary repairs. Sears quickly changed its compensation policy, which had been tied to the amount of money billed by each repair shop, but negative publicity certainly damaged the company's image. Members of the American Marketing Association's Sales and Marketing Council disagreed about whether Sears was guilty of bad ethics or bad management. Judith Bardwick, author of *Danger in the Comfort Zone* and a guest of the council, argued that Sears was guilty on both counts. Noting that the company was in financial trouble, she remarked, "When anxiety is high, people are more willing to fudge the books. The breakdown of ethics was that management did not anticipate the problem."[50]

ETHICS AND COMMUNICATION   The ethics of marketing communication are often tied to the ethics of product strategy, particularly in the case of false or exaggerated claims about a product. Other unethical practices (which may be illegal as well) include bribes, kickbacks, and "bait and switch" advertising. This last practice involves advertising that a product is for sale at a low price, then claiming that it is unavailable and offering a higher-priced item when customers seek to buy it.

Advertising aimed at children—particularly television commercials—has been under intense scrutiny during the last two decades. Believing that children are highly influenced by advertising, the children's advocacy group Action for Children's Television has argued for laws reducing advertising time during children's television programs and has fought programs that are clearly tied to commercial products.

Unethical marketing messages may result in one-time sales, but they are hardly likely to build repeat business. Furthermore, successful business marketer Paul Sherlock believes integrity is essential to any salesperson's success. According to Sherlock, a salesperson who wants to maintain the necessary high energy and positive relationships needed to win business from organizational buyers must believe the product will benefit the customer and that the seller's organization can meet all its responsibilities to the customer.[51]

The Trend toward Increased Ethical Awareness

Perhaps in reaction to the many business scandals that surfaced during the 1980s, the trend today has been toward increased ethical awareness. According to surveys, over three-quarters of major U.S. corporations are trying to promote ethical behavior by their employees.[52] Thus, ethical awareness is supported by business and marketing organizations, as well as the general public.

ETHICS OF EXCHANGE AND COMPETITION

caveat emptor
A legal concept meaning "buyer beware."

The ethics of the exchange process in American business have changed during the last 30 years. Before President Kennedy's statement of the Consumer Bill of Rights, American business practices were largely based on the legal concept of **caveat emptor**, or "buyer beware." In other words, buyers were considered responsible for evaluating the quality of merchandise, truthfulness of promises, and so on; if something was wrong, it was up to the buyer to find out before completing a transaction. But the Consumer Bill of Rights and the quality approach to marketing both take the view that buyers should be pleased with the goods and services they receive. There should be no unhappy surprises about safety, quality, or communication with the seller.

Competition can strain business ethics. In some cases, businesspeople believe (sometimes correctly) that ethical behavior will cost them a sale or prevent them from using an appealing strategy. This belief can lead to such unethical and illegal practices as industrial espionage and bribery.

INDUSTRIAL ESPIONAGE   In industrial espionage, companies steal information about products, clients, or marketing plans from each other. Computers have made this practice easier and blurred the line between ethical and unethical practices. For instance, information and messages carried by a company's electronic mail (e-mail) system are the property of the company. Members of the Information Systems Council recently raised the question of whether a company would be liable if an employee used e-mail to leak confidential information.[53]

BRIBERY   The prevailing standard in the United States is that bribery is unethical. Nevertheless, in many industries organizational buyers are tempted with lavish gifts. Of course, buying from whichever supplier produces tickets to the most exciting sports event is hardly likely to serve the buying organization's best interests. Nor does this sales tactic help the selling organization focus on anticipating and meeting customers' needs.

Foreign Corrupt Practices Act
Act that makes it illegal for American companies to bribe a foreign government official or agency in order to do business in that country.

In some parts of the world, bribery is prevalent, even customary. The U.S. Congress has responded by passing the **Foreign Corrupt Practices Act**. This law makes it illegal for American companies to bribe a foreign government official or agency in order to do business in that country. But while this behavior is now illegal, it may still be expected by foreign governments or businesses.

TECHNOLOGY AND ETHICS

The explosion of technology in the last half of the twentieth century has brought forth new ethical issues. The misuse of electronic information was mentioned earlier. The rapid pace of technological development can tempt marketers to beat competitors by

You Decide

SHOULD DOCTORS PRACTICE SELF-REFERRAL?

Suppose your doctor recommends that you have an X-ray, an MRI, or another diagnostic test. Then you find out that your doctor has a financial stake in the diagnostic facility to which he or she sent you. Self-referral, as this is called, is perfectly legal. But is it ethical? Certainly, it might make you question whether you really need the test.

Some doctors—and patients—view self-referral as a direct conflict of interest that drives up the amount of testing and its cost. Others feel that self-referral allows doctors to have greater control over the quality of testing, and that joint ventures (test equipment and facilities owned by a group of physicians) keep costs down.

The American Medical Association, which debated both sides of the issue for a number of years, has declared self-referral unethical—but with exceptions. For instance, if a patient *clearly* needs a test or procedure, the physician may refer him or her to a facility that the physician owns or works in. Who decides whether the patient clearly needs the procedure? The doctor. But the AMA argues that most doctors can determine objectively whether or not a procedure is necessary and thus ethical under AMA guidelines.

Some doctors have individual guidelines that, they feel, are more appropriate and effective than the general AMA stance. One orthopedist, who owns financial interests in several MRI units, claims that he refers patients to the best one of these units because it is of superior quality and charges less than others in his state.

Some states have begun to take action against self-referrals. The Florida legislature has given doctors an ultimatum: they must either sell their financial interests in testing centers or stop referring their patients to the centers. (In Florida, as of 1991, 40 percent of doctors owned a stake in some type of medical business.)

Do you think self-referral is a matter of greed or good medicine? Should it be banned? If it is permitted, are stricter state regulations needed? If so, what regulations do you think would help keep referrals objective and the quality of patient care high?

Source: Melinda Beck, "Is It Need? Or Is It Purely Greed?" *Newsweek*, December 21, 1992, p. 58.

---

introducing products before the organization has thoroughly tested them to ensure they are safe or perform as promised. Or what about introducing products that make companies more efficient, at the cost of workers' jobs?

Owing in part to technological change, the medical field is fraught with ethical questions: Should physicians be allowed to assist in the death of terminally ill patients? Should experimental drugs for AIDS be given "quick" approval by the FDA? Should organ donors (or their families) be paid? (For discussion of another ethical issue in the medical field, see "You Decide.")

Sometimes a change in both technology and attitudes gives rise to new questions. Take the case of the French drug RU-486, called the "abortion pill." Roussel-Uclaf, the manufacturer of the pill, withdrew the product in response to worldwide outcries about the ethics of marketing a pill that could be used to terminate a pregnancy. The French government ordered the pill back on the market. The company complied but halted worldwide marketing of the product because of the controversy, which exceeded Roussel-Uclaf's expectations. Chairman Edouard Sakiz explained, "When we developed the compound, abortion had been legal in France for 15 years. We never thought we would create an ethical dilemma."[54]

code of ethics
Written statement of an organization's ethical principles and standards of conduct.

ORGANIZATIONAL CODES OF ETHICS

Many organizations, concluding they must take a formal stand requiring ethical behavior by their employees, have established a **code of ethics**. Such a code is a written statement of the organization's ethical principles and standards of conduct. These codes usually cover confidentiality, conflicts of interest, relationships with other organizations in the marketing channel (such as the propriety of giving gifts to buyers of the company's services), payments to government officials (say, to speed up bureaucratic processes), and other areas. The Code of Conduct for the Colgate-Palmolive Company details standards of behavior for employees' relationships with fellow employees, the company, suppliers and business customers, consumers, the government, society, the environment, and shareholders.

Recognizing the importance of ethical codes in marketing, the American Marketing Association (AMA) established its own written code of ethics, reprinted in Figure 3.7. The AMA provides guidelines for ethical behavior in the areas of marketers' responsibilities, honesty and fairness, the exchange process (including the marketing mix), and organizational relationships. (For more on the AMA Code of Ethics, see "Put It into Practice.")

PERSONAL VERSUS ORGANIZATIONAL ETHICS

Just as an organization has a written or informal code of ethics, so each of its employees has personal ethics. Sometimes the two come into conflict. For example, in the case of RU-486, sales of the product could benefit thousands of women, reaping hundreds of millions of dollars for Roussel-Uclaf.[55] But other consequences include the deaths of embryos, the diversion of funds from the possible development and manufacture of medication to fight a deadly disease, and negative publicity and possible lawsuits against Roussel-Uclaf. One employee might conclude that the company is obligated to its shareholders or to women to make the product available; another may have a strong moral belief that he or she should not be involved in marketing the product.

One reason for conflict is that ethics may be based on three different philosophies:

moral idealism
A philosophy of ethics that focuses on individual rights and duties regardless of the consequences.

utilitarianism
A philosophy of ethics that adheres to the idea of the greatest good for the greatest number.

altruism
Unselfish devotion to others.

1. **Moral idealism** focuses on individual rights and duties regardless of the consequences. A person with strong moral idealism might be a "whistle blower," alerting authorities to an employer's unethical or illegal practices. Such a person is apt to have little sympathy for most managers' desire to balance concern for social responsibility with concern for profits.
2. **Utilitarianism** upholds the greatest good for the greatest number. Simply put, if the benefits (to society, to the organization) exceed the costs (socially, financially), then the practice is ethical. If the costs are higher than the benefits, then the practice is unethical. A drawback of this philosophy is that it's not always clear what the benefits and costs are or how to measure them.
3. **Altruism** is unselfish devotion to others. Giving something away with no thought of receiving something in return is an altruistic act. Many acts that appear altruistic are not purely so. A hospital's donation of supplies to a relief agency is not purely altruistic if the firm is partly motivated by its ability to take a tax deduction and receive favorable publicity. Since marketing is based on exchanges, it is difficult to imagine a purely altruistic marketing activity.

How does an organization deal with differing individual viewpoints? It is not enough to uphold absolute standards such as altruism. Rather, marketers need the authority to work creatively with their coworkers to devise practical solutions. For example, a team might observe the organization uses environmentally damaging but cheap processes. It could study whether customers could be persuaded that an environmentally friendly version of the product is worth a higher price.

One consultant advises, "We can learn how to look at the ramifications now and over the longer term, and we can go on to learn how to better argue about the right-

FIGURE 3.7

Code of Ethics of the American Marketing Association

Code of Ethics

Members of the American Marketing Association are committed to ethical, professional conduct. They have joined together in subscribing to this Code of Ethics embracing the following topics:

Responsibilities of the Marketer
Marketers must accept responsibility for the consequences of their activities and make every effort to ensure that their decisions, recommendations, and actions function to identify, serve, and satisfy all relevant publics: customers, organizations and society.

Marketers' professional conduct must be guided by:
1. The basic rule of professional ethics: not knowingly to do harm;
2. The adherance to all applicable laws and regulations;
3. The accurate representation of their education, training and experience; and
4. The active support, practice and promotion of this Code of Ethics.

Honesty and Fairness
Marketers shall uphold and advance the integrity, honor, and dignity of the marketing profession by:
1. Being honest in serving consumers, clients, employees, suppliers, distributers, and the public;
2. Not knowingly participating in conflict of interest without prior notice to all parties involved; and
3. Establishing equitable fee schedules including the payment or receipt of usual, customary and/or legal compensation for marketing exchanges.

Rights and Duties of Parties in the Marketing Exchange Process
Participants in the marketing exchange process should be able to expect that:
1. Products and services offered are safe and fit for their intended uses;
2. Communications about offered products and services are not deceptive;
3. All parties intend to discharge their obligations, financial and otherwise, in good faith; and
4. Appropriate internal methods exist for equitable adjustment and/or redress of grievances concerning purchases.

It is understood that the above would include, but is not limited to, the following responsibilities of the marketer:

In the area of product development and management,
- disclosure of all substantial risks associated with product or service usage;
- identification of any product component substitution that might materially change the product or impact on the buyer's purchase decision;
- identification of extra cost-added features.

In the area of promotions,
- avoidance of false and misleading advertising;
- rejection of high pressure manipulations, or misleading sales tactics;
- avoidance of sales promotions that use deception or manipulation.

In the area of distribution,
- not manipulating the availability of a product for purpose of exploitation;
- not using coercion in the marketing channel;
- not exerting undue influence over the resellers choice to handle a product.

In the area of pricing,
- not engaging in price fixing;
- not practicing predatory pricing;
- disclosing the full price associated with any purchase.

In the area of marketing research,
- prohibiting selling or fundraising under the guise of conducting research;
- maintaining research integrity by avoiding misrepresentation and omission of pertinent research data;
- treating outside clients and suppliers fairly.

Organizational Relationships
Marketers should be aware of how their behavior may influence or impact on the behavior of others in organizational relationships. They should not demand, encourage or apply coercion to obtain unethical behavior in their relationships with others, such as employees, suppliers, or customers.
1. Apply confidentiality and anonymity in professional relationships with regard to privileged information;
2. Meet their obligations and responsibilities in contracts and mutual agreements in a timely manner;
3. Avoid taking the work of others, in whole, or in part, and represent this work as their own or directly benefit from it without compensation or consent of the originator or owner;
4. Avoid manipulation to take advantage of situations to maximize personal welfare in a way that unfairly deprives or damages the organization of others.

Any AMA member found to be in violation of any provision of this Code of Ethics may have his or her Association membership suspended or revoked.

AMERICAN MARKETING ASSOCIATION

Source: Reprinted with permission from "AMA Adopts New Code of Ethics," *Marketing News* (September 11, 1987), pp. 1, 10; published by the American Marketing Association.

Put It Into Practice

APPLY THE AMA CODE OF ETHICS	Take another look at the American Marketing Association's Code of Ethics in Figure 3.7. Read it carefully. Think about your experiences as a consumer: • Has a marketer ever broken the code of ethics in order to sell a product to you? (For example, have you ever been the victim of high-pressure manipulation or misleading sales tactics?) • Conversely, have you had an exceptionally good encounter with a marketer because that person seemed to have a high standard of conduct? How did these experiences make you feel? Discuss your experiences with classmates.

---

ness or wrongness of proposed actions." The key, according to this consultant, is learning to communicate our ethical positions more effectively. "When we do that," he says, "there's the possibility of debate and clarification."[56]

Diversity

The population of this land has never been uniform. Even before the first Europeans arrived, there were many tribes and nations composed of all ages and both sexes. Today, however, the diversity of the population is greater than ever. Immigrants continue to arrive in the United States from all parts of the globe, speaking many different languages and bringing different values. As described in Chapter 2, family structure has grown more varied as well.

People tend to prefer the company of others like themselves, however, and various forms of discrimination persist. For example, Sidney T. Bowers, founder of United Energy of Wisconsin, has found that being African-American has made it difficult for him to get credit from banks in spite of his excellent credentials.[57] And Lowell Thompson, a veteran creative director at a Chicago advertising agency, has studied the percentage of African-Americans in the creative departments of ten national agencies. His figures show that African-Americans recently held only 2 percent of such jobs in Chicago, even less than the 5 percent of creative management jobs held by African-Americans nationwide.[58]

Fortunately, many marketers do realize that narrow-mindedness is not only unethical but against their best interests. Marketers and other businesspeople today must recognize the existence and benefits of the population's diversity. Above all, they must appreciate the diversity of the markets they serve and of the work force they participate in.

Issues of diversity are closely tied to issues of ethics and social responsibility. Laws and ethical considerations require fairness in hiring, promotion, and compensation practices. Organizations with operations overseas must contend with the ethical dilemma of how to extend fairness to countries with different, often lower, standards for environmental protection and treatment of workers.[59] In addition, considering the needs of people who make up a market is a key aspect of responsible marketing by large and small organizations. This chapter devotes a separate section to the topic of diversity because it has become so important to the practice of marketing.

DIVERSITY AMONG MARKETS

As examples throughout this book attempt to show, the United States as well as the global marketplace is full of variety. Language, cultural norms and values, geographic

Advertising its Labels for Education program to supermarkets, the company states, "Campbell's Labels for Education program is a straight 'A' promotion that earns us higher sales and, more importantly, highest honors with our consumers." Marketing is based on exchanges, and Campbell's recognizes that even if it is not purely altruistic, its promotion is socially responsible.

location, age, sex, and levels of income and education are just a few of the ways in which people differ. These differences are among the information that marketers should gather through environmental scanning, described in Chapter 2. For example, marketers to consumers will want to know that between 1990 and 2000, the number of African-American households in the United States is expected to grow five times faster than the number of white Anglo households, and the number of Hispanic households is expected to grow even faster.[60] Thus, marketers who think only in terms of white households will miss out on big slices of the consumer pie.

Demographics help identify patterns of diversity so that marketers can target their goods and services appropriately, both in the United States and abroad. For example, in Los Angeles, radio station KLAX-FM, part of the seven-station Spanish Broadcasting System, recently grabbed 7.2 percent of the listening audience—the largest share for radio stations in that area. This success was not only the result of recognizing that there is a large Hispanic market in that area, but of appreciating that many Hispanic listeners are young. To attract young Hispanic listeners, KLAX plays popular Spanish music styles such as *banda, ranchera,* and *nortena.*[61]

Marketers also need to appreciate diversity issues in order to work effectively with their customers. Consider San Diego–based Trader Publications, which publishes a variety of magazines that carry classified advertisements. One of its female employees visited a client, a male car dealer from the Middle East who demanded to be waited on by a male. She handled the situation by proceeding to photograph the car he wanted to sell, as was her usual practice. The client became furious—an outcome the employee might have been able to avoid if she had understood more about the client's culture.[62]

Other chapters in this book, including those on global marketing, consumer behavior, and market segmentation, will take a closer look at diversity among markets.

DIVERSITY AMONG MARKETERS

Just as markets are different, so are marketers. This is because the work force is diverse and growing more so. *Workforce 2000,* a report by a policy research organization

Recognizing diversity among its marketers, Avon salutes five of its African-American district sales managers for their leadership and entrepreneurism. This ad appeared in Ebony *magazine.*

At Avon, Diversity Has Always Been Our Style.

Our District Sales Managers are wearing makeup from the Avon Tones of Beauty collection. Jewelry by Avon.

For over 100 years, Avon has been a leader in diversity and empowerment —the tools of achievement. We're proud of our strong heritage of commitment to the realization of goals and aspirations. And we're proud to have been honored recently in *Black Enterprise* as one of America's "25 Best Places for Blacks to Work." In this spirit, we salute five of our District Sales

Managers, pictured above. They represent the leadership and entrepreneurism that has inspired thousands of our African-American Representatives to achieve their dreams and fulfill their ambitions. If you're interested in learning more about becoming an Avon Representative or would like to know about our earnings opportunities, just call us toll-free at 1-800-821-0400.

Avon District Sales Managers, pictured left to right: Verna Cox, Philadelphia, PA; Audrey A. Burke, Souk Village, IL; Elisia R. Jorge, Los Angeles, CA; Rhea Jones, Flint, MI; Sylvia Coleman, Atlanta, GA.

AVON
SALUTES BLACK HISTORY MONTH

called the Hudson Institute, forecast that 85 percent of the net growth (new hires minus people leaving) in the U.S. labor force by 2000 will be among women, racial minorities, and immigrants.[63] A recent survey of small companies found that nearly half had increased the number of women and racial minorities they employed.[64] As the population ages, more retired people are expected to take part-time jobs or launch second careers. In addition, an increasing number of people with disabilities are able to participate in the work force, thanks to technological developments that have helped them overcome various physical limitations, as well as the Americans with Disabilities Act, which requires employers to make their workplaces accessible.

One sign of diversity is the growing number of businesses owned and run by women and minorities. Statistics show that in the United States women are starting businesses at twice the rate of men. The number of African-American-owned businesses was recently found to have grown at three times the rate of all U.S. businesses. The number of Hispanic-owned businesses, though smaller, has grown at an even faster clip.[65]

The businesses started by these entrepreneurs serve a wide variety of needs and employ all kinds of marketing strategies. "Marketing Movers and Shakers" tells about William C. W. Mow, a native of China and owner of Bugle Boy Industries, a fashion empire with net sales of $470 million in 1992.[66] Donna Salyers's Kentucky-based firm, Fabulous Furs, sells patterns for fake fur clothing. The company's mail-order sales were $1 million in 1992, thanks in part to intense promotion. For example, Salyers wrote to every soap opera, and "Another World" bought a 100-inch-long cape for one of its episodes.[67] Michele's Foods, owned by Michele Hoskins, an African-American, markets a honey-based pancake syrup using an old family recipe. Eight years after Hoskins started the business in her basement, 700 stores were selling the syrup.[68] And on a grander scale, Russell Simmons is on his way to building a giant entertainment empire, including RAL/DefJam, the largest African-American-owned record company, which has produced such star acts as Run-DMC and Public Enemy.[69]

The managers and employees of marketing groups also are an increasingly diverse lot. A notable example is Jan Thompson, vice president of marketing for

Marketing Movers & Shakers

BUGLE BOY'S BILL MOW

Bugle Boy's casual clothes—jeans, shorts, shirts, and activewear—are such a common sight on high-school kids that it's hard to imagine a teenager who doesn't own any. In fact, Bugle Boy's founder and chairman, William C. W. Mow, hopes that Bugle Boy someday becomes to casual clothes what Kleenex is to facial tissues: "When a family goes out shopping, I want them to think, 'Let's get some Bugle Boys.'"

Bugle Boy's success—projected net sales for 1992 hovered around $470 million—came by a roundabout path. Bill Mow, a native of China (his family fled during the communist takeover in 1949), earned his Ph.D. from Purdue University in 1969 and founded Macrodata, a company that

designed and tested semiconductors for computers. He sold the company to a Milwaukee-based conglomerate, which turned around and accused him of doctoring the books. He sued the conglomerate and won, but he had legal bills to pay. So, in 1977, the electrical engineer entered the fashion business.

Bugle Boy, based in Simi Valley, California, made its reputation in pants for young men ages 17 to 35. But, according to Mow, the market has changed. "Right now, anything 17 years and younger is booming," he explains. "We can't make enough of them. And 35 years and older is growing at about 25 percent a year." The company now has seven divisions, coded by age and gender. Each division also has seven product lines, from jeans to knit shirts.

One reason the company does so well is Mow's computer-oriented background. He personally supervised the company's purchase of computers and helped develop software for them. "I know the internal organization of a computer," Mow remarks.

Bugle Boy's competitive advantage lies partly in this computer system. Salespeople carry laptops to depart-

ment stores and can tell managers exactly how much of an item is in stock. And goods are delivered within 72 hours of a store order. Buying fabric cheaply and managing distribution deftly are key factors to staying competitive; the computer system tracks all of this.

Mow also takes his relationship with his retailers personally. Although he does travel to the Orient to check up on Bugle Boy plants there, he spends much of his travel time visiting department stores around the country that carry Bugle Boy products. "It helps stores tremendously and us as well for me to be there," Mow comments. "For a local store in Mississippi to commit 5 or 7 percent of its total volume to us is a little scary for them if they don't know me."

Finally, Mow keeps a curb on prices. "We are the anchor that prevents other people from raising their prices. People cannot just raise their prices. They have to come over our dead body if they want to do it. We are keeping everyone honest."

William C. W. Mow is more than just an example of diversity among marketers. He is the quality approach, with a strong sense of ethics, in action.

Source: Jon Krampner, "Bill Mow: From Silicon Chips to Mass Couture," *Purdue Alumnus,* January/February 1993, pp. 18–23.

Mazda. Thompson directs all marketing activities for the company, including market planning, advertising, merchandising, promotions, motor sports, and sales training. She credits the 40-person marketing team, including both men and women, for the success of her first launch, the Miata.[70]

GLOBAL DIVERSITY Overseas, new marketing faces are emerging as well. Amway Corp. now has representatives in Hungary. "When communism was over, people were free, but what could they do?" notes James Vagyi, an Amway sponsor from Budapest. "The potential was released when Amway started. You have a 90-day, money-back guarantee. Anybody can try it." At a home demonstration, a representative named Noemi Parrag says, "Everybody buys something. We don't push. We just ask. I like making money."[71] And Yang Zhongwei, a former research economist at China's Academy of Social Science, opened the first Pierre Cardin retail store in

 Beijing, on the city's main shopping street. Within a few years, with exclusive rights to sell Cardin items in Beijing and Shanghai, Yang had amassed 12 boutiques.[72]

BENEFITS OF DIVERSITY   Organizations can benefit when their marketing staff and outside marketing experts reflect the diversity of the markets they serve. A diverse work force brings a variety of insights and strengths that can add creativity to decision making and problem solving. In addition, when marketers are diverse, they can better recognize and interpret the needs of more of the population and tailor the features of the marketing mix to such variables as where and when people shop, how they will perceive price discounts, and where they will see or hear advertisements.

AT&T Business Communications Service's San Francisco office seeks to reap these benefits by serving an important customer base: entrepreneurs in the West. These entrepreneurs are increasingly Asian, Hispanic, African-American, and female, so Colleen Mullens, who manages the product line, seeks out employees from these groups. This hiring tactic is part of a larger strategy to forge strong links with the various communities served by AT&T Business Communications Services.[73]

McDonald's Corporation is noted for its appreciation of the value of a diverse work force.[74] When the chain of restaurants expanded into cities from its original suburban locales, the company continued its policy that each store should reflect the community in which it operates. Not only does McDonald's hire and train young people of every race, it hires people with disabilities and provides sensitivity training to coworkers. Through its McMasters program, the company recruits older people, mostly retirees, to work with young crew members and model values of caring and courtesy. As shown in Figure 3.8, McDonald's also communicates its involvement to make sure members of the community know about its actions. When businesses with all kinds of owners burned in the 1992 Los Angeles riot, no McDonald's restaurant was set afire. Explains Edward H. Rensi, president and CEO of McDonald's U.S.A.,

"Our businesses [in South Central Los Angeles] are owned by African-American entrepreneurs who hired African-American managers who hired African-American employees who served everybody in the community, whether they be Korean, African-American, or Caucasian."[75]

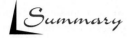

Social responsibility is an organization's acceptance that it is accountable to society for its actions. In marketing, social responsibility to the community can involve stopping a negative activity or promoting a positive activity. For example, marketers practice cause-related marketing by making charitable donations tied directly to the sales of a product. Green marketing refers to efforts to produce and promote environmentally safe products as well as reclaim materials.

Marketing ethics are the principles, values, and standards of conduct followed by marketers. Society expects marketers to adhere to its own values, beliefs, and principles, and criticism of current business practices is often harsh. Laws, like ethics, are based on values and principles, but unlike ethics, laws are enforced by government penalties for noncompliance. A particular marketing practice might be ethical but illegal, or unethical but legal. Ethical issues arise with regard to marketing research and all the elements of the marketing mix: product, pricing, channels of distribution, and communication.

The current trend in business is toward greater ethical awareness. For example, the standard for exchange has moved beyond the historical principle of caveat emptor (buyer beware). The Consumer Bill of Rights established that consumers have rights that marketers must recognize. However, competition can result in at least short-term rewards for engaging in such unethical actions as industrial espionage and bribery. Even so, ethical actions are more consistent with a quality, customer-driven approach to marketing. Technology has brought forth new ethical dilemmas, particularly in the areas of electronic information and medicine. Partly in response to those trends, many organizations have adopted a formal code of ethics. Employees' ability to adhere to such a code depends in part on how well it matches their personal ethics, which may be based on moral idealism, utilitarianism, or altruism. To reconcile any differences, employees can appreciate the consequences of a course of action and discuss the rightness or wrongness of proposed actions.

The population of the United States is becoming ever more diverse. In addition, marketers encounter diversity when they market globally. Thus, marketers need to recognize and respect differences among people in the markets they serve as well as among marketers themselves. Appreciation of diversity helps marketers identify needs and select target markets. Fair hiring of a diverse work force enables marketers to better serve a diverse population.

KEY TERMS AND CONCEPTS

social responsibility (p. 64)
community relations (p. 66)
cause-related marketing (CRM) (p. 66)
green marketing (p. 68)
ethics (p. 72)

marketing ethics (p. 72)
planned obsolescence (p. 75)
price fixing (p. 76)
caveat emptor (p. 78)
Foreign Corrupt Practices Act (p. 78)

code of ethics (p. 79)
moral idealism (p. 80)
utilitarianism (p. 80)
altruism (p. 80)

REVIEW AND DISCUSSION QUESTIONS

1. What evidence of cause-related marketing have you seen recently?
2. What evidence of "green" marketing have you seen recently?
3. Describe the difference between ethical and legal behavior.
4. In the example about Genzyme, did the company act legally? Do you believe it acted ethically or unethically? Explain your answer.
5. What are some of the major ethical issues in product development?

6. Why is advertising aimed at children considered an ethical issue?
7. Technological advances in electronic information and medicine have evoked many new questions of ethics in marketing. In what other areas might technological developments give rise to new ethical questions?
8. Define the three types of personal ethics.
9. Why is an awareness of diversity among markets and marketers important?

Chapter Project
Signing Up for Social Responsibility

Imagine that you've been hired as a marketer by Bill Mow of Bugle Boy. One of the things he wants you to achieve is a heightened image of social responsibility for the company toward both the community and the environment. Think of a plan for a single cause-related marketing effort by Bugle Boy that would benefit the community, the environment, or both. For instance, the company might accept customers' previously worn Bugle Boy clothing in good condition to donate to homeless families.

Think through the specifics of your plan as thoroughly as possible. Answer questions such as how goods might be transported if necessary or which charitable organizations you might deal with. Present your plan in writing and/or to the class.

Case
The Ethics of Waste Handling

Business versus the environment. Versions of this battle are played out around the world. An industry that is particularly vulnerable to attack is waste handling—the toting away and burning, dumping, or burying of massive amounts of garbage created by individuals and organizations.

Take the case of Waste Technologies Industries, which operates an enormous incinerator in East Liverpool, Ohio. The incinerator is capable of burning 60,000 tons of toxic waste a year from industries all around the United States. That might sound insidious to anyone concerned about air pollution. But the WTI plant has highly advanced antipollution technology and smokestack monitors to send emissions data to the Environmental Protection Agency (EPA) on a minute-by-minute basis. WTI spokespeople insist that emissions are well below state limits. Furthermore, WTI has provided more than 100 jobs in an economically depressed town.

But here's the downside. The WTI incinerator lies on the Ohio River floodplain, directly above two aquifers. The nearest homes are only 300 feet away. During the 1980s, when the company applied for its permits, this proximity was legal. Now it's considered illegal; a more recent law requires homes to be at least 2,000 feet from the plant.

So Greenpeace got into the act, along with an EPA whistle-blower named Hugh Kaufman. Kaufman found ten-year-old irregularities in the permit process, and while the EPA concedes their existence, it also believes them to be moot at such a late date. Greenpeace claims that WTI's emissions figures are inaccurate or untrue (much too low), noting that incinerators also emit compounds for which there are no standards or regulations.

Kaufman states, "The children in the area . . . will be paying the price for their whole lives so that a few good men can get paid burger-flipper salaries to poison their neighborhoods." Some residents of the area agree. Hundreds gathered at a local protest rally, allowing themselves to be arrested for criminal trespass.

Such debates are a recurring part of business for WMX Technologies, the largest waste management company in the United States. WMX, parent company of Waste Management International and Chemical Waste Management (Chem Waste), got its start in the local trash-hauling business. It even-

tually expanded into a worldwide provider of "environmental services," including environmental consulting and the design and engineering of waste disposal facilities.

One controversy involving a WMX operation resulted from problems with a Chem Waste incinerator in Chicago. This technologically advanced incinerator designed to burn hazardous waste was one of only three in the nation permitted to burn PCBs, a notorious carcinogen. Chem Waste proudly invited the public to tour this, the nation's largest commercial incinerator, to see how it took care of the serious problem of hazardous waste.

Complaints and problems took their toll, however. In March 1988, Chem Waste admitted to government regulators that it had intentionally shut off pollution monitoring equipment at least four times during the preceding two years. It also admitted to feeding PCB wastes into the incinerator faster than allowed by the plant's permit. Three years later, a container of chemicals exploded in the incinerator's kiln. Chem Waste admitted no wrongdoing in the incident but settled charges from the Environmental Protection Agency by paying $3.5 million. Then, in 1992, Chem Waste revealed that a supervisor had put false labels on up to 100 barrels of toxic waste to avoid safety requirements. The company also admitted to keeping two separate data files on its inventory. State officials launched a criminal investigation, and two months later Chem Waste shut the incinerator, possibly for good.

Such controversy works against the company's expansion plans. Customers hesitate to sign on with a waste handler that might not comply with regulations. For example, Waste Management found that its progress in building a nuclear waste disposal plant in Martinsville, Illinois, slowed because Martinsville officials wanted an accounting of what had happened with the Chicago incinerator. The company faced similar scrutiny in Indiana, where it wanted to expand a hazardous-waste site.

Top management at WMX contends that the problems result primarily from a decentralized style of management that gives local operators a great deal of control. The parent company maintains that it takes a stance of concern for the environment that is consistent with its business objectives. In fact, WMX supports stringent environmental standards for waste disposal because the company's huge size makes it more able than its competitors to afford compliance.

For example, the company early acquired many sites for landfills in the United States and prepared them so that they met or exceeded the EPA's requirements. A showcase is the company's Settler's Hill landfill in Geneva, Illinois. On the half of the fill that is now closed, WMX has constructed a beautiful park and golf course. When the other half is closed, it will build an expanded golf course plus ski slopes and other recreational facilities. At these and other facilities, WMX taps out methane gas (which could explode underground), but instead of burning it off, it uses turbines to generate electricity with the gas. Meeting high environmental standards for landfills was expensive, but it gives WMX a competitive edge as EPA standards take effect and competitors have to upgrade their landfills.

Of course, not everything that is beneficial to the environment is beneficial for WMX. For example, the company's recycling operations have so far been unprofitable. As of now, recyclable materials sell at too low a price to cover the costs of handling them.

As noted earlier, WMX's operations are worldwide, extending to 21 countries. The international business started with a city-cleaning contract in the Saudi Arabian capital of Riyadh. There, Waste Management International recruited, housed, and fed its work force, mainly from Sri Lanka and India. Ignoring the advice of contractors with Middle East experience, Waste Management offered its workers high-quality working conditions, including air-conditioned facilities and training programs. The company justifies this approach by noting that its workers turned out to be highly productive.

WMX's revenues are $10 billion and rising. However, the company's growth has recently slowed. As countries around the world have experienced recessions, they have produced fewer products and less waste. Furthermore, Chem Waste blames the fact that businesses are actively seeking ways to cut the amount of hazardous waste they produce. This benefit to the environment reduces the need for the company's disposal services.

QUESTIONS

1. What are the social responsibilities of WTI and WMX? Have they lived up to some or all of these responsibilities? Is it even possible for a waste management company to do so? Explain.
2. What ethical issues arise in WTI's plans for an incinerator in East Liverpool? Is the problem one of knowing which course of action is ethical, or is it just difficult to accept the costs of taking the obviously ethical course of action? Explain.
3. Suppose you were a marketer for WMX Technologies. Suggest a strategy of green marketing for the company. What would be the basic elements of such a strategy? Do you see any ethical problems with it? Explain.

Sources: Jerry Adler, "It's Not Easy Being Green," *Newsweek,* December 28, 1992, p. 66; Tom Andreoli, "WMX Has a Big Chemical Problem," *Crain's Chicago Business,* September 6–12, 1993, pp. 1, 42; Subrata N. Chakravarty, "Dean Buntrock's Green Machine," *Forbes,* August 2, 1993; Julia Flynn, "The Ugly Mess at Waste Management," *Business Week,* April 13, 1992, pp. 76–77; and "The Money in Muck," *The Economist,* May 29, 1993, pp. 6–8.

CHAPTER 4   *Marketing in a Global Environment*

LEARNING OBJECTIVES

After completing this chapter, you should be able to:

1. Describe the global economy.

2. Identify important characteristics of the major trading partners of the United States.

3. Identify basic measures of a nation's economic condition.

4. Describe political/legal considerations that marketers weigh when deciding whether to enter foreign markets.

5. Explain how foreign languages and cultures affect global marketing efforts.

6. Identify the basic demographic and life-style data considered by marketers serving foreign markets.

7. Discuss ethical issues important to international marketers.

8. Describe the basic mechanisms for entering foreign markets.

Creating Customer Value
Young & Rubicam/Sovero

This is the story of two teams, one American and one Russian, that joined together in a single venture. Under the former Soviet Union's policies of *perestroika* (restructuring) and *glasnost* (openness), in 1988 the prestigious American advertising agency Young & Rubicam announced a joint venture with VTR, an ad agency owned by the Soviet government. Y&R named Gary Burandt, one of its premier admen, to head its new team in Moscow. Yuri Deomidov, director general of VTR, became leader of the Russian group.

From their first meeting in Moscow, the men and women of both teams realized they came from vastly different economies, political systems, and cultures. Yet somehow they'd have to work together to make the venture succeed. For instance, Y&R wanted to establish its office in a building near the U.S. embassy, totally renovating it to meet American standards for business working conditions. But the Soviets preferred that Y&R buy an old mansion for about $1 million (in hard currency only) and restore it for another $1 million. It was unclear whether Soviet regulations would allow Y&R to own the building outright. Young & Rubicam declined.

Burandt writes about his first impressions of the Moscow market, "I quickly realized I was trying to open an ad agency in a country where an important means of trade still is basic barter. . . . This is a city where the notion of the branded product was nonexistent, and the concept of choice—in the marketplace or in politics—virtually unknown." In early discussions about advertising with a Russian newspaper editor, Burandt learned from the editor, "People wouldn't believe ads. They think they're all propaganda."

The American group had to muddle through red tape to obtain everything from multiple-entry visas to living accommodations. Then they hired a mostly Soviet staff. When Y&R/Sovero officially got under way in 1989, it already had contracts from Johnson & Johnson and a Spanish marketer of processed meats.

From the start, the two senior executives—Burandt and his counterpart, Vladimir Vlasov—clashed in styles and values. Burandt's casual, outgoing demeanor contrasted sharply with Vlasov's formal, hard-line mentality. The two

argued over protocol, such as Vlasov's assertion that every Soviet in a joint venture receives a Volvo to drive. But as Burandt learned more about the function of commercial communication in the Soviet Union, he understood some of his colleague's demands and defensiveness. His understanding harkened back to the newspaper editor's comment: commercial communication was not a prestigious occupation but merely the dispensing of political and social messages, such as urging Soviet couples to have children.

Understanding between the team leaders as well as among staff members was crucial to the launch of Young & Rubicam/Sovero, the first such venture in Moscow. As the group began to work a little more smoothly, more contracts came in. They handled more assignments from Johnson & Johnson (dental floss, toothpaste, baby products), did some sampling for Heinz, and worked with Coca-Cola to support the opening of a McDonald's restaurant in Moscow. (Coke is Y&R's customer, and McDonald's is Coke's largest customer.) It's quite possible that the Y&R/Sovero team helped move the then-Soviet (now Russian) economy and political system a little closer to capitalism and democracy.

As you read this chapter on marketing globally, keep in mind how important it is for marketers to listen to the needs and desires of customers in other cultures, economies, and political systems. Try thinking of them not as *foreign* markets, but as segments of a whole market called the world.

Source: Gary Burandt with Nancy Giges, *Moscow Meets Madison Avenue* (New York: HarperBusiness, 1992).

Chapter Overview

Like Young & Rubicam, many organizations have found that they can benefit from taking an active role beyond the borders of their home country. For example, almost half of Johnson & Johnson's sales are to customers outside the United States.[1] Roughly two-thirds of the Coca-Cola Company's revenues come from non–U.S. operations.[2]

Serving customers internationally is a growing practice among U.S. businesses. Between 1970 and 1990, the total value of U.S. exports—products made in the United States and sold elsewhere—rose from under $50 billion to almost $400 billion. The total value of products imported to the United States rose even faster, from less than $50 billion to almost $500 billion. Thus, foreign countries offer U.S. organizations potential target markets and are often the source of major competitors.

The major difference between marketing globally and marketing within the United States is the complexity of the environment. Therefore, this chapter starts by summarizing major trends in the international marketing environment. Then it introduces the many issues marketers must consider when entering a foreign market. Finally, the chapter describes the basic arrangements that businesses set up for operating in foreign markets.

The Changing International Environment

When scanning the marketing environment, marketers need to take a global view. Even when the organization does not have immediate plans to do business outside the United States, marketers need to recognize the business opportunities and threats emerging elsewhere. This discussion summarizes current trends affecting major trading partners of the United States (see Figure 4.1). Of course, changes have continued since this book was written, and marketers must continually update their knowledge.

THE GLOBAL ECONOMY

Today the prevailing view is to think of the U.S. economy as part of a global economy. The actions of U.S. consumers and businesses affect other nations, and the actions of consumers and businesses in other nations affect the United States. This notion of a global economy is not entirely new. In the 1920s, economist Wesley C. Mitchell observed that the Western nations had similar business cycles. In other words, prosperity and recession were occurring at roughly the same time in the United States, European countries, and their major trading partners elsewhere in the world.[3]

Since then, various trends have linked the nations' economies more tightly than ever. One such trend is advances and improvements in the economic infrastructure of many nations. **Economic infrastructure** refers to a country's "internal facilities . . . available for conducting business activities, especially the communication, transportation, distribution, and financial systems."[4] Thus, some components of a nation's infrastructure are telephone systems, highways, railroads, electrical systems, banks, and stock exchanges. Many nations and businesses have improved their infrastructures through such advances as fiber optics, computer networks, satellites, and other technology. As a result, businesspeople can move goods, deliver services, transfer funds, and transmit messages faster and more widely than ever before. Distance has become much less of a barrier to doing business.

economic infrastructure
A country's facilities for conducting business activities, including communication, transportation, distribution, and financial systems.

FIGURE 4.1

**Major Trading
Partners of the
United States
(Imports and Exports
in Millions of Dollars)**

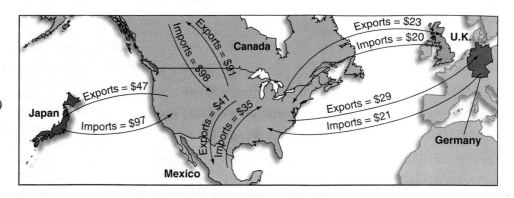

Source: U.S. Bureau of the Census, *U.S. Merchandise Trade,* Series FT 900, monthly.

NORTH AMERICA

The largest and third largest trading partners with the United States are its North American neighbors, Canada and Mexico. More than two-thirds of the products imported by Canada come from the United States, and three-quarters of Canada's exports head for the United States.[5] (Services are the fastest-growing component of U.S.–Canadian trade.[6]) Imports from and exports to the United States constitute an even bigger share of Mexico's trade.[7] Thus, in assessing marketing opportunities in other countries, it makes sense to start by looking at North America.

CANADA   In geographic terms, Canada is enormous, but it is not densely populated, so size is not its major attraction to U.S. marketers. Rather, many U.S. businesses are drawn to Canada by its similarities to the United States. In economic and technological terms, the two countries are similarly advanced. And outside the province of Quebec, most people speak English. Further easing trade between the United States and Canada, the two countries in 1989 signed a free-trade agreement that phases out import taxes (tariffs) for one another's products.

   Together, these characteristics of the Canadian market make it a relatively simple international target for U.S. businesses. For Integrated Computer Solutions, a computer consulting firm, "Canada was simply an extension of the United States in our direct-mail advertising." When Canadian customers started placing orders, the company figured out how to process them.[8]

   There are challenges in doing business across the U.S.–Canadian border, however. Consumers crossing the border still have to stop at customs and declare any purchases they made. Shippers still have to fill out export forms. And marketers must be aware of differences in laws and customs. Unilever found that it can't sell the same formulas of Close-Up and Aim toothpaste in both countries. Canada allows cyclamates but forbids the use of saccharin, whereas U.S. law permits saccharin but not cyclamates.[9]

MEXICO   South of the U.S. border, Mexico also has close ties to U.S. business. Relatively low wage rates and less stringent pollution control regulations have for years made Mexico an attractive location for businesses to set up production facilities. Along the U.S.–Mexico border are roughly 2,000 *maquiladoras,* or factories that assemble U.S components for export.

But perhaps less widely known is that Mexico is an increasingly attractive place to *sell* U.S. products. Consumer demand has risen along with rapid population growth (from 30 million to 81 million in two decades). According to one report, Mexican consumers are more impressed than their Canadian counterparts with things made in America.[10] In the business sector, the Mexican government has privatized, or sold to investors, almost 1,000 organizations once under government control.[11] As these Mexican businesses have prospered, they have become eager to buy U.S. goods and services. Richard Parton, president of a Wisconsin maker of food-processing equipment, was pleased with the million dollars' worth of orders he received from Mexican companies at a trade fair.[12] Today almost 70 percent of the imports sold in Mexico are from the United States.[13]

True, the Mexican culture differs more from mainstream U.S. culture than the Canadian culture does. However, the U.S. companies that act now to learn the culture will likely have the easiest time building brand loyalty in this growing market. Consultant George Muñoz suggests that researching U.S. Hispanic markets is a good way to practice.[14]

NORTH AMERICAN FREE TRADE AGREEMENT   Marketing efforts among Canada, Mexico, and the United States should grow even faster since the three countries signed the North American Free Trade Agreement (NAFTA).[15] This international agreement phases out tariffs and other trade barriers among the three nations, creating what many call the world's largest common market. Besides lifting trade barriers for goods, NAFTA helps service providers serve the three countries by ending requirements that professionals be citizens of the country in which they practice.[16] (Professionals must still comply with any laws regulating how they practice, however.) U.S. banks and securities firms can operate Mexican subsidiaries, and U.S. trucking firms can carry international cargo to Mexico.

Critics of NAFTA have warned that the agreement would cause unemployment as U.S. businesses moved their operations to Mexico. Of course, many businesses—including such giants as Procter & Gamble, PepsiCo, Ford, Chrysler, and General Motors—have already operated in Mexico for decades, a trend that is likely to continue. NAFTA supporters claim that free trade will play a more important role by enhancing Mexico's prosperity. According to the International Trade Commission, NAFTA could lead to a 7 percent increase in Mexican employment and 16 percent growth in wages.[17] As a result, Mexico could become a much bigger customer of U.S. businesses, thus actually creating jobs in both countries. Procter & Gamble predicted that eliminating Mexican duties (taxes on imports) would allow the company to sell a larger range of products in Mexico, thus requiring P&G to increase the number of U.S. jobs by more than 2,000.[18]

THE EUROPEAN COMMUNITY

European Community (EC)
The 12 nations of western Europe that make up a common market.

In an effort to advance their economies by encouraging trade with one another, 12 nations of Western Europe formed a trade group called the European Community (EC). As shown in Figure 4.2, the EC countries are Belgium, Denmark, France, Germany, Greece, Ireland, Italy, the Netherlands, Luxembourg, Portugal, Spain, and the United Kingdom. The agreements creating the EC are designed to lower barriers to trade among member nations. People and products can travel freely across national borders within the community. The EC is also seeking to set uniform tariffs on imports from nonmember nations.

The Nations of the European Community

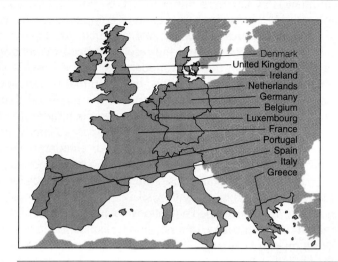

Together, the gross national products of these nations are second only to that of the United States. Thus, the EC is a major force in the worldwide marketplace. In addition, the strengthened trade among EC member nations is likely to make European businesses tougher global competitors. As customers, EC members may be easier to serve. Uniform product standards mean that products do not have to be modified to comply with the laws of each European nation. For example, all motor vehicles sold in the EC must meet the same standards for pollution and noise emissions.[19] Also, the elimination of border checks between member nations has made it easier to transport goods throughout Europe.

In serving the EC, marketers must remember that the community still consists of individual nations. In the words of Andrew Hilton, managing director of Meletai (London) Ltd., "The European Community . . . has at least ten mother tongues, two fundamentally incompatible legal systems, and three major variants of the dominant religion, with Islam making major inroads in France and the United Kingdom."[20] Hilton also notes that nationalism is strong among many Europeans. And in spite of the EC's efforts, not everything about commerce has been standardized. For example, electric plugs and phone jacks differ from one nation to another.[21] A mistaken belief that the European Community would become a single, homogeneous market was behind the failure of Federal Express's attempt to set up a European delivery network like its U.S. system. In contrast, United Parcel Service has succeeded by setting up a network of alliances with local firms in various European nations.[22]

JAPAN

When Americans think of international competitors, they typically think of Japan. In fact, Japan is not only the second largest exporter to the United States, it is also the second largest importer of U.S. products. Thus, U.S. marketers think of the Japanese as not only potential competitors but also potential customers. A significant example is the popularity of the Macintosh computer and of Windows software for IBM-compatible models, which has stimulated sales of U.S. applications software such as Lotus 1-2-3 and dBase. The only major segment of the PC software industry dominated by Japanese rather than U.S. firms is Japanese-language word processing—and U.S. vendors have begun to compete there as well.[23]

In the decades following World War II, the Japanese people worked hard to rebuild their economy, and the result has been tremendous growth. Manufacturers invested heavily in the most modern technology, and businesses promised lifetime employment. In the early 1990s, however, that pattern seemed to have ended. The nation entered a recession, and forecasters predicted that even after the recession ended, the nation's economy would grow much more slowly than it had.[24] Domestic demand has slowed because the typical Japanese family already has many consumer goods. Foreign trading partners have been erecting trade barriers because they see Japan as eager to export its goods but not to buy imported goods.

Japan has a reputation as a difficult nation for outsiders to do business in. Some foreigners are frustrated by the Japanese tendency to postpone business transactions until they have developed a relationship and gained confidence in the quality they will receive. Another source of frustration is distribution in Japan. The country has 13 retail stores (many of them small) for every 1,000 people, versus 6 for every 1,000 people in the United States. Until recently, Japan's small stores had great power to prevent large retailers from opening nearby. The small stores often are controlled by a large manufacturer that dictates product mix based on its own objectives and seldom on consumer research. This system makes it difficult for companies that do not control stores to get their products stocked. However, in the 1990s, Japan reformed its law so that more big retailers could open. The result has been increased retailing competition from chains like 7-Eleven that gather sales data to use in merchandising decisions.[25]

 Not all aspects of Japan's infrastructure make business more difficult, however. The *Washington Post*'s T. R. Reid found Japanese public telephones much easier to use than phones in the United States. They give change and accept a type of charge card. The caller simply inserts the phone card into any pay phone in Japan and dials the phone number. Phone booths near heavy traffic are sound-insulated, and some phone booths are scented. All this, and the cost of a local call is the equivalent of only nine cents.[26]

OTHER NATIONS

The nations discussed so far are currently the biggest trading partners with the United States. However, marketers and other business observers realize that the environment constantly changes. Marketers need to keep their eye on the rest of the world to see where demand is growing and where existing needs create market segments worth targeting.

ASIA/PACIFIC RIM   As more and more mass marketers have recognized, the world's most populous continent is Asia. Besides Japan, the nations with the most potential purchasing power are China and other countries with especially fast-growing economies—Indonesia, Malaysia, Singapore, and Korea (see Figure 4.3). The size of the Asian markets alone is enough to endear them to mass marketers. At its first ten outlets in China, KFC averages four times more customers a year than at its U.S. restaurants.[27]

With 21 percent of the world's population, China cannot be ignored by the world's marketers. Not only does this country have well over a billion people, but their economic status is accelerating in, according to one report, "one of the biggest improvements in human welfare anywhere at any time."[28] The same report observes that if China's economic growth continues outpacing America's as it has for the past 14 years, China will by 2010 become the world's largest economy.[29] This power is especially impressive in light of the country's strengthening economic ties with Hong

FIGURE 4.3

Growth of Asian Economies

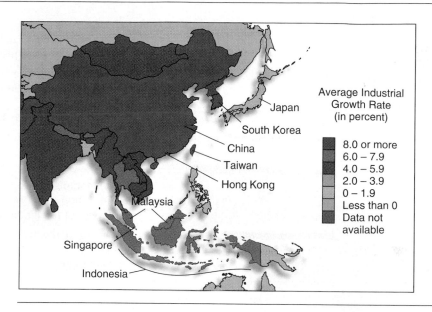

Average Industrial Growth Rate (in percent)

8.0 or more
6.0 – 7.9
4.0 – 5.9
2.0 – 3.9
0 – 1.9
Less than 0
Data not available

Source: Adapted from Philip R. Cateora, *International Marketing* (Homewood, IL: Irwin, 1993).

Korea aims to become a global supplier by targeting niches such as memory chips, video appliances, and aerospace. Korean strategy includes gaining technological expertise from U.S. and European suppliers through alliances such as the one with General Dynamics Corp. to co-produce F-16 fighters.

Kong and Taiwan, which together form a "Greater China."[30] However, China faces a tremendous challenge. No country has ever simultaneously left behind Third World poverty and communist rule. This dual task will have to include overhauling a neglected infrastructure, such as one of the world's smallest railway systems relative to its population.[31]

While the size and growth of China's economy are breathtaking, other Asian economies are expanding as well. Much of that growth is centered in Indonesia, Malaysia, and Singapore.[32] Indonesia—an archipelago of more than 13,000 islands— is the world's fourth most populous nation and is rich in natural resources. According to Indonesian businessman Augusto P. Niko, "Our population is so huge that anything we cannot export can be sold locally."[33] Malaysia is smaller but seeking to become fully industrialized by 2020. Low costs for labor and real estate make Malaysia an attractive location for manufacturing. Singapore boasts not only an advanced economy and management expertise but the busiest port in the world. Like Singapore, South Korea seeks technological leadership. It once did so through such Japanese-style practices as investing massive sums to gain a leading position in particular industries. More recently, Korean businesses are seeking partnerships with foreign companies that can teach useful technologies.[34]

AFRICA   Another region that is significant in terms of population is Africa, the second most populous continent. However, only 1 percent of U.S. exports currently are sold to African buyers.[35] U.S. businesspeople are reluctant to invest in Africa because of its widely held image as a place of poverty and political turmoil. These problems certainly exist, and overall the continent's economic growth has been slow.[36] However, the countries of Africa also have middle-class residents and large, modern cities. According to consultant Michael Sudarkasa, "There are 18 or 19 countries that have gone through democratic elections in the last 18 months. I don't think Americans could name 2 of them."[37] So far, Europeans and Japanese have more actively identified and acted on opportunities for marketing in Africa.

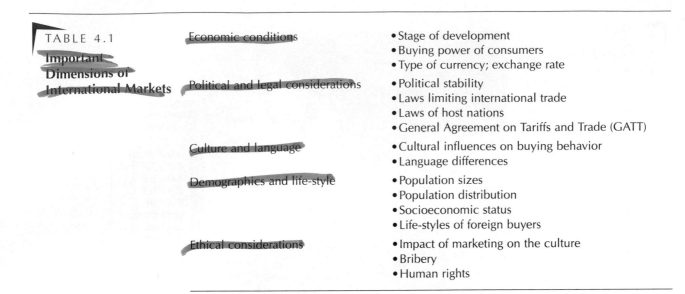

TABLE 4.1

Important Dimensions of International Markets

Economic conditions	• Stage of development • Buying power of consumers • Type of currency; exchange rate
Political and legal considerations	• Political stability • Laws limiting international trade • Laws of host nations • General Agreement on Tariffs and Trade (GATT)
Culture and language	• Cultural influences on buying behavior • Language differences
Demographics and life-style	• Population sizes • Population distribution • Socioeconomic status • Life-styles of foreign buyers
Ethical considerations	• Impact of marketing on the culture • Bribery • Human rights

EASTERN EUROPE   The nations of the former Soviet Union and its European allies have received much attention in recent years. As these nations have moved toward capitalism, marketers have hoped Eastern Europeans would increasingly demand their goods and services. Many have been pleased to find a welcoming market for their products, including basic consumer goods, car repairs, and environmental testing and management.[38] Procter & Gamble and Unilever, for example, have exceeded their sales forecasts for their early years in Eastern Europe.[39] Snickers and Twix candy bars are a high-status treat in Russia.[40]

The unsettled political and economic systems of Eastern Europe can make marketing difficult. For example, one business lost a shipment of leather hides traveling from Russia to Poland when the two countries' port authorities argued about jurisdiction. Before the dispute was settled, the hides rotted.[41] Banking in the former Soviet Union also can be difficult. Most banks charge for basic transactions, and they accept accounts by invitation, which requires connections with bankers.

SOUTH AMERICA   Political upheaval and slow economic growth have in the past dampened marketers' interest in South America. However, there are some signs that these countries have become more attractive markets. They have lifted many restrictions on business and have privatized many government enterprises. Chile has been one of the most attractive South American nations for U.S. businesspeople, thanks to two decades of free-market economics and a decade of economic growth.[42]

Issues in Entering a Foreign Market

As international developments continue to open up opportunities, marketers must be able to evaluate a number of issues that can make global marketing more challenging than domestic marketing. These issues, summarized in Table 4.1, pertain to the dimensions of each country's marketing environment. When marketers identify such issues as differences in economic conditions, laws, and culture, they can identify when and how to tailor their marketing mix to serve target markets in other countries.

FIGURE 4.4

Per Capita Income for Selected Countries*

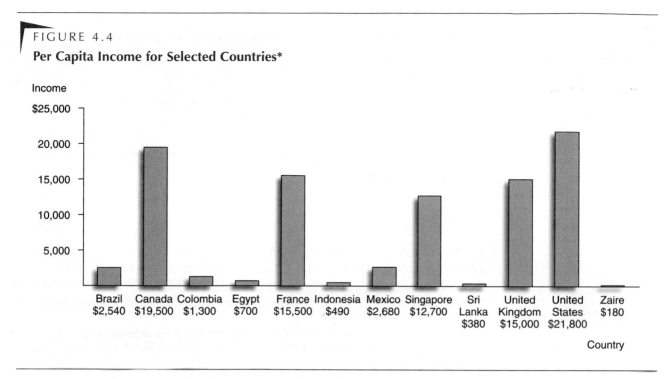

Income

$25,000	
20,000	
15,000	
10,000	
5,000	

Brazil $2,540 Canada $19,500 Colombia $1,300 Egypt $700 France $15,500 Indonesia $490 Mexico $2,680 Singapore $12,700 Sri Lanka $380 United Kingdom $15,000 United States $21,800 Zaire $180

Country

*Per capita gross domestic product, 1990.

ECONOMIC CONDITIONS

As noted earlier, the nations' economies are increasingly intertwined, and business cycles tend to follow similar patterns. However, there are differences, and these may be significant. In learning about particular countries, marketers need to find out such basics as the country's stage of economic development, the buying power of its people, and the strength of its currency.

STAGE OF DEVELOPMENT   To begin comparing countries' stage of economic development, marketers can classify them as developed or developing countries. The so-called **developed countries** have economies in which modern technology allows organizations to produce a wide variety of products and consumers to purchase many services and durable goods. The major developed countries are the United States, Canada, Japan, and most countries in Western Europe. In contrast, the **developing countries** have not fully moved from an agricultural to an industrial economy, though they may be in the process of doing so. Of course, these are very broad classifications and mask many differences among nations.

In general, the buying power of consumers is greater in the developed countries, so these countries interest most marketers. However, a developing nation making significant economic advances may have very strong demand for products that are considered mature in the United States. For example, would you rather sell telephones in the United States or in China, India, and Indonesia, where the combined population of 2 billion people shares only 20 million telephones (one for every 100 people)?[43] In addition, small companies may find a developing country an attractive place for niche marketing. A small company can handle the needs of the market while it is still growing, and big competitors may not be attracted to the market for some time.[44]

developed countries
Countries with the economies and technologies to produce a wide variety of products, as well as consumers who can buy them.

developing countries
Countries in the process of moving from an agricultural to an industrial economy.

	TYPE OF CURRENCY	AMOUNT EQUAL TO ONE U.S. DOLLAR
TABLE 4.2 **Recent Exchange Rates**	Canadian dollar	1.31
	French franc	5.56
	German mark	1.59
	Japanese yen	105.90
	British pound	.65

Source: Adapted from "Key Currency Cross Rates," table in *The Wall Street Journal*, September 16, 1993, p. C15.

BUYING POWER   To look at buying power, marketers can start with such overall measures as gross national product, income per person, and the distribution of income. **Gross national product (GNP)** is the total value of the goods and services produced in a particular country. It is a basic measure of the amount of economic activity going on in the country.

gross national product (GNP)
The total value of the goods and services produced in a particular country.

To get a sense of the buying power of consumers, marketers look at income per person, called **per capita income** by economists and statisticians. Per capita income varies widely from one country to another. Figure 4.4 provides some examples.

per capita income
Income per person.

Almanacs and foreign governments generally publish these data. Besides current figures, marketers will want to look at historical data and forecasts to see whether GNP and earnings are expected to grow at an acceptable pace.

These numbers are, however, just averages that mask the range of incomes within a single country. Studying the distribution of income within the country reveals that even countries with a low per capita income often have a segment of society with much higher earnings. One observer sees signs today of a growing global middle class.[45] For example, almost half the populations of Hong Kong, Singapore, South Korea, and Taiwan are members of the middle class, with tens of millions more in Argentina, Chile, and Mexico.

Furthermore, depending on the economy's structure, an income that is small by U.S. standards may give consumers relatively great buying power. Thus, although Chinese salaries are low, the cost of housing also is low—typically less than 5 percent of household income. As a result, many Chinese consumers have plenty of disposable income.[46] Also, low-income people tend to buy *more* of some products, such as bus service (instead of automobiles). Amparts International, a distributor of parts for trucks and buses, learned that "the bus market in Mexico City alone is much larger than the entire bus market in the U.S."[47]

CURRENCIES   Each nation has its own currency—money that is in general use in that nation. Buyers in the United States use dollars, buyers in Japan use yen, and buyers in Mexico use pesos. Organizations that handle more than one type of currency must understand and keep up with **exchange rates**. Essentially, an exchange rate is the price of a currency. It tells how much of a currency you can get in exchange for another type of currency—for example, how many francs or rubles you can get for $1. Table 4.2 shows some exchange rates recently reported in *The Wall Street Journal*.

exchange rate
The price of a currency.

Exchange rates are continually changing, which creates significant risks for global marketers. Suppose a manufacturer agrees to sell a machine tool for 1.5 million British pounds at a time when the exchange rate is 0.5 pounds for every U.S. dollar.

Then the exchange rate rises to 0.6; in U.S. dollars, the price has fallen from $3.0 million to $2.5 million:

$$\text{Original Price} = £1.5 \text{ million} \times \$1/£0.5 = \$3.0 \text{ million}$$
$$\text{New Price} = £1.5 \text{ million} \times \$1/£0.6 = \$2.5 \text{ million}$$

Because of such risks, many global organizations, including banks, have staff members who try to keep up with exchange rates and trade the organization's foreign currency for the best price possible. Global organizations may also select a bank that can help them handle foreign currencies and exchange rates. The ad in Figure 4.5 describes a number of such services offered by Citibank.

POLITICAL AND LEGAL CONSIDERATIONS

The international political and legal environment can affect a marketing strategy in several ways. In assessing a country, marketers need to consider whether its political system creates an acceptable climate for operating there. Relevant dimensions of the legal environment include laws limiting international trade, laws of host countries, and the General Agreement on Tariffs and Trade.

POLITICAL SYSTEMS   Some political systems favor government control over the freedom of individuals and private organizations. For example, anyone who wants to invest in operations in Indonesia must first get a letter of approval signed by that country's president, a process that takes about nine months.[48] California Sunshine, a caviar producer, struggled with the Russian bureaucracy. The company had for years fished for sturgeon on the Chinese side of the Amur River, so owner Mats Engstrom wrote to the Ministry of Fisheries in Moscow, suggesting a joint venture that would expand fishing to the Russian side. After six months, the ministry wrote that it wasn't interested because there were no fish in the Amur River. After several more frustrating tries in Moscow, Engstrom skipped the national government and negotiated a deal with local officials.[49]

Another political issue is the country's stability. In the United States, the presidency can change hands as often as every four years, and as a result, policies regarding international trade can shift frequently. But although political leaders come and go, the U. S. system itself has endured the Civil War and shows no signs of ending. In contrast, other political systems, such as those of Somalia, Cambodia, and Haiti, stand on much shakier ground.

When a country with an unstable political system is otherwise a desirable place to market, the seller will look for ways to protect its resources. It might insist on being paid quickly, then immediately convert the payment into dollars. The U.S.–based seller might also limit the extent of its operations in the country.

Of course, a country that poses unacceptable risks to one business may be a source of opportunity for another. O'Gara-Hess & Eisenhardt specializes in armor-plating cars. Over half of the cars that receive this protection go to buyers in the Middle East.[50]

LAWS LIMITING INTERNATIONAL TRADE   Nations seek to protect the interests of domestic businesses by limiting the activities of foreign businesses within their borders. An example is antidumping laws, introduced in Chapter 14, which are designed to prevent foreign businesses from harming local competitors by selling at less than cost. Other common laws related to international trade include import restrictions, exchange controls, limits on who may own or work for the organization, and restrictions based on national security.

tariff
The set of duties charged on imported goods and services.

duties
Taxes on imports or exports.

quota
The limit on the amount of a product that may be brought into or taken from a country.

exchange controls
Laws that place a ceiling on the amount of money that may be exchanged for another currency.

hard currency
Currency backed by gold reserves and readily convertible to other currencies.

Import restrictions may take the form of tariffs and quotas. A **tariff** is a set of duties charged on imported goods and services. In this sense, **duties** are taxes on imports or exports. The government may set duties for a type of product at a single rate for all countries, or it may charge different rates to different countries. A **quota** is a limit on the amount of a product that may be brought into or taken from a country. The intent of import restrictions is to give domestic producers an edge within the country. However, they tend to hurt domestic buyers by leading to higher prices.

Exchange controls are laws that place a ceiling on the amount of money that may be exchanged for other currency. Of particular concern is the ability to exchange a country's currency for **hard currency**—that is, currency backed by gold reserves and readily convertible into other currencies. Holders of hard currency can spend it in other countries—say, to invest elsewhere or to pay dividends to the company's owners. Exchange controls may directly state a limit on the amount to exchange, or they may limit exchanges by setting a low exchange rate. China limits exchanges by limiting the amount of hard currency available.[51]

Ownership restrictions may require that a majority of the company's ownership be in the hands of the host country's citizens. Or a majority of the organization's personnel might have to be citizens of the host country. In that case, the organization has to either restrict its operations to countries with enough qualified personnel or arrange to train its employees to make them qualified.

Some marketers also face restrictions related to national security. If the U.S. government determines that selling a particular product to buyers in certain countries poses a threat to national security, the government may prohibit the sale. This type of restriction particularly affects sales of high-tech products such as computers and communications equipment.

LAWS OF HOST NATIONS   U.S. businesses operating in foreign nations must observe those nations' laws. In some cases, business is more regulated in other countries. For example, many European nations specify the days and hours during which businesses may operate. And Germany's strict environmental controls made it difficult for ServiceMaster to get approval for the cleaning products used by its franchisees.

Noted a company spokesperson, "In the United States, everything that isn't expressly prohibited is permissible. In Germany, it's just the opposite."[52]

In other cases, U.S. companies are challenged by operating in a less regulated environment. Many countries allow cartels and unregulated monopolies that are prohibited in the United States. In addition, patents and copyrights are better protected in the United States than in many countries, including India. At least until recently, software developers avoided India because the majority of software obtained there has come from illegal copying of the programs.[53]

Further complicating this picture, marketers must be familiar with any local (as opposed to national) laws regulating business activity. In Canada, businesses must follow the laws of the provinces in which they operate. Thus, in Quebec province, all invoices, catalogs, and product labels must be in French (English translation optional).

 Sometimes an organization finds that a country's laws make that country's market too inhospitable to serve. Coca-Cola Company pulled out of India for 16 years because of a requirement that the company disclose the formula for its concentrate. Rather than give away this closely guarded secret, Coca-Cola stayed away until the requirement was removed.[54]

GENERAL AGREEMENT ON TARIFFS AND TRADE   The laws and regulations governing international trade can make global marketing more difficult. Yet most governments also recognize that when international trade is easy and widespread, domestic consumers can benefit from wider choices and domestic businesses have access to more customers. These benefits are behind a variety of laws and policies designed to promote free trade. For example, Hungary gives a five-year tax break to joint ventures (partnerships between foreign and Hungarian companies formed to carry out specific business activities).[55] In addition, governments promote free trade through such international arrangements as the European Community.

One of the most important efforts to make international trade easier is the **General Agreement on Tariffs and Trade (GATT)**. GATT is an international framework of rules and principles for opening up trade between member nations, backed by an agency that serves as a forum for negotiations. Over 100 nations are GATT member nations. Since the first GATT treaty was signed after World War II, tariff negotiations have taken place in several "rounds," and the average size of tariffs has plummeted (see Figure 4.6). The most recent negotiations were called the Uruguay round because they began in Uruguay in 1986. The Uruguay round reduced or eliminated a number of trade barriers—sharply reducing tariffs worldwide and increasing protection of patents, for example. But it did not meet the impotant goal of broadly opening world markets to trade in services.[56] According to one estimate make during the negotiations, successful completion of the Uruguay round could boost the global economy by $270 billion.[57]

General Agreement on Tariffs and Trade (GATT)
An international framework of rules and principles for opening up trade between member nations, backed by an agency.

CULTURE AND LANGUAGE

Marketers need a basic familiarity with the culture of any nation where they intend to operate. Becoming familiar with a culture is *not* the same as latching on to a few stereotypes and applying them willy-nilly. Rather, marketers should develop a sense of the values and styles of behavior common in various countries so they can recognize cultural differences and work constructively with people of other cultures. Marketers need to know about customs, etiquette, and the dominant religion(s). Some potential areas of difference to be aware of include family roles, personal space, perception of time, individuality versus group identity, and the degree to which the culture emphasizes achievement or relationships.

FIGURE 4.6

Average Tariffs of Industrial Nations

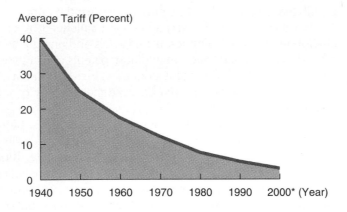

Average Tariff (Percent)

*Projected

Knowledge of and sensitivity to cultural differences can smooth relationships with foreign partners and potential customers. This is especially important for marketing services, because the services marketer typically comes into direct contact with the customer. Thus, a business consultant who repeatedly violates a culture's rules of etiquette is not going to get many referrals or much repeat business.

Learning about a culture can uncover marketing opportunities. For example, the average German employee gets six weeks of vacation time and more than one holiday a month.[58] This suggests a fertile marketplace for consumer products related to leisure time and for industrial products designed to boost productivity. And German retailers' practice of closing at 1:00 p.m. on Saturdays and all day Sundays has created an opportunity for U.S.–based franchises such as McDonald's, which are open seven days a week.[59]

CULTURE AND BUYING BEHAVIOR   Marketers need to learn about cultural influences on consumer behavior. The fact that a product was made in the United States impresses Hungarians, but not French or German consumers.[60] In Asia's fast-food arena, KFC benefits from the fact that chicken is consumed worldwide and is not shunned by certain religions, as are pork (by Muslims) and beef (by Hindus).[61] And when it comes to athletic shoes, Japanese consumers like striking color combinations, such as black and gold.[62]

Cultural differences apply not only to consumers but to the practices of businesses and businesspeople. U.S. salespeople who want to follow proper etiquette in Asia avoid joking around, wearing flashy clothes, giving lavish gifts, and making physical contact (except to shake an extended hand).[63] In making buying decisions, Japanese businesspeople tend to place more importance on their relationship with the vendor than on the product's technical features.[64] In Mexico, people place much emphasis on relationships and especially value family ties. They also tend to value accommodation over winning. Thus, to deal with Mexican businesspeople, marketers can benefit from building relationships and taking time to discuss family.[65]

LANGUAGE   An aspect of culture that affects many marketing decisions is language differences. U.S. marketers in Mexico or Japan have to overcome the hurdle of one different language, but other countries make that challenge look simple. China, for

FIGURE 4.7

The World's Ten Largest Cities

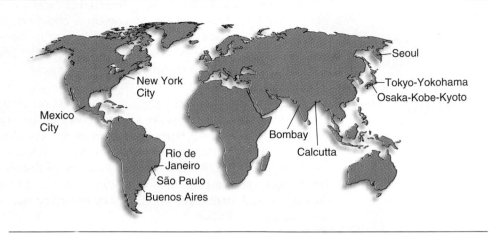

Source: *The World Almanac and Book of Facts* (New York: Pharos Books, 1993), p. 818.

example, has a common written language (Mandarin) but many different spoken dialects. Indonesia has more than 300 different language groups. And even other English-speaking groups have language differences with the dominant U.S. culture. Recently, the British Broadcasting Corporation sought to do away with such Americanisms as *trailer truck* (called an articulated lorry in Britain), *custom made* (bespoke), and the U.S. term for the punctuation at the end of this sentence (a period, something that Britons call a full stop).[66]

Recognizing the extent of language differences helps marketers realize that they must be careful to understand how consumers in other nations are likely to interpret not only their promotional messages but any communications at all, including brand names. No marketer wants to use a brand that sounds to potential buyers' ears as odd as some foreign brands sound to Americans'. Consider, for example, Sweden's Krapp toilet paper, Japan's Homo salami, Italy's Mukk yogurt, and France's Pschitt soft drink.[67]

DEMOGRAPHICS AND LIFE-STYLE

The demographic and life-style data considered by the international marketer are similar to the data collected to evaluate domestic marketing. A good place to start is with population sizes. The world population is roughly 5.4 billion, with less than 5 percent living in the United States. By far, the world population leaders are China (1.15 billion) and India (866 million), followed by the United States, Indonesia, Brazil, and Russia.

More and more of the world's people are living in urban areas. By 2000, almost half are expected to be living in large cities. A marketer looking to serve the biggest cities does well to look beyond the United States. As shown in Figure 4.7, nine out of ten of the world's largest cities are in Asia and Latin America.

AGE   Age segmentation can also lead to valuable insights. For example, data on births show that in the year 2001 there will be over two billion teenagers around the world, most of them in Asia and Latin America. This is 500 times as many teenagers as there were in the United States during the peak years of the baby boom.[68]

Another way to look at these figures is that there are now a lot of children on the planet. In China, kids aged 3 to 16 constitute about one-third of the population, and thanks to government policy, they typically are in one-child families. These data showed Los Angeles–based Nanuet Entertainment that China was a desirable market for toys, including Nanuet's Robotech action figures.[69]

SOCIOECONOMIC STATUS   Demographic data on socioeconomic status also help marketers identify target markets. Marketers rely on such information as income levels and occupational types, or they may ask consumers what social class they belong to. Self–assignments to social class may reflect cultural views of class as well as more objective criteria. In a recent survey of British people, 65 percent called themselves working class, and only 29 percent said they were middle class. Most Americans call themselves middle class, including many who would be ranked as working class in Britain.[70]

LIFE-STYLE   One way around the limits of segmenting on the basis of class is to look instead at life-style. Japanese young adults aged 18 to 21 have demonstrated that they value individuality and practicality. Businesses that have succeeded in selling to this group include L. L. Bean, which offers clothing emphasizing simplicity and value, and Sanyo, which has simplified the controls on a line of appliances such as televisions and washing machines.[71]

In contrast, as capitalism has provided opportunities to Russian and Chinese entrepreneurs, these two nations have seen growth in a group of people who have found business success and seek to flaunt their newly won riches. Those drawn to a life-style of conspicuous consumption are eager to snap up $1,300 Rado watches and six-figure Rolls Royce and Mercedes Benz automobiles.[72]

ETHICAL CONSIDERATIONS

It seems reasonable to assume that ethics requires fair treatment of employees and customers, whatever their national origin. However, putting this principle into practice can be difficult, in part because different nations may have different standards. For example, U.S. consumers set high standards for the accuracy of product claims, but the Chinese so far seem much more willing to allow some truly unbelievable claims. The official *China Daily* carried the following report about a woman who had suffered from hemorrhoids for 20 years: "She smoked 200 Kezhiling cigarettes. They cured not only her piles, but her recurring cough." And at the Beijing International Exhibition of Inventors, Wang Weidong displayed a candy called Civilized Sweet, which, he said, eliminates bad breath and body odor, restores hair to the bald, and turns white hair black.[73] How can a marketer stick to the more mundane claims allowed by U.S. standards and still compete?

For many marketers, the ethical approach is to apply abroad the ethical standards they adhere to at home. Levi Strauss sets standards for its foreign contractors, such as requiring them to pay at least the prevailing local wage.[74] Whirlpool finds that foreign consumers are eager to buy energy-efficient, water-saving appliances, so its concern for environmental issues pays off globally.[75]

IMPACT OF MARKETING   Marketing a product in another culture can sometimes bring about detrimental changes in the targeted group's cultural practices. Asian cul-

Levi Strauss, a company that now manufactures about 50 percent of its jeans and shirts overseas, investigates the wage policies of its 400 foreign contractors. The women in the photograph are sewing Levi products in Costa Rica and earning twice that country's legal minimum wage.

tures have been praised for having diets low in fat, but U.S.–based fast-food chains are introducing Asians to the joys of cheeseburgers and fried chicken. Producers of infant formulas have been criticized for using promotional practices that have the effect of encouraging new mothers, especially in less developed nations, to opt for bottle-feeding rather than breast-feeding, even though the latter is associated with healthier babies. U.S. tobacco companies have been roundly criticized for aggressive marketing tactics in Asia, where cigarette sales had been concentrated in the hands of government monopolies that did little to promote smoking. In many Asian countries, U.S. cigarettes are now seen as glamorous, and there is much less awareness of their health risks than in the United States.[76] From the perspective of quality-driven marketing, one might criticize all these tactics as being based primarily on the business's profit needs rather than on the needs of the customer. (For more on ethical issues related to the impact of marketing, see "Put It into Practice.")

BRIBERY   Another common ethical dilemma in global marketing is the decision whether to engage in bribery. In many countries, it is common practice to bribe officials to cut through a thicket of red tape. Thus, a U.S. business spent weeks negotiating to sell several hundred fax machines to a Russian government enterprise for $300 apiece. The Russian director then asked the U.S. firm to bill the machines at $350 per unit, expecting the business to deposit the extra $50 per unit into the director's personal bank account. When the U.S. firm refused, the deal fell apart.[77]

However tempting it may be to go along with local custom, bribery is illegal even in countries where it is common. The U.S. law prohibiting bribery is the Foreign Corrupt Practices Act of 1977. If a U.S. firm engages in bribery, even if it calls the bribe a "sales commission," it is subject to fines. The individuals responsible for the bribe may go to prison.

HUMAN RIGHTS   Marketers also must consider whether it is ethical to operate in countries that do not offer basic human rights. For example, refusing to do business in South Africa was seen as a way to hasten the end of apartheid there. After the Chinese government suppressed political protests in Beijing's Tiananmen Square in 1992, many people believed U.S. businesses should refuse to operate or invest in China.

CONSIDER THE IMPACT OF MARKETING YOUR PRODUCT

What effect does marketing American products have on people who live in other countries? For this chapter's project, you will be asked to select a product and consider the major issues involved in launching it in a targeted foreign market. When you think about marketing a product in a foreign country, you must learn as much as you can about the impact that product may have on the people who live there. Ask yourself the following questions:

1. Do people in this market need or want the product?
2. Will the product enhance or disrupt their lives?
3. Does the product pose any safety or health risks?
4. Does the product violate any religious or cultural values in the country?
5. Does the product require some prior knowledge or skill on the part of the consumer to use it properly? If so, are members of the market likely to have this knowledge?

Advocates of staying out of these countries have maintained that this is an important way to put pressure on unjust governments. Others believe that businesses operating in these countries can be a force for change.

Mechanisms for Serving an International Market

Creative marketers evaluate the complexities of foreign markets and the needs of foreign buyers, then decide whether and how they can serve those markets effectively. The mechanisms they choose often involve individuals or organizations in the host countries. But while the details vary, the means of serving a foreign market is generally a form of exporting, licensing, joint venture, or direct ownership. Table 4.3 summarizes some pros and cons of each possibility.

EXPORTING

exporting
Producing a product in a manufacturer's own country, then shipping it to another company for sale.

The least risky way to serve foreign markets is to export the organization's products. **Exporting** involves producing the product in the organization's own country, then shipping it to another country for sale. Because this approach involves little change to the organization's way of operating, it is a common mechanism for a first attempt at serving foreign markets. Admiral Screw Company went international by selling its screws to foreign branches of its domestic customers.[78] Inexperienced companies will find many experts who can make the job easier.[79] For example, bankers experienced in international transactions can review letters of credit, and freight forwarders can take care of physical distribution.

trading company
A company that buys a variety of products in one country and resells them in another.

Some organizations use an even simpler version of exporting; they use an intermediary to ship the product overseas and sell it there. An example is a **trading company** which buys a variety of products in one country and assumes the risks of reselling them in other countries. The producer gets a guaranteed price from the trading company. This lowers the risk but also places a ceiling on the producer's profits if the product is a hit.

A twist on exporting that is becoming more popular is international mail order. Fast door-to-door deliveries by services such as Federal Express and DHL make it

	MECHANISM	ADVANTAGES	DISADVANTAGES
TABLE 4.3 **Mechanisms for Serving International Markets: Some Pros and Cons**	Exporting	Simple; minimal financial risk	May be less profitable than other mechanisms
	Licensing	Minimal capital outlay; useful for serving countries with import restrictions	Difficult to control licensee; when licensing agreement ends, licensee may become a competitor; may be less profitable than other mechanisms
	Joint venture	Risk limited to the organization's share in the venture; foreign partner contributes expertise the organization lacks; useful when the host country limits foreign ownership	Share control with venture partner; partner may learn technology or secrets that it uses to compete with the organization
	Direct ownership	Maximum control over foreign operations; ability to be close to customers	Expensive to set up; requires extensive knowledge of foreign markets and contacts overseas

Source: Based in part on information in Philip R. Cateora, *International Marketing,* 8th ed. (Homewood, Ill.: Irwin, 1993), pp. 325–334.

easy for a retailer to have goods shipped worldwide. Computer magazines in Japan carry advertisements with ordering information, and U.S. dealers that have targeted Japan have staff who can communicate in Japanese via fax or telephone.[80]

LICENSING

licensing
Granting another organization the rights to use a trademark or a patented product or process.

Small organizations often opt for licensing arrangements. **Licensing** is granting another organization the rights to use a trademark or a patented product or process. In exchange for these rights, the organization that holds the license pays a fee. Kidsports International granted Tokyo's Urban Planning Development a license to build a fitness and play center in Tokyo bearing the Kidsports name.[81]

A popular form of licensing is franchising, formally defined in Chapter 16. Many franchises are based in the United States. In the United Kingdom, for example, over 100 of 755 chains are U.S.–based.[82] Baskin-Robbins, the fifth largest franchisor in the world, serves up ice cream at over 3,500 stores in more than 45 countries.[83] (See Figure 4.8 for a sample foreign ad for a U.S.–based franchise.) A relatively recent user of international franchising is Anita Roddick of The Body Shop (see "Marketing Movers & Shakers").

Granting a license carries a risk because the licensor gives up control over how the product is made and how the customer is treated. And when the licensing agreement ends, the licensee may use its newfound expertise to become a tough competitor. Furthermore, licensing is typically the least profitable way for an organization to enter a market.

Still, the benefits outweigh the risks for some marketers. Licensing is less costly than developing the expertise and resources to plan and implement an international

FIGURE 4.8

**Marketing a
U.S.–Based Franchise
in Santiago, Chile**

 marketing strategy. Also, it enables the marketer to readily adapt the product to serve markets with different tastes and needs. Thus, Marvel comic books are produced by foreign licensees in 22 different languages.[84]

JOINT VENTURES

joint venture
A business agreement in which two or more organizations share management of an enterprise.

A **joint venture** is a business agreement in which two or more organizations share management of an enterprise. In the case of a U.S. organization that wants to enter a foreign market, it would enter into a joint venture with an organization from the targeted country or with experience operating there. Joint ventures can benefit organizations that are strong in some areas but not others. They seek a partner that has the strengths they lack. Thus, a joint venture between Lockheed and Russia's Khrunichev Enterprise to provide rocket launch services combines Russian rocketry expertise with U.S. marketing skills.[85] (On page 112 "You Decide" describes an attempt at an international joint venture involving businesses and nonprofit organizations.)

A joint venture gives the organization more control than it would have under a licensing agreement. At the same time, the organization does not have to accumulate as many resources or as much experience as it would without its venture partner. Furthermore, some countries, including India and Thailand, encourage the use of joint ventures by requiring that ownership be partly in local hands. Even after China lifted restrictions on foreign ownership, many enterprises launched by foreigners in China continued to be joint ventures. Conveyant Systems, an Irvine, California, maker of telecommunications equipment, finds that its Chinese partners have the connections needed to maintain reliable services such as water and heating fuel.[86]

Joint ventures also have drawbacks. The organization may have to compromise its own objectives when they conflict with those of its partner. Also, the organization may share so much information that its partner can become a formidable competitor. According to one report, the proliferation of alliances between U.S. and Asian companies in the computer industry is allowing Asian organizations to obtain technology

Marketing Movers & Shakers

ANITA RODDICK OF THE BODY SHOP

Anita Roddick isn't what you'd call a beauty queen. She wouldn't want to be called one, either. But she's at the top of the beauty business, at the right place and the right time.

British born, of Italian descent, Roddick is a hippie holdover who got the idea to create and market "natural" cosmetics and skin care products to counterculture types just like herself. In 1976 she got a $7,000 loan from a local bank, hired a chemist to create lotions free of animal fat, and began selling them in cheap, reusable bottles with handwritten labels in a small shop not far from her hometown of Littlehampton, England. Nearly 20 years later her business—called The Body Shop International—consists of 700 shops worldwide, 5,000 employees, and around $200 million in annual sales.

In addition to Anita and Gordon Roddick's flair for marketing and business, the secret to The Body Shop's success lies in its focus on products made from all-natural ingredients and

Anita Roddick's passion for social responsibility. Both of these qualities appeal not only to Roddick's own generation, but also to a younger generation of consumers who want to do the right thing. The Body Shop participates in a variety of socially responsible projects on a worldwide basis, including campaigns to save whales, end cosmetic testing on animals, help the homeless, and save the rain forests.

Further, Roddick doesn't promise that her products will change people's lives or make them younger. "We don't sell products that will keep you young. Nothing will keep you young," she declares. "We don't use words like *rejuvenate*. I'm not part of that dream cream market."

Finally, Roddick's company is run by women and for women, which she believes gives her a decided edge over the competition. "This business is run by a woman. I mean the policy decisions are made by women. All the words are written by women. Product development is controlled by women. So our customer, our female customer, believes that we have a covert understanding of women. It gives us an extraordinary edge. It's the Body Shop secret ingredient," says Roddick.

Roddick's international mystique carries over to the products themselves. For more than 15 years, Roddick has traveled around the world talking with women in developing countries about how they care for their skin and hair. "Women talking to women about their bodies is the easiest entry into social

anthropology ever," she muses. "I'm sitting with the Wayoo tribe a month ago in Colombia, and they're scrunching up cactus plants and washing my hair with it." This is where Roddick gets both her inspiration and her ingredients.

Maintaining control over the quality and service of 700 shops around the world is extremely difficult. Direct ownership is not possible in every company, and a business that starts small like Roddick's can have a tough time entering foreign markets. However, Roddick resisted an obvious route—franchising—for several years, particularly in the U.S. market. She wanted to own her own stores, get to know the unions, regulators, shopping malls, customers. She planned to expand slowly. But larger companies like Estee Lauder, The Limited, and even Kmart latched on to Roddick's product ideas and began to squeeze her out of the market. So in 1990 she decided to franchise. In the United States, 64 of the 78 stores are now franchised. Other franchises now exist around the world, from Sweden to Singapore.

Although the company's stock collapsed in 1992, it has since rebounded. Roddick claims that she didn't care about the stock, and she probably didn't. She really cares about the quality of her products, the quality of life for women around the world, and the quality of the planet.

Sources: Jean Sherman Chatzky, "Changing the World," *Forbes*, March 2, 1992, pp. 83–84; Philip Elmer-DeWitt, "Anita the Agitator," *Time*, January 25, 1993, pp. 52, 54; and "The Beauty Queens," *Vogue*, January 1990, pp. 190–195, 240.

that would have required an investment of billions of dollars and many years of research.[87] Motorola executive James A. Norling advises companies considering a joint venture to establish which technologies are confidential and to control communications so that information about those technologies is not leaked.[88]

You Decide

AT WHAT PRICE CAN THE RAIN FOREST BE SAVED?

You bite into that rich, creamy, crunchy Rain Forest Crunch ice cream cone at your local Ben & Jerry's ice cream stand knowing that you just paid more than you ever thought you would for this simple treat. But you don't mind—the money goes for a good cause. Ben & Jerry's along with several nonprofit organizations—Cultural Survival, the Ford Foundation, the World Wildlife Fund, the Inter-American Foundation, and a Dutch foundation called NOVIB—are banking on your goodwill.

In 1989, these groups banded together to fund a cooperative at Xapuri, Brazil, designed to give rubber tappers in Brazilian forests the incentive to harvest nuts in an environmentally sustainable way by paying them more for the nuts than the low international price. The cost of this subsidy gets passed along to

socially responsible consumers—in this case, those who have a yen for a certain flavor of ice cream.

On paper, the project sounds good—and certainly, so are the intentions of those involved. But financial and administrative snags have highlighted the difficulty of transferring marketing strategies that work in developed countries to developing countries without extensive modification. For instance, consultants familiar with the project say that the Brazilian workers don't realize that Americans will not pay a continually escalating price for gourmet food products just because they are environmentally friendly. The Brazilian infrastructure—its few roads, unreliable or sparse electricity, and unskilled workers—also hinders the

effectiveness of the project. And the factory that shells the nuts hasn't been able to produce enough product to satisfy demand; thus, Cultural Survival has had to buy nearly 50 percent of its nuts on an international market largely controlled by suppliers that the Xapuri cooperative had hoped to put out of business.

The Xapuri cooperative has lost money three of its first four years in operation, and its funding is likely to be cut off if it doesn't show a profit soon. What steps do you think might be taken to save this socially responsible international joint venture? How might project marketers adapt their strategies to meet the needs of the Brazilian workers, American consumers, and the rain forest?

Source: Gary Marx, "Financial Crunch Threatens Green Brazil-nut Program," *Chicago Tribune,* May 30, 1993, sec. 7, pp. 1, 8.

DIRECT OWNERSHIP

An organization may also own production and/or marketing operations in the foreign countries it serves. Such arrangements, called direct ownership, may involve setting up the necessary facilities or acquiring a foreign firm in the same line of business. Loctite Corporation, a maker of industrial adhesives and sealants, uses direct ownership where possible, including subsidiaries in Argentina, Brazil, and Venezuela. The local managers control such decisions as pricing and promotion.[89]

Direct ownership gives the organization maximum control over foreign activities. Setting up operations close at hand may also be a condition of doing business with customers who want fast service. On the downside, direct ownership is expensive. It also requires an ability to handle language, cultural, and other differences. Loctite gains this expertise by hiring locals to run its foreign operations.[90] Because of the drawbacks, direct ownership tends to be most attractive for large firms and organizations that already have global experience.

Of course, direct ownership also occurs when organizations from other countries operate in the United States. For example, Korea's Hyundai Corporation designs and assembles some of its personal computers in San Jose, California, so that its management can more quickly respond to changes in the U.S. market.[91]

As a result of such activities, many marketers today work for foreign-based companies—and many more will tomorrow. Consequently, the most successful marketers of the future will be those with the flexibility and sensitivity required to work with and meet the needs of people from throughout the world.

Summary

The United States is part of a global economy, which affects U.S. marketers even if they have no immediate plans to do business outside the United States. Therefore, marketers need to be aware of potential opportunities and threats to their operations emerging around the world.

America's largest trading partners are in North America, Western Europe, and Japan. In addition, potential for growth comes from Asia, Africa, Eastern Europe, and South America. More than two-thirds of products imported by Canada come from the United States, and three-quarters of Canada's exports head to the United States. In Mexico, low wage rates and less stringent pollution control regulations have attracted many U.S. manufacturers, and consumer demand has increased dramatically, making the country an attractive place to sell U.S. goods. Trading with these nations is likely to accelerate, especially since the signing of the North American Free Trade Agreement.

The European Community (EC) consists of 12 nations of Western Europe with a total gross national product second only to that of the United States. Japan is the second largest exporter to the United States as well as the second largest importer of U.S. products. Asia is of interest to marketers because of its size and explosive growth, especially in China, Indonesia, Malaysia, Singapore, and Korea. Africa is the second most populous continent after Asia, and marketing opportunities are beginning to surface there. With the dissolution of the Soviet Union, Eastern Europe has opened up to trade, and South America—even with its history of political instability—is showing signs of opportunity.

When they consider entering international markets, marketers must identify such issues as differences in economic conditions, laws, and culture in order to tailor their marketing strategies appropriately. Major economic considerations include the stage of a country's economic development, the buying power of its consumers, gross national product, per capita income, and currency strength. Political systems and laws limiting international trade are important as well; the marketer must be familiar with restrictions such as tariffs, duties, quotas, exchange controls, and ownership regulations. Marketers must also be familiar with the culture and language of any nation in which they intend to do business. In addition, they must study international demographics and life-styles. Ethical considerations for international marketing include the impact of marketing on foreign countries, as well as issues of bribery and human rights.

Marketers may decide to serve international markets through one of several mechanisms. They may simply produce domestically and export their products. They may arrange licensing agreements with foreign producers. They may enter into joint ventures, in which they share marketing responsibilities with a foreign partner. Or they may maintain direct ownership of foreign marketing operations.

KEY TERMS AND CONCEPTS

economic infrastructure (p. 92)
European Community (EC) (p. 94)
developed countries (p. 99)
developing countries (p. 99)
gross national product (GNP) (p. 100)
per capita income (p. 100)

exchange rates (p. 100)
tariff (p. 102)
duties (p. 102)
quota (p. 102)
exchange controls (p. 102)
hard currency (p. 102)

General Agreement on Tariffs and Trade (GATT) (p. 103)
exporting (p. 108)
trading company (p. 108)
licensing (p. 109)
joint venture (p. 110)

REVIEW AND DISCUSSION QUESTIONS

1. Based on the information provided in this text (as well as any outside reading you may have done), do you think that NAFTA will offer greater opportunities for U.S. marketers? Why or why not?
2. Although Japan is the second largest exporter to the United States, it is also the second largest importer of U.S. products. However, what are some of the obstacles that U.S. marketers typically face when doing business in Japan?
3. As a marketer for the manufacturer of a moderately priced portable CD player, would you rather sell your product in Japan (a developed country) or China (a developing country)? Explain your answer.
4. What is GATT, and why is it important?

5. Less than 5 percent of the world's population lives in the United States. Where might U.S. marketers of athletic shoes look to expand their customer base? Does your answer depend on whether you are selling basic, low-priced sneakers or high-priced, high-performance shoes? Explain.
6. Why are cultural differences especially important for global marketers of services?
7. Why do you think Levi Strauss set standards for ethical behavior of its suppliers?
8. If you owned a small firm that manufactured a line of casual, moderately priced clothing made from all-natural fibers, what step would you take to enter an international market: licensing or a joint venture? Explain your choice.

9. As a U.S. marketer for the Japan-based Kikkoman Corporation (manufacturer of soy sauce), what steps would you take to make the product attractive to the average American? What information do you think you could provide to Kikkoman's Japanese management that would help its marketing efforts succeed in this country?

Chapter Project
Learning about a Foreign Market

Choose one of the products listed below (or think of one on your own), then select a city from Figure 4.7 to serve. Research the special issues you must consider before entering your chosen market: economic conditions of the city and nation, political and legal considerations, culture and language, demographics, and any ethical issues you can think of (including those you addressed in "Put It into Practice").

Record what you have learned about your chosen market area. Present your findings in writing or to the class.

Product ideas:
- Amusement park
- Taxi service or messenger service
- Hotel
- Bottled water or natural juice
- Computer games
- Baby food
- Bicycles designed for commuting

Case
Colgate-Palmolive Company

In Latin America, consumers buy Fabuloso all-purpose cleaner and Protex antibacterial soap. In Hong Kong, they buy Ajax expert spray cleaner in three different formulas: for windows, kitchens, and bathrooms. All over the world, people recognize and buy Colgate toothpaste. That's Colgate-Palmolive Company's goal for as many of its products as possible.

Colgate-Palmolive has a presence in nearly every corner of the world. The company first entered the Asian and African markets during the 1920s, and today does business in 34 countries with a total population of three billion. The company also does strong business in Latin America, with 16 subsidiaries and sales of around $1.4 billion. Developing countries such as China, India, Botswana, Zambia, Mexico, and Argentina all carry Colgate products, from toothpaste to soap. Developed countries such as Japan, Australia, and the nations of the European Community carry the products as well.

According to a recent annual report, Colgate-Palmolive "researchers create products for the world—not for a single country." Still, its marketers recognize the differing needs of consumers in various countries and develop products accordingly. For instance, Protex is a popular antibacterial soap developed for the warm climate in Latin America. The product does equally well in Asia, which has similar climates and, according to Colgate, similar consumer preferences as well. Another product "transplant" is Ajax Expert spray cleaner, which was originally developed for the European market.

Within a year of its introduction to the Hong Kong market, it had captured 11 percent of the market there.

Colgate tries to focus on developing products with a worldwide appeal. Marketing research is often conducted concurrently in multiple countries that have broad ranges of economic and cultural characteristics. For instance, for its new toothpaste Colgate Total, the company conducted research in Australia, the Philippines, New Zealand, Greece, Portugal, and Colombia. Cross-functional teams that include marketing experts and scientists from around the world work together to develop such products. As it introduces new and existing products worldwide, Colgate also relies heavily on brand-name recognition: practically everyone uses at least one Colgate product, whether it's Ajax cleaning products, Colgate toothpaste, or Palmolive soaps.

Colgate pays close attention to economic and political conditions in markets around the world. The firm has recently invested heavily in China, which has the world's largest population and consumers with increasing buying power. As Latin American economies and governments appear to settle down with freer markets, stabilized currencies, and fewer trade barriers (with the adoption of NAFTA), Colgate hopes to capitalize on the increased purchasing power of that area's 400 million consumers.

Colgate views itself as a worldwide corporation dedicated to shipping high-quality products everywhere on the planet. Notes Reuben Mark, chairman and chief executive officer, "Today virtually every aspect of Colgate's business—from how we organize our operations to how we view new product development to how and where we manufacture—reflects our global orientation." A company that already does business on six continents (it hasn't reached Antarctica yet) and in 75 countries is clearly a global player.

QUESTIONS

1. Why do you think Colgate's approach to developing products with a global appeal has been successful? Do you think this approach would carry over to a complex product such as portable computers? To a service such as consulting? Explain.

2. How do you think the company's use of cross-functional teams is especially helpful in the global marketplace?

3. What differences between the Japanese and Chinese *developing* markets should the company take into account?

Sources: "The Global Reach of Great Ideas," *1992 Annual Report,* the Colgate-Palmolive Company; "Colgate's Latin American Success," *1992 Third Quarter Report,* the Colgate-Palmolive Company; "Colgate's Excellent Growth in Asia," *1993 Second Quarter Report,* the Colgate-Palmolive Company.

Developing and Implementing Marketing Plans

Trek Bicycle Corporation

Customers don't think about marketing plans when they strap on their helmets and bounce along dirt trails on Trek mountain bikes. But Trek Bicycle Corporation of Waterloo, Wisconsin does; in fact, management used strategic planning to turn the company around.

Like many companies, Trek started out small, with four employees working in a tiny, rented warehouse in Wisconsin. The first Trek touring bicycles, made in 1975, were sold to bicycle dealers in the Midwest. Three years later, 5,000 Trek bikes appeared in stores from California to New England.

Its rapid growth meant that Trek had to face technology, volume, and quality issues. How many bicycles could be manufactured with its original production system? If the company went to higher volume, how could it ensure that quality would be maintained? The original Trek road bicycle was made of steel; was this also the bike of the future?

Teams of engineers and production people went to work on all these questions, with some people even tapping the knowledge of members of the aerospace industry to develop a special bonding process for aluminum alloys. In 1985, Trek introduced its first aluminum road bike, soon followed by a carbon composite model. Just a few years earlier, Trek had launched its first mountain bike, making it one of the founding manufacturers of mountain bikes. Trek also expanded its production facilities so that it could turn out 45,000 bikes a year, garnering $20 million in sales. But inventory buildup, slowing sales, heavy development costs, and inefficient operations created a multimillion-dollar loss for the company.

Trek needed a plan. Company officials knew that their bikes still enjoyed a good reputation, but Trek's organization had suffered. So they developed a new strategy, based on the premise that Trek must continue to build a high-quality product but must deliver it on time and at a competitive price. The plan also recognized the need to expand distribution, add new dealers, and increase the level of service to dealers. Finally, the new strategy focused on developing products that markets already wanted rather than trying to predict future market trends.

The plan worked. Not only did Trek curb its losses, it completely turned around, achieving five years of unprecedented growth in what had become a flat market. Today, Trek Bicycle Corporation has nine subsidiaries in Europe and Japan, distributes products in 40 countries, and operates three major distribution centers in the United States. Trek is now the largest manufacturer and marketer of bicycles in America.

Creating a plan for any company, no matter how large or small, is crucial to the company's success, even if customers aren't aware of it as they peddle the product on and off the road.

Source: Promotional material from Trek Bicycle Corporation, Waterloo, Wisconsin.

CHAPTER 5

Strategic Marketing Planning

LEARNING OBJECTIVES

After completing this chapter, you should be able to:

1. Explain how strategic marketing works and why it is important.

2. Describe the process of strategic planning.

3. Discuss the role of marketing in strategic planning as it is carried out traditionally and with cross-functional teams.

4. Identify the functions of marketing management.

5. Describe how marketers develop and evaluate marketing plans.

6. Explain how forecasting supports the process of creating a marketing plan.

Creating Customer Value
King's Medical Company

At King's Medical Company, based in Hudson, Ohio, one reason for success is effective planning. But according to Albert Van Kirk, CEO and one of the company's founders, planning was foreign to him until recently. Instead, he tended to "tell people things in the hall and expect them to get done." In contrast, William Patton, cofounder and general manager, is a planning fanatic. His influence is felt throughout the company.

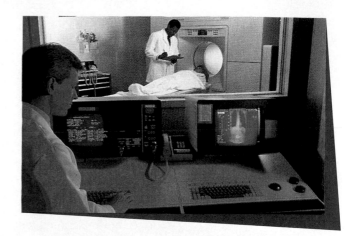

King's Medical Company, founded in 1981, owns and comanages medical equipment such as that used for CAT scans and magnetic resonance imaging (MRI). Strategic planning at King's began with creation of a mission statement, or statement of purpose. A leadership group comprising the company's five board members focused on the company's reason for being in business. Each member of the group wrote down answers to the following questions: What business are you in? Why do you exist? What's unique about your company? How are you different from the way you were three years ago? How will you be different in four years? William Patton, leader of the group, then combined the answers so that the board could hammer out a cohesive mission statement for the company.

The mission statement now contains eight points, including "offering the highest quality support services in the marketplace to ensure that both client and corporate objectives are reached." It is circulated to all employees and even to job applicants. That way, everyone in the company knows exactly why he or she is there.

Periodically, Van Kirk, Patton, and the directors of marketing, sales, territory management, and finance convene to evaluate the industry and the company's position in it. From this evaluation, they can identify ways King's Medical can act on opportunities that arise and create long-term objectives for the company. When they see obstacles, the group looks for ways to overcome those obstacles as a team. Says Van Kirk, "In so many companies, information like this is handed down from the finance department. They'll say, 'You have to sell x, period.'" In contrast, the cross-functional approach at King's Medical helps the company prepare to take advantage of new technology and meet the challenges of its growth.

Finally, the planning team spells out how King's Medical will achieve its long-term objectives. For example, in the company's early years, an objective was to set up a marketing department. The planning team broke that objective down into four tasks: hiring, training, visiting sites, and writing up documents. The team specified how long each of these activities should take, when it should be started and completed, and who was responsible for its completion.

The strategic planning can take months, but it pays off. The company grew 400 percent between 1987 and 1992, from sales of $2.7 million to over $13 million.

As you read this chapter, think about how the planning effort affects an entire organization and the quality of the products it offers to its customers.

Source: Leslie Brokaw, "The Secrets of Great Planning," *Inc.*, October 1992, pp. 151–157.

Chapter Overview

The rapid pace of change in today's world means that marketers must continually think about the future in order to be able to continue meeting customer needs. So that they can be ready to act when changes present problems and opportunities, marketers must decide what needs the organization will meet and how. In other words, marketers must plan. They must set goals and determine how to achieve those goals.

Planning is beneficial to the marketer and to the organization as a whole. It helps managers and employees at all levels prioritize how to spend money and time. By forcing marketers to focus on the future, planning also lessens the chance of their being surprised by a new law, a competing new product, or other changes. Furthermore, planning reduces the chances of making costly mistakes. A carefully thought-out marketing plan is more likely to achieve the desired result than are haphazard marketing activities.

This chapter focuses on the types of planning that are important to the marketing effort. It describes how organizations use strategic planning to chart their overall course and how marketers participate in the process of strategic planning. Next it discusses planning as one of the functions of marketing management. That discussion emphasizes the creation of a marketing plan—the blueprint for aiming a particular marketing mix at a particular target market. Finally, marketing planning requires accurate predictions of future demand. Therefore, the last section in the chapter introduces commonly used forecasting techniques.

The Nature of Strategic Marketing

In many cases successful businesses are started by an innovator who, through luck or insight, happens to offer a new product that generates great demand. Xerox's photocopiers gave millions of offices an attractive alternative to carbon paper. Similarly, many nonprofit organizations flourish because they serve a widespread need. Seeing the popularity of a display of children's creations in a local school gymnasium, Linda Scheck arranged for a permanent site in a park district barn, hoping that a few hundred people would attend during the museum's first months. Thanks to the desire of parents to spend "quality time" with their children in a safe place, thousands came, and within a few years, the Children's Museum and Imaginasium in Hoffman Estates, Illinois, became one of the biggest new children's museums in the United States.[1] Organizations such as Xerox and Scheck's museum owe their early success to being in the right place at the right time.

Yet managers and business owners cannot trust to luck that they will always have just the goods or services that individuals or organizations want to buy. Furthermore, they must recognize that competitors will try to do a better job of delivering the same products. Thus, the organizations that are most successful over the long run make use of **strategic marketing**, or marketing efforts aimed at the accomplishment of particular strategies.

strategic marketing
Marketing efforts aimed at accomplishing particular strategies.

In the original, military sense of the word, a strategy is the way a nation uses its various forces to achieve particular goals related to winning a war. In the business world, managers devise strategies that draw on the organization's resources to achieve high performance, especially relative to competitors.

Nike marketing strategy "in action" is evident in this photo from the 15th annual RUNNER's WORLD/Nike Midnight 5-Mile Run that takes place on New Year's Eve in New York City's Central Park. There is a parade of zany costumes followed by the race's start and fireworks at midnight. More than 5,000 ran in the 1993/1994 race.

STRATEGY IN ACTION: NIKE

One business that takes a strategic approach to deploying its resources is Nike. Developing a careful strategy is critical to the company because the market for athletic apparel is highly competitive. Undoubtedly, strategic thinking is also valued because the company's founder and many employees are former athletes used to trying to beat the competition.

A key part of Nike's strategy is getting widely respected, well-known athletes to wear its products. The best-known example is Michael Jordan, who served as a spokesperson and model for its basketball shoes. Nike recently provided ten top-ranked college football and basketball teams with complete uniforms it planned to market shortly afterward. Of roughly 320 players in the National Basketball Association, 265 wear Nike shoes, half due to contracts with the maker. Nike also has contracts with the coaches of over 60 major colleges. In the National Football League, 275 players wear Nikes, as do 290 major-league baseball players.[2] Such a strategy doesn't leave the competition much room to show off.

Another tactic to gain visibility is the impressive Nike Town store the company operates in Chicago. Nike Town features a three-story courtyard with life-sized figures of athletes suspended overhead. Near the swimsuit section is a 20-foot-long aquarium with fish whose bright colors match the current fashions. In the area displaying Aqua Socks, nine television monitors set into the floor display moving images of a sea floor. According to National Public Radio reporter Alex Chadwick, "This store feels like a theme park or some kind of wild museum of fitness."[3] Soon after its opening, Nike Town had become the most popular tourist attraction in the city.[4] Besides providing consumers with messages about Nike, the store provides a place for the company to learn about consumer tastes and buying behavior.

The strategic approach is working at Nike, at least for now. A Nike-commissioned survey shows that the shoes most desired by over three-quarters of teenage boys in the United States are Nikes.[5] The company's 1990 revenues of $2 billion had almost doubled by 1993, in spite of a recession, and more than one in three pairs of athletic shoes sold in the United States bear the Nike brand.

STRATEGIC QUALITY

In quality-driven organizations, the idea of using strategy to beat the competition is not good enough. Rather, the organization needs to turn the practice of strategic marketing to the task of pleasing its customers. This entails thinking of quality in broader terms than simply eliminating any defects in its products. The organization needs to focus not simply on how products are made, but on what it does and why.[6]

The focus must be on the customer. For example, an organization seeking strategic quality doesn't start with the goal of a 15 percent sales increase, then figure out what product changes would achieve it. Rather, the organization would think about what customers want or need, then ask what the potential increase in sales would be.[7]

To see how strategic quality works, consider the case of Northern Telecom, a Canadian communications company. To achieve its goal of becoming the world's largest supplier of communications equipment, Northern Telecom has charged all of its employees with achieving excellence. The drive to improve therefore extends to all operations, such as a commitment to eliminate the company's use of chlorofluorocarbons (CFCs), which are harmful to the environment. Northern Telecom achieved this objective even before others in the industry thought it possible. One result was "tremendous positive response" from the company's customers.[8] Thus, an activity that didn't involve reducing product defects or setting higher marketing goals wound up helping the marketing effort.

Strategic Planning in the Organization

strategic marketing planning
The development of marketing objectives and strategies

The most effective marketing strategies are those that enable the organization to achieve its overall strategies. Thus, the development of marketing objectives and strategies—a process called **strategic marketing planning**—should support organization-wide strategic planning. At the level of the organization, **strategic planning** consists of all activities that lead to development of a clear organizational mission, organizational objectives, and strategies that enable the organization to achieve its objectives.[9] The focus of strategic planning should be the long term, say, five to ten years.

strategic planning
Activities that lead to the development of a clear organizational mission, objectives, and strategies enabling the organization to achieve its objectives.

Strategic planning lays the foundation for other types of planning in the organization. **Tactical planning** is the creation of objectives and strategies aimed at attaining goals for specific divisions or departments over a medium-range time frame, such as one to five years. Typically, tactical planning is the responsibility of middle management. The creation of marketing plans, described later in this chapter, is a type of tactical planning.

tactical planning
The creation of objectives and strategies aimed at attaining goals for specific departments over a medium-range time frame.

Operational planning is the creation of objectives and strategies for individual operating units over a short time span, usually one year or less. Supervisors and sometimes middle managers are responsible for operational planning. In addition, when workers are involved in planning, they are most often involved in operational planning—say, by setting annual goals for themselves or for their team.

operational planning
The creation of objectives and strategies for individual operating units over a short time span, usually one year or less.

THE PLANNING PROCESS

Planning in the organization begins when management uses information about the environment and the organization's own strengths and weaknesses to develop a long-range vision of where the organization should be going (the mission). From there, the planning process moves to specifying how to fulfill that vision. As shown in Figure 5.1, this process involves creating first a mission statement, then organizational objectives, organization strategies, and a portfolio plan that outlines how the organi-

FIGURE 5.1

**The Strategic
Planning Process**

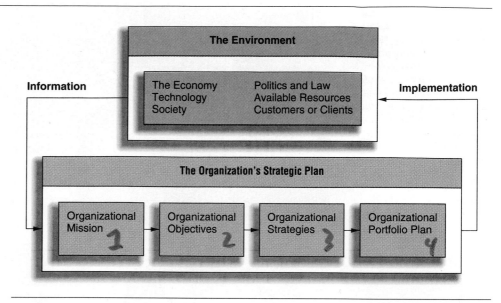

Source: J. Paul Peter and James H. Donnelly, Jr., *A Preface to Marketing Management,* 6th ed. (Burr Ridge, Ill.: Irwin, 1994), p. 10.

zation's product lines fit together. Together these elements form the organization's strategic plan.

Implementing the plan can lead to changes in the environment. Management monitors the environment to observe the changes, which in turn may lead management to modify the strategic plan in the future. Thus, strategic planning is a continuous process.

MISSION STATEMENT   An organization's mission is its purpose—its reason for being. At many organizations, especially relatively young ones, management has not formally thought through what the organization's mission is. Perhaps the person who started a company had an idea for a good or service, and the organization simply grew along with sales of that product. But as the organization grows, the founder's vision is no longer enough to guide the organization's many employees. Or perhaps the organization finds that it has resources to invest but no clear basis for choosing one opportunity over another.

mission statement
A statement of an organization's distinctive purpose.

When management needs a sense of direction and is ready to benefit from strategic planning, it needs to develop a **mission statement**, a statement of the organization's distinctive purpose. In effect, the mission statement answers two questions: (1) What is our business? and (2) What should it be? In "Creating Customer Value," you saw that King's Medical Company used a management team to create and answer such questions. Ameritech has moved beyond the Bell System's past goal of a telephone in every home to a new mission it calls "advanced universal access." By this, the Baby Bell company means that it seeks to provide full-motion video and data access, as well as traditional voice-phone service, to every home and business that wants it.[10]

The mission statement for Auto Research Laboratories Incorporated states: "We will provide testing and technical services to the chemical additive, petroleum, automotive, and heavy equipment industries, and we will seek opportunities to expand our markets or services when our strengths and resources can be employed." A testing and technical services company, Auto Research serves the automotive industry.

Contents   An organization's mission statement should be specific enough to guide its members in deciding what activities to focus on. In addition, the mission statement should describe the organization's purpose in a way that distinguishes it from similar organizations. Thus, the mission of Rodale Press, based in Emmaus, Pennsylvania, is "to show people how they can use the power of their bodies and minds to make their lives better."[11] This guides the company to publish books and magazines on such topics as organic gardening, healthful living, and sports such as running, bicycling, and backpacking. Defining the mission also includes identifying what the organization will *not* do. (For more on writing mission statements, see "Put It into Practice.")

For an increasing number of organizations today, focusing on what they do best means doing only certain core activities while creating alliances with other individuals or organizations to do the rest.[12] (The result may be a "network organization," described in the next chapter.) In France, for example, it is common practice for local governments to stay out of the business of constructing and maintaining their infrastructures such as roads and water distribution systems. Instead, they establish relationships with private companies that specialize in such activities.[13]

At an organization with a marketing orientation, the mission statement will focus on the needs of its markets, rather than on its products. In developing such a mission statement, managers consider who the organization's current and desired customers are and what they value. The mission statement then addresses how the organization will serve those customers. Thus, Rubbermaid defines its mission as offering "simple household problem solutions," not just selling plastic storage containers and wastebaskets.[14] The Leg Room chain of hosiery stores defines its mission as operating "a well-situated, well-edited store that concentrates its efforts on saving its customers time." Leg Room locates its stores en route to many professional women's workplaces, and it offers delivery of its merchandise, primarily pantyhose and socks.[15]

Development   Developing a mission statement is usually handled by the organization's top managers. Thus, in a traditionally structured organization, the vice president

Put It Into Practice

TWO MISSION STATEMENTS

When an organization has a clear, distinctive mission statement, its marketers can plan a strategy that supports the organization's purpose. The following mission statements are for actual companies. Decide whether each statement answers the questions, What is our business? and, What should it be? Does it distinguish the company from other, similar companies? If the mission statement falls short, suggest how to improve it.

Amoco

According to a recent annual report, Amoco's mission is as follows:

> Amoco Corporation is a worldwide integrated petroleum and chemical company. We find and develop petroleum resources and provide quality products and services for our customers. We conduct our business responsibly to achieve a superior financial return, balanced with long-term growth, to benefit shareholders and fulfill our commitment to the community and the environment.

Gateway 2000

The following mission statement was published in a newsletter of Gateway 2000:

> We are Gateway 2000. We share the vision of being our customers' only logical choice.
>
> We care about and respect our customers and do everything within reason to ensure their satisfaction.
>
> We have fun working together to be the most knowledgeable, productive, caring and successful team in the world.
>
> We blend our talents to continually offer higher quality, more innovative and more useful products at a value unmatched by competitors.
>
> We guide our business by common sense, not convention.
>
> We will always be happy, but we will never be satisfied. We will admit and learn from our mistakes and continually improve everything we do.
>
> We will succeed together as a team, sharing our success, offering each other opportunities for growth and enhancing our quality of life.

of marketing would participate in this difficult process. Organizations committed to teamwork and employee involvement may include several, if not all, levels of employees in the process. Government organizations may have their mission spelled out in the law or executive order that created them. The Occupational Safety and Health Administration is charged with defining and enforcing the behavior required by the Occupational Safety and Health Act.

ORGANIZATIONAL OBJECTIVES   A formal mission statement places the organization in the best position to develop organizational objectives. These objectives describe the intended outcomes of carrying out the mission statement. Organizational objectives can describe the organization's desired profit level, market position, reputation, social responsibility, or level of quality. For example, a business might seek to earn profits representing an annual rate of return of at least 15 percent. It might seek to be known as the most environmentally friendly provider of oil changes and other services for automobiles. In the case of Ameritech, whose mission was described earlier, one of its objectives for providing "advanced universal access" is to become a provider of video services such as video links between homes and classrooms.[16]

Objectives should have certain characteristics. As shown in Figure 5.2, they should be written, measurable, clear, specific, and challenging but achievable. Each of these characteristics contributes to making the objectives effective:

• Putting objectives in writing forces the planner to think through the objectives carefully, gives them importance, and helps employees remember them.

FIGURE 5.2

Characteristics of Effective Objectives

- Making objectives measurable—stating them in terms of, say, a dollar amount or market share—allows the planner to assess how close the organization came to meeting them. Part of making objectives measurable is including a time frame for accomplishing them.
- To be clear, objectives are stated in plain language. This helps all employees understand them.
- Specific objectives spell out what is to be done and by whom. For example, an objective might call for the robotics division to increase sales by 6 percent annually over the next five years.
- Challenging objectives—if they are seen as achievable—are more likely than easy objectives to stimulate employees to do their best.

The characteristics of effective objectives apply to objectives at all levels of the planning process, not just to overall organizational objectives.

ORGANIZATIONAL STRATEGIES   When managers know where they want to go, they must figure out how to get there. Organizational strategies describe how the organization intends to achieve its objectives. California Senator Diane Feinstein's campaign strategy described how her campaign intended to achieve the objective of election to the U.S. Senate. Organizational strategies might include how much money to allocate to various lines of business or what activities the organization needs a partner for because they are not areas of distinctive competence. In the case of Ameritech, its strategies include offering demonstrations of the new technology and lobbying for regulatory changes that will make the company's new ventures financially feasible.[17]

Strategies succeed when they lead the organization to achieve its objectives. American Standard Inc., which manufactures bathroom fixtures, air-conditioning units, and automotive braking systems, responded to a cash crunch resulting from a slow economy by setting an objective of reducing inventories of raw materials and finished goods. The company's primary strategy for achieving that objective was to adopt customer-driven manufacturing processes. In other words, the company set up its plants to quickly manufacture whatever products were ordered, rather than trying to predict sales and then manufacture enough to satisfy expected demand. As a result of using this "demand-flow manufacturing," American Standard not only reduced

FIGURE 5.3

Growth Strategies: Product/Market Matrix

Products / Markets	Present Products	New Products
Present Customers	Market Penetration	Product Development
New Customers	Market Development	Diversification

inventories, but it also claims to have boosted efficiency, quality, and responsiveness to its customers.[18]

Growth Strategies   Organizations whose objectives include growth would use one of the strategies identified by the matrix in Figure 5.3. This product/market matrix shows that the organization may grow by selling to new customers and by selling more to its present customers. In addition, the organization may grow by selling new products and by selling more of its existing products. To summarize the four strategies:

market penetration strategies
Strategies for growth by selling more of an organization's existing products to existing customers.

1. **Market penetration strategies** are strategies to grow by selling more of the organization's existing products to its existing customers. For example, makers of breakfast cereal often include recipes on the box so that purchasers will use the cereal as more than a breakfast food. This strategy has led many people to buy Rice Krispies in order to make marshmallow-laden bar cookies. Likewise, the ad for Mott's applesauce in Figure 5.4 shows an additional use for this product: a no-fat alternative to vegetable oil in baked goods.

market development strategies
Strategies for growth by selling existing products to new customers.

2. **Market development strategies** are strategies to grow by selling existing products to new customers. Companies that seek international markets for their products are using a market development strategy. For example, striped, short-sleeved shirts bearing the logo of Hang Ten International were fashionable in the United States during the 1960s and 1970s. When interest in those shirts waned, the company failed to offer successful new designs to men and boys, but it managed to survive by expanding to international markets. Hang Ten now has licensees handling sales and manufacturing for the brand in 35 foreign countries.[19]

product development strategies
Strategies for growth by developing new products to serve existing customers.

3. **Product development strategies** are strategies to grow by developing new products to serve existing customers. For example, Duracell's growth strategies include development of a long-lasting, rechargeable battery, which would be especially useful for powering laptop computers.[20]

diversification
Strategy for growth by serving new customers with new products.

4. **Diversification** is the strategy to grow by serving new customers through the delivery of new products. Diana Stewart is an in-country specialist for the travel industry, meaning that she prepares individualized plans for travelers interested in history, archaeology, and road tours in Cumbria, United Kingdom. To expand her business so that she would be active during the slow periods of the year for travelers, Stewart diversified into publishing a booklet of local events, which she markets to hotels, guest houses, and other clients.[21] Notice that although Stewart's planning and publishing services are sold to different customers, they both build on her expertise in the travel industry.

FIGURE 5.4

Advertising to Support a Market Penetration Strategy

SWOT analysis
The systematic evaluation of an organization's strengths, weaknesses, opportunities, and threats.

distinctive competencies
Things an organization does better than any other organization.

SWOT Analysis To select a particular strategy, management considers the organization's mission and abilities. One way to do this is through the use of **SWOT analysis**, or the systematic evaluation of the organization's internal strengths and weaknesses and external opportunities and threats. SWOT stands for strengths, weaknesses, opportunities, and threats.

To conduct a SWOT analysis, the manager first evaluates the areas of strength and weakness in the organization. Strengths would include patents, customer loyalty, the ability to produce goods or services at relatively low cost, and financial resources available to pursue new opportunities. Some possible weaknesses are high costs, lack of financing, and brands that are not well known or respected. In evaluating strengths and weaknesses, the manager particularly looks for the things the organization does better than anyone else. These are called the organization's **distinctive competencies** (see Figure 5.5 for an example). Especially significant are areas where the organization excels at using its resources to enhance quality, shorten the time it takes to bring a new product to market, and build strong relationships with channel members and end users of its products.[22]

The manager also identifies the opportunities and threats posed by various environments. Opportunities may include unmet demand, new product concepts or technology, or competing organizations that could benefit from better management if they were acquired. Threats might include new or stronger competitors, new laws limiting the organization's activities, and a change in customers' needs or tastes away from the products supplied by the organization. Thus, Jack Rudloe, who operates a nonprofit marine laboratory in Panacea, Florida, identified an opportunity and minimal threats when he observed that the people of many Asian nations enjoy eating dried jellyfish, an animal that populates the waters off Panacea between July and December (the low point of the jellyfish season in Malaysia and Thailand). Inquiries to the National Fisheries Institute and the Commerce Department uncovered no U.S. jellyfish busi-

FIGURE 5.5

Advertising a Company's Distinctive Competency: Providing Snow Shoes That Revolutionized the Sport

nesses to compete with the one Rudloe proposes.[23] (For more on evaluation and marketing techniques at nonprofit organizations, see "You Decide: Can a Museum Benefit from Marketing?")

Of course, what is a threat to one organization may be an opportunity for another. For example, many businesses have viewed compliance with the Americans with Disabilities Act, which requires businesses to be accessible to those with physical disabilities, as a drain on profits. A store owner might worry that the store could not afford to operate if entrances must be modified, aisles widened, and new signs installed. At the same time, other businesses are benefiting by acting on the opportunity to provide goods and services that can help organizations make their facilities more accessible. One such business is Bensenville, Illinois–based Access Specialties and Products, which sells an inexpensive lever handle that can quickly be installed over an existing doorknob to make doors easy to open.

The manager evaluating opportunities and threats should especially look for changes in each dimension of the marketing environment, both domestic and foreign. A change is typically where the most significant opportunities arise. For example, passage of the Americans with Disabilities Act provided many opportunities to companies such as Access Specialties and Products that sell items for making a business more accessible.

The purpose of identifying strengths, weaknesses, opportunities, and threats is to help the manager find organizational strengths that match environmental opportunities, preferably in areas where competitors do not have a similar match. Thus, Jofa, a maker of protective athletic equipment, sees a match between the dangers of skating and its ability to protect the athlete with its technologically engineered products (see Figure 5.6). Likewise, the producer of kits for modifying doorknobs sees a match between the requirements of a federal law and its own ability to design and produce simple but functional products. Another business sees its large pool of funds as a strength enabling it to invest in a new product line with high start-up costs but large

You Decide

CAN A MUSEUM BENEFIT FROM MARKETING?

The notion that museums must adopt business principles rubs some people the wrong way. They believe a museum should be able to operate independent of "business." But like many profit-oriented companies, museums are struggling to survive. Recently, more and more have turned to aggressive marketing and growth strategies, kicking up plenty of controversy.

In Salem, Massachusetts, the Peabody & Essex Museum launched its biggest marketing effort in 1992, centered on an exhibit called "The Great Age of Sail: Treasures from the National Maritime Museum of Greenwich, England." With a budget 50 times larger than spending on past promotions, the museum hired Brown & Yeager Communications to promote the exhibit throughout New England and opened it with a gala fund-raiser, members-only receptions, and a preview for public officials and Boston media. A sailing dory was displayed at a local shopping mall, and public transportation tickets were sold with discount coupons for entrance to the exhibit. In addition, the museum set up a special gift shop devoted to T-shirts, totebags, notepads, and other items representing the exhibit.

"Our mission is to educate and bring the broadest constituency possible here," notes director of exhibitions William Barton. "Everything we have here is for the commonwealth."

"The purpose of the shop is really to continue the education of the museum, and everything we sell has to be related to our mission," continues Danielle Lambrechts, the museum shop manager.

Randolph Barton, chairman of the board of trustees, advocates a financial plan that "over a period of time consolidates, integrates, and upgrades our whole operation. We're programmed to grow, and our major objective here is to make certain we are financially sound."

Similar things are happening on a grander scale at the Solomon R. Guggenheim Museum in New York. The museum's director, Thomas Krens, came to the job with a degree in nonprofit management from Yale. He examined the museum's strengths, weaknesses, opportunities, and threats as well as possible growth strategies. He noted that money was tight and repairs were needed on the building; donors were on the decline. Like the Peabody & Essex, the Guggenheim faced the consequences of a recession. Public funding for art was down, and Americans were less likely to spend money on museum visits and memberships.

Krens took a look at one of the museum's greatest strengths: its collection of nineteenth- and twentieth-century art, and made it part of his strategy. First, he had the building itself restored and expanded. He sold three of the museum's more valuable paintings to raise $30 million to develop a major collection of postwar art. Then he began to establish Guggenheim "branch" or satellite museums around the United States and in Europe to display the overflow from the museum's collection.

Efforts like these have their critics in the museum world. Krens has been accused of creating a "McGuggenheim" chain. "Krens has robbed the museum of all its originality and personality," complains art dealer Sandro Rumney, a descendant of Solomon Guggenheim. "He's just a businessman."

Therein lies the rub. According to William Barton, "Realistically, the environment has forced museums and other nonprofits to be more market aware and get the word out." But traditionalists like Rumney don't buy it.

Do you think that a museum can benefit from a clear mission statement, growth strategy, analysis, and marketing plan in the same way a profit-oriented company can? If not, what different approach would you take? What might be the downside of applying marketing techniques to a museum? What would be the benefits?

Sources: Kathy McCabe, "Marketing Matches Splendor of Great Age of Sail," *The Boston Sunday Globe,* March 7, 1993, p. 10; Alex Prud'Homme, "The CEO of Culture Inc.," *Time,* January 20, 1992, pp. 36–37.

potential profits. (To learn how Pillsbury's Linda Keene found a fit between organizational strengths and environmental opportunities, see "Marketing Movers & Shakers.")

The timing of strategies can be as important as their content. An organization can move too slowly and therefore allow competitors to preempt its plans. At the other extreme, a business that introduces a product before customers are ready to try it may waste many dollars in fruitless promotion. Often an organization's distinctive competencies—its strengths—match an opportunity for only a limited period of time. This time period is known as a **strategic window**. The organization's strategies should lead it to act when strategic windows are open.

strategic window
The time period in which an organization's strengths match its opportunities.

FIGURE 5.6

Promoting an Organization's Strength

ORGANIZATIONAL PORTFOLIO PLAN   Organizations often are in more than one line of business. ConAgra markets prepared foods (such as Healthy Choice frozen entrees and Armour hams), trading and processing services (such as grain milling and commodity trading), and agri-products (such as fertilizers and animal feed). Thus, the organization has a "portfolio" of business units, much as an investor has a portfolio of stocks.

The investor must continually reexamine various stocks and reallocate his or her funds based on their past and expected performance. For example, the investor might buy more of a stock that has been declaring large dividends and sell off a stock that has been falling in price. Similarly, the executives of an organization with a portfolio of business units need to continually reevaluate how those units are performing and allocate resources to them accordingly.

A case in point is W. W. Grainger, which sells maintenance, repair, and operating supplies. In creating a strategic plan, Grainger's managers determined that the company's competitive advantage lay in its fast, service-oriented distribution system. So Grainger dropped its manufacturing businesses, which made such items as electric motors, fans, and pumps. It acquired other distribution companies with lines Grainger lacked. Today Grainger's catalog is well over 2,500 pages long and contains more than 42,000 items.[24]

strategic business unit (SBU)
The part of an organization that has a distinct mission, competitors, and product.

The units of an organization's business that are considered the elements of its portfolio are called strategic business units. A **strategic business unit (SBU)** is a part of the organization that has a distinct mission, has its own competitors, sells one product or a group of similar products, and can be planned for independent of other activities in the organization. Thus, the SBU should have its own management and its own means of obtaining resources. In one organization, management might define an SBU as the part of the organization handling a single product or brand. In another organization, an SBU might be a product line, a division, or even the whole company. The

Marketing Movers & Shakers

PILLSBURY'S LINDA KEENE

When Linda Keene was promoted to vice president of market development and strategic planning for baked goods, Pillsbury had big plans for the division, and it expected results. According to Keene, the company gave her "very aggressive profit goals."

So Keene took a hard look at her division, searching for ways it could grow. "We looked at our core businesses and saw that we had a lot of programs and very strong initiatives under way to grow these businesses," she comments.

One major chance for growth was in market development strategies—targeting new customers for existing products. And the market Pillsbury had failed to target was that of minorities. Keene, an African-American, knew how significant this market was and how many opportunities to reach it Pillsbury had missed. Pillsbury had plenty of strengths, such as a hefty ad budget and products easily recognized by name.

Pillsbury also had weaknesses. The company simply seemed unaware of the huge potential customer base that could be tapped by making some special promotional efforts in its direction. Minneapolis, where Pillsbury is based, "is a city that isn't very diverse. That might have caused us not to be as proactive in, say, Miami or California, where diversity is an everyday reality," says Keene. Keene's superiors told her that since Pillsbury does a huge amount of television advertising, nothing more needed to be done to target these customers.

And the company faced threats. Competitors were already marketing to minority groups. One of them outsold Pillsbury two to one among minorities.

But Linda Keene was determined to make the most of the opportunities she had identified. For instance, she notes, "We found that baking is a very relevant cultural activity in both the African-American and Hispanic markets. Compared with the general population, in which we see declines in baking skills, we have two ethnic groups in which people bake—a lot."

So she took some of Pillsbury's existing products, such as its cornbread twists, and kneaded their marketing position so that it conformed more to African-American and Hispanic values and life-styles. "We'd been marketing the twists as the perfect accompaniment to chili," Keene explains. "While African Americans eat chili, that's probably not the most common way they use cornbread. So we offered a recipe on the package for corn muffins and marketed them as the perfect go-with for greens."

Sales figures were promising, and regional marketing programs were established, with an eye toward the international arena. Keene understood her market, saw potential for growth, and accurately assessed Pillsbury's opportunities. Then she baked all the possibilities into a successful marketing strategy.

Source: "Linda Keene: Making a Stale Business Poppin' Fresh," *Sales & Marketing Management,* April 1992, pp. 38–39.

---

key to identifying SBUs is to look at the organization's activities, not just the formal lines of an organization chart.

At an organization with many products, management may see several levels of SBUs, say, individual products, product lines, and broader categories of business. Grand Metropolitan has three major divisions: Food, Drinks, and Retailing. The Food Division includes such subsidiaries as Pillsbury, Häagen-Dazs, and Green Giant, each offering its own product lines. For example, Pillsbury sells prepared dough, frozen vegetables, frozen pizza, and flour.

The decisions about how much funding to give each of the organization's SBUs form the organization's **portfolio plan**. This plan details which SBUs the organization wishes to build up, maintain, add, or eliminate. The next section describes techniques for preparing a portfolio plan.

portfolio plan
A plan detailing which SBUs an organization wants to build up.

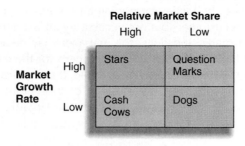

BUSINESS PORTFOLIO ANALYSIS

The basic process for creating a portfolio plan is to rate the performance of each strategic business unit in the organization's portfolio, then determine how to allocate resources to each. Two of the most popular techniques for rating the SBUs in a business's portfolio are the Boston Consulting Group's growth/share matrix and General Electric's industry attractiveness/business strength matrix.

Boston Consulting Group's Growth/Share Matrix   The Boston Consulting Group (BCG) has developed a matrix that classifies SBUs according to two measures: market growth rate (low or high) and relative market share (low or high).[25] The BCG matrix is shown in Figure 5.7. SBUs classified in the matrix are of four kinds:

1. *Stars*—These SBUs have a high share of a market with a high growth rate. Markets that are growing fast tend to attract a lot of competition, so the organization typically must spend heavily if it is to protect the market share of stars.
2. *Cash cows*—These SBUs have a high share of a market that is growing more slowly. The less intense competition coupled with the SBUs' market dominance means that these SBUs generate cash for the organization.
3. *Dogs*—These SBUs have a low share of a low-growth market. Sometimes they are serving a loyal group of customers who make the SBU profitable. However, they tend not to be a major source of cash for the organization, and if they are not generating profits, it is probably not worthwhile to continue funding them.
4. *Question marks*—These SBUs have a low share of a high-growth market. Building market share tends to be costly, but if the organization can do so profitably, these SBUs have great potential.

The manager using the BCG growth/share matrix first uses it to classify the organization's SBUs. This step involves judgment on the marketer's part, as the model does not provide specific criteria for classifying SBUs. For example, is a high-growth market one that is growing at 10 percent a year or more or less? Industry history and expectations will be some guide, but the classification may ultimately be arbitrary.

Then, based on the classification, the manager selects an appropriate objective for each SBU:

- To turn a question mark into a star, the manager may decide to *build* market share. This might involve heavy use of marketing communication or low prices. Such a strategy typically reduces earnings in the short term.

• For a strong cash cow, the manager may decide to *hold* or preserve the existing market share. Thus, the tactics for pricing and marketing communications would be designed to retain customers but not necessarily attract a lot of new ones.
• For question marks and dogs, the manager may decide to *harvest*. This means increasing short-term cash flow without concern for the effect of this strategy on the product's long-term performance. For example, the organization could raise the price.
• For business units that the organization cannot afford to finance for growth, the manager may decide to *divest*. This means the organization sells off the SBU or simply discontinues that line of business. This frees up funds for more attractive SBUs.

Notice that the categories on the BCG matrix and the strategies for managing the SBUs focus on market share. This focus has led to criticism of the BCG portfolio model. The model assumes that a large market share will lead to high profits. However, a large market share is not the only source of profits. That is because a firm may find that it can more profitably serve a smaller niche of the market,[26] or an organization can base a successful strategy on being a follower of or challenger to the market leader. The potential success of an SBU also depends on other factors, including patents, government regulations, and the organization's reputation.

Furthermore, labeling SBUs according to the four categories in the growth/share matrix may overly limit managers' thinking about the possible strategies for SBUs. The standard view is that a successful product goes from being a question mark to a star to a cash cow to a dog, then is discontinued. But there are other possibilities, and an SBU classed as a dog might not be at the end of its usefulness to the organization. For example, Hang Ten's line of men's and boys' sportswear moved to dog status when the brand was no longer considered fashionable. Although sales declined to almost nothing, the company continued advertising in surfer magazines to maintain awareness of the brand. Years later, nostalgic buyers began looking for the shirts again, and Hang Ten began recreating its original shirts, with plans to capitalize on the resurgence of interest by introducing innovative fashions to complement the shirts.[27]

GENERAL ELECTRIC'S INDUSTRY ATTRACTIVENESS/BUSINESS STRENGTH MATRIX
In response to the limitations of the BCG model, General Electric and the consulting firm of McKinsey & Company developed a portfolio model that includes more information about the desirability of markets and the organization's competitive position. As shown in Figure 5.8, the matrix in the GE model compares SBUs with high, medium, or low industry attractiveness and strong, average, or weak business strength. Criteria used to measure industry attractiveness and business strength include:

• market factors such as size of market, the firm's share of market, diversity of market segments, and the firm's participation in diverse segments.
• competitive factors such as types of competitors, level and type of integration, and the firm's level of integration.
• financial and economic factors such as contribution margins, leverage through scale, and barriers to the firm's entry.
• technological factors such as maturity and volatility, the firm's ability to handle change, and the firm's level of technology.

Thus, an industry is most attractive if, for example, it is large, growing, and offers large profit margins. A business (the SBU) is considered strong if, for example, it has a large market share and is a leader in quality and technology.

To use the industry attractiveness/business strength model, the marketing manager first classifies the SBUs along the two dimensions of the matrix. The manager uses

General Electric's Industry Attractiveness/ Business Strength Matrix

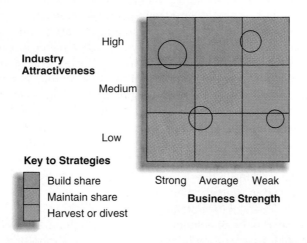

Note: Circles indicate the relative size of the organization's SBUs.

circles to represent each SBU on the matrix, using larger circles for the larger SBUs. SBUs in the upper left of the grid are high in both industry attractiveness and business strength; the organization should *build* market share for these. For SBUs that are in the middle range, the organization should *maintain* share. The organization should *harvest or divest* SBUs that are low in industry attractiveness and business strength.

Although the GE matrix rates SBUs according to broader criteria than the BCG matrix, it too has been criticized for overly emphasizing growth in market share. As noted earlier, devoting resources to high growth is not the only—or even always the best—way to be effective and profitable. Furthermore, portfolio analysis using these matrices does not provide much guidance for selecting the best possible portfolio of SBUs; it is better at simply describing what the organization already has. However, the matrix approaches do provide a helpful framework for beginning to evaluate the organization's portfolio of businesses.

Marketing and Other Functional Areas in the Strategic Planning Process

Strategic planning is considered an activity of the organization's top management. Therefore, except for the vice president of marketing, marketing managers may not be directly involved in creating the organization's strategic plan. Like other managers below the executive level, they are most often charged with planning primarily in their area of responsibility. For example, the human resources manager would be responsible for planning to meet the organization's staffing and training needs, and the sales manager would determine how to meet sales objectives. Marketing managers may, however, be called upon to provide top management with information about markets and the organization's environment. They may be spokespersons for the customer's point of view and for a mission and objectives that put the customer first. In addition, marketing managers need to be familiar with the organization's strategic plan so that the marketing effort supports it.

The precise role of functional managers varies from organization to organization. A small organization might involve every manager in every stage of strategic planning. In a large organization, managers' roles tend to be more specialized. Some organizations encourage a lot of input from employees at all levels, whereas others prefer to let top managers dictate the organization's direction. If the organization carries out activities through strategic partnerships with vendors and others, the marketing department's role extends to helping identify and design desirable relationships.[28]

The role of marketing managers further depends on the organization's view of marketing. In an organization that defines marketing broadly to encompass all efforts to satisfy existing and potential customers, marketing managers are likely to be heavily involved in strategic planning. (In fact, strategic planning in such organizations is virtually identical to strategic marketing planning.) In an organization where marketing is seen only as activities related to planning and executing the marketing mix, marketing managers will more likely play a supporting role in the creation of the strategic plan—for example, by submitting the results of marketing research. And if the organization views marketing primarily as an inflated term for sales management, the marketing manager will probably have little input into the strategic plan.

marketing plan
A blueprint for a particular strategy to reach a particular target market.

Despite these variations, marketing managers usually are expected to support the implementation of the strategic plan by drawing up a marketing plan. A **marketing plan** is a blueprint for a particular strategy to reach a particular target market. It supports the strategic plan by spelling out in detail what marketing actions the organization must take in order to meet strategic objectives. Thus, it includes the avenues for products, pricing, distribution channels, and communication the organization will use to serve the target market. Figure 5.9 provides examples of how objectives in the marketing plan can support the organization's strategic plan.

As defined earlier, the process of creating a marketing plan is known as strategic marketing planning. Whether the marketing manager's role in strategic planning is limited to creation of a marketing plan depends in part on whether marketing has a "traditional" role or participates in cross-functional teams.

TRADITIONAL ROLE OF MARKETING IN THE PLANNING PROCESS

Since the Industrial Revolution, most organizations have been divided according to the functions performed by various employees. Thus, once a company gets big enough, it has a production department, a marketing department, a finance department, a research and development department, and so on. Coordinating the work of these various departments are the company's executives (its top management).

In this kind of functionally organized company, department managers are expected to contribute primarily—or only—in their area of expertise. Thus, the traditional role of the marketing manager might include projecting the number of potential customers for a given product and advising how to promote the product so as to reach them. Top management is not interested in hearing from the marketing manager about how to make the product or improve its quality.

But even in this type of company, organization strategy and marketing strategy overlap to a large extent. Both are concerned with issues such as market share and how best to meet the needs of existing and potential customers. For example, to achieve growth targets for its restaurant chains (Pizza Hut, Taco Bell, KFC), PepsiCo

FIGURE 5.9

Relating the Marketing Plan to the Strategic Plan

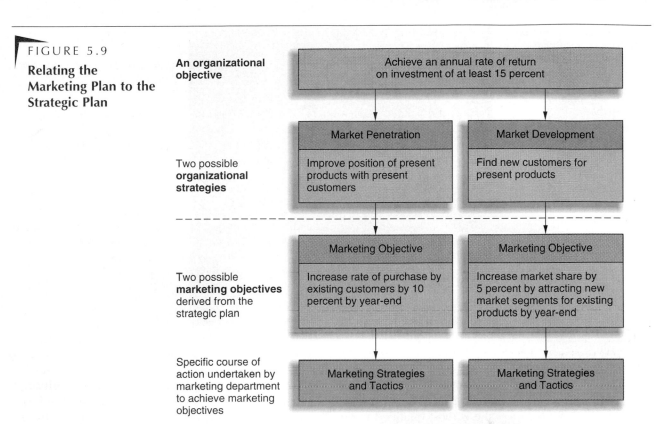

Source: J. Paul Peter and James H. Donnelly, Jr., *A Preface to Marketing Management,* 6th ed. (Burr Ridge, Ill.: Irwin, 1994), p. 28.

has adopted a distribution strategy of making them widely available, including innovative locations such as Minneapolis International Airport, carts at county fairs, and counters in numerous supermarkets.[29] Therefore, even in an organization that limits managers' input to their functional areas, the marketing manager may play an important role as adviser during the strategic planning process.

PLANNING STYLES   The contribution of marketing to planning in a traditional organization depends on the style of planning it uses. If the organization uses *top-down planning,* senior management sets objectives and strategies for all levels of the organization to carry out. The marketing manager would receive broad marketing objectives and would, in turn, develop plans for how to achieve those objectives. The manager would inform all marketing personnel of what they must do to reach the marketing objectives.

Other organizations use *bottom-up planning,* where managers prepare goals for their own units, then submit the goals to higher-level management for approval. The higher-level managers may request that the plans be modified to better fit organizational objectives.

A middle ground is for top management to tell lower-level managers what overall goals they are to achieve, then for the lower-level managers to plan strategies for achieving those goals. At Cadillac, for example, each employee writes individual objectives aimed at helping to meet the company's overall objectives.[30]

Thermos, manufacturer of Thermos bottles, lunch boxes, and gas and electric cookout grills, replaced its more traditional, bureaucratic organization with flexible interdisciplinary teams. Monte Peterson (front), who took over as CEO in 1990, poses with members of the Lifestyle team, which created this hot-selling electric grill. (See Chapter 11 for more on this story.)

ADVANTAGES AND DISADVANTAGES   The basic advantage of the traditional approach to planning is that each person presumably can focus on doing what he or she is most qualified to do. This was long considered the most efficient way to run a business.

On the downside, this approach can limit communication. As a result, lack of information or insight can lead to errors in judgment. Avco Systems Division years ago wasted millions of dollars developing manufacturing capability for an amount of weapons that far exceeded demand.[31] More cooperation between manufacturing and marketing could have prevented this error.

CROSS-FUNCTIONAL TEAMS

More and more organizations are rethinking the traditional role of marketing. Rather than dividing the work according to function, these organizations are bringing together managers and employees to participate in cross-functional teams, described in Chapter 1. These teams might have responsibility for a particular product, line of products, or group of customers.

Because team members are responsible for all activities involving their products and/or customers, they are all responsible for strategic planning. Thus, marketers on a cross-functional team will participate in creating a strategic plan for their business unit as well as a marketing plan for carrying out marketing activities. Furthermore, rather than independently coming up with a marketing plan, they must work closely with team members from other functional areas to devise a marketing plan that addresses their concerns. Thus, if someone from manufacturing says, "That size will be expensive to produce," or if someone from finance says, "We'll never make a profit at that price," the team members from marketing must help resolve the issues before the marketing plan can be considered complete. This approach requires a high degree of cooperation and skill at problem solving.

The greatest advantage of strategic planning with a cross-functional team is the ability of team members to consider a situation from a number of viewpoints. The resulting insights can help the team avoid costly mistakes and less than optimal solutions. Japanese manufacturers are noted for using cross-functional teams to figure out a way to make a desirable product at a given target cost. In contrast, U.S. manufacturers have traditionally developed products by having one group decide what to make, another calculate production costs, and yet another predict whether enough of the product will sell at a high enough price. This approach leads U.S. companies to abandon many product ideas that seem too expensive to make.[32]

When marketers plan as part of a cross-functional team, they are especially suited to contribute in a number of ways. Most obviously, the team will count on members of the marketing staff to provide information and insights drawn from their specialty. For example, it will be primarily the marketers who know how to research the marketplace to learn about wants and needs and who have expertise concerning such technical areas as distribution channels and advertising.

In addition, the marketer can play the important role of advocating the marketing concept. If team members get caught up in the potential for adding features to a product or building in a huge profit margin, the marketer can remind everyone of the need to focus on meeting customer wants and needs. In other words, the strategic plan should be based on how to serve the interests of existing and potential customers, rather than how to persuade them to act in the organization's best interests. Ultimately, the focus on the marketing concept should help the team devise a marketing plan that supports the organization's strategic plan.

Managing the Marketing Effort

marketing management
The process of setting, planning, and executing marketing goals and measuring progress toward their achievement.

Regardless of how the marketing effort is organized, either traditionally or by teams, a marketing manager will typically be responsible for ensuring the marketing effort achieves the organization's strategic objectives. This responsibility, called **marketing management**, is formally defined as "the process of setting marketing goals for an organization (considering internal resources and market opportunities), the planning and execution of activities to meet those goals, and measuring progress toward their achievement."[33] Thus, the marketing manager must determine what the organization's marketing objectives are, decide how to meet those objectives, and see to it that the plans are carried out properly. In addition, when efforts to meet marketing objectives fail, the marketing manager is responsible for making whatever changes are necessary to improve performance.

The marketing manager's position varies according to size and type of organization. In a large corporation, the marketing effort may be headed by a vice president of a marketing division, or each product division may have a marketing manager or marketing vice president. A small company may not have a formal marketing department, relying instead on the sales manager to handle many aspects of marketing.

MARKETING MANAGEMENT FUNCTIONS

As implied in the definition of *marketing management,* the marketing manager carries out several basic functions. These functions, illustrated in Figure 5.10, are setting objectives (goals) and strategy, executing or implementing the strategy, and controlling, which relies on measuring progress. The feedback from controlling provides

FIGURE 5.10

Functions of Marketing Management

information for modifying existing objectives and developing new ones. This chapter addresses the way marketing managers develop objectives and strategies as part of strategic marketing planning. The next chapter describes the other marketing management responsibilities—implementing and controlling the marketing effort.

In all but the smallest organizations, the marketing manager makes these things happen through other people. Thus, another important dimension of the manager's functions includes the activities necessary to obtain qualified people and enable them to carry out their responsibilities. These activities begin with the staffing function: the manager must identify the skills and talents the organization needs in its marketing employees, then find and hire people who meet the requirements. To carry out their responsibilities effectively, most employees will need various kinds of training. Therefore, the marketing manager is responsible for identifying needs for training and seeing to it that these needs are met. The manager also must provide leadership and see that marketing employees are motivated to do good work. Finally, the marketing manager needs to ensure that all employees are receiving feedback on their performance, including formal performance appraisals and informal feedback such as praise for good work. Depending on the organization's size and structure, the marketing manager may carry out these activities independently or with support from the human resources department.

DEVELOPING A MARKETING PLAN

As top management develops the organization's strategic plan, marketing management can carry out the core of its planning process: developing a marketing plan. This process involves several steps:

1. Reviewing the strategic plan
2. Conducting a situation analysis
3. Developing marketing objectives and strategies.

The supplement at the end of this chapter outlines the components of a marketing plan and presents a sample marketing plan for a fictional small business.

Marketing plans can provide a variety of benefits. A thoughtful marketing plan helps all members of the marketing department recognize where their efforts should be focused. It helps the marketing manager observe and best take advantage of opportunities in the marketplace. It provides a means of measuring the marketing department's performance (by comparing results to the marketing objectives). Finally, because marketing plans are typically reviewed by higher-level management, preparing a marketing plan can be a useful activity to promote career advancement.

For action-oriented managers and small-business owners, preparing a marketing plan may seem unduly formal and time consuming. It's tempting to get so busy handling day-to-day concerns that no time remains for planning. However, the lack of a marketing plan can stall even the best operations. When sales don't materialize because markets weren't targeted effectively or the product's package is unappealing, the marketer spends more time fixing the problems than he or she would have spent creating the original plan. Rita Karydas learned that lesson from her initial attempts to market a line of organic skin creams she named Magic Cream. She garnered only modest results from a marketing approach that essentially consisted of picking the first brand name that came to mind, packaging it in a generic white plastic pot, and promoting it by making phone calls, mailing out a homemade fact sheet, and networking.[34] Karydas needs to try planning more formally before she can hope to boost sales significantly.

REVIEW OF STRATEGIC PLAN   To develop the marketing plan, the marketing manager begins by reviewing the organization's strategic plan, including its mission statement and organizational objectives. Sometimes these will provide a clear direction for marketing objectives. In other cases, however, the organization's statement of mission and objectives are ambiguous if they exist at all. In these cases, the marketing manager will have to consult with the organization's executives to try to pinpoint what top management considers the desired direction of the organization to be. In fact, because marketing activities and the marketing philosophy are so central to the success of a strategic plan, top managers and marketing managers may find that they revise their plans several times in light of each other's efforts.

With regard to the earlier example of Magic Cream, Karydas needs to identify specific marketing objectives. She sells Magic Cream as a lip balm, makeup remover, diaper rash treatment, hair conditioner, and soother of sore muscles.[35] Not only is this range of uses likely to strike many consumers as unbelievable, but it implies little about what needs the business is meeting and who would want the product. This definition of the business also focuses on the product, rather than on existing and potential customers and their needs (a marketing focus).

SITUATION ANALYSIS   With the organization's strategic plan in mind, the marketing manager next conducts a situation analysis. The approach is a variation of SWOT analysis. The marketing manager identifies the organization's marketing strengths and weaknesses, such as funds available for a large advertising campaign or high distribution costs. The marketing manager also identifies opportunities and threats in the organization's current and potential markets.

In conducting the situation analysis, the marketing manager often focuses on industry growth and the organization's competitive position. The appropriate marketing strategy will vary depending on how fast, if at all, the industry is growing. A rapidly growing industry tends to attract many new competitors and requires firms to act aggressively if they are to build or even maintain market share. In an industry with little or no growth, a firm that wants to grow will have to do so by taking market share away from competitors.

The other important determinant of marketing strategy is competitive position, or the size of the organization relative to competitors. The market leader tends to enjoy widespread name recognition and has the cash to maintain this position through intensive distribution and communication. A smaller competitor will more likely have to

Fred Levine founded Focus Video Productions with the launch of his first children's video, Road Construction Ahead. *When his initial marketing plan, placing an ad in the* New York Times, *generated little response, he provided videos to reviewers and advertised the enthusiastic reviews. With the revenues that followed each favorable review, Levine ran more ads. Eventually sales of more than 200,000 copies of* Road Construction Ahead *brought in over $3 million—enough to produce Levine's second video,* Fire and Rescue.

compete by offering the lowest price, unique features, or a marketing mix aimed at a single niche of the total market. Thus, followers and niche marketers will have to be particularly aware of their strong points. For Magic Cream, one such strength is the fact that the product is organic, since all-natural products appeal to today's consumers.

MARKETING OBJECTIVES AND STRATEGIES   The analysis of competitive position and market strength leads to creation of marketing objectives and strategies that take advantage of opportunities in the marketplace and strengths of the organization and its marketing department. These objectives and strategies constitute the marketing plan. To create them, the manager takes three steps:

1. Establish marketing objectives.
2. Select the target market(s).
3. Develop a marketing mix to serve each target market.

As stated earlier, the marketing objectives should be consistent with organizational objectives. In addition, they should have the characteristics of effective objectives listed earlier in Figure 5.2. An example is AMP's customer service goal of having less than 1 percent of callers hang up before someone can answer the phone. The customer service department at AMP, which makes connectors and interconnection systems, is divided into work teams, and each team is responsible for trying to meet this goal by answering each call on the first ring. With the help of new equipment, the teams have driven down the "abandon rate" to 0.59 percent.[36]

The strategies for achieving marketing objectives are the choices of target markets and the marketing mix used to serve each target market. In general, the organization must decide whether to use one marketing mix to serve a single broad market or to adapt parts of that mix—the product, price, channels, or communication—to serve one or more segments of the total market. Then the plan spells out what the marketing mix(es) will be. Part of this strategy is a budget for implementing that marketing mix. Chapter 10 discusses selection of target markets, and Chapters 11 through 20 cover various aspects of developing a marketing mix.

The marketing plan for Magic Cream could specify how much growth Karydas wants to achieve over the next one to five years. To achieve that growth, her strategies might include which benefits of the product to emphasize and which consumers to

TABLE 5.1	• What need was the product originally design to satisfy?

TABLE 5.1

Checklist for Evaluating a Marketing Plan

- What need was the product originally design to satisfy?
- Was it successful?
- Is it still competitive?
- What changes have you made or should you make to keep the product up to date?
- What are the specific features of the product?
- Who are your customers?
- Why would they want the product?
- How do the product's features benefit your customers?
- How well do your promotional materials reinforce these benefits?
- Which advertising pieces were most successful? Why?
- Do your promotional materials reach the target market? Can you reach your target market through special-interest organizations or other avenues you are not already using?
- Do your sales presentations cover all the ways your product's features benefit your customers?

Source: Adapted from Martin Edic, "Plan of Attack," *Entrepreneur,* November 1992, pp. 134–135.

target. Karydas might want to consider renaming the product to allude to its natural ingredients and the uses that she decided to emphasize. She probably could benefit from more eye-catching packaging consistent with the rest of her marketing strategy.

IMPLEMENTING THE MARKETING PLAN

Once the marketing plan is complete, the marketing department puts it into action. This implementation process is described in the next chapter. As the marketing plan is implemented, the marketing manager will learn which aspects of the plan are producing the desired results and where problems are occurring. Using this information, the manager can modify the marketing plan so that it achieves the desired results. Answering the questions in Table 5.1 can help the marketing manager evaluate the marketing plan and identify changes that need to be made.

Forecasting

forecasting
Determining what to expect in a market.

market potential
The expected total demand in the market being investigated.

Marketing plans are influenced by expectations of future demand for the organization's goods and services. When marketers' expectations are realistic, their plans will more likely succeed. In contrast, incorrect assumptions about the future can be costly, as Japanese automakers have recently found. Those companies prospered for years by serving a growing market with a variety of models, features, and options produced at modern factories. But recently, sales growth has slumped in Japan and elsewhere, and the investment in innovation has suddenly become hard to afford. As a result, the companies have had to aggressively cut costs. Said Mazda's Executive Vice President Makoto Miyaji, "We expected markets to keep expanding. We're not used to this."[37]

Determining what to expect is known as **forecasting**. Marketers depend on two broad categories of forecasts. First, they are interested in forecasting **market potential**, or the expected total demand in the market they are investigating. For example, Kodak would want to know how many photocopiers businesses will be buying over the next three years. Marketers also need a *sales forecast,* or an estimate of the organization's share of the market potential. In general, the techniques for creating such forecasts involve measuring past and current demand, then using that information to make predictions about the future.

MEASURING DEMAND

demand
The amount of sales of a product at a given price.

The **demand** for a product is the amount of sales of a product at a given price. Thus, when marketers measure existing demand for a product, they measure its sales. They measure sales both in terms of the product's percentage share of the total industry and in terms of its dollar and unit sales. For example, producers of personal computers would want to know both their annual sales and what percentage that represents of all personal computer sales for the year.

To learn current demand for a total industry, the most efficient approach is to use data available from marketing research services and industry trade groups. The organization can purchase the data or look for information in business and trade publications. For example, a recent issue of *The Wall Street Journal* reported that the total market for personal computers worldwide in 1992 was an estimated $46.5 billion. The paper also reported the current and prior-year market shares of the five leading competitors in that market. Thus, from the paper, a reader could learn that IBM's share had fallen to less than 13 percent from 16 percent a year earlier and that Dell's share had roughly doubled, to over 3 percent.[38] For information about sales of the organization's own products, the marketer should be able to use company sales records.

FORECASTING FUTURE DEMAND

Because no one can predict the future perfectly, forecasting future demand is necessarily inexact. Many economists and statisticians specialize in forecasting market potential. Consequently, as is true for measuring current demand, the best sources for forecasts of market potential are trade groups and services that specialize in this type of information.

Several techniques are available to create sales forecasts. Table 5.2 summarizes their benefits and limitations. The techniques based on judgment or opinion are classified as "qualitative." The techniques based on statistical analysis of historical data are classified as "quantitative."

The marketer can use a combination of forecasting techniques to gain a broader perspective on the possible range of demand. In assessing the forecast that results from each technique, the marketer takes into account expected changes in the environment, such as changes in the size of the market to be served or in the economy. These are reported in the business press and in trade magazines. Thus, if *The Wall Street Journal* reports that a recession is apparently ending, the marketer might favor a rosier forecast than if the pace of business is expected to slow.

jury of executive opinion
A group of executives called upon to provide insights from various areas of the organization.

QUALITATIVE FORECASTING TECHNIQUES   The simplest way to arrive at a forecast is to ask "experts" what they predict demand will be. Who might be expert enough to provide a reliable opinion? One approach is to seek the outlook of the organization's executives. Such a **jury of executive opinion** provides insights from people working in a variety of areas, including finance, marketing, and production. The marketing manager can average the estimates to arrive at a single forecast.

The estimates also can come from the organization's salespeople. They are, after all, the organization members who work most closely with customers. In this case, the forecast would be the sum of the estimates. This approach assumes that salespeo-

	TECHNIQUE	BENEFITS	LIMITATIONS
TABLE 5.2 **Forecasting Techniques**	*Qualitative Methods*		
	Jury of executive opinion	Quick; simple; opinions come from executives with expertise in different departments; useful for new or innovative products	Data typically must be broken down by product, region, etc.; consumes time of executives; may not give greatest weight to those with most expertise
	Sales force composite	Providing number can motivate salespeople; salespeople know customers, product, and competitors	Salespeople have a vested interest, so they may give biased estimates
	Survey of buyer intentions	Based on estimates obtained directly from buyers; can provide detailed information; often provides insight into buyers' thinking; can be used for new products	Intention to buy may not result in actual purchase; expensive; time consuming; useful only when there are a few, well-defined potential customers
	Delphi technique	Estimators less likely to succumb to group pressure	Time consuming; expensive
	Quantitative Methods		
	Trend analysis	Quick; inexpensive; effective when demand and environmental factors are stable	Assumes future is continuation of past; does not consider marketing plans or changes in environment; not useful for new or innovative products
	Exponential smoothing	Same benefits as trend analysis but emphasizes more recent data	Same limitations as trend analysis but not as severe because of emphasis on more recent data
	Market tests	Provide more realistic information because based on actual purchases rather than intent to buy; permits assessment of effects of marketing plan; useful for new or innovative products	Time consuming; expensive; alert competition to organization's plans

Source: Adapted from Gilbert A. Churchill, Jr., Neil M. Ford, and Orville C. Walker, Jr., *Sales Force Management,* 4th ed. (Homewood, Ill.: Irwin, 1993), pp. 204–205.

ple will give unbiased estimates. However, if they think their sales forecasts will be the basis for sales quotas they must meet to earn a bonus, salespeople might be tempted to give pessimistic forecasts.

The marketer also can ask people outside the organization. One possibility is to ask the customers themselves, by conducting a survey of the buying intentions of a sample of the target market. This approach assumes that actual buying patterns will match the stated plans of the survey sample. However, people do not always do exactly what they say they will, so this information can be misleading. Industry experts also forecast industry growth, and marketers can get this information from trade groups and business publications. For example, recent articles forecast that sales of ready-to-drink iced teas would grow as fast as 50 to 70 percent a year for a few years, then level off.[39]

Some organizations use a more complex approach to forecasting known as the **Delphi technique**. In this approach, the marketing department sends a survey to experts inside or outside the organization, asking them to provide a forecast. The results are averaged and sent to the experts along with another questionnaire asking them to review the results and provide another forecast. This process is repeated until the experts reach a consensus.

With the exception of the Delphi technique, these qualitative forecasting techniques are relatively simple. Especially when experienced people provide the numbers, they can also be quite accurate. However, inexperience or poor judgment can lead to woefully inaccurate forecasts.

QUANTITATIVE FORECASTING TECHNIQUES   To forecast demand less subjectively, marketers use quantitative techniques such as time-series analysis and market tests. **Time-series analysis** is the use of past data to predict future outcomes. It assumes that demand follows a pattern over time. Thus, it is reliable only if past trends continue into the future.

To use the form of time-series analysis known as **trend analysis**, the analyst looks for the pattern in the data, then uses it to project future demand. For example, if sales have risen an average of 5 percent per year over the past several years, the analyst would predict that they will continue to increase at the same rate. Of course, most patterns are not so obvious. Therefore, computer programs that perform computations like regression are readily available to conduct such forms of trend analysis.

A form of time-series analysis that tries to overcome some limitations of trend analysis is exponential smoothing. **Exponential smoothing** is a form of time-series analysis that gives more weight to more recent data and less to older data by assigning a weight to each year's data. The sales figure for each year is multiplied by the weight assigned. Thus, to analyze sales data for the past three years, the analyst might multiply the current year's sales by 0.8, sales from a year ago by 0.6, and sales from two years ago by 0.4. Then the analyst completes the forecasting by using trend analysis.

Trend analysis and exponential smoothing both require records of past sales. Therefore, they are not useful for forecasting demand for a new product. Marketers of a new product who want to use a quantitative forecasting technique might use a **market test**. This involves offering the product in a few test markets, assuming the response will be similar when the product is offered to the total target market. Market tests are expensive but have the advantage of measuring actual customer behavior.

Note that the quantitative techniques are not a substitute for judgment by the marketer. In fact, they require that the marketer make judgments about many of the figures. For example, to use exponential smoothing, the marketer must decide what weights to assign to each year's data. To use a market test, the marketer must select test markets that he or she believes are representative of the total market. Thus, all of these forecasting techniques are only as good as the judgment of the marketer using them.

EVALUATING THE FORECAST

Before using the numbers generated by a forecast of demand, the marketer should take some time to evaluate the forecast. Because marketing plans are influenced by

Delphi technique
A method of forecasting that surveys experts, averages the results, and repeats the survey.

time-series analysis
The use of past data to predict future outcomes.

trend analysis
Procedure in which an analyst looks for a pattern in data, then uses it to project future demand.

exponential smoothing
Time-series analysis that gives more weight to recent data and less to older data.

market test
The offering of a product in a few test markets.

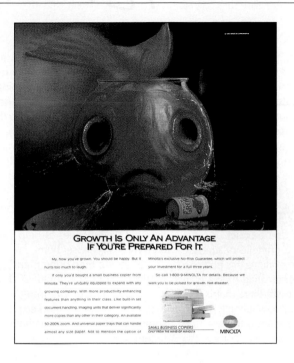
such numbers, the marketer can avoid costly errors by making sure that the forecast is reasonable. The marketer should review the assumptions and judgments used in preparing the forecast. Upon review, do they still seem reasonable? This is especially important given modern use of computer technology to prepare forecasts. Managers should not be so awed by a computer model or detailed spreadsheet that they fail to judge the assumptions underlying them.

The marketer should also look at the results of the forecast. Do the numbers seem realistic? If not, the marketer should review the estimates, judgments, and computations used to arrive at the results. Perhaps the data came from an unreliable source. When a result seems odd, chances are a mistake was made somewhere. It's less costly and embarrassing to prepare a revised forecast than to have to rework the entire marketing plan after trying to implement it.

Finally, the marketer should bear in mind that the accuracy of forecasts cannot be guaranteed. Too many uncontrollable factors may make the future impossible to predict. For example, sales of cold remedies are at the mercy of the length and severity of the cold and flu season. Good news for consumers is bad news for the makers of these products. In one recent year, the cold and flu season got off to a slow start, causing sales of over-the-counter cough and cold medicines to fall 9 percent compared to the previous year.[40] Forecasts for these medicines rely only on more predictable trends, such as the growing strength of private-label products ("store brands"). To cope with the remaining uncertainty, marketers should prepare contingency plans and monitor the environment and the reaction of target markets to the organization's efforts. When marketers observe a development that calls for a change, they must modify their plans. Thus, the planning process continues after the last word of the marketing plan has been typed and evaluated—even after the marketing department has begun implementing that plan (see Figure 5.11).

Successful marketing requires planning. Thus, organizations use strategic planning to develop a clear mission. On a narrower level, strategic marketing planning is the basis for developing marketing objectives and strategies.

The mission statement declares an organization's distinctive purpose. In a marketing-oriented organization, the statement focuses on the needs of markets rather than on products. It also serves as the basis for organizational objectives and the strategies for achieving those objectives. To identify strategies likely to succeed, managers may use SWOT analysis, looking for organizational strengths and weaknesses and for environmental opportunities and threats.

Most organizations offer more than one product or serve more than one market, in effect holding a portfolio of strategic business units. Managers therefore need to evaluate this portfolio and create a portfolio plan. Techniques for creating such a plan include the Boston Consulting Group's growth/share matrix and General Electric's industry attractiveness/business strength matrix.

The result of strategic marketing planning is the creation of a marketing plan. Such a plan spells out the strategy the organization will use to reach a particular target market. To create a marketing plan, many organizations follow the traditional route of assigning planning responsibilities along functional lines. Other organizations use cross-functional teams, which bring varied expertise to the planning process.

Creating a marketing plan is part of managing the marketing effort. To develop a marketing plan, the marketing manager reviews the strategic plan, conducts a situation analysis, and develops marketing objectives and strategies. Other marketing management functions are executing strategies (implementation) and controlling by measuring progress and making changes as necessary. Usually a marketing manager hires employees to help carry out these responsibilities, then must supervise them.

Strategic marketing planning depends on reliable information about the level of demand to expect. Thus, an important part of planning is forecasting. In forecasting, marketers examine market potential and sales, often using some combination of qualitative and quantitative forecasting techniques.

KEY TERMS AND CONCEPTS

strategic marketing (p. 120)

strategic marketing planning (p. 122)

strategic planning (p. 122)

tactical planning (p. 122)

operational planning (p. 122)

mission statement (p. 123)

market penetration strategies (p. 127)

market development strategies (p. 127)

product development strategies (p. 127)

diversification (p. 127)

SWOT analysis (p. 128)

distinctive competencies (p. 128)

strategic window (p. 130)

strategic business unit (SBU) (p. 131)

portfolio plan (p. 132)

marketing plan (p. 136)

marketing management (p. 139)

forecasting (p. 143)

market potential (p. 143)

demand (p. 144)

jury of executive opinion (p. 144)

Delphi technique (p. 146)

time-series analysis (p. 146)

trend analysis (p. 146)

exponential smoothing (p. 146)

market test (p. 146)

REVIEW AND DISCUSSION QUESTIONS

1. Name four or five characteristics of effective organizational objectives.

2. Summarize the four growth strategies that an organization can use to grow by selling new and existing products.

3. What is a SWOT analysis? What are some strengths, weaknesses, opportunities, and threats that a company might face?

4. Suppose you were hired as a marketer for a company that produces customized business forms (such as invoices and personnel records) for organizational buyers in North America and Western Europe.
   a. How would you conduct a SWOT analysis for the company?
   b. What might be some of the company's distinctive competencies?
   c. What factors might come together to become a strategic window for your company?

5. How does the Boston Consulting Group's growth/share matrix work? How does General Electric's industry attractiveness/business strength matrix work? Why do some critics prefer the GE matrix?

6. What are the benefits to even a small company in developing a marketing plan?

7. What are the two qualitative forecasting techniques, and how do they work?

8. What is time-series analysis, and how does it work? What are the two main types of time-series analysis, and how do they work?

Chapter Project
Creating a Successful Marketing Plan

Every organization—even those too small to have a separate marketing department—needs a marketing plan. In this chapter, you have studied a variety of concepts that lead up to developing a marketing plan and you have learned how to create a marketing plan.

Now it's your turn to create a successful marketing plan. Choose one of the following businesses (or come up with one of your own) and develop a written marketing plan for the business. As a guide, refer to the sample marketing plan for Little Learners Parent-Teacher Store following this chapter.

Businesses:

- A chain of flower shops
- A shop that sells memorabilia (sports, television, etc.)
- A limousine service
- A personal shopping service
- A service that organizes conventions for professional groups
- A mail-order gourmet meal provider

Case
Cartoon Corner

After you've read this chapter on planning, it might seem as though marketers just have to plan well enough, and success will fall into place. But according to Ken Veit, owner and operator of Cartoon Corner, achieving success isn't that simple—and planning provides no guarantees.

"Perhaps the most important lesson I've learned is that few plans are ever realized as conceived," writes Veit. "Formal planning and forecasting are largely exercises in reading tea leaves. They must be done, or the business will operate aimlessly. Yet doing them does not increase their chances of coming true."

Veit does concede that planning is necessary. His point is that plans ultimately collide with reality, and his experience as an entrepreneur illustrates this fact.

Veit, a successful insurance executive, was laid off by his employer after 28 years. Unable to find a comparable position during a recession, he evaluated his own strengths—he was a self-professed "product-development wizard . . . global strategist, negotiator, and diplomat." He had experience in every aspect of business, and he loved a challenge. He examined his financial weaknesses and threats—college-age children, a collapsed real-estate market, and worthless, unexercised stock options. It looked like opportunity had come knocking in the form of a franchise retail store called Cartoon Corner, which sold products featuring cartoon characters from the major motion picture studios and was located in a new mall in Scottsdale, Arizona.

So Veit set about analyzing, forecasting, and planning. He evaluated the franchisor. Cartoon Corner, itself a relatively new company, had plans of its own: the company intended to franchise 100 stores during the late 1980s and early 1990s, then go public with a stock offering. Its executives thought they could build a market valuation of $75 million to $100 million by the mid-1990s.

Using Cartoon Corner's sophisticated computer model, Veit calculated his own sales estimates with assumptions about sales, payroll, rent, operating expenses, and the like. He contacted Cartoon Corner's backers and received assurance that the company was healthy. He even hired an independent consultant to analyze the business. Veit calculated his start-up costs to be about $300,000 and projected his sales to be about $350 per square foot of floor space. At that rate, he and his wife could live comfortably in their new home. (They would be relocating to Arizona from Connecticut.)

Veit and his wife sold their house and moved to Scottsdale; there, many of his projections dissolved. He discovered that the new, upscale mall in which his store was located was only partially full and its opening would be delayed. The Gulf War took a toll on mall shopping. Many of Cartoon Corner's backers decided to pull out. The Cartoon Corner company went into liquidation.

So Veit reassessed his plans. He could cut his losses. He'd bought a new house in a soft market, sunk $100,000 into the business, and now assessed himself another $25,000 for his mistakes. He didn't know much about retailing, and he no longer had the support of the franchising organization. But he no longer had to pay a franchise fee, either. And he could buy some of his inventory from Cartoon Corner's corporate stores at liquidation rates. Further, two possible opportunities arose: he might be able to purchase another Cartoon Corner store cheaply with a partner, and one of the company's former vice presidents seemed interested in a joint venture for catalog sales.

Veit stayed in. Reality dealt him more hard blows. All his potential partners backed out. An important supplier of animation refused to deal with him because an existing customer was moving to the same mall. His bank pulled the plug. Much of his inventory arrived damaged. And only 20 of the 240 planned stores actually opened in the new mall.

Veit rode the entrepreneurial roller coaster through his first year, closing out the year at sales of $175 per square foot of floor space. But he decided to continue his business, all the wiser for his experience.

"I began with well-above-average experience, a proven concept, and excellent capitalization, yet in my case, personal bankruptcy remains a distinct possibility. External factors will swing the balance," he comments. "I have discovered that real planning is a learning process, not a means of control. . . . Good planning needs to be done every day. It is more anecdotal than numerical."

Veit continues, "Forecasting begins with the need to produce acceptable numbers and works backward. It is a necessary activity, but it's not what I'd call planning. In my book, planning is about responses to what the real world dishes up." Ken Veit has navigated the bumpy road between the best-laid plans and all the unforeseen circumstances that make the astute entrepreneur shift course to survive.

QUESTIONS

1. Do you think Ken Veit's decision to stay in business after all the obstacles he encountered was a good one? Why or why not? Would you have done the same? Why or why not?
2. Do you think Veit could have avoided some of his problems with better planning? If so, how?
3. How can Veit use some of his real-world experience to combat future obstacles?

Source: Ken Veit, "The Reluctant Entrepreneur," *Harvard Business Review,* November-December 1992, pp. 40–49.

Creating a Marketing Plan

As described in Chapter 5, the result of strategic marketing planning is a marketing plan for a particular product or product line. In the case of a small business, the marketing plan may even cover the marketing activities of the entire firm. The following pages outline the information a marketing plan should contain and present a sample marketing plan for a small business.

In studying this material, keep in mind that managers in various organizations will expect to see specifics in a marketing plan. For example, the procedure at one organization might be to prepare a marketing plan for an entire division, rather than a single product, unless the product is new. Some organizations call for a section analyzing the risks involved in the plan. When preparing an actual marketing plan, the marketing manager should verify exactly what information management wants included.

Components of a Marketing Plan

Although marketing plans need not follow identical structures, the following components constitute a complete marketing plan:

- Title page
- Executive summary
- Table of contents
- Introduction
- Situation analysis
- Marketing planning
- Implementation of the marketing plan
- Summary
- Appendix: Financial analysis
- References.

The sample marketing plan that follows contains the components in this list.

A neat title page gives the marketing plan a professional appearance and makes it easy to identify. The title page should contain the following information:

- The name of the product or brand that is the subject of the marketing plan
- The time period covered by the plan
- The name(s) and title(s) of those submitting the plan
- The person(s), group, or agency to whom the plan is being submitted, for example, a higher-level manager or a lending institution
- The date on which the plan is being submitted.

In preparing the title page, keep in mind that it is the basis for forming a first impression of the overall plan.

The executive summary sums up the contents of the marketing plan in a maximum of three pages. It is a useful source of information for managers who want to be familiar with the plan but do not need to approve its details. The executive summary should state the basic opportunity identified and the overall strategy for taking advantage of that opportunity. A budget summary also is helpful here.

The table of contents lists each section of the marketing plan and its page number. If the marketing plan contains numerous tables and figures, these may be listed after the table of contents. Preparing a table of contents helps the marketer determine that the plan is complete and well organized.

The introduction provides the background necessary to understand the marketing plan. For a new product or strategic business unit, the introduction explains the product concept and the reasons it is expected to succeed. For an existing product or strategic business unit, the introduction summarizes the the product's recent performance. The introduction can also tell the reader what the remainder of the marketing plan will cover.

The situation analysis describes the relevant conditions in the environment. In effect, it describes where the organization is now. This discussion generally includes an "industry analysis"—a section describing the competitive environment. The industry analysis covers such issues as who the competitors are, what market share each holds, what strengths and weaknesses each has, and whether new competitors are likely to enter the market.

Next the marketing plan describes where the organization wants to go. The section on marketing planning covers the marketing objectives, target market(s), and marketing mix and often describes the rationale for each. The section on the marketing mix details the selected strategies for product, price, channels, and communication. The marketing planning section can also include plans for marketing research.

After the objectives and strategy comes a description of how the marketing plan will be implemented and controlled. This description should specify who will be responsible for the efforts and provide a timetable. A marketing plan typically covers one year, though some plans cover a five-year time frame. The discussion of implementation and control also spells out how success or failure will be measured (usually, by comparing the results of implementing the plan with the marketing objectives).

The summary section of the marketing plan is similar to the executive summary. However, it may be somewhat longer and more detailed.

A financial analysis of the marketing plan may appear in an appendix. This should contain at least a sales forecast and an estimate of the marketing costs involved in carrying out the plan. Items to include in a cost estimate are advertising, marketing research, product development, package design, development of distribution channels, and training and compensation of the sales force.

Any sources of information used in compiling the marketing plan should be listed in a section titled "References." Sources may include books, journals, business periodicals, and company reports or memos.

Sample Marketing Plan: Little Learners Parent-Teacher Store

The following pages present a marketing plan for a fictional small business, the Little Learners Parent-Teacher Store. While this plan is shorter and less detailed than an actual marketing plan, it illustrates the basic style of such a plan.

Marketing Plan
Little Learners Parent-Teacher Store
Fiscal Year 1995
Robin Lee, President

Submitted to:

Pat Johnson
Commercial Loan Officer
Commerce National Bank
March 1, 1995

CONTENTS

EXECUTIVE SUMMARY

Little Learners Parent-Teacher Store is an 1,100-square-foot retail store specializing in educational games and teaching aids. Its primary customers are elementary school teachers who want additional resources for the classroom and parents seeking educational resources to supplement their children's learning in school.

In 1995 the owners would like to expand in response to the opportunity presented by a retail vacancy next to the existing store. Expanding into the existing space will increase square footage by approximately 80 percent, to 2,000 square feet. Given the strong demand for the store's products in the first three years of its existence, we expect that an expanded store can boost monthly sales by 55 percent over the previous year, for a total increase of $88,000 in fiscal year 1995. The sales increase would more than offset the additional operating costs. These costs consist of a $1,500-per-month increase in rent and utilities, added annual marketing communication expenses of $5,000, and $16,000 for an additional salesperson. Setting up the new space would involve a one-time cost of $20,000.

The space from the expansion would be used to provide a much broader selection of educational toys and games, which should attract many more parents to the store. To reach the parents, the promotional strategy would emphasize more frequent advertising in the local newspaper, the *Palo Alto Times,* along with sponsorship of quarterly seminars for parents at the Palo Alto Public Library.

INTRODUCTION   Little Learners Parent-Teacher Store is an 1,100-square-foot retail store specializing in educational games and teaching aids. Its best-selling products include workbooks, science experiments, and classroom decorations such as posters and bulletin board art. The store has been in operation since 1992 in the downtown business district of Palo Alto, California. Its primary customers are elementary schoolteachers who want additional resources for the classroom and parents seeking educational resources to supplement their children's learning in school. The owners of Little Learners are two former teachers in the Palo Alto school system. All salespeople in the store have teaching experience, enabling them to better help shoppers evaluate the products for sale.

In each of the first three years of its operation, the store has exceeded its revenue projections. For fiscal year 1994, ending May 31, 1995, the business is expected to post its first profit: $17,500 before taxes. Table 1 summarizes income statements for the past three years. To achieve its sales, the store has relied primarily on recommendations among teachers and weekly advertisements in the local newspaper, the *Palo Alto Times.* Because the store has little direct competition, it has been able to maintain an average 48 percent gross margin, avoiding price reductions except to clear out seasonal items.

The retail space adjacent to Little Learners became vacant in February 1995, when the jewelry store occupying the space relocated. This vacancy presents an attractive opportunity, given the strong sales Little Learners has experienced with minimal advertising. The remainder of this marketing plan details how the owners intend to take advantage of this expansion opportunity.

SITUATION ANALYSIS   Palo Alto, California, is a middle- to upper-class community of mostly professionals. With Stanford University and many research-oriented employers nearby, the people of this community place high value on learning and education.

TABLE 1		FY 1992	FY 1993	FY 1994	FY 1995*
Comparative Income Statements: Fiscal Years 1992–1995	Sales revenue	$86,000	$177,000	$232,000	$321,000
	Expenses:				
	Cost of goods sold	44,000	94,000	119,000	165,000
	Administrative costs	5,000	2,000	2,000	3,000
	Salaries	50,000	66,000	68,000	84,000
	Rent and utilities	20,000	21,000	22,000	40,000
	Advertising and PR	1,500	1,500	2,000	7,000
	Other expenses	1,000	1,500	1,500	2,000
	Income before taxes	($35,000)	($9,000)	$17,500	$20,000

*Projected, with expansion.

Thus, a major environmental opportunity is that this area is a strong supporter of educational resources for parents and teachers, including the Little Learners store.

In fact, we believe that we have only begun to tap the demand for the types of products we sell. Our sales have so far been limited by a small budget for advertising and public relations, as well as space constraints that prevent us from stocking as broad a selection as would interest most parents. A telephone survey of 50 households within a five-mile radius found that only 24 percent were aware of the store, but 43 percent expressed interest in the categories of merchandise offered.

Population trends support the view that demand for a parent-teacher store will continue to grow. Over the last decade, the population of Palo Alto has grown by only 1 percent, but the strongest growth (11.5 percent) was among households with children under 15. Furthermore, most of the population consists of professional people, a group that generally has a sizable amount of disposable income and values high-quality toys and educational opportunities for its children.

INDUSTRY ANALYSIS   Research into the stores located within a 20-mile radius uncovered only one store that directly competes with Little Learners. This store, called Educational Resources, has been operating for ten years in Santa Clara, California. The location is somewhat less desirable, but the costs of operating there are lower. As the store is privately owned, no data are available on its sales volume. However, on a recent Saturday, a steady flow of customers was seen entering the store.

We do not expect major competition from new stores over the near term. Because Educational Resources has operated for ten years without expanding or even, to all appearances, updating its interior, we believe that aggressive expansion is not in its owners' plans. Furthermore, because our own expansion into adjacent space is likely to attract less notice than opening new locations would, we expect that our expansion will attract few, if any, new competitors.

Thus, the major sources of competition for Little Learners are other types of retailers of educational products for children. Examples are toy stores, which sell some toys considered educational, bookstores, catalog retailers, and companies such as Discovery Toys that sell quality products in the home. Despite these environmental threats, we believe that our major strengths—the year-round availability of the store and the expertise of the owners and sales staff—set Little Learners apart as an easy-to-use source of guidance in selecting toys, games, and other materials that enhance learning by children.

4

MARKETING PLANNING

This section describes our growth objective and how we plan to achieve it.

MARKETING OBJECTIVES   Our objective is to achieve a 55 percent increase in sales by the end of fiscal year 1995. The increase is to be achieved by expanding the total square footage of the store to include the vacant space next door, for a total of 2,000 square feet (an increase of approximately 80 percent). The increase in sales is to be measured on a monthly basis in comparison to the previous year. In spite of the costs associated with increased size, we intend to keep our profit margin above 6 percent in fiscal year 1995. We seek to return to our current pretax profit margin of 7.5 percent by the end of fiscal year 1996.

TARGET MARKETS   The target markets for the store have been teachers working within a 20-mile radius of the store and "active parents" living within a 10-mile radius. By "active parents," we mean parents who devote a relatively great amount of time and money to their children's growth and development—for example, signing them up for swimming lessons, sending them to the "best" preschools, selecting toys that purportedly have educational value, joining parents' groups, visiting classrooms.

Active parents are the target market for the store's planned expansion. Not only are they interested in the kinds of products sold by Little Learners, they are willing to spend heavily on such products. They tend to be less budget conscious than the teachers who shop at the store.

MARKETING MIX   To attract the target market of "active parents," Little Learners will use most of the additional space to expand its offerings of educational toys and games. Compared to such materials as workbooks and posters, these are the items most often requested by the parents who shop at the store. The focus will be on top-quality, high-margin items that are hard to find at most toy stores. For example, there will be an extensive line of materials for science experiments, as well as top-quality arts and crafts supplies suitable for children. Top-quality, high-margin items support the store's image as a place to find materials superior to those available at a toy store. This focus appeals to parents who are willing to spend more if it means giving their children an edge.

The strategy to build revenues depends on increasing sales among parents who already visit the store and attracting more of the parents who live within a 10-mile radius. The primary means of increasing sales among current customers is the expanded product line. To attract new customers, we will rely on several types of communications. First, we will increase the frequency of display advertisements the store runs in the *Palo Alto Times* from twice a month to once a week. To build awareness, each ad will feature a different product or product line available at the store, along with the slogan "The Store Dedicated to Joyful Learning."

In addition, Little Learners will sponsor quarterly lectures on topics of interest to parents. The store will arrange for child development experts to speak at the public library. Posters and press releases announcing these events will mention the store's sponsorship.

To supplement these regular communications activities, the store will seek to take advantage of other opportunities to receive publicity. These will include events at the store, such as a writing contest among elementary-school students.

5

FIGURE 1

**Schedule for
Marketing Plan:
Fiscal Year 1995**

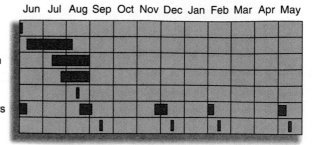

Jun Jul Aug Sep Oct Nov Dec Jan Feb Mar Apr May

Sign new lease
Prepare space
Hire and train new salesperson
Promote expanded store
Open additional space
Plan seminars; line up speakers
Seminars

Itemized costs for this strategy appear in the appendix to the marketing plan.

IMPLEMENTATION AND CONTROL   The owners of Little Learners Parent-Teacher Store will be responsible for implementing this marketing plan. As shown in Figure 1, the timetable for implementing the plan involves occupying the new space by June 1, 1995, and opening for business there by August 15. We expect to achieve the 55 percent increase in sales by the end of the fiscal year (May 31, 1996). Success in carrying out this plan will be measured in terms of completing activities according to the schedule shown in Figure 1 and meeting the objectives of the plan.

If costs should be higher than projected, our contingency plan is to proceed as long as we can keep costs within 15 percent of the projected amount. This will delay our ability to profit from the expansion until fiscal year 1996. If the adjacent retail space should no longer be available, our contingency plan is to forgo expanding the size of the store at the present time and to reevaluate the mix of products offered in the current store. We may be able to increase sales and profits by replacing some current offerings with more of the kinds of products we are planning to sell in the additional space. However, in adjusting the product mix, we will avoid changing in ways that detract from fulfilling our mission of serving teachers as well as parents in their efforts to promote learning.

SUMMARY

Little Learners Parent-Teacher Store is a store specializing in educational games and teaching aids. Its target markets are elementary school teachers who want additional resources for the classroom and "active parents"—those who devote a relatively great amount of time and money to their children's growth and development.

In response to the opportunity presented by a vacancy in the retail space next door, the store seeks to expand in fiscal year 1995. Expanding into the existing space will increase square footage by approximately 80 percent. Our marketing objective is to use this expansion as a means to increase monthly sales by 55 percent over the previous year, increasing total sales for fiscal year 1995 by $89,000. The increase in sales would more than offset the additional operating costs. The additional costs consist of a $1,500-per-month increase in rent and utilities, added annual communica-

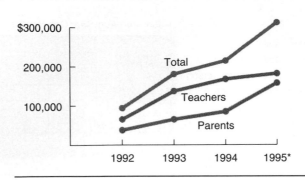

FIGURE 2
Sales History by Category

*Projected.

tions expense of $5,000, and $16,000 for an additional salesperson. The cost to set up the new space would be a one-time expense of $20,000.

The space from the expansion would be used to provide a much broader selection of educational toys and games. This product mix is designed to generate more sales among "active parents." In addition, to draw more active parents into the store, Little Learners plans to increase its budget for marketing communications. The additional funds would be used to double the frequency of advertising in the *Palo Alto Times* and to sponsor public relations activities such as speakers at the public library.

The owners will be responsible for implementing this plan, which calls for opening the new space by August 15, 1995. Success will be measured in terms of meeting the schedule and achieving the sales and profit objectives.

APPENDIX: FINANCIAL ANALYSIS

This appendix presents a sales forecast and budget in support of the marketing plan.

SALES FORECAST   Little Learners Parent-Teacher Store sells to parents and teachers. By offering teachers a free subscription to a company-produced, two-page monthly newsletter, the store can identify which sales go to which category of buyers. Figure 2 shows the pattern of sales to each category during the three years of the store's operations.

The marketing plan targets its expansion efforts at parents. Thus, sales to teachers are expected to follow the historical trend of increasing at an average of 5 percent per year. The additional communications efforts should increase sales beyond historical patterns. A telephone survey of area households found that only about one-quarter were familiar with the store but that almost half were interested in the types of products sold. Therefore, we anticipate that more intensive communications will lead to approximately a 45 percent increase in sales to parents.

BUDGET   The budget for this marketing plan appears in Table 2. The additional salesperson would cost about $16,000 per year, bringing the total cost for sales staff to $34,000. The additional communications expenses would be $5,000, bringing the total

TABLE 2 **Marketing Budget:** **Fiscal Year 1995**	**MARKETING EXPENSES**	
	Sales staff	$34,000
	Advertising, newspaper	6,300
	Seminar speakers (4 @ $100)	400
	Other, including posters, in-house PR	300
	Total marketing expenses	$41,000
	COSTS FOR ADDITIONAL SPACE	
	Preparation of space	$20,000
	Additional rent and utilities @ $1,500 per month	18,000
	Total for additional space	$38,000

budget for promotion to $7,000. The total costs to expand into the new location are $20,000 to prepare the space, plus an additional $1,500 per month in rent and utilities.

REFERENCES

Churchill, Gilbert A. Jr., and J. Paul Peter, *Marketing: Creating Value for Customers.* (Homewood, Ill.: Austen Press, 1995).

CHAPTER 6

Implementing and Controlling the Marketing Effort

LEARNING OBJECTIVES

After completing this chapter, you should be able to:

1. Describe the basic ways in which marketing groups can be organized.

2. Identify techniques for coordinating marketing activities.

3. Describe how marketing managers can motivate their employees.

4. Describe how marketers can communicate effectively.

5. Identify the steps in the control process.

6. Explain how marketers evaluate performance in terms of customer satisfaction, sales, and profits.

7. Discuss the use of marketing audits.

Creating Customer Value
Burlington Northern

Every kid dreams of riding the rails on a freight train, perhaps across the Great Plains, up the Pacific Coast, or through the lush Deep South. Before the railroad industry was deregulated in 1981, most railroad workers were engineers, logisticians, and other specialized employees who kept the railway system in tune. They moved their freight cars along a maze of tracks, intent only on performing their individual jobs. It never occurred to them that their functions might broaden. And they certainly wouldn't have predicted that within a few years, they'd be working side by side with their adversaries in the trucking business.

But with deregulation came change, and Burlington Northern met the change head on. The new laws allowed railroad companies to engage in "intermodal" business—that is, link themselves with other modes of transportation, such as trucks and ships, in order to improve service by speeding up delivery of goods. So Burlington Northern created its Intermodal Team, a new business unit within its marketing division.

The team drew members from various backgrounds, including operations and strategic planning. Bill Greenwood, the team leader, knew that Burlington Northern already had more than 160 ramps that could physically connect its trains to trucks. But he didn't know how his team was going to implement the plan or what results they'd get.

The core Intermodal Team established a larger task force, consisting of more than 40 people from various functions and business units at Burlington Northern, to carry out a three-stage plan. First, task force members consolidated the ramp connections to focus on the interstate highway system, which streamlined the link to the trucking industry. Then they updated all necessary equipment. Finally, they encouraged the company to develop new intermodal products and services tailored to customers' needs.

Meanwhile, the Intermodal Team capitalized on its members' strengths and struggled to overcome obstacles to teamwork. Ironically, none of the team members had a marketing background. However, each had expertise in a certain area and the willingness to perform as a team member. As each member's strengths emerged, the team members contributed different *types* of leadership—intellectual, social, and so forth.

"We were coming into a marketing group," noted one participant, "but none of us had ever been in marketing before. I think that worked to our advantage because we brought fresh perspective and didn't carry any baggage. Moreover, it was clear to all of us that we had to restructure the way the business operated in order to make it marketable."

Once the main strategy was in place, the team members focused on details. They stepped up advertising, featuring trucks in the ads. They painted their boxcars green, when the rest of the industry painted theirs white. They aggressively tried out the newest equipment.

A year and a half after the Intermodal Team began its mission, Burlington Northern was first in intermodal business in the railroad industry. It was setting records in the trucking industry as well. "We far exceeded what this network ought to have produced," says Bill Greenwood. "The numbers would just blow our minds."

As you study the concepts of implementation and control in this chapter, think about how teamwork can facilitate both. The strength of a team can put into action a far-reaching plan and produce results that exceed expectations.

Source: Jon R. Katzenbach and Douglas K. Smith, *The Wisdom of Teams* (Boston: Harvard Business School Press, 1993), pp. 28–42.

Chapter Overview

In the story of Burlington Northern, a team of marketers not only implemented a plan, it revolutionized the railroad freight business. At other organizations employees specialize in carrying out individual marketing functions, rather than serving on a team. Either way, marketing managers are responsible for seeing that the activities called for in marketing plans are performed in a way that achieves marketing objectives. In other words, marketing managers are responsible for implementing and controlling the marketing effort.

This chapter introduces basic issues related to implementation and control. It begins by explaining ways in which marketing groups are organized so that people can work together efficiently. Then the chapter describes the coordination, motivation, and communication needed to make implementation succeed. (The various implementation activities, such as product planning, pricing, and physical distribution, are covered in later chapters.) Once employees begin to carry out marketing activities, the marketing manager is responsible for seeing that they lead toward achievement of marketing objectives. Thus, the last section of the chapter describes how managers use controlling to identify needs for improvement in the marketing plan or its implementation.

Organizing Marketing Groups

organize
To structure a group by defining areas of authority and working relationships.

Except at the smallest companies, marketing efforts are carried out by a group of employees. An important management task is to **organize** this group; that is, to structure the group by defining areas of authority and working relationships. To an employee with limited responsibilities, such as analyzing prices or selling a product line, it may seem unimportant whether the marketing group has one structure or another. However, employees will work together most efficiently if the group is organized logically and in accordance with the marketing objectives established during the planning process.

CENTRALIZED VERSUS DECENTRALIZED ORGANIZATIONS

centralized organization
An organization in which most decisions and authority lie with top management.

Generally speaking, the marketing group and the organization of which it is a part may be centralized or decentralized. A **centralized organization** is one in which relatively few people hold authority and responsibility. In practice, this means that a large share of decisions are made by top management. In a centralized organization, for example, marketing staff will probably have to get the approval of top management before hiring a new advertising agency or changing the price of a product. A centralized structure makes it easier for management to coordinate the work of various departments.

Typically, a centralized organization has many layers of management. Procter & Gamble once had as many as ten layers between entry-level employees and its chief executive. Some of these managers supervised only two or three people.[1] Such an arrangement tends to be expensive. To cut costs, Procter & Gamble has eliminated some layers so that each entry-level employee is seven or fewer layers away from the CEO.[2] In its sales department, P&G has eliminated a layer of management by making managers responsible for teams of employees organized around customers.[3]

decentralized organization
An organization in which a relatively great number of people hold authority and make decisions.

When organizations eliminate layers of management, the outcome tends to be a more decentralized structure. In **decentralized organizations** a relatively great number of people hold authority and responsibility. Because there tend to be fewer layers of

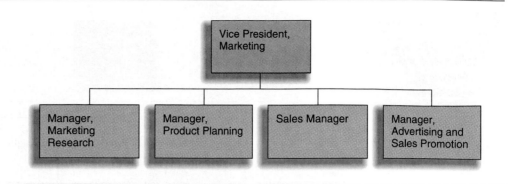

FIGURE 6.1

Marketing Department with Functional Organization

management, middle and lower-level managers—and even operative employees—have authority to make decisions about their areas of responsibility. For example, Macy's recently adopted a more decentralized structure that allows individual stores to tailor the goods they carry to the customers they serve.[4]

A decentralized structure enables the organization to benefit from the expertise and decision-making skills of more of its employees. Also, fewer levels of managers can mean lower costs. Because decentralized organizations allow employees and lower-level managers to make more decisions without first requesting approval, they can more quickly get a product to market or respond to changes in the environment.

Given these benefits, some managers today are seeking to create organizations that are almost "flat"—that is, almost lacking in hierarchy. Such organizations give their employees broad latitude in making decisions, often as part of a team. At Indus Group, a San Francisco maker of management software, the 250 staffers work in teams on particular projects, such as customer support or product development. At the end of each week, all 250 Indus employees type one-page summaries of their accomplishments for the week and their plans for the next week. The company's president reads each summary on the company's electronic bulletin board.[5]

Whether they are centralized or decentralized, traditionally structured companies cluster marketing personnel in a group. The marketing group may be organized by function, product, or geographic location. Other companies more directly attempt to organize the marketing group in a way that positions them to meet customer needs.

ORGANIZING BY FUNCTION

Just as an entire company might be divided into functions, such as marketing, production, finance, and research and development, the marketing group can be organized by function. Thus, as shown in Figure 6.1, the marketing department can be divided into specialized groups handling such marketing functions as marketing research, product planning, sales, and advertising and sales promotion.

A functional organization may be effective when all the company's products have similar marketing needs, such as when all products are directed to the same target market. This type of organization may also be appropriate for a small company with one product or a few similar products. Employees who handle a single marketing function become expert at it. The marketing manager must coordinate everyone's work to make sure it meets the organization's overall marketing objectives. This may work well in a small organization or one with limited offerings, but coordination may become overly complex in an organization with a variety of marketing plans to execute.

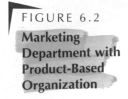

FIGURE 6.2

Marketing
Department with
Product-Based
Organization

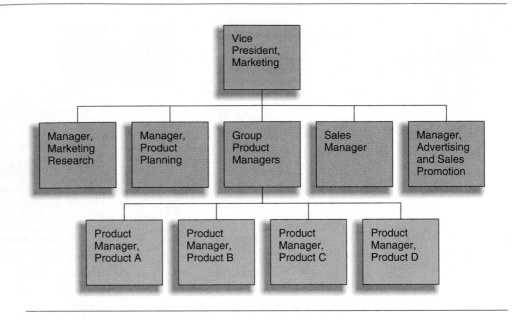

ORGANIZING BY PRODUCT

product-based organization
An organization in which
managers have responsibility for all marketing activities
pertaining to a particular
product.

product managers
Managers who oversee
employees and activities
pertaining to the marketing
of a particular product.

In some marketing groups, managers have responsibility for all marketing activities pertaining to a particular product. Figure 6.2 illustrates such a **product-based organization**.
Reporting to each of these managers, known as **product managers**, are the employees
who carry out the specific activities needed to implement the marketing plan. The group
product managers, in turn, report to the organization's vice president of marketing.
The vice president also oversees some functional groups that cannot be efficiently divided among products. For example, the company might have a single sales force, rather
than paying two different groups of salespeople to sell two different products to the
same customers.

If the organization handles many products that fall into several categories, it may
need an additional layer of management: a product group manager. This person coordinates the work of several product managers.

A product-based organization makes sense when the marketing mix and target
market vary significantly from one product to the next. Employees become experts in
their product and the needs of its target market. They can therefore quickly identify
and respond to needs as they arise. Also, because product managers handle a variety
of responsibilities, the organization develops talented marketing managers. However,
because each product needs marketing employees with expertise in various functions, this type of organization can be expensive.

ORGANIZING BY GEOGRAPHIC LOCATION

The marketing group also may be organized by geographic location. A company serving a global marketplace might have separate marketing divisions for North America,
Asia, Europe, and Africa. The Olive Garden division of General Mills Restaurants is
organized into three groups: restaurants serving the northeastern, western, and southern regions of the United States.[6] Often a portion of the marketing group, such as the
sales or advertising department, is organized geographically.

Armstrong Floors, a manufacturer and marketer of interior furnishings, initiated the "SMART" program for servicing consumers. (SMART is an acronym for sales, merchandising, advertising, retail support, and tactics.) Armstrong invited nearly 1,700 retailers (resellers) of its floors to visit the company's headquarters to learn more about the product and service their customers better. Sherry Qualls, Armstrong residential floors advertising manager, addresses "SMART" issues with resellers.

Organizing by geographic location makes sense when the company's markets are significantly different from one location to another. When the needs and values of customers vary among locations, the company can benefit from having people paying attention to each group. An employee handling distribution in Asia would probably approach the task differently than the person handling distribution in Europe. Likewise, a chain of home improvement stores would want to feature and stock different products in the South than in the Northeast.

ORGANIZING FOR CUSTOMER SATISFACTION

The competitive pressures generated by new technology and increased international competition have led some companies to seek ways to organize that put customers first. Such a company is Motorola, where many of the employees have been organized into work teams dedicated to improving performance quality and customer satisfaction. Thanks to the flexibility of the team approach, Robert Galvin, chairman of Motorola's executive committee, believes the company can double in size every year without becoming stifled by bureaucracy. Galvin describes this future Motorola as "a corporation that will look gigantic but have the dynamics of little teams."[7]

In many cases, these organizations group people according to the customers they serve so that employees can be well acquainted with their customers' needs. Hewlett-Packard assigns salespeople to serve particular industries, rather than geographic territories. H-P salespeople are expected to become experts in the industry they serve as well as in the products they sell.[8] At KPMG Peat Marwick, the biggest international accounting firm, employees are organized into cross-functional teams serving particular lines of business, such as clients in government, health care, or education.[9] In other cases, cross-functional teams are formed to meet specific needs, then disbanded when the needs have been met.

Applying a quality orientation and teamwork to the task of organizing may lead to creation of a "network organization." As shown in Figure 6.3, in a network organization the operations are carried out by independent business units interacting with one another.[10] These business units may take the form of functional groups or cross-functional teams. The ways they cooperate may range from a long-term buying and selling arrangement to a strategic alliance, in which organizations contribute their

FIGURE 6.3
**Basic Form of a
Network
Organization**

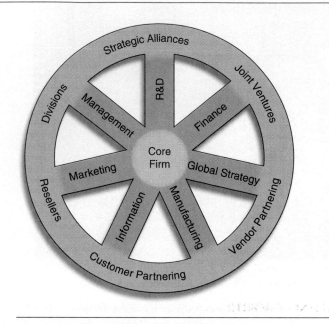

Source: Frederick E. Webster, Jr., "The Changing Role of Marketing in the Corporation," *Journal of Marketing* (October 1992): p. 9. Reprinted with permission of the American Marketing Association.

core competencies to carry out a venture designed to benefit all the participants. Moreover, the individual firms typically have few layers of management.

The network organization places less importance on hierarchical reporting relationships, relying instead on cooperation among equals. At McKinsey & Company, a major consulting firm, success depends on the ability of employees to share their specialized knowledge with clients and one another, not so much on management's ability to supervise the employees.[11] Because network organizations are flexible and flat, they allow the organization to be in touch with customer needs and competitive forces so that it can respond quickly to new needs and opportunities. "Looking Ahead" at the end of this book takes a closer look at network organizations.

Implementing the Marketing Plan

Whatever way the marketing group is organized, its core activities are directed toward implementing the marketing plan or plans for which it is responsible. For the sake of clarity, this chapter describes implementation as if one marketing group carries out one marketing plan. The chapter focuses on general principles of successful implementation. The remaining chapters in this book discuss how to implement the various marketing activities, including marketing research and decisions related to the four elements of the marketing mix (product, price, channels of distribution, and communication).

Implementation is where a quality focus will be most apparent to current and prospective customers. A marketing organization with this orientation will seek to carry out the marketing plan in a way that achieves excellence and pleases customers. Therefore, employees at all levels must seek to continuously improve implementation. For example, a team developing a new product will focus on satisfying the needs of the target market, perhaps giving customers even more than what they thought to ask for. The order-fulfillment department will continuously look for ways to ensure that orders are filled quickly and without errors. Salespeople will focus on providing such excellent service that prospective customers will *want* to buy from the company.

When the implementation process succeeds, the marketing group achieves the objectives laid out in the marketing plan. Successful implementation depends on coordinating work, motivating employees, and communicating with people inside and outside the organization.

COORDINATION

No marketer can succeed in isolation. Even the most brilliant and hardworking marketing experts need help in carrying out their marketing plans. And even a small company needs employees or contractors to handle at least some marketing activities—say, designing a logo or distributing goods. In addition, the success of the marketing effort depends on cooperation from nonmarketing personnel. Therefore, implementing the marketing effort requires that the marketing manager coordinate the work involved by setting priorities, scheduling activities, and building cooperation.

SETTING PRIORITIES   Because employees in different departments have different, even conflicting, concerns, priorities can be difficult to agree on. For example, production managers can minimize mistakes and maximize productivity when the company makes a moderate amount of a single product. However, sales managers can boost earnings by offering a variety of products—and the more they sell, the better. Even within the marketing group, there are disagreements over priorities. If the head of marketing research is convinced that spending more on research will enable the company to target its product so well that it can afford to cut back on promotion, the head of promotion will almost certainly object.

How can the marketing manager set priorities in light of these conflicts? The manager can either impose priorities or lead the group in reaching a consensus. The latter approach can be more difficult and tends to require more patience, but it is likely to result in greater commitment to the priorities agreed on. Whether the manager sets priorities alone or leads the group in doing so, the focus should be on doing what is necessary to achieve the objectives of the marketing group and the organization.

SCHEDULING   Implementing any marketing plan requires carrying out many activities. To make sure that they are done on time, the marketing manager must schedule them. Scheduling requires identifying what needs to get done, who will perform each task, how long each task will take, and when it must be completed. For example, a company launching a new service will want much of its advertising to take place around the time the service begins. If the company advertises too far in advance, people will become discouraged when they can't buy the service, and they may have lost interest by the time the service *is* available.

Scheduling activities is easier when the manager uses some of the techniques and tools developed for that purpose. One such tool is the **Gantt chart**, which lists the activities to be completed and uses horizontal bars to graph how long each is to take. Figure 6.4 shows a sample Gantt chart of the type AutoResearch Laboratories Inc. (ALI) would use to upgrade one of its services (some form of test to measure the performance of petroleum products). By looking at the chart, the manager can easily see what needs to be done at any given time. In the example, upgrading a service involves four functional areas at ALI—marketing, operations, engineering, and purchasing—so the chart is coded to show which function(s) are responsible for each activity.

Gantt chart
A chart that lists marketing activities and uses horizontal bars to graph the time allotted to each.

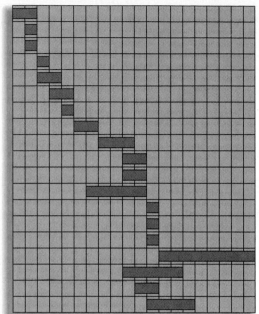

FIGURE 6.4
Sample Gantt Chart

Project: Automated Single-Cylinder Engine Tests
Tasks (Responsibility)*

Determine Customer Requirements (M)
Survey Competition (M, E)
Determine Industry Standards (E)
Specify Hardware (E, O)
Specify Software (E, M)
Procure Prototype Materials (E, P)
Evaluate Prototype Materials (O)
Develop Prototype (O, E)
Test Prototype (O)
Revise Prototype (E, O)
Obtain Customer Input (M, E)
Obtain Operator Input (O, E)
Finalize Design (E)
Procure Final Design Materials (P)
Subcontract Construction (E, P)
Install Final Design (O)
Operator Training (O)
Client Service Training (E, M)
Promote New Test (M)

*M = Marketing; O = Operations; E = Engineering; P = Purchasing

Source: Auto Research Laboratories, Inc.

critical path method (CPM)
A method using a network of circles and arrows to chart the schedule of marketing activities.

Another way to record activities to be scheduled is to use the **critical path method (CPM)**. To use this method, the manager creates a network with circles representing the tasks that must be completed and arrows between the circles representing the activities required to carry out each task. Thus, to complete a project, the employees must move along the arrows through the network. The sequence of tasks that will require the greatest amount of time is called the critical path. For the project to be completed on time, the manager must make sure that activities along the critical path do not fall behind.

Another resource for scheduling is computer software. Today a variety of project management programs are available to help with scheduling on a personal computer. These include Superproject for Windows, Project Scheduler 5, and Time Line. Among other applications, they allow the user to create and update Gantt charts, look at cost-and-time graphs, and schedule multiple projects, allowing for the relative priority of each project.[12]

BUILDING COOPERATION   To get their work done, managers and employees alike need the cooperation of others. In general, people tend to cooperate when they understand the need to do so and when they respect the person seeking their cooperation. Thus, a general guideline for building cooperation is to make sure others understand what it is you're trying to do and why. For example, when requesting help from the company's accountant in developing sales and cost records for each product line, the marketer can explain, "This kind of information will help us make sure we are emphasizing the most profitable products." In addition, any employee or manager who wishes to receive respect must earn it by being ethical, considerate, and fair and by striving to do excellent work.

Mitsuru Sato coordinates teamwork by managing Honda and Chrysler's joint effort to market four-wheel-drive jeeps in Japan.

Another way to build cooperation is to be aware of the concerns and goals of employees in different functional areas and to realize how marketing activities can affect them. Corning Glass Works once learned that Ford Motor Company, a major purchaser of Corning's ceramic substrate used in emission-control systems, was going to require that Corning beef up its quality efforts. This meant that for the company to meet the sales objective of keeping one of its biggest customers, the whole production department would have to meet the quality requirements imposed by Ford. The effort succeeded, with the result that Corning increased its U.S. market share for substrate so much that it had to reopen a factory.[13] Thus, the success in quality improvement and marketing led to more work for the production department (not a bad thing, of course, but an added challenge nonetheless).

COORDINATING TEAMWORK   Coordination is especially important when the marketing plan is implemented by a team. In organizations that rely on teamwork within and across departmental and organizational lines, success depends on the ability to work cooperatively with one's equals, not on the ability to give or follow orders. In managing Honda and Chrysler's joint effort to market four-wheel-drive Jeeps in Japan, Mitsuru Sato must get managers from both companies to appreciate each other's concerns. In particular, Sato works hard to convince Chrysler to make quality improvements, while winning over Japanese car dealers so that they will give the Jeeps favorable treatment.[14]

At the Dow Chemical Company's plastics group in Midland, Michigan, the challenge was to get members of a cross-functional product development team to overcome functional rivalries. Researchers wanted to proceed carefully over several months to examine all options. Manufacturing managers wanted to stick to a slight variation of an existing product. The two factions wouldn't compromise, so they worked independently. As a result, the project bogged down until a new team leader got everyone talking at a barbecue he organized for the team.[15]

For team members to coordinate their work, they must all understand what they can and should be doing. Are they an advisory group, for example, or are they expected to make and carry out decisions? Team members need to know about the objectives and performance of the team itself and of the organization as a whole. Management and the team leader must work together to ensure that this information is getting to the team. (For a discussion on being a team member, see "Put It Into Practice.")

Chances are, you won't jump straight from college into the marketing world as a marketing manager. Nor will you always be designated a team leader. In many cases, you'll be a team member. Being a good team member is an extremely important skill to have. For any team to function effectively, all members must be doing their jobs to their full capacity.

An effective team member needs good communication skills, flexibility, an understanding of priorities and goals, commitment to the job at hand, and acceptance of agreed-upon incentives.

As you work on your Chapter Project for this chapter, implementing and controlling a marketing effort, consider all of the people who would be involved in the real-life campaign. Put yourself in their shoes: What would *they* think is the best way to carry out their responsibilities? What resources and incentives do they need? How would you function in each of their roles? Polishing your skills as a team member will help you become an effective—and desirable—potential employee in the marketing workplace.

Because team members depend so heavily on one another to achieve their objectives, teams need to take time to evaluate their progress and whether they are achieving the results they are supposed to. The team leader needs to make sure that all team members are participating in meetings and other teamwork. Signs that team members are working well together are open debate and disagreement on issues coupled with comfort in working toward resolution of the issues.

To develop such a team, the team leader needs to take on a coaching role, rather than simply telling team members what to do. When problems arise, the team leader helps employees find a solution by asking them questions to keep the discussion moving forward, rather than issuing directives. Teamwork is most likely to succeed when there are cooperative goals and open discussion of opposing viewpoints.[16] Thus, the team leader should try to keep team members focused on a common objective, such as delighting customers.

COMMUNICATION

Imagine a marketing department in which the employees responsible for advertising don't understand who the target market is, or where half the team members don't show up for meetings because the meeting announcements are missing the date. Getting people to work together to implement the marketing effort requires good communication. The marketing manager must make sure that employees know what they are supposed to be doing. Employees and managers alike must be able to share ideas and to give and follow instructions. They must be able to discern the wants and needs of their existing and potential customers. They must be able to explain how the organization's products can satisfy those wants and needs.

For example, implementing the marketing plan for Seattle-based Merchant du Vin, an importer of high-quality beers, depends on a variety of communication skills. Charles Finkel, the company's founder, had to start by persuading small European breweries to brew traditional beers—including wheat beers, an oatmeal stout, and an ale flavored with peaches—many of which had long been unavailable. In setting up channels of distribution, Finkel had to persuade stores to carry his offerings and educate beer lovers about the products. Finkel also has visited brewers, given speeches at industry events and consumer tastings, and helped restaurant owners develop lists of beers to complement menu offerings.[17]

As Finkel no doubt realizes, his success requires that he have skills in speaking, writing, listening, and nonverbal communication. These skills are important for all marketers.

SPEAKING SKILLS   Communication through the spoken word is known as oral communication. Marketers use oral communication in meetings, on the phone, and when giving speeches or other presentations. To use oral communication effectively, it is important to speak in a moderate tone of voice and to tailor the message to the audience. What words will the listener understand? What are the listener's values and interests?

One of the advantages of communicating through the spoken word is that you can get immediate feedback. For example, when a suburban bank first installed automated teller machines (ATMs), it stationed an employee by the machines to offer help and answer questions. When this employee explained a procedure, she could watch the customer to see whether he or she understood.

When you use oral communication, look for clues about whether the listener understands your message. Some clues are whether the listener looks confident or confused, whether the listener has questions, and whether the listener behaves in a way that shows he or she understood the message. In the case of the bank employee helping customers use the ATMs, she might have told the customer to enter his or her personal identification number, then watch to make sure the customer didn't stare blankly at the machine or try to enter a checking account number instead. Another way to get listener feedback is to invite questions, giving the listener plenty of time to think of some.

Making sure the listener understands is especially important when speaking to someone whose first language is not English.[18] To do this, speak slowly (not loudly), and use simple words. Check for understanding by asking, "What did you hear me say?" The following clues indicate a listener may need more help in understanding your message:

- Nodding and smiling in a way that is not directly connected to what you are saying
- Not interrupting at all
- Trying to change the subject
- Not asking any questions at all
- Laughing at inappropriate times.

Conversely, it may be hard to understand someone whose native language is not English. If you are having trouble understanding a word, try asking the person to spell it for you. If you make a genuine effort at understanding, your example can help to create a positive climate for cross-cultural or international communication.

WRITING SKILLS   Marketers need writing skills for a variety of kinds of messages. They write memos, reports, advertisements, press releases, letters, and many other materials conveying information about their product or marketing activities. Three key guidelines are essential to effective writing:

1. Know your audience.
2. Keep it simple.
3. Get organized.

Try to understand the viewpoint of those who will read your message, then write from that viewpoint. For example, when making a proposal to a higher-level manager, keep in mind what that person's objectives are, then describe how your idea will support achievement of the manager's objectives. Likewise, when telling prospective customers about your product, focus on explaining how the product will meet their needs, not on listing the features of the product that you consider miracles of modern design. Figure 6.5 shows how advertising copywriter Jerry Fisher applied this principle to an ad for a mobile disc jockey business in Connecticut.

Keeping it simple means writing the way you talk. If you're not sure the person receiving the message will understand a particular word, choose a simpler word. Keep sentences and paragraphs short.

FIGURE 6.5

Communicating from the Viewpoint of the Message Receiver

Careful writers also plan. Determine just what your main point is. Then organize your thoughts to support that point. Typically you would put your main point in the first paragraph or section, then start each of the following paragraphs or sections by making a supporting point.

LISTENING SKILLS   Some people think that a good talker makes a good salesperson. However, it is at least as important to know what other people are thinking as it is to get one's own point across. The salesperson who listens to customers is able to recognize their needs and show them how the organization's goods or services can address those needs. Not only in sales but in any other aspect of marketing that involves working with people, effective listening is an important way to receive knowledge.

To foster good communication by listening effectively, you must go beyond just hearing people talk. You must make an active effort to understand the message. Try following these ten rules for good listening:[19]

1. Remove distractions, and give the speaker your full attention.
2. Look at the speaker most of the time.
3. When the speaker hesitates, give a sign of encouragement such as a smile or nod.
4. Try to hear the main point and supporting points.
5. Distinguish between opinions and facts.
6. Control your emotions.
7. Be patient; don't interrupt.
8. Take notes.
9. At appropriate times, ask questions to clarify your understanding.
10. Restate what you think the speaker's point is, and ask if you heard correctly.

These tips apply when listening to formal communications, such as a speech, as well as to less formal messages, such as a customer complaint or an employee suggestion.

NONVERBAL COMMUNICATION SKILLS   While we usually think of communication in terms of words (verbal communication), the majority of the information we get through interpersonal communication is nonverbal.[20] People send messages through their posture, gestures, facial expressions, style of dress, tone of voice, and distance from the listener. Through experience, we learn what these messages mean in our culture. For example, in the dominant American culture, a speaker who does not make eye contact with his or her audience is thought to be hiding something. In other cultures, avoiding eye contact is seen as a sign of respect.[21]

When nonverbal cues such as these are inconsistent with the verbal message, people tend to believe the nonverbal message. (Recall the familiar saying, "Actions speak louder than words.") Thus, if a restaurant adopts the slogan "Where service is more than just a word," yet its servers are grumpy and slow, customers will come to believe that service really is just a word at that establishment. As a result, marketers who are preparing messages for customers or coworkers must make sure that their nonverbal communication matches the intended message.

OVERCOMING COMMUNICATION BARRIERS   Even a person with a variety of communication skills will encounter barriers to communication. Effective communication depends on overcoming these barriers when possible.

One barrier to communication is information overload. This occurs when people are so overwhelmed with information that they miss hearing the message. Marketers need to be concerned with information overload when they are preparing an advertising strategy. For example, television viewers see so many advertisements that it is important to test a new ad to make sure it will attract enough notice. Likewise, when preparing a report for management, the marketer must make it easy to read and should place an executive summary at the front.

Misunderstandings are another barrier to communication. These occur when the message is overly complicated, the sender of the message has not thought it through carefully, or the receiver is not really paying attention. Some ways to avoid misunderstandings are to choose words carefully when speaking or writing and to listen or read with care when receiving a message.

Prejudices, too, interfere with communication. Making broad generalizations about the speaker or writer can lead the receiver to misinterpret a message. For example, someone who believes that young people like change for change's sake may disregard the suggestion of a younger colleague, even if it is beneficial. The sender of a message can also let prejudices interfere with good communication. For example, prejudices about a target market could lead to the creation of an inappropriate advertising message. The most basic way to avoid letting prejudices become a barrier to communication is to be aware of one's own prejudices.

FORMAL AND INFORMAL COMMUNICATION   Effective managers know that their employees do not receive all of their information through memos, meetings, and management directives. Rather, within the organization, communication may be formal or informal. *Formal communication* flows along the lines of the organizational chart and is directed toward accomplishing organizational objectives. For example, a marketing research report is a type of formal communication, and so is a team meeting to discuss the pricing of a product. *Informal communication* is directed toward meeting the individual needs of the people who use it. Informal communication often takes the form of gossip or rumors. The paths it follows are known as the *grapevine*.

FIGURE 6.6

A Misguided Approach to Motivation

DILBERT

MOTIVATION

motivation
inspiring people to act in desired ways.

Through coordination and communication, the marketing manager makes sure employees know what they are supposed to be doing. If they have the proper training and education, the employees should also know how to carry out their tasks. For implementation to succeed, the remaining element is **motivation**—that is, inspiring people to act in desired ways.

For example, to attract a loyal and committed work force, Starbucks Coffee Company offers a package of employee benefits that is exceptionally generous among food retailers. All employees, even those who work part time, receive health insurance, stock options, training programs, career counseling, and product discounts. Howard Schultz, the chief executive of Starbucks, explains the marketing benefits of this approach: "More than half of our retail sales force is part-time workers. That tells me that the majority of our customers are coming into contact with part timers. How we treat our people is directly related to how we treat our customers and the quality of our product."[22]

PRINCIPLES OF MOTIVATION   To motivate employees, the marketing manager must recognize that different people are motivated by different things at different times. One employee may want to earn a lot of money, whereas another is more interested in professional growth. According to various theories of motivation, some of the incentives that may motivate employees are money, security, interesting work, relationships with coworkers, esteem, the opportunity to realize one's potential, and opportunities to be creative or to be promoted. Though his tactics are questionable, the manager pictured in Figure 6.6 appears to be well aware of what motivates his employees. (In "Marketing Movers & Shakers," see how Carol Bartz not only motivates employees, but also implements an aggressive marketing program.)

The manager's behavior also can motivate employees. Employees are more likely to be motivated when they see that their boss is fair and follows the same rules they are expected to adhere to. Furthermore, the manager can motivate by treating employees with respect and by communicating what is expected of them.

Not only must rewards be attractive to employees, but employees must believe they can achieve them. For example, if the marketing department bases a bonus on its goal of total customer satisfaction, employees must believe they have the power to do the things customers want. Even if the manager is confident that employees can achieve a reward, motivation will not work unless the employees themselves share this belief. At the same time, however, one of the ways a manager can inspire people to do excellent work is to have high expectations (a self-fulfilling prophecy). In sum, the manager's job as motivator is to provide rewards for objectives that are challenging but achievable.

Marketing Movers & Shakers

CAROL BARTZ AT SUN MICROSYSTEMS

Carol Bartz doesn't want to hold your hand. And she doesn't want her salespeople to, either, even if you're a loyal customer of hers. But she does want her sales force to be the best at selling computer workstations and solving customers' problems with them.

Until 1992, Bartz was head of worldwide field operations at Sun Microsystems, a manufacturer of computer workstations that has outsold Hewlett-Packard, Digital Equipment Corp., and IBM because it offers systems that adapt easily to competing hardware and software, at a low price. She is now CEO of Autodesk, Inc., which produces software.

Bartz knows how to implement aggressive marketing plans, oversee an equally aggressive sales force, listen to customers, and motivate employees. Between the time she joined Sun in 1983 as customer marketing manager and when she left, she directed a work force totaling 6,000. "What accounted for my success at Sun is the fact that I'm fairly outspoken and like to tackle issues and problems," Bartz comments. "I like to make decisions. I don't couch things."

Bartz initiated Sun's Passport Program for the company's overseas sales accounts. Through the program, international customers could receive the same terms, delivery, and service no matter where they were located. (Previously, each international agreement had to be negotiated separately, so a Sun customer with offices in several countries had a nightmare of paperwork.) The program meant that overseas customers would receive the same exceptional treatment that local customers received.

Sun's sales force is known throughout the industry for being aggressive, even arrogant. Bartz acknowledges this. "Part of the downside of the kind of sales force I'm talking about is the fact that they don't spend the same amount of time hand-holding the customer as some of the competition. That's a serious downside, and I don't mean to minimize it." But she's quick to point out that Sun's sales force

listens to customers, understands their problems, and works hard to offer the best solutions. And, she feels, these are the qualities that count. She leaves the soft follow-up—the hand-holding, the phone call asking, "Hi, how are you?"—to Sun's dealers and distributors.

Bartz believes in empowering and motivating employees in two ways: with a hands-off policy, allowing people the freedom to do their job, and with money. "I believe very, very strongly in letting my field managers run the sales force. . . . I don't meddle. I'm very, very proud of that. My field management knows that their job is to sell. Period." At Sun, she kept the compensation plan simple: "We had a 'the more you sell, the more you earn' philosophy."

To motivate the overseas branches, which previously had *too much* autonomy, to participate willingly in the Passport Program, she decided the answer also involved money. International executives previously earned bonuses based simply on revenues and other performance goals. When the Passport Program was instituted, the compensation formula was much more biased toward group goals.

Carol Bartz left her mark at Sun, and she marches ahead to meet new challenges. If she doesn't hold anyone's hand, at least she's got both hands free to do her job.

Source: "Carol Bartz Watches Sun's Rise," *Sales & Marketing Management,* July 1992, pp. 36–37.

MOTIVATING TEAMS   A recent study of teams at 500 organizations found that at a majority of organizations, the teams were not as effective as desired. The most common barrier to team performance was lack of motivation. At 80 percent of the organizations, compensation and rewards were based solely on individual, rather than group, performance.[23]

To motivate employees to work as a team, the manager needs to offer rewards for group achievements rather than just for individual accomplishments. For example, a **group incentive system** is a compensation method based on paying a bonus to members of a group that achieves specified objectives. Thus, after a team launches a new product on time and under budget, each team member might receive a bonus representing a share of the first year's profits generated by the new product. Of course,

group incentive system
A compensation method that pays a bonus to group members based on the group's achievements.

many marketing managers have little input into their employer's compensation plan, but they can be careful to apply the same standards to all rewards, including praise and positive performance appraisals. For example, if marketing employees are assigned to cross-functional teams, the marketing manager must uphold team goals, rather than fostering an us-versus-them attitude toward employees in other functional areas.[24]

Trying to motivate a team may seem daunting when the teams have a great deal of authority. With no supervisor to crack the whip, who—or what—will keep employees in line? Certainly, the risks are real. After XEL Communications, a maker of telecommunications equipment, began using self-managing teams, it seemed to the company's manufacturing vice president as though "you'd go out there on a Friday afternoon, and half a team would be gone." But soon team members saw how their performance affected goal achievement and rewards, and they began working harder, and smarter, than ever.[25]

Controlling The Marketing Effort

When the marketing group begins implementing the marketing plan, the manager needs to know whether the plan is obtaining the desired results. The Danish Pharmaceutical Association, a network of 300 privately owned pharmacies, devised a strategy to reposition Danish pharmacies as a comprehensive source of health care information and services, rather than just a place to buy drugs and related goods. To implement this strategy, the pharmacies expanded their products to include health and diet foods, herbal medicines, and skin-care products. They improved their information services to include publication of self-help books and preventive-care pamphlets and a computer system that accesses health information. They started an antitobacco campaign that included selling antismoking chewing gum and offering stop-smoking classes. They also developed packages of health care supplies such as a home health care package for patients discharged from the hospital.[26]

The results of implementing this strategy were not all as the association had intended. Others in the health care industry saw many of the tactics as infringing on their territory. Hospitals wouldn't recommend the home health care packages, for example. Doctors objected to the stop-smoking courses, which were eventually discontinued.

As in this case, when a marketing strategy does not perform as expected, the marketer needs to find out where problems lie. Somehow, the marketing group will have to make changes to bring performance and standards into line. For example, the Danish Pharmaceutical Association turned its efforts to improving relations with others in the health care industry so that they could collaborate on achieving mutual goals. The process of measuring performance and making corrections as needed is known as **controlling**.

controlling
The process of measuring the performance of a marketing effort and making necessary corrections.

THE CONTROL PROCESS

Controlling involves three steps, shown in Figure 6.7. First, the manager measures the results being obtained. Then the manager compares those results with the standards that have been set (these should be spelled out in the marketing plan). Finally, when performance is close to or superior to the objectives, the manager reinforces performance. For example, in the first year Starbucks Coffee offered stock options to all employees based on the company's performance, Starbucks exceeded its profit objective by 20 percent. In response, management made the formula for awarding stock options more generous for future years.[27] When performance is significantly below the objectives, the manager

FIGURE 6.7

Steps in the Control Process

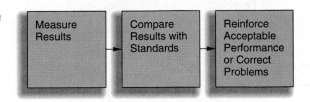

takes corrective action. At TGI Friday's restaurants, the percentage of sales that come from bar orders has plunged, so the chain repositioned itself as a place for families to enjoy a meal, rather than a spot for singles to drop in after work.[28]

PROBLEM SOURCES   The type of action taken in response to unacceptable performance depends on the source of the problem. The basic causes of unacceptable performance are problems with the plan, with the way it is being implemented, or with both.[29]

Problems with the plan arise when the plan was not well prepared, or—as with TGI Friday's—a change in the environment requires a change in the plan. Thus, a sales target may be unrealistic, or a new highway may make a store's location less desirable so that the store will have to move, work harder to draw in customers, or accept lower revenues. In such situations, the manager needs to review and modify the objectives in the plan.

Problems with how the plan is being implemented can arise in several areas. Perhaps not enough resources are being directed toward one area. Or the problem may lie with employees who don't understand what they are supposed to be doing or aren't putting forth enough effort. At Enrich International, the problem was poor communication between the product development and order-processing groups. The company would tell its distributors about new products, but not its order takers. When orders for the new products came pouring in, the order takers were annoyed and confused.[30]

In general, when performance suffers from problems with implementation, the response should be to identify and solve those problems. For Enrich International, this included creating a communications team with members from both departments who prepared a definite schedule of new-product rollouts. The team had the added benefit of becoming a forum for ideas on how order takers could promote other products when they handled calls.

When there are problems with both the plan and the implementation, the plan fails, and the manager must start the planning process from the beginning. This has arguably been the case with the merchandising group of Sears, Roebuck and Company in recent years. Management has attempted a variety of responses to declining sales and profits, including redefinition of Sears's target market (women with families, rather than men), returning more decision-making power to store managers, increasing the share of the business devoted to apparel, and abandoning the attempt to follow an "everyday low price" strategy.[31]

CONTROL AND THE QUALITY APPROACH   The need to start over from scratch should be rare, especially in organizations with a total quality philosophy. First, such an organization would focus on continuous improvement, not just wait to spot problems to correct.[32] For example, employees at a company that successfully practices TQM wouldn't ask, "Why aren't small companies buying our service?" Rather, they would ask a positive question such as "How can we better identify the needs of small companies?"

The need to start over from scratch in a business plan is rare; however, many organizations have recently developed plans for reengineering their processes. Reengineering involves rethinking and redesigning to organize around outcomes (such as customer satisfaction) rather than around functions (such as production and sales). In this ad, Ernst & Young recognizes the importance of implementing the reengineering plan and offers its consulting expertise.

Furthermore, the focus on continuous improvement should apply to strategic marketing planning, so that marketing plans increasingly meet the criteria of being challenging but achievable. With input from the employees, management would continually be fine-tuning the marketing plan and the process of implementing it. This means control is not something that happens only after implementation is complete. Instead, management seeks information to measure performance throughout the implementation process. (See "You Decide," which focuses on a company that jumped straight to the implementation phase without a plan, and think about what measurements you would use in the control process.)

FOCUS OF THE CONTROL PROCESS   Much of the marketing control effort focuses on financial performance—that is, the money spent and generated by the marketing department. If marketing costs bring about the desired results, they are effective. The basic measures of effectiveness are sales analysis and the measurement of profitability. The manager wants the marketing effort to be efficient as well as effective. To find out whether it is efficient, the manager can conduct cost analysis. But financial analysis is not the only way to evaluate marketing efforts. The manager should also make sure that customers are satisfied.

CUSTOMER SATISFACTION

Especially at an organization with a quality orientation, one of the most important performance measures will be customer satisfaction. The marketing manager needs to determine whether customers are pleased with the goods and services they receive.

MEASUREMENT   While customer satisfaction is not the easiest outcome to measure, the manager and all employees of the marketing department can continuously improve methods for receiving feedback from customers. For example, all employees

You Decide

HOW SMART IS SMARTFOOD'S KEN MEYERS?

This is the story of an entrepreneur who practiced the *opposite* of what we discuss in this chapter. Ken Meyers, one of the founders of the Smartfood popcorn company, used "guerrilla" tactics to push his products into the marketplace and into people's mouths.

"In the beginning, at least, we didn't have a grand plan," explains Meyers. "We were outsiders without a lot of money, and we were just trying to get some attention."

Meyers tried the traditional marketing campaign, using local advertising and a budget of $100,000. His money didn't buy him much. Advertising agencies laughed at the paltry sum. Distributors and retailers wouldn't pay attention to him. But Meyers knew he had a good-quality product and that if people had a chance to taste Smartfood, they'd like it.

So Meyers launched his guerrilla campaign. With the help of friends, he sewed several bedsheets together and painted the word "Smartfood" on them. Then he hired a small plane to fly the Smartfood flag up and down the New England coast. While the plane flew over beaches, Meyers and friends handed out free samples of Smartfood to sun worshippers.

Then Meyers headed to the slopes, where he hired some skiers to dress in giant popcorn bags and ski the slopes at several New England ski areas. Of course, he handed out free samples of Smartfood.

People began talking about Smartfood, and Meyers's unusual campaign got publicity (read: more visibility). As sales of Smartfood began to take off, Meyers eventually hired an advertising agency, but stuck to quirky, funny ads. The Mullen advertising agency came up with "bubblehead" ads, in which one of two characters in each ad was pictured with a thought bubble above his or her head containing—what else?—Smartfood.

Only a few years after the company got started, Frito-Lay bought the whole thing. Meyers stayed on for awhile, but Frito-Lay practiced a more traditional promotional approach. Meyers eventually decided to leave because he missed the fun of the original Smartfood efforts.

"I'm an entrepreneur and marketing person," he notes. "Frito-Lay was very good for me, but I spent a lot of time in management and integration-type things." Recently, Meyers has started his own consulting company.

Ken Meyers didn't have a formal marketing plan, yet his product became a huge success. He simply jumped to the implementation stage. Do you think his success was pure luck? Do you think he should have followed a plan? How might you incorporate some of Meyers's spontaneity—and zaniness—into the implementation of a formal marketing plan? If you were Meyers, what aspects of the guerrilla marketing campaign would you have examined as a controlling effort?

Source: "Kernels of Wisdom from Ken Meyers," *Sales & Marketing Management*, March 1991, p. 24.

may be trained to observe and report feedback from customers. Packaging for consumer goods may display a toll-free customer hotline. Publishers of computer software often include in their manuals a toll-free number for help. The organization may conduct various types of surveys as well, such as by giving customers cards to fill out with their comments or complaints about service. At American Express Travel Related Services Company, the quality assurance departments gather this information by listening to phone calls, reading correspondence from customers, and conducting surveys of customers' satisfaction with individual transactions.[33]

MARKETING RESPONSES   The marketing group can use customer feedback in two basic ways. First, the feedback can uncover needs for improvement. Thus, if many of the callers to a software company's toll-free number are asking the same few questions, the company might conclude that it needs to improve the way certain features are explained in its manual. This type of response improves the quality of the organization's future goods and services.

Customer feedback is also an opportunity for the organization to communicate with its customers. For example, customers are more likely to be understanding about a delay or a price increase if someone from the organization explains the reason for it.

TABLE 6.1		1993	1994	1995
Income Statements: Simplified Kurt's Klip Shop	Revenues	$66,200	$87,100	$81,000
	Expenses	60,900	81,000	74,500
	Profit	$ 5,300	$ 6,100	$ 6,500

In fact, if someone from the organization takes the initiative to keep the customer informed, the customer may actually be more satisfied with the organization than before, even if the news is bad. *Inc.* senior writer John Case forgave software publisher Intuit for putting him on hold, because the recorded message apologized and explained what the company was doing to correct the problem.[34] T. Scott Gross, author of *Positively Outrageous Service,* advocates the following approach:[35]

- When in doubt, apologize.
- Apologize even when the customer doesn't know you goofed. This really makes an impression.
- Make amends to the customer in excess of the slipup.
- Empower employees to solve problems.

Occasionally, communicating with customers results in an opportunity to provide exceptional service. At AT&T's Universal Card Services (UCS), customer service associate Ed Richardson received a call from a customer whose wife, who has Alzheimer's disease, had disappeared during a summer vacation. Since the man's wife was an authorized user of his AT&T Universal Card, this customer hoped that UCS could help. After finding no record that the card had been used recently, Richardson called the customer back and suggested he avoid using his card for a while. Richardson put a code on the account requiring that a merchant call for verification if the card were used, arranging for the call to come to him, day or night. A few days later, a merchant called to say a confused woman had presented the card. Richardson called the husband and the police, and the wife was taken to a hospital.[36]

SALES ANALYSIS

sales analysis
Gathering, classifying, comparing, and studying company sales data.

As mentioned earlier, financial performance is a basic way to evaluate the results generated by implementing a marketing plan. One method for evaluating financial performance is to conduct **sales analysis.** This type of analysis consists of "gathering, classifying, comparing and studying company sales data."[37] Thus, the owner of the fictional hair salon Kurt's Klip Shop can begin by looking at total revenues for the shop. The data in Table 6.1 show that sales increased from 1993 to 1994, then declined slightly in the following year. (We are using a fictional example to keep the numbers simple. The details of analyzing financial data for actual companies are beyond the scope of this book.)

The definition of sales analysis implies that it requires planning the kinds of information the marketing manager will need for the control process. This information will include records of what goods were sold or what services were delivered. The records should include any other information needed to classify the sales data, such as the price and the buyer's address. At most organizations, this information will be stored on a computer so that the marketing manager and other interested employees can retrieve and analyze it as needed.

After the organization has set up a system and begun gathering sales information, the marketer can classify, compare, and study it. Marketers classify past and present sales in a variety of ways:

- By product, package size, model, grade, or color
- By customer type or size
- By geographic region
- By price or type of discount
- By method of sale, such as direct sales or mail order
- By method of payment, such as cash or charge
- By size of order
- By commission to be paid to salesperson
- By reason for purchase.

By classifying sales according to customer type, catalog retailer Talbots learned that sales of its children's clothing were growing at around a 15 percent rate in a recent year, faster than its companywide sales increase of 9 percent.[38]

Classifying sales helps marketers identify problems to solve or opportunities to act on. Total sales at the Northshore men's clothing store in Rumson, New Jersey, were down, but rugby jerseys bearing the letters and colors of various colleges were popular. So the store's owner, Brian George, created a whole new product line, named Varsity Raggs. The products bearing this name include school blankets, towels, varsity jackets, sweaters, and caps, sold mostly through colleges. These products are responsible for most of the recent rise in sales and profits at George's company.[39]

MEASUREMENT OF SALES   There are several ways to measure sales for a sales analysis. Each provides only a partial picture of the organization's performance. The most common measures of sales are unit volume, dollar volume, and market share.

unit volume
The number of goods or units of service sold by an organization.

Unit Volume   To determine **unit volume**, the marketer finds the number of goods or units of service that the organization has sold. Following the launch of SnackWell's Devil's Food Cookie Cakes, the company reported consumers were buying more than one million cookie cakes a day.[40] Unit volume is useful for identifying the organization's most popular products and for measuring the demand for its products. When unit volume is increasing, the marketer knows that the organization is selling more goods and services than in the past.

However, unit volume cannot indicate whether the organization is making a profit or growing as fast as its competitors. If costs are too high or the price too low, the organization can sell a lot of products and still lose money. If competitors are growing faster than the organization, it may be losing market share even while it grows.

dollar volume
The dollar value of the total sales of a product.

Dollar Volume   Another way to measure total sales is to find their **dollar volume**, or their value in dollars. In a recent year at Armco, sales from the specialty flat-rolled steel SBU totaled $625 million, sales of the grinding systems SBU totaled $372 million, and sales of the fabricating and processing SBU totaled $400 million.[41] To find dollar volume, the marketer multiplies unit volume by the price for each unit of product.

Whereas unit volume tells only the number of products sold, the dollar volume takes into account the different prices of the organization's products. For example, the number of wills prepared at a family law practice might be much greater than the number of divorce cases negotiated. However, the dollar volume of handling a divorce is usually higher because it requires more time than preparing a standard will. The marketer needs to know dollar volume to evaluate the organization's profitability, as described in the next section.

FIGURE 6.8

Market Share for Makers of Cellular Phone Hardware

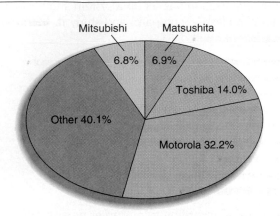

Source: G. Christian Hill and Ken Yamada, "Motorola Illustrates How an Aged Giant Can Remain Vibrant," *The Wall Street Journal,* December 9, 1992, p. A14. Reprinted by permission of *The Wall Street Journal,* © 1992 Dow Jones & Company, Inc. All rights reserved worldwide.

Market Share   Finally, the marketer measures sales volume in terms of market share. To compute market share, divide total sales of the product by the industry's total sales for the product type to come up with a percentage. Figure 6.8 shows the market share for various makers of cellular telephone hardware.

 The marketer can look at changes in market share over time or compare market shares to find the organization's rank in the marketplace. For example, Charles Finkel's beer-importing company, Merchant du Vin, is the number-one importer of specialty beers in the United States, but Pike Place Brewery, which Finkel recently opened in Seattle, is only the 79th largest brewery.[42]

Market share shows the marketer how well the organization is performing compared with competitors. Thus, if sales are rising more slowly than they were in past years but market share is steady or rising, the marketer can conclude the growth in the market has slowed. The marketer can adjust the strategy to make it suitable for a slow-growth market or seek ways to stimulate growth for the category of product, not just the organization's brand.

CONTROLLING WITH SALES DATA   To use sales data in the control function, the marketing manager disaggregates it (breaks it down) to see whether the organization is meeting its sales objectives. If the organization has a sales force with individual quotas to fulfill, the manager will want the data broken down by salesperson. If the marketing department has set targets for specific products or geographic regions, the manager will need sales figures broken down by product or region. In Figure 6.9, sales for Kurt's Klip Shop are broken down by customer type.

The marketing manager compares the disaggregated data with the sales objectives to identify needs for correction and praise. In the case of data broken down by salesperson, most likely some members of the sales force will need rewards for high performance and others will need to improve. Disaggregating sales by product might show that the reason an organization has exceeded its total sales target is that one product performed much better than expected. In the case of SnackWell's Devil's Food Cookie Cakes, the maker has to consider alternatives such as investing in more factories to make the cookie cakes faster or communicating with consumers to persuade them to try other kinds of SnackWell's cookies.

FIGURE 6.9

Dollar Volume by Customer Type: Kurt's Klip Shop

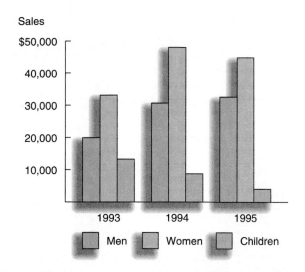

Sales

MEASUREMENT OF PROFITABILITY

The basic measure of a business's success is its profitability—how much it earns after expenses. Thus, for controlling in a business, an important type of information is the profits generated by particular products or by sales to particular customer groups. For example, a marketing manager at General Mills might compare the profitability of its new cereal brands with the profitability of Cheerios, or a manager at Humana might compare the profitability of hospitals located in different regions of the United States.

profit margin
The result of profits divided by revenues.

A basic measure of profitability is the **profit margin**, or profits (that is, revenues minus expenses) divided by revenues. The profit margin is expressed as a percentage. For example, to find the profit margin for Kurt's Klip Shop in 1993, refer to the numbers in Table 6.1. Divide the 1993 profit of $5,300 by revenues of $66,200; the answer is .08, or a profit margin of 8 percent. The profit margins for the following two years are 7 percent and 8 percent, respectively. The numbers suggest that to achieve the jump in sales between 1993 and 1994, the hair salon incurred some extra expenses—perhaps for additional promotions and advertising—which caused the profit margin to shrink a bit.

In general, profit margins that are growing or are greater than competitor's are a sign of financial health. Starbucks Coffee originally sold only coffee beans. Adding brewed coffee boosted profit margins by 5 percent, confirming that this was a profitable direction in which to expand.[43]

As in the case of analyzing sales, the marketing manager will need to see profit margins broken down in various ways, such as by product or by market. The manager can disaggregate the data in the ways listed for sales analysis. The manager might use this information to decide which products or target markets should receive the most resources. Or the manager might use the information about profits to adjust the marketing mix—say, to reconsider the price of an unprofitable product or make sure the most profitable items are widely available.

MARKETING COST ANALYSIS

To interpret profitability, it helps to understand how much the organization is spending and for what. For example, if a particular market segment is generating relatively

TABLE 6.2		1993	1994	1995
Marketing Costs by Functional Account: Kurt's Klip Shop	Advertising			
	Newspaper	$3,000	$4,600	$3,400
	Yellow Pages	1,200	1,400	1,500
	Promotions			
	Discounts to men (10% off on Thursdays)	500	700	800
	Balloons for kids	100	—	—
	Owner's time spent on marketing activities	1,200	1,500	1,600
	Research			
	(in-store cards asking for customer comments)	100	100	100
	Total marketing costs	$6,100	$8,300	$7,400

cost analysis
A study of the size and type of costs involved in a marketing effort, as well as any change in costs.

natural accounts
Traditional categories for financial accounting.

functional accounts
The allocation of costs to correspond to specific marketing activities.

low profits, the marketing manager may seek to identify areas where the marketing group can boost profits by cutting costs incurred to serve that market segment. To do so, the marketing manager conducts **cost analysis**. This involves identifying the size and type of costs incurred to carry out the marketing effort, as well as how these costs have changed over time.

ALLOCATION OF COSTS   Accounting systems are set up to measure various costs, such as those for supplies, inventory, rent, and salaries. These usual categories for financial accounting are known as **natural accounts**. Marketing cost analysis calls for reallocating the costs in natural accounts so that they correspond to specific marketing activities, such as order entry, transportation, selling, and advertising. The resulting accounts are called **functional accounts**. Table 6.2 shows functional accounts for marketing at Kurt's Klip Shop. The marketing manager needs to ensure that the organization's accounting system is set up so that it is possible to create the functional accounts. Allocating the costs may require studying how employees use their time, measuring space, counting units of product, and making estimates.

Each of the functional accounts is further allocated among product types or market segments. In general, the manager needs to categorize costs according to the objectives laid out in the marketing plan. Thus, if the organization seeks to achieve a given level of profits for each product, the manager will want to study costs for marketing each product. If the organization seeks to lower distribution costs for certain regions, the accounting system will have to be capable of providing cost information by region. In the case of Kurt's Klip Shop, the owner decided to build the share of business coming from men and not to focus on cutting children's hair. Therefore, the share of the budget for promotions directed at men has been increasing while the share directed to children has been eliminated.

ACTIVITY-BASED COSTING   An increasing number of U.S. organizations—including Motorola, Harley-Davidson, Dell Computer, Coca-Cola Company, and the Internal Revenue Service—are adopting a fresh approach to understanding costs. Called *activity-based costing*, this accounting system itemizes all costs associated with producing and marketing a particular product for a particular market. Activity-based costing can help managers see which products are profitable and can suggest areas where reducing costs can have the most impact. Northwestern University Professor

Results of a marketing audit at The Bombay Company would likely be outstanding, identifying the product as home furnishings with fashion and value that promotes impulse buying. Robert E. M. Nourse opened his first store in April 1980 in Toronto. In 1992, net sales were 176 million with pretax income at $15.7 million—8.9 percent of sales. Robert Nourse was chosen Inc. *magazine's 1993 Entrepreneur of the Year.*

Bela Belachandran gives the example of a company that makes toothpaste and sells it to Wal-Mart and Kmart for $2.50 a tube. Suppose that Wal-Mart wants certain things done in terms of packaging and shipping that bring the manufacturer's total cost to $2.20, compared to only $1.60 for selling to Kmart.[44] The marketing manager can see how much more profitable it is to sell to Kmart and will be able to see if the costs ever exceed the selling price for that product.

While many observers of U.S. business view activity-based costing as the hottest new idea since total quality management, most Japanese corporations have been using a form of it for decades. All employees are made aware of their contribution to product costs, so they can be sensitive to ways of keeping those costs down. This approach fits well with the Japanese use of teamwork. As described in the previous chapter, cross-functional teams work together to develop new products so that they can be made and sold for a "target cost." In contrast, the typical American approach has been to design a product, then see how much it will cost, proceeding with it only if the costs are acceptable. The increasing use of cross-functional teams in the United States may spur a move to this new way of looking at costs.

THE MARKETING AUDIT

To get a broader perspective on the success of the organization's marketing activities, the marketing manager will want to occasionally evaluate the organization's total marketing effort. To do this, the manager requests a **marketing audit**. This is an in-depth, systematic review of an organization's or strategic business unit's marketing environment, objectives, strategies, activities, and personnel. It is the most thorough approach to evaluating the marketing effort.

marketing audit
A systematic review of an organization's marketing environment, objectives, strategies, activities, and personnel.

For more objective results, the audit may be conducted by an outside consultant. If that is too expensive, the marketing manager may assemble a team of auditors from within the organization.

CONTENT   To begin a marketing audit, the auditors plan what kinds of information to gather and how. Table 6.3 lists basic questions that can be asked in the course of a marketing audit. The questions should cover how well the marketing group is carrying out its activities and whether those activities are the right ones to be doing. In addi-

TABLE 6.3

Questions to Include in a Marketing Audit

Products: The Reason for Existence

1. Is the product free from deadwood?
2. What is the life-cycle stage?
3. How will user demands or trends affect you?
4. Are you a leader in new product innovation?
5. Are inexpensive methods used to estimate new product potentials before considerable amounts are spent on R&D and market introduction?
6. Do you have different quality levels for different markets?
7. Are packages/brochures effective salespeople for the products they present?
8. Do you present products in the most appealing colors (formats) for markets being served?
9. Are there features or benefits to exploit?
10. Is the level of customer service adequate?
11. How are quality and reliability viewed by customers?

Customer: User Profiles

1. Who is the current and potential customer?
2. Are there geographic aspects of use: regional, rural, urban?
3. Why do people buy the product; what motivates their preferences?
4. Who makes buying decisions; when, where?
5. What is the frequency and quantity of use?
6. Are intermediaries making money from the line?

7. Can the product support marketing communications programs?
8. Will the manufacturing process require more volume?

Distribution Channels: Selling Paths

1. Does the system offer the best access to all target markets?
2. Do product characteristics require specials?
3. What is the most profitable type of presentation for each market: direct vs. reps, master distributors or dealers, etc.?
4. What are the trends in distribution methods?

Sales Administration: Selling Efficiency

1. Are customers getting coverage in proportion to their potential?
2. Are sales costs planned and controlled?
3. Does the compensation plan provide optimum incentive and security for reasonable cost?
4. Is performance measured against potential?
5. Are selling expenses proportionate to results and potentials within markets or territories?
6. Are there deficiencies in recruitment, selection, training, motivation, supervision, performance, promotion, or compensation?
7. Are effective selling aids and sales tools provided?

Source: Adapted from Hal W. Goetsch, "Conduct a Comprehensive Marketing Audit to Improve Marketing Planning," *Marketing News,* March 18, 1983, p.14. Reprinted with permission of the American Marketing Association.

tion, the marketing audit should look at policies related to marketing and how the marketing group is organized.

The focus of the audit may be horizontal or vertical. In a horizontal marketing audit, the auditors look at all the elements of the marketing mix and how they are related. In a vertical marketing audit, the auditors analyze only one part of the marketing mix, such as the total personal selling effort.

When the auditors have decided what to study and gathered the information, they discuss the marketing effort with managers, employees, distributors, and customers. The auditors describe what the marketing group is doing and where it can make improvements.

APPLICATIONS   A complete marketing audit is difficult and time consuming. Therefore, it is not a suitable part of the ongoing control process. Rather, the marketing manager uses it periodically—say, every three to five years—to supplement routine control activities such as sales and cost analysis. If the auditors are impartial and complete, the marketing manager may find that the audit uncovers some points that are surprising and useful in tailoring the marketing plan more closely to the achievement of organizational objectives.

Markets: Where Products are Sold

1. Have you identified and measured major segments?
2. Are small, potential market segments overlooked in trying to satisfy the majority?
3. Are the markets for the products expanding or declining?
4. Should different segments be developed; are there gaps in penetration?

Competitors: Their Influence

1. Who are the principal competitors, how are they positioned, and where are they headed?
2. What are their market shares?
3. What features of competitors' products stand out?
4. Is the market easily entered or dominated?

Pricing: Profitability Planning

1. What are the objectives of current pricing policy: acquiring, defending, or expanding?
2. Are price policies set to produce volume or profit?
3. How does pricing compare with competition in similar levels of quality?
4. Does cost information show profitability of each item?
5. What is the history of price deals, discounts, and promotions?

Advertising: Media Program

1. Are media objectives and strategies linked to the marketing plan?
2. What are the objectives of the advertising program?
3. How is media effectiveness measured?
4. Is advertising integrated with promotion and sales activity?
5. Is the ad agency's effectiveness periodically evaluated?
6. Do you dictate copy theme and content to the agency?
7. Are you spending realistically, in relation to budget?

Sales Promotion: Sales Inducement

1. Does the sales promotion support a marketing objective?
2. Is it integrated with advertising and selling activities?
3. How is it measured for results?
4. Are slogans, trademarks, logos, and brands being used effectively?
5. Is point-of-sale material cost effective?
6. Are you effectively using couponing, tie-ins, incentives, sampling, stuffers, combination effects?
7. How do you evaluate trade shows for effectiveness?

Summary

A marketing group and the company to which it belongs may be a centralized or decentralized organization. The marketing group itself may be organized by function, product, geography, or cross-functional teams.

Once a marketing plan has been established, the marketing manager must implement it by coordinating the necessary activities, communicating with employees and customers, and motivating employees. Coordination involves setting priorities, scheduling activities, building cooperation, and coordinating teamwork. Communication necessitates good speaking, writing, and listening skills, as well as effective nonverbal cues. Marketers may have to overcome barriers to communication such as information overload, misunder-

standings, and prejudice. Marketing managers motivate employees by offering incentives that encourage them to act in a desired manner. In addition, good marketing managers treat employees fairly and also abide by their own rules and standards of conduct.

The process of measuring and correcting the performance of a marketing plan is called controlling. In the control process, the marketing manager obtains and measures results, compares those results with set standards, and corrects problems or reinforces the performance. Measures of success include customer satisfaction, sales, and profitability. A more complex and far-reaching way to measure performance is to conduct a marketing audit.

KEY TERMS AND CONCEPTS

organize (p. 162)
centralized organization (p. 162)
decentralized organization (p. 162)
product-based organization (p. 164)

product managers (p. 164)
Gantt chart (p. 167)
critical path method (CPM) (p. 168)
motivation (p. 174)

group incentive system (p. 175)
controlling (p. 176)
sales analysis (p. 180)
unit volume (p. 181)

dollar volume (p. 181)
profit margin (p. 183)

cost analysis (p. 184)
natural accounts (p. 184)

functional accounts (p. 184)
marketing audit (p. 185)

REVIEW AND DISCUSSION QUESTIONS

1. Describe the four basic methods for organizing a marketing team.
2. If you were hired as a marketing manager by a mid-sized recording company that produced country music, folk, and pop vocals, as well as sheet music for some of its recordings, which method of marketing organization would you prefer? Why?
3. As you coordinate the marketing plan for one of your new artists at the recording company, how would you go about setting priorities, scheduling activities, and building cooperation? Would you use the Gantt chart, critical path method, and/or computer software in your scheduling?
4. Why are good speaking skills, listening skills, and writing skills especially important to marketers?
5. A toy company makes inflatable balls with handles. Children use the toys by sitting on the ball, holding the handle, and jumping. The instruction sheet that comes with this product contains the following warning:

   Warning: Do not over inflate. Service station line pressure varies. Over inflation and rapid deflation (explosion) can result. Do not exceed maximum shown above [in a table of acceptable pressures].

   a. What does this message mean in plain English?
   b. Is the wording of such information a proper area of concern for marketing? Explain.

6. What are some of the ways a marketing manager can successfully motivate employees?
7. Suppose you were assigned to manage a product development effort in a country whose culture valued group harmony over individual achievement. In this culture, being singled out for public praise is considered an embarrassment. How would you motivate this group of employees? In particular, how could you reward good performance?
8. As a marketing manager, if you discovered that the performance of a particular marketing effort fell significantly below the objectives of the marketing plan, what three potential causes would you investigate?
9. In what ways can marketers measure customer satisfaction?
10. Name and define the three most common sales measures.
11. Refer to the marketing objectives mentioned for Kurt's Klip Shop on page 184. Based on the disaggregated sales data shown in Figure 6.9, what is your opinion of this business's performance? Do you think Kurt's Klip Shop is meeting its objectives? What other measures of performance would be important?
12. As a marketing manager, how would you use marketing cost analysis to interpret the profitability of a product for which you are responsible?

Chapter Project
Implementing and Controlling a Plan

Start with your answers to Review and Discussion Questions 2 and 3. You are the marketing manager for a mid-sized recording company that produces country music, folk, and pop vocals, and some sheet music. You've chosen the method of marketing organization you prefer and begun implementation of your marketing plan by setting priorities, scheduling activities, and building cooperation. Now you need to follow through the rest of the implementation and control for your plan. You want to make your company (and your artists) the hottest in the music business.

- State how you would use coordination, communication, and motivation.
- Decide how you will control your marketing effort by measuring customer satisfaction, using sales analysis, measuring profitability, and using marketing cost analysis. (You won't have actual numbers, but you can create your own scenario.)

You'll need to use your imagination for this project, creating various specific scenarios. You can do this project alone or in teams, whichever you and your instructor prefer. *Alternative:* Go back to the marketing plan you developed as a Chapter Project for Chapter 5, and use it for this project.

Case
Illinois Bell/Ameritech

With a budget of only $75,000, Sara Foley swung her marketing plan into action. In 1991, when Foley was division manager for employee communications at Illinois Bell (now part of Ameritech), she created a program called "Winning the Business: Be a Product Pro," or "Product Pro" for short. The program included all of the company's 21,000 employees. Her objective was to convince employees that they each played an important part in generating sales for Illinois Bell—and get them to act on that belief.

Foley began implementing her plan by communicating with employees, building cooperation among them, and motivating them. Referring to each employee as a "sales ambassador," she launched the program with two-hour product presentations given by 150 volunteer presenters right at employees' work sites. Explained Foley, "We knew from previous research that employees prefer to receive information in an interactive setting at their work site." Thus, she demonstrated to employees that she had listened to them.

After the initial presentations were completed, Foley coordinated further communication about Illinois Bell goods and services that employees could be offering customers. This communication took several forms: monthly follow-up videos, messages sent via electronic mail, news bulletins, and articles in the company newspaper.

In addition, Foley's program taught employees more about the telephone business. For instance, many employees were unaware that the company's number one source of income was telephone usage charges. They might have thought that a fax or answering machine manufactured by a competitor such as Panasonic represented business lost by Illinois Bell. Wrong. Both machines generate usage of Bell's telephone lines, so employees were encouraged to find ways for customers to increase this usage. Such communication with customers also made possible another benefit: Bell employees could get feedback about their products.

Another facet of the Product Pro program, called "Adopt-A-Garage," involved linking garage customer service technicians with marketers from Illinois Bell and its then–parent company, Ameritech. For example, Judy Kearney, director of marketing communications at Illinois Bell, rode with service technicians as they made calls. She also improved relations by returning technicians' phone calls quickly and answering their questions immediately. When Illinois Bell introduced its new Caller ID product, she took the equipment to her "adopted" garage and demonstrated it herself.

By various measures, the program was a success. Product Pro provided a 50 percent increase in the number of employee-initiated sales leads. It generated $63 million in additional business for Illinois Bell.

Perhaps one reason for Product Pro's success is that Foley devised a way to make corrections in the program midway through its implementation. She held three employee contests designed to test their knowledge of the products they were selling. If a majority seemed to lack knowledge in a certain area, she could fill the gap with an article in the company newspaper or via eletronic mail.

QUESTIONS

1. Why was Foley's inclusion of all employees in the Product Pro marketing plan important?
2. How did Foley assess the program's success in teaching employees while the program was still under way? What other control methods might have been useful?
3. If you were a marketer working with Sara Foley at Illinois Bell, what new marketing programs might you suggest for the company, building on the success of Product Pro?

Source: "Illinois Bell's Sara Foley Dials for Dollars," *Sales & Marketing Management,* November 1992, pp. 28–29.

3

Customers and Markets

Setting the Stage

Gateway 2000

Imagine being able to call a company, make a suggestion or request for improvement in its products, and see the results. As a Gateway 2000 customer, you can do that. The company, which sells personal computers, is based entirely on its customers' needs. And it finds out about many of those needs through marketing research.

The seven-member marketing research staff at Gateway 2000 conducts surveys constantly, asking about 3,200 randomly selected customers a month to answer questions. People respond. According to Mike McClendon, marketing research supervisor, "Due to the vested interest Gateway 2000 customers have in the company, our survey results are unusually accurate. The average turndown rate for surveys in general is about 90 percent—ours is only 2 percent. The people we call want to talk to us, and they give us straight answers."

McClendon explains that Gateway 2000 has three main reasons for conducting these surveys: (1) "to gather information necessary to track Gateway's performance through our customers' eyes in areas such as sales, customer service, technical support

and shipping"; (2) to find out "what customers are looking for in hardware and software and how much they would like to pay for new products"; and (3) to gauge customer satisfaction with existing products and features. According to Dave Berger, director of marketing programs, when Gateway 2000's marketers "combine information on how satisfied customers are with existing products and then look at their needs for the future, we can make better decisions about introductions."

Gateway 2000 is the brainchild of 31-year-old Ted Waitt, who got the idea in 1984 while working as a sales clerk in a computer store. "I became fascinated with the idea that if you knew what you were talking about, you could sell somebody a $3,000 product over the phone in a 20-minute conversation." Gateway 2000 was launched with a $10,000 bank loan and run from an old South Dakota farmhouse, owned by Waitt's father. Today the company is among the leading direct sellers of personal computers; earnings recently hovered around $100 million on sales of nearly $1.7 billion.

Gateway 2000 can put its marketing research to work on a customer-by-

customer basis because it practices "bundling," in which customers can pick a complete system from Gateway's catalog (Most computer sellers now do this, but Gateway was one of the first.) In addition, the company stocks computer components rather than finished computers, so that customers can custom order exactly what they want. When an order comes in, technicians quickly assemble the finished machine, tailored to the customer's needs.

Gateway 2000 plans to take its marketing research even further. For instance, the marketing research group intends to conduct demographic surveys to obtain information about the life-styles of customers. Mike McClendon says, "The Market Research Council has a principle called YOC, which stands for 'Your Opinion Counts.' And it's true . . . . Gateway customers are driving what we offer and how much they pay for it."

Source: Brian Dumaine, "America's Smart Young Entrepreneurs," *Fortune,* March 21, 1994, p. 36; annual report from Gateway 2000, 1993.

CHAPTER 7   *Marketing Research*

Information and Technology

LEARNING OBJECTIVES

After completing this chapter, you should be able to:

1. Identify the basic types of information useful in marketing research and some places to find such information.

2. Discuss why and how marketing researchers need to begin research by formulating the problem.

3. Describe basic types of research design and approaches to collecting data.

4. Explain how marketing researchers go about analyzing and interpreting data.

5. Describe principles for preparing a marketing research report.

6. Explain how modern technology has affected the process and use of marketing research.

7. Discuss ethical considerations of marketing research.

8. Identify issues that arise in international marketing research.

Creating Customer Value
Whirlpool

In 1989, government regulation changed the temperature of the refrigeration industry: beginning with 1993 models, all refrigeration products had to conform to new standards that phased out the use of chlorofluorocarbons (CFCs) in the cooling process. When Whirlpool got the word, the company knew it had three years to design and produce a completely new line of refrigerators. Then things got even more exciting. The Natural Resources Defense Council and a group of 24 electric utilities decided to spur greater improvements by awarding a $30 million prize to the company that could not only eliminate CFCs but boost energy efficiency by at least 25 percent. To meet the challenge, Whirlpool used three of its most important weapons: customer research, cross-functional teams, and a commitment to quality.

"Quality is an integral part of our strategy," explains Jerry Weinstein, vice president of refrigeration manufacturing and technology at Whirlpool in Evansville, Indiana. "It's part of what we call our platform—one of the bases on which all our marketplace strategies are built. It permeates all our planning. . . . Quality, for us, is meeting and exceeding all our customers' expectations."

Part of exceeding customers' expectations involves marketing research, or learning about customers. Even before the 1989 edict, Whirlpool had in place a variety of methods for doing this. The company conducts an ongoing survey which it calls Standardized Appliance Measurement Satisfaction (SAMS). This survey of 180,000 households provides an idea of how satisfied consumers are with Whirlpool products and those of competitors. If consumers rate a competitor's product higher than Whirlpool's, engineers at Whirlpool tear apart the competing product to find out why.

Whirlpool also hosts focus groups across the United States and abroad. At these wide-ranging discussions, small groups of consumers discuss face to face with Whirlpool's marketers their level of satisfaction and their ideas for new features and products.

In addition, Whirlpool operates a Usability Lab in Benton Harbor, Michigan. There, customers use computer simulations to try out existing and future Whirlpool product designs. Whirlpool uses this research to make certain that its products are accessible to everyone who wants to use them, including those in wheelchairs.

But consumers don't always make their desires perfectly clear, and marketers must listen carefully. In the words of marketing vice president John Hamann, "The consumer speaks in code." One survey showed that people wanted "clean refrigerators." What did this mean? After asking more questions and interpreting the data, marketers concluded that people wanted refrigerators to have a clean appearance. So Whirlpool's newer models have stucco-like doors and sides that hide fingerprints.

To bring its research talents to bear on the challenge of product development, Whirlpool uses cross-functional teams. Explains J. C. Anderson, divisional vice president of refrigeration manufacturing in Evansville, "We have more component parts, more assemblies, more manufacturing processes that we need to control than probably any other product line. And this necessitates real teamwork—a tremendous level of cooperation between engineering, marketing, and manufacturing." In fact, Whirlpool's team organization may be more formal (and permanent) than at other companies, due to unionization. At the Evansville plant, a formal labor-management council with a steering committee made up of twelve representatives (six from labor and six from management) meets each month to address a variety of operational situations. Whirlpool uses employee empowerment and a gain-sharing program, meaning that employees are involved in all activities at the plant, and everyone shares the gains. For the refrigerator project, the development team called itself the Golden Carrot Project Team.

It's an approach that gets results. Whirlpool recently captured the $30 million prize for developing the most energy-efficient, environmentally sound refrigerator. From an environmental standpoint, the 25 percent reduction in energy use is significant, since refrigerators are responsible for about 20 percent of the energy use in most U.S. homes. The new model also offers an important benefit to consumers: $20 to $40 savings in electric bills each year.

As you read this chapter on marketing research, note how communication with customers includes receiving messages from them in the form of research data. Think about how the marketing concept and the quality approach, by their very nature, mean listening carefully to what customers say, and interpreting correctly what they need and want.

Sources: Robin P. Bergstrom, "Where Nothing Constant Remains Unchanged," *Production,* February 1993; David Leonhardt, "Whirlpool Wins Fridge Contest," *Boston Globe,* June 20, 1993; Sally Solo, "How to Listen to Consumers," *Fortune,* January 11, 1993, p. 77; and James B. Treece, "The Great Refrigerator Race," *Business Week,* July 5, 1993, pp. 78–81.

↙ *Chapter Overview*

marketing research
The function that links the consumer, customer, and public to the marketer through information.

The story about Whirlpool described how the company uses marketing research to improve existing products and develop new ones. The American Marketing Association defines **marketing research** as "the function that links the consumer, customer, and public to the marketer through information—information used to identify and define marketing opportunities and problems; generate, refine, and evaluate marketing actions; monitor marketing performance; and improve understanding of marketing as a process."[1] In other words, for marketers to anticipate or respond to customer needs, they need to know about their current and prospective customers and about the success of their own practices. They get much of this knowledge through marketing research.

Researching markets and topics of interest to marketers may be the responsibility of one member of the organization or of a marketing research department. When an organization focuses on its distinctive competencies, it may find that the best way to handle research activities is to hire an outside firm that specializes in marketing research. (As described in "Looking Ahead" at the end of this book, the marketing organization can form a "strategic alliance" with the research firm.) Either way, an organization with a quality focus will expect that researchers will continuously seek to improve the way they do their work so that the users of the research are satisfied with the results. Satisfaction with marketing research depends on its usefulness for improving marketing decisions.

This chapter provides an overview of what marketers can expect in working with marketing researchers and marketing research. It describes the kinds of information marketing researchers provide and the places they find it. The chapter then describes the steps in the process of marketing research. Next the chapter explores the impact of technology on marketing research and examines some ethical issues that may arise when an organization conducts marketing research. The chapter closes with an introduction to issues that arise in international marketing research.

Using 12 weeks of marketing research data gathered by Nielsen Marketing Research's Scanatrak, Gold Bond-Good Humor Ice Cream advertises that it is the market leader in frozen novelties.

Information for Effective Marketing

Who buys our product? What price should we charge? Is our advertising getting results? Are customers happy with the services we provide? These are just a few of the questions marketers face as they plan, implement, and control the marketing process. To find the right answers, marketers need to know about the environment, customers, and the organization itself.

INFORMATION VERSUS DATA

data
Facts and statistics.

information
Data presented in a useful way.

Marketers need information, not just data. **Data** are simply facts and statistics. Examples include the number of people living in Dallas, the average price of a new luxury car, or the number of calls received each day last week by the reference department of the public library.

In contrast, **information** refers to data presented in a way that is useful for making a decision. Generally, this means that the data are presented to show the presence or absence of some trend, relationship, or pattern. A store's computer might produce data about how much of which items sold each day, week, and month. A researcher could evaluate these data to look for such relationships as the kinds of customers who make the biggest purchases. Or the researcher could plot the sales of certain product categories on a month-by-month basis. In these cases, the researcher is converting the data into information.

Such information, in turn, is useful for decision making. Thus, knowing which customers buy the most would be useful in identifying a target market for the store or in planning advertising or store hours that would be attractive to the biggest customers. And knowing sales trends could help with such decisions as which products to stock or how often to order more.

Before computers made it easy to record, sort, and analyze data, marketers generally had difficulty getting enough information to make decisions. Today, however, the typical marketer is overwhelmed with facts, reports, and analyses. The necessary information is available, but it can be hard to find. Marketers have five complaints about the information that crosses their desks:[2]

1. There is too much marketing information of the wrong kind and not enough of the right kind.
2. Marketing information is so dispersed throughout the company that great effort may be needed to locate simple facts.
3. Vital information is sometimes suppressed by other executives or subordinates for personal reasons.
4. Vital information often arrives too late to be useful.
5. It is often difficult to know whether information is accurate, and there is no one to turn to for confirmation.

The best defense against these problems is a thoughtful and thorough approach to conducting marketing research and to setting up and using a system for gathering marketing information. Such an approach begins with identifying the kinds of information needed and its sources.

TYPES OF INFORMATION NEEDED

Marketers need information about their environment, especially target markets, customers, and competitors. They want to know how target markets are responding to the current marketing mix and how they would react to changes in the marketing mix. They want to know how well competitors are doing and what competitors plan to do next. Therefore, they turn to marketing research to provide information about all areas of marketing, especially their own and their competitors' market share, the market potential of current and potential products, and characteristics of the consumers and organizations in their markets. Table 7.1 lists basic questions marketers ask to help plan, solve problems, and control marketing activities.

INFORMATION FOR THE QUALITY APPROACH   In quality-driven organizations, information about customers is especially important. If the organization is to provide goods or services that customers perceive to be of high quality, it needs to know what customers want and whether they think they are getting what they want from the organization's products. Thus, information from satisfied and dissatisfied customers, as well as defectors to competing products, can help marketers ensure that products have the right quality and features.[3] (To learn how a company used information about customers to enhance their satisfaction with a good *and* a service, see the "Marketing Movers & Shakers" story about Doug Burgum of Great Plains Software.)

Marketers especially need information about new and unfamiliar groups of customers. To help its members tap the giant Chinese market, the Chocolate Manufacturers Association hired Gallup China Ltd. to obtain such basic information as whether the Chinese like and eat chocolate.[4]

marketing database
A system for organizing marketing data so that they are easy to store and retrieve.

MARKETING DATABASES   To make sense out of the information they receive, marketers need it organized into a **marketing database**, that is, a system for organizing marketing data so that they are easy to store and retrieve. It is possible to create a database with index cards or file folders. Today, however, most databases are computerized, because most organizations can afford a powerful enough computer to

TABLE 7.1

Questions Marketing Research Can Help Answer

I. Planning
    A. What kinds of people buy our products? Where do they live? How much do they earn? How many of them are there?
    B. Are the markets for our products increasing or decreasing? Are there promising new markets that we have not yet reached?
    C. Are the channels of distribution for our products changing? Are new types of marketing institutions likely to evolve?

II. Problem Solving
    A. Product
       1. Which of various product designs is likely to be the most successful?
       2. What kind of packaging should we use?
    B. Price
       1. What price should we charge for our products?
       2. As production costs decline, should we lower our prices or try to develop higher-quality products?
    C. Channels of Distribution
       1. Where, and by whom, should our products be sold?
       2. What kind of incentives should we offer the trade to push our products?
    D. Communications
       1. How much should we spend on marketing communications? How should it be allocated to products and to geographic areas?
       2. What combination of media—newspapers, radio, television, magazines—should we use?

III. Control
    A. What is our market share overall? In each geographic area? By each customer type?
    B. Are customers satisfied with our products? How is our record for service? Are there many returns?
    C. How does the public perceive our company? What is our reputation with the trade?

Source: Table from p. 9 of *Basic Marketing Research,* Second Edition by Gilbert A. Churchill, Jr., copyright © 1992 by The Dryden Press, reproduced by permission of the publisher.

perform that capability. Later, this chapter discusses in greater detail the use of computers in marketing research.

SOURCES OF INFORMATION

Marketing researchers can get information from inside or outside the organization. Furthermore, they can generate information designed to answer a particular question, or they can read the results of previous data-gathering efforts. In either case, a wide variety of tactics are available.

INTERNAL SOURCES OF INFORMATION   The marketer can find a wealth of data within the organization itself. For example, sales records can tell which products are selling best and who is buying them. Accounting data can indicate which products are the most profitable. Inventory data can indicate how fast goods are moving off the shelves. By creating special discount programs for frequent shoppers, a seller can gather basic data about what kind of customers it has and where they are located.

When marketers determine that they need internally generated information, they should ensure that the organization's record-keeping systems provide it. Waste Management of Illinois West is testing trucks with on-board computers that record

Marketing Movers & Shakers

DOUG BURGUM, GREAT PLAINS SOFTWARE

Doug Burgum, owner of Great Plains software in Fargo, North Dakota, doesn't simply ask his customers to "stay in touch." He requires them to. He's not jealous, just possessive. He wants his customers to be up to date on improvements to Great Plains accounting software. He wants to know how *they* think he can improve his product. He wants them to be satisfied. And he doesn't want them to think about defecting to another company's software.

Because early software often contained bugs, Burgum needed a way to notify customers of corrections. So beginning in the early 1980s, Great Plains wrote into each module a code that blocked further work after 50 transactions. To unlock it, customers had to register with Great Plains for certain numerical "keys." When cus-

tomers phoned in for keys, Great Plains asked them 20 or so questions on such topics as their location and company size, using the answers to compile buyer profiles.

Great Plains still uses this system, and customers are happy with it. They get regular updates on their software and get a chance to offer their insights and opinions about the company's software and service. Great Plains saves every customer idea in a suggestion database, and the product-marketing team reviews them all at least several times a year. Often, ideas from customers end up as new features in Great Plains software.

When a new customer comes to Great Plains, marketing research manager Catherine Bickle includes the new firm in her annual new-customer survey. During the survey, customers who have owned Great Plains products for between six and twelve months participate in 20-minute phone interviews, answering questions from a 14-page questionnaire. According to Bickle, this helps Great Plains forecast what customers' needs will be in the next five years.

Lori Laub, head of the technical-support staff, devised a unique call-distribution system for technical support built on the customer database. When a customer calls Great Plains and punches in an account number, the system instantly knows who the customer is, which software

modules the customer owns, and which support plan he or she uses. So when a technical specialist answers the phone call, he or she is already looking at a computer screen with information on previous problems or questions the customer has had, and there's no need to recap prior contacts.

Back to Doug Burgum. How did he build a philosophy for such an intensely customer-driven staff and company? It started with his boyhood on the Great Plains. His family owned and ran a grain elevator business. "When you've got a grain elevator, the people you serve are landowners, and they move the ownership of that land from father to son," he says. "My cousins are serving the grandsons of the people my grandfather served. That was the only business example I grew up with. You served customers for a lifetime. There was no such thing as a quick buck. . . . When we bought Great Plains I was 27, and I figured we had a great opportunity to build something where we'd instill in people that long-term mentality."

Burgum takes the long view, much like that across the Great Plains itself. He's taken the time to build a customer base, fine tune his products and service, and continually look for ways to improve quality. It's paid off. During the past 10 years, Great Plains grew every quarter. And in surveys of CPAs who evaluate PC-based accounting systems, the company took top honors for at least five years running.

Source: Jay Finnegan, "Taking Names," *Inc.*, September 1992, pp. 121–130.

---

how long the truck spends at each stop, how much it collects, and comments about the site, including any problems the driver encounters. According to Frank McCoy, the division president and general manager of Waste Management of Illinois West, "The whole idea is to get closer to the customer and know his waste stream and the time it takes to handle it."[5] At Dell Computer, employees at all levels review customer complaints in order to find ways to improve service. When one customer complained of receiving a Word for Windows License Pack after ordering a Word for Windows software package, employees redesigned an internal form to more clearly distinguish

TABLE 7.2	SOURCE	EXAMPLES
External Sources of Data	Business and industry publications	*Million Dollar Directory* (details about companies with assets over $500,000); *Directory of Mailing List Houses* (sources of mailing lists); *Sales & Marketing Management; The Wall Street Journal; Encyclopedia of Associations*
	Research services	A.C. Nielson Co., Arbitron Co., IMS International, Information Resources, Inc.
	Trade groups	American Medical Association; National Association of Realtors; National Association of Retail Dealers of America
	Customer surveys	Mail surveys, telephone surveys, personal surveys (including mail intercepts, focus group interviews, and in-home interviews)
	Government reports	*Statistical Abstract of the United States; Survey of Current Business;* state employment and economic data; *United Nations Statistical Yearbook* (worldwide data)
	Computer databases	NEXIS (full text of articles from 125 periodicals); LEXIS (legal cases and documents); PATSEARCH (U.S. patents filed since 1975); CompuServe; Dow Jones News/Retrieval; Dialog; The Source; Mead Data Central

the two products. Such changes have helped to cut errors in filling orders from 30 percent to only 3 percent.[6]

EXTERNAL SOURCES OF INFORMATION   Of course, as described in earlier chapters, marketers also need to know what is going on outside the organization. They need to know about the economy, the legal environment, their current and hoped-for customers, and much more. Therefore, marketers also need external sources of information. Such sources include business and industry publications, research services, trade groups, customer surveys, government reports, and computer databases (see Table 7.2 for examples). Spartan Motors, which builds chassis for heavy-duty vehicles, gathers information about customer needs, competitors, and technology by sending representatives to industry trade shows. Spartan designers at one show learned that fire fighters were falling out of speeding fire trucks, so the company introduced the first enclosed cab, now the industry standard.[7]

For companies that market consumer goods, an important source of external data is suppliers of single-source data. **Single-source data** refers to a single database containing data on sales by product and brand, coupon usage, and exposure to television advertising. The data on sales and coupon usage come from checkout scanners that read Universal Product Codes (bar codes), and the data on advertising exposure come from recording devices installed on the televisions of participating households. Figure 7.1 illustrates the process of collecting single-source data for a service known as Infoscan, offered by Information Resources Inc.

Single-source data can be useful for making a variety of decisions. The data on product sales can help producers and retailers learn which products sell best in particular locations. Tying sales data to coupon usage helps marketers decide whether coupon offers are effective in generating sales for particular products. If not, the mar-

single-source data
A single database containing data on sales by product and brand, coupon usage, and exposure to television advertising.

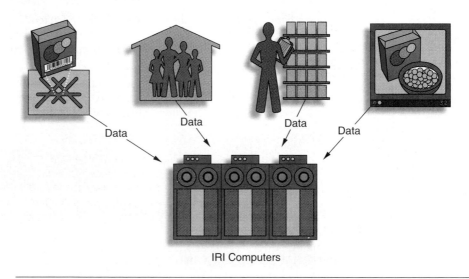

FIGURE 7.1

Collecting Single-Source Data: InfoScan

*Universal Product Codes (**UPCs**) for each grocery item are scanned at checkout. Information is sent from store to chain and on to Information Resources Inc. (IRI) via telecommunication systems.*

*   *Household panel members present an identification card at checkout, which identifies and assigns items purchased to that household. Coupons are collected and matched to the appropriate UPC. Information is electronically communicated to IRI computers.*

*   *IRI field personnel visually survey stores and all print media to record retailers' merchandising efforts., displays, and ad features. Field personnel also survey retail stores for a variety of custom applications (e.g., average number of units per display., space allocated to specific sections, and number of facings). Results are electronically communicated to IRI computers.*

*   *Household panel members are selected for television monitoring and equipped with meters that automatically record the set's status every five seconds. Information is relayed back to IRI's computers.*

Data   Data   Data   Data

IRI Computers

Source: Adapted from William R. Dillon, Thomas J. Madden, and Neil H. Firtle, *Essentials of Marketing Research* (Homewood, Ill.: Irwin, 1993), p. 122.

keter may wish to find other means to stimulate sales, or may consider making the coupons worth more or publishing them in other media. Tying sales data to advertising exposure helps marketers evaluate the effectiveness of their advertising campaigns. They will want to stick with advertising that is associated with strong sales and modify ad campaigns that do not generate results.

Furthermore, marketers can carry all of these efforts a step further by conducting experiments and using single-source data as a measure of the results. Thus, they can use different ad campaigns or coupon programs in different locations. They then compare the sales volume in the locations to find which communications efforts seem most effective.

PRIMARY DATA   When the marketing researcher conducts a telephone poll, tries selling a new service in a few selected areas, or listens to a group of consumers discussing what they look for in camping equipment, the researcher is gathering primary data. **Primary data** are data "collected specifically for the purpose of the investigation at hand."[8] When Marriott was planning to launch a chain of budget hotels, it gathered

primary data
Data collected specifically for a particular investigation.

primary data about competitors' strengths and weaknesses by sending a team of employees around the United States to stay in economy hotels and record data about the hotels' facilities and services. The information helped the new chain, Fairfield Inn, achieve an excellent occupancy rate in its first year.[9]

Statistical Inference   Most often primary data are used to infer something about a population, such as all small businesses or all teenage girls in the United States. The researcher questions or observes a sample of the population, then uses statistics to reach conclusions based on the data gathered about the sample. If 37 percent of the teenage girls surveyed say they plan to see a particular movie, the researcher might conclude, considering the size of the sample, that it is likely that 35 to 39 percent of all teenage girls in the United States would have the same intentions. This process of using data from a sample to draw conclusions about an entire population is known as **statistical inference**.

statistical inference
The process of using data from a sample to draw conclusions about an entire population.

Interestingly, statistical inference can be more accurate than a survey of the entire population (a "census"). The major reason is that surveying an entire population is such a big task that more errors can occur. Also, collecting the data can take so long that changes occur in the population during the research.

Sampling   For statistical inference to produce accurate results, the sample should be representative of the population. For example, if the researcher wants to know about all small businesses in the United States, the sample should not be limited to manufacturers or to businesses whose owner the researcher knows. Likewise, if the organization wants to know whether its target market is satisfied with its products, it should not limit its research to existing customers. Doing so omits those who are so unimpressed with the organization's quality or price that they will not buy its goods or services.[10]

Keep this principle in mind when you hear the results of so-called surveys that consist of an open invitation to register an opinion. Typically, the respondents use a fax machine or a 900 telephone number to send in their views on a particular topic, such as a current event. Such methods do not generate representative opinions, but only responses from those who feel strongly enough to pay the phone or fax charge.

probability sampling
Selecting research subjects in such a way that each member of the population has a known chance of being selected because the subjects are selected randomly.

The usual way to make the sample representative is to use **probability sampling**. This is a process of selecting research subjects in which each member of the population has a known chance of being selected because the subjects are selected randomly. In addition, the larger the random sample, the more representative of the total population it will be.

benchmarking
Identifying organizations that excel at carrying out a function and using their practices as a springboard for improvement.

Benchmarking   One way in which quality-driven organizations have sought primary data is through the practice of **benchmarking**. This involves identifying one or more organizations that excel at carrying out some function and using their practices as a source of ideas for improvement. For example, L. L. Bean is noted for its excellent order fulfillment. During one spring, the company reportedly mailed 500,000 packages, with every order filled correctly. Even during the busy Christmas season, the company claims, it fills 99.9 percent of its orders correctly.[11] Therefore, other organizations have sought to improve their own order fulfillment by benchmarking L. L. Bean.

The organization carries out benchmarking through such activities as reading about other organizations, visiting or calling them, and taking apart competing products to see how they are made. In effect, benchmarking is an information source because the process generates ideas for improving marketing and other activities. The

FIGURE 7.2

Benchmarking and the Ford Taurus

process of benchmarking varies according to the information needs of the organization and the resources available. However, some basic principles apply:[12]

- *Plan your approach.* Pick a specific area to improve. Study your own procedures and identify companies that do the process well.
- *Get the implementers involved.* The people who will have to make the changes should be the ones who do the investigating.
- *Be prepared to exchange information.* The organizations you investigate will likely have questions for you.
- *Avoid illegal activities.* Don't get into discussions that might be interpreted as price fixing, market allocation, or other illegal actions.
- *Keep confidential data confidential.* Especially avoid giving information about a company to any of its competitors.

Benchmarking can deliver results, but only under certain conditions. It is most useful for learning about existing (rather than new) products and about business practices, including ways of satisfying customers. Organizations are less willing to reveal much about new products or to disclose their strategies to competitors. In addition, research into the success of implementing total-quality efforts suggests that benchmarking leads to improved performance only when the organization already has a comprehensive quality program. When organization members aren't yet focused on quality improvement, trying to adopt the practices of the top performers is simply disruptive.[13]

Xerox is widely credited with the first benchmarking project in the United States. In 1979, Xerox studied Japanese competitors to learn how they could sell midsize copiers for less than what it cost Xerox to make them. Today many companies including AT&T, Eastman Kodak, and Motorola use benchmarking as a standard management tool. In designing the Taurus, Ford Motor Company listed about 400 features customers said were most important, then identified the car with the best of each and tried to match or top it. Figure 7.2 shows the Nissan Maxima taillight style that Ford benchmarked for the Taurus. Pittsburgh's Mellon Bank started benchmarking to improve the way it handled customer complaints about its credit card billing. Mellon benchmarked seven companies, including credit card operations, an airline, and a competing bank, by visiting three companies and phoning four. The bank learned a

TABLE 7.3	POPULATION	HOUSING
Information Available from the 1990 Census Population	*All Persons and Housing Units*	
	Household relationship	Number of units in structure
	Sex	Number of rooms in unit
	Race	Unit owned or rented
	Age	Vacancy characteristics
	Marital status	Value of owned unit or rent paid
	Hispanic origin	
	Sample of Persons and Housing Units	
	Education—enrollment and attainment	Source of water and method of sewage disposal
	Place of birth, citizenship, and year of entry	Autos, light trucks, and vans
	Ancestry	Kitchen facilities
	Language spoken at home	Year structure built
	Migration	Year moved into residence
	Disability	Number of bedrooms
	Fertility	Farm residence
	Veteran status	Shelter costs, including utilities
	Employment and unemployment	Condominium status
	Occupation, industry, and class of worker	Plumbing
	Place of work and commuting to work	Telephone
	Work experience and income in 1989	Utilities and fuels

number of ways to improve its use of computers and personnel; as a result, Mellon cut its time to resolve a complaint from an average of 45 days to 25 days.[14]

SECONDARY DATA   Sometimes the researcher can obtain needed information—or at least narrow the search for it—by using data collected for some other purpose. The original purpose of the Census Bureau's count of the U.S. population each decade was to determine how many U.S. representatives each state will send to Congress. For that purpose, the census data are primary data. But many marketers use these population counts and other Census Bureau data to learn about the size and composition of the marketplace (see Table 7.3). They are using the data as **secondary data**, that is, data "not gathered for the immediate study at hand but for some other purpose."[15]

secondary data
Data gathered for some purpose other than the immediate study at hand.

Kenneth Seiff used secondary data to arrive at a basic marketing strategy for his new company, Pivot Corporation, which makes golf-related sportswear. Statistics from the National Golf Foundation told the company's under-30 founder that the largest age segment of U.S. golfers were in their twenties. Yet it was easy to see from current products that makers of golf apparel were targeting golfers over 50. Other data indicated that about half of golfers play less than seven times a year. Together, these statistics told Seiff that there was opportunity in producing youthful designs and making them available in department stores, rather than country club pro shops.[16]

An enormous variety of secondary data is available, much of it at little or no cost. One of the most important sources for data about the United States is the U.S. Bureau of the Census. Every five years the Census Bureau conducts eight economic censuses, which cover retail trade; wholesale trade; service industries; transportation, communications, and utilities industries; financial, insurance, and real estate indus-

Put It Into Practice

USING DATABASES FOR MARKETING RESEARCH

You don't need to trot off to the library or make a hundred phone calls to do marketing research. Instead, you can use a computer and modem to gather a wealth of information from on-line databases. Companies offering databases do charge fees, usually based on time, which vary from a few dollars per month to more than $100 per hour. There are four main database companies that are especially relevant to sales and marketing. Keep this information at hand for your own marketing research projects.

CompuServe. CompuServe offers databases such as Business Database Plus; Magazine Database Plus (about 90 business and consumer periodicals, as well as the Associated Press news wire); CENDATA (from the U.S. Census Bureau), with information on housing starts, population, etc.; and SUPERSITE, which shoots out statistics on zip codes, states, counties, TV markets, and the like. CompuServe is one of the least expensive databases, and very easy to use.

NEXIS. NEXIS allows the user to search using English commands or special codes. (Using the latter provides more specific results.) Some of its databases include Analyst Research; Consumer Goods; Marketing (information from trade publications and other sources); PROMT/PLUS (overview of markets and technology).

Dialog. Users can access Dialog without codes, but the database may seem a little more complicated than that of either CompuServe or NEXIS. A sampling of sources and files includes Worldwide Sales Prospecting (sorting companies by geography, size, etc.), Worldwide Corporate Intelligence; Kompass International Directories; ABI/INFORM (information on business management and administration); Moody's Corporate Files; and D&B-Donnelly Demographics.

Dow Jones News/Retrieval. Dow Jones News/Retrieval is one of the more expensive services and may seem somewhat complicated to use. But it does offer a lot of relevant information, much of it exclusive (not found on other databases), most especially *The Wall Street Journal* and *Barron's*. Some of its databases are Comprehensive Company Reports (financial and business information on public companies), Dow Jones Business Newswires, Japanese Business News, and Statistical Comparisons of Companies and Industries.

Source: Christel Beard and Betsy Wiesendanger, "Marketer's Guide to Online Databases," *Sales & Marketing Management,* January 1993, pp. 37–41, 86.

tries; manufacturers; mineral industries; and construction industries. Each business must report such basic operating statistics as number of employees, annual payroll, and the value of goods and services produced in the year of the census.[17] Until recently, such extensive data were useful primarily to big organizations with mainframe computers. Today, however, a personal computer with a good-sized memory and a CD-ROM drive can get the information from CD-based software selling for about $1,000—well within the range of most small businesses.[18]

A few private sources of data include MRI, Simmons, and the *Buying Power Index.* The Prizm database (from Claritas/NPDC in Alexandria, Virginia) can identify clusters of consumers by a variety of criteria, including life-style and demographic segments. To learn about organizational buyers, a marketer might tap into Dun's Business Locator, an index on CD-ROM that provides basic data on over ten million U.S. businesses.[19] In addition, the "Put It into Practice" box describes the wealth of secondary data available from on-line databases. Note that these are only some of the possibilities; a complete listing of secondary sources is beyond the scope of this chapter.

Secondary data may be too old or not targeted enough to the problem at hand. However, because gathering secondary data tends to be less expensive than conducting primary research, an efficient research strategy is to begin by collecting secondary data. The information that results can narrow the focus of any primary research—or even eliminate the need to obtain primary data. Mike and John Schroll, who own Schroll Cabinets in Cheyenne, Wyoming, keep abreast of market trends by reading

FIGURE 7.3

Steps in the Marketing Research Process

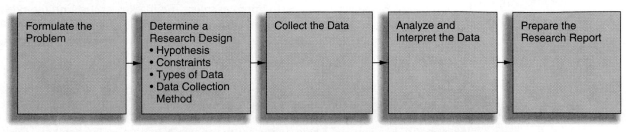

industry publications. In this way, they learned that white-painted cabinets were becoming popular on the coasts and correctly forecasted—ahead of their competitors—that demand for such cabinets would soon grow in the Cheyenne area.[20]

The Marketing Research Process

Carrying out the function of marketing research involves several steps. First, the researcher formulates the problem to be solved. Then the researcher determines a research design appropriate for solving the problem. Using the tools specified in the research design, the researcher collects the data. The researcher analyzes and interprets the data, then communicates the findings by preparing and submitting a research report. Figure 7.3 summarizes this process, and the following sections describe it in greater detail.

FORMULATING THE PROBLEM

The marketing research process begins when someone in the organization sees a need for information. The marketer may want to evaluate new possibilities or improve current practices. Perhaps a product development team wonders what price buyers will be willing to pay for a new car stereo with a given set of features. Or perhaps an advertising manager wonders whether an ad campaign is getting the anticipated results. A small-business owner might wonder whether her product was selling better in department stores or in specialty shops. Marketers expect that research will help them answer such questions.

When a marketer needs information, he or she must formulate the problem to be solved. For example, the marketer might have to improve the performance of the sales force or decide the best distribution channels for a new product. Sometimes marketers confuse problems with symptoms. A *problem* is a situation requiring some type of action, whereas a *symptom* is merely evidence that a problem exists. Thus, a number of years ago, Xerox was concerned that it was rapidly losing photocopier sales to Japanese competitors. That was the symptom. After some investigation, it became clear that Xerox's marketers were focusing on what features they could add to their copiers to make them more desirable, whereas customers mainly wanted copiers that would break down less often. The problem was product quality. Xerox management realized that to compete, it would have to review data not just on sales and profits, but also on product performance and customer satisfaction.[21]

Focusing on symptoms rather than formulating the true problem can lead to vague, unhelpful research. In the case of declining sales, it is not enough to say that the purpose of the research will be to improve sales. The marketer must find the problem, then investigate how to improve sales. However, sometimes research is needed to help with problem formulation. In such situations, the marketer might use exploratory research, described in the next section.

DETERMINING A RESEARCH DESIGN

"We need to do a survey." Often, when someone needs marketing information, this is the solution proposed. In the view of many, the core job of the marketing researcher is to conduct surveys and interpret their results. However, the appropriate tools for solving a particular marketing problem may not include a survey. To get the best information at the lowest cost, the marketing researcher needs to select the type of research tools most appropriate for solving the problem that has been formulated. The plan for how to collect and analyze the data is known as a **research design**.

research design
The plan for how to collect and analyze data.

The researcher is in the best position to design the research when the marketer has carefully defined the kinds of information needed. Researchers are rarely in a position to define the problem on their own. Therefore, the marketer must be clear about what problem needs to be solved. One of the most valuable roles the researcher can play is in helping the manager or decision maker define the problem in terms research can help solve.

hypothesis
A tentative assumption to be tested by research.

One of the most productive ways of framing a problem or question is as a hypothesis. A **hypothesis** is a tentative assumption to be tested by research. For example, a hypothesis for marketing research might be that notebook computers (small, portable computers) are most likely to be purchased for business use by salespeople and other businesspeople who travel frequently. The researcher would conduct a study that identifies who buys this product category and for what uses. If the research supports the hypothesis, the marketer of this product will create a marketing mix to appeal to salespeople and business travelers, showing how notebook computers can benefit their work.

BASIC RESEARCH DESIGNS   Based on the problem definition, the researcher selects one or more of the basic research designs; these are exploratory, descriptive, and causal research.

Exploratory Research   When researchers seek to discover ideas and insights, they are conducting **exploratory research**. In general, it is used for generating hypotheses and identifying areas to study further. For example, the researcher might ask consumers to describe their ideal vacation. This could give a travel agency ideas for assembling tour packages, or it could give an advertising agency ideas for images to test in planning an ad campaign for a resort.

exploratory research
Research that seeks to discover ideas and insights.

Exploratory research gathers information from whatever sources are likely to provide useful insights. Thus, the researcher tends to be less concerned with probability sampling and more concerned with opening communication lines to those with something to say. A case in point is the use of toll-free numbers to learn about customer satisfaction by making it easy for customers to contact someone at the company. The Subway chain of sandwich restaurants has its phone number printed on its napkins.

The 100 or so callers each week aren't necessarily a representative sample of customers, but they do keep the company aware of what issues they feel strongly enough to call about.[22] Some of those issues presumably would merit further investigation.

Descriptive Research   Studying how often something occurs or what, if any, relationship exists between two variables is called **descriptive research**. The researcher might seek to learn whether men or women more often select vacation destinations. Or the researcher might test whether significantly more people select a cruise package from a brochure whose front cover shows a photo of people swimming and dancing or one that shows bountiful buffets. In the latter case, the researcher is looking for a relationship between the brochure design and the success of the communication effort.

As with exploratory research, the results of descriptive research may become the basis for further investigation. At Marsh Supermarkets, researchers in the catwalks watched the movements of shoppers and learned that they tended to buy mostly from goods displayed at the periphery of the store. Shoppers often avoided going up and down the aisles, where dry goods were stocked. So the researchers experimented with varying display space, repositioning various products, and installing TV monitors in the periphery that play ads for center-store items.[23]

Causal Research   The follow-up experiments at Marsh Supermarkets were a type of causal research. **Causal research** looks for cause-and-effect relationships. In other words, it doesn't just investigate whether there is a relationship between two variables, such as brochure design and vacation purchase. Rather, it seeks to find whether the design *causes* people to choose the cruise package.

Not surprisingly, cause-and-effect relationships can be hard to demonstrate. In the case of the cruise brochure, one possibility would be to ask vacationers why they made the choices they did. In that case, the researcher would hope that the vacationers really know what motivated them. Another possibility is to set up an experiment in which exposure to the brochure is systematically varied.

Experiments   An **experiment** is a research design that involves manipulating one or more variables while keeping the others constant and measuring the results. The research described in the "You Decide" box is a type of experiment. A lot of the marketing experiments in the recent past have involved testing consumer reactions when a marketer varied the amount or content of advertising for a particular product. Overall, that body of research has tended to show that changes in advertising content make more difference than changes in frequency of exposure.[24]

Maritz Motivation Company conducted an experiment using equipment that tracked the eye movements of consumers viewing mailers printed in one, two, or four colors (that is, full color). The researchers found that the subjects were most likely to pick up and look at the four-color mailer. When the researchers contacted the subjects with follow-up questions 24 hours later, the subjects were most likely to remember the company name that was printed on the four-color mailer. The researchers concluded that the use of color improves the effectiveness of a mailer.[25] Eye-tracking equipment is also useful for comparing reactions to different versions of advertisements.

Marketing experiments do not have to involve fancy equipment, just careful records of the variables. United Airlines keeps track of what food it serves on each flight, as well as ongoing surveys of customer satisfaction. Whenever United makes changes in food service, the company looks for corresponding changes in customer satisfaction. This information plays a key role in the menu planning by United's Food Services Division.[26]

descriptive research
Research that studies how often something occurs or what, if any, relationship exists between two variables.

causal research
Research that looks for cause-and-effect relationships.

experiment
Research that involves manipulating one or two variables while keeping others constant, and measuring the results.

You Decide

SHOULD SUPERMARKETS PUT SALES ABOVE CUSTOMER SATISFACTION?

Have you ever hit the supermarket running, with no time to spare, and been stopped short because you couldn't find anything? One brand of cornflakes sits at one end of the cereal aisle, while another hides at the other end, so it's harder to compare prices and ingredients. Razor blades are nowhere near the shaving cream. Bins of produce change constantly: one week, the apples are on the far side of the aisle, and the next week they're right up front.

Marketing researchers at the University of Chicago wondered whether such challenges hurt supermarket sales. To find out, they rearranged shelves in real supermarkets. General Mills, Procter & Gamble, and Kraft General Foods funded the study because they could apply the results to the distribution of their goods.

The research team looked at "micromerchandising," which involves customizing the selection and display of products from store to store, so that each store meets the needs of the particular area it serves. Thus, the results of the study may affect how supermarkets display, price, and promote their products. "We think one can increase sales by . . . going from a mass-marketing mentality toward the mom-and-pop approach," remarks Stephen Hoch, project director and professor of marketing and behavioral science at the University of Chicago.

Conducting their study in 90 supermarkets in the greater Chicago area, the team divided the stores into four types: ethnic, urban, established suburb, and growing suburb. They tabulated scanner data for each type to find which products were selling well. Products that perform poorly, such as Scott Paper's four-packs of tissue in urban areas, lose shelf space in those stores or are pulled altogether. Products that do well, such as single rolls of tissue in urban stores, may get more shelf space.

The researchers also evaluated whether rearranging products as well as cross-merchandising products (such as razors and shaving cream) would increase sales and profits. Oddly enough, they found that alphabetizing soups (making them easier for customers to indentify and locate) decreases sales. That may be because a random grouping forces customers to take notice of other soups they might not have thought about—and perhaps buy a few. Clustering cereals by types rather than brand has a comparable effect. But when researchers placed toothbrushes in the middle of the toothpaste section, brush sales—with their relatively high profits—increased. In the soft-drink section, researchers first displayed the drinks by container size (all the two-liter bottles together, for instance), then they rearranged the drinks by brand. When the drinks were arranged by brand, they sold better. An added benefit was that arrangement by brand made restocking easier.

If you were evaluating the results of this study, how would *you* interpret the results? Would you conclude that the increase in sales translated to more satisfied customers? Why or why not? If customers complained about the arrangement of products, would you change it even if the current arrangement boosted sales?

Sources: Laura Duncan, "How the GSB Is Bringing Science into the Grocery Store," *GSB Chicago* (University of Chicago Graduate School of Business), Winter 1991, pp. 15–17; and Richard Gibson, "The Fine Art of Stocking a Supermarket's Shelves," *The Wall Street Journal*, October 5, 1992, pp. B1 and B10.

test marketing
Offering a product in limited geographic areas and measuring how target markets and competitors respond to the mix.

Test Marketing   Among the most common ways marketers use experiments is in test marketing. To conduct **test marketing**, the organization offers a product in limited geographic areas, known as test markets, so that it can see how target markets and competitors respond to the marketing mix. For example, BirdsEye used test marketing to introduce the first frozen foods to consumers. In 1930 BirdsEye placed specially-built storage cases for frozen foods in 18 grocery stores in Springfield, Massachusetts. Salesmen gathered data by interviewing customers in their homes to get detailed reactions to the first frozen products: chicken, haddock, sirloin steak, and strawberries. At the end of the 40-week test period, marketers concluded that frozen foods had strong potential—if the company could solve problems of product refrigeration, transportation, and selection.[27] See Figure 7.4 for some BirdsEye products currently available.

If the response in test markets is different than was anticipated in the marketing plan, the organization can adjust the marketing mix before offering the product to the

FIGURE 7.4

Test Marketing Revealed a Strong Potential for Frozen Foods

entire target market. The results of test marketing can also influence other marketing decisions, such as the creation of advertising messages.

Test marketing is especially important as a way to forecast sales of a new product. It could have saved Pillsbury the costly mistakes it made in introducing Oven Lovin' cookie dough, packaged in a resealable tub. A similar product had been a hit in Britain, and U.S. consumers told researchers they liked the idea. But the consumers either followed the common pattern of saying what they thought the interviewers would like to hear or else thought they would use just part of the dough at a time. Instead, consumers baked all the cookies at once or ate the leftover dough raw, so the expensive packaging proved unnecessary, and consumers wouldn't pay the price again. Pillsbury had to eat its heavy advertising expenses and withdraw the product from the majority of U.S. stores.[28]

Problems with the research design can make the results of test marketing difficult to interpret. First, the researcher should select test markets that are representative of the total market to be served. If the total market is diverse, this may be difficult to do, and other portions of the target market may respond differently than the test markets did. Furthermore, uncontrollable events, such as bad weather or retaliation by a competitor, may make it difficult to assume that performance in the test market is representative of how the product will perform in the entire market. Finally, it is difficult to ensure that the organization performs the same way in the test markets as it will following the test marketing. For example, not all salespeople will perform in the same way, and it is tempting to overpromote a new product during test marketing in order to make it look good and avoid "wasting" the time spent developing it.

CONSTRAINTS ON RESEARCH DESIGN   In designing the research, the researcher needs to take into account the amount of time and money available for collecting and analyzing the data. These become constraints on the research options. Generally, when the consequences of a decision are great, the organization will be willing to spend more money on the research than when the consequences are slight. It doesn't make sense, for example, to spend $50,000 on a study to show how to boost sales by $30,000. The time available will depend not only on the importance of the decision, but also on the consequences of delaying a decision. For example, if a competitor is

FIGURE 7.5

**Top Sources of
Marketing Research
for New Products**

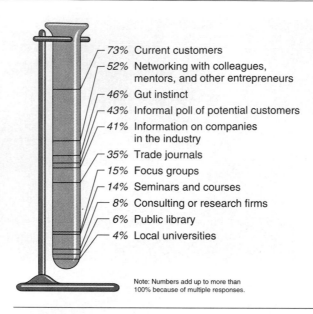

- *73%* Current customers
- *52%* Networking with colleagues,
  mentors, and other entrepreneurs
- *46%* Gut instinct
- *43%* Informal poll of potential customers
- *41%* Information on companies
  in the industry
- *35%* Trade journals
- *15%* Focus groups
- *14%* Seminars and courses
- *8%* Consulting or research firms
- *6%* Public library
- *4%* Local universities

Note: Numbers add up to more than
100% because of multiple responses.

Source: Reprinted with permission, *Inc.* magazine, June 1992. Copyright 1992 by Goldhirsh Group, Inc.,
38 Commercial Wharf, Boston, MA 02110.

likely to launch a new product soon, the organization might want to act quickly to beat the competitor.

Even when marketing research seems expensive, however, the potential benefits can make it an important investment. That was the case with Biosite Diagnostics, a San Diego biotechnology company that spent $150,000 to hire a research firm to survey potential users of its planned first product, a disposable diagnostic test called Triage. The research showed that the target market—hospital emergency room physicians—was very interested in Triage, which enabled the unproven company to attract investment funds for production. Research results also helped the company refine its marketing strategy in two ways. First, the results showed that lab technicians, not doctors, made the purchase decisions for lab tests. Second, Biosite learned that the potential market was so big it should rely on distributors to handle selling activities. So Biosite arranged with one distributor to sell Triage in the United States and another to handle European sales.[29]

Marketing research need not be sophisticated and expensive to be worthwhile, however. A survey of small to midsize companies conducted by *Inc.* magazine found that nearly 40 percent spent less than $1,000 to conduct their marketing research.[30] As shown in Figure 7.5, the top sources of information were current customers and colleagues.

Deck House, an Acton, Massachusetts–based designer and manufacturer of post-and-beam houses, collects customer information at minimal cost. The company dedicated one of its existing toll-free numbers to a customer service line. One staff person, Eric Stacy, handles all the calls to that number with the aid of a database that includes job numbers, model numbers, the builder's name for each job, and a record of any problems that have occurred. After helping the customer, Stacy asks some questions designed to learn about customers' wants and needs. For example, by

TECHNIQUE	ADVANTAGES	DISADVANTAGES
Observation	Accurate and objective	Limited to measurement of behavior and a few demographic characteristics; much time usually required
Surveys	Versatility; ability to uncover motivations, attitudes, beliefs; relative speed	Possible failure of subjects to report their attitudes, beliefs, behavior accurately; likelihood that some people will decline to participate

TABLE 7.4
Basic Research Techniques

having Stacy ask customers how they would organize a house, the company learned that people in New Jersey want all their bedrooms upstairs, while those in Virginia want the master bedroom downstairs.[31]

COLLECTING DATA

Depending on the research design, collecting data may involve a variety of activities, from looking up articles on a computer database to watching a sample of consumers try out a product prototype to asking questions over the telephone. Whatever activities are involved, data collection requires personnel. They may be employees of the organization using the research, or the organization may contract with a research service. In either case, the accuracy of the data depends in part on hiring qualified people to do the collection and on supervising these people effectively.

Whenever a research project involves collecting primary data, some errors are bound to occur during data collection. For example, some members of a random sample may refuse to participate, survey respondents may provide incorrect answers, or research staff may make mistakes when coding data to be entered into the computer. The researcher cannot prevent errors completely but should have plans for minimizing them.

TYPES OF DATA TO GATHER   Given the hypothesis and the constraints, the researcher must decide whether to use primary data, secondary data, or some combination of the two. As noted earlier, secondary data tend to be easier and cheaper to gather. However, secondary data may not be tailored to answering the question at hand. Therefore, one common approach is to start the research effort by analyzing secondary data and using it to develop a plan for later gathering primary data. Thus, the collection and analysis of secondary data is used for exploratory research. When the research involves collecting secondary data, the researcher must evaluate the sources of data to make sure that they truly address the research objectives and to check whether they are likely to be accurate.

If the researcher decides to gather primary data, he or she needs to select the technique or combination of techniques that will be most suitable. The basic possibilities are observation and surveys. Table 7.4 lists advantages and disadvantages of using each.

OBSERVATION   Sometimes people don't do exactly what they say they will, and sometimes users of a product can't fully describe their experiences with it. For these reasons, researchers may use **observation**, or the collection of data by recording

observation
The collection of data by recording actions of customers or events in the marketplace.

actions of customers or events in the marketplace. For example, a supermarket scanner that records what each consumer buys is recording actual behavior. A toy maker might have experts observe children playing with various toys in order to see what features attract them. Thus, observation is a useful tool for research.

Uses of Observation   Observation can be useful for learning about competitors and their products. The marketer can keep records of what competitors are doing in terms of product offerings and communications. Also useful in such a database would be notes on what competitors' people say in speeches to trade groups. To learn about competing software and service, CE Software of West Des Moines, Iowa, buys the software, tries it, then calls the maker's technical support department with a few questions. Pamela Kelly, who operates Rue de France, a catalog company that sells lace curtains, places difficult orders with competitors and observes how those orders are handled.[32]

Among the biggest uses of observation is the measurement of television viewing habits. To record what television shows are being broadcast in participating homes, and who is watching, A. C. Nielsen Company uses a "people meter." Each member of the participating household has his or her own viewing number. The viewer is supposed to enter his number into the people meter whenever he turns on the set or changes the channel. Nielsen uses the resulting data to produce its Nielsen ratings of TV shows. Arbitron Company is working on a competing device—a portable, passive people meter that each member of the household would wear or carry around. The device would measure TV viewing and radio listening by picking up audio signals encoded in the programs being broadcast.[33]

Advantages and Disadvantages   Observation techniques have the advantage that the researcher can see what subjects are doing, rather than relying on their memory or truthfulness in reporting their behavior. Thus, researchers using observation can collect data independently of subjects' self-perception, which tends to make the results more objective and accurate. This benefit of observation is apparent to a small southern California company that sells windows and doors for installation in new homes. Every two months this company's 70 employees gather to eat pizza and watch videotapes of their customers hanging their doors and windows. Applying what they learn to improving their products has reduced customer complaints by 60 percent.[34]

On the downside, observation can be time consuming. A researcher could conduct several surveys in the time it takes to watch a single consumer making an automobile buying decision or trying to operate a new product. Furthermore, observation can only measure people's overt behavior and a few kinds of demographic data such as gender, not such hidden information as motives, beliefs, and attitudes, which may be important to the marketer.

SURVEYS   To learn the beliefs and thoughts of the people being studied, the researcher uses some type of survey. A **survey** is the collection of data through use of a questionnaire. The researcher can conduct a survey through the mail, by telephone, or in person.

Surveys are a major form of research in the United States. One study showed over 40 percent of respondents had participated in a survey during the past year. About three-quarters had participated in a survey at some time.[35]

Uses of Surveys   Surveys are especially important for marketers using the quality approach, because they can help the organization move beyond knowing whether its products have defects to knowing whether customers are delighted. The Fort Sanders Health System—six health-care facilities serving the Knoxville area—conducted a

survey
The collection of data through use of a questionnaire.

survey of customer satisfaction and learned that some of the measures of quality it considered most important were not what mattered most to hospital patients. Many hospitals have tried to upgrade and promote their meals, but patients ranked food 32nd out of 34 items in terms of importance. And employees place importance on good clinical care, but patients take that for granted. What patients pay most attention to are the quality and degree of personal attention they receive from personnel in all areas of the hospital.[36]

While surveys are versatile and can generate important information, the researcher must contend with the drawback that some respondents will fail to answer some questions completely and accurately. Even well-intentioned respondents may not know the answers to some questions—and may not even realize that they don't know. If you ask consumers whether they will buy possible new products, for example, they tend to respond most favorably to product concepts that are somewhat familiar. However, good product design and marketing communication may actually lead consumers to buy something completely new. Veteran marketer Al Ries observes, "If you said to a consumer, 'We're thinking about coming out with a Honda Deluxe or an Acura. Which would you rather buy?' 98 percent would say the Honda Deluxe. But a Honda Deluxe would have died in [my] opinion."[37] Further skewing the results of surveys, some people will refuse to respond at all.

Developing a Survey   When the researcher's job includes developing a survey, he or she can use some techniques for ensuring that the survey will work as intended. One important step is to test the questionnaire. The researcher should ask a few people to try answering the questions. The researcher can observe whether the subjects are confused by certain questions, for example. Careful researchers do not trivialize this step. When Compaq Computer Corporation worked with Yankelovich Clancy Shulman to develop an international survey of customer satisfaction with Compaq products, they spent many hours writing, testing, and rewriting each of the survey items to make sure it was precise and would deliver useful information.[38]

Also important is to see whether people take much longer to complete the survey than anticipated. The biggest objection people have to completing surveys is the length of time involved. Refusal rates increase dramatically when surveys require more than 12 minutes to complete.[39] Therefore, researchers do well to consider this factor if they want people to participate. Ben & Jerry's uses short questions, multiple choices, and visuals to ensure that its survey will work as intended. (See Figure 7.6.)

In addition, the researcher should compare the structure of the survey with the kinds of information to be provided by the research. The data generated by the survey should be relevant to providing that information. To test whether the data will be relevant, the researcher can begin planning the format for reporting the data and make sure the survey will gather data that fit the format.

Mail Surveys   To reach a large number of widely dispersed people, a mail survey can be effective. Surveying people by mail is useful when they might have to look up information or might be uncomfortable discussing it with strangers. For example, the review of a textbook manuscript is done by mail, enabling the instructor reviewing the manuscript to read it and then refer back to it when making comments. On the downside, conducting a survey by mail can be time consuming. Subjects may not get around to replying for weeks or months, during which time the researcher cannot be sure whether they will reply at all.

Telephone Surveys   To get an immediate response, the researcher can use a telephone survey. This is an efficient way to contact a large group of people. Also, people

FIGURE 7.6

A Survey That Takes Less Than 12 Minutes to Complete

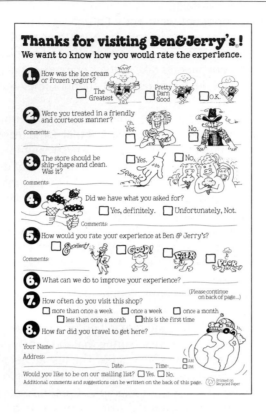

are more apt to participate in a telephone survey because it seems easier than filling out forms.

Drawbacks of a telephone survey include the inability to show products over the phone or to reach people who have no phone or no listing of their phone number. Also, today many consumers are better able to screen their calls, thanks to answering machines and "caller I.D." If many of them choose not to take calls from researchers, the research sample may not be representative. Figure 7.7 shows the many possible outcomes of attempting to interview a subject by phone.

Personal Surveys   To discuss issues in depth, researchers usually use personal surveys, because these enable the interviewer to probe for further information. Thus, this type of survey is suitable for complex or emotional issues. It also allows the interviewer to present visual information such as a sample product or advertisement. However, personal surveys tend to be time consuming and expensive. Also, the subjects may be influenced by their perceptions of the interviewer's reactions. Popular forms of personal surveys are mall intercepts, focus group interviews, and in-home surveys.

A **mall intercept** is a personal survey in which the interviewer stands in a shopping center, stops consumers, and asks them to participate. This is presumably an effective way to find potential purchasers. However, the sample of respondents may be biased. Only certain types of people may be willing to take the time to participate—notably, people with few other obligations. Also, interviewers may tend to ask certain kinds of people—say, those who look the friendliest or the least busy.

A **focus group interview** is a personal interview of a small group of people in which the interviewer poses open-ended questions and encourages group interaction. In a typical focus group interview, six to twelve people participate for one or two

mall intercept
A personal survey in which the interviewer stands in a shopping center and asks consumers to participate.

focus group interview
A personal survey of a small group of people in which the interviewer poses open-ended questions.

FIGURE 7.7

Possible Outcomes When Attempting to Contact Respondents for Telephone Survey

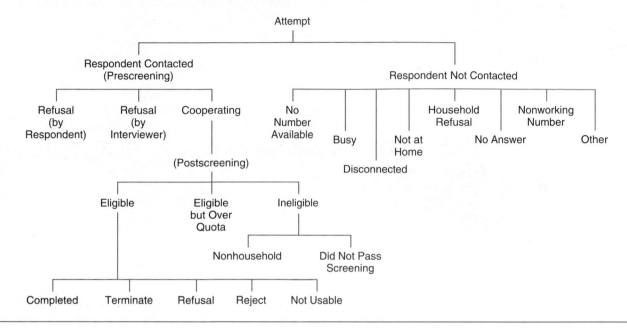

Source: Frederick Wiseman and Philip McDonald, *Toward the Development of Industry Standards for Response and Nonresponse Rates* (Cambridge, Mass.: Marketing Science Institute, 1980), p. 29. Reprinted with permission.

hours. Researchers may observe the interview through a one-way mirror, although more marketers are finding it helpful to be present to participate in a dialogue with customers.[40] The interview is usually taped so that it can be studied later. Focus groups are useful for identifying issues to explore in more directed follow-up studies. The success of the focus group depends on the ability of the interviewer to encourage the discussion and the ability of the researchers to interpret the results. Researchers must be careful not to treat the opinions of one or a few focus group participants as being representative of an entire target market.

in-home interview
A personal survey in which the interviewer goes door to door to visit subjects at their homes.

In-home interviews are surveys in which the interviewer visits subjects at their homes. In Eastern Europe, Procter & Gamble researchers visited consumers and learned that many of the locally made detergents smelled terrible and worked so poorly that clothes had to be soaked all day. P&G concluded, correctly, that consumers would be willing to switch to its Ariel detergent.[41] In-home interviews give researchers a chance to learn a lot about consumers. However, they depend on a representative sample being at home when the interviewer seeks them out, as well as on their willingness to talk to a stranger in their home. Because of the drawbacks, in-home interviews are the least-used type of survey.[42]

ANALYZING AND INTERPRETING DATA

To turn the collected data into information, the researcher must analyze the data. When data are recorded on a questionnaire or other form, the researcher first reviews each form to make sure it has been filled out completely and properly. Then the

EMS, a research service in the supermarket industry, offers next-day, store-specific information.

coding
Assigning numeric symbols to the data collected.

tabulating
Counting the number of cases that fall into each category of response.

researcher codes the data; **coding** means assigning numeric symbols to the answers. The researcher's next step is **tabulating** the data, which means counting the number of cases that fall into each category of response. For example, if the research involves watching people try out computer software, tabulation might include counting the number of times each user consults the reference manual. Or if the research is a mail survey asking for demographic information about magazine subscribers, tabulation could include counting the number of subscribers in each income category.

STATISTICAL ANALYSIS   When the data have been tabulated, the researcher performs various kinds of statistical analysis. The analysis may be as basic as computing the average response to a question, or the researcher may use a computer to perform a variety of sophisticated techniques. Modern personal computers are powerful enough to handle many kinds of data analysis. The selection of techniques should be based on which will best help the marketer solve the problems the research was designed to help with.

INTERPRETATION   Before preparing a final report, the researcher should evaluate the results. Do they seem logical and reasonable? If not, part of the researcher's job is to review the assumptions behind the research as well as the process of arriving at the result. The researcher's logic and experience can allow him or her to spot mistakes that could prove embarrassing and costly. Using sophisticated analytical techniques or state-of-the-art computer systems will not prevent errors from faulty assumptions, a poor research process, or even mistakes in data entry. At Oscar Mayer, researchers use data to generate models of what results to expect from various courses of action. If the results predicted by the model don't seem to make sense, the researchers take another look at the model to find problems there. If they don't see anything wrong with the model, they proceed with caution, perhaps testing the recommended course of action on a small scale.[43]

Evaluating the results can uncover situations where the researcher can provide more helpful information by modifying the research design. Campbell Soup Company set up a sophisticated test panel in which consumers evaluated a proposed lower-sodium version of V-8 juice. The consumers in the test panel—men and women who had drunk a similar product in the previous six months—gave the new product poor ratings; they preferred their current product. However, the company was committed to developing a reduced-sodium version of V-8 and wanted to know how to make that effort succeed, so the researchers investigated further. They learned that most loyal drinkers of this type of product tended not to be very health conscious and were therefore happy with regular V-8 juice, salt and all. The researchers set up another test panel, this time selecting as panelists consumers who used the type of product and also were sensitive to health issues. In this case, the test panel preferred the lower-sodium version, so Campbell targeted Light 'n Tangy V-8 juice to this type of consumer.[44]

PREPARING THE RESEARCH REPORT

Finally, the researcher puts the information generated by the analysis into a report. The report should begin with a concise summary of what the research was designed to do, what the results were, and what these results mean in terms of making marketing decisions. Supplementary information in the report then describes the research in greater detail, including the method and limitations. Statistical information, sample forms, and the like would appear in an appendix at the end of the report. Besides a written report, the marketer may request one or more oral reports.

A thorough research project may require much technical expertise and sophisticated statistical analysis. Nevertheless, the marketer may reasonably require that the report be understandable. If it is not useful as an aid to decision making, the report does not fulfill the ultimate goal of the marketing research.

USING MARKETING RESEARCH

While the definition of marketing research does not explicitly describe the role of those who receive the research reports, the way they respond affects the value of the research. First, the user of marketing research needs to consider whether it is accurate and useful. Suppose a consulting firm wants to estimate the potential demand for seminars on injecting humor into speeches. The firm could conduct a telephone poll of executives, asking them if they would send their managers to such a seminar. Do their responses predict their actual behavior? If not, the research did not accurately measure their intentions. The user also needs to assess whether the results are useful. Do they answer the objectives for the research and imply how to proceed?

Furthermore, the user needs to incorporate sound judgment when applying the research results. The marketer has experience and intuition, which should supplement the research information. For example, intuition and industry knowledge, not statistical analysis, led Hewlett-Packard to recognize a rival was about to launch a competing product ahead of H-P. Hewlett-Packard's market intelligence included a tip-off from its travel agent that the rival had booked conference rooms around the country, as well as knowledge that the rival had been developing a similar product. H-P announced its new product earlier than planned, thus beating its rival to the market.[45]

Applications of New Technology

Marketing research and information processing in general are areas that clearly benefit from the use of computers. As computer technology has advanced, marketers have become able to obtain and use information with greater ease and sophistication. Of course, marketers must continue to use their judgment and expertise in deciding what kinds of information they need and how they will apply it.

MARKETING INFORMATION SYSTEMS

marketing information system (MIS)
A set of methods and procedures for gathering, sorting, storing, and distributing information used in making marketing decisions.

Computer technology makes it easier to organize data into a **marketing information system (MIS)**. This is a set of methods and procedures for the regular gathering, sorting, storage, and distribution of information to be used in making marketing decisions. The MIS continually takes in data from internal sources such as sales records and from external sources such as publications and research. An MIS may give a competitive advantage in France to IMR Finance, a wholesaler of pharmaceuticals in that country. IMR has a database containing information about the French drug market. It plans to put this database to use as a way to help drug companies see where their products will sell best.[46]

A significant advantage of an MIS over merely gathering information when requested and writing a report is that the people who can use marketing information are able to get it quickly and easily. The information also should be up to date. United Airlines regularly asks a percentage of its flyers to fill out questionnaires concerning customer satisfaction, then stores the results in a computerized database. Managers routinely use the data to see whether the company's activities in a given area, such as baggage handling or food service, are satisfying its customers.[47]

An MIS is most useful when its users see to it that they get the kinds of information they really need. Therefore, marketing managers must be clear about the kinds of information that can help them make decisions. Then they must ask the designers of the system to include the capability of collecting and delivering those kinds of information. The people who design such systems cannot be expected to anticipate every need of the user.

One company that has a useful MIS is SKI Ltd., an operator of ski resorts in Vermont and California. It maintains a database of customer information, including such data as the home address, skiing ability, and past skiing expenditures of over 2.5 million skiers. The data come from a variety of sources, including SKI's lodging facilities, ski school, and rental shops; requests for brochures; and surveys of customers. SKI uses the data to identify groups to target for particular promotions. For example, it mailed 90,000 cards offering midweek discounts on lift tickets to skiers who lived at least a three-hour drive away and normally came only on weekends. SKI credits this mailing with unusually high levels of midweek skiing at its resorts.[48]

MARKETING DECISION SUPPORT SYSTEMS

marketing decision support system (MDSS)
A coordinated collection of data, system tools, and techniques with supporting software and hardware so that an organization can interpret information and use it to make management decisions.

Today the management information systems in many organizations contain a **marketing decision support system (MDSS)**. Such a system consists of "a coordinated collection of data, system tools, and techniques with supporting software and hardware by which an organization gathers and interprets relevant information from business and the environment and turns it into a basis for making management decisions."[49] Thus, the MDSS not only provides information, it does so in a form designed to assist the decision maker during the process of making a decision.

This means that the MDSS requires three types of software:

1. Database management software for sorting and retrieving data from internal and external sources

2. Model base management software that contains routines for manipulating the data in ways that are of interest to the marketer

FIGURE 7.8

Basics of a Marketing Decision Support System (MDSS)

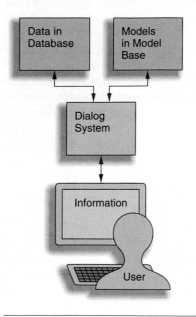

3. A dialog system to permit the marketer to explore the database and use the models to produce reports that address his or her questions.

Figure 7.8 shows the basic setup of an MDSS.

Typically an MDSS allows the user to conduct "what if" analysis. This means the user can ask the computer to show the likely outcome of changing a certain variable in a certain way. For example, the marketer might ask what will happen if the advertising budget is doubled or if the number-three competitor drops out of the market.

The ability to perform "what if" and other kinds of analysis is not built into a computer, of course. The organization must enter a great deal of internal and external data as well as the models and assumptions to be used. Consequently, creating an MDSS is time consuming and expensive. However, the ability to get fast answers to specific marketing questions is enough to make the effort worthwhile at a growing number of organizations.

THE INFORMATION TECHNOLOGY REVOLUTION

Much as technology is enabling many organizations to tailor their offerings to the needs of individual customers, it enables the marketing researcher to meet the unique needs of individual users within the organization. The user of a personal computer in a network can retrieve the data relevant to a particular problem and easily manipulate the data to provide a variety of types of information. Thus, one user might tap into the database to determine when to restock inventory, another might look up data to quote prices or delivery dates to a prospective customer, and a third user might identify the regions in which a new product was selling the most.

One of the chief benefits of the user's ability to extract and analyze data is that the user can get just the information he or she needs. In contrast, the old-fashioned approach of having staff experts prepare reports for various managers was much less efficient. To be sure of covering all the bases, the staff person would be likely to include unnecessary information. The manager would have to wade through pages looking for the relevant material, which, despite the best efforts of the report's author, might be missing.

COMPUTER MAPPING   A computer application that is helping marketers identify and learn about potential customers is computer mapping. Mapping software (at its most sophisticated called a "geographical information system," or GIS) combines various kinds of demographic data with the ability to draw and manipulate maps. Thus, the user can draw a map showing average income levels of a county, then zoom closer to look at particular towns in more detail. Seeing the information on a map can be more useful than merely reading tables of numbers. At PepsiCo, a GIS enables marketers to analyze traffic patterns and consumer demographics to identify the best sites for new Taco Bell and Pizza Hut restaurants.[50]

Two leading sellers of GIS software are Environmental Systems Research Institute and Intergraph. For $15,000 to $45,000, Dun & Bradstreet sells software that produces maps of business and consumer characteristics.[51] Other suppliers of such software target smaller users. MapInfo, a program sold by a company of the same name, starts at $1,000 and breaks the United States down into individual street maps. With demographics such as Census Bureau data, the user can create detailed maps of various consumer characteristics such as income and ethnicity.[52]

VIRTUAL REALITY   Another computer capability that is being applied to marketing research is virtual reality. This technology enables users wearing special goggles and gloves to see and manipulate objects in three dimensions, as if the objects were actually there. Virtual reality enables marketers to display potential new products or product displays without going to the expense of physically building all the possibilities under consideration. MarketWare Corporation has developed Visionary Shopper software to use in consumer shopping experiments. The subject can remove products from the shelf, examine labels, and react to such variables as price or packaging by choosing whether to place the items in a shopping cart. The software developers hope that the results of experiments using Visionary Shopper will be more realistic than answers to a survey.[53]

technical-market research
Research incorporating customers by demonstrating a product on a computer screen and asking customers to evaluate it.

A major application of virtual reality to marketing research is known as **technical-market research**.[54] This type of research incorporates customers into the process of product design by demonstrating the product on a computer screen and asking customers to evaluate it. The software shows the product in three dimensions, models how it will behave, and quickly demonstrates how changes in the product's design will affect performance. This process enables an organization to anticipate customer needs that the customers have not yet envisioned because they are unfamiliar with the potential of the organization's technologies. General Motors uses this technology to test consumers' reactions to being in the front seat of a new car in the showroom of a dealership.[55]

When companies use technical-market research, they bring together the efforts of personnel in marketing and in research and development (R&D). Such teamwork enables the organization to use the full potential of its technological expertise in serving the interests of its customers. Furthermore, teamwork between marketing and R&D enables the organization to move quickly from concept to distribution of the product. In the tire industry, such a collaboration led to development of the all-season tire, which frees customers from having their tires changed every winter and spring. In addition, Goodyear Tire & Rubber Company has used technical-market research to work with automobile manufacturers to develop a variety of tire improvements.[56]

Technical-market research begins when a cross-functional team including members from marketing and R&D establishes goals and plans the research. Then, com-

TABLE 7.5	ACTIVITY	EXAMPLES
Researchers' Own Perceptions of the Four Most Difficult Ethical Problems They Face*	Maintaining their research integrity	Deliberately withholding information, falsifying figures, altering research results, misusing statistics, ignoring pertinent data
	Treating outside clients fairly	Passing hidden charges to clients, overlooking violations of the project requirements when subcontracting parts of the project
	Maintaining research confidentiality	Sharing information among subsidiaries in the same corporation, using background data developed in a previous project to reduce the cost of a current project
	Balancing marketing and social considerations	Conducting research for companies that produce products hazardous to one's health or research that improves the effectiveness of advertising to children

*Based on responses to the question, "In all professions (e.g., law, medicine, education, accounting, marketing, etc.), managers are exposed to at least some situations that pose a moral or ethical problem. Would you briefly describe the job situation that poses the most difficult ethical or moral problem for you?"

Source: Developed from information in Shelby D. Hunt, Lawrence B. Chonko, and James B. Wilcox, "Ethical Problems of Marketing Researchers," *Journal of Marketing Research,* 21 (August 1984): pp. 309–324.

bining information about customer needs and perceptions with possible product attributes, team members develop computer models and identify target markets. Engineers and marketing researchers together interview targeted customers, using computers to show them what the potential product will look like and how it will perform, with and without modifications suggested by the customers. Further work on the computer enables the team to develop a prototype, which can be used to complete the product development process as described in Chapter 11.

Ethical Considerations

Information is so important to gaining a competitive edge that it can be tempting to overstep ethical boundaries to get additional information. Table 7.5 summarizes some areas in which marketing researchers have said they most often face ethical problems. Despite the temptation to behave unethically, marketers must consider the consequences of their actions for the parties involved.

In many cases, there are no firm standards for deciding whether a particular practice is ethical. However, several questions can help the marketer decide:[57]

- Is the action or anticipated action arbitrary or capricious? Does it unfairly single out an individual or group?
- Does the action or anticipated action violate the moral or legal rights of any individual or group?
- Does the action or anticipated action conform to accepted moral standards?
- Are there alternative courses of action that are less likely to cause actual or potential harm?

When the answers to these questions suggest that a course of action is unethical, it is up to the researcher to decide whether the benefits of the action are really worth

losing clients' and research participants' trust and respect for the individual researcher, his or her employer, and the marketing research profession in general. (For a marketing research issue with ethical implications, refer again to the "You Decide" box on stocking supermarket shelves.)

DECEIT AND FRAUD IN MARKETING RESEARCH

Suppose your boss asks you to do a survey of consumer interest in a potential new product that you know your boss is enthusiastic about. In fact, your boss has been speaking highly of this product to the company's executives. Do you care what the results of the survey will be? Most likely, you hope that the results will support the boss's viewpoint, since that will please him or her. What if the results are ambiguous or show a distinct lack of interest in the new product? At such times, it can be tempting to make some "adjustments" so that the data produce the desired result. Or when time is running short and many research subjects have failed to respond, it can be tempting to compromise the integrity of the survey in order to produce a report that makes the research effort look complete. Bowing to such temptations, of course, would be unethical. Users of marketing information depend on the researcher to provide accurate information so that they can make informed decisions.

In other situations, researchers may be tempted to misrepresent the truth to participants. One such temptation is making false claims about the research project. Figure 7.9 shows a particularly egregious example of such deception. Or the researcher may promise subjects that their responses will be anonymous so that they will participate without fear of injury or embarrassment. Secretly marking the responses and later determining the identity of the subjects breaks that promise.

Another kind of false claim is to ask people to participate in a research project that is really just a front for a sales pitch. Such experiences lead people to distrust marketing researchers and to avoid participating in research projects in the future. This poses a real problem for marketing researchers. Over the last decade, the proportion of people

FIGURE 7.10

Reasons Given for Refusing to Participate in Research

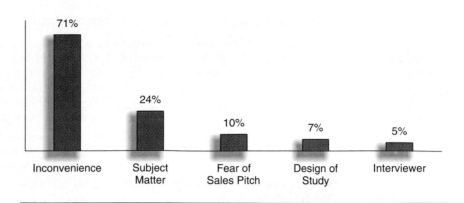

Source: Walker Industry Image Study, 10th ed. (Indianapolis, Ind.: Walker Research & Analysis, 1992), p. 3.

contacted who have refused to participate in a research study has more than doubled, to over 30 percent.[58] Figure 7.10 summarizes their reasons for refusing.

INVASION OF PRIVACY

If research is not handled carefully, it can invade people's privacy. In planning a research effort, the researcher should identify ways in which privacy may be invaded and seek to minimize the problem. For example, participants are likely to feel their privacy has been invaded if they haven't fully given consent to participate. Thus, it may be an invasion of privacy for a researcher to observe consumers shopping without first asking their permission. The situation becomes even more sensitive if the researcher videotapes the consumers or if the researcher is observing the purchase of items such as condoms that consumers consider private. Two ways to minimize this type of invasion of privacy are to post notices stating that researchers are observing customers on the premises and to approach each consumer after the observation and ask for permission to use the data gathered from observing him or her.

A related issue involves industrial espionage, or efforts to secretly determine what a competitor is doing. Some ways of learning about a competitor, such as reading magazine articles or taking apart and studying the competitor's existing products, are considered acceptable. Some organizations will even let competitors visit to benchmark areas of operation that are not considered proprietary. However, researchers should avoid collecting data through deceptive practices such as having a researcher pose as an employee of a competing organization. Likewise, it is unethical for a researcher to share with a client information the researcher collected for or about a competitor of the client.

Implications for Global Marketing

The differences among countries make marketing research especially important when the marketer considers targeting consumers or organizations in other countries. Global marketers generally follow the standard research tactic of starting with secondary data and following up with primary research as needed. They use secondary sources to study such dimensions of the marketing environment as laws, demograph-

TABLE 7.6 **Selected Information Sources: Secondary Data on International Markets**	**INFORMATION SOURCE**	**TYPES OF DATA**
	The Export Connection, a National Trade Databank service of the U.S. Department of Commerce (Washington, D.C.)	Monthly series of CD-ROM disks containing data from 15 U.S. government agencies, including marketing research reports, information about specific countries and their economies, and a listing of foreign importers of U.S. products
	Global Market Surveys	Detailed surveys for given industries such as graphics, computers, medical equipment, industrial equipment
	Dun & Bradstreet's *Principal International Business*	Names, addresses, number of employees, products produced, and chief executive officer, up to 6 SIC classifications (4-digit) for each organization; over 144,000 business units classified by 4-digit SIC and alphabetical order
	Moody's International Manual	Company histories, descriptions of business, financial statistics, management personnel
	Overseas Business Reports	Monthly reports provide information for marketing to specific countries (e.g., "Marketing in Pakistan," "Marketing in Nigeria")
	The Exporter's Guide to Federal Resources for Small Business (Washington, D.C.: U.S. Government Printing Office)	Reference guide to export assistance available from the U.S. government
	Automated Trade Locator Assistance System (district offices of the Small Business Administration)	Results of current marketing research about world markets
	Small Business Foundation of America, export opportunity hotline: 800–243–7232	Answers to questions from small businesses interested in exporting
	Hotline sponsored by AT&T and seven other organizations: 800–USA–XPORT	Free exporter's kit and data on 50 industries and 78 countries
	International trade fairs (sponsored by many industry organizations and national governments, including the U.S. Small Business Administration)	Products and needs of existing and potential buyers and competitors from around the world

Source: Giordano A. Chiaruttini, "Brave New World," *Entrepreneur,* May 1993, p. 156; George Gendron, "FYI: Foreign Affairs," *Inc.,* June 1993, p. 14; "Going Global: Canada," supplement to Inc., June 1993; Aimee Stern, "Do You Know What They Want?" *International Business,* March 1993, pp. 102–103; Robert W. Hass, *Industrial Marketing Management* (Boston: PWS–Kent Publishing Company, 1989), p. 435.

ics, and culture. They also explore product needs in the countries they study. Table 7.6 lists some of the many sources of information about international markets.

CULTURAL DIFFERENCES

The basic principles for conducting primary research are the same for international as for domestic markets. However, the researcher needs to be aware of differences among countries that should affect research design.[59] For example, in Latin America, Russia, and China, telephone interviews are impractical because too few people have phones. But in Saudi Arabia, door-to-door interviewing is illegal. To interview Saudi males, the researcher can meet with businessmen in their offices; to interview females, the researcher can ask to be introduced to businessmen's wives and their friends.

Researchers must be aware of cultural differences in communication styles. By mainstream U.S. standards, Italians, Spaniards, and Latin Americans may seem to be effusive and to overstate their answers. By the same standards, Germans and the English may understate their enthusiasm, and Asians may say what they think the interviewer wants to hear. In China, Gallup China Ltd. found that subjects were brought up short by follow-up questions asking why they had answered a previous question the way they had. After a pause, most subjects would reply, "Because it's true, that's why."[60]

 In spite of the challenges, Procter & Gamble has effectively used marketing research to help it enter the Russian market. For example, it hired local researchers to conduct door-to-door interviews about hygiene and household cleaning practices. P&G learned that Russians typically store detergent in their small bathrooms, so the company made sure its detergent boxes could withstand water damage. P&G also gave samples to hundreds of Russian consumers, then interviewed them two weeks later, asking about the products and P&G's advertising. Among other information, the company learned Russians prefer that products be labeled in English alone, because they associate this with higher quality.[61]

INTERNATIONAL MARKETING RESEARCHERS

 Fortunately for small or inexperienced marketers, some research firms are set up to handle international assignments. These include Research International (based in New York City), Burke International (New York City), Starch INRA Hooper Inc. (Mamaroneck, New York), SRG International (North White Plains, New York), and A. C. Nielsen (Chicago). Other, smaller firms specialize in particular regions. For example, OmniTrak Group, based in Honolulu, specializes in Asia.

Marketing research is the function that links consumers, organizational buyers, and the general public to marketers. Thus, the information that marketing research generates is a vital tool for marketers. Marketers need more than just data—facts and statistics—they need useful information that shows trends and relationships. To make sense of the information they receive, marketers can have it organized into a marketing database.

Marketers can get information from internal sources (sales figures, accounting and inventory data) or external sources (business publications, research services, customer surveys). They can collect primary data through their own surveys or observations, including benchmarking. They can obtain secondary data from a multitude of published sources.

To be effective, marketing research begins with formulation of the problem. Next, the careful researcher creates a research design, using exploratory, descriptive, or causal research. Then the researcher collects data through observation or surveys. The next step is analyzing and interpreting data. Finally, the researcher prepares and submits a research report. When managers or other decision makers review the final research report, they must evaluate whether the results meet their needs.

Computer technology has made it easier to organize data into a management information system (MIS). A more sophisticated approach is a marketing decision support system (MDSS), which brings together three types of software: database management, model base management, and a dialog system. Another application of technology is that marketers today can engage in technical-market research by demonstrating a product on a computer screen while asking customers to evaluate it.

There are many ethical considerations in marketing research. These include deceit, fraud, and invasion of privacy. Marketers must evaluate whether their actions are ethical, and act accordingly.

When marketers consider serving customers in other countries, they especially need marketing research. Global marketers usually start by using secondary sources to scan the marketing environment. Then they follow up with primary research. The research design may have to be modified to reflect differences in values, customs, and technology. Many organizations have their international marketing research handled by firms that specialize in that type of work.

KEY TERMS AND CONCEPTS

marketing research (p. 194)

data (p. 195)

information (p. 195)

marketing database (p. 196)

single-source data (p. 199)

primary data (p. 200)

statistical inference (p. 201)

probability sampling (p. 201)

benchmarking (p. 201)

secondary data (p. 203)

research design (p. 206)

hypothesis (p. 206)

exploratory research (p. 206)

descriptive research (p. 207)

causal research (p. 207)

experiment (p. 207)

test marketing (p. 208)

observation (p. 211)

survey (p. 212)

mall intercept (p. 214)

focus group interview (p. 214)

in-home interview (p. 215)

coding (p. 216)

tabulating (p. 216)

marketing information system (MIS) (p. 218)

marketing decision support system (MDSS) (p. 218)

technical-market research (p. 220)

REVIEW AND DISCUSSION QUESTIONS

1. Why is marketing research important to organizations that are dedicated to total quality?

2. What are some of the complaints marketers often have about the kinds of marketing information they receive?

3. If you were a marketer in a company that was too small to hire an outside marketing research firm and your company was developing a new line of "healthful" dog food, what internal and external sources of information might you use to conduct your own marketing research?

4. Why is it important for the marketing problem to be clearly formulated before marketing research begins? What is the role of exploratory research in this regard?

5. If you were a marketer for a developer that was considering building a new shopping mall, how would you use observation as part of your marketing research?

6. Suppose you are conducting research for a movie distributor by preparing a survey that asks for demographic information about moviegoers in India.
   a. What types of data might be useful?
   b. What are some issues related to the marketing environment that you might need to consider?

7. What are the three types of software necessary for a marketing decision support system (MDSS), and what do they do?

8. Suppose you were asked to conduct a survey of potential users of a walk-in health care facility. What questions would you ask yourself to make sure your survey—and the information it provides you—is ethical?

Chapter Project
Design an Observational Research Project

Suppose you have been hired by the developer of a new shopping mall to determine who has buying influence in a family. Your hypothesis is that children exert quite a bit of buying influence on their parents. Using what you've learned in this chapter as well as your own imagination, formulate a research project in which you observe the behavior of parents and their children as they make purchasing decisions in a shopping mall.

Note characteristics of their behavior on your survey. For instance, who pays for products that children want? Do children argue with their parents over purchases? How much time does the family spend in a single store? Present your findings in writing and/or to the class.

Case
Chemical Bank

Every time you use your ATM card, open a checking account, or respond to a mailing from your bank, the marketing staff at the bank learns something about you. The marketing objectives of such information typically include maintaining a long-term relationship with you as a customer by satisfying your banking needs. Chemical Bank in New York has elevated this sort of marketing research nearly to an art.

With the deregulation of the financial services industry in the 1980s, banks began to compete more vigorously with each other for customers. To do so successfully, they needed to learn more about their customers. Thomas C. Werbe, vice president of marketing information services at Chemical Bank, recalls, "In early 1987 Chemical had no centralized marketing database." But now, under Werbe's direction, the bank has the capacity to collect and store millions of pieces of data about its customers.

Chemical Bank obtains data about customer banking behavior through branch and ATM transactions, as well as through responses to mailings and telemarketing. The bank stores the data in three categories: (1) by the *type* of account (such as checking or savings); (2) by *customer*, defined as anyone who has a financial relationship with the bank; and (3) under a single *household ID* for all customers having the same last name and address.

Chemical Bank also gathers and stores demographic data about its customers. To obtain the data, the bank matches customer information from internal sources with data from external sources. For example, motor vehicle registrations and county real estate records provide information about customers' assets and where they live. Based on customers' addresses, the information system can make predictions about values and life style.

Chemical Bank's information system also helps analyze response to direct mailings. It does so by answering a variety of questions: How many people responded? How many responses were converted to sales? How much did each sale cost the company? How much profit was generated?

The marketing information system at Chemical Bank is designed so that other departments besides marketing can use it. The result is cross-functional cooperation. Explains Werbe, "The branch people and the marketing people are working much closer together, and I think that one of the reasons that they are is because we have information like this." However, the marketing group oversees the design, function, and application of the system. In addition, information that might violate a customer's privacy is not available to all employees. Thus, employees at the bank's branches have access to only about half the information about customers that Werbe and his staff do.

As for the qualities of the marketing staff that works with the marketing database, Werbe observes that they are young, enthusiastic professionals. "You try and hire young people that are pretty bright who have an interest in this and then you bring them in and you try to retain them because they're pretty valuable people and will be more so in the 1990s." He also notes that the system can empower marketers but requires that they bring varied skills to their jobs: "You really need the marketing person who understands the technical aspects and also understands the applications as well. . . . It's a whole new career for people that can translate the needs between marketing applications and the technical side."

QUESTIONS

1. How does the information system described in this case help Chemical Bank serve its customers more completely? As a bank customer, do you think such a system would improve the services you receive? Explain.

2. Might large databases such as this violate customers' privacy? Explain. What steps might a bank take to prevent invasion of privacy?

3. How might Chemical Bank use a focus group interview to obtain additional information for its database?

Source: Thomas C. Werbe, "Chemical Bank's Marketing Database," presentation at American Marketing Association's Marketing Research Conference, September 23–26, 1990.

CHAPTER 8

Consumer Behavior

LEARNING OBJECTIVES

After completing this chapter, you should be able to:

1. Identify societal influences on consumer behavior, including those of culture, subculture, and social class.

2. Describe how reference groups affect consumer behavior.

3. Explain how perceptions, motivations, attitudes, and life-style influence consumer behavior.

4. Describe the basic steps in the decision-making process of consumers.

Creating Customer Value
MasterCard

"MasterCard. It's not just a credit card. It's smart money." The new MasterCard slogan is a long way from its 1980s "Master the Moment" and an even greater distance from Visa's "Visa. It's everywhere you want to be" and Amercian Express's "Membership has its privileges." And the '90s MasterCard advertisements are set in the most mundane of shopping spots—the supermarket. What's going on? Aren't credit cards for those big-ticket, luxury items like CD players and diamond rings? Or for use on vacation, so you don't have to carry cash? Of course, but the marketers at MasterCard (and its competitors) want consumers to think of credit cards in a new way.

Alex W. ("Pete") Hart was drafted from MasterCard's board of directors to head up the organization at the tail end of the glitzy 1980s. The economy was beginning to slide, along with consumer attitudes toward spending. Hart had to change the way MasterCard did business and change the way consumers thought about MasterCard. Unlike his predecessor, he threw open his door to input from employees and MasterCard member banks and businesses. He delegated more of MasterCard's processing to outside companies. And he formed a team of 35 people to develop programs to entice nontraditional businesses such as dentists, fast-food restaurants, and supermarkets to accept credit cards.

To smooth the way for fast-food restaurants, the team instituted a computer system that could accept small purchases without a signature. It made an agreement in California whereby people could renew their driver's licenses by phone with a MasterCard. Team members are working on making it possible to charge speeding tickets with the card. They've also pioneered "co-branding" programs with non-

bank companies such as AT&T and General Motors, which are the fastest growing segment of the credit card market.

As of 1993, 10,000 supermarkets accepted credit cards, up from 800 in 1991. MasterCard provided the stores with discounts on card terminals and assisted with marketing. Supermarkets could also issue co-branded MasterCard accounts tied to a frequent-shopper discount program.

Such efforts are designed to get the consumer to view the MasterCard as an efficient way to organize personal finances and keep track of household spending, including grocery bills. Hart and his team want consumers to use the card as a daily tool—one that's better than cash or checks—rather than save it just for luxury purchases. He knows consumers are looking for value, and he wants them to think of their cards that way: "When I came here, I said the watchword is value."

As you read this chapter, you'll learn more about consumer buying behavior. Think about your own buying habits. Would you take your credit card to the supermarket?

Source: Saul Hansell, "The Man Who Charged Up MasterCard," *New York Times,* March 7, 1993, sec. 3, pp. 1, 8.

Put It Into Practice

USE YOUR POWERS OF OBSERVATION

Marketers are constantly observing consumers in a variety of ways to determine consumer buying behavior and how they can influence it. For a few hours, do some observing of your own; tune your own powers of observation to who buys what. Go to a department store, shopping mall, or downtown shopping district and take a notebook.

Watch people. Who goes into the expensive fashion boutique? Who stops to look in the pet store window? Who eats lunch at the diner? Who attends the movie matinee? Who browses in the home furnishings shop? Note such characteristics as apparent age group, ethnic or racial group, sex, and social class. Do they appear to be purchasing things or just window shopping? Are they shopping alone or with friends or family? Do they seem to be discussing purchases together? Do the behaviors you observe differ according to the characteristics you have noted?

Jot down as many details as you can observe. Later, compare notes with classmates. Simply by sharpening your powers of observation, you can learn about the consumers you want to reach as a marketer.

Chapter Overview

consumer
Someone who buys goods and services for his or her own or for household use.

The ultimate customers that MasterCard markets to and needs to understand are consumers. As described in Chapter 1, a **consumer** is someone who buys goods and services for his or her own or for household use, rather than to make something to sell. Many marketers target consumers, offering an enormous array of products from financial planning to answering machines to snacks. When an organization's target markets include consumers, its marketers need to understand why consumers buy certain products and not others.

consumer behavior
The way in which external and internal forces shape people's exchange activities.

To obtain this understanding, marketers study **consumer behavior**, or the way in which external and internal forces shape people's exchange activities. As implied by the definition, the study of consumer behavior is concerned with external forces, such as family and culture; internal forces, such as attitudes; and behavior in the form of participation in exchange activities. This chapter introduces these three aspects of consumer behavior, by discussing the consumer's place as a member of society, the consumer as an individual, and the process by which consumers make buying decisions.

The Consumer in Society

"Think for yourself." "Do your own thing." Many of us grew up hearing such sayings that uphold the importance of the individual. But no matter how much we emphasize the individual, the fact is that each person is influenced by various groups. Most notable are the broad groupings of culture, subculture, and social class, as well as a person's reference groups, including the family. ("Put It into Practice" addresses the importance of observing these and other consumer traits.)

CULTURE, SUBCULTURE, AND SOCIAL CLASS

Each of us is a member of a culture, various subcultures, and a social class. Those groups influence our behavior by providing direct messages about specific activities. For example, someone whose family and friends are football fans is likely to hear that sport described in glowing terms and is likely to buy tickets to football games or to watch them on television. Culture, subculture, and social class also influence con-

core values

TABLE 8.1

Summary of Mainstream U.S. Cultural Values

VALUE	GENERAL FEATURES	RELEVANCE TO MARKETING
Achievement and success	Hard work is good; success flows from hard work	Acts as a justification for acquisition of goods ("You deserve it")
Activity	Keeping busy is healthy and natural	Stimulates interest in products that are time savers and enhance leisure-time activities
Efficiency and practicality	Admiration of things that solve problems (e.g., save time and effort)	Stimulates purchase of products that function well and save time
Progress	People can improve themselves; tomorrow should be better	Stimulates desire for new products that fulfill unsatisfied needs; acceptance of products that claim to be "new" or "improved"
Material comfort	"The good life"	Fosters acceptance of convenience and luxury products that make life more enjoyable
Individualism	Being one's self (e.g., self-reliance, self-interest, and self-esteem)	Stimulates acceptance of customized or unique products that enable a person to "express his or her own personality"
Freedom	Freedom of choice	Fosters interest in wide product lines and differentiated products
External conformity	Uniformity of observable behavior; desire to be accepted	Stimulates interest in products that are used or owned by others in the same social group
Humanitarianism	Caring for others, particularly the underdog	Stimulates patronage of firms that compete with market leaders
Youthfulness	A state of mind that stresses being young at heart or appearing young	Stimulates acceptance of products that provide the illusion of maintaining or fostering youth
Fitness and health	Caring about one's body, including the desire to be physically fit and healthy	Stimulates acceptance of food products, activities, and equipment perceived to maintain or increase physical fitness

Source: Leon G. Schiffman/Leslie Lazar Kanuck, *Consumer Behavior,* 4th ed. © 1991, p. 424. Reprinted by permission of Prentice-Hall, Inc., Englewood Cliffs, New Jersey.

sumer behavior indirectly by helping to shape the values and attitudes that influence purchase decisions. For example, a teenager whose social class values planning ahead and taking charge of one's life will believe it prudent to take college preparatory classes in high school and to save money for college.

culture
The learned values and behaviors shared by a society and designed to increase the probability of the society's survival.

CULTURE   One of the most important means by which a society influences the behavior of individuals is through its culture. A **culture** is "the complex of learned values and behaviors that are shared by a society and are designed to increase the probability of the society's survival."[1] In mainstream U.S. culture, people learn to sympathize with the underdog, to dress up for a job interview, and to blow out the candles after our friends have sung "Happy Birthday." The society conveys information about such values and behaviors through the family and through religious and educational institutions.

core values
Values that are pervasive and enduring.

    A particularly important component of a culture is its **core values**, the ones that are pervasive and enduring. Chapter 2 mentioned some core values of mainstream U.S. culture. Table 8.1 provides a more complete listing.

TABLE 8.2
Types of Subcultures

DEMOGRAPHIC CHARACTERISTIC	EXAMPLES OF SUBCULTURES
Age	Adolescents, young adults, middle aged, elderly
Religion	Jewish, Catholic, Mormon, Buddhist, Muslim
Race	African-American, Caucasian, Oriental
Income level	Affluent, middle income, poor, destitute
Nationality	French, Malaysian, Australian, Canadian
Gender	Female, male
Family type	Single parent, divorced/no kids, two parents/kids
Occupation	Mechanic, accountant, priest, professor, clerk
Geographic region	New England, Southwest, Midwest
Community	Rural, small town, suburban, city

Source: J. Paul Peter and Jerry C. Olson, *Consumer Behavior and Marketing Strategy,* 3d ed. (Burr Ridge, Ill.: Irwin, 1993), p. 469.

To know the core values of the cultures they are interested in serving, marketers must research those cultures, rather than assuming that the values listed in Table 8.1 are universal. Such investigation would show, for example, that as many adults in recent years have taken on the responsibilities of owning a home and raising children, they have come to place a lower value on buying products for their status. They are more interested in getting their money's worth in terms of product performance.[2] Marketers interested in this group must therefore make it clear why their products are a good buy.

Value differences can be especially notable in international marketing, as Procter & Gamble learned when it began marketing diapers in China and Korea. In those countries, P&G offers white unisex diapers, rather than the pink and blue versions popular in the United States, because consumers there don't want to show (by buying pink) that their child is a daughter.[3]

subculture
A segment within a culture that shares values and patterns of behavior that distinguish it from those of the overall culture.

SUBCULTURES   As described in Chapter 3, the population of the United States has been becoming more and more diverse. One way to understand the diverse groups is in terms of various subcultures. A **subculture** is a segment "within a culture that shares distinguishing values and patterns of behavior that differ from those of the overall culture."[4] Table 8.2 shows some ways in which the population is divided into subcultures.

These categories apply outside of the United States as well. Western Europe and the United States both have fast-growing Muslim communities, where many of the values are conservative and family oriented. Clearly, given the degree of diversity that exists, this chapter can cover only a few subcultures of particular importance to marketers.

Because each subculture has its own set of values and desirable behaviors, a marketer might find that it can better meet the needs of particular subcultures than of the entire culture of a nation or region. Or the marketer may wish to adjust the marketing mix for various subcultures—say, distributing through different types of stores in Hispanic neighborhoods or using different advertising media to reach younger adults.

The U.S. subcultures representing various racial and ethnic groups are of particular interest to marketers because of their size. By 1990, almost one-quarter of the people in the United States were members of racial and ethnic minorities. That proportion could increase to almost one-third by 2030 and to one-half by 2050.[5]

In describing these groups, it is important to keep in mind that marketers can identify only *patterns* of values and behavior; the descriptions do not apply to every individual within a subculture. Furthermore, because a person is a member of more than

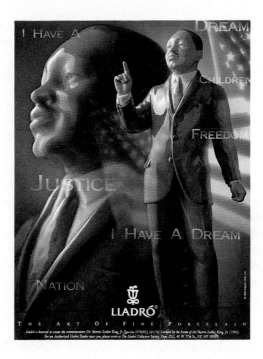

Recognizing the African-American consumer, Lladró has created this porcelain figurine of Dr. Martin Luther King, Jr., and advertises in Ebony magazine.

one subculture—for example, a young Jewish Easterner, a middle-aged Mexican-American Catholic—the degree to which each person is influenced by each subculture will vary. Thus, in reading the following descriptions of subcultures, bear in mind that these are overall patterns that do not apply uniformly to all members of the subculture.

European-American Consumers The majority of people living in the United States today are of European descent. However, European-Americans do not typically think of themselves as a subculture. If they think of themselves as part of an ethnic group, it is more likely to be in terms of their roots in a particular country, say, Ireland or Italy. Because European-Americans are the dominant group, their values and practices tend to match the overall values and practices of the U.S. culture. This makes it easy to ignore or forget the fact that the European-American subculture is, in fact, a subculture. But, to use a broad example, European-American teenagers would typically listen to different music and dress differently to go to a party than would their counterparts from other U.S. subcultures.

The majority of marketers are part of this subculture that tends not to recognize itself as a subculture, so it is not surprising that marketing strategies often ignore the importance of subcultures. The most direct effect is that marketing efforts often satisfy only a portion of the customers they are intended to serve. Providing quality to all members of the organization's target market requires that marketers learn about the different subcultures of the countries they serve.

African-American Consumers The largest racial or ethnic minority subculture in the United States is African-Americans, with 30 million people in 9.3 million households.[6] While a relatively large share of African-Americans are poor, about two-thirds are not,[7] and in total black consumers spend an impressive $172 billion a year.[8] Blacks tend to spend a higher proportion of their income than whites do, partly because they have less long-term debt and partly because, research shows, they worry less about economic uncertainty.[9]

Until recently, what little consumer research had been done on the buying patterns of blacks and whites showed mostly similarities between the two groups when differences in socioeconomic status were accounted for.[10] However, marketers have begun to research this group more carefully and have noted some distinctive characteristics. A study consisting of over 1,000 in-home interviews found that nearly half of blacks say they are "not too happy," more than three times the rate among nonblacks, a pattern that did not change when researchers adjusted for age and economic status.[11] This is significant to marketers because it suggests there are attitudes held in common by blacks, regardless of their class. Other differences uncovered by the survey are that African-Americans are more often willing to put up with a boring job in exchange for good pay, rely more heavily than others on advertising when they make product choices, and place higher value than others on religion, sense of duty, self-confidence, and individuality.[12]

In terms of consumer behavior, African-Americans spend more on clothing and personal-care products than the general population and make the majority of their charitable donations to their churches.[13] Blacks tend to watch television and listen to the radio more than whites, and a smaller percentage reads newspapers.[14] African-Americans are drawn to products and advertising that appeal to black pride and reflect their heritage. Thus, marketers do well to learn about and respect this subculture.

Two companies that have done just that are Johnson Publishing Company, publisher of *Ebony* and other magazines targeting African-Americans, and Spiegel, the giant catalog retailer. The two have entered into an agreement in which Spiegel uses ads in *Ebony* and the *Ebony* subscriber list to promote and distribute a catalog called *E Style,* which offers clothing and accessories designed for black women. The clothing features dramatic design, warm and bright colors designed to flatter darker skin tones, and some items with an African flair. There's also a variety of hats, a fashion accessory purchased much more often by black women than by women of other subcultures. Research into the needs of the target market included not only focus groups but also measurements of 1,300 black women to ensure that the clothing would properly fit the proportions of these customers.[15]

Hispanic Consumers With the largest numerical growth among racial and ethnic groups in the United States, Hispanics are expected to become the biggest ethnic minority group in the United States by the middle of the next century.[16] Much of the future growth is expected to occur in California, Florida, New York, Texas, and the Southwest.[17]

This subculture includes people who trace their roots to Spanish-speaking countries, including Mexico, Puerto Rico, Cuba, Central and South America, and the Dominican Republic. By far the largest Hispanic group in the United States is Mexican-Americans. Because Hispanic Americans come from so many different nations, they actually represent many subcultures and even have language differences. They often think of their ethnic identity in terms of their national origin, rather than the broad umbrella of "Hispanic" or "Latino." However, these groups do share some common values, such as a strong family orientation.

In general, the socioeconomic status of Hispanic Americans is related to immigration.[18] About one-quarter of Hispanics in the United States are poor, but these are mostly recent immigrants. Those who have been in the United States for several generations are typically much better off economically. The Census Bureau found that in 1989, 42 percent of Hispanics owned or were buying a home, for example. Furthermore, although the Spanish language is the basis for classifying Hispanic Americans as a single subculture, by their third generation in the United States, most

FIGURE 8.1

Social Classes in the United States

Upper Americans: Range from high-income elite to managers and professionals; value high quality, prestige, spending with good taste.
Middle Class: Average-pay, usually white-collar workers who live on the "better side of town," try to do what's proper, and emulate Upper Americans.
Working Class: Average-pay, blue-collar workers who depend heavily on relatives, have relatively limited horizons, and are concerned with pursuing ease of labor and leisure.
Lower Americans: May be poor or just above poverty; may or may not be employed; may or may not seek instant gratification.

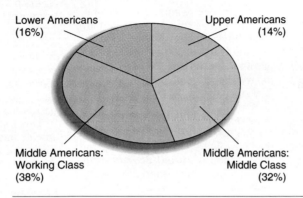

Lower Americans (16%)

Upper Americans (14%)

Middle Americans: Working Class (38%)

Middle Americans: Middle Class (32%)

Source: Adapted from Richard P. Coleman, "The Continuing Significance of Social Class to Marketing," *Journal of Consumer Research* (December 1983):, pp. 265–280.

speak only English.[19] Presumably, then, while Spanish-language advertising would reach many Hispanics, it would not be appropriate for marketing upscale products.

Asian-American Consumers While Asian-Americans constitute the smallest of the three ethnic groups described here (6 million households), they are an important subculture to marketers, especially because their average educational attainment and household income are the highest among all groups, including whites.[20] This group is also experiencing the fastest rate of growth, having increased 108 percent during the 1980s.[21] Most Asian-Americans live in the West, particularly in California, and in urban areas.[22]

Like Hispanic Americans, Asian-Americans are highly diverse, tracing their ancestry to many different countries, including China, Japan, the Philippines, and Korea. This variety is made even more challenging by the fact that recent immigrants speak many different languages. However, some common traits include hard work, strong family ties, and a high value placed on education.[23]

SOCIAL CLASSES   In spite of the value placed on equality in the United States, consumers here as well as in other countries are of different social classes. Social class refers to people who have not only similar income levels, but also comparable wealth, skill, and power. The most reliable way to rate these is by occupation. Thus, a surgeon, a sales manager, and a data-entry clerk are considered to be members of different social classes. (The social class of a college student has more to do with the occupation of the student's parents and the student's career plans than with his or her part-time job flipping hamburgers.)

While there is no hard-and-fast rule for identifying social classes in the United States, marketing analysts typically divide the U.S. marketplace into the class groupings shown in Figure 8.1. These groupings show not only income differences, but also

social class
A grouping of people with similar income levels, wealth, skill, and power.

Marketing Movers & Shakers

RUTH OWADES OF CALYX & COROLLA

Ruth Owades' business depends on feelings. She's the owner of Calyx & Corolla, an elegant mail-order florist. She understands her customers, the way they feel about flowers, and the message they want those flowers to convey. "It's an emotional purchase," admits Owades.

Calyx & Corolla is not Owades' first business venture; rather, it follows her successful entry into mail-order entrepreneurship, Gardener's Eden, which she sold to Williams Sonoma in 1982. But Owades pioneered a new way of selling an ancient product that had to stay fresh. She wanted to offer consumers flowers straight from the farm (and thus fresher than those found at local florists), so she convinced both growers and Federal Express to team up with her. Federal Express made special arrangements for handling the perishable flowers, and the growers found a way to handle orders instantly.

Still, Owades had to consider who her customers would be and what their attitudes toward flowers were. She learned that Americans spend only half as much as Europeans do on flowers. She also found that Americans don't often treat themselves to flowers; they use flowers as gifts or messages of congratulations, sympathy, and the like. But those attitudes and habits are changing. Owades says that now "Americans are learning to enjoy flowers and learn more about them." To satisfy this curiosity (and drum up more interest), Calyx & Corolla includes a detailed care card in every shipment, which has a toll-free service line providing advice. There's even a separate number for the Plant Doctor, who answers questions from puzzled or concerned customers.

In consideration of who her customers are, Owades notes that price is very important. For instance, business customers like to give flowers because they create the right impression without appearing to be extravagant. On the other hand, someone with more extravagent tastes can order exotic flowers and containers that range from baskets to garden buckets to unusual glass and pottery vases.

The catalog itself reflects an upscale, tasteful image that acknowledges the emotional nature of the purchase. "Long-stemmed roses are an unforgettable expression of love or appreciation, and our roses are the loveliest and longest-lasting you will find," boasts one entry. "They are cultivated by the world's finest growers and are air-shipped in bud, surrounded by fluffy white baby's breath." You can order these roses arranged in a monogrammed, silver-plated champagne cooler. It's a lovely way to say, "I'm sorry."

Sources: "Ruth Owades—A Budding Entrepreneur," *Sales & Marketing Management,* June 1992, pp. 32–33; Calyx & Corolla catalog, Early Spring 1993, p. 5.

differences in values and behavior. For example, people in the lower classes tend to have a relatively strong focus on the short term, to think in relatively concrete terms, and to be relatively emotional in their decision making. Consumers in the upper classes, by contrast, tend to be more abstract and future oriented in their thinking.[24]

Given differences such as these, people of different social classes tend to make different choices regarding their clothing, home furnishings, use of leisure time, choice of media, and patterns of saving and spending. If marketers determine that their product is most likely to appeal to members of certain classes, they can develop a mix that takes into account some of these differences. An example is the advertising of luxury goods on classical radio stations. (For another example of appealing to an upscale market, see "Marketing Movers & Shakers" about Ruth Owades.)

REFERENCE GROUPS

Besides sharing the values of a culture, subculture, and social group, consumers consider or consult with various groups when making purchase decisions. These groups

TABLE 8.3

Methods Used by Reference Groups to Influence Consumer Behavior

METHODS	DEFINITIONS	EXAMPLES
Reporting	Talking about preferences and behaviors	"All of us drink Budweiser."
Recommendations	Suggesting appropriate behaviors	"You should get a Schwinn High Sierra."
Invitations	Asking for participation in events	"Do you want to go to the Lionel Ritchie concert with us?"
Requests	Asking for behavior performance	"Would you run down to the corner and get me a newspaper?"
Prompts	Suggesting desired behaviors	"It sure would be nice if someone would buy us a pizza!"
Commands	Telling someone what to do	"Get me some Kleenex, and be quick about it!"
Promises	Offering a reward for performing a behavior	"If you'll go to Penney's with me, I'll take you to lunch later."
Coercion	Threatening to punish for inappropriate behavior	"If you don't shut up, I'm going to stuff a sock in your mouth!"
Criticism	Saying something negative about a behavior	"Quit hassling the salesclerk. You're acting like a jerk."
Compliments	Saying something positive about a behavior	"You really know how to shop. I bet you got every bargain in the store."
Teasing	Good-natured bantering about behavior or appearance	"Man, that shirt makes you look like Bozo the clown!"

Source: J. Paul Peter and Jerry C. Olson, *Consumer Behavior and Marketing Strategy,* 2d ed. (Burr Ridge, Ill.: Richard D. Irwin, 1990), p. 370.

reference groups
Groups consumers use as a reference point for evaluating their own beliefs and attitudes.

serve as the consumers' **reference groups,** or groups they use as a reference point for evaluating their own beliefs and attitudes. For example, teenagers typically use their friends as a reference group for deciding what clothes are attractive or whether it's smart to use drugs.

TYPES OF REFERENCE GROUPS   Most people have several reference groups, including family, friends, clubs and professional organizations, and individuals that they consider to have expertise in some area. For example, the patron of a hair salon might take the recommendation of another, very stylish patron who suggests buying a certain type of brush or shampoo. As in this example, a person need not be a member of the reference group that he or she consults.

Reference groups that the consumer is a member of are called *membership groups.* A consumer may seek or wish to be a member of a reference group, in which case it is called an *aspiration group.* Baseball players are an aspiration group for many of the boys who start using snuff or chewing tobacco. Makers of these products capitalize on that when they feature athletes in their ads for smokeless tobacco. Finally, the consumer may wish to keep his or her distance from a group, in which case it is called a *dissociative group.* Marketers want to make certain that targeted consumers do not link their products to dissociative groups. Thus, ads for Honda have shown "you meet the nicest people" (not scary Hell's Angels) riding Honda motorcycles.

REFERENCE GROUP INFLUENCES   Reference groups can influence consumer behavior in a variety of ways. Table 8.3 provides some examples. In most cases, the refer-

ence groups do not tell the consumer what to do; rather, the consumer is influenced by respect for the group's opinion or concern for group members' feelings. Figure 8.2 shows a magazine advertisement that capitalizes on this influence. The ad humorously reflects the fact that as we grow up, our parents are both an associative and a dissociative group. They can be embarrassing, yet the urge to be just like Mom or Dad runs deep. The ad encourages young adults to act on that impulse and try a drink that was popular with an older generation.

Reference groups have the most impact when consumers are unfamiliar with a product and find the reference group especially believable or attractive (as in the case of friends). Also, consumers are most likely to consult a reference group regarding purchases of items that are noticeable to others, as in the case of clothing and cars. Thus, the pressure to affiliate with a gang extends to the colors of clothing worn by gang members. Some socially responsible retailers respond to this undesirable type of reference group by not stocking clothing in gang colors, or at least advising customers on buying colors that are not associated with gangs.

FAMILY INFLUENCES

From the time our parents set such limits as "You may choose *one* candy bar" or "You can buy that game if you save half the money yourself," our family has influenced our purchase decisions. Thus, the family is among the most important reference groups for most consumers. Furthermore, marketers in some cases consider families (in the form of households), rather than individuals, as the basic unit for measuring consumption. That is because family members often make purchase decisions and purchases for one another. For example, a parent might ask a child to run to the store for some bread, a roommate might offer to pick up a video on the way home, or one spouse might buy the other one flowers for Valentine's Day.

FAMILY DECISION MAKERS   Marketers want to know who makes the purchases in a family and which family members influence those purchases. If the typical purchaser of a product is the wife, the marketer will create a different marketing mix than if the typical purchaser is the husband or a teenager. Likewise, if certain family members tend to have a significant voice in making a purchasing decision, the marketer will probably want to promote to them as well as to the actual buyer.

In past decades, the usual approach was to assume that the female head of household (the wife and mother) bought most household products, with her husband buying certain items such as automobiles and insurance. Today marketers realize not only that many households do not contain both a man and a woman, but that adults of both sexes are involved in purchasing a variety of products. Especially in two-career households, the husband or both spouses together might do the grocery shopping. And although men are more likely than women to be patients in a recovery program for substance abuse, the person who actually buys this type of service (for self or significant other) is more often a woman. Thus, one tactic to promote such programs is to advertise on late-night television, when wives are waiting for substance-abusing husbands to come home.[25]

Furthermore, thanks to busy parents and part-time jobs, children now do a significant share of the shopping. The ad for Cheerios in Figure 8.3 reflects the expanded influence of children in making purchase decisions. With so many possible influences, marketers have to research who the buyers and influencers are for specific products.

FAMILY LIFE CYCLES   The needs of a family and the ability to satisfy those needs change throughout the various stages of the family's existence. Together these stages are known as the **family life cycle**. A traditional view of the family life cycle includes the following stages:

- Bachelor stage—young, single people living away from their parents
- Newly married couples with no children
- Young married couples with youngest child under six
- Young married couples with youngest child six or older
- Older married couples with dependent children
- Older married couples still in labor force but with children living independently
- Retired married couples with children living independently
- Solitary survivor in labor force
- Solitary survivor retired.

Of course, not every person or family passes through all these stages or passes through them in this order, especially given the variety in the structure of the modern family. Figure 8.4 shows an attempt to portray a modern family life cycle in all its complexity. Even this diagram fails to cover all the possibilities, such as never marrying.

Despite its limitations, the family cycle is a useful starting point for identifying ways in which needs change as families mature. For example, young married people tend to spend more on luxuries because usually both spouses are working and they don't have the expenses related to child rearing. As they get older and take on more responsibilities, their buying habits change. Thus, Melba Turner told a reporter, "I used to buy everything I wanted and never worry about price. When we [Turner and her husband] turned 30 we faced the reality that our resources are limited."[26] Parents of young children make many of their purchases to care for their children—for example, buying children's clothing and life insurance.

This change from conspicuous consumption to family-oriented spending is particularly important today, because parents of young children are primarily the huge age group known as baby boomers. In response, many companies have tried to attract

family life cycle
The various stages of a family's existence.

FIGURE 8.3

An Ad That Recognizes the Active Role of Children in Household Purchases

buyers by appealing to family ties. For example, brokerage house Shearson Lehman shifted advertising messages, changing from ads emphasizing its financial expertise to an ad featuring a two-career couple planning for the wife to stay home with a newly adopted baby.[27]

As parents grow older, their financial position tends to improve, so they are more apt to spend money on leisure activities and home improvements. Older adults make purchases related to retirement and buy gifts for younger relatives. They also may be heavy consumers of health services.

When marriages don't last, one consequence is that household finances are often strained. Thus, the prevalence of divorce in modern society means that marketers can't count on the trend toward increased spending predicted by the traditional family life cycle. Anne McBride found that because of her divorce, the need to save for her teenage son's college expenses, and the requirements of caring for elderly parents, she must do her shopping at discount stores.[28]

The Consumer as Individual

While external forces in society help to explain consumers' behavior, internal forces are important as well. Each individual consumer is influenced by his or her perceptions, motivations, attitudes, and life-style.

PERCEPTION

perception
The way people gather and record information.

One reason that consumers respond differently to the same external forces is that they perceive those forces differently. **Perception** refers to the way people gather and

FIGURE 8.4

A Modern Family Life Cycle

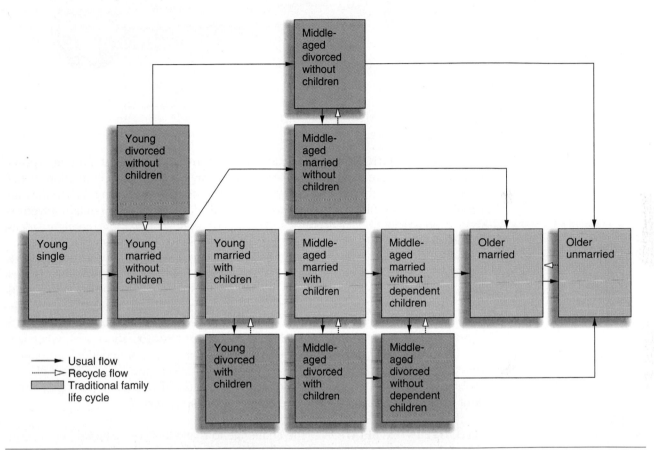

Source: Reprinted with permission from "A Modernized Family Life Cycle," by Patrick E. Murphy and William A. Staples, in the *Journal of Consumer Research* (June 1979): pp. 12–22. University of Chicago Press.

record information. To illustrate the importance of perception to marketers, Douglas F. Haley of marketing research firm Yankelovich Clancy Shulman relates an anecdote about the Empire State Building. Customers were complaining that the elevators were too slow, so the building's management drew on its engineers' expertise to make them 50 percent faster. But customers still complained, so management brought in experts to do a sophisticated computer analysis of usage patterns. Elevator operations were fine-tuned, and waiting times fell another 25 percent. But customers continued complaining, so management tried installing mirrors on the elevator doors. The complaints stopped. Evidently, when people could look at themselves, they stopped paying attention to the time they spent waiting.[29]

This story has an important message for marketers practicing the quality approach. It's not enough to make an excellent product. Rather, for customers to be satisfied or delighted, they must perceive that the product is excellent. Figure 8.5 summarizes forces that influence what consumers perceive and how they perceive it.

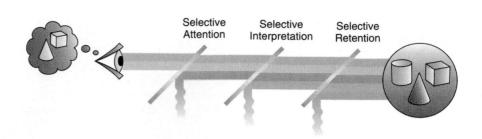

Selective Attention   Selective Interpretation   Selective Retention

SELECTIVE ATTENTION   For people to perceive something, they first must be exposed to it. Consumers are exposed to an enormous array of marketing information. When they are shopping, they see product displays and attractive packaging. When they are traveling, they see billboards, signs, and other displays. Magazines contain advertisements and articles about categories and brands of products. The mass media broadcast many advertising messages every hour. Even bills contain advertising messages.

Among all the messages that consumers are exposed to, they pay attention to only some. Such **selective attention** occurs so that we don't feel bombarded by too much information. Thus, Jay Schulberg, executive creative director of ad agency Bozell, criticizes the widespread popularity of the "family values" theme in advertising, saying the ads "all look the same, and no one is making an impression."[30] Instead, people pay attention only to what seems the most interesting or relevant. That's why, when you decide to buy a car, it suddenly seems as though there is a tremendous amount of newspaper and magazine articles, conversation, and advertising on the subject of automobiles. It's not that all of a sudden publishers have decided to cover the topic; rather, your interest has led you to be aware of the existing messages.

SELECTIVE INTERPRETATION   The challenge to marketers goes beyond getting consumers' attention. Marketers must also contend with **selective interpretation**—the tendency to hear and interpret things in a way that fits existing beliefs and values. For example, someone who believes computers are difficult to use will tend to remember all the stories he or she hears about systems crashes or jargon-loaded users' manuals. To improve the likelihood that consumers will interpret a message as intended, marketers can keep the message simple and focus on a single main point.

SELECTIVE RETENTION   Marketers want consumers to remember their messages. However, through **selective retention**, people tend to remember only certain information, typically information that matches their beliefs and values. Thus, selective retention and selective interpretation together favor marketers who can describe their products in a way that is consistent with the beliefs and values of their target markets.

In an effort to do just that in England, Colgate has used an advertising campaign that reflects the frustration of British women that most of them are alone responsible for cleaning their bathroom, even though many hold down full-time jobs as well. The ads show brawny men handling cleaning chores and headlines such as "How to Save Time Cleaning. Get Him New Ajax Liquid." And to break through the clutter of advertising messages to get (female) consumers' attention, the ads make the first-ever use of male sexuality in advertising such products in England, showing only the male models' naked torsos. An Ajax spokesperson refers to the photos as "an aesthetically pleasing image."[31]

selective attention
The way people attend only to certain messages.

selective interpretation
The tendency to hear and interpret things in a way that fits existing beliefs and values.

selective retention
The tendency to remember only certain information, typically that which matches existing beliefs and values.

FIGURE 8.6

Maslow's Hierarchy of Needs

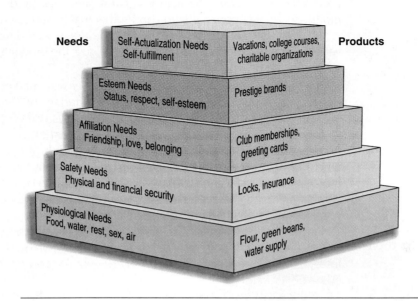

Needs

Self-Actualization Needs
Self-fulfillment

Esteem Needs
Status, respect, self-esteem

Affiliation Needs
Friendship, love, belonging

Safety Needs
Physical and financial security

Physiological Needs
Food, water, rest, sex, air

Products

Vacations, college courses, charitable organizations

Prestige brands

Club memberships, greeting cards

Locks, insurance

Flour, green beans, water supply

MOTIVATION

motivation
The inner drive that propels people to fulfill a need.

When consumers perceive that they have a need, the inner drive that propels them to fulfill the need is called **motivation**. Marketers want to know what motivates consumers so that they can appeal to those motives. The advertising agency BBDO Worldwide has developed a marketing research tool it calls Personal Drive Analysis. This tool is the result of studying what kinds of drives motivate consumers and identifying 74 personal drives. For example, in buying athletic shoes, consumers motivated by status or winning would be motivated to buy Nike shoes, whereas consumers associate LA Gear with sexiness and indulgence, Keds with family and simplicity.[32]

MASLOW'S HIERARCHY OF NEEDS   Psychologist Abraham Maslow postulated that what motivates people to act is unfulfilled needs and that people meet certain basic needs before being highly motivated to meet other needs. Thus, Maslow ranked needs in a five-level hierarchy, shown in Figure 8.6. In general, according to Maslow's theory, people first try to meet the needs at the bottom of the hierarchy—the physiological needs, such as the needs for food and rest. As the needs in the bottom categories become satisfied, people move on to fulfilling needs in the higher categories, that is, the needs for safety, affiliation, esteem, and self-actualization.

While Maslow's hierarchy of needs has been criticized as lacking research to support its accuracy, it can be helpful to a marketer in several ways. First, it suggests some of the many needs that may motivate consumers to enter into an exchange. For example, makers of clothing need think not only in terms of meeting consumers' need for something to wear. They can serve affiliation needs (and have reaped big profits) by selling T-shirts imprinted with logos and slogans related to big sports events, rock concerts, and hit movies. In the words of Kirk Beaudin, president of Sara Lee's knitwear division, "You may not be an athlete, but you can associate yourself with athleticism" by paying $10 for a Nike or Dallas Cowboys T-shirt.[33]

In addition, Maslow's hierarchy can help with the selection of target markets. Makers of a subcompact car might position the product to meet the basic need for transportation. Makers of a luxury sedan would seek to identify consumers who are more concerned about affiliation and self-actualization needs.

Finally, when marketers position their products according to needs, they can motivate consumers to purchase by telling them how the products will meet their needs.

UTILITARIAN AND HEDONIC NEEDS   Another way marketers think of motivation is in terms of satisfying needs that are either "utilitarian" or "hedonic." **Utilitarian needs** are related to basic functions and material benefits. When your hands are dirty, you want something that will help to fulfill the function of washing them. When you are thirsty, you are motivated to find something to drink. When people are motivated to meet utilitarian needs, they tend to be rational about their choices. For example, a recent study of consumers' views about buying automobiles shows that they are primarily interested in such utilitarian criteria as performance, reliability, and ease of maintenance, rather than a fancy exterior.[34]

In contrast, **hedonic needs** are related to the desire for pleasure and self-expression. People like to shower with a soap that smells good. They like to sing and listen to music that moves them. Decisions about meeting hedonic needs tend to be relatively emotional.

Notice that, as in the example of soap that smells good, the same product can meet both utilitarian and hedonic needs. Likewise, the Seiko watch advertised in Figure 8.7 meets the utilitarian need to tell time and the hedonic needs to wear stylish accessories and support worthy causes such as the U.S. Olympic team. These are powerful combinations for the marketer, because consumers may react to such products both rationally and emotionally. Thus, in advertising its ThinkPad portable computer, IBM calls it "seven and a half pounds of brains and beauty." The ad not only details the degree of resolution of the computer's display, but calls the screen "a thing of almost aching beauty." If users of ThinkPad find that it meets their hedonic as well as utilitarian needs, IBM will truly have delivered quality in their eyes.

The degree to which each type of need is important to consumers may change over time. The skin-care industry used to sell what was called "suntan lotion" and emphasized how sexy a suntan was (to meet hedonic needs). Today, exposure to the sun has been linked to skin cancer, and the products, now generally called "sunscreen," emphasize utilitarian needs such as degree of protection from ultraviolet rays.[35]

ATTITUDE

When people are motivated to meet a need, the way they meet that need depends on their attitudes toward the various alternatives. An **attitude** is the combination of a person's beliefs about and evaluations of something, leading to a tendency to act in a particular way. Many consumers today think fresh produce is more nutritious than frozen vegetables (belief), and they consider nutritiousness to be a good thing (evaluation), so sales of frozen vegetables have plummeted (tendency to act).[36] Of course, many consumer attitudes are positive as well. Imagine that Myrna Lowe believes the Goodyear mechanics at the service station in her town are capable and honest (belief). She considers those traits important (evaluation), so she always has her car serviced by Goodyear and recommends the service station to her neighbors (action).

Because attitudes contain a behavioral component—the tendency to act—they are particularly important for marketers to study and respond to. For example, research shows that women shoppers are increasingly sharing the traditionally male view that shopping is a chore, rather than a source of recreation.[37] This attitude presents an attractive opportunity to companies that sell products through catalogs. For

---

utilitarian needs
Needs related to basic functions and material benefits.

hedonic needs
Needs related to the desire for pleasure and self-expression.

attitude
The combination of a person's beliefs about and evaluation of something, leading to a tendency to act in a certain way.

Advertising That Appeals to Utilitarian and Hedonic Needs

store owners and managers to serve these consumers, they need to find ways to make shopping easy and efficient.

ATTITUDES AND BELIEFS   Sometimes marketing research emphasizes only one component of attitudes—**beliefs**, or a person's views about various subjects. A consumer survey by Grey Advertising found that consumers believe a higher price does not guarantee high quality. According to this and other surveys, consumers today believe value means getting a lot for one's money, so a reasonable price is important. Kenneth Macke, the chief executive of retailer Dayton Hudson, says, "My father bought his first TV set from the local Cadillac dealer because he knew that man knew quality. I bought mine from a department store because of the convenience of delivery. My kids bought theirs from Target [a discount chain]."[38] (For more about the beliefs and attitudes of Macke's children's generation, see "You Decide: What Makes Baby Busters Tick?")

The focus beliefs has an important drawback. In theory at least, beliefs do not necessarily lead to actions. That is because they may not be linked to evaluations—at least not strong enough ones.

CULTIVATING A FAVORABLE ATTITUDE   To cultivate favorable attitudes toward their products, marketers can be most effective when they address all the components of attitudes: beliefs evaluations, and behaviors. Thus, when marketers give away free samples, they hope that by influencing behavior, they will help to create favorable beliefs and evaluations about their product.

When marketers find that consumers' attitudes are unfavorable in some way, they need to change the product or the attitudes. If the marketers determine that the product doesn't satisfy consumers' needs adequately, they will want to modify the product so that it does. Some evidence suggests that a large segment of the American public is fed up with gratuitous sex, violence, and profanity in movies and that Hollywood is begin-

beliefs
A person's views about various subjects.

You Decide

WHAT MAKES BABY BUSTERS TICK?

If you were born between 1964 and 1975, you are—pardon the expression—a baby buster. The term refers to the lower birth rate that created the generation of young adults that has followed the baby boomers. Perhaps because this terms sounds unflattering, the baby buster generation is also called by other names, most popularly Generation X.

Generation X is smaller than the baby boomer group, but it represents a huge number of U.S. consumers—nearly 50 million. As this generation is reaching an age that typically makes some major purchases, it is an important group of consumers for marketers to understand.

According to marketing research, Generation X hates labels. They don't want to be stereotyped, and they aren't interested in products that are directly aimed at them. They prefer products that are simple, of high quality and value, and that have broader appeal than just to their own age group. They are particularly suspicious of messages that appear to be pretentious.

Members of Generation X are cautious about spending money. The uncertain economy and soft real estate markets have had a big influence on the baby busters' spending habits. "Since we're getting paid less, we have less to spend," notes Kasha Cianciara. "What little we have, we use wisely." Luxury autos, expensive vacations, and designer clothes don't have the appeal that they did for an earlier generation.

The slow economy coupled with such problems as AIDS and high divorce rates have created a society in which Xers feel they must overcome many obstacles. Nevertheless, members of Generation X don't necessarily want to dwell on these problems, and the majority are optimistic about their personal future. They may be turned off by marketing messages that have such a heavy social message as to be depressing. The limits on their career prospects may also contribute to the value placed on per-

sonal fulfillment. The typical belief among Xers is that they should keep personal relationships and work commitments in balance.

Many values of Generation X represent high ideals. These consumers have a strong sense of the need for justice in society and for a clean environment. They hate waste—in packaging as well as products themselves. They buy clothing made from natural fibers, spend time outdoors, and avoid flashy cosmetics. They also value relationships—a sense of family and community.

Do you think this description of Generation X is accurate? If not, why not? What values, beliefs, and attitudes might you add? How would you advise marketers to approach this subculture? What types of goods and services do you think would be successful? What reference groups would be important for marketers to consider?

Sources: Erika Kotite, "The Next Generation," *Entrepreneur,* December 1992, pp. 90–94; Nancy Ryan, "20somethings a Market of Contradictions, Tough to Target," *Chicago Tribune,* December 12, 1993, sec. 7, p. 1.

ning to tone down its offerings.[39] Or the product may actually be satisfactory, but the marketer needs to change consumers' beliefs about it. In the sample ad in Figure 8.8, the U.S. Council for energy awareness is trying to change the belief that nuclear power is bad for the environment. Finally, the marketer may try to change consumers' evaluations—say, by associating the product with a good feeling. A classic example is Metropolitan Life's use of Peanuts cartoon characters in its advertising to make life insurance seem like a friendlier product and Met Life like a friendly company.

Of course, even though attitudes contain a behavioral component, a positive attitude is no guarantee of a purchase. Consumers decide to buy only when they also believe they have a need for the product, as well as the means to buy it. Thus, not everyone who has a positive attitude toward the Ritz Carlton will stay there.

LIFE-STYLE

life-style
The manner in which people conduct their lives, including their activities, interests, and opinions.

psychographics
The process of identifying various categories of life-styles.

Consumers' attitudes can influence the life-style they adopt. **Life-style** is "the manner in which people conduct their lives, including their activities, interests, and opinions."[40] The process of identifying various categories of life-styles is called **psychographics**. Psychographics usually focuses on creating profiles of consumers within

FIGURE 8.8

An Advertisement That Seeks to Change Attitudes

each category of life-style. To study consumers' preferences for the colors of products, the Pantone Color Institute and the Cooper Marketing Group categorized consumers according to their shopping habits, as prudent, impulsive, pessimistic, traditional, and confident. For example, the impulsive group tends to shop without a list and to make large and small surprise purchases. Members of this group, who are likely to have some college education, like black, gray, royal blue, and a bright red-orange that Pantone calls "Firewater."[41] Marketers use psychographics because life-style information tells them more about target markets so they can better tailor the marketing mix to meet customer needs. Someone selling a product meant to be purchased on impulse might appeal to the impulsive consumers just described by using a package printed in black and Firewater hues.

A widely used source of psychographic data is SRI International's service called VALS 2 (which stands for values, attitudes, and life-styles). VALS 2 categorizes life-styles as shown in Figure 8.9. Notice that the categories overlap, so the life-styles of some individuals have characteristics of more than one category. The VALS program describes these categories in terms of two dimensions: self-orientation and resources. Self-orientation refers to the pattern of attitudes and activities through which people reinforce their image of themselves. According to VALS 2, people are oriented toward principles, status, or action. The other dimension of these categories describes the amount of resources consumers have, including income, education, self-confidence, health, eagerness to buy, intelligence, and level of energy.

The Consumer's Decision-Making Process

On her way home from work, Tanya Jenkins remembered that she had poured the last of the milk on her raisin bran that morning. She pulled up to the next convenience store she passed, and a few minutes later was on her way with a gallon of milk riding

FIGURE 8.9
**VALS 2 Life-Style
Categories**

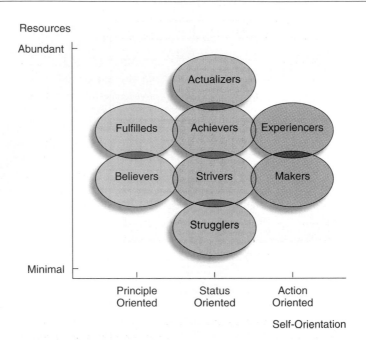

CONSUMER TYPE	PERCENT OF POPULATION	MEDIAN AGE	MEDIAN INCOME	DISTINCTIVE PURCHASE BEHAVIORS
Actualizers	8%	43	$58,000	Possessions reflect a cultivated taste for finer things in life
Fulfilleds	11	48	38,000	Desire product functionability, value, and durability
Believers	16	58	21,000	Favor American products and established brands
Achievers	13	36	50,000	Prefer products that demonstrate success to peers
Strivers	13	34	25,000	Emulate those with impressive possessions
Experiencers	12	26	19,000	Avid consumers of clothing, fast food, music, movies, and videos
Makers	13	30	23,000	Unimpressed by material possessions (except those with a practical purpose)
Strugglers	14	61	9,000	Modest resources limit purchases to urgent needs

Source: Reprinted with permission from SRI International, Menlo Park, CA.

on the seat next to her. Roommates Enrico Suarez and Paul Gangle agreed that they should have a better stereo in their apartment before the party they were planning for next month. They spent hours together poring over back issues of *Consumer Reports* and *Stereo Review,* and they visited a number of stores to price some of the models they were interested in.

As these two examples show, the way in which consumers decide whether and what to buy depends partly on the significance of the purchase. In general, consumers undertake a more formal, lengthy decision-making process when the following conditions exist:

- The product's price is high.
- The product has features that are complex or new.
- There are many brands to choose from.

Thus, consumers give a lot more thought to buying a college education or a vacation trip than they do to buying cheese or a car wash.

A formal decision-making process, such as the one used by Enrico and Paul to buy a stereo, would look something like the process shown in Figure 8.10. This process includes five steps: need recognition, information search, consideration of options, purchase decision, and postpurchase evaluation. Suppose Leslie Braun notices she spilled soup on her silk dress, so she wants to get it dry-cleaned (need recognition). She remembers where the nearest cleaner is (information search) and that it didn't look disreputable (consideration of options), so she takes her dress there (purchase decision). Assuming that she is satisfied with the results (postpurchase evaluation), Leslie may go back to the same laundry the next time she needs to have something dry-cleaned. Consumers making more routine decisions, such as replacing an empty tube of toothpaste, might abbreviate or eliminate some of these steps.

NEED RECOGNITION

The process by which a consumer makes a purchase decision begins when the consumer recognizes a need. This recognition may come from an internal stimulus such as hunger, fatigue, or desire to impress a date. Or it may come from external stimuli such as an invitation to a wedding or a radio advertisement.

At this stage of the decision-making process, the marketer can try to influence consumers by helping them recognize needs that the marketer's products can satisfy. Sometimes this requires explaining a new product to consumers, or it may require changing an attitude or behavior patterns. For example, a decline in sales of window cleaners seems to reflect a trend toward cleaning less.[42] To boost sales, marketers would have to persuade consumers to clean more often or to find more uses for window cleaners.

INFORMATION SEARCH

When consumers have identified a need, they may look for information about how to satisfy that need. A highway traveler who feels hungry might start looking for billboards advertising restaurants near the highway. An office worker who feels hungry might think about where she has purchased a good sandwich lately. Depending on how much experience a consumer has in meeting a particular type of need, the consumer will look for information in up to five kinds of sources:

1. *Internal sources*—These are the sources lodged in a person's memory. If a consumer has satisfied a similar need in the past, he or she is likely to start the search for information by recalling how that need was satisfied. For routine purchases or those made out of habit, this may be the only source of information the consumer uses.
2. *Group sources*—The consumer often consults with other people in his or her reference group. As described earlier, these sources of information may be the most powerful in shaping certain purchase decisions.
3. *Marketing sources*—Consumers also get information from marketers through packages, salespeople, advertisements, product displays, and the like. These sources usually provide information about particular products, including how a product can satisfy a need.

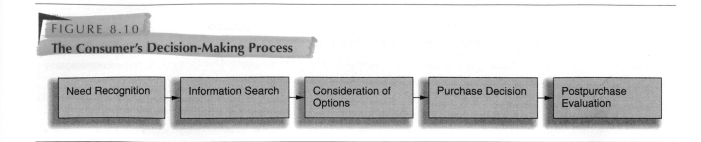

FIGURE 8.10

The Consumer's Decision-Making Process

Need Recognition → Information Search → Consideration of Options → Purchase Decision → Postpurchase Evaluation

4. *Public sources*—These are sources independent of the marketer and the consumer, including media stories about the product and ratings by such independent organizations as Consumers Union, publisher of *Consumer Reports*.
5. *Experiential sources*—The consumer may also be able to experience the product while shopping, for example, by handling it, smelling it, tasting it, or trying it. Because this source of information usually requires that the consumer make a shopping trip, it tends to be the last source the consumer uses.

consideration set
The set of alternatives that the consumer identifies in a purchasing decision.

From all these sources, the consumer usually identifies several alternative ways to satisfy the need he or she recognized. The set of alternatives that the consumer identifies is known as the **consideration set**. As illustrated in Figure 8.11, the consideration set is a subset of all possible alternatives. In most cases, the consumer will not identify all the possibilities. Someone who wants to buy a camera may recall a few brands such as Pentax and Minolta. This consumer may then visit a few camera stores to identify a few models in his or her price range. The cameras that the consumer recalls or learns about constitute the consumer's consideration set. Marketers, of course, look for ways to get their products into the consideration set of the consumers in their target markets. This means that consumers should have a variety of ways to learn about the products.

CONSIDERATION OF OPTIONS

Based on the information gathered, the consumer identifies and evaluates ways to meet his or her need. In general, this step involves deciding what features of the product are important and identifying which of those features each alternative offers. For example, when deciding what to buy for dinner, American consumers are increasingly choosing pasta because pasta dishes are healthful, convenient, and inexpensive.[43] To choose a college, students responding to a recent survey said they considered the tuition, size of the school, its academic reputation, the likelihood of getting a good job after graduation, and the amount of financial help provided.[44] Some of those features will probably be more important than others. In the case of selecting a college, students said academic reputation was most important, followed by likelihood of getting a good job.

Consumers will devote the most time to considering options when a purchase is expensive. They will consider few options for purchases they consider routine or in situations where they feel pressed for time. In those situations, it may be harder to persuade a consumer to spend time learning about a new product.

Knowing what features consumers look for as they consider options helps the marketer identify target markets and develop an appropriate marketing mix. Marketers of cleaning products need to know that consumers today typically care about the

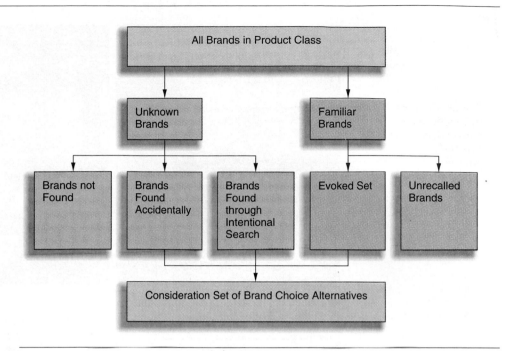

FIGURE 8.11

Forming a Consideration Set for Choosing a Product

Source: J. Paul Peter and Jerry C. Olson, *Consumer Behavior and Marketing Strategy,* 3d ed. (Burr Ridge, Ill.: Irwin, 1993), p. 229.

environmental impact of the products they use, as well as convenience, performance, and price.[45] However, a substantial cost disadvantage for so-called green products leads many consumers to buy on the basis of price.[46] Obtaining knowledge about what customers are looking for is an essential part of the quality approach to marketing. The reason is simple: marketers who want to satisfy consumers must know what is important to them.

PURCHASE DECISION

After considering the possible options, the consumer makes a purchase decision. This step includes deciding whether to buy and, if so, what to buy, where to buy, and when to buy. The consumer's choice will depend in part on the reason for the purchase. Suppose that when Tom O'Neal wants to buy some T-shirts to wear around the house, he is heavily influenced by price, but when he is on vacation, he likes to pick up a T-shirt with a clever design as a souvenir, even though it costs twice as much. And when Becky Khadem buys glassware as a gift, she shops in different stores and makes different selections than when she buys it for her own use. Likewise, Figure 8.12 shows two ads appealing to different reasons for purchasing a Jeep: good gas mileage and advanced features that make driving fun.

Another influence on product choice is the consumer's mood. A consumer who is feeling adventurous is more likely to try something new than one who is worrying how to make ends meet. A consumer who is shopping to cure a case of the blues is more likely to buy luxury goods than someone who is tired and just wants to find a comfortable pair of shoes.

The consumer usually purchases the product selected. This means the consumer has to decide where to make the purchase and how to pay for it. The consumer may

FIGURE 8.12

Two Ads Appealing to Different Reasons for Buying

Reason to buy: Advanced features that make driving fun (ad on left) and good gas mileage (ad on right)

act quickly, especially if the product is on sale, or the consumer may postpone making any purchase. Perhaps none of the options identified really meets the consumer's needs, or perhaps he or she needs to save more money before making the desired purchase. In recent years, this has been happening more often, because consumers have tended to disapprove of the use of credit and to try to reduce their debt burden.[47]

POSTPURCHASE EVALUATION

After buying a product, consumers formally or informally evaluate the outcome of the purchase. In particular, they consider whether they are satisfied with the experience of making the purchase and with the good or service they bought. A consumer who repeatedly has favorable experiences with the same purchase decision may develop loyalty to the brand purchased. Also, in many cases consumers tell their family, friends, and acquaintances about their experiences with buying and using products—especially when those experiences are negative.

EVALUATION AND THE QUALITY APPROACH   This stage of the buying process is particularly important for marketers practicing the quality approach, because their aim is to satisfy or delight customers. If the consumer's postpurchase evaluation is that the transaction was satisfying, the marketer has succeeded. In the case of consumer electronics such as VCRs, cordless phones, and microwave ovens, all too often consumers become frustrated trying to figure out how to operate them. The basic problem, notes Jerry Kalov, head of the Consumer Electronics Group of the Electronic Industries Association, is that producers have let designers add more and more features because they know how, not because most consumers want them. In contrast, Kalov says that when he was involved in product development at Marantz, the company put "all the buttons and dials you could ask for" in its stereo system "behind a little glass door where all the aficionados could reach them if they wanted to." On the front they put just two knobs: one to turn the power off and on, and one to control the volume.[48]

COGNITIVE DISSONANCE   In the case of large-ticket items, a common response is for the consumer to wonder whether the alternative chosen was really the best alternative. This feeling is called **cognitive dissonance** by psychologists or "buyer's remorse" by many salespeople. It may result because of the difficulty—even impossibility—of fully considering every possible alternative course of action. Furthermore, some of the alternatives *not* chosen may have attractive features, so that the correctness of the choice is not obvious. Cognitive dissonance is most likely to occur for major purchases that are difficult to select and undo.

> **cognitive dissonance**
> Uncertainty whether the chosen alternative was the best; often called "buyer's remorse."

People tend to resolve the discomfort of buyer's remorse by seeking information to support their decision and by becoming more critical of the alternatives they rejected. Marketers can help consumers feel good about major purchases by providing reassurance after the sale is complete. For example, a salesperson might send a thank-you letter that restates many of the benefits of the product selected.

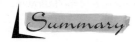

Summary

To understand why consumers buy certain products instead of others, marketers study consumer behavior—the way in which external and internal forces shape people's exchange activities. The study of consumer behavior comprises external forces such as family and culture, internal forces such as attitudes, and behavior in the form of participation in exchange activities.

At the societal level, culture and subculture influence consumer behavior through direct and indirect messages that shape values. People also are influenced by their social class, the group of people who have similar income levels and comparable wealth, skill, and power. Reference groups are groups people use as a basis for evaluating their own beliefs and attitudes. One of the most important reference groups is the family. Marketers are interested in knowing which family members make buying decisions, as well as which types of purchasing decisions are associated with various stages in the family life cycle.

At the individual level, consumers are influenced by their perceptions, motivations, attitudes, and life-styles. Therefore,

marketers are interested in how consumers gather and process information, as well as the drives that propel them to fulfill a variety of needs. To predict buying behavior, marketers study attitudes, or the combination of beliefs about and evaluations of something that leads to a tendency to act in a particular way. Marketers study consumer life-styles through the use of psychographics, which categorizes people according to the way in which they conduct their lives.

Consumer buying decisions may result from formal or informal decision making. Consumers are most likely to use a formal decision-making process when the price is high, the product is complex, and there are many alternatives. Consumers may look for information about products from internal sources, group sources, marketing sources, public sources, or experiential sources. Once they have chosen a product, especially a big-ticket item, they may experience cognitive dissonance, or a loss of confidence in their choice. Marketers can counter this by providing support after a buying decision has been made.

KEY TERMS AND CONCEPTS

consumer (p. 230)

consumer behavior (p. 230)

culture (p. 231)

core values (p. 231)

subculture (p. 232)

social class (p. 235)

reference groups (p. 237)

family life cycle (p. 239)

perception (p. 240)

selective attention (p. 242)

selective interpretation (p. 242)

selective retention (p. 242)

motivation (p. 243)

utilitarian needs (p. 244)

hedonic needs (p. 244)

attitude (p. 244)

beliefs (p. 245)

life-style (p. 246)

psychographics (p. 246)

consideration set (p. 250)

cognitive dissonance (p. 253)

REVIEW AND DISCUSSION QUESTIONS

1. If you were a marketer who planned to test a new line of baked goods in Santa Fe, New Mexico, what subcultures and social classes would be important for you to consider?

2. Suppose you wanted to promote a line of costume jewelry to middle- or upper-middle-class teenaged girls.
   a. What reference groups would you study to determine their influence on teens in the United States?
   b. Would your answer be different if you were interested in Japanese teenagers? Explain.

3. Summarize Maslow's hierarchy of needs. How can marketers apply this theory?

4. As a marketer, how would you cultivate a favorable attitude among consumers toward a line of fruit drinks?

5. Using Figure 8.9—the VALS 2 life-style categories—determine which type of consumer(s) would be apt to buy each of the following products:
   a. a foreign-made luxury automobile
   b. the latest CD equipment
   c. classic, American-made clothing
   d. the lowest-priced brand of margarine

6. What are the five steps involved in formal decision making by consumers?

7. If you were marketing a new development of condominiums, which information sources would you expect potential buyers to use in making their decision? How do you think they would use each one?

Chapter Project
A Generation X Sales Pitch

If you read the "You Decide" box in this chapter, you've already started thinking about the generation from which most college students are drawn—baby busters or Generation X—as an important group of consumers. Now take your thinking a few steps further. Design a plan to address and influence the buying decisions of Generation X consumers for one of the following (or choose a product or service of your own):

- a catering service
- a line of business clothing
- home furnishings
- a nightclub
- bicycles built for commuting

In pitching a product to this group, you'll need to consider culture, subculture, and social class; reference groups such as family and friends; motivation; beliefs and attitudes; life-style; and the type of decision-making process that will be most common for your product or service.

Case
Promoting a New Image for the Prune

What do you think of prunes? Most likely, you don't think about them at all. Generally speaking, consumer perception of prunes is reflected in a giggle or a blank stare. That's the challenge the California Prune Board has faced for years: to change that perception, create a primary demand for prunes, and usher in, as one writer puts it, the "Prune Age." To that end, the board has hired Ketchum Public Relations to improve the prune's image.

Consumer attitudes toward the prune as weird or funny, as good only for its natural laxative properties, have certainly affected buying behavior. But the prune business (now a $200 million industry) is responsible for that reputation. Starting in the early 1920s, Sunsweet ran ads that read, "Prunes are a natural laxative from Nature's own pharmacy," and "Shake hands with health every day." The industry dug itself even deeper into the hole with its 1970s campaign for the prune as the "funny fruit." No wonder people didn't think about prunes unless they were desperate.

In the 1980s, when Ketchum Public Relations took on the prune account, consumers were becoming increasingly health conscious, and the cancer-preventing characteristics of fiber were getting a lot of media and marketing attention. Ketchum launched a program of sampling, trials, coupons, and brochures for consumers as well as the medical community. Consumers started to view the prune as not only good medicine, but perhaps even a life-prolonging food. Sales began to rise.

But eventually people got tired of hearing about fiber. Mirroring that trend, Ketchum is seeking to make consumers think of the prune as *food,* not just a source of fiber. Sunsweet wants to cultivate a favorable attitude toward the prune as "the fruit for the '90s."

That may happen, in an odd sort of way. Food-technology consultants Creative Food Consultants have discovered that the chemical composition of prunes causes them to hold moisture in baked goods, much as shortening or butter do. Therefore, prune puree is a low-fat substitute for shortening and butter in many baking recipes. Believe it or not, brownies and chocolate-chip cookies taste great made with prune puree. Baking with prune puree also prolongs shelf life—an obvious plus for bakers.

But will the marketers of baked goods be eager to offer consumers cakes and cookies made with prunes instead of more conventional ingredients? The prune board needs to sell the prune's image not only to consumers but to the baking industry. Jim Degen, a marketing consultant for the board, comments, "Things in the baking industry move unbelievably slowly. . . . We have to sell [prunes] to the marketing guys, and the marketing guys are all about 30 years old and under. When they hear *prune,* they just stop listening." Prune promoters respond to the reluctance by suggesting that marketers can always refer to prunes as "dried plums." Maybe consumers would be more attracted to a cake with that item in the ingredients list.

QUESTIONS

1. How have consumer attitudes toward prunes changed over the years described? What attitude is the prune board seeking to cultivate?
2. What external influences on consumer behavior should the prune board consider?
3. As a marketer for the prune board, what would *you* do to cultivate a favorable attitude toward prunes? How would you "undo" the prune's negative image?

Source: Marialisa Calta, "Pitching the Prune," *Eating Well,* September/October 1992, pp. 18–22.

CHAPTER 9   *Organizational Buying Behavior*

LEARNING OBJECTIVES

After completing this chapter, you should be able to:

1. Identify the categories of organizational buyers.

2. Discuss marketing issues regarding the buying behavior of foreign organizations.

3. Describe how marketing to organizations is affected by demand, competition, and technology.

4. Describe how organizational purchasing decisions are carried out.

5. Discuss the nature of interactions between marketers and organizational buyers.

6. Explain what buying centers are and how they affect the marketing effort.

Creating Customer Value
ENSERCH Environmental Corp.

Cleaning up the environment sometimes seems like too huge a task for anyone. Yet ENSERCH Environmental (formerly the Environmental Division of Ebasco) has taken on that task. The firm, headquartered in Dallas, has offices in Boston, Atlanta, Denver, Columbus, and Lyndhurst, NJ, as well as in other locations.

ENSERCH Environmental, a multinational, billion-dollar corporation, markets its capabilities to many organizations, both governmental and industrial. If there's a site that needs cleaning up, whether it's contaminated wells or a landfill, ENSERCH Environmental has the engineers, scientists, and managers to do it.

In the environmental engineering industry, teamwork is essential. Complex government regulations on safety, cost, scheduling, and the specifications and site conditions of a particular clean-up job alone require a team of experts to work together on lengthy proposals to win government contracts. Recently, the U.S. Army Corps of Engineers requested proposals for a multimillion-dollar project involving clean-up of civilian and military hazardous waste sites. ENSERCH Environmental pulled team members from its environmental and construction sections in Denver, Atlanta, New Jersey, Virginia, and Boston to produce a six-volume sales presentation to the U.S. Army Corps of Engineers. Chemists, geologists, engineers, field construction managers, and cost management specialists all contributed to the report, which won the contract.

At ENSERCH Environmental and other environmental engineering firms, marketers must have technical expertise. For instance, the federal facilities marketing coordinator for ENSERCH in Boston, Richard Gleason, has a master's degree in geology. Other managers who handle marketing duties for ENSERCH have degrees in science and/or engineering. Their clients—both the government and industry—expect them to know their business from the inside out. Thus, marketing proposals are backed by technical expertise.

Why does ENSERCH Environmental go to so much trouble and expense (sometimes tens of thousands of dollars) to win a contract from the government? Environmentalism is big business. Contracts with the Environmental Protection Agency (EPA), Department of Energy, military, or NASA can run into the millions of dollars. ENSERCH recently completed a five-year contract with the EPA that was worth over $150 million.

All of this was beyond the scope of the original company, called Electric Bond and Share Company (Ebasco), formed as a holding company in 1905 for General Electric. Back then, GE was just trying to push electricity into rural America. But perhaps it was not beyond the imagination of its founder, Thomas Edison. As you read this chapter, consider the complexities of marketing to the government and other large clients as well as the importance for marketers of technical knowledge in a given field. But don't be afraid of a marketing task that seems vast; after all, the rewards can be even greater.

Sources: Ebasco annual report, 1990; interview with Boyd Allen III, principal hydrogeologist, ENSERCH Environmental Corporation.

Chapter Overview

The story of ENSERCH Environmental shows how teamwork helped to meet the needs of organizational buyers. In this and other ways, marketers seek to provide goods and services to organizations to help them carry out their own missions. Marketers who serve organizational buyers—in addition to or instead of consumers—must understand the behavior of these buyers.

This chapter provides an introduction to organizational buying behavior. It describes the scope of organizational markets and examines several basic categories of organizations. The chapter also considers how three forces—demand, competition, and technology—play a role in organizational buying decisions. Then the chapter describes the nature of purchasing decisions in organizations, including the types of purchases made and the ways organizational buyers decide to purchase. Finally, the chapter discusses the interactions among the people involved in organizational buying: first, the interactions between buyer and seller, and second, the interactions among the employees involved in making a purchase.

The Scope and Size of Organizational Markets

When we think of marketing, the first examples that come to mind usually involve consumer goods such as soap, televisions, and athletic shoes. However, the biggest exchanges between buyers and sellers involve marketing to organizational buyers such as businesses and government agencies. Organizations buy goods and services to help them carry out their missions. For example, Ford Motor Company buys spark plugs in order to make cars, and all kinds of organizations pay for temporary secretarial help so that they can get work done when employees are on vacation or leaves of absence. (For a closer look at the types of organizations one company serves, see the "You Decide" box.)

CATEGORIES OF ORGANIZATIONAL BUYERS

To appreciate the extent of organizational purchasing, it helps to think of organizational buyers in terms of four broad categories: producers, intermediaries, governments, and other institutions. Marketers serve these types of buyers in both domestic and foreign markets.

producers
Organizational buyers that buy goods and services in order to produce other goods and services for sale.

PRODUCERS   When Detroit Edison sells electricity to Ford Motor Company or when a proofreader sells proofreading services to Austen Press, they are selling to **producers**, also known as the industrial market. This type of organizational buyer consists of businesses that buy goods and services in order to produce other goods and services for sale. Thus, Ford uses electricity to produce automobiles to sell, and Austen Press uses proofreading to produce textbooks to sell.

Producers are engaged in many different industries, ranging from agriculture to manufacturing, from construction to finance. Together, they constitute the largest segment of organizational buyers. Figure 9.1 compares the number of companies and employees in each of the major categories of producers identified by the Census Bureau. (It also shows the categories of intermediaries, discussed in the next section.)

Producers of goods (manufacturers) have some different characteristics and needs than do producers of services. Manufacturers tend to be larger and more concentrat-

You Decide

HOW CAN CAREMARK SERVE ITS MANY MARKETS?

The biggest exchanges between buyers and sellers involve sales to organizations. Often, these exchanges take place in a complex environment. For instance, a single marketer may serve several different *types* of organizations. Take the case of Caremark International Inc., an Illinois-based firm that offers health care plans through its own and other facilities.

First, Caremark needs to convince physicians it is a high-quality, up-to-date health care company that health care professionals would want to be affiliated with. Caremark is best known for its leading role in establishing alternative-site care (care outside of hospitals) for patients with HIV/AIDS, cancer, hemophilia, organ transplants, high-risk pregnancies, and other ongoing conditions. It also has a state-of-the-art system for monitoring patients over a long period to see which treatments work and which do not.

Second, Caremark has to sell itself to traditional care facilities such as hospitals. For these members of its target market, Caremark seeks to position itself as a high-quality company dedicated to providing top notch service at the lowest cost.

A third target for Caremark is the employers who buy health care plans for their employees. The concern for this group is to obtain the best care for their employees at the lowest possible cost. Addressing employers, Caremark promotes its patient-monitoring system as a major factor in reducing long-term costs.

Fourth, Caremark markets itself to pharmaceutical companies. It seeks to create arrangements to offer necessary drugs to patients at low prices.

Finally, of course, Caremark has to appeal to the needs of patients, who like the convenience of alternative-site care and the variety of services available at these sites, including low-cost prescriptions. They also expect to receive these services at as low a cost as possible.

Although patients are not organizational buyers but consumers, they are an important component of Caremark's marketing effort to employers. If patients don't elect the Caremark program, it will not succeed at that particular organization.

Thus, to carry out its mission to provide the highest-quality health care at the lowest price, Caremark serves five different groups. In what basic ways would you expect the marketing mix to be different for each group? Do you think cross-functional teams would help Caremark's effort to serve these different types of customers? Explain.

Source: Caremark International Inc., 1992 Annual Report.

---

ed geographically than services businesses. There are many more services firms in the United States (see Figure 9.1), but they tend to be smaller. Therefore, advertising plays a relatively heavy role in reaching services firms. Marketers that serve manufacturers rely more on personal selling. Advertisements aimed at manufacturers seek to develop a good image of the marketer's organization. An example is the advertisement in Figure 9.2, where transportation company ZIM Container Service describes how it protects customer's shipping interests, much as a mother bear protects her cubs. Then the sales force works with interested shippers to identify specific needs and ways to meet those needs.

intermediaries
Resellers that purchase goods to sell at a profit.

INTERMEDIARIES Other organizational buyers, called **intermediaries** or resellers, purchase goods to resell at a profit. They may be retailers (businesses that sell to consumers) or wholesalers (businesses that sell to retailers or other businesses). Crown Books is a retailer; it purchases books and periodicals from a number of publishers and resells them to consumers in its stores. Wholesaler McKesson Corporation buys drug products from producers and resells them to drugstores. Chapter 17 takes a closer look at the role of intermediaries.

Intermediaries typically carry a large number—thousands or even hundreds of thousands—of different products. Once an intermediary decides to carry a particular item, the company tends to reorder it automatically as long as customers keep buying it. Thus, the biggest challenge in marketing to intermediaries is to convince them that a new product will appeal to their customers.

FIGURE 9.1

Number of Establishments and Employees: Producers and Intermediaries

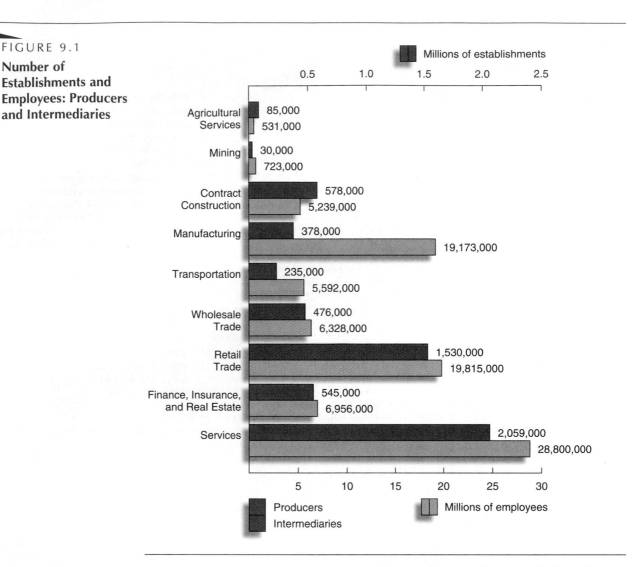

Source: U.S. Department of Commerce, *Statistical Abstract of the United States,* 113th ed. (Washington, DC: U.S. Government Printing Office, 1993), p. 538. Data are for 1990.

For example, when Kenneth Cole wanted to introduce his new high-fashion shoe company at the Fashion Footwear Association of New York's trade show, he couldn't even afford a booth. So he got a city permit to park a film production van outside the exhibit. A camera operator and director pretended to be filming "The Beginning of a Shoe Company." Adding to the sense that something exciting was happening were the police officers there for crowd control and the limits on visitors—only one allowed inside at a time to see the models wearing Cole's line of shoes. In two days, Cole sold 40,000 shoes and created an identity for Kenneth Cole Productions.[1]

Besides buying goods for resale, intermediaries buy products needed to operate. For example, Crown Books buys not only books and magazines for resale but also cash registers and advertising services. Crown won't resell the cash registers, of course, but will use them to produce the service of making publications available to consumers.

FIGURE 9.2

Advertising Aimed at Promoting a Good Image to Buyers

GOVERNMENTS In the United States, government organizations operate at the federal, state, and local levels. The Census Bureau estimates that there were over 86,000 governmental units in the United States in 1992.[2] Together they spend almost $2.4 trillion a year on a variety of products, including machinery, equipment, facilities, supplies, and services.[3] More than half of this money is spent by the federal government, making it the world's biggest customer.[4]

Government agencies tend to be low-risk customers, unlikely to declare bankruptcy. In recent years, however, governments at all levels have sought to cut their spending. This trend is actually an advantage to private businesses that can provide at a lower cost services traditionally provided by governments, such as collecting garbage or operating prisons. In addition, businesses that are flexible can prosper even in the face of budget cuts. The National Institutes of Health asked Arlington, Virginia–based Technautics to conduct a survey of career opportunities for minorities in the field of biomedical research—a far cry from the company's experience in providing engineering and technical support to weapons programs. But Technautics marshaled its resources, satisfied its new customer, and grew quickly by providing a variety of research services to the government.[5]

Selling to the government can be relatively complex. A variety of policies and regulations dictate the supplier's activities in the exchange and in day-to-day operations. For routine purchases, the marketer must provide a product that meets a set of specifications. Usually several potential suppliers submit bids, and the government agency buys from the organization that bids the lowest amount. In spite of the paperwork involved, many organizations are eager to service government accounts because they can be so large. Harris Corporation worked for six years to win the Federal Aviation Administration's contract to modernize air-traffic communications systems. But Harris expects the $1.7 billion contract to provide it with revenues over a 15-year period.[6] Also great are the challenges and rewards of serving foreign governments. Harris spent two years developing a custom radiation-hardened circuit to meet the specifications of Japan's space agency. Harris expects this product to be its ticket to a sizable chunk of Japan's space business.[7]

Many resources are available to help marketers who wish to sell to the federal government:

- The U.S. Government Printing Office (GPO) offers a variety of publications that spell out guidelines for selling to the government. These include the Federal Acquisition Regulations and guidelines for selling to specific government agencies, including the military.
- For invitations to bid on federal government purchases, marketers should consult *The Commerce Business Daily,* also printed by the GPO.
- For advice on selling to the government, marketers can consult with the Business Service Center of the Government Service Administration and refer to the Small Business Administration's (SBA's) *U.S. Government Purchasing and Sales Directory.*
- For small businesses, another resource is an SBA database called the Procurement Automated Source System (PASS). Over 900 federal purchasing agents and prime contractors use the database to identify companies to work on federal projects. Small businesses can be listed on PASS for free by contacting the SBA.[8]

Also, a variety of books and articles have been published on this topic.

OTHER INSTITUTIONS   Besides the business and government organizations described so far, the marketer may wish to target other institutions such as hospitals, museums, universities, religious organizations, and political parties. To gauge the size of these markets, consider that the Census Bureau counted almost 170,000 firms exempt from federal income tax in 1987 (the most recent year for which this information is available). These not-for-profit institutions generated receipts of more than $267 billion—substantial buying power, to say the least.[9] To operate, these institutions need to buy a variety of goods and services. Their buying behavior resembles that of business and government organizations.

BUSINESS CLASSIFICATIONS

Marketers can gain further insights about their business customers by identifying types of businesses in greater detail. Often this means focusing on the products they offer. Thus, steelmakers and photography studios will have different needs.

Marketers that recognize differences can identify ways to modify the marketing mix. That was the experience of NIR Systems, a Silver Spring, Maryland, maker of measurement devices for industrial use. An NIR sales rep visiting a pharmaceutical company saw one of NIR's devices upside down on a lab bench; the customer's technicians said it worked better upside down. So NIR pleased its pharmaceutical customers by developing a modified version of the product for their use.[10]

The most common ways to classify businesses according to products or services produced are to use SIC codes or the *Thomas Register.*

Standard Industrial Classification (SIC) codes
Codes assigned by the U.S. Office of Management and Budget to categories of businesses.

SIC CODES   The **Standard Industrial Classification (SIC) codes** are codes assigned by the U.S. Office of Management and Budget (OMB) to categories of businesses. Most codes have four digits, which identify a major group, industry group, and specific industry. Figure 9.3 provides an example. Every 10 or 15 years, the OMB updates the categories. It assigns at least one code to each U.S. company.

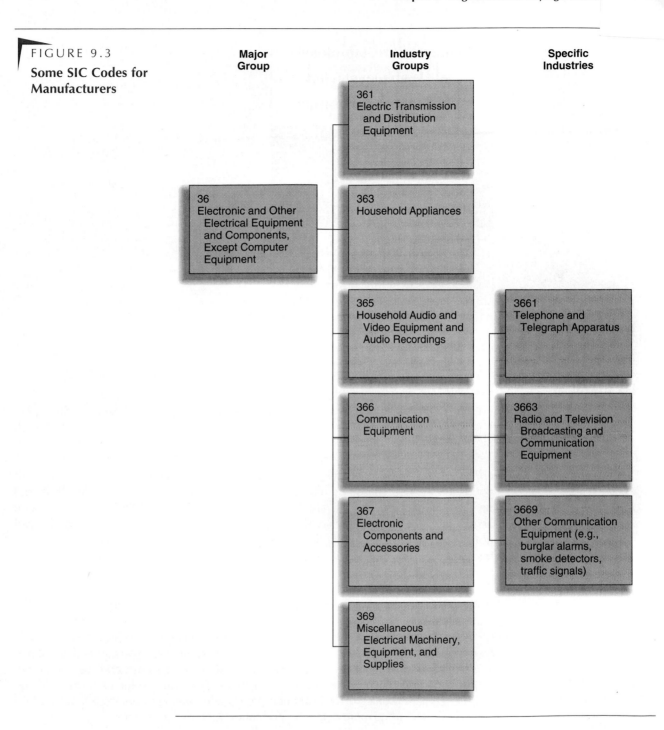

FIGURE 9.3

Some SIC Codes for Manufacturers

Marketers use SIC codes to identify the organizations they wish to do research on or communicate with. Thus, organizations that sell mailing lists of businesses will allow the marketer to specify mailing labels for organizations with particular SIC codes. When the marketer specifies zip codes as well, it is possible to target potential organizational buyers with a high degree of precision. Also, in analyzing data about

In this advertisement that appeared in Restaurant Business *magazine, the Norwegian Seafood Export Council humorously promotes its quality, availability, and management skills to the restaurant business (SIC code 5812).*

Last week restaurateur Sal Bambacci started buying cod from Norway.

This week he won the lottery.

When your customers taste Norwegian cod, great things will happen to you too. After all, our quality assurance, government inspection, consistent availability, and resource management are the best in the business. For this kinda luck, call *1-800-328-7256*.

Cod from Norway

You gonna tell us there's no connection?

organizations, the marketer may review government data categorized by SIC code. The marketer could use such data to answer a variety of questions, including which SIC categories are largest and which are growing fastest.

There are some drawbacks to using SIC codes. Because the categories are updated only occasionally, it is hard to keep up with industries producing new kinds of goods and services. Also, the marketer targeting customers by SIC code may miss out on some organizations that are in more than one industry; they may have been assigned a code for an industry the marketer is not targeting. Finally, marketers will not be able to get four-digit codes for every industry in every geographic area. This is because the government will disclose the data only when more than two organizations exist in an area.

THOMAS REGISTER   Another often-used source of information on business types is the *Thomas Register,* a set of over 20 reference books. The majority of the volumes contain names and advertisements for over 52,000 types of goods and services, alphabetized by type of product. Thus, under the listing for "Adhesives, silicone," you can find about two pages of suppliers listed by state and city. Listings show a company's address, sometimes a phone number, and a rating of the company's size. Some volumes in the *Thomas Register* contain profiles of 145,000 companies and catalog pages from almost 2,000 companies, providing more detailed information for these companies.

INTERNATIONAL TRANSACTIONS

Many marketers serve foreign as well as domestic organizations. Marketers serving a mature, slow-growth industry in the United States often find that the same industry is relatively young and faster growing in other countries. And just as foreign consumers are attracted to many U.S. brands, including Coca-Cola and Levi's, foreign businesses are eager to snap up U.S. technology in a variety of products, such as computers.

Meeting the needs of foreign organizations can require product modifications. For example, most of the world's buyers specify dimensions with metric measurements. And one reason given for the difficulty U.S. automakers have had in selling cars in Japan has been their slowness to offer cars with the steering wheel on the right, the standard in that country.

Besides selling to foreign business, marketers can often find substantial opportunities with foreign governments. To protect national security, the U.S. government imposes some limits on what products may be sold to foreign governments. These limits typically involve military products or products that may be converted to military uses. To learn about specific restrictions, the marketer can consult the Department of Commerce's *Commodity Control List.* A marketer that produces products on this list may have to apply for special export licenses or may be unable to sell them to a foreign government at all.

Major Forces in Organizational Markets

Zebra Technologies Corporation sells bar code printers to industrial users. For example, a manufacturer might buy a printer from Zebra to make bar code labels for tracking parts and inventory. In targeting industrial applications, Zebra chose to avoid selling to retailers because they are the most visible users of bar codes and therefore the most competive part of the industry. In contrast, says Edward L. Kaplan, one of the company's founders, only 20 percent of the potential industrial uses for bar codes have been implemented, meaning there is great potential for growth in demand. By helping customers apply the technology of bar codes to their operations, Zebra has successfully responded to the opportunities and limitations of the forces of demand, competition, and technology.[11]

DEMAND

Organizational buyers demand goods and services that will help them make a profit and meet the needs of their own customers. Their demand shifts in response to changes in the various dimensions of the marketing environment, as described in Chapter 2. For example, when President Clinton signed the Family and Medical Leave Act in 1993, the requirement that businesses provide unpaid leave for a variety of family emergencies was expected to generate at least a modest increase in the demand for temporary help from agencies such as Manpower and Western Temporary Services.[12]

derived demand
Demand dependent on another source, as the demand for organizational goods depends on the level of demand for consumer goods.

DERIVED DEMAND   The demand of organizational buyers is **derived demand**; in other words, the demand for organizational goods depends on the level of demand for consumer goods. The amount that an organization buys depends on how much customers will buy from that organization. Thus, the amount of invoice and purchase order forms an electrical supply house orders from a printer depends on how much the store expects electricians to buy, which in turn depends on consumer demand for remodeling and new homes. In the Northwest, the boom in consumer demand for espresso has led to surging sales of espresso carts. In Yakima, Washington, alone, over 20 espresso carts and stores are positioned on city streets and in shopping malls and the lobbies of office buildings.[13]

Derived demand means that marketers serving organizational markets must be concerned not only with the demand of those organizations, but also with the demand of consumers for their customers' goods and services. Therefore, when the

Consumer demand for new homes influences the demand for the many goods sold to housing contractors, such as land, building materials, fixtures, and appliances.

end products or consumer segments are uniform enough, marketers to organizations try to stimulate consumer demand. For example, consumer demand for new homes affects the demand for goods and services sold to housing contractors. An increase in the demand for new homes leads housing contractors to buy land, fixtures, and appliances.

acceleration principle
The principle stating that a small change in consumer demand for a product results in a major shift in the demand for goods and services used to produce the product.

ACCELERATION PRINCIPLE   Consumer demand is especially important because of the strength of its effect on organizational buying. According to the **acceleration principle**, a small change in consumers' demand for a particular product can result in a major shift in the demand for the goods and services that go into that product. Suppose a real estate developer learns that the demand for housing is expected to slow somewhat over the coming months. Rather than building many houses and being out millions of dollars while waiting for consumer demand to pick up, the developer decides to hold off on any new construction, concentrating instead on selling the few vacant homes in existing subdivisions. When the developer learns that demand for new homes is picking up again, the developer might take out a construction loan and start to work on a new subdivision, leading to a big jump in the use of construction services, building materials, and home appliances. Thus, the demand for these goods and services takes major swings in response to moderate shifts in consumer spending patterns. The result is that the demand of organizational buyers is more volatile than consumer demand.

COMPETITION

Existing and potential competitors are, of course, an important part of the marketing environment for any marketer. However, competition keenly affects those serving organizational buyers because of the relatively small numbers of buyers and the relatively great size of their purchases. Whereas losing one consumer to competing preparers of tax returns might cost an accountant several hundred dollars, the loss of a big corporate customer could cost tens or hundreds of thousands.

sole sourcing
Routine purchasing from a
single supplier.

SOLE SOURCING   Often an organization routinely makes a particular type of purchase—say, of office supplies—from a single supplier. This practice is called **sole sourcing**. Sole sourcing is certainly a desirable arrangement for the seller, which can concentrate more resources on pleasing customers, than on convincing them to buy. Therefore, some marketers make it an objective to be the sole source.

A case in point is Wabash National, a Lafayette, Indiana, maker of truck trailers. Wabash seeks to build long-term relationships through a willingness to innovate in order to meet customer needs. Thus, when Dart Transit Company asked its supplier to develop a trailer with thinner walls, that supplier told Dart the change was impossible. However, Wabash worked with Dart to develop a design that met Dart's needs. Such attention to quality and customer satisfaction has enabled Wabash to travel far toward its goal of being the sole source for all of its customers.[14]

Sole sourcing, coupled with human beings' normal tendency to resist change, can make it especially difficult for a marketer to win business away from a competitor. To overcome this challenge, marketers to organizations need to be well aware of what the competition is doing. Often, what they learn is that their competitors aren't really delivering value to their customers. In Western Europe, a survey of 1,000 business customers found that they most valued a salesperson who keeps promises and a product that arrives on time and performs as expected. What they say they are most likely to get is a trustworthy organization and one with a good reputation, as well as courteous customer service—not bad things, but not the most important to them.[15]

IDENTIFYING CUSTOMER NEEDS   To gain a competitive advantage, suppliers must be familiar with their target markets and what they need. While surveys and focus groups may be sufficient for learning about consumers, the smaller number of organizational buyers makes it feasible to learn more about specific organizations. With regard to the physical distribution industry, David Pope, director of international marketing at CSX Intermodal, observes, "In the past, too many carriers fell into the trap of trying to guess what would be considered value." Intense competition has since spurred CSX and a number of its competitors to ask customers what services they want. As a result, they now provide a wide variety of services to make it easier for producers to distribute their goods overseas.[16]

Not only salespeople but employees throughout a customer-oriented company may visit current or potential buyers. These visits enable the supplier's employees to learn what their customers need and to think of ways the supplier can help meet those needs. DuPont's "Adopt a Customer" program encourages blue-collar workers to visit a customer once a month, learn the customer's needs, and act as the customer's representative on the shop floor.[17]

SOLVING CUSTOMER PROBLEMS   An important way that marketers can learn about their customers is to have a team from the selling organization solve problems with a team from the customer organization. Often such teams are cross-functional, drawing together employees from, say, purchasing and manufacturing at the customer organization and sales and engineering at the seller. Such efforts are the essence of the quality approach to marketing.

Harris Semiconductor initiated team problem solving when Ford Motor Company, a major customer, learned that its assembly employees were dissatisfied with the integrated circuits (microchips) they were getting from Harris. Ford's equipment was rejecting the chips, even though Harris was sure they were meeting specifications.

Harris managers and line workers commuted to the Ford assembly plant, where they investigated the problem along with Ford production workers and engineers. They learned that the color and reflectivity of the Harris chips were confusing Ford's robots. Rather than blaming the robots, the Harris team modified the chips and also made further improvements based on what they learned about Ford's manufacturing process. The Ford workers, impressed, asked that Harris be made the sole suppliers of the microchips.[18]

TECHNOLOGY

As technology advances, marketers must stay ahead of or at least keep up with the changes. This is especially true when the marketer's use of technology enables its customers to operate more effectively or more efficiently.

TECHNOLOGY OF THE MARKETER'S PRODUCTS   Organizational buyers expect their suppliers to have expert knowledge of the products the suppliers sell, including technological expertise. One of the reasons for the success of Zebra Technologies has been its ability to see ways in which bar code technology can help its industrial customers work more efficiently. Other marketers can similarly look for ways in which their technology can help customers.

Taking this principle a step further, marketers must recognize opportunities for advancing the technology they sell. They must understand technological developments and incorporate them into their products. They must be able to help the organizations in their target markets understand these developments and show how to benefit from them. Few organizational buyers can afford to ignore uses of new technology. Therefore, marketers who want to keep existing customers and attract new ones must help them keep up to date.

Raychem, a high-tech pioneer in the use of heat-shrinkable plastic tubing, has successfully done this by viewing prospective customers as partners in applying the company's technology. Raychem Vice President Michael Sullivan advocates his company's approach of meeting with prospects and presenting not a particular good or service, but the company's capabilities. If the salesperson listens to the prospect's problems, together they can explore ways to apply the marketer's technology to solve those problems.

Thus, Raychem showed shrinkable tubes to an English electrical utility and learned that, with modifications, such tubing would be useful to insulate underground cables. Telephones have underground cables, too, so Raychem visited the telephone utility in England and learned what product modifications it would require. In China, Raychem sold similar tubing but modified it so workers could insert pressurized air into the cable. In Saudi Arabia, Raychem learned that the problem was many workers were untrained, so the company sold training services along with tubing to join pipelines.[19]

TECHNOLOGY OF THE MARKETER'S PROCESSES   Marketers also must use new technology appropriately within their own organizations. For example, the typical organizational buyer expects to be able to fax in an order. Buyers of more and more types of manufactured goods expect their suppliers to produce short runs of just enough of a product tailored to their specific needs. Retailers look for computer links with suppliers that enable them to replenish inventory on short notice (see Chapter 17). Buyers in many kinds of organizations expect salespeople to provide the kinds of fast answers that require the use of portable computers.

FIGURE 9.4

The Process of Organizational Buying Decisions

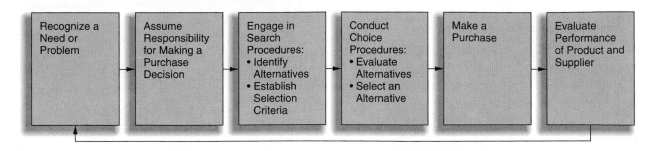

Suppliers that lack such technological resources will lose business to competitors that have them. That was the case when Loveda McNair of McNair Amusements, a traveling carnival, needed a gear reduction motor to repair a children's roller coaster called the Go Gator. The ride broke down near Milledgeville, Georgia, on a Friday night. McNair started calling industrial supply companies around Atlanta. No one could help her, so she called the toll-free national hotline for industrial supplier W. W. Grainger. Grainger's central computer used satellite links with its individual outlets to determine that the motor McNair needed was available in Grainger's facility in the Chicago suburb of Niles. At 8:45 that evening, Grainger paged a customer service representative, who took the motor to an air-freight company. McNair picked it up at the Atlanta airport the next morning, and the Go Gator was up and running later that day.[20]

The Purchasing Decision

At Elk Grove, Illinois–based Groen, which manufactures commercial food preparation and processing equipment, Louise E. O'Sullivan-Oshin has always focused on what customers need. For example, she got the idea for the company's Combo oven/steamers from European equipment, which she had to redesign for the U.S. marketplace. Explains O'Sullivan, "European equipment . . . was made for chefs who lovingly take care of their equipment. We design our equipment for 16-year-old kids behind the counter or prisoners working in a prison kitchen." O'Sullivan's familiarity with customer needs propelled her through the ranks of marketing and sales at Groen to a position as its president. In that position, she continues to devote half her time to visiting and discussing needs with Groen customers, including hospitals, hotels, manufacturers, and schools. The company as a whole has profited from the customer focus; five of its six major products are the market leaders.[21]

Like O'Sullivan, marketers serving organizational buyers can benefit by understanding what their customers are looking for and how they make decisions. In general, organizational buying decisions follow the process shown in Figure 9.4. First, someone in the organization recognizes a need or a problem to be solved. Next, one or several people assume responsibility for making a purchase decision to meet the need or solve the problem. The buyer or buyers within the organization then engage in search procedures to identify alternatives and establish criteria (such as product

---

TABLE 9.1

Types of Organizational Purchases

PURCHASE TYPE	COMPLEXITY	TIME FRAME	NUMBER OF SUPPLIERS	APPLICATIONS
Straight rebuy	Simple	Short	One	Frequently purchased, routine products, such as printer ribbons
Modified buy	Moderate	Medium	Few	Routine purchase that has changed in some way, such as air travel (new fares, flights, destinations)
New task purchase	Complex	Long	Many	Expensive, seldom-purchased products, such as new location for a department store

---

specifications) for making a selection. The organizational buyer(s) conduct choice procedures, including evaluation of the alternatives and selection of one. The buyer(s) make the purchase, then evaluate the performance of the product and its supplier.

TYPES OF PURCHASES

The specific way in which organizational buyers follow these steps depends in part on the complexity of the purchase to be made. The possibilities are summarized in Table 9.1. They are the straight rebuy, modified rebuy, and new task purchase.

STRAIGHT REBUY   The simplest and most common type of purchase is called a **straight rebuy**. This type of purchase involves routinely reordering from the same supplier a product that has been purchased in the past. Many of the organizations that buy fortune cookies from Chicago producer Noodles of China use straight rebuys. For example, a Wisconsin bar owner maintains an ongoing supply of cookies with risqué messages. The only changes to his orders are to occasionally suggest messages he finds amusing.[22]

Organizations use a straight rebuy when they are experienced at buying the product, have an ongoing need for it, and have regular suppliers of it. In many cases, organizations have computer systems that automatically reorder certain commonly used products. Organizations use this simple approach to purchasing because it is fast and requires relatively few employees.

To retain customers who use straight rebuys, the marketer needs to maintain a high quality of products and reliable service so that the customers will continue to be satisfied with their purchases. That did not happen to the Minnesota electric power plant that had fortune cookies from Noodles of China at its board meeting. The cookies got mixed up at the producer's warehouse, and the power plant directors mistakenly received a batch with the risqué messages. The chairman of the board was reportedly displeased, which no doubt affected any future purchase decisions.[23]

Straight rebuys are common among organizations that practice **just-in-time inventory**, or a system of replenishing parts or goods for resale just before they are needed. Such buyers do not have time to hunt around for potential suppliers and solicit bids. Instead, they regularly place their orders with a supplier whose quality and timely delivery they can count on. If a supplier delivers items that are late or of unacceptable quality, these buyers will not have a reserve in inventory to draw on.

straight rebuy
Routine reordering from the same supplier of a product that has been purchased in the past.

just-in-time inventory
A system for replenishing parts or goods for resale just before they are needed.

Therefore, organizations that use just-in-time inventory tend to favor suppliers with a strong commitment to quality.

MODIFIED REBUY   When some aspects of the buying situation are unfamiliar, the organization will use a **modified rebuy**. This type of purchase involves considering a limited number of alternatives before making a selection. Organizational buyers follow this approach rather than a straight rebuy when a routine purchase changes in some way—for example, a supplier discontinues a product or stops satisfying the customer, the price of a usual product rises, or a new product becomes available to meet the same need. Thus, the Minnesota power company that had the awkward experience with fortune cookies would probably use a modified rebuy for its next purchase of refreshments.

In such situations, the organizational buyer considers the new information and decides what changes to make. If the change proves satisfactory and the product is one needed routinely, the buyer may then make it part of a straight rebuy. Marketers seek to win new organizational customers by giving them reasons to change from a straight rebuy to a modified rebuy in which they consider the marketer's products.

NEW TASK PURCHASE   Organizations purchase some products only occasionally, especially in the case of large investments such as machinery, equipment, and real estate. In those cases, the organization may use a **new task purchase**. This type of purchase involves an extensive search for information and a formal decision process.

New task purchases are most often used for big-ticket items, so the costs of a mistake are great. Therefore, a new task purchase is time consuming and involves a relatively large number of decision makers, who consider many alternatives. This is the type of purchase decision that is most likely to rely on a cross-functional team, because many kinds of expertise are required to make the best decision.

A new task purchase is an opportunity for the marketer to learn about the needs of the organizations in its target market and to discuss with the organization ways to meet its needs, such as through the use of new products and technology. This is the approach used by AutoResearch Laboratories Inc. (ALI), which provides testing and evaluation services to companies that develop and/or market petroleum products. When an ALI customer wants to conduct a new kind of test, ALI's marketing department arranges a meeting of both companies' technical people (engineers or chemists) at ALI's facilities. The ALI technical staff seek to demonstrate that they can run the needed test flawlessly. In deciding whether to give the work to ALI or one of its competitors, customers also consider such criteria as price, timely delivery of the final report, and willingness to handle special requests.[24]

BUYING CRITERIA

As in the example of ALI, organizational buyers consider several criteria when making a buying decision. These include price, performance, reliability, and ease of purchase. Because organizational buyers often make much larger purchases than consumers, they may give great weight to some criteria. For example, the price of a pad of paper is much more significant to a buyer who will be purchasing pads by the carton than to a buyer purchasing one or two.

ECONOMIC CRITERIA   Because businesses operate to make a profit, they place importance on criteria related to profitability. In today's economic environment, this often translates into cost consciousness. For example, General Electric Company

---

modified rebuy
Purchase that involves considering a limited number of alternatives before making a selection.

new task purchase
Purchase that results from an extensive search for information and a formal decision process.

recently called together over 300 suppliers to its appliance division and announced an initiative called Target 10. Under Target 10, GE planned to cut its supplier costs by 10 percent, meaning that suppliers wanting to continue doing business with GE would have to cut their prices.[25]

Although organizational buyers are concerned about price, they may be willing to pay more for a product if it will enable the company to boost profits by improving efficiency or increasing output. Figure 9.5 shows an advertisement designed to appeal to the desire to improve profits by lowering costs. Similarly, Illinois Tool Works has seen consistent profits from its strategy of developing a variety of industrial products, many specifically designed to save its customers money. Explains Senior Vice President Michael W. Gregg, "We develop products that make our customers more efficient. As they make more money, we make more money."[26]

value analysis
A comparison of the costs of a potential purchase with the benefits the product is expected to provide.

To evaluate economic criteria, members of the buying organization may prepare a **value analysis**. This is a comparison of the costs of a potential purchase with the benefits the product is expected to provide. The potential buyer weighs the cost to acquire and use products against productivity improvements the products are expected to deliver.

Part of the value analysis may be a consideration of whether to make, buy, or lease the products that will meet the organization's needs. Consumers also make such decisions, of course. They decide whether to make dinner or send out for pizza; they decide whether to buy or lease a car. However, make-buy-lease decisions can be a more prominent part of decision making for organizations, because they typically have greater access to the resources needed to make a variety of goods and services.

The selection of making, buying, or leasing depends on a variety of factors, including the organization's capabilities and the impact of the alternative on the organization's income taxes. An increasing number of organizations today are choosing to buy or lease rather than to make many goods and services. This frees them to concentrate on what they do best.

QUALITY AND SERVICE CRITERIA   Trends such as the desire to operate with lean inventories and to bring products to market faster have made today's organizational buyers more concerned than ever with the quality of the products they purchase. Marketers must be able to convince their customers that they will reliably deliver the desired level of quality. To this end, it helps to have a record of high performance, as well as a formal commitment to quality products and processes.

Meeting quality criteria entails knowing what organizational buyers are looking for. In the case of supplying seeds to farmers, suppliers know that most farmers are looking for varieties of fruits and vegetables that yield a uniform size at a uniform time, because it is most efficient to harvest everything at once. Farmers also are looking for fruits and vegetables that will meet government standards for size, weight, grading, and color. Interestingly, none of these criteria has anything to do with taste, but this is not a problem for farmers or retailers because consumers, in turn, usually select fruits and vegetables based on their appearance.[27]

Sometimes marketers are surprised by the quality standards set by foreign customers. That happened to Giddings & Lewis Measurement Systems Inc., which makes precision measuring devices used in automobile production. Technological developments enabled the company to offer greater accuracy at a lower price than competitors, but European automakers didn't bite. Giddings & Lewis sent Vice President John Bosch to the Stuttgart Works of Daimler-Benz to find out why. There he was told in no uncertain terms that the device's unattractive casing demonstrated a lack of concern for quality and customer needs. So Giddings & Lewis hired a design firm to develop a new cover for the device, and worldwide sales soared to $50 million.[28]

For many, if not all, buyers, quality does not mean just goods that are defect free or aesthetically pleasing, it also includes service geared toward helping the organizational buyer solve its problems. Minneapolis-based Kurt Manufacturing built its reputation on its skill in manufacturing precision parts and assemblies, but today its customers expect more. As Kurt's customers try to get new products to market quickly, they do not have time to draw up detailed blueprints of the parts they need and send them out for bids. Instead, they look for dependable partners such as Kurt to work with them in turning performance requirements into products. Thus, Kurt shares design responsibilities with these customers. Says CEO Bill Kuban, "We are a manufacturing arm for our customers, not just a job shop."[29] (To learn about another marketer who places importance on the quality of services provided to clients, see "Marketing Movers & Shakers: Rosemary Maniscalco and Uniforce.")

vendor analysis
Procedure in which the buyer rates each potential supplier on various performance measures.

VENDOR ANALYSIS   When buyers are using a formal decision process, they need a method for weighing the various criteria they have established. One approach is to conduct a **vendor analysis**. This is a procedure in which the buyer rates each potential supplier on various performance measures such as product quality, on-time delivery, price and payment terms, and use of state-of-the-art technology. Figure 9.6 provides an example.

The result of conducting a vendor analysis is generally a list of approved vendors. General Electric, for example, works only with the vendors that are top-rated in an analysis of quality, technology, price, and other factors. The company finds regular vendor analysis a more efficient way to ensure quality than waiting to inspect parts when they are received.[30]

Marketing Movers & Shakers

ROSEMARY MANISCALCO AND UNIFORCE

"Previously the temporary employment business was a reactionary one," says Rosemary Maniscalco, chief operating officer of Uniforce Temporary Services in Hyde Park, New York. "Today, it's part of a planned program, one that takes advantage of the changes everywhere in business."

Foremost among those changes is the importance placed on cost control. Slow economic growth and intense foreign competition have led organizations to look for ways to keep a lid on personnel costs. As a result, many employers—the customers of temporary-help services such as Maniscalco's—rely on a skeletal work force supplemented with temporary help as needed.

Maniscalco describes Uniforce's marketing efforts as "day-in and day-out niche marketing in hundreds of different niches nationwide." In other words, Uniforce caters to a variety of organizational buyers, appreciating and serving their different needs. She further notes that her company's marketing philosophy is "to show our client companies that we will go the extra mile for them through our services, that we will be there when they need us for whatever reason."

Maniscalco herself knows the rigors of the temp business. After graduating from the Fashion Institute of Technology in New York, she wound up temping for Olsten, the third largest agency in the business. She worked in a variety of assignments and locations. Eventually, she joined Uniforce, and she is now one of its executives.

She feels that her experience on the front lines of temping has given her important, firsthand knowledge. Certainly, she understands the dynamics of relationships among members of the buying center in any given company: Who needs the temporary help? Who decides the specifications of what help is necessary? Who controls the flow of information? Who OKs the decision to hire a temp?

It's important to keep track of these issues in such a competitive industry. "But we don't intend to ever stumble," says Maniscalco. "We offer more than any other temporary services company in the industry because we intend to be the best temporary services company within it."

Source: "Rosemary Maniscalco: May the Uniforce Be with You," *Sales & Marketing Management,* September 1992, pp. 38–39.

As the use of vendor analysis is taking hold in the health care industry, it is shaking up pharmaceutical firms. One of the largest and most influential buyers of drugs is the Kaiser Permanente health maintenance organization. A staff of Kaiser physicians studies various categories of drugs and chooses the effective ones that cost the least. The chosen drugs go on a list, called a formulary, of drugs Kaiser encourages its doctors to prescribe. Kaiser encourages drug companies to offer discounts in exchange for selection over competing products. It has a staff of pharmacists that educates its physicians about drugs on the formulary. As a result, 96 percent of Kaiser's prescriptions are for drugs on the formulary.[31]

In serving organizations such as GE and Kaiser Permanente that use vendor analysis, a key marketing objective is to get on the list of approved vendors. The organizations most likely to get on approved-vendor lists are ones that are quality driven. They must be adaptable enough and customer oriented enough to identify and meet the criteria buyers develop.

For more on buying criteria, see the "Put It into Practice" box.

CHARACTERISTICS OF ORGANIZATIONAL BUYERS

The way organizational buyers make purchasing decisions varies from one organization to the next. The differences are especially varied because not only do organiza-

FIGURE 9.6

Sample Vendor Analysis Form

	5 Excellent	4 Good	3 Satisfactory	2 Fair	1 Poor	0 N/A

Supplier Name:_____   Type of Product:_____
Shipping Location:_____   Annual Sales Dollars:_____

Quality (45%)
Defect rates
Quality of sample
Conformance with quality
  program
Responsiveness to quality
  problems
  Overall quality

Delivery (25%)
Avoidance of late shipments
Ability to expand production
  capacity
Performance in sample
  delivery
Response to changes in
  order size
  Overall delivery

Price (20%)
Price competitiveness
Payment terms
Absorption of costs
Submission of cost savings
  plans
  Overall price

Technology (10%)
State-of-the-art components
Sharing research &
  development capability
Ability and willingness to
  help with design
  Responsiveness to
  engineering problems
  Overall technology

Buyer:_____ Date:_____
Comments:_____

Source: Chrysler Corporation.

tions differ in their needs and methods of operating, but the individuals who make the buying decisions within the organization also differ.

CHARACTERISTICS OF ORGANIZATIONS   The way an organization makes buying decisions depends in part on the organization's size. At a large organization, there are more likely to be formal procedures for making purchase decisions, and those decisions are more likely to involve a group of people (called a buying center, described

---

Put It Into Practice

DETERMINING BUYING CRITERIA

For marketers to sell to organizational buyers, each party must have a clear understanding of buying criteria: price, performance, reliability, and ease of purchase. As an individual consumer, you can see how important these criteria are to your own purchases before you ever have a chance to engage in selling to an organization.

Consider the most recent large purchase you made; it may have been a bicycle, a car, a piece of furniture, a stereo, or some other item. Make a chart with the following headings: "Price," "Performance," "Reliability," and "Ease of Purchase." Under each heading, comment on how well your purchased item met the criterion. Then comment on how well a competing product that you considered buying did or did not meet each criterion. Chances are, the purchased item met the criteria more successfully than the competing item. When you market goods and services to organizations, organizational buyers will consider these four criteria in making their buying decisions.

---

later in this chapter). At small organizations, purchase decisions are more often quick, informal, and carried out by one or a few people.

Marketers also need to know whether the organization is highly centralized. At a centralized organization, purchases are more likely to be handled by one or a few people. At a decentralized organization, many people may be authorized to make purchase decisions. To serve a decentralized organization, the marketer may have to work with a variety of people in different departments or locations of the same company.

The type of industry in which the organization operates influences the kinds of products it needs and where it is located. For example, law offices tend to use different types of computer software than mining operations do. And while dry-cleaning businesses are spread throughout the United States, manufacturers of dry-cleaning equipment are concentrated near the Great Lakes and in the Atlantic states.

CHARACTERISTICS OF BUYERS WITHIN THE ORGANIZATION Controller Mercedes D'Agostino believes that her successful career has been the result of caution and careful planning. When she reviews requests to purchase machinery, D'Agostino wants to see at least three bids from vendors with a long and favorable track record, and she is reluctant to award a contract to any but the lowest bidder. In contrast, Sid Greenspan, who heads research and development, believes that the company's success depends on quickly generating innovations. He considers himself an excellent judge of potential suppliers' credentials, and when he approves of a salesperson or company, he is eager to hear the representative's new ideas. These two hypothetical managers take markedly different approaches to their buying decisions. The differences stem partly from their differing roles in the organization and partly from who they are as individuals.

Position in the Organization The criteria used by organization members making buying decisions, as well as the kinds of decisions they make, depend in part on their position in the organization. One reason is that buyers have different degrees of power. The individual's degree of power depends in part on his or her place on the organization chart. Organizational politics also affects the power of individuals. Randy Bradley, whose NetPro software company makes half of its sales to the government, maintains that political issues are especially relevant to the buying behavior of government officials. Bradley advocates learning who is in power, what their constituency is, and what the marketer's place is in that picture.[32]

TABLE 9.2	FUNCTIONAL AREA	KEY CONCERNS IN PURCHASE DECISION MAKING
Functional Areas and Their Key Concerns about Buying	Design and development engineering	Name reputation of vendor; ability of vendors to meet design specifications
	Production	Delivery and reliability of purchases such that interruption of production schedules is minimized
	Sales/marketing	Impact of purchased items on marketability of the company's products
	Maintenance	Degree to which purchased items are compatible with existing facilities and equipment; maintenance services offered by vendor; installation arrangements offered by vendor
	Finance/accounting	Effects of purchases on cash flow, balance sheet, and income statement positions; variances in costs of materials over estimates; feasibility of make-or-buy and lease options to purchasing
	Purchasing	Obtaining lowest possible price at acceptable quality levels; maintaining good relations with vendors
	Quality control	Assurance that purchased items meet prescribed specifications and tolerances, governmental regulations, and customer requirements

Source: Reprinted with the permission of Macmillan College Publishing Company from *Industrial and Organizational Marketing* by Michael H. Morris. Copyright © 1988 by Macmillan College Publishing Company, Inc.

Employees in different departments tend to have different concerns, as shown in Table 9.2. Ideally, everyone is working toward the achievement of organizational goals. But even while doing so, people with different responsibilities and areas of expertise are inclined to concern themselves with different areas of performance.

One advantage of using cross-functional teams in marketing to organizational buyers is that the marketer can draw on the expertise of people from various disciplines to recognize and interpret the concerns of organizational buyers from different functional areas. Thus, a finance person on the team will be sensitive to financial issues at the client organization, and a production person will be sensitive to the needs of production at the client organization.

Personal Characteristics   Although an organizational purchase is, in the legal sense, an action of an organization, the actual process of selecting what to buy and placing an order is carried out by human beings. Chapter 8 identified some internal forces that motivate consumers in making purchase decisions. These forces also operate on buyers within organizations.

For example, organizational buyers are subject to a variety of motives. One is, or should be, helping the organization meet its goals. Thus, organizational buyers are motivated to weigh economic factors, such as the return on investment in a piece of machinery.

Many comparisons of consumer and organizational buying imply that these kinds of rational, analytical factors are the primary force behind organizational buying decisions. However, organizational buyers are also influenced by other, more personal motives, including friendship, professional pride, fear and uncertainty, and personal ambition.[33] In marketing to corporate CEOs, Marguerite Sallee, who heads Corporate

FIGURE 9.7

**Advertising Aimed at
the Personal Motives
of Organizational
Buyers**

Child Care Management Services, says her company learns about what goals are important to each executive, then tries to show how the company's services can help the CEO succeed.[34] Figure 9.7 shows an ad that appeals to the pride of a business owner, as well as to the practical benefits of having a business look well established. The seeming reliance on analysis in organizational buying may simply reflect the effort of employees to behave as expected. Organizational culture requires that decisions be analyzed and justified, so organizational buyers expend more energy in rationalizing their intuitive or emotional choices.[35]

Like many individual consumers, many organizational buyers are risk averse; that is, they seek to avoid risks. Making the wrong decision can be costly to the organization and to the career of the decision maker. Risk aversion is probably a factor behind the results of a British study showing that organizational buyers tend to prefer large, well-known suppliers and to use the same supplier even when they have good reason to change.[36] Sticking with familiar suppliers and products doesn't guarantee that the employee is making the best choice, but it provides some security that he or she will avoid making a poor choice. Marketers to organizations will find that buyers are especially cautious when a product has a high price, lacks a performance record, or requires a great deal of training to use.[37] The marketer of such products will have to work harder to demonstrate the expected benefits of purchasing them.

Cultural Influences The individuals who make purchase decisions within an organization, like individual consumers, are shaped by their culture. Thus, marketers to organizations in foreign countries may encounter individual responses that surprise them if they are not familiar with the culture. Raychem's Michael Sullivan tells of the time he tried to work with a Japanese colleague to serve that man's largest customer. Sullivan wanted his colleague to call the customer's purchasing director, but the man refused. Arguing made no difference, so Sullivan, frustrated, called the purchasing director himself. Fortunately, the purchasing director spoke English, and they made an appointment. Afterward, Sullivan realized that his colleague was saying he *could not* call the customer, not that he was unwilling to do so. The reason was that Sullivan's colleague had a lower status than the director of purchasing, so the phone call would have been improper in his culture. Sullivan could get away with it because his job title and gray hair made him seem senior enough.[38]

THE NATURE OF ORGANIZATIONAL TRANSACTIONS

Organizational transactions vary widely, depending in part on the size and type of organization. However, some characteristics of organizational transactions distinguish them from purchases by consumers. For example, as noted earlier, organizations tend to make bigger purchases than consumers. Also mentioned earlier is that economic factors may weigh more heavily in organizational than in consumer buying decisions.

To evaluate and select the products they buy, organizational buyers (and consumers too) use one of these approaches:

- *Inspection buying*—Making a selection and purchase based on looking at each item to be sold. For example, before leasing factory space, the organization's representatives would want to see the building.
- *Sampling buying*—Making a selection and purchase based on looking at part of the goods to be sold. The chef of a restaurant might look at a sample of asparagus before purchasing a few crates of it.
- *Description buying*—Making a purchase based on written or oral specifications for the product. A buyer might use a catalog to select ribbons for computer printers or might tell the representative of a temporary-services firm what skills are needed. As in the latter example, description buying is the usual way to purchase standardized services.
- *Contract buying*—Negotiating the terms of a purchase agreement, including product specifications, price, and timing of payments. This approach is common for purchasing customized products, as in the case of a construction project or professional services.

competitive bidding
Inviting several potential suppliers to offer a price and other terms of sale for a product meeting given specifications.

When buyers are clear on the specifications they will require, they often use **competitive bidding**. This involves inviting several potential suppliers to offer price and other terms of sale for a product meeting given specifications. When the buyer believes that the suppliers will be able to provide similar quality, the buyer may select on the basis of the price bid. Government agencies seek competitive bids for most purchases by publishing requests for bids like the one shown in Figure 9.8. After receiving bids, the government agency selects the organization that offers to supply the product meeting the bid specifications at the lowest price.

Interactions with Organizational Buyers

In marketing to organizations, moreso than in marketing to consumers, the exchange process may be a collaborative effort. A salesperson or team of employees works with a buyer or team of employees to identify ways the marketer can meet the potential buyer's needs. The marketer can benefit from seeing its role as one of problem solver, rather than simply seller of a particular type of goods or services. At Zebra Technologies, described earlier, Edward L. Kaplan says, "Originally, we really viewed ourselves as a provider of computer printing hardware. But the customer is not looking to buy a

FIGURE 9.8

Sample Request for Bids

CHICAGO TRANSIT AUTHORITY
Advertisement for Bids for Material and Equipment
Sealed proposals will be received for the following by Chicago Transit Authority at Room 738, Merchandise Mart Plaza, Chicago, Illinois 60654, until 2:00 P.M. on Friday, May 14, 1993, at which time and place all such proposals will be opened publicly and read aloud:
Req. G23327U, Spec. No. CTA-6024-93.
Two Units of Class 1A Flammable Material Storage Sheds for Skokie Shops Unit One.
PROPOSAL GUARANTEE: NONE
Any contract resulting from this solicitation is subject to a financial assistance contract between the Chicago Transit Authority and the United States Department of Transportation and the Regional Transportation Authority.
The contractor will be required to furnish certified copies of any and all Insurance Policies required in relation to this contract prior to CTA's execution. Contractor will be required to comply with all applicable Equal Employment Opportunity laws and regulations and affirmative action requirements of the Federal Transit Administration and the Illinois Human Rights Commission. All bidders will be required to certify that they are not on the Comptroller General's list of ineligible contractors.
Any contract resulting from this advertisement will be awarded to the lowest responsive and responsible bidder.
Chicago Transit Authority hereby notifies all bidders that it will affirmatively ensure that in regard to any contract entered into pursuant to this advertisement, Disadvantaged Business Enterprise and Women's Business Enterprise will be afforded full opportunity to submit bids in response to this invitation and will not be discriminated against on the grounds of race, color or national origin in consideration for an award.
The right is reserved to accept any bid or any part or parts thereof or to reject any and all bids. Acceptance of any bid is subject to concurrence by the Regional Transportation Authority and the United States Department of Transportation.
All inquiries should be directed to and copies of the documents obtained for the Materials Management Department, Room 725, Merchandise Mart, Chicago, Illinois 60654.
CHICAGO TRANSIT AUTHORITY
By: Edward L. Gronkowski
General Manager, Purchasing
April 30, 1993

piece of hardware. What the customer is looking to do is solve a labeling problem. . . . So we shifted the focus of the company . . . to being a solutions provider."[39] This strategy has worked so well that in a recent year Zebra was on *Forbes'* list of 200 best small companies and *Business Week*'s list of hot growth companies.

BUYER-SELLER INTERACTIONS

For many organizational purchases, a strong relationship between buyer and seller is important. The buying organization depends on both parties to create exchanges that will help the organization meet its goals. Thus, all but the smallest organizations assign the buying duties to employees with expertise in carrying out that function. These employees may be called **purchasing agents**. A large organization may have purchasing agents who specialize in different categories of products. For large or complex purchases, they may engage in lengthy negotiations with suppliers to arrive at contract terms.

purchasing agents
Employees responsible for carrying out buying duties.

For their part, marketers that serve organizational buyers tend to depend relatively heavily on each customer, so they cultivate long-term relationships with their customers, often employing salespeople to phone or visit them. Amp, Inc., which markets an extensive line of electronic connectors, outdoes its competitors by involving its own sales engineers in its clients' projects. When an Amp customer is developing a new product, the Amp engineer serving that company is there to show how Amp products can add value.[40] As described in "Looking Ahead" at the end of this book, these relationships may extend beyond simply buying and selling to become strategic alliances, cooperative relationships in which each organization contributes what it does best in order that all members of the alliance may successfully carry out their mission.

The cooperative nature of long-term buyer-seller relationships such as strategic alliances leads buyers as well as sellers to take an active role in strengthening these relationships. A notable example is Wal-Mart, which several times a year conducts

In this ad, Mitsubishi tells manufacturers why they should use its CNCs (sophisticated computerized numerical controllers for machine tools). The primary reason is Mitsubishi's commitment to maintaining long-term relationships with its customers. The company promises to customize the CNC and provide three days of free training.

two-day management seminars at its headquarters in Bentonville, Arkansas. Besides flying in store managers, Wal-Mart invites five of its major suppliers, offering them time with top managers. The suppliers not only learn about Wal-Mart from their meetings with managers, they also spend four hours brainstorming ways in which their own knowledge could benefit the retailing giant. They flesh out a few of their ideas and present them to Wal-Mart. In one case, a team identified an unneeded form; by eliminating its use, Wal-Mart estimated it could save $500,000 a year in managers' time. Also, suppliers and Wal-Mart managers participate in team exercises during the seminar. In so doing, the suppliers develop relationships with store managers—relationships that presumably help the two companies work better together over the coming years.[41]

DEVELOPMENT OF LONG-TERM RELATIONSHIPS   Developing an ongoing relationship with a customer can take a lot of work. The marketer may invest significant time and money before getting an order. When International Jensen Inc. (IJI) sought to supply car stereo speakers to Honda Motor Company, Honda responded by requiring the company to duplicate the speakers it was already using. Despite the difficulty of duplicating an existing product, IJI took on the challenge and won a contract to supply two of the four speakers being installed in Hondas built in Marysville, Ohio. Later, IJI negotiated for business with Mazda Motor Corp. After an all-day Friday meeting in Hiroshima, Mazda allowed IJI to submit a bid—to be written in Japanese and delivered by the following Monday morning. Thanks to months of preliminary planning, IJI was able to submit the winning bid that Sunday evening.[42]

For large, regular, or highly technical purchases, the organizational buyer expects ongoing support after making the purchase. For example, the buyer of a computer system may expect assistance in selecting, installing, learning to operate, and maintaining the system.

The quality approach to marketing demands that sellers be certain their customers are getting value from their products. At Pacific Bell, this includes providing training to organizational buyers of voice mail systems. The training helps buyers use the systems in ways that enhance their image, rather than upset customers by greeting them with an endless recording.[43]

ETHICAL ISSUES   The heavy investment marketers make in their organizational customers can make unethical behavior tempting. Salespeople seek to win the loyalty of organizational buyers through many means, including large and small gifts, especially around the December holidays. Customers who make large purchases often receive invitations to lunches in fancy restaurants and tickets to shows or sports events. Even smaller customers may be offered lunch.

Different organizations have different standards for what constitutes acceptable relationship building. Some prohibit their employees from receiving any gifts at all. In such situations, the marketer does well to respect that standard and avoid putting employees in an awkward position. In other organizations, going out to lunch is viewed as a good opportunity to discuss business, and small gifts are seen as perks of the buyer's job. North American telephone companies, the major customers of telecommunications firms such as Canada's Northern Telecom, expect seminars and trips from their suppliers, not just for the fun, but because these activities are an opportunity to learn about the complex products they buy.[44]

Despite the variations in standards, it raises ethical questions when buyers make purchase decisions based on favors received from the seller, rather than on the organization's need for the goods and services. Gifts that induce such behavior may be considered bribes in some cases. However tempting bribery may seem as a sales tactic, offering high quality at a reasonable price is a much more effective way to maintain long-term goodwill and repeat business.

SOURCE LOYALTY   Thanks in part to the efforts of marketers to provide service before and after a purchase, organizational buyers tend to have stable, long-term relationships with their suppliers. This characteristic of buyer-seller interactions is known as **source loyalty**. Repeatedly giving business to the same few suppliers limits the search for alternatives, which means the buyer may be missing out on the best choice at times. However, there are potential benefits of source loyalty, including good communications with suppliers, products well adapted to customer needs, and preferred status with the supplier in case of a shortage.[45]

source loyalty
Stable, long-term relationships between organizational buyers and their suppliers.

RECIPROCITY   In some instances, the sales departments of two organizations seek to establish an arrangement called **reciprocity**. In such an arrangement, the two organizations agree to purchase one another's products. Marketers will find it hard to compete with an organization engaged in a reciprocity arrangement unless they can clearly demonstrate a price or quality advantage.

reciprocity
An arrangement in which two organizations agree to purchase one another's products.

Marketers who are interested in entering reciprocal buying arrangements should do so with caution. The U.S. Department of Justice has challenged them as a form of restraint on trade. Furthermore, such arrangements may not be in the organization's best interests. Will the organization be buying inferior products or paying too much for them as a result of an agreement designed to boost sales? Reciprocity can create an ethical problem in which the need to sell conflicts with the need to buy the best products at the best price.

THE BUYING CENTER

When marketers serve organizational buyers, the exchange process can involve several individuals. The various organization members who have a role in selecting, pur-

FIGURE 9.9
Roles in the Buying Center

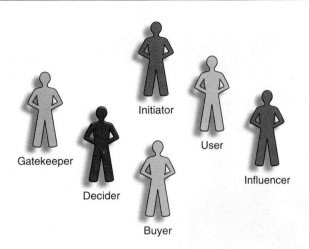

buying center
Organization members who have a role in selecting, purchasing, and using a product.

chasing, and using a product are known as the **buying center** for that product. The buying center is not a formal group, but merely the people who communicate with one another regarding the purchase.

ROLES IN THE BUYING CENTER   As summarized in Figure 9.9, the people in a buying center fill six roles:

1. *Initiators*—People in the organization who identify a problem or need that can be resolved with a purchase.
2. *Users*—People in the organization who actually use the product. In the case of a photocopier for a department, there may be many users. In the case of furniture for an office, there is a single user.
3. *Influencers*—People who affect the buying decision, usually by helping to develop specifications for the product. For example, a designer or production editor might develop specifications for typesetting a book, or an engineer might write specifications for machining a part.
4. *Buyers*—People with the authority and responsibility to select a supplier and negotiate contract terms. Medium-sized and large organizations generally give these duties to a purchasing department.
5. *Deciders*—People with the formal or informal power to select or approve the selection of a supplier. If a purchase is technical, the purchasing department may rely on the expertise of an employee in the research or engineering group.
6. *Gatekeepers*—People who control the flow of information into the buying center. Such employees may include secretaries, technical experts, and purchasing personnel.

These roles may be filled by six or more individuals, or one person may fill multiple roles.

Marketers to the organization need to know which employees play each role in the buying center. Compaq Computer Corporation recognizes that the buying centers of its customers include the actual users of its computers, some of whom have strong enough opinions that they also act as influencers. The buyers are managers who write the checks but may not get involved in evaluating products, beyond noting that a brand is one they are comfortable with. The buying centers served by Compaq also

FIGURE 9.10

Ad Targeted to Users in the Buying Center

include information systems professionals who typically focus on whether a system under consideration is capable of doing the job well. Thus, their role tends to be that of decider.[46]

Members at the client organization will probably be willing to disclose information about who is involved in the buying decision, because doing so will help the marketer cooperate with them. However, the marketer must be careful in interpreting information provided by organization members; their perceptions are not always unbiased. For example, a study of purchasing agents found that they had a higher estimate of their responsibility and control over decisions than did others.[47]

To implement the quality approach to marketing, it is necessary to identify and meet the needs of all members of the buying center. Different members will place varying amounts of emphasis on personal needs, economic concerns (cost, return on investment), technical features, and reliability and ease of use. The ad in Figure 9.10 reflects the likelihood that healthcare workers who handle hypodermic needles (the users in the buying center) are most concerned about meeting safety needs. At AutoResearch Laboratories, marketing personnel must convince their clients' technical staff of the company's expertise in carrying out the desired testing program. ALI also must convince clients' management that its price is competitive, its billing terms are reasonable, and the company is dependable.[48]

A company that seeks to meet multiple buying center needs is Rite-Hite, a Milwaukee manufacturer of loading-dock equipment. Rite-Hite not only works with purchasing agents, it invites prospective customers' quality and safety teams and product users to tour its factory to learn about the products of Rite-Hite and its competitors. The tours are designed to help the prospective customers' employees identify needs and explore solutions. Of the businesses that send employees on the tours, about 90 percent eventually make a purchase from Rite-Hite. In one recent year, 353 companies sent visitors and purchased $12 million worth of equipment.[49]

INTERACTIONS IN THE BUYING CENTER   To understand the interactions in the buying center, the marketer needs to identify its members and how they are related. Several terms describe the dimensions of these people's are involvement:[50]

- *Vertical involvement*—The number of levels of the organization represented in the buying center. For example, the purchase of expensive machinery may require the approval of top management, while the users of the machinery are operative employees.
- *Lateral involvement*—The number of departments or divisions that participate in the buying center. Routine buying decisions may involve only one or two people in one or two departments. But for many decisions at an organization that uses cross-functional teams, the lateral involvement may be great.
- *Extensivity*—The number of people in the buying center. This number may be as small as 1 or as large as 50 and varies according to the type of purchase. The buying center tends to be largest for purchases of novel products, for complex purchasing decisions, and for purchases likely to have a large impact on the organization.
- *Connectedness*—The extent to which members of the buying center interact with one another with regard to the purchase. For example, getting approval may be a mere formality, or those who want to make the purchase may have to make a detailed presentation supporting their view.
- *Centrality*—The importance of the purchasing agent in the buying center. The purchasing agent may be heavily involved in selecting a model or a supplier, or that person may simply place the order. When the purchasing agent's importance is relatively low, the marketer will have to invest more effort in identifying and working with other members of the buying center.

The relative importance of buying center members will vary according to the type of purchase. For a straight rebuy, the person placing the order will have a relatively great degree of control. However, for most new task purchases, a variety of people will be heavily involved. In the case of a novel and highly technical product, such as a new computer or communications system, the person with the most technical expertise will likely play a significant role as influencer.

BUYING CENTERS AND THE QUALITY APPROACH   The concept of a buying center is especially important in working with organizations that are emphasizing customer responsiveness and total quality.[51] The demands of such an emphasis require that more people be involved in a variety of decisions, including what and how much to buy. Buying center members in an organization that practices total quality management might include employees whose primary responsibility is for materials management, operations management, and quality assurance. They and the other members of the buying center are likely to interact with one another extensively.

Summary

The biggest exchanges between buyers and sellers involve marketing to organizational buyers, so it is important for marketers to understand this type of buying behavior. Organizational buyers fall into four general categories—producers, intermediaries, governments, and other institutions (such as hospitals or universities).

Major forces that influence organizational buying behavior are demand, competition, and technology. The demand of organizational buyers is derived demand; that is, it depends on the level of demand for consumer goods. According to the acceleration principle, a small change in consumers' demand for a product can result in a major shift in the demand for the goods and services needed to produce that product. Competitors are especially important to marketers serving organizational buyers because each customer has a relatively great impact on such marketers' total sales. Marketers cannot afford to lose organizational buyers to the competition, so they must excel at delivering value to their customers. The importance of technology to organizational buyers means that marketers serving them must know the technology of their products, recognize opportunities for advancing the technology, and use technology appropriately within their own organizations.

Organizational purchases are of three main types: straight rebuy, modified rebuy, and new task purchase. To make these purchases, organizations may engage in inspection buying, sampling buying, description buying, or contract buying. The way organizations make purchases depends in part on organizational characteristics such as size and degree of centralization, as well as on characteristics of the people who are making the decision, such as their motives and their role in the organization.

Because the organizational purchase is often so large and complex, most organizations assign the responsibility for purchasing to purchasing agents. Marketers seek to cultivate long-term, cooperative relationships with organizational buyers and their purchasing agents. Source loyalty and reciprocity are examples of this type of relationship, although the latter is often found to be a form of restraint on trade. Together, the individuals involved in the buying decision at an organization are called a buying center. The marketer must identify who these individuals are, which roles they play, and how they interact.

KEY TERMS AND CONCEPTS

producers (p. 258)	**sole sourcing (p. 267)**	**vendor analysis (p. 273)**
intermediaries (p. 259)	**straight rebuy (p. 270)**	**competitive bidding (p. 279)**
Standard Industrial Classification (SIC) codes (p. 262)	**just-in-time inventory (p. 270)**	**purchasing agents (p. 280)**
derived demand (p. 265)	**modified rebuy (p. 271)**	**source loyalty (p. 282)**
acceleration principle (p. 266)	**new task purchase (p. 271)**	**reciprocity (p. 282)**
	value analysis (p. 272)	**buying center (p. 283)**

REVIEW AND DISCUSSION QUESTIONS

1. Name and describe the four broad categories of organizational buyers.
2. Why is selling to the government a complex process? Why do marketers seek government contracts anyway?
3. If during a sluggish economy people still eat out but shift from a relatively upscale restaurant chain to a less-expensive, family-oriented one, what principle goes into effect? Who is affected, besides the restaurant owners?
4. Suppose you are responsible for marketing machines that process payments by debit cards at stores such as supermarkets.
   a. How much would your sales representatives need to know about the machines in order to sell them successfully? What strategies might you use to provide potential customers with enough information?
   b. What additional considerations should you take into account if your target market includes stores in Western Europe as well as the United States?
5. When purchases take the form of a modified rebuy, how can marketers gain new organizational customers?
6. As a marketer, what characteristics of an organization (and the people within it who are involved in buying decisions) must you be aware of in order to serve that organization successfully?
7. Name and define the four different approaches to organizational transactions.
8. As a marketer for a health care plan, you attend a meeting at a company that is considering adopting your plan. There are about a dozen people at the meeting, serving a variety of roles in the decision-making process. It's up to you to determine who they are. In this scenario, note which role in the buying center is played by each person (named in boldface).

   "We need a new plan that's available to people where they live, not one that is only near this office," states **Mary**, a manager.
   "I will work with you to develop the specifications of the plan so it will be appropriate for our employees," notes **Dominick**, the human resources director.
   "I want to be able to choose my own physician," says **Ida**.
   "I will distribute copies of the plan to various managers," offers **Sean**, an administrative assistant.
   "I will review the plan and let you know what our decision is," concludes **Angela**, the chief executive officer.

Chapter Project
Buying and Selling in Teams

This is your chance to practice organizational buying and selling. Create at least two organizations in your class by dividing into pairs of teams: one that will try to sell a product and one that will make the decision whether to buy. Each team should consist of four to eight members.

The selling team may choose one of the following goods or services, or come up with one on its own:

- trash removal service
- groundskeeping service
- catering service
- video recording equipment
- office furniture.

The two teams should agree on what type of buying they plan to negotiate—inspection, sampling, description, or contract. Then the buying team should determine which members play which roles in organization (their function and level) and in the buying center (initiators, users, influencers, buyers, deciders, or gatekeepers). The selling team should determine how it plans to present the product to the buying team. (If the buying team is a government agency, the selling team should determine which rules and regulations are pertinent to the sale.)

Each buying and selling team negotiates in front of the class. When the team has completed a transaction or reached an impasse, the class discusses the results. What were the objectives of each side? (Were those objectives clear, or did you have to guess?) Was the selling effort appropriately tailored to the type of purchase? Did the selling team address the needs of the individual buyers and the buying organization as a whole? How could both teams better have achieved their objectives?

Case
Flying High With Flight Time

"We found a niche in the aviation industry, acted on it, and focused our company and employees on service," says Dara Zapata, president and one of the three women who founded Flight Time. Their Boston-based company keeps track of the availability of chartered aircraft and arranges chartered flights for customers. The founders' business timing and philosophy have served them well.

In 1985, with airline deregulation opening the door to new competition in flight, Zapata, Patricia Zinkowski, and Jane McBride, all with experience in the travel industry, launched Flight Time. "Luckily for us," explains Zinkowski, chief financial officer of the company, "people were hungry for a company like ours in 1985. The airlines were just going through deregulation, so there were many start-ups seeking new business channels. And since we worked directly with them *and* travel agents, we provided them with clients through our chartering service."

Relying on referrals from airlines as well as other contacts, the three women compiled a mailing list and sent a marketing package to potential business customers. They also sent a newsletter to potential clients, focusing on their European contacts for international appeal.

Within six years, Flight Time's revenues sailed to over $6 million. The company regularly handles 100 business and celebrity clients, including *Fortune* 500 companies. Its 24-hour, toll-free number, virtually a hotline, makes it possible to service businesses and other groups on short notice. Once it got a call from a frantic secretary for a college football team, which needed a flight for 100 players and cheerleaders on a Sunday night—immediately. Flight Time booked them.

During the Gulf War, when many commercial airlines stopped transporting passengers to the Mideast, Flight Time stepped in. "We found out that some airlines decided to hang in there, however," explains Zinkowski. "So we set up charter arrangements with them and began marketing Flight Time to oil companies, many of whom had employees in the Middle East."

Flight Time also handles more mundane travel arrangements. Wayland Millwork, a distributor of doors, took its chief executive and a group of employees on a tour of suppliers in Marlborough, Massachusetts; Peoria, Illinois; Waterloo, Iowa; Oshkosh, Wisconsin; Minneapolis; and Cincinnati. Wayland's main reason for chartering a Lear jet through Flight Time was cost. The charter totaled $2,000 below the less convenient alternative of booking a series of commercial flights.

To operate this type of business, Flight Time's founders must keep current on airline regulations, both in the United States and abroad. They need to be skilled at marketing to large and small organizations, as well as individuals (who have included Henry Kissinger and the late Malcolm Forbes). They need to be able to deliver service fast, often on the spur of the moment. So far, their business is traveling faster than the speed of sound.

QUESTIONS

1. What customer needs does Flight Time have to keep in mind when marketing to potential business clients? What competitive advantage(s) can the company offer them?
2. What do you think is the secret of the company's success?
3. In addition to providing fast and flexible service, how might Flight Time increase its business worldwide?

Sources: "Flying to the Top with Flight Time," *Sales & Marketing Management,* March 1992, pp. 22–23; Robert A. Mamis, "Charter Is Cheaper," *Inc.,* October 1993, p. 47.

CHAPTER 10   *Market Segmentation*

LEARNING OBJECTIVES

After completing this chapter, you should be able to:

1. Define market segmentation, and explain why marketers use it.

2. Describe when organizations use market segmentation.

3. Identify approaches to segmenting consumer markets.

4. Identify approaches to segmenting organizational markets.

5. Describe the steps in the market segmentation process.

6. Explain how marketers use market segmentation to position products.

Creating Customer Value
Verifone

According to Hatim A. Tyabji, chairman of the board, president, and CEO of California-based Verifone, his company is committed to "product innovation, employee empowerment, fiscal and environmental responsibility, and responsiveness to changing customer needs." Quality is paramount at Verifone, a manufacturer of transaction automation systems (automatic debit and credit machines): "More than an abstract principle, excellence is a choice, reaffirmed daily in countless individual and collective decisions in Verifone offices around the world," continues Tyabji.

Verifone relies heavily on employees around the world to serve its many international markets. In Western Europe, South America, and the Philippines, for example, Verifone "brings the market to the product" with a program called Omnihost. This program overcomes poor phone transmissions that often block automatic transactions. Having established that there was a market for transaction automation in these countries and having positioned itself as the company to provide it, Verifone went the extra step to coordinate employees in its offshore offices to make sure customers received the product.

In addition, Verifone believes that internationally, local employees can ferret out and serve new markets efficiently, sometimes just by speaking the language. Local employees also understand telephone infrastructure and different transaction regulations. Marius Carloganu, research and development engineer in Paris, says, "As a European, I understand how the market here differs from the U.S. market." His group noted the problem of variations in infrastructures and transaction regulations so that Verifone could develop an operating system that could be adapted for use in each country.

Because the Verifone work force is so widely dispersed, it needs an easy way to stay in touch in order to function effectively as a team. An electronic mail system takes care of that, linking all thirty offices worldwide and all 1,500 employees, regardless of their position in the company. By using their computers to send and receive messages at their convenience, employees operating in different time zones can collaborate without losing hours or days. Notes Guy Lang, a senior software engineer in Dallas who swiftly completed a project with employees located in London and Paris, "When I went home every evening, they were just coming in, so I could send them the work I did on e-mail and they picked up where I left off."

As you read this chapter on market segmentation, you'll get a feel for how quality comes into play in the innovative ways a company meets the needs and desires of the market segments it wants to serve. Verifone has already got the idea, and it's off and running.

Source: Verifone 1992 Annual Report, pp. 1–16.

Chapter Overview

market
The individuals or organizations with the desire and ability to buy a product.

By empowering its employees worldwide to learn about and address the needs of its customers in various countries, Verifone tailors its efforts to meet the needs of particular groups of potential buyers. In other words, the company divides the total **market**—the individuals or organizations with the desire and ability to buy a product—into relatively homogeneous segments. This process is known as market segmentation. Based on the results, the company decides which of those segments to serve, and how.

This chapter discusses why and when organizations use market segmentation instead of simply assuming they should serve an entire market with a single marketing mix. It describes the process of market segmentation and the criteria used to select target markets, or market segments to serve. Finally, it tells how organizations "position" their products, that is, how they design and promote them in a way that leads a particular market segment to see the products as satisfying important wants or needs.

The Need for Market Segmentation

One of the oldest and most commonly told stories of the need for market segmentation involves the early auto industry. By focusing on the economies of mass production, Henry Ford developed the Model T into a car intended to satisfy everyone. Said Ford, "They can have it in any color, as long as it's black." In contrast, General Motors' Alfred P. Sloan, Jr., had GM's engineers come up with several models, each designed to satisfy the needs and tastes of a different group of customers. This strategy helped GM become the nation's leading automaker.

Like Sloan, marketers have recognized for many years that a single marketing mix seldom is adequate to address the wants and needs of an entire market for a product. For example, not every consumer wants the same features in a home, nor does every business want to own the most advanced form of inventory management software. Similarly, buyers learn about products from different sources (such as friends and coworkers, *Consumer Reports* magazine, and television commercials, in the case of consumers). They place different values on low price (one organization might consider the latest technology to be a sound investment, whereas another is concerned with cutting costs). And different customers prefer to buy in different places (a catalog, a charming boutique, an outlet mall for consumers; over the phone, at a warehouse club, at a trade show for organizational buyers). Such variations among individual and organizational buyers are the main reason for market segmentation.

Furthermore, from the seller's standpoint, serving only a portion of the total market is often the most efficient strategy. That is certainly the case when a portion of the market accounts for a disproportionate share of sales for a product. One reason that printer and catalog producer R. R. Donnelley failed in introducing a catalog to Japan was that it ignored this principle. Although Donnelly's catalog was in English, the company did not limit its mailing to Japanese consumers who knew the language. When the sales response to the catalog was disappointing, Donnelley shut down the project.[1] In contrast, it makes sense for the organization to devote its marketing resources to the portion of consumers or organizational buyers most likely to purchase the product.

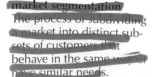

market segmentation
The process of subdividing a market into distinct subsets of customers that behave in the same way or have similar needs.

WHAT IS MARKET SEGMENTATION?

Formally defined, **market segmentation** is "the process of subdividing a market into distinct subsets of customers that behave in the same way or have similar needs."[2]

Murphy Insurance Services, an independent commercial service agency in Waunakee, Wisconsin, uses niche marketing by catering to the needs of specific industries. This allows the agency to offer the best deals, because they become top suppliers for their clients as well as top producers for the insurance companies they represent. Shown here are Joan Ogden, Patrick Murphy, and Steven Murphy, key people behind the success of Murphy Insurance.

Thus, the individuals or organizations in each subset, or market segment, have common needs and similar responses to a particular marketing effort. Businesses use this information to decide what segment(s) of the market they can serve most profitably. Nonprofit organizations use the information to determine what segment(s) of the market they can serve most effectively and efficiently.

WHEN DOES AN ORGANIZATION USE SEGMENTATION?

In some cases, organizations find it advantageous to develop a single marketing mix to serve a single market segment. This approach tends to be least costly and to give potential customers the clearest sense of the organization's specialty.

Thus, although Fisher-Price markets over 400 products, the company focuses on moderately priced toys for children six and under[3]—a focus that is well known among toy buyers in the United States. Other organizations find it more beneficial to use their own version of GM's strategy of developing several marketing mixes to serve several segments. This approach is more complex and more costly, but it can enable the organization to appeal to more customers and therefore generate larger earnings. Even when an organization decides to try serving the entire market with a single marketing mix (or not to enter the market at all), market segmentation is important. Only when marketers know about the existing market segments can they determine whether their strategy will be the most successful one.

niche marketing
Tailoring the elements of the marketing mix to attract a single market segment.

SINGLE-PRODUCT STRATEGIES   When an organization has a single type of good or service to sell, it may use market segmentation to find which categories of individuals or organizations are most likely to be interested in the product and to find it superior in some way to any competing products. The most profitable strategy may be to concentrate on selling the product to a single market segment, tailoring the elements of the marketing mix to attract that segment. This approach is known as **niche marketing**.

America Online, based in Vienna, Virginia, has used niche marketing to sell on-line information services to various categories of customers. For example, the company has arranged for a group called SeniorNet, which encourages older consumers to use computers, to promote America Online to its members. In return the company designs services to appeal to these consumers—for example, bulletin boards with news on topics such as health care and sex among people over 50. This strategy has been more profitable than market leader Prodigy's efforts to appeal to consumers generally.[4]

Because niche marketing can be done successfully with a relatively small investment, it is an attractive strategy for small organizations. It also allows a firm to achieve strong sales from loyal customers by specializing in serving their specific needs. Cheryl Shuman successfully launched an eyewear business by serving the needs of movie and TV producers. Shuman works with prop people to select the right frames, and she makes up the glasses with different lenses for different camera angles. Charging $300 an hour for her time, plus the price of the glasses, Shuman earned $14,000 in her second month in business.[5]

Niche marketing is relatively risky, however. A change in the demand of the single market segment can cause the organization's overall sales to plummet. That happened early in the century to Imperial Broom Company, a Richmond, Virginia company founded to make brooms for an African-American wedding tradition called "jumping the broom." This custom, based on the broom's being a symbol of the home in parts of Africa, was started by slaves (who couldn't legally marry) and involves the couple jumping into marriage over a broom lying on the ground. Soon after Imperial's founding, the company had to diversify into selling brooms for more mundane uses. Today, interest in African goods and services has renewed demand for bridal brooms, but Imperial's current president is wary about the long-term prospects for this market niche.[6]

In other cases, as already mentioned, a single product may appeal broadly to a market. Selling a single product line to all customers with a single marketing mix is known as **mass marketing** or undifferentiated marketing. In contrast to America Online, Prodigy has spent about $1 billion to sell on-line information services to a mass market.[7] Mass marketing is a viable choice under one of these conditions:

- The total market is too small to divide into segments.
- There are so many heavy users that they are the only group worth targeting.
- The brand already has such a large share of the market that targeting specific segments would be uneconomical.

mass marketing Selling a single product line to all customers with a single marketing mix.

Before deciding to use mass marketing, marketers need to carry out the research involved in market segmentation. They need to determine whether the conditions are right for mass marketing to be profitable. Besides looking for the conditions just listed, marketers must be able to appeal to a broad spectrum of buyers, keeping costs low enough to generate large sales. When Western Publishing launched its line of Little Golden Books over 50 years ago, the company knew it would have to sell 50,000 copies of its first 12 titles in order to mass-market these children's books at 25 cents each. This was a daring move, since the children's books of the time were strictly expensive niche items. However, the company sold more than a million books in the first six months. Today, Little Golden Books have become a "literary institution," having sold more than 1.5 billion copies to purchasers of all income groups.[8]

MULTIPLE-PRODUCT STRATEGIES   Many organizations today sell multiple versions of a product, each designed to appeal to a different market segment. In Europe, Electrolux varies its household appliances according to national tastes and customs. It offers 120 basic refrigerator designs with 1,500 variants. The refrigerators are large in northern Europe, where consumers shop once a week, and small in southern Europe, where consumers are apt to visit the market every day. In the north, the freezers are on the bottom, and in the south, the freezer goes on top. In Britain, consumers eat a lot of frozen food, so some units there are 60 percent freezer space.[9] In variations of this strategy, organizations adjust other elements of the marketing mix to reach several market segments. For example, a company may use different advertising messages and media to reach customers in different market segments. In either case, this strate-

FIGURE 10.1

**Supporting
Differentiated
Marketing of Musical
Theater**

differentiated marketing
Selling multiple versions of
a product to different
market segments.

gy is called **differentiated marketing**. Figure 10.1 shows differentiated marketing of musical theater involving product and price variations. Product variations include first-run shows in London and on Broadway, touring productions, local productions, and audio and video recordings. Prices vary among these offerings and tickets to most shows are available at several price levels.

By meeting the needs of various segments, a differentiated strategy should produce greater sales. However, as many a production manager has been quick to tell the organization's marketing people, serving a variety of market segments is more difficult and expensive than producing a single product intended for everyone. That has been the case with Electrolux, whose profits have suffered from the costs of keeping its product line diverse.[10] Therefore, when marketers consider a differentiated strategy, they must work closely with production personnel and other functional areas to ensure that the extra costs generate additional profits.

Marketers also must be careful to avoid differentiating so much that potential customers aren't clear what a company or its brands stand for. This is the major risk Mercedes-Benz faces in seeking to develop car models to serve all segments of the automobile market. Critics warn that Mercedes could lose its prestigious reputation.[11]

Some observers think that marketers have taken differentiated marketing too far. For example, 250 models of cars and trucks are available in the United States, and there are variations within these models. This degree of choice can leave consumers confused and suspicious of individual product claims. Says Susan Small-Weil, chief planning officer for the ad agency Warwick Baker & Fiore, "People in the 1990s don't want to . . . juggle all the complexities created in the 1980s."[12] One company that has tried to simplify by limiting choices is Alamo Rent A Car, which reduced its numerous rental options to a three-tier plan. Notice that such a change does not necessarily eliminate segmentation altogether; rather, it involves a simpler segmentation strategy.

Approaches to Segmenting Consumer Markets

Marketers can choose from among a variety of ways to segment markets. In choosing a basis for segmentation, the marketer relies on his or her existing knowledge about

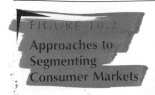

FIGURE 10.2

Approaches to
Segmenting
Consumer Markets

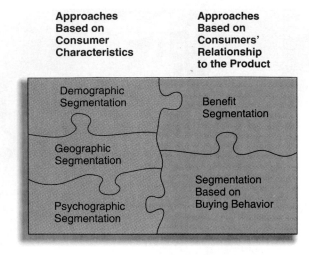

the market, current trends in purchases, and his or her best judgment. For example, a marketer might know that food preferences vary among regions of the country. He or she might conclude that Midwesterners would prefer a different type of barbecue sauce than Southerners.

For consumer products, marketers can use two basic categories of segmentation. They can segment the market according to characteristics that describe consumers (such as demographic or psychographic data). They also may use segmentation based on consumers' relationship to the product (what benefits they are looking for, how much they buy, how loyal they are to a particular brand). Figure 10.2 illustrates the basic types of segmentation for consumer markets.

CONSUMER CHARACTERISTICS

In earlier chapters, you have seen that there are many ways to categorize consumers. Demographic data describe populations in terms of such variables as age, gender, race or ethnic group, and socioeconomic status. Geographic data describe people's location—the nations, regions, and more specific areas where they live. And psychographic data provide insights into various life-styles.

demographic segmentation
Division of the market on the basis of population characteristics.

DEMOGRAPHIC SEGMENTATION   The most common way to segment consumer markets is to use **demographic segmentation**, or division of the market on the basis of population characteristics. This approach segments consumers according to such variables as gender, age, race or ethnicity, income level, occupation, education level, and household size and composition.

Segmentation by Gender   Segmenting based on gender is appropriate when a product is likely to appeal more to one gender than to the other, or when members of each gender are likely to respond differently to other aspects of a marketing mix. For example, the marketers of a cruise line might find that men and women tend to look for different things in a vacation. The cruise line can make sure it offers some of what each gender is looking for, and it might promote its cruises in different ways to attract each

You Decide

TARGETING YOUNG CONSUMERS—IT'S PROFITABLE, BUT IS IT ETHICAL?

Age segmentation has uncovered the buying power of today's kids. According to some estimates, big allowances and odd jobs give U.S. preteens $9 billion to spend each year. More significantly, estimates James McNeal, marketing professor at Texas A&M University, 4- to 12-year-olds influence purchases worth over $130 billion.

Behind this huge influence lie the time pressures of modern parents. With many households headed by a single parent or by two employed parents, many shopping tasks are delegated to children. An increasing number of teenagers, especially girls, are doing the family shopping. According to one study, one-third of 12- to 15-year-olds shop for the family's groceries weekly.

Marketers are taking advantage of this buying power. For example, many candy makers are targeting kids with a variety of novelty products. Product introductions have included candies designed to dye the inside of the mouth bright colors and a fizzy gumball called Mad Dawg that causes the young consumer to foam at the mouth. Perhaps typical of these

products' consumers is Bob Yu, age 11, who says, "I buy what I want. I just eat it before I get home."

One way to reach children is to create clubs for them to join, thereby getting their names on a mailing list. Hyatt Hotels Corporation offers kids' programs called Camp Hyatt, including sports lessons, movies, pottery classes, and video games. Hyatt later sends participating children news about events and attractions. Delta Air Lines has a Fantastic Flyer club with 700,000 children enrolled. Burger King has a Kids Club with 2.7 million members, each of whom receives a newsletter, iron-on T-shirt logos, and activity booklets. Buyers of Kids University shoes can sign up for a free newsletter and Kids U. pennant. The kids like getting the mail, and marketers appreciate the chance to develop brand loyalty at an early age.

Other companies are appealing to children through the schools. For example, Apple Computer promotes its products to schools, not only because schools are themselves a good market, but also because kids using their programs may influence their parents' buying decisions. Ten-year-old Laurence Faust uses an Apple comput-

er at school, and his father bought another for their home. Laurence wants AppleWorks software so he can write a book on the home computer, and his father plans to buy it.

Some people question the values being taught to children by these marketing efforts. They fear that children are learning that the path to satisfaction is to buy things. And giving in to the demands of today's kids can be expensive. For example, Bausch & Lomb's Killer Loop sunglasses, popular among California teenagers, cost $120.

Based on the information in this story, what are three products you think could be successfully promoted to children under 16? Name products not mentioned in the story. If you were the parent of a 9-year-old, how would you feel about your child watching TV ads for fast food that were targeted to him or her? Under what conditions do you think it is ethical to market consumer products to children? Under what conditions is it unethical?

Sources: Susan Greco, "Smart Marketing to Kids," *Inc.,* November 1992, p. 30; Laurie McLaughlin, "Tweens Blossom as Consumer Group," *Advertising Age,* October 14, 1991, p. 33; Christopher Power, "Getting 'Em While They're Young," *Business Week,* September 9, 1991, pp. 94–95; and Pauline Yoshihashi, "New Candies for Kids May Seem Tasteless to Adults," *The Wall Street Journal,* April 8, 1993, pp. B1, B9.

gender. Or it might determine whether men or women are more apt to make the decision to take a cruise, then focus its efforts on whichever gender makes the decision.

Segmentation by Age. People's needs and tastes change as they grow older, so many marketers segment on the basis of age. Rubbermaid, a company that in the past has focused on an older age group of consumers, has sought to increase its customer base by targeting young adults. The company seeks to persuade them that its products have many uses in today's homes.[13] And the "You Decide" box discusses efforts to appeal to the tastes and interests of children.

Marketers are interested in knowing which age groups are increasing in the population and which are declining. Figure 10.3 shows the age distribution of the U.S.

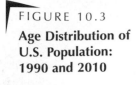

FIGURE 10.3

Age Distribution of
U.S. Population:
1990 and 2010

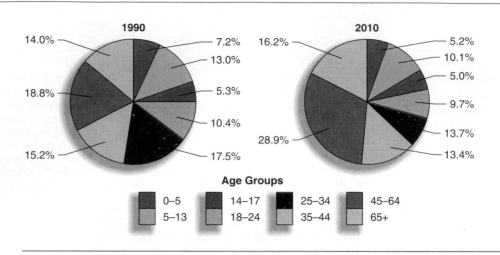

1990

14.0% — 7.2%
13.0%
18.8% — 5.3%
10.4%
15.2% — 17.5%

2010

16.2% — 5.2%
10.1%
5.0%
9.7%
28.9% — 13.7%
13.4%

Age Groups

▮ 0–5	▮ 14–17	▮ 25–34	▮ 45–64
▯ 5–13	▯ 18–24	▯ 35–44	▯ 65+

Source: Gregory Spencer, *Projections of the Population of the United States, by Age, Sex, and Race, 1988 to 2080,* U.S. Department of Commerce, Bureau of the Census, May 1989, p. 8.

population as it was in 1990 and is expected to be in 2010. As indicated in the figure, a notable trend in the United States is that the oldest segments of the population are growing fastest.

This trend, often referred to as "the graying of America," has inspired a variety of companies to direct their efforts toward older market segments. Levi Strauss & Co. developed its Dockers line of casual, roomy men's trousers to appeal to consumers who are significantly older than buyers of its traditional jeans.[14] Cane & Able, based in Edison, New Jersey, has developed retail displays of elder-care products such as canes, magnifying lenses, and heat packs.[15]

As with other forms of segmentation, the marketer appealing to particular age segments must not fall victim to stereotypes. Burger King's effort to win over Generation X with "BK Tee-Vee" spots was a flop.[16] And contrary to the usual stereotypes, one survey found that most consumers 50 and over are physically fit, have a positive outlook, and are open to new experiences. Thus, an inappropriate line of products for older consumers was Gerber's Senior Citizen line of pureed foods (too embarrassing to buy). A better approach was the British ads for Ubuleve, a rub for rheumatism sufferers, which showed active adults engaged in such pursuits as cycling.[17] General Motors has found that the so-called mature consumer does not want to be set apart strictly by age but does appreciate cars with certain comfort and safety features such as large, easy-to-read controls and a system for enhancing night vision.[18]

Segmentation by Race or Ethnicity   Sometimes marketers find it profitable to segment the market according to race or ethnic group. They believe that their product will appeal to one or more of these groups. Market segmentation can help marketers avoid the often incorrect assumption that European-American tastes, values, and needs define the whole market.

Increasingly often, segmentation by race or ethnicity leads marketers to focus on serving African-Americans, Hispanics, or Asian-Americans. J. C. Penney appealed to African-Americans' pride in their heritage by opening in-store boutiques selling authentic African clothing, housewares, and art. Sales were double what had been forecast, and customers even called the store to say thank you for making the products available.[19] Kentucky Fried Chicken has been testing additions to its menu designed to appeal to the ethnic mix of consumers near its restaurants. At 300 restaurants in predominantly African-American neighborhoods, KFC has begun offering such traditional soul food as collard greens, black-eyed peas, and candied yams. These restaurants have also switched employee uniforms from polo shirts to vests, ties, and hats made of traditional African kente cloth. With sales up following the menu additions, KFC made plans to test a Hispanic menu, including plantains, flan, and black beans and rice.[20] Carnival Cruise Lines is another company targeting Hispanics. Its FiestaMarina cruise division is offering cruises on which the staff speaks Spanish and the menus and entertainment have Hispanic themes.[21] To reach Asian immigrants in their native languages, companies including AT&T advertise on sideband radio, which involves broadcasters' leasing unused portions of other stations' FM channels to run programming in foreign languages.[22]

To serve racial or ethnic market segments (as when serving any kind of market segment), marketers need to move beyond relying on assumptions and stereotypes about these groups. They need to do their homework to learn what the consumers in the segment really need. When marketing consultants Don Coleman & Associates developed a database about the car-buying preferences of upscale African-Americans, they found influential new-car buyers with tastes sharply different from those of whites. In the past, decisions on marketing automobiles to African-American had been based on zip codes and guesswork, with frustrating results. In the words of Jerome Williams, a marketing professor at Penn State University, "When people talked about the black market, they were really talking about the ghetto."[23] Similarly, Bill Daniel, one of three black owners of Equinox Advertising, says ads targeted to black consumers are stereotypical, even when produced by black agencies, because such appeals are "easier to sell to white marketing departments."[24] More research into racial and ethnic subcultures, coupled with greater sensitivity, can avoid such marketing goofs as the Revlon advertisement in which Nat "King" Cole sings "Unforgettable" while viewers see a series of "unforgettable" women—all white.[25]

Marketers that use segmentation based on race or ethnic group must be careful to make sure their efforts are authentic as well as accurate. J. C. Penney's attempt to serve black consumers stirred protests among some black leaders, who complained that the retailer should instead work on getting more blacks into management positions at the company.[26] And Hispanic Americans often view as condescending marketing materials that simply translate English messages into Spanish, rather than reflecting knowledge of Hispanic culture.[27]

Segmentation by Socioeconomic Variables   Segmenting by income level helps marketers determine which consumers are likely to respond to a particular combination of price, style, and quality. Presumably, low-income consumers will be especially interested in bargains, whereas high-income consumers will be willing to spend extra for prestigious or high-quality products. Segmenting by education level or occupation are other ways to explore the socioeconomic status of various market segments. American Express does this by marketing its credit card to college students through direct mail and displays in bookstores. In that way, the company reaches a segment that averages substantially higher lifetime earnings than does the general population.[28]

Segmentation by Family Types   Demographic segmentation can also involve various ways to categorize households by size, composition, or stage in the family life cycle. For example, large families are likely to be attracted to big boxes of laundry detergent or an amusement park with a single admission price for a whole family. People who

live alone are apt to prefer smaller packages of many items, especially those that can spoil before they are used up.

Trends in family composition have led marketers to find ways to appeal to a variety of family types. One change is that as fewer families include a full-time homemaker, many parents rely on their children to take an active role in handling chores. The ad in Figure 10.4 appeals to this type of family.

Some products and marketing strategies will appeal to consumers at particular stages of the family life cycle. For instance, when their children grow up and leave home, many couples consider selling their house and moving into a home that is smaller and easier to care for. Consequently, ranch homes are popular among empty nesters. As this market segment has grown, so has the demand for these houses.[29]

geographic segmentation
Dividing the total market into groups according to location.

metropolitan statistical area (MSA)
An urbanized area of at least 50,000 people, encircled by nonmetropolitan counties.

primary metropolitan statistical area (PMSA)
An MSA with at least one million people.

consolidated metropolitan statistical area (CMSA)
A metropolitan area made up of two or more PMSAs.

GEOGRAPHIC SEGMENTATION   To use **geographic segmentation**, the marketer divides the total market into groups according to location. To look at national buying patterns, the marketer might divide the continental United States into regions, such as Northeast, Southeast, Midwest, Southwest, and West. A marketer who plans to serve a regional market might use geographic segmentation to further divide the market within a single state or metropolitan area. Marketers might also segment the market on the basis of counties or zip codes.

A marketer interested in segmenting urban areas of the United States needs to be familiar with the Census Bureau's terminology for metropolitan areas. According to the Census Bureau, a **metropolitan statistical area (MSA)** is an urbanized area of at least 50,000 people that is encircled by nonmetropolitan counties and is neither socially nor economically dependent on another metropolitan area. A **primary metropolitan statistical area (PMSA)** is an MSA with at least a million people. A **consolidated metropolitan statistical area (CMSA)** is a metropolitan area made up of two or more

PMSAs. The five largest CMSAs are the New York, Los Angeles, Chicago, Philadelphia, and San Francisco areas. These terms reflect the fact that a metropolitan area can cross political boundaries, such as state lines.

One kind of information associated with geographic segmentation is statistics reflecting changes in population. For example, a marketer can learn which states, regions of the country, or nations of the world have the fastest-growing populations. States expected to see the fastest population growth in the United States are California, Texas, and Florida.

In addition, marketers can compare the needs and preferences of various geographic segments in order to look for differences. Haggar Apparel, a maker of mid-priced men's clothing, learned that Mexican consumers have relatively little access to quality clothing, compared to consumers in the United States and Canada. The company therefore sees Mexico as an attractive source of sales growth.[30] In Europe, a custom is to restrict eating to mealtimes; consumers snack much less than Americans. U.S. potato chip makers PepsiCo and General Mills hope this preference translates into an opportunity to get in on the ground floor of building demand.[31]

One basis for differences among geographic segments is variations in climate. For example, in most parts of the United States, the demand for bowling products begins to peak when the weather turns cold and people are looking for indoor activities. But in Phoenix, bowling products sell best in the summer, when people find it too hot to go outside. Therefore, Kmart stores in most of the country stock bowling products in late summer or early fall, but in Phoenix the stores introduce the products in the spring.[32]

PSYCHOGRAPHIC SEGMENTATION   While demographic and geographic segmentation are relatively simple, straightforward ways to segment markets, they do not directly address the needs and wants that lead people to make buying decisions. In an attempt to more specifically identify the consumers who would be interested in particular products, marketers have developed **psychographic segmentation**. This is segmentation based on consumers' activities, interests, and opinions (their life-styles) measures through psychographics.

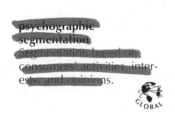

psychographic segmentation Segmentation based on consumers' activities, interests, and opinions.

A variety of psychographic data is available. Advertising agency Backer Spielvogel Bates conducts a yearly study it calls Global Scan, which studies the attitudes, life-styles, and product usage of consumers in 13 countries (using eight languages). Global Scan places international consumers into five psychographic categories it has named Strivers, Achievers, Pressured, Adapters, and Traditional.[33]

To use psychographic segmentation, the marketer appeals to consumers with particular combinations of activities, interests, and opinions. Thus, the TV ads for Rib Ticklers barbecue sauce (see Figure 10.5) are directed toward consumers who like to toss some meat on the grill and slather it with barbecue sauce. These consumers aren't likely to have a very high opinion of vegetarianism. So the memorable ad starts with a sweet portrayal of a cow, a chicken, a lamb. The music swells. Then comes a shot of a barbecue grill, and the announcer exclaims, "Hey! Here's an idea. Let's eat 'em!"[34]

CONSUMERS' RELATIONSHIP TO THE PRODUCT

Marketers can also look at consumers' relationship to the brand or category of product they offer. One such approach is to categorize consumers in terms of the benefits they seek from a particular type of product. Marketers also can segment on the basis of such buying behavior as quantity purchased or loyalty to a particular brand.

benefit segmentation
Segmenting a market
according to desired
benefits.

FIGURE 10.5

Advertising to a Psychographic Segment: Consumers Who Unabashedly Barbecue Meat

BENEFIT SEGMENTATION   Segmenting a market according to the kinds of benefits desired is known as **benefit segmentation**. To use benefit segmentation, the marketer must know about consumers' values and their perceptions of various existing products. The primary way to gather this information is through surveys, but the marketer may sometimes be familiar enough with an industry and its customers to identify unmet needs. This was the case with Jose Cordova, who knew that tortillas are a basic part of the cuisine of the Southwest and that the all-purpose flour sold in U.S. stores makes dough that is more suitable for bread. So Cordova reopened the Valencia Flour Mill, started by his grandfather in Jarales, New Mexico, and soon met success by selling tortilla flour to supermarkets and tortilla makers in New Mexico.[35]

Apple Computer applied its strength in developing user-friendly computers to marketing its PowerBook portable computer. The company learned that people are especially interested in size and weight of this type of computer, so it developed a small, light model with such comfort features as palm rests. Apple's marketing communications were directed at anyone on the go who might use a computer, and the ads described the many ways PowerBook owners could use the machine's capabilities.[36]

SEGMENTATION BASED ON BUYING BEHAVIOR   Often the consumers most likely to purchase a product are those who have purchased the same or a similar product in the past. Therefore, marketers also segment markets on the basis of product purchases. They might divide the market for, say, airline tickets into heavy, moderate, and light users. Then they would find a way to attract and keep heavy users or to develop a product that would satisfy an unmet need of moderate or light users, thereby making them heavy users of the new product.

brand loyalty
the consistency with which a consumer continues to buy the same brand of a particular product.

One measure of whether consumers might be heavy users of a particular brand is their **brand loyalty**. This refers to the consistency with which a consumer continues to buy the same brand of a particular product. Some shoppers always buy the same brand of laundry detergent, whereas others check prices and buy whatever is cheapest. The former group would be considered more brand loyal. All other things being equal, marketers can get the best return on their promotion dollar by serving brand loyal customers who are heavy users. (For more on brand loyalty, see "Put It into Practice.")

To make its marketing efforts more efficient, Campbell Soup Company conducted research into the usage patterns of its customers. The company used this information to divide the customers into four groups:

1. Most profitable—These consumers are the most loyal, frequent, and consistent customers.
2. Profitable—These consumers ranked second in each category.
3. Borderline—These consumers ranked lower than the profitable customers.
4. Avoid—These consumers are least likely to buy, and they probably select the product on the basis of price.

Campbell's researchers concluded that the most profitable group was over three times as profitable as the borderline group, making it the group on which to focus marketing efforts.[37]

Approaches to Segmenting Organizational Markets

As with consumer markets, choosing methods for segmenting organizational markets is a judgment call. Marketers usually rely on geographic segmentation, segmentation based on customer type, and segmentation based on end use of the product. Figure 10.6 illustrates these typical approaches to segmenting organizational markets.

GEOGRAPHIC SEGMENTATION

In some cases, marketers find it helpful to segment an organizational market geographically. As with marketing to consumers, it is often most profitable to concentrate on areas with high growth rates or where the climate or population creates strong demand for a particular type of product. Thus, a company that supplies the construction industry might want to concentrate on expanding in areas of high growth. Or a start-up consulting firm may want to keep its initial costs down by locating near many businesses that might buy its services.

 Geographic segmentation also can help marketers evaluate the desirability of serving various international markets. Marketers can compare the size and needs of markets in various countries, then select countries that can be profitably served. For example, a company that sells high-tech diagnostic equipment to hospitals would

FIGURE 10.6

Approaches to Segmenting Organizational Markets

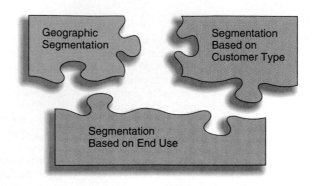

Geographic Segmentation

Segmentation Based on Customer Type

Segmentation Based on End Use

want to target countries that have the reliable electricity and trained personnel necessary to use the equipment.

SEGMENTATION BASED ON CUSTOMER TYPE

Another way to segment organizational markets is by type of customer. Different types of buyers will want different types of products and services. Flowers Industries provides various types of baked goods to market segments it calls frozen retail (such as supermarkets that carry its frozen carrot cake), foodservice (such as fast-food restaurants that use its Kaiser rolls), and deli/bakery (such as stores with facilities to bake its braided breads on site). Flowers' Kwik Kakes line of snack cakes was developed for convenience stores.[38] Figure 10.7 provides a humorous look at how another organization targeted buyers based on their expected need for paper shredders. If this organization's marketing strategies were quality driven, not based on the cynical thinking shown in the cartoon, how do you think it might address its customers' problem that they receive a "high volume of needless paper"?

FIGURE 10.7

Segmentation Based on Type of Organizational Buyer

Marketing Movers & Shakers

TOM CARNS AND PDQ PRINTING

A year after moving to Las Vegas, Tom Carns used $25,000 in working capital to open PDQ Printing, a quick-printing shop located in an 1,100-square-foot space. His net income for the first month was a measly $82. However, Carns's business sense eventually made him a leader in the industry.

One ingredient in the success of PDQ Printing was rapid growth in Las Vegas, but Carns's marketing savvy was even more important. Before he opened PDQ Printing, Carns visited every quick-printing shop in town. Said Carns, "Most shops were dirty and disorganized. The people were sloppy dressers. They played loud rock music at the back of the shop. They were definitely lacking in customer service and commitment." He concluded that there was room in town for a print shop with a different approach.

Defining quick-printing as a "custom-manufacturing business," Carns observed that customers' needs vary widely. He decided to segment the market according to type of needs and to serve those who demand customer service and professionalism—and are willing to pay for it. As his target market, he selected small and medium-sized white-collar service companies. Small companies, reasoned Carns, are more likely than big ones to rely on the expertise of their printer. And white-collar service companies, such as accounting firms, medical offices, and law offices, rely more on accurate and timely printing than do other kinds of businesses. Carns's next step was to learn more about the demands of specific types of businesses.

Carns learned that medical offices must complete vast amounts of paperwork, often using forms they purchase as part of a package of services needed to keep their offices running. The companies that sell those services often fail to keep up with the need for new forms. So PDQ went to medical offices and offered to print replacement forms.

He learned that in law offices paralegals are the people who buy printing and that their major concern is maintaining confidentiality. Days before opening a new office in a building containing several law offices, PDQ distributed a brochure that had its cover stamped with the word *confidential*. Attached to the brochure was a copy of a contract all PDQ employees were required to sign, promising to keep confidential all documents they handled, as well as a statement holding PDQ liable for any breach of confidentiality. PDQ also ran an ad in the newsletter for local paralegals and distributed doughnuts to the largest litigation firms in town. In its first full month of operation, PDQ's new office grossed an impressive $64,000.

To position itself as a high-service, professional firm, PDQ requires that all employees dress neatly and forbids them from playing radios. Employees who do not work directly with customers accompany a salesperson on calls one day each quarter, and each salesperson must visit competitors one day a year. In addition, the company keeps records of all forms printed, assigning each a job number that the customer can use for calling to request refills. PDQ also takes the unusual step of assuming responsibility for proofreading.

Even though the quick-printing business is crowded, Carns's tactics have led to profits of about $1 million a year. PDQ generates about $5 million in sales—about 19 times the industry average.

Source: Edward O. Welles, "Quick Study," *Inc.*, April 1992, pp. 67–76.

Furthermore, different kinds of users within organizations often have different needs and preferences. In this regard, there is good reason for IBM's strategy to promote its O/S 2, 2.0 operating system for personal computers first to data-processing managers and then to a broader business audience.[39] Presumably, data-processing managers would be the users who are most interested in the latest technology and most willing to be creative in adapting new software to their needs. In contrast, most other businesspeople would prefer to wait for the operating system to be time-tested and have the capability to run many popular programs. (To learn how one marketer successfully segmented by type of customer, see the "Marketing Movers & Shakers" box about Tom Carns of PDQ Printing.)

SEGMENTATION BY SIZE   One way to identify different types of organizations is by looking at their size. Thus, the marketer might segment organizations by the amount of their annual sales. Amdahl's strategy is to serve the information-processing needs of the largest users of computer technology.[40] These buyers are the ones most apt to be interested in Amdahl's relatively sophisticated computers.

Not only do bigger organizations tend to place bigger orders, but their buying procedures themselves may vary. A large corporation might have a formal process that requires vendors to talk to buyers as well as users of the product.

SEGMENTATION BY SIC CODE   Another way to identify organization types is to use SIC codes. As described in Chapter 9, these codes identify the principal product sold by a business. A marketer can look up the types of organizations that have codes similar to current customers' and investigate whether they share needs the marketer's organization is well equipped to serve. Or if many of the marketer's current customers have SIC codes in common, the marketer can investigate whether the organization is effectively reaching and serving those industries.

SEGMENTATION BY END USE

The way customers will use a particular product is another basis for segmenting organizational markets. Raw materials, in particular, may be used in a variety of ways. For example, plastics are used for packaging, industrial products, and consumer products. Many types of machinery and equipment also have varied uses; computers are a notable example. An innovation in that industry is pocket-sized computers that respond to commands entered by writing on the screen with a pen-sized stylus. Experts predict three categories of end uses:[41]

1. Replacements for paper forms, such as order pads used by servers in restaurants.
2. Portable personal computers for such applications as spreadsheets; the user can use the stylus to enter numbers into the spreadsheet.
3. Sale to consumers who want to own the latest gadget.

Because the small size of these computers limits the number of applications that can be designed for them, marketers, designers, and people in other functional areas must work closely together to decide which of these uses to address.

The Market Segmentation Process

In general, to carry out market segmentation, an organization has to identify what the possible market segments are, then gather information about the level of demand in each segment. After that, the organization decides which segment(s) it can serve best. The process is similar whether the markets studied are domestic or international.

To see how this works, consider the Florida Marlins baseball team. With fewer Americans having watched the World Series in 1993 than in the preceding year, the team's management might have ended that year—its first season—doubting the sport's future. However, the Marlins are one of several teams attracting fans to their stadiums at the rate of over 3 million a season. Market segmentation provides some clues: the ethnic segment of Hispanics and the geographic segments of the nations in and around the Caribbean both are rich sources of baseball fans. Most of the fans attending Marlins games are from metropolitan Miami, which has a large Hispanic population. To reach Hispanics in the United States, the team aims Spanish-language

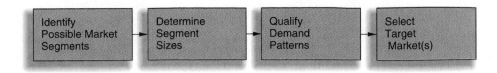

FIGURE 10.8

The Process of Market Segmentation

Identify Possible Market Segments → Determine Segment Sizes → Qualify Demand Patterns → Select Target Market(s)

broadcasts south toward Miami in addition to the English-language broadcasts it beams northward.

The Marlins have determined that international market segments also are significant: the population of Puerto Rico, the Dominican Republic, Venezuela, and Panama is about 30 million, or six times that of metropolitan Miami. The Marlins entered into negotiations for broadcasting rights to those countries, worth an estimated $20 million (on top of the team's $45.5 million share of U.S. broadcasting rights). Seeking to become "the team of the Americas," the Marlins even has a director of international marketing, Hall of Famer Tony Perez.[42]

STEPS IN THE PROCESS

More formally defined, the process of market segmentation follows the steps shown in Figure 10.8. These steps are to identify possible market segments, determine the size of each segment, qualify the pattern of demand in various segments, and select one or more target markets (segments to serve).

IDENTIFY POSSIBLE MARKET SEGMENTS   First the marketer explores various ways to divide the market into segments. There is no foolproof, scientific way to decide what categories to use for creating market segments. Marketers generally rely on experience and intuition to decide which approaches to try.

In identifying segments, marketers should make decisions that support the organization's mission or objectives. For example, at a retailer whose objective is to sell goods at the lowest price in the area, marketers would focus on segmenting in ways that help them identify and learn about customers who value low prices. Their efforts would probably include segmentation on the basis of income level.

Meaningful Bases for Segmentation   After trying one or more approaches to segmentation, the marketer determines whether the results are meaningful—that is, whether they will help the marketer make a good decision concerning what segments to serve. The marketer can conclude that the basis for segmenting the market is meaningful if the market segments meet the following criteria:

- The size of the segment can be measured or estimated with acceptable accuracy.
- The segments are large enough that it is theoretically possible to make a profit serving them.
- Within each segment, the potential buyers have similar needs.
- The needs of potential buyers in different segments are different. (If they are not, the segmentation approach may be appropriate, but the marketer may simply have created too many segments.)
- The organization can reach at least one segment through marketing activities.

An example of segmentation that met these criteria was the determination by Kendall-Futuro, maker of Curad adhesive bandages, that 60 to 70 percent of adhesive bandages are used by children. The company concluded that it could win some of Band-Aid's big market share by offering the young market segment brightly colored, pint-size bandages (see Figure 10.9). Curad made the idea succeed through other marketing tactics such as a licensing agreement in which bandages imprinted with Ronald McDonald were inserted into Happy Meals.[43]

If the segments do not meet the criteria for meaningful segmentation, the marketer should adjust the categories or try other approaches to segmentation until he or she finds a meaningful basis for segmentation. Only when the categories are meaningful should the marketer move on to the remaining steps in the segmentation process.

Combined Approaches to Segmentation   Ultimately, marketers often combine several approaches to segmentation to describe market segments. For example, the marketer gets only limited information by dividing a consumer market into urban, suburban, and rural consumers. The marketer could develop more meaningful segments by adding other characteristics, such as age and brand loyalty. Thus, the marketer might be interested in suburban adults who are not loyal to their current brand. To decide whether to use the additional categories, the marketer applies the criteria just described for determining whether segments are meaningful.

DETERMINE SEGMENT SIZES   Once the market is divided into segments, the marketer determines the size of each segment. These efforts focus on each segment's **market potential**—the total amount of product that buyers in the segment will purchase during a specified period of time, given a specified level of marketing activity. The marketer can estimate market potential in terms of dollars of sales or units of

market potential
The total amount of product that buyers in the segment will purchase during a specified period of time, given a specified level of marketing activity.

product. Thus, a publisher might predict that a book will generate revenues of $75,000 or sell 5,000 copies.

The marketer cannot control such variables as the marketing efforts of competitors, so market potential must be an estimate based on experience with the same or similar products. For instance, a marketer might use industry data to determine the current sales volume at a type of restaurant. Then the marketer predicts the percentage changes that can be expected in a given period of time—say, the percent by which sales should grow in one year.

QUALIFY DEMAND PATTERNS   Besides the size of the segments, marketers want to know more about the patterns of demand for their product among segments. Thus, once they have segmented the market, they conduct research to qualify their expectations about demand. An art museum might want to test the assumption that gifts to such institutions increase with the age of the donor. The museum would look at the giving patterns within each age-based segment to see whether the relationship between age and size of donations holds. Then the institution would couple that information with its estimates of the size of each market segment to see which were worth pursuing most actively. Thus, if 35- to 45-year-olds are one of the largest segments, they might be an important one to focus on even if an older but smaller segment is more generous.

The point of qualifying demand patterns is learning which segments are or could be the greatest source of meeting profit or other objectives. A financial services company found that offering money-market checking accounts was not profitable, so the company planned to stop providing this service. However, research showed that the company's best customers highly valued the accounts. Rather than lose these important customers—and the profits they generated—the company decided to keep offering the money-market accounts.[44]

target markets
Market segments on which an organization focuses its efforts.

SELECT A TARGET MARKET   The information the marketer has gathered about market segments enables him or her to select one or more market segments to concentrate on. A business using market segmentation would concentrate its efforts on the market segments it can serve most profitably. A nonprofit organization focuses on the market segments it can serve most efficiently or most consistently with its objectives. (Notice that these goals involve profits, efficiency, and effectiveness, rather than necessarily getting the most customers possible.) The market segments on which an organization focuses its efforts are known as the organization's **target markets**, even though they are technically market *segments.*

There is no one best way to select a target market. To identify segments where they can maximize profits or effectiveness, marketers typically rely on the following criteria:

- *Size of the segment*—Depending on the organization's product, capacity, and access to resources, a bigger market segment may be more attractive than a small one. IBM's OS/2, 2.0 operating system for personal computers must win a substantial share of the market for operating systems at large and medium-sized businesses so that software companies will want to develop many products that run on OS/2, 2.0.[45] A tiny market segment often is not worth the cost to serve, although an organization that can do so profitably may reap great rewards from a loyal clientele.
- *Expected growth of the segment*—Even relatively small market segments may be attractive if they are expected to grow. The organization that enters a small but growing market has a chance to perfect its products and build brand loyalty before competitors are attracted to this target market. Conversely, a large market segment may not be economical to target if it is expected to shrink.

Recent growth in the number of consumers who consider themselves environmentally active has attracted many marketers. One is EcoVillage, an experimental housing project in Ithaca, New York. Plans for EcoVillage include fish ponds and orchards instead of yards; private kitchens, bathrooms, and bedrooms; and semi-private and public areas for meetings. Solar energy will decrease the need for electricity. Here, Ray and Maria Gasser and their two children plan their move to EcoVillage.

• *Competition in the segment*—It's harder to make a profit when a lot of businesses are competing to serve the same customers. For a market leader, however, competition can be a plus if it means that smaller competitors are devoting a lot of their resources to fighting over what remains of the pie. In either case, the marketer needs to consider the amount of competition in the market segment.

• *Cost of reaching the segment*—Some target markets are difficult to reach at a reasonable cost. For example, a company that wants to sell to fans of pro football may find that TV commercials during games and ads in *Sports Illustrated* are too costly, given the profits the company expects to earn from that market segment. In such a case, the organization needs to consider other target markets or to seek more creative ways of reaching the otherwise desirable segment.

• *Organizational objectives, resources, and strengths*—An organization should target a market only when doing so is compatible with the organization's objectives and feasible in light of the amount of resources available. To meet its growth objectives, Nike needs to target a segment where there is room for growth. Because the company already has a strong share of the market for men's athletic shoes, Nike started targeting the market for women's athletic shoes.[46] In addition, the unique strengths of an organization may make some market segments more attractive than others. For example, a location near an airport would likely lead a hotel to target business travelers rather than, say, families on vacation.

Along with selecting the target market or markets that meet these criteria, the organization chooses a marketing mix that is designed to appeal to the target markets. To appeal to the U.S. Hispanic market, Gerber introduced a line of tropical baby foods and a line of baby-care products called Tropical Tesoros. (Hispanic parents commonly call their babies *tesoros,* meaning "little treasures.") These products are packaged in bright colors, with labels in both Spanish and English. Because Hispanic customers often shop at small neighborhood grocery stores called *bodegas,* Gerber focuses on those distribution channels for Tropical Tesoros. Since buyers for *bodegas* select products themselves at cash-and-carry stores, the Tropical Tesoros line is packed in clear plastic, rather than brown paper bags, so that buyers can see what they are purchasing.[47]

INTERNATIONAL IMPLICATIONS

In segmenting and targeting markets, marketers with a global perspective may use geographic segmentation and identify particular countries to serve. Such an approach can make sense with widely used consumer goods such as cars or shampoo. It also is appropriate when a particular country has a need that affects a sizable portion of the population. Comverse Technology targets Mexicans for its "virtual telephone service," a system for taking phone messages and letting customers retrieve their messages from pay phones. This system meets the need for phone service in a country where telephone installation is expensive and can take months.[48]

Another approach is to use other bases for segmentation and target the needs of segments within various countries. The Sierra Medical Center in El Paso, Texas, uses direct mail to reach wealthy Mexicans; such patients are desirable customers because they are likely to pay cash rather than rely on insurance or government programs.[49] Massachusetts-based Stratus Computer markets fault-tolerant computers (that is, computers with extensive backups to prevent the system from crashing). To enter Asian markets, Stratus first targets three industries likely to have great potential: financial services, travel services, and telecommunications.[50]

global marketing
Using a single marketing strategy to serve domestic and foreign markets.

GLOBAL MARKETING   As the organization evaluates market segments, it must make a decision comparable to the choice between mass marketing and target marketing: the organization must decide whether to devise a single marketing strategy to serve domestic and foreign markets or to use a different strategy in each country. Using a single marketing strategy is often called **global marketing** or operating as a global corporation.

Organizations that pursue such a strategy include Coca-Cola and Levi Strauss. Cable News Network uses its English-language programming throughout the 142 countries it serves. Ford brought together designers from Italy, Germany, and the United States to develop a "world car" to be sold in both Europe and the United States.[51]

A global strategy is most effective under certain conditions. First, potential customers in various countries should have the same kinds of needs. The organization should be in basically the same competitive position in each country. The same elements of the marketing mix (including the product's brand name) should be effective in all the countries.

multinational marketing
Using different marketing strategies to serve buyers in different nations.

MULTINATIONAL MARKETING   In contrast, using different strategies to serve customers in different nations is often called **multinational marketing**, or operating as a multinational corporation. This strategy works best when customer wants or needs are different from one country to another. Preferences in food and drink are common examples. Kraft sells four different formulations of its cheese slices in Europe, varying them according to the dominant preference in each country.[52] And consumers outside the United States have a low opinion of diet soft drinks; a common view is that they taste terrible and are meant for sick people. To sell a sugar-free cola to health-conscious consumers outside the United States, Pepsi has therefore developed Pepsi Max, which contains only one calorie but has a decidedly non-wimpy name. Differing tastes in soup have led Campbell Soup Company to offer split pea with ham in Argentina, cream of chile poblano in Mexico, *flaki* (a peppery tripe soup) in Poland, and watercress and duck gizzard soup in China.[53]

Tailoring a marketing strategy to diverse needs does not have to prevent an organization from having a global outlook, however. Raychem customizes its vast array of high-tech goods to meet the needs of its organizational customers around the world. Yet Raychem vice president Michael Sullivan says, "Raychem is a global company, and therefore it has no foreign customers. . . . They just happen to be everywhere in the world."[54] And as Figure 10.10 shows, a global outlook can be a major competitive advantage.

FIGURE 10.10

Advertising CitiBank's Global Expertise

AND EVERYWHERE IN BETWEEN

From São Paulo to Singapore, more people around the world choose Citibank than any other bank.

BECAUSE Citibank's experience and expertise in emerging markets is unequalled—over 90 years in Asia and 75 years in Latin America. **BECAUSE** Citibank has the largest worldwide branch network, offering millions of clients the most advanced and effective banking services available today.

BECAUSE Citibank is the leading global private bank, providing investment management services with a distinctly international focus. **BECAUSE THE CITI NEVER SLEEPS.** *CITIBAN©*

Positioning the Product

product positioning
Adapting a marketing mix so that the target market will see the product as meeting important wants or needs.

A fundamental part of serving a particular target market is **product positioning**. This involves adapting a marketing mix so that the target market will see that product as meeting important wants or needs. The result—the product's position—is the potential customers' view of the product's attributes. For example, an automobile might be positioned as sporty and high performing, as safe and reliable, or as economical and practical. When it added calcium to its Sunny Delight and Hawaiian Punch fruit drinks, Procter & Gamble sought to position them as healthful beverages for growing children and adolescents.[55]

From a quality perspective, the key issue with regard to positioning is that the product must actually deliver what it is positioned to deliver. If a car is positioned as safe and reliable, its performance should measure up in that regard. If Sunny Delight Plus Calcium drinks are positioned as providing an important nutrient, they should at a minimum deliver that nutrient. Many would add that the drinks also should truly be a nutritious beverage; dietitians complain people would get more food value from drinking milk and real fruit juices.[56]

For positioning to succeed, potential customers also must have a way to learn about the product and the needs it is designed to meet. This entails communicating effectively with the target market, making the product available through channels that support the positioning strategy, and setting a price that matches the product's position as well as the value placed on the product by the target market. To support its position as delivering old-fashioned value, the Wendy's chain of fast-food restaurants used advertising in which Wendy's folksy founder, Dave Thomas, says, "I guess I'm old fashioned" for believing that fast food should be good food and that people should be able to eat good food without spending a lot.[57]

BUYER PERCEPTIONS

To position a product, marketers need to know how consumers or organizational buyers in its target market perceive products in that category. After sales growth of its cream soda slowed, A&W Brands conducted research to learn why. The results showed that consumers didn't know what flavor cream soda was. They tended to think of it as being related to root beer.[58]

Based on what they have learned about their target markets' perceptions, marketers determine whether they must make changes to satisfy their target markets. They may identify a need for a new type of product or for modifications to an existing product. They may learn that members of the target market don't know (or don't believe) that the organization's product actually meets the need it was positioned to meet. In that case, the problem is not with the product, but with other elements of the marketing mix.

In the case of A&W, the company saw a need for several changes to the marketing mix for its cream soda. A&W added vanilla to strengthen its taste, began running ads that stress the product's "cold, sparkling, vanilla taste," and redesigned the packaging to better differentiate the cream soda from A&W root beer. In addition, the company saw these efforts to educate consumers as an opportunity to broaden its target market to attract 12- to 24-year-olds.[59]

To use another example, the prime customers for Turtle Wax, Inc., which makes car-care products, are men aged 18 to 35, followed by women in the same age group. Research shows that people in this age group are strongly concerned about the environment. Thus, if the company decides to position itself on the basis of being the environmentally responsible alternative, these consumers should be receptive to Turtle Wax's 20-year history of selling only biodegradable products packaged in recyclable containers.[60]

RELATIONSHIP TO COMPETITION

In positioning a product, the marketer also has to consider the relationship of the product's position to that of competing products. Is the product the market leader or a follower? Or perhaps the product is so innovative (or protected by a patent) that there is little if any close competition. This information influences the kind of marketing strategy that is most likely to succeed.

In the case of MasterCard, the credit card had lost much of its market share to Visa and to Sears's Discover card. So MasterCard has sought to distinguish its card by positioning it as the most useful credit card for everyday transactions—a way to organize one's finances and pay routine expenses. To make it easy for fast-food restaurants, parking lots, and movie theaters to accept charge cards, MasterCard developed a computer system that handles small purchases quickly without a signature. The company offers supermarkets discounts on credit-card terminals, help with marketing, and a program for linking MasterCard accounts to a program for frequent shoppers. In California, the company has arranged with the state to allow renewal of driver's licenses over the phone by credit card and is planning a system for paying traffic tickets on the spot. To inform consumers of MasterCard's positioning as a convenience for routine purchases, the company has run ads that show MasterCard used for buying groceries. The announcer says, "It's smart to use your monthly statement to keep track of your monthly grocery shopping."[61]

A product that is the market leader or holds a strong share of the market might need to compete directly with other leading products in the marketplace. For a product without a big market share, it may be less risky to use niche marketing, described earlier in the chapter. To position a product with this strategy, the marketer looks for ways to create a unique marketing mix. For example, almost 25 years ago, two American importers learned of a Japanese car with great traction. They targeted the car, which they named Subaru, to snowy, rainy regions of the United States. Today Subaru's top dealer is in Anchorage, Alaska.[62]

In seeking to distinguish the organization and its products, marketers with a quality approach will care about more than the image they create, cautions consultant Peter Laundy.[63] Today's media-savvy buyers are not easily fooled by organizations that simply trumpet such claims as meticulous workmanship or concern for the environment. In contrast, the organizations that are building an enduring reputation for value and trustworthiness—companies like Ben & Jerry's, Apple Computer, and Starbucks Coffee—focus on expressing their true character. Although they are aware of what their competitors are doing, they chart their own course by focusing on their founders' values and their customers' wants and needs. According to Laundy, this approach has the practical benefit that an organization's unique character (as opposed to an artificially generated image) is hard to copy.

POSITIONING MAPS

An important application of market segmentation is to identify needs for new products or for repositioning existing ones. The marketer can identify segments that are not being well served by an existing product. Then the marketer can decide whether it is economically feasible to serve one of those segments by developing a new product or by adjusting the marketing mix for an existing product.

positioning map
A diagram of how consumers perceive various brands in terms of specific attributes.

A useful tool for making such decisions is the **positioning map**. This is a diagram of how consumers perceive various brands in terms of specific attributes. Figure 10.11 shows a positioning map for major brands of automobiles. To create such a map, the marketer uses three kinds of information from potential customers:

1. Evaluations of the important attributes of a class of products.
2. Judgments of the degree to which existing brands have these attributes.
3. Ratings of the degree to which an "ideal" brand would have these attributes.

The marketer can review the map to make sure that his or her product has the attributes deemed important and that customers realize it has those attributes. The marketer can see whether the marketing mix must be revised to adjust the product's position. Depending on the marketing strategy chosen, it might be beneficial to introduce or reposition a product in a less crowded area of a positioning map. In making such decisions, the marketer weighs the previously discussed criteria for selecting target markets.

Sometimes the way to find an uncrowded spot is to think of new product attributes to offer. Parke-Davis advertises that Nicotrol is "the first [nicotine] patch worn only during waking hours."[64] Thus, the company positions this stop-smoking aid in a unique category, with all other patches being worn around the clock.

FIGURE 10.11

Sample Positioning Map: Automobiles

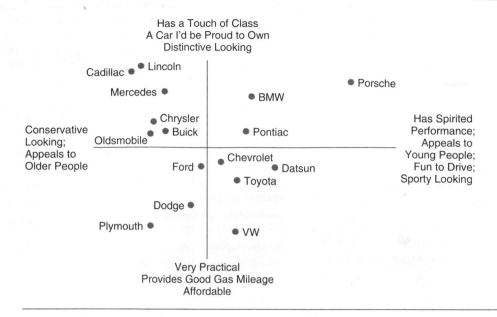

Source: John Koten, "Car Makers Use 'Image' Map as Tool to Position Products," *The Wall Street Journal* (March 22, 1984), p. 31. Reprinted by permission of *The Wall Street Journal,* © 1984 Dow Jones and Company, Inc. All Rights Reserved Worldwide.

Summary

Market segmentation is the process of subdividing a market into distinct subsets of customers that behave in the same way or have similar needs. Marketers use segmentation because a single marketing mix seldom is adequate to address the wants and needs of an entire market for a product. Also, it is often most efficient to serve only a subset of the total market.

Organizations use segmentation when they need to determine which portion(s) of the total market they can serve most profitably or effectively. Market segmentation helps the marketer select and plan a strategy of niche marketing, mass marketing, or differentiated marketing.

For consumer markets, the organization may base segmentation on characteristics that describe consumers themselves or on consumers' behavior with regard to the organization's brand or type of product. Forms of segmentation based on consumer characteristics include demographic segmentation (based on population characteristics such as gender, age, or income level), geographic segmentation (based on where consumers live), or psychographic segmentation (based on activities, interests, and opinions). To segment on the basis of consumers' relationship to the product, the marketer may consider benefits desired, product usage, or brand loyalty.

One approach to segmenting organizational markets is geographic marketing. The marketer might also segment organizational markets according to type of customer, measured in terms of size or SIC code. Finally, the marketer may segment on the basis of the end use of the product.

The market segmentation process begins when the marketer identifies possible market segments. Then the marketer determines the size of the segments, measured by their market potential. The marketer qualifies demand patterns among segments in order to investigate which segments are or could be most profitable to serve. Finally, the marketer selects one or more target markets. A target market should be of a size the organization can serve profitably, its expected growth and level of competition should be acceptable, the cost of reaching the segment should be reasonable, and serving the segment should be compatible with the organization's objectives, resources, and strengths. For marketers with a global perspective, the process is basically the same, except that it includes the decision of whether to use a global marketing or multinational marketing strategy.

Positioning involves adapting the marketing mix so that the target market will see the product as meeting important wants or needs. To do this, marketers investigate how consumers or organizational buyers perceive their product and others in the same category. This helps them recognize any adjustments they need to make to their marketing mix or the perceptions of the target market. Marketers also assess their product's position relative to that of competing products. A useful tool for viewing the product's position in terms of cus- tomer perceptions and competing products is the positioning map. This type of diagram shows how consumers perceive various brands in terms of specific attributes. The marketer can use positioning maps to identify any unmet needs that might be served with a new product or with modifications to an existing one.

KEY TERMS AND CONCEPTS

market (p. 290)

market segmentation (p. 290)

niche marketing (p. 291)

mass marketing (p. 292)

differentiated marketing (p. 293)

demographic segmentation (p. 294)

geographic segmentation (p. 298)

metropolitan statistical area (MSA) (p. 298)

primary metropolitan statistical area (PMSA) (p. 298)

consolidated metropolitan statistical area (CMSA) (p. 298)

psychographic segmentation (p. 299)

benefit segmentation (p. 300)

brand loyalty (p. 300)

market potential (p. 306)

target markets (p. 307)

global marketing (p. 309)

multinational marketing (p. 309)

product positioning (p. 310)

positioning map (p. 312)

REVIEW AND DISCUSSION QUESTIONS

1. What is market segmentation? For each of the following products, describe what types of market segmentation could be helpful.
   a. haircuts
   b. wheat
   c. symphony concerts
   d. word-processing software

2. What is mass marketing? When would an organization use such a strategy?

3. A neighborhood movie theater has four screens. How could this theater use a strategy of differentiated marketing?

4. A daily newspaper serves the metropolitan Philadelphia area. Would you expect it to use geographic segmentation of that market? Explain.

5. Give an example of when it would be appropriate to use each of the following types of segmentation when marketing to organizational buyers.
   a. geographic segmentation
   b. customer-based segmentation
   c. segmentation by end use

6. What are the criteria for determining whether an approach to segmenting a market is meaningful?

7. What is meant by a segment's market potential? In general, how do marketers determine market potential?

8. A for-profit hospital is considering building and running a center for providing services to the elderly. The center would be located near the hospital and would serve the same community. It would contain offices for doctors specializing in care of the elderly, a pharmacy, an adult day-care center, and rooms for meetings and recreational activities.

   Consider the list of criteria for identifying target markets. How can the hospital apply these criteria to determine whether it is considering an appropriate target market?

9. For each of the following products, would you recommend a strategy of global marketing or multinational marketing?
   a. automated teller machines (ATMs)
   b. pickles
   c. compact discs (CDs)

10. Review the positioning map shown in Figure 10.11.
    a. Identify a product on the map that is probably using niche marketing.
    b. Identify two products that seem to be competing directly for the same target market.
    c. If you were to create a new product in this category, where would you position it? Why? (Make whatever assumptions you like in answering this question, but do state your assumptions.)

Chapter Project
Market Segmentation for Shoes

On your own or in a group, list all the categories of shoes you can think of (for example, men's athletic shoes, steel-toed work shoes, baby shoes). Use a format such as the worksheet shown in Table 10.1. In the second column, indicate what market segments each of these kinds of shoes is designed to appeal to.

Visit a shoe store or the shoe department of a department store. Then complete the remainder of Table 10.1 by answering the following questions:

• Which of the categories on your list are available at that store or department?

• Where would you expect to find the kinds of shoes in the remaining categories?

TABLE 10.1

Worksheet for Chapter Project

STORE VISITED:

SHOE CATEGORY	MARKET SEGMENTS	AT STORE? (YES/NO)	WHERE ELSE AVAILABLE
_____	_____	_____	_____
_____	_____	_____	_____
_____	_____	_____	_____
_____	_____	_____	_____
_____	_____	_____	_____

In your group or in class, discuss the following questions:

• Imagine that shoe manufacturers all adopted a strategy of mass marketing. What do you think the shoes would be like?
• What would happen to the price of shoes?
• Do you think consumers would be better off or worse off in this situation? Why?

Case
Swatch

By combining innovation in production with innovation in marketing, the Société Suisse de Microélectronique et d'Horlogerie (SMH) led the revival of the Swiss watch industry. Out of loyalty to his homeland, SMH's chairman, Nicolas Hayek, did not want to abandon production in high-wage Switzerland. So SMH found a more creative alternative. The company developed a manufacturing technique that cut the number of parts in watches and allowed fully automated assembly while maintaining high quality. These improvements allowed SMH to charge a low price for its new brand, called Swatch.

To make the most of low price plus high quality, SMH used exciting watch designs and advertising geared to a youthful, stylish clientele. Thus, its watches were positioned as a fun fashion accessory. With this marketing strategy, Swatch has become the world's biggest- and fastest-selling timepiece.

The Swatch brand has some variations, including the Flik-Flak, a watch designed for children. And the Swatch line itself accounts for only a quarter of SMH's sales and half of its output. The company also is among the world's biggest producers of luxury watches, sold under the brand names Omega, Longines, and Rado. In addition, SMH produces components for other watchmakers to assemble.

The strategy of selling a variety of products to meet different needs is directed toward achieving the corporate strategy spelled out by Nicolas Hayek: attacking Japanese competition directly in all segments of the market for watches. The wide price range of the watches has been credited for the company's strong performance in recent years.

The world market for watches is expected to grow slowly, so Hayek's latest corporate plan involves looking for other consumer products where a similar blend of design and marketing innovation could work. To that end, the company is seeking to introduce a Swatch car in 1995. This would be a cheap, ecological car that uses electricity but has the performance and safety features of a conventional gasoline-powered automobile. The car's design may be as exciting as that of Swatch watches—it may even be transparent, hints an SMH spokesman. Critics wonder whether consumers will view the car negatively, associating the brand with disposability. Nevertheless, SMH has entered into a joint venture with Volkswagen and has been testing a prototype.

QUESTIONS

1. What are some of the market segments that SMH targets for its watches?
2. What do you think would be the best approach toward segmenting the potential market for the Swatch car?
3. How do you think SMH's marketers should use market segmentation to position the Swatch car?

Sources: "Ambitious," *The Economist,* April 18, 1992, pp. 74–75; Peter Laundy, "Image Trouble," *Inc.,* September 1993, pp. 80–82, 84; Margaret Studer, "SMH Leads a Revival of Swiss Watchmaking Industry," *The Wall Street Journal,* January 20, 1992; Laurel Touby, "Swatch Winds Up for Car Making," *Marketing,* October 18, 1990, p. 14.

Product Development and Management

Setting the Stage

Bellcore (Bell Communications Research)

It's hard to remember a time when Ma Bell was one company. In the early 1980s, as a result of a major divestiture agreement, local operating firms were spun off from AT&T, creating what sometimes appears to be a tangled web of telephone service companies. One of these is Bellcore (Bell Communications Research), which develops telephone services for local phone companies.

From the beginning, officials at Bellcore had to fill a tall order: they had to jump into an existing market with existing products as well as develop new products as quickly as possible. Leo T. Mariani, director of new product development, explains that the company's job is "to make use of those [ideas] in the imbedded base [current network] as well as to make sure that technology is ready to support the next set of new ideas coming down the road. Part of our work is not only to support [local phone companies'] near-term revenue objectives . . . but also to influence the technology which is a couple of years down the road."

Bellcore now has a systematic process for new-product development: Network Service and Technology Process, or NSTP. NSTP is a lot like the development process used for new consumer products. A proposal stage generates ideas; a concept development stage involves market analysis; a product planning stage includes the business plan; and a development and deployment stage test markets and launches the product.

One new product that was ferried through this process is voice-activated dialing, first offered in New York by NYNEX. The local phone company spearheaded much of the marketing research, and Bellcore implemented its own NSTP. The company undertook an "Opportunity Proposal and Analysis," focusing on qualitative and quantitative marketing research. Then Bellcore fully developed the concept using all of the criteria in its concept-planning stage; came up with a business plan in its product-planning stage, and wrote all of the technical specifications during the development and deployment stage. "This is a model for success, when the client comes to us with a clear customer need," comments Mariani. "It still requires a systematic analysis as we did in the NSTP because it impacts the technology required to provide the service."

NYNEX has led the way with voice-activated dialing but Mariani believes that other local phone companies are likely to expand the service to other regions of the country in the near future. "Once the technology is in place, there are many business applications for it." Or a consumer can program the home phone to "Call Pizza Hut." Not a bad idea, for business and consumer alike!

Source: Interviews with Leo T. Mariani, director of new product development, Bellcore; and Dr. Donald G. Norris, associate professor of marketing, Miami University, Ohio.

CHAPTER 11   *New Products*

LEARNING OBJECTIVES

After completing this chapter, you should be able to:

1. Define ways in which products may be classified.

2. Explain what makes a product "new."

3. Identify the steps in developing a new product.

4. Discuss why many new products fail.

5. Describe ways in which companies organize to carry out the product development effort.

6. Describe approaches to shortening the time required for developing new products.

Creating Customer Value
Motorola

Motorola teams are everywhere: literally thousands of them are scattered around the world. They research and develop new products, improve production, and manage inventory. The company's executives envision Motorola doubling in size every five years. By the end of this century, they predict, Motorola will be "a corporation that will look gigantic but have the dynamics of little teams."

Motorola has proved that it has the ability to anticipate change in technology and the marketplace, which is crucial in the fast-moving industries where Motorola operates: information and communications, systems technology, and automotive and industrial electronics. In the 1930s and 1940s, founder Paul Galvin saw his company pioneer several new products, including two-way radios and the walkie-talkie. In 1949, Galvin and his son Robert shifted the company's emphasis to semiconductors, based on the belief of Motorola's engineers that these products would revolutionize communications. They were right. Today the company is the world market leader in cellular phones, pagers, two-way radios, and some types of microchips.

Motorola's ability to anticipate change and develop new products stems in part from its use of teams. The company also invests substantial sums in research and development, and it encourages the free flow of ideas. Engineers and others are allowed to coax along previously neglected projects if they think the projects are worthwhile. Company managers believe that the conflict and pressure of argument about projects actually inspires good ideas.

Sometimes the openness to conflicting views results in an astonishing turnaround for a product idea. For instance, a computer microprocessor called 68000 received little initial support, but a team that believed in the concept continued to work on it. Ultimately, the team developed the chip that became the "brains" of Apple Computer's popular Macintosh.

Another team working in the company's small government electronics division in Arizona came up with a huge, costly product that management rejected. However, when Robert Galvin heard the team's presentation, he gave the product the go-ahead. The product is called Iridium, after

the element. Iridium is intended to consist of 66 communications satellites circling Earth, linking special hand-held, portable phones as well as personal computers, fax machines, and pagers around the world. Because of the project's complexity, scope, and enormous cost (an estimated $3.4 billion), Motorola's willingness to proceed with the Iridium project depends on the company's ability to find other firms to join it in bringing the new product to the marketplace. Besides sharing expenses, Motorola's 12 partners—which include Lockheed and Sprint in the United States, BCE Mobile in Canada, and China Great Wall Industry Corporation in China—share expertise in different fields and access to many markets worldwide.

Besides the Iridium project, Motorola has formed alliances with companies to develop and market other products. Under an agreement with Arrow Electronics, Arrow distributes Motorola's Series 8000 line of RISC-based network servers and multiuser systems in the United States and Canada. And Motorola invested in a small firm called In Focus Systems Inc., which manufactures liquid crystal display (LCD) technology, an important move against Pacific Rim competitors.

Winner of the 1988 Malcolm Baldrige National Quality Award, Motorola has a deep commitment to quality. This commitment is embodied in its Total Customer Satisfaction teams, which have authority to make changes in production or procedures when they anticipate or recognize problems. In 1987, Robert Galvin instituted productivity goals that seemed nearly impossible: to reduce Motorola's defect rate from 6,000 per million parts to 3.4. In other words, he wanted near perfection, which he called "six-sigma quality," using statistical terminology. Motorola itself might be called the six-sigma company.

As you read this chapter, consider how the process of developing new products can be enhanced when employees or organizations team up to share their strengths. Also keep in mind how the organization can maintain a focus on introducing products that meet customer needs.

Sources: G. Christian Hill and Ken Yamada, "Taming the Monster," *The Wall Street Journal,* December 9, 1992; Thomas McCarroll, "Betting on the Sky," *Time,* November 22, 1993, p. 57; Lois Therrien and Mark Lewyn, "Motorola's Iridium," *Business Week,* November 23, 1992, pp. 116–120; Ronald E. Yates, "Motorola Enters LCD Market," *Chicago Tribune,* August 21, 1992, p. B-1; Motorola, Inc. 2nd Quarter Report, 1992, p. 4; and personal correspondence from John M. Windolph, director of corporate communications, Iridium Inc., Washington, D.C., December 9, 1993.

Chapter Overview

Motorola's ability to develop high-quality products in a volatile industry has been an important ingredient in its success. Like Motorola, organizations that want to grow need to develop new products regularly. Because of stiff competition from around the world, organizations that fail to innovate will lose ground to those that find better ways to meet customers' needs.

The industry leaders in terms of sales growth and profitability get almost half their revenues from products developed within the preceding five years. In contrast, the least successful get only 11 percent of their sales from new products.[1] Because new products are so important, many organizations set objectives for product development. For example, 3M Corporation requires that 25 percent of each division's annual sales be generated by products developed within the past five years.[2]

This chapter begins discussing the elements of the marketing mix with an examination of products. The chapter describes general ways of classifying products, including the characteristics that make a product "new." The remainder of the chapter addresses issues related to new products. It describes the process of new-product development, then turns to a discussion of why new products fail. The chapter ends by examining ways in which organizations seek to prevent new-product failure, using organizational structure and efforts to speed up the development process.

Product Classifications

As Chapter 1 explained, a product in the marketing sense includes not only a tangible item for sale, but also packaging, service, and whatever other aspects of the product add to the user's satisfaction in using it. In addition, the products offered by many marketers are totally or largely made up of services rather than goods. To help in planning the marketing mix, organizations classify their products in various ways.

PRODUCT MIX AND PRODUCT LINE

product mix
The full set of products offered for sale by an organization.

Most organizations market more than one product. The full set of products offered for sale by an organization is known as the organization's **product mix** or product assortment.[3] Figure 11.1 shows some of the elements of the extensive product mix for Fisher-Price.

FIGURE 11.1
Product Mix for
Fisher-Price

Infant Toys	Preschool Toys	Juvenile and Licensed Products
Baby's First Blocks Puffalump Kids Baby Basketball Pick Up 'n Go Dump Truck etc.	Fun Hydrant Sprinkler Flip Track Rail & Road Set Tumbling Racers Dino-Roarrrrrs Magic Burner Kitchen Center etc.	Nursery monitor Youth beds Car seats Books Eyeglasses etc.

Source: Fisher-Price 1992 Annual Report.

When the organization has many products, grouping them helps the marketer plan strategies. Therefore, marketers in multiproduct companies think in terms of **product lines**, or groups of products that share common characteristics, customers, or uses. In Figure 11.1, the product lines are infant toys, preschool toys, and juvenile and licensed products. Commonly, products in the same product line are distributed through the same channels and are similarly priced. Because of these ways in which products in a product line are related, it can be beneficial for a single member of the organization to hold responsibility for marketing the entire product line. Such a person often has the title "brand manager."

The next chapter discusses product mix and product line in greater detail.

CONSUMER PRODUCTS AND INDUSTRIAL PRODUCTS

Marketers must consider whether their target market consists primarily of consumers or organizational buyers. Logically, goods and services sold to consumers are known as **consumer products**. Goods and services sold to organizations are known as **industrial products** or business products. If the marketer is selling the same product to consumers and organizations, the product will need different marketing mixes for these different types of customers. Chapters 8 and 9 address some of the issues that arise in serving consumers and organizational buyers, respectively.

CONSUMER PRODUCTS   Goods and services targeted to consumers are as varied as cars and concerts, swimwear and stereos. Considering the breadth of possibilities, it can be helpful to think of consumer products in terms of the following categories:

- **Convenience products** are inexpensive consumer products that are purchased frequently and with minimal effort. Examples include food, socks, and dry cleaning.
- **Shopping products** are consumer products purchased after spending some effort comparing various alternatives. For example, consumers typically do some shopping before buying electronic equipment, day-care services, and many kinds of clothing. A major reason that consumers put more effort into selecting shopping products is that these goods and services tend to cost more than convenience products. Thus, the consequences of a mistake are greater.
- **Specialty products** are relatively expensive consumer products that are unique in some way. As a result, consumers are willing to make a special effort to obtain them. Examples include college educations and paintings by Vincent Van Gogh.

Figure 11.2 shows a sample of each of these categories.

product lines
Groups of products that share common characteristics, customers, or uses.

consumer products
Goods and services sold to consumers.

industrial products
Goods and services sold to organizations.

convenience products
Inexpensive consumer products that are purchased easily and often.

shopping products
Consumer products purchased after consideration of alternatives.

specialty products
Expensive, unique consumer products.

FIGURE 11.2
The Three Categories of Consumer Products

Convenience Product   Shopping Product   Specialty Product

In deciding what category best describes their products, marketers have a great deal of freedom. They need not simply assume that because they have a particular product (say, pens), it must be in a particular category (convenience products). While disposable pens are a convenience product available in many outlets including supermarkets, drugstores, and office-supply stores, other pen manufacturers create distinctive pens with special features, higher prices, and more limited distribution. Paris-based Recife produces a line of environmentally friendly fountain, rollerball, and ballpoint pens encased in ebonite, a vulcanized rubber that is tapped harmlessly from trees in rain forests. The pens cost $78 to $200 each and are available in specialty stores and a few upscale department stores.[4]

Even a single product may fall into different categories for different consumers in varying circumstances. A Brooks Brothers shirt could be a convenience good for a business traveler whose luggage was lost en route to an important meeting, a shopping good for a comparison shopper preparing for a job interview, and a specialty good for someone who only wears Brooks Brothers pinpoint oxfords.[5] However, to devise a strategy that meets the needs of a target market, marketers must keep in mind how the product would be categorized for most consumers in the target market. Thus, Timex Corporation's past loss of market share to competitors has been blamed on its failure to observe that consumers had switched from viewing watches as functional objects to seeing them as fashion accessories. Its revenues jumped after Timex introduced its more exciting Indiglo line.[6]

Marketing Mix Knowing which of these categories their products fall into helps marketers devise an appropriate marketing mix. If they are selling convenience prod-

An example of accessory equipment, this automated guided vehicle from Saurer Automation Systems, Inc., can be quickly adapted to changes in any production floor plan.

ucts, marketers need to keep the price low and make the products widely available and easy to purchase on impulse. Attractive and informative packaging also is important for convenience products, since they are so often selected at the point of purchase. Marketers selling shopping products need to offer them in selected places and provide information that will help consumers choose the products. Marketers selling specialty products will want a price high enough to support the notion of prestige, and they can be less concerned about easy accessibility.

Marketing Strategy   The categories of consumer products can also help marketers evaluate whether they are pursuing the most profitable strategy for their products. For example, repositioning a convenience product as a shopping product enables the marketer to charge a higher price. Thor-Lo Inc. of Statesville, North Carolina, found success in selling athletic socks by creating sport-specific socks with dense padding in areas where the foot takes the most stress during the particular sport. The company has thus turned its product from a convenience product into a shopping product.[7] This type of repositioning may also be advantageous for a marketer with limited distribution. By distinguishing the product as offering a special benefit, the marketer can position it as a specialty product and distribute it through limited channels.

INDUSTRIAL PRODUCTS   Organizational buyers purchase raw materials, parts, machinery and equipment to make their products, and supplies and services to operate their business. These are all industrial products. As with consumer products, it is useful to think of them in terms of basic categories:

installations
Nonportable industrial goods.

accessory equipment
Portable equipment and tools.

component parts and materials
Processed items formed into finished products.

- **Installations**—These are "nonportable industrial goods such as furnaces and assembly lines that are major, and that are bought, installed, and used to produce other goods or services."[8] For example, Pitney Bowes's Mail Center 2000 is a computerized mailroom system that weighs, stamps, and prepares mail of any size or shape in a matter of minutes.[9]
- **Accessory equipment**—This consists of "portable factory equipment and tools that are used in the production process and do not become part of the finished product."[10] Examples include desks, screwdrivers, and calculators.
- **Component parts and materials**—These are processed items that are made into finished products. Owens-Corning Fiberglas Corporation is developing fiberglass walls and panels for refrigerators and water heaters.[11]

	CATEGORY	TYPE OF PURCHASE DECISION	IMPORTANCE OF LOW PRICE	MAJOR TYPE OF COMMUNICATIONS
TABLE 11.1 **Basic Categories of Industrial Products**	Installations	Complex; infrequent; lengthy; multiple members of buying center	Not as important	Personal selling
	Accessory equipment	Less complex and lengthy; few members of buying center	May be important	Advertising
	Component parts and materials	Less complex; frequent; several members of buying center	May be important	Personal selling
	Raw materials	Frequent; complexity varies	Very important	Personal selling
	Supplies	Simple; frequent; may be a single buyer	Important	Advertising
	Business services	Varies	Varies	Varies

raw materials
Unprocessed items made into component parts or finished products.

supplies
Consumable industrial goods.

business services
Support services for the organization.

- **Raw materials**—These are unprocessed items that are made into component parts or finished products. Examples are wheat, copper, and cotton.
- **Supplies**—These are "industrial goods that are consumed in the process of producing other products."[12] Examples are light bulbs and pens.
- **Business services**—These are services that support the organization's activities. The trend among organizations today is toward the purchase of many professional services, ranging from marketing research and advertising to engineering and accounting. In addition, organizations pay for a variety of more routine services such as cleaning and package delivery.

Table 11.1 summarizes characteristics of these categories.

As with consumer products, the category of product influences the marketing mix. For example, installations tend to be very costly, so buyers make long, involved purchase decisions. Therefore, marketers of installations emphasize personal selling to help buyers make the right selection. For less costly, more routine purchases, personal selling is less important. Low price is an important part of the marketing mix for supplies and raw materials, where substitutes tend to be readily available. In contrast, many kinds of equipment and business services offer unique benefits for which customers will pay a premium.

Industrial products, in general, are designed to help their buyers succeed in meeting the needs of their own customers. In part, this means that industrial products are attractive when they boost profits by helping the customers to operate at a lower cost. The ability to operate a mailroom efficiently is the major selling point of the Mail Center 2000 mailing system, which is higher priced than a simple postage meter. Also, especially at quality-driven organizations, buyers of industrial products are interested in how products will help them better meet their customers' needs. Fiberglass walls on refrigerators are relatively expensive, but they provide insulation as well as structure. Therefore, manufacturers don't need to use an extra layer of insulation and can offer consumers more storage space.[13]

DURABLES AND NONDURABLES

When we buy certain consumer goods, we expect them to last for years after we buy them. For example, when we buy a car or mattress set, we expect to get years of use

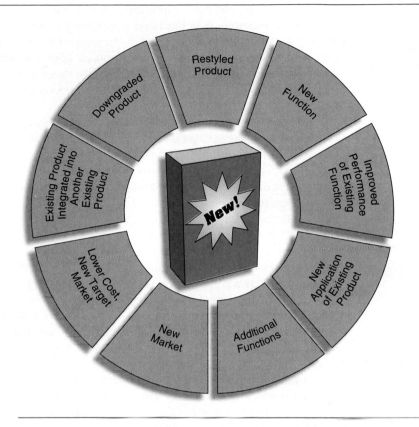

FIGURE 11.3

Types of Innovation That Can Lead to a New Product

Restyled Product

New Function

Improved Performance of Existing Function

New Application of Existing Product

Additional Functions

New Market

Lower Cost, New Target Market

Existing Product Integrated into Another Existing Product

Downgraded Product

New!

---

durable goods
Goods that are used over an extended rather than a brief period of time.

nondurable goods
Goods that are used over a brief time period.

from it. Consumer goods "used over an extended rather than a brief period of time" are known as **durable goods**.[14] Typically, durable goods are considered to be those that are used for at least three years.

When we buy other goods, we don't expect them to last for three years. In the case of some products, such as restaurant meals or gasoline, we might not even expect them to last for three days. Consumer goods that are used over a brief time period are called **nondurable goods**.

Buying durable goods involves different concerns than buying nondurables. Buyers who expect to use the product over the course of several years will be concerned about the product's reliability and the seller's willingness to service the product. Because durable goods tend to be relatively costly, consumers tend to spend time researching these purchases. Therefore, personal selling plays a significant role in promoting durable goods. In contrast, buyers of nondurables tend to place greater emphasis on price and convenience. Marketers of nondurable goods focus on making them readily available to the consumers in their target markets.

NEW PRODUCTS

new product
A product that is new to the marketing organization in any way.

This chapter emphasizes a particular type of product: those that are new. But what makes a product "new"? For our purposes, consider a **new product** to be one that is new to the marketing organization in any way. This means that several types of innovation can lead to a new product.[15] The possibilities are summarized in Figure 11.3.

The most obvious type of innovation is that the product may do something entirely new. For example, IBM has been developing a thin computer monitor called the TFT-LCD monitor, which can convert television signals into digital form so that they can be used to create vivid graphics displays. IBM is seeking to have airlines install these on seat backs so that passengers can use them to watch TV movies, play video games, participate in interactive computing, and connect to the Prodigy electronic bulletin board service.[16]

Another type of innovation is that the product may perform a function that other products already do, but perform it better. The Snakeboard skateboard made by San Diego–based Skateboard USA has two independently pivoting platforms, making the Snakeboard much easier to maneuver than a standard skateboard.[17]

The innovation may be a new application of an existing product. In other words, when people use an existing product in a new way, the product is essentially new for that application. Sales of Skintastic skin lotion took off when it became known as a repellant for flies and other insects.

Similarly, when a product is modified so that it can do more, it becomes new with regard to the additional functions. AT&T's VideoPhone 2500 is the first telephone to display a color motion picture of the person at the other end of the line.[18]

When the marketer offers an existing product to new target markets, the product is in effect new for the new markets. Gillette's Sensor razor blade was such a success, grabbing 17 percent of the U.S. market in three years, that the company began targeting women as well as men. Sensor for Women uses the same type of cartridge but has a wider handle for easier gripping in the shower.[19]

Lower cost can be a type of innovation when it enables the marketer to reach more customers. The marketer can use cost savings to lower the price, making an existing product newly available to some buyers. Advances in manufacturing efficiency over the past few years have driven down the cost of making contact lenses from $2 or more a pair to less than 50 cents. Makers of contact lenses have responded by offering lenses that are essentially identical but sold in different packages at different prices. What distinguishes the lenses is the length of time the company recommends buyers use them. For example, Bausch & Lomb's Optima FW lenses cost about $70 a pair and are recommended for replacement every year, its Medalist lenses cost $15 to $25 and are recommended for replacement at least every three months, and its SeeQuence 2 lenses cost $7 to $9 per pair with recommended replacement every week or two.[20] (What do you think of the ethics of this tactic? Is the company just offering consumers more payment options, or is it tricking them? A Bausch & Lomb spokesperson says the price differences reflect a "volume discount" for buying lenses more often—albeit a "discount" that leaves the frequent buyer with a higher annual tab.)

An existing product may be integrated into another existing product to form a new offering. In effect, the marketer upgrades the product by combining the features of two products into one. Thus, Rollerblade's Metroblade in-line skates contain a removable athletic shoe liner. The wearer can skate on the wheels or slip them off and walk on the shoes.[21] Motorola is developing tiny versions of its pagers that can be incorporated into pocket computers and cellular phones.[22]

A downgraded product may be a type of innovation. If a product has a lower price and also lower quality, it may become affordable to new segments of the market. This type of innovation is a hallmark of product strategy at L'Oréal, the French cosmetics giant. The company first launches its innovations as luxury products, then simplifies them and relaunches them in the mass market. For example, its Niosôme face cream to fight wrinkles is available in exclusive beauty shops. In supermarkets

You Decide

ARE CLEAR PRODUCTS CLEARLY NEW?

When the makers of Ivory Liquid, Tab cola, and Amoco gasoline wanted to perk up sales, how did they innovate? The same way makers of Pepsi cola, Palmolive dishwashing liquid, and Ban antiperspirant did. They created "clear" products. "Clear represents the biggest trend in consumer products since the 'lite' products craze of the eighties," proclaimed Michele Szynal, a Gillette spokesperson. (Gillette has introduced Gillette Series ClearGel antiperspirant.)

Why clear? Why not some other color, or some other way to restyle these products in order to offer them as new? Some observers believe that companies hope consumers will equate "clear" with "green," or environmentally sound. Or that we will think of clear products as natural, and thus good for us (or our dishes and cars). Notes Northwestern University business professor Dipak Jain, "[The idea is] we drink clear water, so the car should drink natural things, too."

But does clear necessarily mean better? That depends on what con-

sumers view as an improvement. Clear doesn't necessarily mean fewer calories or no preservatives. Tab Clear has the same ingredients as traditional soda, without the caramel coloring. SunSprings, another clear drink, contains between 110 and 130 calories per 11-ounce bottle.

Technically, making a formerly colorful product clear is a way to make it new. It is an attempt to update the product and make it more attractive to potential buyers. Marketers hope the change will enhance and extend the popularity of their products. But Ross Goldstein, a San Francisco marketing consultant, warns that if these new products are to survive in the market, they can't just *look* new; they have to *offer* consumers something new.

In many cases, that has not happened. Just a few years after clear products began coming on the market, observers were calling the concept a fad—and one that was ending. Sales of

heavily promoted Crystal Pepsi lagged company forecasts. Sales of Ivory clear dishwashing liquid and Mennen Lady Speed Stick Crystal deodorant plummeted. Miller took its clear beer off the market. The decline in clear products was blamed on products that did not fit the "clear" image (as in the case of beer and gasoline) and on consumers' reluctance to pay more for products with fewer ingredients.

Recall the categories of "new" products listed in the chapter. In which category(ies) would you place clear versions of a product? Do you think the strategy of removing color from products is likely to recover and succeed in the long run? Why or why not? Do you think that making a clear version of a product and calling it "new" is ethical? Why or why not?

Sources: Annetta Miller and Karen Springen, "Clear, and Cashing In," *Newsweek,* February 15, 1993, p. 52; Barbara Carton, "All Clear," *The Boston Globe,* March 3, 1993, p. 32; and Kathleen Deveny, "Anatomy of a Fad: How Clear Products Were Hot and Then Suddenly Were Not," *The Wall Street Journal,* March 15, 1994, pp. B1, B5.

and discount stores, consumers can find L'Oréal's Plénitude cream, which offers the same benefits at one-sixth the price.[23]

Finally, a restyled product may be considered new. Restyling seldom changes the uses of a product, but it may make the product more attractive to potential buyers. For example, joining the trend toward clear products, Procter & Gamble changed the color of its Ivory dishwashing detergent from ivory to clear. (For more on clear products, see "You Decide: Are Clear Products Clearly New?")

Another way to think of the possible kinds of new products is in terms of the organizational growth strategies introduced in Chapter 5. Thus, an organization can seek growth from market penetration, product development, market development, or diversification.

GOVERNMENT REGULATION This discussion takes a broad view of what constitutes a new product. However, through the Federal Trade Commission (FTC), the federal government limits the use of the term *new* when describing a product to the public. First, the FTC says when an organization somehow modifies an existing product and calls it "new," the product must be changed in a "functionally significant or

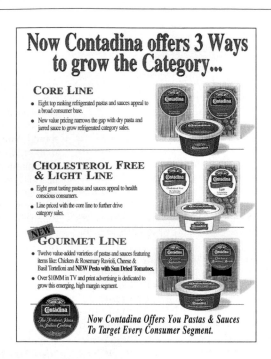

Now Contadina offers 3 Ways to grow the Category...

CORE LINE
- Eight top ranking refrigerated pastas and sauces appeal to a broad consumer base.
- New value pricing narrows the gap with dry pasta and jarred sauce to grow refrigerated category sales.

CHOLESTEROL FREE & LIGHT LINE
- Eight great tasting pastas and sauces appeal to health conscious consumers.
- Line priced with the core line to further drive category sales.

NEW GOURMET LINE
- Twelve value-added varieties of pastas and sauces featuring items like: Chicken & Rosemary Ravioli, Cheese & Basil Tortelloni and **NEW Pesto with Sun Dried Tomatoes.**
- Over $10MM in TV and print advertising is dedicated to grow this emerging, high margin segment.

Contadina
The Freshest Ideas in Italian Cooking

Now Contadina Offers You Pastas & Sauces To Target Every Consumer Segment.

substantial respect." In addition, as was the case with New Coke, the product may be called new for only six months. Thus, Contadina could run the ad in Figure 11.4 for six months before modifying it so the gourmet line of pasta and sauces is no longer called new.

PRODUCT LINE EXTENSIONS   A new product may represent a move into an entirely new product line. But as in the case of Contadina's pastas and sauces, new products are more often extensions of an existing product line. In other words, the length of the product line increases. Polaroid recently began offering a camera, developed under the code name Joshua, that rolls instant prints into a storage compartment, rather than ejecting them from the camera. It also is more compact than the company's other instant cameras.[24]

As noted earlier, offering a greater variety of products may increase the number of customers served by the organization. Introducing products in the form of **product line extensions**, or new products added to existing product lines, can offer additional benefits. Most notably, buyers are already familiar with the existing brand and products, so they will more readily understand and appreciate the new products added to the line. In the case of Polaroid's new camera, people are already familiar with the notion of instant cameras and associate them with the Polaroid brand. Thus, the company can focus on promoting the benefits of the particular product. A related advantage of product line extensions is that resellers are apt to see them as less risky and therefore to stock them.

Furthermore, if the producer has a number of product line extensions, it may claim more shelf space or more pictures in a catalog for its products than if it had a single offering in a product category. Consider the lowly paper clip. An office supply retailer will allocate only so much space on its shelves or in its catalog to display boxes of paper clips. That space will be greater in order to show smooth and textured

product line extensions
New products added to existing product lines.

FIGURE 11.5
The New-Product Development Process

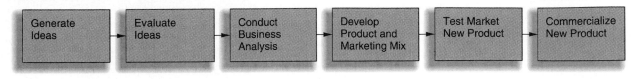

styles, various sizes, and rainbow-colored, vinyl-covered clips. The greater amount of display space should enhance the likelihood that customers will select one of the producer's offerings.

The Development Process

In one form or another, new products can be the key to a company's growth and success. Consider the case of Charles M. Harper, president of ConAgra. After Harper suffered a heart attack, he directed his research and development staff to explore the idea of developing a line of foods with reduced sodium, fat, and cholesterol levels that would also taste good. Besides developing the food products, ConAgra prepared other elements of the marketing mix, including selection of a brand name, Healthy Choice. Marketers settled on green packaging that would stand out in grocery frozen-food cases, and they planned distribution through traditional channels rather than health food stores. After a year of work, ConAgra's employees had a line of products ready for test marketing.

Consumers were impressed with the taste. ConAgra began distributing Healthy Choice, and within four years, the brand was enjoying a 40 percent share of the market for frozen dinners and entrees. ConAgra didn't stop there, but continues to think of new products to carry the Healthy Choice label.[25]

There is no practical way to be sure that all new products will succeed as the Healthy Choice line did. However, being systematic about developing new products will lessen the number of mistakes. Figure 11.5 shows a logical process for developing new products.

GENERATING IDEAS FOR NEW PRODUCTS

The marketer starts with an idea. Many new-product ideas come from customers, the sales force, and other employees. Table 11.2 lists basic sources of new-product ideas. Among the outside sources of ideas listed in the table, one of the most common is competitor's products. When a competitor introduces a new or improved good or service, marketers usually look for a way to match or improve on the innovation.

Ideas for new products can arise from all dimensions of the marketing environment. For example, it was a retailer that led Southern Audio Services to its current product strategy. The retailer asked owner Jon Jordan why he was entering the highly competitive market for home loudspeakers instead of targeting an underserved niche

TABLE 11.2 Sources of New-Product Ideas	SOURCE	EXAMPLES
	Sales force	Knowledge of customers' needs; inquiries from customers or prospects; knowledge of the industry and competition
	Research and development	Application of basic research; original or creative thinking; testing existing products and performance records; accidental discoveries
	Other company sources	Suggestions from employees; use of by-products or scrap; specific market surveys
	Outside sources	Inventors; stockholders; suppliers or vendors; resellers; advertising agencies; customer suggestions; competitors' products; patent abstracts; trade shows and journals

Source: Adapted from J. Paul Peter and James H. Donnelly, Jr., *A Preface to Marketing Management,* 6th ed. (Burr Ridge, Ill.: Irwin, 1994), p. 135.

like speakers for pickup trucks. Jordan took the advice, and his sales of truck speakers doubled every year thereafter.[26] Many businesses reaped sales as a result of observing a phenomenon in the social environment: Americans' enthusiasm for cats, which received an extra boost with the move of Chelsea Clinton's cat, Socks, into the White House. Culver City, California, retailer Street Kids enjoyed heavy demand for its Socks key rings and its stuffed cats resembling the First Feline.[27]

According to some estimates, an organization needs 60 or 70 ideas to come up with one viable new product. This means that marketers must constantly seek ideas. Some of the techniques they use are brainstorming described in the chapter project, employee suggestion boxes, and customer surveys. David Blohm, who heads MathSoft, a software company in Cambridge, Massachusetts, gets ideas from participating in industry conferences. He finds that attending the meetings is an efficient way to keep up to date on new technology.[28] Table 11.3 describes some of the techniques marketers use to generate product ideas.

IDEAS FROM CUSTOMERS   At an organization with a total-quality focus, it is especially important that the search for new ideas include exploring with customers what their needs are. Deere did this when it asked farmers to describe their dream tractor. Then the company gave them what they asked for: strong and safe machines with soundproof cabins, seats offering back support, more headlights for improved night vision, and more glass for greater visibility.[29] Successful marketer Paul Sherlock advocates developing long-term relationships with customers and listening to them, especially when they say they have a problem. Sherlock suggests that whenever a salesperson suspects there is an opportunity to meet a need with a new product, the salesperson should take a creative technical person to visit the customer and become involved in solving the problem.[30]

Communicating with customers is also important in serving the consumer marketplace. For example, 3M Company listened to complaints that steel scouring pads were apt to rust and splinter after just a few uses. The company responded with a new soap-filled scouring pad, Scotch Brite Never Rust.[31] And Ukiah, California–based Real Goods Trading Corporation includes political articles and commentary in its catalog of energy-saving products. The editorial content generates customer letters, many of which give the company ideas for new products to make or distribute.[32]

TABLE 11.3	TECHNIQUE	DESCRIPTION
Techniques for Generating Ideas	Delphi	A panel of experts fills out a questionnaire; a researcher tabulates the results and sends them to panel members. Repeat the process until the panel reaches a consensus or an impasse.
	Benefit analysis	List all the benefits customers receive from the product under study. Think of benefits that are currently missing from the list.
	Use analysis	Ask customers how they use the product under study. List the various uses.
	Relative brand profile	Ask target markets whether the brand name makes sense for other product categories under consideration. A stretch of the brand name that makes sense to potential buyers can be the basis for a new product.
	Unique properties	List all the properties held in common by a product or material currently on the market. Look for unique properties of the organization's product.
	Achilles' heel	List the weaknesses of a product or product line (for the organization and its competitors). Prune the list to the one or two weaknesses most likely to inspire a response from competitors. Identify product concepts that could result from correcting these weaknesses.
	Free association	Write down one aspect of the product situation—a product attribute, use, or user. Let the mind roam, and jot down every idea that surfaces. Repeat the process for other aspects of the product situation.
	Stereotype activity	Ask, "How would _____ do it?"—referring to how a member of some group or a particular person would use the product. Example: What type of bicycle would a senator ride? Can also ask what the stereotype would *not* do.
	Study of other people's failures	Study products that have failed. Look for ways to solve the problems that led to failure.

Source: Adapted from C. Merle Crawford, *New Products Management,* 3rd ed. (Homewood, Ill.: Irwin, 1991), pp. 519–522.

International Customers   Learning about customers and their needs is especially important in devising a product strategy to serve international markets. The basic choices for international product strategy are to offer the same product worldwide, to adapt it for foreign markets, or to create a completely new product to serve foreign markets.

Some single-product strategies are well known. The Coca-Cola Company finds that people around the world enjoy Coke, and Levi's jeans are popular on every continent. Hayes Microcomputer Products, best known for its modems, learned the hard way that it needed a single-product strategy. Originally, Hayes developed modems for the U.S. market, then became frustrated trying to sell them in other countries, each of which had its own regulatory standards for access to telephone lines. So Hayes revamped its product development process to start by learning customer needs—in this case, the standards in force in 30 target countries. The company developed a product that could meet all the standards; as a result, it now successfully sells modems in 63 countries.[33]

Other organizations find success in adapting the product mix. Retailer Pier 1 does so to maintain its position as a seller of the exotic—which, by definition, varies

FIGURE 11.6

R&D Expenditures by U.S. Industry

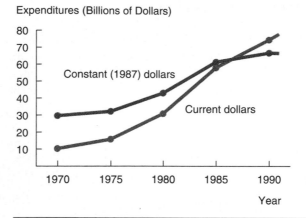

Source: U.S. Department of Commerce, *Statistical Abstract of the United States,* 113th ed. (Washington, D.C.: U.S. Government Printing Office, 1993), p. 595.

from one country to another. In its existing and planned European and Asian stores, Pier 1's merchandising strategy is to include a variety of Americana, such as posters of U.S. pop stars. Instead of chopsticks, sold in U.S. stores, Asian stores will carry Native American artifacts.[34]

Differences among countries may dictate some basic product modifications. For instance, electric appliances used in Europe must operate on different voltages than in the United States, and cars driven in Japan and England require steering wheels on the right side. The fact that most countries, unlike the United States, use the metric system makes it necessary to modify many U.S. goods. Services, too, may require modification. An example is checking accounts, which would be structured differently in Greece (where checkbooks are rarely used) than in the United States.[35]

In some cases, the organization moves beyond adapting a product and invents one to serve the needs of a foreign target market. For example, because tastes in food vary so widely, food producers often must create products that match local eating habits. To serve the Ivory Coast, Nestlé has developed a version of a local yam dish that it calls Bonfoutou.[36]

IDEAS FROM RESEARCH AND DEVELOPMENT   Another source of ideas related to technology is research and development (R&D) activities. U.S. companies have been criticized for not devoting enough of their resources to R&D. This may be true, but as Figure 11.6 shows, U.S. industry has continually increased the amount of money it spends on R&D (even when adjusting for inflation). Furthermore, the amounts shown in the figure represent only what U.S. *businesses* have spent. Other R&D funding comes from the government, colleges and universities, and other nonprofit institutions. Together, all organizations spent $157.4 billion on R&D in 1992.[37]

Large organizations and those that depend heavily on technology set up their own laboratories to expand and apply technical knowledge in their industry. Corning's R&D staff conducts research to make the company a leader in all aspects of glass technology. The company spent millions of dollars to fund research in such areas as methods to make high-quality car windshields. The results of that project led to the development of glass for the flat-panel displays used in laptop computers. Then, applying the principles of total quality management, Corning's R&D staff continuously seeks ways to improve these displays and the other products it has developed.[38]

Sometimes the investment in R&D is the source of an organization's competitive advantage. Illinois Tool Works keeps its customers happy through its ability to innovate with products that help buyers keep their costs down. Worldwide, the company holds over 4,450 patents.[39] Reebok's R&D department includes an Advanced Concepts Group, which designs products for the distant future. An example of a product developed by this group is the Pump Fury, which seeks to lighten the runner's load by removing 25 percent of the weight of each shoe, including the middle third of the midsole, the laces, and most of the upper. What keeps these shoes on your feet? A bladder inflated with a Pump button or a CO_2 cartridge.[40]

For global marketers, an important decision related to research and development is whether to set up R&D facilities in one location—say, at their headquarters—or to operate nearer their various market segments. To serve consumers in over 140 countries, Procter & Gamble has chosen a middle route by operating technical centers in the United States, the United Kingdom, Belgium, Germany, Venezuela, and Japan.[41] Setting up research facilities overseas requires that the organization's knowledge of other parts of the world include recognizing the strengths and weaknesses of the foreign country's engineering and science talent. To serve the rapidly growing Chinese market, Motorola hires hundreds of engineers there but finds that Chinese graduates are much stronger in basic sciences than in technological applications. As a result, Motorola provides its Chinese engineers with extensive training at its facilities in the United States, Singapore, and Hong Kong.[42]

Besides coming up with ideas through their own primary research, R&D personnel can generate ideas by learning from their colleagues at other organizations. When scientists attend conferences, for example, they share ideas with others in the field. Thus, Samuel H. Fuller, vice president for corporate research at Digital Equipment Corporation, says, "We treat university research as a virtual research lab."[43]

When the organization cannot afford its own research laboratory, it may form strategic alliances with others that specialize in research.

EVALUATING PRODUCT IDEAS

Next the organization must evaluate the ideas that have been generated, deciding which are worth pursuing. This step involves determining whether the product idea will help achieve the objectives of the marketing department and the organization. The marketer should consider whether pursuing the idea makes use of the organization's strengths. AT&T seeks to identify innovations that enable it to participate in marketing all kinds of communications terminals, from telephones to televisions to computers. Such innovations enable the company to make the most of its vast communications network.[44] If an idea is outside the organization's area of expertise but meets its customers' needs, the organization might consider pursuing a strategic alliance with another firm.

Evaluation should cover a variety of other issues as well. Table 11.4 shows a checklist of criteria used for evaluating new-product ideas at Johnson Wax. The marketer will want to consider whether the product idea is really innovative and whether it can be protected with a patent or copyright. The marketer also will need to consider legal and ethical issues such as whether the product will be safe to use. The safety issue has been a prominent one in evaluating possible new products for use with microwave ovens. For example, researchers are exploring the development of massage creams and hair oils that would be warmed in the user's microwave. However, because the ovens heat products unevenly, companies are concerned that consumers could easily burn themselves.[45]

TABLE 11.4	ELEMENT	YES	NO
Checklist for Evaluating New-Product Ideas at Johnson Wax	1. The idea represents high value-added products, not commodity-type products.	_____	_____
	2. It requires consumer-oriented development and presentation of products using existing marketing capabilities.	_____	_____
	3. The idea has high advertising or promotional content that allows for intensive communication.	_____	_____
	4. It's not a major capital investment for the consumer (such as appliance or motor home).	_____	_____
	5. There is opportunity for developing logical extensions.	_____	_____
	6. The product offers a significant "plus" that is discernible by a large majority of consumers.	_____	_____
	7. There is an opportunity to expand into many overseas markets.	_____	_____
	8. The idea ties in with existing key Johnson's functions—technology, marketing, sales force.	_____	_____
	9. Labor will be of average or lower intensity relative to national norms.	_____	_____
	10. Capital will be of average or lower intensity relative to national norms.	_____	_____
	11. The product is compatible with Johnson's physical packaging capabilities.	_____	_____
	12. The product is preferably nonperishable.	_____	_____
	13. The idea is related to entomology, microbiology, polymer chemistry, emulsion or film formation, or substrate technology.	_____	_____
	14. The product uses existing distribution channels.	_____	_____
	15. There is an extended product life cycle (that is, years versus months).	_____	_____
	16. The product can be a building block for a multiproduct line or business.	_____	_____

Source: Adapted from Rodger L. DeRose, "New Products—Sifting through the Haystack," *Journal of Consumer Marketing* (Summer 1986): p. 83. Reprinted by permission of Marketing Journals Publishing Company.

CONDUCTING BUSINESS ANALYSIS

Typically, only a few ideas survive the evaluation stage. The marketer then conducts a more rigorous analysis of these ideas, to see whether they make business sense. In particular, at a business, marketers will want to know whether pursuing the ideas will be profitable and, if so, which ideas will be the most profitable. Therefore, marketers need to predict sales and costs for the proposed product. The marketer should continue to develop a product idea only if the forecast shows the organization can afford to make it a success.

PREDICTING SALES   Marketers need some idea of the sales a new product will generate. Forecasting demand for a new product can be tricky, because there are no historic data for that product to use as a basis for making projections. For example, many businesses are eager to become involved in interactive media such as devices that allow people to use their television to order pizza, comment on programs, or download video games. The success of such enterprises depends in part on how much time consumers want to spend in front of their TV set instead of elsewhere, say, at the mall or library.[46] Since consumers' opportunities in this area are still limited, marketers have little basis for predicting behavior except what consumers say they will do.

To get a sense of the possible demand for a new product, the marketer often uses **concept testing**. This involves asking potential customers to evaluate pictures or written descriptions of the product. For complex products, marketers and designers may work

concept testing
Asking potential customers to evaluate pictures or descriptions of a new product.

Put It Into Practice

CONCEPT TESTING   Marketers use concept testing—asking potential customers questions about pictures, computer simulations, written descriptions, or other renderings of a new product—to get a sense of possible demand for it. Choose one of the companies from the list in the chapter project on page 347 (or make up one of your own). Develop questions that you could use to test the concept of a new good or service to be offered by that company. (Later, you can incorporate your concept testing into the chapter project.)

together to present computer models of the product and make immediate changes to the model in response to customer feedback. Concept testing usually concentrates on getting reactions from the ultimate consumers of a product, but the organization that is considering producing the product should remember to test the concept on resellers as well. (For more on concept testing, see the "Put It into Practice" box.)

Marketers use sales forecasts and concept testing to identify product ideas for which there is strong or potentially strong demand. Makers of ready-to-eat cereal are extending their product lines to snacks with products such as Fingos, Chex Snack Mix, and Rice Krispies Treats. One reason is that many consumers already eat cereal as a snack food, so demand already exists. Another is that Americans spend more than three times as much on snacks as they do on cereal.[47] Thus, the potential market is huge relative to the market for the companies' existing products. In the pharmaceutical industry, demand depends in part on the prevalence of various illnesses. Thus, Merck's strategy is to concentrate on developing drugs to treat chronic diseases of the elderly because that age group is growing. By 2000, an estimated one out of five people in the United States will be old enough to receive Medicare.[48]

PREDICTING COSTS   To predict whether the product can be profitable, the marketer subtracts expected costs from forecasted sales. This means that the marketer must be clear enough about the product's features to estimate production costs. Will the organization be able to use existing personnel and facilities? What materials and training will be required? The marketer also must estimate the marketing costs. This means he or she must have a general plan for the marketing mix, including such variables as packaging, channels of distribution, and communications. Thus, the marketer must consider whether the product will be sold through existing channels or whether new ones must be developed. The marketer must decide whether to advertise heavily. For example, 3M launched Scotch Brite Never Rust scouring pads with a $9 million advertising campaign, in contrast to competitors' total lack of advertising for several years.[49]

Sometimes the cost of bringing a product to market alone is too great, but doing so with another firm is economically attractive. IBM decided it should use a technology called advanced liquid-crystal displays in its display screens. To keep costs under control, the company entered into a joint venture with Toshiba Corporation. IBM contributed its expertise in materials, Toshiba its superior manufacturing capabilities.[50]

DEVELOPING THE PRODUCT AND MARKETING MIX

If business analysis predicts that the product will be profitable, the marketer moves on to developing the product concept. This involves designing and testing the product. In organizations that practice total quality management, an important aim of continuously improving processes is to seek ways to speed up this development stage. Organizations can gain an important edge in serving their customers by being the first to introduce products that meet customer needs.

In the late 1970s, Heida Thurlow, a mechanical engineer from Germany, was unable to find work in the United States and conceived the idea of Chantal Cookware. This colorful enamel-on-steel cookware features patented stay-cool handles, plus tempered glass lids rimmed in stainless steel. A niche player in an industry dominated by multinationals, Chantal has grown from a two-product line into a company with sales of about $10 million a year.

concurrent engineering
Linking product design with manufacturing engineering.

PRODUCT SPECIFICATIONS   In the standard process of developing the product concept, marketers and other members of the product development team begin by developing specifications for the product. These spell out in detail what the product will consist of. For tangible products, the specifications would include such information as materials, size, weight, and performance requirements.

Modern organizations are increasingly realizing that they can benefit from linking product design (what the product will be like) with manufacturing engineering (how it will be made). By combining these tasks through teamwork, in a practice known as **concurrent engineering**, they make sure the organization is using its production resources efficiently. Organizations that use concurrent engineering are in a position to make goods faster and at a lower cost than their competitors, which is often a significant marketing advantage. Invacare Corporation, an Elyria, Ohio, maker of home medical devices, uses such an approach. At the concept stage of the development process, Invacare assembles a team of employees from its marketing, quality, manufacturing, purchasing, engineering, and financial functions. The group evaluates product specifications, thereby preventing mistakes further down the line and also getting the product to the manufacturing stage faster.[51]

PROTOTYPE   The development step also includes building a prototype of the product, then testing the prototype to ensure it performs up to standards. Actually building and testing the product is the surest way to see whether it works as planned. Thus, Chrysler tested a prototype of its battery-powered minivan by having engineers drive it the 2,700 miles from Detroit to Los Angeles. Along the way, engineers were able to identify ways to improve the minivan. Not incidentally, the project also generated publicity for Chrysler's efforts to produce an environmentally friendly product.[52] For many consumer goods, the marketer will also need to prepare samples of the packaging.

The organization may have a sample of potential customers test the prototype by using it in their home or workplace. This can be an important way to keep product development focused on customers and their needs. To this end, General Motors enlisted 1,000 consumers to test-drive its 30 prototype battery-powered cars for periods of two to four weeks. Explained Kenneth Baker, vice president of GM's R&D center, "We want to know what's desirable and what isn't about electrics, and we want to gain experience in the real world before we come up with an actual production date for the cars."[53]

TEST MARKETING NEW PRODUCTS

During the preceding steps of the development process, the organization tries to keep its ideas a secret. At some point, however, the organization needs to know how its target market will react. That knowledge requires test marketing. Chapter 7 introduced the basics of test marketing. Because competitors as well as potential customers can see and evaluate the marketing mix at this time, the organization should have refined it thoroughly during the preceding steps of product development.

During test marketing, the marketer offers the product for sale in a limited area and measures the response. The marketer evaluates not only the product, but all elements of the marketing mix. Based on the results of test marketing, the marketer determines how the marketing mix should be adjusted before a full-scale launch. Thus, after testing pizza as a dinner item, McDonald's concluded from the unimpressive results that it should use the product as a specialty menu item for airports, train stations, and shopping malls. The company also concluded that for pizza to sell in its other outlets, it would have to change the atmosphere—say, by dimming the lights—to make it more relaxing.[54]

Test marketing can be an expensive and time-consuming stage of the development process. For General Mills, testing and refining its chain of Olive Garden restaurants required five years and about $28 million. The company may well devote at least that much to test marketing its new restaurant concept: a chain of Chinese-American restaurants called China Coast. The company opened test restaurants in Orlando, Florida, where the large proportion of tourists gives management a chance to gauge reactions from a broad cross section of the U.S. population. Customers completing taste tests and questionnaires allowed the company to distinguish between consumers' stated preferences and their actual behavior. For example, consumers said they favored light, healthful dishes but tended to order the menu items highest in fat, sugar, salt, and sauces. They said they wanted authentic Chinese cuisine but made selections along the lines of fried rice.[55]

TEST MARKET LOCATIONS   Ideally, the test market should reflect the target market for the product. For that reason, organizations seeking to serve a U.S. mass market are interested in knowing which cities have populations most like that of the country as a whole. A study by Donnelley Marketing Information Services found that the most typical American cities in terms of age distribution, racial mix, and housing prices are those shown in Figure 11.7. Topping the list was Tulsa, Oklahoma. This city is especially attractive as a test market because Tulsans are more likely than other Americans to agree to participate in a marketing survey. Consequently, an increasing number of marketers are testing their products in Tulsa. However, many still prefer the older approach of favoring medium-sized cities in the Midwest that they feel are typically American.[56]

USES OF TEST MARKETING   Because test marketing is expensive and provides so much information to competitors, organizations use it only for certain products. It is most effective for products that cost much less to develop than to market. Thus, if a consumer product requires extensive distribution and a nationwide television advertising campaign, it might make sense to try the product in a few local markets to see whether consumers are responding as expected. In contrast, test marketing is not appropriate when competitors will be able to make a few quick modifications and launch a superior competing product. After all, an important source of new-product ideas is watching for test marketing by competitors.

Nonetheless, it is wise for marketers to skip test marketing only when they have a firm expectation of success. For products that are truly innovative, it is risky to skip

FIGURE 11.7
**The Most Typical
American Cities***

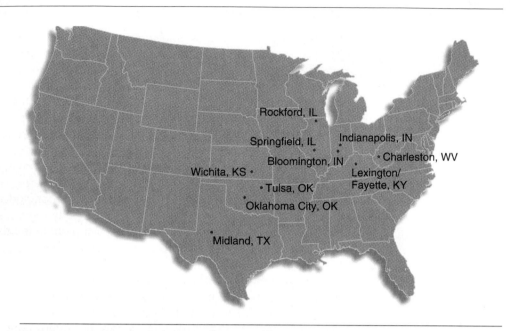

*Based on a study of cities with more than 50,000 people by Donnelley Marketing Information
Services. "Typical" means they come closest to meeting the national averages for age distribution,
racial mix, and housing prices.
Source: Steve Lohr, "Test It in Tulsa—It'll Play in Peoria," *Chicago Tribune,* June 7, 1992, sec. 7, p. 3.

this chance to see how the product performs. Thus, Time Warner is offering consumers in Longwood, Florida, a chance to subscribe to its interactive cable television network. Those who do will be able to try out such services as home shopping, selecting movies and video games to play on their TV set, and transmitting cellular phone calls over cable lines. However, many competitors are hot on the heels of Time Warner, and they will inevitably be able to refine their own products based on Time Warner's experience in Longwood.[57]

Organizations that want to avoid some of the shortcomings of test marketing may set up purchase laboratories. These are essentially experiments in which a sample of consumers has an opportunity to select products from mock grocery shelves. In a typical experiment, interviewers ask consumers in a shopping mall whether they use a particular class of product. Those who do are invited to the purchase laboratory, where they are asked about their product usage and preferences. The consumers see sample advertisements for the new brand and competing brands, then receive money, which they may use to buy this type of product from the mock grocery shelf. Those who buy the test product answer further questions about the reasons for their purchase.

COMMERCIALIZING NEW PRODUCTS

commercialization
Launch of a new product.

Product development ends with the launching of the new product. During this step, known as **commercialization**, the organization commits to selling the product and starts full-scale production, distribution, and promotion. During commercialization, the marketer may still need to make adjustments to the product mix. For example, problems that result from full-scale production may require changes in product design.

Commercialization does not have to be a headlong plunge into the marketplace. Especially when the costs of marketing a product are high, the organization might gradually roll it out. This means the organization introduces the product gradually, city by city or region by region, until the whole target market is being served. Frito-Lay first sold its Doritos Tortilla Thins exclusively in Tulsa and Omaha, with plans to expand distribution to the rest of the United States months later.[58] Procter & Gamble launched its disposable training pants in Holland and the United Kingdom, expanding from there to Canada and the United States.[59]

The way the organization handles commercialization can influence responses from the target market and from competitors. The marketer might actively promote its plans so that targeted buyers are aware of and interested in the new product by the time the organization has spent money to produce it. Or the marketer might try to downplay the product under development so that competitors are caught off guard when commercialization begins. In the case of Apple Computer's Newton palm-top computer, the company was criticized for overpromising on its capabilities and launch date. Initial reviews and sales of the product were disappointing, and competitors had made progress on alternative products by the time the Newton was launched. In contrast, Apple's earlier development of the Macintosh personal computer had been cloaked in secrecy, and the initial reaction to the unveiling of that product was awe at its capabilities.[60]

Prevention of New-Product Failure

The effectiveness with which organizations introduce new products varies widely. However, it is common for a new product to fail in the marketplace. According to estimates, failure rates for product development range from 33 percent to 90 percent. Furthermore, of the time that engineers and scientists devote to technical development of new products, about 80 percent is spent on products that do not achieve commercial success.[61] (For the story of one entrepreneur whose new product did succeed despite a number of obstacles, see the "Marketing Movers & Shakers" story about Sheri Poe of Ryka.)

WHY NEW PRODUCTS FAIL

Research into marketing practices has found that the primary reason for the failure of new products is inability of the selling company to match its offerings to customer needs.[62] Organizations lack this ability when they do not thoroughly research customer needs, when they fail to stick to what the organization does best, and when they do not provide better value than competitors. These mistakes can lead to such problems as poor-quality products, too-small target markets, and failure to understand the needs of a target market. The NeXT desktop computer was slow and initially came only with an optical drive, rather than the floppy disk drive most customers considered useful. And La Choy's Fresh and Lite frozen egg rolls couldn't be cooked in a microwave oven because the shells would get soggy.[63]

In contrast, the organizations at which new products succeed emphasize planning, organization, and cooperation among various functions.[64] One way to put this emphasis into action is through the use of cross-functional teams. The company can also encourage cooperation by getting everyone focused on delivering quality. At Fuji Xerox, development of the successful 3500 copier brought together the efforts of corporate planners, design and manufacturing engineers, parts suppliers, and sales and services personnel.[65] OXO International, a maker of kitchen utensils, designs such high-quality products that they succeed with virtually no advertising. Despite their moderate price, OXO tools are a pleasure to use and are striking to see.[66]

Marketing Movers & Shakers

SHERI POE OF RYKA INC.

In 1987, Sheri Poe stepped into the athletic shoe arena to fight the big guys. She had the idea that women's athletic shoes should be lightweight and comfortable, designed for women's feet. Her timing, in an uncertain economy, was terrible. Bank lenders laughed her out of their offices, warning her that there was no way she could compete with Nike and Reebok. One female investment banker (like Poe, an aerobics enthusiast) did pay attention, and helped Poe's new company, Ryka Inc., raise capital by selling shares to the public.

The first shoes Ryka produced were tripped up by poor quality, and Poe was forced to change factories and shoe models. Then, in 1990, she was invited to appear on "The Oprah Winfrey Show," during which Oprah tossed Ryka shoes into the audience, asking, "Do you believe how light they are?" (The Ryka 975 Step-Lite weighs just under seven ounces.) Overnight, the shoes sold out.

Poe's story sounds like an entrepreneur's dream come true, and it is, in many respects. Certainly, not every marketer gets a shot at free publicity in front of 14 million viewers on television. But Poe's success has come from hard work, harsh experiences, and even crises. These experiences have formed a savvy businesswoman with a vision combining a high-quality new product and social responsibility toward women.

Poe's desire for a better women's athletic shoe came from her own aches and pains. Exercising as part of an effort to recover a sense of well-being after having been raped, Poe found that wearing shoes designed for men gave her chronic backaches. She knew the idea of a shoe for women was a good one, so she was determined to overcome the obstacles of uninterested lenders, inadequate production, and the closed doors of retailers. She offered certain aerobics instructors deep discounts on the shoes and got the attention of such chains as MVP Sports and Lady Foot Locker. She also chose to market herself as the only female owner of a manufacturer of women's athletic shoes. She notes that professional and amateur women athletes are much more likely to buy shoes made by a company run by a woman.

In 1992, Poe announced the establishment of the Ryka ROSE (Regaining One's Self-Esteem) Foundation, which is devoted to helping women who, like Poe, are survivors of rape and other violence. During the first year, Ryka donated 7 percent of its pretax profits to the foundation. This was an extremely important move. The market's response to the foundation has been overwhelmingly positive. Retailers such as Lady Foot Locker, Foot Locker, Champs, and Athletic X-press all declared their enthusiasm, and *Newsweek* and "Dateline NBC" requested interviews with Poe. Poe feels that the foundation strikes a chord with consumers too. "They want their buying dollar to help other women. Our company is about an athletic shoe with a soul." Fashion model Kimberly Collier echoes Poe: "Even if the shoe wasn't as good, I'd still buy it because I think it's a very, very good cause."

Nike and Reebok haven't yet suffered from Ryka's entry into the market; they are still the giants in the athletic shoe industry. But Ryka boasts over $13 million in annual sales for its targeted product line (several models of Ryka shoes designed for different activities). Its image is bolstered by the ROSE Foundation, which helps keep the company's name in people's minds in a distinctive way. And Sheri Poe? She's running hard on the heels of her competitors.

Sources: Carolyn Friday, "A Lightweight Takes on the Big Boys," *Newsweek,* August 24, 1992, p. 55; "A Ryka Rose," *Sporting Goods Dealer,* p. 72; Nora Lockwood Tooher, "A Company for Women, and Sharing," *The Providence Journal-Bulletin,* December 15, 1992, pp. F-1, F-12; "Step On It," *American Health,* January/February 1993; and "Ryka Founder Steps with Purpose in Footwear Business," *Chicago Tribune,* November 8, 1993, p. 6.

Besides the product itself, other elements of the marketing mix may be the source of product failure. For example, marketing messages may not reach the target market, or distribution channels may not be appropriate. The initially poor sales of Sony's MiniDisc, a portable audio system, were blamed largely on poor distribution. The product was launched during the busy Christmas selling season, but deliveries were late and supplies minimal. Resellers as well as consumers were disappointed. DOW Stereo/Video, based in San Diego, heavily advertised its plans for the first live radio demonstration of MiniDisc, but Sony failed to deliver a model on time, so the demo had to be canceled at the last minute.[67]

Sometimes new products fail because the organization didn't bring them to market fast enough. A competitor has a similar idea or learns of the organization's plans, then beats the organization to market. Buyers in the target market become loyal to the competing product before the organization has a chance to grab market share. Or market conditions change so that the product is no longer needed. The U.S. automotive industry has suffered from long cycle times relative to its Japanese competitors. While U.S. automakers take an average of 48 to 60 months to redesign and begin producing a new car, Japanese companies do it in 30 months. As a matter of fact, a competitive strength of the Japanese is their product development time. They often offer consumers the latest technology before businesses in other countries do.[68]

Marketers can't prevent every problem that leads new products to fail. Instead, they can take certain actions that minimize the chance of failure. As mentioned earlier, one of these is to be systematic about product development. However, methodically following the steps of the development process may take too much time in rapidly changing industries.[69] In such situations, marketers may need more streamlined approaches such as the use of venture teams and other tactics that shorten development time.

ORGANIZING FOR SUCCESS

The work of developing a new product is typically handled by employees from various departments in the organization. Often it even involves representatives from external organizations such as advertising agencies and research laboratories. For new products to succeed, these diverse people must be organized in such a way that their efforts can be coordinated and directed toward achieving compatible goals.

Organizing is especially challenging for global marketers. Should the company keep its costs down by conducting all product development at a single facility? Or should it stay more in tune with customer needs by having these activities take place in each country it serves? For some types of products, the answer is a combination of centralized and localized activities—say, soliciting product ideas from local employees and conducting technical research in a central laboratory.

ORGANIZATIONAL FORMS   For organizing the people involved in developing new products, the choices boil down to the five possibilities shown in Figure 11.8:[70]

new-product committee
A committee consisting of representatives from various functional areas who regularly meet to discuss the progress of one or more new products being developed.

- A *functional* organization is one in which employees primarily carry out particular functions, such as sales or finance. The company assigns employees from the necessary functions to spend part of their time working on tasks related to developing a new project. They may be assigned to serve on a **new-product committee**, which regularly meets to review progress on one or more products under development. The functional organization typically is used for relatively minor innovations such as product improvements or new package sizes.
- In a *functional matrix,* people from various functions are assigned to represent their department on a team or committee charged with developing the new product.
- With a *balanced matrix,* employees report to a functional manager and a project manager. The hope is that they will care about how both the project and the function contribute to the organization. Of course, their divided loyalties may also get them bogged down in confusion and uncertainty.
- When the company wants greater loyalty to the project, it can use a *project matrix.* This is a variation of the matrix arrangement in which employees are expected to emphasize their role in developing the new product.

FIGURE 11.8

Organizational Forms for New-Product Development

Options				
Functional With or without committee	Functional matrix	Balanced matrix	Project matrix	Venture Inside Outside

0%_____20%_____40%_____60%_____80%_____100%

Degree of Projectization*

*Defined as the extent to which participants in the process see themselves as independent from the project or committed to it. Thus, members of a new-product committee are almost totally oriented (loyal) to their functions or departments; spin-out (outside) venture members are almost totally committed to the project.

Source: C. Merle Crawford, *New Products Management,* 3d ed. (Homewood, Ill.: Irwin, 1991), p. 411.

spin-out
A new-product venture that has been separated from the parent organization; also called a venture group.

- With a *venture,* the company puts employees to work full time on the new product. The venture may operate as part of the company, or it may be set up as a separate organization—maybe in a separate part of the building or even in another city or state. A venture that has been separated from the parent organization is called a **spin-out** (or, more commonly in the past, a venture group).[71] The cost of setting up a venture and dedicating employees' time to a new product is great, but it can get employees to devote themselves to the product's success.

The term "projectization" in Figure 11.8 may look intimidating. It simply describes the degree to which employees focus on their role as part of the development project, rather than their role in carrying out a particular function.

Which organizational form is best? It depends on the type of innovation desired. In an organization that is basically content with its product line but wants to make some adjustments, the least costly approach is the functional one. But if a new product is critical—and especially if management expects functional members to oppose the changes—more projectization will enhance commitment to the new product's success.[72] Logically then, companies where innovation is viewed as a key to success often set up some type of venture organization. And in one study, the venture organization was associated with the greatest rate of successful new products (see Table 11.5).

venture team
A cross-functional team responsible for all steps in the development of a particular product.

VENTURE TEAMS   Modern organizations are increasingly bringing together people from many functions to serve on venture teams. A **venture team** is a cross-functional team responsible for all steps in the development of a particular product. The team may turn over responsibility for the product following commercialization, or it may assume responsibility for managing the product as a separate business. Companies that have used venture teams include Exxon, IBM, Motorola, and Xerox.

Venture teams operate independently from the organization's functional departments, such as marketing or finance. At Hewlett-Packard, teams are responsible for designing and executing the generation of new products. These product-generation teams report to a product-generation manager rather than a functional manager.[73]

The team members come from several functions. A typical venture team includes engineers for designing the product and developing a prototype. Staff from the mar-

TABLE 11.5

Performance of the Basic Organizational Forms for New-Product Development

ORGANIZATIONAL FORM	PERCENT OF PROJECTS	PERCENT RATED SUCCESSFUL	PERCENT RATED EITHER SUCCESSFUL OR MARGINALLY SUCCESSFUL
Functional	20%	32%	63%
Functional matrix	34	41	79
Balanced matrix	23	58	88
Project matrix	20	62	92
Venture	14	62	94
Total	100%		

Total projects: 540

Source: Reprinted by permission of the publisher from "Organizing for Product Development Projects," Erik W. Larson and David H. Gobeli, *Journal of Product Innovation Management,* September 1988, pp. 180–190. Copyright 1988 by Elsevier Science, Inc.

keting department develop tests of the product concept, conduct test marketing, forecast sales, and plan the marketing mix. Accountants analyze costs and evaluate profitability. At 3M Corporation, researcher Dick Patterson formed a team to develop a sophisticated mechanical splice for optical cables. The team included a senior design engineer (who drew up detailed product designs), a senior engineer (who produced molds, dies, and prototypes), an advanced physicist (who handled testing and evaluating), and a sales and marketing manager (who figured out how to sell the splice, including arranging for a demonstration at a trade show).[74]

Venture teams are especially useful for developing products that are completely new to the company (that is, new product lines) or that involve new technology. Successfully launching such products typically requires more time and money than managers of existing products are willing to risk.[75] In contrast, the leader and members of the venture team will be primarily committed to the success of the new products.

SHORTENING DEVELOPMENT TIME

Organizations can also boost the likelihood their new products will succeed by shortening the time they spend developing them. Getting products to market faster leaves competitors less of a chance to beat the organization to market. Also, the conditions giving rise to a need in the target market are less likely to have changed by the time the product is available. Three major ways to shorten product development time are using teamwork, delegating authority, and building on a base of specialized knowledge.

USING TEAMWORK   The ability to handle functions simultaneously is a major benefit of teamwork. It is the reason for the use of product development teams at Geo. A. Hormel & Company. Hormel's teams include members from research, engineering, operations, and marketing.[76]

Chrysler has not only started using teamwork to shorten the development process but has built the Chrysler Technology Center (CTC) so that all employees working on product development can work in one location.[77] 3M Corporation also built a product development facility. It has two wings, one for the research department, the other

FIGURE 11.9

A New Product Built on Specialized Knowledge

for marketing. Where the wings meet, there are large conference rooms intended to encourage meetings between members of the two departments.[78]

DELEGATING AUTHORITY   An organization that can move quickly is typically one in which decision-making power is delegated. Middle managers at Johnson & Johnson have relatively great power to make decisions. Even if top managers are unimpressed with a new-product idea, they often let unit managers pursue it. If the idea fails, J&J is not punitive. Explains Ralph S. Larsen, the company's chairman, "Growth is a gambler's game."[79] Decentralized management is credited in part for the company's many successes, which include disposable contact lenses and Retin-A skin cream.

BUILDING ON SPECIALIZED KNOWLEDGE   Another way to shorten development time is to devise marketing strategies that involve building and taking advantage of a base of specialized knowledge.[80] The organization seeks to master knowledge of a particular technology, a market segment, and its own strengths or weaknesses. One way marketers do this is to involve members of target markets in designing new products.

 Also, an organization practicing this strategy would build relationships with suppliers and other outside organizations. That approach paid off for Joseph Jarke, who wanted to develop a product to ease the challenge of airline travel by people who, like Jarke, are wheelchair users. Jarke took his product concept—a wheelchair that can fold up to the size of a briefcase—to United Airlines for input from a potential user and to GE Plastics for expertise in selecting materials. Both companies were impressed with Jarke's SeatCase Travel Chairs and willing to help him get his venture off the ground. Today SeatCases are available on a dozen airlines and on Japan's bullet trains.[81]

 Building on a base of specialized knowledge should speed development by reducing the time it takes for the organization to figure out what customers want and how to meet those needs. As the organization builds its experience in serving particular customers along with its suppliers and resellers, it gains insights that will improve decision making about new products and other areas of marketing. The product expertise of Rollerblade's engineers and the skill of the top boot designers at Italy's Nordica made a strong team to improve the safety of the braking system for in-line roller skates. Skaters using Rollerblade's new Active Brake Technology stop by rolling the boot—not the whole skate—forward, which moves a lever that lowers the brake. Theoretically, this method of braking is easier and more natural than the original method (see Figure 11.9).[82]

PUTTING IT ALL TOGETHER   Shortening product development time is often one of the quality goals at organizations practicing total quality management. Thus, employees' efforts at continuous improvement include speeding the development process. Their tactics may include all of those discussed here and more.

At Schaumburg, Illinois–based Thermos, innovative product development saved the company from stagnating. Recognizing that consumers expect more than a clever advertising message or a pretty new color, Thermos's chief executive, Monte Peterson, sought a commitment to true innovation by turning away from the company's previous reliance on functional departments. Peterson assembled a cross-functional team of six middle managers to look at the market for grills.

The team named itself the Lifestyle team and assigned itself to study people's cookout habits and find a need Thermos could meet better than its competitors. Leadership of the team rotated, depending on which task was most urgent at any point. For example, the marketing manager led the team during the consumer research. During that phase, the team conducted focus groups, visited homes, and videotaped barbecues. They learned that more women were barbecuing than in the past, that many cooks were getting tired of handling dirty charcoal, and that many homeowners were building fancy decks and wanted the grill on their deck to look good.

From their research, the team came up with a broad concept: a grill that looks like a handsome piece of furniture, doesn't require environmentally unfriendly charcoal lighter, and cooks food that tastes good. To be safe for apartment dwellers, the grill would have to be electric. With these criteria, the team developed a prototype. The team got outside expertise from Fitch Inc., an Ohio industrial design firm, which assigned about ten members to the Thermos team.

While marketing research was being conducted, the engineers were studying ways to improve the technology of electric grilling, and personnel in manufacturing had been studying ways to make the new grill at a reasonable price. The solution to the engineering group's greatest challenge—how to make an electric grill that reaches high enough temperatures to really grill rather than bake—lay in Thermos's core competency, vacuum technology. The engineers found that a domed vacuum top could do this by keeping the heat in the grill, the way a Thermos bottle keeps coffee hot. The manufacturing people kept costs in line through such input as insisting that tapered legs would be needlessly expensive to make.

Final testing by consumers and Thermos employees resulted in a product that the company could roll out with pride. Peterson credits new products such as the electric grill with generating much of the company's newfound growth. And the success of the teamwork has led Thermos to apply the same approach to developing additional products.[83]

Summary

Since most organizations market an assortment of products, known as their product mix, they usually group their products according to product lines. Products may be consumer products (sold to consumers) or industrial products (sold to organizations). Consumer products fall into the categories of convenience (inexpensive, frequent purchases), shopping (more expensive purchases based on comparisons among alternatives), and specialty (expensive and unique purchases). Industrial products may be installations (nonportable industrial goods), accessory equipment (portable equipment and tools), raw materials (unprocessed items), supplies (consumable industrial goods), and business services (support). Goods may be either durable (lasting at least three years) or nondurable (lasting less than three years).

A new product is one that is new to the marketing organization in any way. It may perform a new function, improve performance, provide a new application or function, be integrated into another product, be downgraded or restyled, have a lower price, or be offered to a new market. Government regulations stipulate that the term "new" may be applied to a product for only six months.

Companies can enhance their chances of success with a new product if they are systematic about developing it. The process of development begins with idea generation. Ideas for new products can come from many sources, including customers, the sales force, and other employees. The organization must evaluate the ideas to be sure that they meet the objectives of the marketing department and company. Next the marketer conducts a business analysis to see whether predicted sales and costs are acceptable. If so, the process continues with development of the product and other elements of the marketing mix. Usually the organization test markets the product to see whether it is received and used as expected. If the results of test marketing are acceptable, the development process ends with commercialization.

Although there is no way to guarantee the success of a new product, companies that emphasize planning, organiza-tion, and cooperation among various functions usually have the lowest rates of failure. Two important ways to avoid fail-ure are to select the most appropriate form of product devel-opment organization and to look for ways to speed up development. The people responsible for product develop-ment may have responsibility along functional lines, project lines, or some balance between the two (such as a matrix structure). An increasingly popular way to organize is to use a venture team, which is a cross-functional team responsible for all the steps in the development of a product. Ways to shorten product development time are to use teams, delegate decision-making power, and build on a base of specialized knowledge.

KEY TERMS AND CONCEPTS

product mix (p. 320)
product lines (p. 321)
consumer products (p. 321)
industrial products (p. 321)
convenience products (p. 321)
shopping products (p. 321)
specialty products (p. 321)
installations (p. 323)

accessory equipment (p. 323)
component parts and materials (p. 323)
raw materials (p. 324)
supplies (p. 324)
business services (p. 324)
durable goods (p. 325)
nondurable goods (p. 325)

new product (p. 325)
product line extensions (p. 328)
concept testing (p. 334)
concurrent engineering (p. 336)
commercialization (p. 338)
new-product committee (p. 341)
spin-out (p. 342)
venture team (p. 342)

REVIEW AND DISCUSSION QUESTIONS

1. Sometimes a consumer product can encompass more than one category, such as convenience and shopping, depending on how it is produced and marketed. As a marketer for a company that manufactures shaving razors, how would you produce and present the razor as a convenience product? How would you produce and present it as a shopping product?
2. As a marketer for an office-cleaning company, as what type of product would you present your service to busi-nesses? What issues do you think would be important to potential customers?
3. Name the nine ways a product might be considered "new" (not including the FTC regulation).
4. Why is time and money spent on research and develop-ment important?

5. Assume a company that produces cameras has an idea for an entirely new and superior type of film, but busi-ness analysis shows that the cost of taking it to market by itself is prohibitive. How might the company consider going ahead with the product? Elaborate on how this might work.
6. When is test marketing most effective? What are the short-comings of test marketing? How can they be avoided?
7. Assume a U.S.–based company markets a line of outdoor clothing, specializing in clothes for skiing and hiking. The company wants to expand its market to serve Japan, China, and Western Europe. As a marketer at this company, what steps would you take to prevent failure of the new line?
8. How would you use a venture team to carry out the steps you plan to take in question 7? Who would be on the team?

Chapter Project
**Product Development
in Teams**

Choose one of the following companies, then generate and evaluate ideas for a new product of that company. Use any of the techniques in Table 11.3 you think will be helpful. (You can com-bine this project with the "Put It into Practice" box on concept testing.)

Next form a team with about four other classmates and repeat the process of generating ideas. To do so in your "venture team," try brainstorming or a technique from Table 11.3. To brainstorm, appoint one member of the group to record your ideas. Then the group members state ideas as they think of them, without worrying at this stage about logic or practicality. No one is to criticize an idea at this stage, only to contribute additional ideas. When your group is done coming up with ideas, the group evaluates the ideas and refines or discards them. At this stage, you are seeking a concept to test.

Write a report on the discussions and findings of your team or present them in class. In your report or as a class, discuss the process of generating and evaluating ideas. Did you get the most creative ideas when you worked alone or in a group? What different insights did group members bring to bear on this task? Which approach—working alone or in a group—was more difficult to use? What did this project show you about developing a product as part of a cross-functional team?

Company ideas:
- Taxi service
- Resort near the ocean
- Producer of games
- Maker of uniforms
- Radio station

Case
WaterBabies

Imagine an old-fashioned doll: one that doesn't cry, feed, or crawl. One that doesn't need batteries. Dan Lauer, a young former banker, remembered such a doll from his childhood. With six children in his family, there wasn't a lot of money for elaborate toys. So his three sisters would fill rubber gloves or balloons with water, paint faces on them, dress them up in doll's clothes, and play with them. About 25 years later, Dan remembered those dolls as he longed to become an inventor.

With $100 in capital, Lauer made the leap into entrepreneurship, founding Lauer Toys in 1987. He wrote 700 letters to toy companies, including Hasbro and Mattel, trying to get them interested in his new dolls, called WaterBabies. "I found that toy companies get 400 letters a week from guys like me," Lauer remarks.

Richard Sallis, president of the U.S. subsidiary of Playmates Ltd. (Hong Kong), which also produces Teenage Mutant Ninja Turtles, recalls the WaterBaby prototype that Lauer sent him. The body was made of two water-filled balloons, and the arms and legs were condoms. "It leaked all over my desk. They said, 'Can you imagine this as a doll?' I said 'No, I can't. Get it off my desk.'"

By 1989, Lauer had run up about $10,000 in debt. But he caught the attention of George Martin, an entrepreneurial law student who compiled an equity investment that allowed Lauer to leave the bank and devote full time to Lauer Toys. Later, Lauer sold stock in his company to local investors, including his mother. But he still couldn't license his WaterBabies design to a toy company, so he decided to produce it and market it himself.

Stores didn't want to bother with a toy from an unknown inventor. But Lauer talked one toy buyer for Venture Stores of St. Louis into taking the toy home and "testing" it on his daughter. She and her friends loved it. Gradually, Venture, Wal-Mart, Toys "R" Us, Target, and Kay-Bee stores agreed to a test market in their St. Louis–area stores. The test began just before Thanksgiving, and Lauer hoped to sell about 5,000 dolls for Christmas. He sold 15,000. After a few more hurdles, Mattel, Hasbro, and Playmates were clamoring for Lauer's attention.

Lauer signed on with Playmates because he believed that the company needed his toy more than the others did and would work harder to promote it. By 1992, Playmates estimated sales of WaterBabies would be around four million in the United States, and the firm planned to sell the dolls in Europe and Japan.

What's the appeal of these "new" dolls called WaterBabies? They're old-fashioned in the sense that they don't have moving parts or require batteries. "The good thing about the doll is that it forces you to interact with it," notes Lauer. But they are also extremely realistic. Filled with warm tap water and dressed in sleepers designed by one of Lauer's sisters, they feel like hot water bottles—or real babies. So this new product draws not so much on technology (except that required to keep the bodies from leaking) as on a simple idea. Its market test was a good predictor of success; children loved it, and parents didn't have to worry about a complicated or dangerous toy. It's likely that Dan Lauer has more new ideas for old toys from his childhood.

QUESTIONS

1. Did the process Lauer used to develop WaterBabies match the process for new-product development described in this chapter? Explain.
2. Why do you think the test market for WaterBabies was so important?
3. Can you think of an old toy from your childhood that could be reworked or refined to make a new product? How would you go about developing it?

Source: Subrata N. Chakravarty, "The WaterBabies Story: Persistence," *Forbes,* May 11, 1992, pp. 198, 200.

CHAPTER 12

Existing Products

LEARNING OBJECTIVES

After completing this chapter, you should be able to:

1. Describe the stages of the product life cycle.

2. Describe variations of the product life cycle: renewed expansion, fashions, fads.

3. Discuss the process by which products are adopted by increasingly large numbers of buyers.

4. Discuss how various characteristics of products play a role in marketing.

5. Define brands and describe issues marketers consider in devising a branding strategy.

6. Describe the basic types of decisions marketers must make with regard to product lines and product mix.

Creating Customer Value
Harley-Davidson, Inc.

To bikers, HOG doesn't mean what it sounds like. It's a club for owners of motorcycles—Harleys, to be precise. HOG stands for Harley Owners' Group, and its members are as devoted to their bikes as Porsche owners are to their cars.

With its corporate headquarters in Milwaukee and its manufacturing plants in Wisconsin and Pennsylvania, Harley-Davidson is the only U.S. manufacturer of motorcycles. The company has traveled a bumpy road. But with ingenuity and a commitment to quality, teamwork, and customer satisfaction, Harley has managed to hang in there for the rough ride.

The company was founded in 1903 by Bill Harley and three Davidson brothers, who thought there would be a market for a motor-driven bicycle. That first year, they produced three motorcycles. More than 90 years later, 80,000 Harleys a year cruise out of the plants. According to Jim Paterson, executive vice president of the Motorcycle Division (Harley also makes accessories), the goal is to produce 120,000 per year.

In 1969, when Harley-Davidson merged with American Machine and Foundry Corp., the founding families lost most of the control over the manufacture of their motorcycles. Quality plummeted. The bikes leaked oil and broke down. According to William G. Davidson (known as "Willie G." to Harley enthusiasts), now vice president of styling, "numbers were very important then. There were different people running the company with different goals. I think we were trying to make too many vehicles and we were losing track of our quality." Not only that, Japanese bikes were gaining ground fast. They cost half as much, they were mechanically reliable, and they didn't have that Harley "growl." By 1980, Harley was clearly in trouble. The company's American market share for super heavyweight bikes had plummeted from 77.5 percent in 1973 to 30.8 percent.

The next year, a group of 13 managers from Harley (including Willie G.) pulled off a coup, securing financing for a leveraged buyout of the company. They appealed to the Reagan administration for stiff tariffs on imported bikes,

which were granted. The tariffs bought them time, and they launched their quality campaign. Ironically, Harley management looked to Japanese methods, including just-in-time manufacturing and employee empowerment. By 1986, Harley's performance had improved so much that management actually requested a lifting of the trade tariffs six months before their expiration date. The Harleys were rolling, and they weren't about to be stopped.

Harley-Davidson now cites three main company objectives: (1) to create market demand for 120,000 bikes per year; (2) to have the capacity to build 120,000 bikes; (3) to be first in customer satisfaction. In addition, Paterson notes, Harley strives to be "the most respected brand in the world." Respect, of course, is a direct outcome of the product's quality. Paterson defines several dimensions of quality, including innovation and a product that can be trusted to meet expectations. Harley-Davidson wants its customers to be satisfied with price, delivery, reliability, and performance.

The company has already succeeded at the satisfaction objective so well that dealers can't keep up with the demand. Nevertheless, the company is increasing output at a conservative pace. It does not want to risk hurting quality and the reputation it has worked so hard to build. A key tactic for boosting output has been to assemble teams of employees charged with continuous improvement in the way things are done at Harley—getting people "to work smarter, not harder," according to one executive. The teams look for ways to get many operations under the control of one operator, enabling that person to evaluate processes, decrease time wasted, increase productivity, and thus produce more vehicles.

If this sounds like a sweatshop, it's not. Employees are encouraged to take control of quality in every aspect of their jobs. Harley now uses a "real-time quality system" and "statistical process control." This means that individual employees use computers and continuously generated statistics to evaluate the quality of a process or product at any time. Operators of all production machines are trained in whatever technology is necessary to put them in charge of their processes. "When you work here, you are a part of the whole Harley family," explains Don Kieffer, manager of manufacturing and quality engineering. "The motorcycle ties together the customer to the management to the salaried people to the production workers in a way that no other company can."

To meet the objective of creating demand, Harley is making a big push to go global, targeting Europe and the Pacific Rim. Harley's market share overseas averages only about 15 percent, so there is plenty of room to grow. As in the United States, much of the challenge involves increasing production while maintaining the quality that delights Harley customers. The demand is already intensifying. In Japan, waiting lists for Harleys can lead to waits as long as six months in spite of price tags as high as $25,000.

Undeterred by the production challenges, the company has exceeded expectations. Between 1980 and 1992, its U.S. market share rose 97 percent, productivity 50 percent, U.S. revenues 80 percent, and international revenues 170 percent. "We're *not* like other companies, damn it," exclaims Rich Teerlink, CEO and president. "We rose from the ashes, no matter what mistakes management made over the years, because the riders, dealers, and suppliers refused to let the company die."

Sources: Charles Leroux, "Full Throttle," *Chicago Tribune Magazine,* June 6, 1993, pp. 14–18; Kevin Kelly and Karen Lowry Miller, "The Rumble Heard Round the World: Harleys," *Business Week,* May 24, 1993, pp. 58–60; Gary Slutsker, "Hog Wild," *Forbes,* May 24, 1993, pp. 45–46; "Willie G. Davidson: Born to Ride," *Sales & Marketing Management,* April 1991, pp. 26–27; and promotional video produced by Harley-Davidson, Inc.

Chapter Overview

Harley-Davidson managed its products effectively, bringing a declining product line back to life by injecting an emphasis on quality through teamwork and employee empowerment. Deciding what to do about a product for which sales are no longer growing is only one of the many decisions involved in managing the products in an organization's product mix. Marketers also make such decisions as how to package the product and what sales support to provide.

This chapter introduces some basic considerations marketers face in product management. The chapter begins by describing the typical life cycle of a product, from its introduction to its decline and possible removal from the product mix. Then the chapter addresses the many dimensions of a product—quality, features, design, branding, packaging, and product safety. It discusses ways in which marketers decide how these dimensions of the product can meet the needs of their target markets. The chapter closes by moving from consideration of individual products to a look at the overall product mix. This section of the chapter introduces issues involved in deciding what assortment of products and product lines to offer.

The Product Life Cycle

The marketing strategies that work best for telephones are not the same as those for fax machines. There are many reasons for the differences, of course, but one important source of differences is that these products are at different stages of their life

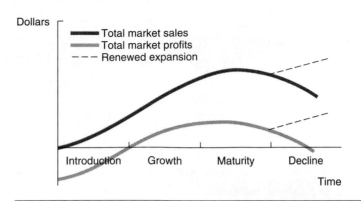

FIGURE 12.1

The Product Life Cycle

product life cycle
The four stages in a product's sales and profit history: introduction, growth, maturity, decline.

cycles. In a sense, products, like living beings, pass through certain life stages. The **product life cycle** is a model of the stages in a product's sales and profit history.

LIFE CYCLE STAGES

The details of the product life cycle vary among different industries, products, and markets. However, the basic model describes a product's life cycle in terms of four stages. As shown in Figure 12.1, the stages in the product life cycle are introduction, growth, maturity, and decline. The two curves in the figure show the pattern of industry sales and profits throughout these stages. During the final stage, the marketer may try to stimulate new demand or may stop offering the product.

INTRODUCTION During the introduction stage of the product life cycle, a new product enters the marketplace. (Consider a "new" product to be a good or service that is innovative enough to not have direct competition yet.) Sales start out low but begin to climb. Production costs are usually high because the producers do not yet have experience in making the product. Marketing costs tend to be high because sellers must devote resources to educating target markets about what the new product is and how it will benefit them. The objective is for target markets to be aware of the product and to try it. These efforts emphasize building desire for the type of product, rather than for a specific brand.

Because costs are high and sales only beginning to build, industry profits tend to be low, if they exist at all. Thus, one of the biggest challenges of the introduction phase is to keep enough money coming in to cover the expenses of building demand. Depending on its size and reputation, the producer may also have difficulty persuading resellers to handle the product or give it enough attention. Fortunately, the organizations that operate in this stage of the product life cycle tend to face little competition. If they can protect some aspect of the product with a patent or copyright, they can maintain their position as sole producer of the product for years. The lack of competition often leads a marketer to set a relatively high price.

An example of an industry in the introduction stage of the product life cycle is recyclers of used motor oil. This industry lost $10 million between 1987 and 1992. One problem was high development costs, and another was the marketing error of charging less for oil collection than it cost to provide this service. However, future prospects are expected to be bright for the three U.S. firms in the industry so far.[1]

Perfume is in the maturity stage of the product life cycle. For particular brands, the marketer's challenge is to set the brand apart by creating an image for the brand.

Vanilla Fields. For Women.
Only Nature Could Inspire
So Perfect a Fragrance.

VANILLA
FIELDS

GROWTH   During the growth stage, sales climb the most rapidly as more and more buyers begin trying the product. Profits also rise as sellers learn to make best use of their production facilities and distribution channels. The challenges of this stage include keeping up with demand and fending off competitors, who are attracted to the market because of its growth. The increase in competition may lead sellers to lower prices and to look for ways to add services that will enhance the product's value.

One business in the growth stage is comic book stores. With 1992 sales double annual sales of four years earlier, this type of business has attracted increasing competition. The early comic book stores were primarily set up by people with a fascination for the product. The newer entrants to the market more often have expertise in retailing. These entrepreneurs have forced the original stores to adopt more businesslike practices in order to keep up.[2]

MATURITY   In terms of the product life cycle, a product is mature when it has become a familiar offering and when its success during the growth stage has led many competing firms to enter the marketplace. Because many buyers already own the product, sales growth slows and may even begin falling. Competition causes profits to rise more slowly than sales. This is because keeping up with competitors may require reducing prices, improving quality while holding the line on price, or increasing spending for promotion. In the mature U.S. market for personal computers, prices were recently reported to be falling an average of 8 percent every three months. In Japan, U.S. marketers of PCs made inroads by slashing prices by as much as 30 percent.[3] Price-oriented advertising is common for a product in the maturity stage.

Another example of a product in the maturity stage is pagers, more commonly called beepers. Over the past decade, prices of this product have fallen from $400 to just $60 to $120. The lower prices have extended the appeal of the products beyond businesspeople to consumers. For example, teenagers buy beepers so their friends can reach them while they are out. To further appeal to consumers, beepers now come in bright colors and are available in many outlets, including Kmart and some supermarkets.[4]

Bottled water, too, is in the maturity stage in the United States and United Kingdom. In the United States, growth in annual sales has slowed to 3 percent, way down from 500 percent a decade earlier. U.S. consumers can choose from 700 brands, each struggling to convey a sense that it comes from an especially pristine source.[5] Growth in sales to British consumers has plummeted to 8 percent a year, down from an astonishing annual growth rate of over 1,000 percent in the previous decade.[6]

DECLINE Eventually the sales volume for most products begins to fall. There are many possible reasons for a decline in sales. Perhaps new technology has led to a superior alternative. In a recent year, CD players outsold turntables 8 to 1, and sales of turntables are expected to begin falling soon.[7] Needs or values may change so that the product is no longer relevant or appealing. For example, a decline in sales of ground decaffeinated coffee has been attributed to consumer dissatisfaction with the product's taste.[8] People who want to avoid caffeine are switching from coffee to other kinds of drinks such as soft drinks. Decaf makers blame the decline on a trend toward drinking soft drinks instead of coffee, but critics of decaf's taste point out that sales of gourmet coffee are on the rise.[9]

Marketers may respond to the sales decline by seeking ways to keep the product profitable. An obvious approach is to cut costs. In the case of turntables, makers are doing so by limiting the number of models. Also, if a niche market continues to demand a product, customers may be willing to pay a higher price. This, too, appears to be the case with some buyers of turntables, while other consumers are snapping up rebuilt models so that they can keep using their record collections.[10] If the product is no longer profitable, sellers may want to discontinue it altogether. Later, this chapter discusses the decision to discontinue a product.

PROS AND CONS OF THE MODEL

The life cycle model has several limitations. First, it applies better to categories of products (say, personal computers) than to individual products (for example, the IBM PS/2). Also, the life cycle varies from one type of product to the next and may not describe some products very well. Such limitations make it impossible for marketers to use this model to forecast how a product will perform in the future or when it will enter the next stage of its life cycle. In other words, it is a "post hoc" model; it describes the past, rather than predicting the future.

Given the limitations of this model, why do marketers care about the product life cycle? It is useful for helping them envision ways in which to adapt marketing strategy to changing conditions. For example, it reminds marketers of a new product with rapidly growing sales that they can expect more competition and probably reduced profits unless they can find ways to protect their share. Table 12.1 summarizes typical strategies appropriate for each stage of the product life cycle. Many were alluded to earlier in this section and will be covered in more detail in the chapters that cover the relevant aspects of the marketing mix. Keep in mind that the strategies summarized in the table are just general guidelines; it would be impossible to cite a single strategy that would succeed for every type of good and service.

Some critics warn that the life cycle model can become a self-fulfilling prophecy. They say that marketers who believe their product is "mature" may give up on finding ways to make it grow. But more positively, if the product's behavior really does show signs of maturity, the model can remind marketers that it is important to consider innovation as a way to keep the product vital.

TABLE 12.1

The Product Life Cycle's Implications for Marketing Strategy

STRATEGY DIMENSION	LIFE CYCLE STAGE			
	INTRODUCTION	GROWTH	MATURITY	DECLINE
Basic objectives	Establish a market for product type; persuade early adopters to buy	Build sales and market share; develop preference for brand	Defend brand's share of market; seek growth by luring customers from competitors	Limit costs or seek ways to revive sales and profits
Product	Provide high quality; select a good brand; get patent and/or trademark protection	Provide high quality; add services to enhance value	Improve quality; add features to distinquish brand from competitors	Continue providing high quality to maintain brand's reputation; seek ways to make the product new again
Pricing	Often high to recover development costs; sometimes low to build demand rapidly	Somewhat high because of heavy demand	Low, reflecting heavy competition	Low to sell off remaining inventory or high to serve a niche market
Channels	Limited number of channels	Greater number of channels to meet demand	Greater number of channels and more incentives to resellers	Limited number of channels
Communication	Aimed at early adopters; messages designed to educate about product type; incentives such as samples and coupons to induce trial	Aimed at wider audience; messages focus on brand benefits; for consumer products, emphasis on advertising	Messages focus on differentiating brand from its competitors; heavy use of incentives such as coupons to induce buyers to switch brands	Minimal, to keep costs down

VARIATIONS OF THE PRODUCT LIFE CYCLE

Of course, the pattern of industry sales and profits need not follow this model from start to finish. Sometimes insightful marketing tactics or even good luck can bring a declining product back to life. And some products follow the stages of fashion or fad rather than the life cycle shown in Figure 12.1.

RENEWED EXPANSION   Instead of letting sales decline and eventually discontinuing the product, the marketer may see a way to bring about renewed expansion in sales and profits. To do this, the marketer makes the product "new" in some way. As described in Chapter 11, there are several ways to make an existing product new. Basically, marketers can improve the product (say, by adding features or improving quality), find new uses for the product, or find new markets to serve with it (reposition the product). In any case, the result should be continued growth in sales and profits. In effect, the marketer extends the life cycle for the product.

Himmel Nutrition Inc. did this with Ovaltine milk modifier, a chocolate-flavored powder popular during the 1940s. Himmel communicated the fact that, unlike competing products such as Nestle's Quik, Ovaltine is fortified with vitamins, thus positioning the product to appeal to health-conscious consumers. Sales have jumped in response to the effort, and Himmel is researching ways to improve the product to stimulate even more demand.[11]

FIGURE 12.2

Variations of the Product Life Cycle

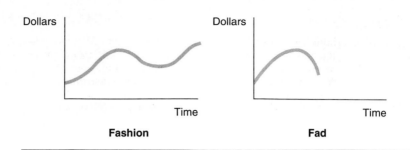

In the industrial marketplace, steelmakers are looking for new uses for their products. For example, the industry is trying to persuade homebuilders to construct steel-frame houses, which are lighter, more flexible, and more recyclable than wood houses.[12]

Sometimes a marketer can renew a product simply by recognizing and responding to renewed interest. This requires that the marketer be aware of changes in the marketing environment that might make the product more appealing. For example, water shortages and restrictions on water use have stimulated new interest in collecting water with rain barrels—a product that hasn't seen widespread use in generations.[13] The resurgence of interest in the classic two-speed Waring Blendor (the company's spelling) has been credited to consumers' move back to the basics and their belief that such products represent old-fashioned quality. And according to Mary Gillespie, a spokesperson for the Association of Home Appliance Manufacturers, blenders in general outlasted the trend toward food processors because blenders are better for pureeing big batches of liquids.[14]

When a marketer is looking for new target markets, international marketing is often appealing. However, marketers must be careful to avoid assuming that people in another nation or culture will understand what the product is and how to use it. A firm that introduced baby food to several African nations evidently didn't consider that there could be more than one explanation for what is in a jar with a picture of a baby on it. Consumers in those nations reached the logical but disturbing conclusion that the jars contained ground-up babies.[15]

FASHIONS AND FADS   Some products tend to follow two variations of the basic product life cycle. These variations are fashions and fads. Figure 12.2 illustrates the general pattern of these two life cycles.

fashions
Accepted and popular product styles.

Fashions are accepted and popular product styles. Their life cycle involves a stage of distinctiveness in which trendsetters adopt the style, followed by a stage in which more customers emulate the trendsetters. Next, the style becomes widely available at mass-market prices, then eventually becomes phased out. This happened to the so-called grunge look. It moved from Seattle rock bands to college campuses. In a single year, U.S. sales of sturdy, no-nonsense Doc Martens shoes and boots—a staple of grunge—doubled.[16] When department stores began featuring flannel shirts and ripped jeans, musicians and students were ready to move on. Many fashions, such as skirt lengths, lose popularity, then regain it again. As in these examples, the fashion cycle is typical of clothing. Other products that follow this cycle are hairstyles and cosmetics.

fads
Products that experience an intense but brief period of popularity.

Fads are products that experience an intense but brief period of popularity. Their life cycle resembles the basic product life cycle but in compressed form. It may be so brief that few competitors have a chance to capitalize on the fad. An example of a fad product is liquid-diet plans. Consumers rushed to them because they looked like an easy way to lose weight. Sales really took off in 1988 after talk-show host Oprah Winfrey credited use of Optifast with her loss of 67 pounds. But like Winfrey, most people failed to achieve long-term weight loss, and the federal government began to investigate the claims made for the products. Sales tumbled, but industry observers expect that it's only a matter of time before frustrated dieters try another fad.[17] In the meantime, makers of liquid-diet products can take heart from the tendency of many fads to repeat their popu-larity after years of decline. That was the case with troll dolls, which were popular in the 1960s and 1990s. (For more on fads, see "Put It into Practice.")

PRODUCT DIFFUSION

Throughout the product life cycle, a product enters the homes and workplaces of more and more buyers. Thus, not so many decades ago, few households had televi-sion sets. Those few had the discretionary income and imagination to buy the new technology, and the neighbors would gather to watch with the proud owners. Then as more and more consumers appreciated TV programming or wanted to emulate their neighbors, and as TV prices fell, they bought sets of their own. Today at least one tele-vision is in every American home—well, almost every home. The authors know of one writer in the Chicago area without a television, and there may be a few other holdouts here and there.

As in this example, the buyers who try the product early in its life cycle tend to have different characteristics than those who buy later. Also, to some extent, the behavior of early buyers tends to influence those who buy later. The model that describes this process is called **product diffusion**.

product diffusion
The process through which a product is adopted by increasing numbers of buyers, with early buyers influencing later ones.

innovators
The earliest buyers of a product.

THE DIFFUSION PROCESS   The process of product diffusion starts when a few mem-bers of the market, known as **innovators**, try buying the product. When innovators are consumers, they tend to be people who are adventurous and willing to take risks. For example, the first car owners to install neon lights on the underside of their vehicles were so impressed with the eerie effect that they were willing to risk generating some less than favorable reactions. Explains Pete Santoro, the Kansas City distributor for Motion Neon, "The police officers around here . . . when they see some car going down the street with lights underneath it, they freak out. The first thing they've got to do is catch it."[18] When innovators are organizational buyers, they tend to be organiza-tions that seek to distinguish themselves through use of the latest technology and ideas. Ingersoll Milling Machine Company, a maker of customized machines for heavy indus-try, is committed to the idea that using the latest machinery can improve its productiv-ity. Ingersoll has a rule that when its machines reach 10 years old, they must be replaced unless someone can justify keeping them. This commitment to modernizing has enabled the company to double its output with half the number of machines.[19]

early adopters
The second category of buyers to try a product; they tend to buy after they see a product will work.

If the experience of innovators shows that the new product works, **early adopters** begin to buy. These buyers appreciate the latest product ideas, and they are often

FIGURE 12.3

An Unflattering Portrait of an Early Adopter

respectable and influential. Figure 12.3 is a humorous representation of this group of buyers.

Influenced by what early adopters have, the rest of the market begins to get interested in the product. The biggest category of buyers is divided into groups called the early majority and late majority. Members of the **early majority** tend to avoid risk and to make purchases carefully. Members of the **late majority** not only avoid risks, but are cautious and skeptical about new ideas. Eventually the product becomes commonplace, and even the laggards are ready to buy. **Laggards** are reluctant to make changes and are more comfortable with tradition. An example is the writer mentioned earlier, who still isn't sure why she needs a television just yet.

early majority
Buyers who are next after early adopters to try a product; they are among the majority of buyers.

late majority
Buyers who are more cautious; they try a product after the early majority.

laggards
The last buyers to try a product.

APPLICATIONS   Appreciating that different groups of customers buy at different stages of the product's life helps the marketer to devise a marketing strategy that will appeal to the group likely to buy at any given point. Marketers assume that these groups fall into a normal distribution such as the one shown in Figure 12.4. Thus, during the introduction stage, marketers would seek to win over the 16 percent of the market that consists of innovators and early adopters. When the majority starts buying, the product has entered the growth stage. When laggards buy, it is in the maturity and decline stages.

FIGURE 12.4

Groups of Buyers during Product Diffusion

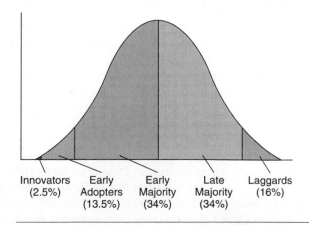

Innovators (2.5%)   Early Adopters (13.5%)   Early Majority (34%)   Late Majority (34%)   Laggards (16%)

Managing Individual Products

In devising a product strategy at any stage of the life cycle, marketers must consider the quality, features, and design of the product itself. But as noted in Chapter 11, there is more to a product than just a tangible good with certain features. Therefore, marketers also must consider such product-related concerns as packaging, product safety, and sales support.

QUALITY, FEATURES, DESIGN

Think about your parents' car and about the one you own (or would like to own). How are they similar, and in what ways are they different? Chances are that, in answering this question, you thought of the cars in terms of their quality, features, and design. These are basic ways to describe products.

QUALITY   Perhaps more than ever, today's consumers and organizational buyers are looking for quality. At a minimum, they want products that meet their specifications. In other words, products should do what buyers want them to do, and do it well. For customers of Rally's fast-food restaurants, quality means "a fully dressed burger, a 16-ounce Coke, and good-sized fries for $1.97, in 45 seconds."[20] Employers, seeking to get the most for the health care dollars they spend on their employees, want to identify which hospitals provide good care efficiently. A group called Cleveland Health Quality Choice has sought to meet that need locally by preparing regular ratings of the 31 Cleveland-area hospitals' patient satisfaction, general medical services, general clinical services, and intensive care. The report notes whether performance is at, above, or below predicted levels of death rates and length of stay.[21]

Quality, in the mind of today's customer, means getting good service along with a tangible product. This may explain Burger King's success with its dinner menu. Besides offering fried chicken, shrimp, steak sandwiches, and baked potatoes, Burger King provides table service to its evening customers. While they wait for their food, customers can enjoy free popcorn and free refills on their soft drinks.[22]

Solutions   Buyers want more than just features—they want products that fulfill their needs or solve their problems. In the case of complex products, providing solutions often involves helping customers use what they buy. Marketers serving organizational buyers may train the buyers' employees in using their products. Or a consumer goods company might staff a toll-free line for customers to call with their questions or complaints.

In both cases, good service includes responsiveness when a customer encounters problems with a product. Even if the marketer suspects the problem was the buyer's fault, good long-term relationships depend on getting the buyer's problem fixed first. Then the marketer can help identify the source of the problem. Involving buyers (such as an organization's technical staff) in diagnosing the problem makes it more likely they will recognize and accept any role they had in causing the problem. And keeping customers happy is almost always more valuable than being right about problems with a product's performance.[23]

Marketers fail to provide quality not only when their products don't work as intended, but also when their products do not really meet a need. One product that has been criticized in this regard is Potato Perfect, which bakes potatoes in half the time of a conventional oven but with tastier results than when preparing them in a microwave. Gary Stibel, managing partner of the New England Consulting Group,

FIGURE 12.5

Using a Guarantee to Promote a Quality Image

questions whether this product will succeed. Says Stibel, "I don't think many people are having a baked-potato problem right now."[24]

Warranties and Guarantees   An important indicator of quality is a warranty for the product. A **warranty** is the producer's statement of what it will do to compensate the buyer if the product is defective or does not work properly. Lanier Worldwide offers its customers a refund if its copiers do not meet their guaranteed uptime of 98 percent (that is, if the copiers are out of order more than 2 percent of the time).[25] In many instances, the courts will also hold that businesses have *implied warranties,* or unstated promises to compensate the buyer if their products fail to perform up to the basic standards of the industry or to do what the seller says they will. Of course, like Lanier, an organization that wants to convey its concern for quality will offer customers more than implied warranties enforced by the courts.

Many sellers offer a guarantee instead of or in addition to a warranty. A **guarantee** is a promise that the product is as represented and will perform properly. Typically, if the product fails to perform, the organization making the guarantee replaces the product or refunds its cost. These promises imply that the manufacturer is confident in the products' quality.

Customers tend to have a more favorable view of products with generous guarantees and warranties. Thus, to keep its customers "for a lifetime," Lanier offers a 100 percent uptime guarantee for its digital dictation systems.[26] And as shown in Figure 12.5, McDonald's builds a quality image with a guarantee of hot food, fast and friendly service, and accuracy of drive-thru orders. On the reverse of the handout shown in the figure, the company promises, "If you're not satisfied, we'll make it right. Or your next meal is on us."

Global Implications   High quality is one of the most important aspects of an international product. A high-quality product is most likely to succeed in spite of the difficulties

warranty
The producer's statement of how it will compensate the buyer if the product is defective.

guarantee
A promise that the product as it is represented will perform properly.

of marketing to buyers in another country. For example, when tariffs lead a marketer to set a higher price for a product than domestic competitors charge, buyers may still choose the product if its quality is superior. A high-quality product is also more likely to meet various nations' product standards. In determining how loud its copiers can be, Xerox meets European noise requirements—the world's most stringent.[27]

ISO 9000
A series of five standards for the processes an organization uses to ensure quality.

The importance of quality has led an increasing number of U.S. organizations to pursue a quality standard known as ISO 9000. **ISO 9000** is a series of five standards for the processes an organization uses to ensure quality. These standards, created by the International Organization for Standardization, cover such practices as how the organization designs, produces, and packages its products. ISO 9000 has been adopted as a quality standard by the European Community and has become a part of the requirements of some U.S. government agencies, including the Federal Aviation Administration, the Food and Drug Administration, and the Defense Department. Therefore, businesses selling in Europe or to the U.S. federal government are especially concerned about demonstrating that they can meet ISO 9000. They do this through a process called registration, which involves undergoing an extensive audit. Over two-thirds of companies fail the first such audit.[28]

U.S. companies have been slow to register under ISO 9000. In contrast to over 20,000 companies in EC countries, roughly 600 U.S. companies had registered by the end of 1992.[29] Some managers have not even heard of ISO 9000, and others have put off registering because it is expensive and time consuming. However, companies that have done so find it worth the effort. DuPont has registered over 100 facilities in Europe and several more in the United States. It credits this effort for such improvements as an increase in on-time delivery at one plant and the generation of more business from European customers.[30] Houston-based Precision Tube Technology also saw its sales increase after registering. Precision's quality-assurance manager explained, "This registration really set us apart because our competitors are not registered."[31]

FEATURES   Häagen-Dazs Triple Brownie Overload ice cream contains chocolate ice cream, pecans, fudge, and pieces of brownie. It also contains over 20 percent more calories than plain chocolate Häagen-Dazs ice cream.[32] These are examples of this product's features. A product **feature** is "a fact or technical specification about [the] product."[33]

feature
A fact or technical specification about a product.

In an organization with a marketing orientation, marketers select product features by determining what it is that customers want their products to offer. Thus, when developing a line of automobiles, they might ask consumers in the car's target market whether they are interested in such features as antilock brakes, a stereo with a cassette deck, and a rear-window defroster. Then they balance the answers with cost and pricing considerations. In the automobile example, if consumers say that all of these features are important but that they don't want to pay more than $20,000 for a new car, the marketer may have to make some trade-offs between features and price.

Organizations with a quality focus take this process a step further. They attempt not only to ask potential customers what they want, but to learn what these customers are likely to *need*. The marketer in such an organization may identify a need for features that target markets have not yet thought of and may not yet even understand. This has evidently worked in the toothbrush industry, where producers have added a variety of features, helping to stimulate a 30 percent increase in sales despite higher prices. For example, SmithKline Beecham's Flex toothbrush has a tiny spring in its handle to help prevent overly vigorous brushing from damaging gums. Gillette Company's Oral-B toothbrushes include a patch of blue bristles that gradually fade to white, indicating that it's time to replace the brush.[34]

According to Business Week . . . *"Design-driven products are transcending the traditional norms of market success." An example is My First Sony (pictured here), a traditional boom box redesigned with bright colors and rounded shapes that are appealing to and safe for young children. The design helped to create a whole new product category: tape players for preschoolers.*

DESIGN   A well-designed product is pleasing to look at and easy to use as intended. If a videocasette recorder is well designed, it should not only look good on the shelf, it should be easy to program. Designing products for both ease of use and aesthetic appeal can be difficult, but it can set products apart. A reporter found a recent version of Honda's CRX practical, "exquisite" in its engineering, and fun to drive with the top removed and packed away.[35] Likewise, the school products made by Creative Works are not only attractive but durable and safe. The compass, for example, has a patented point that does not easily penetrate skin.[36]

Given that the purpose of design is to make products a pleasure to use, good design is clearly a key part of the quality approach to marketing. Quality-driven design begins with learning who uses a product and what users' needs are. The Power Tool Division of Ingersoll-Rand Company sent a team to factories where its tools would be used. The company learned that half the people using wrenches on an auto assembly line were women, so it recognized a need for a tool that could be used by workers with a wide range of hand sizes. The result was a two-size, variable-grip wrench. Not only did the wrench meet the needs of workers on the assembly line studied, but it turned out to be popular in Japan, where hands tend to be smaller.[37] Note that design is most likely to have such an impact when designers have a say early on, as when they participate in cross-functional teams.

COST ISSUES   A well-designed product can please customers without necessarily costing more to make. This is especially true when the organization uses cross-functional teams to develop its products. If employees from engineering, marketing, and manufacturing work together on what the product will look like and how it will operate, they can create a design that is easy and economical to make as well as use.

That was the case at Westinghouse several years ago, when the company faced declining sales of a mature product, electrical panelboard and switchboard products sold to electrical contractors. The products also had become expensive to make because customers selected from over 2,400 possible components in many different configurations. To revamp the entire product line, Westinghouse set up a team of employees from its engineering, manufacturing, marketing, process planning, and information systems departments. The team redesigned the product, improving it by making the units smaller and using half the number of possible components. The team also researched customer needs and learned that just eight configurations would satisfy over 90 percent of the market's requirements. This knowledge helped the team improve the efficiency of purchasing, stocking parts, manufacturing, and processing orders.[38]

Color   Part of designing a product is deciding what color or colors it should be. A product's color can influence how people perceive it and, thus, whether they buy it. Igloo Products Corporation attributes an increase in sales of its cooler to adding new colors. Color consultant Patricia Verlodt told the company that its red and blue coolers were boring, and she suggested that the company add turquoise- and raspberry-colored products. After that change, sales rose 15 percent.[39]

When a hot-dog chain called Wienerschnitzel wanted to boost sales, color consultant Carlton Wagner recommended adding orange to the chain's magenta-and-red color scheme. Wagner believes that people associate orange with cheapness, so the change was intended to signal that the hot dogs are low priced. The company added orange to a prototype store's color scheme, and sales grew 7 percent.[40] Color consultants come up with such recommendations through such standard marketing research tools as observation, focus groups, and surveys.

PACKAGING

The packages in which goods are sold serve several purposes. First, packaging is functional. Many kinds of products, such as soup, laundry detergent, and lubricating oil, must be carried in some type of container. Furthermore, customers may expect the package to have some kind of seal or other device to show that it has not been tampered with. In many cases, resellers want products to have some sort of antitheft device as well (see "You Decide").

Packaging also can be used to promote the product. Colorful, attractive packaging helps a product stand out in the eyes of buyers, and it can include labels that provide information to help with purchase decisions and make the product's brand easy to identify. Coca-Cola has long identified its product by a curvy bottle that has been known as the "contour" bottle, the "hobble skirt" bottle, and the "Mae West" bottle. The company continued featuring this bottle in its advertising even after most consumers began buying soft drinks in cans or two-liter plastic bottles. Recent advances in plastics technology have allowed Coca-Cola to begin selling Coca-Cola Classic and Diet Coke in a 20-ounce plastic version of the contour bottle. Marketing research showed that older consumers associate the shape with quality, while young consumers see it as distinctively modern.[41]

Finally, distinctive packaging can be a product feature that sets the product apart from the competition. This is the case with fancy perfume bottles designed to reflect the image of a particular fragrance. And the Colgate-Palmolive Company recently replaced Colgate toothpaste's pump dispensers with a tube called the Stand-Up that rests on its cap. Colgate wants consumers to choose Stand-Up because it uses less packaging and costs less than pump dispensers and rival Crest's Neat Squeeze (but more than traditional toothpaste tubes).[42]

The use of packaging to distinguish a product may be an important part of the marketing mix for reaching certain target markets. For example, to target elderly consumers, the marketer will want packages that are easy to open. To target single people, the marketer might want to offer small or single-serving packages.

PACKAGING STRATEGIES   The way in which a package is designed depends on the marketer's goals. For the consumer products classified as convenience goods, packaging needs to be eye-catching or to look like the market leader (as in the case of store-brand shampoo in bottles that resemble those of a major brand). Consumers often

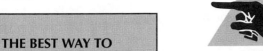

You Decide

WHAT'S THE BEST WAY TO CATCH A THIEF?

As conditions in the marketing environment change, existing products must be updated or changed to meet new demands. In the case of operating a store, one condition that has changed is that many of the goods sold have less packaging than before. As a result, attaching devices to the goods to deter shoplifters requires more ingenuity.

What's the best way to catch a thief nowadays? According to several electronics manufacturers, the answer is to place the antitheft device on the product itself, called "source embedding." Knogo Corporation is one of these companies. The firm makes a magnetic strip that can be embedded right in lipstick tubes, book covers, and the soles of shoes. Knogo's magnetic strips have caught on in Europe much more quickly than in the United States. The company regularly sells them to distributors and retailers in Scandinavia, the Netherlands, and France. In addition, Knogo is working with a compact disc manufacturer in Germany to figure out a way to embed its device in a CD.

Another firm, Sensormatic Electronics Corporation, places a plastic tag—called a chiclet—on the product. The chiclet is deactivated by a salesclerk at the point of purchase. Using radio frequencies, the magnetic material inside the tag vibrates, setting off an alarm if the product is removed from the store before deactivation.

If you were a manufacturer, what packaging strategies might you use to incorporate the need for antitheft devices? Do you think the placement of antitheft devices on the products themselves is practical? Why or why not?

Sources: Stephanie Strom, "Putting the Tag on Shoplifters," *The New York Times,* May 16, 1993, p. F11; "Strips: The Next Generation," *The New York Times,* May 16, 1993, p. F11.

---

select convenience goods while they are at the store, so the product needs to attract shoppers. If a product is fragile, the functional aspects of packaging are especially important to protect the product.

In selecting packaging, the marketer must consider the costs of the various alternatives. Making the packaging as attractive, protective, and convenient to use as possible would be very expensive. Therefore, marketers try to determine how much of these benefits are needed to satisfy their customers, then limit the packaging on that basis.

With noncost issues as well, marketers must respond to customer wants and needs. In the case of soft drinks, consumers in the United States have become unwilling to drag empty bottles back to the store where they bought the drinks. Thus, however environmentally desirable or attractively priced glass bottles may be, they are no longer feasible for soft drinks sold in the United States. In Egypt, however, 90 percent of Coke products are sold in refillable bottles, as are 99 percent in the Philippines.[43]

Figure 12.6 offers ten tips for developing effective packaging.

PACKAGING AND THE ENVIRONMENT   With all the talk about overflowing landfills, it seems clear that the design of packaging can have a major impact on the environment. Thus, a significant balancing act for marketers is that between using a lot of packaging to keep products safe and make them attractive and finding ways to keep packaging materials to a minimum. Marketers also have choices as to the materials used. For example, aseptic packaging, such as juice boxes, has been criticized because it is made of materials that are difficult to recycle.

As noted in Chapter 3, packaging decisions increasingly reflect concern about the impact on the environment. Because people in their roles as consumers and organizational buyers also tend to be concerned about environmental issues, marketers let them know about environmentally friendly packaging decisions. For example, packaging made of recycled paper is often branded with the arrows in a circle that symbolize recycled materials.

FIGURE 12.6

Ten Tips for Developing Effective Packaging

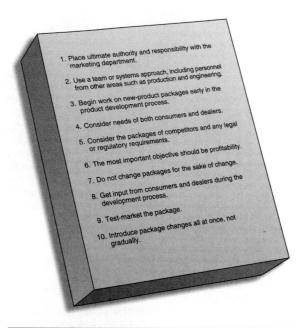

1. Place ultimate authority and responsibility with the marketing department.

2. Use a team or systems approach, including personnel from other areas such as production and engineering.

3. Begin work on new-product packages early in the product development process.

4. Consider needs of both consumers and dealers.

5. Consider the packages of competitors and any legal or regulatory requirements.

6. The most important objective should be profitability.

7. Do not change packages for the sake of change.

8. Get input from consumers and dealers during the development process.

9. Test-market the package.

10. Introduce package changes all at once, not gradually.

Source: Reprinted from *Business Horizons,* January–February. Copyright 1988 by the Foundation for the School of Business at Indiana University. Used with permission. Reported in Steven J. Skinner, *Marketing* (Boston: Houghton Mifflin Co., 1990), p. 262.

LABELING   An important part of most packages is some kind of labeling. A label can be as small and simple as a sticker on an apple identifying it as a Royal Gala apple from New Zealand. It can be as complex as the information taped to the window of new cars on a dealership lot.

Labels can work with packaging to support the organization's promotional effort. If promotion emphasizes certain product features or quality messages, these can be reinforced on the labels. The dust jackets or covers of trade books contain messages written to entice readers to buy the books.

Labels can provide information helpful to resellers and consumers. For example, resellers typically expect that labels will carry a universal product code (UPC), or bar code. The UPC identifies the product by inventory number and size or weight. Consumers, in turn, expect that the labels on products will help them make buying decisions by indicating the contents of the products. Labels may also contain instructions to help buyers use the product correctly, as in the case of washing instructions on clothes labels.

In some cases, the government requires that products bear labels containing certain information. Clothing labels must indicate fiber content, and the labels on prepared foods must list the ingredients in order of weight. Under the Nutrition Labeling and Education Act of 1990, the Food and Drug Administration (FDA) allows labels to make health claims only when they are scientifically valid. For example, a manufacturer of frozen entrees may not claim they prevent heart disease simply because they have less saturated fat than competing brands.

GLOBAL IMPLICATIONS   In developing packaging for international markets, marketers must consider a number of issues. One is that the package may have to be durable enough to withstand transportation over greater distances or via a less reliable

When Jerry "Guido" Smith developed BCD (biodegradable cleaner degreaser), which lacks synthetic dyes or fragrances and is pH-balanced, he needed a fitting package. Smith visited trade shows and supermarkets, judging packaging forms for usage and shelf appeal. The standup pouch, a concept used mostly in Europe and Japan, was the final choice. The pouch requires 70 percent less plastic than a bottle with the same volume. The flat pouch is also cheaper to ship and less bulky in landfills.

infrastructure than in the United States. Also, the marketer must take into account language differences. When several target markets speak different languages, it may be more efficient to use several languages on one package than to print several versions of the package. To sell its candy in Europe, M&M Mars prints as many different languages on each candy wrapper as will fit.[44] Freeman Cosmetic Corporation, based in Beverly Hills, California, has learned that Mexican consumers like products that look as though they are from the United States, so the company prints the front label in English and the back label in Spanish.[45]

Packaging should be consistent with local wants and needs. Phoenix-based Penn Racquet Sports had trouble selling its tennis balls in Japan until the company realized that customers didn't like buying three balls in a can, the standard packaging in the United States. The company did much better with a two-ball canister.[46] Most consumers in China find Procter & Gamble's shampoo a luxury, so the company has had success selling single-use pouches of shampoo for the equivalent of 14 cents apiece.[47]

Organizations marketing to the European Community should be familiar with the EC's regulations designed to encourage the use of environmentally friendly products and packaging.[48] Under the eco-label program, products deemed friendly to the environment qualify to bear a special label. (However, the criteria for products to receive the label have not yet been established.) Also, a proposed EC regulation seeks to protect the environment by, among other things, setting packaging requirements that will make the packaging materials easier to recycle. The environmental concern of many Europeans is mirrored by U.S. consumers, so many U.S. businesses already have experience in this area that can help them compete in Europe.

PRODUCT SAFETY

The safety of the organization's products is both an ethical and a practical issue for the marketer. From the standpoint of ethics, manufacturers and resellers must come to terms with the prevailing view that customers should not be harmed by using a product as intended. At least in some cases, people might argue that customers should not be harmed even when misusing a product—say, using a hair dryer in the bathtub.

The practical issue related to product safety is that when users get harmed by a product, they will avoid buying it in the future, tell family and friends to avoid the product, and perhaps sue the company that made or sold it. Lost sales and a damaged reputation are hard to reclaim. And it is tremendously expensive to defend and pay damages in a product liability lawsuit—that is, a case in which the user seeks compensation for injuries resulting from using the product.

Besides relating to the products themselves, safety issues extend to their packaging. For products that are risky to handle, safety requires that the packaging be reliable in protecting those who come into contact with the products. The packaging materials themselves also must be safe to use. During the 1980s, for example, concern arose that some packages of foods to be heated in a microwave oven contained materials that allowed possible carcinogens to seep into the food when heated.[49] The source of the problem was metal and plastic strips used to cause the food to brown. A number of manufacturers began looking for alternatives.

Another safety issue related to packaging is that consumers want to know whether products—especially food and drug items—have been tampered with. Marketers have responded with a variety of seals that customers must remove before using the product. While such devices make it easier to detect whether a product has been tampered with, consumers must remember that producers cannot make packaging that completely prevents tampering.

Branding

Often buyers don't just choose a type of product to buy, they choose a brand. They say, "I'd like to buy a Jaguar," or, "I have a craving for a Big Mac," or, "We could really improve our reports if we would do them on a Macintosh." In these examples, it is to the sellers' advantage that the potential customers are interested in a Jaguar, Big Mac, and Macintosh, rather than just an automobile, sandwich, and computer. Not only are the customers interested in the products, but they would probably pay more to satisfy their desires than they would to buy just any product in the three categories.

When marketers consider whether they can benefit from this phenomenon, they are considering branding. A **brand** is "a name, term, design, symbol, or any other feature that identifies one seller's good or service as distinct from those of other sellers."[50] Examples include the name Cirrus for that network of automated teller machines and the symbol of the peacock for NBC. Even the appearance of a pill (its shape and color) can be protected as part of the brand.[51]

A variety of terms describe the elements of a brand more precisely. A **brand name** is "that part of a brand which can be spoken."[52] Thus, it consists of letters, numbers, or words, such as Clinique, Tylenol, and 7-Up. A **brand mark** is the part of a brand that cannot be spoken. It generally consists of a symbol or graphic design such as the example shown in Figure 12.7. To obtain the legal right to use the brand exclusively, its owner must register it with the U.S. government. Then the brand becomes a **trademark** or, if it refers to a service, a **service mark**. (Don't confuse trademarks and brand names with trade names. A *trade name* is the legal name under which a company operates. Thus, Ralston Purina Company is the trade name of a company that owns many brand names, including Corn Chex.)

brand
The name, term, or symbol that identifies a good or service as distinct from all others.

brand name
The part of a brand that can be spoken.

brand mark
The part of a brand that cannot be spoken.

trademark
The legal right to use a product brand exclusively.

service mark
The legal right to use a service brand exclusively.

BENEFITS OF BRANDING

As indicated earlier, using a brand is a way to distinguish products in the minds of potential buyers. They may put forth extra effort and spend additional money to buy a particular brand. Commitment to buy a particular brand is called *brand loyalty*. The majority of consumers are loyal to one brand when they purchase certain products, including cigarettes (such as Marlboro), mayonnaise (Hellman's), and toothpaste (Crest). For other products, such as garbage bags and canned vegetables, only about

In this
directe
Gener
benefi
manuf

FIGURE 12.7

Example of a Brand Mark: The Starkist Tuna

one-quarter of consumers are brand loyal.[53] By protecting its brand with trademark or service mark status, the organization also creates an element of the product that competitors may not copy.

When an organization assigns a brand to a product, it seeks to create associations between the brand and a particular image and collection of benefits. Pepsi's "Be young, have fun, drink Pepsi" message seeks to link the soft drink with the pleasures of youth.[54] The ad in Figure 12.8 builds on the bulldog symbol for Mack trucks and the strength and tenacity that animal evokes. When such an effort succeeds, customers' perceptions about the brand make it a powerful marketing tool. AT&T's Alan Schultheis credits AT&T's reputation as innovative and service oriented for the success of the company's Universal Card.[55]

privat
A bra
the re:

FIGURE 12.8

Advertising Message That Builds on a Brand's Image

gener
Produ
only b

FIC

Ty

brand
Using
name

family
Brand
produ

manu
A bra
the pi

STRATEGIES FOR BRAND TYPES   Retailers enjoy several benefits from offering private and generic brands. Perhaps most important, these products can be more profitable than manufacturer's brands because the store spends less to promote them. Also, the retailer enjoys great control over the marketing mix, including product quality, promotion, and pricing. Finally, brand loyalty to a private brand benefits the retailer directly because customers must buy from the store in order to get the brand.

To counter the popularity of private brands, manufacturers have to continually innovate and show how their products offer extra value. Procter & Gamble introduced Charmin Spacemaker and White Cloud Spacemaker toilet tissue, which offer the same amount of product as do competitors but in compressed packaging.[64] Toy makers are typically able to convince children to ask for their products by brand, so Toys "R" Us stocks only brand-name toys.[65]

Also, as will be discussed in Chapter 14, manufacturers can compete with private and generic products by cutting the price of their brand-name goods. Procter & Gamble responded to the popularity of private-brand and generic alternatives by lowering the price of its Tide laundry detergent. For similar reasons, Philip Morris cut the price of Marlboro cigarettes. In summary, manufacturer's brands are most likely to do well relative to private brands when they are priced low, when buyers don't want to risk quality (as in the case of baby food), and when the products are innovative.[66]

Often the makers of generic and private-label products are the same ones who produce the familiar manufacturer's brands. Why would they make generic and private brands to compete with their own brands? There are several explanations:

- A manufacturer may have excess production capacity, making it more economical to produce these goods. Merck decided to enter the market for generic drugs for that reason. At its plant in West Point, Pennsylvania, Merck makes the Dolobid brand of arthritis drug and its generic equivalent, diflunisal, thereby keeping product volume high and unit costs low.[67]
- Resellers of private and generic brands tend to place large and predictable orders. Therefore, they may be an important source of business.
- Choosing not to produce these products does not necessarily eliminate the competition they present. Presumably, the resellers that want private brands or generic goods will simply order them from someone else. When a brand-name company declined to make baby bottles for Toys "R" Us, Gloucester, Massachusetts–based NutraMax got the contract.[68]

SELECTING A BRAND

Decisions related to branding are critical to the success of the marketing effort. A good brand name can set the product apart from the competition and give rise to such positive feelings as trust, confidence, security, and strength.[69]

SELECTION CRITERIA   To select a brand name, the marketer can consider a variety of criteria. These should reflect the following four concerns:[70]

1.   The brand name should imply the benefits delivered by the product. For example, Easy Off oven cleaner implies that the product will simplify this nasty chore; Sure deodorant sounds as though it delivers reliable protection.

2.   The brand name should be positive, distinctive, and easy to remember. Examples include U-Haul truck rental and Air Jordan athletic shoes. While it is helpful for the name to generate positive associations and feelings, it can be difficult to find a term that can do this internationally without having negative connotations in some languages or cultures. By avoiding controversy, an easy-to-pronounce name with little or

A bright yellow cake named "Cuscuz" is a traditional breakfast food in Northeast Brazil. Vitamilho was the brand name chosen for the corn meal used to make this food. In Brazil, vita *means "life" and* milho *is a Portuguese word for corn.*

no meaning—for example, Exxon—may be more beneficial to an international company than a name with more meaning.

3.   The name should be consistent with the image of the product or organization. Thus, to promote the image of healthfulness, makers of breakfast cereal are giving their products names that avoid any mention of sugar but imply sweetness in other ways. Thus, heavily sweetened cereals bear such names as Wheaties Honey Gold, Frosted Flakes, and Honey Bunches of Oats.[71]

4.   The name should be legally permissible. Most importantly, this means that the name should not violate the trademark status of another organization's brand.

These four criteria for choosing a brand imply that marketers need to be as familiar with the marketing environment when devising a brand name as when designing a product. Thus, a crackdown by the Food and Drug Administration on foods making health claims has led to fewer applications for trademark status for names containing the words *heart, pure,* and *fresh.* But continuing consumer interest in healthful products is behind a surge in trademark applications for foods containing the words *light* or *lite* and *nature* or *natural.* Also, in the apparent belief that U.S. consumers want to "buy American," companies requested trademarks for over 1,200 brand names containing the words *America* or *American* in the first two years of this decade.[72]

SELECTION PROCESS   A typical approach to selecting a brand name begins when members of the organization contribute ideas. The organization may also get suggestions from outside sources such as its advertising agency. Then the list is pared down. In the auto industry, the group that does this typically includes executives, ad agency representatives, and others. When only a few ideas remain, the organization conducts marketing research to test how the name is perceived. When Mercury wanted to name a minivan, it was considering the name Columbia, hoping consumers would appreciate the connection to the space shuttle. But research showed that consumers linked the name to Colombia and that country's drug trade. So Mercury called its minivan the Villager instead.[73] As in this example, the organization uses research to further pare its list. It conducts legal research on the remaining ideas, weeding out any names likely to fail a legal challenge. If more than one name survives, the final choice is apt to be an intuitive one.

Sometimes an organization seeks help in naming its brands from a brand-naming service such as Name Lab or Interbrand Group. For example, Nigerian Breweries (NB) asked Interbrand to come up with a name for a new beer, a stout that was to compete with Guinness in Nigeria. Through discussions and brainstorming, Interbrand came up with a number of possible names. The firm checked to make sure that none of them had a negative meaning in Swahili. Of the possibilities Interbrand suggested, NB approved ten. Interbrand checked the trademark status of these and conducted marketing research to see how consumers reacted to the names compared to Guinness. Finally, Interbrand recommended the name *Legend* because "it had global credibility."[74]

PROTECTING TRADEMARK RIGHTS

As mentioned earlier, organizations may obtain legal protection for their brands by registering them with the U.S. government. Registering the brand—making it a trademark or service mark—gives the owner the exclusive right to use it.

To further protect the trademark or service mark status of a brand, the organization should use it and identify it as a brand. The basic way to do this is to use the symbol ® following a trademark or service mark. When a brand is still being registered, the organization can use the ™ symbol to show that the brand is the organization's exclusive property. The brand name should always be capitalized, and the organization should never change its spelling.

In spite of these efforts, people may intentionally or unintentionally misuse the trademark. This is a particular problem in international trade, where 5 percent of all goods are counterfeit.[75] When misuse occurs, it is up to the owner to take legal action to protect its rights. General Mills had its lawyer write to Gag Foods Company when that business began marketing Roadkill Helper in boxes that resemble those of General Mills's Hamburger Helper mixes. The company's owner agreed to stop making the product after its current inventory ran out.[76]

Organizations that fail to take such measures risk having the brand lose its protection as a trademark or service mark. Some former brand names that have become generic are *aspirin, escalator,* and *thermos.* Sometimes the public uses a brand name as if it were generic, and the owner has to work hard to protect its rights to the trademark. Two such terms are Xerox and Realtor. The owners of these terms place advertisements reminding people to use the terms properly.

Managing the Product Mix

Marketers have to make decisions not only about the organization's individual products, but also about its products as a group. Marketers evaluate the organization's product mix by considering its width, depth, and consistency. Width of the product mix refers to the number of product lines handled by the organization. Depth refers to the average number of products in each product line. Consistency refers to the similarity of the product lines. For example, IBM PC Company has three basic product lines: entry-level computers (brand name PS/1), high-end personal computers (the PS/2), and the aggressively priced ValuePoint line, positioned between PS/1 and PS/2.[77] These product lines are consistent (all personal computers), and each contains a variety of products, including processing units, keyboards, and monitors for the various computers.

A narrow and consistent product mix lets the organization specialize in some types of products. Such an organization can build a reputation as an expert in a particular area. Thus, IBM is known as a computer expert, and people go to concerts by the Kronos Quartet when they want to hear chamber music by twentieth-century composers.

However, a wider product line can be useful when an organization wants to increase sales by serving more customers. Carlson Companies enjoys this benefit. The Carlson Travel Group, which includes a large network of travel agents, encourages clients to stay at the hotels and resorts that are part of the Carlson Hospitality Group (including Radisson Hotels and Colony Hotels & Resorts). And the clients for the varied marketing services of Carlson Marketing Group include the travel agents and hotels in the other two groups, helping the Carlson marketing Group develop a reputation for expertise in serving the hospitality industry.[78]

Offering many kinds of products also can protect the organization from a big drop in sales if customers lose interest in one product. Japan's Itochu Corporation enjoys this type of diversification. Its operations extend to numerous industries, including textiles, steel, food products, real estate, and entertainment.

cannibalization
One product taking sales away from another in the product mix.

Similarly, deep product lines allow the organization to appeal to more customers. However, when there are many choices within a single product line, the organization runs a greater risk of **cannibalization**. This refers to one product taking sales away from another in the product mix. Thus, when Campbell Soup Company introduced its Healthy Request line of soup, it risked having people switch from its basic Campbell's soup line (perhaps motivated in part by doubts as to whether those red-and-white cans were somehow an "unhealthy" item to request).

PRODUCT LINES

As described in Chapter 11, a product line is a group of products related in some way. Marketers evaluate and forecast the performance of entire product lines as well as individual products. This information may lead the marketer to add or delete an entire product line or to vary the offerings within that product line. Pepsi-Cola North America's goal to become a "total beverage company" has led that company to add product lines, including Lipton iced tea, All Sport sports drink, and bottled water distributed under the Avalon and H2Oh! brands.[79]

line extension
Adding new products to an existing product line.

One way to vary the offerings within a product line is to make it deeper, also called "stretching" the product line. To stretch a product line, marketers use a strategy called **line extension**. This strategy involves adding new products to an existing product line. Bayer has responded to weakness in sales of its aspirin by stretching its product line to include nonaspirin pain relievers under the brand Bayer Select.[80]

The criteria for adding, deleting, or changing product lines are basically the same as those for altering the number and types of individual products within the marketing mix. These criteria are introduced in the next section. In applying them to the product line, the marketer considers whether the product line as a whole meets the criteria.

THE PRODUCT MIX

Marketers must consider the relationships of all the products sold by the organization. The total collection of products sold by an organization is known as its product mix or product assortment. When marketers think about whether the marketing mix is enabling the organization to achieve its objectives, they may refer to the product mix as a "product portfolio." As described in Chapter 5, when marketers think of their products in terms of a portfolio, they think of ways to balance the risks and returns of various products to improve the organization's performance.

Sales at the Hills Pet Nutrition division of Colgate recently increased by 11 percent to almost $800 million. One of the reasons for the profitable growth was the introduction of three new product lines including a line of nutritionally balanced snacks for dogs.

To manage the product mix, marketers may modify, discontinue, or add products and product lines. Marketers should choose these options when they help to meet the objectives of the product team, marketing department, or organization as a whole.

Of course, it's important to remember that there are times when the best strategy is to make no changes in the product mix. This is true for marketers who are happy with niche marketing of a high-quality product that its customers are pleased with. The owners of Kelchner's Horseradish in Dublin, Pennsylvania, are proud that the horseradish is still trimmed and scraped by hand, not using chemicals. And Mike Dieter, general manager of the New Braunfels Smokehouse, located in the Texas town of New Braunfels, declines to expand his distribution channels. Says Dieter, "We don't want to be Mr. Smoked Meat of the world."[81] Such companies keep their customers happy with high quality and keep the profits coming through conservative spending.

MODIFYING PRODUCTS   Marketers may modify any aspect of a product, including features of the product itself, the packaging, or services provided to customers. To build market share for Hawaiian Punch, Procter & Gamble introduced new flavors of the drink, based on its successful Fruit Juicy Red. The new flavors, clearly designed to appeal to kids, are Fruit Juicy Blue, Fruit Juicy Yellow, Fruit Juicy Orange, and Fruit Juicy Green.[82] (To learn about a restaurateur who has continually made changes to maintain customer loyalty, see "Marketing Movers & Shakers.")

Modifications are important when a product is still profitable but some change in the environment makes the current form of the product less than optimal. For example, the government may set new safety or environmental standards, or a competitor may introduce a product that is similar but easier to use. In the shopping center industry, overbuilding has led to a decline in construction. Therefore, developers are rehabilitating existing shopping centers, focusing on the kinds of stores in which consumers are demonstrating an interest (such as discount stores).[83]

Internal changes also may lead the organization to modify its products. An example is when a manufacturing employee on a product team notes that some changes to the product will reduce the cost to produce it without sacrificing quality.

DISCONTINUING PRODUCTS   Before removing a product or product line from the organization's offerings, the marketer should consider whether doing so will be more

Marketing Movers & Shakers

SARI ABUL-JUBEIN OF CASABLANCA RESTAURANT

In Casablanca, patrons relax in cool wicker chairs, dining beneath the gentle breeze of ceiling fans. Or they lean against the brass-railed mahogany bar modeled after Rick's Café Americain in the classic movie *Casablanca*. Murals depicting scenes from the film sweep across the walls. But this Casablanca isn't in Morocco. It happens to be a landmark restaurant in Cambridge, Massachusetts, where professors, students, artists, politicians, and businesspeople have enjoyed good food and conversation since 1955.

"I'm here [at the restaurant] a lot because I like being here, acting as host, maître d', joking with people,

picking on people," says owner Sari Abul-Jubein. Together, Casablanca and Abul-Jubein have created a history—and nearly cult status in Cambridge. Abul-Jubein, born in Palestine, raised in Syria, and later educated in New England, started at the restaurant fresh out of college in 1971. As a waiter, he enthusiastically worked "day and night." When the manager died in 1972, Abul-Jubein took over. And when the original owner decided to sell the restaurant in 1976, Abul-Jubein found a way to buy it. Immediately, he made changes based on good marketing instincts that were designed to please customers and to allow for growth.

He enlarged the restaurant, shifting the emphasis from a bar atmosphere to good food. "I've had a knack for food ever since I was a kid," he explains. "I knew when I bought [the restaurant] that the only way to grow was through food, not liquor." More than 15 years later, 60 percent of Casablanca's sales are in food rather than alcohol. Mindful of the restaurant's link to the film whose name it bears, Abul-Jubein carefully weaves appropriate ethnic foods into the menu, creating a sense of romance and mystery not only with atmosphere but also with flavors.

Specialties include Abul-Jubein's favorite foods from his childhood in Syria—hummus, tabbouleh, feta cheese, olives, and Syrian bread, as well as Moroccan seasoned skirt steak. Abul-Jubein also added northern Italian dishes and—of course—Casablanca Burgers.

In 1990, the restaurant closed for renovation, and with tight financing as well as delays, Abul-Jubein grew nervous. Not the least of his problems was how to move—and preserve—the spectacular David Omar White murals of *Casablanca* from the old space to the new. If Abul-Jubein is the heart of Casablanca, White's murals are its soul, and the restaurateur found a way to save them: "We cut entire walls, studs and all. How they didn't break is beyond me." Once the murals were installed in the renovated restaurant, the artist retouched them where necessary and then expanded on them.

When the restaurant reopened in 1991, it was to rave reviews and the support of loyal customers. Sari Abul-Jubein had proved that by continually modifying an existing high-quality product—his restaurant—the Casablanca in Cambridge could have just as long a run as its classic namesake.

Source: Leanne Star, "From Colby to Casablanca," *Colby,* March 1993, pp.16–23.

beneficial than some other strategy. The marketer should have a set of criteria for making such decisions. As a start, the marketer can consider whether sales and profits are likely to improve and where the product is in its life cycle. Table 12.2 provides some specific questions to answer. For example, if new technology has made a product obsolete and higher costs have all but eliminated profits, the product is probably not worth keeping.

Deciding to discontinue a product is difficult because such a decision has a potentially great impact. Customers will be disappointed that the organization has stopped offering a product that they presumably have grown to need or at least like. When Volkswagen dropped its popular Bug in 1975, its sales went on a decline that the company is now trying to reverse by introducing a new version of that car.[84] Discontinuing a product may also mean laying off the employees who produced and sold it. Furthermore, discontinuing a product does not necessarily free a company from all expenses related to that product. For example, the organization may still

TABLE 12.2	AREA OF CONCERN	QUESTIONS
Deciding Whether to Discontinue a Product: Some Questions to Answer	Sales trends	How have sales moved over time? What has happened to market share? Why have sales declined? What changes in sales have occurred in competitive products both in our line and in those of other manufacturers?
	Profit contribution	What has been the profit contribution of this product to the company? If profits have declined, how are these tied to price? Have selling, promotion, and distribution costs risen out of proportion to sales? Does the product require excessive management time and effort?
	Product life cycle	Has the product reached a level of maturity and saturation in the market? Has new technology been developed that poses a threat to the product? Are there more effective substitutes on the market? Has the product outgrown its usefulness? Can the resources used on this product be put to better use?

Source: J. Paul Peter and James H. Donnelly, Jr., *A Preface to Marketing Management,* 6th ed. (Burr Ridge, Ill.: Irwin, 1994), pp. 117–118.

need to offer customer service to owners of the product, and it may need to provide a supply of replacement parts.

Nevertheless, discontinuing a product at the end of its life cycle may be the least costly alternative and allows the organization to devote more of its resources to more profitable products. When the organization is no longer spending as much money to support a poor performer, its overall profitability may improve. This is the aim of Procter & Gamble in reducing the variety of products it offers. Through such changes as eliminating the White Cloud brand of toilet tissue in favor of Charmin Ultra and Puritan oil in favor of Crisco, P&G hopes to reduce production and marketing costs.[85]

ADDING PRODUCTS   An important source of sales growth is adding new products to the product mix. The organization may do this by developing products or by acquiring the rights to market products developed elsewhere. In some cases, the organization adds products because customers ask for them. Consulting firm Step Associates, based in Laramie, Wyoming, conducts surveys of clients who attend its seminars. Clients at seminars on facilities management asked for training in management skills, so Step added those services. Then participants in the training seminars started asking for consulting services, and Step again responded by broadening its product mix.[86] Assuming the organization can maintain high quality and acceptable profits, adding goods and services customers ask for makes good marketing sense.

The new products may be line extensions or they may be a whole new product line. When an organization sees a need for a particular product that serves an existing target market or is related to an existing product, a line extension is probably most appropriate. When the organization needs more diverse offerings, it focuses on adding new product lines. Mr. Coffee has been focusing on new-product development to allow the company to diversify beyond coffee makers. Heavy competition for coffee makers has made that market less attractive, so the company is considering adding such products as Potato Perfect, described earlier in the chapter, and a water-filter pitcher that filters two quarts of tap water in up to one minute.[87]

Adding new products to develop the best strategic mix has allowed Airbus Industrie to achieve a 30% share of the international civil aviation market. There are seven members of the "Airbus family—including the world's largest twin-aisle twin and the longest range jetliner in aviation history."

In determining whether and how to add products to the product mix, the marketer should consider using brand extension, described earlier in this chapter. General Mills has done this by sweetening and flavoring Cheerios in various ways, creating Honey Nut Cheerios and Apple Cinnamon Cheerios.[88] Similarly, Kellogg Company has modified Rice Krispies to create Cocoa Krispies, Fruity Marshmallow Krispies, Frosty Marshmallow Krispies, and Rice Krispies Treats cereal.[89] Brand extension provides the benefit of using customers' good associations with the existing brand to interest them in trying the new product.

Brand extension has some disadvantages, however. If the new product does not serve the same target market or carry the same image, the brand's image may become weak or confusing. This is the risk that Aston Martin faces in introducing a less expensive, more routinely manufactured automobile than its existing top-of-the-line models. While $110,000 for the new car may not seem cheap to most car buyers, it is only about half what the company charges for its more expensive models.[90] Another potential drawback of brand extension is that if customers have a bad experience with one product carrying the brand, the negative feelings will carry over to the other products as well.

Summary

Marketing strategies differ among the wide variety of goods and services offered. One explanation is that products pass through stages of a product life cycle at different rates and times. During the introduction stage, a new product enters the marketplace with little or no competition, and marketers must convince the target market that it can meet their needs. During the growth stage, sales climb rapidly as more buyers try the product, and the growth attracts competition. When a product reaches maturity, it is familiar to its widest group of buyers and has attracted many competitors. When sales begin to fall, the product enters decline. Marketers can discontinue the product or attempt renewed expansion. This model has limitations—most notably that it has no predictive powers—but it is useful as a framework for selecting a marketing strategy. Some products follow fashion or fad cycles rather than full product life cycles. A fashion is an accepted and popular style; a fad is a product that experiences intense and brief popularity.

Buyers who make purchases at different stages of a product's life cycle tend to have varying characteristics. Early buyers influence later buyers; the model that describes this phenomenon is called product diffusion. Innovators are the first to try a new product. Early adopters follow innovators. Most buyers are either the early majority (who avoid risk and make their purchases carefully) or the late majority (who are more cautious and skeptical). Laggards resist making changes; they are more comfortable with tradition.

In devising a product strategy, the marketer considers the product itself, as well as other dimensions of the product mix. With regard to the product itself, three important characteristics are quality, features, and design. Buyers have expectations for the quality of the product itself and for the service that accompanies it. Features are the technical specifications of a product. These should meet actual wants and needs of the buyer. Good design gives products a pleasing appearance and makes them easy to use. Another element of the product mix is packaging, which meets functional needs and also can be used to promote the product. Out of a commitment to social responsibility or to meet increasingly stringent laws worldwide, marketers today look for ways to keep packaging materials to a minimum and, if at all possible, recyclable, reusable, or biodegradable. Product safety is another element of the product mix that has ethical as well as practical implications.

A brand is a word, design, symbol, or other feature that distinguishes a seller's product from its competitors'. By developing positive associations with their brands, marketers seek to make members of their target markets loyal to their brands. Types of brands are manufacturer's brands (owned and used by the producer of a product), private brands (owned and used by the reseller), and generic products (goods or services named only by generic class, without a brand name or brand mark). In choosing a brand, marketers consider several criteria: (1) it should imply the benefits delivered by the product; (2) it should be positive and distinctive; (3) it should be consistent with the product and company image; and (4) it must be legally permissible.

Marketers describe an organization's product mix in terms of its width, depth, and consistency. When considering whether to modify, discontinue, or add products, they must keep in mind the relationships among products in the organization's product mix. Modifying a product because of a change in the environment may help renew sales. Discontinuing a product may allow an organization to devote more resources to more profitable products. But discontinuation may disappoint some loyal customers, require employee layoffs, and force the company to continue to provide service to customers who already own the product. Adding products is an important source of growth, if doing so does not weaken the brand's or organization's image or ability to maintain high quality.

KEY TERMS AND CONCEPTS

product life cycle (p. 351)

fashions (p. 355)

fads (p. 355)

product diffusion (p. 356)

innovators (p. 356)

early adopters (p. 356)

early majority (p. 357)

late majority (p. 357)

laggards (p. 357)

warranty (p. 359)

guarantee (p. 359)

ISO 9000 (p. 360)

feature (p. 360)

brand (p. 366)

brand name (p. 366)

brand mark (p. 366)

trademark (p. 366)

service mark (p. 366)

brand extension (p. 368)

family brand (p. 368)

manufacturer's brand (p. 368)

private brand (p. 369)

generic products (p. 369)

cannibalization (p. 373)

line extension (p. 373)

REVIEW AND DISCUSSION QUESTIONS

1. Name and describe briefly the four stages of the product life cycle, as well as marketing objectives for each.

2. Suppose you are a marketer for a manufacturer that produced manual lawnmowers (not powered by gas or electricity). You have decided there might be renewed interest for the product because it does not burn fuel or use electric power and has minimum impact on the environment.
   a. What steps might you take to bring about renewed expansion for the mower?
   b. In what countries do you think your product strategy might be effective?

3. Think of a fad you have observed or experienced in your lifetime. Describe briefly the product, what it was used for, approximately how long its popularity lasted, and why you think it was popular.

4. According to the model of product diffusion, what are the characteristics of the five different types of buyers?

5. Find two advertisements for similar products (such as two checking accounts, two types of soap, two automobiles). Compare them to determine differences in quality, features, and design for each product. Which product would you buy, and why?

6. Compare the brand names of the two products you evaluated in question 5. How effective are they? Do they imply benefits delivered by the product? Are they positive and distinctive? Are they consistent with the image of the product or company?

7. How can packaging help or harm the sales of a product?

8. What are the difficulties involved in discontinuing a product?

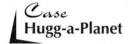
Creating a Product Brand

Branding is one of the key decisions involved in marketing a product. Marketers hope to achieve brand loyalty for their products.

Choose a product from the list of ideas below, use your product idea from the Chapter 11 project, or come up with one of your own. Create a brand for your product, including a brand name and brand mark. If your product is an entire line, give the line a family brand. To select and evaluate your brand, use the four main criteria discussed in the text.

Write a description of your decision process. Present your brand—as well as your rationale for choosing it—to the class.

Note: You can expand on this project by designing a package for your product, incorporating your brand name and brand mark.

Product ideas:
- Healthful desserts
- Furniture designed to fit dorm rooms or small apartments
- An outdoor game designed for the beach
- Tools for left-handers
- A chain of health clinics located in large office buildings and industrial parks

Case
Hugg-a-Planet

Globes have been around ever since the Western world discovered that the earth wasn't flat. But Angela Forenza, along with her son Robert and her daughter Patricia, have put a new spin on the product. One day, Angela got the idea that it might be nice if someone manufactured a "user friendly" globe. Traditionally, globes have been made of wood, metal, or plastic—materials that are hard to the touch. Most are set on stands, which remove them somewhat from their owners. And they signify history or geography class to many former students who were forced to memorize names of rivers and capitals of countries.

Robert Forenza agreed with his mother: why not make a globe that's soft and cuddly, like a spherical pillow? He arranged to have a prototype made. He hired a Korean factory to manufacture the covers and found someone in New York to stuff them.

Hugg-a-Planet (the brand name for the Forenzas' globe) was a tough sell at first. Robert explains, "When I described Hugg-a-Planet over the phone, it was tough for prospects to envision. After a while, I figured out that all I had to do was send them a sample. They'd keep it around their office, play with it while they were on the phone, roll it across their desk, and eventually fall in love with it." He was right. Only a few years after its inception, the company's total revenues hovered around $1 million.

The Forenzas have since expanded their product line to fifteen items including a 6-inch-diameter Baby Hugg-a-Planet, a Hugg-a-Star, and a 2-foot-diameter Super Hugg-a-Planet. The product mix has expanded as well to include a quilt and tote bag. All the products have a global, environmental motif.

Time will tell whether Hugg-a-Planet products are mere fads. Certainly the sudden intensity of their popularity reflects a faddish craze. But with the tremendous growth of the environmental movement into mainstream awareness, Hugg-a-Planet, which is perceived as an environmentally friendly product, is likely to hang in there.

This fact has not been lost on the Forenzas. "The environmental cause is certainly something we've embraced and tried to get the most out of, but we've also tried to be true to it," notes Patricia. "Over the years, we've been involved with most of the major groups: Audubon, Sierra Club, Greenpeace, to name a few." Hugg-a-Planet products are packaged in cardboard boxes, and the globes themselves are stuffed with garment industry scraps, both acceptable to environmental groups.

The Forenzas plan on slow, methodical growth for their company. They don't view their enterprise as faddish at all. They plan on being in business for a long time. Perhaps they take their cue from the real prototype for their product: the earth.

QUESTIONS

1. Do you think Hugg-a-Planet products will prove to be a fad? Why or why not?
2. Do you think that "Hugg-a-Planet" is an effective brand name? Why or why not?
3. What new product *lines* could you see coexisting successfully in the Forenzas' company with the Hugg-a-Planet products?

Source: "The Forenzas: Global Marketing Goes Soft," *Sales & Marketing Management,* September 1991, pp. 30-31.

CHAPTER 13   *Services*

LEARNING OBJECTIVES

After completing this chapter, you should be able to:

1. Discuss the importance of marketing in the service economy.

2. Identify characteristics of services.

3. Describe ways marketers classify services.

4. Describe the process for making decisions about purchasing services.

5. Discuss issues that arise in devising a marketing mix for services.

6. Discuss issues that arise in various types of nonbusiness marketing.

Creating Customer Value
AT&T

After the federal government chopped the giant AT&T monopoly into Ma Bell and seven Baby Bells in 1984, the company initially shed more than a hundred thousand jobs and lost billions of dollars. With long-distance phone service a maturing product and phone equipment an unreliable source of profits, AT&T's future was uncertain. But now AT&T's top executives—and many of its customers—believe that divestiture was the best thing ever to happen to the company. AT&T has turned around thanks to clear vision, customer focus, employee empowerment, teamwork, and the leadership of Robert Allen, CEO since 1988.

Allen is a hands-off manager who believes that the employees who are closest to customers can make the best judgments about how to meet their needs with the highest-quality services. He also believes that teams can most effectively carry out the company's main goals: "to bring people together and give them easy access to each other and to the information they want and need—anytime, anywhere." Under Allen, AT&T established teams throughout the company, even at the highest level.

Instead of designating a president or chief operating officer, Allen created a team comprising the heads of AT&T's four major business groups—the telephone network, network equipment, end-user products, and NCR (the computer maker it acquired in the biggest takeover in that industry's history)—plus the chief financial officer. The chairmanship of that top-level team, called the Operations Committee, rotates yearly. The Operations Committee meets several days a month to oversee the company's day-to-day operations. A New York consultant who helped Allen design the team calls it "a team that's unique at this level in corporate America."

The members of the Operations Committee take their roles seriously and depend on each other's expertise in making decisions that affect AT&T as a whole. Their bonuses are tied to the performance of their group. "Our committee is the point at which the aspiration of the corporation meets the practicality of the business unit," notes Robert Kavner, committee member for end-user products.

Allen and the Operations Committee have set up other teams as well, such as those that are now exploring and developing six specific areas of potential growth for the company: video, wireless, data transmission, voice recognition and processing, messaging, and scalable computing (large and small computers built around the same microprocessors). Like the Operations Committee, each of these exploratory teams has members from the four major business groups. Each team has a connection to the Operations Committee, to make sure that communication is open and everyone is talking.

Of the team strategy, AT&T executive Richard Bodman says, "Organizations that develop an army, an air force, a navy, and marines can face the threats of the world more securely than those that only have one. The trick is to get all those folks to hit the beach at the same time."

When it comes to relationships with customers, one executive notes, "It takes teamwork to offer the breadth of our products to customers who come in through the conduit of the long-distance business." But none of these teams means a thing if AT&T's services are of less than the highest quality. Its customers must receive good value for their money.

Allen says that his customers are all the people who work for him. In this spirit, AT&T reinforces teamwork by empowering employees to evaluate their boss's performance. Since the early 1990s, more than 800 company executives have had the opportunity to deliver such "upward feedback." This approach, which effectively turns the organizational chart upside down, supports both managers and employees.

AT&T runs a complicated business of providing both goods and services to its customers (such as the "*i* plan" and "Picasso," a telephone capable of transmitting full-color, high-quality images during a conversation). Sometimes this puts the company in the difficult position of selling hardware to companies that compete with AT&T's services. But Allen believes that operating in both domains is an advantage. "We can show customers what's possible on the telecommunications network as well as with our terminal devices, like phones and computers. By running the network we also get a better understanding of technical engineering requirements—the way things work together."

As you read this chapter, you'll see how many companies face the challenges of marketing services, or some combination of goods and services. The next time you pick up the phone, think about one large company that not only offers communications services to businesses and individuals throughout the world, but continues to innovate—developing new services and the equipment to support them. Ma Bell refuses to hang up.

Sources: David Kirkpatrick, "Could AT&T Rule the World?" *Fortune,* May 17, 1993, pp. 55–66; Josh Hyatt, "800 Calls Without AT&T," *The Boston Globe,* April 28, 1993, pp. 31, 37; "New AT&T Phone Carries Still Video Images, Sound," *The Wall Street Journal,* May 12, 1993, p. B6; and Bart Ziegler, "AT&T's Bold Bet," *Business Week,* August 30, 1993, pp. 26–30.

Chapter Overview

services
Products that are purely or mostly intangible.

In the opening story about AT&T, teamwork helped employees deliver high-quality communications services. According to the American Marketing Association, **services** are "products, such as a bank loan or home security, that are intangible, or at least substantially so."[1]

This chapter introduces the marketing of services. The chapter describes the role of services in the U.S. economy and the nature of marketing services as opposed to tangible goods. Then the chapter describes special considerations in developing a marketing mix for services. Finally, the chapter examines characteristics of nonbusiness marketing, which typically involves providing some type of services. This discussion covers marketing by nonprofit organizations, public service marketing, and marketing for political uses.

Our Service Economy

In recent decades, the U.S. economy has been referred to as a "service economy." That is because the production and marketing of services has taken on an increasingly larger role relative to that of tangible goods. Figure 13.1 illustrates the growing role of the service sector in the U.S. economy. By the most recent Census Bureau estimates, the service sector accounted for 54 percent of the U.S. gross national product (value of goods and services produced) and 77 percent of U.S. nonfarm employment.[2] In other words, over half of the nation's products are services, and three out of four employees work in the service sector.

CAUSES OF GROWTH

The growth of the service sector has several causes. One is that people are most apt to buy services when they can afford more than such basic needs as food, clothing, and

FIGURE 13.1

The Growing Proportion of the Gross Domestic Product Attributed to Services

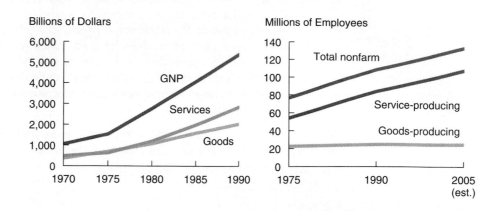

Source: U.S. Bureau of Economic Analysis, *National Income and Product Accounts of the United States:* Volume 2, 1959–1988, and *Survey of Current Business,* March 1993.

shelter. Thus, as national economies develop, services tend to play a larger role. In the United States, baby boomers are in their peak earning years, so a large segment of society is able to pay for vacations, financial advice, and entertainment. They also buy more goods such as appliances and VCRs, and these purchases fuel the need for repair services. The changing family structure also has led to increased demand for services. Since fewer households contain a full-time homemaker, Americans are pressed for time. They hire help to handle child care, housekeeping, repair jobs, and more. And when some consumers want to buy a car, they hire a service called Car Bargains to gather competing bids.[3]

In the business sector, too, changes have led to increased demand for services. Thanks to restructurings and other efforts to keep costs down, businesses are operating with minimal staff and need to hire contractors to handle peak periods or special projects. The increased complexity of modern business also has generated a need for various experts. For example, to automate, firms turn to experts in computers and robotics. To compete internationally, they turn to experts in foreign markets and international marketing.

RELUCTANCE TO ADOPT MARKETING PRINCIPLES

The size and growth of the service sector make the marketing of services particularly important. However, until relatively recently, few service providers have fully applied marketing principles to their operations. There are at least five reasons for this slowness in adopting marketing principles:[4]

1. *Limited view of marketing*—Many services businesses held onto a sales orientation for years after goods producers were embracing the marketing concept. For example, the telecommunications industry broadened its concept of marketing only after deregulation in the mid-1980s.
2. *Limited competition*—Many services businesses, including banking, railroads, and public utilities, have been regulated or have for other reasons faced relatively little competition. They have therefore had little incentive to broaden their view of marketing.
3. *Lack of creative management*—Critics have accused the managers in many service industries of failure to act creatively.

4. *No obsolescence*—Many services are less subject to obsolescence than are goods. This reduces the urgency to make changes.
5. *Lack of innovation in the distribution of services*—As will be discussed later in this chapter, marketers of services have identified few ways to distribute them. The assumption has been that the nature of services requires that its producer deliver it directly to buyers in a limited area. While the theory may be sound in a general sense, it has discouraged marketers of services from thinking creatively about channels distribution.

In spite of these sources of resistance to change, more and more service organizations are using marketing principles and tactics. The remainder of this chapter includes examples of how they are doing so.

The Nature of Marketing Services

The marketing of services in many ways resembles marketing tangible products (goods). That is because goods and services aren't dramatically different from a marketing standpoint. They both are offerings designed to meet a customer need in exchange for payment. They both must be offered in a convenient location at a price the customer considers reasonable. The marketer uses various kinds of communications to inform the target market about either type of product and to stimulate a purchase. Finally, as discussed later in this chapter, many products have both tangible and intangible components, so it is hard to conceive of pure goods or pure services.

Thus, whether selling goods or services, the marketer needs to gather and interpret information about what potential buyers want and need. Then the marketer creates a marketing mix designed to meet the needs of the mass market or one or more target markets. Marriott Corporation learned from research that its customers primarily want a fast check-in; cleanliness; a friendly staff; a fast, high-quality breakfast; and value for their money. In response to the first need, Marriott introduced an express check-in program called "first 10." Customers who make reservations in advance are greeted when they arrive, handed room assignments and keys, and escorted to their room.[5]

Because the basics of marketing goods and services are the same, most chapters of this book apply to both types of product. But while the basic process of identifying and meeting the needs of target markets is the same for goods and services, some distinct characteristics apply more to services. The nature of services creates special challenges for marketers. Therefore, marketers of services need to be aware of the characteristics typical of services, some ways to classify services, and the nature of the buying decision for services.

CHARACTERISTICS OF SERVICES

Several characteristics distinguish services from goods. Services are distinguished by their intangibility, inseparability of production and marketing, involvement of the customer, variability of quality, perishability, use of highly differentiated marketing systems, and use of a client relationship. These characteristics influence the decisions involved in developing a marketing mix.

goods-services continuum
The range that measures whether products are tangible or intangible.

INTANGIBILITY   In terms of how tangible they are, products span a range of possibilities, shown in Figure 13.2. This range, which extends from entirely tangible to entirely intangible, is called the **goods-services continuum**. Most products contain some of both characteristics. For example, the price of a suit may include alterations; a restau-

FIGURE 13.2

The Goods–Services Continuum

Copper Wire, Salt	Oil Change, Restaurant Meal	Teaching, Financial Advice

100%
Goods

100%
Services

rant meal contains food, atmosphere, and the work of the serving staff; and a seminar includes instruction and usually written materials to take back to the workplace.

With developments in information technology, many organizations that traditionally offered tangible products are finding it logical and profitable to add information to their product mix. Their innovations may be either enhancements of the organization's original products or entirely new products. An example of the former is Matsushita/Panasonic's bicycle division in Japan, which offers customization as a product feature. At bicycle stores, the company collects details about each customer and uses the data to build whichever of several hundred thousand models is needed. An example of a service being a separate new product is the interactive computer network Inland Steel set up to keep its customers informed about their orders. The knowledge Inland began accumulating in this way eventually led the company to offer such services as consulting on specifications for technical products.[6]

In Figure 13.2, the products considered services are the ones on the right side—the ones that are mostly or entirely intangible. For instance, airline transportation is a service based on something intangible: moving people from one destination to another in an airplane. Modern air transportation may also include other services for business travelers; an example is hookups for laptop computers that allow the passenger to play computer games, look up stock market quotes, and make hotel reservations.[7] Also, air transportation typically includes such tangibles as food and drinks on the plane, as well as magazines to read and perhaps take home.

The intangibility of services poses some special problems for the marketer. When potential buyers cannot see, touch, smell, or taste the service before buying it, they have a harder time evaluating it and appreciating its benefits. For example, music lovers cannot hear a concert until they attend it, so they must rely on promises and their expectations to decide whether it will be worthwhile. This means that having a good reputation is especially important for a service provider. (For more on evaluating an organization's reputation, see "Put It into Practice.")

Marketers can address this difficulty by finding tangible ways to represent service features and benefits. For example, Prudential's brand mark, the rock of Gibralter, symbolizes strength and solidity. And when business consultant Tom Crum conducts workshops on handling conflict, he appears wearing the traditional garb for practicing aikido, the Japanese art of self-defense and mind-body coordination. Crum uses aikido exercises in his workshops to help participants learn on a physical as well as intellectual level.[8] Thus, his clothing symbolizes his training techniques in a way that participants will long remember (see Figure 13.3).

INSEPARABILITY   Primarily because services are intangible, they may be produced and marketed simultaneously. A consumer thinking of having cosmetic surgery meets with the surgeon for a consultation. A business owner who wants a loan goes to the bank and discusses his or her needs with a loan officer. This link between production and marketing means that marketing issues play a part in decisions as to where and how services will be produced.

Put It Into Practice

EVALUATING AN ORGANIZATION'S REPUTATION

A good reputation is important to any organization, but it is vital to the survival of an organization that provides a service. That is because reputation is one of the few characteristics on which potential customers can base their purchase decision for a service.

Consider your own response to a service business's or nonprofit organization's reputation. Choose a service provider that you are aware of or familiar with. (You might want to select the nonprofit organization you plan to focus on for your chapter project.) Ask yourself what *you* consider the organization's reputation to be. Then determine the basis for your opinions: Do you know the organization firsthand? Do you know people who have used its services? Does the organization produce high-quality advertising or receive favorable publicity? Has the organization been in operation for a long time?

Discuss your evaluation with your class. You may find that classmates who also know the organization have a different opinion of it.

From the standpoint of quality, buyers of a service are not only evaluating what was produced, but also *how* it was produced. Thus, the quality of a hotel visit depends not only on whether the mattress was comfortable and the room quiet, but also on how polite and helpful hotel employees were toward the guests. Once again, this means that marketing should play a role in setting production standards.

Inseparability may mean that customers not only want a particular type of service, they want it to be provided by a particular person or group of persons. For example, if you bought a ticket to see Prince, you would probably be disappointed to see Willie Nelson walk out on stage. Besides entertainers, this principle applies to professionals and craftspeople such as doctors, lawyers, financial advisers, clothing designers, painters, writers, and chefs. The risk of having the service equated with its provider is that if the customer is disappointed with the service, he or she is likely to have a poor opinion of the provider and to avoid seeking out any more services from that organization. On the positive side, the service provider who makes customers happy will generate a loyal clientele.

It is, of course, possible to separate some aspects of marketing from some aspects of production, even for the most intangible services. One way to do this is to sell a

FIGURE 13.3

A Tangible Way to Represent Service Features and Benefits

FIGURE 13.4

Product Requiring Customer Involvement: Museum Exhibits

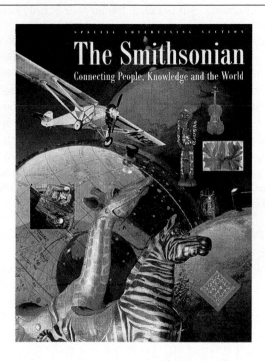

contract in which the seller promises to deliver the service in exchange for the customer's payment. To represent his or her rights to the service, the buyer might receive a ticket, a credit card, or a signed contract. Or the buyer might make an appointment for later delivery of services such as filling a tooth or moving furniture.

INVOLVEMENT OF THE CUSTOMER   One implication of inseparability is that customers are involved to a relatively great degree in the production and marketing of many kinds of services. If you want to get your hair permed, you have to plan on spending a sizable chunk of time at the hair salon letting someone work on your hair. If you want to enjoy an exhibit at the Smithsonian, you have to walk around the museum and pay attention to what is on display (see Figure 13.4). And if an organization wants to buy the services of an advertising agency, it will have to assign employees to work with the agency, conveying what the organization's product and target market are, reviewing the agency's ideas, and making the final selections.

Of course, not every service requires the same degree of involvement. Your involvement with the company that issues your Visa card may not go much beyond pulling out your card to make purchases and pulling out your checkbook once a month to pay the bill. Likewise, an organization may or may not become very involved in the activities of its law firm when all its legal matters are routine.

VARIABILITY OF QUALITY   Because services are produced and consumed at the same time, the quality can vary more than is likely with goods. Most organizations that produce goods have procedures to prevent, identify, and correct defects. If those procedures are working at all, the customer is not likely to see any gross errors because the company won't offer defective products for sale. The company may even have a goal of zero defects. But the more intangible a product, the harder it is to put such controls in place. If the product is investment advice, for example, the customer depends on the adviser to be thinking clearly and knowledgeably at the time he or she is giving the advice. But because the adviser is only human, he or she is likely to have some bad days.

This characteristic of quality drives home the importance of ensuring that the people who deliver services be well qualified and highly motivated to satisfy their customers. Total quality management, with its emphasis on continually improving processes, can help. Some organizations are trying to eliminate errors from service delivery by mapping the customer's and service provider's activities throughout a service operation.[9]

But as the other chapters should have made clear by now, attention to quality is crucial to marketing goods as well. Poor legal advice can ruin an organizational client of that lawyer, but so can a computer system that goes down at a busy time. An error during surgery can do great personal harm, but so can improper wiring in a house, leading to a major fire. The obvious conclusion is that producers of both goods and services can benefit from a focus on quality.

PERISHABILITY   Services are also perishable. In other words, if a service is not used when offered, it cannot be used at all. If no one makes an appointment to see the massage therapist on Thursday at 4:00 p.m., no massages will be provided at that time. If no one buys 10 percent of the tickets for a basketball game, those seats cannot be used to see the game at another time. In contrast, goods are less perishable. If a car sits in a used-car lot for a week, someone may buy it the next week. And even such goods as milk and tomatoes have some shelf life.

Because most services are perishable, it is especially important to plan for fluctuations in demand. For most services, demand shifts according to season, day of the week, or time of day. The demand for attending a play is strongest in the evening. The demand for tax preparation services is strongest between mid-February and mid-April.

HIGHLY DIFFERENTIATED DISTRIBUTION CHANNELS   Established distribution channels are in place for handling many kinds of tangible goods. For example, makers of food products typically sell to certain categories of wholesalers, which sell to supermarkets and other stores where consumers expect to find food. Someone who comes out with a new type of food would use the same channels. Likewise, when musical recordings are introduced in new formats, their makers tend to offer them in the same kinds of stores where consumers have come to expect to find music on records and cassettes.

In contrast, the marketing systems for services differ more widely. For example, savings and loan institutions try to reach customers with convenient branches and hours for delivering their mostly standardized products. Airlines must offer their services through established airports, and they focus on communications, appealing to travel agencies and the flyers themselves. Hospitals depend heavily on their relationship with physicians in the community, who treat patients at the hospital(s) where the doctors have privileges.

CLIENT RELATIONSHIP   In many cases, marketers of services view the buyers as clients, rather than customers. In other words, the buyer sees the seller as someone the buyer can lean on for advice and help. This relationship is especially likely when the provider of the service is a professional, such as a doctor, lawyer, or financial adviser. The client relationship tends to be personalized and ongoing.

As a result, the success of a service organization depends in part on its employees' ability to develop client relationships as well as provide the basic service such as diagnosing an illness or recognizing a good investment. More simply put, service marketers depend on their ability to retain, not just attract, customers.[10] Marketing efforts designed to create and maintain loyalty among existing customers are called **relationship marketing**. Relationship marketing focuses on such concerns as pre-

relationship marketing
Marketing efforts designed to create and maintain loyalty among existing customers.

paring to correct mistakes,[11] building trust, and demonstrating commitment to the customer.[12]

Organizations that keep track of their customers' purchases know that relationship marketing makes good economic sense. Home Depot stores, for example, have determined that while a shopper spends only $38 on a single visit, the typical shopper visits the store 30 times a year. Throughout a lifetime, that typical customer will spend $25,000.[13] The flip side of this equation is that alienating a Home Depot customer on his or her first visit would cost the store not $38, but $25,000. In that same vein, the Boston-based consulting firm Forum Corporation has found that the typical consumer tells nine people about a bad experience before telling the company.[14] Again, the costs of an error in service are greater than they might seem on the surface.

CLASSIFICATION OF SERVICES

Classifying services helps marketers recognize the kinds of marketing strategies likely to succeed. Services may be classified in several ways. These include the way the services are delivered, the types of organizations providing the service, and the types of customers they target.

MEANS OF DELIVERY As shown in Figure 13.5, services may be equipment based or people based. In other words, they may be delivered primarily by equipment, as in the case of movie theaters and airlines. or they may be delivered primarily by people, as in the case of janitorial services and accountants.

The means of delivery influences where quality is most at stake in the product mix. For equipment-based services, marketers must be concerned that the equipment is of good enough quality to meet customers' needs. They must ensure that the employees who keep the equipment operating or come into contact with users are skilled and interested in meeting customer needs. Thus, the quality of computer programming services depends on both the computers used and the programmers themselves. In Russia, few sophisticated computers have been available, so programmers themselves have had to be more sophisticated. Today Russian programmers are noted for their talent in writing amazingly complex programs that use relatively little computing power. According to Michael Friend, who manages Boeing's Russian operations, "They can do things on a PC that we would use a [much larger] mainframe for."[15]

For people-based services, the level and consistency of quality depend almost entirely on the training and motivation of the people providing the services. Thus, Robert Carlson, a retired CEO of Pratt & Whitney, helps Russian factory directors plan how to restructure their operations.[16] The quality of this service depends on Carlson himself, not on any inanimate objects. Especially for such people-based services, the ability of service providers to maintain good customer relations is a key to success.

TYPE OF PROVIDER Another way to classify services is in terms of the kind of organization providing them. Service providers include businesses, government, and nonprofit organizations. Most of the examples in this book involve businesses—organizations that offer goods and services in order to earn a profit. Marketing is also important for many government services, including mass transportation, state colleges and universities, state lotteries, and the military. Nonprofit organizations from the American Cancer Society to the Brookfield Zoo use marketing to help them identify needs and target services, build support for causes, and solicit contributions. A particular type of nonprofit organization that uses many marketing tactics is the political campaign. The nonbusiness categories of marketing are described further in the last section of this chapter.

FIGURE 13.5

Categorizing Services by Means of Delivery

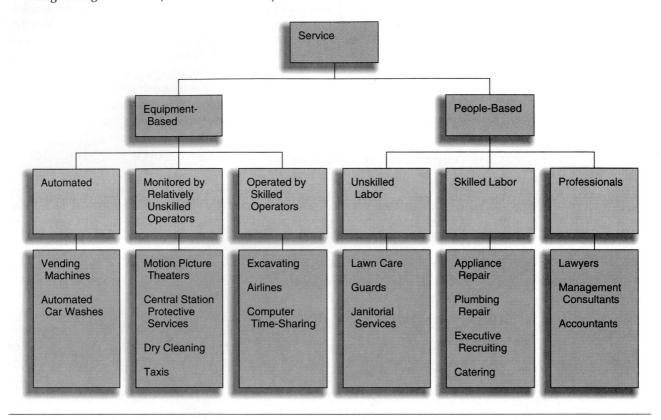

Source: Reprinted by permission of *Harvard Business Review*. An exhibit fom "Strategy Is Different in Service Businesses," by Dan R. E. Thomas, *Harvard Business Review* (July/August 1978) p. 161. Copyright © 1978 by the President and Fellows of Harvard College; all rights reserved.

Different types of organizations may provide similar types of services. For example, the U.S. Postal Service competes with UPS for package delivery services. Karen L. Meyer once directed a nonprofit organization, the National Center for Access Unlimited, which helped corporations understand their responsibilities under the Americans with Disabilities Act. Today she provides similar consulting services as president of her own business, Karen L. Meyer & Associates.[17]

Another way to think of service providers is in terms of the kind of customers they serve. Basically, the organization may provide services to consumers, organizations, or both. For example, as explained by the ad in Figure 13.6, Ameritech not only provides phone service to consumers and businesses, it also helps consumers *become* part of the business market. Ameritech helps people set up home offices by offering a variety of services, including second and third phone lines, cellular communications, enhanced faxing, electronic mail, and consultations on setting up a home workplace.

An organization marketing to consumers will need to consider not only the special characteristics of marketing services but also the information about consumer behavior described in Chapter 8. An organization marketing to organizational buyers will need to consider the characteristics of marketing services and the nature of organizational buyers, introduced in Chapter 9.

FIGURE 13.6

A Service Business Serving Consumers and Organizations

FIGURE 13.6

A Service Business Serving Consumers and Organizations

THE PURCHASING DECISION FOR SERVICES

Chapters 8 and 9 described the way in which consumers and organizational buyers make purchasing decisions. Those general models apply to services. For example, the Tortilla Factory restaurant of Herndon, Virginia, bought third-party delivery services from Takeout Taxi because the services reduced the company's risks and added to its profits. Tortilla Factory wanted to add home delivery of its food but had been concerned that the added revenues would not offset the cost of hiring additional staff and buying the necessary insurance. Takeout Taxi handles order taking, delivery, and promotion of the restaurant, all for a share of the sales.[18] Despite the similarities of the purchase decisions, however, the characteristics of services require some modifications to the process.

IDENTIFYING AND EVALUATING ALTERNATIVES   One area of difference involves the way potential buyers gather information and evaluate the alternatives. For tangible products, it is relatively easy to think of criteria to look for, then to examine various product offerings and determine whether each meets those criteria. That's what you do when you select the reddest strawberries or the used car that handles best. As products become less tangible, it becomes harder to evaluate alternatives without consuming the products.

Sources of Information   For marketers, this limitation in purchasing services has some important implications. One is that buyers of services look for information about alternatives from a variety of sources besides the product itself. The specific sources vary from one type of service to another, but some common ones include advertising, news accounts, members of reference groups (such as family and friends), employees of service providers, and referrals from colleagues of the service provider.[19]

Marketers who are looking to build a client base would do well to learn what sources are used in their industry. It makes good sense to be sure that the most impor-

and Tokyo. In each city, Ruggeri selects a site close to commercial districts and prestigious stores. That way, when the city's trendsetters move on to another spot, the restaurant can still do a brisk business with businesspeople and shoppers.[27]

As with the buying process for services, the marketing mix is basically the same as that for goods. However, the characteristics of services give rise to special needs in preparing the marketing mix.

DEVELOPING AND TARGETING THE SERVICE

To provide quality services, the organization must tailor these products to the needs of specific customers. In other words, services seldom can be highly standardized. Thus, while Pepperidge Farm can decide exactly what ingredients will go into each loaf of whole-wheat bread and what every label will look like, an appliance repairperson must look at each appliance to see what work is needed. Furthermore, the repairperson must respond courteously to the varying comments and questions from each customer.

The individual nature of each transaction often means that a service provider has to consider whether each transaction is a good fit with its product mix. Sometimes the organization's services are not the best way to meet a customer's needs. Explaining that fact to the customer can be part of good relationship marketing. Millington McCoy, managing director of Gould & McCoy, a New York executive search firm, tells of the time a division president on the West Coast asked her to fly to California and conduct a search to fill a fairly low-level position. McCoy suggested that the California executive could get more for his money—and make a better impression on his employer—by using a local firm.[28]

 Tailoring a service to customer needs is even more complex when the targeted group is multinational or multicultural. With demand for television services exploding throughout Asia, a number of satellite broadcasters and cable networks are moving in. However, providing programming is difficult. In Asia more than on other continents, consumers differ in terms of language, religion, and social systems. India is unusual in that it has a large English-speaking population interested in reruns of U.S. programs.[29]

QUALITY OF SERVICES   The intangible and individualized nature of services can make it difficult to develop objective standards for measuring their quality. A good start is to consider what customers look for in deciding whether they have purchased a high-quality service. Broadly speaking, to evaluate whether a service is of high quality, customers look for the characteristics listed in Table 13.1.

An organization that clearly provides a quality product is Phelps County Bank (PCB) of Rolla, Missouri. PCB's strategy is to take on its two rivals in town by offering a level of service that is the envy of the industry. The lobby opens five minutes early and closes five minutes late each day so as not to annoy customers whose watches are a couple of minutes off. Customer service reps and tellers have authority to resolve customer problems on the spot. Happy customers love to tell their stories: A florist who was short of cash to pay a refrigerator repairman called the bank while the repairman waited. A loan officer hand-delivered a loan to the flower shop. A university professor got approval for a mortgage loan before moving to town. Later bank employees helped him resolve a dispute with an insurance company that deducted an automatic monthly payment for a policy it had canceled. This level of service brings in profits as well as customers. PCB charges relatively high rates on its loans, but customers consider its services good value. In recent years PCB's assets and deposits have surpassed those of its competitors.[30]

To see whether they are satisfying customers by meeting quality standards, marketers need to ask their customers how the organization is doing. Unfortunately,

TABLE 13.1
Criteria for Evaluating the Quality of Services

CRITERION	DESCRIPTION
Reliability	Customers want performance to be consistent and dependable.
Responsiveness	Customers must see service providers as ready and willing to perform.
Competence	Service providers should have the skills and knowledge needed to perform the service properly.
Access	Customers want the service provider to be approachable and easy to contact.
Courtesy	Service providers should be polite, respectful, considerate, and friendly.
Communication	Customers want the service provider to listen to them, keep them informed, and use language they can understand.
Credibility	Service providers should be trustworthy, believable, and honest.
Security	Customers want the service provider to protect them from danger, risk, or doubt. The service provider should show customers that he or she will respect the confidentiality of personal information.
Understanding	Service providers should try to understand what their customers want and need.
Tangibles	Customers look for quality in the equipment, facilities, and communications materials used to provide the service.

Source: Adapted from J. Paul Peter and James H. Donnelly, Jr., *A Preface to Marketing Management,* 5th ed. (Homewood, Ill.: Irwin, 1991), pp. 207–208.

reports marketing researcher Leonard Berry, they often fail to do just that. Berry says marketers assume they know what their customers want; even when they do ask, they conduct a single survey, rather than systematically listening to them. Explains Berry, "Any single service quality study provides only a snapshot at one point in time. Only when companies take snapshots regularly and from different angles do they learn what is actually happening, why, and what priorities should be."[31] The First National Bank of Chicago asked customers what they wanted from the bank. First Chicago learned that customers want employees to return calls when they say they will and to offer an explanation when problems occur. So the bank included these criteria in its performance standards.[32]

Standards for Quality   How can the organization make sure that its employees are providing quality service time after time? One approach is to include quality measures in the company's performance standards, as First Chicago does. The organization can also have employees practice focusing on quality by setting the standard that each employee must satisfy his or her "internal customers"—those in the organization who use the employee's work.

For example, at Creative Professional Services, a Woburn, Massachusetts, provider of marketing services, the salespeople offered a guarantee to the company's account managers, who are responsible for producing materials for clients. If a salesperson turns over incomplete or incorrect specifications to the account manager, the account manager can invoke the guarantee, selecting a form of payment from the salesperson. This might involve the salesperson taking the account manager to lunch or doing some of the work on the job himself or herself. Since Creative Professional Services started using the internal guarantees, the company has streamlined its procedures, which in turn should improve the services it sells its clients.[33]

Employee Empowerment   Another approach to improving service that is derived from total quality management is giving employees the power to satisfy customers.

Marketing Movers & Shakers

TEDD SAUNDERS OF THE SAUNDERS GROUP

Walk into the lobby of the posh Park Plaza Hotel in Boston, and you probably won't notice a thing. Ditto in the lobbies of the Lenox and the Copley Square. All three are owned by the Saunders family's company, the Saunders Group. And all three have undergone a nearly invisible transformation by 32-year-old Tedd Saunders, who is director of environmental affairs at the Park Plaza and now President of Eco-Logical Solutions, a consulting company working on environmental issues for service industries.

"Initially, it was pure idealism," explains Saunders. "I knew this was the right thing to do. What really made this possible . . . was being able to bring this to a language that a businessperson could rationalize and understand." During the early 1990s, Saunders brought his commitment to the environment to his family business, convinced that he could make environmentally friendly changes in the way the hotels operate without slipping in service. Saunders had the giant chandelier in the Park Plaza lobby cleaned ultrasonically, avoiding harsh chemicals. He insisted the hotel use shredded office paper instead of foam peanuts for packing boxes. He ordered the installation of low-flow showerheads, faucets, and toilets. He installed thermopane windows and dispenser systems for shampoo and soap in showers, removing the tiny trial-size plastic containers. And he switched entirely from plastic to reusable cutlery and dinnerware in the employee cafeteria, which serves 100,000 meals annually. He even added recycling bins camouflaged with rosy pleated skirts that match the lobby decor.

Saunders then went further, forming a Green Team and offering $100 rewards to employees who came up with good ideas for environmentally sound changes. (One employee suggested reusing old, stained tablecloths by turning them into chefs' aprons.) The Green Team, made up of 18 volunteer employees, meets each month to bat around new ideas.

When asked about the changes in his hotels, Saunders replies, "In all cases, our goal is to respond to an increased awareness on the part of our guests for us to act environmentally responsibly. Our goal has been to create an environmental policy which guides all our decision making to balance our economic viability with environmental action." Saunders showed that not only could his customers and the environment coexist peacefully, he could serve them both equally well.

Source: Mary Sit, "The Green Team Has Checked In," *The Boston Globe,* May 10, 1993, pp. 11–12.

Empowering its employees is behind the quality strategy at the Ritz-Carlton. Thus, if a front-desk clerk sees that a bill contains an error, the clerk fixes it without consulting a supervisor. To help employees use this power effectively, the company gives each employee over 100 hours of training in quality each year.[34] (For more on delivering high-quality service—and in an environmentally responsible way—see "Marketing Movers & Shakers.")

Supplementing these ideas, Table 13.2 presents ten principles for a quality approach to marketing services.

LACK OF PATENT PROTECTION   One of the ways marketers of goods set their products apart from the competition is by introducing innovations that can be patented. A patent gives the manufacturer exclusive rights to use the innovation for 17 years. In contrast, services cannot be patented.

To counter this drawback, marketers of services must continually innovate and improve. Only through continuous improvement can they continue to distinguish themselves from the competition. Hertz does this by offering a program called the #1

TABLE 13.2 **Ten Principles for a Quality Approach to Marketing Services**	
	1. Quality service means never having to say, "That's not my job."
	2. The delivery of quality service is never the customer's job.
	3. Customers should never be inconvenienced because of company policies that are known only to employees and do not become known to customers until they are used against them.
	4. Customers should never be required to restate their request or complain to several people before having it resolved.
	5. You will never treat your customers better than you treat each other.
	6. How your employees feel is eventually how your customers will feel.
	7. Never allow an employee's work to interfere with his or her job.
	8. If you establish negative expectations for your customers, you will always meet them.
	9. A great many customers will not return bad service with bad behavior. They are always polite, never get loud, cause a scene, or scream for the manager. They just never come back.
	10. When you lose a customer because of poor service, chances are you will never know it.

Source: Adapted from James H. Donnelly, Jr., and Steven J. Skinner, *The New Banker* (Homewood, Ill.: Dow Jones–Irwin, 1989), Chap. 3.

Club Gold. Customers who join the program by paying $50 can avoid waiting in lines to get a car. Instead, they call ahead to reserve a car, get on the courtesy bus when they arrive at the airport, tell the driver their last name, and ride directly to their car, which an attendant has already started. How do you know it's the right car? Your name is blazing above it in lights.[35] At Sea-Land Service, which ships containers of goods across the oceans, continuous improvement comes from empowering employees to resolve problems. For example, if a clerk sees that a shipper has classified goods into a needlessly expensive category, the clerk can call the shipper and arrange to reclassify the goods. Not only is the customer pleasantly surprised by the call, but Sea-Land spends less money pleasing the customer this way than it would making changes later when the customer figures out the mistake.[36]

MANAGING FLUCTUATING DEMAND   When marketers plan how much of a service to make available, they think in terms of the amount of time the organization should be open and the number of people on hand to provide the service. Long hours and adequate staffing for peak periods will enable the organization to serve all potential customers. However, this level of staffing is likely to result in **idle time**, or time during which service providers have no clients to serve. (Some services will measure excess capacity in other ways, such as empty seats.) Idle time is expensive, so this strategy is not suitable for all products or organizations. At the same time, understaffing or limiting hours can result in disgruntled customers.

idle time
Time during which service providers have no clients to serve.

Various tactics are available for managing fluctuations in demand. Paying staff on commission helps to keep costs in line with sales. Closing the business during certain times can reduce the amount of idle time. A seaside resort might close for the winter. Another way to manage slow periods is to stimulate demand, as in the case of a beauty shop that offers a lower "senior citizens' rate" during a time when other customers are at work. If there is enough demand, an organization might let customers wait for service during busy periods. For example, many popular restaurants will not take reservations.

PRICING THE SERVICE

One of the most noticeable characteristics of pricing for services is the many ways to refer to price in the service sector. Prices may be called charges, fees, fares, rates, or

For a price of $699 per couple, the honeymoon getaway at Napili Kai in Maui, Hawaii, includes ocean view rooms, white sand beaches, a Jacuzzi, tennis, golf, and swimming for four days and three nights. The resort's advertising spells out all of these features.

premiums. Whatever the name, the price set for services is designed to fulfill the same basic objectives described in Chapter 14—notably, to cover costs and generate a profit. When the Delahaye Group sets prices for its service of tracking the effectiveness of public relations, the company considers the amount of time expected to be required, expected changes that will affect future costs, and industry pricing practices.[37]

Because of the intangible nature of services, part of the pricing job may involve making sure both parties understand what is included in the product. The seller must understand what the customer wants, and the customer must understand what the seller is offering. Customers are most apt to be pleased with the value of a service if they can look at an itemized bill and see that they got a lot of work for their money. At CMG Health, an Owings Mills, Maryland, packager of mental health care for insurance agencies and health maintenance organizations, salespeople ask customers to explain their assumptions about what will be included and what they will pay. This not only helps the company avoid underpricing, it also leads to more satisfied clients.[38]

Besides this economic function, pricing also influences how buyers perceive the product. When customers have few cues for judging quality, they may evaluate it on the basis of price.[39] Because services are often hard to evaluate, price therefore plays a particularly important role in this regard. For example, imagine that you were a manager trying to decide between a $50-per-hour consultant and a $200-per-hour consultant to advise you on setting up a new marketing decision support system. Which consultant would you assume had the greatest expertise? And could you really prove it?

Because of the perishable nature of services, marketers use pricing to limit idle time. For example, the organization may use **off-peak pricing**. This consists of charging different prices during different times or days in order to stimulate demand during slow periods. Thus, a cruise line might offer a lower price during the off-season, and many hotels offer special packages on weekends, when business travel is at a minimum. (For more on pricing as well as managing fluctuating demand, see the "You Decide" box).

off-peak pricing
Charging lower prices during slow periods to stimulate demand.

You Decide

WHAT'S THE RIGHT MARKETING MIX FOR INDOOR PLAYGROUNDS?

At Fun Centers (owned by Chicago-based Discovery Zone), kids shoot down slides, wriggle through mazes, and climb ropes. At Gymboree sessions (owned by a Burlingame, California, company), tots and parents play together with group leaders. And at McDonald Corp.'s Leaps & Bounds, youngsters blow off steam by leaping and bounding around on play equipment.

The idea behind these fast-growing indoor play centers is a "structured environment in which the adult can feel comfortable. You're having a parent-child experience take place in a kind of amusement park," explains Leo Shapiro, head of his own marketing research firm in Chicago. "It's an extraordinarily positive experience."

There certainly seems to be a market for organized indoor play. The most recent U.S. Census counted 47.4 million children aged 12 or younger and predicted that by the year 2000, there could be more than 51 million children living in the United States. Some analysts view shopping malls as ideal locations for new play centers because recession-battered rents are low and people still need to shop. Discovery Zone agrees and is aggressively trying to capture the market. Linda Killian, an analyst with Renaissance Capital in Greenwich, Connecticut, says, "If Discovery Zone is able to position itself as the child's entertainment outlet in a mall, there may be no need for other entrants."

Some of these "playgrounds" charge flat fees, such as Gymboree's rate of $7 to $14 per twelve- to fourteen-week "semester." Discovery Zone's Fun Centers cost $4.95–$6.95 per child for two hours of play, whereas the $5.95 per child for each visit to Leaps & Bounds has no time limit. Of course, customers will decide whether these prices are fair. One mother notes, "The boys have a great time; there are lots of smiles and lots of sweat." But with entrance fees as well as charges for food and tokens for special games, "the costs can get up there."

The indoor play centers have peak and off-periods, following the days of the week as well as weather. Extremely cold or hot weather tends to drive people inside. Ultimately, prices could reflect this.

How do you think marketers of the play centers could capitalize on peak periods and stimulate demand during slower periods? In addition to shopping malls, what other types of locations would be good for play centers? Do you think these indoor play centers will survive as services in the long run? Why or why not?

Source: Daniel M. Gold, "It's Pay-for-Play—Health Clubs for the Toddling Set," *The New York Times,* May 16, 1993, p. 14.

DISTRIBUTION CHANNELS FOR THE SERVICE

Because the production and marketing of services are difficult to separate, distribution emphasizes finding ways to provide the services conveniently to customers. As mentioned earlier, the producer of services rarely relies on resellers to bring its products to buyers. Rather, the marketer seeks ways to make the services easily accessible. Examples of conveniently available services include automatic teller machines for round-the-clock access to certain banking transactions and the automatic ticket machines that enable flyers to buy a ticket on Southwest Airlines in just 20 seconds.[40]

Distribution strategy can help a service provider position itself. To attract a mass-market clientele, Memphis-based National Commerce Bancorporation opened branches in supermarkets. The branches keep the same hours as the stores and make loans as well as cash checks. To support this distribution strategy, the branches promote their services throughout the store with signs, flyers, and other techniques.[41]

A common approach to distributing services to a broad consumer market is through **franchising**. This method of distribution is based on a contract in which a franchisor gives franchisees the right to operate a business under the franchisor's trade name. In exchange, the franchisees pay a specified amount and operate the business according to a plan specified by the franchisor. Franchising is most suitable for businesses where it is possible to spell out rules for day-to-day operations. Thus, hotels, oil-change facilities, printshops, and fast-food restaurants are often franchises (see Figure 13.8).

franchising
An agreement in which franchisees receive the right to operate a business under the franchisor's trade name in exchange for paying a fee and operating according to a specified plan.

Furthermore, increasing competition has made marketing not only useful but necessary for survival in many industries. For example, not only do health care providers have to contend with competitors, but they have to accommodate the reduced demand that results when insurers limit what they will pay for. In the case of addiction treatment, insurance companies are not as generous as they once were, so addiction treatment centers are turning to advertising to help fill their beds. Parkside Medical Services of Park Ridge, Illinois, reports that 40 to 50 percent of its inpatients learn about the organization through advertising. Creating advertising messages for such services involves striking a balance between compassion and the firmness necessary to break through the typical addict's denial.[45]

SPECIAL CHALLENGES   Some characteristics typical of nonprofit organizations make marketing challenging. One is that providers of funds to the organization are often different from users of its services. This means that the organization has two major groups to satisfy, and their needs and wants may differ. Thus, donors to a museum may wish that the funds would be used to make some important acquisitions, whereas visitors might wish the money would enable longer evening hours (and the museum's management might want to replace a worn roof). Serving diverse groups can also result in a complicated organizational structure.

The lack of a profit objective can complicate the task of identifying a useful measure of success. Thus, it may be difficult to establish marketing objectives consistent with the organization's overall mission. London's two opera houses—the English National Opera (ENO) and the Royal Opera House—are struggling to create viable marketing mixes. To broaden its customer base, the ENO charges £42 ($72) or less for its seats, performs operas in English, and encourages the audience to dress comfortably. To uphold its high reputation, the Royal Opera charges three times as much for seats and experiments more with new productions to please its more sophisticated audience. Both organizations seek corporate and government sponsorship as well as ticket sales. Whether one strategy is more appropriate than another depends in part on such unanswered questions as why the government should subsidize these organizations—to broaden the appeal of opera or to maintain British opera's artistic standards and reputation?[46]

Also, marketing objectives may not always involve generating financial transactions (getting people to buy the organization's goods and services). Instead, the organization may be seeking to recruit volunteers or to get people to do a particular thing, such as write to the president or avoid cocaine use.

PUBLIC SERVICE MARKETING

Public services are those provided by government agencies at the federal, state, and local levels. They include street sweeping, highway patrols, and Medicaid benefits. In fact, all branches and agencies of government provide services. To build awareness of their activities, to encourage citizens to behave in certain ways, or to better target their services, government agencies use marketing.

When the government agency is seeking to promote awareness among the general public, it may use advertising. The Army's "Be all you can be" campaign is a widely familiar example. (See the ad from *Rolling Stone* magazine in Figure 13.9.) Advertising is an effective communication strategy for a lot of public service marketing because the targeted group is often huge.

In some cases, however, a government agency finds it is more effective to communicate through some other means. To obtain a commitment of time or money may require a more direct appeal, especially when addressing groups not used to mass communications. The Unit Trust of India (UTI) is selling mutual funds to the people of that country in

FIGURE 13.9

Advertising a Public Service: U.S. Army

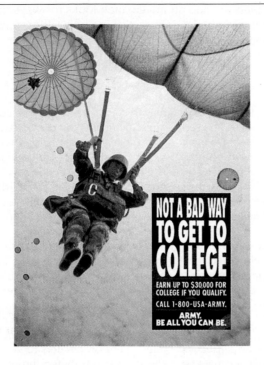

order to guide funds into investments that are productive. To reach India's large and far-flung rural population, UTI relies on 90,000 sales agents, paying them commissions of 1–2 percent of each investment they bring into the fund. Many of them work for UTI part–time and hold other jobs. One of UTI's best-selling products is a dowry fund, so that parents of a daughter can plan ahead for this huge marriage expense.[47]

Sometimes government agencies undertake more targeted communications activities as well. For example, by asking consumers to vote on which picture of Elvis Presley should appear on a stamp, the U.S. Postal Service generated a list of consumers with some interest in stamps. The 800,000 people who gave their names when voting received a catalog containing a variety of items, including a sheet of 40 stamps in a protective sleeve designed to resemble a record dust jacket.[48]

Of course, the other elements of the marketing mix also are important. Thus, to compete with other carriers of messages, the U.S. Postal Service has to consider the location and hours of its post offices. The Postal Service also has broadened its product offerings to include overnight and two-day mail service, as well as self-adhesive Christmas stamps. With regard to distribution, the Postal Service has sought to make stamps more easily available through outlets such as supermarkets.

MARKETING FOR POLITICAL USES

The application of marketing to politics is the primary use of person marketing, introduced in Chapter 1. Running for public office is essentially an exercise in marketing. In one sense at least, it is more complex than marketing goods: the candidate is seeking financial contributions, campaign volunteers, and votes. Political marketing may also take the form of idea marketing. For example, a local group might organize to build support for a referendum increasing taxes for the schools.

Political marketing includes the various aspects of marketing used for other services. The candidate and staff conduct research to identify the concerns of the public and the segment(s) of the public likely to appreciate the candidate's views. The candidate crafts a platform and an image, then looks for ways to present them to potential voters. Typical communications tactics include rallies, fund-raising events, publicity, brochures, and bumper stickers.

Summary

Services are products that are purely or mostly intangible, such as travel and health care. In the United States, the service sector accounts for more than 70 percent of employment and over half of the gross national product. Despite the importance of services to the economy, service providers in the past have neglected to apply marketing principles to their operations. The reluctance to adopt marketing principles stemmed from a limited view of marketing, limited competition, lack of creative management, the lack of obsolescence of services, and lack of innovation in the distribution of services. Today, however, services are more actively marketed.

Services tend to be different from goods in several ways. First, they are largely intangible. Services generally are produced and marketed simultaneously, making the two processes inseparable. Customers tend to be heavily involved in the production and marketing of services. The quality of services tends to vary more than the quality of goods. Services are perishable; that is, if a service is not used when it is offered, it cannot be used at all. Distribution channels for services differ more widely than they do for goods. Finally, the relationship between buyer and seller of a service is usually thought of in terms of a client relationship—one that is personalized and ongoing.

Marketers classify services by delivery, by the type of organization providing the service, and by the type of customers targeted.

In making a purchasing decision for services, buyers often evaluate the service by trying it, then deciding whether to use the service again. This involves a certain amount of risk, so buyers look for ways to reduce this risk. Marketers may try to make buyers more comfortable by offering limited trials, information on credentials, or testimonials.

The marketing mix for services has some special characteristics. First, services are seldom highly standardized and it is difficult to develop objective standards for quality. Service organizations can set standards for satisfying internal customers and empower employees to make decisions and correct problems for clients. Services cannot be patented, so marketers must continually innovate and improve their product. Managing fluctuating demand is also an objective for marketers of services. Pricing services is tricky because they are so hard to evaluate. Both parties must be clear about what is offered. In addition, marketers may use off-peak pricing to stimulate demand during slow periods. In planning distribution channels, marketers focus on finding ways to provide the services conveniently to clients. The producer of a service rarely relies on resellers to get the product to buyers. Many services are distributed through a franchising arrangement. Marketing communications, especially in the form of personal selling, is often closely linked to providing the service.

Nonprofit organizations provide services that can be marketed; in fact, competition often requires marketing. Even government agencies and political candidates must build awareness of their activities through marketing. Sometimes the providers of funds to the organization are different from the service users; marketing must satisfy both groups. The lack of a profit goal can make it difficult to measure success objectively. Also, marketing objectives for these organizations don't always involve a financial transaction.

KEY TERMS AND CONCEPTS

services (p. 382)
goods-services continuum (p. 384)
relationship marketing (p. 388)

idle time (p. 397)
off-peak pricing (p. 398)
franchising (p. 399)

public service announcement (PSA) (p. 401)

REVIEW AND DISCUSSION QUESTIONS

1. Why has the service sector in the United States grown so much in recent years?
2. Why have service providers been reluctant to engage in marketing until recently?
3. Where would you place the following products on the goods-services continuum, and why?
   a. a Japanese restaurant
   b. television repair
   c. marriage counseling
   d. a guided tour of Yellowstone National Park

4. If you wanted to market a car wash, what steps would you take to help potential customers make their purchasing decisions and, ultimately, come to your car wash?
5. Which three criteria from Table 13.1 might potential buyers rely on most when evaluating each of the following services? Discuss the reasons for your choices.
   a. a divorce attorney
   b. overnight parcel delivery to the Middle East
   c. a cooking class
   d. a carpenter

6. If you wanted to market a weekend workshop on how to invest money, would you price it high or low? Why?

7. Why is personal selling such an important method of communications for services?

8. What are some of the special challenges to marketing faced by nonprofit organizations?

Chapter Project
Marketing a Nonprofit Organization's Services

Most of the projects in this book have focused on profit-centered organizations. In this project, however, you have a chance to think about promoting a nonprofit organization that provides a service.

Choose an existing government agency (local, state, or federal) or national or international nonprofit organization (such as the Red Cross or local fund-raising group for schools) that interests you. If you can, gather some information about the organization, including communications such as magazine ads. First, analyze the special characteristics of your organization that make marketing its services a challenge. Then decide what steps you could take to make the "purchasing decision" (for users and donors or volunteers) most comfortable. Finally, decide whether you would use advertising or personal selling—or both—to communicate your organization's services.

Present your findings either in written form or to your class.

Case
KLM Royal Dutch Airlines

In 1920, the first KLM DeHavilland aircraft soared into the sky from Amsterdam to London. That year, the new airline carried 345 passengers and 25 tons of freight and mail. More than 70 years later, KLM circles the globe with a fleet of passenger jets and freight aircraft, carrying more than eight million passengers and 385 tons of freight and mail annually. Its cargo department handles everything from fresh flowers to racehorses. KLM is now the oldest international scheduled airline in the world that still operates under its original name.

How has KLM managed to stay airborne when so many other airlines have crashed financially? One reason may be its quality program, which has been in effect since 1984. The quality program includes all 25,000 employees and states succinctly that KLM will provide customer service with reliability, punctuality, care, and friendliness. (Note how these qualities relate to the criteria for evaluation in Table 13.1.) These standards apply both to passengers and cargo.

Of course, KLM customers want their flights to depart and arrive on schedule, serve the locations they find convenient, and operate safely. And they get more. Like many other large companies, KLM offers a variety of services within the larger service of transport. One of these is catering.

The KLM Catering Services department must coordinate and supervise worldwide catering services for KLM; manage production facilities; research and develop new recipes and menus, including diet meals, while ensuring high quality during travel; and serve the needs of around 20,000 passengers per day. Early in air travel, airline catering consisted of snacks and drinks; in the 1990s, part of an airline's marketing effort often includes the food as well as service behind the food. The catering department makes sure that meals are not duplicated on certain routes so that frequent fliers are not confronted with the same menu twice on a round trip. The department also selects magazines and newspapers appropriate to each flight and offers tax-free items for sale during the flight.

According to KLM Catering, service is "mostly a matter of the personal touch. The hallmark of quality is that service is individual." The company treats requests for "special" meals with equanimity, supplying passengers with individualized meals meeting dietary or religious requirements. In addition, the company strives to keep pace with differing cultural attitudes toward food, from flavors to items served.

To help ensure quality at KLM Catering Services, a meals development group researches new recipes; a selection group chooses the wines served on board; other groups make sure that the flight is provisioned on time and that all meals are prepared and stored hygienically. Thus, individual service on KLM flights is provided by groups of employees dedicated to pleasing each customer.

QUESTIONS

1. As competition among airlines grows more intense, what other aspects of service (in addition to schedule and food) might become increasingly competitive?

2. Since KLM's catering service cannot be patented, how might marketers continue to innovate and improve it?

3. How might marketers best promote the service aboard KLM?

Source: Promotional material, KLM Royal Dutch Airlines, June 1992 and January 1993.

5

Pricing

TOYS "R" US

At the grand opening of a new Toys "R" Us store in Spain, a little boy stands poised against the long pink tape with a pair of scissors, ready to snip it. A huge stuffed giraffe with long eyelashes and a polka dot ribbon plastered to its forehead looms behind him. At another grand opening, in Japan, a line of executives in dark suits grip their scissors with white gloves, awaiting the signal to slice the tape. American and Japanese flags fly side by side on mauve flagpoles just outside the store. The excitement among children and adults is tangible. Who can wait to dash into the huge store filled with treasures?

Marketing toys is serious business in the United States and abroad. Behind the shelves stocked with Lego and Play Doh, Toys "R" Us is fighting hard to maintain its dominant 20 percent share of the $15 billion U.S. toy market while it launches into new markets worldwide. By 1992, the company had 126 locations in Canada, France, Germany, Hong Kong, Japan, Malaysia, Spain, Singapore, Taiwan, and the United Kingdom. (In each case, overall management in a country or region is conducted by someone native to the area.) Earnings at the international division passed the $1 billion mark early in this decade. In the company's words, Toys "R" Us had become "the world's largest and fastest-growing children's specialty retail chain in terms of both sales and earnings."

Pricing is a key factor in the company's strategy and success as well as its difficulties. Toys "R" Us originally made its mark by sticking to "everyday low pricing" rather than having huge sales and other promotions, thus building loyalty among customers who might otherwise shop department stores and small specialty stores. But then the rules of the pricing game changed as huge discounters like Wal-Mart and Kmart muscled their way into the toy market. Between 1985 and 1992, Wal-Mart doubled its market share, and Kmart saw its toy sales increase 25 percent in 1992 alone. (One tactic Kmart has found successful is stocking more low-priced toys during the Christmas season, to attract more shoppers.) "If Wal-Mart and the other discounters weren't around, Toys 'R' Us would have the toy market virtually to itself," remarks Greg Simpson of A.G. Edwards & Sons Inc. Toy prices at these discounters are consistently a few cents lower than they are at Toys "R" Us.

Toys "R" Us responded by offering to match the price advertised by any competitor on any toy. During the 1991 Christmas season, the company began giving away catalogs containing nearly $200 worth of coupons for everything from diapers to strollers to toys. Will these strategies help Toys "R" Us regain its stronghold in the U.S. market? Will pricing strategies have the same ramifications in international markets? As the company goes global, so its pricing practices must meet the challenges of its new markets. Executives at Toys "R" Us would probably agree that selling toys is not child's play.

Source: Toys "R" Us/Kids "R" Us Annual Report Year Ended February 1, 1992; "Brawls in Toyland," *Business Week*, December 21, 1992, p. 36.

CHAPTER 14

Fundamentals of Pricing

LEARNING OBJECTIVES

After completing this chapter, you should be able to:

1. Describe the role of pricing in the marketing mix.

2. Explain the economic principles that link price to sales and profits.

3. Describe approaches to pricing based on cost, profit, competition, and customer perception.

4. Compute prices based on markup and markdown pricing.

5. Execute a breakeven analysis.

6. Discuss legal and ethical issues surrounding pricing.

Creating Customer Value

Saturn

It was a bold move by the world's largest car maker. Suffering a hemorrhage of sales and workers, GM had to do something. So top executives asked the company's Advanced Product and Design Team, "Can GM build a world-class-quality small car in the United States that can compete successfully with the imports?" The team focused on a small-car project and cleaned the slate of traditional approaches to car design and manufacture. In time, the new car idea was dubbed the Saturn Project.

From the original Saturn team sprang another crucial team, intended to develop better business and better relations with labor. This new Group of 99 included plant managers, superintendents, production workers, skilled tradespeople, committee personnel, and staff from the United Auto Workers (UAW). In an unprecedented arrangement, the Group of 99 enabled GM management and the UAW to work toward the same business objectives. In January 1985, these two major teams—the Saturn Project and the Group of 99—became a separate subsidiary of GM called the Saturn Corporation. A totally new method of producing American automobiles was under way at a single plant in Spring Hill, Tennessee.

Quality has been a top priority at Saturn. Since the first cars rolled off the assembly line and into the driveways of American car buyers in 1991, Saturn has done a remarkable job of satisfying its customers. According to J.D. Power & Associates, the following year, Saturn rated third in customer satisfaction behind Lexus and Infiniti. It placed ahead of Acura, Mercedes-Benz, and Toyota.

Potential Saturn buyers aren't that easy to win over. They want the contemporary design and performance of a Japanese car. (Saturn's own research reveals that 70 percent of its buyers would not have bought another GM product instead of a Saturn.) "Saturn is a consumer-driven proposition, which makes it different then anything in the history of GM or Detroit," explains Laurel Cutler, vice chairman of FCB/Leber Katz Partners in New York. Teamwork and Saturn Corporation's establishment of "no-haggle" value pricing have contributed to this superior quality and high rate of customer satisfaction.

On the production end, the unique agreement between labor and management puts all workers on salary with a 20 percent bonus linked to quality, productivity, and profitability. It gives workers a voice in how the cars are built and the authority to solve problems. For instance, the team of line workers that assembles fixtures on the left side of each Saturn hires workers, approves parts, selects equipment, and handles its own budget. Regarding the relationship between Saturn and the UAW, Anthony Mills, a UAW business unit coordinator, says, "The union here is assuming that people who come to Saturn are accountable for their own actions."

Customers love the new pricing policy. When they walk into a Saturn store, they know how much the cars cost, instead of preparing themselves for a showdown with a traditional dealer. In fact, dealers are called "retailers" instead of "dealers" because, as Thomas Shaver, former director of marketing services, says, "We [are] in the retail business, not the deal business, where you had horrible negotiations over price." Saturn prices start at just $9,195, way below those of Lexus and Infiniti, the only two brands to top Saturn in the customer-satisfaction ratings. This gives the retailer an average gross profit of just under $1,300 per car.

The Saturn value-pricing method has been so popular that other car makers are following suit. Some GM lines, such as Chevrolet and Pontiac, now follow the new pricing policy. Ford Motor Co. assigns a single low price to all versions of a car (such as the Escort subcompact) equipped with a standard set of options—those that are traditionally most popular, such as air conditioning and power steering. In addition, many of the companies are producing *fewer* models and option packages, but overall better-equipped cars so that buyers are less confused about their choices (and prices) when they enter a store.

Saturn's method of building, pricing, and selling quality cars has indeed sparked a revolution in the American auto industry. Its approach got the company off to a fast start: by its second model year, it had attained a 2.1 percent share of the U.S. car market. Saturn alone can't save the aging, giant

industry. But it offers what American consumers value: excellent products at a fair price. As you read this chapter on the fundamentals of pricing, see how pricing reflects the philosophy of a quality organization such as Saturn.

Sources: Joseph B. White, "GM to Stress Value Pricing for '94 Models," *The Wall Street Journal,* July 12, 1993, pp. A3, A9; Raymond Serafin, "The Saturn Story," *Advertising Age,* November 16, 1992, pp. 1–4; Kathleen Kerwin, Larry Armstrong, and Thane Peterson, "The Big Three Think They Smell Blood," *Business Week,* September 28, 1992, pp. 34–35; David Woodruff, James B. Treece, Sunita Wadekar Bhargava, and Karen Lowry, "Saturn," *Business Week,* August 17, 1992; Richard LeFauve and Arnoldo C. Hax, "Managerial and Technological Innovations at Saturn Corporation," *MIT Management,* Spring 1992, pp. 8–18.

Chapter Overview

price
The amount of money, goods, or services that must be exchanged for ownership or use of a product.

Saturn's success shows that a high-quality product and a fair approach to pricing are important to success in marketing a product. A **price** is the amount of money, goods, or services that must be given to acquire ownership or use of a product (good or service). In the cities of Eastern Europe, the price of a taxi ride might be measured in packs of American cigarettes.[1] But in most cases, a price is stated in terms of money—say, $12 for a haircut or $9,200 for a Saturn car.

This chapter introduces the basic principles of pricing that marketers must rely on when they set prices. It begins with a general look at the role of pricing in the marketing mix. The chapter then describes economic concepts concerning price. Next, the chapter discusses the basic approaches to pricing: setting prices based on cost, profit, competition, and customer perceptions. Finally, the chapter addresses legal and ethical issues related to pricing.

The Role of Pricing in the Marketing Mix

The price of a product plays two major roles in the marketing mix. These two roles make setting the price for a product among the most important marketing decisions.

Like the other elements of the marketing mix, pricing influences how much of a product consumers or organizations purchase. In general, potential customers look for a price that reflects the benefits they think they will receive from the product. They also consider the price of the product relative to that of competitive offerings.

Price also influences whether selling the product will be profitable for the organization. (In the case of a nonprofit organization, it influences whether enough money will be raised to enable the organization to continue carrying out its mission.) A study of over 2,000 companies found that increasing price by 1 percent (assuming no loss in sales volume) has over three times the impact on operating profits of a 1 percent increase in unit sales volume. The effect on profits is much greater than the companies could realize from cutting their costs by the same percentage.[2] Of course, price increases usually lead to at least some drop in sales, so the pricing decision is as complex as it is important.

FIGURE 14.1

Marketing Communications Supporting a High-Price Strategy

CONSISTENCY WITH OTHER ELEMENTS OF THE MARKETING MIX

A marketing strategy is most effective when the price of a product is consistent with the other elements of the marketing mix. The product element of the marketing mix influences price by determining the product's quality, the cost to produce it, and the benefits it will deliver to customers. Furthermore, as described later in this chapter, the price typically shifts as the product moves through various stages in the product life cycle.

Moving a product through distribution channels also has several possible links to pricing. One is that a decision to use resellers means the producer usually gives up some control over pricing. For example, even if a producer puts an item in a package marked with a suggested retail price, a store owner might decide to put it on sale at a lower price. Resellers also contribute to the image of the product. Thus, items sold through discount stores are expected to cost less than the same category of item at more prestigious retailers. And transporting goods adds to their cost. Marketers must decide what pricing strategy will best take transportation costs into account. For example, transporting very bulky or heavy items is expensive, so the marketer might charge separately for shipping.

Marketing communication affects pricing strategy by influencing how potential customers perceive the product. If a marketing message emphasizes some way in which the product is outstanding, customers will tend to expect a higher price. Figure 14.1 illustrates this type of strategy for Parker Duofold pens. When marketing messages emphasize value or thriftiness, customers will expect a price no higher than that of competitors.

FIGURE 14.2

Sample Demand Curve

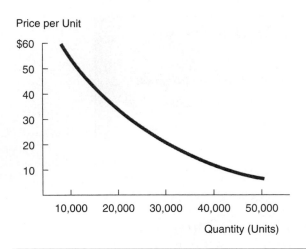

Price per Unit

$60, 50, 40, 30, 20, 10

10,000 20,000 30,000 40,000 50,000

Quantity (Units)

PRICE AND POSITIONING

A price consistent with the other elements of the marketing mix helps position the product. Nissan Motor Company's Altima is positioned as an excellent value—as well made as a luxury car but selling at a much lower price. Initially priced at $13,000 for the base model, the Altima was soon attracting more sales than had been forecasted. In the words of Christopher W. Cedergren, senior vice president of the marketing research firm AutoPacific Group, "Nissan's hit a home run, and the reason is price."[3]

Economics of Pricing

Price is the element of the marketing mix that links marketing considerations to economic considerations. To set a profitable price, marketers must be able to apply such economic concepts as demand curves and marginal analysis. These may seem largely theoretical. However, marketers are able to use marketing research to learn enough about patterns of demand to estimate some economic solutions.

DEMAND AND REVENUE

demand curve
The graph that shows the quantity of a product demanded at various prices.

To select the most profitable price, the marketer needs to know how much prospective customers will buy at various prices. In general, as shown in Figure 14.2, the lower the price of a product, the greater the demand for it. A graph such as this, which shows the quantity demanded at various prices, is called a **demand curve**. Each product has its own demand curve, and most follow the general pattern of sloping downward. This means that when the seller changes the price of a product, the amount demanded also changes. Thus, when Kraft cut cheese prices 8 percent, sales volume increased 5 percent.[4]

The shape of a demand curve for an individual firm is influenced by the market structure in which the organization is operating. As described in Chapter 2, a market structure may be a pure monopoly, an oligopoly, monopolistic competition, or pure competition:

- In a pure monopoly, a single firm sells a product for which there are no good substitutes. The firm has the market for the product to itself, so the demand curve for the firm is identical to the demand curve for the product. Thus, the monopolist typically is able to exert some influence on the price and quantity demanded of the product.
- In an oligopoly, the number of sellers is small enough for the activities of a single seller to affect other firms and for the activities of other firms to affect it. While the products the firms sell are often differentiated from one another, they are also good substitutes for each other. Because of the availability of attractive substitutes, the demand curve for the oligopolist will be fairly elastic.
- With monopolistic competition, there are many sellers of the product, but the product of each seller is in some way differentiated in customer's minds from the product of every other seller. Because of this product differentiation, the firm has some discretion in setting price and output. However, the availability of similar products means pricing discretion is limited and the demand curve faced by the firm will be highly elastic throughout its relevant range.
- With pure competition, there are many firms selling identical products, with no one firm large enough relative to the entire market to be able to influence market price. Under these circumstances, the firm can sell its entire output at the prevailing market price, and nothing above that price. it has virtually no pricing latitude and simply accepts the prevailing market price as a given.

In addition, a product's demand curve is likely to undergo changes throughout the life of the product. Effective promotion can shift the demand curve to the right, meaning that more of the product will be demanded at any price. Or the entry of new competitors into the market can change the slope of the demand curve. That is because potential buyers will be more reluctant to buy at a high price when they can take their business elsewhere. Changes in tastes and technology also lead to shifts in demand curves as customers become more or less interested in the product. For example, there has recently been a surge in the popularity of the paintings of Latin American artists such as Fernando Botero, Diego Rivera, and Frida Kahlo, resulting in record prices for their works.[5]

ESTIMATING DEMAND   How do marketers know what the demand will be at each possible price? The answer is that they don't know with certainty; rather, they make estimates. Their estimates are based on demographic and psychological factors of their target markets and on estimates of how sensitive sales of the product are to its price. These demand factors affect the shape of the demand curve for a particular product.

Consider the auto industry. Demographic data show that car prices have been rising faster than consumers' incomes. Psychological data suggest consumers are looking for a low price and don't want to assume the risks that accompany haggling with a car dealer. Car makers are responding with "value" prices—single, no-hassle prices on models equipped with a generous package of options. List prices for those packages are lower than before, but basic models are no longer available, leading to a slight boost in the overall prices paid.[6]

Demographic Factors   The demographics of the target market are useful in estimating demand by indicating how many potential buyers there are and whether they have the resources to buy at a particular price. Some specific questions marketers ask in this regard are the following:[7]

- How many potential buyers are there in the target market?
- What is the location of these potential buyers?
- Are they organizational buyers, channel members, or consumers?

- How much is the average buyer likely to spend?
- What is the economic strength of potential buyers?

Chapter 7 presented some guidelines for finding the answers to questions such as these.

When the marketer determines that potential customers are organizational buyers, this analysis needs to take a broad view of what constitutes demographic factors. The marketer looks at trends in the industry being served. Pharmaceutical companies are thus studying trends in drug purchases. They have noted that purchase decisions have shifted from individual physicians to large buyers such as health maintenance organizations and mail-order drug retailers.[8]

Psychological Factors   Marketers also consider psychological factors, that is, how potential buyers will perceive various prices or changes in price. They ask questions such as the following:[9]

- Will potential buyers use price as an indicator of the product's quality?
- Will they be favorably attracted by odd pricing such as 99 cents instead of $1, or $177 instead of $180?
- Will potential buyers perceive the price to be too high relative to what the product delivers?
- Are potential buyers concerned enough with prestige to pay more for the product's image?
- How much will potential buyers be willing to pay for the product?

In the case of marketing drugs, pharmaceutical companies have noted that buyers are placing more importance on low price. The traditional approach was to spend heavily to have salespeople (called detailers) visit doctors, explain particular drugs' advantages, and drop off free samples. Since the doctors didn't have to pay for the drugs they prescribed, performance easily outweighed price. In contrast, HMOs and mail-order pharmacies are less impressed by prestige and thus insist on lower prices.[10]

To find the answers to questions about psychological factors requires substantial marketing research. Even then, the information gathered may not accurately predict actual buying behavior. However, to accurately predict demand, marketers should at least consider psychological factors such as those addressed by the preceding list of questions.

price elasticity
A measure of the sensitivity of demand to changes in price.

Price Elasticity   A third basis for estimating demand is the product's price elasticity. **Price elasticity** is "a measure of the sensitivity of demand to changes in price."[11] Stated mathematically, it is the percentage change in the quantity demanded divided by the percentage change in price, or:

$$e = \frac{\Delta Q/Q}{\Delta P/P}$$

When $e > 1$, demand is said to be *elastic.* This means that a small change in price results in a large change in the quantity demanded. When a small change in price yields a smaller change in the quantity demanded ($e \leq 1$), demand is *inelastic.* Demand for a product is most likely to be inelastic if the product has few substitutes, is a necessity, and costs relatively little. Examples are gasoline and telephone service; most people keep driving and making phone calls even when prices go up.

Knowing the product's price elasticity helps marketers predict patterns in total revenue. In general, for a product with elastic demand, total revenue increases when the product's price declines. For example, if the cost of a European vacation were to fall, many consumers would decide that this is the year to vacation in Europe. The increase in the number of tourists would be great enough to generate more total rev-

FIGURE 14.3

Sample Demand Curves Showing Different Price Elasticities

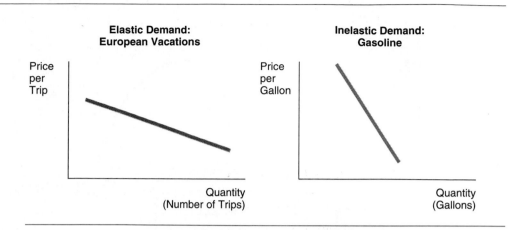

enue, even though the average tourist would spend less. If a product has inelastic demand, total revenue increases when the product's price increases. Thus, if the price of a loaf of bread goes up by a dime, most consumers will keep buying about the same amount of bread, and the seller can enjoy greater earnings. Figure 14.3 shows these relationships.

Sometimes marketers conduct research to learn about the price elasticity of their products. When Approach Software, based in Redwood City, California, prepared to introduce its first product, a database program, marketing director Jaleh Bisharat interviewed 30 prospective customers. Bisharat learned that they expected to pay at least $149. Then she sent a mailing to 50,000 prospects, offering each prospect the software at one of three prices: either $99, $129, or $149. Sales at the top price almost equaled those at $129, so the company tested an even higher price, $199. At that price, demand fell off. So Approach launched the software at an introductory price of $149.[12]

Often, conducting this type of research to determine price elasticity is considered too costly and time consuming. How can a marketer estimate price elasticity without offering the product at many different prices? One approach is to look at historical data and see how the quantity purchased varied as the product's price changed. When Bernard Chaus Inc. raised the prices of its women's clothing to match those of Liz Claiborne, sales revenues declined 20 percent, and the company went from generating profits to losing money. Chaus later lowered prices and found that unit sales went up more than enough to make up for the lower price per unit of clothing.[13] Another approach is to compare data across sales districts where different prices were charged. While these estimates have limitations, they can give marketers a sense of how potential customers will respond to different price levels.

ESTIMATING REVENUE   Demand curves and the theory related to them help marketers estimate the revenue that products are likely to generate at various prices. In making these estimates, marketers use three basic measures of revenue: total revenue, average revenue, and marginal revenue.

total revenue
The total amount of money received from the sale of a product.

Total revenue refers to the total amount of money received from the sale of a product. To find the total revenue (*TR*) associated with a given price, multiply the price (*P*) by the number of items sold (*Q*):

$$TR = P \times Q$$

FIGURE 14.4

Sample Total Revenue Curve

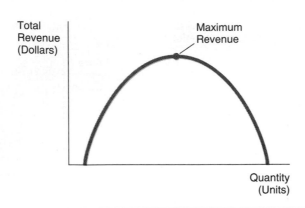

At some price, represented by the peak of the curve in Figure 14.4, the revenue reaches its maximum amount. Assume that a shoe store could sell 1,000 pairs of shoes a week at $5 each, 100 pairs of shoes a week at $75, and 10 pairs of shoes a week at $500. Multiplying quantity by price gives total revenues of $5,000, $7,500, and $5,000, respectively. Of these three pricing choices, $75 would yield the greatest revenues—$2,500 more than if the shoes were priced at either $5 or $500. From this example, you can see why cutting prices does not always generate greater revenues, even when more of the product is sold. This concept is important for the marketer to remember when it is tempting to stimulate sales with a price cut.

average revenue
The average amount of money received from the sale of one unit of a product.

Average revenue is the average amount of money received from the sale of one unit of a product. Assuming that the product sells at a single price, the average revenue would equal the price of one unit. To find average revenue (AR), divide total revenue (TR) by the quantity of units sold (Q):

$$AR = \frac{TR}{Q}$$

marginal revenue
The change in total revenue that results from selling one additional unit of a product.

Marginal revenue (MR) is the change in total revenue (ΔTR) that results from selling one additional unit of a product (ΔQ):

$$MR = \frac{\Delta TR}{\Delta Q}$$

If a museum that has sold 5,000 membership subscriptions can sell one more for $50, its marginal revenue would be $50 (that is, 50/1). To sell 5 million subscriptions, the museum would probably have to set a lower price, so marginal revenue at the greater quantity would be lower. Thus, the marginal revenue curve slopes downward because to sell more and more of a product, the organization has to offer it at a lower and lower price.

PROFIT MAXIMIZATION AND MARGINAL ANALYSIS

profit
The difference between the revenues generated by a product and the costs it incurs.

The measurements just described are important for identifying the price at which the organization will earn the greatest profit. A business's **profit** is the difference between the revenues it generates and the total costs it incurs:

Profit = Total Revenues – Total Costs

FIGURE 14.5

Types of Graphs Used for Marginal Analysis

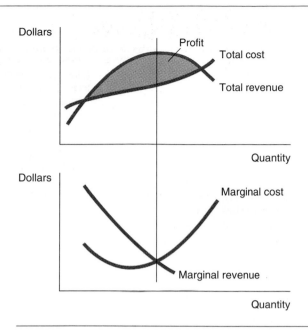

If the organization sells a number of units of product at the same price, its total revenues equal the number of units sold times the price per unit. For such a situation, the profit equation can be stated as follows:

Profit = (Number of Units × Price per Unit) − Total Costs

Suppose an office-cleaning service charged its customers $12 per hour and handled 100 hours of work in one week. If its total costs for that week were $1,000, its profits for the week would be (100 hr. x $12/hr.) − $1,000 = $200.

A general economic principle is that a business seeks to maximize the profit side of this equation. Raising the price higher and higher would have this effect if such changes did not affect the amount sold or the expenses incurred. However, the problem is more complex because price does affect the other numbers in the equation. Recall that demand curves slope downward; a lower price means that more units will be sold. Also, the more units sold, the greater the total costs to produce and market the products.

At what level of sales (and price) will the organization earn the greatest profit? One way to determine the answer is to use **marginal analysis**, or the technique for finding the greatest profits by measuring the economic effect of producing and selling each additional unit of product. To conduct marginal analysis, the marketer begins by looking at how costs and revenues change in response to changes in quantity.

The basic pattern of these relationships looks like the graph at the top of Figure 14.5. Total costs increase along with an increase in the quantity produced and sold. The costs increase fastest when the quantity is small (because the organization is getting the hang of production) and when the quantity is very large (because the organization has to devote more expensive resources, such as personnel working overtime and machinery that is wearing out). Total revenue rises to a peak and then falls off, because to sell the largest quantities, the organization would have to charge lower prices.

The bottom portion of Figure 14.5 shows how this pattern is reflected in marginal cost and marginal revenue. (In mathematical terms, these represent the slopes of the

marginal analysis
The technique for finding the greatest profits by measuring the effect of producing and selling each additional unit of a product.

Put It Into Practice

INTERVIEW A LOCAL BUSINESSPERSON

As you've seen, there are several ways to set a price for a product. To give yourself an idea of how real-world businesses set prices for their products, form a team of three or four class-mates and interview several businesspeople who are accessible to you. Choose local businesses, such as a pharmacy, car dealer, clothing shop owner, insurance broker, or carpenter (or someone else you know)—whoever is willing to discuss with you how he or she arrives at a price for goods or services.

Ask about any regulations that restrict pricing in the particular business. Ask what approach (or approaches) each businessperson uses to set a price, and why. Ask about any products that were particularly successful or unsuccessful due to their price.

After conducting the interviews, meet as a team to discuss your findings. What differences and similarities did you find among the businesses? For instance, did the economic climate in a particular area influence how the businesspeople their set prices? Present your findings and conclusions to the class.

---

two curves on the top.) Where profits reach their peak (total revenue is the farthest above total cost), marginal cost equals marginal revenue. Thus, if the marketer can estimate the organization's marginal cost and marginal revenue, he or she will be able to identify the quantity at which profits will be the greatest. By referring to the demand curve for the product, the marketer can identify the price at which this quantity will be demanded.

Approaches to Pricing

While marginal analysis is the rational way to price products from an economic standpoint, gathering the precise information needed can be difficult and costly, even for the basic equations presented in this chapter. Further complicating the task, in the real world, there are more variables than in these equations. Compaq Computer Corporation found that when it lowered the price of its computers, it didn't simply sell more of those models. Rather, many customers used the same amount of money to buy more sophisticated computers. Thus, at the lower price level, the company generated more dollars per order—but not of the same products.[14]

Given the challenges of using marginal analysis, marketers in practice approach the pricing decision in various ways. The basic approaches are based on cost, profit, competition, and customer perception. These approaches are not mutually exclusive. In fact, the marketer can benefit from considering all of them: the minimum charge to cover costs and earn a profit, an amount that matches or beats competitors' prices, and an amount that equals customers' perceptions of what the product is worth. A simplified version of this approach is being used by the Vermont grocery store owner who told one of his suppliers' salespeople, "What you charge tells me how low I can go. What my competitor sets prices at is how high I can go. I just pick a place in between, and that's my price."[15] (To gain more insight into how real-world marketers approach pricing, see "Put It into Practice.")

fixed costs
Expenses that remain unchanged over a wide range of quantities of a product.

PRICING BASED ON COST

As a general rule, the price of a product must be high enough to cover the total cost of production, communications, and channels of distribution. The total cost includes fixed and variable costs. **Fixed costs** are the expenses that remain the same over a wide range

Marketing Movers & Shakers

WALTER MINNICK AND TJ INTERNATIONAL

The northern spotted owl and the forest products industry have been locked in a struggle. Both the industry and the owl needed the timber in the Pacific Northwest in order to survive. Federal plans to protect the bird severely restricted the harvest of the old-growth forests. Lumberjacks and management alike felt threatened by new environmental policies and concerns.

An exception was Walter Minnick, the 50-year-old president and CEO of Boise, Idaho's TJ International Inc. (whose partner is the Canadian firm MacMillan Bloedel Ltd., a $3 billion wood and paper company). Why is

Minnick unperturbed? "We and others have developed a way to build houses out of forestry resources that are independent of the spotted-owl forest," he explains.

TJ International produces "engineered wood," a product that is manufactured from strips of wood or veneer that are laminated together with resins, forming structural beams something like the I-beams used in construction. TJ's beams are just as strong as those made from regular lumber, but of higher quality because they neither warp nor have knots. In addition, TJ doesn't have to depend on old-growth forests for its materials; the wood strips and veneer come from small, fast-growing trees. Minnick says, "Engineered wood is an example of using technology to help solve a very sharp public-policy issue."

Where does price enter the arena? The fact is, engineered wood has in the past cost up to 90 percent more than real lumber. Builders and contractors have been reluctant to try the new product because of its unfamiliarity and high price. But with the new restrictions on the harvest of old-growth forests and a gain in housing starts, the price of lumber itself soared

90 percent between October 1992 and March 1993, bringing the prices of the two products very close to one another. Larry Zarker of the National Association of Home Builders notes, "You could see the market [for engineered wood products] explode."

TJ International's marketing challenges are not over, of course. The company depends on lumber in order to manufacture its beams, so the high price of lumber means high costs for TJ. In addition, new competion has appeared: major lumber companies such as Louisiana-Pacific, Georgia-Pacific, and Boise Cascade have all started making their own engineered wood products.

Still, TJ owns a healthy market share (sales recently topped $400 million) and is somewhat protected by its partnership with MacMillan Bloedel, not to mention the fact that TJ has a head start on technology and experience. It also has Minnick at the helm, an avid outdoorsman who hikes, backpacks, and serves on the council of the Wilderness Society. He genuinely wants to preserve U.S. forests. Not many lumbermen have the opportunity to coexist so peacefully with the spotted owl.

Source: Dori Jones Yang, "A Lumberman Goes Against the Grain," *Business Week,* March 29, 1993, pp. 52–53.

---

variable costs
Costs that change along with changes in quantity of a product.

of quantities. A major fixed cost is the production facility. Only after production increases by a very large amount will an organization build another factory. **Variable costs** are the costs that change along with changes in quantity. For example, materials and labor costs are greater when the organization produces or sells more goods or services.

Failure to cover total cost means the organization will be losing money on the product. In an effort to ensure that revenues will cover costs, marketers use some form of cost-oriented pricing. These techniques basically involve determining the cost to produce and sell a product, then making sure the selling price is higher. A former approach to pricing at Compaq Computer Corporation was to find the total cost of all the features on a particular computer model, then determine what suppliers would charge for all the necessary parts. Then the company would add on a profit margin of, say, 40 percent. The result was the price charged to dealers, who would tack on another markup of their own.[16] (For another example of how the cost of manufacturing a product affects its price, see "Marketing Movers & Shakers.")

TABLE 14.1

Typical Markup Percentages

TYPE OF PURCHASE	MARKUP PERCENTAGE*
Shoes	48.55%
Women's dresses	47.13
Men's wear	38.24
Sporting goods	28.98
Books and magazines	27.50
Auto accessories	27.01
Records and tapes	25.14
Tobacco	13.13

*Percent of original retail price.

Source: Gene A. German and Debra J. Perosio, *Operating Results of Mass Retail Stores* (Washington, DC: International Mass Retail Association, 1989–1990), p. 67.

ADVANTAGES   Cost-based pricing is relatively easy to use. This makes it popular among sellers who handle many different products. The emphasis on covering costs also makes it appealing for pricing nonroutine jobs such as construction and the development of military weapons. AutoResearch Laboratories Inc. (ALI) uses a cost-based approach to set prices for its customized testing services. When preparing to bid on a job, ALI conducts a detailed analysis of all the costs it expects to incur. It adds a fixed percentage to the total cost. If the result is higher than competitive prices for services of the same quality, ALI considers adjusting the percentage it adds to its costs. However, ALI rarely lowers the percentage below what it considers its base profit margin.[17]

LIMITATIONS   When using cost-oriented pricing techniques, the marketer must be aware of their limitations. Perhaps most important, these techniques do not consider the effect of price on demand. Thus, an organization might find that a price high enough to cover costs and deliver a comfortable profit is so high that buyers turn to competing or substitute products. If, as a result, sales are lower than expected, profits may suffer as well.

Cost-oriented pricing also fails to take into account what competitors are charging. To compete profitably, the organization might have to lower its costs rather than charge enough to cover high costs. Or the organization might have to distinguish its product in some way to match the price it wants to charge. Another way to make cost-based pricing more responsive to demand is to add on a smaller percentage for products that are price sensitive.

markup pricing
Adding a percentage or dollar amount to a product's cost to arrive at a selling price.

MARKUP PRICING   To use **markup pricing**, the marketer adds a percentage to the product's cost in order to arrive at a selling price. There are two basic ways to state the markup percentage:

1. The easiest markup percentage to understand is a markup stated as a *percentage of the cost* to the reseller. If the reseller pays $9 for a compact disc and sells it for $15, the markup of $6 is 66.7 percent of the cost ($6/$9 = .667).
2. More typically, however, the markup percentage is stated as the *percentage of the selling price* that is added to the cost to get the selling price. In the case of the compact disc, the markup as a percentage of the selling price is $6/$15 = .40, or 40 percent.

Table 14.1 shows some typical markup percentages, stated as a percentage of selling price.

A variation of this approach is to add on a dollar amount rather than a percentage to arrive at the selling price. For example, a contractor might set a price for a project $10,000 above the expected cost. This variation of markup pricing is sometimes called cost-plus pricing.

Markup pricing is common among resellers. This approach is often more practical than analyzing the market forces for each of hundreds or thousands of products.

RATE-OF-RETURN PRICING A variation of cost-based pricing commonly used by manufacturers is **rate-of-return pricing**. This pricing technique involves determining total costs, then adding a desired rate of return on the investment to produce the product. The marketer may add either a percentage return or a particular dollar amount. For example, return on investment (ROI) is the profit as a percentage of the capital invested in the operation.

rate-of-return pricing
Determining total costs, then adding a desired rate of return on the investment.

To apply rate-of-return pricing, the marketer uses a formula such as this:

$$\text{Price} = \text{Total Cost/Unit} + \text{ROI(Investment/Unit)}$$

The total cost per unit includes both the variable costs to make each unit (notably, the labor and materials devoted to producing it) and a share of the fixed costs. Suppose a manufacturer is planning to produce 10,000 skateboards at a total cost of $60,000. The required investment to fund this operation is $450,000, and the company seeks a 25 percent return on its investment. The company would compute the price to charge resellers as follows:

$$\text{Price} = \frac{\$60,000}{10,000} + \frac{.25(\$450,000)}{10,000} = \$6 + \$11.25 = \$17.25/\text{Unit}$$

From this example, you can see how failure to meet sales forecasts can hurt profits. At a price of $17.25 but sales of only 5,000 skateboards, ROI falls to less than 6 percent. This is not much more than the company could earn by leaving its funds in a bank savings account.

 ## PRICING BASED ON PROFIT

Of course, for a business to prosper, it has to think beyond its costs to its profits. Southwest Airlines has achieved exceptional profits with a low-cost, low-price strategy. The company keeps its costs down by avoiding such amenities as serving meals, offering assigned seats, and making connections with other airlines. Instead, Southwest offers low fares coupled with frequent service out of relatively small airports on one type of aircraft. Notes an observer, "Wherever Southwest goes, three things quickly happen: fares come down, traffic usually triples, and the airline rouses a rabid following."[18]

A logical way of pricing based on profit is to use marginal analysis to identify the point at which profits will be greatest—the point at which marginal costs equal marginal revenues. Unfortunately, in practice it is difficult to construct accurate demand curves and to accurately identify the total costs associated with each product. The limitations of marginal analysis lead marketers to seek other ways of identifying a profitable price. One such technique is breakeven analysis.

breakeven analysis
The technique for identifying the sales volume at a given price needed to cover costs.

breakeven point
The level of sales at which total revenues equal total costs.

Breakeven analysis is a technique for identifying the sales volume at the price needed to cover costs ("break even"). The level of sales at which total revenues equal total costs is called the **breakeven point**. Rhino Records has a breakeven point of just 15,000 copies of an album. It keeps its costs low by focusing on reissues while its big competitors are trying to go platinum with new recordings.[19]

FIGURE 14.6

**Sample Graph for
Breakeven Analysis**

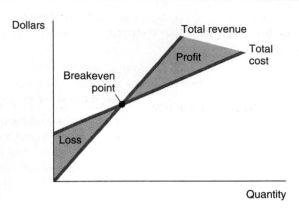

FINDING A BREAKEVEN POINT   To conduct breakeven analysis, the marketer can construct graphs such as the one shown in Figure 14.6. *For a given price,* the marketer estimates the revenues that would be earned at various quantities. Then the marketer graphs the total costs of producing and marketing those quantities. This graph makes some assumptions commonly used to simplify breakeven analysis. First, it assumes that the curve for total revenues will be a straight line; in other words, each unit is sold at the same price. It also assumes that the total cost curve will be a straight line. In other words, the cost to produce each additional unit is the same. The point at which these two curves intersect is the breakeven point. The marketer would want to offer the product at the specified price only if the organization expects to sell more than the quantity at the breakeven point.

An alternative to using the graphs is to use the following formula for computing a breakeven point (in units):

$$\text{Breakeven Point} = \frac{\text{Fixed Costs}}{\text{Price} - \text{Variable Cost per Unit}}$$

Thus, in the earlier example of skateboards, assume that the total cost of $60,000 to produce 10,000 units included fixed costs of $17,500 and variable costs of $4.25 per unit. At a price of $18.25, the breakeven point would be computed as follows:

$$\text{Breakeven Point} = \frac{\$17,500}{\$18.25 - \$4.25} = 1,250 \text{ units}$$

If the cost estimate were correct and the organization in fact sold 1,250 units, it would break even.

APPLYING BREAKEVEN ANALYSIS   As in this example, once the marketer has estimated the breakeven point, it's necessary to consider whether it is likely to sell that quantity at the given price. The marketer might compare the breakeven points for several prices to see which breakeven points the organization seems likely to be able to meet or surpass. The more familiar the marketer is with the demand curve for the product, the more accurate this analysis can be. Thus, the marketer combines breakeven analysis with analysis of customer demand.

Of course, the marketer doesn't want merely to cover costs; the price should also be set at a level that will generate a profit. The marketer can incorporate the specific profit objective into breakeven analysis. To do this, the marketer adds the desired level of profits to the total fixed costs in the preceding equation. In the previous example, the marketer might seek to earn a $21,000 profit. Thus, the equation would be revised as follows:

$$\text{New Breakeven Point} = \frac{\text{Fixed Costs} + \text{Desired Profit}}{\text{Price} - \text{Variable Cost per Unit}}$$

$$= \frac{\$17,500 + \$21,000}{\$18.25 - \$4.25} = 2,750 \text{ Units}$$

As this example shows, the organization has to sell more units at a given price to meet the objective of earning a profit rather than just covering costs. With this revised equation, the marketer can determine the breakeven point for achieving the desired profit level.

PRICING BASED ON COMPETITION

Marketers also must take the competition into account when setting prices. They must be able to meet competitors' prices or show why their own product is worth more. Competitors' prices are especially important under the following conditions:

- There are many competitors.
- Competitors are large.
- It is hard to create distinctive differences among products.
- Competitors are a convenient source for customers in the target market.

For example, when the product is hard to set apart, as in the case of rubber bands or coal, the organization will usually match competitors' prices.

COMPETITIVE ENVIRONMENT   As noted earlier, the competitive environment influences how the marketer considers competitors when selecting a price. Sometimes the marketer must simply accept the going price rather than use some of the pricing approaches described earlier. In such cases, management will want to make sure that if the organization is not operating at a profit, it is looking for ways to keep costs down.

Even if the organization does not currently have much competition, marketers must keep in mind that the situation can change. Especially if marketing the product proves highly profitable, competing organizations are likely to enter the market. Also, the marketer must expect competition if the market is relatively easy to enter. For years, Procter & Gamble was able to enjoy the rewards of pricing its Pampers and Luvs diapers 33 to 35 percent above discount alternatives. However, consumers found high quality in private-label diapers, and sales of P&G's diapers suffered. So the company has countered with price cuts. A recent cut of 5 percent for Pampers and 16 percent for Luvs represented the third time in ten months that P&G cut diaper prices.[20]

COMPETITION-BASED PRICING TACTICS   There are four basic approaches to setting prices relative to the competition:

follow-the-leader pricing
Pricing tactic of following any price changes made by the industry leaders.

1. **Follow-the-leader pricing**—This pricing approach consists of following any price changes made by the industry leaders. This is typical of an oligopoly, that is, a

FIGURE 14.8

**Value Pricing
Promoted in an Ad**

Presenting the world's only American made, suspension ready, epoxy bonded, Easton Aluminum racer with full Shimano STX Special Edition and a lifetime warranty.

At under $700, it's a value as clear as black & white.

Trek 7000 Performance Aluminum. The difference is higher performance and a lower price.

Trek Aluminum Mountain. There is no frame of reference.

TREK USA

value
The ratio of perceived benefits to price.

VALUE PRICING   Most potential customers are looking for **value**, that is, the ratio of perceived benefits to price.[27] Mathematically, this relationship is shown as follows:

$$\text{Value} = \frac{\text{Perceived Benefits}}{\text{Price}}$$

From this ratio, you can see that a product's value is greater when customers perceive greater benefits or when the price falls.

value pricing
Setting a price so that a product's value is higher than the value of competing products.

To respond to the interest in value, marketers may engage in **value pricing**. This strategy involves setting the price so that the product's value is higher than the value of competing products. Value pricing may entail setting a low price, the marketer may promote high perceived benefits of the product, or the strategy may emphasize both high benefits and low price. Quality inspectors at J. C. Penney compared the store's girls' turtlenecks with similar sweaters from Lands' End, The Gap, and L. L. Bean and found Penney's sweaters were inferior. Designers at Penney's responded by setting more stringent specifications for fabric, fit, and construction. Then the store priced the improved turtlenecks 38 percent below the ones sold at The Gap. As a result, sales of the sweaters tripled. Similar tactics throughout the store have caused its sales growth to outstrip that of competitors.[28] Bicycle manufacturer Trek® USA has also adopted a form of value pricing (see Figure 14.8).

As indicated earlier in the chapter, price and perceived benefits are not always independent of one another. Sometimes higher-priced products are perceived as having greater quality. Therefore, setting the price too low may lead customers to conclude that the product offers relatively few benefits, so that its value is also low. To uncover such views, marketers engage in marketing research.

Value pricing is most likely to succeed when the organization focuses on identifying customer needs. Such a quality-driven approach starts by finding out what customers need and how much they value a product that meets those needs. Then the organization

TABLE 14.2 **Laws Limiting Pricing Practices**	LAW	LIMITED PRACTICES
	Sherman Antitrust Act	Price fixing
	Consumer Goods Pricing Act	Resale price maintenance
	Federal Trade Commission Act	Deceptive pricing practices
	Robinson-Patman Act	Price discrimination that lessens or damages competition; discrimination in the use of promotional pricing
	Laws of most countries	Dumping

seeks to develop a marketing mix that includes a price reflecting the value the customer places on the product. To do this profitably, the organization can use cross-functional teams to control costs at all stages of development, production, and marketing.

Thus, an organization that practices the quality approach to marketing is particularly well positioned to benefit from value pricing. By giving customers what they want, this organization can provide value even at a comfortable markup. For example, the marketer may be able to show organizational buyers that a product will save them more money than they paid for it.

Legal and Ethical Issues in Pricing

The ways in which marketers use price to achieve various objectives should be legal and ethical. The government has created a number of laws and regulations that limit prices and pricing activities. In addition, some ethical considerations suggest issues of concern to marketers.

GOVERNMENT REGULATION OF PRICING

To promote fair trade, federal and state governments impose some limitations on pricing decisions. As summarized in Table 14.2, the U.S. government has limited price fixing, deceptive pricing, price discrimination, and dumping. State laws and the laws of other countries vary. Therefore, the marketer should consult a lawyer about regulation of prices in the states and countries where the organization operates.

price fixing
The practice of sellers' making agreements with competitors or distributors about the final price of a product.

Sherman Antitrust Act
The law banning price fixing.

Federal Trade Commission Act
The law that prohibits deceptive pricing practices.

PRICE FIXING   Sellers may not make agreements about the final price with competitors or distributors of their products. Such practices are known as **price fixing**. The U.S. law that banned this practice is the **Sherman Antitrust Act**.

Producers have often tried to use a form of price fixing known as "resale price maintenance." This involves forming agreements with retailers under which the retailers must sell the producer's products at prices set by the producer. Producers have argued that resale price maintenance enables them to maintain a price that supports the positioning strategy for the product. However, it also limits the ability of retailers to compete on the basis of price. For that reason, resale price maintenance was declared illegal under the Consumer Goods Pricing Act of 1975.

DECEPTIVE PRICING   The **Federal Trade Commission Act** prohibits deceptive pricing practices. An example would be to mark goods with an extremely high price, then announce a "price reduction" and sell the product at the normal price. Likewise, a

When Japanese firms were accused of dumping microchips in the United States, Intel and other U.S. companies began developing more sophisticated chips to meet special needs. Intel recently launched a chip four times bigger than Intel's previous chip, the 486. Pictured is the Pentium chip and Vino Dham, who managed the final stages of the 486 project and led the team that developed the Pentium chip.

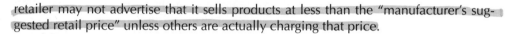

retailer may not advertise that it sells products at less than the "manufacturer's suggested retail price" unless others are actually charging that price.

PRICE DISCRIMINATION   Other restrictions have to do with charging different prices to customers when the price difference does not reflect a cost difference to the seller. Such a practice is called **price discrimination**. Price discrimination that lessens or damages competition is prohibited by the **Robinson-Patman Act.**

This prohibition applies only to goods, not services, and covers products of the same grade and quality. For example, a seller that uses promotional pricing, such as special discounts, free goods, or merchandising service, must offer them to all customers on equal terms in proportion to the size of their purchases.

price discrimination
The practice of charging different prices to customers when the price difference does not reflect a cost difference.

Robinson-Patman Act
The law that bans price discrimination when it damages competition.

dumping
The practice of pricing a product below cost or below the going price in the domestic market.

DUMPING   Imports are subject to antidumping laws in the United States and most other countries. In fact, the latest international agreement under the General Agreement on Tariffs and Trade preserves the right of member nations to act on complaints of dumping. **Dumping** is the practice of pricing a product below the cost to produce it or below the going price in the domestic market. Presumably, an importer might use dumping to gain market share in the foreign market, thereby taking business—and jobs—away from domestic manufacturers.

Of course, forbidding dumping means that customers will pay higher prices than they otherwise might. Recently, the U.S. International Trade Commission (ITC) found that steel imports from 16 countries were priced unfairly. As a result, some imported steel would be subject to stiff duties (taxes on imports). The higher costs resulting from this decision could cause U.S. consumers to pay $1 billion in higher prices.[29]

Antidumping policy also seems to be based on the view that domestic sellers can't find creative ways to respond to a low-price strategy of a foreign competitor. But around the time Japanese firms were being accused of dumping semiconductors (microchips) in the United States, Intel and other U.S. companies began developing more sophisticated "design-rich" chips to meet special needs. This gave U.S. firms the lead in the high-profit end of the market for microchips.[30] Likewise, Motorola once faced a plunge in the price of Japanese pagers to a level so low Motorola's managers were convinced their foreign competitors were dumping. Motorola responded by meeting its competitors' prices and by working with its employees and suppliers to aggressively cut costs. Rather than cutting costs by sacrificing quality, Motorola discovered it could save money by eliminating defects.[31]

IS CREATIVE PRICING SNEAKY OR SMART?

You Decide

Small businesses get hit hard by big changes in the economy. During the recession of the early 1990s, some just didn't survive. When the economy began to make a tentative recovery, those that did were reluctant to jeopardize their reprieve by raising prices. But for some, raising prices was an absolute necessity—as long as they followed certain rules of thumb, such as not publicizing the event. "You don't want to call attention to yourself," notes management consultant H. Gene Berger, "especially if you're running a little company that relies on a small number of customers."

How did some of these companies go about increasing prices without losing customers? One home health care firm hired Berger's agency (Jay Ile Associates, in New Jersey) to determine whether it could raise its prices selectively. In studying the firm's pricing structure, Berger learned that in some cases the company was actually charging as little as one-third of its competitors' rates. So Berger recommended that the company gradually raise prices for those customers by up to 50 percent over an 18-month period. In the end, the firm's prices remained below the competition's. Customers didn't complain because they knew they were still getting the best price for the service.

Another small company, Algoma Hardwoods Inc. of Algoma, Wisconsin, estimated that it could increase its revenues by introducing a new line of premium products at a premium price. The company began to manufacture the specially made, high-quality doors and windows that are now required in some buildings by the Americans with Disabilities Act. During the first half of 1993, the product line increased the company's total sales of doors and windows by up to 30 percent. By setting a premium price on a premium (and necessary) product, Algoma Hardwoods raised its revenues.

A third company, California-based American Lock & Supply Inc., reorganized its pricing structure to tailor hundreds of different pricing programs to its different buyers. Discounts vary according to such characteristics as order size and the customer's need for customized services. Some customers complained, but the company's president stressed that prices were still competitive. Few customers actually left for the competition.

Do you think these three companies practiced smart or sneaky pricing tactics? If you see a difference among the three companies, explain why. Which of the three would you say probably take(s) a quality approach, and why?

Source: Michael Selz, "Small Firms Use Variety of Ploys to Raise Prices," *The Wall Street Journal*, June 17, 1993, pp. B1–B2.

ETHICS OF PRICING

The laws just described ban a number of pricing tactics. For the most part, these tactics are both illegal and unethical in the United States. However, some pricing tactics are legal but of dubious ethical value.

UNETHICAL PRACTICES Prices that confuse customers may be unethical. For example, some prices, such as air fares, have such a complex structure that they can be overwhelming. If potential customers can't figure out how to get a lower price, they may spend more than they have to. Or the pricing structure may encourage customers to buy features they don't really need. For instance, car rental companies used to add on a charge for insurance, even though most renters would already be covered by insurance on their own cars. For more on the ethics of pricing, see "You Decide."

Also, customers may interpret claims of low prices more literally than they may be intended. Thus, Wal-Mart once used the slogan "Always the low price. Always." Concern that customers might take this statement literally as a legally binding promise that Wal-Mart would have the lowest price on every item in the store helped to motivate management to tone down the wording. Wal-Mart now says, "Always low prices. Always."[32]

Sometimes marketers set a high price as an indicator of quality and exclusivity. But what if the product isn't really superior to the competition's? Is the high price misleading? Are customers getting anything extra for the greater expense? If not, perhaps customers are being cheated.

At the other extreme, some stores advertise very low prices for certain products in order to attract customers to the store. Then the store's salespeople tell the customers about the limitations of the low-priced products and steer them to higher-priced models or brands. The salespeople may even report that the lower-priced models are out of stock. Using such pricing tactics as a basis for educating customers may not seem so bad, but the practice is often used in a deceitful way. In its negative form, this pricing practice is called **bait and switch**. Bait-and-switch tactics are illegal as well as unethical.

bait and switch
The practice of advertising low prices for certain products, then claiming that the low-priced products are of poor quality or unavailable.

ETHICAL PRACTICES   On a more positive note, there are many ways to use pricing fairly. Pricing tactics may even be an extension of social responsibility. After Hurricane Andrew devastated South Florida, Home Depot stores declined to raise their prices, even though some suppliers reacted to the intense demand for building materials by jacking up prices as much as 40 percent. By refusing to take advantage of their customers' plight, Home Depot stores were practicing relationship marketing—focusing on building long-term relationships with customers, rather than simply on the profit to be derived from individual transactions. Observed Kerry Herndon, a flower grower in Homestead, Florida, "If they had spent $50 million on advertising, they couldn't have bought the good will they got" by holding the line on prices.[33]

This and the next chapter introduce basic considerations that marketers can use to price their products profitably *and* ethically. Perhaps the most rewarding approach is to use the quality approach to marketing. That is, marketers can offer products that meet customers' needs so well that they will be delighted to pay the asking price in exchange for the product's benefits.

Summary

The price of a product plays two major roles in the marketing mix. It influences how much of the product customers will purchase, and it influences whether selling the product will be profitable. The price of a product should be consistent with other elements of the marketing mix.

To set the best price for a product, marketers must try to find out how much of the product customers will buy, and at what prices. The demand curve illustrates the relationship between price and quantity demanded. Marketers try to estimate demand based on demographic and psychological factors that affect price elasticity and total demand. The demand curve also helps marketers estimate the revenue a product is likely to generate, including total revenue, average revenue, and marginal revenue. Estimates of revenue help marketers determine potential profits. To determine at what level of sales and price the company will earn the greatest profit, marketers can use marginal analysis.

The approaches to pricing are based on cost, profit, competition, and customer perception. Pricing based on cost can take the form of markup pricing or rate-of-return pricing. Pricing based on profit often uses breakeven analysis to determine the breakeven point, where total revenues equal total costs, and additional sales constitute profit. Marketers must be able to meet competitors' prices or show why their product is worth more. To set prices based on competition, marketers may use follow-the-leader pricing, adaptive pricing, opportunistic pricing, and predatory pricing. Finally, pricing based on customer perception involves learning as much about the customer as possible in order to set a price that represents what customers think the product is worth. When setting prices based on customer perception, marketers can use demand-backward pricing or value pricing.

Of the legal and ethical issues that surround pricing, many are strictly regulated by the government. The Sherman Antitrust Act, Consumer Goods Pricing Act, Federal Trade Commission Act, and Robinson-Patman Act were passed to curtail price fixing, price discrimination, and dumping.

KEY TERMS AND CONCEPTS

price (p. 410)

demand curve (p. 412)

price elasticity (p. 414)

total revenue (p.415)

average revenue (p. 416)

marginal revenue (p. 416)

profit (p. 416)

marginal analysis (p. 417)

fixed costs (p. 418)

variable costs (p. 419)

markup pricing (p. 420)

rate-of-return pricing (p. 421)

breakeven analysis (p. 421)

breakeven point (p. 421)

follow-the-leader pricing (p. 423)

adaptive pricing (p. 424)

opportunistic pricing (p. 424)

predatory pricing (p. 424)

reference price (p. 425)

demand-backward pricing (p. 425)

value (p. 426)

value pricing (p. 426)

price fixing (p. 427)

Sherman Antitrust Act (p. 427)

Federal Trade Commission Act (p. 427)

price discrimination (p. 428)

Robinson-Patman Act (p. 428)

dumping (p. 428)

bait and switch (p. 430)

REVIEW AND DISCUSSION QUESTIONS

1. In what ways is the price of a product intertwined with the marketing mix?
2. According to the general pattern of demand curves, would demand be relatively high or low for the following products?
   a. Diamond earrings that cost $2,000
   b. Single-serve nonfat yogurt with a price recently cut by 5 percent
   c. Cowboy boots that cost $75, in a region where there is a surge of interest in country music and dancing
   d. A guided tour of several national parks, after an effective advertising campaign
   e. Office furniture, six months after several new competitors have entered the market
3. Imagine you are a marketer responsible for recommending a price for an organic deterrent to garden pests (insects or rodents).
   a. What demographic and psychological factors might you consider in estimating demand for your product?
   b. How would you expand your analysis if you were targeting Britain and Canada as well as the United States?
4. For each of the following examples, compute the price elasticity and indicate whether demand for the product is elastic or inelastic.
   a. Dr. Koo is a family physician in rural West Virginia. When his insurance costs went up, he raised his basic charge for an office visit from $20 to $25. The number of patients who came for office visits in a month declined from 200 to 180.
   b. When ABC Supermarkets marked one-pound bags of M&Ms candies down to $1.50 from $2.50, sales rose by 65 percent.

5. An office-supply catalog lists cork bulletin boards with oak frames for $60 each. Last year it sold 480 of these.
   a. What was the retailer's total revenue from the bulletin boards?
   b. What was the average revenue?
   c. What was the marginal revenue at 450 bulletin boards?
6. Which basis for pricing (cost, profit, competition, or customer perception) would you use for the pest-control product in question 3? Explain your choice. Remember that you can use a combination of approaches if you think that will work best.
7. A hardware store buys padlocks for $4 each and marks them up by 25 percent of cost.
   a. What is the selling price for the padlocks?
   b. What is the percentage markup based on selling price?
8. A clinic provides the immunizations required for Americans who want to travel abroad. It calculates that its total cost to provide this service to 1,000 patients is $9,000, including $4,000 in fixed costs and average variable costs of $5 per patient.
   a. At a price of $20 per patient, what would the clinic's breakeven point be?
   b. Assume the clinic wants to earn a $10,000 profit on this service. Compute a new breakeven point that accounts for the desired level of profits.
9. Name and describe briefly the four basic approaches to setting prices relative to the competition.
10. Why is an organization that practices the quality approach to marketing well suited to use value pricing?
11. Name and describe briefly the four pricing practices that have been limited by the U.S. government.

Chapter Project
Pricing a Product

As you've learned in this chapter, setting a price for a product requires careful analysis. For this project, choose one of the products listed below (or one of your own) and conduct your own analysis to determine the best price for your product.

First, research regulations in your product's industry to find out whether there are particular constraints on pricing. Then decide what your best basis for pricing would be: cost, profit, competition, customer perception, or some combination of these. Use any information you can obtain about similar, existing products (from news sources, journals, annual reports, etc.) to determine the best price for your product.

Describe your product and the reasoning behind the price in a written report or to your class. (Note: You can expand on this project by actually estimating demand and revenue, then conducting marginal analysis.)

Product ideas:

- A tour package
- A messenger service (providing quick local deliveries)
- A cooking-demonstration video
- A house-sitting service
- A bicycle helmet

Case
Philip Morris/Marlboro Cigarettes

Forget your opinion of cigarettes and cigarette smoking. You may feel uncomfortable about marketing a product that, if your efforts are successful, can addict its buyers and ultimately seriously harm their health. For this case, you are not being asked to condone the marketing of cigarettes. Instead, try to view the plight of Marlboro as a marketing problem to see what you can learn.

Philip Morris Companies Inc. makes Marlboro cigarettes, the world's most successful brand (with 21 percent of the U.S. market). The company also markets a host of other consumer products in the United States, including Kraft cheeses, Sealtest ice cream, Post Raisin Bran, Sanka, Lender's bagels, and Parkay margarine. Internationally, it offers such food products as Gevalia coffee and Toblerone chocolate. In addition, Philip Morris owns the Miller Brewing Company and interests in Molson Breweries and Oscar Mayer.

With so many products under its roof, Philip Morris commands attention from the marketing world—and Wall Street. So when the company announced a temporary price cut on Marlboros in April 1993, investors dumped Philip Morris stock, causing its price to plunge. In fact, many investors were worried that the price cut signified a nosedive for brand loyalty toward a variety of products, so they also sold off their stock in such companies as RJR Nabisco, Procter & Gamble, H.J. Heinz, Quaker Oats, Coca-Cola, and PepsiCo.

Just what happened to Philip Morris that caused such a stir? Shipments of Marlboro cigarettes to resellers had dropped a substantial 8 percent in the first quarter of 1992, signaling that the resellers weren't moving the cigarettes off their shelves fast enough. To stimulate greater demand, the company slashed the price of Marlboros by 40 cents a pack (from $2.15 to $1.75). Roger Enrico, chief of PepsiCo's Frito-Lay subsidiary, noted, "In the annals of business history, Philip Morris's action is bigger than New Coke. MBAs will study this decision for the next century."

The price cut was significant for several reasons:

1. The Marlboro cigarette brand alone inhales more U.S. revenues than such companies as Campbell Soup, Kellogg, and Gillette.

2. The change was responding to a dramatic shift in consumer buying habits: more consumers are buying according to price rather than brand preference. Although Marlboro has long been the leader in full-price cigarettes (ahead of RJR's Camel and Winston), discount brands have taken a firm hold in the market. Discount cigarettes made up 36 percent of the market in 1993 and are expected to capture an estimated 50 percent by the century's end. One confirmed smoker who switched from Camels to a cheaper discount brand remarked, "A cigarette is a cigarette."

3. The price cut took effect just when the federal government was considering raising the excise tax on cigarettes. "Obviously, this move makes it easier to raise cigarette taxes because it won't have as great an impact on the consumer," explained one Clinton administration official.

4. The cut triggered a price war, a situation feared by marketers in any industry. Even when a price war is short lived, it can seriously damage competition and an industry as a whole. As one tobacco industry executive said, "Thanks a lot. Now [Philip Morris] has established a floor. People don't understand why they did it."

Defending the company's action, Michael A. Miles, chairman and CEO, explained, "We announced a significant change in pricing strategy designed to make our premium products more affordable, and thus encourage consumers to make purchase decisions based on brand preference rather than price." Philip Morris's rationale, according to William I. Campbell, head of Philip Morris USA, is, "When we make Marlboro more affordable, it will grow." Many marketers, investors, and financial analysts aren't buying that explanation. Instead, they believe Philip Morris is trying to correct past mistakes.

In the view of the critics, Marlboro had been raising its prices too fast. Demand for tobacco products has historically been inelastic; once you start smoking it's hard to stop, even if the price goes up. And an extraordinarily successful marketing effort has positioned Marlboro as the cigarette of the rugged American individualist. With these points in its favor, Philip Morris raised prices sometimes as often as twice a year (without improving the product), confident that smokers would stand by their brand. Evidently, some of them didn't.

At the time Marlboro announced the price change, Philip Morris called the lower price temporary, saying that it would promote the change only in store displays, not in advertising. However, a few months later, the company ran an ad for its premium brands under the headline "Premium Quality. New Low Price." It also sent a letter to smokers on its mailing lists, advising them about reduced prices. Critics observed that the ad did nothing to distinguish the company's brands.

QUESTIONS

1. Do you think cutting the price of Marlboro cigarettes was a good marketing decision? Why or why not? If your answer is "no," what steps would you have taken instead?
2. If you were the marketer responsible for rival Camel cigarettes, how would you handle the pricing of your product in light of Marlboro's price?

3. Why is the consideration of such marketing environment conditions as excise taxes important in establishing price?

Sources: Eben Shapiro, "Marlboro Price, Already Cut, May Remain So," *The Wall Street Journal,* July 19, 1993, pp. B1, B6; Ira Teinowitz, "PM Feeds the Pricing Fire," *Advertising Age,* June 7, 1993, p. 4; Patricia Sellers, "Fall for Philip Morris," *Fortune,* May 3, 1993, pp. 68–69; Paula Dwyer, Maria Mallory, and Dave Lindorff, "Lots of Puffing But Less Profit in New Markets Overseas," *Business Week,* May 3, 1993, p. 132; "When Smoke Got in Their Eyes," *The Economist,* April 10, 1993, pp. 65–66; Eben Shapiro, "Price Cut Raises Chance of Boost in Tobacco Tax," *The Wall Street Journal,* April 7, 1993, p. A3; Eben Shapiro, "Price Cut on Marlboro Upsets Rosy Notions About Tobacco Profits," *The Wall Street Journal,* April 5, 1993, pp. A1, A6; Gary Levin, "PM Shores up Marlboro," *Advertising Age,* April 5, 1993, pp. 1, 44; *PM/Quarterly,* April 1993, pp. 4–5; *Philip Morris Companies Inc. Annual Report,* 1992, pp. 16–23; Kevin Goldman, "Philip Morris Ad about Price Cuts Is Considered Risky by Strategists," *The Wall Street Journal,* August 5, 1993, p. B3.

CHAPTER OUTLINE

CHAPTER 15

Pricing Goods and Services

LEARNING OBJECTIVES

After completing this chapter, you should be able to:

1. Describe the major categories of pricing objectives.

2. Identify the steps in the pricing process.

3. Describe pricing strategies for different types of products.

4. Identify methods for adjusting prices.

5. Discuss the ways marketers evaluate and control pricing.

Creating Customer Value
United Parcel Service

"We run the tightest ship in the shipping business," declared the old ads for United Parcel Service (UPS). Although the ads have changed and the corporation has altered its structure, it is still one of the most efficient—and largest—shippers in the world. The difference is a new emphasis on employee participation and empowerment, new technology, and a new pricing strategy.

United Parcel Service, based in Atlanta, ships nearly 3 billion parcels and documents a year (more than 11 million a day), serves 1.2 million regular customers, and employs 286,000 people worldwide. That's a lot of packages, customers, and workers to keep track of. How does the company do it?

"I'd have to attribute the company's success to our employee partnership concept and long-term approach to business," explains John Alden, senior vice president of business development for the company. "Because our employees know their jobs are secure and their opportunity to rise to a management position is great, it gives them the added incentive to go that extra mile." Employees participate regularly in team meetings called Communications Meetings, Service Involvement, and KORE sessions as part of a company program called "Delivering Our Future." The meetings give drivers and others who have direct contact with customers a chance to understand UPS's overall mission and business challenges. They also provide the company with important information about its customers and their geographic areas.

Drivers may team up with account executives for a day to make sales calls. Under the Service Involvement program, employees work together to devise measurable ways of improving the company's service. Training is another key element for all employees. For example, the sales force is expected to understand the technology that creates better service to UPS customers. UPS sent its 150 sales managers through a logistics training course especially designed for them by Michigan State University. Eventually, the company wants to send all district and regional managers as well as national operators through the program. In addition, UPS

has expanded its marketing team from 7 employees, adding 175 people to handle questions from customers and survey them for new ideas.

Other quality improvements involve UPS's processes and products. The company has adopted state-of-the art technology, such as its TotalTrack system, which monitors shipments around the clock and can confirm delivery in seconds. It has added new services, including 3-Day Select, which guarantees delivery anywhere coast to coast in the United States within three business days. UPS recently started offering corporate customers flexible pickup and delivery times and customized shipment plans. These developments have helped UPS expand aggressively around the world. The company has distribution centers in Europe, a joint venture in Japan, and a subsidiary in Britain.

But UPS needed to revamp its pricing structure. Many corporate clients complained that the company refused to offer any kind of discount for high-volume shipments. By 1990, UPS was losing business to Federal Express and Roadway Package System, both of which offered organizational buyers a better deal. Under chief executive Kent C. Nelson, UPS responded by adjusting its prices to offer quantity discounts to corporate clients. This was not an easy decision, for it undercut one of the company's founding philosophies: "We'd always prided ourselves on saying your grandmother paid the same price General Motors did," notes Nelson.

Home deliveries had been the staple of UPS's business. But harsh realities dictate that it simply costs more per item to deliver a single package to one consumer than it does to deliver 50 of them to a store or other business. To reflect the greater profitability of serving organizations, UPS has raised residential rates about 11.4 percent a year. Commercial rates have grown only about 3.4 percent annually.

Catalog retailers get the tightest squeeze. Some, such as Lillian Vernon Corp., have reduced the amount of shipping they do via UPS. But others, such as Lands' End Inc., have negotiated an attractive contract with UPS that is helping keep rates down. In fact, Lands' End switched its overnight shipping service from Federal Express to UPS as a result of a new agreement.

In the end, UPS must be able to provide not only fast, accurate delivery of goods, but also a good price to its customers. As you read this chapter about managing prices, note how price is related to profits, to the other elements of the marketing mix, and, ultimately, to customer satisfaction.

Sources: Chuck Hawkins and Patrick Oster, "After a U-Turn, UPS Really Delivers," *Business Week,* May 31, 1993, pp. 92–93; "UPS Delivers More to its Customers," *Sales & Marketing Management,* September 1992, p. 64; *United Parcel Service 1992 Report to Shareholders,* pp. 24–25; *Cargovision,* March/April 1993; other press materials from UPS.

Chapter Overview

The previous chapter introduced basic principles of pricing. This chapter extends that discussion by explaining the ways in which marketers create specific pricing strategies for the organization's goods and services.

The chapter does this by describing the basic pricing objectives marketers pursue through the selection of various tactics. Then it describes a model for the pricing process. Next, the chapter turns to strategies marketers typically use for pricing new products, existing products, and product lines. It covers ways in which marketers adjust the basic price through discounting, psychological pricing, and geographic pricing, as well as forms of price discrimination to avoid. Finally, the chapter addresses the evaluation and control of pricing through observing and reacting to the responses of competitors and customers.

Pricing Objectives

The pricing strategy used for particular products and product lines should support the marketing objectives developed during strategic marketing planning. Motorola, for example, is seeking to challenge Intel as the leading producer of microprocessors by developing a rival chip called the PowerPC. Says Motorola's marketing director, "Our goal is to make the PowerPC a standard in the computer industry."[1] To meet this objective, Motorola has selected a pricing objective of using low prices to win market share. Specifically, the PowerPC was introduced at less than half the price Intel was expected to charge for a competing microchip. In general, the most common pricing objectives include achieving a desired level of sales, competing in terms of relative price or market share, earning a targeted level of profits, enabling the organization to survive, and measuring up to a standard of social responsibility.

POSITIONING OBJECTIVES

When it is consistent with the other elements of the marketing mix, price supports the organization's effort to position the product to serve particular market segments. Price

Hey Ewe! is the call in this appeal for subscribers to Mountain Bike *magazine by offering 40 percent off newsstand prices. Many magazines offer discounts, but the ad combines humor with the "shear" size of the ad.*

influences which potential customers will buy the product. Some people will seek out the lowest price for a category of goods or services. Others will pay more but conclude that they cannot afford a product when it is priced above a certain level. Therefore, the price level helps the marketer attract particular target markets.

Price also may convey information about the product. When potential buyers are unable to directly evaluate the product's benefits relative to the competition, they may use price as an indicator of quality. This is often the case with services.

SALES OBJECTIVES

The objective of setting a particular price may be to achieve a specified level of sales. The level of sales may be measured in terms of the units of product sold, such as hours billed by a lawyer or sets of steak knives sold in a department store. Or sales may be measured in terms of dollar volume.

A high level of sales is an important objective of the Resolution Trust Corporation (a government agency formed several years ago as part of the federal government's bailout of the savings and loan industry). The RTC is charged with selling off assets of failed S&Ls to help cover their debts. The longer these assets remain unsold, the greater the cost to taxpayers. Taxpayers should therefore be grateful for the rapid pace of sales in the RTC's Texas region, where the agency is selling almost $150 million worth of assets a week. Carmen Sullivan, who heads the Texas region, credits flexible pricing tactics for the quick sales. On some properties, for example, she holds auctions with no minimum bids.[2]

Sales objectives are easy to measure, and growing sales are one indicator that the organization is offering an attractive marketing mix. However, success in meeting sales targets does not always translate into success in terms of other objectives, such as profits. For example, AT&T could sell an enormous number of telephones by putting them on sale at $5 each. But this would not likely help the company achieve its profit objectives.

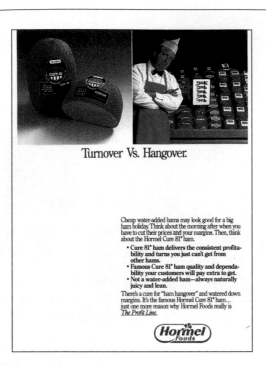

COMPETITION-RELATED OBJECTIVES

Part of setting price is to consider where the organization is and wants to be relative to competition. Thus, the marketer considers the organization's relative share of the market, as well as how the organization's products are priced relative to the competition's.

COMPETITORS' PRICES   When several competitors offer basically the same product, customers may make selections based on price. In this case, sellers must meet each other's prices. Charging more would mean that customers buy from someone else. Charging less would mean that the organization unnecessarily sacrifices some profits.

In other cases, the marketer is interested in charging a price different from that set by competitors. Thus, in a competitive bidding situation, the seller will want to set the lowest price. In contrast, if the organization wants its products to be viewed as prestigious, it will want to set its price higher than that of its run-of-the-mill competition. Thus, in Figure 15.1, Hormel tells its supermarket customers that the high quality and good reputation of its hams means consumers will pay more for them than for competing products.

MARKET SHARE   Stating objectives in terms of market share is a variation on measuring sales. The marketer divides the sales of its own product by the sales of all such products. The result is the percentage of sales for the particular product. In general, to achieve high market share, the marketer sets the price low relative to that of competitors.

Market share objectives have the same limitations as sales objectives. For example, a high price coupled with high quality might give the organization a low market share but an extremely profitable segment of the total market. In general, however, there may be a link between high market share and high profits. Research by the Marketing Science Institute found that the greatest returns on investment were earned by companies with market shares of more than 40 percent. Businesses with smaller market shares tended to earn lower profits.[3]

PROFIT OBJECTIVES

Businesses often seek to set the price that gives them the highest profit. At times, they hope that another objective, such as an increase in sales or market share, will eventually lead to greater profits. At other times, the profit level is the specific focus of the pricing strategy.

When the objective is specifically profit related, marketers seek the price that will help the organization achieve a given profit objective. The organization's top management may agree on a desired return on investment (ROI). Then the marketer identifies the price that is likely to result in the specified ROI.

SURVIVAL OBJECTIVES

Ideally, the organization is able to charge a price that achieves objectives for sales and profits. However, market conditions may be such that the organization's short-term goal is simply to survive until conditions improve. For example, stiff competition in the face of low demand means that sellers probably have to charge a low price in order to win over the few buyers in the marketplace. In the case of the Big Three automakers, one way to avoid the expense of closing factories in response to weak demand in recent years was to sell cars to rental companies at or even below cost. A typical practice was to sell at a price just over dealer cost, then to pay a cash incentive of $400 to $1,400 for each car delivered, and finally to buy the cars back at only slightly less than the purchase price just four months later. Eventually, however, big losses led the manufacturers to abandon this strategy.[4]

Survival objectives typically include setting a price at or below cost as the only way to win customers or sell enough to cover variable costs. Organizations forced to use such tactics would also look for ways to help improve conditions so that they are no longer limited to survival objectives. They might stimulate demand through advertising or product improvements, or they could cut costs until the low price level becomes profitable.

SOCIAL RESPONSIBILITY OBJECTIVES

Economic objectives, such as those just described, are of primary importance to most businesses. However, in setting prices, the marketer may also weigh issues related to social responsibility. Manufacturers of prescription drugs and vaccines have been criticized for charging too much. The prices are thought to be too high because some of the people who would benefit from these products are unable to afford them. This view implies that for essential products, one objective should be to make the products affordable. However, the cost to develop new drugs is high, and the potential liability involved in selling them can be enormous. Society's need for widely available medicine must somehow be balanced against the sellers' need to cover costs.

Social responsibility objectives often play a major role in the pricing decisions of the government and many nonprofit organizations. For example, a counseling service may have a sliding scale based on ability to pay, so that anyone who needs the service can benefit from using it. Or a city may charge households for garbage pickup on the basis of the volume of garbage each produces. While the record keeping is more complex than for charging a flat fee, this pricing policy is designed to reduce the environmental impact of garbage by encouraging households to reduce consumption and to reuse and recycle materials.

government may also have to follow specific guidelines for how to set prices. In addition, governments sometimes limit price changes. Utilities such as electric companies must get government approval for any rate increase, and governments sometimes impose general wage and price controls. At the other end of the spectrum, government action may keep prices from falling below a certain level. The U.S. government has propped up the prices of citrus products by limiting the amounts that may be sold in California and Arizona. In 1993, when the Agriculture Department suspended the quotas in response to complaints of cheating, that year's record-breaking harvest drove prices to their lowest level in seven years.[7]

Finally, marketers are limited by the prices competitors are charging. If the marketer wants to charge a higher price than are competitors, the organization will have to convince the target market that the product is superior in some way. W. W. Grainger can charge relatively high prices for maintenance, repair, and operating supplies because its efficient ordering systems can lower the organizational buyer's total cost of placing an order.[8] In the United Kingdom, Procter & Gamble has made its Fairy dishwashing soap a success by developing a formula that washes more dishes per drop of soap and is milder to the hands.[9] If distinguishing the product is impossible, it must be priced at the same or a lower price than the competition.

ANALYZE PROFIT POTENTIAL   Based on the pricing objectives and constraints, the marketer develops a sense of what range of prices will make sense. The marketer then must analyze the potential profits associated with the range of prices being considered. To do this, the manager gathers information about the pattern of demand. Then such techniques as marginal analysis can give the marketer information about the links between price, demand, and profits.

SET INITIAL PRICE LEVEL   Now the marketer is ready to set a basic price. To do this, the marketer uses pricing methods based on some combination of cost, profit, competition, and customer perception. In addition, the marketer takes into account the way the price fits with the other elements of the marketing mix. Thus, if the product is intended to be sold to discount stores, the marketer will have to keep the price low. If the marketer is planning communications that emphasize how the product is superior to its competitors, the marketer may be able to set a relatively high price.

The term used to refer to the initial price level varies from industry to industry. Often it is referred to as the list price. A **list price** is "the selling price for an item before any discounts or reductions in price."[10]

list price
The selling price for an item before discounts or reductions are taken.

MAKE PRICE ADJUSTMENTS AS NEEDED   There are many reasons for adjusting the list or quoted price. The marketer may want to provide a temporary price promotion to attract buyers to the product. See Figure 15.3 for an example of how Parsons Green Reproductions Ltd., in London, advertises its annual January sale. Or the marketer may want the price charged to various groups of customers to reflect the costs of serving them (as in the case of offering quantity discounts). Deciding when and how to offer the various types of price adjustments is the last step in the pricing process. The basic alternatives for adjusting prices are described later in this chapter.

PRICING NEW PRODUCTS

Among the pricing objectives for a new product, two are common: to get many members of the target market to try the product and to quickly recover the costs of developing the product. Admittedly, these two objectives are incompatible to some degree.

FIGURE 15.3

Ad for Price Reductions to Attract Buyers

Persuading people to try a product calls for a low price, and quickly recovering costs implies a higher price.

penetration pricing
Setting a low price to attract the target market to a new product.

PENETRATION PRICING   When the marketer charges a relatively low price to induce members of the target market to try a product, the marketer is using **penetration pricing**. Approach Software offered its database program at an introductory price of $149 for six months before raising the price to $399.[11] A marketer is most likely to choose penetration pricing when he or she expects competitors to enter the market soon and when demand for the product is price elastic.

Although charging a low price may seem to hurt the organization's profits, it does provide some economic advantages. It helps the organization quickly build up to the volume at which it can operate most efficiently. Also, if the marketer's strategy is to appeal to a mass market, penetration pricing enables the organization to achieve the necessary market share. Furthermore, competitors may be more reluctant to offer competing new products if customers are used to paying low prices.

A company that has enjoyed the benefits of penetration pricing is Southwest Airlines. Its approach to entering a new market is to offer introductory fares well below those being charged by competitors. When Southwest started offering flights out of Baltimore, for example, it charged $39 for a ticket to Chicago and just $19 for a ticket to Cleveland. Once the company has attracted a lot of attention and passengers, it raises fares somewhat. Thanks to low overhead (through such cost-saving tactics as flying modern aircraft and not serving meals), Southwest can keep even its regular fares low and still earn a profit.[12]

skimming
Setting a high price to recover quickly the costs of a new product.

SKIMMING   When the marketer's objective is to quickly recover the costs of the new product, the marketer sets the price relatively high. This pricing strategy is known as **skimming** (as in skimming the cream off the milk). An organization is most likely to use skimming when demand is inelastic and the organization has a temporary monopoly on the product, as when it holds a patent. Eventually, competitors are likely to enter the marketplace—attracted in part by the high prices. In response to the competition, the marketer will probably have to lower prices somewhat. Skimming strategies are also useful when the organization wants demand to build gradually while it increases production capacity. As it lowers the price, the organization markets the product to more price-sensitive target markets.

An organization considering a skimming strategy should proceed with caution. In some industries, such as semiconductors, this practice is widely accepted.[13] When it is not, however, the high prices may offend potential customers, generating ill will instead of profits. That has happened in the case of pharmaceutical companies selling drugs for rare diseases at very high prices.

PRICING EXISTING PRODUCTS

In pricing existing products, the marketer considers various characteristics of the product. These include how perishable and distinctive the product is, as well as what stage in the life cycle the product has reached.

PERISHABILITY   Some kinds of products, like houses and tractors, are likely to last a long time. Others, like bananas and medicine, have a shorter life before they are no longer usable. In addition, some products are perishable in other ways. Sometimes demand for a product runs out after a time. This is the case for Christmas cards and high-fashion clothing. Or products may become unavailable for other reasons. For example, concert tickets are useful only until the concert has begun.

The degree to which a product is perishable in any of these ways influences the pricing strategy. The marketer will want to price perishable products so that they are sold before they spoil or lose their appeal or usefulness. Doing this might involve setting a low price or setting a moderate price with a plan for slashing prices if necessary to sell the product quickly.

DISTINCTIVENESS   Marketers are able to create a distinctive image for some products, such as cars and consulting, more readily than for others, such as paper clips and dry cleaning. In the case of distinctive products, the marketer is able to use such means as quality, branding, design, and features to distinguish them from their competitors. If the target market views the product as superior, the marketer can charge a higher price than can competitors. Thus, to enjoy the "environmental correctness" of wearing natural cosmetics, such as those sold by Body Shop or Bath & Body Works, consumers pay prices that reflect profit margins of 15 to 20 percent, compared to 5 to 8 percent margins for the mainstream competition.[14] It is with such distinctive products that the marketer is most obviously able to enjoy a profit advantage as a result of a commitment to quality.

In contrast, for homogeneous products, the marketer must generally set the price equal to that of competitors. To induce customers to buy the product, the marketer may also offer various types of discounts, as well as maintain reliably high quality. If the pricing strategy is to build market share or maintain a large share, the marketer may routinely use a below-market price. In effect, the marketer is using penetration pricing for an existing product. (Conversely, see "Marketing Movers & Shakers" to learn about a marketer who prices a perishable but distinctive product above the competition.)

LIFE CYCLE STAGE   The most effective pricing strategy often varies with stage in the product life cycle. The typical pricing strategies for the introduction stage were

Marketing Movers & Shakers

STEVEN JUDGE OF VERMONT MILK PRODUCTS

Imagine drinking a glass of milk that is truly farm fresh, sweeter and smoother than any you've had in a very long time. True, it costs more. But not only is the milk of the highest quality, you know the profits go directly to the group of family farms that provide the milk, allowing them to survive. And you know that not only are the cows that produce the milk treated well, the farmers also work hard to improve the soil, prevent erosion, and avoid water pollution. So you decide the higher price for this superior product is worthwhile.

Steven Judge and Vermont Milk Producers are banking on it. Judge, who owns a small, 300-acre dairy farm with 50 cows in Vermont, is hoping to make his milk part of a premium beverage industry. After all, water and coffee, which once were seen as commodities, each now enjoy a thriving "gourmet" market.

The demand for milk as a commodity increases only about 1 percent a year, while supply goes up between 2 percent and 3 percent. This means continual downward pressure on milk prices. Through the federal Farm Bill, the U.S. government has historically subsidized the milk industry by purchasing surplus dairy products, but that changed during the 1980s. Slowly, farmers were squeezed out of business.

Other changes have shaken the marketing environment in which Judge operates. During the late 1980s, the National Dairy Promotion and Research Board began to promote a scientific discovery that injecting cows with growth hormones would increase their milk production by 10 percent. The board estimated that demand for milk would drop 15 percent initially due to consumers' distaste for the idea, but that eventually the public would come around.

That's when Steven Judge and his wife, Wendy, nearly out of business themselves, got angry. They hated the idea of treating their cows with hormones. They figured consumers would as well. And their business couldn't take a 15 percent drop in demand. So they began to wonder: why wouldn't consumers who rejected the the hormone-contaminated milk pay a little more for milk that was guaranteed to be fresh and pure?

Steven Judge organized a group of ten small farms, which agreed to produce the highest-quality milk (using the fastest and most expensive processing) in return for a higher price. The group was called Vermont Milk Products, and the milk itself would be sold under the brand Vermont Family Farms. With a little marketing research, Steven Judge discovered that even with the trend toward low-fat foods, more than 45 percent of all milk sold is still whole milk. So Judge's group decided to stick with whole milk.

The pricing strategy of Vermont Milk Products was to charge a higher price for better milk. The high price would cover VMP's payments to processors and grocery stores, which were required to handle the milk as quickly as possible to ensure freshness. Profits for the farmers would be just enough to keep them going. To keep the farmers from increasing production (and thus perhaps reducing demand), Judge contracted to buy only as much milk as the farmer was already producing. Ironically, although VMP was setting a premium price for a premium product, it was also practicing survival pricing.

As Vermont Family Farms milk made its way to groceries around the Boston area (Judge chose local outlets to guarantee the freshness of the milk), farmers received 77 cents per half gallon from the milk processor, which sold the milk to stores for about $1.50 per half gallon. Stores charged consumers about $1.99. (For generic milk, farmers receive about 57 cents per half gallon, which winds up on grocery shelves at about $1.00.)

Consumers began to buy the milk in cardboard cartons printed with the picture of a gentle dairy scene (cows grazing, red barn, rolling hills, blue sky). Sales reached $268,000 in the first year and were projected to triple in the second year. Judge hopes to expand to include 75 farms within the first six years, paying farmers as much as $20 per hundred pounds of milk, as opposed to the $16 per hundred pounds that they now receive.

Already, Judge has accomplished a variety of goals: By providing consumers with a desirable product at a price they are willing to pay, he has helped his own farm and others stay in business. He has created a true brand where only a generic commodity once existed. And he has approached a traditional industry in a whole new way, finding creative solutions that benefit everyone, from cows to consumers.

Vermont Milk Products is still only a part-time venture for Judge. His other business—dairy farming—demands dawn-to-dusk commitment. After all, those cows need to be milked and fed, calves need attention, the barn needs cleaning, and the herd needs to be moved from pasture to pasture. But it's the farm that puts the fresh, sweet milk on the shelves.

Source: Elizabeth Conlin, "Milking the Profits," *Inc.,* July 1993, pp. 92–98.

described in the section on pricing new products. As the product enters the growth stage, competitors are entering the market, so sellers price their products at or below the competition to gain a greater share of the growing market. Thus, consumer-goods giant Kao Corporation introduced the first concentrated laundry detergent to Japan. Its Attack detergent sold at a premium price for years, until such big competitors as Procter & Gamble entered the Japanese market.[15]

Low price becomes even more important during the maturity stage. To grow, marketers must win customers from competitors or win over new target markets that had been uninterested in buying at a higher price. When sales of audio books slowed after a decade of rapid growth, publishers tried to reach a broader market by producing cheaper versions of the originals—typically abridged versions in plainer packaging, selling for under $10.[16]

During the decline phase of the product life cycle, the marketer may reduce prices further in an effort to keep sales strong. However, such a strategy may damage profits. If so, the marketer may hold prices steady and perhaps develop a strategy for serving a niche market with relatively low sales but high profits.

PRICING PRODUCT LINES

When a product is part of a product line, the marketer will want to consider not only the price of each individual product, but the pricing strategy for the entire line. The price for each product in the line should be consistent with the overall image of the line. To lure cash-strapped consumers, Fort Worth, Texas, furniture retailer Bombay Company keeps prices of its products under $500, and most items sell for less than $200.[17] Each price should also reflect the relative value of the various products. Thus, the item with the greatest prestige or most features would probably be the most expensive in the product line.

Establishing pricing objectives for the product line as a whole gives the marketer some flexibility in setting prices. For example, if the marketer is seeking to earn maximum profits for the product line, one way to do this may be to seek a greater return on some items than on others. For products with many competitors or few special features, the marketer would expect lower profits. The organization may be able to charge a higher price for the items that have few competitors and offer distinctive benefits.

price lining
Setting several pricing points and pricing each product at one of those points.

PRICE LINING   One approach to pricing a product line is to set several pricing points and price each product at one of those points. NorthWord Press publishes $40 and $50 nature books, shorter books selling for $9.95 to $19.95, $9.95 nature calendars, and nature recordings priced at $9.95 for a tape and $15.95 for a compact disc.[18] This pricing technique is called **price lining**.

Such a tactic is thought to help prospective customers by limiting the choices they have to make. This benefit is most relevant to shoppers in a store, and price lining is used most often by retailers. Thus, imagine that you were preparing a catalog of books and related materials on health and nutrition. For three of these books, you must pay wholesale prices of $10, $11, and $12. What will you charge your customers? If you simply use a markup of 50 percent of the retail price, you will charge $20, $22, and $24. But if you want to use price lining, you will choose a single price for all three books. You might decide that if the markup results in a price between $20 and $24, you will charge $22 or perhaps an odd amount such as $21.95.

uniform pricing
Charging a single price for an entire product mix.

UNIFORM PRICING   Sometimes a marketer uses **uniform pricing**—charging a single price for an entire product mix. The $5 Clothing Store, located on the West Coast,

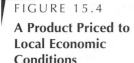

FIGURE 15.4

A Product Priced to Local Economic Conditions

sells discounted and overstocked clothing for $5. The Motel 6 chain bears that name because it originally offered no-frills rooms for only $6 a night. As in these examples, this single-price strategy is especially appropriate for sellers competing on the basis of low price.

STRATEGIES FOR GLOBAL MARKETERS

The pricing strategies of marketers serving international markets are basically the same as for domestic marketing. However, the task is complicated by such economic and political factors as tariffs, currency differences, and laws restricting pricing decisions. Recently the high value of the Japanese yen relative to the U.S. dollar has made it difficult for Japanese marketers to price their products attractively in the United States. Japanese car makers are raising prices 5 to 10 percent a year just to earn the same number of yen per car. The price of a typical Japanese compact car has risen from $2,000 less than a comparable U.S. model to $2,000 more. Fortunately for the Japanese auto companies, they have been building some cars in the United States, thereby somewhat avoiding the problem with currency exchange rates.[19]

A country's economic conditions, too, play a role. In recent years, rapid inflation in Russia has made pricing difficult. Procter & Gamble has responded to inflation of 10 percent a week by raising its prices almost weekly. As a result, its consumer goods are the highest-priced brands, affordable by only 5 to 10 percent of Russians.[20] In contrast, one of the reasons for the popularity of U.S. candy bars in Russia is that their 25-cent price makes them the least expensive Western status symbols.[21] In Brazil, few parents have been able to afford disposable diapers, so Procter & Gamble trimmed the cost of marketing there by offering a unisex style it calls Pampers Uni, which P&G can price lower than a gender-specific product line (see Figure 15.4).[22]

Difficulties in exchanging currencies may affect pricing strategy. The marketer may decide to require payment in dollars, rather than accepting the currency of the nation where the product is sold. Or the marketer may use **countertrade**, that is, bartering goods and services rather than selling them for money. Ben and Jerry's Homemade Ice Cream makes and sells its premium ice cream in Russia. The company uses the rubles it earns there to buy Russian walnuts, honey, and *matryoshky* (Russian nesting dolls) to sell in the United States.[23]

countertrade
Bartering goods and services rather than selling them for money.

PepsiCo has devised a creative solution to the limits the Chinese government places on currency exchange. Its various divisions in China coordinate their activities so that divisions needing to import supplies use the hard currency generated by divisions that export. One of these importing divisions is Pizza Hut, and an exporting division is a joint venture with Hua Chang Toy Company to make toys and promotional items for sale abroad.[24]

Adjusting Prices

The final step in setting prices is to select various ways to adjust the list or quoted price. The basic options are to use some combination of discounting, psychological pricing, and geographic pricing. (For a way to organize thinking about price adjustments, see "Put It into Practice.")

    The marketer should adjust the price in ways that support the overall marketing strategy. Honda Motor Company recently did this by offering dealers an incentive of $400 to $1,000 for selling certain models. The company paid this money to dealers instead of consumers in order to maintain the brands' image by keep the price constant. Dealers, of course, could negotiate lower prices with their customers.[25]

DISCOUNTING

discount
A reduction in price.

market price
The price actually paid by the customer.

rebate
A refund of part of the price of a product.

A **discount** is, quite simply, a reduction in price. Subtracting any discounts from the list price results in the **market price**, or the price actually paid by the customer. The seller may subtract the discount before the customer pays, or the seller may offer a **rebate**, that is, a refund of part of the price. Marketers offer discounts to encourage desirable behaviors, such as buying in quantity.

    Discounts have an important effect on the market price. According to one report, it is not uncommon for discounts of various types to consume around 20 percent of the product's list price.[26] The effect of such discounts is especially great in the case of products sold through intermediaries. However, marketers often devote little attention to the use of discounts. The major reason is that most accounting systems track sales in terms of list price, not market price, so marketers don't realize the significance of decisions about discounts. A practical consequence is that these decisions are often made by a variety of employees, including salespeople and clerks processing orders. This means that marketers looking for a way to boost profits would do well to look at the organization's discount policies, making sure they serve the organization's marketing objectives and incorporate the incentives that matter to buyers.

    Commonly used types of discounts include quantity discounts, seasonal discounts, trade discounts, cash discounts, allowances, promotional discounts, and loss leaders.

TABLE 15.1	TYPE OF PRICE ADJUSTMENT	PROS AND CONS FOR MY PRODUCT
Worksheet for Making Price Adjustments	Quantity discounts	
	Seasonal discounts	
	Trade discounts	
	Cash discounts	
	Allowances	
	Promotional discounts	
	Loss of leaders	
	EDLP	
	Odd-even pricing	
	Bundle pricing	
	FOB origin pricing	
	Uniform delivered pricing	

Source: Michael D. Mondello, "Naming Your Price," *Inc.*, July 1992, pp. 80–83.

quantity discount
A reduction in the price per unit for purchases of a minimum quantity.

QUANTITY DISCOUNTS   A **quantity discount** is a reduction in the price per unit for purchases of some minimum quantity. *The Cotton Quarterly,* the first journal of fiction to be printed on T-shirts, is priced at $20 per issue (one shirt) or only $75 for a year's subscription of four issues.[27] The main reason for offering quantity discounts is that for many products, it costs less per unit to fill large orders. A buyer who purchases small quantities in effect pays the seller extra for the service of holding merchandise until the buyer needs more.

Quantity discounts may be cumulative or noncumulative. A noncumulative quantity discount is a price reduction determined on the basis of each purchase. The office products catalog for Office Essentials includes rolls of calculator paper at the following prices: a pack of 3 rolls for $2.95 ($.98 each), a pack of 12 rolls for $9.95 ($.83 each), and a case of 100 rolls for $75.00 ($.75 each). A buyer who wants 100 calculator rolls per year can pay a smaller price for each roll by ordering them all at once.

A cumulative quantity discount reduces prices according to the amount purchased over a period of time. A manufacturer might give a rebate of 5 percent to buyers whose annual purchases were greater than, say, $50,000. Some shoe stores give consumers a price break after they have purchased a given number of pairs, say 25 percent off on the tenth pair. As both examples illustrate, cumulative quantity discounts are designed to encourage customers to keep buying from the same source. Because the cost savings to the seller are less obvious for this type of discount, sellers using cumulative quantity discounts should consider whether they can defend their use within the limits of the Robinson-Patman Act.

Quantity discounts may make big purchases affordable for potential customers. Monterey, California–based Edutech, a software distributor, found that schools couldn't handle the retail price of many software packages. For example, 500 copies of a major word-processing program at $500 each would be a huge cost for a college. So Edutech instead sells the school a license to make its own copies of the software. The cost of the license depends on the number of expected users, with a minimum of 100. Edutech prices the software at an 85 percent discount and provides manuals for each user.[28]

seasonal discount
A price reduction offered during times of slow demand.

SEASONAL DISCOUNTS   A **seasonal discount** is a price reduction offered during times of slow demand. For example, a manufacturer of snowblowers or beach balls

FIGURE 15.5
**Sample Trade
Discount**

would offer wholesalers and retailers a price break for ordering the product early. This enables the manufacturer to smooth out its production schedule and rewards buyers for keeping the products in inventory until demand picks up.

The perishability of services makes pricing an important tactic for selling them at times when they otherwise might go unused. Airlines, for example, want to fill as many of their seats as possible during each flight. For that reason, seasonal discounts in airfares are common each fall, following peak summer travel.

trade discount
A percentage reduction from the list price, offered to resellers.

TRADE DISCOUNTS   Manufacturers also may offer resellers **trade discounts**. These discounts in effect reward the resellers for the various functions they perform. Trade discounts are stated in terms of percentage reductions from the list price. A typical way to quote such a discount is shown in Figure 15.5. In this case, the manufacturer sells to wholesalers, which sell to retailers. The discount to the retailer is 30 percent of the $50.00 list price, or $15.00. Thus, the retailer pays $35.00. The wholesale discount is 10 percent of the selling price to the retailers, or $3.50. Subtracting the two discounts from the list price results in a $31.50 selling price charged by the manufacturer.

Some industries, such as hardware, food, and drugs, use traditional percentages for trade discounts. However, a seller may offer a different discount schedule if the competition warrants it.

cash discount
An incentive for buyers to pay quickly, or a lower price for payment in cash.

CASH DISCOUNTS   Sometimes the marketer offers a **cash discount** as an incentive for buyers to pay quickly. A typical example of the terms for a cash discount offered to an organizational buyer is stated "2/10 net 30." This means that a buyer who pays within 10 days can take a 2 percent discount. Otherwise, the total amount of the bill is due within 30 days. Thus, if the total invoice is for $5,000, a buyer who pays within 10 days will be able to take a discount of $100 (.02 x $5,000) and send only $4,900. Buyers who pay after 30 days are subject to interest penalties.

A 2 percent discount may not sound like much. But think of it this way: skipping this discount is the cost of using the money for an extra 20 days—the difference between paying within 10 days and paying within 30. This "interest rate" of 2 percent for 20 days is equivalent to 36 percent per year (assuming a 360-day business year). Stated mathematically, .02/20 = .36/360. Thus, not taking advantage of the cash discount is quite expensive for buyers, and offering it is costly for sellers. Many buyers would rather borrow money from a bank to be able to pay within 10 days than pay later at the higher rate.

Cash discounts offered to consumers are more often stated in terms of a lower price for payment in cash rather than on credit. Such discounts reflect the lower cost of handling cash than processing credit payments. Gas stations frequently offer this type of discount.

FIGURE 15.6

Promotional Discount in the Form of a Coupon

Introducing the sweetener that topped the leader.

Enjoy the sweet, satisfying taste of new SugarTwin Plus, the only blend of the leading sweeteners. It tastes more like sugar, without all the bitter aftertaste of the leading brand. Taste tests prove it. So compare it for yourself, send for your free sample today!

Sample it. Free.

Save 30¢
On new SugarTwin Plus 100 ct.

Void

Void

trade-in allowance
A discount for providing a good or service, along with a monetary payment.

promotional allowance
A price reduction in exchange for the reseller performing certain promotional activities, such as advertising the product.

promotional discount
A short-term discount to stimulate additional sales or to induce buyers to try a product.

loss leader pricing
Setting prices near or below cost in order to attract customers to a store.

ALLOWANCES   The seller may offer a type of discount called an "allowance" to buyers in return for a good or service provided. For example, car dealers offer **trade-in allowances** to buyers who provide a used car along with their monetary payment. The advantage to the seller is that the list price basically remains the same; in bargaining with each customer, the seller starts at this higher price.

Manufacturers may offer resellers a **promotional allowance**. This is a price reduction in exchange for the reseller performing certain promotional activities, such as advertising the product. This pricing tactic combines the communications and pricing elements of the marketing mix.

PROMOTIONAL DISCOUNTS   Sometimes sellers offer a discount only temporarily, as a way to stimulate additional sales or to induce potential customers to try a product. Such discounts are called **promotional discounts**. When retail stores place goods "on sale," these are promotional discounts. Coke and Pepsi have used this type of discounting so frequently that consumers hold off on buying when these drinks are at full price—not the most desirable outcome of such a strategy, of course. Another approach to promotional discounts is the use of coupons good for a price reduction, as in the example in Figure 15.6 where Alberto-Culver introduces its new product Sugar Twin Plus with two coupons, one for a free product sample and another for a discount on a product purchase. By offering a promotional discount instead of a lower price, the seller avoids creating ill will by raising the price when the promotion ends.

LOSS LEADERS   A retailer may use discounting to draw customers into the store. In some cases, the retailer prices some products below or near cost in order to attract customers, so that they will buy other products as well. This pricing tactic is called **loss leader pricing**. Some states prohibit retailers from selling at less than cost, so retailers should use loss leaders with caution. In Arkansas, three independent drugstores sued Wal-Mart, alleging the chain had sold more than 100 products below cost with the intent to destroy competition.[29]

The items selected for loss leader pricing should be those that will attract many members of the target market. At a supermarket, a low price on milk, apples, or a popular brand of laundry detergent is likely to attract many consumers. At Goody's Family Clothing, based in Knoxville, Tennessee, a regular loss leader is blue jeans. Goody's displays them in the back of its stores, and customers who come to buy jeans often leave with higher-margin clothing they see when they shop.[30]

every-day low prices (EDLP)
Prices consistently set below the competition's rather than occasional discounts on items.

DISCOUNTING VERSUS EVERY-DAY LOW PRICES   As an alternative to offering promotional or seasonal discounts, some sellers have adopted a strategy called **every-day low prices** (EDLP). This strategy involves consistently setting prices below the competition, rather than occasionally discounting certain items. An EDLP strategy is one of the features of Wal-Mart's marketing mix, and that chain's success has led other retailers to try a similar pricing strategy. Manufacturers—notably Procter & Gamble—also have experimented with EDLP. One attraction is that demand should be more stable, which should reduce production costs. Quaker, for example, has reported savings of $5 million to $10 million.[31] Other savings should result from cuts in promotional expenses. P&G, for example, boosted profits by cutting costs after it adopted EDLP.[32]

The results of using EDLP have been mixed. At first, P&G lost market share in 10 of 11 product categories surveyed by Salomon Brothers. Competing brands as well as private labels picked up the loss.[33] Eventually, however, the company reported that its "value-priced" brands were doing better than brands not using the EDLP strategy.[34] In general, it may be that some products perform better under EDLP, whereas others—such as products bought on impulse—benefit from the promotional efforts that accompany a temporary price reduction. Likewise, unfamiliar brands may benefit from the attention generated by special deals.[35]

At the retail level, research casts some doubt on the benefits of EDLP. A Houston-area study by Southwest Information Resources found that 75 percent of consumers believed the prices of retailers with an EDLP strategy were comparable to those of other retailers, and about half said they thought a claim of every-day low prices is just a sales gimmick.[36] Researchers at the University of Chicago conducted an experiment in which some stores in the Dominick's supermarket chain used every-day low prices in 19 product categories, while other stores used the standard "high-low" prices, or list prices coupled with periodic discounts. The stores that used EDLP generated slightly more sales but substantially lower profits. Stephen J. Hoch, the marketing professor who headed the study, noted that whether stores can benefit from using promotions for particular products depends less on what competitors do and more on the importance of price to consumers. Retailers, said Hoch, "ought to pay more attention to the people coming into their stores"—the essence of the quality approach to marketing.[37]

PSYCHOLOGICAL PRICING

psychological pricing
Tactics designed to make a price look more appealing to buyers.

Often, the way the marketer adjusts prices is designed to add to the product's appeal. Pricing tactics designed to make a price look more appealing to buyers are known as **psychological pricing**. Psychological pricing for a product line may include price lining, described earlier. For product lines or individual products, the marketer may use prestige pricing, odd-even pricing, and bundle pricing.

PRESTIGE PRICING   Buyers may see a high price as a sign that a product is exceptionally fine. Setting a high price to convey an image of high quality and exclusivity is

FIGURE 15.7
Odd-Even Pricing at the Grocery Store

prestige pricing
Setting a high price to convey an image of high quality or exclusivity.

known as **prestige pricing**. This pricing strategy is used for some lines of cars, clothing, perfume, jewelry, cosmetics, wine and liquor, and crystal and china.

When these items are expensive, the price reinforces the notion that the goods are something special enjoyed by a privileged few. The marketing manager for a company that sells luxury goods noted, "Our customers do not want to pay less. If we halved the price of all our products, we would double our sales for 6 months and then we would sell nothing."[38] In other words, a low price would attract a broad segment of the market, and then the wide ownership of the product would make it less prestigious. This seems to have happened to Tiffany's in Japan. Sales at that upscale jeweler plunged in the 1990s; some observers believed that so many Japanese consumers bought jewelry from Tiffany's during the preceding decade that the name lost some of its status.[39]

odd-even pricing
Setting prices a few dollars or cents below a round number.

ODD-EVEN PRICING   Every day we encounter examples of **odd-even pricing**, that is, prices set a few dollars or cents below a round number (see Figure 15.7). On a recent day, one newspaper advertised bacon at 79 cents a pound, Delco car batteries at $37.88, and "luxurious waterfront condominiums" starting at $134,990. Why did the advertisers select these prices instead of 80 cents, $40, and $135,000? Presumably, they thought members of their target markets would perceive the prices as lower. Thus, bacon consumers would think of a pound of bacon as costing "seventy-something cents," rather than "about 80 cents."

As an astute college student, you probably noticed that the Delco car battery was advertised at almost $40, not $30. Wouldn't most consumers notice, too? Yet marketers continue to use this tactic. To see whether odd-even pricing really works, researchers studied the effect on sales of food products when prices ended in 9 rather than another number. The study found sales to be 10 percent higher when the price ended in 9. Research into the ways consumers perceive prices has found that they tend to see items with prices ending in 9 as being low priced—and sometimes lower in quality as well.[40] Consequently, there may be some benefit to using odd-even pricing when the marketing strategy is to emphasize low price rather than top quality.

bundle pricing
Offering several products as a package at a single price.

BUNDLE PRICING   Another way that marketers can convey the idea that their products are a good value is to use **bundle pricing**. This entails offering several products as a package at a single price. Hotels and travel agencies offer vacation packages that include travel, accommodations, and entertainment. Everex uses bundle pricing for its personal computers. The company has offered a complete computer system (hardware, software installed, and warranties) for $2,999 with the advertising message, "All you do is plug it in and use it."

Bundle pricing assumes that customers will appreciate being able to receive a variety of products by making a single purchase. In fact, the convenience of making a single purchase may make the package worth more together than as individual parts. Adding to the marketer's advantage, it may be less costly to sell the products as a package than individually.

GEOGRAPHIC PRICING

geographic pricing
Pricing a good or service according to where it is delivered.

The cost to provide a good or service can vary according to where it is delivered. For example, it costs more to ship a printing press to a printer several states away than to one in the same city. And it costs more to provide copies of *People* magazine to subscribers in Australia than to subscribers in Atlanta. Therefore, marketers sometimes use **geographic pricing** to adjust the price to reflect these cost differences. In doing so, they must keep in mind that if they charge more to ship to distant customers, they will be at a disadvantage relative to competitors who are closer to those buyers.

There are several approaches to geographic pricing. One approach is simply to add on the cost of transporting the product. For example, a consultant might pass along the cost of traveling to a client's workplace. The marketer also might use FOB origin pricing or some form of uniform delivered pricing.

FOB origin pricing
Geographic approach to pricing in which the seller's price is for the good at the point of shipment, where the title passes from seller to buyer.

FOB ORIGIN PRICING   The abbreviation FOB stands for "free on board." With **FOB origin pricing**, the seller's price is for the good at the point of shipment, where title passes from seller to buyer. In other words, the buyer is responsible for selecting a means of transporting the goods, choosing a specific carrier, handling any claims for damage in shipment, and paying for shipping. A seller using FOB origin pricing typically names the location of the point of shipment, expressed as the location of the factory or warehouse. For example, the seller might specify "FOB factory" or "FOB St. Louis." This type of pricing is most attractive to buyers located near the seller and set up to handle the responsibility of shipping goods.

uniform delivered pricing
Geographic approach to pricing in which the seller's price includes shipping; title passes where the buyer receives the goods.

UNIFORM DELIVERED PRICING   In contrast, other sellers use **uniform delivered pricing**, which means the seller's price includes shipping. On a contract, such a pricing arrangement could be called "FOB buyer's location" or "FOB destination." Title passes where the buyer receives the goods. The seller arranges for transportation, is responsible for any damage that occurs during shipment, and pays the freight charges. Some types of uniform delivered pricing are single-zone pricing, multiple-zone pricing, FOB with freight allowed, and basing point pricing.

Single-zone pricing means that all buyers pay the same price for the goods, including delivery. A catalog retailer might add on a $2.50 delivery charge for any purchase under $50. The delivery charge is the same no matter what state the buyer lives in. In effect, the seller charges each buyer the average amount to ship to its customers. The resulting price is most advantageous for the most distant customers, who wind up paying less than the cost to ship to them.

Multiple-zone pricing involves dividing the selling area into regions, or zones. Each zone has its own delivery price. The different charges reflect the differences in the cost to deliver to each zone. For example, an MCI user in Los Angeles pays a different

rate to call Sacramento than would an MCI user in Miami. However, all Los Angeles buyers of the same MCI package would pay the same rate to call Sacramento.

FOB with freight allowed means that the seller allows the buyer to deduct shipping costs from the list price of the goods. The seller typically quotes such a price as "FOB plant—freight allowed." In this case, the buyer arranges for transportation of the goods, but the seller bears the cost.

In the case of **basing point pricing**, the seller bases the price on one or more geographic locations where the product is produced (called basing points). The delivered price is the list price plus the cost of delivering from the basing point to the buyer. The goods may actually be shipped from a location other than the basing point. In some cases, then, customers will pay a freight charge that exceeds the actual transportation costs; the cost difference is called phantom freight.

Buyers don't want to pay phantom freight, so basing point pricing is relatively uncommon. However, it has been used in some industries with high freight expenses—for example, cement, lumber, and steel. The rationale for using basing point pricing is to give distant suppliers the ability to compete by offering comparable transportation rates.

FOB with freight allowed
Type of uniform delivered pricing in which the seller allows the buyer to deduct shipping costs from the list price of a product.

basing point pricing
Type of uniform delivered pricing in which the seller charges the list price plus the cost of delivering from one or more geographic points where the product is produced (basing points).

Evaluation and Control of Pricing

As with other dimensions of marketing strategy, the marketer needs to evaluate how well the chosen pricing strategy is working. Competitors and target markets will respond to this and other aspects of the marketing effort, and these responses will require that the marketer make adjustments. The cartoon in Figure 15.8 shows two young marketers evaluating a disappointing level of customer response.

COMPETITOR RESPONSES

Whether competitors respond as expected can determine whether the pricing strategy succeeds or fails. Unfortunately, competitors do not always respond as expected. The marketer simply must monitor competitors' pricing strategies and continually adapt the organization's own prices.

price war
Repeated price reductions by competitors in an effort to undercut one another's prices.

RESPONSES TO LOW PRICES When the organization uses a price reduction or a low-price strategy, competitors may respond by reducing their own prices. Unless the marketer has determined that the organization can afford lower price levels, the result may be that everyone is hurt financially. Sometimes a **price war** results; com-

You Decide

HOW SHOULD HEALTH CARE PRICES BE DETERMINED?

Patients are fed up. No longer do they view their physicians as kindly members of the family. More and more, they are becoming savvy consumers who insist on shopping around for the best care at the best price.

In the first two years of this decade, health care expenditures rose 37 percent to top $800 billion. It's no wonder that health care consumers are feeling tapped out. "My parents always said the doctor is the lifeline of the family—don't ask about prices. It was a taboo thing to do," comments Ron Pollack, executive director of Families USA, a health care consumer advocacy group based in Washington, D. C. That attitude is gone.

"Don't get me wrong, I like doctors," explains arthritis patient Louis Ullman. "But we all need to rely more on ourselves and our knowledge. My philosophy is that I'm paying the doctor to be an expert; and if I don't at least listen, I'm wasting my money and time. But I have no problem asking questions and deciding myself what to do with the results." Ullman's doctor prescribed an anti-inflammatory medicine that costs around $144 a month; Ullman decided to take aspirin instead, which costs around $7 a month and gives him the same results without side effects.

Doctors, many of whom have accepted the notion that one of their jobs is to market their services, are responding in different ways. Many practice a form of price discrimination, determining prices by a patient's ability to pay. While a sliding scale may meet some objectives of social responsibility, it means that patients who are privately insured pay the most for the same care. Jane Orient, president of the American Association of Physicians and Surgeons, notes that in these cases, patients could plead poverty, pay the lower rate, file a claim for the full price, and pocket the difference. Of course, the flip side of this situation is that the physician who is paid less for a procedure by Medicaid or Medicare can bill the private insurance company of another patient more for the same procedure.

Other doctors are responding to their newly cost-conscious patients by simply posting price lists of procedures in their waiting rooms. That way, people know exactly what treatments will cost. Families USA's Pollack likes this idea, saying, "We need one set of prices for everyone."

Do you agree with Pollack, or do you feel that price discrimination in health care is legitimate? Why? Do you think that patients who shop around for quality care at the best prices will ultimately hurt or help the health care industry? How do you think doctors can best respond to their patients' concern about price?

Source: Wendy Bounds, "Sick of Skyrocketing Costs, Patients Defy Doctors and Shop for Cheaper Treatment," *The Wall Street Journal,* June 16, 1993, pp. B1, B8.

could confuse customers by signaling that the product no longer offers the same level of quality.

There are steps to make a price change work. One is to time any increase to coincide with improvements to the product.[49] The marketer can make sure that the communications effort supports the change by explaining to potential customers why they will continue getting good value. The marketer can also communicate with resellers and big customers to make sure they aren't caught by surprise. The marketer should be able to explain to them the reasons for the change.

AVOIDING ILLEGAL PRICE DISCRIMINATION   In using the various options for adjusting the price, the marketer should take care to avoid illegal price discrimination. As defined in Chapter 14, price discrimination is the practice of charging different prices to customers when the price difference does not reflect a cost difference to the seller. Recall that the forms of price discrimination prohibited by the Robinson-Patman Act are those that substantially interfere with competition. This means there are some legitimate reasons for charging different prices. The price differences may reflect differences in the cost to produce, sell, or deliver goods. Price differences may result from meeting changes in market conditions and moving seasonal merchandise, including perishable goods. Also allowed are price differences intended to meet the competition. (For more discussion of price discrimination, see "You Decide.")

One way to avoid charges of illegal price discrimination is to be evenhanded in applying the various means of adjusting prices. For example, any customer purchasing a given quantity could be eligible for a quantity discount. Or all customers could be quoted prices FOB with freight allowed. Likewise, sellers offering promotional allowances must offer them to all distributors in proportion to the amount purchased. MCI offered 20 percent discounts to the millions of customers who participate in its Friends & Family program.[50] Other MCI customers paid more, but this is not illegal price discrimination, because they, too, could encourage family members and friends to sign up with MCI.

Summary

Marketers create specific pricing strategies—any of which should support marketing objectives—in a variety of ways. Generally, pricing objectives include achieving a desired level of sales, being competitive in terms of price or market share, earning a targeted level of profits, enabling the organization to survive, and achieving a standard of social responsibility.

The way a marketer prices the organization's products varies according to organizational and marketing objectives as well as the unique nature of the product and its target markets. Ideally, marketers should follow a logical pricing process in which they (1) set pricing objectives; (2) evaluate demand and other pricing constraints; (3) analyze profit potential; (4) set the initial price level; and (5) adjust the price as needed.

When pricing a new product, marketers are generally trying to get as many members of the target market to try the product as soon as possible and to recover the costs of developing the product as soon as possible. Several methods may accomplish this. Marketers may try penetration pricing—setting a low price to attract potential customers. They may resort to skimming—setting the price high in order to recover production costs quickly.

When pricing an existing product, marketers must consider such characteristics as perishability, distinctiveness of the product, and stage in the life cycle. If the product is part of a product line, marketers consider the price of each individual product as well as the pricing strategy for the entire line.

Marketers may use either price lining or uniform pricing for the line.

Sometimes prices need adjustment. Marketers often use a combination of discounting, psychological pricing, and geographic pricing. Discounts—price reductions—may come in the form of quantity discounts, seasonal discounts, trade discounts, cash discounts, promotional discounts, allowances, or loss leaders. (Or marketers may switch to every-day low pricing.) Psychological pricing comes in the form of odd-even pricing (such as $7.99 versus $8.00) and bundle pricing (offering several products in one package). Geographic pricing includes FOB origin pricing and uniform delivered pricing.

Marketers need to evaluate how well the chosen price strategy is working by determining how the competition and the target market are responding. For example, if the company reduces prices, competitors may respond with low prices of their own or try to distinguish their products as being of higher quality (and thus worth a higher price). If customer response is less than satisfactory, the price may need further adjustment; if it is greater than expected, the company may have to increase production to meet demand. If outside factors influencing the initial price level change, marketers will have to consider new prices. It is best if a price increase coincides with improvements in the product itself. If marketers opt for some type of price discrimination, they should be certain that it is legal.

KEY TERMS AND CONCEPTS

list price (p. 442)

penetration pricing (p. 443)

skimming (p. 443)

price lining (p. 446)

uniform pricing (p. 446)

countertrade (p. 447)

discount (p. 448)

market price (p. 448)

rebate (p. 448)

quantity discount (p. 449)

seasonal discount (p. 449)

trade discount (p. 450)

cash discount (p. 450)

trade-in allowance (p. 451)

promotional allowance (p. 451)

promotional discount (p. 451)

loss leader pricing (p. 451)

every-day low prices (EDLP) (p. 452)

psychological pricing (p. 452)

prestige pricing (p. 453)

odd-even pricing (p. 453)

bundle pricing (p. 453)

geographic pricing (p. 454)

FOB origin pricing (p. 454)

uniform delivered pricing (p. 454)

FOB with freight allowed (p. 455)

basing point pricing (p. 455)

price war (p. 455)

REVIEW AND DISCUSSION QUESTIONS

1. What basic categories of pricing objectives do marketers have?
2. Name the five steps of the pricing process.
3. If you were involved in marketing bottled water in Europe, what pricing constraints would you face?
4. If you were pricing a new product line of kites—of varying sizes and shapes, with different levels of performance sophistication—what strategies might you use to arrive at the best price? (Consider issues related both to new products and product lines, as well as characteristics of existing products that may apply.)
5. What, if any, kinds of discounts would you expect to consider or use for each of the following products? Explain your choices.

a. cotton balls
b. mainframe computers
c. haircuts

6. Do you think odd-even pricing would be effective for bread at a supermarket? Why or why not? For an accountant's services? Why or why not?
7. Why is a price war considered to be a negative situation from the marketer's standpoint?
8. If customer demand for the kites in question 4 is greater than you expected, what steps might your company take either to meet the demand or level it off? What factors would you consider before deciding which path to take?
9. Is price discrimination ever legitimate? If so, when?

Chapter Project
Adjusting the Price of a Product

In your project for Chapter 14, you determined the best approach to pricing a product, then set your price. For this project, you will reevaluate your product's list price and make necessary adjustments based on possible competitor and customer responses. (You may study the pricing history of an actual, similar product.)

To carry out the project, answer the following questions with regard to the list price you set in the Chapter 14 project: Do you need to offer discounts? Consider odd-even, geographic, or every-day low pricing? If your product is part of a product line, have you made appropriate use of price lining or uniform pricing? Also take into account the life cycle stage of your product. To help systematize your thinking, use the worksheet described in "Put It into Practice" and provided in Table 15.1.

Write a report explaining the reasons for any adjustments you feel you need to make in your product's price. In a typical organization providing this type of product, who would you expect to make decisions about these price adjustments? What should be the marketer's role in controlling the use of these adjustments? Present your findings in class.

Case
Europe's Discount Wars

Price wars aren't unique to the American marketplace; they happen all over the world. In Europe, the fight between discounters and traditional retailers is fierce. Leading the offensive are German discounters such as Aldi, Spar Handels, and Lidl & Schwarz, which together control about one-fourth of Germany's food retailing industry.

These "hard" discounters do business by renting small, inexpensive stores on urban street corners where everyone can reach them by foot or by public transportation. They employ as few people as possible and sell goods right out of the boxes they've been shipped in. They offer a small range of products—usually private label—and sell only the cheapest, fastest-moving goods they can get their hands on.

Among themselves, the discounters are tough competitors. Aldi, with 3,360 stores in seven European countries, offers about 600 products. Of these, 200 are sold under Aldi's own label. Spar Handels offers the same 200 products under its own store brand at prices that match Aldi's.

Of course, the discounters are also competing with traditional retailers. These stores are trying to meet the price challenge. They have begun to offer not only less expensive goods than their standard offerings, but goods that are actually of lower quality so that prices can drop through the floor. Some of the supermarkets practice geographic pricing and promotional pricing as well. Others respond by making adjustments to their product mix as well as their price.

In spite of their efforts, supermarkets are struggling to remain profitable in the face of relatively high operating costs. The average operating margin for a traditional supermarket in Britain is about 6.5 percent, whereas the margin for discounters is around 1 percent. That gives discounters plenty of room to earn a profit at lower prices.

In the middle are so-called "soft" discounters, providing less service and sometimes lower quality than the supermarkets yet charging higher prices than the hard discounters like Aldi. Kwik Save, Britain's largest discount chain, stocks 2,500 products (compared to Aldi's 600), and its stores are larger. That means overhead is greater, and the store can't offer the deep discounts that Aldi does. On the other hand, it can't compete with the more prestigious stores.

In Europe, the discount war takes on slightly different proportions than a price war in the United States. The competition from discounters has led food retailers to seek more efficient ways of operating. As a result, more and more are entering into mergers, acquisitions, and alliances with food retailers in other European countries. In 1989, only one such link existed; three years later, there were 13, accounting for about $519 million in sales.

And the grocery business is not the only one getting into the discount battle. Warehouse clubs are appearing on the scene, enabling shoppers to buy a membership that entitles them to purchase items in bulk at rock-bottom prices. For example, American-based Costco and the British wholesaler Nurdin & Peacock are both planning to open warehouse clubs in Britain.

QUESTIONS

1. If you were a marketer for an American discount chain that planned to open stores in Europe, how would you study the competition to determine the prices of your products?
2. What strategies might European supermarkets use to compete against the discount chains?
3. Do you think the German style of discount store would be successful in the United States? Why or why not?

Sources: Cacilie Rohwedder, "Deep-Discount Fight Consumes Much of Europe, *The Wall Street Journal,* June 18, 1993, p. A5C; "Europe's Discount Dogfight," *The Economist,* May 8, 1993, pp. 69–70.

Channels of Distribution

Setting the Stage

Micro Warehouse

With all the choices available to organizations and consumers looking to buy computers, companies that sell them face stiff competition. The three founders of Micro Warehouse, all formerly in the computer publishing industry, know this well. In 1987, they realized that there were virtually no computer catalogs available to the general public. Most mail-order resellers just advertised in special publications and waited for customers to call. In addition, there was little or no service backing these sales. Buying a computer was confusing and difficult for most customers because technology and products were constantly changing, and retail distribution of up-to-date products was often weak. Micro Warehouse set out to change that.

Micro Warehouse jumped into the computer-selling business by offering a monthly catalog of major brand-name products at prices generally 30 to 60 percent off the manufacturer's suggested retail price. They offered comprehensive promotional and informational literature, a toll-free number staffed by knowledgeable telemarketing teams, and free technical support both before and after each sale. Of course, they also offered the convenience of catalog shopping.

Because Micro Warehouse makes overnight delivery commitments (customers who order before midnight can receive products the next day), the company moved its distribution facility to Wilmington, Ohio, where Airborne Express is based. It now maintains 100,000 square feet of warehouse space there and $45 million worth of inventory so that orders can be filled quickly and efficiently. Micro Warehouse works closely with Airborne, verifying Airborne's on-time delivery performance and surveying customers to make sure they are satisfied with delivery. Micro Warehouse charges only $7 for overnight delivery of its products.

Micro Warehouse views its main competition as the retail superstores, such as CompUSA. While it's true that superstores can maintain a large inventory and sell it at low prices, Micro Warehouse relies on its efficient distribution, quick delivery, and convenience to maintain its competitiveness. The company's formula must be working: the telephones at Micro Warehouse ring 30,000 times a day.

Source: Promotional material from Micro Warehouse and Hershey Consulting Services, Highlands, N.C.

CHAPTER 16   *Managing Distribution Channels*

LEARNING OBJECTIVES

After completing this chapter, you should be able to:

1. Describe the nature of distribution channels and how they meet marketing needs.

2. Identify the basic types of distribution channels for consumer and industrial goods and services.

3. Describe some variations of the basic channels.

4. Explain how marketers use traditionally structured channels and alternatives to those structures.

5. Discuss principles for selecting distribution channels and working with channel members.

6. Evaluate legal and ethical considerations in distribution.

Creating Customer Value
Ben & Jerry's Homemade

Chunky Monkey. Rainforest Crunch. Cherry Garcia. Chocolate Chip Cookie Dough. Everyone knows what these names stand for—flavors of that sweet, rich, incredibly delicious, all-natural ice cream made by two "counterculture" businessmen who settled in Vermont and decided that ice cream might be cheaper to produce than bagels. (By the time they learned that ice cream was actually more expensive, they were well into manufacturing it and had headed for success.) Ben Cohen and Jerry Greenfield have become household names, their ice cream is household ice cream, and their way of doing business has become a household example to many larger companies.

Ben & Jerry's started as a small company, with a small-company atmosphere. In 1988, the organization still operated out of one major business site, with 150 employees and $32 million in sales. Today the firm operates four major business sites, employs 500 people, and draws in sales of $130 million. As the company grew, distribution had to expand, and its owners chose a team organization to accomplish this while maintaining their firm's focus on the importance of its people.

When it became evident that the ice-cream producer needed a new distribution center, Ben & Jerry's selected a cross-functional team to carry out the tasks of planning and designing it (instead of hiring an outside agency). The eight-member team, consisting of employees from marketing, sales, finance, and other departments, scouted other plants around the country, then reported what they concluded Ben & Jerry's needed. Management gave them the go-ahead. In 1992, the $3.5 million distribution center opened in Bellows Falls, Vermont. At the same time, Ben & Jerry's adopted the use of just-in-time manufacturing, receiving deliveries as needed rather than bearing the cost of holding an inventory of materials.

With the success of the first team, Ben & Jerry's established another team to design a manufacturing plant. Explains company president Chuck Lacy, "The passion you

get by doing things in-house overcomes the expertise you can buy on the outside."

Employee empowerment through the use of cross-functional teams is helping Ben & Jerry's grow, not only in its distribution and production capabilities but in other areas as well. Now the company has what it calls "Big Nine" process teams—nine groups of employees that meet on a regular basis to find solutions to everything from training problems to flavor selection. At one point, distributors complained that they couldn't get enough of the right flavors for their customers. Employees, rather than upper management, solved the problem. Decision making at all levels is paramount. "The name of the game is creating more ownership at all levels in the mission of the company, which consists of a profit-making component and a social responsibility component," explains Elizabeth Bankowski, who holds the title of Director, Social Mission Development.

As you read this chapter, you'll see how cost-effective, efficient channels of distribution are vital to the success of a product. You'll see how teamwork and a customer focus can help make distribution as smooth as what some people believe is the very best ice cream in the world.

Source: Robert J. Sonenclar, "Ben & Jerry's: Management with a Human Flavor," *Hemisphere,* March 1993, pp. 25–26.

Chapter Overview

As explained in Chapter 1, among the four elements of the marketing mix is channels of distribution, or getting the product to the target market so that it will be convenient to buy. Thus, when a marketer has developed an efficient distribution system, the organization makes its products available to customers when and where they want to buy them, while keeping distribution costs to a minimum. For example, thanks to effective teamwork, Ben & Jerry's developed an efficient approach to distribution.

This chapter introduces the basic concerns of marketers in setting up and using a strategy for channels of distribution. The chapter begins by describing basic types of distribution channels—the networks of organizations that distribute goods and services. The chapter then discusses how marketers select the members of distribution channels and how the channel members work together. Finally, the chapter covers legal and ethical considerations related to channels of distribution.

Channels of Distribution

What do you do when it's time for lunch? Maybe you head over to a nearby Wendy's franchise and order a hamburger and a soft drink. Or maybe you open your refrigerator and pull out the Pepperidge Farm bread, Smuckers peanut butter, and Dannon yogurt you bought during a recent trip to the supermarket. Suppose you were a buyer for Smuckers. How would you get the glass jars and the peanuts your employer needs to produce peanut butter? Surely you wouldn't have to drive a pickup to the peanut farm or a trailer truck to the glassmaker every week. No, these suppliers use various resellers to make it easy for you to send in your orders and receive deliveries at your factory.

channel of distribution
An organized network of entities that perform all the activities required to link producers with users of products.

The ways in which producers make their products available to you, the buyer, involve channels of distribution (or distribution channels for short). A **channel of distribution** is "an organized network (system) of agencies and institutions which, in combination, perform all the activities required to link producers with users to accomplish the marketing task."[1] Thus, the Wendy's restaurant, the supermarket, and the distributor of glass jars are all members of distribution channels.

THE NATURE OF DISTRIBUTION CHANNELS

As you can see from the definition, a channel of distribution consists of whichever organizations are responsible for getting goods and services from producers to their ultimate users. In some cases, a channel of distribution may simply be the producer carrying out the distribution functions described later in this chapter. Other distribution channels consist of the producer plus one or more resellers. In these channels, the resellers handle some of the distribution functions.

intermediary (middleman)
An independent business specializing in linking sellers with consumers or organizational users.

The resellers in a distribution channel are called intermediaries. An **intermediary**, or **middleman**, is an independent business that specializes in linking sellers with consumers or organizational users. Thus, The Gap, Musicland, and other stores are a type of intermediary (retailers) because they buy goods from a variety of sources and make them available to consumers in one place. This and the next chapter introduce some of the many types of intermediaries.

TABLE 16.1

Functions Performed by Intermediaries

Transactional Functions

Buying	Purchasing products in order to resell them
Selling	Promoting products to potential customers and soliciting orders
Risk taking	Assuming business risks by owning goods that can deteriorate, be damaged, or become obsolete

Logistical Functions

Concentration	Bringing goods from various places together in one place
Storing	Maintaining inventories and protecting goods in a way that meets customer needs
Sorting	Purchasing in quantity and breaking into amounts desired by customers; includes: • *Accumulation*—bringing similar goods from multiple sources together into a larger homogeneous supply • *Allocation*—breaking a homogeneous supply into smaller lots • *Assorting*—building an assortment of products from several sources to serve customers • *Sorting out*—breaking down a heterogeneous supply into separate, relatively homogeneous stocks
Transporting	Physically moving goods from where they were manufactured to where they are to be bought or used

Facilitating Functions

Financing	Providing credit or funds to facilitate a transaction
Grading	Inspecting products and classifying them into categories based on quality
Marketing research	Gathering data on market conditions, expected sales, consumer trends, and competitive forces; reporting information on these topics

THE NEED FOR INTERMEDIARIES

Intermediaries are important because they have expertise in performing some or all of the distribution functions. When producers lack expertise or efficiency, they ask intermediaries to take on these tasks.

DISTRIBUTION FUNCTIONS   To identify the many distribution functions, it is helpful to think of them in terms of three categories: transactional, logistical, and facilitating functions. Table 16.1 lists the activities involved in carrying out these three types of functions. Which functions a particular intermediary performs depends on the type of intermediary and its agreement with the seller.

By performing *transactional functions,* such as buying products for resale or selling the products they have purchased, intermediaries bring together sellers and buyers. When intermediaries carry out these functions, the producer can reach the entire target market with a minimum number of sales contacts. For example, suppose you started a company that makes bicycle helmets. Selling to every bike rider in the United States or even in your county would be difficult and expensive. But suppose you instead sold the helmets to bike shops and to sporting goods stores such as SportMart. As shown in Figure 16.1, you could drastically cut the number of sales

FIGURE 16.1

**How Intermediaries
Reduce Necessary
Sales Contacts**

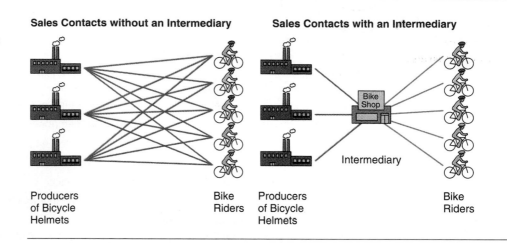

FIGURE 16.1

**How Intermediaries
Reduce Necessary
Sales Contacts**

contacts needed for making your product available to interested consumers. Furthermore, bike riders would know where to go to find a product such as yours.

Transactional functions provide other benefits as well. First, they keep distribution costs down by standardizing exchanges. In other words, when fewer but larger sales take place, prices, delivery schedules, and payment terms tend to be more uniform and more favorable to the buyer. Also, when intermediaries buy from producers, they take on some of the risk that the products may deteriorate, become obsolete, or suffer damage.

In essence, the *logistical functions* involve moving goods around and combining them in quantities that make them easy to buy. For example, through the concentration function, a supermarket makes peanut butter, bread, yogurt, and many other items available in one place. The supermarket stores these products in the appropriate facilities and displays them on shelves with other, like items. And it sells bread by the loaf, rather than by the case. The wholesaler that trucks these products to the store also is carrying out logistical functions.

By performing *facilitating functions,* intermediaries make buying and selling easier. These functions include financing transactions, grading product quality, and gathering market information. Sales forecasts, competitive analyses, and reports on market conditions provided by intermediaries help producers find out what customers want. In developing its DeWalt line of power tools, Black & Decker consulted with several big home improvement chains to learn what consumers were asking for.[2]

INTERMEDIARIES AND COSTS   Although intermediaries perform a variety of services, they are sometimes seen as a source of unnecessary costs. "Buy from us and save!" go the ads from discounters. "Eliminate the middleman!" But the savings are real only if buyer and seller are willing to absorb the cost of intermediaries' services themselves. In other words, eliminating the middleman does not eliminate the functions performed by intermediaries.

The aim is to locate distribution functions where they can best meet the needs of sellers and their target markets. For example, buying from a factory outlet can be a good deal for consumers who don't mind the time and expense of driving to a relatively remote location and don't mind going elsewhere when they want to see another manufacturer's products. Other consumers prefer to pay a retailer for providing the service of making a wider selection available at a more convenient location.

TABLE 16.2	Agent or Broker	An intermediary that negotiates purchases or sales but does not take title to the products it handles
Types of Intermediaries	Dealer	Distributor, retailer, or wholesaler
	Distributor	An intermediary—typically a wholesaler—that performs a variety of distribution functions, including selling, maintaining inventories, and extending credit; often serves industrial markets
	Retailer	An intermediary that sells to consumers
	Wholesaler	An intermediary that sells to other intermediaries; the term is most commonly applied to consumer markets

Likewise, a producer might find that an intermediary can store and transport its goods more efficiently than the producer can. This is the case for McKee Foods, whose Little Debbie brand of snack cakes is the nation's top seller in terms of unit volume. The company's tactic is to sell at a price 50 to 70 percent below the competition. McKee can afford to do this because it trucks cakes to the central warehouses of distributors (wholesalers), which efficiently handle the tasks of serving individual stores; McKee's competitors bear such expenses themselves.[3] Clearly, in such cases, intermediaries meet important needs.

The Organization of Distribution Channels

To understand the possible ways to make products available to potential users, the marketer needs to know the ways most distribution channels are organized. A marketer who is familiar with channel organization can make an informed choice about distributing a particular product. That choice may involve one or more of the basic channel organizations or the use of more innovative organizations, such as strategic alliances or reverse channels.

BASIC TYPES OF DISTRIBUTION CHANNELS

Several basic ways to organize channels are common. These channels use the types of intermediaries defined in Table 16.2.

direct marketing
A distribution channel that has no intermediaries.

CHANNELS FOR CONSUMER GOODS Consumers buy goods from retailers or directly from the manufacturer. Figure 16.2 shows the four most common distribution channels for consumer goods. In Channel A, there are no intermediaries. This type of channel organization is called **direct marketing**. Corky's Bar-B-Q restaurant in Memphis, Tennessee, uses direct marketing to sell ribs at its drive-through window and through overnight mail delivery, as well as to diners in its restaurant.[4] Later, this and the next chapter take a closer look at various means of direct marketing.

In Channel B, goods move from producer to retailers to consumers. Some big retailers like J. C. Penney, Wal-Mart, and Safeway buy in such large quantities that producers will sell directly to them. These stores, in turn, sell the goods to the consumers who shop there.

Channel C is the most common channel for consumer goods. In this channel, the producer sells to wholesalers, which sell to retailers, which in turn sell to consumers.

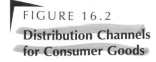

FIGURE 16.2

Distribution Channels for Consumer Goods

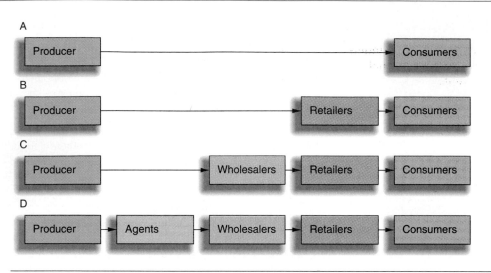

Kellogg produces many brands of cereal, which it sells to food wholesalers. The wholesalers sell the cereal to many stores, mainly supermarkets and grocery stores. In general, this is the most practical way to achieve the widespread distribution necessary to reach the huge target markets for most consumer goods. Dealing with millions of consumers or even thousands of retailers would be difficult for most small producers and inefficient even for large ones. Retailers also tend to benefit from this channel because it enables them to rely on the wholesaler's familiarity with a variety of products.

Channel D is the most indirect channel. Goods pass from producer to agents to wholesalers to retailers and then to consumers. Unlike many other types of intermediaries, agents do not take title to the products they distribute. They coordinate a large supply of goods when there are many small manufacturers and retailers. Small manufacturers that lack the capital for their own sales force use agents, often called manufacturer's representatives, to serve as an independent sales force to contact wholesalers.

CHANNELS FOR ORGANIZATIONAL GOODS   As noted in Chapter 9, the total number of organizational buyers is much smaller than the total customers for consumer goods. In addition, organizational buyers are more concentrated geographically, and they often buy in relatively large quantities. Many industrial goods, such as computer systems or sophisticated medical equipment, need a great deal of service before and after the sale. Because of these characteristics of selling organizational goods, distribution channels for these products are usually shorter than those for consumer goods. Figure 16.3 illustrates the four most common channels for organizational goods.

The most common channel for organizational goods is Channel A, a direct channel from producer to organizational buyers. A direct channel is most efficient when buyers are large and well defined, when selling requires extensive negotiations, when the price per unit is high, and when the product requires extensive service and support. For complex, sophisticated products, not only may the company's own salespeople with technical expertise be best equipped to help prospects see the value of the product, but organizational buyers may look for this expertise and be unwilling to rely on—or buy from—independent sales representatives.[5] Mitsubishi customizes

FIGURE 16.3

Distribution Channels for Organizational Goods

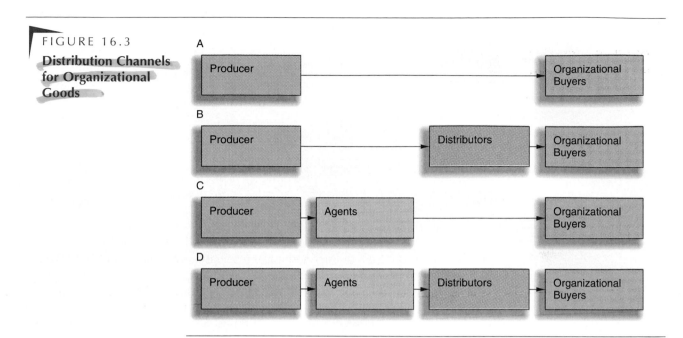

each CNC (computer numerical control—a kind of control panel for machine tools) and provides free training after the sale.

In Channel B, goods flow from the producer to a distributor. A **distributor** is a wholesale intermediary typically serving organizational markets, offering a variety of services, and providing strong promotional support for a product. Using a distributor is efficient for producers of products targeted to a large number of organizations that buy in small quantities, as in the case of building materials and software packages.

In Channel C, the intermediaries are agents instead of distributors. Channel C is often the choice for a producer that does not have a marketing department but needs market information, is too small to field its own sales force, or wants to introduce a new product or enter a new market without using its own salespeople. For example, manufacturers of food-processing equipment often use agents.

In Channel D, agents bring together producers and organizational distributors. Thus, agents seek a market for a producer's output and locate sources of supply for a buyer. A manufacturer without a sales force may rely on agents to sell to large wholesalers if the organizational buyers purchase the product in small quantities or if customers must make frequent repurchases.

CHANNELS FOR SERVICES Because most services are produced and consumed at the same time, services are distributed through short channels. Thus, to buy a car wash or financial advice, you must go to the people providing those services. Figure 16.4 illustrates the typical channels of distribution for services.

The most common distribution channel for services is the direct one (Channel A). For example, cat owners who want their pets neutered or vaccinated go directly to the veterinarian. Business managers who want temporary secretarial services deal directly with Kelly, Manpower, or some other organization that provides such services.

When service firms use intermediaries, these are usually agents or brokers, as shown in Channel B. An example is travel agents, who act on behalf of their cus-

distributor
A wholesale intermediary that services industrial markets, offers a variety of services, and provides promotional support for a product.

FIGURE 16.4

Distribution Channels for Services

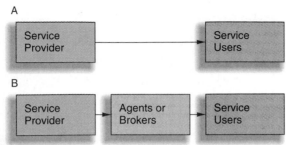

A

Service Provider → Service Users

B

Service Provider → Agents or Brokers → Service Users

tomers to buy tickets from airlines and make reservations at hotels. And Ticketmaster acts as an agent by selling tickets to performances at many venues, including concerts at Chicago's Riviera Theatre and Aragon Ballroom. Computers have lessened the use of agents in many channels. For example, a corporate travel department can make reservations through a link with American Airlines' SABRE reservation system rather than by calling a travel agent.[6]

VARIATIONS OF THE BASIC CHANNELS

The basic distribution channels described so far are the most common options available. However, creative marketers see these choices as only a starting point in planning this element of the marketing mix. Sometimes the distribution strategy that best meets marketing objectives includes other twists such as multiple channels, alliances with channel members, and reverse channels.

MULTIPLE DISTRIBUTION CHANNELS   To reach diverse markets, a producer might use several channels of distribution for a single product. Clambake Celebrations, based in Orleans, Massachusetts, sells lobster dinners, steamer clams, clam chowder base, and clambake dinners through a local retail store and also through direct channels, including a catalog.[7] A producer might use one type of marketing channel to serve consumers and another to serve organizational buyers.

In some instances, organizations use multiple channels to fit a multibrand strategy. Under one brand name, the product is distributed through one channel, and under another brand name, the product is distributed through another channel. Whirlpool makes appliances under its own name to distribute to consumers and under the Kenmore name to sell to Sears.

dual distribution
The use of two or more distribution channels to provide the same basic product to a target market.

The use of two or more types of distribution channels to provide the same basic product to a target market is called **dual distribution**. Producers use dual distribution to maximize coverage in the marketplace or to make the marketing effort more cost effective. Thus, the Quaker Oats Company gets its breakfast products to consumers through supermarkets, restaurants, warehouse clubs, in-store bakeries, and meals in airplanes, schools, and hospitals.[8]

STRATEGIC CHANNEL ALLIANCES   Building a channel of distribution is difficult and time consuming, especially when it involves international marketing. For this reason, channel members may seek to build a close relationship that meets mutual needs.

strategic channel alliance
A relationship between two channel members that meets mutual distribution needs.

Such a relationship is called a **strategic channel alliance**. For example, this was the approach used by cut-flower retailer Calyx & Corolla (see "Marketing Movers & Shakers" in Chapter 8). From the start, founder Ruth Owades knew that the concept of delivering cut flowers direct from grower to consumer depended on close partnerships with the growers and the shipper. Therefore, she included Federal Express and a number of growers in the process of planning how they would work together to achieve both speed and high quality.[9] "Looking Ahead," which follows Chapter 20, discusses strategic alliances in greater detail. (To see how Rykodisc used this type of relationship, see "Marketing Movers & Shakers.")

REVERSE CHANNELS   Traditionally, channels of distribution have moved products from producer to end user. However, sometimes it is important to move goods in the opposite direction. A distribution channel from end user to producer is called a **reverse channel**. Members of the reverse channels for used computers include Advanced Recovery and the East-West Education Development Foundation (EWEDF). Advanced Recovery takes computers apart, then sells the semiconductor chips to parts wholesalers and maintenance shops and extracts valuable metals such as aluminum and gold, also for resale. The EWEDF fixes up used computers and gives them to worthy organizations in 130 countries.[10]

reverse channel
A distribution channel that goes from end user to producer.

Recycling   Reverse channels have gained attention with the growth of recycling efforts and consumer interest in the environment. For example, consumers in many communities separate their empty bottles and cans from the rest of their trash. These containers move through a reverse channel when recycling companies pick them up, sort them, and sell them to the manufacturers that make new products with them. As more and more communities set up recycling programs, reverse channels should grow in importance.

In Germany, laws that require producers to reclaim and recycle their packaging are to be gradually expanded to include certain products themselves—electronics equipment and automobiles. For this reason, Volkswagen has already learned to strip down a car in 20 minutes. It will reclaim and recycle the latest European version of the Golf for free.[11] Other manufacturers that want to market in Europe will have to plan reverse channels and product design accordingly.

The growth of reverse channels also accompanies the demand for ways to use recycled materials. The California Recycling Company uses recycled plastic to make durable, waterproof building materials that resist graffiti. Its customers include the State of California and the Southern California Rapid Transit District.[12] The determination of Julie Lewis to develop a business using recyclable materials led her to form shoemaker Deja Inc. of Tigard, Oregon. The Deja Shoe has a recycled fabric covering and recycled rubber soles. The materials are produced from such waste materials as milk jugs, file folders, tire rubber, and wetsuit trim. Even the shoeboxes are made from recycled cardboard.

Recalls   Another type of reverse channel is the system set up for product recalls. If a manufacturer discovers a problem with its products, it may notify owners to bring their products to the seller for refund or replacement. Or owners might return to the manufacturer to have the product repaired.

Such reverse channels are used when car makers find a defective part that must be replaced or when toy makers learn that a product is unsafe. When automaker Saturn learned of a problem with faulty generator wires, it announced a voluntary recall. Customers were to take their cars to Saturn dealers, where the company would replace the wires with safer ones. In planning this reverse channel, Saturn considered customer

Marketing Movers & Shakers

DON ROSE'S RYKODISC USA

The world's first company devoted entirely to producing CDs started with a couple of guys sitting around a cafe during the Cannes Music Festival in 1983, scribbling some ideas on a cocktail napkin they now refer to as the "sacred napkin."

"The essence of Rykodisc is we're all music fans," explains Rykodisc USA's CEO Don Rose, speaking of his colleagues. "Essentially, music ruined our lives, and this is our way of getting back at it." What he's talking about is his ten-year-old company (based in Salem, Massachusetts), whose name in Japanese means "sound from a flash of light," a reference to CD laser technology. During the early 1980s, none of the big record companies paid much attention to the new CD technology, favoring instead the established long-playing records and cassette tapes. CD players then cost between $700 and $900 and industry marketers assumed they'd only appeal to hardened audiophiles.

So Don Rose (then owner of Eat Records), Don's brother-in-law Rob Simonds (a record importer), Doug Lexa (another record importer), and

lawyer Arthur Mann gambled that the industry was wrong. They started with a jazz CD by Jim Pepper called *Comin' and Goin'*, then went on to blues and acoustic-music samplers. "We thought the best place to start was compilations, since there was little of anything from those genres on CD then," notes Rose.

Rykodisc established itself in the business of CD reissues—finding the best recordings available, remastering, and adding new tracks to CD reissues. From the start, Rose and his colleagues stuck with the quality focus, viewing their audience as "a more discerning audience than the majors—a committed, intelligent clientele."

Ultimately they drew the attention of big-name artists who wanted their recordings reissued by Rykodisc. In 1985, Doug Rose landed the CD rights to Frank Zappa's work. Two years later, the late Jimi Hendrix's manager approached Rykodisc to issue Hendrix's never-before-released *Live at Wonderland*. A year after that, Rose promised David Bowie better quality and service (such as new cover art, posters, and the like) than the musician had received from his major record label, EMI. Rose got the contract.

One of the biggest nightmares in the recording industry is distribution, especially for a small, independent company like Rykodisc. By the late 1980s, the regional distribution system used by many of the independents had just about collapsed. One of the largest and oldest distributors went bankrupt owing Rykodisc $200,000. Large, powerful retailers like Musicland and Tower Records are now demanding slotting allowances, which the major record labels

are paying. Says Jac Holzman, chairman of Discovery Records (part of Time Warner), "Rykodisc's problems are like those of every other independent. They will always be outspent by the majors."

Doug Rose is undaunted. Rykodisc recently entered an alliance with Rounder Records (a folk and blues label based in Cambridge, Massachusetts), East Side Digital, and Precision Sound. Together, they formed a national distribution network called The REP Co. With 34 sales reps working from Kansas City, Minneapolis, Seattle, and Cambridge, Rose hopes he'll be able to distribute his CDs cost effectively at the optimum level of coverage. With this alliance, Rose has a direct connection between sales and distribution.

Rykodisc isn't confining itself to the United States. The company has acquired a popular folk and world-music label in Britain called Hannibal. Artists include Trio Bulgarka, Kanda Bongo Man, Kate and Anna McGarrigle, and the noted Richard Thompson. In addition, the company is developing new artists, such as Sugar (although reissues still account for 50 percent of sales).

Rykodisc's numbers remain solid in this volatile industry. Revenues approached $18 million in 1993, up from $11 million in 1989. Rose remains as committed to the quality of his work force as he is to his releases. "When hiring," he says, "we never look for college degrees or major-label experience. The most important question in our job interview is, 'What's the last record you bought?'"

Sources: Judy Temes, "Sneaking up on the Big Boys," *The Boston Globe,* September 1, 1993, pp. 42–43; Bruce Sylvester, "Rykodisc: Ten Years," *Pulse!,* October 1993, pp. 51–52.

satisfaction with more than wiring. Dealers offered convenient hours, soft drinks, and door-to-door pickup service in some cases. Saturn's continued focus on the customer was credited for the fact that the recall did not seem to be hurting sales.[13]

Gannett newspapers, the largest U.S. newspaper group, is at the end of a reverse channel that starts with consumers who sort their garbage for recycling. For several years, every Gannett newspaper has used some recycled newsprint. The company deals only with newsprint manufacturers that are able to provide a recycled product.

To notify customers about a recall, the manufacturer needs a reliable way to identify and reach them. The manufacturer might rely on sales records (in the case of cars), refer to warranty cards sent in by purchasers (in the case of appliances), or post notices at stores and other locations (in the case of toys or other products for children).

The Structure of Channels

The structure of a channel of distribution depends on the members of that channel and the extent of their relationship. Products may be sold through traditional channels, or distribution efforts may be coordinated through some type of channel integration, described later in this section. If the producer uses direct marketing, the marketer may set up the channel to reach customers through some combination of mail, telephone, television, or personal contacts.

TRADITIONAL DISTRIBUTION CHANNELS

The traditional channels of distribution described so far represent independent producers and intermediaries. Each organization has its own objectives, and these tend not to be entirely compatible. For example, a producer wants end users to buy its products, not some other producer's. A distributor, in contrast, wants buyers to select whatever products it carries (but especially the most profitable ones). It is therefore to the distributor's advantage to carry many competing offerings, so as to have something of interest to all buyers. To seek to achieve their objectives, the members of a distribution channel enter into formal and informal agreements with one another.

Under these traditional arrangements, one way to ensure that all members of the channel are satisfied is for them to practice the quality approach to marketing. If customers are so impressed with the product and with the ease of purchasing it that they seek out the particular brand and the intermediaries in the distribution channel, then all channel members can meet their marketing objectives. Of course, many organizations fall short of this ideal. To resolve some of the shortcomings of traditional arrangements, they seek to modify channel structure. The usual modification is some form of channel integration.

FIGURE 16.5

Types of Vertical Marketing Systems

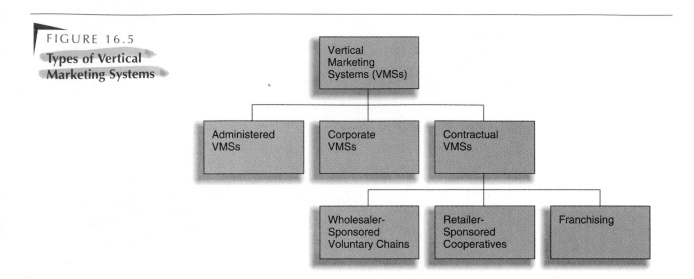

[Handwritten note in margin: retailer sponsored cooperative]

HORIZONTAL INTEGRATION

The organization may combine with others at the same stage in the distribution channel. Often this involves buying or merging with these other organizations. The owner of a dry-cleaning shop might, for example, buy several existing dry-cleaning establishments, or two distributors might merge into one. Although horizontal integration may add to the organization's strength in the marketplace, it is not always the most effective way to improve distribution. Problems that may result include those associated with corporate growth—for example, decreased flexibility and difficulties in coordination and planning.

VERTICAL CHANNEL INTEGRATION

Members at different levels of a distribution channel also may coordinate their efforts to reach a desired market. Such coordination is called vertical channel integration. It most often takes the form of a vertical marketing system.

vertical marketing system (VMS)
A distribution channel that is centrally managed and designed to achieve efficiency with a maximum marketing impact.

VERTICAL MARKETING SYSTEMS   A **vertical marketing system (VMS)** is a distribution channel that is centrally managed and designed to achieve efficiency with a maximum marketing impact. The members of the VMS may, but need not, be part of the same company. By combining what were once several intermediaries into a single system with central management, the VMS saves money by avoiding duplication. And the larger size that results from combining several organizations is what gives the VMS its impact. As summarized in Figure 16.5, vertical marketing systems are one of three types: administered, corporate, or contractual.

Administered VMS   With an *administered vertical marketing system,* separate companies develop a comprehensive program for distributing a line of products. A dominant channel member exercises power by administering the VMS so decisions take into account the channel as a whole. Members of an administered VMS may agree, for example, to adopt similar accounting and ordering procedures and to cooperate in marketing communications. The Quaker Oats Company administers such a VMS through a program called Total Customer Development. Quaker Oats works with its customers (stores) to develop programs for marketing Quaker's products to consumers, to identify ways to make the distribution process more efficient (such as by eliminating paperwork), and to improve the profits of all channel members.

Corporate VMS   In a *corporate vertical marketing system,* a single corporation owns all or a share of each organization in the distribution channel. A typical arrangement consists of a corporation that owns and operates production facilities, warehouses, and retail stores. Starbucks Coffee Company buys green coffee beans, roasts them, and sells them in its own retail stores. Bill and Sylvia Varney run a corporate VMS that started out as simply a small shop, Varney's Chemist Laden, which originally sold toiletries ordered from outside producers. Bill planted a small herb garden outside the shop, and the two experimented to see what products they could make from the herbs. Eventually, the store began selling the teas, soaps, wreaths, and other products the Varneys made. Then, adding to production and retailing, the Varneys hired a sales representative to handle wholesaling of their herbal creations. They later expanded the wholesale system and added direct marketing through catalogs to the retail operation.[14] On a larger scale, manufacturer Nike has opened Nike Town retail stores to showcase its athletic shoes and sportswear.

Operating a corporate VMS gives the firm a great degree of control over the entire distribution system. And when one part of the channel flourishes, others can benefit. The Varneys found that when wholesaling got their products into stores in other cities, customers would see the company's address on the packages and contact the company to ask for a catalog.[15] Along with control, of course, comes a need for the resources and expertise to run the system efficiently.

Contractual VMS   To maintain formal control without the need for expertise in all stages of distribution, the organization might participate in a *contractual vertical marketing system.* Such a VMS consists of channel members linked by formal agreements specifying each member's responsibilities. These contracts formalize the link between channel members and outline the rights and duties of each member. Thanks to the combination of explicitly defined responsibilities and shared expertise, contractual vertical marketing system is the most popular type of VMS. As shown in Figure 16.5, contractual vertical marketing systems fall into one of three categories:

1. *Wholesaler-sponsored voluntary chain:* A wholesaler establishes a contractual relationship with independent retailers to standardize and coordinate efforts at making purchases, managing inventory, and deciding what to buy and how to promote those products. Examples include IGA (Independent Grocers' Alliance) Food Stores and Associated Druggists.
2. *Retailer-sponsored cooperative:* Retailers jointly own and operate a wholesale facility. Members of a retail-sponsored cooperative may also choose to use a common store name so that they can benefit from sharing advertising expenses. Examples of retailer-sponsored cooperatives include Associated Grocers and Certified Grocers.
3. *Franchising:* Business operators pay to join the parent company's distribution system. As this is the most visible form of VMS, it is covered in greater detail in the next section.

franchising
A contractual distribution system in which a parent company (the franchisor) gives franchisees the right to operate the business according to the franchisor's marketing plan and to use its trademark.

FRANCHISING   The form of contractual VMS known as **franchising** is a contractual distribution system in which a parent company, the franchisor, gives one or more franchisees the right to operate the business largely according to the franchisor's mar-

For The Price Of A New Car, You Can Drive Your Own Business.

Two days before their wedding, Phil and Carmen Linthicum started down the road to happiness by purchasing a ServiceMaster franchise. For about the cost of a new family car (approximately $6,500 down plus working capital), they became the owners of a fulfilling business that can grow with their family. When you purchase a ServiceMaster franchise, you'll share the resources of the largest professional cleaning company in America. We invest more in training and development than any other company in the industry. And our local distributors have an active interest in your success.

The service industry is the fastest growing segment of our economy. So there's definitely a place for you. Choose a ServiceMaster franchise and you'll be in the driver's seat. *ServiceMASTER.* (800) 752-6688

keting plan and using the franchisor's trademark.[16] Along with the right to operate the business, the franchisee typically receives a variety of marketing, management, and technical services.

To receive these benefits, the franchisees pay a fee to the franchisor. The cost of purchasing a franchise varies widely. At the low end, the total investment to start up an AIMM franchise (which rents audiovisual and other equipment to business travelers) is $12,000 to $30,000. In contrast, the total investment for a McDonald's franchise is $220,000 to $265,000 and for a Blockbuster Video Superstore is $447,000 to $775,000.[17]

With roughly 2,500 franchisors and more than 540,000 franchise outlets in the United States, franchising is responsible for over $750 billion in annual sales.[18] Some of the most familiar U.S. franchises are McDonald's, Burger King, Holiday Inn, Weight Watchers, Century 21, and H&R Block. Franchising also accounts for a growing share of retail sales abroad. About 400 U.S. firms have franchises in other countries. Most foreign franchises are formed under a master license in which a U.S. franchisor authorizes a foreign firm or entrepreneur to operate franchise units in a given country or geographic area. The master licensee subfranchises individual units or owns and operates them all.

Advantages   Franchising has advantages to the franchisor and the franchisee. For the franchisor, the benefits include a ready source of funds for expansion coupled with the ability to establish policies for operating each franchise. For franchisees, the advantages include greater name recognition, participation in advertising programs, better prices from suppliers, and business advice (see Figure 16.6).

Because of such advantages, owners of existing independent businesses are often interested in operating as a franchisee. To become a franchisee and get these advantages, an independent business undergoes a process called franchise conversion. This involves entering into a franchise agreement and changing over to the franchise's name and operating formula. Brad Amrhein entered into a franchise conversion for his family-owned drugstore, which was struggling to compete in a part of Scott City, Missouri, that had become economically depressed. By converting to a Medicap franchise, Amrhein got not only a more familiar name for the store, but also help in borrowing money to finance a move to a more prosperous locale. Within a year of conversion, the store's sales doubled, and profits rose as well.[19]

Drawbacks   Of course, franchising arrangements do not always work out. From the franchisor's standpoint, it can sometimes be hard to find enough qualified franchisees. Also, the activities of franchisees are harder to control than those of employees. For the franchisee, this type of arrangement can be frustrating when the franchisor does not provide adequate support such as effective advertising or seems to lack understanding of the franchisee's local market.

DIRECT MARKETING

direct marketing
Using direct channels of distribution, such as catalogs or door-to-door selling.

→ Internet
→ 1-800 #'s

Increasingly, firms serve buyers with direct channels. Using direct channels of distribution is called **direct marketing**. This distribution strategy changes the method of performing certain marketing functions but cannot eliminate the need for them. For example, a manufacturer or service provider that uses direct marketing will have to handle such activities as processing orders, keeping adequate inventory on hand, transporting products to buyers, and maintaining hours convenient to members of the target market.

The usual methods of distribution through direct marketing are to offer products through the mail (as in the case of catalogs), by telephone, through door-to-door selling, or on televised shopping channels. Chapter 17 discusses the practice of using such channels to offer products to consumers. In addition, Chapter 18 covers the use of mailings to promote products, and Chapter 20 examines personal selling via telephone. The uses of direct marketing are often quite sophisticated. In Japan, Amway has become the fastest-growing foreign firm by setting up a network of 700,000 independent agents armed with fax machines, computers, and telephones. They sell about 150 household items, most imported from the United States. Using its three automated distribution centers, which have on-site customs inspection, Amway can deliver orders in only two days.[20]

Even when direct marketing is not the most efficient channel of distribution, producers of a new product many use it to build demand in order to persuade intermediaries to carry their product. Intuit Inc. initially could not persuade retailers to stock its personal finance software, called Quicken. So Intuit sold Quicken directly to consumers by placing ads in computer magazines. This approach was so successful that Egghead Software asked to stock Quicken.[21]

A producer that uses direct marketing may combine it with other channels of distribution. For example, small record labels are compensating for the difficulty of getting their recordings onto the shelves of retail stores by finding high-tech modes of direct marketing. Subscribers to *Nautilus,* an electronic monthly published on compact disc, can hear samples of music available from Windham Hill Records. They can order CDs of the music they like simply by entering a command on their computer.[22] However, as discussed later in this chapter, combining direct marketing with other channels may lead to friction between the producer and other channel members.

Managing Channels of Distribution

Whether the producer owns its distribution channel or arranges with independent businesses for these services, managing the channel is critical to the product's success. From the intermediaries' perspective, channel management is also important for making sure that everyone's efforts are directed toward satisfying customers. For example, if a retailer advertises a special price on a product, the retailer depends on others in the distribution channel to make that product available on time. Thus, all the participants in the distribution channel are concerned that the channel operate effectively.

SELECTING A DISTRIBUTION CHANNEL

The process of channel management begins with selection of a type of channel and of the specific organizations that will distribute the product. The right channel members will know how to get the product to places where the target market will buy it. In contrast, with the wrong channel members, interested buyers might never encounter the product. Considering that changing a distribution channel can be difficult and expensive, the selection of a channel is a critical part of marketing planning.

While this discussion emphasizes the role of the producer in selecting a distribution channel, keep in mind that other channel members also make decisions about which sellers to represent and which target markets to serve. Randall Bourne decided to start a catalog business to sell fancy picture frames to consumers. To launch this retail business, called Expressions, he built up a network of suppliers by attending trade shows, studying magazines, and visiting manufacturers, then overcoming their reluctance to sell to him. Through research and experience, Bourne determined that the most profitable target market for Expressions was parents looking for ways to display photos of their children.[23]

As summarized in Table 16.3, marketers should base the selection of a distribution channel on characteristics of the target market, the organization's marketing objectives, the nature of the product itself, the intermediaries, and the marketing environment. (See also "Put It into Practice: Create Your Own Table of Considerations.") In addition, the control process includes monitoring these characteristics to identify changes that may warrant a new distribution channel.

TARGET MARKETS   Especially when the organization is committed to the quality approach to marketing, the marketer must consider the target markets when selecting distribution channels. A customer orientation is as important to channel decisions as it is to other areas of marketing strategy. The marketer should select channels that will please customers in terms of product availability, convenience, and price. For example, increasing concern about cost containment among consumers and insurance companies has fueled the success of efficient mail-order pharmacies such as Medco Containment Services of Montvale, New Jersey.[24]

Sometimes changes in target markets require changes in channel strategy. Thus, because of the shrinking number of households with an adult home full time, Fuller Brush found that it could no longer prosper by selling its merchandise door to door. And as a target market grows, longer channels may be necessary to reach a greater number of people more efficiently.

Another concern related to target markets is the distance of the target market from the producer. When members of the target market are far away, the distribution

TABLE 16.3	BASIC CONSIDERATION	ISSUES TO CONSIDER
Criteria for Selecting a Channel of Distribution	Target market(s)	Number Geographic dispersion Purchasing patterns Susceptibilities to different selling methods
	Organization's marketing objectives	Efficiency Intensity of distribution
	Product characteristics	Perishability Bulkiness Degree of standardization Installation and maintenance services required Unit value Stage in life cycle Image
	Intermediary characteristics	Availability Willingness to accept product or product line Strengths and weaknesses
	Marketing environment	Competitors Economic conditions Laws and regulations

Source: Adapted from J. Paul Peter and James H. Donnelly, Jr., *A Preface to Marketing Management*, 6th ed. (Burr Ridge, Ill.: Irwin, 1994), p. 195.

channel also tends to be long. That is because an intermediary can often transport goods more efficiently than a producer can.

MARKETING OBJECTIVES   As with all elements of the marketing mix, the distribution strategy, including the choice of channels, should support the marketing objectives. Two major issues are which channels will be most efficient and which will provide the level of coverage desired.

Efficiency   To achieve profit objectives, marketers look for channels that can distribute the product efficiently. In many cases, this means relying on the expertise of intermediaries. A small or new organization with limited financial resources may also rely on intermediaries as a way to share the financial risk and cost of distributing products. Rather than needing cash to build transportation systems and stores, the producer in effect allows the intermediaries to share in the sales revenues.

To measure the efficiency of a particular channel, the marketer needs to be able to figure the total distribution cost in that channel. These are the major costs of distributing products:[25]

- Transporting the product
- Processing orders
- Losing orders when the organization is unable to meet demand
- Carrying inventory (including the costs of storage space, capital invested, taxes, insurance, and wearing out of the inventory)
- Packaging the product for shipment
- Handling materials.

CREATE YOUR OWN TABLE OF CONSIDERATIONS

As a marketer, whenever you set out to choose the best channel(s) for distribution of a product, you need to begin with a systematic evaluation of factors. Overall, you'll want to base your selection on: (1) characteristics of the target market; (2) your company's marketing objectives; (3) the nature of the product itself; (4) which intermediaries (if any) you may choose; and (5) the marketing environment. To cover each of these areas in an organized manner, try making a list of the five general considerations, in the form of a table like Table 16.3. Then fill in the right side of the table with pros, cons, and other issues or observations about each consideration. You'll be asked to create a table like this as the first step in your project for this chapter.

Sometimes cutting costs in one area (say, carrying inventory) can lead to higher costs in another area (lost orders). The marketer therefore has to look at the whole distribution system when measuring its efficiency.

Distribution Intensity   A marketing strategy typically includes objectives for how intensively the product will be distributed. Marketers think of distribution intensity as falling along a continuum ranging from intensive through selective to exclusive distribution.

intensive distribution
Distribution through all wholesalers or retailers that will carry a product.

Intensive distribution is distribution through all wholesalers or retailers that will carry the product. This is the approach that supports a mass marketing strategy. It is especially suitable for products that have a low cost per unit and are purchased frequently.

selective distribution
Distribution through a limited number of intermediaries.

Selective distribution is distribution through a limited number of intermediaries. The marketer selects the intermediaries that best meet the various criteria summarized in this section of the chapter. This approach tends to be less expensive than intensive distribution and enables the members of the distribution channel to have a deeper relationship. It is an appropriate way to distribute shopping goods or luxury goods because customers are willing to go to a particular store.

exclusive distribution
The use of a single wholesaler or retailer to serve each territory.

Exclusive distribution is the use of a single wholesaler or retailer to serve each territory. Thus, it is the most limited form of distribution. Exclusive distribution is appropriate when the product requires a special effort by salespeople or when the intermediary must have large or unique facilities to carry the product.

THE PRODUCT   Marketers need to ask whether the nature of the product lends itself to a particular type of distribution channel. In some cases, a product-related characteristic may override other factors in channel selection. For example, a highly perishable product such as most services may require a direct channel. Direct channels are also appropriate for complex products. The producer can train its own sales force to explain how the product works and what benefits it can provide.

Life cycle stage also is important. Notably, a new product may require established intermediaries to give it credibility. However, if intermediaries are unwilling to risk handling a new product made by a new or small company, the producer may have to be innovative in developing distribution channels. The producer may use a direct channel, as described earlier, or forge a partnership with a more powerful organization. Maxis, a developer of toys using simulation software, couldn't get its first product, SimCity, into stores, so the company assigned distribution rights to Broderbund, a larger software producer.[26]

The desired image of the product and customers' actual perceptions also are related to channel selection. Making a product available only through a few prestigious retailers, for example, supports an image of the product as luxurious or exclu-

FIGURE 16.7
**Product Using
Selective Distribution**

sive (see Figure 16.7). In contrast, when Gitano Group made its jeans and sportswear available to low-priced retailers like Wal-Mart and Kmart, full-priced retailers no longer wanted to carry the products for fear of hurting the image of their stores.[27]

INTERMEDIARIES   The marketer can in many cases narrow the selection process by asking what intermediaries are already serving the marketer's industry. Many industries have traditional channels of distribution—channels that have developed over many years and become the accepted practice. These traditional channels are not always the best choice, but the marketer would do well to consider why they are so widely used and whether they offer important efficiencies.

Before designing a detailed distribution strategy, it is wise to find out whether the necessary intermediaries exist and are willing to carry the product. If so, the marketer needs to evaluate the prospective intermediaries. Some background information worth acquiring includes the intermediary's sales and profit history, its clientele, and the other goods and services it handles.

Especially when entering a foreign market, a producer cannot assume that intermediaries are necessarily eager to carry its product. When American Standard, the world's largest maker of plumbing fixtures, initially entered South Korea, it found that local manufacturers controlled that country's channels of distribution. If distributors took on the American Standard line, they risked being cut off by their big local suppliers. American Standard therefore looked for a distributor that had a long-standing relationship with the big South Korean producers and so was less likely to be cut off. It succeeded by looking outside Seoul (the country's largest city as well as its capital) and signed up with a South Korean distributor called Home Center that had been in business for almost three decades. The combination of Home Center's reputation, American Standard's quality, and South Korea's booming construction market eventually led to strong growth in American Standard's earnings and profits.[28]

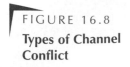

FIGURE 16.8

Types of Channel Conflict

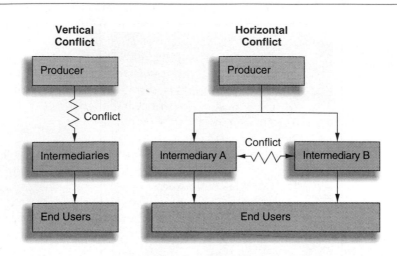

THE MARKETING ENVIRONMENT Many factors in the marketing environment can influence which channel will be most effective. Some of the major environmental influences are competitors, the economy, and laws and regulations pertaining to distribution.

Marketers do well to observe what channels competitors are using. It may be hard to compete if the product is not available in the same places. On the other hand, the marketer may observe a way to gain an advantage by making the product available somewhere that competitors do not have their products.

Changes in the economic climate tend to influence where consumers make their purchases. During a recession, they are more likely to restrict their shopping to retailers that specialize in low prices or high value. Thus, if it does not hurt the product's image, the producer may do well to see that its products are distributed in such stores during economic slowdowns. During recessions the producer may also find that intermediaries are more conservative about taking on new products. This means that the maker of a new product may have to rely on short or direct channels because intermediaries are reluctant to handle it.

The law places some limits on which channels may be chosen and how the channel members must be treated. Major federal laws affecting distribution are described later in this chapter.

CONFLICT, COOPERATION, AND LEADERSHIP

Once a distribution channel is in place, the members of that channel must cooperate to get the product to market. Channel members must strive to achieve the general goal of distributing the product profitably. However, as noted earlier, channel members also find that differences in their specific goals cause their interests to conflict at times. Conflict arises whether or not the members of the channel are part of the same formal organization. Conflicts involve such issues as how to allocate profits, which channel members will perform which services, and which channel members will make certain decisions about marketing the product.

TYPES OF CONFLICT As shown in Figure 16.8, some of the conflict that occurs in channels of distribution is vertical. Vertical conflict occurs between channel members at different levels—for instance, between a wholesaler and a retailer. One source of vertical conflict involves a channel member bypassing another member. Wal-Mart created this type of conflict by working directly with producers, rather than following the industry practice of buying from wholesalers. The giant record companies are upset about a reverse channel being created by compact disk retailers. With the cost of CDs high and the durability of these recordings great, many retailers are buying CDs back from customers, rather than limiting their purchases to the record companies. Producers have retaliated by refusing to contribute advertising dollars to any retailer that sells used CDs.[29]

Vertical conflict also may arise when one channel member believes another is not doing its job. A producer, for example, may believe intermediaries are not giving its products enough advertising support, shelf space, commitment from the sales force, or other forms of attention. Other vertical conflicts have included such issues as what prices may be charged (a big price discount could hurt a product's image) and how much inventory an intermediary should be willing to carry.

Horizontal conflict also may occur among channel members. This type of conflict involves channel members at the same level, such as two or more wholesalers or two or more retailers. Horizontal conflict arises because different marketing intermediaries handle similar products. For example, personal computers are sold through five types of retailers: local (small) dealers, large dealers such as MicroAge and ComputerLand, computer superstores such as Computer City SuperCenters, mail-order houses, and computer shows.[30] Conflict was expected when Grid Systems Corporation, a PC manufacturer, began offering an on-line ordering service through which buyers can order computers directly from Grid's manufacturing facility. Grid was originally part of Tandy Corporation, which owns Radio Shack stores. It would not use its innovative direct channel until after being divested from Tandy, so as not to undercut Radio Shack when the two were part of the same company.

Horizontal conflicts may occur when one intermediary seeks to gain sales at the expense of the others. They also may arise when an intermediary believes that its objectives are hurt by another channel member's carrying the same product. As in the case of Gitano jeans, department stores may object to carrying a brand that is also sold at discount stores.

COOPERATION AND CONFLICT RESOLUTION   Although there is no single method for resolving channel conflict, channel members are most likely to prosper when they appreciate that they depend on one another for their success. Ideally, channel members cooperate by recognizing their differences and negotiating a resolution. Formal agreements about the roles of each member can reduce conflicts.

Forms of Cooperation   Channel members are increasingly moving beyond mere conflict resolution to building mutual trust as the basis for cooperation. For example, when channel members agree on serving a common target market by providing high-quality goods and services, their quality focus can be a basis for cooperation. The channel members can do more than simply conduct transactions; they can forge long-term relationships, perhaps even partnerships or strategic channel alliances.[31]

Producers can strengthen these links by learning the needs of their intermediary customers as well as the end users of their products. Thus, intermediaries might want producers to share information about how to match product characteristics to the needs of end users.[32] Shared information is at the heart of VF Corporation's links with close to one-third of its retail customers. The company, which makes a variety of clothing lines, including Lee and Wrangler jeans, uses an electronic linkup with the stores to learn which products are selling best and when items need to be automatically resupplied.[33]

channel captain
The leader in a distribution channel (may be the producer, wholesaler, or retailer).

Channel Leadership   In spite of this ideal, cooperation today still tends to result from the leadership of one member of the distribution channel. This leader is referred to as the **channel captain**. The channel captain may be a producer, wholesaler, or retailer. Which member of the channel becomes captain depends on which has greatest power in the form of economic strength, expertise, size, or reputation. Stated more theoretically, a channel member's power may be of several types:

• Reward power arises from the channel member's ability to give other channel members something desirable. Wal-Mart, for example, can place giant orders with producers.
• Coercive power derives from fears that a channel member can do harm. Thus, if a channel member is not offered a price as low as its competitors paid, the channel member might threaten a lawsuit for illegal price discrimination.
• Legitimate power stems from the position of the channel member. A franchisor, for example, has certain rights spelled out in the franchise agreement.
• Referent power arises from the emotions inspired by a channel member. Channel members will likely want to work with producers that have a reputation for fairness.
• Expert power comes from the channel member's knowledge or skills. Many potential franchisees will want to sign up with a franchisor known to effectively support its brands, and retailers will like buying from wholesalers with a clear knowledge of their product line.
• Information power stems from the channel member's possession of information valued by others in the channel. An example is a wholesaler with a sophisticated database of marketing information.

In general, some marketers believe the producer or the owner of the brand name should be the channel captain because that channel member has the most to lose if the channel fails to perform. The producer also is most familiar with the product. Procter & Gamble's large size, well-known brands, and marketing expertise give it substantial strength relative to the intermediaries that carry its products. Thus, when supermarkets were unhappy with P&G's switch to "value pricing" (see Chapter 14), they could threaten to discontinue some P&G items, but no one would stop doing business with P&G altogether. If a producer's brand is not well recognized, however, the producer is relatively weak because resellers can more easily reject the product in favor of one with a lower price or other advantages.[34]

Wholesalers may become leaders when their size and familiarity with the marketplace give them an advantage. In the pharmacy industry, wholesaler McKesson is a leader for these reasons. It pioneered the technology of placing in drugstores computer terminals linked to McKesson's central computer. The wholesaler uses the system not only to improve the efficiency of order processing but to collect sales data and produce daily reports, which the drugstores buy for help in store management.[35]

Large retailers have increasingly taken a leadership role in distribution channels. One reason is that retailers are the closest link to the end user. Also, the retailing industry has consolidated in recent years, so that there are fewer but larger retailers.[36] Thus, a number of supermarket and drugstore chains—including Lucky Stores and Sav-On in California and Nevada, Jewel Food Stores in the Midwest, and Acme Markets in Pennsylvania—have come under the umbrella of American Stores Company. American Stores is using the clout that comes from large size to negotiate better prices from its suppliers.[37] Finally, as described later in this chapter, technology has made it easy for channel members to share information, so retailers today can learn directly about customers.[38] For example, Wal-Mart's chief executive, David Glass, claims, "We're probably in a better position to determine specifically what the customer wants to buy than is the manufacturer."[39]

FIGURE 16.9

Common Distribution Channels for Serving International Markets

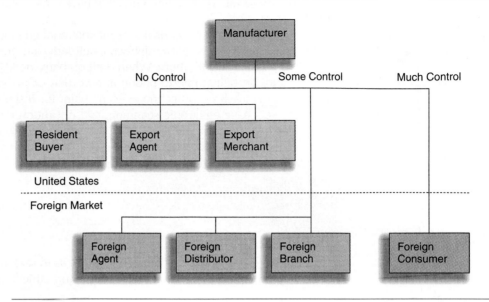

Source: J. Paul Peter and James H. Donnelly, Jr., *A Preface to Marketing Management,* 6th ed. (Burr Ridge, Ill.: Irwin, 1994), p. 258.

IMPLICATIONS FOR GLOBAL MARKETING

The channel element of the marketing mix can be a particularly challenging aspect of international trade. Even when the organization uses a single strategy for product and communications, different kinds of intermediaries may be needed in each country. Transportation distances may be greater. Cultural differences may also affect channels of distribution. In Moscow, retailers who ran out of Wrigley's Spearmint gum didn't call the distributor to reorder because they assumed, incorrectly, that they would have to wait months for delivery. Quite simply, Russian retailers are not used to thinking that reordering is worth the trouble.[40]

Some marketers handle the distribution challenge by making a concerted effort to learn about foreign markets and by exerting great control. Others prefer to arrange for outside experts to handle some or all distribution functions. Small businesses such as Hamilton Manufacturing Corporation, which makes machines that give change for paper money, often arrange for intermediaries to buy their goods at a discount and resell them to customers in foreign markets.[41] To introduce its software to international markets, NovaSoft Systems sought deals with foreign distributors serving the kinds of businesses the company considered its prime targets.[42] Figure 16.9 shows common distribution channels for international marketing.

When the marketer manages channels of distribution in the foreign market, its people must be familiar with the strengths and limitations of the country's infrastructure. This is especially important in less-developed areas, including the former Soviet Union, where marketers may have to create their own distribution systems from scratch.[43] Mexican law prohibits foreign truckers from operating in that country, so shipments must be transferred to another trucker at the U.S.–Mexico border. Furthermore, Mexico's private toll roads are so expensive that most truckers avoid them, sticking to the secondary roads, which are in such poor condition that fragile cargo may arrive damaged. Until the roads improve, U.S. firms distributing goods in

Mexico tend to rely on trucking firms that have close relationships with counterparts in Mexico.[44]

Thus, for the marketer considering international channels of distribution, there are many questions to answer: Are highways, railroads, airports, and the like adequate for handling physical distribution? When the company needs to replenish its inventory, can it count on being able to phone in an order, or is the telephone system unreliable? What is the level of technology? In Spain, for instance, less than one-fourth of hypermarkets have electronic scanning, and not much more than one-third of large supermarkets can scan purchases.[45] If the infrastructure makes rapid ordering and transportation of goods unreliable or impossible, the organization may not be able to benefit from such strategies as just-in-time inventory management, described in the next chapter.

Legal and Ethical Considerations

In resolving disputes and building cooperation, as in seeking a competitive advantage, channel members must be aware of the legal and ethical considerations that arise.

LEGAL PRINCIPLES

Suppliers have a legal right to select the intermediaries that carry and represent their products. The courts have upheld that right to do business with some and refuse to do business with others. However, companies may not engage in practices that are unfair or stifle competition. Such practices would violate the Sherman Act and the Clayton Act. A variety of anticompetitive activities would be illegal:

- Setting up a vertical marketing system in order to drive out of business the intermediaries that currently handle the company's products.
- Refusing to deal with a particular intermediary as a way to coerce that intermediary into a certain type of behavior.
- Agreeing with other, competing businesses—say, a group of wholesalers—to limit sales by territory or customer. For example, competing wholesalers may not agree that one will serve stores east of the Mississippi River while the other sells only west of the Mississippi.

An attempt to drive them out of business was the basis for a lawsuit filed by distributors of Canada Dry and Coors in the New York area. The distributors charged that Canada Dry Bottling Company of New York hired truck drivers and began selling directly to former customers of the distributors. They also claimed that Canada Dry New York used tactics such as withholding discounted products during promotions in an effort to force the distributors to charge certain prices. Canada Dry New York and other bottlers being sued contested the charges.[46]

Many of the legal issues surrounding distribution involve exclusive distribution. Like other distribution arrangements, exclusive distribution is legal so long as it does not interfere with free trade. Problems may arise in three areas: exclusive dealing agreements, closed sales territories, and tying agreements.

exclusive dealing
A restriction imposed by a supplier forbidding the customer from purchasing some type of product from any other supplier.

EXCLUSIVE DEALING   The first problem area, **exclusive dealing**, is "a restriction which is imposed by a supplier on a customer forbidding the customer from purchasing some type of product from any other supplier."[47] Electronic Liquid Fillers (ELF), which makes packaging systems, uses independent agents to sell its products in foreign countries. It will not sign agreements with sales reps that are working for a direct competitor of ELF.[48]

The Clayton Act specifically prohibits exclusive dealing when it lessens competition. This may occur if an exclusive-dealing agreement blocks competitors from the market or if the sales revenue involved is a sizable percentage of total sales in the market. In contrast, exclusive dealing is legal if intermediaries and end users in a given market have access to similar products, if sellers are initially entering a market, or if the exclusive-dealing contract strengthens an otherwise weak competitor.

CLOSED SALES TERRITORIES   Sometimes producers grant intermediaries closed or exclusive sales territories. In other words, the producer specifies the geographic area to be served by each intermediary and has only one intermediary serve that area. This policy is designed to improve the intermediary's ability to market the product in its territory. When closed sales territories diminish competition, they are generally illegal.

tying contract
An agreement under which the seller will sell a particular product only if the buyer also purchases another, specified product.

TYING AGREEMENTS   A **tying contract** is an agreement under which the seller will sell a particular product only if the buyer also purchases another, specified product. In the lawsuit filed by the Canada Dry distributors, they claimed that Canada Dry New York required them to join a particular Teamsters local, lease overpriced trucks, and buy insurance at inflated prices.[49] Tying contracts are common in franchising. A franchise agreement might, for example, dictate where restaurant franchisees buy ingredients and other supplies. Franchisors justify the policy as necessary for quality control and protection of the franchisor's reputation.

full-line forcing
An arrangement in which an intermediary that wants to carry a particular product must buy the entire line.

Another kind of tying arrangement is **full-line forcing**. Under full-line forcing, an intermediary that wants to carry a particular product must buy the entire product line. Purposes of such restrictions include ensuring that intermediaries accept new products, ensuring that a suitable range of products is available to customers, and moving weaker products along with more popular items.

Tying contracts are illegal when they reduce competition. The courts do, however, accept tying contracts when three conditions are met:

1. The supplier alone can provide products of a certain quality.
2. The intermediary is free to carry competing products.
3. A company has just entered the market.

THE GRAY MARKET

Another legal and ethical issue involves international business transactions. As described in Chapter 4, U.S. businesses sometimes expand into foreign markets by selling foreign companies a license to produce and sell products with the U.S. companies' brands. The licensing agreement forbids the foreign producer from selling these products in the United States. However, the distributors of these products are under no such restrictions. Some foreign distributors have taken advantage of this loophole to sell the foreign-made versions of U.S. products in the United States. The market for such goods is known as the **gray market**, and the goods themselves are called gray goods or parallel goods.

gray market
The market in which foreign distributors sell foreign versions of U.S. products in the United States.

The gray market is a problem for U.S. producers. First, the foreign distributors are often able to sell gray goods at a lower price than can sellers in domestic distribution channels. This undercuts the channels that domestic producers have worked hard to establish, and it may mean that goods wind up being sold by retailers that do not fit the producer's marketing plan. Gray goods also may hurt the product's image if they

Unethical actions by one channel member can hurt the others in the distribution channel. The United States recently recalled several brands of crayons made in China because they contained potentially hazardous levels of lead. The producers' decision to sell such a product resulted in unfavorable publicity to the crayons' distributors and to the stores that stocked the crayons.

are sold at a price well below that of the producer's pricing strategy or if the foreign-made versions differ from the version developed for the U.S. market. However, there is not much that producers can do about this, because the Supreme Court in 1988 ruled that items made under legitimate license are legal, no matter what country they are from. But although it is legal for retailers to buy gray goods, some might question the ethics of doing so.

ETHICS AND CHANNEL POWER

As noted earlier, the channel captain of a distribution channel is typically the member with the greatest power to influence the behavior of other members. A channel captain can use power with integrity to benefit the channel as a whole. The result is a shared vision of channel goals and a coordinated effort to serve customers. However, ethical dilemmas arise when the channel members encounter ways in which they can achieve short-term gains at the expense of other channel members.

These issues are especially likely to come up when a dominant channel member sees a need to make a change that shuts out another channel member or increases the competition faced by channel members. Such actions can cost the good will of the other members of the distribution channel.

slotting allowance
A fee paid by producers to retailers in exchange for the stores' carrying a new product.

A significant example is slotting allowances. Supermarkets often demand that producers pay a **slotting allowance** in exchange for their carrying a new product. This fee is typically in the range of $50 to $500 per store, or $50,000 to $100,000 for a 100-store chain.[50] In addition, producers are expected to provide a case or two of samples for test marketing and, if they want prime shelf space, to pay an additional promotional allowance.

This approach bases product decisions not on consumer needs but on the store's ability to bring in extra money. It places a relatively great burden on small producers, which may prevent some desirable products from becoming available. Mo Siegel, for example, has found it more expensive to enter channels today with his line of Earth Wise environmentally friendly products than he did years ago with Celestial Seasonings tea. Slotting allowances certainly create negative feelings among producers. However, store managers complain that there are so many new products (some barely different from the old ones) that this is the only realistic way to cope with limited shelf space. Furthermore, they contend, putting an untried product into valuable shelf space involves providing a service to the producer that it should pay for.

You Decide

ARE SLOTTING ALLOWANCES JUSTIFIED?

Felix Sanchez's Puebla Foods, Inc. produces Mi Pueblito tortillas, the leading brand in New York City's corner stores. He began selling his fresh tortillas in 1977. Driving from his base in Passaic, New Jersey, Sanchez sold his fresh tortillas door to door in Mexican neighborhoods.

At first he earned about $350 a week. Eventually he developed a customer base and was earning $1,000 a week, and a few neighborhood stores began to stock his product. Over the next four years, Sanchez continued to add customers to his "tortilla route." This method of direct marketing—with no intermediaries—helped keep Sanchez abreast of changes in the marketing environment, such as which blocks shifted in population from Puerto Rican to Mexican. He was aware at all times of his target market—in many cases, he met his consumers personally.

Sanchez's persistence, along with a high-quality product that consumers wanted to buy, paid off. A decade and a half after he started, Puebla Foods reached sales of almost $4 million and locked in a majority of the local retail tortilla market.

But for all their popularity, Mi Pueblito tortillas were not sold in a single supermarket. There is only so much room available on supermarket shelves for products (already 26,000 different items at the typical supermarket), and getting space for a new product can be difficult for small producers. In recent years, supermarkets have doubled the number of different items they carry, yet producers just keep on introducing new products.

Big producers such as General Mills and Procter & Gamble enter into powerful vertical channel relationships with supermarkets. Small producers such as Puebla Foods, however, have limited power, so retailers leverage the imbalance by demanding large slotting allowances. Supermarkets will waive fees for large companies with well-established products and the ability to safeguard the success of new products with extensive market research and heavy advertising. As noted in the chapter, supermarket managers justify slotting allowances as a way to limit the number of new products crowding already overcrowded shelves. They say the fees cover the costs of accounting and placing the products in inventory, as well as cover the risk of placing an untried product onto valuable shelf space.

None of this helped Sanchez, whose small company was effectively locked out of the supermarket channel. So Sanchez formed a strategic alliance with New York's biggest Latino food distributor, Goya Foods. Now packaged under the Goya Foods label, Sanchez's fresh tortillas are available in supermarket chains like Grand Union and Pathmark. For Sanchez, the numbers add up to fresh revenues: his company gets $1 million a year for 1,000 cases of tortillas a week.

Do you think slotting allowances are justified? Do you believe adding Goya Foods to his distribution channel was the right move for Sanchez to make? Why or why not? What other distribution channels might Sanchez have tried instead of entering the alliance with Goya?

Source: "The Streets Were Paved with Tortillas," *Forbes,* May 25, 1992, p. 272.

Producers that can't or won't pay slotting allowances look for other ways to distribute their goods, such as through specialty stores or the few supermarket chains that charge low or no slotting allowances. These stores, in turn, are able to offer their customers goods that are unavailable elsewhere. (For more on slotting allowances, see "You Decide: Are Slotting Allowances Justified?")

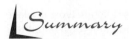

Summary

Channels of distribution are the means by which marketers get their products to the target market so that they will be convenient to buy. Channels of distribution perform all the activities required to link producers with users of products. Intermediaries are separate businesses that specialize in carrying out many of the distribution functions. These functions may be of three types: transactional, logistical, and facilitating.

Distribution channels may be organized in a few basic ways. Channels for consumer goods include direct channels (direct marketing) in which products move directly from producer to end user. Other channels include those in which goods move from producer to retailer to consumer, and from producer to wholesaler to retailer to consumer (this is the most common). Finally, goods may pass from producer to agents to wholesalers to retailers to consumers. Distribution channels for services and industrial goods are usually shorter than those for consumer goods. Marketers may decide that variations on the standard types of distribution are better suited to their products and markets, and thus use multiple distribution channels, strategic channel alliances, or even reverse channels (as in the case of recycled goods) to best serve their markets.

Distribution channels may be organized vertically or horizontally. A vertical marketing system (VMS) is centrally managed and designed to achieve efficiency with a maximum marketing impact. Franchising is an example of a VMS. Direct marketing is another means by which the producer sells directly to the consumer (such as by catalog).

Managing the distribution channel is vital to a product's success. Marketers should select the channel based on characteristics of the target market, the organization's marketing objectives, the nature of the product itself, the intermediaries, and the marketing environment. The channel must be efficient and provide the level of coverage desired by the producer. The product's life cycle stage should be considered, as well as its image. Changes in the marketing environment—such as regulations and the economic climate—are also key factors.

Conflict between channel members may arise over such issues as allocation of profits and decision making. Channel members should remember that they depend on one another for success. Cooperation often depends on the establishment of a channel captain (producer, wholesaler, or retailer) who will manage distribution. Channel strategy is particularly complex for global marketers, who must contend with such issues as the possible need for different types of intermediaries, longer transportation distances, cultural differences influencing the behavior of intermediaries, and inferior infrastructure.

Legal and ethical considerations arise with regard to channels of distribution. Companies may not engage in practices that are unfair or stifling to competition. Exclusive dealing, closed sales territories, and tying agreements may be legal in some instances and illegal in others. The gray market, in which foreign-made versions of U.S. products are marketed in the United States, is a problem for American producers because foreign distributors are often able to undercut American prices. However, thus far the gray market is legal. Channel members may face ethical dilemmas when they encounter ways to achieve short-term gains at the expense of other channel members. Such dilemmas arise with regard to slotting allowances.

KEY TERMS AND CONCEPTS

channel of distribution (p. 466)
intermediary (middleman) (p. 466)
direct marketing (p. 469)
distributor (p. 471)
dual distribution (p. 472)
strategic channel alliance (p. 473)
reverse channel (p. 473)

vertical marketing system (VMS) (p. 476)
franchising (p. 477)
direct marketing (p. 479)
intensive distribution (p. 482)
selective distribution (p. 482)
exclusive distribution (p. 482)

channel captain (p. 486)
exclusive dealing (p. 488)
tying contract (p. 489)
full-line forcing (p. 489)
gray market (p. 489)
slotting allowance (p. 490)

REVIEW AND DISCUSSION QUESTIONS

1. What marketing functions might a producer use an intermediary for and why?
2. Your company produces clothing with special fasteners for people who have difficulty with buttons and zippers. As a marketer, would you consider dual distribution for your product line? Why or why not?
3. What is the most common distribution channel for services, and why? Give an example.
4. Suppose you ran a shop that sold homemade sauces, baked goods, baby foods, and other specialty foods, all produced by local cooks. You decided to expand your business and felt it would benefit from the establishment of a vertical marketing system. What type of VMS would you set up, and why?

5. What are the two major issues linking marketing objectives to distribution? Why are they important?
6. Suppose you were a marketer for a line of moderately priced basic household tools (screwdriver, hammer, pliers, wrench, etc.) and became embroiled in horizontal channel conflict because the tools were sold through several different types of retailers. Do you think a channel captain could resolve this situation? Explain.
7. What additional challenges do marketers typically face when using channels of distribution in foreign countries?
8. Do you agree with the 1988 Supreme Court ruling that gray market items should be legal? Why or why not?

Chapter Project
Choosing a Distribution Channel

Imagine that you are the marketer in charge of choosing the best distribution channel(s) for a line of stuffed toys (dolls and animals) made entirely of recycled fabric. First, create a table as suggested in "Put It into Practice," listing the five general considerations for selection of a distribution channel on the left side of the table. Then fill in the blank side of your table as you evaluate each consideration.

Next, think through more specific considerations, such as whether you'll need a reverse channel; whether direct marketing (such as through a catalog) would be effective; and whether you want to engage in full-line forcing. Note these decisions as well.

Decide which distribution channel(s) would be best for your line of stuffed toys and how you would apply a cross-functional approach to the task of physical distribution. Present your conclusions in writing or to your class.

Case
Nu Skin International, Inc.

To some people, it sounded too good to be true. Nu Skin International, founded in 1986 in Provo, Utah, by members of the Roney family, was somehow paying its independent distributors millions of dollars a year only a few years after its start-up. Nu Skin makes high-quality skin and hair-care products, which it distributes through a system called multilevel or network marketing. This means that independent distributors sell its products directly to consumers for a commission; to get bigger commissions, the distributors recruit more people to sell Nu Skin products. By keeping distribution channels short, Nu Skin seeks to cut costs, increase efficiency, and provide better service to consumers. Instead of paying the costs associated with selling through retail stores, Nu Skin allocates more money to its distributors for their selling efforts.

"When we started sending out big checks to our distributors," explains president Blake Roney, "that was a big test for the seven [Nu Skin] stockholders. Many distributors were making millions of dollars, but we were barely making enough money to live on. We could have gone out of business at any moment, and yet we had distributors who were multimillionaires."

By 1991, that seemed to be the least of the company's distribution problems. "In multilevel marketing, you find people who want to get rich quick," continues Roney. "They wanted Nu Skin to be a pyramid." Distributors had allegedly violated state business practice laws in Ohio, Michigan, Illinois, Florida, Connecticut, and Pennsylvania. Some were accused of representing earnings as greater than they really were in order to recruit new distributors. Others allegedly made unreasonable claims or representations about the products or company.

The red flags went up, and state attorneys general began investigating. The situation was complex because multilevel marketing practices are governed by the laws of the various states, rather than federal law. Eventually, Nu Skin voluntarily agreed to change some of its sales and marketing programs. In effect, it began monitoring its distributors more closely and supporting them in ways that discourage unethical or illegal practices.

The company weathered the media and legal storm. It helped that Nu Skin cooperated with regulators and took corrective steps. But beyond that, the company learned something from its own managers' and its distributors' mistakes. Says executive vice president Steve Lund, "The scrutiny caused (1) our distributors to further emphasize retail sales and product marketing, (2) Nu Skin to make its marketing organization leaner, and (3) Nu Skin to better teach its distributors what they

can and can't say. As a result, we are more credible. None of our distributors has survived this experience without paying more attention to legalities, ethics, and morality—and that's a positive thing." In addition, in 1991 Nu Skin International joined the Direct Sellers Association (DSA), which represents network marketing and direct sales companies worldwide, promoting ethical business practices. Finally, publications such as *Success* and *Forbes* examined the company and found it in good health. (In the case of *Forbes,* the magazine followed up an initially negative piece with positive comments.)

Meanwhile, the company has continued to upgrade its physical distribution system, opening a state-of-the-art warehouse and distribution center in Provo. "It's so efficient that people come from all over the United States to study it," declares Blake Roney. Around 50,000 orders can be processed in a single day in the 200,000-square-foot facility. A $20 million computer system maintains constant communication between U.S. operations and those around the world (Nu Skin has offices in Canada, Hong Kong, Taiwan, Australia, and New Zealand). Thus, distributors can obtain current sales information, order directly from the company, and automatically receive paychecks in the currency of their country of residence.

Nu Skin International made a fast start out of the gate—perhaps too fast—but by the mid-1990s began to regain its positive image. In 1992 sales hovered around $600 million, with 3,000 employees, and the company had opened several foreign offices. It had launched a new product line called *Interior Design,* a series of nutritional products. Nu Skin says that *"Interior Design* is skin care from the inside out." By working from the inside out to make positive changes, there's a good chance that Nu Skin will survive and prosper.

QUESTIONS

1. How might Nu Skin have avoided some of the legal and ethical problems it encountered with its independent distributors?

2. What further steps can the company take to restore its image?

3. Do you think network or multilevel marketing should be federally regulated? Why or why not?

Sources: Ken Shelton, "Nu Skin International: Beauty and the Beast," *Utah Business,* October/November 1992, pp. 20–26; Nu Skin International promotional booklet, 1992, pp. 4–12.

CHAPTER 17

Wholesaling, Retailing, and Physical Distribution

LEARNING OBJECTIVES

After completing this chapter, you should be able to:

1. Discuss the role of wholesaling and retailing in distribution.

2. Identify basic categories of wholesalers.

3. Describe various types of store and nonstore retailing.

4. Discuss tactics used by wholesalers and retailers in their marketing strategies.

5. Describe trends in wholesaling and retailing.

6. Identify the tasks in the physical distribution process.

7. Discuss trends in physical distribution.

Creating Customer Value
Home Shopping

Imagine a new TV network that doesn't sell advertising. Instead, it offers products directly to consumers by phone or computer. The network, to be called Best TV, buys and broadcasts what it considers to be the best programs created by other cable TV channels. In traditional advertising slots, it runs shopping segments much like those seen on Home Shopping Network and QVC. This new idea in retailing is the brainchild of TV mogul Barry Diller, who made a success of the Fox network and now runs the QVC shopping channel. (QVC stands for Quality, Value, Convenience.)

Home television shopping involves viewers watching products displayed and described during specified segments, then using their phone to order the products they want. This method of retailing has taken off, becoming a $2.5 billion industry with an annual growth rate of about 20 percent. Compared with all shoppers, TV shoppers tend to be young, educated, and fashion conscious.

Thus, although many people still snicker about home television shopping, marketers cannot ignore it. In the past few years, premier clothing designers such as Diane Von Furstenberg and Bob Mackie have teamed up with the shopping channels to sell their garments. (In her debut, Von Furstenberg sold $1.2 million worth of dresses in two hours.) IBM sells some of its personal computers via TV. Novelist Barbara Taylor Bradford bypassed the traditional selling circuit to introduce a new novel on QVC. Prestigious retail stores such as Saks Fifth Avenue have allied themselves with QVC; Saks sold out $570,000 of its Real Clothes line in its first one-hour slot. Thus, this ten-year-old method of retailing will most likely establish itself just as firmly as catalogs and department stores did in earlier decades.

This major new way to bring goods to consumers requires teamwork in the form of alliances between suppliers and retailers. For instance, Macy's has planned the launch of its own show, "TV Macy," with help from Home Shopping Network (HSN). Catalog giant Spiegel Inc. is interested in a home shopping relationship as well. "We're in the retail business to provide consumers with a convenient way to shop. If that's the new avenue, then we'll use it," remarks Debbie Koopman, a spokeswoman for Spiegel.

Arrangements between the shopping networks and their suppliers vary. A home shopping channel may buy the goods directly from either the manufacturer or a wholesaler, just as a traditional retailer would. If a manufacturer wants to buy time for an infomercial, it simply pays a fee for the air time. Volvo Cars of North America Inc. recently drove the latter route, airing two half-hour infomercials showcasing the safety features of their cars and ending with a toll-free phone number designed to lure customers into a nearby showroom.

Back to Best TV. With QVC already doing about $1 billion worth of business each year, Barry Diller merged it with HSN, its smaller competitor. The result is a home shopping network available to over 60 million viewers—about two-thirds of all television households in the United States. Producers and suppliers are overjoyed because, before the merger, QVC and HSN each required suppliers to give it exclusive rights to sell products via home shopping.

Diller is a past master at pulling together the major players in various aspects of the communications industry into a single winning team, resulting in some of the top cable programming companies, including TBS and Discovery. If he can get cable programmers and operators, traditional retailers, manufacturers, and wholesalers together in a venture that benefits them all as well as the consumer, he will have a major marketing force. "Overnight, the network could be in more homes than Fox is," says John Motavelli, editor of *Inside Media*. "It's a bid for building a national network without spending $4 billion to buy NBC."

Diller's vision doesn't stop there. He has negotiated to broadcast in Japan and Canada. In an alliance with British Sky Broadcasting, he has arranged to broadcast to Britain, Ireland, and parts of Europe. With Grupo Televiso, QVC will broadcast in Mexico, Spain, Portugal, and Latin America in Spanish and Portuguese.

How do marketers envision the home shopping networks of the near future? Many believe the networks will operate multiple channels that recreate the shopping mall experience. Users will be able to switch channels to visit different "stores," as well as ask for information, place orders, and pay for their purchases. "They'll have something for everyone," predicts Wendy Liebmann of WSL Marketing in New York. As you read this chapter, look ahead to such possibilities.

Sources: Julie Hatfield, "Dial M for Merchandise," *The Boston Globe,* July 14, 1993, pp. 35, 39; Kevin Maney and Ellen Neuborne, "New Network Looms Behind QVC Deal," *USA Today,* pp. 1–2B; Pat Slogan and Kate Fitzgerald, "Macy's Rings up Home Shopping," *Advertising Age,* June 7, 1993, p. 8; Frederic M. Biddle, "Retailing's Future Vision?" *The Boston Globe,* May 2, 1993, pp. 78–79; Annetta Miller and Seema Nayyar, "Highbrow Goes Lowbrow," *Newsweek,* pp. 48–49; Laura Zinn, "'Retailing Will Never Be the Same,'" *Business Week,* July 26, 1993, pp. 54–60.

Chapter Overview

As you learned in the previous chapter, many producers rely on wholesalers and retailers to get their products to the consumers and organizational buyers in their target markets. They must decide not only whether to use these intermediaries, but also which specific types to use. Furthermore, the wholesalers and retailers themselves must devise a marketing strategy.

This chapter formally defines wholesalers and retailers. It takes a more in-depth look at the role of these intermediaries and the many forms they take. The chapter also considers wholesalers' and retailers' marketing strategies—that is, their selection of target markets and creation of a marketing mix. Next, the chapter discusses current and future trends in wholesaling and retailing, such as those discussed in the story about home shopping. When wholesalers and retailers are part of a distribution channel, goods must be physically moved from the producer to these intermediaries. Thus, the chapter ends by introducing basic considerations related to the physical distribution of goods.

The Role of Wholesaling and Retailing in Distribution

Ideally, the role of wholesalers and retailers is to handle the distribution functions more efficiently and effectively than producers can. These intermediaries play a valuable role when they can save the other channel members money through such activities as physically moving goods to a convenient location, assuming the risk of managing large inventories, and operating during hours convenient to the ultimate buyers of the products. They also may offer expertise not only in saving money but in finding new or better ways to make products available to customers.

Thus, a wholesaler is behind the success of the video rental department of the Omaha-based chain of Baker's supermarkets. The wholesaler, Video Home Theater, provides Baker's with a leasing package that includes not only the videos but fixtures for displaying them, training of Baker's staff, computer systems, setup, and promotion of the department. Louis Stinebaugh, general merchandise director at Baker's, says, "We believe we have the best of all worlds—very little risk, minimal investment, excellent service, and access to lots of expertise."[1]

Wholesalers and retailers carry out their role effectively when they deliver high quality, meeting the needs of others in the distribution channel. At the retail level,

United Stationers is the largest wholesale distributor of office products in North America. Offering more than 25,000 items, the company sells retailers products from over 400 manufacturers. It also provides overnight delivery from its regional distribution centers and local distribution points.

Commuter Cleaners meets commuters' need for a truly convenient way to get their clothes to and from the dry cleaners. Rather than simply opening at a busy street corner, Commuter Cleaners operates trucks that meet commuters at the train station each morning and evening.[2] Specialty toy shops help producers develop demand for their products by giving shelf space to untried but appealing items and providing demonstrations of toys that can't be explained in a short advertisement (as was the case with Erector sets years ago). This level of service is so important to some producers, including Geobra Brandstaetter, German maker of Playmobil construction toys, that they shun the big chains altogether.[3] At the wholesale level, in Europe so-called smart distribution centers are winning business customers by providing such services as final assembly or customization of the product, testing, repairs, and multilingual hot lines—whatever customers need to make the products work.[4]

The specifics of the distribution role vary somewhat depending on whether the intermediaries are wholesalers or retailers. But in distinguishing wholesalers and retailers, keep in mind that some organizations serve both roles. For example, Smart & Final operates over 100 stores that sell food and food-related products. It looks like a retailer. However, over 60 percent of Smart & Final's sales are to small businesses, community organizations, and church groups. Beauty parlors buy coffee supplies and shampoo; catering trucks use the store's hamburger buns and napkins.[5] Because the majority of its sales are to organizational buyers, Smart & Final is primarily in the wholesaling business. Similarly, the Staples chain of office-supply stores targets small businesses (wholesaling) but also sells to consumers (retailing).

WHOLESALING

wholesaler
A business that buys, takes title to, stores, and resells goods to retailers or organization buyers.

A **wholesaler** is a business that "is primarily engaged in buying, taking title to, usually storing and physically handling goods in large quantities, and reselling the goods (usually in smaller quantities) to retailers or to industrial or business users."[6] Although most consumers have little contact with wholesaling activities, wholesaling is a major business. The Census Bureau estimates there were 466,700 wholesale establishments operating in the United States during 1987 (the most recent year for which statistics are available). They employed roughly six million people.[7]

Wholesalers perform some or all of the distribution functions introduced in Chapter 16. For example, they may transport and warehouse goods, exhibit them at

FIGURE 17.1

Sales by Major Types of Retailers

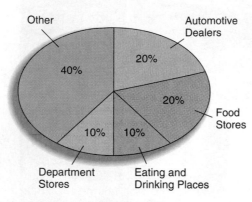

Other

Automotive Dealers

20%

40%

20%

Food Stores

10%   10%

Department Stores

Eating and Drinking Places

Total Retail Sales: $1.96 trillion

Source: U.S. Department of Commerce, *Statistical Abstract of the United States,* 113th ed. (Washington, D.C.: U.S. Government Printing Office, 1993), p. 776.

trade shows, and tell store managers which products are moving the fastest. Stores that carry a wide selection of merchandise often like the convenience of dealing with wholesalers, which often make many different products available from a variety of sources. Producers may appreciate such benefits as expertise in locating retailers or other organizational buyers. Bob Trinchero, chief executive of Sutter Home Winery, says that an important factor in his company's success has been the ability to choose and work cooperatively with wholesalers.[8]

RETAILING

retailer
An intermediary that sells primarily to ultimate consumers.

Often wholesalers sell merchandise to retailers. A **retailer** is an intermediary "engaged primarily in selling to ultimate consumers."[9] Retailers may buy from either producers or wholesalers. The most obvious examples of retailers are stores, but any organization in the business of selling to consumers is engaged in a form of retailing, whether or not it operates a store. Audrey Evans sells troll dolls and collectible dolls from a kiosk located in the Gurnee Mills mall in Gurnee, Illinois.[10] And Anyone Can Whistle uses a catalog to sell user-friendly musical instruments and related products such as wind chimes. The products are displayed in the catalog, and consumers who want to hear what the instruments sound like can request a free 30-minute cassette tape that corresponds to the catalog.[11]

Retailing is even bigger business than wholesaling. According to the Census Bureau, almost three times as many people worked in retail trade as in wholesale trade in 1990.[12] In 1992, retailers rang up sales of almost $2 trillion, or roughly $7,700 for each person in the United States.[13] Figure 17.1 shows which types of retailers accounted for the largest segments of the total.

Retailers provide a convenient way for producers to make their products available to consumers. From the consumer's perspective, retailers offer a variety of benefits. They make goods available at convenient hours and during the desired seasons or times of day. Retailers also seek to operate in locations convenient to the customer—some will even come to the consumer's home. Retailers make products easier to purchase by accepting credit cards or offering layaway plans. They also may modify products to make them more valuable to consumers, as in the case of monogramming luggage or slicing salami.

Types of Wholesalers and Retailers

Identifying the basic types of wholesalers and retailers helps intermediaries position themselves in the complex and fast-changing distribution business. It gives marketers a sense of the possible ways to distribute goods and services through intermediaries. In particular, it can help marketers select the type(s) of intermediaries that can best handle their products. Yaleet Inc., a shoe marketing company based in Syosset, New York, distributes its retro, Sixties-style Naot sandals and shoes through health food stores, in-line skating stores, bike shops, and surf shops, as well as through shoe stores. By using non-shoe retailers, the company keeps competition to a minimum and reaches its typical customers, who tend to be interested in health and the environment.[14]

In contrast, Huffy Corporation, learned the hard way about thinking through its choice of intermediaries. When Huffy launched its Cross Sport, a combination of sturdy mountain bike and lightweight racing bike, it distributed the bikes through its usual intermediaries—mass marketers such as Kmart and Toys "R" Us. Unfortunately, the bikes were more expensive than the rest of Huffy's line and targeted to an older market, thus requiring more sales support than the stores could provide. A year after the Cross Sport was launched, Huffy cut back production by 75 percent.[15]

TYPES OF WHOLESALERS

There are so many types of wholesalers that to have a general sense of their roles, it is helpful to think of them in terms of three categories: merchant wholesalers, manufacturers' wholesalers, and brokers and agents. Table 17.1 identifies the major types of wholesalers in each of these categories and describes what they do. Because the mix of services provided by each type of wholesaler meets different needs, certain wholesalers are common in some industries but not others. Therefore, a producer selecting a type of wholesaler does well to begin by learning what distribution channels are already common in his or her industry.

merchant wholesaler
A wholesaler that is independent of producers and takes title to the products it handles.

MERCHANT WHOLESALERS   The American Marketing Association definition of *wholesaler* (the one used for this text) best fits the category known as **merchant wholesalers**. These wholesalers are independent of the producer(s) of the products they handle, and they take title to those products. Merchant wholesalers are by far the largest category of wholesalers, accounting for over 80 percent of all wholesaling establishments. Distributors are a type of merchant wholesaler.

Full or Limited Service   Producers selecting a merchant wholesaler will consider how many distribution functions these intermediaries will handle. Basically, this depends on whether the wholesaler is a full-service or limited-service wholesaler. Full-service wholesalers perform all the channel functions. They may be called "general merchandise wholesalers" (which carry a broad range of products) or "specialty wholesalers" (which carry a narrow range but much selection within their category). General merchandise wholesalers typically handle hardware, drugs, or clothing. Specialty wholesalers handle such products as automobile parts or health foods.

As their name implies, limited-service wholesalers perform only some of the distribution functions. There are four basic types:

rack jobber
A wholesaler that performs most distribution functions in addition to providing and stocking racks for merchandise.

1. **Rack jobbers** perform most distribution functions except sometimes marketing research and grading of products. The rack jobber gets its name from its addition-

TABLE 17.1

Major Types of Wholesalers

TYPE	DEFINITION
Merchant wholesalers	Wholesalers that take title to the products they sell
Distributors	Wholesale middlemen, especially in lines where selection or exclusive agency distribution is common at the wholesale level and the manufacturer expects strong promotion support; often a synonym for wholesalers
Full-service wholesalers	Wholesalers that perform all the channel functions
General merchandise wholesalers	Wholesalers that carry a variety of goods in several distinct and unrelated lines of business
Specialty wholesalers	Wholesalers that stock a narrow range of products
Limited-service wholesalers	Wholesalers that perform only some of the distribution functions
Rack jobbers	Wholesale intermediaries operating principally in the food trade, supplying certain classes of merchandise that do not fit into the regular routine of food store merchandise resource contacts; commonly place display racks in retail stores, provide an opening inventory on a consignment or guaranteed-sale basis, periodically check the stock, and replenish inventories
Cash-and-carry wholesalers	Wholesalers that carry a limited selection of products and do not provide transportation for the goods they sell; customers must pay cash and transport their purchases
Drop shippers	Wholesalers that deal in large lots shipped direct from the factory to the customer of the drop shipper, take title to the goods, assume responsibility for the shipment after it leaves the factory, extend credit, collect the account, and incur all the sales costs necessary to secure orders
Truck jobbers	Wholesalers that operate a small warehouse and stock trucks that carry the goods to retailers, where they are sold in their original packages to the retailers
Manufacturers' sales branches	Captive wholesaling operations owned and operated by manufacturers; perform the functions of full-service wholesalers
Manufacturers' sales offices	Captive wholesaling operations owned and operated by manufacturers; perform selling functions and do not carry inventory
Agents	Business units that negotiate purchases, sales, or both but do not take title to the goods in which they deal
Brokers	Intermediaries that serve as "go-betweens" for the buyer or seller, assume no title risks, do not usually have physical custody of products, and are not looked upon as permanent representatives of either the buyer or seller
Auction houses	Business establishments engaged in selling merchandise on an agency basis by the auction method; goods are sold to the highest bidder at a sale that is usually publicized in advance or held at specific times well known in the trade

Source: Most definitions from Peter D. Bennett, ed., *Dictionary of Marketing Terms* (Chicago: American Marketing Association, 1988).

cash-and-carry wholesaler
A wholesaler that carries a limited selection of products and does not transport those products.

drop shipper
A wholesaler that takes title to products but does not handle physical distribution.

al service of providing and stocking the racks (shelves) on which the merchandise is displayed in stores. The products rack jobbers handle include magazines, hosiery, and health and beauty aids.

2. **Cash-and-carry wholesalers** carry a limited selection of products and do not provide transportation for the goods they sell. Their customers must go to them, pay cash, and transport their own purchases. These wholesalers commonly handle office supplies, hardware, electric supplies, and groceries.

3. **Drop shippers** take title to the products but do not handle physical distribution. They get orders for the merchandise, then have the producer deliver the products

Nifda, a company made up of independent foodservice distributorships, advertises its ability to provide service, quality, and quick deliveries to restaurants and institutions serving food.

truck jobber
A wholesaler that operates a small warehouse and trucks that carry goods to retailers.

to the customer. They sell goods that would be expensive to transport—for example, coal, grain, and lumber.

4. **Truck jobbers** operate a small warehouse and stock trucks that carry the goods to retailers, where they are sold in their original packages to the retailer. These wholesalers typically handle perishable or fast-moving items such as baked goods, meat, and fresh produce.

Number of Products Represented   Another consideration is whether the wholesaler will represent one, a few, or many producers. From the producer's standpoint, a wholesaler that sells for few, if any, other producers will give the product a lot of attention. Reef Brazil, which exports (from Brazil) sandals targeted to surfers, has had the greatest success in countries where it had to set up distributorships from scratch. The reason is that these new distributors generally handle fewer product lines, so they work harder for Reef Brazil.[16]

On the other hand, retailers may be most interested in the kinds of service they can get from a wholesaler that represents many producers. For example, Lotus Light Enterprises, based in Silver Lake, Wisconsin, handles 7,500 different natural foods and health and beauty aids for about 400 companies. Lotus Light's sales and marketing coordinator, Michael Charney, says, "Our most important service is providing a forum for our customers' products. We show their products to retailers and exhibit them at trade shows."[17] Lotus Light also provides such services as shipment of orders within 24 hours and a toll-free number for retailers to call when placing orders.

MANUFACTURERS' WHOLESALERS   Sometimes the producer sets up its own wholesaling operation. This operation may take the form of a branch office, which performs the functions of a full-service wholesaler, including carrying inventory. Or the manufacturer's wholesaling operation may be a sales office, which just performs the selling functions and does not carry inventory. The producer sets up its own wholesaling operation when a direct or short channel is appropriate.

BROKERS AND AGENTS   Some intermediaries that handle sales to retailers and organizational buyers do not take title to the products. Often, they do not take possession of the goods either. Instead, they bring together the producer and customer by arranging for a sale. These intermediaries are called **agents** or **brokers**, with the exact title varying from one industry to another. Since agents and brokers can't earn money by selling at a higher price than they paid (they never bought the products), they charge the producer a fee or commission. Agents are commonly used in the distribution of services.

Some agents or brokers represent several noncompeting producers, and others sell on behalf of a single producer. They may represent the producer for a single transaction (as in real estate), or they may have an ongoing relationship with the producer (as is common in the food business). A low-service, low-cost approach is to sell through an auction house, which simply brings together buyers and sellers.

agent/broker
An intermediary that does not take title but brings together the producer and customer.

TYPES OF RETAILERS

In general, retailing occurs either in stores or through a variety of types of nonstore retailing ranging from vending machines to catalogs. For example, the National Cheerleading Association offers cheerleading-related merchandise in catalogs and in the NCA Super Center stores it owns in Houston.[18] Table 17.2 describes the major types of retailers.

STORE RETAILING   Marketers divide stores into a number of categories based on such characteristics as the variety of their product mix, degree of convenience, and overall price level. (The distinctions among the categories can be blurry, so some stores are easier to classify than others.) Producers seek to have their products distributed through the types of stores that have characteristics consistent with their marketing strategy. And retailers try to operate stores of the types they think will best meet the desires of their target markets.

When consumers are looking for a big selection of some type of product or when they want to draw on the expertise of salespeople, they tend to shop at specialty stores. In today's environment, some of the most successful retailers are the big limited-line stores featuring low prices. These stores are called **category killers** because their extensive merchandise and low prices make them tough to compete wtih in the category of products they offer. Examples are Crown Books and Toys "R" Us. (To learn about a retailer who successfully uses a specialty store to exploit a niche marketing strategy, see the "Marketing Movers & Shakers" box on Carol Konop.)

category killer
A large, limited-line store featuring low prices.

In contrast, consumers sometimes want the convenience of being able to buy several kinds of products at the same store. They visit stores that have used some degree of **scrambled merchandising**, or offering products from two or more unrelated product lines. For example, shoppers at Walgreens can buy potato chips and magazines along with their cough medicine. Supermarkets were early adopters of the scrambled merchandising strategy. More recently, their bigger competitors, such as superstores and hypermarkets, have taken scrambled merchandising a step further, developing an even broader product mix. From the retailer's perspective, scrambled merchandising offers a way to draw more potential customers into a store and to offer products that can be sold at a higher markup. Wal-Mart reports that over 80 percent of the customers of its huge Supercenter stores shop in both the grocery and general merchandise sections.[19]

scrambled merchandising
Offering products from two or more unrelated product lines.

Retailers that want to target consumers looking for the lowest possible price have several store types to choose from. Most of these stores use **mass merchandising**,

mass merchandising
Seeking a high volume of sales by charging low prices.

TABLE 17.2

Major Types of Retailers

TYPE	DEFINITION	EXAMPLE(S)
Specialty stores	Stores that handle a limited variety of goods; may cater to narrowly defined target markets	Coconuts Music and Video
Limited-line stores	Stores that offer a large assortment of one product line or a few related lines	The Gap
Single-line stores	Stores that offer a single product line	Pizza Hut
Category killers	Big, low-priced limited-line stores	Toys "R" Us
Supermarkets	Large, departmentalized retail establishments offering a relatively broad and complete stock of dry groceries, fresh meat, perishable produce, and dairy products, supplemented by a variety of convenience, nonfood merchandise and operated primarily on a self-service basis	A&P, Safeway
Convenience stores	Retail institutions whose primary advantage to consumers is locational convenience; high-margin, high-turnover retailers	7-Eleven
Variety stores	Establishments primarily selling a variety of merchandise in the low and popular price range, such as stationery, gift items, women's accesories, toilet articles, light hardware, toys, housewares, and confectionary	Woolworth
Department stores	Retail establishments which carry several lines of merchandise, such as women's ready-to-wear and accessories, men's and boys' clothing, piece goods, small wares, and home furnishings, all of which are organized into separate departments for the purpose of promotion, service, accounting, and control	Macy's, Nordstrom
Mass merchandisers	Retailers offering a wide but shallow mix of products	Sears
Discount stores	Large retail stores which incorporate aspects of supermarket merchandising strategy to a high degree, attempt to price merchandise at a relatively low markup, carry stocks, and render only limited customer service, usually on the basis of a specific extra charge	Wal-Mart, Kmart, Target
Warehouse stores	Retailers that offer certain types of merchandise, particularly groceries, drugs, hardware, home improvement products, and home furnishings, in a warehouse atmosphere; facilities are typically in low-rent, isolated buildings with a minimum of services offered, and the consumer performs the bulk of the functions in a self-service mode	Price Club, Sam's Warehouse
Superwarehouses	Large stores that feature low prices and carry more items than supermarkets, but often no perishable items	Cub Foods
Off-price retailers	Retailers that offer lower price for goods late in the season or with a limited selection of colors and sizes	T. J. Maxx, Filene's Basement
Hypermarkets	Unusually large limited-service combination discount store, supermarket, and warehouse under a single roof; typically sells both food and nonfood items at 10 to 15 percent below normal retail prices	Bigg's, American Fare
Catalog showrooms	Retail outlets that consumers visit to make actual purchases of articles described in catalogs mailed to their homes	Service Merchandise
Nonstore retailers	Retailers that use vending machines or direct marketing	ARA Services, Lands' End

Source: Most definitions from Peter D. Bennett, ed., *Dictionary of Marketing Terms* (Chicago: American Marketing Association, 1988).

meaning they seek a high volume of sales by charging low prices. Among retailers using this strategy, a general merchandise retailer might operate variety stores or discount houses. Or by asking customers to forgo some services, the retailer can sell at a

Marketing Movers & Shakers

CAROL KONOP AND THE SHIRT STORE

The Shirt Store specializes in one product: men's shirts. The shop's designer and owner, Carol Konop, makes certain those shirts are the best in the business. Konop designs the shirts herself and has them manufactured by the Barnesboro Shirt Co., Inc., in Pennsylvania, about 300 miles from the shop in New York City. She knows the manufacturer—Yale Shanfield—personally, and phones the factory up to five times a day to check on her products. (Shanfield, too, is a bug about quality—he insists that his shirts be inspected four times before being shipped.)

Konop also believes in quality of service. The eight employees at the Shirt Store are ready to help customers select shirts as well as accessories such as ties and suspenders. "My customers can afford to shop at such famous stores as Brooks Brothers and Paul Stuart, but they like my prices and they like my service," notes Konop.

Konop started as a bookkeeper for a shirt manufacturer and retailer in New York. She loved the customers, as well as the flamboyant garment industry itself. "I was hooked," she remembers. She worked her way up through the ranks until, years later, she decided to leap into business for herself as a designer, manufacturer, and retailer of men's shirts.

As a retailer, Konop decided to eliminate an intermediary and deal directly with a labor contractor, who makes garments for small businesses that sell their own products but don't manufacture them. (Thus, she maintains high quality and charges about 25 percent less for her shirts than do her larger competitors.) She called Shanfield, with whom she had worked in the past.

Konop has four rules for maintaining a successful relationship with a supplier. First, choose a supplier that delivers high-quality goods on time. Second, establish terms of payment clearly and pay the supplier promptly. Third, try to plan orders ahead to avoid putting unnecessary pressure on the supplier. Fourth, don't shop around; switch suppliers only if a new one can improve the business.

Konop found an excellent site for The Shirt Store: across from Grand Central Terminal in midtown Manhattan, directly in the path of hundreds of thousands of commuters. Shoppers can drop in to browse, order shirts, or pick them up without detouring on their way to or from work. The store offers 100-percent cotton shirts in a wide range of styles, colors, and sizes. It holds about 1,200 dozen shirts in stock. In addition, The Shirt Store takes orders for custom-made shirts.

The Shirt Store sells about $1 million worth of shirts each year, and Konop ploughs almost half of that money back into manufacturing. Her marketing budget is slim. Most of it goes for a monthly mailing (four newsletters and eight postcards a year) to the store's 11,000 regular customers.

Konop plans to expand her retail business by opening another local store and licensing products (about 12 percent of her current revenue comes from the sale of accessories, which she acquires from sources around the world). Eventually, she'd like to go global. If American customers can buy shirts imported from other countries, why not sell hers abroad?

Source: Corinne K. Hoexter, "A Shirt Tale," *Your Company,* Spring 1993, pp. 22–25.

low price in a warehouse club, off-price store, or catalog showroom. The large volume purchased by category killers allows them to obtain merchandise at a lower cost and, therefore, charge low prices. Hypermarkets, too, seek this size advantage, only with a broader selection of merchandise.

NONSTORE RETAILING   Not all retailing takes place in stores. Every day consumers select merchandise in catalogs, on television screens, and in vending machines, among other places. The two basic types of nonstore retailing are vending machines and direct marketing.

Vending Machines   The practice of selling through vending machines, sometimes called "automatic merchandising," is useful for products that can be sold via credit card or for relatively small amounts of cash. Some products sold this way are soft

FIGURE 17.2

A Company Specializing in Direct Selling on a Global Scale: Avon Representatives in China

drinks, snack foods, stamps, photocopies, and telephone calls. Automatic teller machines (ATMs), which make limited banking services available around the clock, are another form of vending machine.

For products that do not require sales help or the need to touch the merchandise before a purchase, vending machines make shopping convenient. Travelers can use electronic ticketing machines (ETMs) to buy airline tickets and boarding passes. Airline Computerized Ticketing, based in Santa Ana, California, has installed these machines in major office buildings, hotels, airports, and other facilities. Customers must first make a reservation through a travel agent, then can choose to pick up the tickets at the nearest ETM if that is more convenient than other arrangements.[20] Music lovers at various locations in southern California (including AMC theaters) can buy CDs from vending machines. They push an album cover on the machine, which causes a 30-second music sample to play. They can then ask to see a listing of the songs on the CD or to purchase the CD, paying with cash, credit card, or bank automated teller card.[21]

direct marketing
Marketing efforts that use direct selling, direct mail, telemarketing, and the like to solicit orders from consumers.

Direct Marketing   **Direct marketing** consists of marketing efforts that use direct selling, direct mail, telemarketing, direct-action advertising, catalog selling, cable selling, or other media to solicit orders from consumers. Milkmen working for home-delivery dairies such as Oberweis Dairy in the Chicago area and Smith Brothers based in Kent, Washington, not only bring milk and eggs to consumers' doorsteps, they also take orders for a variety of products such as muffins, coffee, bacon, and even pizzas.[22] Direct marketing offers convenience because the consumer can make purchases and receive products without leaving home. It is especially useful for serving consumers who find it difficult to shop in stores because they are disabled, need to care for children, or simply have many other responsibilities.

direct selling
Selling in which a sales representative gives consumers a personal explanation and demonstration of a product.

Direct selling refers to a sales representative giving consumers a personal explanation and demonstration of the product, often in their homes. Direct selling is the way Tupperware, Amway Corporation, Mary Kay Cosmetics, and Encyclopedia Britannica distribute their products. So does Avon, the world's largest cosmetics company, which generates more than half of its sales outside the United States (see Figure 17.2). Brazil's

320,000 Avon Ladies—including 60,000 in the Amazon—see hawking the company's cosmetics and cologne as a good opportunity to raise their standard of living. In some Brazilian river villages, Avon products arrive by kayak, and the Avon Ladies arrange barter deals—say, 20 pounds of flour for a bottle of cologne. More often, payments are in the form of gold nuggets or powder.[23]

direct mail
The mailing of brochures, letters, etc., that describe a product and ask the consumer to order it.

Direct mail is the mailing of brochures, letters, and other materials that describe a product and ask the consumer to order it. Geerlings & Wade, a direct-mail retailer of wine, sends its customers a four-page brochure every few weeks describing a type of wine and the vineyard where it is produced.[24] Although people often refer to direct mail as "junk mail," many consumers look forward to opening the mail each day and enjoy receiving sales literature. Sales resulting from direct mail have grown fast in Japan, where marketing via mail works particularly well for fashion accessories, jewelry, cameras, ladies' wear, and furniture.[25]

Direct mail often uses catalogs to present product offerings. Over 8,000 different catalogs are competing for U.S. consumers' attention.[26] They are produced by giant retailers like Spiegel and J. C. Penney as well as by such entrepreneurs as Stringham and Smith Company, which earns a five-figure income selling brownies and desserts.[27] According to a recent survey, almost half of all mail and telephone orders were in response to catalog marketing.[28] In recent years, the growth in catalog retailing has outpaced that of store retailing, but starting up a new catalog business can be tricky. The large number of competitors makes it difficult to stand out from the crowd, and the proportion of the population that buys from catalogs remains relatively constant.[29]

telemarketing
The selling of a product by telephoning prospects, describing the product, and asking for an order.

Telemarketing is the selling of a product by telephoning prospects, describing the product, and asking for an order. Alta-Dena Dairy of Chatsworth, California, used a telemarketing service to sign up new customers for its routes.[30] Selling through telemarketing allows for more personal contact than selling through direct mail or catalogs. However, this form of retailing does not allow the consumer to see the product, and some consumers are annoyed by the phone calls.

Direct-action advertising refers to advertisements that contain ordering information such as a number to call, or an address to send an order. Figure 17.3 shows an example of such an advertisement from Manhattan Beach Blading Company that appeared in *Inline* magazine. Besides magazines, direct-action advertising may also be displayed on billboards, broadcast on radio or television, or printed in newspapers.

In recent years, electronic and broadcast media have become increasingly important in direct marketing. As described in the story at the beginning of this chapter, home shopping channels are growing fast. In this type of retailing, television channels broadcast shows that demonstrate products and provide a phone number to call with an order. A possibility for the future is that interactive TV will allow viewers to skip the phone call and place orders using their remote control.

Computer networks also offer information about a variety of products. With a modem (a device that sends computer messages over phone lines), consumers can place an order and charge it to a credit card. However, the limitations of displaying products on computer screens and the view of most consumers that using a computer is work have kept the role of on-line retailing small. In a recent year, on-line services sold only $100 million worth of merchandise, compared to over $2 billion for TV home shopping channels.[31] On-line services are hoping that they will have more success participating in interactive TV, which combines features of home shopping channels and on-line shopping. An exception to the poor performance of on-line shopping is PC Flowers of Oakton, Virginia. By enabling users of the Prodigy service to have

FIGURE 17.3
Example of Direct-Action Advertising

cool stickers
for your skates

URBAN SKRATCH
crack & peel stickers
....

1.800.945.MBBC

manhattan beach blading company
1142 manhattan ave., suite 21
manhattan beach, ca 90266 usa

flowers delivered, PC Flowers has become one of the biggest florists in the United States. One reason given for the success of this business is the fact that men—the major users of on-line services—are major buyers of flowers.[32]

Of course, a retailer is not limited to just direct marketing, or even to a single form of direct marketing. In fact, combining modes of direct marketing can increase the performance of the overall marketing effort. Considering all the modes of direct marketing and combining several in a single effort is called **integrated direct marketing**.[33] For example, the marketer might forecast that 2 percent of consumers receiving a direct-mail piece will place an order. By adding a toll-free telephone number and training staff to handle the resulting calls, the marketer might add another 1 or 2 percent. The marketer might also use follow-up phone calls to reach consumers who thought the product looked interesting but didn't get around to responding. That effort, the marketer might predict, could add another 2 to 14 percent, for a total response rate two and a half to nine times greater than from direct mail alone.

integrated direct marketing
Combining more than one mode of direct marketing in a single effort.

Marketing Strategies for Wholesalers and Retailers

Two decades ago, Walgreen Company settled on a two-pronged marketing strategy that still drives the drugstore chain's marketing mix. Walgreens decided to focus on health care and convenience. The focus on health care shapes product mix, including the decision to sell off the Wag's restaurant chain and Sanborns, a chain of Mexican department stores. The emphasis on convenience guides planning of store locations, including the move away from shopping malls and into freestanding neighborhood stores. Walgreen's president, L. Daniel Jorndt, comments, "Would you walk 600 yards across a parking lot and then through a mall to buy a paper or get a prescription?"[34]

The product mix at Albertson's stores is carefully designed to provide one-stop shopping convenience. To provide customer satisfaction, the stores couple the basics—grocery, general merchandise, meat, and produce—with service departments like pharmacy, video rental, floral, bakery, and deli.

Expanding on both the health care focus and convenience, Walgreen is test marketing pharmacy-only stores called RxExpress, which feature drive-through windows.[35] Walgreen and other wholesalers and retailers benefit when they create a marketing mix that serves the needs of well-selected target markets.

TARGET MARKETS

Wholesalers serving organizational buyers typically segment their markets as described in Chapter 10: by geographic area, type of buyer, or end use of the product. Steel distributor Anko Metal Services targets Denver-area growth industries. Thus, when commercial construction slowed in the 1980s, Anko shifted from an emphasis on that industry to targeting the defense industry. Then cutbacks began shrinking national defense, and public sector construction took off with the construction of a new airport, a convention center, and prisons. So Anko began targeting public sector construction, emphasizing commodity-grade metals.[36]

For wholesalers serving retailers, the traditional approach to marketing has been a kind of mass marketing that treats all stores in the same way. However, wholesalers are becoming more sophisticated and are segmenting retailers, say, by size or product selection. They can then target specific mixes of goods and services to separate market segments.

Retailers, too, have increasingly benefited from selecting particular target markets to serve. Like other organizations that market to consumers, they may consider geographic, demographic, and psychographic criteria to identify market segments. A grocery chain that has made a notable success of target marketing is The Vons Companies, which operates in the highly competitive Southern California market. Based on information gathered from surveys, sales data, and demographic data, Vons adapts each store to the tastes of the neighborhood it serves. Customers in Hispanic neighborhoods find more varieties of chiles, and stores in upscale neighborhoods find more sushi and stuffed sausages. In addition, to serve the most price-conscious shoppers, Vons has opened Expo and Super Combo warehouse-type stores.[37]

PRODUCT STRATEGIES

Wholesalers and retailers both need to make decisions about their product mix. They also need to determine the level of service they will offer their customers.

SELECTION OF PRODUCTS   In the case of wholesalers, the product mix depends largely on the kinds of customers they serve. For example, supermarkets or hardware stores will want to work with wholesalers that offer a wide variety of product types. However, specialty stores or business buyers may be more interested in the wholesaler's in-depth knowledge and selection in a particular area.

In retailing, decisions about what products and product lines to carry are called **merchandising**. (This term has broad meaning and also applies to certain promotional activities.[38]) A retailer's merchandising decisions should be based on the wants and needs of its target market.

Sometimes this involves adding products and product lines, as in the case of supermarkets offering carryout foods and cafés where customers can buy and eat prepared items. Not only do these offerings appeal to consumers who are pressed for time, they also tend to be relatively profitable.[39] Catalog retailer L. L. Bean has sought to boost its flagging sales by updating and expanding its product offerings to include childrens' clothing. Now owners of its durable clothing and sporting goods have a reason to buy something new for themselves—and perhaps to try the new line of children's clothing.

In contrast, other merchandising decisions involve avoiding or discontinuing products that are incompatible with marketing objectives. Thus, to maintain Crate & Barrel's position as a specialty store with stylish offerings, its managers change up to 40 percent of its selection of housewares and furniture each season.[40]

merchandising
Retail decisions about which products and product lines to carry.

LEVEL OF SERVICE   For a wholesaler, level of service primarily refers to the number of distribution functions the wholesaler will perform. It can also refer to the amount of intangibles offered with the sale of tangible goods. Lanier, the world's largest independent distributor of office products, offers not only an extensive line of photocopiers, but "total copier support and service." In an agreement with Du Pont Corporation, Lanier manages Du Pont's total in-house U.S. copying needs, providing more than 3,000 copiers, service, and toner supplies. The companies are planning to expand this agreement to cover Du Pont's global operations.[41]

For retailers, service decisions concern how easy the retailer will make the consumer's effort to obtain what he or she needs. Retailers especially must seek ways to offer a level of service that does not cost so much that they must charge more than the target market will pay. But whatever the number of functions performed by either type of intermediary, a quality focus demands that the wholesaler or retailer do the job courteously and accurately and select the services that meet customer needs.

According to a recent survey, the most important measure by which consumers rate a shopping experience is the time involved. In particular, they don't want to spend a lot of time waiting to pay for their purchases. Next most important was whether consumers perceived they had been treated well by store employees.[42] Thus, to a large degree, the level of service offered by a retailer reflects the number of sales personnel available to help customers, the salespeople's training, and their authority to make decisions related to satisfying customers. The retailer's policy for accepting returns and exchanges also affects the service level. At the Value Village chain of for-profit resale stores, goods that still have a price tag attached may be returned for store credit within seven days of purchase. This policy is based on what the chain's owners learned from a manager of the Nordstrom department stores: for every dollar Nordstrom refunds for returned merchandise, the customer spends another three dollars.[43]

Depending on the target market and product mix, additional services may be appropriate. For example, full-service retailers may offer tailoring, gift wrapping, gift registries, play areas for children, and delivery and installation of merchandise. For a nonstore retailer, a high level of service may include knowledgeable order takers who can help with purchase decisions, enough inventory to ship most orders right away, and a policy that makes it easy to return unwanted merchandise. Lands' End offers 24-hour-a-day operators to take phone orders, "specialty shoppers" to help customers who want advice, and full refunds with no questions asked. Especially in December, when many purchases are Christmas gifts, catalog retailers are seeking an edge by offering guaranteed delivery within a short time frame so that the gifts will arrive for the holiday.[44]

Exceptional service may be the basis of a retailer's competitive advantage. The Kenyon College Book Shop, located in Gambier, Ohio, has earned national recognition and growing revenues by operating a coffee shop, hiring extra sales staff, and providing chairs and sofas in which to thumb through its books.[45] At Galloway Lumber, located in Kirksville, Missouri, when a customer reports a problem, one of the Galloways calls later the same day to make sure the problem is being solved to the customer's satisfaction. While other businesses in town are closing, Galloway's continues to expand.[46]

At the other extreme, self-service retailers seek to keep costs down by limiting the services they provide. Customers of a warehouse store may select products displayed in the cartons in which they were shipped. The customers may use scanners to record their own purchases, then pack the merchandise in bags they brought from home. Even among consumers with much discretionary income, few are interested in the high level of service (and high prices) associated with couture salons such as Martha, once located on Park Avenue in New York. The wealthy women who shopped at Martha didn't have to hunt through the racks of $12,000 gowns; the gowns would be brought out three at a time, then ironed between fittings. Did the customer need matching shoes? Owner Martha Phillips would go out and buy them. However, today even rich shoppers have simpler tastes and are more comfortable shopping in more casual surroundings, so the Park Avenue store recently shut its doors.[47]

PRICING

For wholesalers, the nature of the pricing decision varies depending on the type of wholesaler. Merchant wholesalers generally can charge their customers whatever price they wish. However, not only do their customers want a low price, but so do the producers that supply them. When wholesalers charge a relatively low price, the product will be more attractive to the ultimate buyers. But when wholesalers provide extensive services, the price they charge needs to reflect this.

In the case of manufacturers' wholesalers, the wholesaler has little if any control over the price. The producer makes this decision as part of its own marketing mix.

Agents and brokers have wide latitude in pricing decisions. Often, their payment is a commission based on the selling price. Therefore, these wholesalers have an incentive to arrange sales at as high a price as buyers will pay.

As described in Chapter 14, retailers typically base their prices on a markup over the price they pay to acquire the merchandise. The resulting price should reflect the level of service provided by the retailer as well as the value consumers believe they are getting. Retailers also must decide if and when to discount or mark down the price of

Besides markups and markdowns, retailers often use price lining. American Greetings supports a price lining strategy by offering product lines sold at three price groups: "value products," sold at the lowest price, "core products," offered at a moderate price, and "premium products," priced higher than the other two categories. The company also provides a product mix analysis that enables stores to customize their offerings from the three price categories.

merchandise. Markdowns are most common when it is difficult to forecast just how much of a product consumers are likely to buy. For example, changes in fashion as well as changes in season require that sellers of clothing frequently slash prices to make room for new merchandise.[48] However, regular discounts cut into profits and may encourage consumers to delay purchases until after the product goes on sale.

An alternative to frequent discounting is every-day low pricing, described in Chapter 15. But as noted in that chapter, evidence suggests that this pricing tactic is not always the most profitable. Traditionally, many retailers have profited from the high regular prices and low sale prices offered by their suppliers. Important sources of profit include two popular practices among intermediaries:

1. Through *forward buying,* retailers buy a big supply of a product when the supplier offers it at a reduced price. They sell some of the product at the special low price the producer is seeking to encourage. Then, when the promotion is over, they mark the remainder of the merchandise up to the full price, enjoying a heftier markup percentage.
2. Through *diverting,* retailers buy more than they need when the product is offered at a low price, then resell what they don't need to other retailers at a higher price.

One impact of these practices is that consumers don't get the full impact of the price reductions producers are trying to stimulate. This works to the disadvantage of brand-name products relative to their private-label competition, which is why some big producers such as Procter & Gamble are trying to encourage every-day low pricing.[49]

DISTRIBUTION

Wholesalers and retailers make distribution decisions on two levels. First, as participants in the marketing channel, they make some or all of the decisions concerning marketing functions. They must be concerned about issues of channel management. For example, a large wholesaler might seek to develop its expertise in order to take on

Shopping Miami is a retail store in Brazil marketing U.S. consumer goods to the Brazilian customer. The company uses a unique form of distribution whereby customers select purchases from samples on display in the Saõ Paulo store, then the order is faxed to Florida, where distributors Suzanne and Dick Zimmerman have the items shipped to Brazil.

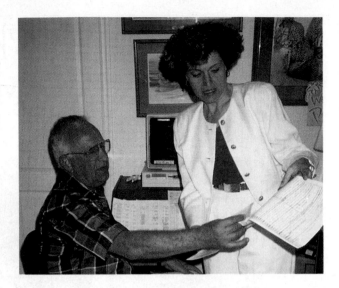

a leadership role in the channel. If the intermediaries' activities include physical distribution, they must make decisions in this area as well. For example, wholesalers and retailers are often concerned about inventory management and warehousing. Southland Corporation, which owns 7-Eleven convenience stores, recently began using an inventory management program from Japan. Called Accelerated Inventory Management, the system is designed to provide store managers with fast, precise knowledge about what products are selling.[50]

On another level, intermediaries are producers of distribution services. As such, they must distribute their own services to their customers. Mighty Eagle Travel Inc., based in Winter Park, Florida, has a distribution strategy that includes the use of drive-through windows. When the travel agency moved into a former bank building, it decided to keep the existing window. Customers mainly use it for such routine services as picking up tickets.[51]

SITE SELECTION   For a store retailer, one of the most important distribution decisions is site selection, or deciding where to locate the store. In general, retailers want a location that is easy to get to and well traveled so people will notice the store. The retailer considers how far consumers are willing to travel for the types of merchandise the store carries, as well as how many competitors serve the same area. One of the most creative companies in terms of site selection is PepsiCo, which continually develops nontraditional sites for its Taco Bell, Pizza Hut, and KFC restaurants. The company recently opened a kiosk in a Moscow subway station to sell Pepsi's soft drinks along with food from Taco Bell.[52]

In the past, the logical choice was simply to find an affordable spot in the business district of the area being served. However, today's widespread reliance on the automobile has made the choice more complex by increasing the distance buyers will travel to many types of stores. Convenience often means easy access to parking—say, the huge parking lot of a suburban mall or the nearby parking spaces of a strip shopping center. Convenience can also mean locating the store where members of the target market are already passing by, as in the case of Eateries Inc.'s strategy of locating its Garfield's restaurants near such mall attractions as movie theaters.[53] Locating in a shopping center is a way to select a site where consumers will come for a variety of reasons: the majority of shopping trips are for multiple purposes.[54]

FIGURE 17.4

**Communicating a
Retailer's Image**

However, some retailers might choose a remote location in order to minimize costs and, therefore, the price of merchandise.

In some cases, particular locations offer additional benefits to the retailer. For example, a mall or business district might conduct promotional efforts to attract customers. The attraction of entertainment at a big regional mall brings in consumers who may be in the mood to spend money at the mall's stores. The 78 acres of Minneapolis's Mall of America include a miniature-golf course, a 14-screen theater, and an amusement park called Camp Snoopy.[55] Similarly, bargain-hunting consumers are drawn to outlet malls, where sales are outpacing those at more traditional mall formats.[56] In fact, department stores such as Saks Fifth Avenue, R. H. Macy & Company, and Bloomingdale's are opening clearance centers in outlet malls to carry unsold merchandise from their other stores.[57] A mall can be an expensive location, but some big developers offer assistance programs to small retailers in an effort to create a varied mix of tenants.[58]

MARKETING COMMUNICATIONS

For intermediaries, marketing communications also take place on two levels. The wholesaler promotes its services to the producers or intermediaries that supply it with merchandise. This effort primarily relies on using the wholesaler's sales force to reach potential suppliers. The wholesaler may back up this personal selling with ads placed in the trade magazines that serve the target market. The wholesaler must also promote the products it handles to potential buyers.

Retailers promote both themselves and the merchandise they carry. Marketing communications about the retailer seek to build an image of the retailer that will be attractive to its target market. Thus, the ad in Figure 17.4 projects an image of Penney's as a place to find stylish clothing. These messages also provide information such as a store's hours and location. Messages about the merchandise seek to lure members of the target market to the store to buy the advertised items and other items as well. The specific types of merchandise promoted should be consistent with the store's desired image.

IMAGE AND ATMOSPHERE

As noted in the discussion of target markets, part of positioning the intermediary to serve a particular target market is to create an image for that intermediary. Benetton has sought to move from an image of "one big teenage sweaterfest" to being a place for adults to shop. The change has included higher prices, wider aisles, and wood shelving in place of metal fixtures.[59]

In planning and evaluating image, the marketer must bear in mind that from the customer's standpoint, image is not a collection of unrelated characteristics. Thus, each time you enter a store, you don't mentally measure the aisles, note the type of shelving used, evaluate the color scheme, and so on. Rather, judging stores is so routine that we have a mental model (called a "schema" in psychological jargon) that describes a whole category such as a supermarket or boutique, a hot dog stand or French restaurant.[60]

What this means for marketers is that they need to think about not just the specific tactics they can use to create and adjust an image, but also the nature of the schema their target market has for the particular store. In the case of the hot dog stand, the operator would consider that people who go to a hot dog stand are expecting to find such features as simple decor, a limited menu, and low prices. If they find something with these or similar characteristics, they are likely to be satisfied. To distinguish the stand from its competitors, the operator would have to do more than make minor adjustments to this formula (such as adding hamburgers or brownies to the menu). If the operator of the hot dog stand installed thick carpeting, hired a pianist, and began serving complimentary oysters, people would notice and remember that this hot dog stand is something different. Of course, the operator then risks losing customers who like hot dog stands in order to attract new customers.

atmospherics
Factors such as architecture, lighting, and layout that attract attention and stimulate sales.

STORE RETAILING   The basic way a store retailer creates and maintains a particular image is through the store's atmosphere. Retailers' decisions about store atmosphere involve **atmospherics**, or "store architecture, layout, lighting, color scheme, temperature, access, noise, assortment, prices, special events, etc., that serve as stimuli and attention attractors."[61] Table 17.3 summarizes some broad alternatives for atmospherics. Again, remember that these alternatives do not function independently but as part of people's schemas for types of stores.

As with other dimensions of the marketing mix, atmospherics should be consistent with attracting and meeting the needs of the store's target market. An example of a retailer that uses atmospherics consistent with serving its target market is Sunglass Hut's Greenwich Village store. A feeling of being outdoors makes it easier to sell sunglasses, so the store has a boating theme. The refinished hardwood floor resembles a boat deck, and the cases for displaying the glasses look like lifejacket compartments. Several strips of track lighting supplemented with suspended lamps make the store bright.[62]

Good store design can boost sales. The Gap positions a table inside the front door angled to appear as a diamond. This positioning is intentional, based on research that indicates customers entering the store turn right 80 percent of the time. At the Gap, consumers are guided by the table's angle to a collection of full-priced, newly arrived clothing.[63] The videos playing on a large screen at the back of each Disney Store lure customers with familiar songs from Disney movies. By the time customers have

TABLE 17.3

Atmospherics: Some Broad Possibilities

COMPONENT OF ATMOSPHERICS	SOME VARIABLES	EXAMPLES
Architecture	Imposing room heights and elegant details; period architecture such as colonial look; small or large rooms; modern or old fashioned	Warehouse look of stores emphasizing low price; waterfalls, pillars, and mosaics in upscale department stores
Layout	Basic grid of straight aisles; clustering of related goods into "boutiques"; main aisle as a loop with merchandise along walls and in center	Grid pattern of most supermarkets (easier to catch shoplifters); boutique pattern of upscale gift shops (encourages browsing)
Lighting	Bright or dim; purely functional or attention getting	Bright lights to stimulate sales in a supermarket; dim lighting with special effects to create an exciting atmosphere in a nightclub
Color scheme	Warm colors to draw in customers and stimulate quick decisions; cool colors to relax customers	Fast-food restaurant decorated with heavy use of red and yellow; elegant restaurant decorated in blues and grays
Sounds	Music (loud or soft, fast or slow); high or low noise level	Pianist playing soft music at Nordstrom's to create sense of elegance; loud music to generate excitement and fast turnover at Hard Rock Cafe

returned to the door—usually by a different route—they have often spotted something to buy.[64] (For more on atmospherics, see "Put It into Practice.")

NONSTORE RETAILING   Nonstore retailers also must be concerned about image. In the case of vending machines, the retailer needs to be sure they are easy to use and in good working order. The retailer also must consider whether the machines will be appealing to target markets and whether they display the merchandise attractively.

With regard to direct marketing, creating and maintaining an image depends on the type of media used. Sales representatives who contact consumers in person or over the phone must be well trained and should convey a level of professionalism appropriate to the product. Written materials used in direct marketing should be attractive, and their message should be clear. Creating a catalog that is appealing to its target market is essential to the success of this type of retailer.

Trends in Wholesaling and Retailing

Economic and technological changes have made wholesaling and retailing more competitive than ever. This means that the survival of modern wholesalers and retailers depends on their ability to recognize and meet their customers' needs. The principles of target marketing and total quality management are becoming as essential to intermediaries as to other marketers. So are the many ways that wholesalers and retailers can team up with others in the marketing channel to keep their customers happy.

A case in point is 800-Flowers, which arranged with United Parcel Service to be able to handle a flood of orders for Valentine's Day candy and flowers. 800-Flowers stockpiled two-pound boxes of chocolates and bunches of long-stemmed roses at UPS's Louisville distribution center. When 800-Flowers was reaching capacity for handling orders during the week of Valentine's Day, its representatives could offer the

OBSERVE THE SHOPPING ATMOSPHERE

When you shop, as a consumer you are affected by a variety of factors intended by retailers to entice you to buy their products. Atmospherics—elements such as store design, lighting, color scheme, noise, and even temperature—can influence your decision to buy.

For this chapter's project, you'll be choosing a site location and "designing" a retail store using atmospherics. Before doing so, visit a number of different stores with your eyes, ears, and even nose open to sensation. Be keenly aware of retailers' use of atmospherics, and evaluate the effect on you. Which types of atmospherics make you want to linger? Which make you want to buy? Do you think the store could sell more by moving customers through quickly or by encouraging them to stay and think about the products for sale? Keep track of these observations for your chapter project.

option of having roses or chocolates delivered via UPS Next Day Air. The orders were transmitted directly to the Louisville facility, where computers printed shipping labels, monitored inventory, and kept records.[65]

WHOLESALING TRENDS

With many producers using shorter channels, often the intermediaries that get eliminated are wholesalers. One study predicts that the wholesaler's share of products sold in the United States will fall from 42 to 46 percent to as low as 36 percent by 2000.[66] Midsized wholesalers are the biggest losers. The wholesalers expected to survive are the ones that offer a level of service difficult to obtain through other sources.

One way they have done this is through leadership in technology. Distributor W. W. Grainger, Inc. offers same-day delivery of 53,000 different maintenance, repair, and operating supplies. The computer technology that makes this possible includes a system for more accurately forecasting sales and one for closely tracking the movement of products from supplier to regional distribution center to branch location to customer. Through a satellite network, Grainger branches can share information about what each has in stock. Also, an Electronic Catalog on CD makes it easier for Grainger's customers to locate and order the items they need (see Figure 17.5). Customers using a system called Grainger Express can use their computers to hook up with a branch computer and learn product price and availability, place orders, check the status of their orders, and leave messages for Grainger branch employees.[67]

Some wholesalers have remained competitive by adopting a quality orientation and a focus on the customer. Darter Inc., which distributes mill supplies, paper products, and janitorial supplies, among other goods, does more than fill orders; it sends product representatives to factories to show how the company can help these customers cut costs.[68] A customer focus may also include market segmentation, as noted earlier. Also important are efforts to build long-term partnerships with other channel members. The wholesaler that focuses on delivering quality seeks to identify its customers' needs. For example, store managers may appreciate information about how much of each product their customers are buying. Or they may want an easy and fast way to reorder merchandise.

RETAILING TRENDS

Major trends in retailing include shifts in which stores are most popular with consumers. Also, technology has brought retailers new opportunities and challenges. In

FIGURE 17.5

Using Technology to Facilitate Direct Sales

many cases, adapting to these trends has meant offering better prices. As a result, more and more organizational buyers are making purchases from retailers rather than through more traditional channels of distribution.

COMPETITION   In recent years, an economic slowdown coupled with stiff competition has reduced the number of major retailers. Especially vulnerable are supermarkets and department stores. During the last decade, half of the top 12 supermarkets were acquired by other companies. Some of the best-publicized department store closings included B. Altman and Bonwit Teller in New York and Sakowitz in Houston. Sears has closed stores and laid off thousands of employees. The main reason given for why consumers are deserting department stores is that they believe they can get better value elsewhere. According to retail consultant Elizabeth Eagles, "Shoppers believe that by walking into a department store they are automatically going to have to overpay for their purchase."[69]

The consensus among observers of retailing seems to be that this value consciousness will continue and will keep weeding out all but the retailers that best meet consumers' desire for value. According to a study by Columbus, Ohio–based Management Horizons, half of today's retailers will be out of business by 2000.[70] Among retailers of food, drugs, and household items, supermarkets have lost half their market share to their bigger, often lower-priced competition (see Figure 17.6). The major winners appear to be the discounters, most notably Wal-Mart.[71] That trend has occurred not only in the United States, but also in Europe and Japan.[72]

Recently, not only have department stores lost market share to discounters, but so have specialty stores serving the middle of the market—for example, The Gap and The Limited.[73] (The Gap has responded by opening Gap Warehouse stores.) However, the *Ready-to-Wear Review* predicts that the discount department store will peak in the mid-1990s, then begin to decline.[74] This view is based on the belief that consumers will increasingly demand more service than they can get at a factory outlet or other low-price store.

In the meantime, some big suppliers are helping such midprice retailers as supermarkets look for ways to keep costs down so they can offer lower prices. These

FIGURE 17.6

Sales of Retailers Classified by the Census Bureau as Supermarkets

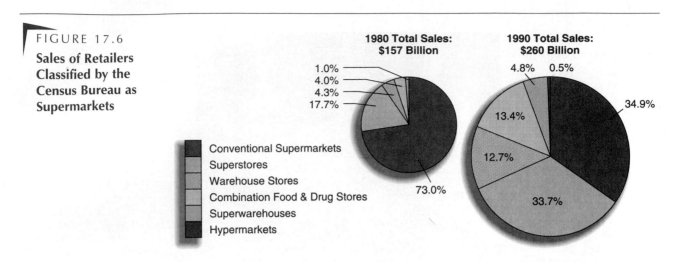

1980 Total Sales: $157 Billion

1.0%
4.0%
4.3%
17.7%
73.0%

Conventional Supermarkets
Superstores
Warehouse Stores
Combination Food & Drug Stores
Superwarehouses
Hypermarkets

1990 Total Sales: $260 Billion

4.8%   0.5%
34.9%
13.4%
12.7%
33.7%

Source: U.S. Department of Commerce, *Statistical Abstract of the United States,* 113th ed. (Washington, D.C.: U.S. Government Printing Office, 1993), p. 778.

efforts, called *efficient customer response,* include Scott Paper Company's work with supermarkets, such as helping them reduce inventory. Keyes Fibre has helped supermarkets by developing "family packs," which are smaller than the giant sizes of paper goods available at warehouse clubs yet big enough to sell at a low unit cost.[75]

Although individual stores have closed and some chains have gone out of business, there are still a lot of places to shop. In fact, there is twice as much retail sales space per person now than 15 years ago—18 square feet for every U.S. citizen.[76] Many experts have concluded that too much retail space was built during the 1980s. Some malls have less than 70 percent of their stores occupied.[77] Not only have developers had difficulty finding tenants for some shopping centers and malls, but when new stores do fill the space, they find it harder to succeed with so much competition.

Discounters are not the only retailers that have succeeded in recent years. Industry analysts have observed that consumers are increasingly choosing either to shop at a discount store or a high-end retailer offering special goods or services.[78] Thus, retailers that don't want to compete with a low-price strategy may find success by offering something distinctive. This was the strategy adopted by a number of retailers in Bath, Maine, when they learned Wal-Mart planned to open a nearby store. Knowing that they couldn't beat Wal-Mart's price on high-volume goods, they sought other sources of competitive advantage. For example, Gediman's Appliance Store set up a room where people can sit in easy chairs and view the televisions, and it eliminated the low end of its inventory where price competition was most important.

TECHNOLOGY   Probably the most significant technological advances affecting modern retailing have to do with gathering and sharing information.[79] As described in Chapter 16, retailers can use scanners to keep track of what is selling, enabling them to order merchandise as needed. The scanner systems can also print out cents-off coupons for products related to the ones just purchased. Furthermore, retailers can use modern information systems to learn about who their customers are. For instance, they can link customer data collected by scanning the codes on "frequent shopper" cards to the product data collected with scanners. Technology can also add to shoppers' convenience. In the not-too-distant future, service-oriented retailers may use portable terminals to ring up sales anywhere in the store. The store employee uses a

You Decide

WHAT'S WRONG WITH ON-LINE SHOPPING?

It seems so easy. You turn on your computer, punch a few buttons on the keyboard, and order anything from contact lenses to groceries. That's the dream of marketers for companies such as CompuServe (which offers Electronic Mall), and Modem Media Inc. (which specializes in interactive marketing) and organizations like CUC International (founded 20 years ago to promote on-line shopping). But on-line shopping—ordering products through computer services—has been something of a dud, and marketers are trying to find out why.

For one thing, the majority of people who frequently go on-line aren't heavy shoppers. Most users are male, but most shopping dollars are spent by women. Although he's a self-described "on-line junkie," one potential shopper (who happens to be a market researcher) admits that he "never bought a thing on-line." He explains that written descriptions and crude graphics aren't enough to make him buy; further, the prices aren't that great. "With such a direct connection to the vendor, it should be the cheapest possible price," complains this consumer. "The prices are competitive, but they aren't compelling." Other home computer users are retirees on fixed incomes or students with little spending money.

Another problem with on-line shopping is that it isn't much fun. Many Americans shop as recreation. They like to stroll the aisles, handle products, try on clothes. Not only does most on-line shopping disallow this, but the computer is generally associated with work, not leisure. One software developer says, "I'm not a very on-line person. I log on at work, not at home. [Besides], I can't buy a flannel shirt unless I know what it looks like."

On-line shopping does have its adherents. One investor relations director remarks, "It's easier for me to punch a few keys on a keyboard than it is to fill out a form for a catalog." But isn't it easier still to phone the toll-free phone number for the catalog?

Some marketers have caught on to the idea that shoppers like the experience, or sensations, of shopping. For instance, potential home buyers can tour available homes by computer, then choose those that they want to see in person. And a company called MarketWare Corp. has developed software called Visionary Shopper, which allows consumers to "stroll" through store aisles via computer screen, examine packages and even "place" them in a shopping cart. So far, the software has been used mostly for marketing research, but the implications for on-line shopping are obvious. In addition, marketers of on-line shopping services are exploring possibilities with interactive TV. (Prodigy Services Co. says it is developing its own interactive TV services and plans to handle orders placed by customers over cable TV.)

What do you think the future of on-line shopping will be? In addition to the problems mentioned above, what others can you see? What steps should marketers (and designers) take to make the on-line shopping experience more appealing to consumers?

Sources: William M. Bulkeley, "Online Shopping Fails to Fulfill Promise," *The Wall Street Journal,* June 21, 1993; Howard Schlossberg, "Shoppers Virtually Stroll Through Store Aisles to Examine Packages," *Marketing News,* June 7, 1993, p. 2.

---

scanner on the portable terminal to read the bar code on the product and the magnetic stripe on the customer's credit card, then produce a receipt. The customer doesn't have to stand in line at a checkout counter.

Modern technology is also improving retailers' ability to share information with others in the distribution channel. A notable application is electronic data interchange. Communication is also enhanced with the variety of ways now or soon available for sharing information, including voice mail, electronic mail, and fax machines. A number of supermarket chains let consumers fax them a grocery list; store personnel then fill the order.

As noted earlier, technology can expand the use of nonstore retailing. It can help nonstore retailers target distribution through traditional modes such as catalogs. Modern printing technology makes it possible not only to tailor the mailing list but to produce several versions of a catalog or other written materials to match the needs and interests of various groups. Technology can provide new mechanisms for displaying and ordering merchandise. So far, few consumers have taken advantage of the existing technology to make purchases via their computer (see "You Decide: What's

FIGURE 17.7
**The Physical
Distribution Process**

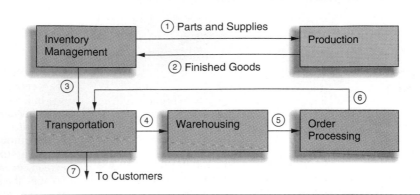

Wrong with On-Line Shopping?"). However, many observers of the retailing industry predict that electronic shopping will eventually become more popular through more user-friendly means, perhaps interactive television.

Kmart has been a leader in applying technology to retailing.[80] Satellites transmit sales data nightly from each store to the company's headquarters in Troy, Michigan. The company uses this data to continuously adjust prices to the most profitable level. The nightly sales data also enable Kmart's buyers to see which products are selling well in which stores and therefore to place orders and adjust inventory levels at the chain's regional distribution centers. Kmart stores also are testing ceiling-mounted scanners that track the number of customers entering and leaving the store. The scanners are part of a system that notifies personnel when a particular department needs more sales personnel or when customers are headed for the checkout lanes. Also, by measuring overall store traffic each day, the system provides evidence for whether promotional efforts are succeeding.

Physical Distribution

physical distribution
Moving and storing goods
to get them efficiently to the
end user.

As goods move through distribution channels, one of the major activities that takes place is the physical movement of the goods from one place to another. The goal of this movement is to get the goods efficiently to the end user. Moving and storing goods for this purpose constitute the process of **physical distribution**.

THE PHYSICAL DISTRIBUTION PROCESS

Physical distribution comprises the functions of transportation, warehousing, inventory, and order processing.[81] These functions occur in a process such as the one shown in Figure 17.7. To carry out this process, producers and intermediaries may obtain support from other organizations such as transportation companies, public warehouses, insurance companies, and fulfillment companies. Thus, many catalog retailers contract with a fulfillment company to handle such functions as storing goods, taking orders, and shipping the products to the buyers. And over the last decade, Safeway has found that hiring outsiders to manage its warehouses can cut its costs.[82]

FIGURE 17.8

Proportion of Goods Carried by Each Mode of Transportation*

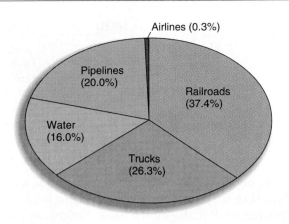

*As measured in ton-miles.

Source: U.S. Department of Commerce, *Statistical Abstract of the United States,* 113th ed. (Washington, D.C.: U.S. Government Printing Office, 1993), p. 610.

TRANSPORTATION   The function of transportation involves actually moving goods from seller to buyer. The basic choices, or modes of transportation, are motor carriers (trucks), railroads, air carriers, water carriers, and pipelines. Figure 17.8 shows the proportion of goods transported by each of these modes. To select a mode of transportation, the marketer considers various factors, especially the relative costs, speed, and flexibility of each. Table 17.4 summarizes some of these criteria. The marketer also weighs whether to own the mode selected (say, a fleet of trucks), rather than contracting with someone else to transport the goods. In selecting a specific carrier for that mode of transportation, the marketer considers costs, quality, and areas of specialization. Martinair Holland is a specialist in transporting animals. It offers customized shipping of animals, from cattle to whales to ostriches.[83]

intermodal transportation
Transportation that combines several modes.

piggyback service
Intermodal transportation of truck trailers via train to a station near their ultimate destination.

Besides the individual alternatives, the marketer may select some form of **intermodal transportation**, that is, transportation combining more than one mode. One version is **piggyback service**, whereby a railroad picks up truck trailers, loads them onto flatcars, and carries them to a station near their ultimate destination. The trailers are then delivered by truck to the buyer. Ships offer a similar service. Intermodal transportation can offer a degree of flexibility and efficiency unavailable with individual modes of transportation. This is important for Robbins Company, which ships large machinery and needs to move machines quickly to its customers around the world. In a typical month, Robbins ships three or four containers of parts by train from Kent, Washington, to New York. There the containers are loaded onto ships, which deliver them to Liverpool. From there they travel by truck to the company's assembly plant.[84]

Many businesses that serve global markets use intermodal transportation to handle the complexities of international physical distribution. Intermodal systems have become increasingly reliable, thanks in part to strategic alliances among transportation companies and fast electronic access to information. Lufthansa Airlines, the Maersk Inc. steamship line, and San Francisco–based Aeroground Inc. work together to carry containers from Asia to Europe by air, sea, and truck.[85]

The selection of how to transport goods is somewhat different when the shipments are small. For example, the marketer isn't going to be choosing between trains

TABLE 17.4	MODE	COST	SPEED	LOAD FLEXIBILITY
Characteristics of Transportation Modes	Motor carriers	High	Fast	Moderate
	Railroads	Moderate	Moderate	High
	Air carriers	Very high	Very fast	Low
	Water carriers	Very low	Very slow	Very high
	Pipelines	Low	Slow	Very low

freight forwarder
A company that gathers small shipments from various organizations and hires a carrier to move them as larger lots.

and boats to ship a manuscript, a report, or a computer diskette—or, for that matter, the small packages typically sent out by a catalog retailer such as Lands' End or Smith & Hawken. For small packages, the usual choices are government post offices, package delivery services such as United Parcel Service, and express delivery services such as Federal Express.

For some companies with small shipments, it is advantageous to use a **freight forwarder**. Such a company gathers small shipments to be sent to other cities from various organizations. The freight forwarder hires a carrier to move them as larger lots, usually at a lower rate than would be charged the small lots. Besides the possible cost advantage, the freight forwarder offers the convenience of picking up and delivering the packages. Their expertise makes freight forwarders popular for handling international shipments, including such related tasks as obtaining export licenses and taking care of foreign banking activities. The problems freight forwarders can solve range from the routine to the unusual, as in the case of a load of pipes to be flown to Saudi Arabia. There seemed to be no way to fit the pipes on the plane until freight forwarder Union Transport suggested removing the plane's front windows. The pipes were loaded through the cockpit and into the cargo area.[86]

WAREHOUSING   After transportation, the most costly function of physical distribution is warehousing, or holding a stock of the product while it awaits sale or transfer. Besides making the product available within a reasonable distance of the intermediary or end user, warehouses provide a location for sorting and consolidating goods. Organizations need to warehouse goods when it is more efficient or reliable to produce or buy large quantities, rather than just what is needed immediately. They also need to warehouse goods that can only be produced during part of the year, as in the case of crops. Conversely, some goods can be produced year round but are mainly purchased during part of the year. Examples include swimming pool filters and artificial Christmas trees.

To plan for warehousing, the marketer must decide how many warehouses will be used and where they will be located. These decisions should depend on customers' expectations and the importance of rapid transportation to the overall marketing strategy. As noted earlier, holding a lot of inventory is costly, but losing sales because goods are unavailable also is a cost to the organization. In selecting the locations of the warehouses, the marketer will also consider the likely transportation routes for the goods.

Buyers and sellers can benefit from using teamwork to set up a warehouse system. GE Supply, a distributor of electrical products, worked with a building contractor to set up mini-warehouses in trailers at construction sites. A computerized catalog in each trailer lists the various materials the contractor requires, including a

The CA-Warehouse Boss™ is software designed to improve warehouse efficiency. This integrated warehouse management system can link scanners, conveyors, and other devices. It tracks products from arrival to departure, enabling users to keep accurate inventory records.

picture and description of each. When workers need products, they walk to the trailer, select them from bins, and use a scanner to read the bar code on each. Each day the computer system creates reports of product usage, which GE Supply uses in determining what to deliver the next morning. The contractor has estimated that this approach saves about 20 percent over a more traditional warehousing system.[87]

Another warehousing decision is whether to use public or private warehouses. **Public warehouses** are businesses that offer space and inventory support services for a rental fee. This approach is flexible because the renter pays only for the space and services used. Other organizations find that it is more efficient to own their warehouses. These private warehouses give their users greater control over warehouse operations. Also, some products, such as hazardous or sterile materials, may not be suitable for public warehouses.

public warehouses
Businesses that offer space and inventory support services for a rental fee.

INVENTORY MANAGEMENT   Most producers and resellers of tangible goods carry some inventory of the goods. One reason is that they don't want to risk being out of stock when a customer orders the goods. Another reason is the belief that production can be more efficient if the organization produces a lot of one type of good before switching over to producing something else. The organization may also be seeking to protect itself against such potential supply problems as strikes or equipment breakdowns.

However, balanced against these possible advantages are the costs of carrying inventory. The organization must pay for the storage space and insurance for the goods. Also, the money spent in these ways is unavailable for investment in potentially profitable ventures. The organization therefore seeks to manage its inventory by maintaining just enough to provide the benefits it seeks. At the Quaker Oats Company, this trade-off between inventory and other costs is just one of the areas of distribution costs that fall under its Supply Chain Management program. Supply Chain

FIGURE 17.9

Reading Bar Codes in Industrial Settings

Management is a continuous effort that examines the whole production and distribution process and identifies ways to improve quality and lower costs.[88]

To keep track of inventories, organizations today often use Universal Product Codes (UPCs), commonly called bar codes. A laser beam in a scanner (such as the one advertised in Figure 17.9) reads the black-and-white stripes of these codes, and the scanner translates the information into computer code identifying the product. This process is much faster than keeping written records. However, an inventory management system based on UPCs requires that these codes be accurate. Anyone who has stood in a checkout line while a clerk struggles to get the price on an item with a faulty bar code knows how frustrating such mistakes can be. Many retailers, including Kmart and Wal-Mart, therefore set quality standards for UPCs and fine the supplier whenever a bar code is missing or inaccurate.[89]

ORDER PROCESSING   To process an order, someone in the organization receives the order and enters it into the processing system. The system then notifies production or warehouse personnel to fill the order. The employee who is to fill the order checks inventory. If the goods are in stock, the order is filled. If not, the goods must be produced or back-ordered. In the meantime, others in the organization check the buyer's credit (for a purchase on credit) and send out a bill or process the payment. Usually most of this work is done with a computer system. Then the information about the purchase can also be readily available for use in planning and marketing research.

Companies with a quality focus seek to identify and meet customers' wishes in this area. This is the goal of giant wholesaler McKesson Corporation's total-quality effort. McKesson's Millbrook Distributors unit is seeking a goal of 100 percent accuracy in filling orders, which saves customers time and money they would otherwise spend checking orders. The McKesson Drug unit surveyed its customers and learned that the

*Micro Warehouse Inc.,
publisher of the
MacWarehouse® catalog,
stands out in terms of
product availability. The
company, which sells
computers and software by
mail order, focuses on
customer service as a key
to success.*

service improvement they most wanted to see was faster credits for any merchandise they returned. So McKesson Drug challenged its employees to find ways to speed up that process, and they did, cutting credit-processing time from 19 days to 7.[90]

As noted earlier, some organizations find they can cut costs by hiring an outside service to process orders. However, as with so many other ways of cutting costs, there is a risk that customer service will suffer. When the producer's or intermediary's own employees take orders, the organization maintains greater control and closer contact with customers. The seller can identify unmet needs and build long-term relationships. By being more familiar with customers and the organization's products, employees are better able to identify ways in which the organization can serve its customers. Therefore, sellers may find that to achieve a desired level of customer service, they want to handle at least part of the order-processing function. Fortunately, a great deal of computer software is available to help in this area.[91]

EVALUATION AND CONTROL

The organization relies on physical distribution to make its products available to customers when and where they are ready to buy. Most physical distribution objectives call for achieving this at the lowest possible cost. In general, this means balancing the cost of carrying inventory with the cost of lost sales. In terms of transportation, it also requires that the marketer consider trade-offs between speed and cost.

In effect, this means that the marketer must decide what level of customer service is desirable, given that superior customer service costs more. A high level of customer service would involve quickly transporting whatever products were desired and guaranteeing delivery as needed. It also would involve easy communication between buyer and seller about the product and its distribution. Superior customer service would make distribution convenient for the customer—for example, deliveries would arrive at a time specified by the customer. Such a focus on superior customer service has been the key to success for Micro Warehouse, which sells computers and software through mail order. If customers have a problem or change their mind about an order, the company gives them a shipping number to have the product returned at no charge.[92]

A cross-functional view of physical distribution can help lead the organization to the best trade-offs between cost and customer service. In the past, the norm was to divide responsibility for the different aspects of physical distribution. Thus, one person might handle inventory management and another person shipping, without the two being responsible for seeing how those functions affect one another or the organization's total costs. In contrast, forward-thinking organizations today are linking responsibility for these activities with one another and with production functions. This cross-functional approach enables the organization to ensure that the performance of the physical distribution system supports the overall performance of the organization. McKesson Water Products Company assembled a cross-functional team to study inventory control. The team introduced the use of hand-held computer terminals, which route sales representatives use to enter data about what is loaded on their trucks and what they sell. This system is more accurate than the previous paper-and-pencil approach and saves hundreds of hours of record-keeping time.[93]

TRENDS IN PHYSICAL DISTRIBUTION

As noted earlier, one trend in physical distribution is to plan it as an entire system, rather than a series of discrete functions. Besides this cross-functional approach, another trend is improving the efficiency of physical distribution. Many firms are taking advantage of the ability to process a lot of information quickly and easily with computers. Computer technology helps firms by enabling them to conduct more sophisticated planning and control of the distribution effort.

just-in-time (JIT) inventory management
A system of holding little inventory and requiring suppliers to provide the exact quantity needed according to a precise schedule.

JUST-IN-TIME INVENTORY MANAGEMENT   Since the last decade, many organizations have sought to hold down inventory costs by adopting an approach called **just-in-time (JIT) inventory management**. Brought to the United States from Japan by auto and other manufacturers, JIT consists of holding little inventory and requiring suppliers to provide the exact quantity needed according to a precise schedule. By receiving products just as they are needed, the buyer minimizes the cost of carrying inventory. The supplier shoulders the responsibility for delivering acceptable-quality products on time—perhaps even several times a day for large buyers.

For JIT to deliver the benefits of low cost and high quality, buyers have to be able to accurately predict what they will need and when. Suppliers must be able to provide fast, reliable delivery. The quality of their products also must be high, because a JIT schedule allows no time for replacing defective goods.

JIT works best when suppliers are located near the buyer. For example, Toyota's Kentucky plant sends trucks to pick up parts from some suppliers as often as 16 times a day. Each truck stops at several suppliers' plants. Clearly, this is practical only because suppliers are close at hand. Along with geographically close relationships, teamwork with suppliers also helps a JIT system run smoothly. Fountain Valley, California–based Kingston Technology Corporation has developed a strong reputation for integrity in dealing with its suppliers. Companies that supply parts to Kingston, which makes product upgrades for computers, are so satisfied in their dealings with the company that they will give Kingston preferred service—even shipping products to Kingston ahead of other customers. "We will deal with a vendor only as a long-term partner," explains David Sun, one of the company's founders.[94] Also, the buyer should be certain that the reduction in warehousing costs is greater than the increased cost of frequent, fast deliveries.

APPLICATIONS OF NEW TECHNOLOGY   Modern computer technology helps marketers carry out the detailed planning and coordination needed for strategies as com-

FIGURE 17.10

Using Technology to Manage Transportation

Calms children.   Calms adults.

Life.   Auto.   Home.   Career.

plex as JIT distribution. It also provides other forms of useful information. Marketing information systems and marketing decision support systems (see Chapter 7) routinely include information about physical distribution—what products have been ordered, what orders have been shipped, what items are on back order, and the inventory level of each product. United Parcel Service uses bar codes to regularly update data on the location of each package it handles (see Figure 17.10).

Perhaps most important, computer technology can make many distribution functions more efficient, increasing profits and perhaps making it possible to serve smaller customers. When Timberland realized that small boutiques were responsible for an increasing share of sales of Timberland shoes, the company determined how to use technology to make these customers more profitable to serve. By using scanners to track inventory and create shipping bills, Timberland cut the cost of small shipments, and by setting up a system for customers to send orders directly to its computers, Timberland allows for sales to increase faster than its sale force.[95]

It has become commonplace for organizations to use such information internally. A relatively new development, called electronic data interchange, now makes it possible for the various organizations in a marketing channel to share information. As defined by the American Marketing Association, **electronic data interchange (EDI)** is a "communication system which allows direct electronic transfer of information between two enterprises."[96] Instead of sending one another paper documents such as purchase orders and shipping reports, channel members that use EDI can make the information available electronically. This gives EDI users more flexible and up-to-date information. Warehouse managers can see what orders are being processed by the manufacturer. Or they can check the computer system of their trucker or air carrier to see where a particular shipment is and, thus, when it is likely to arrive. A common use of EDI is for inventory control. Retailers share sales data with suppliers so that they know when to ship more of a product and what to produce or buy more of.

electronic data interchange (EDI)
A communication system that allows direct electronic transfer of information among enterprises.

Wal-Mart is linked in this way with over half of its 5,000 suppliers, and Kmart with 2,600 of its 3,000 suppliers.[97]

The easy and continuous flow of information supports the trend toward close and cooperative relationships among channel members. In Framingham, Massachusetts, stereo-speaker producer Bose Corporation arranged for a steamship line, a domestic trucker, and a freight forwarder to set up an integrated EDI system linked to Bose. The companies also supply Bose's plant with staff to monitor and expedite the movement of cargo. This arrangement has allowed Bose to minimize inventory levels and achieve an exceptional rate of on-time deliveries.[98] To lower the costs and improve the reliability of shipments from foreign vendors, London-based Woolworth PLC set up an arrangement with P&O Containers Ltd., which had experience with EDI as well as the willingness to tailor a system to Woolworth's needs. P&O not only manages the logistics of handling cargo from order to delivery (even making sure production is on schedule), it also has a few staffers working full time in Woolworth's British offices and in the Far East, where much of the production takes place. In its first year, this setup has saved Woolworth $1.5 million.[99]

Another way in which computers are modernizing physical distribution is through software that helps users select the optimal solution to a complex problem. Software such as Roadshow by Routing Technology Software identifies the delivery route that offers the best combination of speed and low cost. Simulation software can help managers with the design and layout of warehouses. Other packages help users compute the necessary inventory levels for providing a given level of customer service.[100]

To help with controlling physical distribution of goods, satellites make it possible to navigate and communicate with carriers worldwide. On-board computers provide a record of the carrier's performance. Such advances are particularly important for distributing goods to customers that use JIT inventory management. In general, these and other advances in information technology have enabled producers to handle distribution more efficiently and thereby offer end users faster service through shorter channels.

Summary

The role of wholesalers and retailers is to handle distribution functions more efficiently and effectively than producers can. Although the roles of each vary somewhat, some organizations do serve both roles. A wholesaler is a business that buys, takes title to, stores, and resells goods to retailers or industrial users. A retailer primarily sells to ultimate consumers. Retailing is by far a larger business than wholesaling, employing about three times as many people.

In general, wholesalers fall into three categories: merchant wholesalers, manufacturers' wholesalers, and brokers/agents. Merchant wholesalers, which are independent of producers, are the largest category (about 80 percent) of wholesalers.

Retailing occurs either in stores or through nonstore avenues ranging from vending machines to direct marketing (catalogs, direct mail, telemarketing, direct-action advertising, television selling, and on-line selling). Many direct marketers use a combination of methods in a single marketing effort called integrated direct marketing.

When devising marketing strategies, wholesalers and retailers must identify their target market(s). They also need to determine the level of service they must offer to customers,

characteristics of the product itself, price, and channels of distribution (including site selection). In their marketing communications, they must promote the services they offer as well as the products they carry.

Economic and technological changes have made wholesaling and retailing increasingly competitive. Because many producers now use shorter distribution channels, wholesalers are being eliminated, so they must offer a distinctive level of service, both through technology and the quality focus necessary to build long-term relationships. The sluggish economy during the early 1990s has reduced the number of major retailers, especially supermarkets and department stores. Retailing analysts believe that value-conscious consumers will continue to weed out all but the retailers that best meet their needs. Technological advances have allowed retailers and wholesalers to gather and share crucial information that helps get the products that consumers want into their hands as efficiently as possible.

Physical distribution is the actual moving and storing of goods in order to reach the end user. Transportation, warehousing, inventory, and order processing are all part of physical distribution, and their cost and efficiency must be considered by marketers. Some quality-based organizations have moved toward using just-in-time (JIT) inventory practices in order to cut physical distribution costs and meet consumer demand. Teamwork is vital in this case. Electronic data interchange (EDI), another development in distribution, allows the electronic sharing of information (such as inventory information) between two enterprises, such as channel members.

KEY TERMS AND CONCEPTS

wholesaler (p. 497)

retailer (p. 498)

merchant wholesaler (p. 499)

rack jobber (p. 499)

cash-and-carry wholesaler (p. 500)

drop shipper (p. 500)

truck jobber (p. 501)

agent/broker (p. 502)

category killer (p. 502)

scrambled merchandising (p. 502)

mass merchandising (p. 502)

direct marketing (p. 505)

direct selling (p. 505)

direct mail (p. 506)

telemarketing (p. 506)

integrated direct marketing (p. 507)

merchandising (p. 509)

atmospherics (p. 514)

physical distribution (p. 520)

intermodal transportation (p. 521)

piggyback service (p. 521)

freight forwarder (p. 522)

public warehouses (p. 523)

just-in-time (JIT) inventory management (p. 526)

electronic data interchange (EDI) (p. 527)

REVIEW AND DISCUSSION QUESTIONS

1. Which single type of retailer accounts for the largest segment of the total retail trade?
2. If you were a marketer for the producer of a line of trendy, brightly colored socks, what type of wholesaler might you choose and why?
3. Name and define the two basic types of nonstore retailing. Give examples of products sold through each. (Try to think of some not mentioned in the text.)
4. If you were the agent for several young artists (sculptors and painters) who wanted to sell more of their work to the public, would you approach one of the home shopping channels? Why or why not?
5. Assume you own a local appliance shop (selling TVs, dishwashers, washing machines, microwaves, air conditioners, and small appliances such as vacuums and food processors). One of the large category killers (like Circuit City) recently opened just a few miles from your shop. What steps would you take in order to remain competitive? (Use your imagination!)
6. In which of the following locations would you place a kiosk selling moderately priced gloves and hats, and why?
    a. inside a shopping mall, a few paces from the entrance to a major department store
    b. on a busy urban street corner (such as in New York City) where a lot of commuters walk by every day
    c. at a ski resort

7. What type of image should be presented by a sales representative who practices direct sales for financial services (such as investments)?
8. As a consumer, do you prefer shopping in specialty stores, department stores, or discount outlets? Why? Does your preference depend on the type of product you are shopping for?
9. For each of the following products, what mode(s) of physical distribution do you think would be most efficient? Why?
    a. apples bound from Washington State farms to Midwestern supermarkets
    b. blood samples being analyzed by a genetics laboratory in another state
    c. natural gas being delivered to homes and workplaces around a major city
10. What are some ways in which marketers can apply the quality approach to marketing to the function of order processing?
11. What are some benefits and pitfalls of just-in-time inventory management? Would you recommend this tactic for a computer wholesaler serving North America and the Pacific Rim? Why or why not?
12. How is technology influencing physical distribution today?

Chapter Project
Siting and Designing a Retail Store

Assume you've decided to become an entrepreneur, opening your own retail store. Choose a type of store from the list below, or come up with one of your own. (Have in mind one or more specific products you will sell. For example, if you choose a bookstore, will you also sell magazines and greeting cards?)

Based on your observations of similar existing stores (see "Put It into Practice"), choose a location, such as downtown, shopping mall, concession in a park, etc. Then draw up a floor plan for your store, and describe how you would use atmospherics to create and maintain the image you want for your store and products.

Present your new store to your class. Invite reactions from your classmates: Would they shop there? Does your store fit their schema for this type of retailer? How is it the same or different?

Store ideas:
- vintage clothing shop or costume shop
- a category killer that sells sports equipment
- a shop that sells high-quality crafted items
- a healthful fast-food restaurant
- a bookstore

Case
Sears, Roebuck and Co.

January 1993 marked the end of an era. Sears, Roebuck and Co., the giant American retailer, announced it was closing the Big Book—the Sears general merchandise catalog. The Big Book had survived for more than 100 years. From its pages, customers could buy their family's entire wardrobe plus just about everything they needed to start and maintain a home. In fact, from 1908 to 1937, they could buy the house itself, offered in kit form for around $1,500. Other notable bygone products included a 4-oz. bottle of Laudanum (opium), an automatic revolver, and a motor car. More recently, shoppers could order a computer, washing machine, or mountain bike.

The Sears catalog was first published in 1886, offering only watches. Eventually it became a staple of American life, particularly in rural areas where no other shopping was available. It was said of rural Americans that they read just two books, the Sears catalog and the Bible.

But by today's retail standards, the Big Book was hardly user friendly. For instance, only in 1992 did Sears begin taking orders through a toll-free number. Customers had to mail in their orders. Nor did the company offer home delivery. Customers had to travel to the nearest Sears store or catalog center to pick up their purchases. No wonder modern consumers preferred to place their orders with Spiegel or Lands' End. Although the catalog was generating annual revenues of around $3.3 billion, it had been a money loser for a number of years.

Still, the Big Book had many loyal followers whose families had shopped its pages for generations. When the last catalog was published, many bought extras as souvenirs. "It's a memory thing," says customer Alyce Smudde. "I'm gonna keep it."

The poor performance of the Big Book was only one of the many problems at Sears. Disappointing sales at its stores caused the giant retailer to fall from its number-one spot in U.S. retailing to third place behind Wal-Mart and Kmart. A brief attempt at every-day low pricing did nothing to help matters. To cut costs, the company laid off 50,000 employees and closed 239 stores. Its board of directors admitted the failure of the store's past insistence on selling only private brands and its efforts to diversify into services (by acquiring the Dean

Witter Reynolds investment firm and the Coldwell Banker real estate brokerage). Sears has since sold off these interests.

According to Arthur C. Martinez, chairman of Sears's Merchandise Group, the company's newest strategy will be to focus on its retail stores. Most of the stores are located in shopping malls, so the future of Sears depends in part on the health of the shopping mall concept itself. Some experts predict malls are on the decline, but Martinez states, "The death of the mall is a myth. . . . We have the best store locations in the country, and we'll focus on our profitable core retail activities in those malls. . . . Mall shoppers still make up the largest shopping component."

To lure more shoppers, Sears is upgrading its stores' appearance, expanding its clothing lines, and maintaining a good selection of brand-name appliances and electronics. "Sears will continue to serve middle America with quality goods and services at moderate prices," declares Martinez. "We'll sharpen our merchandising mix in apparel, products and services for the home, and in automotive."

To encourage women to spend more on clothing—an important source of profits—Sears launched an ad campaign touting the "softer side of Sears." These advertisements link clothing to items that sell well. For example, in one ad, a woman in an evening dress says she went to Sears to buy a Die Hard (battery) but bought a dress "to die for." This marketing message and the merchandising changes are intended to work together to create a more fashionable image of Sears. In the initial months of the change in strategy, Sears began showing strong increases in sales.

And catalogs are not completely out of the picture. The old Big Book indirectly has continued as a source of revenue because Sears has sold its giant mailing list to other catalog retailers for a share of their catalog revenues. Furthermore, a year after discontinuing the Big Book, Sears entered into an agreement with Hanover Ventures under which Hanover will produce at least three specialty catalogs for over 24 million Sears customers. The initial three catalogs in this venture—seen as presenting little risk to Sears—are called Show Place (offering bed and bath accessories), Great Kitchens (containing kitchen accessories and small appliances), and Beautiful Style (featuring women's clothing in large sizes). In addition, Sears plans to continue direct marketing through two other specialty catalogs: Craftsman Tools and Smart Choice.

QUESTIONS

1. Do you think that closing the Sears catalog division was a smart marketing move? Why or why not?
2. Can Sears regain its position as a strong retailer by focusing on its department stores? Why or why not?
3. If you were a marketer for Sears, what additional steps would you recommend to Martinez for the retailer's comeback?

Sources: Howard G. Haas, "Diversification: Wrong Tack for Sears," *GSB Chicago* (University of Chicago Graduate School of Business), Spring 1993, p. 11; Paul Gray, "An Ode to the Big Book," *Time,* February 8, 1993, p. 66; George Lazarus, "Cuts in Promotion Made Catalog Sales an Uphill Battle," *Chicago Tribune,* January 26, 1993, sec. 3, pp. 1, 4; John Schmeltzer, "Sears Closing The Book," *Chicago Tribune,* January 26, 1993, sec. 1, pp. 1, 10; Bill Barnhart, "Markets' Response Is Muted," *Chicago Tribune,* January 26, 1993, sec. 1, p. 8; John Schmeltzer, "Sears Back in Catalogs," *Chicago Tribune,* January 11, 1994, sec. 3, pp. 1–2; John Schmeltzer, "Sears Momentum Continues While Sales Crawl for Others," *Chicago Tribune,* December 3, 1993, sec. 3, pp. 1, 4; Gregory A. Patterson, "Sears to Show 'Softer Side' in Fall Ad Blitz," *The Wall Street Journal,* August 24, 1993, p. B6; and Sunita Wadekar Bhargava, "After the Big Book, the Big Race," *Business Week,* September 20, 1993, p. 106E-2.

7

Marketing Communications

Setting the Stage
National Basketball Association

Twenty years ago, pro basketball was nearly dead. The NBA was near financial collapse, and basketball players were hardly media stars. Today, basketball business is soaring through the hoops. With better management and aggressive marketing, the NBA has achieved a major turnaround. Total attendance during a recent season was nearly 18 million; new expansion teams are in the works; and names like Larry Bird, Magic Johnson, and Michael Jordan are household words even after the players' retirement.

How does the NBA promote itself? First, there are the players. Though giants such as Bird, Johnson, and Jordan have moved on, "we have renewable resources with the NBA draft every year," notes David Schreff, vice president and general manager of the NBA Marketing Group. "Players come with their own level of fame and marketability. And that is why our sponsors remain with us."

Second, there are those sponsors. Essentially, the NBA serves as a broker for deals between television networks and advertisers. For instance, the NBA was instrumental in a $125 million deal between Miller Brewing and NBC. "Business is better than ever," accord-

ing to Schreff. "We continue to add world-class companies to our deliberately small roster of sponsors." Those sponsors include heavy hitters such as AT&T, Coca-Cola, McDonald's, Bausch & Lomb, and IBM. And although the NBA's about American basketball, the league and its sponsors recognize the value of marketing abroad. "We're with the NBA for the long haul," comments Jackie Woodward, senior manager for sports marketing at McDonald's. "Our customers are NBA customers, not only in the U.S., but all over the world."

Third, because of its major sponsors and the popularity of the game, the NBA is a hot property for television. For instance, Turner Sports recently signed a four-year deal with the NBA for $352 million. NBC signed a $725 million agreement for four years.

Fourth, there are the fans. Marketers at the NBA know that basketball "delivers a young audience and you can't get that anywhere else," according to Steve Auerbach, executive vice president–national broadcast at DeWitt Media in New York. And 40 percent of that audience is female. Advertisers love it. "This allows us to go after the male group we want without completely abandoning the female group,"

says Glenn C. Van Deusen, a marketing director for Bausch & Lomb.

Other marketing pluses for the NBA include its shrewd decision to limit the number of sponsors it signs to avoid overcommercializing the sport, as David Schreff explains. Then there's the promotion of special events and concepts, such as the Olympic Dream Team.

Not everyone is pleased with the new NBA. Sportswriter Scott Ostler complains, "The old NBA was gyms and arenas . . . . The new NBA is closed practices, designer ice cream on the team plane, *fan*tastic TV commercials, $50 cheap seats, salary-cap discussions, and games in Tokyo." Maybe so. But NBA marketers sure know how to deliver a slam dunk.

Sources: Kevin Goldman, "NBA Advertisers Face Life after Jordan," *The Wall Street Journal,* November 29, 1993, p. B9; Al Harvin, "NBA Crowds up in Preseason," *The New York Times,* November 7, 1993, sec. 8, S5; "NBA Makes It Official: Toronto to Join in '95–'96," *The New York Times,* November 5, 1993, B18; Scott Ostler, "Homogenized Basketball," *Sport,* February 1993, p. 10; Gary Levin, "NBA Is Real Pro in Scoring Sponsorships," *Advertising Age,* November 9, 1992, pp. 3, 41.

CHAPTER 18   *The Communications Mix*

LEARNING OBJECTIVES

After completing this chapter, you should be able to:

1. Discuss the function of marketing communications, including the importance of setting clear objectives.

2. Describe the process of communication.

3. Identify the possible elements of the communications mix.

4. Explain criteria for selecting the right communications mix.

5. Describe ways that marketers create a budget for communications.

6. Describe how marketers evaluate and control the communications effort.

7. Discuss ethical issues in communications.

Creating Customer Value
Chart House

"We have been around a long time, and we have become part of the landscape," says Michael Plant, vice-president of marketing for Chart House, a 65-unit chain of restaurants based in Solana Beach, California. But blending in is the kiss of death for a restaurant. So the company laid out a $1.5 million plan for marketing communications designed to stabilize the chain's sales by bringing in new customers and making them repeat customers. Chart House used print and public relations, outdoor, and radio advertising as well as sales promotions, and the staff was empowered to improve the quality of service.

First, the company contracted with an outside agency, EvansGroup (based in Portland, Oregon), to develop the plan for marketing communications. The agency came up with the slogan "Where's the nearest Chart House?" Then it placed magazine ads in in-flight publications as well as upscale consumer magazines like *Architectural Digest, Forbes, Inc.,* and *New Yorker.* One ad features a woman telling her husband they are having twins; another features the signing of a business deal. Billboards and radio commercials followed. In addition, Chart House launched the Aloha Club, a frequent-diner program, intended to entice customers back to the restaurant and thus make them loyal diners. Finally, Chart House installed a national toll-free phone number for directions to, locations of, and reservations at the various restaurants.

Once the communications effort was under way, it was clear that neither the restaurant's refurbished image nor its promises to customers would work without the support of employees. "One of our biggest challenges is communicating the program in-house," noted Plant. "Managers have to have faith in the program, and the staff has to be able to sell it as well as be empowered to fix problems; or better yet, spot them before they occur."

So the Chart House chain instituted a total quality management program that includes retraining staff members at all levels to participate actively in achieving the restaurant's goals of better service (and, ultimately, increased sales). The quality program also helps with evaluating and controlling the communications effort. "It doesn't take a brain surgeon to figure out that incremental increases in frequency [of dining per customer] will have a tremendous impact on the bottom line," Plant remarks. "The response to the Aloha Club has so far exceeded our wildest expectations."

As you read this chapter, you'll see how marketers strive to combine various tools for communicating with current and potential buyers in order to build and maintain the desired level of sales. Like Chart House, organizations that use the quality approach in their communications do so with their customers' needs in mind.

Source: Theresa Howard, "Chart House Retools Image with First National Ads," *Nation's Restaurant News,* July 26, 1993, p. 12.

Chapter Overview

marketing communications
The element of the marketing mix that involves informing target markets about a product and influencing them to buy it.

The Chart House restaurants use a number of methods to inform potential diners about the high quality of their food and service. Before consumers or organizational buyers can purchase a restaurant meal or any other product, they need to know about it. They need to know what the product is, how it will benefit them, and where they can find it. Providing this information is the goal of marketing communications. **Marketing communications** is the element of the marketing mix that involves communicating with target markets to inform them about a product and influence them to buy it.

This chapter introduces the issues and activities involved in carrying out marketing communications. It begins by describing the basic functions of this element of the marketing mix. Then the discussion moves to the process of communication itself—what it is and how messages are transmitted from one party to another. Next, the chapter defines the elements of the communications mix—the various means of carrying out a communications strategy. Then the chapter explores activities involved in managing a domestic or global communications effort, including setting objectives, selecting the communications mix, budgeting, and evaluating and controlling. The chapter closes with a discussion of ethical and social issues in marketing communications.

The Functions of Marketing Communications

Marketing communications is the basic way in which organizations deliver messages to their target markets. From the organization's standpoint, this information may serve several purposes. It may increase awareness of the product. It may increase demand for a product, perhaps by providing incentives to buy it or by distinguishing it from competing products. Marketing communications may enhance the value of the product, increasing the likelihood that members of the target market will be favorably predisposed toward it. Sometimes the organization uses marketing communications to stabilize sales.

Customers need to know about a product in order to be interested in buying it. Marketers get the word out in a variety of ways—through print and broadcast advertising, by knocking on doors and phoning customers, by mailing coupons and samples, and by seeking out media coverage of their activities, just to name a few. Some products, such as new cereals or soaps, don't require much explanation; a catchy print advertisement with a coupon lets consumers know the product is available and gives them an incentive to try it. But others, such as a new kind of office equipment or a new magazine, need more. Potential subscribers to a new magazine need to know whether the articles and ads will interest them, how often the magazine is published, and how much a subscription costs. To get this information across, marketers might decide to offer a free trial issue to interested readers.

STIMULATING DEMAND

Before they will buy a good or service, potential customers must feel they need or want it. As discussed earlier, the desire for the product, coupled with the ability to buy it, is called demand. Marketers are interested in stimulating what they call primary and selective demand.

Stimulating Selective Demand

When Quality Time Is The Only Time You Can Afford,

It Better Be Bell.

PRIMARY DEMAND   When potential buyers demand a good or service, they are sometimes thinking just in terms of a general category such as lawn mowers, party catering, or vacations. This level of demand is called **primary demand**. For marketers to sell their particular products, there must be enough primary demand for the product category.

primary demand
The desire for a general category of a good or service.

When Johnson & Johnson introduced its Acuvue disposable contact lenses, it sought to increase primary demand for disposable contact lenses. To do so, Johnson & Johnson offered free trials through coupons and a toll-free number. Each coupon included a brief survey asking potential customers what type of eyewear they currently used and whether they had ever tried contact lenses before.

SELECTIVE DEMAND   New Balance promoted its running shoes with the slogan "A shoe that fits better, performs better." This message was designed to tell consumers already interested in running shoes why they should demand shoes made by New Balance, which offers a variety of widths. The ad was seeking to stimulate **selective demand**, or the demand for a specific brand of product.

selective demand
The desire for a specific brand of good or service.

Similarly, Bell Helicopter's advertising seeks to set its helicopters apart from other aircraft. (See Figure 18.1.) The ad explains that not only are Bell Helicopters reliable and economical to operate, they come with extensive training and support. In this way, the ad is designed to entice people who purchase helicopters to choose Bell instead of the competition.

Stimulating selective demand requires distinguishing one brand from another. U.S. consumers in particular are bombarded with choices; how do we decide which products and services to buy? Which brand of blue jeans? Which type of tomato plants for the vegetable garden? Which movie or video should we see tonight? Where should we go to college? Which lawyer should we hire to represent us in a particular legal case?

The objective, then, is to convince potential buyers that the product offers value—ideally, greater value than competing products. In doing this, financial adviser Rita Mitchell faced the unfortunate challenge that many consumers are slow to trust her with their investments because she is a black woman. Mitchell has successfully built credibility in the face of such attitudes by sending out a regular newsletter featuring tax tips and financial advice.[1] Another way to demonstrate value is to describe product benefits, such as ease of use, low impact on the environment, low cost per unit, or sturdy construction. Bumkins diaper company (which manufactures a variety of cloth diaper products) includes in its store display a poster that compares the low cost of using cloth diapers as opposed to disposable ones. Its packaging touts the environmental advantage of using the product.

STABILIZING SALES

Marketers also use communications to stabilize the sales of a product. Once a new customer has tried the product, marketers want to make that customer a loyal user. Many magazines continue to offer "low" subscription rates to renewing subscribers. *Runner's World* also offers a variety of free running-related books to subscribers who renew.

Sales of some goods and services may fluctuate naturally by season or cycle, so marketers try to increase sales during slow periods. For example, ice cream sales may increase during the summer and decrease during winter. Reservations at a ski resort will increase during the winter and decrease during the summer unless effective communications alerts potential vacationers to summer attractions at the resort such as golf, tennis, horseback riding, hiking, and swimming.

QUALITY IN MARKETING COMMUNICATIONS

In providing quality to customers, marketing communications has a complementary role to that of the product itself. From the customer's perspective, quality describes the fit between expectations about the product and perceptions of the outcome of buying and using the product.[2] In other words, when the customer's experience with the product meets or exceeds expectations, the customer is satisfied with the quality. Marketing communications has a direct role in shaping one side of this equation: expectations. Thus, in a quality-driven marketing effort, communications will build realistic expectations about what the product can do for the user. In addition, by conveying the marketing message clearly, the marketer will better enable the target market to know about, and thus benefit from, the product. The ad in Figure 18.2 does this by focusing on the unique features of Cherokee shoes: ribbon laces, a sole you can see through, and comfort.

The key to quality in marketing communications is to get everyone in the communications effort to focus on customers and on meeting customer needs. This may seem obvious, but it doesn't always happen. In creating an advertising message, for example, it can be tempting to focus more on being artistic or on inducing people to buy something whether they need it or not. Advertising great David Ogilvy observes, "I am worried about the kind of advertising that is in fashion today. Too much of it is pretentious nonsense, highbrow and incomprehensible." He adds, "I once got a new client who told me to create a campaign for him that would make his friends at his country club congratulate him on his clever, amusing advertising. I refused. I just gave him a campaign that increased his sales."[3]

FIGURE 18.2
Advertising Designed to Build Realistic Expectations

"They have ribbon laces, a sole you can see through and they're really comfortable. No wonder chicks love 'em."

CHEROKEE.
Make yourself comfortable.™

For information, call (800) 824-1932
Clothes, footwear and accessories for men, women and children

When everyone involved in marketing communications is focused on satisfying customers, the various elements of this effort are most apt to support one another. A common scenario is for an organization to place ads in trade magazines to generate mailed-in responses from interested prospects; the sales department is supposed to follow up on these inquiries. In one study, researchers sent in thousands of such responses to ads for products priced at $5,000 or more. Only about three-quarters of their inquiries generated a follow-up in the form of printed materials, and only one in eight generated a phone call from a salesperson. The printed materials took an average of 58 days to arrive, and the phone calls straggled in 89 days after the inquiry was made.[4] The logical conclusion is that the organizations studied are losing a lot of customers because their marketing communications effort is not cohesive.

Communication: How Messages Work

communication
The transmission of a message from a sender to a receiver.

For marketing communications to be effective, they must meet the standards of any effective communication. Defined formally, **communication** is the transmission of a message from a sender (or source) to a receiver. In successful communication, the sender and receiver share the same meaning of the message. Thus, a print advertisement, coupon, television commercial, or other marketing communication should convey a message that means something positive to the target market.

source
The sender of a message.

THE COMMUNICATION PROCESS

encode
To convert a message to a group of symbols that represent images or concepts.

Communication is a process. The **source** (such as a company or an individual) **encodes** the message, converting it into a group of symbols that represent images or

TABLE 18.1

Marketing Communications: Three Examples

SOURCE	ENCODING	MEDIUM OF TRANSMISSION	RECEIVER	DECODING	NOISE	FEEDBACK
Universal Pictures	preparation of ad	newspaper ads for *Schindler's List*	newspaper readers	reading the movie listings	ads and reviews for other movies	readers go to see *Schindler's List* and other shows
Joslyn Power Products Corp.	preparation of sales presentation	presentation by salesperson	buyers at electric utilities	listenting to the presentation	interruptions; fatigue	some buyers place orders for switching gear
General Motors	writing press release	press release mailed to news media	auto writer at *Chicago Tribune*	reading the press release	huge stack of press releases from other organizations; deadline for column	auto writer prepares article about plans to test electric car

medium of transmission
The mode that carries a message, such as television, radio, print, live speech, or music.

receiver
The person or group for whom a message is intended.

decode
To convert symbols to the images or concepts contained in a message.

noise
Physical sounds, misunderstandings, or other distractions that cause a receiver to fail to decode a message properly.

feedback
The receiver's response to a message.

concepts. Through a **medium of transmission**—such as television or radio, written words, photographic images, live speech, and musical sounds—the source sends the message to the **receiver**, the person or group for whom the message is intended. The receiver then **decodes** the message, converting symbols to the images or concepts contained in the message. If the receiver does not or cannot decode the message to mean what the source intended, then **noise** exists. Noise can take the form of physical sound—such as radio, telephone, or television static—or it can be the receiver's misunderstanding of the sender's language, a printing error, or a distraction such as a customer's dislike of a salesperson's mannerisms or dress.

Feedback is the receiver's response to the message. In a sense, feedback begins the communication process all over again: the receiver now becomes the sender and the sender becomes the receiver. In marketing communications, feedback takes two main forms: the potential customer either accepts the product or rejects it (see Table 18.1). It may also take a more subtle form in change of attitude, either toward a specific product or toward a general category of products.

It's easy to see how crucial all of these stages are to the marketing effort, and how a breakdown in any one of them can cause havoc in the communication between a company and its potential customers. The choice of a single word—such as a product name—is an example of encoding a message. In the perfume industry, creators of a new cologne decided to call it Santa Fe, banking on positive associations that people have about the Southwest: its rugged, open country and artsy sophistication. If potential customers receive this message correctly, they may send positive feedback by purchasing the cologne. Such issues apply equally to serving foreign markets. Many Japanese consumers love anything to do with the American West but might not be familiar with Santa Fe. "Texas" might convey a clearer message. Conversely, marketers know that naming a line of formal clothing "California" would be a lost cause because of the informality associated with California. But naming such a line of clothing "Boston" might prove successful, for Boston conveys the message of formality and elegance, as well as a bit of stuffiness.[5]

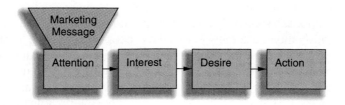

FIGURE 18.3
The AIDA Model

THE AIDA MODEL

As implied by the preceding examples, marketing communications succeed when they achieve certain basic results. Ultimately, of course, the marketer wants receivers of the message to respond by buying the product or brand being offered. However, to get to that result, some other things must happen to the receiver first. As summarized by the model in Figure 18.3, the message must achieve first attention, then interest, desire, and action.

What this means for the marketer is that each message must first break through the clutter of other communications so that the intended audience notices the message. Messages are most likely to receive attention when they are distinctive and relevant to the needs of the audience. Thus, marketers who focus on their customers' needs are in the best position to accomplish this first goal of communication.

Next, the communication aims to generate interest in the organization and/or its products (goods or services). In general, this means letting the receiver of the message know how the organization or its products can help to meet a need of the receiver. The basic way to do this is to focus on the product's benefits, not just its features. Thus, a letter in which a marketing research company says, "We can help you know your customers and their needs" (a product benefit) should generate more interest than one that says, "Our staff of Ph.D.'s can perform the most sophisticated statistical analyses" (a product feature). If the information about benefits is successfully presented, many receivers will also have a desire for the products described.

The last stage of the AIDA model—action—is the one that most directly benefits the organization. However, it can be the hardest step to achieve. Potential buyers may resist making the effort to buy even if they agree they will be better off with the good or service. After all, some effort and risk are involved in making any purchase. For this reason, marketing communications often include incentives to stimulate a purchase. Coupons, for example, reduce the financial risk. Free coffee at a bank makes the trip there a bit more pleasant.

COMMUNICATION AND THE TARGET MARKET

Effective communication is designed so that it is understandable and appealing to the target market. This means the marketer must know what vocabulary will be clear to members of the target market. The marketer must know how the target market will interpret images and sounds used in the message as well.

The marketer also must know where members of the target market are likely to encounter marketing messages. Will targeted consumers watch television? Which programs? Do they clip coupons? Read labels on packages? Do targeted organizational buyers attend trade shows? Read trade magazines? Do they have time to meet with a salesperson? Answering questions such as these can help marketers begin to satisfy their customers before those people even make a purchase.

For Southwest Airlines, communication with the target market is part of its overall marketing philosophy. "Fundamental to our success," notes the company's director of marketing, "is an identification of a very solid niche and staying with it—then communicating that to our customers in a very memorable way."[6] Deborah Zizmore of the Direct Mail Marketing Association in New York comments about the new wave of catalogs that include magazinelike feature articles: "This is another communications vehicle that helps solidify the relationship between the company and consumer, just like the way the companies have service representatives, not just telephone operators, taking orders."[7]

COMMUNICATION AND THE MARKETING TEAM

Not only does communication need to take place between a firm and its customers, it also needs to take place among members of the organization. Members of the marketing team need to communicate with one another and with employees in other departments. They need to communicate with other members of the distribution channel as well. Carrying out these communication activities is often called **internal marketing**.

internal marketing
Marketing communications among various members of the organization and the distribution channel.

Probably the most important internal marketing communication between manager and staff members is a clear marketing plan, detailing objectives and tactics for all the elements of the marketing mix. If noise exists in the form of vague objectives, disorganized ideas, or misunderstood language, feedback may be negative—and the marketing effort may fail. Continued communication, both written and oral, among marketing research, advertising, sales, legal, and technical staff throughout the marketing effort will help ensure success.

One way a large marketing group can keep in touch with its own members as well as the rest of the company is through a marketing newsletter.[8] A newsletter can keep readers informed of new developments in products and services as well as changes in personnel and the marketplace. Graphics, photos, brief features, events calendars, and a readers' column (and/or letters to the editor) all foster communication. A readers' or letters column allowing staff members to air ideas and constructive criticism completes the circle of communication: the receivers become senders.

Options in the Communications Mix

communications mix
The blend of advertising, personal selling, sales promotion, and publicity that makes up a communications strategy.

The **communications mix** blends together several different elements to create the overall strategy for marketing communications. The elements of this mix may include advertising, personal selling, sales promotion, and publicity. These elements can be more generally categorized as *personal selling* and *nonpersonal selling*. Personal selling is conducted on a person-to-person basis, whereas nonpersonal selling encompasses advertising, sales promotion, and publicity.

Marketers strive for the right mix of communications elements to make sure that the product is well received. If the product is new, the effort will probably rely heavily on advertising and sales promotion, in order to get the word out and entice people to try the product. If the product is more established but the objective is to stabilize sales during a weak season, the mix will most likely contain a healthy dose of sales promotions, or short-term incentives for people to buy the product immediately. If the product

TABLE 18.2

Elements of the Communications Mix

ELEMENT	STRENGTHS	WEAKNESSES
Advertising	Efficient for reaching many buyers simultaneously; effective way to create image of the brand; flexible; variety of media to choose from	Reaches many people who are not potential buyers; ads are subject to much criticism; exposure time is usually short; people tend to screen out advertisements; total cost may be high
Personal selling	Salespeople can be persuasive and influential; two-way communication allows for questions and other feedback; message can be targeted to specific individuals	Cost per contact is high; salespeople may be hard to recruit and motivate; presentation skills vary among salespeople
Sales promotion	Supports short-term price reductions designed to stimulate demand; variety of sales promotion tools available; effective in changing short-term behavior; easy to link to other communications	Risks inducing brand-loyal customers to stock up while not influencing others; impact may be limited to short term; price-related sales promotion may hurt brand image; easy for competitors to copy
Publicity	Total cost may be low; media-generated messages seen as more credible than marketer-sponsored messages	Media may not cooperate; heavy competition for media attention; marketer has little control over message

is highly technical and needs a lot of explanation, the mix will probably contain more personal selling, so that potential buyers can ask questions of a salesperson.

Of course, there are advantages and disadvantages to each type of marketing communications. (See Table 18.2 for an overview.) For example, advertising reaches many people at once, but its costs are high and feedback can be difficult to evaluate. Publicity, on the other hand, is virtually free but is difficult to control.

ADVERTISING

When people think of marketing messages, they usually think of advertisements. *Advertising* is "paid, nonpersonal communication through various media by [organizations that] are in some way identified in the advertising message and who hope to inform and/or persuade members of a particular audience."[9] (Advertising is covered in greater detail in Chapter 19.)

When deciding how advertising fits into the communications mix, marketers consider such issues as budget and which media to use: television, radio, print, direct mail, or outdoor (billboards). Each medium has its advantages and disadvantages, and the medium (or blend of media) that is most appropriate for one product may not be suitable for another. For instance, a national television commercial can reach most U.S. households at once—not a practical way to advertise a sale at a local department store. When choosing when, where, and how to use advertising, marketers using the quality approach decide which method will communicate the message about the product most effectively and efficiently.

PERSONAL SELLING

personal selling
Selling that involves personal interaction with customers.

As mentioned earlier, **personal selling** is selling that involves personal interaction with the customer.[10] Personal selling can take place face to face, by phone (telemarketing), by video, even by fax or computer. Personal selling provides immediate feedback to the seller, which allows the seller to adjust communication to meet the needs of the situation. If noise in the communication process exists—from other people in the room, ringing telephones, static, misunderstood language, and so forth—the seller can probably correct it immediately. Thus, if a customer does not understand how a particular feature on a lawn mower works, a face-to-face seller can correct that through in-person demonstration. If a telemarketer gleans that he or she has called a potential customer at an inconvenient time, the phone call can be rescheduled.

On the downside, personal selling costs more per customer contact than any other type of marketing communication, and the "personal touch" provided by personal selling can sometimes backfire. Also, one salesperson may present the message more clearly and in a more appealing manner than another. Thus, personal selling, even by highly trained professionals, is inconsistent.

SALES PROMOTION

When marketers want a quick rise in sales to result from their communications efforts, they often use some form of sales promotion. *Sales promotion* is "media and non-media marketing pressure applied for a predetermined, limited period at the level of consumer, retailer or wholesaler in order to stimulate trial, increase consumer demand or improve product availability."[11] For instance, a free sample of a product induces many consumers to try it. Note from the definition that sales promotion may be directed toward ultimate users or intermediaries. (Sales promotion is covered in more detail in Chapter 19.)

At the consumer level, promotion typically takes the form of coupons, limited-time discount offers, free samples, tie-in "gifts," two-for-one pricing, rebates, contests or sweepstakes, special events, or similar efforts. Sales promotion usually takes place in conjunction with advertising or personal selling. For example, a coupon may appear in a newspaper ad or in a piece of direct mail. Sometimes companies team up in a single sales promotion intended to capture customers for both businesses.

Sales promotions directed toward intermediaries are called *trade promotions.* These activities include providing displays highlighting the product, awarding intermediaries prizes based on sales performance, and displaying products at trade shows. A manufacturer may also stimulate sales with price breaks in the form of trade allowances.

Sales promotions are designed to produce quick results that, marketers hope, will not only boost sales in the immediate future, but will translate to loyal customers in the long run. However, sales promotions can't be conducted on a continuous basis, because eventually they become ineffective. A perpetual "sale," a coupon with no expiration date, the continuous offer of the same gift with purchase all can cause the consumer to delay purchase. After all, there is no sense of urgency in these promotions. Thus, to be truly effective, the sales promotion must be short and sweet: offered for a limited time and perceived to have value. (See "Put It into Practice: Make Sales Promotions Work.")

PUBLICITY

Finally, a communications mix may include efforts to generate publicity. *Publicity* is "non-paid-for communication of information about the company or product, generally in some media form."[12] This type of communications is covered in more detail in Chapter 19.

Publicity can appear in a variety of forms. The most common are news stories (print or broadcast). Other types of media coverage include reviews (say, of a restau-

Put It Into Practice

MAKE SALES PROMOTIONS WORK

According to *Nation's Business,* "a well-chosen promotional gift can strengthen the relationship between a business and its customers." In addition, the gift should distinguish the company from others in the market. The magazine suggests "choosing items that stimulate interest or have special significance to the customer" and that are tied to the overall marketing plan. Finally, the magazine recommends choosing good-quality gifts in order to maintain the image of the product or company as one of high quality.

For this chapter's project, you will be designing a sales promotion for a supermarket's dairy, deli, bakery, or coffee shop. As part of your promotion, come up with a promotional product that fits the criteria suggested above; it may be a T-shirt, a mug, a package of napkins, a cheese knife (or other cutlery, such as a slotted spoon or pasta fork), or the like. Decide whether the item will carry a slogan or your store's name. Draw up specifications for the item, such as its materials (plastic, wood, etc.), its color, and so forth. If your item is a T-shirt, sketch the design you plan to use on the shirt. State how your promotional gift will meet the criteria suggested above.

Source: "Make Promotional Products Work for Your Company," *Nation's Business,* September 1993.

rant, hotel, or music recording) and broadcasts of speeches. To get media coverage, the marketer may use press releases, press conferences, and a variety of events intended to draw attention. In the apparel industry, fashion shows are an important source of media attention. Italian designer Gianni Versace not only stages dramatic fashion shows (he was the first to use "supermodels") but also clothes popular rock stars for free.[13] (To learn how Nicholas Graham used trade publicity in place of an advertising budget, see "Marketing Movers & Shakers.")

Another example of publicity resulted in a *Newsweek* article for a new product designed to alert suntanners when they've had enough sun. With widespread concern about the dissipation of the ozone layer and the effects of ultraviolet rays on skin and health, *Newsweek* decided that the new product was newsworthy. The biotech firm that created the product got favorable publicity for the cost of letting the magazine know about its product.

Publicity also has its downside. The marketer has little or no control over what is said in the story or review, and there is no way to target an audience. In addition, coverage is not continuous. A press conference may not be attended by the media, or a press release may go unnoticed. Noise also is difficult to control. Distractions such as broadcast technical problems and misunderstood language can certainly take place in publicity. Since the marketer does not participate in the process of editing a news story, press conference, or review, certain remarks may be taken out of context altogether, creating confusion, misunderstanding, or a poor view of the good or service.

But even the downside of publicity has an advantage: because the public knows that the seller is not controlling the story, consumers are more likely to believe what is said (which can be a boon when the news is favorable). Thus, for a new or small company or a nonprofit organization with a tight communications budget, a bit of good publicity can be very helpful in promoting a good or service.

Managing the Communications Mix

The planning, implementation, and control activities involved in managing a marketing effort also apply at the level of communications strategy. The marketer's planning includes setting objectives and selecting what elements to include in the communica-

Marketing Movers & Shakers

NICHOLAS GRAHAM OF JOE BOXER

You'd think the guy who walks around department stores with a pair of boxer shorts on his head was named Joe Boxer. In some respects, he really *is* Joe Boxer, but his name is Nicholas Graham, and he is the 35-year-old founder and owner of the San Francisco-based Joe Boxer Corporation. Graham, a native of Canada, moved to San Francisco in the early 1980s to try making it in music and avant garde performance art. The money didn't exactly roll in, so Graham followed up on his interest in art on fabric and began designing funny neckties. In 1984 a buyer for

Macy's in San Francisco suggested he try designing funny underwear; after all, consumers had nothing to choose from but plain white.

So Graham started with buffalo-check boxers (with detachable raccoon tails), which sold out of Saks in two days. His boxers flew off the racks at Macy's, Bergdorf Goodman, and Barney's as well. Soon his shorts sported pink pigs, running dogs, garden hoses, chili peppers, and even glow-in-the-dark lips. Even the most conservative customers loved them. "What we did was create an item that couldn't be seen," Graham says. "You could have a pin-striped suit on and be wearing something really funny underneath."

How did Graham handle communications? He didn't have much of a budget, but he had plenty of imagination. He created and participated in his own in-store promotional events, sometimes simply strolling the aisles with a pair of boxers perched on his head. People laughed and bought pairs of shorts. He used the push strategy to get the attention of retailers, who agreed to carry his product. He livened up meetings with retailers simply by relying on his own antics,

and buyers soon looked forward to seeing him. His reputation got him attention in the trade as well as general press, publicity that he couldn't afford to buy with advertising.

Graham is a savvy businessman who realizes that he isn't promoting underwear. "We're really more of a graphic design and marketing firm than an apparel company," he notes. "Underwear is a great vehicle for our graphics because it's funny, but the real product is the design."

Joe Boxer has branched out to include sleepwear, children's and women's underwear, bedding, beach towels, and even tablecloths and placemats. By 1992, the company's nationwide sales had topped $24 million. The company has gone global, with licensing agreements in Canada, Australia, New Zealand, and the United Kingdom. It also distributes some products in Mexico, Belgium, and the Netherlands.

Even as Joe Boxer Corporation expands, Graham realizes that he must maintain a high standard of quality in his designs in order to keep them both imaginative and funny. "It's like a big performance piece that's never finished," he explains. "There's always the next thing."

Source: Gayle Sato Stodder, "Boxer Rebellion," *Entrepreneur,* August 1993, pp. 88–92.

tions mix. In addition, the marketer must prepare a budget for marketing communications. When the effort has begun, the marketer must evaluate its success and make adjustments as needed.

SETTING OBJECTIVES FOR COMMUNICATIONS

As at every other level of planning, the marketer seeks to devise objectives that are clear, specific, and challenging but achievable. An example is the objective set by Glen White, who owns Fort Worth–based Scientific Information Services (SIS), a firm that consults on matters related to hazardous-waste regulations. When his advertising and personal selling efforts proved disappointing, White set a goal of sending out a monthly newsletter that would provide targeted customers with information about laws and trends, thereby giving them an idea of how SIS could help them.[14]

Communications objectives should also support the overall marketing objectives. In the case of SIS, White set the goal of generating six new contracts a month. Likewise, if the overall marketing objective is to serve a particular target market, the communications objectives should include communicating with members of that market. As noted earlier, the marketer needs to know where and when to reach those potential buyers. If objectives include a particular level of sales, the communications objectives should include reaching enough potential buyers to generate that level of sales.

Gillette matched communications strategy to marketing objectives when it successfully launched its Sensor razor in America and Europe. The company considered and rejected the usual approach of launching the razor in selected markets to build awareness, then adjusting strategy before a full rollout. Instead, Gillette decided on a more dramatic strategy of simultaneously launching the Sensor on both continents. The communications objectives included a massive advertising campaign. First the company laid the groundwork by spending double its previous-year ad budget on a campaign that bolstered Gillette's company image with the slogan "Gillette—the best a man can get." Then Gillette actually launched the product with commercials that were identical from country to country except for language. This tactic was intended to attract the most attention and create a single broad image for the product. Besides the $100 million it spent on the commercials, the company spent another $75 million on public relations, packaging, and design. The PR campaign's successes included stories about the Sensor on the CBS evening news and in dozens of European magazines.[15]

As in the Gillette example, communications objectives include the basic message to be used. If the marketing objectives involve expanding sales for a long-standing product, the communications objectives would probably involve telling target markets why the product will meet their needs better than its competitors can. To that end, the ad in Figure 18.4 describes how commuting on a BMW motorcycle is exhilarating, especially compared to driving a car. In another case, the message might emphasize that low price makes the product a better value. Or if the marketing objectives include positioning the product as a prestige item, the message should convey that image.

SELECTING THE RIGHT MIX

None of the elements in the communications mix functions alone; instead, they all work together toward the success of the overall marketing effort. Hyatt Hotels has put that principle in action by linking the efforts of its sales force with other areas of marketing. The company's marketing researchers and the salespeople who service Hyatt's big accounts share information with one another so that they can identify the best sources of business. Others in the marketing department devise direct mail, promotions, and publicity to meet the needs of targeted groups. Thus, when members of the sales staff recommended creation of a meeting package in which customers buy air travel as well as accommodations, others in marketing created the Destination Hyatt package and arranged a press conference to announce it. Taking such efforts the logical next step, Hyatt has also set up cross-functional teams that bring together employees from sales, marketing, operations, and finance to address the needs of particular market segments.[16]

Keeping in mind the interdependence of marketing and other activities, the marketer must select the right mix of communications elements. To do so, the marketer evaluates the contributions advertising, personal selling, sales promotion, and publicity can make to achieving communications objectives, as well as the objectives of the overall marketing plan. The marketer also should research whether the communications strategy is likely to succeed. The marketer can ask a sample of the target market to view a prototype of the message and report their reactions. They might do so in conjunction with evaluating the product itself. Publishers of new magazines often do this by producing two or three different covers for the magazines, then distributing them in different geographical areas and monitoring market response.

NATURE OF THE TARGET MARKET(S)   The marketing manager must never lose sight of the target market(s) for the product. The size of a target market, its geographic distribution, and such characteristics of group members as their income, age, occupation, religion, and culture—all can help determine the best communications mix. Suntory Water Group, a division of Japan's Suntory International, considered target markets in devising its communications mix. Suntory targeted its 10-K sports drink to children aged six to twelve and wanted a relatively low-cost way to reach that audience. So Suntory decided to rely heavily on publicity: 10-K sponsored a trip by four college students across the United States to visit 28 Major League baseball parks in 28 days to see 28 games. Suntory theorized that college students would be an aspirational reference group for its young target market. The trip by the young men—who wore 10-K caps and T-shirts—was also a fund-raiser for charity, so the event appealed to the mass media as well.[17]

For marketers targeting consumers in the Western world, several trends are influencing the success of communications strategies.[18] One is that most consumers feel inundated by advertising. By a recent estimate, typical U.S. consumers encounter up to 3,000 marketing messages a day.[19] On television, the shift to 15-second commercials has caused the number of ads to skyrocket, and consumers are zapping them with their remotes, tuning them out, or just plain mixing them up. A notorious example is the series of ads for Eveready batteries that feature a marching rabbit. Critics and consumers alike praised these ads, but almost half of consumers surveyed thought they were for Duracell—and Duracell's market share grew. Along with being over-

FIGURE 18.5

**Conveying the
Tangible Benefits of
a Service**

whelmed by ads, consumers are increasingly demanding goods and services that meet their particular needs. This means marketers cannot just talk *to* their customers, they must communicate *with* them, learning customers' needs and adapting their products accordingly.

The consequence of all this is that modern marketers cannot rely as much as they once did on the one-way communication of advertising. They must find ways to incorporate more personal communication into the mix. They may train salespeople and others to receive feedback. And they may use direct mail or similar means to reach precisely targeted buyers with a marketing mix tailored to their needs.[20]

For a product with several target markets, such as one marketed in various countries, the marketer may have to tailor communications to reflect significant differences. When Coca-Cola introduced its Coca-Cola Light reduced-calorie soda in China, its communications efforts ran into trouble. While the appeal of a "light" or "diet" Coke in the United States and Western Europe was obvious, it wasn't so in China, where food supplies are limited and Coke is a status symbol. In China, "less" Coke was less appealing to consumers, and the availability of two similar Coke products was confusing. The company therefore returned to selling just Coca-Cola Classic in China.[21]

NATURE OF THE PRODUCT   The product itself also helps determine the most effective communications mix. For starters, whether a product is a good or a service will make a difference. Because potential buyers cannot see, hear, touch, taste, or smell services before purchasing them, marketers try to use the elements of the mix that make features most tangible or that provide a comfortable basis for a purchase decision (see Figure 18.5). Often the message focuses on building a good image or reputation, because sometimes that is the only way for customers to evaluate a service before buying it. The Massachusetts-based Tufts Health Plan sponsors a 10-kilometer road running race for women each year, called the "Tufts 10-K." Over its lifetime, the race has become an increasingly well-publicized and well-attended event and will probably remain in the HMO's promotional plan for quite some time.

A highly technical or highly specialized product will require types of communication that enable the marketer to explain the product's benefits. Often, this means more personal selling to trade and organizational customers rather than consumers. Innovative marketers can find other, less expensive ways to communicate about the product. One tactic is to put information about the company and product on a computer diskette. The diskette might demonstrate a service, building customer involvement by asking the customer to answer various questions that tailor the electronic presentation to his or her situation.[22]

Price is another consideration. A low-priced convenience or disposable product usually does best with advertising and sales promotions such as coupons. For automobiles, personal selling supports the demand generated by advertising; in recent years, price-related promotions such as cash-back incentives and rebates have become popular as well. Personal selling fits the mix for other expensive items, too, such as fine jewelry, furniture, and many purchases by organizational buyers.

PRODUCT ADOPTION PROCESS AND PRODUCT LIFE CYCLE   Another factor that affects the communications mix is the product's stage in its life cycle. As described in Chapter 12, that life cycle includes the stages of introduction, growth, maturity, and decline:

* When a new product comes on the market, one of the main communications objectives is to introduce it to the public through advertising, free samples, direct mail, news stories, and the like.
* Once the product reaches the growth stage, the marketer's objective is to get customers to buy it rather than another brand. Advertising and personal selling can help differentiate the product from other brands.
* Once the product is mature, or established in the market, the marketer seeks to retain loyal customers while attracting new ones, as illustrated by the Rolex ad in Figure 18.6. Advertising reminds customers that the product is still available and attractive; sales promotions can rejuvenate demand for the product. It is vital at this stage for the sales force to satisfy intermediaries with excellent service.
* Finally, when a product begins to decline, so typically does the communications budget; the product will probably be phased out over a period of time. Expensive personal selling and sales promotions are usually cut from the mix, but advertising—perhaps even cooperative advertising with an intermediary—can be beneficial.

PUSH STRATEGY VERSUS PULL STRATEGY   When thinking about the communications mix, the marketing manager needs to evaluate whether a push strategy or a pull strategy will work best for the particular good or service. A **push strategy** directs marketing communications to the next step in the marketing channel, such as a wholesaler or retailer. When Procter & Gamble decided to discontinue Citrus Hill orange juice, marketers of the Minute Maid brand sought to take over Citrus Hill's shelf space through a push strategy. Minute Maid spent a substantial amount on incentives to grocers—payments to get grocers to stock the product. Minute Maid also arranged to fill in with special promotions, such as samples, where Citrus Hill bowed out.[23]

A **pull strategy** attacks the problem from the opposite end, by communicating directly with the ultimate user. This is designed to stimulate demand for the product, which causes channel members to respond by carrying it. Tropicana used a pull strategy in its own response to the demise of Citrus Hill. It had ready a list of middle-class

push strategy
Directing marketing communications to the next step in the marketing channel.

pull strategy
Directing marketing communications to the ultimate user.

households that were likely buyers of Citrus Hill orange juice. Just weeks after P&G announced the product's withdrawal, Tropicana had sent coupons to the homes on its list. Tropicana also boosted its spending on TV ads by $1.2 million.[24]

In many cases, marketers rely on both push and pull strategies to promote their products. They might place a heavier emphasis on one than the other, given the nature of the product, market, and so forth. When Snapple, which sells juice, soda, and iced tea, was first seeking distribution through supermarket chains, it couldn't rely on a push strategy because the chains demanded big slotting allowances that Snapple couldn't afford. However, Snapple built consumer demand, and supermarkets responded by carrying its product lines. Now that Snapple's success has attracted competition, it not only must continue advertising to consumers but also must maintain its positioning in the eyes of retailers through such tactics as coupons and joint advertising projects (called "co-op advertising").[25]

BUDGETING

Establishing a budget for marketing communications can be as tricky as targeting a market and evaluating the overall effectiveness of the communications effort. Depending on the size and structure of the company, the marketing manager will have a greater or lesser say in the absolute dollar amount allocated to marketing communications. But he or she typically will be responsible for deciding how much of the department's resources to allocate to a single communications effort and how much to designate for each element in the communications mix.

Budgeting for communications is an ongoing process as the product moves through its life cycle. During the introduction stage, sales typically lag behind dollars spent on communications. The target market is just becoming aware of the product, and intermediaries may need time to accept the product and make it available.

TABLE 18.3

Methods for Setting Communications Budgets

METHOD	ADVANTAGES	DISADVANTAGES
Percentage of sales	Simple to use; marketer likely to benefit from increasing the budget during times of rising sales	Budgeting based on expected sales implies communications can't improve sales performance; doesn't provide a way to allocate resources among elements of the communications mix
Fixed sum per unit	Same as for percentage-of-sales method	Same as for percentage-of-sales method
Meeting the competition	Takes into account competitors' activities; amounts budgeted will be reasonable if competitors are budgeting effectively	Can lead to a situation where no marketer gains market share; can lead to ever-increasing communications budgets; assumes competitors have the same objectives
All you can afford	Takes into account limited resources; may stimulate creativity in making funds work hard	Doesn't consider marketing objectives; borrowing may be worthwhile to fund some communications strategies
Objective task	Based on achieving communications objectives; focusing on objectives uses funds most efficiently	No basis for setting priorities among objectives; treats all objectives as equally worthy of funding; hard to estimate what it will cost to achieve a particular objective

During the growth and maturity stages, the budget for communications may very well stabilize at a desirable level relative to sales. During the decline stage, sales may fall in spite of the communications effort. If so, the organization will have to decide what level of communications is profitable.

While the marketer is establishing objectives for the communications plan, thinking about budget has already begun. Of necessity, knowledge of available resources helps shape the communications strategy. And when the marketing manager takes into account all the issues related to selecting a communications mix, as well as the actual cost of the various elements, the budget begins to come into focus. Common budgeting techniques marketers use to arrive at the final numbers include the percentage-of-sales method, the fixed-sum-per-unit method, meeting competition, the all-you-can-afford method, and the objective-task method (see Table 18.3).

percentage-of-sales method
Establishing a communications budget based on a specified percentage of actual or estimated sales.

PERCENTAGE-OF-SALES METHOD   With the **percentage-of-sales method**, the communications budget is based on a specified percentage of either actual or estimated sales. Assume a company decides to spend 5 percent of forecasted sales on marketing communications. If the company forecasts $500,000 in sales for a product during the coming year, it would allocate $25,000 (that is, .05 × $500,000) to marketing communications.

This relatively simple method may be effective when a product is in the growth or maturity phase of its life cycle. If sales are growing or have stabilized at a fairly high rate, the increased allocation of resources to communications likely will not hurt the product's sales performance.

But the method has its drawbacks. In a sense, it requires that the tail wag the dog, relying on the predicted results to dictate strategy intended to improve the outcome. In other words, if marketing communications are supposed to boost sales, couldn't the organization earn more by increasing its budget for such communications as advertising? Furthermore, sales may not meet predictions, and they may dip and rise according to a number of variables, including where the product lies in its life cycle.

If sales drop due to seasonal fluctuations or new competition, does it make sense to withdraw the communications effort?

A final drawback is that the percentage-of-sales method doesn't provide a way to allocate resources among the elements of the communications mix. For example, personal selling is very expensive, but it may be the best way to promote a certain product. Local advertising might not cost much, but it also might fail to reach the targeted market.

fixed-sum-per-unit method
Allocating a fixed sum to the communications budget for each unit to be sold or produced.

FIXED-SUM-PER-UNIT METHOD   A marketer using the **fixed-sum-per-unit method** allocates a fixed sum for communications based on each unit of product sold or produced. Imagine that a producer of bicycles decides to spend $20 on communications for each mountain bike it sells. The company predicts it will sell 80,000 mountain bikes, so it budgets $1.6 million for marketing communications.

While this method gives marketers a place to start with a budget, like the percentage-of-sales method it doesn't take into account many variables affecting the communications mix, such as product life cycle, nature of market and product, and the cost of the individual elements of the mix itself. Nor does it take into account the role of marketing communications in building sales. However, if the market is easily identified and the product has a clear position in that market, the fixed-sum-per-unit method can be a convenient way to track and control costs for marketing communications.

MEETING COMPETITION   Some marketers simply try to meet the competition. In other words, they match competitors' communications budgets. If Competitor A spends $1 million on TV ads, so do they.

This tactic can result in a deadlock between organizations, with neither advancing in its share of the market. Often, organizations won't reveal exactly how much they are spending on communications, or they may reveal an overall budget (possibly in order to intimidate competitors) but decline to discuss budgeting methods or the amount spent on each element of the communications mix. When Chesebrough-Pond's relaunched its Vaseline Intensive Care lotion (the leading skin lotion, with 28 percent of the $683 million market), the company announced that it would be spending $38 million in advertising and $21 million in sales promotions. But it wouldn't reveal the percentage of increase these figures represented.[26]

Like the previous three methods of budgeting, meeting the competition doesn't necessarily address the objectives of the communications plan or the product's communications needs vis-à-vis market, life cycle, and so forth. It only ensures that the organization will spend as much as its competitors. Furthermore, this tactic can lead marketers into a vicious cycle of ever-increasing communications budgets. In these cases, competing marketers may try to call a moratorium on increased spending.

In the early 1990s, Kellogg Company's chairman and chief executive officer, Arnold G. Langbo, did just that. To win back its U.S. market share, Kellogg had exceeded its previous-year ad spending by as much as $100 million per quarter. General Mills boosted its spending to support its fall advertising campaign, and Quaker Oats Company invested heavily in advertising for new products. Langbo called for a leveling off of marketing expenditures, but he also declared that Kellogg would take all necessary steps to maintain its large market share leads in Europe. "Our strategy is to leave no area of the market uncovered," Langbo remarked.[27]

ALL-YOU-CAN-AFFORD BUDGETING   Another approach to budgeting is *all-you-can-afford budgeting.* This method consists of deciding what the organization can afford to spend on communications, then allocating that amount among the various elements of the communications mix. The all-you-can-afford method is common among small companies.

FIGURE 18.7

Budgeting with the Objective-Task Method

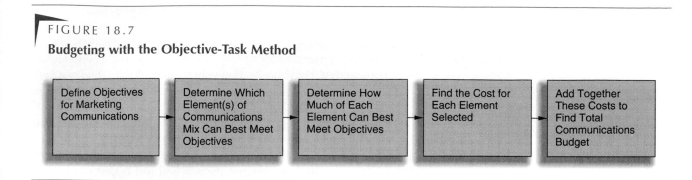

This type of budgeting does ensure that the company won't spend too much. However, it doesn't take into account how much money is necessary to achieve marketing objectives such as breaking into a new market or maintaining market share. On the other hand, this way of planning helps a small company with limited funds focus on spending that money more resourcefully than a large company might be inclined to do. Thus, a small budget may force a creative organization to come up with inexpensive—but unique and successful—advertising.

objective-task method
Quantifying communications objectives, determining the communications mix required to meet those objectives, and budgeting the cost of that mix.

OBJECTIVE-TASK METHOD   The **objective-task method** is the only budgeting formula based on the marketer's communications objectives and thus custom designed to meet the communications needs of the product. Figure 18.7 shows how it works. To implement the objective-task method, the marketing manager must define the goals of the communications mix: Do they include a 30 percent increase in brand awareness? Do they necessitate a 15 percent increase in distinction (in consumers' minds) between this product and those of competitors?

Quantifying objectives this way helps determine the communications mix and the budget required to execute the communications plan. Once objectives have been quantified, the marketer evaluates each element in the communications mix and decides how much of which elements can best meet the objectives. When this has been determined, a dollar amount can be assigned to each element in the mix. The total for the elements is the overall communications budget for the product.

The objective-task method does have shortcomings. It provides no basis for setting priorities among objectives. This can be a problem when funds are limited, especially when a competitor spends substantial sums on communications. Also, by treating all objectives the same way, the objective-task method implies that every objective is equally important. Obviously, this is rarely if ever the case. Money spent to achieve some communications objectives will have a bigger impact on profits than money spent on other objectives. Even so, a budget method that is tied to objectives should be most effective, with the fewest wasted dollars of any of these methods.

EVALUATION AND CONTROL

Feedback is as important in marketing as in other uses of communications. It is the basis of evaluating the marketing communications effort. Even before fully implementing a communications plan, marketers seek feedback in the form of evaluations from a variety of sources. These may include marketing researchers, experts familiar with the product, legal staff, and members of the target market. They also evaluate the communications efforts of their competitors, trying to gauge the size and intended purposes of these efforts.

Once the communications effort is under way, the marketing team uses a number of tools to monitor it. Team members track sales to look for changes that seem to be responses to the communications. They watch for reactions in their competitors' communications activities. And they conduct research to learn whether members of the target market have heard or seen their messages, what they recall about them, and how (if at all) the marketers' communications have affected their beliefs and attitudes.

 CONTROLLING WITH SALES DATA   Sales data are a logical way to measure whether communications efforts are working as intended. Sales below forecasted levels indicate a problem—and so might higher-than-expected sales. Hoover Ltd., a British unit of Maytag Corporation, suffered because of an overly enthusiastic response to a sales promotion. The company offered free airline tickets to qualified buyers of its appliances. So many consumers applied for the tickets that the promotion was much more expensive than anticipated, and the company couldn't even keep up with processing the requests. Maytag reported a $30 million charge against its earnings to cover the unexpected costs, and it fired three executives under whom the promotion had been launched.[28]

One of the most advanced companies in terms of evaluation and control of marketing communications is Nabisco, which manufactures such products as Oreos, Chips Ahoy!, Fig Newtons, and Ritz crackers. During the mid-1980s, the company began to focus its selling efforts on its retail customers. Nabisco's 2,800 sales reps not only stack the cookies and crackers on store shelves, they also carry hand-held computers that collect sales data for stores and use laptop computers to help retailers strategically place products on the shelves. Thus, up-to-date information about sales and promotional efforts is available at all times not only to Nabisco but to the company's customers, helping both parties adjust promotional efforts to meet current needs.[29]

The *single-source research system* (introduced in Chapter 7) is a useful application of technology in this area. Scanner-generated buying information at large stores such as supermarkets is combined with consumer demographic studies and data on communications efforts, such as advertising or in-store sales promotions. Marketers use this information to measure the success of their communications strategies by quantifying consumer response to ads and sales promotions and to measure the profitability of these efforts.

CONTROLLING WITH CONSUMER RESEARCH   Another way to evaluate the effectiveness of marketing communications is to go straight to consumers themselves to learn their attitudes about the good or service. One of the benefits of going straight to customers is that it places the focus of evaluating marketing communications on the customer.

Several tactics are available for doing this. The simplest is just to ask customers how they learned about the organization and its products. The marketing team may mail out surveys or set up conferences called *customer roundtables* with consumers, resellers, or representatives of organizational buyers. In the survey or during the roundtable, the marketers ask how these customers view the product. Marketers may ask direct questions about price, packaging, and features of the product. Marketers may rely on customer recall or unprompted responses. *Recall* seeks to learn how much consumers remember about the product or an advertisement about the product. Research using *unprompted response* analyzes consumers' comments without directly asking, "What do you remember about product (or advertisement) X?"

An important way to evaluate the effectiveness of marketing communications is to do customer research. Survey Sampling, Inc. helps with that job by selling phone numbers of consumers. The "refreshing" idea described in this ad refers to the fact that phone numbers in each sample are retired from use for twelve months to reduce the possibility that consumers on the list will be fed up with frequent surveys.

Other types of consumer research focus more on buying behavior than on attitudes. The key is to find a way to link the message and the response. The Barn Nursery & Landscape Center, located in Cary, Illinois, prints coupons for the items featured in its monthly newsletters (sent in response to customer requests). By tracking the number of coupons redeemed, the store can see how many sales the newsletter is stimulating. One month, the Barn promoted tree wraps; that month its sales of that product equaled the usual sales for an entire year.[30]

IMPLICATIONS FOR GLOBAL MARKETERS

In devising a global communications strategy, the marketer must not only weigh the issues described so far, but also cultural and economic factors related to the countries being served. These can influence whether the communications process succeeds in delivering the intended message.

CULTURAL CONSIDERATIONS   The marketer must take into account language differences. Advertisements must be understandable by their audience, of course, but other aspects of marketing communications are important as well. Foreign publications are unlikely to bother with public relations materials unless they are in the publication's language; publishers may even be insulted if the marketer hasn't bothered to translate a press release. For any marketing message, mere word-for-word translations almost guarantee embarrassing mistakes. The organization needs to use people who are fluent in the languages of potential customers and who understand the marketer's industry.

The marketer also must ensure that messages reflect the culture of the people being addressed. Again, mistakes can be embarrassing. For example, although Muslims and Jews are forbidden to eat pork, promotional materials for refrigerators being introduced into Middle Eastern countries used a photo of a refrigerator stocked with food items that included a large ham.[30] When Procter & Gamble launched its

Hitachi uses billboard advertising along the streetcar line in Warsaw, Poland.

Wash & Go shampoo and conditioner in Eastern Europe, its ads showed a woman hopping into the shower and saying, "Take two bottles in the shower? Not me! I just want to wash my hair and go." Unfortunately, these ads were directed to people who take baths, not showers, and who had never used—or heard of—conditioner. Soon, the "Not me . . . " line from the ad became an all-purpose punch line used to answer all kinds of questions in Czechoslovakia. And Polish bars began serving a drink called Wash & Go—a shot of vodka with a water chaser.[32]

ECONOMIC AND LEGAL CONSIDERATIONS   The marketer also must consider economic constraints on communications strategy. For example, the choice of advertising media may be more limited in developing nations than in the United States. U.S. consumers have 86 televisions in use for every 100 people, but only 11 televisions are in use for every 100 Chinese.[33] Therefore, in China a mass marketer probably would not want most of its advertising to be on television; posters or billboards might be more effective.

   With any type of communications, the marketer must be aware of any legal and political restrictions as well. France limits the amount an organization may spend on sales promotion.[34] Valérie Banino of the L'Oréal group, marketers of skin-care and related products, reports that free samples in stores are unwise in much of Africa "because you may unleash a disturbance"; L'Oréal instead includes samples in magazines.[35]

   Because of all these concerns, many international marketers prefer not to rely on an advertising agency whose experience is limited to the United States. For a global strategy, they might use a multinational advertising agency. Coca-Cola works with McCann-Erickson Worldwide, which uses what it calls a "borderless" agency plan. Under this plan, the agency encourages its creative directors from around the world to collaborate, contributing to efforts outside their own geographic areas.[36] Or marketers might turn to foreign agencies for each country in a multinational strategy.

   In either case, the growth in global marketing gives an edge to advertising people with skills in communicating internationally. When Foote, Cone & Belding was looking for a director to handle its Colgate-Palmolive account, the agency wanted an American who had lived abroad, was multilingual, and could tackle traveling to 36 countries. The person for the job was Edwin M. Wiley, who speaks six languages and has marketing and advertising experience in several countries in Europe.[37]

You Decide

WHAT'S BEHIND YOUR DOCTOR'S ORDERS?

When your doctor writes you a prescription, you expect him or her to know the facts, including the pros and cons, about the medication being prescribed. You don't expect the doctor's prescription to be solely the result of a response to advertising rather than familiarity with the product, and you certainly aren't thinking about whether advertisements for the drug are misleading. You just want the medication to relieve your symptoms safely.

But a study recently conducted by researchers at UCLA indicates that 92 percent of the prescription drug advertisements from ten of the leading medical journals violate federal regulations prohibiting misleading claims by drug companies. The study concludes, "Until existing regulations are applied rigorously, the public is at risk." UCLA researchers asked experts to rank 109 ads for educational value, scientific rigor, and compliance with FDA standards. After tabulating the experts' comments, the researchers found that 100 ads contained "deficiencies in areas for which the FDA has established explicit standards for quality."

One of these standards is the "fair balance" rule, which requires that drug advertisers present a balanced view of a product's risks and benefits. The fair balance rule prohibits use of false statistics, misleading headlines, and graphics that can't be supported by scientific literature. The UCLA researchers found that 40 percent of the ads examined failed the fair balance test by inflating a drug's benefits and minimizing the risks or side effects. Thirty percent presented faulty or inconclusive statistics, and 30 percent used misleading visual aids.

It's true that many of these ads are accompanied by fine-print explanations, footnotes, and disclaimers. But doctors often fail to read the ads as carefully as would be necessary to sort through all the information, put the ad in perspective, and make a thoroughly informed decision about a product. So the product winds up in the consumer's medicine cabinet, whether it belongs there or not.

Do you think the advertising of medical products should be held to a higher standard than other advertising? Why or why not? Do you think the consumer (patient) has a responsibility in this situation? If so, what is it? Do you think that the "fair balance" rule is fair to advertisers? Why or why not?

Source: "Not What the Doctor Ordered," by Geoffrey Cowley, *Newsweek,* June 8, 1992, p. 54.

Ethical and Social Issues in Marketing Communications

Marketing communications is a constant balancing act of the message, ethics, and social values. Because the power of marketing communications through its use of mass media has been abused many times, the general public often views such activities with cynicism. Misleading advertisements, sweepstakes in which prizes were not awarded (or that required payment for the "prize"), money-back guarantees that were not honored, gifts promised in exchange for customer effort and time (say, for touring a timeshare development) that turned out to be of minimal value or never awarded at all, and services promised but never provided are just some of the unethical, if not illegal, shortcomings of communications efforts in the eyes of the consumer.

Truth in advertising has long been a concern of marketers and their customers. Some banks advertise "free" checking accounts, neglecting to mention that they require a relatively high minimum balance. The customer in effect pays by parking money in the checking account, rather than by using it to earn higher interest elsewhere. "You Decide: What's behind Your Doctor's Orders?" addresses this issue with regard to the advertisement of drugs. Apparently, many pharmaceutical companies don't go as far as they should to present a balanced view of their products. So far, no action has been taken by the Food and Drug Administration to enforce existing guidelines.

REGULATION OF THE COMMUNICATIONS EFFORT

Abuses of marketing communications have caused agencies like the Federal Trade Commission (FTC) to set strict guidelines for some types of communications. In general, these regulations as well as various laws are designed to protect consumers. In the case of sweepstakes, for example, the FTC has issued guidelines to ensure that prizes promised are actually awarded. In addition, consumers have grown more wary, sometimes even cynical, in their scrutiny of marketing messages.

Sometimes business is called to task for its actions through simple embarrassment. The Center for Science in the Public Interest issues annual "awards" for the ads it deems most unfair, misleading, and irresponsible. "Winners" in a recent year included Old Milwaukee beer's "Swedish bikini team" ads, for linking beer drinking to sexual conquest, and Whittle Communications' supposedly educational poster on how the heart works, which included ads for fast food and candy bars directly alongside.[38]

Different media may be under different legal and ethical constraints. For a number of years, U.S. law has prohibited TV ads for cigarettes and liquor (except for beer), but print and outdoor ads for these products abound. In Europe, however, many countries broadcast cigarette and liquor commercials. And while it is acceptable in the United States to present a print advertisement of a woman in a bikini smoking a cigarette, this would be totally unacceptable in an Islamic country such as Saudi Arabia.[39]

COMMUNICATIONS DIRECTED AT CHILDREN

Marketing communications directed at children are especially loaded with ethical and social implications. Children are avid consumers of television. The average American child, who watches more than 20 hours of TV each week, sees more than 20,000 commercials in a year. If that weren't enough, the Turner Broadcasting Network has tried airing a 14-hour marathon of cartoons on its three cable networks, during which viewers would be exposed to 700 commercials from toymaker Hasbro.[40] Thus, children are aware of many products and want to have them. Some children's advocacy groups have lobbied to limit these marketing efforts, including cartoon programs that require the use of interactive toys or are thinly veiled ads for the toys that appear as characters in the cartoons.

Some advertising that influences young people has even raised health and safety concerns. Two characters that appeal especially to youngsters—Spuds Mackenzie, the mascot for Budweiser beer, and Joe Camel, the mascot for Camel cigarettes—are major examples. Both companies came under attack for their portrayal of drinking and cigarette smoking in a way that is appealing to young consumers; both denied that the characters were created to entice young people to buy their products. But it was clear that youngsters had latched on to the characters as mascots, and the connection between the mascots and the products was undeniable.

Finally, the creation of Channel One has brought TV (and its advertising) to the school classroom on a regular basis. Channel One is a for-profit cable television company owned by Whittle Communications. On a contract basis, Channel One provides a 12-minute videotape each weekday to participating schools. The tape contains a 10-minute newscast of current events, with 2 minutes of advertising. The advertising often promotes snack foods, candy, and similar products. Currently, Whittle Communications professes to reach 7.8 million students each day.[41] Because the Channel One contract requires schools to guarantee that a certain percentage of students will watch the program each day, the company's marketers can approach potential advertisers with a clearly targeted market and a guaranteed audience.

Chapter Project
Design a Sales Promotion Event

Every year, the International Dairy-Deli-Bakery Association and *Progressive Grocer* cosponsor a series of awards for retailing excellence, in which entrants are judged on the quality of the sales promotions. Past winners have included Finast Supermarkets of Maple Heights, Ohio, which tied its "Carnival of Cakes" promotion to Mother's Day. Finast ran a full-page color ad with 15 varieties of layer cakes and several coupons, and gave away plastic cake servers with each purchase. The stores were decorated with balloons, carousels, and canopies, and staffers dressed as carnival clowns. Another winner was the deli at Raley's supermarket in Sacramento, California, which ran a promotion for cheese from Switzerland. The staff created a huge mural of the Swiss Alps and suspended it above the deli cases. A white pavilion with Swiss flags, wines, and cheeses welcomed shoppers; a refrigerated case resembling a Lake Lucerne steamboat held more cheese. Consumers registered for cash giveaways and were offered recipes featuring the cheese.

Imagine that you're in charge of the dairy, bakery, deli, or coffee shop in a supermarket. Design a sales promotion event tying your products to an event, place, season, holiday, or other theme. Use your imagination to come up with specific ways to draw consumers into your store.

Source: Lee W. Dyer, "Making It with Merchandising," *Progressive Grocer*, July 1993, pp. 139–143.

Case
Elvis Presley Enterprises

Each year, 680,000 Elvis Presley fans stream through the gates of Graceland, the late legend's estate in Tennessee, searching for everything from trinkets to proof that the King is still alive. Most of us would assume that all the manager of his giant empire would have to do to make money would be to make enough Elvis dolls available to satisfy the crowds and rake in the royalties on the songs. Not so. When Elvis died in 1977, he was broke and addicted to prescription drugs. He (or his former business manager) had squandered his enormous wealth, and his total estate was worth less than $5 million. Just maintaining it would have run the well dry within a few years. But Priscilla Presley, who had divorced Elvis in 1973 but remained close to him because of their daughter, was aware of how devoted his fans were and saw a chance to rejuvenate not only his tarnished image but also the empire itself.

As comanager of the estate (along with Elvis's accountant and a Memphis bank), Priscilla founded Elvis Presley Enterprises (EPE). She realized that she wasn't promoting goods or services; those were tangential. She was promoting the image of a late, great star—hardly a tangible product. But she used goods and services to create the product: the aura of Elvis. She hired a CEO, Jack Soden, to help her run the company. He wasn't an Elvis fan. "I liked that," she explains. "It indicated to me that all the B.S. would be out of the way."

Priscilla and Soden kept information about the company very private. But they went very public with their marketing communications. EPE refurbished Graceland, the 23-room Georgian mansion that Elvis lived in for 20 years and that so many fans now visit. (Priscilla was unhappy with Elvis's taste in decorating, so she returned the decor in the first-floor rooms to the style she'd surrounded herself with when she lived there.)

Now, tourists come to see Elvis's grave, eat in the Heartbreak Hotel Restaurant, see movies about Elvis, and gawk at his car collection and two jets. (Each exhibit costs a separate fee.) They shop in the eight gift shops for Elvis potholders and baseball caps.

Regarding the promotional items, Priscilla seems to have mixed feelings. She must recognize that she is very different from many of her customers. She wants to sell higher-quality, more tasteful goods in the stores, such as a coffee-table book on Graceland and a slick Elvis tour jacket. But she comments, "The thing that my staff tries to convince me of is that the stuff is selling, and we certainly don't want to put a stop to that."

Graceland is only one facet of Elvis Presley Enterprises. There is also a division that licenses Elvis's name worldwide and acts as a watchdog over the use of his image, as well as a music-publishing group that, in conjunction with RCA, watches over the release of Elvis's songs. Because Elvis's image is key to the entire promotion effort at EPE, the company keeps a close eye on those who try to sell unauthorized merchandise or who use the King's name in vain. (EPE once considered suing the television sitcom

"Designing Women" for airing an episode that was unflattering to Elvis.)

In addition to keeping tight control of Elvis's image, Priscilla likes to maintain a bit of the mystique. She is close-mouthed about certain plans for the future, such as what will be done with the sealed second floor of the Graceland mansion, where Elvis died. She knows that many of Elvis's fans still believe that he is alive and well, and living on that second floor. The tourists are tantalized, and maybe they'll come back. It's hard to sell a ghost to the general public. But Priscilla Presley is doing it.

QUESTIONS

1. How did the nature of the product and the nature of the target audience affect some of Priscilla Presley's communications decisions?
2. In what ways do you think EPE could effectively use socially responsible marketing communications?
3. Why is it so important for Priscilla Presley and EPE to maintain as much control as possible over Elvis's image?

Source: Suzanna Andrews, "Making Elvis Pay," *Working Woman*, September 1993, pp. 52–55+.

CHAPTER 19

Advertising, Sales Promotion, and Publicity

LEARNING OBJECTIVES

After completing this chapter, you should be able to:

1. Describe functions of advertising.

2. Identify basic advertising techniques.

3. Discuss ethical issues in advertising.

4. Describe how marketers design an advertising campaign.

5. Discuss how marketers evaluate and control the advertising effort.

6. Identify major techniques for sales promotion.

7. Discuss the value of sales promotion and how it can be done ethically.

8. Identify the types and uses of publicity.

9. Explain how to manage bad publicity.

10. Discuss ethical issues surrounding publicity.

Creating Customer Value
The *Tallahassee Democrat*

Newspapers, like most other publications, depend on advertising for much of their revenue. The *Tallahassee Democrat,* a Knight-Ridder paper, is no exception. This is the story of advertising from both sides of the fence:

- Marketers who need attractive, accurate advertising and who in this case become the newspaper's customers.
- A team at the *Tallahassee Democrat,* which sought to satisfy its customers—the marketers—with the best ads possible.

During the 1980s, the *Democrat* suffered from a dismal customer service record but remained fairly healthy because it was the only paper in town. Fred Mott, the *Democrat's* general manager, knew this had to change if the paper were going to survive over the long haul. So he began instituting teams at the top level, through which managers met regularly and got to know each other. As top managers forged a stronger alliance, they began to focus on customer satisfaction and ways to integrate the paper's different functions: production, circulation, and advertising.

The first try involved setting up a new Advertising Customer Service department. The idea was to pull together artists, production people, clerical and billing employees, as well as accountants who were involved in advertising. The department fell flat. Errors in advertisements continued to proliferate, and sales reps complained that they had no time to spend with customers. Through customer surveys, the department learned that advertisers believed the *Democrat* was much more concerned with its own internal protocol than with customers and the quality of ads. One particular ad was so poorly prepared that employees said it looked like a "rat had run across the page." The ad was dubbed the "rat tracks fax" and came to represent the challenge *Democrat* managers knew they had to face.

So Fred Mott appointed Doris Dunlap (a top manager) to lead a cross-functional team that was to turn around *Democrat* advertising. The team was named ELITE, for "ELIminate The Errors." She gathered a group of twelve employees from different departments at the paper and set about to improve the quality of advertising. Within a year,

advertising accuracy had soared above 99 percent, and lost revenue from ad errors was next to nothing. Customer surveys showed that advertisers were happy.

To achieve this success, the ELITE team examined the process by which ads were created at the paper. Team members determined this process could be improved with some simple applications of technology: cellular phones and portable fax machines so ad reps could submit orders throughout the day; desktop computers and publishing software so the ads could be created in-house.

But paying attention to customers became the top priority. "People in the building who get a piece of paper began to realize that that piece of paper, whether it be a bill or an ad layout or whatnot, is no longer just a piece of paper," recalls one team member. "It is the customer. I think that transformation was the hardest and most eye-opening event for me. People cradled that piece of paper and took care of it in a way they never had before."

Customers, who pay for and rely on those ads to improve their own businesses, responded with enthusiasm. One restaurant manager rejected an ad so late in the day that it previously would have been left out of that edition of the paper. But with up-to-date communication and computer capabilities, the ad rep and artist were able to come up with a new ad in a half hour. The restaurant manager was astonished—and thrilled. He became one of the *Democrat*'s most faithful customers.

With the success of the ELITE team, the *Democrat* has a new way of selling, creating, producing, and billing for advertisements. Because of the team, the paper now has an excellent relationship with its customers, and the quality of advertisements is as high as customer satisfaction. As you read about advertising in this chapter, think about how many people are involved in the ad process and how important each person's contribution is along the way.

Source: Jon R. Katzenbach and Douglas K. Smith, *The Wisdom of Teams* (Cambridge, Mass.: Harvard Business School Press, 1993), pp. 67–72.

Chapter Overview

When you think of advertising, you might think of Madison Avenue. High-fashion magazines. Television. Celebrity endorsements. Simulated rock videos. Simulated car crashes. Simulated house burglaries. Real testimony to the superior taste of cereal, soda, margarine. But as you've seen in the story about the *Tallahassee Democrat,* advertising is hardly all glitz and glamour. Still, no matter how mundane the details, advertising has an important role to play in creating exchanges that will please the marketer's customers.

This chapter looks at advertising and two other elements of the communications mix, sales promotion and publicity. It explains what advertising does and what basic techniques are available. Then the chapter takes you through the steps involved in designing a domestic or global advertising campaign and discusses ways to evaluate and control the campaign. Next, discussion turns to sales promotion: types of sales promotion, the value it provides to marketers, and ethical considerations. Finally, the chapter examines publicity: ways to generate publicity, methods for managing negative publicity, and ethical issues surrounding publicity.

Advertising

advertising
Paid, nonpersonal communication through various media by organizations that are identified in the message and seek to inform and/or persuade members of a particular audience.

As you learned in Chapter 18, **advertising** is paid, nonpersonal communication through various media by organizations that are identified in the message and seek to inform and/or persuade members of a particular audience. Advertising serves a number of functions, both for marketers and their target markets. The functions that support a particular marketer's objectives will help that marketer select the types of advertising to use.

FUNCTIONS OF ADVERTISING

The overriding function of advertising is to inform potential customers about a product and persuade them to buy it. It can also remind customers about a product, and it can convey information about the organization itself or issues important to the organization. Advertising can inform a large number of people with a single message. Good advertising can create or enhance perceptions of the quality or reliability of a product, thus encouraging customer loyalty and repeat purchases.

In most cases, advertising seeks to reach potential customers and entice them to spend money on the advertiser's products. But advertising itself costs money. Compared to personal selling, advertising costs less per person reached. Even so, the money spent on advertising by U.S. companies alone is astronomical: the annual budget for advertising in the United States is more than $20 billion.[1] The country's leading advertiser is Procter & Gamble, with an advertising budget in the United States alone of more than $2.1 billion per year. Philip Morris also spends more than $2 billion a year; General Motors and Sears each spend over $1 billion.[2]

TYPES OF ADVERTISING

Because advertising can serve a variety of purposes, marketers have come to assign specific terms to ads with certain broad categories of objectives. Knowing the basic types of advertising can help the marketer recognize the options available and select the form of advertising that will most likely help meet communications objectives.

product advertising
Advertising that attempts to lead members of the target market to buy the advertiser's product.

institutional advertising
Advertising that promotes an organization's image or philosophy.

PRODUCT VERSUS INSTITUTIONAL ADVERTISING   Advertising messages may emphasize a product or the organization behind the product. **Product advertising** attempts to lead members of the target market to buy the advertiser's goods or services. Apple Computer runs ads to encourage people to buy its Newton notebook computer. And Fantastic Sam's advertises to persuade people to get haircuts from its stylists.

In contrast, **institutional advertising** promotes an organization's image or philosophy. Organizations often use institutional advertising to improve public relations through positive messages. An example is Ford's advertising based on the slogan, "Quality is Job 1." This focuses on the company's concern for quality rather than on the features of particular automobiles.

pioneering advertising
Advertising that seeks to develop primary demand (demand for a product category).

competitive advertising
Advertising that attempts to develop secondary demand (demand for a particular brand of product).

comparative advertising
Advertising that compares one specific brand to another.

OTHER CATEGORIES   Advertising can be further divided into four subcategories: pioneering, competitive (including comparative), advocacy, and reminder advertising. **Pioneering advertising** seeks to develop primary demand, that is, demand for a product category—say, dairy products, beef, or, as in the case of Figure 19.1, plastics—rather than a specific brand. Pioneering advertising is especially important for introducing an innovative product or one that is new to the target market. In Russia, for example, consumers until recently had little access to the wide variety of goods available from Western companies. Marketers to Russian consumers therefore need to explain what their products are and how to use them.[3]

Competitive advertising attempts to develop secondary demand—demand for a particular brand of product. Such ads are especially important for established products and when competition is heavy. Thus, in the cutthroat marketing environment for bottled water, Evian tries to maintain its position as something special by using competitive advertising stressing the benefits of drinking Evian water.[4] Britain's Virgin Atlantic Airways distinguishes itself from the competition through ads describing Virgin's amenities, including roomy seating, individual videos to watch, and limousine transportation to and from the airport.[5]

Comparative advertising is competitive advertising with a bite. These advertisements pit one brand against another, making comparisons to specific competing brands. Comparative advertising is prohibited in some countries, but those restrictions are changing. Japan relaxed its guidelines in the mid-1980s, and the United States, which had similar restrictions, eased them in the 1970s. However, a 1988 revision of the Lanham Act now prohibits advertisers from tarnishing the image of competitors by unfairly representing "another person's goods, services, or commercial activities" as being of poor quality.

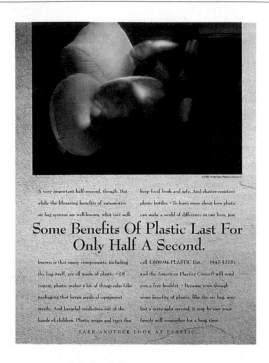

Some Benefits Of Plastic Last For Only Half A Second.

TAKE ANOTHER LOOK AT PLASTIC

advocacy advertising
Institutional advertising that supports socially responsible messages, activities, or causes.

Advocacy advertising is institutional advertising that supports socially responsible messages, activities, or causes. Retailer Benetton once ran an ad campaign showing its founder, Luciano Benetton, naked behind a bold headline reading, "I want my clothes back." The ad was soliciting donations of used clothing to be distributed to poor people through the Red Cross and other organizations.[6] Nonprofit organizations such as Mothers Against Drunk Driving (MADD) and the National Rifle Association (NRA) rely heavily on advocacy advertising to promote their causes.

reminder advertising
Advertising that seeks to keep a product's or organization's name in the public eye.

When a product or organization is already well known, the marketer may use **reminder advertising**. Such advertising seeks to keep a product or organization's name in the public eye, reinforcing its identity. In Sacramento, California, Worthington Chevrolet has for over two decades run a series of TV ads to remind consumers about the dealership. The ads started as a takeoff on a competitor's commercials in which that dealer posed with his imposing German shepherd. To poke fun at him, Cal Worthington began starring in ads along with what he called "my dog Spot." In each ad, Spot was actually a pig, a chicken, a tiger—any animal but a dog. Aside from Spot's presence, each ad is different. In one, Worthington stands on his head and sings; in another, he stands on a flying biplane. Says Worthington, "I never intended to continue the commercials, but I got such great feedback on them, I couldn't stop."[7]

cooperative advertising
Advertising in which manufacturers and channel members team up for one campaign.

Advertisers may use one or more of the above types of advertising in conjunction with another technique: **cooperative advertising**. Cooperative advertising involves manufacturers and channel members or franchisers and franchisees teaming up for one advertising campaign. By collaborating on cooperative advertising, manufacturers and channel members can reach the target market more efficiently than they could if each acted alone. And by advertising the same products and slogans, as well as special promotions—like a burger of the month—franchise operations benefit from unity within the overall marketing strategy.

This British magazine ad grabs the reader's attention with its humor and serves as reminder advertising for Harvey Nichols' home furnishing division, keeping the name in the public eye.

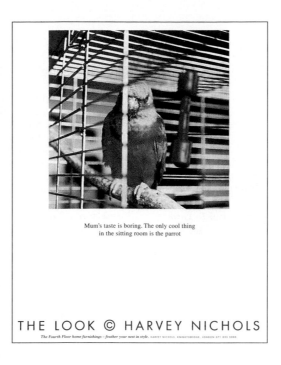

Mum's taste is boring. The only cool thing
in the sitting room is the parrot

THE LOOK © HARVEY NICHOLS

The Fourth Floor home furnishings – feather your nest in style. HARVEY NICHOLS, KNIGHTSBRIDGE, LONDON 071 235 5000.

LEGAL AND ETHICAL ISSUES IN ADVERTISING

In the United States, advertising is regulated by the Federal Trade Commission (FTC). The FTC's domain includes guarding against unethical, unfair, or deceptive advertising as well as regulating advertising aimed at children. Thus, after Eggland's Best advertised that its eggs did not contain cholesterol, the company was required to stop advertising this claim when studies revealed that the eggs were no different from other eggs. If the FTC finds an advertising claim is misleading, it may require **corrective advertising** to retract or clarify the original ads.

corrective advertising
Advertising that retracts or clarifies previously misleading claims.

If FTC regulations seem strict, they are much more relaxed than those of some other countries. Sweden and Canada have banned all advertising aimed directly at children. Switzerland does not allow an actor to portray a consumer. Both Switzerland and New Zealand place limits on TV political ads.

Although government regulations give marketers guidelines to follow in deciding what advertising practices are ethical, there certainly are gray areas. As social attitudes change, so do attitudes about certain types of advertisements. (See "You Decide: Do Infomercials Belong on the Air?")

Fortunately, marketers have sources of help in this area. The National Advertising Division of the Council of Better Business Bureaus offers guidelines that many advertisers willingly follow. Consumers, fellow advertisers, and government agencies are all encouraged to complain to the NAD about possible unethical advertising practices. The NAD enlists the aid of experts in the advertising industry as well as consumer groups to make decisions in its cases, and it opens its findings to the public.

In addition, advertisers with a quality focus reduce their risk of running afoul of ethical and legal guidelines because they seek success through customer satisfaction. Ethical advertising efforts are honest, and they may be a valuable source of information. Ringer, an Eden Prairie, Minnesota, marketer of natural lawn and garden products, educates consumers with a catalog that devotes six pages to detailed information about controlling plant diseases and pests without chemicals. The catalog

You Decide

DO INFOMERCIALS BELONG ON THE AIR?

In the summer and fall of 1992, presidential candidate Ross Perot hit the airwaves with his famous charts and graphs explaining how he could tame the national debt if he was elected. By October, he had bought $2.5 million worth of prime time to air half-hour infomercials touting his candidacy.

In doing this, Perot joined the likes of actor John Ritter, who appears in a 30-minute infomercial selling study tapes for children; Victoria Jackson, whose infomercials sell her line of cosmetics; and the infamous Ron Popeil of Ronco. How did infomercials—30-minute advertising spots that pose as talk shows or news—grow into a billion-dollar industry?

Cable television unleashed many more channels than could be filled with programming, creating hundreds of hours of "dead time." In 1984, deregulation allowed stations and cable networks to sell half-hour segments of airtime to advertisers. So they sold the dead time—such as late night or Sunday morning—cheaply, sometimes for as little as a few hundred dollars for a half hour (compared to $300,000 for a 30-second network spot during prime time). In addition, infomercials are much less expensive to produce than glitzy, glittery prime time commercials. So money rolled in fast to the makers of infomercials.

Not surprisingly, the Federal Trade Commission has since clamped down by reregulating the cable industry and pursuing cases of alleged deceptive advertising in infomercials. Under FTC guidelines, whenever infomercials provide ordering information, they must disclose that the ad is paid programming. In addition, some observers think that the popularity of infomercials among big marketers will make this type of advertising more respectable (and more creative). For many advertisers, the infomercial format serves the legitimate purpose of being a way to present more detailed factual information than they can in a standard commercial.

One of the main problems with the infomercial business is the wide range of perception of just exactly what an infomercial is. An increasing number of marketers are using the format of a news story to talk about their own commercials. Dial Corp. calls its infomercial tracing the history of Breck shampoo girls a "documentary." "Honestly," gushes a company spokeswoman, "the Breck girl thing is beyond advertising. This wonderful story should be told about how the Breck girls were selected. It is a nostalgic love story that supersedes commercialism." In the food industry, commercial deals made between famous chefs and makers of everything from processed food to food processors are by now almost taken for granted. Is a cookbook (or cooking demonstration) that suggests using Swanson's chicken broth or Wilton insulated baking sheets an infomercial? "These are products that we recommend," says *The Frugal Gourmet* author Jeff Smith. "I don't like the word *endorse*." But Smith earns money from the products he advertises.

Consumer groups want to clear up some of this uncertainty, so that viewers realize they are watching an advertisement whenever they tune in an infomercial. If viewers tune in partway through the half hour, how do they know whether they are seeing a talk show or an infomercial? One suggestion has been for infomercials to display a small logo, like the closed-caption logo, on the screen at all times.

Do you think infomercials serve a legitimate purpose for marketers and consumers? Why or why not? What steps, if any, do you think should be taken to regulate them?

Sources: Scott Donaton, "Time Warner Studying Infomercials on Cable," *Advertising Age,* June 7, 1993, pp. 3, 46; David J. Jefferson and Thomas R. King, "Infomercials Fill up Air Time on Cable, Aim for Prime Time," *The Wall Street Journal,* October 22, 1992, pp. A1, A4; Gary Levin, "Big Marketers Will Reshape Infomercials," *Advertising Age,* May 24, 1993, p. 46; Laura Shapiro, "Commercially Speaking," *Newsweek,* June 15, 1992, pp. 56–57; "A Pressing Issue," *Sales & Marketing Management,* January 1992, p. 45.

not only shows uses for Ringer's products, it builds an image of the company as credible and concerned about the environment.[8]

When well done, an ethical approach to advertising works. The widely admired advertising campaign for Absolut vodka is built around the company's support for the arts. Ads showing artworks commissioned by Absolut not only draw attention, they position Absolut as a drink for people with sophisticated tastes.[9]

In evaluating the ethics of advertising, it is, of course, important to remember the purpose of advertising. The advertiser is seeking to sell something, and the public is well aware of the advertiser's intentions. Thus, it is reasonable to ask that advertisers refrain from lying and from hurting their customers. Professor Theodore Levitt makes the point well:[10]

FIGURE 19.2

Process for Designing an Advertising Campaign

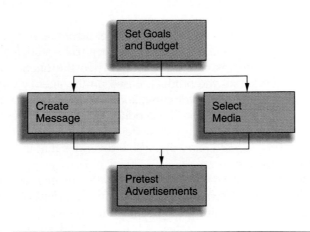

If people in business can respond professionally to . . . wants and wishes without violating society's generally accepted standards of decency, taste, and appropriateness, and their own moral codes, so they can go home at night to their families without guilt, apology, or embarrassment—confident and comfortable—then that is all anybody can rightfully ask of anyone.

Designing an Advertising Campaign

When marketers have decided their communications mix should include advertising, they must design the advertising campaign. This task includes the steps summarized in Figure 19.2: setting goals and budget, creating the message, selecting the appropriate media, and pretesting.

Developing the campaign requires teamwork, even in an organization that is not formally organized into teams. In small organizations, the advertising staff might be one or two people working with the organization's chief executive. Large organizations often have an advertising group under the umbrella of a marketing department. Members of an advertising group might include researchers, artists and designers, copywriters, and media analysts. Marketing managers and top executives also are typically involved in decisions about advertising. Other employees with input include product experts (such as engineers) and administrative personnel concerned with the impact of advertising on the organization's finances.

advertising agency
A firm devoted to planning and preparing advertising campaigns for other organizations.

Often an organization arranges to have many of the tasks related to advertising handled by outside specialists: an **advertising agency**. An advertising agency is a firm devoted to planning and preparing advertising campaigns for other organizations (the advertisers). In such cases, teamwork involves collaboration among staff within the agency, among employees within the client organization, and between agency and client.

WORKING WITH AN ADVERTISING AGENCY

When an organization decides to employ an advertising agency to design and produce advertisements, two sets of marketers come together:

1. Advertisers—those from the organization needing advertisements to stimulate sales of its products
2. The ad agency—those representing an organization that markets advertising services.

If each is practicing the quality approach to marketing, then each must focus on satisfying its customers' wants and needs.

The advertising agency seeks to meet advertisers' needs by offering a variety of services.[11] In a typical case, the agency begins by studying the advertiser's product to identify its strengths and weaknesses. Then the agency analyzes the existing and potential market for the product. Based on the agency's knowledge of the product's sales, the channels of distribution, and the advertising media available, it next develops a plan for advertising the product to intermediaries or end users. Finally, the agency executes that plan. It writes, designs, and produces the advertisements, arranges for media to carry the ads, and verifies that the ads actually ran where they were supposed to.

Besides these tasks, today's advertisers are increasingly looking for advertising agencies to provide what is called *integrated marketing*. In a nutshell, integrated marketing involves planning and implementing the whole communications mix. Often, it involves direct marketing activities like mailing advertising to a target market and maintaining a database of responses. Cathay Pacific, a Hong Kong–based airline, ended a decade-long relationship with the Leo Burnett agency because it was dissatisfied with Burnett's integrated marketing capabilities in Asia.[12] In contrast, McKinney Advertising and Public Relations, based in Philadelphia, impressed a small client with limited funds by devising three possible low-cost communications strategies: a quarterly newsletter, a public relations campaign, and a direct-mail advertising campaign.[13]

With so many crucial tasks in the hands of the advertising agency, communication between the advertiser and the ad agency is vital. The agency must have complete knowledge of its client's product, competitors' products and advertising strategies, and media available for disseminating ads. The agency should also understand its client's philosophy, objectives, and image, as well as the target market for the product.

EVALUATION OF THE AGENCY RELATIONSHIP   Once the advertiser begins working with an ad agency, it must begin formally and informally evaluating how well the two organizations work together. Sometimes it takes a few tries before the agency hits on an idea that pleases the client. Nevertheless, the advertiser will want to consider whether the relationship is resulting in effective communications with the advertiser's target markets. After all, one of the benefits of using an agency is that if the results are disappointing, it is relatively easy to end the relationship and find another agency. To evaluate the agency's performance, the advertiser might use a form such as the one shown in Figure 19.3.

CHARACTERISTICS OF AD AGENCIES   A small ad agency may consist of only a few staff members doing a variety of jobs. But large advertising agencies employ creative staff, production staff, account executives, and marketing personnel. Figure 19.4 illustrates the organizational chart of a typical medium-sized or large advertising agency. The account executives are responsible for setting up and implementing contracts with the agency's clients. The creative services group prepares the actual advertisements. The marketing services group selects media and places the ads, and it may conduct various types of research as well. The management and finance group provides support services to the advertising agency.

Global marketers also may need to be familiar with the practices of advertising agencies in other countries. In Japan, the biggest advertising challenge is getting a share of limited ad space, so the most value is placed on close links with the media. The lesser prestige of creating ads, coupled with the need to stand out from the clutter of many short commercials, has resulted in Japanese advertising that can only be described as bizarre. In an ad for Giga television, a man sits in a dark house, eating a

FIGURE 19.3

Checklist for Evaluating an Ad Agency's Performance

Rate each agency on a scale from 1 (strongly negative) to 10 (strongly positive).

General Information

☐ Agency size compatible with our needs.
☐ Strength of agency's management.
☐ Stability of agency's financial position.
☐ Compatibility with type of clients agency handles.
☐ Range of services agency is able to offer.
☐ Cost of agency services; billing policies.

Marketing Information

☐ Agency's ability to offer marketing counsel.
☐ Agency's understanding of the markets we serve.
☐ Agency's experience dealing in our market.
☐ Agency's success record; case histories.

Creative Abilities

☐ Well-thought-out creativity; relevance to strategy.
☐ Agency's art strength.
☐ Agency's copy strength.
☐ Overall creative quality.
☐ Effectiveness compared to work of competitors.

Production

☐ Faithfulness to creative concept and execution.
☐ Diligence to schedules and budgets.
☐ Agency's ability to control outside services.

Media

☐ Existence and soundness of media research.
☐ Effective and efficient media strategy.
☐ Ability to achieve objectives within budget.
☐ Strength at negotiating and executing schedules.
☐ Attitude toward periodic review of plan and budget.

Personality

☐ Agency's overall personality, philosophy, or position.
☐ Compatibility with client staff and management.
☐ Willingness to assign top people to account.

References

☐ Rating of agency's work by current clients.
☐ Rating of agency's work by past clients.
☐ Rating of agency's reputation by media.
☐ Rating of agency's strength by financial sources.
☐ Overall rating of agency's people or attitude by references.

Additional Considerations or Comments

_____
_____
_____
_____
_____
_____

Source: William F. Arens and Courtland L. Bovée, *Contemporary Advertising,* 5th ed. (Burr Ridge, Ill.: Irwin, 1994), p. 97.

banana and staring at a static-filled TV screen. In an ad for a food product, a tribe chases a moa (a giant extinct bird) to the edge of a cliff. The moa jumps into the air, the tribesmen rush off the cliff, and an announcer proclaims, "Hungry? Cup Noodles!"[14]

Whatever its variations around the globe, advertising is big business. In the past, an advertising agency simply received a 15 percent commission from the advertiser. Today, competition has made agencies more flexible. Many work on a guaranteed-profit basis, while others are willing to base the advertiser's payment on performance. Small organizations can find agencies willing to bill for a single short campaign, rather than a year's effort. However agencies choose to handle their billing, it adds up to nearly $100 billion per year, worldwide. Ranked in terms of their billings, the top three ad agencies in the world are WPP Group, based in London ($19 billion), Interpublic, New York ($13 billion), and Omnicon, also based in New York ($13 billion).[15]

SETTING GOALS AND BUDGET

Whether working with an agency or developing an ad campaign in-house, advertisers must set their goals and budget before proceeding with the campaign.

target audience
The group toward which an advertisement is directed.

GOALS Advertising can cost a lot, and establishing specific goals helps to ensure that every dollar is spent wisely. First, marketers must identify the **target audience**,

FIGURE 19.4

Typical Structure of an Advertising Agency

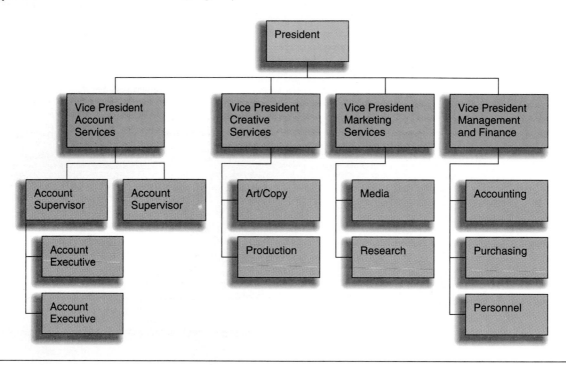

Source: William F. Arens and Courtland L. Bovée, *Contemporary Advertising,* 5th ed. (Burr Ridge, Ill.: Irwin, 1994), p. 95.

that is, the group toward whom the advertisements will be directed. Usually this is the same group of buyers identified as the target market for the product.

Then advertisers must ask themselves, What do we want to accomplish with this ad campaign? Ultimately they want people to buy the product, of course, so most advertising campaigns have sales objectives. In such cases, a good advertising campaign takes the target audience through at least some of the steps in the AIDA process:[16]

- *Attention:* noticing the advertisements
- *Interest:* desire to learn more about the product
- *Desire:* favorable attitudes including a wish to own or use the product
- *Action:* trying or repeatedly buying and using the product

To have practical value for advertising strategy, advertising goals need to be specific. They must address the role the ads will play in stimulating sales. For example, the ad campaign might seek to introduce a new product to a target market or tell customers where they can buy the product. In many cases, the goal of advertising is to break the ice for salespeople by making the target audience aware of the product's name and its features. Sometimes the goal is to get people to buy the product immediately, and other times—say, for infrequently purchased items—the advertiser tries to get people to buy in the future.

In devising advertising strategies for international markets, marketers have three basic options:

1. An advertising strategy may use essentially the same media and message to reach target markets in each country served. Coca-Cola used the same ad (except for language) to reach viewers of the Winter Olympics in 131 countries, and Seagram used a global billboard ad for Chivas Regal scotch.[17]
2. A basic strategy may be modified for different countries. To advertise Dove soap in Australia, France, Germany, and Italy, Unilever uses models from the country in which the ads run.[18]
3. Each country may have a unique strategy. Procter & Gamble needs to vary its ads for laundry detergent according to the knowledge and customs of each country's consumers. Few families in Russia have washing machines, so commercials there are directed to women who wash clothes by hand in buckets.[19]

Whether to use a single advertising strategy or to vary it depends on how target markets in the countries served are expected to respond to the strategy.

BUDGET   The advertising goals and budget are closely linked aspects of the plan for the ad campaign. Companies have a wide range in the level of funds available to them for advertising. Caribou Kayaks spends almost nothing on advertising, whereas some consumer goods giants are unfazed by the $900,000 cost of a 30-second TV ad during the Super Bowl.[20] If goal setting precedes budgeting, the goals can influence the amount of money budgeted. And if budgeting must come first, it will dictate some limits to the choices available for advertising.

There are several ways to set a budget. The basic alternatives were described in Chapter 18.

CREATING THE MESSAGE

"Where's the beef?" (Wendy's); "It's the real thing" (Coca-Cola); "Celebrate the moments of your life" (General Foods International Coffees); "We run the tightest ship in the shipping business" (UPS); "What you want is what you get" (McDonald's). All of these famous advertising slogans contain messages—the advertisers wanted you to remember not only the slogan, but what the slogan said about the good or service. Nonprofit advertisers also rely on memorable slogans, such as "This is your brain on drugs" (Partnership for a Drug-Free America).

Of course, the most effective advertising is more than a catchy slogan. It is information that the target audience cares about—the name of a good restaurant, the new-car models available this year, the current exhibit at a local art museum. To establish and build long-term relationships, it can be helpful to include useful general information in the advertising message. The Barn Nursery & Landscape Center publishes a newsletter full of gardening advice. The newsletter builds business because customers can see a benefit from reading it, and it then reminds them about the store.[21] In contrast, a brochure or print ad headlined simply with the company's name will generate less attention than an ad headline addressing a need. And the Miller Lite slogan "It's it and that's that" was roundly criticized—and quickly dropped—for telling consumers nothing.[22] (For more on slogans, see "Put It into Practice.")

APPEALS   The message is the guts of an advertisement. It must inform people about the product and persuade them to buy it. In addition, to move the target audience on

RECALL AND RECORD ADVERTISING SLOGANS

The heart of an effective advertising campaign is the message it sends to the target audience. A good slogan—one that packs a punch and makes the audience remember the product—contains the message. In this chapter's project, you'll begin planning your own advertisement. Part of that will be devising a slogan for a good or service.

Make yourself aware of various slogans in ads from different media. Which ones do you remember? Which ones are forgettable? How effective are they at conveying their message? Keep a journal in which you record the slogans you observe or recall over the next two weeks. By the time you're ready to come up with one of your own for the chapter project, you'll be able to evaluate it with a critical eye.

a more emotional level, a message can use any of several different types of appeals. Figure 19.5 illustrates one of the possibilities.

A *fear appeal* suggests that the advertiser is offering the target audience protection from some source of fear or unpleasantness. Thus, people can prevent a bad situation (say, financial ruin) by making a certain purchase (such as life or health insurance). Or people can improve an existing unpleasant situation (such as injuries from an auto accident or the need to care for an ill and aging parent) through a purchase (hiring an attorney or placing the parent in elder care).

Sex appeals suggest that purchasing a product will make the consumer more attractive. Products such as makeup and shampoo are obvious candidates for such appeals. They are also used for automobiles, alcohol, and even real estate.

Humor appeals rely on the target audience's sense of humor. In general, they are extremely effective for a short period of time, but they must be replaced often because jokes wear out quickly. (Part of the success of a joke is its surprise; once consumers have seen or heard the commercial, or read the ad, the joke becomes old rapidly.)

These are major categories, but many other appeals are used as well. Common examples include appeals to nostalgia, status, a sense of justice, and family values.

WORD CHOICES   Not only are certain appeals successful in getting the message across to consumers, but there are trends in particular words that help sell a product. These words change rapidly. For instance, the association of the word "clear" with products skyrocketed in the early 1990s. A review of applications for food and drink trademarks showed growing use of the words "light" or "lite," "nature" or "natural," "quality" and "value." In contrast, applications for trademarks using the words "heart," "pure," and "fresh" declined.[23] Presumably, such trends are responses to what consumers care about. Thus, it's important for marketers and members of the advertising industry to spot such trends and even to play a role in establishing them.

WRITING AD COPY   Usually, creating the message is the job of copywriters at ad agencies. These people must somehow convey the product's benefits in a way that catches and holds people's attention. While this demands a good deal of creativity, it also requires that the copywriter be sensitive to the needs of the client (advertiser) and understand the target audience. Thus, the vocabulary should be familiar to the target audience, and the benefits featured should be important to it.

The copywriter also should take into account the strategy for positioning the product. The message needs to reflect the product's intended image. To take a broad example, the message for a prestige product would emphasize not price but the product characteristics that make it distinctive.

The Designer Bag from Ruffies.

Next time you take out the trash, why not go out in style? With Ruffies® Color Scents®. A collection of designer-color trash bags with deodorizing potpourri scents. Now made with a stronger, concentrated plastic. And all for a price that's less than most plain, frumpy bags. Look for the new package design.

RUFFIES

COLOR SCENTS®

It's more. For less.

SELECTING THE MEDIA

Marketers want to choose the best media to reach their audience with their advertising message. Often, if they can afford it and it will be effective, marketers will select a mix of several media in order to reach the most people in the right audience. To make decisions about media, marketers must be familiar with a few basic terms used in media buying:

- *Reach*—the number of different people who will be exposed to an advertisement
- *Rating*—the percentage of households in a market that are tuned to a TV show or radio station
- *Frequency*—the average number of times a person in the target audience would be exposed to an advertisement
- *Cost per thousand*—the cost of reaching 1,000 people or households with an advertisement in one medium.

The decision about which medium (or media) to use must be based not only on cost but on who the target audiences are and where their members are located. The marketer also must consider which media best suit the positioning and type of product. For example, some products require extensive explanation or use of color. The basic media choices are television, radio, print, direct mail, and outdoor advertising.

TELEVISION   By far, television reaches the most people at once. A television commercial could potentially reach 95 percent of the households in the United States.[24] A TV commercial appeals to the senses through the use of music, voices, and other sounds as well as colorful pictures. Through the effective use of pictures and sounds, you can almost smell a Big Mac and feel the baby blanket softened in Downy fabric softener.

Television commercial campaigns are costly, but they reach a wide audience, potentially 95 percent of U.S. households. Burger King, however, has suffered through the past eight years with seven unsuccessful, and mostly unmemorable TV ad campaigns from "Herb" to "BK TeeVee." A recent campaign strategy is to go back to 1974 with Burger King's, "Have It Your Way."

But television has its downside, one being its high cost. Not only do networks charge an average of more than $100,000 for a 30-second spot in prime time, but there are production costs as well. Dave Thomas, founder of Wendy's International, points out that "a typical four- or five-day production for a series of television commercials costs about a million dollars."[25] Thus, its reach, rating, and frequency would be high, but so would its cost per thousand, depending on its time slot and whether it is shown only on a local station or nationwide. Its wide coverage can also be a drawback. The advertiser must pay to reach everyone who is watching, instead of just those people in the target audience. Finally, a viewer's exposure to a television commercial is short—usually 15 or 30 seconds. And the life of a commercial isn't very long—perhaps a few months. Part of the appeal of a new television commercial is its freshness and surprise, which quickly fade.

A relatively new twist on television is the infomercial, introduced earlier in "You Decide." These 30-minute blends of information and advertising enable the marketer to explain a product in greater depth than the standard TV commercial allows. Thus, they make television advertising suitable for more products and messages. When American Harvest, based in Chaska, Minnesota, introduced its Jet-Stream Oven, a "cyclonic cooking oven," it needed to explain this new type of product, so it used infomercials. And McDonald's aired an infomercial on Black Entertainment Television to provide information about the company's efforts to be socially responsible to the African-American community. Explains Stephanie Skurdy, McDonald's director of communications, "[African-American consumers] want to know what we are doing to support the community, and you can't tell it in 30 seconds."[26]

RADIO   It may seem as though radio is television's poor relation in many respects, struggling to stay alive. But there are many more radio stations in the United States than there are television stations. It costs much less to advertise on radio than it does on television, and advertisers are much more apt to reach their target audience—say, listeners who like country music, late-night talk shows, or business news. Radio is often effective for local businesses, from car dealerships to hardware stores.

True, radio commercials lack the visual effects of television. But a great deal of drama and illusion can be created with voices, music, and other sounds. Like television commercials, radio ads live a short life, and it is difficult to convey information that is abstract or complex. But an imaginative copywriter can streamline the message so that, with effective delivery, the audience understands and remembers it.

PRINT   Newspapers and magazines, depending on their content and circulation, can provide either broad exposure or exposure to a very specific market. Daily newspapers have the unique ability to give retailers the opportunity to advertise immediate events such as one-day sales. Airlines also frequently advertise short-notice fare changes in newspapers. Weekly sections on travel or food carry advertisements geared toward readers of those sections (for restaurants, hotels, and the like). The reach and cost for newspaper advertising can be very good, but frequency depends on how often the advertiser wants the ad to run as well as how often the newspaper is published (daily or weekly).

Magazines also are a healthy medium for advertisers: during the 1980s, 2,800 new magazines went on the market.[27] It's true that not all will survive, but magazines do have a large and varied audience. Advertisers can reach many thousands of readers in magazines like *Time* or *People* or more precisely target a category of consumers with specific interests in magazines like *Antique Monthly, Popular Photography,* and *Golf Digest.* Trade publications such as *Electrical Contractor* and *Convenience Store News* are an important way to reach organizational buyers in particular industries.

National magazines also allow advertisers to target a more specific audience within a larger audience. Sometimes national magazines publish special advertising sections. Ads in such a section reach an audience interested in the particular topic. Or the advertiser can reach selected geographic segments by running its ads in zoned or geographic editions of the national magazine. Thus, only some copies of the magazine will carry these advertisements, so the advertiser pays less than for full coverage and avoids wasted circulation.

Magazines reproduce color more effectively and precisely than do newspapers, and a magazine advertisement lasts longer than a newspaper ad if the magazine is published monthly, bi-monthly, or even quarterly. In addition, advertisers have opportunities to use attention-getting gimmicks such as pop-ups or sample packets of a product (such as hand lotion). But a magazine advertisement must be submitted weeks or even months in advance of publication, and the advertiser usually has little control over where the ad is placed in the magazine. A magazine ad also usually costs more than a newspaper ad, and often more than radio as well.

A form of print advertising that can be very effective for organizations serving a local market is the Yellow Pages. One advantage of advertising in the Yellow Pages is that individuals and organizations hang on to their copies for a year—far longer than they keep looking at a magazine. Another is that when people look in the Yellow Pages, they are generally planning to make purchases. And marketers can target their audience by more than geography; many specialized listings are available. Members of the Yellow Pages Publishers Associations publish directories in a variety of languages, including Chinese, Farsi, Korean, Russian, and Spanish.[28] A major disadvantage of Yellow Pages advertising is that it is hard to create an ad that stands out from the many others on the same page.

DIRECT MAIL   With direct mail, marketers can reach an audience targeted as most likely to be interested in a particular good or service. Probably everyone receives at least one piece of direct-mail advertising a day: catalogs, invitations to join nonprofit organizations, campaign flyers, newsletters, and advertisements for everything from credit cards to power tools. A piece of direct mail contains more information than a television commercial or magazine ad, which is helpful in describing complex or big-ticket items. And although many people claim to throw away most of the direct mail they receive, more than 90 million consumers in the United States responded to

As seen in this historical photo of Yankee Stadium, outdoor advertising has been very popular at baseball games and other sporting events.

advertisements they received in the mail in a recent year. They spent more than $180 billion on mail-order products.[29]

OUTDOOR   Outdoor advertising—billboards and posters such as those found on buses and in subway tunnels—has had its ups and downs in popularity. It has gone from the days of the historic Burma Shave billboards (which spelled out their message in progressive signs along the road) to today's clash with environmentalists who want outdoor advertising banned. From the 1920s to the 1960s, outdoor advertising was considered the most effective way to reach American consumers in rural regions. During the late 1960s, Ladybird Johnson's campaign to "beautify America" (thus eradicating billboards), along with corporate consolidation and restrictions on liquor and tobacco advertising, shoved outdoor advertising into decline. But billboards and transit ads remained strong in cities, and in 1990 gross billboard revenues totaled nearly $1.5 billion.[30]

The outdoor industry continues to struggle, looking for different types of advertisers. According to Tom Teepell, senior vice president of the Institute of Outdoor Advertising (IOA) in New York, "Industrywide, the big boom in both transit advertising and billboards seems to be in retail. Suddenly, we're seeing major chains like Introspect and Benetton—as well as your local merchants—becoming heavy users of outdoor."[31] In addition, marketers for regional tourism and the entertainment business are using outdoor more frequently. Cher Suserud, vice president of communications at Gannett Outdoor, notes that "more and more studios—Paramount, Warner Bros., United Artists—have started buying outdoor all across the country to promote their movies to the general public."[32]

Therein lies one of the advantages—and disadvantages—of outdoor advertising. A poster or billboard reaches many people. But it does not target an audience, except by geographic location. A good billboard must be eye-catching to drivers without completely distracting them, and since drivers see it for only a few seconds, written copy must be kept to a minimum.

Most outdoor ads are on posters. One reason may be that billboards aren't cheap. Depending on location as well as the complexity of producing the board itself (if it has lights or moving parts), it can cost as much as a television commercial. Universal Studios in Florida has some billboards that cost $100,000 each: one with King Kong shaking his fist and another on which E.T.'s finger lights up and his eyes roll around.[33]

OTHER MEDIA   Creative marketers—especially those trying to stretch a small budget—don't have to stop with the basic options. A familiar alternative is to place the company's name on athletes and their equipment. According to one account, placing a logo on a NASCAR race car would get the sponsor "exposure time" equivalent to over $200 million in advertising.[34] Audio Computer Information grabs attention for its weekly radio program by promoting it through Western Union's DeskMail. The company's cofounder, John Stewart, prepares one-page messages on his computer and sends them via modem to Western Union, which formats and sends them telegram-style.[35] To announce the opening of a store in Sunnyvale, California, J. C. Penney sent local households a 4½-minute videocassette showing off the store.[36] And a Roswell, Georgia, company called Space Marketing arranged with NASA to place advertising on the side of a rocket used to launch a satellite. The advertiser got 58 feet of ad space for about $500,000.[37]

Several programmers have been developing screen-saver software that includes advertising. The software displays moving images when the screen has been unchanged for some time, so that the constant images won't burn a permanent image into the user's computer screen. Such software has existed for some time. What is new is that these versions feature brand-name images. Software by PC Dynamics of Westlake Village, California, shows the Energizer Bunny marching across the screen. Home Run Software Productions has developed a version featuring Nike athletic shoes.[38] The question is whether these are an effective way to bring reminder advertising to computer users—or simply a way to annoy them. (That same issue has limited the use of advertising in movie theaters, a practice that has annoyed most patrons.)

PRETESTING

pretest
The testing of one or more versions of an advertisement before launching the whole campaign.

Once the goals and budget have been set, the message has been created, and the media have been selected, marketers often decide to **pretest** one or more versions of the advertisement. This involves observing a test audience's responses to the advertisement before completely launching the ad campaign. If the target audience for the pretest doesn't respond as expected, the marketers can modify the ad campaign before bearing the total expenses involved.

The marketer can choose from among several types of pretests. In a *portfolio test,* participants read a portfolio that contains the ad along with other ads and written material. Then the researcher questions them about the ad: Was it memorable? Was it informative? In a *jury test,* a panel of consumers views an ad and then rates it according to how attractive and informative it is, as well as how successfully it catches attention. *Theater tests* are a little more involved. Consumers watch new television shows or movies in which the new ads are also shown, then indicate their reactions to the advertisements with small recording devices or fill out questionnaires after the preview.

Evaluation and Control

Once the ad campaign has been launched, the advertiser's job turns to evaluating its effectiveness and making any necessary changes. The basic approach to evaluation is to conduct posttesting. The changes may take the form of reallocating resources or conducting follow-up advertising.

posttest
Testing that evaluates the success or failure of an ad after it has run.

POSTTESTING

Several types of **posttests** help marketers quantify the success of an ad by evaluating the ad after it has run.[39] With *aided recall,* marketers show consumers an ad, then ask

FIGURE 19.6

Starch Readership
Report

where consumers have seen it in the past: Was it something they read? Something they heard? Something they saw? A popular variation of this type of test is the *Starch Readership Report.* Interviewers for Starch ask readers of selected magazines whether they remember certain ads in those magazines. For large ads, the interviewer asks about specific parts of the ad, using a copy of the magazine as an aid for doing so. The results of the Starch Readership Report are presented as scores reflecting the percentage of respondents who read the ad as a whole and each part of the ad (see Figure 19.6).

With *unaided recall,* marketers simply ask participants what ads they saw recently. In a quarterly survey, Video Storyboard Tests asks consumers, "What is the most outstanding TV commercial you've seen in the last four weeks?" The answers enable marketers to determine whether participants are aware of any advertising messages without leading them to report ads they would not have remembered without a reminder. However, it can be harder for the marketer to gather reactions to a particular ad, because many participants may not recall it. Also, with both types of recall tests, the marketer is not measuring the ad's effect, if any, on buyer behavior.

Attitude tests are designed to measure how effective the advertising campaign is in creating a favorable attitude toward the product or organization. A typical approach is to conduct a survey asking members of the target audience to rate the ad, the organization, and its products relative to competitors. The assumption is that people with a favorable attitude toward the product will be likely to buy it.

To more directly measure buying behavior, the marketer may use *inquiry tests.* To conduct such tests, the marketer includes in the advertisement an offer that requires some type of response. The offer might be for free information, samples, coupons, or other promotional items. The number of inquiries (or sales in the case of coupons) that result is used as a measure of the ad's effectiveness in generating a response.

Sales tests involve an effort to find a link between the advertisement and the level of sales. Thus, the marketer might conduct an experiment using outdoor advertising in one area and radio advertising in another. Or the marketer might use two different versions of the same print ad or compare sales levels with an old and new ad campaign. In all these cases, it is difficult, even impossible, to control all the variables. Thus, differences in weather patterns or the economy can lead to shifts in sales volume that are unrelated to the advertising campaign.

Another type of sales test is to combine the advertising with a promotion that allows the marketer to link responses to the ads. Direct Tire Sales, located near Boston, promised in its radio ads that it would donate 3 percent of all radio-generated sales to a local charity. Customers were happy to help the charity by telling Direct that they were responding to the ads.[40]

Just as it is important for marketers to choose the right media for an advertising campaign, so it is important for them to try to choose the best method of posttesting to get an accurate reading of the effectiveness of an ad. For instance, sales tests, while elaborate, are also expensive; marketers might be able to get equally useful information by using one of the other methods.

FOLLOW-UP ADVERTISING

After evaluating an advertising campaign, marketers may decide to make some changes. If posttests show that consumers aren't responding to posters in a certain area, marketers can reduce the emphasis on outdoor advertising. If tests show that the message simply isn't getting across, marketers may decide to rework it or scrap it and start again with a new message. If tests show that more television exposure is essential, marketers may shift the budget to accommodate this.

In essence, evaluation and control is like a post-game analysis: marketers determine which plays resulted in a touchdown or field goal and which ended in a fumble.

Sales Promotion

sales promotion
Media and nonmedia marketing effort applied for a predetermined, limited period at the level of consumers or intermediaries in order to stimulate trial, increase consumer demand, or improve product availability.

Marketers often think of sales promotion as a supplement to other elements of the communications mix. **Sales promotion** is media and nonmedia marketing effort applied for a predetermined, limited period at the level of consumers or intermediaries in order to stimulate trial, increase consumer demand, or improve product availability. One example is the sweepstakes advertised in the Kawasaki *Good Times* publication in which a Nissan 4×4 SE-V6 King Cab and a Kawasaki motorcycle or Jet Ski® SuperSport Watercraft were the prizes (see Figure 19.7).

Sales promotions do have their drawbacks. They are short-lived. Marketers may also find it difficult to limit the sales promotion to a target market. For example, many different types of consumers are exposed to supermarket coupons. Another challenge with sales promotions is making comparisons among competitors' activities because sales promotions take many different forms, from a trade show exhibit to a banner flying behind an airplane to a clown waving people into a shopping mall. In addition, some sales promotions are costly, and the publicity they can generate is out of the marketer's control. In Nicaragua, Coca-Cola used a sweepstakes with a cash prize worth about $8,250. A local newspaper printed the wrong winning number, and 3,000 people tried to claim the prize, mobbing a local bottling plant. Coke refused to pay, and many consumers responded with a boycott.[41]

A Sales Promotion in the Form of a Sweepstakes

A frequent concern about sales promotions is that because many involve a short-term price break, they erode brand loyalty by encouraging customers to make selections based on price. This view was supported by a drop in consumers' brand loyalty over the last decade, just when price-related promotions were assuming a major role. According to marketing researchers at NPD Group, though, promotions have little effect on brand loyalty over the long run; brands that are well supported by advertising remain strong.[42]

On the other hand, sales promotions tend to garner quick results—in most cases, much faster than advertising. And just as the uniqueness of a sales promotion may render it difficult to pin down for evaluation, it can also lead to enormous success, imprinting the product's name in customers' minds. Entrepreneurs who are creative by nature can make valuable use of sales promotions on a tight budget, as did Ken Meyers, creator of Smartfood popcorn. Meyers hired skiers to dress in giant popcorn bags and ski the slopes of several New England resorts while he handed out free bags of Smartfood at the base.

TYPES OF SALES PROMOTION

In general, sales promotion may be consumer oriented or trade oriented. This means that the techniques the marketer selects will depend in part on whether the sales promotion is aimed at end users (consumers) or intermediaries (the trade).

consumer promotion
Sales promotion directed toward consumers of a good or service.

CONSUMER PROMOTIONS   Sales promotions may be directed toward the consumers of a good or service. These promotions are used to bolster the organization's advertising and sales efforts. Most **consumer promotions** take the forms summarized in Table 19.1: coupons, deals, premiums, samples, contests and sweepstakes, and

TABLE 19.1	TECHNIQUE	PRIMARY OBJECTIVE(S)
Techniques for Consumer Sales Promotions	Coupons	Stimulate demand through a temporary price cut; encourage retailer support
	Deals	Stimulate demand through a temporary price cut
	Premiums	Attract new customers; build goodwill
	Contests and sweepstakes	Build awareness and sales of the product
	Samples	Encourage product trials by minimizing the risk to consumers; especially useful for new, low-cost, and frequently purchased products
	Point-of-purchase displays	Increase trials and sales by drawing attention to the product in the store; educate consumers about the product; especially useful for convenience goods and impulse purchases
	Rebates	Encourage sales through a temporary price cut

rebates. Each type has its advantages and disadvantages, and marketers must determine which is the best method for reaching consumers and enticing them to buy.

Coupons   Coupons are one of the most-used types of consumer sales promotion.[43] In a recent year, U.S. consumers redeemed 7.7 billion coupons, with an average face value of 58 cents.[44] The use of coupons is growing in the United States and in many other countries, including Canada and the United Kingdom. In contrast, coupons are rarely worth using in Germany, where the law limits coupon discounts to 1 percent of the product's value.[45] Because coupons offer a price break, they are particularly effective during times when economic growth is uncertain or sluggish.

Coupons can work for both large and small businesses, in a variety of ways. Most coupons are printed on freestanding inserts, the usually glossy sheets that fall out of your Sunday paper. Others are distributed on the product packaging, in magazines and newspapers, and in the store. When the objective of coupons is to get consumers to switch brands, in-store distribution can be effective. Some checkout systems can be programmed to print a coupon whenever the scanner reads that the consumer is purchasing a competing brand.[46] "Direct mail to your local area is probably the best way to reach local customers," claims Bob Bennett, vice president of marketing at Promotion Fulfillment Corp. in Camanche, Iowa.[47] But this method is expensive. Marketers with tighter budgets can leave coupons on the windshields of parked cars, slip them onto doorknobs, or in the case of store retailing, hand them to customers who walk into the business.

To be effective, a coupon has to offer something the consumer wants, at an attractive savings. "Nothing works as well as the word *free*," notes Bob Bennett. "Offers of 'buy one, get one free' or 'buy one, get french fries free' get the best response."[48] According to NCH Promotional Services, the largest coupon processor and promotion information manager in the world (based in Lincolnshire, Illinois), coupons that grant cents off on the product should offer at least a 40 percent savings if the goal is to get consumers to try something new.[49]

Marketers that use coupons should track the rate at which they are redeemed so that they can evaluate the success of the promotion. Many retailers today gather this information by reading the bar codes on the coupons and including coupon redemption information in their scanning databases. Quaker Direct, a direct marketing arm of

The Vision Value Network, at some grocery store checkout areas, is a compact, in-store system that allows a retailer to deliver promotions and instant savings with paper and paperless coupons, personalized letters, sweepstakes, and even video messages.

The Quaker Oats Company, took a sophisticated approach to coupon tracking. Quaker had embedded in each coupon a number identifying the household to which it was sent. Within a few months, Quaker could track which coupons were redeemed by which household. This information enables the company to better tailor its future mailings.[50] Many producers arrange for service bureaus to handle the tasks of processing coupons and collecting data on their redemption.

Another control issue is whether the coupon is generating sales from new customers or merely enabling existing customers to buy at a lower price. According to a recent study, 99 percent of households surveyed reported using a coupon in the preceding year. Of these, 90 percent used them for products they usually buy, and only 32 percent used them to try new brands.[51]

Deals   A deal is simply a short-term price reduction. Your local supermarket may feature a two-day special, such as two boxes of macaroni-and-cheese dinner for the price of one. Not only does a deal like this move inventory off the store's shelves, it keeps the consumer's kitchen stocked. As a result, the consumer is likely to use the product more often and is less apt to buy a competitor's macaroni-and-cheese dinner.

Premiums   Another sales promotion technique is to offer merchandise for free or at a very low price. These free or low-cost items are called premiums. Gas stations hand out free glassware with fill-ups, and fast-food restaurants sell small toys (such as dolls that tie in with popular movie characters) for a minimum price with the purchase of a meal. Direct Tire Sales generated sales by offering $80 in ski lift tickets with the purchase of a set of new tires.[52]

Another type of premium is the advertising specialty, an item imprinted with the organization's name. Many items are used as specialties; some common examples are calendars, pencils, golf balls, and refrigerator magnets. This approach to using premiums is common for marketing to organizations as well as consumers. The marketer may have salespeople leave the specialties with prospects they call on, or it may send them to its customers or prospects.

FIGURE 19.8

**An Example of a
Point-of-Purchase
Display**

Contests and Sweepstakes   Although both give consumers a chance to win prizes, contests and sweepstakes are different. To be eligible to win a prize in a contest, consumers must complete a task, such as answering trivia questions or drawing a picture. In Calgary, Alberta, Melitta (producer of coffee makers) sponsored a contest in which a radio station broadcast actors speaking lines from famous movies. Callers who identified the name of the actor and movie were eligible to win Melitta products. To enter a sweepstakes drawing, consumers need only complete an entry form; the sweepstakes is purely a game of chance.

Contests and sweepstakes in the United States are regulated by the Federal Trade Commission. FTC regulations are designed to ensure that contests and sweepstakes are fair, that the odds for and against winning are presented clearly, and that prizes are actually awarded to winners.

Samples   Probably every consumer has received free samples of products in the mail: shampoo, toothpaste, laundry detergent, cereal, even diapers. In addition, when you open many magazines, you are sure to find tiny packets of makeup and envelopes of perfume attached to advertisements. The intent of these samples is for consumers to try the product, like it, remember it, and buy it. To reach college students, many marketers provide samples at party-style marketing events with names such as College Fest and Campus Fest, where students can enjoy live music along with the sales pitches.[53]

Sampling is expensive. Therefore, marketers are most apt to give away samples of products that are new, cost little to produce, and are purchased frequently. For these products, inducing a trial is likely to have a great impact on sales.

Point-of-Purchase Displays   To draw shoppers' attention to a product once they are in a store, marketers use point-of-purchase (POP) displays. These are in-store signs, bins, or other devices that hold and advertise a product at the same time. Figure 19.8

shows an example. Sometimes the displays are accompanied by an in-store demonstration or free samples such as crackers, appetizer dip, or bottled sauces.

Point-of-purchase displays help a product to stand out from others on the shelves. According to a study by Information Resources Inc., POP displays boosted sales of laundry detergent by 207 percent, sales of frozen dinners by 245 percent, and sales of soft drinks by 138 percent.[54] POP displays introducing Doodle O's cheese snacks were so effective they sometimes had to be refilled daily rather than weekly, as planned.

Rebates   Rebates are a return of money with proof of purchase of a product. Manufacturers of everything from autos to hair dryers to light bulbs use rebates to entice consumers to buy their products. Buyers are more apt to take advantage of a rebate on a big-ticket item such as an automobile, but often they don't bother to clip a proof-of-purchase seal, fill out a mailing label, and spend extra money on postage to mail in a rebate offer on an inexpensive, frequently purchased product such as shaving lotion or film. As a result, manufacturers of these products can induce consumers to buy without actually paying the rebates.

trade promotion
Sales promotion directed toward wholesalers or retailers.

TRADE PROMOTIONS   Other sales promotions, called **trade promotions,** are aimed at intermediaries: wholesalers and retailers. Although these efforts are largely invisible to most consumers, they are significant to marketers. Over the last decade, producers of consumer goods have been spending more on trade promotion than on advertising. Some types of consumer promotions, such as samples and deals, are also used as trade promotions, but others are unique to the trade.

Allowances   Trade allowances are of several kinds. A *merchandise allowance* is paid to a retailer for featuring a product prominently. A *case allowance* is a straight discount on a case of the product ordered by the retailer or wholesaler. A *finance allowance* covers expenses related to consumer promotions. And many retailers require *slotting allowances* in exchange for adding a new product to their shelves.

The nature, quantity, and timing of allowances are often a matter of industry practice. However, a creative marketer can make these types of trade promotion a basis for competitive advantage. The marketer can learn which types of allowances are most significant to its intermediaries and make sure to offer and communicate these. The Quaker Oats Company took a fresh look at its use of trade allowances and realized it could get more value by adjusting the way it timed them. Now Quaker times trade allowances to reflect patterns in consumer demand. Offering greater allowances when demand is lower enables Quaker to even out demand, thereby reducing production and distribution costs. Intermediaries are happy, too, because this tactic helps them keep their inventories lower.[55]

Cooperative Advertising and Sales Support   Marketers may also engage in cooperative advertising with retailers and/or help train a distributor's sales force to sell the product more effectively. This last effort is most important in the case of goods or services that require technical knowledge.

Trade Shows   Marketers in many fields participate in trade shows, events that are designed to bring marketers and customers together in one location over a short period of time—usually three or four days. Thousands of such events take place each year in the United States alone. At trade shows, marketers exhibit their goods and services to potential customers in the trade. Trade shows are also useful for reaching organizational buyers, especially for marketers of big-ticket items. In addition, marketers working at a trade show have a chance to see what their competitors are doing.

According to the Trade Show Bureau (TSB), customers attend these events for two main reasons: to update their knowledge in the field and to shop for the goods and services they need.[56] (The same TSB survey says that eight out of ten attendees are there to keep current on industry changes; seven out of ten make actual purchasing decisions; nine out of ten use the shows to gather information that will lead to later purchases.[57]) Although exhibiting in a trade show may be expensive, and certainly marketers should choose carefully which shows are likely to be beneficial, the returns can be lucrative.

ETHICAL ISSUES IN SALES PROMOTION

As with advertising, sales promotion in the United States is regulated by the Federal Trade Commission. As mentioned, the FTC regulates sweepstakes and contests for fairness and legitimacy. Of course, as in other areas, avoiding legal problems is a minimal standard of ethical behavior.

Marketers that want to offer premiums should keep in mind that the item they offer for little or nothing may be a product that other organizations are in business to sell for a profit. The popularity of videos as a sales promotion, for example, probably cuts into video dealers' sales. A few Decembers back, McDonald's offered cassettes of *Dances with Wolves* for $7.99 to customers who also bought food. The Video Software Dealers Association complained that some dealers were stocking up on the video at McDonald's outlets without a food purchase. Said an association spokesperson, "If you can buy a brand new Academy Award–winning movie for $8, you put in the consumer's mind that's all it's worth."[58] Is this type of promotion unethical or just smart marketing strategy?

Sampling can pose ethical problems when access to the product should be limited. Sampling of cigarettes poses obvious problems because these can fall into the hands of minors, and tobacco companies have come under fire for allegedly promoting smoking among young people. Is it the tobacco company's responsibility to ensure that the cigarettes are given only to adults who smoke? If so, how can it do this? Similar issues arise with other products that should have limited access—say, over-the-counter medicines or previews of R-rated movies.

In the case of rebates, an ethical issue arises with regard to the likelihood a real benefit is offered. A marketer might make obtaining the rebate so inconvenient or complicated that many consumers just don't bother. Marketers must ask themselves whether such a consequence is deliberate—and possibly unethical.

In situations that are not strictly regulated by the government, marketers must use their own judgment. If there is any doubt about the ethics of a certain promotion in the mind of the marketer, it's a good idea to check the promotion carefully.

Publicity

publicity
Non-paid-for communication of information about the organization or product, generally in some media form.

Whether or not they think of it as part of the communications effort, all organizations are concerned about the kind of publicity they generate. **Publicity** is non-paid-for communication of information about the organization or product, generally in some media form. At a large organization, generating favorable publicity is usually the job of a public relations director. In smaller companies, publicity can be the job of marketers, the owner, and other employees. Indeed, in a quality-focused organization, publicity—presenting a positive image of the company—is the job of all employees.

Because it is nonpaid and usually reported by the media as news (and therefore considered objective), publicity carries a lot of weight with the general public. Good publicity can greatly enhance the image of a company. Bad publicity, on the other hand, can cause real damage.

TYPES OF PUBLICITY

Publicity comes in many forms. The most common are news stories and public service announcements. News stories initiated by the media themselves allow the marketer little, if any, control over the message. Therefore, public relations people (or company spokespeople) must be able to think on their feet, conducting interviews calmly and confidently.

Public service announcements (PSAs) are free space or time donated by media to nonprofit organizations for socially responsible messages. Partnership for a Drug-Free America, United Negro College Fund, the Red Cross, and Save the Children are just a few of the organizations that rely on public service announcements for publicity.

GENERATING PUBLICITY

Marketers generate news stories in whatever ways are likely to attract favorable media coverage. The simplest approach is to circulate press releases. Marketers may also host news conferences and stage attention-getting events.

PRESS RELEASES   A press release (also called a news release) is an article written by company members and distributed to the media—newspapers, magazines, and television and radio stations. A press release is like a mini–news story; it provides the media with information about the organization or product as well as names and phone numbers of marketers (or public relations people) at the company who can be contacted for further details.

A press release gives the marketer some control over news coverage by allowing the marketer to decide when to make an announcement and what information to include. It does not, however, guarantee that the media will publish or broadcast a story. Nor does it ensure that the media will present the story exactly as the press release does.

Some organizations hire an outside publicist to generate publicity, but this activity can be carried out within the communications or marketing team. The person assigned to the job should be familiar with different reporters and their reporting and writing styles. The press release should be directed to the reporters most likely to be interested in the type of news it contains. In preparing a press release, the following tips can help:[59]

- Keep it short. A single page is best.
- Use clear, concise language, avoiding jargon.
- Polish up the lead (first sentence or paragraph) so that it grabs the reader's attention.
- Cite major facts or statistics.
- Include the name and phone number of the person on the publicity team who can be contacted to verify the story.

Also, because reporters receive many more press releases than they can or want to use, marketers keep looking for ways to make their press releases stand out. To get publicity for his Great Scott! fudge, Jim Scott includes a sample with the press releases he sends. The fudge has been featured in *Bon Appétit, Food & Wine, Chocolatier,* the *Los Angeles Times,* and the *New York Times.*[60]

NEWS CONFERENCES   The marketer can also communicate with the media through news conferences (also called press conferences). The marketer invites reporters to the news conference and usually provides them with advance information. A spokesperson for the organization may read a prepared statement, answer questions from the media, or both. Again, this gives the company some control over coverage, but there is no guarantee that the media will attend or will ask questions that the spokesperson wants to answer.

ACTIVITIES AND EVENTS   The media see more than enough stories about new products, modifications to products, and newly hired executives. To break through the clutter, marketers may stage events designed to attract the attention of the media as well as the public. To draw attention on its tenth anniversary, a law firm in Orlando commissioned two photographers to create photos celebrating 20 local companies, 10 of which were the law firm's clients. Not only did the resulting exhibit receive favorable publicity in the local press, but the local historical museum added the photos to its collection.[61] On a sillier note, British Knights, a marketer of sneakers, sponsored what it called the "World's Smelliest Socks Contest." The prize? A free pair of sneakers, of course.[62] As in these examples, the key is to create events that are somehow favorably linked to the organization or its products.

In addition, marketers keep alert for opportunities to inform the media about activities involving the organization or its product in interesting ways. Following an oil spill in Tampa Bay, Tri-State Bird Rescue & Research concluded that Procter & Gamble's Dawn dishwashing detergent was the best product for cleaning oil off birds. P&G responded by sending 30 cases of Dawn to Florida to help with the rescue effort.[63]

Thus, there are as many ways to generate publicity as there are ideas in the minds of marketers. "Marketing Movers & Shakers" tells about ways that Barry Buchanan, owner and designer of Caribou Kayaks, uses his imagination to generate publicity. For instance, he once sold a kayak to the associate director of a new museum in Atlanta, who then exhibited the kayak in the museum's rotunda.

MANAGING BAD PUBLICITY

In June of 1993, a consumer claimed to have found a syringe in a can of Diet Pepsi. Over the next few days, more consumers across the United States made similar claims. No one could figure out how a person could tamper with a sealed can of soda. Even at the plant, the open cans were only exposed for less than a second before being sealed. Based on evidence, Pepsi-Cola Company declared the claims to be a hoax. The company turned out to be correct, and sales were largely unaffected. If the claims had been true, or the incident had been less effectively managed, the negative publicity could have been devastating for Pepsi-Cola. Recalling cans of soda and managing bad news at the start of the summer season could have caused the company significant losses.[64]

Depending on the severity of the event, it can take time for a company's damaged image to recover. These days, no one thinks twice about using Tylenol, but in the late

Marketing Movers & Shakers

BARRY BUCHANAN'S CARIBOU KAYAKS

Spectators crane their necks and squint as the tiny kayaks inch into view, their owners paddling furiously. On a hot July day, racers in the Blackburn Challenge maneuver their sea kayaks along the Massachusetts coast. Kayaking, an ancient mode of travel, has become a popular sport in rivers and along coastal waters.

Thirty-five-year-old entrepreneur Barry Buchanan is counting on the sport's increasing popularity. He is the creator of Caribou Kayaks, custom-built sea kayaks of his own design. Seven of his boats, paddled by customers, are in this year's Blackburn Challenge. He wants a winner.

Buchanan, who has always loved fine carpentry, learned to build boats at The Hinckley Company, maker of luxury wooden sailing yachts in Bar Harbor, Maine. While employed at Hinckley, he did a few of his own backyard boat projects; when he built a dory in his living room from plans in a book and sold it, he knew he wanted his own business. He'd taken up sea kayaking (rather than whitewater kayaking) because he lived close to

the ocean. He couldn't afford to buy a kayak, so he built one. Besides, he had some ideas for improving on sea kayak design.

A friend put up the money for a couple of boats, and Buchanan's new kayak appeared in a local boating magazine. Suddenly, Caribou Kayaks —a one-man company with a name that evokes Maine—was afloat.

"I placed an ad once," recalls Buchanan when asked about his advertising budget. He operates on a shoestring, relying on Yankee ingenuity for publicity and other types of marketing communication. He knows he's got a high-quality, distinctive product: the Caribou has a unique design, lightweight construction, and colorful paint finish (each unique) that sets it apart from other sea kayaks. Buchanan is a perfectionist, spending many weeks on each boat. He's also a savvy marketer who says he has "no background in business or marketing." His publicity efforts include:

- Contacting the local newspaper and TV station often. He maintains a good relationship with reporters and editors. For instance, Buchanan knew that the television assignment editor was from Buchanan's own town of Bass Harbor. So he mailed the editor a letter and pictures of his boats. A reporter went to Buchanan's workshop and did a human-interest piece on him. The newspaper periodically covers developments at Caribou—updates in design, races, and so forth.
- Calling and writing to any publication with boating or Maine subject matter, even driving the boats to the offices of some publications for editors to see.

- Starting the Acadia Sea Kayak Club—organizing meetings, speakers, and paddling expeditions. He also attends meetings of other sea kayak clubs, along with gatherings hosted by outdoor organizations such as the Appalachian Mountain Club.
- Writing directly to potential (and past) customers, personally visiting as many as possible.
- Producing a homemade promotional video of Caribou Kayaks in action.
- Giving away Caribou Kayaks hats and T-shirts.
- Leaving business cards on parked cars that have kayak racks on their roofs.
- Participating in special paddling efforts, such as an organized circumnavigation of Mt. Desert Island, to raise money for awareness of charitable causes.

Customers themselves provide excellent publicity. "I was actually paddling the most natural-feeling, stable boat that I'd ever been in," wrote customer Jim Skeen of the Caribou in an article for *ANorAK*, a kayaking publication. Skeen also happens to be associate director of Fern Bank Natural History Museum in Atlanta, and arranged to showcase his Caribou in the rotunda shortly after the museum's opening.

Then there are the sea kayak racers who glide into the limelight in their Caribous. One of those paddlers in the Blackburn Challenge hopes to make a bid for the 1996 Olympics. Others slice through the surf simply chasing after a personal best, which is what Caribou Kayaks is all about.

Sources: Personal interview with Barry Buchanan, creator and owner of Caribou Kayaks; Tamsin Venn, *Sea Kayaking Along the New England Coast* (Boston: Appalachian Mountain Club Books, 1991), pp. 15–18; Jim Skeen, "My Boat—The Caribou," *ANorAK*, April/May 1992, p. 15.

1970s, when a number of consumers died after ingesting Tylenol capsules that had been tampered with, the manufacturers of Tylenol surely wondered whether the product would survive. A catastrophic event such as this can, in fact, bring about some good changes in industry: now, many products carry tamper-resistant seals.

Decisions made by Pepsi CEO Craig Weatherup are credited with bringing the hoax that there were syringes found in cans of Diet Pepsi to a swift end.

Managing this type of publicity may seem like an impossible task, but for a company that believes in quality, it should be a matter of common sense. Marketers should not be defensive or panicky. They should tell the truth, presenting the necessary facts. The company should act in the most socially responsible way possible, then take the opportunity to let the media—and the public—know what positive changes have been made. When presidential candidate Bill Clinton had his personal integrity questioned by a woman who claimed to have had an extramarital affair with him, Clinton managed the bad publicity by acknowledging former problems in his marriage but refusing to offer details. He and his wife, Hillary Rodham Clinton, granted interviews to let the public know that their marriage was now secure. By doing this, Clinton made himself seem more human, less like a polished politician; thus, American voters were quick to forget the issue and move on to real election concerns.

Finally, a marred relationship with the press itself can cause problems. When Wal-Mart Stores suddenly stopped its twice-weekly ads in the *Nashville News,* the publisher was stunned and angry. During the four years the store had been in the area, its competitors had dropped out, so the paper had come to depend on frequent advertising from Wal-Mart. Publisher Louis Graves didn't take the blow lightly, stating that every press release received from Wal-Mart would go "right into the trash. I don't give free publicity to companies that don't help pay the light bill around here." The situation is similar in Snyder, Texas, where Wal-Mart distributes advertising circulars by mail rather than through the local *Daily News.* Publisher Roy McQueen admitted openly that the company's refusal to advertise in the *Daily News* affected his coverage. When Sam Walton, founder of Wal-Mart, visited the local store, McQueen declined to cover the event: "I told them, 'Thanks but no thanks.' If we don't have a readership worth advertising to, why should they want us to run a photograph?"[65] Perhaps both parties are right. Wal-Mart should not be forced to advertise if it doesn't need to, but neither are newspapers required to cover all stories. Wal-Mart will have to assess the price of no publicity in small towns.

ETHICAL ISSUES IN PUBLICITY

This section has already touched on one ethical issue in publicity: managing negative publicity truthfully. Telling the truth also applies to positive publicity. Just as in advertising, press releases and news conferences should state nothing that is misleading, unfair, or possibly detrimental to the consumer. Further, to maintain credibility, a publicity message should say something of substance rather than just be a transparent attempt to get the attention of the media. A company that practices quality marketing should have no problem maintaining high ethical standards when it comes to publicity.

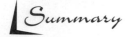

Summary

The main function of advertising is to inform customers about a product and persuade them to buy it, but advertising may also be used to remind consumers about a product. Product advertising attempts to sell a product and is aimed at either end users or channel members. Institutional advertising promotes an organization's image or philosophy.

A company may produce its own advertising or work with an outside advertising agency to develop an advertising campaign. Either way, advertisers must first set the goals and budget for the campaign. Next, they create the message, which is the heart of the campaign, and the slogan, which carries the message. Then they select among media for the mix best suited to the product and market: television, radio, print, direct mail, and outdoor. Just before the campaign is fully launched, advertisers conduct pretests to determine the effectiveness of the ad. Finally, after the ad has run, posttests are conducted to quantify its success.

Sales promotion is media and nonmedia marketing effort applied for a predetermined, limited time period at the level of consumers or intermediaries in order to stimulate trial, increase consumer demand, or improve product availability. Sales promotion may be directed to consumers or the trade. Consumer promotions include coupons, deals, premiums, contests and sweepstakes, samples, point-of-purchase displays, and rebates. Trade promotions (aimed at wholesalers and retailers) may use variations of consumer promotions as well as merchandise allowances, case allowances, finance allowances, and trade shows.

Publicity is the non-paid-for communication of information about the organization or product, generally in some media form. The most common forms of publicity are news stories and public service announcements. Marketers can generate publicity by distributing press releases, hosting news conferences, and staging special events. However, the media decide whether and how to cover a story. Because publicity is nonpaid and considered more objective than advertising or sales promotion, publicity carries a lot of weight with the public. Negative publicity may be damaging to an organization's image, but it can be managed effectively by ethical marketers.

KEY TERMS AND CONCEPTS

advertising (p. 566)

product advertising (p. 567)

institutional advertising (p. 567)

pioneering advertising (p. 567)

competitive advertising (p. 567)

comparative advertising (p. 567)

advocacy advertising (p. 568)

reminder advertising (p. 568)

cooperative advertising (p. 568)

corrective advertising (p. 569)

advertising agency (p. 571)

target audience (p. 573)

pretest (p. 581)

posttest (p. 581)

sales promotion (p. 583)

consumer promotion (p. 584)

trade promotion (p. 588)

publicity (p. 589)

REVIEW AND DISCUSSION QUESTIONS

1. Do you think regulations governing comparative advertising should be stricter in the United States or more relaxed than they already are? Why?
2. If you were a marketer planning an ad campaign for a line of frozen yogurt, what would be some of the specific goals you might set?
3. What type of budgeting would you use for your frozen yogurt ad campaign, and why? (Take into consideration the size of your company and your goals.)
4. Which type of appeal do you think would work best for your message about frozen yogurt? Why?
5. What are some advantages and disadvantages of the following advertising media?
   a. television
   b. newspapers
   c. outdoor

6. How does posttesting help the overall ad campaign?
7. Imagine you are a marketer for a chain of sporting goods stores. Your communications objective is to increase sales by bringing in new customers.
   a. What, if any, kinds of sales promotions would you use? How would you use each choice?
   b. What additional issues would you consider if your chain operated in Europe as well as the United States? How would these issues affect your choice of sales promotions?
8. In what ways could you generate good publicity about the sporting goods store and bring in new customers?
9. An accounting firm decides to target small businesses in the local community. How might it use advertising, sales promotion, and publicity to generate business from its target market?

Chapter Project
Create Your Own Advertisement

This is a chance for you to be creative. Make your own advertisement. Choose a good or service from the list below, one from a previous chapter project, or one of your own. First, set your goals and budget. Next, work on your message and slogan. Select a medium for your advertisement (print, direct mail, or outdoor would work best for this project). Then design your ad. (You don't have to be an artist or graphic designer to do this.)

With your ad, grab the audience's attention and make people remember your product. Use an appeal of fear, nostalgia, or humor if you think it is appropriate; use a drawing or photograph if it is eye-catching and relevant. Above all, use your imagination and good marketing sense!

Show your ad to two members of your target audience. Ask them for their reactions. Does their understanding of the ad match your intended message?

Product ideas:
- A line of greeting cards
- Sunglasses for children
- Party supplies
- A hotel geared toward business clients
- A catering service specializing in exotic or ethnic foods

Case
Wendy's International

Clara Peller frowned at the hamburger and complained, "Where's the beef?" That line launched her—and Wendy's International—to fame and fortune. Before that television commercial was aired in 1984, only 34 percent of Americans surveyed said they had even heard of Wendy's restaurants. By the end of the second "Where's the beef?" ad campaign, consumer awareness of Wendy's was up to 60 percent.

"Where's the beef?" is one of those all-time favorite slogans that people remember and quote, perhaps because it not only refers to hamburgers, it refers to situations in daily life. "Where's the beef?" we ask—in relationships and in work. (Walter Mondale even used the slogan during his 1984 presidential campaign.) It also typifies what we Americans like to think of as our indigenous spunk.

Ironically, the writers at the agency Dancer Fitzgerald Sample who created the "Where's the beef?" slogan were surprised by the way it caught on. They had thought the lines in the commercial about "the big, fluffy bun" were more funny and memorable.

Despite its popularity, the "Where's the beef?" campaign was not without controversy for Wendy's, something that founder Dave Thomas thrives on and even encourages. Senior citizens groups claimed that the commercials were stereotypical and demeaning to the elderly. (Clara Peller was a senior citizen at the time she made the ads.) But Peller countered, "If other older people can do what I do, more power to them."

This wasn't the first time Wendy's had become embroiled in controversy. In 1981, Wendy's and Dancer Fitzgerald Sample had introduced a campaign with the slogan, "Wendy's. Ain't No Reason to Go Anyplace Else." The campaign itself was successful: in the first quarter after the campaign was run, sales increased 24 percent and earnings went up 40 percent. But English teachers, students, and journalists wrote letters and articles complaining about the company's use of "ain't." "I hope your food is better than your language," and "Bad language is no way to sell hamburgers," they said. Finally, Dave Thomas called a press conference. "We used the word *ain't* to attract attention," he explained. "We weren't trying to tell people that *ain't* is right to use." The controversy had kept the company in the spotlight even after the campaign was over.

Thomas is quick to say that although controversial commercials can be a positive way to draw attention to a company, "You have to walk the line and try to be controversial without really insulting people. We weren't disrespectful. Mostly, we were just the first ones to get on TV and say what people were really thinking."

QUESTIONS

1. Do you think the controversial Wendy's commercials were appropriate? Why or why not? If not, how would you have changed them?
2. How would you have managed the bad publicity generated by the commercials?
3. In general, do you agree with Dave Thomas's belief that controversy—if used properly—can be a positive marketing tool? Why or why not?

Source: R. David Thomas with Ron Beyma and Mary Maroon Gelpi, *Dave's Way* (New York: Berkeley Books, 1991), pp. 167–171.

CHAPTER 20

Personal Selling and Sales Management

LEARNING OBJECTIVES

After completing this chapter, you should be able to:

1. Discuss the role of personal selling in the organization.

2. Describe the various tasks involved in personal selling.

3. Explain the importance of relationship selling to organizations that practice quality marketing.

4. Identify the steps in the selling process.

5. Describe the activities involved in managing a sales force.

6. Discuss ethical issues in personal selling.

Creating Customer Value
Xerox

"Team Xerox" is the name of a company that prides itself on its relationship with customers and high customer satisfaction ratings.

In 1959, Xerox essentially invented a new industry: the photocopying business. But by the early 1980s, the company's customer satisfaction rating was diminishing and it found that it was losing customers, mostly to Japanese competitors.

Xerox learned its lesson from the Japanese focus on quality, and established its Leadership Through Quality program, in which it began to listen to customers (through the Customer Satisfaction Management System), cut costs, benchmark, and empower employees. Teamwork began at the company that now calls itself "Team Xerox." (About 75 percent of Xerox employees are involved in a team at any given time.)

Formal teams are now an integral part of the Xerox Group, which is made up of three companies; U.S.–based Xerox Corporation, United Kingdom–based Rank Xerox, and Japan-based Fuji Xerox. Fuji Xerox is known worldwide for its high-quality products, as evidenced by its being awarded the Deming Prize in 1980. In their sales territory (district), which includes South Korea, Taiwan, and the Philippines, Fuji Xerox teams have created a strong network with associated companies in Asia.

How do teamwork and personal selling fit together at Xerox? Xerox has two different types of formal teams: full-time teams and cross-functional teams. Members of full-time teams (called family groups), such as those who work in the telemarketing centers, work together on a daily basis. Cross-functional teams come together to address a specific issue, such as a customer service problem. One customer service team cut its average response time nearly in half.

Members of the sales staff may be asked to serve on cross-functional teams completely outside their daily domain, such as distribution or inventory. In one case, a team made up of members from sales, accounting, distribution, and administration was able to cut inventory costs by $200 million a year when it discovered that each department was ordering extra inventory so as not to be caught short. The team examined the whole inventory chain, then streamlined and reorganized procedures so that anyone who needed copiers could get them as quickly as possible.

Teams at Xerox aim at building a relationship with the customer. To this end, a team made up of employees from distribution, accounting, and sales developed a system that tracks distribution more efficiently, boosting its customer satisfaction to 90 percent and solidifying the company's relationship with customers. As in this example, personal selling at Xerox is focused on satisfying the customer.

Sources: Brian Dumane, "The Bureaucracy Busters," *Fortune,* June 17, 1991, pp. 36–46; "Quality, a Race Without a Finish Line," *Xerox Annual Report,* 1992.

Chapter Overview

personal selling
Selling that involves direct interaction between salesperson and customer.

A salesperson at Xerox can be any member of a team that sells to and services Xerox accounts. These people are all engaged in some form of **personal selling**. This element of the communications mix involves direct interaction between a salesperson and a customer, face to face, by telephone, or even by computer link.

This chapter describes the nature of personal selling—its important role in the organization, as well as the different tasks involved in the job and the increasing importance of developing long-term relationships between buyer and seller. Next, the chapter outlines the steps of the personal selling process. Then the chapter turns to a description of managing the domestic or international personal selling effort. The chapter concludes with an examination of some ethical issues involved in personal selling.

The Nature of Personal Selling

Gone is the Avon lady who rang the doorbells of U.S. homemakers in order to sell them cosmetics. Gone is the Electrolux salesman who relied on the tried-and-true sales tactic of dumping dirt on your carpet and suctioning it up with a high-powered Electrolux vacuum cleaner. Yet both companies are still very much in business, and both rely heavily on the abilities of their salespeople. Today, however, Avon representatives in the United States often sell to career women in the workplace. And Sweden-based Electrolux now sells a variety of appliances not only in the United States, but throughout Europe as well, so its sales force must be able to meet the needs of diverse groups of customers.[1]

The nature of personal selling has changed to keep pace with rapidly changing markets and customer needs. The best salespeople communicate effectively with both the company they represent and their customers, helping customers make wise purchasing decisions and providing feedback to manufacturers who produce the goods and services customers want. Figure 20.1 shows how a typical salesperson spends an average 45½-hour workweek.

In addition, personal selling is a solid stepping stone on a marketer's career path, and it can be a challenging and exciting career itself. About 60 percent of marketing graduates in the United States begin their marketing careers in sales.[2] And nearly 30 percent of the top executives in the 1,000 largest American corporations have spent at least part of their careers in sales and marketing.[3]

THE ROLE OF PERSONAL SELLING IN THE ORGANIZATION

Personal selling may be an organization's largest single operating expense. At the very least, it is most likely the largest marketing expense. According to a recent account, the cost of a face-to-face sales call is roughly $300.[4] For that reason alone, it is critical that the organization's personal selling get results.

COMMUNICATION WITH CUSTOMERS   An organization's salespeople are its direct link to customers. Salespeople communicate the organization's messages to customers and receive feedback; they also communicate customers' needs to the organization. In the case of international selling, this requires that salespeople be able to understand not only customers' language but also cultural nuances. For example,

FIGURE 20.1

How Salespeople Spend Their Time

The average salesperson spends nearly six hours a day on some form of selling, including service calls.

Breakdown of an Average 45.5-Hour Workweek

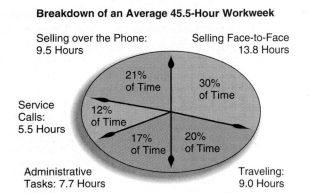

Selling over the Phone: 9.5 Hours

Selling Face-to-Face 13.8 Hours

Service Calls: 5.5 Hours

21% of Time

30% of Time

12% of Time

17% of Time

20% of Time

Administrative Tasks: 7.7 Hours

Traveling: 9.0 Hours

Source: "Sales Force Compensation," a survey of 250 U.S. companies, 66 percent with sales of less than $25 million. Courtesy of The Dartnell Corporation, Chicago, 1992.

French customers tend to be put off by boasts that a product is the biggest or greatest and by salespeople who address them by their first name. They tend to respond well to salespeople who focus on the big picture first, then move on to the details. Business lunches are typically reserved for celebrating the closing of a sale with a customer after the salesperson has worked with the customer for a long time.[5]

Salespeople present the organization's (or the product's) image to customers. Customers may even confuse a sales representative with the organization or product itself, blaming the rep for inadequacies in the product or its availability. In the case of a company like Mary Kay Cosmetics, products are sold to men and women by independent beauty consultants under the supervision of company sales directors. Sales directors and beauty consultants are expected to maintain a certain level of personal grooming consistent with the company's image.[6] Like Mary Kay, organizations that rely heavily on a strategy of communications through channel members need an effective sales force to present products to potential customers successfully.

The sales force not only communicates about the organization's own products, it also gets the news about competitors. In talking with customers, a salesperson may be the first person in a firm to hear about innovations in a competing product or the communications strategy of a competitor. Thus, the organization's salespeople are not only responsible for generating sales, they play a role in marketing research. Organizations that seek to be close to their customers and meet their needs must have a way to readily receive this information from their sales force. A typical way of doing so is to have salespeople include such information in their routine reporting of sales calls. If salespeople believe that no one wants to hear what they have learned in the field, the organization loses out on one of its most important sources of information.

Because of their communications activities with customers, salespeople are said to have a boundary-spanning role. This means that the role of the salesperson extends across the organization's boundary with the external environment. The salesperson links customers outside the organization with employees inside the organization, especially those involved in marketing. The boundary-spanning role of the sales force means the organization depends heavily on the performance of these people.

TABLE 20.1
Varieties of Sales Tasks

1. Selling function
Plan selling activities
Search out leads
Call potential accounts
Identify decision makers
Prepare sales presentation
Make sales presentation
Overcome objections
Introduce new products
Call new accounts

2. Working with others
Write up orders
Expedite orders
Handle back orders
Handle shipping problems
Find lost orders

3. Servicing the product
Learn about the product
Test equipment
Supervise installation
Train customers
Supervise repairs
Perform maintenance

4. Managing information
Provide technical information
Receive feedback
Provide feedback
Check with superiors

5. Servicing the account
Stock shelves
Set up displays
Take inventory for client
Handle local advertising

6. Attending conferences/meetings
Attend sales conferences
Attend regional sales meetings
Work at client conferences
Set up product exhibitions
Attend periodic training sessions

7. Training/recruiting
Recruit new sales reps
Train new salespeople
Travel with trainees

8. Entertaining
Entertain clients with golf and so forth
Take clients to dinner
Take clients out for drink
Take clients out to lunch
Throw parties for clients

9. Traveling
Travel out of town
Spend nights on the road
Travel in town

10. Distribution
Establish good relations with distributors
Sell to distributors
Handle credit
Collect past due accounts

Source: Adapted from William C. Moncrief III, "Selling Activity and Sales Position Taxonomies for Industrial Salesforces," *Journal of Marketing Research* (August 1986): pp. 266–267, published by the American Marketing Association. Reprinted with the permission of the American Marketing Association.

DECISION MAKING   Although sales representatives may be assigned territories, products, or specific customers, good reps must be able to formulate their own strategies for personal selling. In organizations that empower their employees, salespeople may have the authority to adjust prices or payment schedules or to offer customers other beneficial arrangements. They may also work with their customers after the conclusion of a sale, helping them use the product or quelling any doubts about the purchase selection.

VARIETIES OF SALES TASKS

The job of most salespeople is demanding and varied. Table 20.1 summarizes the types of activities involved in selling. To describe each in detail would require too much space. But to get a general overview of personal selling, it is helpful to think of it as involving three basic tasks: order getting, order taking, and supporting.

order getting
Developing business by seeking out potential customers, providing them with product information, and persuading them to buy.

ORDER GETTING   When people think of personal selling, the activities that most often come to mind are those involved in order getting. **Order getting** is developing business by seeking out potential customers, providing them with necessary information about products, and persuading them to buy. Order getters may be positioned inside a store (such as an appliance salesperson for Sears) or outside (such as a sales rep for Snap-On Tools, who visits auto mechanics at their shops).

A good order getter knows the products he or she is selling, knows the customers' needs, and can find creative ways to solve customers' problems better than the competition. Winning over buyers of a competitor's product can require a sizable dose of creativity. According to one survey, "Buyers are basically lazy, continuing to use the same suppliers despite good reason to change."[7] Overcoming this challenge requires showing how easy—and profitable—it is to change.

"Buyers like to be sold," notes Pam Lontos, a sales trainer based in California. "They will buy, but you've got to help them get beyond their indecision and fears."[8] In an organizational buying situation, the effective order getter addresses the general business concerns as well as specific purchasing concerns of the customer, helping the customer make the best buying decision. In a consumer buying situation, an order getter may address specific concerns such as the safety features of a car, the horsepower of a snowblower, or the durability of a carpet fabric. Helping buyers to make decisions that meet their needs is part of the quality approach to selling.

ORDER TAKING   A successful order getter generates sales that require the tasks involved in order taking. **Order taking** is the routine completion of sales (orders and reorders) to customers who have already decided to buy a product. While this activity may sound like little more than a rote transaction, it is an important part of the sales process. (After all, if no one completes the purchase transaction, the sale has not taken place.)

Order takers must be equipped to answer questions, make price or payment adjustments, handle complaints, and inform customers of changes in the product itself or its supporting services. A well-trained order taker may alert the company to possible order-getting situations. An order taker may also be an order getter, as in the case of representatives for mail-order catalogs such as Lands' End or L.L. Bean. The manner in which these order takers handle phone calls can influence whether a customer decides to buy not only the sweater or pair of boots he or she intended to buy, but perhaps a wool hat or socks as well.

SALES SUPPORT   **Support salespeople** help order getters and order takers in a variety of ways but do not conduct actual sales transactions with the organization's customers. There are two main types of support salespeople: missionary salespeople and technical specialists.

Missionary salespeople (also called *merchandisers* or *detailers*) work for producers, calling on channel members and peforming promotional activities. These salespeople develop good relationships with channel members and perform tasks that help stimulate greater demand for their products. For instance, a missionary salesperson for Nabisco might deliver a special display for SnackWell's cookies to a supermarket, set up the display, and suggest that a supermarket employee hand out free samples to shoppers. This person would not, however, take orders for the products. Just calling a retailer's or wholesaler's attention to a product can increase sales appreciably.

Technical specialists (called *sales engineers* in some industries) provide salespeople with assistance in the form of technical expertise. Technical specialists are important to pharmaceutical companies, environmental engineering firms, manufacturers of building products, and other marketers of complex goods and services. At Ebasco Services, geologists, chemists, and engineers serve as technical specialists in a team marketing effort.

order taking
The routine completion of sales to customers who have already decided to buy.

support salespeople
Those who assist both order getters and order takers but do not conduct sales transactions themselves.

missionary salespeople
Those who work for producers, calling on channel members and performing promotional activities.

technical specialists
Those who assist salespeople by providing technical expertise.

In this ad that appeared in Grocery Marketing magazine, General Mills promotes its highly developed customer service center system of sales support.

OTHER SELLING ARRANGEMENTS   Some organizations combine these sales tasks in various ways to serve the needs of their customers. Widely used selling arrangements include team selling, conference selling, and seminar selling.

team selling
Use of a team of sales professionals working together to sell and service a company's major customers.

Team Selling   In **team selling**, a team of sales professionals works together to sell and service an organization's major customers. A selling team may include order-oriented salespeople as well as missionary and technical support people, along with employees from other parts of the company, including finance and operations. Black & Decker has seen sales to Wal-Mart and Home Depot climb since it set up divisions to work as teams in serving these big customers. Each division includes salespeople, a marketer, an information systems expert, a sales forecaster, and a financial analyst, who collaborate on selling and promotional activities for their client.[9]

This type of selling is very effective for products that are complex and require support following the sale. Some team members can help the prospective client understand what the product is and how it can help meet the client's needs, and others can provide any necessary after-sales support. Team selling may be essential for serving organizations that use teamwork for making purchase decisions, as is often the case for buying computer hardware and software.

conference selling
Personal selling in which a salesperson and other pertinent employees meet with customers to work out problems or discuss future arrangements.

Conference Selling   In **conference selling**, a salesperson and other pertinent employees (perhaps from production or customer service) meet with customers. Together, they work out problems or discuss possible future arrangements. This technique supports efforts to build long-term relationships with customers.

Creative Staffing, a Miami provider of temporary staff, often fields an impressive team of employees to meet with prospective customers. In such a conference, the participants from Creative Staffing might include the chief financial officer, sales director, sales rep, operations manager, and the employee who will service the account. Explains Ann Machado, the firm's CEO, "When you explain what each person does, it gives you more credibility."[10]

At Kiwi International, all 550 employees, from flight attendants to mechanics, sell for the airline. Each employee is given a two-hour sales training seminar and is asked to devote four unpaid hours a month to sales activities. Even pilots make sales calls.

seminar selling
An educational program conducted by a company team to inform a customer's technical staff about product development or innovation so that they will recommend a purchase.

Seminar Selling Organizations offering innovative or complex products may use seminar selling. **Seminar selling** is an educational program conducted by a company team. The members of this team inform a customer's technical staff about innovations in an existing product or the development of a new product. The objective of this approach is to get the technical people interested in the product so that they will persuade those with purchasing authority to buy it.

RELATIONSHIP SELLING

relationship selling
Personal selling in which salespeople and customers develop long-term, mutually beneficial relationships.

Many quality-oriented firms practice **relationship selling**, in which salespeople develop long-term, mutually beneficial relationships with customers. Today, customers expect a more complex relationship than simple order taking. They want to collaborate with a salesperson who can provide in-depth counseling on purchasing decisions, can help find imaginative solutions to problems, is willing to be an advocate for them within the company, and subscribes to high ethical standards.[11] For instance, customers may be able to negotiate better terms with a seller who is trying to build a long-term relationship with them.[12] The benefit to the seller is retaining the buyer's business. Relationship selling is a major dimension of relationship marketing, introduced in Chapter 13.

Relationship selling is not new. In fact, it appears in the promise made by L.L. Bean in his original catalog for boots, more than 80 years ago: "Everything we sell is backed by a 100% guarantee. We do not want you to have anything from L.L. Bean that is not completely satisfactory. Return anything you buy from us at any time for any reason if it proves otherwise."[13]

Relationship selling is especially important given the intense competition of today's global marketplace. Large corporations searching for ways to cut costs turn to suppliers that can help them streamline operations.[14] Those suppliers must employ a sales force skilled in identifying and solving customers' problems.

Bose, a $500 million manufacturer of acoustic speakers, asked that neighboring G&F, a small manufacturer of molded plastic parts, assign a full-time employee to work at the Bose plant, thus eliminating regular sales calls by G&F and allowing Bose to cut the cost of employing buyers and planners. This not only solidified the relationship between G&F and Bose, it changed the way G&F viewed personal selling. "This

FIGURE 20.2

Steps in the Selling Process

has changed our whole way of doing business, but I never thought it would work this well," says G&F president John Argitis. "Instead of spending time trying to get new accounts, we concentrate solely on servicing and pricing. You don't really sell, you look for opportunities."[15]

Steps in the Selling Process

The usual way to describe the process of personal involves seven steps. As shown in Figure 20.2, these steps are prospecting, preparation, approaching the customer, presentation, overcoming objections, closing, and follow-up. A successful salesperson will follow all of these steps in some fashion, but the boundaries between them may be blurry.

PROSPECTING

prospecting
Identifying potential customers.

Personal selling begins with **prospecting**, or identifying potential customers. Since there can't be any sales without customers, salespeople must locate individuals or organizations that might be interested in buying their products. These potential customers fall into three categories, ranked from largest to smallest:

1. *Leads*—individuals or organizations that might be customers
2. *Prospects*—individuals or organizations that already have an interest in the product
3. *Qualified prospects*—individuals or organizations that want the product, can afford to buy it, and have the authority to make a purchase decision.

Obviously, the last category is the most valuable to the salesperson, but people in that category are the hardest to identify. The salesperson might start out with a long list of leads, narrow it down to prospects, and narrow it further to a few qualified prospects.

SOURCES OF PROSPECTS   Salespeople may get leads and prospects from a number of sources. Commonly used possibilities include mailing lists, databases, trade shows, previous customers, suppliers, and personal contacts. Referrals from existing customers are often among the most valuable prospects, and the salesperson can get them just by asking. A creative salesperson will use these and other sources. A book called *Cole's Directory* uses U.S. Census Bureau statistics and other data to classify streets and neighborhoods in the United States by income. The average income on what the directory calls an "$A" street is in the top 20 percent for that particular region.[16] Salespeople for luxury products would focus on these streets and neighborhoods.

FIGURE 20.3

Sample of Partial Information from Dun's Market Identifiers

```
  9/5/1
 0213235     DIALOG File 516:  D&B Duns Market Identifiers
 Allied Warehousing Service Inc
 Abbott Labs
 20 26th St
 P O Box 1700
 Huntington, WV  25703-1233

 TELEPHONE: 304-523-2131
 COUNTY: Cabell      MSA: 3400  (Huntington-Ashland, WV-KY-OH)
 REGION: South Atlantic

 BUSINESS: Public & Contract Warehousing

 PRIMARY SIC:
  4225        General warehousing and storage, nsk
   42250000   General warehousing and storage, nsk
   42259901   General warehousing

 LATEST YEAR ORGANIZED: 1980   OWNER CHANGE DATE:          NA
 STATE OF INCORPORATION: WV    DATE OF INCORPORATION: 09/26/1980
 ANNUAL SALES REVISION DATE: 01/02/1994
                             LATEST            TREND         BASE
                             YEAR              YEAR          YEAR
                                              (1992)        (1990)

 SALES           $    2,700,000E  $         NA  $         NA
 EMPLOYEES TOTAL:           41              41            50
 EMPLOYEES HERE:            20

    SALES GROWTH:  NA %  NET WORTH: $         NA
    EMPLOYMENT GROWTH:  -18 %

 SQUARE FOOTAGE: 650,000  RENTED
 NUMBER OF ACCOUNTS: NA
 BANK: Twentieth Street Bank (Inc)  BANK DUNS: 00-794-5066
```

Source: Used by permission of Dun and Bradstreet Information Services.

cold canvassing
Locating prospects from a phone book or other source and calling on them.

Salespeople may try **cold canvassing** (or cold calling) by simply getting lists of names. To reach consumers, they might pick names and addresses from a phone book. Sellers to organizations might turn to Dun's Market Identifiers, an information service of Dun & Bradstreet. Figure 20.3 shows an example of the type of information provided by this service on a computer file. Generally, the refusal rate with cold canvassing is high, but some marketers have found it to be successful.[17]

 In Japan, however, cold canvassing is difficult because formal introductions and relationship building are so important there. One U.S. company found that Japanese consumers resented sales calls from strangers even in response to a request for information. To reach Japanese businesses, marketers sometimes try sending direct-mail advertising first, to serve as a kind of introduction.[18]

Prospecting, even with solid leads, can be intimidating. "Fear of rejection is the number-one barrier to effective selling, but the cure is easy," claims Dave Grant, a sales trainer based in California. "When I'm afraid of being rejected, I'm afraid that when the buyer says no, I lose. But if what I'm offering is in the buyer's best interests, and he says no, he's the one who loses. If you really believe in your product or service, you'll never experience rejection."[19] Therefore, a salesperson who practices the quality approach of identifying a potential customer's needs and making the best attempt to meet those needs with the right product need not fear the prospecting process.

qualifying
Determining whether a prospect is in a position to buy a product.

QUALIFYING PROSPECTS Prospects should be qualified. **Qualifying** a prospect involves determining whether the prospect is in a position to buy the product. This determination is important because not everyone who wants a product can afford it or has decision-making authority. The prospect who wants to buy a luxury automobile may not be qualified to do so because of income. The employee who wants to have a personal computer at his or her desk may not be authorized to make that buying decision.

PREPARATION

preparation
Learning more about a qualified prospect's needs.

Before trying to make a sale with a prospect, the effective salesperson carries out the next step: preparation. **Preparation** means doing homework. The salesperson finds out more about the qualified prospect's needs and, if necessary, more about technical aspects of the product. "Salespeople blow it when they haven't done their homework," warns Jeff Salzman, cofounder of Colorado-based Career Track, a sales training company. "Before coming in to see me, do your research. Know my problems; know who my competitors are. Put yourself in my head. Tell me how you can help me, and I'm all ears."[20]

The salesperson can accumulate information about the prospect's needs directly from the prospect as well as from outside sources (without invading the prospect's privacy). Granted, this information gathering will continue throughout a selling process that uses a quality approach. But it should begin in earnest during the preparation stage.

Finally, at this point the salesperson should learn the best time to approach the prospect—for instance, during evenings at home or during the business day at work.

APPROACHING THE CUSTOMER

approach
Initial formal contact with the qualified prospect.

Once the salesperson has completed preparations, he or she plans an **approach** to the qualified prospect (initial contact), with the goal of learning more about the customer's needs, gaining attention, and stimulating interest. The most foolproof way to get a prospect's attention and interest is to be genuinely interested in his or her needs. After all, it's only normal for people to want their problems solved. And most buyers are smart enough to see through a salesperson who only pretends to be interested.

Thus, during the approach, the salesperson continues to ask questions and gather information from the potential customer. Some marketers also recommend establishing rapport with the customer by "smiling, keeping a relaxed posture, maintaining eye contact, and using the customer's name. On the phone, put a smile in your voice, use the customer's name, maybe talk for a minute about personal issues."[21]

PRESENTATION

presentation
Communication of the sales message to the customer.

The **presentation** communicates the sales message to the customer, with the goal of stimulating further interest in the product. During the presentation, the salesperson describes and sometimes demonstrates specific attributes of the product. As in every stage of the selling process, however, it is important that communication flow in two directions. The salesperson needs to go beyond delivering a sales pitch to observing and listening to the prospect. The presentation, like every stage of the process, is an opportunity to learn more about how the organization can help prospects meet their needs.

stimulus-response presentation
Sales presentation that provides a stimulus with the goal of influencing the customer to buy the product.

TYPES OF PRESENTATIONS   The three main types of sales presentation are the stimulus-response format, the formula selling format, and the need-satisfaction format. These are summarized in Figure 20.4.

Stimulus-Response   In the **stimulus-response presentation**, the salesperson assumes that if he or she provides the appropriate stimulus, the customer will buy the product.

FIGURE 20.4

Types of Sales Presentations

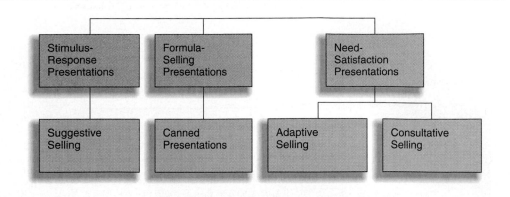

Thus, the salesperson might try several different angles before hitting the one that causes the customer to make the purchase. *Suggestive selling,* in which a catalog sales rep asks a telephone customer if he or she would like to hear about a special offering, or a restaurant waiter asks patrons if they would like to see the dessert menu, is a form of stimulus-response presentation. Furniture-kit manufacturer Cohasset Colonials practices a form of suggestive selling through its catalog pages by offering "go-togethers"—two or more of its products sold at a slight discount.

formula selling presentation
Sales presentation of product information in a thorough, lockstep format.

Formula Selling   The **formula selling presentation** is somewhat more rigid, based on the idea that product information must be provided in a thorough, lockstep format. Although the sales information is conveyed somewhat formally, the good salesperson is at least flexible enough to answer questions on the spot or stop during the presentation to explain a product feature more thoroughly at a customer's request. An advantage of this type of presentation is that it reduces the risk of the salesperson omitting important information. The Ohio-based Longaberger Basket Company uses the formula method to sell its baskets through independent sales consultants who conduct presentations in customers' homes. (See "Marketing Movers & Shakers.")

canned presentation
A memorized, standard sales message given without deviation to all prospects.

Canned presentations, which are memorized, standard sales messages presented without variation, are often used by telephone salespeople. Many prospects are put off by canned presentations, but telemarketing consultants believe this is due to poor scripting and delivery. Judy Lanier, a partner at Softel Systems in California and author of *The 11 Best Kept Secrets of Successful Scripts,* says goal setting is just as important in writing sales scripts as in other aspects of marketing. "You really have to know your objective before you start writing," she emphasizes. She comments further, "Presentation is everything." In other words, the best-written script will fall flat with a bad delivery.[22] And as with the formula selling presentation, canned presentations provide some insurance against the omission of important information.

need-satisfaction presentation
Sales presentation that includes asking questions and listening to customer's answers in order to identify needs and desires.

Need Satisfaction   Finally, the **need-satisfaction presentation** emphasizes asking questions and listening to a customer's answers in order to nail down his or her needs and desires. Need satisfaction is the format most geared to identifying and solving problems for the customer. In *adaptive selling,* a form of need-satisfaction selling, the salesperson adjusts the presentation to fit the selling context, which dictates whether more questions should be asked or solutions offered. In *consultative selling,* the salesperson acts more directly as an expert who can recognize and solve a customer's problems. "You must know much more about the problems your customers are trying

Marketing Movers & Shakers

DAVE LONGABERGER OF THE LONGABERGER COMPANY

In a living room filled mostly with women, an independent sales representative makes a sales presentation about handmade baskets. Surrounded by handsomely woven and stained maple baskets of all shapes and sizes, with names like "gathering basket," "market basket," and "tea basket," the sales consultant gives prospects a brief history of the company that makes the baskets and pottery and then launches into a description and demonstration of each one. An hour or so later, the rep hands each person an order form and a "Wish List" (catalog with prices), then takes orders. A Longaberger party has concluded.

Baskets are big business, at least in Dresden, Ohio, where The Longaberger Company has been handweaving them since 1972. Dave Longaberger started this family-run operation that now employs 4,000 people and boasts an annual growth rate of 40 percent, with $200 million in annual sales. How did he do it?

As a child, Longaberger worked at a corner grocery and a restaurant. Later, he started his own restaurant and bought his own grocery store. But his true inspiration for a family-based business came from his own family

history. Longaberger's father, J. W., had learned basket weaving from *his* father; the family was poor, so during the day J. W. worked at the local paper mill, and at night he wove baskets to sell to farmers and housewives. Dave and his eleven brothers and sisters learned the craft as children.

During the early 1970s, J. W. still made baskets and sold them for about $1.50 apiece. But by then, Dave Longaberger had noticed how popular foreign-made baskets had become. So he asked his father for a dozen to see if customers would pay $10 for a basket in a store. They did.

Although Longaberger launched the company through retail shops, he couldn't sell enough baskets to make ends meet. A basket enthusiast told Dave that she was buying his baskets and selling them to friends, thus the idea for the home show was formed. After that Longaberger baskets were no longer sold through retail outlets. The business took off. "When [customers] come to a Longaberger party, we pretty well know that 95 percent of them are going to buy something." (This figure contrasts with the 20 percent of customers who buy something in a retail store.) The company now contracts with more than 20,000 sales consultants nationwide, who sell Longaberger baskets, pottery, and accessories at $3.95 to $100 apiece.

Even in a sluggish economy, Longaberger baskets—although they sell at a higher price than others—have a distinct appeal. Each is handwoven and signed by a craftsperson. All are constructed of maple and are designed to be functional as well as decorative. They not only represent value to recession-strapped customers, but they have an heirloom quality. And the cozy,

comfortable atmosphere created by personal salespeople who not only get and take orders but also engage in relationship selling (they are often friends, neighbors, and relatives of customers) clinches the sale. Dave Longaberger is keenly aware of the importance of this relationship. "McDonald's doesn't sell hamburgers and french fries," he says bluntly. "They sell compassion and feeling."

It's tough to maintain a large force of independent sales consultants, but Longaberger offers positive motivation, recognition, and compensation. His favorite principle of management is, "Listen—learn—lead. If you are willing to *listen* to people, willing to *learn* from what you listen to, then, and only then, will you learn how to *lead* them." The fact that reps set their own hours, make the formula presentation in their own style, are compensated immediately upon a sale, and have opportunities to attend such functions as the "Bee" in Ohio (where they obtain recognition and can learn how to weave their own baskets) is attractive to many. They also know they are selling a high-quality product.

In 1990 the company introduced its own line of pottery and dinnerware, as well as various accessories. In the long run, Dave Longaberger hopes to see his organization expand into furniture construction, real estate, and even an educational theme park. By the year 2010, he envisions a company that employs 30,000 people.

Could so many customers be interested in baskets? In 1993, 300,000 tourists visited Dresden from all over the United States, mostly because of Longaberger baskets.

Sources: Sharon Nelton, "A Basket Maker with Vision," *Nation's Business,* July 1993; Longaberger Wish List (catalog), The Longaberger Company, 1992.

to solve, and be creative in figuring out how your product or service can help them achieve their goals," says John Sample, CEO of Texas-based Business Interiors.[23] The need-satisfaction format most obviously fits the quality approach, but salespeople whose organizations use other formats still can practice quality selling by listening to their customers.

PRESENTATION FORMATS   The salesperson can use the various types of presentation in person or to sell over the phone. Either way, the salesperson can benefit from a quality focus.

Selling Face-to-Face   When selling in person, physical appearance is important, as noted earlier. The prospect will form an impression of the salesperson and his or her organization based on appearance. In addition, the salesperson should bring along any materials likely to be necessary for explaining the product and answering questions. The salesperson should acknowledge and greet everyone attending the presentation, clearly describe the product and its benefits, then encourage the prospect to discuss how the product might be relevant to his or her needs. Successful marketer Paul Sherlock notes, "There is something more important than what you are saying— that is, what the *customer* has to say."[24]

telemarketing
Conducting sales presentations over the phone.

Selling over the Phone   Organizations are increasingly beating the high costs of sales calls by having salespeople make their presentations over the telephone. Such selling efforts are called **telemarketing**. Salespeople using telemarketing can reach many more customers at a lower cost in less time than with face-to-face selling. This makes telemarketing attractive to organizations that otherwise believe they cannot afford personal selling. To generate customers for her Keiser, Oregon, chimney sweep business, Katherine Moser used telemarketing with a recorded message. As impersonal as that technique might sound, it was far more successful than the advertising Moser had tried before.[25]

In addition, the efficiency of telemarketing can enable the organization to provide a level of sales service that might otherwise be too expensive. Summit Racing Equipment, which sells performance auto parts, takes orders over the phone 24 hours a day. This not only enables U.S. consumers to order parts when they work on their cars at night, it allows overseas customers to reach Summit at times convenient for them.[26] Union Pacific Railroad began serving its 20,000 smallest accounts with telemarketing from Omaha. The telemarketers interact with those customers much more than traveling sales reps ever could, and a higher proportion of customers are impressed with the service they receive.[27]

In spite of these advantages, telemarketing is viewed as a nuisance by many on the receiving end. Complaints about abuses of telemarketing have led to various restrictions. In the United States, the Telephone Consumer Protection Act of 1991 requires that telemarketers maintain a "no solicitation" list and avoid any wire solicitation— such as by telephone, fax, or computer modem—of anyone on the list. (The ban on unsolicited faxes has been challenged but still stands as of this writing.[28]) In addition, many states have restrictions, such as a requirement that telemarketers obtain a license. (For more on ethical issues related to telemarketing, see "You Decide.")

Salespeople who use telemarketing make their impression with their voice and telephone etiquette. Therefore, telemarketers should have a confident and pleasant manner and should speak clearly in a style appropriate to the audience.

OVERCOMING OBJECTIONS

objections
A prospect's resistance to making a purchase.

In the sales situation, **objections** are a prospect's resistance to making a purchase. Objections usually involve a product's features and price. They may also be based on the fact that the prospect simply does not need or want the product at this time.

IS TELEMARKETING CONSISTENT WITH THE QUALITY APPROACH?

You Decide

As a consumer, you know the calls. If you are at home, you get them during the day. You certainly get them at dinner time, and sometimes late into the evening. When you answer the phone, the unfamiliarity of the voice tips you off that a sales pitch is coming. It could be for financial services, magazine subscriptions, theater tickets. But if you are like many consumers, you don't want to hear it. Businesspeople also get these calls at the workplace, and they can get just as annoyed.

What especially annoys people is getting a call not just from a stranger, but from a stranger's computer. Such calls come from autodialers—computers that automatically dial phone numbers, deliver a recorded message, and allow recipients to leave messages in return. The A-Aa-1 Lucky Leprechaun Co., a chimney-sweeping business started by Kathryn and Ronald Moser, improved sales by using an autodialer that could call about 400 numbers a day. "In the first week, we recovered the full $436.50 monthly rental fee," says Kathryn Moser.

In 1989 the Mosers decided to move, with their business, from Salt Lake City, Utah, to Portland, Oregon. Two months after they moved, a new Oregon law required the Mosers to shut off their autodialer. Frustrated and angry, they approached the American Civil Liberties Union to launch a federal lawsuit. To finance the process, they gathered together other small businesses in the same fix to form the National Association of Telecomputer Operators. Recently, however, the U.S. Supreme Court

upheld the right of states to ban autodialed sales pitches.

The Mosers' battle is uphill all the way. Lobbyists and lawmakers alike have been besieged with complaints from angry consumers. "People are terribly annoyed that this new technology is being used to invade their privacy," notes Gene Kimmelman, legislative director for the Consumer Federation of America. At latest count, over 40 states had restricted or banned the use of autodialers to deliver recorded sales messages.

In response to the critics, Lucky Leprechaun says it limits telemarketing to the hours of 9 a.m. to 8:00 p.m., Monday through Saturday. Its system blocks the phone numbers of hospitals, government agencies, and businesses as well as consumers who ask to be left alone.

The lawyer who argued state and federal lawsuits for the company says to disgruntled consumers, "Hang up your phone." But that remedy still does not address the inconvenience and even distress that can arise from a phone ringing at the wrong time (say, when waiting for the results of a parent's surgery or when trying to sleep after a stressful day or night). In contrast, a sales message that arrives by mail can be examined at a convenient time or thrown away without the discomfort of directly turning down an offer.

But no matter how annoying it is to get a call from a telemarketer, that person's job can be trying, too. A recent account about telemarketing firms that sell magazine subscriptions

reports that these telemarketers work in shifts of about four hours each, with many working double or triple shifts. At some companies, they must punch time clocks and ask permission for bathroom breaks. The employees may not bring food or drinks into their cubicles. As telemarketers make calls, supervisors walk the floor, listening in on cordless phones. Discipline for failure to meet high sales quotas includes not receiving the guaranteed wage. Most of these jobs provide health benefits to supervisors only.

Indeed, turnover in this business is high. A survey at one company revealed that 88 percent of telemarketers had held their jobs less than a year. At another company, turnover among those who had completed the training program was 100 percent within a year. "There's a tremendous amount of stress, work pressure and performance pressure," remarks Michael Smith, a professor of industrial engineering at the University of Wisconsin–Madison. "They're turn-of-the-century factory workers, but they're educated and have technology."

If telemarketing annoys many prospects, why do you think some marketers use this type of personal selling? What can marketers do to ensure that telemarketing generates customers who are satisfied, even delighted? What steps would help to make telemarketing treat employees and prospects more ethically?

Sources: Dana Milbank, "New Collar Work," *The Wall Street Journal,* September 9, 1993, pp. A1, A8; Mary Lu Carnevale, "Telemarketers Fight Banning of Autodialers," *The Wall Street Journal,* January 20, 1993, pp. B1–B2; "Ban on Automatic-Dial Phone Pitches Upheld," *Chicago Tribune,* March 30, 1993, sec. 3, pp. 1, 6.

A skilled salesperson knows when objections are valid and shows respect for the prospect's wishes by backing off. Perhaps that prospect will become a customer in the future. But the same salesperson also recognizes when objections become an opportunity to further showcase the product's attributes, demonstrating how it can benefit

Korean businesses are the world's "toughest," says Yong K. Kim, president of User Technology Associates (UTA), Arlington, Virginia, a computer services and training enterprise with sales in Korea. According to Kim, "Koreans are very impatient at business, very results-oriented, and they want everything now."

the prospect. For instance, if the prospect compares the product unfavorably to the competition, the salesperson can show ways in which the product is better suited to the prospect's needs. Or the salesperson can illustrate how a weakness that bothers the prospect is outweighed by other strengths. Finally, if the prospect voices concern about price, the salesperson might demonstrate that the product is priced competitively or is made of higher-quality materials than a competing product.

In some situations, the prospect uses objections as a negotiating tactic to lead the salesperson to sweeten the deal. Such customers exist around the world, but it can be helpful for the global marketer to be familiar with the negotiating tactics typical of prospects in a particular country being served. In France, for example, business customers are known as clever and dramatic negotiators. The successful salesperson is patient and demonstrates interest in, but not an overwhelming need for, the client's business.[29]

CLOSING

closing
The point at which the prospect makes a purchase commitment.

The point at which the prospect makes a commitment to purchase a product is called the **closing**. In most cases, the salesperson must initiate the commitment. This may seem obvious, but according to marketing experts, many sales are lost because a salesperson doesn't ask for an order. "Plenty of salespeople don't make the sale because they don't ask for it," remarks Michael LeBoeuf, author of *How to Win Customers and Keep Them for Life.* "How can you get the order if you don't ask?"[30]

There are a few standard techniques for closing. In the *trial close,* the salesperson asks the prospect to make a decision about a particular aspect of the purchase, such as the color of a car or the model of a refrigerator. In the *assumptive close,* the salesperson discusses such issues as financing or delivery, making the assumption that the prospect is going to buy. In the *urgency close,* the salesperson impresses upon the prospect the need for an immediate decision, say, because interest rates have been increasing, airfares are going up, or the popularity of the item means it may go out of stock.

The salesperson who practices the quality approach uses these techniques only when they are appropriate to the situation. For example, a travel agent uses an urgency close only if he or she has accurate information that airfares or hotel rates are indeed expected to increase. An appliance salesperson uses the assumptive close only when it is obvious that the new homeowner needs and wants the washing machine and dryer. Otherwise, these techniques may be perceived as a "hard sell" and may backfire.

FOLLOW-UP

follow-up
After-the-sale activities designed to make sure the customer is satisfied with the product purchased.

The closing is not the end of a sale. Instead, the person who practices quality selling engages in **follow-up**, making sure that the customer is satisfied with the good or service. Follow-up may involve a phone call to learn whether the sofabed was delivered on time and undamaged, to find out if the new photocopier is functioning properly, or to be sure that the surgical outpatient is resting comfortably at home. Also helpful is to mail or provide written information on how to get the most from the product or even to offer a training program for users. The marketer may ask customers to complete a brief survey to assess their satisfaction and identify any problems that can be resolved before the customer becomes dissatisfied.

Follow-up goes a long way toward maintaining a good relationship with the customer. It is especially important in the case of big purchases, where the customer often feels some doubts about the purchase decision (called "buyer's remorse" or "cognitive dissonance"). Effective follow-up can alleviate such feelings. And some researchers have learned that conducting the follow-up necessary to obtain repeat sales from existing customers costs about half the amount needed to close a sale with a new customer.[31]

Sales Management

sales plan
A formal statement of selling goals and strategies.

sales management
Formulation of a sales plan and overseeing its implementation.

Personal selling happens in an organized manner. As in other aspects of marketing, the selling effort is driven by a **sales plan**, or formal statement of selling goals and strategies. Formulating and overseeing the implementation of the sales plan are the basic activities of **sales management**.

In the typical medium-sized or large organization, sales management is the responsibility of a sales manager. Sales managers typically perform the traditional managerial functions of organizing and supervising the sales force. In companies that use team selling or other types of cross-functional teams, the sales manager's role is particularly important. He or she must have the knowledge and skills to create effective teams that may have members both inside and outside the company. In companies engaged in international selling, the sales manager may be required to coordinate sales forces from different parts of the world.

ORGANIZATIONAL STRUCTURE AND USE OF TECHNOLOGY

To decide how to get the most from their salespeople, be they employees, independent reps, or manufacturer's reps, sales managers must decide how to organize the sales force. Just as managers at other levels decide on an organizational structure, so must the sales manager.

sales territory
Group of present and potential customers assigned to a particular salesperson, branch, dealer, or distributor.

SALES TERRITORIES   The basic decision about organizing a sales force is how to set up **sales territories**. These are groups of present and potential customers assigned to particular salespeople, branches, dealers, or distributors.[32] As shown in Figure 20.5,

FIGURE 20.5

Common Ways of Organizing a Sales Force

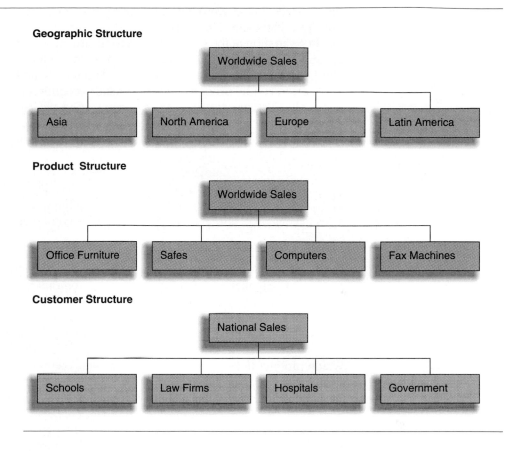

Geographic Structure

Worldwide Sales

Asia | North America | Europe | Latin America

Product Structure

Worldwide Sales

Office Furniture | Safes | Computers | Fax Machines

Customer Structure

National Sales

Schools | Law Firms | Hospitals | Government

most companies organize their sales force in one of three ways: by geography, by product, or by customer.

In a geographic structure, individual salespeople are assigned geographic territories to cover. The salesperson calls on all prospects in the territory and usually represents all of the company's products. For example, a salesperson might be assigned to cover targeted business buyers in Chile, the southwestern United States, or a smaller region such as metropolitan Miami. A geographic structure provides the practical benefit of limiting the distance each salesperson must travel to see customers.

In a product structure, each salesperson is assigned to prospects and customers for a particular product or product line. A product structure is beneficial when the sales force must have specific (often technical) knowledge about a product in order to sell it effectively. However, this structure can result in a duplication of sales efforts (more than one salesperson calling on a single customer), so it tends to be costly.

A customer-organized structure assigns a salesperson or selling team to serve a single customer or single type of customer. It works best when different types of buyers have large or significantly different needs. When this structure involves devoting all of a salesperson's time to a single customer, it is costly, but the long-term results can be worthwhile if the customer's purchases are large enough. As mentioned earlier in this chapter, the small plastics manufacturing firm G&F assigned a full-time salesperson to work at the Bose speaker plant so that G&F could thoroughly meet

Bose's needs. In the five years after making this arrangement, G&F's annual sales grew from $3 million to $15 million.[33]

major account management
The use of team selling to focus on major customers in an effort to establish long-term business relationships.

In a variation of the customer-organized structure, a company may employ **major account management**, or the use of team selling to focus on major customers in an effort to establish long-term relationships. Procter & Gamble, whose sales force used to be organized by product, shifted to major account management, which the company calls Customer Business Development. "Our new structure is more flexible and customer focused," notes P&G executive E. A. Lennon. "Our primary choice is to align our sales and other functional resources primarily by customer, with geography as a subordinate principle."[34]

The customer-organized structure is well suited to the use of cross-functional teams and to the quality approach's customer orientation. Nevertheless, geographic and product territories can also be managed with a quality focus. For this to happen, sales management and the sales force must concentrate on meeting customers' needs.

TECHNOLOGY IN THE SALES ORGANIZATION   One reason that team structures are getting results is that they are able to make good use of modern information technology. Today's smaller, cheaper, more powerful computers enable salespeople to share information with customers, other members of the marketing organization, and other organizations in the distribution channel. Ideally, for example, sales reps could check their computer files to learn whether the customer they are about to call on has just complained to someone in customer service. Or a wholesaler might tell a retailer which product lines are selling best in similar communities. At software developer Qualitas, based in Bethesda, Maryland, customer service reps maintain a database of customer information and daily give the company's salespeople about 30 qualified leads from current and prospective customers.[35]

There are many ways to use computer technology to assist personal selling, but a few applications are most typical. The organization may use a database to keep track of its leads, prospects, and customers, making it easy to identify and study various categories of potential, current, and past customers. Many salespeople travel with a laptop or notebook computer to make notes while on the road. They can hook up by phone to the organization's computer to tap into its marketing information system or marketing decision support system and to send and receive messages. The salesperson can easily learn which products are selling (in total or through a particular intermediary) or where a customer's order is in the production process. Sales reps for Genentech can even access the latest articles on issues of interest to their customers and can send technical questions directly to company specialists at headquarters.[36]

A case in point is Leegin Creative Leather Products, a belt manufacturer based in Industry, California. Leegin pulled out of years of stagnating sales by empowering its sales force with information technology. When a Leegin sales rep calls on a store, he or she takes inventory, then uses a laptop computer to record the numbers of each style. Using the new data, the computer quickly provides the salesperson with information: the store's total orders for the past year, a comparison of current and past sales volume, and the number of belts sold, categorized by color, style, or whatever the sales rep and store manager wish. With this information, the sales rep is in a position to recommend what the store should order. Seeing the data behind the recommendations tends to make store managers trust Leegin's sales reps, and relying on the sales reps' insights increases customers' ability to profit from carrying Leegin's products. Each night, Leegin's sales reps send their orders electronically to the company, along with whatever messages they want to send to employees there. They can also use their computers to get information from the company—say, availability of

Computer and communications technology now provide worldwide assistance for salespeople. When on the road, salespeople keep in touch by using modems and fax machines. This WorldPort™ fax/data modem is compatible with all international standards and connects easily to all laptop computer brands.

types of belts, records of customer payments or credit problems, and notes about what competitors are doing.[37]

What are the practical implications of information technology for salespeople? Obviously, they must be comfortable learning how to use the latest computer and communications technology. They must have skills in collaborating with others, as the ability to share information makes it imperative to act as a team member with those handling other functions. And many sales managers expect that, freed of the need to process a lot of paper, the sales reps of the future will increasingly be based in their homes, rather than in a branch office.[38]

RECRUITMENT

How does a sales manager recruit salespeople who are bright, creative, motivated, and willing to stay on the job? The recruitment process involves a number of activities, from deciding whether to hire salespeople or contract with independent representatives to selecting the individuals who will sell the product.

independent sales representatives
Professional salespeople who act as independent contractors, paid entirely on commission.

INDEPENDENT REPS VERSUS EMPLOYEES   First, the sales manager must determine whether to hire independent sales representatives or a full-time sales force. **Independent sales representatives** are professional salespeople who act as independent contractors and who are paid entirely on commission. Examples are the sales consultants for companies like Mary Kay Cosmetics and the Longaberger Basket Company.

Using independent reps has advantages in a variety of situations. It quickly gives selling clout to smaller companies and those that are just starting out. According to Bill Kinard, owner of a California-based manufacturing company, contracting with reps "enables you to get fairly rapid coverage without the heavy initial outlay of money needed to support a direct sales force."[39] Organizations that sell in foreign

countries can benefit from local reps' understanding of their country's business cul-

Put It Into Practice

WHAT MAKES YOU A GOOD SALES CANDIDATE?

People often say they could never be salespeople. But think about it. You engage in selling all the time, whether you are arguing a point with a friend, asking someone on a date, presenting your ideas about a subject in class, or going on a job interview.

Think of yourself as a potential sales recruit, and list six qualities you have that would make you a good candidate for hire. To get your imagination going, you might consider how you would handle the different steps of the selling process. Later, if you decide to develop a résumé for a career in sales or marketing, you will have already gotten a start.

ture and avoid the gaffes that can result from managing employees in another country. The flip side, of course, is that the sales manager has less control over the performance of individual salespeople.

Hiring a sales force gives the organization more control over the selling of its products. This can be especially important for highly technical or proprietary products where the sales force needs inside, detailed knowledge. To market its sophisticated motion control products in 58 countries, Parker Hannifin Corporation operates sales offices in locations from Prague to Taipei.[40] However, staffing an inside sales force requires much work as well as money. The organization has to figure out what kinds of people are likely to sell its products effectively and how to identify those people. It has to supervise them, which may require a small company to hire a new manager as well as the salespeople themselves. And if certain salespeople don't work out, the organization has to bear the frustrations and expenses of losing these employees and trying to find more suitable replacements.

SEARCH FOR CANDIDATES   Whichever route the organization follows in setting up a sales force, the sales manager must find the people who will represent the organization's products. The manager may start the search simply by tapping his or her own industry contacts. To find experienced independent reps, the manager may prospect at trade shows or run classified ads in trade journals. Some organizations use *network selling,* also known as multilevel marketing, in which independent reps can increase their own earnings by recruiting and supervising other sales reps. This is the tactic used by Amway, Shaklee, and many other organizations.

There are many ways to identify candidates for an inside sales position. A good place to start may be to ask current employees for suggestions. Employment agencies, which prescreen applicants, are another source of candidates. Colleges and universities can provide the names of candidates who are educated and typically enthusiastic, ready to be trained. Although recent graduates may lack on-the-job experience, that is not necessarily a drawback. (See "Put It into Practice: What Makes You a Good Sales Candidate?") Barry Farber, president of Farber Training Systems in New Jersey, says emphatically, "I'd hire a rep without experience or knowledge of the industry who's willing to give one hundred and ten percent effort, versus someone who's experienced and highly skilled, but who is unmotivated."[41]

These are just a few of the possible sources of candidates. Creative sales managers need not limit themselves to the possibilities identified. "You can't lock yourself into just one [recruitment method]," notes Dirk Beveridge, president of Beveridge Business Systems of Illinois. "I view the recruiting process as having a quiver full of arrows on my back. One arrow in the quiver is newspaper advertising; another is talking to other salespeople and suppliers, and so on."[42]

SALES CANDIDATE PROFILE   Before sales managers can evaluate candidates fairly, they need a clear sense of what they are looking for. A systematic approach is to start by understanding the selling job. The sales manager conducts a job analysis and prepares a job description. A job analysis is an investigation of the activities, tasks, responsibilities, and environmental influences involved in the job. A job description is a detailed report of these findings.

Based on the job description, the sales manager can create a sales candidate profile—a description of ideal characteristics or qualifications. Typically, these characteristics include indicators of ability such as intelligence, verbal and math skills, and some measure of sales aptitude. In addition, many organizations are looking for certain personality traits thought to be related to success in selling. These organizations might look for someone who is responsible, sociable, creative, and has high self-esteem. Finally, the profile might specify certain skills, such as technical knowledge related to the product, ability to make an effective sales presentation, and interpersonal skills. (A variety of tests are available to measure all of these criteria.) If the profile is accurate, it will predict the ability to carry out the responsibilities in the job description and will help the sales manager identify the right person for the sales job.

The criteria to include in the profile depend in part on the nature of the product being sold. For instance, a potential candidate for a job selling pharmaceuticals to veterinarians should have at least some familiarity with and liking for animals. After all, the salesperson may have to spend hours tromping in and out of barns and animal hospitals. But especially in organizations that want to practice relationship selling, many of the vital characteristics of the good salesperson focus on customer relations. Dirk Beveridge calls the ideal salesperson a "sustaining resource." This salesperson builds a good emotional relationship with the customer, knows the product thoroughly, can identify the customer's needs from the *customer's* point of view, and ultimately becomes "like an unpaid member of your customer's staff."[43]

 The optimal criteria may also vary according to the country in which the salesperson will be operating. Personality traits or selling skills that work well in one country may be a hindrance in another. For example, a salesperson with a casual and friendly style may put U.S. customers at ease but insult prospects in a country that, like France, places more importance on formality and respect. Furthermore, selection criteria that are acceptable and even encouraged in one country (say, ethnic background in Malaysia) may be inappropriate or even illegal in others (as is ethnic background in the United States).[44]

SCREENING CANDIDATES   When the sales manager has identified candidates and decided on the criteria for selecting them, he or she is ready to screen the candidates. The basic techniques are to review résumés or written forms of application, administer aptitude and/or personality tests, and conduct interviews.

Many sales managers have their own tactics for screening candidates. Some call a candidate back for a more thorough interview outlining territory, responsibilities, and so forth, then ask the candidate to outline what he or she expects to accomplish in the job over a certain period of time.[45] Others provide a candidate with product and company information, asking him or her to give a sales presentation a week or so later. Some managers have candidates travel with company representatives on sales calls for a day, then ask their reps to report on the candidates' skills, attitude, motivation, and so forth.[46]

All of these tests are designed to see candidates in action in order to evaluate how well they will do on the job. These situations also give candidates a chance to decide whether they indeed want the job. In the end, both sales manager and sales candidate want a good match.

With a selection of over 3,200 name-brand products, Circuit City provides its sales counselors extensive training to help them match product features with customer needs. Programs include a two-week initial training period in existing products, five weeks in new markets, and ongoing training in every store, every week.

TRAINING AND SUPERVISION

Once salespeople have been hired, the sales manager must train and supervise them. These activities are important even for experienced salespeople.

TRAINING SALESPEOPLE Training costs an organization money and salespeople time, so both want it to be effective. The sales manager wants the sales force to be unified, whether in team or individual sales efforts. Training helps achieve this goal. Sales training involves more than learning the steps in the selling process. According to one study, average training programs spend 35 percent of their time on product information, 30 percent on sales techniques, 25 percent on market and general company information, and 10 percent on topics such as ethical selling practices.[47]

Much of the training for new sales recruits comes on the job, sometimes in "apprenticeship" with experienced salespeople. But many companies now go further than that. Seminars, classes, workshops, videos, and even interactive computer programs provide training. Some organizations have their own sales training staff; others hire outside firms that specialize in sales training to get new recruits up to speed and foster ongoing education for experienced salespeople. WilTel, an Oklahoma-based subsidiary of The Williams Companies that employs telephone salespeople, sends each new hire to Washington University in St. Louis for a two-week course in telecommunications technology. Then trainees spend two days at the University of Tulsa to polish up their writing and presentation skills.[48]

Today it is still uncommon to find salespeople who are already experienced in total quality management and team selling. Therefore, organizations that adopt these practices need to train sales and other employees in them. Kraft General Foods trains its salespeople to take a customer focus by having teams play a computer simulation game in which they pretend to sell to a traditional supermarket chain, a discounter, and a distributor that serves independent grocers. Early on, the trainer asks, "Which retailer has a competitive advantage?" The answer, which consistently surprises trainees, is that it is their job to help *all* the customers find a competitive advantage."[49]

Cross-functional training is beneficial not only for companies involved in team selling, but also for firms that simply want their sales force to be linked closely to the rest of the organization. Robinson Brick Co., a Denver manufacturer of residential brick, requires that salespeople take one other employee out into the field with them each month.[50] At Global Mail Ltd., which delivers international mail, sales trainees start by spending a few days with employees in customer service, accounting, operations, and telemarketing. They see firsthand how actions by salespeople affect other activities in the company.[51]

SUPERVISING A SALES FORCE   In many cases, ongoing training of salespeople is part of supervising them. The job of supervision basically entails enabling the salespeople to do their jobs and then seeing that the work gets done up to standards. Thus, supervision also includes motivation and compensation, covered in the next section, as well as evaluation, controlling, and leading. John Sample, CEO of Business Interiors, notes with insight, "Salespeople, especially successful ones, are entrepreneurs. And they are used to doing things on their own and having control of what they do, and they like to look at a job from start to finish."[52] How does a sales manager rein in these lone rangers, especially when it's necessary to create a team?

One important principle is the recurring one of focusing on customer needs. Some management experts advise that a sales manager in a customer-driven organization be not a gatekeeper for the sales force, but rather an advocate for the customer.[53] Others emphasize the importance of managers staying in touch with the sales force by traveling with it: "Sales management is a field job," writes Jack Falvey, contributing editor of *Sales & Marketing Management*.[54] Falvey explains that by talking with salespeople and accompanying them on visits to customers, the sales manager learns how the organization can help salespeople do their job well. In sum, to supervise the sales force effectively, the sales manager should be in constant contact with both the force and its customers.

MOTIVATION AND COMPENSATION

motivation
The positive or negative needs, goals, desires, and forces that impel an individual toward or away from certain actions.

Motivation is "the positive or negative needs, goals, desires, and forces that impel an individual toward or away from certain actions."[55] In terms of the sales force, motivation is the "fire within" that keeps salespeople productive year after year. How do successful salespeople stay motivated? "The answer is that they enjoy the challenge of working with customers and being paid well for their ability to produce business through creativity, knowledge, trust, and integrity," writes Jack Falvey. "To motivate such salespeople, managers must treat them as contributors. This will keep their productivity up and turnover and lost business down."[56]

To be sure, a sales manager looks for self-motivation in the new recruit before hiring. But the salesperson must also be presented with a clear job description, work under fair management, receive fair compensation, and be rewarded for a job well done. A good sales manager meets those needs and also knows how to challenge and stimulate the sales force to continue selling in a sluggish economy or a declining market.

CLEAR AND FAIR EXPECTATIONS   To meet the expectations of sales management, the salesperson needs to know what those expectations are. The most basic way to communicate these expectations is with a clear job description. The organization should spell out just what activities the salesperson should do and how performance will be measured. The activities specified might include those listed earlier in Table 20.1. Table 20.2 provides examples of common performance criteria.

Dan Vena, director of sales at Da Vinci Systems, a marketer of electronic mail systems, took a fresh look at expectations after four months of sales far below targeted levels. First, he asked each salesperson to describe his or her responsibilities and learned that none of them really knew what was expected. Next, Vena asked each employee for three suggestions as to how they could be more effective. Finally, he

TABLE 20.2

Common Performance Criteria for Salespeople

1.   Total sales volume and increase over last year.
2.   Degree of quota attainment.
3.   Selling expenses and decrease versus last year.
4.   Profitability of sales and increase over last year.
5.   New accounts generated.
6.   Improvement in performance of administrative duties.
7.   Improvement in service provided customers.
8.   Improvement in customer satisfaction.

Source: Gilbert A. Churchill, Jr., Neil M. Ford, and Orville C. Walker, Jr., *Sales Force Management,* 4th ed. (Homewood, Ill.: Irwin, 1993), p. 409.

made sure that the goals he set were measurable. Following those actions, sales rose almost immediately.[57]

Expectations and company policies for salespeople must not only be clear; they also must be fair. Good salespeople are eager to meet a challenge, but an impossible goal is more likely to discourage than to motivate. And salespeople will want to feel that they all have a chance at the rewards the organization offers.

COMPENSATION   The usual ways to compensate salespeople are to pay a straight salary, a straight commission, or a combination of salary and commission. A **salary** is a fixed payment made to an employee on a regular basis (say, at the beginning and the middle of each month). A **commission** is payment tied directly to the sales or profits from sales that a salesperson completes. Table 20.3 summarizes uses, advantages, and disadvantages of each of these compensation methods.

Commissions are usually paid on a percentage of sales basis. For example, if a sales rep who earns a 5 percent commission closed a $50,000 sale, the sales rep would earn a commission of .05 × $50,000, or $2,500. Laws governing compensation of sales representatives vary from state to state, and the sales manager must be familiar with the laws governing the organization's representatives. Generally, state laws cover the way a sales rep's commission is computed, when the commission must be paid— including payment upon termination—and the penalties for late payment.[58]

In the case of team selling, fair compensation can become a bit complicated. If the whole team does well, does everyone deserve equal compensation? Likewise, if the team does poorly, should every member suffer? Traditionally, people in the service and support area (even of major accounts) are paid less than order-getting salespeople. But organizations that recognize the efforts of the total team in the sales effort are beginning to even out the compensation.[59] One way some firms are doing so is by paying straight salaries, with bonuses based on the organization's profits.[60]

RECOGNITION   Providing recognition and appreciation of excellence on the job is not only good motivation, it helps promote quality in selling. Recognition may come in the form of tangible compensation such as money, travel, or merchandise, or it may be public appreciation of a salesperson's contribution to the sales effort (such as being named salesperson of the month). In many cases, recognition is a combination of both money and appreciation.

Procter & Gamble, explains a P&G executive, differentiates between "rewards (pay and promotion), which are administered by function, and recognition, which is usually non-monetary and can be more spontaneous in nature."[61] P&G doesn't have

salary
A fixed payment made to an employee on a regular basis.

commission
Payment tied directly to the sales or profits from sales that a salesperson completes.

TABLE 20.3

Comparison of Major Compensation Methods

COMPENSATION METHOD (FREQUENCY OF USE)	ESPECIALLY USEFUL	ADVANTAGES	DISADVANTAGES
Straight salary (12%)	When compensating new sales reps; when firm moves into new sales territories that require developmental work; when sales reps must perform many nonselling activities	Provides sales rep with maximum amount of security; gives sales manager large amount of control over sales reps; easy to administer; yields more predictable selling expenses	Provides no incentive; necessitates closer supervision of sale reps' activities; during sales declines, selling expenses remain at same level
Straight commission (5%)	When highly aggressive selling is required; when nonselling tasks are minimized; when company cannot closely control sales force activities	Provides maximum amount of incentive; by increasing commission rate, sales managers can encourage reps to sell certain items; selling expenses relate directly to sales resources	Sales reps have little financial security; sales manager has minimum control over sales force; may cause reps to provide inadequate service to smaller accounts; selling costs less predictable
Combination (85%)	When sales territories have relatively similar sales potentials; when firm wishes to provide incentive but still control sales force activities	Provides certain level of financial security; provides some incentive; selling expenses fluctuate with sales revenue; sales manager has some control over reps' nonselling activities	Selling expenses less predictable; may be difficult to administer

Source: Gilbert A. Churchill, Jr., Neil M. Ford, and Orville C. Walker, Jr., *Sales Force Management,* 4th ed. (Homewood, Ill.: Irwin, 1993), p. 591.

separate monetary reward systems for its customer teams, but performance against business objectives is linked indirectly to salary.

Motivation on a day-to-day basis can take many forms. A sales manager who empowers salespeople is engaging in motivation that usually pays off. Ways to do this daily include asking for and actively listening to sales reps' opinions, praising sales efforts that are in progress, and acknowledging staff for hard work and positive results.

It's probably tempting to enroll in the many motivational workshops, seminars, and retreats available. These vary in quality and effectiveness. Certainly, they can be helpful in the right place, with the right group of people, at the right time. But no seminar is a cure-all or a substitute for good management.

EVALUATION AND CONTROL

sales quota
Sales goal used for managing selling efforts.

The measures for evaluating and controlling efforts by the sales force are both quantitative and qualitative. Quantitative evaluation of a salesperson's performance is usually based on whether he or she has achieved a **sales quota**, or a sales goal used for managing selling efforts.[62] Sales quotas may be expressed in dollars, units, or points (that is, a predetermined number of points may be allotted for each dollar or unit sale).[63]

To retain customers and build loyalty, Albertson's Inc. has initiated the Service First Program. This program emphasizes the importance of quality service and gives managers a chance to empower their employees.

The sales manager's job usually includes setting sales quotas, perhaps in a joint effort with the salespeople who are expected to meet those quotas. Because they are supposed to motivate salespeople, quotas should, like all objectives, be challenging but achievable. This usually means setting them at least as high as the sales forecast for the salesperson's territory, but lower than the total potential sales that theoretically could be achieved.

Whether or not the salesperson meets his or her quota typically has a heavy influence on the commission, bonus, or raise the salesperson will receive. Consequently, from a management perspective, it is crucial to be sure that the quotas are stimulating the kinds of activities desired. At an organization that claims to emphasize quality and customer service, high quotas without measures of satisfaction can actually work against the organization. One company set quotas for selling service agreements along with its goods. Salespeople secretly included service agreements in most customers' contracts, knowing that they would meet their quota even if the customers later called to have the agreements voided.[64] The company said it cared about serving customers, but what it evaluated was the level of its sales.

MEASURING QUALITY IN SELLING   At an organization that uses the quality approach to marketing, simply measuring sales volume is not an adequate measure of the salesperson's success. Quality-driven organizations place at least as much emphasis on retaining customers and building loyalty. They need to know such information as sales levels of existing customers and the number of customers who have stopped buying.

Customers will be repeat buyers if they are delighted not only with the product itself, but with the service they receive from the sales force. Measuring customer satisfaction or delight with the sales effort is especially important in serving organizational buyers, who often rely on salespeople to provide information and help them solve problems. The challenge is that customer satisfaction can be difficult to quantify. The organization may rely on more qualitative information such as regular customer surveys, or it may track measures such as the number of merchandise returns and the number of customer complaints received. In either case, where customer satisfaction is part of the basis for rewarding employees, employees naturally put effort into that area.[65]

PERFORMANCE APPRAISALS   Most companies require the sales manager to conduct some type of periodic performance review of each sales representative. The sales manager evaluates each salesperson on the basis of goals achieved, level of selling skills, knowledge of the product, and so forth. The performance evaluation should give the salesperson and sales manager a chance to discuss achievements, areas that need improvement, performance objectives for the future, and the salesperson's career goals.

Ethical Issues in Personal Selling

Since personal selling is based on interactions and relationships between people, it is not surprising that this area of marketing gives rise to many ethical issues. Generally speaking, many of the ethical dilemmas that arise involve conflicts between the sales a salesperson might be able to generate by taking advantage of prospects and the benefits of building positive relationships with prospects. The reason these areas come into conflict is that sometimes the benefits of deceptive practices are immediate, whereas the benefits of ethical behavior may come more gradually, over the long run.

No matter how tempting the immediate rewards of unethical selling tactics, unethical behavior is unwise on practical as well as moral grounds. Research supports the commonsense notion that buyers are more likely to make purchases from organizations whose representatives behave ethically.[66] FMC's Alan Killingsworth has made the following observations about running that company's petroleum equipment group:[67]

> In my tenure internationally, I never lost an order because we refused to compromise our ethics. I will say we had to sell a little harder in some cases and had to continue to focus the customer on the benefits and features of our product, services, and company. We sold to an organization and not to an individual. This limited any attempt by an individual making a purchasing decision to evaluate FMC on anything but our features and benefits.

As more and more organizations focus on delivering customer value, salespeople should increasingly find that unethical tactics are not tolerated, much less rewarded.

MANIPULATION OF PROSPECTS

Many people have a negative view of personal selling because of the manipulative tactics of some salespeople. Most of us have at some time encountered an overeager salesperson who attempted to push us into buying something we weren't sure we really wanted. Some salespeople make outrageous claims for their products. Broadly speaking, when a salesperson makes a false claim about the significant features or benefits of a product, the salesperson's behavior is illegal as well as unethical.

An example of a false claim would be to say an investment is sure to earn the investor at least 10 percent a year. In fact, the returns on most kinds of investment aren't guaranteed, as many investors in Prudential-Bache energy partnerships recently learned to their dismay. Pru-Bache salespeople have been accused of using the Prudential name, and its image as solid and dependable, to lead investors to believe the partnerships were a safe investment. But, as limited partnerships of this type tend to be, these were risky, and some investors lost their retirement savings. Without admitting wrongdoing, Prudential has agreed to pay well over $300 million to settle investors' claims.[68]

Sometimes a claim is clearly an exaggeration. For example, the maker of a food processor might say, "This is the last appliance you'll ever need to buy for your kitchen." Such claims are considered a selling tactic called puffery. Puffery is legal, but it tends to leave prospects wondering whether they can believe anything the salesperson says.

A salesperson should in no way try to manipulate a prospect into a sale, especially if it is clear that the sale will not deliver value to the prospect. In the end, such tactics generate ill will and undermine the reputation of the salesperson and his or her employer. Thus, neither the customer nor the salesperson will benefit.

BRIBERY

bribes
Money, goods, or favors offered in exchange for influence.

In many instances, salespeople give gifts to customers or receive gifts from them. However, this practice may border on the unethical and illegal practice of taking or giving **bribes**—money, goods, or favors given in exchange for influence. Even if a gift is not intended as a bribe, it may be perceived as one, so the salesperson should consider his or her actions carefully. For example, sending holiday greeting cards to customers is a friendly gesture that could not be misconstrued as a bribe. But presenting expensive gifts of food, liquor, entertainment, or even cash might very well get both parties into trouble.

Many salespeople have felt pressure to use bribery because "everyone else is doing it." If competitors are treating prospects to fancy meals and box seats at baseball games, salespeople might fear that the prospects will not want to do business with them unless they do the same. In such situations, sales managers can do much to encourage ethical behavior by making the organization's standards clear, using rewards for generating satisfaction as well as sales, and fostering a climate in which customer value is everyone's top priority.

Part of the difficulty in avoiding bribery is that the difference between a friendly gesture and a bribe is unclear and varies from one situation to another. As in all other areas of marketing, however, if you have any doubts about the ethics of an action, don't go ahead with it.

Summary

Personal selling involves direct interaction between salesperson and customer—face to face, by telephone, or by computer link. Salespeople present the organization's image and products to customers and get news from customers about competitors.

There are three basic sales tasks. Order getting involves developing business by seeking out potential customers, providing them with product information, and persuading them to buy. Order taking is the routine completion of sales to customers who have already decided to buy a product. Support salespeople assist order getters and order takers but do not conduct sales transactions themselves. In team selling, a team of sales professionals works together to sell and service a company's major customers. Many quality-oriented firms practice relationship selling, in which salespeople and customers develop long-term, mutually beneficial relationships.

The personal selling process begins with prospecting, or identifying potential customers. Then it moves to preparation, or learning more about a prospect's needs. Next is the approach, or initial contact with a qualified prospect. Then the salesperson makes a presentation, communicating the sales message to the prospect. At some point, the salesperson may have to handle the prospect's objections, or resistance to making a purchase. The next step is the close, or the point at which the prospect makes a commitment to purchase. Finally,

the process is completed with follow-up, in which the salesperson makes sure that the customer is satisfied with the purchased product.

Management of the personal selling effort is often the job of a sales manager. This job begins with organizing the sales force, typically by dividing responsibilities into geographic, product, or customer sales territories. The sales manager must also ensure there is a skilled and motivated sales force. The manager may hire independent sales representatives or a full-time sales force. Doing so involves specifying the characteristics of the job and the employee, then identifying and screening candidates for the position. Training new recruits is important in unifying the sales force; it is also expensive for the company, so training efforts must be effective. Ways to motivate the sales force effectively include fair treatment, clear expectations, and fair compensation.

Evaluation and control of efforts by the sales force can be both quantitative and qualitative. Quantitiative evaluation of a salesperson's performance usually involves measuring achievement of a sales quota. Periodic performance reviews usually include qualitative measures of selling skills, knowledge of the product, and so forth.

Ethical issues are especially important in personal selling because of the personal interactions and relationships involved. One major area in which ethical issues arise is the temptation to manipulate prospects into buying, perhaps by providing misleading or inaccurate information. Salespeople are also sometimes tempted to use bribery to induce prospects to buy. Such tactics may offer short-term benefits, but they detract from the effort to build a mutually beneficial relationship with buyers by delivering value to them.

KEY TERMS AND CONCEPTS

personal selling (p. 598)
order getting (p. 600)
order taking (p. 601)
support salespeople (p. 601)
missionary salespeople (p. 601)
technical specialists (p. 601)
team selling (p. 602)
conference selling (p. 602)
seminar selling (p. 603)
relationship selling (p. 603)
prospecting (p. 604)
cold canvassing (p. 605)

qualifying (p. 605)
preparation (p. 606)
approach (p. 606)
presentation (p. 606)
stimulus-response presentation (p. 606)
formula selling presentation (p. 607)
canned presentation (p. 607)
need-satisfaction presentation (p. 607)
telemarketing (p. 609)
objections (p. 609)
closing (p. 611)

follow-up (p. 612)
sales plan (p. 612)
sales management (p. 612)
sales territory (p. 612)
major account management (p. 614)
independent sales representatives (p. 615)
motivation (p. 619)
salary (p. 620)
commission (p. 620)
sales quota (p. 621)
bribes (p. 623)

REVIEW AND DISCUSSION QUESTIONS

1. Name and define the three basic sales tasks.
2. If you were a sales manager for a company that manufactured equipment for office phone systems, how would you use team selling to sell the product? Do you think conference selling or seminar selling would work? Why or why not?
3. As the owner of a small firm that writes and produces direct-mail marketing material for other companies, how would you use relationship selling to build your business?
4. As the owner of a small business that does historic restoration and renovation of commercial and residential buildings, what sources might you use in prospecting?
5. If you were a real estate agent, what type of sales presentation would you use to sell homes to qualified prospects? Why?

6. As a salesperson, in what instances might you decide to accept a prospect's objections and not try to close the sale?
7. Why is follow-up an important part of the selling process?
8. If you were a sales manager, what methods would you use to determine whether a potential sales recruit was right for the job?
9. Suppose you are a sales manager for a sales force that has been fighting a sluggish economy and has thus been plagued by low sales and low morale.
   a. What steps would you take to motivate your force?
   b. Suppose your sales force served business clients in Japan and Germany as well as the United States. How would this affect your approach?
10. What ethical issues arise with regard to personal selling?

Chapter Project
A Personal Selling Exercise

Divide the class into pairs. Each pair should have a qualified prospect and a salesperson. The pair should decide what type of goods or services the salesperson is selling and the prospect is considering buying.

The prospect then makes a list of his or her needs and desires with regard to the product. (If the prospect represents a business, perhaps there is a problem that needs to be solved.) The salesperson next meets with the prospect to identify those needs, then makes a brief sales presentation. The prospect voices some objections, the salesperson handles them, and hopefully the prospect becomes a customer. This project can be done in class as a dialogue, or offered in writing.

You can adapt this project to team selling, conference selling, or seminar selling.

Case
Hewlett-Packard Company

"We strive to understand what our customers want, how they want it, and when they want it," says Manuel Diaz, general manager of Hewlett-Packard's computer systems, organization, worldwide sales, and marketing. "Then we come up with the products, programs, and marketing activities to satisfy them. It all starts with the customer." That's the philosophy of the California-based company that recently became the second-largest computer systems organization in the world.

Personal selling is critical to H-P's success because most of the company's customers are businesses. So, in 1992, H-P reorganized the sales force to assign salespeople to industries—a form of customer organization—rather than geographic territories. "We've organized our whole sales and marketing effort around listening to customers and understanding their industries," explains Diaz.

Training is a key aspect of this new organization. For instance, salespeople who now call on the financial services sector of H-P's market are required to take about two weeks of classroom training to learn the basics of finance. "They learn all the fundamentals, from banking to what happens on the trading floor," notes Diaz.

As for supervision, H-P calls one of its methods "Management by Wandering Around." The method is exactly what it sounds like: managers informally keeping up to date with employees. The company also has an open-door policy that allows employees to air grievances and discuss career possibilities. All of these training and supervision policies are designed to empower the employee to contribute effectively to the organization.

H-P strongly believes in relationship selling, as is stated in a recent annual report: "H-P's view of its relationships with customers has been shaped by two basic beliefs. First, we believe the central purpose of our business—the reason H-P exists—is to satisfy real customer needs. Second, we believe those needs can be fully satisfied only with the active participation and dedication of everyone in the company."

To that end, the company also practices a form of major account management, which it calls its "global accounts program." In this program, top-level managers act as liaisons with major customers in each of the industries that H-P serves. Those managers develop sales and marketing plans, meet with the customers, and are expected to deliver on projected revenues. "They are the eyes and ears that connect us to our major customers," remarks Diaz. "They are our antennae."

All of the information gathered from customers by salespeople and managers goes directly back to the H-P factories, where products are designed and manufactured specifically to meet customers' needs. One of H-P's hottest products has been the OmniBook 3000, which *The Wall Street Journal* calls "the first PC small enough and with good enough battery life to let you work with Windows software all the way through a cross-country plane flight without hassles." Another is its now-classic H-P Laser Jet printer series, launched in 1984. Because of continuous improvement, the series has for a decade maintained its 50 percent market share.

Besides being organized by customer type, many of H-P's sales reps serve on cross-functional teams. These support the company's total-quality effort by looking for ways to improve processes. With regard to sales, cross-functional teams have looked for ways to improve the use of customer feedback, studied the way H-P's customers make buying decisions (so the company can better approach them), and investigated ways to ensure customers get everything they need, not just everything they ordered.

Selling is a global issue at H-P. By the year 2000, the organization predicts that 70 percent of demand for its products will come from overseas. Currently, H-P has at least some presence (through joint ventures and other alliances) in Taiwan, Hungary, India, Italy, Spain, and Japan. A reflection of H-P's view that boundaries—geographic, technological, and service—exist to be broken is the company's simple slogan: "Think again."

QUESTIONS

1. What form of organization (sales territories) does H-P use for its sales force? Does this form of organization support its objectives as stated in the case?
2. In addition to classroom training, what other methods might help H-P salespeople learn about the industries they serve?
3. Would you like to work for H-P as a salesperson? Why or why not?

Sources: Margaret Kaeter, "Adding Quality to Sales," *The Quality Imperative,* September 1992, pp. 29–32; "Business to Business Product: Hewlett-Packard," *Sales & Marketing Management,* August 1993, p. 42; *Hewlett-Packard in Brief* (company report, n.d.), pp. 3, 5, 15.

Looking Ahead

Maintaining Competitive Advantage

The changing marketing environment is forcing marketers to reconsider how they approach their task. Such critical thinking is already beginning to reshape marketing. This discussion summarizes some major trends that are leading to innovative approaches to marketing. We also will describe how marketers are responding to and anticipating change by stretching their definitions of teamwork and quality.

A New Marketing Environment

Throughout this book, we have looked at many ways in which the marketing environment has changed. Thanks especially to advances in information technology, modern marketers are linked more closely than ever before to their suppliers and customers throughout the world. Such changes are timely for U.S. marketers, who increasingly find that their growth comes from foreign customers.

EMERGING MARKETS AROUND THE WORLD

As noted in Chapters 2 and 4, the fastest economic growth is occurring in parts of Asia. Economic prospects are expanding in Latin America, too. Marketing professor Ravi S. Achrol proposes that the world is becoming more uniformly developed, creating a global economy characterized by greater diversity and faster change than in the U.S. marketplace.[1] Thus, marketers have to broaden their scope beyond the slower-growing economies of the United States, Germany, and Japan. Forward-thinking marketers have already begun to do so.

Most notably, marketers will be affected by economic activity in China. They must ask, as did one recent commentator, "What will happen when a fifth of mankind, already the biggest producers of large numbers of industrial and food products, really start industrializing and exporting? When they start affording the big consumer and infrastructure goods like cars and telecoms systems?"[2] Marketers that don't ask these questions may find themselves cut off from their biggest geographic market segment. They may also find themselves unaware of some of their newest and biggest future competitors. Stated broadly, the successful marketers will be those that think in terms of global, rather than domestic, markets.

ECONOMIC SHIFTS IN THE UNITED STATES

The most important reason that tomorrow's marketers must think of their markets in global terms is that the U.S. economy no longer provides the demand needed to keep big corporations growing. Such giants of U.S. commerce as AT&T, General Motors, and IBM have announced layoff after layoff. Profit margins are shrinking, and sales growth is slowing at one company after another. The cause? Many analysts suggest that the U.S. economy has "matured." The rapid growth that followed World War II is not expected to return anytime soon. Furthermore, as other nations' technology has advanced, they have produced tougher competitors for U.S. businesses.

REACTIONS TO SLOWER GROWTH   Slower economic growth means that marketers cannot boost sales simply by spending more to make and promote their products. The initial response to this reality has been for businesses to look for ways to save money. Typically the savings have come from laying off as many employees as possible and restructuring the organization, so that the remaining employees can carry on.

When modern organizations need more staff or expertise, they are increasingly likely to contract with temporary workers, rather than hiring employees. By one estimate, half of the work force will be contingent workers (temporary or part-time employees or independent contractors) by the year 2000.[3] Already, the nation's largest employer is Manpower Inc., a temporary employment agency.[4]

THE INFORMATION AGE   One area in which U.S. economic growth has remained strong is in the exchange of information. Some people say that we live in an information age. A variety of computer, telecommunications, and other firms are already constructing a kind of information superhighway. "Traveling" this superhighway with computers, telephone hookups, satellite transmissions, and cellular devices, consumers, marketers, and businesspeople will be able to send and receive text, pictures, and entertainment. The implications for marketers are as diverse as enjoying easier communication with salespeople and figuring out how to get messages to consumers who can select 500 television channels with their remote controls.

Information technology also affects the product mix. Some products based on information are investments, wholesaling services, and research services. Producers of goods, too, rely on information to help them tailor their products to individual customers' needs. When a marketer relies heavily on information, the marketer's product tends to have a short life cycle, reflecting feedback from customers that leads to changes.[5]

CONSEQUENCES FOR MARKETERS   These trends mean that for organizations to move beyond mere survival, marketers must continually look for needs they can satisfy, both in the United States and abroad. And when marketers identify a need, the organization must be able to move quickly to meet it. Therefore, while a key issue for organizations in the recent past was efficiency, the foundation for success in the future will be adaptiveness.

Teamwork in the Twenty-first Century

The organizations that move quickly enough to survive in the future will use teamwork. Consultants Jon R. Katzenbach and Douglas K. Smith predict that "teams will become the primary unit of performance in high-performance organizations."[6] Teams help the organization move quickly and adapt to new needs and demands. In contrast, the prototype of success from the Industrial Revolution was to gain a competitive edge by efficiently producing goods in large volumes. The massive size of mass manufacturers required (or seemed to require) centralized, hierarchical management. But the resulting bureaucracy also slows an organization down and distances many of its employees from its customers. Such arrangements will work against big corporations.[7]

Another trend working against big hierarchical organizations is the growth in the proportion of workers known as technical workers. These people don't fit into the old classifications of white collar or blue collar. They might dress like white-collar workers, and they tend to be well educated and handle complex decisions. At the same time, they use tools and instruments, work with their hands, and make or repair things. Examples include computer programmers, copy machine repair technicians, and X-ray technicians. Under current projections, technical workers will be the largest segment of the work force by the year 2000.[8] Because of their technical expertise, they don't fit easily into a hierarchical organization, where managers more often are experts in the rules and policies of their organization.

These trends mean that successful organizations will be leaner and will have a flatter structure (fewer layers of management). Often cross-functional teams of technical workers will work under the direction of a manager whose primary responsibility is to coordinate their efforts and build cooperation. A classic example is Xerox, which went from four functional divisions to nine product divisions. Cross-functional teams in each of these divisions work together to make sure the division is producing what its customers want.[9] Carrying such arrangements a step or two further, more and more organizations are being structured as strategic alliances and virtual corporations.

STRATEGIC ALLIANCES

Until recently, the method of choice for handling uncertainty has been to become vertically integrated. As described in Chapter 16, vertical marketing systems give the organization a degree of control over its suppliers and customers. However, vertical integration will not be a flexible enough arrangement to handle the increasing diversity of markets and fast pace of change. Vertical integration also becomes less necessary as advances in information technology make it easier and faster to communicate with other organizations.[10]

Thus, the future is likely to see the opposite trend: small organizations working together as needed to meet common objectives. Instead of emphasizing ways to beat the opposition, tomorrow's organizations will more often be seeking to manage ongoing, mutually beneficial relationships with one another.[11] Already organizations are getting smaller. IBM's work force is three-quarters of its 1985 size; Digital Equipment Corporation has shrunk from 126,000 to 98,000 employees. And research by MIT professors Erik Brynjolfsson and Thomas W. Malone found that although the average number of employees per company grew until the 1970s, it has since been declining.[12]

strategic alliances
Long-term partnerships designed to accomplish the strategic goals of both parties.

When tomorrow's smaller companies need more expertise, they are apt to form **strategic alliances**. These are long-term partnerships designed to accomplish the strategic goals of both parties. Instead of being controlled through the power of a hierarchy, the group's activities are largely controlled by shared norms, such as a high value on commitment, trust, and shared benefits.[13] Motorola seeks out and builds relationships with suppliers that share its concern for "total customer satisfaction."[14]

A common criticism of strategic alliances is that the sharing of information can enable partners to become tough competitors. But believers in strategic alliances maintain that sharing information also is a necessary part of the drive to achieve superior quality. With regard to the electronics industry, Ernst & Young's Stephen Almassy observes, "Companies are breaking down corporate barriers in order to achieve world-class product development and delivery."[15]

core competencies
The few processes central to the organization's success.

CORE COMPETENCIES   To plan strategic alliances, the organization has to know what its **core competencies** are. These are the few processes central to the organization's success. In a well-planned strategic alliance, each member focuses on carrying out its core competencies. Genentech's core competency is advanced genetic research, and it forms strategic alliances with firms such as Corning to apply the results of its work.[16] Apple Computer combined its easy-to-use software (but shortage of manufacturing facilities) with Sony Corporation's skills in manufacturing and miniaturization. Sony made 100,000 PowerBook notebook computers for Apple under its strategic alliance.[17]

CHOOSING A PARTNER   The depth of commitment required to make a strategic alliance work makes it crucial to choose partners that will be able to give both parties a real advantage. According to consultant Ram Charan, this means looking for more than an arrangement that will save money. Rather, the partner should be able to provide "access to a new market or a special expertise, or [enable the organization] to beat others to market."[18] To extend its service to international markets, MCI Communications Corporation has entered into a strategic alliance with British Telecommunications. Many other telephone companies are expected to seek similar arrangements to serve new geographical markets.[19]

Milestone Media and DC Comics' strategic alliance to market comic books featuring black superheroes also meets these criteria. Milestone Media benefits from its larger partner's strength and expertise in producing and distributing comic books. DC Comics, in turn, sought out an organization that would help it broaden its product line in terms of ethnic diversity. According to DC publisher Paul Levitz, "By reaching to an outside structure, you can tap into a passion that you couldn't pull together on demand."[20]

Another strategic alliance that involves sharing expertise to tap new markets consists of AT&T, Sega of America (which makes machines that play electronic games), and PF. Magic, a small producer of computer games. AT&T determined that it would be profitable to sell more long-distance phone service by allowing its customers to play interactive computer games over their phone lines. However, although the big corporation knew a lot about marketing telephone service, it was unfamiliar with computer games. Sega used its expertise in game-playing machines to develop a machine that can be hooked up to a phone line. PF. Magic provided the games, and the packages were distributed through AT&T stores.[21]

In addition, members of each organization must trust members of the other. Building trust generally requires that the parties forming a strategic alliance do so in a spirit of collaboration, emphasizing the common good. Trust building also requires a long-term effort to seek ways to work together. For today's marketers, the greatest challenge that results from working in strategic alliances may be learning to focus on building these long-term relationships, rather than focusing on individual sales of some product.[22]

A related issue is that the members of the alliance must trust that the others will deliver an acceptable level of quality. In Washington, D.C., John Cotter put together an alliance of nine local companies that handled various kinds of home improvements. The object of the alliance was to share communications activities and customer lists in order to build business. The biggest concern among businesses considering membership in the alliance was whether poor work by another contractor would hurt their own reputation. To make sure that their partners would be acceptable, representatives from the companies met extensively and visited one another's job sites. Eventually nine companies formed an alliance called the Quality Group, and they have found the joint effort to be beneficial.[23]

Because of the sometimes great differences in marketing from one country to another, global marketers often find strategic alliances attractive. The marketer finds an organization in the target country to handle marketing functions for which its local presence gives it an edge. According to one report, such global strategic alliances increased 20 to 30 percent per year during the late 1980s and early 1990s.[24]

MAKING STRATEGIC ALLIANCES WORK   Because strategic alliances are designed to achieve strategic goals, the basic measure of their success is whether they improve the competitive position of the organizations entering into the alliance.[25] In a study of 49 strategic alliances, the McKinsey research firm found that about one-third fell short of the parent companies' expectations.[26] One reason that so many failed is that managing a strategic alliance is complex. Not only must the alliance's activities be controlled, but positive relationships among individuals from two different organizations must be cultivated. When conflicts arise, there frequently is no one manager with the authority to dictate a solution. Rather, parties from both sides must work together to resolve each conflict. Thus, the individuals who form and operate a strategic alliance must have skills in preventing and resolving conflicts.

Another pitfall to avoid is that of the members of the alliance becoming so tightly bound together that they lose their flexibility and innovativeness. For example, if a supplier becomes focused on its strategy in supplying another member of the network, it may customize its facilities to serve this single customer so much that it can't compete in serving other customers. It may even lose its ability to innovate. As a result, even its customer in the strategic alliance may eventually drop this supplier. And the buyer in a strategic alliance may become overly involved in a supplier's management decisions, to the extent that it is stretching its resources beyond its core competencies. Harley-Davidson avoids such problems by using a simple, flexible contract with its suppliers, making it easy for both parties to escape the arrangement.[27]

An essential tool to prevent problems is a well-written agreement that provides clear direction but allows the alliance enough flexibility to respond to changes in the marketing environment. When conflicts do arise, the members must seek a solution that benefits both parties. Some members may find that it helps to be systematic about evaluating their alliance. Procter & Gamble and Genta, a San Diego biotechnology company, use a consultant to help them manage their strategic alliance. First, managers from each company rate the performance of both partners in a variety of areas. Then they meet with the consultant to discuss how they can use greater cooperation to benefit both parties.[28]

Experience has also shown that in successful strategic alliances, the partners must work cooperatively, rather than trying to dictate what to do. The opposite happened in an alliance between TRW and Fujitsu in which TRW was to sell some Fujitsu products in the United States. The products didn't sell, and TRW blamed Fujitsu for failing to adapt them to the U.S. marketplace. Fujitsu, in turn, complained that it lacked a say in decision making, and the alliance fell apart.[29]

Glass and ceramics maker Corning is one company that has made strategic alliances work. The company credits its success to its long-term view. In the words of Corning vice chairman Van Campbell, "We're looking only for lifetime associations, because you have to invest an enormous amount of energy to make a partnership work."[30] Such an investment, says Campbell, is not worthwhile for an alliance that will last only a few years.

VIRTUAL CORPORATIONS

virtual corporation
A network of alliances in which each member shares its expertise in a particular area.

Some organizations not only enter into strategic alliances, but use that type of relationship as a model for their overall operating structure. These organizations create what have come to be called virtual corporations. A **virtual corporation** is a network of alliances in which each member shares its expertise in a particular area. In the purest form of a virtual corporation, the member organizations are small and streamlined, contributing only their core competencies. The virtual corporation may form quickly in response to a market need and end when that need disappears.[31]

To move quickly, share risks, save money, and bring together creative people, Paul Farrow set up Walden Paddlers as the core of a virtual corporation. Farrow, Walden's only employee, saw a need for a high-quality kayak designed for beginners and made out of recycled plastic. He arranged a manufacturing alliance with Hardigg Industries, a plastics molding business that was seeking to do custom work and was one of a handful of companies with the necessary facilities. The kayaks are designed by Jeff Allott of General Composites, a design firm that was seeking to reposition itself away from the defense industry and more toward sporting goods (an industry about which Allott and his partner had a passion). To build relationships with dealers, Farrow supplied each with a demo kayak for 30 days; the dealers quickly sold the first 100 boats produced. Eventually Farrow plans to create an alliance with a major national distributor that has expertise in promoting sporting goods. Walden Paddlers also relies on the expertise of an outside banker, lawyer, and packaging designer.[32]

According to one account,[33] the key characteristics of a virtual corporation include a high level of trust among members, sharing of information through electronic linkups, and fuzzy boundaries between members and their suppliers, competitors, and customers. Such an organization is most likely to succeed when members can work cooperatively and when each member has identified its true core competencies.

BENEFITS OF VIRTUAL CORPORATIONS   Why form a virtual corporation rather than hire the employees needed to operate a traditional corporation? A single big organization tends to move more slowly than the small organizations that join together in a virtual corporation. Thus, the virtual corporation can offer the responsiveness and adaptability so necessary in today's rapidly changing environment. In addition, a virtual corporation has more resources than any of its member organizations would have alone. And by specializing in their core competencies, the members direct their resources to where they can have the most impact.

Furthermore, the activities and products of a virtual corporation can be excellent because each member draws on its area of expertise. Thus, to develop his idea for a hand-held, pen-based computer, Ron Oklewicz formed TelePad, staffed with a few designers and engineers. For help with product design and development, TelePad linked up with GVO Inc., an industrial design firm. To work out some bugs in engineering, the organization brought in a team from Intel Corporation. The computers are made in an IBM plant that had extra capacity, and the production workers are paid with checks issued by a data-processing firm. Oklewicz himself offers expertise in selling to the government, one of TelePad's target markets. He believes that this business arrangement enables him to benefit from the expertise of thousands of highly trained people. For example, he credits Intel's team with solving in a week problems that would have taken his own employees months to resolve.[34]

CHALLENGES OF VIRTUAL CORPORATIONS   Of course, coordinating the activities of several virtual corporation members in different locations is a complex task. What will make it a viable one is further advances in information technology. Roger N. Nagel, operations director for Lehigh University's Iacocca Institute, envisions a "national information infrastructure" that will make it easy for organizations to connect with one another at will. Different organizations' computers and machine tools would be linked by this network, and an information clearinghouse would make it easy for organizations to identify who provides the services they need.[35] In addition, the federal government is planning a National Research and Education Network, which would enable scientists and engineers in different research labs to share and manipulate computer simulations and computerized product designs.[36] An information infrastructure with such capabilities would make it possible for people to work in cross-organizational as well as cross-functional teams. In other words, people from more than one organization could work on the same project at the same time, rather than shipping the work from one organization to another.

VIRTUAL CORPORATIONS AND THE CONTINGENCY WORK FORCE   The virtual corporation is one of the trends behind the growth in the contingency work force. The culture of a virtual corporation supports the practice of expanding or contracting to meet fluctuating needs by hiring and releasing contractors and temporary employees as the work load requires. Prophet Market Research consists of Scott Galloway and R. Ian Chaplin, who work out of their San Francisco homes and contract with M.B.A. and Ph.D. students on 40 campuses. Prophet notifies these researchers of assignments via messages on the Internet computer network, then sends a laptop computer loaded with the necessary background material.

As in this example, contingency workers serve not only as production workers and secretaries but in such specialized roles as engineers, medical technicians, and paralegals. Glasgow design consultants John Reid and Bill Mather have found strong demand for their business, called The Edge. What attracts their organizational customers is the ability of The Edge to act as part of the customer's marketing group, handling everything from selecting a brand name to training salespeople to directing an advertising campaign.[37]

In effect, an organization that uses such services has a "just-in-time" work force. Of course, not all of these contingency workers are equally happy and motivated by such arrangements. A likely ethical issue of the twenty-first century will be the treatment of contingency workers.

Quality and Value

One of the potential benefits of teamwork within and among organizations is that it can put the focus on customers. In contrast, notes consultant John W. Humphrey, "The command-and-control structure of many companies made managers responsible to each other instead of to customers."[38] Whether through employee empowerment, strategic alliances, or virtual corporations, successful managers are seeking to move away from hierarchy to partnerships designed to satisfy their customers.

What this means for the quality movement is a shift in focus from error-free products to customer value.[39] Instead of focusing internally on the organization's processes, successful organizations are learning to look outside, to their customers. They derive their competitive advantage from providing customer value, that is, goods and services that meet customers' needs at a fair price. To determine how well the organization is performing, its managers and employees do not rely on internal measures, but ask customers.

Sometimes this means creating partnerships with customers in order to develop ways to satisfy their needs. Gibbs and Associates, a Moorpark, California, company that develops software for computer-aided manufacturing, teamed up with Fadal Engineering Company to develop software that would control Fadal's machining centers. Users of Fadal's machines would be machining relatively simple parts and would be more comfortable looking at pictures than at the text displayed by many software programs. So Gibbs came up with software that uses two- and three-dimensional illustrations to show users clearly what they are doing. Users can easily see if problems will result from programming the machine in a particular way.[40]

Focusing externally—that is, on the customer—requires that marketers ask basic questions about what customers want and need. They need to take a fresh look at whether the organization is meeting those wants and needs. Consultant Edith Weiner illustrates how this might apply to retailing. A clothing store sells many items, such as pants and coats, but these items are available through many outlets. Some, like catalogs, can be more convenient. Why would anyone bother going to a store? One reason might be to try on, say, a pair of pants before buying. If so, it doesn't make sense for fitting rooms to be tiny, uncomfortable stalls stuck at the back of the store. In the future, a clothing store might be able to gain a competitive advantage by providing big fitting rooms where customers can sit, move around, and get a good look at how the clothes fit.[41]

In the words of consultant Tom Peters, this value-driven approach amounts to a change from "doing things perfectly" to "doing things well."[42] As an example, Peters cites the development of Ingersoll-Rand's Cyclone Lightning Grinder, a tool for removing metal burrs from equipment such as engine parts. Ingersoll-Rand teamed up with the Group Four industrial design firm to make a product that not only removed burrs effectively but also was comfortable to use and attractive. When a distributor took hold of a prototype, he exclaimed, "Wow!" Said project leader Jim Stryker, "I've put 'Wow' on my short list of future new-product criteria."

This external focus is, in effect, the true meaning of the marketing orientation.

KEY TERMS AND CONCEPTS

strategic alliances (p. 630)
core competencies (p. 630)
virtual corporation (p. 632)

Career Opportunities in Marketing

Throughout this book, you've seen how a variety of people have achieved success in marketing: as entrepreneurs, as executives of large companies, as businesspeople in the United States and abroad. Both men and women have succeeded, including those from a variety of cultural and racial backgrounds.

These marketers believe—formally or informally—in delivering value to customers. In this section, you'll learn some of the career opportunities that exist in marketing and how to begin your job search. But don't limit yourself to the ideas presented here; as a potential successful marketer, use your imagination!

Types of Career Opportunities in Marketing

You've studied chapters on marketing research, managing new and existing products, distribution channels, and communication. You've read about profit-centered and nonprofit organizations. Maybe you already have a sense of what type of marketing opportunity you'd like to pursue. Or perhaps you want to try to do them all and become an entrepreneur.

Below is a broad accounting of the major career opportunities that exist for marketers not only in the United States, but in other countries as well. For instance, 3M employs marketing staff in more than fifty countries.[1] Seventy-five percent of The Gillette Company's personnel is employed abroad (although these are not all marketing staff), embodying the company's philosophy of "world-class brands and world-class products, made possible by our world-class people."[2] Toys "R" Us, Inc. operates more than 120 stores in ten countries, including Canada, Europe, the United Kingdom, Japan, and Malaysia.[3] Lotus Development Corporation has offices—and related marketing opportunities—in Japan, Singapore, and China.[4]

MARKETING RESEARCH

Marketing researchers are responsible for gathering and analyzing all kinds of information useful for planning, implementing, and controlling the marketing effort. Marketing research is a popular field: more than 30,000 people are employed in it.[5] Some marketing researchers work for the companies that actually manufacture and sell the goods and services they are researching; some work for advertising agencies; others work for or operate their own, independent research firms.

Opportunities exist for marketing researchers both in the United States and abroad. The Dun & Bradstreet Corporation routinely conducts research on a global basis. According to the company's annual report, "our divisions have unparalleled capabilities to provide comprehensive local, regional and global information services to customers throughout the world."[6] And Henkel KGaA, the German manufacturer of hair-care products, toiletries, and cleansers, works "closely with Nielsen to harmonize our marketing-research information across Europe."[7]

Marketing research can be an exciting entry into the world of marketing for recent graduates. Monitoring trends and identifying business opportunities, designing surveys, interviewing consumers, tabulating data, and writing reports are just a few of the tasks that researchers with various levels of experience undertake.

PRODUCT MANAGEMENT

The process of managing new and existing products has undergone significant change with the establishment of cross-functional teams at many companies. Still, other companies successfully use the traditional hierarchy in which the management of a product is overseen by a brand manager. Naturally, a brand manager or other type of marketing manager is not an entry-level position, but support positions, ideal for recent college graduates, do exist.

CHANNELS OF DISTRIBUTION

A wide variety of opportunities—and positions—exist in the area of distribution channels. For instance, an operations manager supervises physical distribution functions such as warehousing. The traffic manager weighs the pros and cons of different types of transportation. People in inventory control forecast customer demand for goods and monitor levels of stock. Many organizations have a customer service department linked to distribution, designed to make sure the needs of customers are met promptly and effectively.

RETAILING

Many people begin their careers in marketing through retailing; more than 4.5 million people work in retail sales in the United States.[8] People interested in a career in retailing can concentrate on either merchandise management (products themselves) or store management. Those who want to enter merchandise management generally do so as buyer trainees, then work their way up through assistant buyer and buyer to merchandise division manager. Those interested in store management start as management trainees, then move up through assistant department manager, department manager, and on to store manager. Many larger stores such as department store chains have their own training programs for both career paths.

ADVERTISING

Many people view advertising as the glamour end of marketing. In a sense, they're right: advertising gets the attention of consumers or organizational buyers. It can make or break a product, can even make or break careers.

There are many types of advertising, sales promotion, and publicity, and advertising is originated in different ways (by manufacturers, service providers, independent advertising agencies) through a variety of media. The career opportunities for those who are imaginative and persistent may be limitless. Students who excel in writing may want to pursue careers in copywriting or direct marketing, while those who have artistic talent may be interested in the art department; still others may find they have a talent for media buying.

One successful direct marketer founded her company, Letterworks International, because she needed a job. "The reality of the way this business started was that I couldn't get a job," says Heidi Neumann Hansen. "I was doing free-lance writing for people, and they needed these services, and the ad agencies weren't doing it. I took advantage of an opportunity."[9]

Entry-level jobs in advertising aren't easy to come by, and because of their popularity the pay is often lower than in other marketing fields. If you want to pursue a career in advertising, you must be willing to start at the bottom of the hierarchy and work hard through its different levels—or, with at least some professional experience, strike out on your own.

PERSONAL SELLING

Entering the field of marketing via personal selling has two advantages. First, you may find that you're good at it, like it, and decide to make it a career. As a sales representative, you have the potential to earn a good salary, set your own hours, engage in a certain amount of regional, sometimes national, or even international travel, and advance at a fairly rapid rate. Second, personal selling provides you with excellent training to move on into other areas of marketing if you so choose.

As a recent graduate, you may land a job in order getting, order taking, or even missionary selling. You may be prospecting for customers and demonstrating products or answering questions and attending to complaints from existing customers. You may attend trade shows, sales meetings, and motivational conferences. To be successful you must be self-disciplined and highly motivated, because a supervisor will not be watching you at all times.

If you decide to pursue a career in sales itself rather than move into other areas of marketing, you may aspire to become a sales manager or director of sales, managing the organization's sales force. A sales manager's job generally entails a mixture of travel (visiting salespeople in their territories, as well as major customers), people management, and business responsibilities.

NONPROFIT ORGANIZATIONS

As you've read throughout this book, nonprofit organizations are engaging in increasingly sophisticated marketing efforts. Like profit-centered organizations, they are competing for dollars through membership, donations, and the like. Nonprofit organizations as diverse as the Appalachian Mountain Club and Childreach International have employees engaged in marketing actitivities.

Many of these activities mirror those of profit-centered organizations, such as conducting surveys, using direct mail advertising, even merchandising. In addition, nonprofit organizations often engage in fund-raising by approaching potential individual donors or members as well as corporations, or by applying for government grants or other public funds. Fund-raising itself can be an exciting, challenging career that combines good writing skills and business sense with polished interpersonal skills.

ENTREPRENEURSHIP

You think you've got good business sense and a great idea for a product, or the thought of owning a franchise appeals to you. You've got drive and self-discipline, and you want to control your own destiny; you want no limits on your career advancement or earning potential. You think you want to be an entrepreneur.

Your aspirations are admirable, and there are opportunities in the marketplace for entrepreneurs. Entrepreneurship can generally be divided into two categories: franchise ownership and outright business ownership. (Of course, there are variations on these.)

In a franchise agreement, the entrepreneur (franchisee) enters into a business relationship with a franchisor, agreeing to certain terms such as the price at which a product will be sold and from whom supplies will be bought. In turn, the franchisor offers benefits (such as the value of an established product name and chances to participate in widespread promotional campaigns) to the entrepreneur.

The entrepreneur who starts his or her own business takes all the risks but has the freedom and potential to gain more. We all hear stories about successful businesses that started in someone's living room or garage, with just a few dollars in capital (Heidi Neumann Hansen, mentioned earlier, founded her company with an investment of $500.[10]) But many entrepreneurs must find some type of financial backing. And while there are examples of recent college graduates who instantly grab success as entrepreneurs, in many cases successful entrepreneurs have at least some professional experience. A good job with a company that is already established provides you with priceless training, contacts with people in the industry, and a chance to learn from your mistakes without losing your entire business. John Guardiola, owner of a Duraclean franchise, states in a magazine ad, "In my opinion, IBM is a superb organization. I wouldn't trade my 15 years there for anything. Yet, in spite of all the benefits a large, successful corporate structure can offer, I came to the conclusion it was time to go into business for myself."[11] Guardiola made his decision to buy a franchise *after* spending 15 years learning about business as an employee at IBM.

Of course, there are entrepreneurs who simply refuse to follow the traditional path, and you may be one of them. Sophia Collier and Connnie Best, two such entrepreneurs, started an alternative soft-drink company in 1977, when they were both in their early twenties. Soho Soda began because "there was no alternative beverage on the market," says Collier.[12] Her sum total of business experience was managing a food cooperative in Portland, Maine; Best had no real experience at all. They encountered plenty of obstacles but pushed through to success. Two vital factors in their achievement were their persistence and the fact that they came up with the right product at the right time to meeting consumers' needs.

Another example is Russell Simmons, founder and head of the two largest African-American-owned record/entertainment companies in the United States: RAL (Rush Associated Labels)/DefJam and Rush Communications. Simmons, in his mid-thirties, is known in the industry as the "Godfather of Rap" and has produced a score of superstar rap acts, including Public Enemy, LL Cool J, and Run-DMC. He left college to found Rush Management in 1979, promoting local rap groups, including his brother Joey's group, Run-DMC. He says he learned the business by "hangin' out" and "getting flavorful," immersing himself in the whole culture of rap.[13] Simmons started with a clear goal in mind and learned everything he could, not only about the kind of music he was promoting, but also about his customers. When rap music reached the mainstream, he set new goals (entering film, radio, and even fashion). The continual shift toward new objectives is the mark of a true entrepreneur.

Conducting Your Job Search

This section takes you on a brief walk through your search for a job in marketing. Don't rely on this text as your only source for career planning, but instead use it as a starting point.

CHARACTERISTICS OF A GOOD MARKETER

What makes a good marketer? Certainly, not all marketers are alike, just as not all marketing jobs are alike. But successful marketers generally agree that the following traits are the mark of a good marketer:

- Someone who works well with other people
- Someone who uses his or her imagination to solve problems
- Someone who is self-motivated and self-confident
- Someone who is willing to take appropriate risks
- Someone who can spot trends
- Someone who enjoys a fast-paced working environment

As you begin your job search, ask yourself whether any or all of the above characteristics apply to you.

Remember that not all marketing jobs require all these traits. For instance, a person interested in writing advertising copy doesn't need as strong a desire to spend time with other people as does someone who wants to begin a career in personal selling.

Further, some marketing fields require specialized skills and education. Thus, an advertising art director needs a background in commercial art. Someone who conducts cost analysis of physical distribution systems must be comfortable with math. An advertising account executive or director of marketing may be required to obtain an M.B.A. Learning what skills, education, and personality traits are expected of marketing professionals in different jobs will help you decide which job is best for you.

RESEARCHING THE RIGHT JOB

Finding the right job takes work. First, you need to evaluate your own strengths, weaknesses, and interests, as discussed above. Then you need to identify resources that can help you pinpoint which companies or nonprofit organizations have training programs or entry-level positions to fill.

CAREER PLACEMENT OFFICE   Haunt the career placement office at your college. Learn what information is available to you and how to obtain and use it. If possible, arrange an interview with someone in the office to help you focus your search. If you attend a medium-sized or larger school, chances are recruiters from different companies will visit the college to scout for good employment candidates. Even if you are only mildly interested in a particular company, try to speak with the recruiter. The interview will give you valuable information and experience.

In addition to company listings, many colleges also have listings of alumni who are willing to speak with or correspond with graduating seniors interested in careers in their particular field. These can be valuable contacts, not only for specific jobs, but for current information about the marketing field.

EMPLOYMENT AGENCIES   Employment agencies, or "headhunters," can help you launch your career by helping you focus your search, providing you with an introduction to a company, and arranging interviews for you. An employment agency is paid a fee by the company that does the hiring and wants to place as many qualified job candidates as possible. Many agencies now specialize in certain fields, and some only accept candidates at a certain level (for example, middle management and above), so when you phone an agency to ask about employment opportunities, ask whether the agency handles recent graduates in your field of interest.

When you consider using an employment agency for your full-time job search, don't rule out contacting an agency that handles temporary assignments. A temporary agency's customers require qualified candidates only for a specified period of time—for instance, to handle a holiday rush or to replace a permanent employee who is temporarily disabled. A temporary assignment can be valuable in two ways: (1) it gives you immediate working experience in your field of interest; (2) it may lead to full-time employment later on.

Don't forget the state employment office, which lists job openings only in your state, and at which you may find different job listings than exist at private agencies or the college career office.

WANT ADS   The competition for jobs listed in the newspaper want ads is usually fierce, but don't hesitate to respond. Also, at the library, read sales and marketing trade publications as well as business magazines, which often contain job listings. These give you an idea of what types of entry-level positions are currently available, as well as what salary you can expect to earn.

PERSONAL CONTACTS   Friends, relatives, and acquaintances may be your most valuable resource as you look for a job. A personal introduction to a company by one of its employees helps distinguish you from other applicants. Don't be shy about contacting people you know, even if it's just to ask for information about a certain field in marketing. Most people who are established in their careers are happy to help students by answering questions and passing a résumé to the proper department, even if a specific job is not readily available. If you present yourself in a professional manner and convey your genuine interest in the person's field or organization, chances are you'll at least get a friendly reply; perhaps you'll even get an opportunity for an interview.

WRITING YOUR RÉSUMÉ

One of the most important aspects of your job search is writing your résumé. A good résumé actually markets your strengths to your customer: your potential employer. Your résumé should present your qualifications clearly in a well-organized format.

There are three résumé formats: (1) the chronological format, which presents your work experience and education in the sequence in which they occurred; (2) the functional format, which groups your experiences according to relevant skills; and (3) the targeted format, which emphasizes skills that apply to specific jobs. The chronological and functional formats are often most useful for recent graduates, who are still in the process of targeting their careers.

Whichever format you choose, your résumé should contain the following information:

- Full name, address, and telephone number. If you have a school address and home address where you can be reached, include both.
- Your highest and next-highest level of education, including relevant courses taken.
- Your work experience, including summer jobs and campus jobs, focusing on any experience related to aspects of marketing.
- Relevant extracurricular activities and interests, including any awards or honors you have earned.
- A statement that personal and professional references will be available upon request.

One final note about résumé writing. While your résumé should present your strengths and qualifications to their best advantage, it should not misrepresent them. In other words, don't claim experience you don't have, job titles you haven't earned, skills you haven't mastered, or courses you haven't taken. Doing so is not only unethical, it will catch up with you, perhaps costing you a job you wanted badly. Instead, emphasize your existing experience and your willingness to learn. No one expects a recent college graduate to know everything about the field he or she wants to enter.

WRITING YOUR COVER LETTER   When you submit a résumé, it should be accompanied by a cover letter, which introduces you to a potential employer. In your cover letter, state your purpose (inquiring about employment), list two or three of your main qualifications, and refer to the enclosed résumé. If you were referred to the organization by someone you know, mention the person's name and the nature of your relationship (friend, relative, etc.). Close the letter by politely requesting an interview and thanking the reader for his or her consideration.

Don't be tempted to be cute or outrageous in your cover letter in an effort to gain attention. Your effort will certainly attract attention, but it will probably land your letter and résumé in the wastebasket. Instead, adopt a professional, courteous tone, and keep the letter brief.

THE SUCCESSFUL JOB INTERVIEW

You may be granted an informational interview or an interview for a specific job. An informational interview is just what it sounds like—it provides you with a chance to learn more about the company and the types of positions that may become available. Although it is not an interview for a specific job opening, it is just as important, for it gives you the opportunity to create a favorable impression with a potential employer. So treat the informational interview and the specific job interview as equally important.

When you've been granted an interview, write down the date, time, address, and name of the person to whom you are to report for your appointment. Ask for directions to the company if necessary.

Then do your homework. Find out as much about the organization in advance as possible. This indicates to the interviewer your genuine interest in the firm as well as your self-motivation. If you know someone who works at the company, call and ask about the company's best-selling products or services, as well as qualities the company considers important in its employees. Ask the person to send you a copy of the firm's annual report or other pertinent written material, if possible. (You can also request this from the personnel department.) Consult general publications such as *The Wall Street Journal* or trade publications for any news information about the company.

Next, prepare *yourself* for the interview. Review in your mind your strengths, weaknesses, and relevant experiences. Think through carefully and clearly why you would want to work for the organization, and why you would want this particular job. Ask yourself what you expect to learn from the job and what you think you can contribute. Ask yourself what your general and specific career goals are. An interviewer will most likely ask you all of these questions.

The day of the interview, be sure to arrive a few minutes prior to the time scheduled for your appointment. You don't need to invest in a new wardrobe, but wear simple, appropriate business clothes. Pay attention to good grooming. During the interview, be alert but try to relax; the interviewer wants to learn about you, not trip you up. Listen to the questions you are asked, and answer honestly, maintaining a positive attitude. Don't be afraid to ask questions of the interviewer, about the company, the position, the working environment, expectations of employees, and the like.

Even if the interview seems to go well, it's unlikely you will be offered the position after the initial interview. But if you are, be prepared to accept if you know you want the job. If you truly feel you need time to consider the offer, ask for a day or two. Regardless of how the interview went, thank the person as you leave. Within a day or so, follow up with a thank-you note to the interviewer and anyone else within the company with whom you had significant contact (such as someone who referred you to the firm). The thank-you note not only establishes you as someone who is professional and courteous, it marks you as someone who follows through to the end.

If you don't get the job, don't be heartbroken. Most people experience some disappointments during their job search. Review what you learned from the job application process and use that knowledge to improve your job-hunting skills. Move on to the next application and interview with enthusiasm. If you persist, your job search will pay off. If you are offered a job, congratulations! You are on your way toward a career in marketing.

APPENDIX: *Mathematics Used in Marketing*

In a business, the ultimate test of a marketing strategy is whether it satisfies customers and is profitable. Even nonprofit organizations need to ensure that marketing decisions are economically viable. Thus, marketers must be able to work with the financial numbers that help predict the success of plans and measure the success of operations. This appendix describes some techniques for doing so.

The Operating Statement

operating statement
Financial statement that summarizes revenues and expenses for a specified period of time; often called an income statement or profit-and-loss statement.

In general, as discussed in the chapters on pricing, a business's profit is the difference between its total revenues and its total expenses. But where do marketers actually get such numbers? Most often, accounting and financial personnel report revenue and expense figures in the form of an **operating statement**, often called an income statement or profit-and-loss (P&L) statement. The operating statement summarizes these performance figures for a specified period of time, typically a quarter or full year.

Operating statements appear in the annual reports of publicly held companies. The organization also distributes this type of information to managers (and sometimes to all employees) to help them control their group's activities. For example, comparing operating statements over several periods shows whether some categories of expenses are growing too fast and whether profits are keeping pace with sales increases. Marketers who can interpret the information on an operating statement have the basic tools for evaluating their organization's profit performance.

LITTLE LEARNERS PARENT-TEACHER STORE
OPERATING STATEMENT
FOR THE FISCAL YEAR ENDED MAY 31, 1995

Sales Revenue:			
Gross sales		$244,000	
Less: Returns and allowances		12,000	
Net sales			$232,000
Cost of Goods Sold:			
Beginning inventory	$ 35,000		
Purchases	126,000		
Cost of goods available for sale		$161,000	
Less: Ending inventory		42,000	
Cost of goods sold			119,000
Gross Margin			$113,000
Expenses:			
Selling expenses:			
Sales salaries	$ 45,000		
Other marketing	2,000		
Total selling expenses		$ 47,000	
Administrative expenses:			
Administrative salaries	$ 23,000		
Office supplies	1,500		
Other administrative expenses	500		
Total administrative expenses		25,000	
General expenses:			
Rent and utilities	$ 22,000		
Miscellaneous general expenses	1,500		
Total general expenses		23,500	
Total expenses			95,500
Net Profit (Loss) before Taxes			$ 17,500

CONTENTS OF THE OPERATING STATEMENT

Thanks to standards adopted by the U.S. accounting profession, operating statements in the United States all follow a similar format. Table A.1 provides an example, using Little Learners Parent-Teacher Store, the business introduced in the marketing plan that followed Chapter 5. Some people think operating statements are hard to understand. It may help to keep in mind that they are just a listing of how much money came in (revenues), how much went out (expenses), and the difference between those amounts.

As you review this sample, keep in mind that bigger organizations will have more complex and detailed operating statements. Furthermore, the specific items on the statement will vary somewhat from one industry to another. For example, a manufacturer's or a bank's operating statement will have about the same broad categories but will differ as to specifics.

SALES REVENUE   The operating statement begins by reporting how much money the organization brought in from selling goods or services. *Gross sales* refers to the total amount paid by all customers during the accounting period. However, as any business owner knows, customers sometimes want to return merchandise. Therefore, the accountant subtracts an amount for **returns and allowances**. A return occurs when the customer brings or sends back the goods. An allowance occurs when the business responds to a dissatisfied customer by allowing the customer to keep the goods but not charging for them. The amount of sales revenue that remains after subtracting returns and allowances is called *net sales.* In Table A.1, the calculation is as follows:

$$\text{Net Sales} = \text{Gross Sales} - \text{Returns and Allowances}$$
$$= \$244{,}000 - \$12{,}000 = \$232{,}000$$

returns and allowances
An accounting adjustment to sales for items brought back by customers for a refund and items for which customers received a credit even though the items were not returned.

COST OF SALES OR GOODS SOLD   Next, the operating statement shows the total cost to produce or acquire the products the organization sold during the accounting period. Depending on the nature of the product, this amount may be called the **cost of sales** or the **cost of goods sold**. A manufacturer would report the total cost to make the goods it sold. A service business uses the cost to perform the service. For an intermediary, cost of goods sold means the cost to acquire the inventory that the wholesaler or retailer sold to its customers.

How can the company's accountant keep track of this amount? The usual approach is to use some basic arithmetic. First, record the cost of the inventory on hand at the beginning of the accounting period, called *beginning inventory* in Table A.1. Then add the total amount spent to acquire more inventory throughout the accounting period, including any shipping charges. The sum of these two numbers is the *cost of goods available for sale* during the accounting period:

$$\text{Beginning Inventory} + \text{Purchases} = \text{Cost of Goods Available for Sale}$$
$$\$35{,}000 + \$126{,}000 = \$161{,}000$$

cost of sales
The total cost to produce or acquire the products sold by an organization during an accounting period.

cost of goods sold
The cost of sales for tangible goods.

But not all of the inventory that was purchased during the year was sold. Some goods are still on the store's shelves and in its storeroom. To find the cost of what was purchased, subtract what remains unsold:

$$\text{Cost of Goods Available for Sale} - \text{Ending Inventory} = \text{Cost of Goods Sold}$$
$$\$161{,}000 - \$42{,}000 = \$119{,}000$$

For a manufacturing business, the calculations will be similar. Instead of an inventory of goods to be resold, the manufacturer has an inventory of parts and materials. The manufacturer also has partly completed products (called *work-in-progress inventory*) and finished goods in stock. As in the retailing example, the manufacturer finds the total cost of these items at the beginning of the accounting period, then adds the total spent during the year and subtracts what remains unsold. In addition, the manufacturer adds in the cost of the labor used to produce the goods, as well as the overhead costs of running the factory.

GROSS MARGIN   Unless an organization can make or buy products for less than the price it charges to sell them, it cannot hope to make a profit. Thus, the first measure of a business's profitability is its gross margin (or gross profit). **Gross margin** is the difference between sales revenue and the cost of sales. In Table A.1, the gross margin is computed as follows:

gross margin
The difference between sales revenue and the cost of sales.

$$\text{Gross Margin} = \text{Net Sales} - \text{Cost of Goods Sold}$$
$$= \$232,000 - \$119,000 = \$113,000$$

To earn a profit, the store must keep its expenses less than the gross margin amount of $113,000.

EXPENSES   Accountants divide organizations' operating expenses into three major categories called *selling expenses, administrative expenses,* and *general expenses.* Selling expenses refer to the organization's marketing communications. For a store such as Little Learners, the major communications expense is for the salaries of its salespeople. In addition, Little Learners spent $2,000 in fiscal year 1994 on newspaper ads and public relations efforts.

Administrative expenses are the costs to manage a business. They include managers' salaries, office supplies, the wages of office help, and any other expenses in this area. For Little Learners Parent-Teacher Store, the major administrative expense is the owner's salary. The owner of this small business handles most administrative activities single-handedly. Other small-business owners use a part-time bookkeeper.

General expenses, as the name implies, cover any operating expenses not included in the other categories. The biggest general expense for Little Learners and many other businesses is rent and utilities. Other expenses that fall into this category include insurance, interest paid on loans, and maintenance of machinery and equipment.

NET PROFIT BEFORE TAXES   Subtracting total expenses from gross margin results in the "bottom line"—the company's net profit or loss before taxes. In fiscal year 1994, Little Learners Parent-Teacher Store earned a profit:

$$\text{Gross Margin} - \text{Total Expenses} = \text{Net Profit}$$
$$\$113,000 - \$95,500 = \$17,500$$

Some operating statements also show the amount of income taxes paid and the amount of profit remaining after taxes. The usual way to report a loss—that is, the difference when total expenses exceed the gross margin—is to place the amount of the loss in parentheses.

OPERATING RATIOS

operating ratios
Ratios of operating statement items to net sales.

The most common way to evaluate the data in an operating statement is to use **operating ratios**. These are ratios of operating statement items to net sales. In other words, the person analyzing the operating statement thinks of the items on the statement as a percentage of net sales.

To find such a ratio, divide the item by the amount of net sales ($232,000 in the case of Table A.1). For example, selling expenses as a percentage of net sales at Little Learners Parent-Teacher Store would be computed as follows:

$$\text{Selling Expense Ratio} = \frac{\text{Total Selling Expenses}}{\text{Net Sales}}$$
$$= \$47,000/\$232,000 = .203 = 20.3\%$$

If Little Learners' owner wanted to evaluate whether the store was using its sales dollars effectively, she could look at the selling expense ratio over several years to see whether it was falling. (A falling operating ratio means the organization is getting more sales for its money in that area.) Or the owner could compare the selling expense ratios at other stores to see how Little Learners is performing relative to the competition.

MAJOR TYPES OF RATIOS

Three types of operating ratios provide a broad overview of a business's financial performance. These are the gross margin ratio, the net profit ratio, and the operating expense ratio. The **gross margin ratio** is the organization's gross margin divided by its net sales. For Little Learners, the computation would be as follows:

gross margin ratio
The ratio of gross margin to net sales.

$$\text{Gross Margin Ratio} = \text{Gross Margin/Net Sales}$$
$$= \$113,000/\$232,000 = .487 = 48.7\%$$

This figure is also called the gross profit ratio and the gross margin percent.

The **net profit ratio** is the organization's net profit or loss divided by net sales. Here is the net profit ratio for Little Learners:

net profit ratio
The ratio of net profit (or loss) to net sales.

$$\text{Net Profit Ratio} = \text{Net Profit/Net Sales}$$
$$= \$17,500/\$232,000 = .075 = 7.5\%$$

The **operating expense ratio** is the organization's total expenses divided by its net sales. Here is the computation for Little Learners:

operating expense ratio
The ratio of total expenses to net sales.

$$\text{Operating Expense Ratio} = \text{Total Expenses/Net Sales}$$
$$= \$95,500/\$232,000 = .412 = 41.2\%$$

The operating expense ratio is a quick check as to whether the organization is keeping its expenses under control. If this ratio seems high, or if the analyst is interested in a particular area of expenses, the analyst can compute operating ratios for specific types of expenses. An example is the selling expense ratio computed earlier.

EVALUATING THE RATIOS   The way to evaluate any of these ratios is to make comparisons. The analyst can see whether the organization's performance is improving by looking at the same ratio over several accounting periods. To see whether an organization is performing better or worse than average, the analyst can compare the ratios for several organizations in the same industry. Sources of operating ratios for typical firms in various industries include trade associations, Robert Morris Associates, and Dun & Bradstreet. In general, high gross margin ratios and high net profit ratios are signs of good performance: the organization is turning a lot of its sales into profits. Conversely, low expense ratios are good because they suggest the organization is generating sales with minimal expenses.

Other Performance Measures

Of course, the operating statement doesn't provide the whole picture of whether the organization's marketing and other efforts are a financial success. Some other widely used performance measures include return on investment or assets, inventory turnover, and market share.

RETURN ON INVESTMENT OR ASSETS

Do profits of $1 million a year mean a business has performed well? If you said, "It depends," you're on the right track. The corner gas station might be pleased to earn a million dollars, whereas that figure would be disappointing at Standard Oil. One way to get a context for a profit figure is to use the net profit ratio to see whether profits are a large share of sales dollars. Other ways to analyze profits include determining how much was generated by the owners' investment in the company or by the company's assets.

return on investment (ROI)
Net profit from an enterprise divided by the amount invested to conduct that enterprise.

RETURN ON INVESTMENT (ROI)   The figure that evaluates profits in terms of the owners' investment is called **return on investment (ROI)**. ROI is the net profit from an enterprise divided by the amount invested to conduct that enterprise. In the case of Little Learners Parent-Teacher Store, assume the owner has so far invested $200,000. The store's ROI for fiscal year 1994 would be computed as follows:

$$\text{Return on Investment} = \text{Net Profit/Investment}$$
$$= \$17,500/\$200,000 = .088 = 8.8\%$$

The owner can compare this figure with the earnings she could get from investing $200,000 in other ways.

From a purely economic standpoint, it makes sense to invest in the enterprises that will generate the highest ROI. When the ROI for an enterprise is not attractive, the owner can either look for ways to operate more profitably or find another use for the funds invested.

A marketer may be interested in the profitability of particular marketing activities, such as the launch of a new product. In that case, the "investment" part of the ROI formula would be the funds used to carry out those activities. For example, the expenses for launching a new product would include product design, marketing research, and marketing communications. To see how this works, assume that a bank spent $630,000 on planning and communications for a new type of credit line for consumers in its area. In the first year the bank offered this credit line, many consumers applied for and used the new service, generating $120,000 in profits from fees and interest payments. Here is the bank's return on investment:

$$\text{ROI} = \text{Net Profit/Investment}$$
$$= \$120,000/\$630,000 = .190 = 19.0\%$$

Similarly, a retailer might want to find the ROI of opening or operating particular stores.

return on assets (ROA)
Net profit from an enterprise divided by the total assets used to conduct that enterprise.

RETURN ON ASSETS (ROA)   Another way to think of profits is in terms of the amount of assets used to generate those profits. Whereas the investment measure in ROI refers to what the owner has put into the enterprise, "assets" refers to what the business itself owns, such as its buildings, equipment, supplies, and cash. The way to measure income in terms of assets is to find the **return on assets (ROA)**. ROA is the net profit from an enterprise divided by the total assets used to conduct that enterprise. Total assets are reported on a financial statement known as a balance sheet.

In the case of Little Learners Parent-Teacher store, assume that its assets (mainly its inventory and some equipment) total $400,000. Its ROA would be as follows:

$$\text{Return on Assets} = \text{Net Profit/Total Assets}$$
$$= \$17,500/\$400,000 = .044 = 4.4\%$$

An increase in this ROA would signal that the store is using its resources more effectively.

INVENTORY TURNOVER

inventory turnover
The number of times an organization sells an average amount of inventory during a specified period of time; also called merchandise turnover rate or stockturn rate.

For marketers of goods, an important performance measure is **inventory turnover**, also called the merchandise turnover rate or the stockturn rate. Inventory turnover measures the number of times an organization turns over (sells) an average amount of inventory during a specified period of time. This measure shows whether goods are selling fast enough to keep inventory costs low. A high turnover rate also alerts marketers to items that may go out of stock at times, resulting in lost sales. In contrast, a falling rate of inventory turnover may signal that the target market is no longer as interested in the product.

To measure inventory turnover, the analyst may use two formulas. The first is based on the cost of the inventory:

$$\text{Inventory Turnover} = \frac{\text{Cost of Goods Sold}}{\text{Average Inventory at Cost}}$$

The simplest way to find the average inventory at cost is to take the average of the beginning and ending inventory figures on the operating statement. Using Table A.1 as an example, simply add together the beginning inventory and the ending inventory, then divide by 2:

$$\text{Average Inventory} = \frac{\text{Beginning Inventory} + \text{Ending Inventory}}{2}$$

$$= (\$35,000 + \$42,000)/2 = \$38,500$$

Then plug in the numbers to find the turnover for the fiscal year:

$$\text{Inventory Turnover} = \$119,000/\$38,500 = 3.09$$

In other words, by this measure, Little Learners turned over its inventory about three times in fiscal year 1994.

The second formula for inventory turnover measures inventory in terms of units sold:

$$\text{Inventory Turnover} = \frac{\text{Net Units Sold}}{\text{Average Inventory (in Units)}}$$

This makes sense in computing the turnover for a particular type of product. For example, suppose a maker of office supplies sells 650 cartons of yellow legal pads every month. Its average inventory of these pads is 800 cartons. Here is the turnover rate:

$$\text{Inventory Turnover} = 650 \text{ cartons}/800 \text{ cartons} = 0.8$$

Some of this manufacturer's money is being spent on carrying an inventory of yellow pads that doesn't sell out every month.

MARKET SHARE

market share
The sales of an organization's product as a percentage of all sales of such products.

Most marketers are concerned with the market share held by their products. **Market share** represents the sales of an organization's product as a percentage of all sales of such products. In other words, it tells what percentage of a market the company's product represents—how big its slice of the total pie is. For example, if Little Learners Parent-Teacher Store and its direct competitor, Educational Resources, both sell the same amount, they would each have half the "pie," or a 50 percent market share.

To compute market share, the analyst needs to know the sales for the total market and for the organization's own product. The analyst uses those figures in the following formula:

$$\text{Market Share} = \frac{\text{Sales of Organization's Product}}{\text{Total Sales for Product Type}}$$

Sales may be stated in terms of dollar volume or the number of units sold. Suppose an aircraft corporation sold 25 jumbo jets, out of industrywide total sales of 300. Its market share for jumbo jets would be as follows:

$$\text{Market Share in Units} = 25 \text{ units}/300 \text{ units} = .083 = 8.3\%$$

Also suppose that these are state-of-the-art aircraft selling for $5 million apiece, compared to an industry average of $3 million. In terms of dollar volume, the company's market share is greater:

$$\text{Market Share in Dollars} = \$125,000,000/\$900,000,000$$
$$= .139 = 13.9\%$$

FIGURE A.1

Example of Markups
(in Dollars)

Manufacturer
Cost to Make: $35
Selling Price: $50

Wholesaler
Cost to Buy: $50
Selling Price: $75

Retailer
Cost to Buy: $75
Selling Price: $125

Consumers
Cost to Buy: $125

Manufacturer's
Markup = $15

Wholesaler's
Markup = $25

Retailer's
Markup = $50

A service provider sometimes cannot measure sales in terms of units. In that case, market share may be measured as the number of customers served relative to the size of the target market.

Marketers should interpret market share figures with caution. A large or growing market share suggests that an organization is providing the value customers are looking for. However, it does not indicate whether the organization is profiting or whether it could do even better with some other marketing strategy.

Wholesale and Retail Pricing

The pricing chapters introduced a variety of approaches to setting prices for goods and services. This appendix takes a closer look at the computations involved in two pricing tactics used often by wholesalers and retailers. These tactics are price markups and markdowns.

MARKUP

As a product moves through a distribution channel, each channel member charges the next a somewhat higher price. The channel members are said to "mark up" the price of the product. The percentage by which the price is increased is called, logically enough, a **markup**. Figure A.1 provides an example. There are two ways to state these markups as percentages—either as a percent of the cost or as a percent of the selling price.

markup
The percentage by which channel members increase the price of a product when they sell it; may be stated as a percentage of cost or a percentage of selling price.

MARKUP BASED ON COST   The easiest types of markups to understand are those based on the product's cost—that is, the price the channel member paid to acquire the product. To find the percentage of a markup based on cost, simply divide the amount of the markup by the amount of the cost:

$$\text{Markup Based on Cost} = \frac{\text{Markup in Dollars}}{\text{Cost in Dollars}}$$

This is the way many wholesalers and some small retailers express their markups.

In Figure A.1, for example, the wholesaler bought televisions from the manufacturer for $50 each. The wholesaler will sell them to retail stores for $75, a markup (in dollars) of $25. The wholesaler's percentage markup is therefore $25/$50, or 50 percent.

MARKUP BASED ON SELLING PRICE   Most retailers state markups as a percentage of the price at which they *sell* merchandise to their customers. This approach uses the following formula:

$$\text{Markup Based on Price} = \frac{\text{Markup in Dollars}}{\text{Selling Price in Dollars}}$$

Thus, in Figure A.1, when the wholesaler bought televisions at $50 and resold them at $75, the markup based on price would be $25/$75, or 33 percent.

CONVERTING MARKUP PERCENTAGES   Sometimes the marketer knows the markup computed in one way but wants to convert it to the other type of markup. Some basic formulas are again useful. The following formula converts markup based on cost to markup based on price:

$$\text{Markup Based on Price} = \frac{\text{Markup Based on Cost}}{100\% + \text{Markup Based on Cost}}$$

Using the earlier example of the television wholesaler, you would make the conversion as follows:

$$\text{Markup Based on Price} = \frac{50\%}{100\% + 50\%} = \frac{50\%}{150\%} = 33\%$$

The following formula converts markup based on price to markup based on cost:

$$\text{Markup Based on Cost} = \frac{\text{Markup Based on Price}}{100\% - \text{Markup Based on Price}}$$

Here is the computation for the example of the wholesaler:

$$\text{Markup Based on Cost} = \frac{33\%}{100\% - 33\%} = \frac{33\%}{67\%} = 50\%$$

MARKDOWN

To stimulate more sales of a product, resellers may decide to reduce the price they are charging. Thus, a store might hold a clearance sale near the end of the summer, or a wholesaler might offer reduced prices on merchandise damaged in a flood. To arrive at the new price, wholesalers and retailers use markdowns. A **markdown** is the percentage by which a price is reduced. For example, CDs may go on sale at 20 percent off the full price.

markdown
The percentage by which the full price of an item is reduced in order to stimulate sales.

FINDING THE MARKDOWN   The following formula computes the markdown percentage:

$$\text{Markdown} = \frac{\text{Markdown in Dollars}}{\text{Original Price}}$$

Suppose that a hotel wants to attract weekend visitors and offers rooms for $79, down from the usual price of $198. This markdown is $198 – $79 or $119, and $119/$198 equals .60, or 60 percent.

markdown ratio
The ratio of total markdowns (in dollars) for a group of products to total sales (in dollars) for those products.

FINDING THE MARKDOWN RATIO   When the seller uses markdowns, some units of the product are sold at full price and others at the reduced price. From a financial standpoint, the marketer wants to know more than the size of the markdown on a single unit. The marketer is interested in the overall effect of the markdown on earnings from the product. Therefore, the marketer computes the **markdown ratio**, which compares total markdowns for a group of products to total sales volume for those products. Here is the formula:

$$\text{Markdown Ratio} = \frac{\text{Total Markdowns in Dollars}}{\text{Total Sales in Dollars}}$$

To see how this works, consider again the hotel offering a price discount on weekends. Suppose that in a month the hotel had booked 100 nights at the reduced rate ($79) and 200 nights at the full rate ($198). For that month, its total markdowns would be the amount of the markdown ($198 – $79) times the number of rooms booked at the reduced rate (100):

$$\text{Total Markdowns in Dollars} = 100(\$198 - \$79)$$
$$= 100 \times \$119 = \$11,900$$

The hotel's total sales would be as follows:

$$\text{Total Sales in Dollars} = 100(\$79) + 200(\$198) = \$47,500$$

With these numbers, you can find the markdown ratio:

$$\text{Markdown Ratio} = \$11,900/\$47,500 = .251 = 25.1\%$$

In other words, the special weekend rate resulted in an overall markdown ratio of 25.1 percent. Booking more rooms at full price would reduce this ratio.

Markdown ratios can help marketers control their pricing strategies. By analyzing markdown ratios, the marketer can determine whether discounts are taking too big a bite out of profits for a particular product or product line. For example, large retailers review markdown ratios for each department of the store.

KEY TERMS AND CONCEPTS

operating statement (p. 643)

returns and allowances (p. 645)

cost of sales (p. 645)

cost of goods sold (p. 645)

gross margin (p. 645)

operating ratios (p. 646)

gross margin ratio (p. 647)

net profit ratio (p. 647)

operating expense ratio (p. 647)

return on investment (ROI) (p. 648)

return on assets (ROA) (p. 648)

inventory turnover (p. 648)

market share (p. 649)

markup (p. 650)

markdown (p. 651)

markdown ratio (p. 651)

REVIEW AND DISCUSSION QUESTIONS

Table A.2 shows an operating statement for Drafting on Demand, a temporary services agency that provides drafters to engineering departments that need extra help with projects. This business employs five drafters, all with experience in computer-aided design as well as in drawing blueprints. Use the operating statement in Table A.2 to answer questions 1 through 4.

1. Fill in the missing amounts (indicated by letters in parentheses).
2. Did the business have a profit or a loss for this reporting period?
3. Compute the following ratios:
   a. gross margin ratio
   b. net profit ratio
   c. operating expense ratio

4. To evaluate the financial performance of Drafting on Demand, what information would you want besides the ratios you computed in question 3? Explain.
5. A popular Thai restaurant decides to open a second location. The restaurant's owners forecast that setting up the restaurant will cost $430,000 and that in its first year it will earn a profit of $8,600.
   a. What is the expected return on investment for the new restaurant?
   b. Does this ROI look favorable? Can you suggest why this new restaurant might look like a good investment to its owners?
6. Can you compute inventory turnover from the operating statement in Table A.2? Explain.

TABLE A.2

Sample Operating Statement for Review and Discussion Questions

**DRAFTING ON DEMAND
OPERATING STATEMENT
FOR THE YEAR ENDED DECEMBER 31, 19XX**

Sales Revenue:			
Gross sales		$395,000	
Less: Allowances		1,000	
Net sales			$394,000
Cost of Sales:			
Direct labor		$140,000	
Overhead		70,000	
Cost of sales			210,000
Gross Margin		(a) _____	
Expenses:			
Selling expenses:			
Sales salary	$60,000		
Advertising	5,000		
Total selling expenses		$ 65,000	
Administrative expenses:			
Administrative salaries	$85,000		
Office supplies	2,500		
Other administrative expenses	1,000		
Total administrative expenses		(b) _____	
General expenses:			
Rent	$ 9,000		
Utilities	2,500		
Interest	2,000		
Other general expenses	1,000		
Total general expenses		(c) _____	
Total expenses			(d) _____
Net Profit (Loss) before Taxes			(e) _____

7. According to the operating statement for Big Sound Audio Equipment, the company started the year with inventory of $600,000 and ended with inventory of $700,000. The cost of goods sold for the year was $7,800,000. What was the inventory turnover rate?

8. From an industry trade magazine, marketing manager Jon Bretts learns that European organizations bought $4 million worth of electric pencil sharpeners last year. They are expected to spend at least $4.2 million on the machines this year. Jon's company sold $800,000 worth of electric pencil sharpeners in Europe last year and is trying for a 10 percent increase in sales.

a. What was the company's European market share last year?

b. If Jon's company meets its sales goal for this year and total sales are as forecast, what will the company's market share be?

9. Solve the following problems using the data in Figure A.1.

a. Find the retailer's markup percentage based on cost.

b. Find the retailer's markup percentage based on selling price.

10. To make room for its spring clothes, Big Value Store reduced the price of $100 sweaters to $65 at its East

Towne and West Towne locations. The East Towne store sold 50 sweaters at full price and 40 at the reduced price. The West Towne store sold 35 sweaters at full price and 100 at the reduced price.

a. What was the markdown percentage for the sweaters?

b. What was the markdown ratio for the East Towne store?

c. What was the markdown ratio for the West Towne store?

d. Compare the performances of the two store locations.

Appendix Project
Analyzing Operating Statements

Obtain annual reports (for the same year) for two organizations in the same industry—say, two airlines or two universities. You should be able to find annual reports in your local library, or you can request them by contacting the companies you're interested in.

Look up the operating statement in each annual report. Remember, it may be called by another name, such as income statement or profit-and-loss statement. Under whatever name, it will be the table that shows revenues, expenses, and profit or loss.

For each company, find the gross margin ratio, net profit ratio, return on investment (or assets), and any other figures you think are important for this type of industry. Based on this information, at which of the two companies would you rather hold a marketing job? Why?

Notes

CHAPTER 1

1. Peter D. Bennett, ed., *Dictionary of Marketing Terms* (Chicago: American Marketing Association, 1988), p. 117.
2. "The Commuter's Choice," *Newsweek,* August 3, 1992.
3. Lands' End catalog, 1991.
4. See Joseph M. Juran, "Made in the U.S.A.: A Renaissance in Quality," *Harvard Business Review,* July-August 1993, pp. 42–47, 50.
5. Howard Schlossberg, "Dawning of the Era of Emotion," *Marketing News,* February 15, 1993, pp. 1–2.
6. John Hillkirk, "New Award Cites Teams with Dreams," *USA Today,* April 10–12, 1992, p. 1A.
7. See Iris Mohr-Jackson, "Broadening the Market Orientation: An Added Focus on Internal Customers," *Human Resource Management* (Winter 1991): pp. 455–467.
8. Kaoru Ishikawa, *What Is Total Quality Control? The Japanese Way* Englewood Cliffs, N.J.: Prentice-Hall, 1985).
9. Neil A. Morgan and Nigel F. Piercy, "Market-Led Quality," *Industrial Marketing Management* 21 (1992): 111–118.
10. "TQM and the Bottom Line," *Supervisory Management* (July 1992): p. 12.
11. Black & Decker 1992 Annual Report, p. 5.
12. "The Cracks in Quality," *The Economist,* April 18, 1992.
13. Otis Port, "Quality: Small and Midsize Companies Seize the Challenge—Not a Moment Too Soon," *Business Week,* November 30, 1992, pp. 66–72.
14. "Customers: The Missing Ingredient in TQM?" *Quality Digest,* February 1993, p. 9.
15. Gilbert Fuchsberg, "Small Firms Struggle with Latest Management Trends," *The Wall Street Journal,* August 26, 1993, p. B2.
16. Phaedra Hise, "Pushing the Customer-Service Envelope," *Inc.,* July 1993, p. 24.
17. "Study Shows Strong Evidence That Participative Management Pays Off," *Total Quality Newsletter,* September 1992, pp. 1–4.
18. Jerry Bowles, "Quality '93: Empowering People with Technology," *Fortune,* September 20, 1993, special advertising section, p. 147.
19. Shelby D. Hunt and John J. Burnett, "The Macromarketing/Micromarketing Dichotomy: A Taxonomical Model," *Journal of Marketing* (Summer 1982): pp. 9–26.
20. George Gendron, "FYI: Standing Room Only," *Inc.,* March 1992, p. 11.
21. James McGregor, "Chinese City Has One Ideology: Profit," *The Wall Street Journal,* December 10, 1992, p. A12.
22. Annetta Miller and Karen Springen, "Egg Rolls for Peoria," *Newsweek,* October 12, 1992, p. 59.
23. Nina Darnton, "Dining-room Boutique," *Newsweek,* October 12, 1992, p. 94.
24. Bennett, *Dictionary of Marketing Terms,* p. 117.
25. "Death Struggle in the Sky," *Newsweek,* June 15, 1992, p. 43.
26. Philip Kotler and Sydney J. Levy, "Broadening the Concept of Marketing," *Journal of Marketing* (January 1969): pp. 10–15.
27. James T. Bennett and Thomas J. DiLorenzo, *Unfair Competition: The Profits of Nonprofits* (Lanham, Md.: Hamilton Press, 1989), p. 11.
28. David J. Luck, "Broadening the Concept of Marketing—Too Far," *Journal of Marketing* (July 1969): pp. 53–55.
29. "Think New Zealand," *Forbes,* June 8, 1992, p. 74.
30. Louise Kiernan, "Ads Fight to Liberate Smokers," *Chicago Tribune,* April 26, 1993, sec. 2, pp. 1, 4.

31. Frederick E. Webster, Jr., "The Changing Role of Marketing in the Corporation," *Journal of Marketing* (October 1992): pp. 1–17.
32. *Ibid.,* p. 7.
33. Charles R. O'Neal and William C. LaFief, "Marketing's Lead Role in Total Quality," *Industrial Marketing Management* 21 (1992): 133–143.
34. See Jeen-Su Lim and David A. Reid, "Vital Cross-functional Linkages with Marketing," *Industrial Marketing Management* 21 (1992): 159–165.
35. See Webster, "The Changing Role of Marketing"; and Stanley F. Slater and John C. Narver, "Superior Customer Value and Business Performance: The Strong Evidence for a Market-Driven Culture," Report No. 92–125 (Cambridge, Mass: Marketing Science Institute, 1992).
36. CPC International Inc., 1991 Annual Report, pp. 16–17.
37. Slater and Narver, "Superior Customer Value," p. 8.
38. Haller M. Moyers, "Making Cross-Functional Teams Work," *Manufacturing Engineering,* December 1992, p. 176.
39. Lim and Reid, "Vital Cross-functional Linkages with Marketing."
40. Roger A. Kerin, Vijay Mahajan, and P. Rajan Varadarajan, *Contemporary Perspectives on Strategic Marketing Planning* (Boston: Allyn & Bacon, 1990), Chapter 1; Harper W. Boyd, Jr., and Orville C. Walker, Jr., *Marketing Management* (Homewood, Ill.: Richard D. Irwin, 1990), Chapter 2; and Philip Kotler, *Marketing Management,* 7th ed. (Englewood Cliffs, N.J.: Prentice-Hall, 1991), Chapters 2 and 3.
41. V. Daniel Hunt, *Quality in America* (Homewood, Ill.: Business One Irwin, 1992), pp. 138–139.
42. *Ibid.,* pp. 140–141.
43. Michael Oneal, "Pizza Pizza, and Tigers Too," *Business Week,* September 14, 1992, pp. 108–109.
44. *Ibid.*

CHAPTER 2

1. "A Little Advice for the New CEO," *Newsweek,* November 19, 1992.
2. Burt Nanus, "Visionary Leadership: How to Re-Vision the Future," *The Futurist,* September-October 1992, pp. 20–25.
3. Patricia Saiki, "Rising Force," *Entrepreneur,* December 1992, p. 176.
4. See, for example, Kenneth L. Fisher, *The Wall Street Waltz* (Chicago: Contemporary Books, 1987).
5. Toshiyuki Matsuura, "Current Trends and Developments in the Amusement Industry," *Japan 21st,* July 1993, pp. 45–50.
6. Kathleen Deveny, "Firms See a Fat Opportunity in Catering to Americans' Quest for 'Easy' Lunches," *The Wall Street Journal,* November 2, 1992, pp. B1, B4.
7. Kathleen Deveny, "Man Walked on the Moon but Man Can't Make Enough Devil's Food Cookie Cakes," *The Wall Street Journal,* September 28, 1993, pp. B1, B12.
8. Fabian Linden, Gordon W. Green, Jr., and John F. Coder, *A Marketer's Guide to Discretionary Income* (Washington, D.C.: U.S. Government Printing Office, 1984).
9. Wendy Bounds, "Fighting Bugs with Garlic and Peppers," *The Wall Street Journal,* July 12, 1993, p. B1.
10. Peter D. Bennett, ed., *Dictionary of Marketing Terms* (Chicago: American Marketing Association, 1988), p. 76.
11. Craig Canine, "The FDA Gets Fresh," *Eating Well,* September/October 1991, p. 105.
12. "FDA Test Passed," *Progressive Grocer,* July 1993, p. 10.
13. Institute of Financial Education (IFE), *Retail Banking* (Chicago: IFE, 1990), Chapter 8.
14. Interview with Russell C. Buchanan, retired senior vice president, Midlantic Corp.
15. John J. Keller, "Cellular Industry Group Acts to Avert Crisis by Research into Phones' Safety," *The Wall Street Journal,* February 1, 1993, p. B6.

16. David W. Cravens and Gerald G. Hills, "Consumerism: A Perspective for Business," *Business Horizons,* August 1970, p. 21.
17. Peter Brimelow and Leslie Spencer, "Ralph Nader, Inc.," *Forbes,* September 17, 1990, pp. 117–121.
18. *Ibid.,* p. 118.
19. Paul M. Barrett, "Supreme Court Ruling Makes It Tougher for Workers to Win Job-Bias Lawsuits," *The Wall Street Journal,* June 28, 1993, p. A18.
20. Dorothy J. Gaiter, "Court Ruling Makes Discrimination Studies a Hot New Industry," *The Wall Street Journal,* August 13, 1993, pp. A1, A10.
21. Miriam Jordan, "Cathay Air Acts to Adopt Chinese Flavor," *The Wall Street Journal,* August 23, 1993, p. A6.
22. Cathy Taylor, "California Retailer Barks up Wrong Tree," *Chicago Tribune,* October 11, 1992.
23. "Learning to Trust American Cars," *American Demographics,* October 1992, p. 20.
24. Dr. Demo, "What Is a Demographer?" *American Demographics,* October 1992, p. 6.
25. Deveny, "Firms See a Fat Opportunity."
26. *Statistical Abstract of the United States,* U.S. Department of Commerce 1989, p. 13.
27. "It's Not Like Mr. Mom," *Newsweek,* December 14, 1992, p. 70.
28. *Ibid.*
29. Judith Waldrop, "Secrets of the Age Pyramids," *American Demographics,* August 1992, pp. 46–52.
30. See, for example, Erika Kotite, "The Next Generation," *Entrepreneur,* December 1992, pp. 90–94.
31. Ford S. Worthy, "A New Mass Market Emerges," *Fortune,* Special issue (Fall 1990), pp. 51–55.
32. *Ibid.*
33. Leon G. Schiffman and Leslie Lazar Kanuck, *Consumer Behavior,* 4th ed. (Englewood Cliffs, N.J.: Prentice-Hall, 1991), p. 424.
34. For numerous examples, see Sondra Thiederman, *Bridging Cultural Barriers for Corporate Success: How to Manage the Multicultural Work Force* (New York: Lexington Books, 1991).
35. Alecia Swasy, "Don't Sell Thick Diapers in Tokyo," *New York Times,* October 3, 1993, p. F9.
36. Judie Lannon, "Brands across Borders: Do Advertising Ideas Travel?" Presentation at Attitude Research Conference of the American Marketing Association, January 20–23, 1991.
37. Margaret Ambry, *The Almanac of Consumer Markets* (Chicago: Probus Publishing, 1990).
38. Amy Feldman and Joshua Levine, "Sprucing Up the Cocoon," *Forbes,* January 4, 1993, pp. 64–65.
39. Bill Saporito, "Unsuit Yourself: Management Goes Informal," *Fortune,* September 30, 1993, pp. 118–120.
40. Surita Wadekar Bhargava, "Gimme a Double Shake and a Lard on White," *Business Week,* March 1, 1993, p. 59; Richard Gibson, "Too Skinny a Burger Is a Mighty Hard Sell, McDonald's Learns," *The Wall Street Journal,* April 15, 1993, pp. A1, A6; and Gabriella Stern, "In a Turnabout, Fast-Food Fare Becomes Fattier," *The Wall Street Journal,* August 23, 1993, pp. B1, B6.
41. Sandra D. Atchison, "Move Over, Jane Fonda, Here Comes Pudgeball Nation," *Business Week,* April 19, 1993, p. 29.
42. "Discarded Packaging Has Declined," *Boston Globe,* March 11, 1993.
43. Philip R. Cateora, *International Marketing,* 8th ed. (Homewood, Ill.: Irwin, 1993), pp. 507–508.
44. Bernard Baumohl, "Are Banks Obsolete?" *Time,* June 28, 1993, pp. 49–50.
45. Saiki, "Rising Force."
46. Thomas McCarroll, "How IBM Was Left Behind," *Time,* December 28, 1992, pp. 26–28.

47. "A Close Look at Five Countries," *The Grocer,* September 12, 1992, p. 50.
48. "Can Korea Unite and Conquer?" *International Business,* November 16, 1992, p. 54.
49. "PepsiCo Inks Deal to Open Pizza Huts in the Ukraine," *Nation's Restaurant News,* November 2, 1992.
50. Sharon Begley and Carolyn Friday, "Nature at the Patent Office," *Newsweek,* December 14, 1992.
51. "Jumping Ahead by Going High Tech," *Fortune* (issue date not supplied).
52. *Ibid.*
53. Michael Clements, "Granite Rock: Concrete Improvement," *USA Today* (issue date not supplied).
54. Manjeet Kripalani, "Electric Utilities," *Forbes,* January 4, 1993, pp. 134–136.
55. Leon Jaroff, "A Thirst for Competition," *Time,* June 1, 1992, p. 75.
56. Michael E. Porter, *Competitive Strategy* (New York: The Free Press, 1980). Also see Michael E. Porter, *Competitive Advantage: Creating and Sustaining Superior Performance* (New York: The Free Press, 1985); and Michael E. Porter, *The Competitive Advantage of Nations* (New York: The Free Press, 1990).
57. Roger Eglin, "BT Prepares to Beat the World," *Management Today,* July 1993, pp. 9, 12.
58. John R. Emshwiller, "Solar Dish Inventor Has Difficulty Marketing Product," *The Wall Street Journal,* June 22, 1993, p. B2.
59. Jeffrey A. Tannenbaum, "More U.S. Franchisers Are Looking to Expand Abroad," The Wall Street Journal, November 13, 1992.
60. *Ibid.*
61. "Learning to Trust American Cars."
62. Bradley A. Stertz, "Detroit's New Strategy to Beat Back Japanese Is to Copy Their Ideas," *The Wall Street Journal,* October 1, 1992, pp. A1, A10.
63. "Learning to Trust American Cars."
64. "Saturn," *Business Week,* August 17, 1992, p. 86.

CHAPTER 3
1. Rosemary St. Léger, "Bright Idea Plugs into Potential of Inner City," *GSB Chicago* (University of Chicago Graduate School of Business), Summer 1992, pp. 10-13.
2. Jerry Bowles, "Quality '93: Empowering People with Technology," *Fortune,* September 20, 1993, p. 144.
3. Michael p. Cronin, "Volunteering Your Company," *Inc.,* September 1993, p. 31.
4. Ellyn E. Spragins, "Making Good," *Inc.,* May 1993, pp. 114-118+.
5. "FCC Tags Stern Revolting; He's Appealing," *Newsweek,* December 28, 1992, p. 65.
6. Spragins, "Making Good."
7. The Home Depot, "1992 Corporate Social Responsibility Report."
8. "The Environment: The Grass Can Be Greener," *Earth's Best Family Times,* 1(2): 1993.
9. Richard A. Marini, "In Search of the Perfect Bean," *Frequent Flyer,* August 1993, pp. 24-25.
10. Wilson Ring, "Lobster Dives Bring Profits—and Death," *Chicago Tribune,* April 26, 1992, sec. 1, pp. 23-24.
11. Michael Schroeder, "Charity Doesn't Begin at Home Anymore," *Time,* February 25, 1991, p. 91.
12. "Smart Businesses Are Saving the Planet and Lots of Money, Too," *Total Quality Newsletter,* October 1992, pp. 1-4.
13. Procter & Gamble, "Total Quality Environmental Management: A Systemic Approach to Continuous Improvement," company brochure.
14. John E. Ettlie, "The Manufacturing Ecology Imperative," *Production,* February 1993, p. 28.
15. *Ibid.*
16. Robert A. Mamis, "Waste Not," *Inc.,* May 1993, p. 48.
17. Allan J. Magrath, "The Marketin' of the Green," *Sales & Marketing Management,* October 1992, pp. 21-22.
18. "Smart Businesses Are Saving the Planet," p. 3.
19. Robin Yale Bergstrom, "Environmental Affairs," *Production,* April 1993, pp. 36-47.
20. Judith Gaines, "Levi's Leftovers Get a New Lease on Life," *The Boston Sunday Globe,* February 21, 1993, pp. 34-35; Frank Edward Allen, "We Knew There Was a Reason to Save Our Tattered Dungarees," *The Wall Street Journal,* November 30, 1992, p. B1.
21. "Smart Businesses Are Saving the Planet," p. 3.
22. Ettlie, "The Manufacturing Ecology Imperative."
23. Martha H. Peak, "From Catchword to Content," *Management Review,* November 1992, pp. 34-38.
24. *Ibid.*
25. Allan J. Magrath, "The Marketin' of the Green."
26. *Ibid.,* p. 21.
27. Laura Bird, "Detergent Industry Spins into New Cycle," *The Wall Street Journal,* January 5, 1993, pp. B1, B4.
28. "Veterinary Product Companies Take the Green Road," VPN Staff Report, Public Relations Office, Merck AgVet, division of Merck & Co., Inc.
29. Patagonia catalog, Fall/Winter 1992.
30. Mamis, "Waste Not."
31. The Home Depot, "1992 Corporate Social Responsibility Report."
32. "Smart Businesses Are Saving the Planet," p. 4.
33. Michael p. Cronin, "Green Marketing Heats Up," *Inc.,* January 1993, p. 27.
34. "Smart Businesses Are Saving the Planet," p. 3.
35. See, for example, Magrath, "The Marketin' of the Green," pp. 21-22.
36. Patagonia catalog, Fall/Winter 1992.
37. "Can You Afford to Be Ethical?" *Inc.,* December 1992, p. 16.
38. *Webster's New Collegiate Dictionary* (Springfield, Mass.: G. & C. Merriam Company, 1973). See also Gene Lazniak and Patrick E. Murphy, *The Higher Road: A Path to Ethical Marketing Decisions* (Boston: Allyn & Bacon, 1992), chapter 1.
39. Robert McGarvey, "Do the Right Thing: Ethics and Your Bottom Line," *Entrepreneur,* October 1992, pp. 140-143.
40. Scott Cook, "The Ethics of Bootstrapping," *Inc.,* September 1992, pp. 87+.
41. "Business Week/Harris Poll: Is an Antibusiness Backlash Building?" *Business Week,* July 20, 1987, p. 71; and "Looking to its Roots," *Time,* May 27, 1987, pp. 26-29.
42. John Schwartz and Carolyn Friday, "Beating the Odds in Biotech," *Newsweek,* October 12, 1992, p. 63.
43. See Andrew Stark, "What's the Matter with Business Ethics?" *Harvard Business Review,* May-June 1993, pp. 38-40+.
44. "Tactics and Dirty Tricks," *The Economist,* January 16, 1993, pp. 21-22.
45. Gregg Cebrzynski, "TV Station Sued Over Alleged Phoney Survey," *Marketing News,* August 28, 1987, pp. 1, 42.
46. Martha Brannigan, "Pseudo Polls: More Surveys Draw Criticism for Motives and Methods," *The Wall Street Journal,* January 27, 1987, p. 27.
47. "Raising Static about Kids' TV," *Boston Globe,* March 11, 1993.
48. Phone and mail interview with E. A. Lennon, Senior Manager, Business Systems Development, Procter & Gamble.
49. The Home Depot, "1992 Corporate Social Responsibility Report."
50. Peak, "From Catchword to Content," pp. 34-35.
51. Paul Sherlock, *Rethinking Business to Business Marketing* (New York: The Free Press, 1991), pp. 6-7.
52. Stark, "What's the Matter with Business Ethics?"
53. Peak, "From Catchword to Content," p. 34.

54. McGarvey, "Do the Right Thing," p. 141.
55. *Ibid.,* p. 142.
56. *Ibid.,* p. 143.
57. St. Léger, "Bright Idea."
58. Leon E. Wynter, "'Whitelist' Spotlights Ad Industry Hiring," *The Wall Street Journal,* February 2, 1993, p. B1.
59. See, for example, Brian Dumaine, "Exporting Jobs and Ethics," *Fortune,* October 5, 1992, p. 10.
60. "Minority Households Head for Big Gains in the 1990s," *Business Week,* December 7, 1992, p. 24.
61. Andrea Gerlin, "Radio Stations Gain by Going After Hispanics," *The Wall Street Journal,* July 14, 1993, pp. B1, B8.
62. Sharon Nelton, "Winning with Diversity," *Nation's Business,* September 1992, pp. 18-24.
63. *Ibid.,* p. 19.
64. "The Diverse Work Force," *Inc.,* January 1993, p. 33.
65. Patricia Saiki, "Rising Force," *Entrepreneur,* December 1992, p. 176.
66. Jon Krampner, "Bill Mow: From Silicon Chips to Mass Couture," *Purdue Alumnus,* January/February 1993, p. 19.
67. Erle Norton, "Entrepreneur's Tenacity Becomes a Pattern for Success," *The Wall Street Journal,* January 14, 1993, p. B2.
68. "Black Firms Nibble at Ethnic Food Market," *The Wall Street Journal,* November 16, 1992, p. B1.
69. Bob Weinstein, "Rap Master," *Entrepreneur,* September 1993, pp. 87-91.
70. "'Drive,' She Said: Mazda's Jan Thompson," *Sales & Marketing Management,* November 1991, pp. 30-31.
71. Barry Newman, "Hungarians Seeking to Find a New Way Find Instead Amway," *The Wall Street Journal,* January 15, 1993.
72. James McGregor, "China's New Rich Seek the Good Life," *The Wall Street Journal,* January 13, 1993, p. A10.
73. "M. Colleen Mullens: Passionate about Diversity," *Industry Week,* March 2, 1992, pp. 26-27.
74. Edwin M. Reingold, "America's Hamburger Helper," *Time,* June 29, 1992, pp. 66-67.
75. *Ibid.,* p. 66.

CHAPTER 4
1. Elyse Tanouye, "Johnson & Johnson Stays Fit by Shuffling Its Mix of Businesses," *The Wall Street Journal,* December 22, 1992, pp. A1, A4.
2. George Gourlay, "Quality's Cultural Foundation," in *Making Total Quality Happen,* ed. Frank Caropreso (New York: The Conference Board, 1990), pp. 71–74.
3. See Kenneth L. Fisher, *The Wall Street Waltz* (Chicago: Contemporary Books, 1987), pp. 146–147, citing Wesley C. Mitchell, *Business Cycles, The Problem and Its Setting* (New York: National Bureau of Economic Research, 1927).
4. Peter D. Bennett, ed., *Dictionary of Marketing Terms* (Chicago: American Marketing Association, 1988), p. 65.
5. "Going Global: Canada," *Inc.* advertising supplement, June 1993, p. 1.
6. Reginald Biddle and Toni Dick, "Selling Services to Canada," *Business America,* May 31, 1993, pp. 2–5.
7. Andrea Dabrowski, "Mexico, Sí," *International Business,* March 1993, pp. 54–57.
8. Albert Warson, "Tapping Canadian Markets," *Inc.,* March 1993, pp. 90–91.
9. G. Pierre Goad, "Freer, but Not Free," *The Wall Street Journal,* September 24, 1992, p. R18.
10. "Profiles in Marketing: Frank Bracken," *Sales & Marketing Management,* April 1993, p. 10.
11. Dabrowski, "Mexico, Sí."
12. *Ibid.,* p. 57.
13. "Going Global: Mexico," *Inc.* advertising supplement, September 1993, p. 1.
14. Nancy Ryan, "Head Start Urged on Mexico Business," *Chicago Tribune,* January 17, 1993, sec. 7, p. 4.

15. See, for example, Paul B. Carroll and Dianne Solis, "From U.S., Mexican Executives Hear Sound of an Opening Bell," *The Wall Street Journal,* November 18, 1993, p. A14; "Business Expects NAFTA Will Bring Host of Benefits," *The Wall Street Journal,* November 19, 1993, p. A3.
16. Biddle and Dick, "Selling Services to Canada."
17. Dabrowski, "Mexico, Sí," p. 57.
18. "Business Expects NAFTA Will Bring Host of Benefits."
19. Catherine Vial, "Why EC Environmental Policy Will Affect American Business," *Business America,* March 8, 1993, pp. 24–27.
20. Andrew Hilton, "Mythology, Markets, and the Emerging Europe," *Harvard Business Review,* November-December 1992, pp. 50–54.
21. Margot Hornblower, "No One Ever Said It Would Be Easy," *Time,* March 1, 1993, pp. 32, 41.
22. "All Strung Up," *The Economist,* April 17, 1993, p. 70.
23. Andrew Tanzer, "Software on Black Ships," *Forbes,* December 21, 1992, pp. 300–301.
24. Clay Chandler, Jacob M. Schlesinger, and John Bussey, "Japan Economy, Built on Rapid Expansion, Faces Wrenching Shift," *The Wall Street Journal,* December 7, 1992, pp. A1, A9.
25. "Taking Aim," *The Economist,* April 24, 1993, p. 74.
26. T. R. Reid commentary on "Morning Edition," National Public Radio, September 9, 1993.
27. Andrew Tanzer, "Hot Wings Take Off," *Forbes,* January 18, 1993, p. 74.
28. "China: The Titan Stirs," *The Economist,* November 28, 1992, pp. 3–6. See also Brenton Schlender, "China Really Is on the Move," *Fortune,* October 5, 1992, pp. 114–116+; "China Can't Restrain Growth," *The Wall Street Journal,* April 26, 1993, p. A9; Andrew Tanzer, "This Time It's for Real," *Forbes,* August 2, 1993, pp. 58–61.
29. "China: The Titan Stirs," p. 5.
30. Pete Engardio, "'Greater China' Could Be the Biggest Tiger of All," *Business Week,* September 28, 1992, p. 58; Louis Kraar, "A New China without Borders," *Fortune,* October 5, 1992, pp. 124–126+.
31. "The Faltering State," *The Economist,* November 28, 1992, pp. 8–9.
32. Louis Kraar, "Asia's Hot New Growth Triangle," *Fortune,* October 6, 1992, pp. 136–138+.
33. *Ibid.,* p. 138.
34. Pete Engardio and Neil Gross, "Asia's High-Tech Quest," *Business Week,* December 7, 1992, pp. 126–130.
35. Robert C. Schmults, "The African Market: A Lion Awakes," *Insight,* August 9, 1993, pp. 18–21.
36. See, for example, "Africa's Growth Outlook Damped," *The Wall Street Journal,* April 28, 1993, p. A11.
37. Schmults, "The African Market," p. 21.
38. Jeannette R. Scollard, "Road to Russia," Entrepreneur, March 1993, pp. 114–119.
39. Gail E. Schares, "Colgate-Palmolive Is Really Cleaning Up in Poland," *Business Week,* March 15, 1993, pp. 54, 56.
40. Neela Banerjee, "Russia Snickers after Mars Invades," *The Wall Street Journal,* July 13, 1993, pp. B1, B10.
41. Scollard, "Road to Russia."
42. Gary Marx, "'Bullish on Latin America': Foreign Money Pours in as Growth Takes Off," *Chicago Tribune,* June 20, 1993, sec. 7, pp. 1, 4.
43. "Dossier: Telecommunications in Asia: Malaysia-Thailand," *International Business Newsletter,* June 1993, pp. 12–13.
44. See, for example, Scollard, "Road to Russia."
45. "Selling to the New Global Middle Class," *Business Week,* October 25, 1993, p. 152.
46. Valerie Reitman, "Enticed by Visions of Enormous Numbers, More Western Marketers Move into China," *The Wall Street Journal,* July 12, 1993, pp. B1, B6; Tanzer, "This Time It's for Real," p. 59.

47. "Going Global: Mexico," p. 5.
48. Louis Kraar, "Indonesia on the Move," *Fortune,* September 20, 1993, pp. 112, 114, 116.
49. Armin A. Brott, "How to Avoid Bear Traps," *Nation's Business,* September 1993, pp. 49–50.
50. Jerry Flint, "Opportunities in Terrorism," *Forbes,* February 15, 1993, pp. 193–194.
51. Hal Plotkin, "In the China Shop," *Inc.,* September 1993, pp. 108–109.
52. Donald L. Baron, "European Vocation," *Entrepreneur,* January 1993, pp. 117–122.
53. Sunita Wadekar Bhargava, "Software from India? Yes, It's for Real," *Business Week,* January 18, 1993, p. 77.
54. Suman Dubey, "After 16-Year Dry Spell, Coca-Cola Co. Will Bring 'the Real Thing' Back to India," *The Wall Street Journal,* October 22, 1993, p. B7C.
55. Albert Warson, "Exploring Hungarian Opportunities," *Inc.,* June 1993, pp. 96–97.
56. Philip R. Cateora, *International Marketing,* 8th ed. (Homewood, Ill.: Irwin, 1993), pp. 49–51.
57. Lawrence Ingrassia and Bhushan Bahree, "NAFTA Victory Keeps GATT's Chances Alive," *The Wall Street Journal,* November 19, 1993, p. A9.
58. Daniel Benjamin, "Germany Is Troubled by How Little Work Its Workers Are Doing," *The Wall Street Journal,* May 6, 1993, pp. A1, A7.
59. Jack Hayes, "No Bratwurst on Saturday: Big Macs Reign in Germany," *Nation's Restaurant News,* November 2, 1992, p. 18.
60. Susan Greco, "Will Your Product 'Travel' Overseas?" *Inc.,* July 1992, p. 118.
61. Tanzer, "Hot Wings Take Off."
62. Randall Johnson, "Superior Product Quality Can Smash Any Trade Barriers," *Total Quality Newsletter,* June 1992, p. 5.
63. Madeline E. Hutcheson, "When in Asia . . . ," *UPS International Update* (United Parcel Service), Spring 1993, p. 4.
64. Robert A. Mamis, "Not So Innocent Abroad," *Inc.,* September 1993, pp. 110–111.
65. "Going Global: Mexico," p. 2.
66. Kevin Helliker, "They're Sore Because They Know the Irish Speak English the Best," *The Wall Street Journal,* July 13, 1993, p. B1.
67. "A Task for Two: Invent a Brand," *The Grocer,* September 12, 1992, pp. 48–49.
68. "Growing Your Business by Going Global," *Inc.,* September 1993, p. 107, citing Peter Schwartz, *The Art of the Long View.*
69. Andrew Tanzer, "China's Dolls," *Forbes,* December 21, 1992, pp. 250, 252.
70. "The Class of 1992," *The Economist,* September 5, 1992, pp. 62–64.
71. Karen Lowry Miller, "You Just Can't Talk to These Kids," *Business Week,* April 19, 1993, pp. 104, 106.
72. James p. Gallagher, "Russia's New Wealthy Are Happy to Spend Their Money," *Chicago Tribune,* September 12, 1993, sec. 1, p. 16; James McGregor, "China's New Rich Seek the Good Life," *The Wall Street Journal,* January 13, 1993, p. A10.
73. Uli Schmetzer, "Chinese Capitalism: Mother of Inventions," *Chicago Tribune,* October 11, 1992, sec. 1, p. 23.
74. Brian Dumaine, "Exporting Jobs and Ethics," *Fortune,* October 5, 1992, p. 10.
75. John N. Maclean, "Whirlpool Thriving on Energy Efficiency," *Chicago Tribune,* July 5, 1992, sec. 7, p. 5.
76. Stan Sesser, "Opium War Redux," *The New Yorker,* September 13, 1993, pp. 78–89. See also Paula Dwyer, "Lots of Purring but Less Profit in New Markets Overseas," *Business Week,* May 3, 1993, p. 132.
77. Brott, "How to Avoid Bear Traps."
78. Jerry DeMuth, "Stop-and-Go Exports," *International Business,* July 1993, pp. 66, 68.
79. Jeffrey J. Ake, "Easier Done than Said," *Inc.,* February 1993, pp. 96–99.
80. "Home Delivery Services: Convenience for Consumers," *International Business Newsletter,* June 1993, pp. 9–10.
81. Stephanie Losee, "New U.S. Export: Destressing Kids," *Fortune,* February 8, 1993, p. 10.
82. Baron, "European Vocation," p. 117.
83. "Variety Is the Ice of Life," *Business Franchise* (Britain), July/August 1993, pp. 36–37.
84. Dave Savona, "Global Go-Getters: Marvel Entertainment Group," *International Business,* September 1993, p. 20.
85. "Fruits of Socialism," *Time,* January 11, 1993, p. 10.
86. Plotkin, "In the China Shop."
87. Robert Neff, "Multinationals Have a Tiger by the Tail," *Business Week,* December 7, 1992, pp. 131–133.
88. "Motorola," *Fortune,* August 24, 1992, global business advertising section, pp. S-6–S-7.
89. Tim Smart, "Why Ignore 95% of the World's Market?" *Business Week,* Reinventing America 1992 special issue, p. 64.
90. *Ibid.*
91. Paul M. Eng, "Made in the U.S.A. . . . by Hyundai," *Business Week,* October 26, 1992, p. 96.

CHAPTER 5
1. Michael A. Lev, "Children's Museums Are Coming Out from Behind the Displays," *Chicago Tribune,* February 14, 1993, sec. 2, pp. 1, 3.
2. Fleming Meeks, "'Be Ferocious,'" *Forbes,* August 2, 1993, pp. 40–41.
3. National Public Radio, "Weekend Edition Saturday," December 19, 1992.
4. Donald Katz, "Triumph of the Swoosh," *Sports Illustrated,* August 16, 1993, pp. 54–73; National Public Radio, "Weekend Edition Saturday," December 19, 1992.
5. Katz, "Triumph of the Swoosh."
6. Michael E. Raynor, "Quality as a Strategic Weapon," *Journal of Business Strategy* (September/October 1992): pp. 3–9.
7. William Keenan, Jr., "Drawing the Line," *Sales & Marketing Management,* August 1993, pp. 32, 34–36, interviewing marketing consultants Al Ries and Jack Trout.
8. Raynor, "Quality as a Strategic Weapon."
9. J. Paul Peter and James H. Donnelly, Jr., *A Preface to Marketing Management,* 6th ed. (Burr Ridge, Ill.: Irwin, 1994), p. 9.
10. Jon Van, "'Universal Access' Ameritech's Big Picture," *Chicago Tribune,* February 14, 1993, sec. 7, pp. 1, 4.
11. Rodale Press brochure.
12. Frederick E. Webster, Jr., "The Changing Role of Marketing in the Corporation," *Journal of Marketing* 56 (October 1992): pp. 1–17.
13. Richard Normann and Rafael Ramírez, "From Value Chain to Value Constellation: Designing Interactive Strategy," *Harvard Business Review,* July-August 1993, pp. 65–77.
14. "Rubbermaid: Breaking All the Molds," *Sales & Marketing Management,* August 1992, p. 42.
15. Susan Reda, "Store Sells Time, Hosiery Too," *Stores,* August 1993, pp. 64–65.
16. Van, "'Universal Access.'"
17. *Ibid.*
18. Michael Barrier, "When 'Just-in-Time' Just Isn't Enough," *Nation's Business,* November 1992, pp. 30–31.
19. John R. Emshwiller, "Hang Ten International Rides Forward by Looking Back," *The Wall Street Journal,* December 30, 1992, p. B2.
20. Julie Tilsner, "Duracell Looks Abroad for More Juice," *Business Week,* December 21, 1992, pp. 52–56.
21. David Askham, "Market Research Paved Way for Specialist Holidays in Cumbria," *London Times,* September 4, 1992, p. 22.
22. George S. Day, "Marketing's Contribution to the Strategy Dialogue," University of Pennsylvania, n.d.

23. Eric Morgenthaler, "U.S. Has Jellyfish That Nobody Wants Except Maybe in Asia," *The Wall Street Journal,* December 19, 1992, pp. A1, A5.

24. David Young, "Grainger Retools Strategy, Gets Faster, Busier, Bigger," *Chicago Tribune,* July 18, 1993, sec. 7, pp. 1, 6.

25. Boston Consulting Group, *The Product Portfolio* (Boston: BCG, 1970).

26. Robert Jacobson and David A. Aaker, "Is Market Share All That It's Cracked Up to Be?" *Journal of Marketing* (Fall 1985): pp. 11–22; Carolyn Y. Woo and Arnold C. Cooper, "The Surprising Case for Low Market Share," *Harvard Business Review,* November-December 1982, pp. 106–113; and Stephen J. Markell, Sue E. Neeley, and Thomas H. Strickland, "Explaining Profitability: Dispelling the Market Share Fog," *Journal of Business Research* 16 (1988): 189–196.

27. Emshwiller, "Hang Ten Rides Forward."

28. Webster, "The Changing Role of Marketing," p. 11.

29. Amy Barrett, "Detergents, Aisle 2. Pizza Hut, Aisle 5," *Business Week,* June 7, 1993, pp. 82–83.

30. "Overrating Appraisals," *Total Quality Newsletter,* November 1992, p. 8.

31. Jeen-Su Lim and David A. Reid, "Vital Cross-Functional Linkages with Marketing," *Industrial Marketing Management* 21 (1992): pp. 159–165.

32. Ford S. Worthy, "Japan's Smart Secret Weapon," *Fortune,* August 12, 1991, pp. 72–75.

33. Peter D. Bennett, ed., *Dictionary of Marketing Terms* (Chicago: American Marketing Association, 1988), p. 116.

34. Frances Huffman, "Marketing Makeover," *Entrepreneur,* November 1992, pp. 129–133.

35. *Ibid.*

36. Dick Schaaf, "Complex Quality," *The Quality Imperative,* September 1992, pp. 16–18+.

37. Karen Lowry Miller, "Overhaul in Japan," *Business Week,* December 21, 1992, pp. 80–83, 86.

38. Data presented in a graph in *The Wall Street Journal,* January 7, 1993, p. B4.

39. Kevin Goldman, "Ads Seek to Make Iced Tea the Hot Drink," *The Wall Street Journal,* August 17, 1993, p. B8; and Joshua Levine, "Watch Out, Snapple!" *Forbes,* May 10, 1993, pp. 142, 146.

40. Kathleen Deveny, "Cold Remedies Take a Turn for the Worse," *The Wall Street Journal,* November 17, 1992, pp. B1, B11.

CHAPTER 6

1. Procter & Gamble report of its Meeting for Financial Analysts, July 15, 1993.

2. *Ibid.*

3. Gabriella Stern, "P&G Starting to Cut as Many as 10,000 Jobs," *The Wall Street Journal,* June 24, 1993, pp. A3, A7.

4. Joyce M. Rosenberg, "New Macy's Slashing 'Pomposity, Baloney,'" *Wisconsin State Journal,* November 27, 1992, p. 10C.

5. Leslie Brokaw, "Thinking Flat," *Inc.,* October 1993, pp. 86, 88.

6. "Olive Garden Restructures Marketing Department," *Nation's Restaurant News,* May 24, 1993, p. 6.

7. G. Christian Hill and Ken Yamada, "Motorola Illustrates How an Aged Giant Can Remain Vibrant," *The Wall Street Journal,* December 9, 1992, pp. A1, A14.

8. "Playing to Win," *Sales & Marketing Management,* August 1993, p. 42.

9. Jerry Bowles, "Quality '93: Empowering People with Technology," *Fortune,* September 20, 1993 special advertising section, p. 142.

10. Frederick E. Webster, Jr., "The Changing Role of Marketing in the Corporation," *Journal of Marketing* (October 1992): pp. 1–17; "The Network Organization: Managing in the 21st Century," *Supervisory Management,* March 1992, p. 2.

11. Walter Kiechel III, "How We Will Work in the Year 2000," *Fortune,* May 17, 1993, pp. 38–42+.

12. Henry Fersko-Weiss, "Project Managers: A New Focus on Graphics and Resource Controls," *PC Magazine,* February 11, 1992, pp. 38–39.

13. Richard Dulude, "Quality and Market Share," in *Total Quality Performance,* eds. Lawrence Schein and Melissa A. Berman, Research Report No. 909 (Washington, D.C.: The Conference Board, 1988), pp. 22–25.

14. Karen Lowry Miller, "The Man Who's Selling Japan on Jeeps," *Business Week,* July 19, 1993, pp. 56–57.

15. Aimee L. Stern, "Managing by Team Is Not Always as Easy as It Looks," *New York Times,* July 18, 1993, p. F5.

16. Dean Tjosvold, Valerie Dann, and Choy Wong, "Managing Conflict between Departments to Serve Customers," *Human Relations* 45 (1992): 1035–1053.

17. "Charles Finkel Brews a Taste for Beer," *Sales & Marketing Management,* August 1992, p. 32.

18. The guidelines in this paragraph are from Sondra Thiederman, *Bridging Cultural Barriers for Corporate Success: How to Manage the Multicultural Work Force* (New York: Lexington Books, 1991).

19. Samuel C. Certo, *Supervision* (Burr Ridge, Ill.: Austen Press, 1994), p. 160.

20. Albert Mehrabian, "Communication without Words," *Psychology Today,* September 1968, pp. 53–55.

21. For excellent examples of different cultures' communication styles, see Thiederman, *Bridging Cultural Barriers for Corporate Success.*

22. Matt Rothman, "Into the Black," *Inc.,* January 1993, pp. 59–65.

23. "Work Teams Have Their Work Cut Out for Them," *HRFocus,* January 1993, p. 24.

24. See Clay Carr, "Planning Priorities for Empowered Teams," *Journal of Business Strategy* (September-October 1992): pp. 43–47.

25. John Case, "What the Experts Forgot to Mention," *Inc.,* September 1993, pp. 66–68+.

26. Richard Normann and Rafael Ramírez, "From Value Chain to Value Constellation: Designing Interactive Strategy," *Harvard Business Review,* July-August 1993, pp. 65–77.

27. Rothman, "Into the Black," p. 65.

28. Ron Ruggles, "TGI Friday's: Changing with the Times," *Nation's Restaurant News,* March 29, 1993, p. 51.

29. Thomas V. Bonoma, "Making Your Marketing Strategy Work," *Harvard Business Review,* March–April 1984, pp. 69–76.

30. Mark Henricks, "All Together Now," *Entrepreneur,* April 1993, pp. 42, 45, 47.

31. John Schmeltzer, "Execs Unveil Road Map for a 'New Sears,'" *Chicago Tribune,* February 12, 1993, sec. 3, pp. 1–2.

32. See, for example, "Better Questions," *Total Quality Newsletter,* October 1992, p. 8.

33. Maryanne E. Rasmussen, "Measuring Bottom-Line Impact of Customer Satisfaction," in *Making Total Quality Happen,* ed. Frank Caropreso, Research Report No. 937 (Washington, D.C.: The Conference Board, 1990), pp. 55–59.

34. George Gendron, "FYI," *Inc.,* May 1993, p. 9.

35. Cited in T. Scott Gross, "Outrageous! Master the Art of Everyday Showmanship," *Success,* March 1992, pp. 40–42.

36. Jerry G. Boales, "Leaders Build Organizational Capital," *Fortune,* September 20, 1993, special advertising section.

37. Peter D. Bennett, ed., *Dictionary of Marketing Terms* (Chicago: American Marketing Association, 1988), p. 176.

38. Gregory A. Patterson, "Holiday Hopes of the Catalog Industry: Merrier Christmas, Happier New Year," *The Wall Street Journal,* December 2, 1992, pp. B1, B8.

39. Brent Bowers, "A Clothier Discovers a Sideline Can Dress Up Results," *The Wall Street Journal,* December 7, 1992, p. B2.

40. Kathleen Deveny, "Man Walked on the Moon but Man Can't Make Enough Devil's Food Cookie Cakes," *The Wall Street Journal,* September 28, 1993, p. B1.

41. Armco annual report (Parsippany, N.J., 1991).

42. "Charles Finkel Brews a Taste for Beer."
43. Rothman, "Into the Black."
44. Ronald E. Yates, "New ABCs for Pinpoint Accounting," *Chicago Tribune,* January 24, 1993, sec. 7, pp. 1, 4.

CHAPTER 7

1. Peter D. Bennett, ed., *Dictionary of Marketing Terms* (Chicago: American Marketing Association, 1988), p. 117.
2. J. Paul Peter and James H. Donnelly, Jr., *A Preface to Marketing Management,* 6th ed. (Burr Ridge, Ill.: Irwin, 1994), pp. 39–40.
3. See Neil A. Morgan and Nigel F. Piercy, "Market-Led Quality," *Industrial Marketing Management* 21 (1992): 111–118.
4. Jennifer Cody, "They Hired Someone to Find Out if People Really Like Chocolate?" *The Wall Street Journal,* November 26, 1993, p. B1.
5. Casey Bukro, "Garbage Collection Goes On-Line," *Chicago Tribune,* March 17, 1993, sec. 3, pp. 1–2.
6. Stephanie Anderson Forest, "Customers 'Must Be Pleased, Not Just Satisfied,'" Business Week, August 3, 1992, p. 52.
7. Edward O. Welles, "The Shape of Things to Come," *Inc.,* February 1992, pp. 66–69+.
8. Bennett, *Dictionary of Marketing Terms,* p. 151.
9. Stanley F. Slater and John C. Narver, "Superior Customer Value and Business Performance: The Strong Evidence for a Market-Driven Culture," Report No. 92-125 (Cambridge, Mass.: Marketing Science Institute, September 1992).
10. "Shrewd Thinking . . . about Market Surveys," *Boardroom Reports,* September 1, 1992, p. 15, quoting *Marketing News.*
11. Otis Port, "Quality: Small and Midsize Companies Seize the Challenge—Not a Moment Too Soon," *Business Week,* November 30, 1992, pp. 66–72.
12. Jeremy Main, "How to Steal the Best Ideas Around," *Fortune,* October 19, 1992, pp. 102–106.
13. Port, "Quality," p. 68.
14. Main, "How to Steal."
15. Bennett, *Dictionary of Marketing Terms,* p. 182.
16. Fleming Meeks, "And then the Designer Left," *Forbes,* December 7, 1992, pp. 162+.
17. Brad Edmondson, "Get Ready for the Other Census," *American Demographics,* November 1992, pp. 14+.
18. James Coates, "Low-Cost Software Brings Census Closer to Home," *Chicago Tribune,* May 2, 1993, sec. 7, p. 6.
19. William Bak, "Thoroughly Modern Marketing," *Entrepreneur,* May 1993, pp. 58, 60–61.
20. Richard J. Maturi, "Time for a Change?" *Entrepreneur,* September 1993, pp. 160, 162–163.
21. Joseph M. Juran, "Made in U.S.A.: A Renaissance in Quality," *Harvard Business Review,* July-August 1993, pp. 42–50.
22. Peter O. Keegan, "Operators Are All Ears with New 800 Numbers," *Nation's Restaurant News,* March 29, 1993, p. 15.
23. Michael J. McCarthy, "James Bond Hits the Supermarket: Stores Snoop on Shoppers' Habits to Boost Sales," *The Wall Street Journal,* August 25, 1993, pp. B1, B8.
24. Charlie Etmekjian, "Experiments: Their Changing Nature and Why They'll Still Be with Us during the 1990s," presentation at American Marketing Association's Behavioral Research Conference, January 24-27, 1990.
25. Matthew D. Shank and Raymond LaGarce, "Study: Color Makes Any Message More Effective," *Marketing News,* August 6, 1990, p. 12.
26. Bruce W. Mainzer, "Consumer Research at United: The Only Good Research Is Research That's Available Now!" presentation at American Marketing Association's Attitude Research Conference, January 26-29, 1992.
27. David Powers Cleary, "BirdsEye Frozen Foods," *Great American Brands: The Success Formulas That Made Them Famous,* Fairchild Publications, New York, N.Y. Copyright 1981, pp. 7–12.

28. "Failure of Its Oven Lovin' Cookie Dough Shows Pillsbury Pitfalls of New Products," *The Wall Street Journal,* June 11, 1993, pp. B1, B8.
29. Udayan Gupta, "Costly Market Research Pays Off for Biotech Start-Up," *The Wall Street Journal,* August 2, 1993, p. B2.
30. "What's the Best Source of Market Research?" *Inc.,* June 1992, p. 108.
31. Michael p. Cronin, "An 800 Number Dedicated to Tracking Customers," *Inc.,* June 1992, p. 108.
32. "Gathering Intelligence Any Way You Can Get It," *The Office Advisor* (*Inc.* magazine newsletter), Spring 1993, p. 4.
33. "Nielsen Rival to Unveil New 'Peoplemeter,'" *The Wall Street Journal,* December 4, 1992, p. B8.
34. Robert Lee, "What Business Customers Have to Say: Listening to Our Leaders," presentation at American Marketing Association's Business-to-Business Conference, March 28-30, 1993.
35. Walker Industry Image Study, 10th ed. (Indianapolis: Walker Research & Analysis, 1992).
36. "Data Drives Hospital System's 'Triage' Quality Improvement," *Total Quality Newsletter,* August 1993, pp. 5–6.
37. William Keenan, Jr., "Drawing the Line," *Sales & Marketing Management,* August 1993, pp. 32–36.
38. Douglas F. Haley and Andrea Z. Morgan, "From Bean Counting to Marketing Intelligence: Transforming a Customer Service Scorecard into a Blueprint for Marketing Action," American Marketing Association and American Society for Quality Control's joint conference on Customer Satisfaction and Quality Measurement, April 7-9, 1991.
39. Walker Industry Image Study.
40. See, for example, "Taking a Long Look at Focus Groups," *Sales & Marketing Management,* April 1993, p. 9; Laura Bird, "Marketers Come Out from Behind the Mirror," *The Wall Street Journal,* June 23, 1993, p. B1; and Phaedra Hise, "Mailing Makeover," *Inc.,* September 1993, p. 26.
41. Annual Report of Procter & Gamble Company, 1993, p. 6.
42. Walker Industry Image Study.
43. Etmekjian, "Experiments," pp. 3–4.
44. Bickley Townsend, "Market Research That Matters," *American Demographics,* August 1992, pp. 58–60.
45. Slater and Narver, "Superior Customer Value and Business Performance," p. 4.
46. Dave Savona, "A French Pair," *International Business,* July 1993, p. 89.
47. Mainzer, "Consumer Research at United."
48. David H. Freedman, "An Unusual Way to Run a Ski Business," *Forbes ASAP,* December 7, 1992, pp. 27–28+.
49. Bennett, *Dictionary of Marketing Terms,* p. 53.
50. Eric Schine, "Computer Maps Pop Up All over the Map," *Business Week,* July 26, 1993, pp. 75–76.
51. William Bak, "Hot Spots," *Entrepreneur,* June 1993, pp. 54, 56–57.
52. Coates, "Low-Cost Software Brings Census Closer to Home."
53. Howard Schlossberg, "Shoppers Virtually Stroll through Store Aisles to Examine Packages," *Marketing News,* June 7, 1993, p. 2.
54. See Antonio S. Lauglaug, "Why Technical-Market Research?" *Journal of Business Strategy* (September/October 1992): pp. 26–35.
55. Phil Guarascio, "How GM Targets 'Mature' Market Niche," *Advertising Age,* January 11, 1993, p. 26.
56. Lauglaug, "Why Technical Market Research?"
57. Gilbert A. Churchill, Jr., *Basic Marketing Research,* 2d ed. (Fort Worth, Tex: Dryden Press, 1992), p. 58.
58. Walker Industry Image Study.
59. The examples in this paragraph are from Aimee Stern, "Do You Know What They Want?" *International Business,* March 1993, pp. 102–103.
60. Cody, "They Hired Someone to Find Out if People Really Like Chocolate?"

61. Valerie Reitman, "P&G Uses Skills It Has Honed at Home to Introduce Its Brands to the Russians," *The Wall Street Journal,* April 14, 1993, pp. B1, B10.

CHAPTER 8

1. Peter D. Bennett, ed., *Dictionary of Marketing Terms* (Chicago: American Marketing Association, 1988), p. 50.
2. Bill Kelley, "The New Consumer Revealed," *Sales & Marketing Management,* May 1993, pp. 46+.
3. Alecia Swasy, "Don't Sell Thick Diapers in Tokyo," *New York Times,* October 3, 1993, sec. 3, p. 9.
4. Bennett, *Dictionary of Marketing Terms,* p. 196.
5. Tim Bovee, "Hispanics Poised to Become Largest Minority in U.S.," *Wisconsin State Journal,* September 29, 1993, p. 1; William Dunn, "The Move toward Ethnic Marketing," *Nation's Business,* July 1992, pp. 39–41.
6. Dunn, "The Move toward Ethnic Marketing."
7. J. Paul Peter and Jerry C. Olson, *Consumer Behavior and Marketing Strategy,* 3d ed. (Homewood, Ill.: Irwin, 1993), p. 482.
8. Dunn, "The Move toward Ethnic Marketing."
9. Laura Bird, "Marketers Miss Out by Alienating Blacks," *The Wall Street Journal,* April 9, 1993, p. B8.
10. See Jerome D. Williams and William J. Qualls, "Middle-Class Black Consumers and Intensity of Ethnic Identification," *Psychology and Marketing,* Winter 1989, pp. 263-286; John C. Mowen, *Consumer Behavior,* 2d ed. (New York: Macmillan, 1990), p. 628; James F. Engel, Robert D. Blackwell, and Paul Miniard, *Consumer Behavior,* 6th ed. (Hinsdale, Ill.: Dryden Press, 1990), pp. 91–95.
11. Nancy Millman, "Blacks Put a Value on Accurate Portrayal in Ads," *Chicago Tribune,* April 25, 1993, sec. 7, pp. 1, 6.
12. *Ibid.*
13. Wilma Randle, "Closer Look at Black Spending," *Chicago Tribune,* August 25, 1993, sec. 3, pp. 1–2.
14. "'Black Pride' Plays Role in Buying Goods," *Marketing News,* February 19, 1990, p. 11.
15. Pamela Patrick Novotny, "Spirited Style," *Chicago Tribune,* August 15, 1993, sec. 6, p. 7; John Schmeltzer, "Ebony Good Fit at Spiegel," *Chicago Tribune,* July 26, 1993, sec. 4, pp. 1, 4.
16. Bovee, "Hispanics Poised"; Dunn, "The Move toward Ethnic Marketing."
17. Bovee, "Hispanics Poised."
18. Peter Brimelow, "The Fracturing of America," *Forbes,* March 30, 1992, pp. 74–75.
19. *Ibid.*
20. Dunn, "The Move toward Ethnic Marketing."
21. Bovee, "Hispanics Poised"; Dunn, "The Move toward Ethnic Marketing."
22. Peter and Olson, *Consumer Behavior and Marketing Strategy,* p. 486.
23. *The Asian-American Market* (New York: FIND/SVP, 1990); Bryant Robey, "America's Asians," *American Demographics,* May 1985, pp. 22–29.
24. Donald W. Hendon, Emelda L. Williams, and Douglas E. Huffman, "Social Class System Revisited," *Journal of Business Research* 17 (1988): pp. 259–270.
25. Patricia Braus, "Selling Self-Help," *American Demographics,* March 1992, pp. 48–52.
26. Faye Rice, "What Intelligent Consumers Want," *Fortune,* December 28, 1992, pp. 56–60.
27. "Marketers of Luxury Goods Are Turning from Self-Indulgence to Family Values," *The Wall Street Journal,* October 22, 1992, pp. B1, B10.
28. Rice, "What Intelligent Consumers Want."
29. Douglas F. Haley and Andrea Z. Morgan, "From Bean Counting to Marketing Intelligence: Transforming a Customer Service Scorecard into a Blueprint for Marketing Activity," Presentation at American Marketing Association's Customer Satisfaction and Quality Measurement Conference, April 7-9, 1991.

30. "Marketers of Luxury Goods Are Turning from Self-Indulgence," p. B1.
31. Virginia Matthews, "Ajax's Beefcake Meant to Spur Men to Clean Up," *Marketing* (Canada), June 28, 1993, p. 34.
32. Pat Baldwin, "Ad Firm Links Brand Choice to Motivation," *Chicago Tribune,* August 9, 1992, sec. 7, p. 9.
33. Richard Phalon, "Walking Billboards," *Forbes,* December 7, 1992, pp. 84, 86.
34. "Keeping the Customer Satisfied," *Adweek,* August 24, 1992, pp. 40+.
35. Pat Sloan, "Getting a Tan, Family Style," *Advertising Age,* January 25, 1993, p. 12.
36. "Sales of Prepared Frozen Vegetables Melt," *The Wall Street Journal,* December 15, 1992, p. B10.
37. Mike Dorning, "For Women, Shopping Is Not Just an Adventure, It's a Job," *Chicago Tribune,* January 20, 1993, sec. 3, pp. 1, 3.
38. Rice, "What Intelligent Consumers Want," pp. 57–58.
39. Norm Alster, "A Few Good Films," *Forbes,* April 26, 1993, pp. 58+.
40. Bennett, *Dictionary of Marketing Terms,* p. 106.
41. Lisa Anderson, "'Prudent' Shoppers True Blue," June 7, 1992, sec. 7, pp. 1, 7B.
42. "Sales of Prepared Frozen Vegetables Melt."
43. "Shoppers in Middle America Are Trying 'Exotic' Italian Foods, and That's *Amore,*" *The Wall Street Journal,* October 6, 1992, pp. B1, B7.
44. Diane Crispell, "People Patterns: Students Picking College Bank on Reputation," *The Wall Street Journal,* May 12, 1993, p. B1.
45. Kathleen Deveny, "For Growing Band of Shoppers, Clean Means Green," *The Wall Street Journal,* April 6, 1993, pp. B1, B7.
46. Kelley, "The New Consumer Revealed."
47. "Consumers: Debt Is a Dirty Word," *Fortune,* November 1992, pp. 23–24, 26.
48. James Coates, "It's High Noon in Showdown over Electronics Simplicity," *Chicago Tribune,* January 24, 1993, sec. 7, pp. 1, 5.

CHAPTER 9

1. Bob Weinstein, "Head Over Heels," *Entrepreneur,* May 1993, pp. 116–121.
2. U.S. Department of Commerce, *Statistical Abstract of the United States,* 113th ed. (Washington, D.C.: U.S. Government Printing Office, 1993), p. 291.
3. U.S. Department of Commerce, *Statistical Abstract of the United States,* p. 293.
4. See Clinton Crownover and Mark Henricks, "Patriot Games," *Entrepreneur,* September 1993, pp. 105–109.
5. Susan Greco, "Breaking Away," *Inc.,* October 1993, pp. 84, 86.
6. Harris Corporation Annual Report 1993, p. 8.
7. *Ibid.,* p. 14.
8. Erskine Bowles, "Uncle Sam on RAM," *Entrepreneur,* August 1993, p. 138.
9. U.S. Department of Commerce, *Statistical Abstract of the United States,* p. 775.
10. Elizabeth Ehrlich, "The Quality Management Checkpoint," *International Business,* May 1993, pp. 56–58+.
11. Jaclyn H. Park, "Animal Logic," *GSB Chicago* (University of Chicago Graduate School of Business), Winter 1993, pp. 21–24.
12. Michael Selz and John R. Emshwiller, "Few Attempts Seen to Avoid New Law," *The Wall Street Journal,* February 8, 1993, pp. B1–B2.
13. Nicholas K. Geranios, "'Everyone Has the Fever' for Specialty Coffees," *Chicago Tribune,* December 6, 1992, sec. 7, p. 12.
14. Edward O. Welles, "Least Likely to Succeed," *Inc.,* December 1992, pp. 14+.
15. Dirk Dusharme, "News You Can Use," *Quality Digest,* May 1993, p. 8.
16. John Morris, "Customized Services Boost Competitiveness," *International Business,* November 1993, pp. 48ff.
17. Stanley F. Slater and John C. Narver, "Superior Customer Value and Business Performance: The Strong Evidence for a Market-

Driven Culture," Report No. 92-125 (Cambridge, Mass.: Marketing Science Institute, 1992), p. 3.

18. Employee Empowerment: It's an Interdependent Relationship," *FYI* (Harris Corporation), Spring 1993, pp. 6–7.

19. Michael Sullivan, "Translating the Voice of the International Customer," presentation at the American Marketing Association Business-to-Business Conference, March 28–30, 1993.

20. David Young, "Grainger Retools Strategy, Gets Faster, Busier, Bigger," *Chicago Tribune,* July 18, 1993, sec. 7, pp. 1, 6.

21. ary Cobb Sullivan, "Groen President's Close Customer Contact Keeps Product Innovation Cooking," *GSB Chicago* (University of Chicago Graduate School of Business), Winter 1993, p. 35.

22. Evelyn Lauter, "'We Have to Keep Coming Up with New Ideas and New Flavors,'" *Chicago Tribune Magazine,* January 31, 1993, p. 36.

23. *Ibid.*

24. Personal correspondence from Jerry Keller, AutoResearch Laboratories Inc., December 23, 1993.

25. Kevin Kelly and Zachary Schiller, "Cut Costs or Else," *Business Week,* March 22, 1993, pp. 28–29.

26. David Young, "Illinois Tool Still Fastened to Keep-It-Simple Formula," *Chicago Tribune,* April 26, 1993, sec. 4, pp. 1, 4.

27. Steven Pratt, "At What Price Perfection?" *Chicago Tribune,* April 29, 1993, sec. 7, pp. 1, 6, 8.

28. Ehrlich, "The Quality Management Checkpoint," p. 58.

29. Gary S. Vasilash, "Making It in the 1990s as a Supplier," *Production,* January 1993, pp. 46–48.

30. Robin Yale Bergstrom, "Hanging a Vision on Quality," *Production,* July 1993, pp. 56–61.

31. Shawn Tully, "Why Drug Prices Will Go Lower," *Fortune,* May 3, 1993, pp. 56–58+.

32. Crownover and Henricks, "Patriot Games," p. 109.

33. J. Paul Peter and James H. Donnelly, Jr., *A Preface to Marketing Management,* 6th ed. (Burr Ridge, Ill.: Irwin, 1994), p. 80.

34. Susan Greco, "Marketing through Employers," *Inc.,* June 1993, p. 29.

35. See Paul Sherlock, *Rethinking Business to Business Marketing* (New York: Free Press, 1991), pp. 22–23.

36. Richard Watson, "Facing Up to Problems," *Business Franchise,* July/August 1993, pp. 39+.

37. Roger W. Brucker, "Merchandising: The Hit-and-Run of a Guerrilla Marketing Tactic," *Business Marketing,* April 1987, pp. 76+.

38. Sullivan, "Translating the Voice of the International Customer," p. 12.

39. Park, "Animal Logic," p. 23.

40. Robert Lee, "What Business Customers Have to Say: Listening to Our Leaders," presentation at the American Marketing Association's Business-to-Business Conference, March 28-30, 1993.

41. Example provided by Dr. S. J. Garner, Richmond, Kentucky.

42. John S. McClenahen, "Sound Thinking," *Industry Week,* May 3, 1993, pp. 24, 28.

43. Lee, "What Business Customers Have to Say," pp. 6–7.

44. Lawrence Surtees, "Northern Telecom: The Morning After," *Report on Business,* July 5, 1993, sec. B, pp. 1, 4.

45. Haken Hakansson, ed., *International Marketing and Purchasing of Industrial Goods* (New York: Wiley, 1984).

46. Douglas F. Haley and Andrea Z. Morgan, "From Bean Counting to Marketing Intelligence: Transforming a Customer Service Scorecard into a Blueprint for Marketing Action," presentation at the American Marketing Association and American Society for Quality Control joint conference on Customer Satisfaction and Quality Measurement, April 7-9, 1991.

47. Peter and Donnelly, *A Preface to Marketing Management,* p. 82.

48. Personal correspondence from Jerry Keller, ALI, December 23, 1993.

49. Susan Greco, "Making Company Tours Pay Off," *Inc.,* February 1993, p. 26.

50. Wesley L. Johnston and Thomas V. Bonoma, "The Buying Center: Structure and Interaction Patterns," *Journal of Marketing* (Summer 1981): pp. 143–156.

51. Charles R. O'Neal and William C. La Fief, "Marketing's Lead Role in Total Quality," *Industrial Marketing Management* 21 (1992): pp. 133–143.

CHAPTER 10

1. Aimee Stern, "Land of the Rising Mail," *International Business,* November 1993, pp. 28, 30.

2. Peter D. Bennett ed., *Dictionary of Marketing Terms* (Chicago: American Marketing Association, 1988), p. 114.

3. Fisher-Price Annual Report 1992, p. 4.

4. Mark Lewyn, "For America Online, Nothing Is as Nice as a Niche," *Business Week,* September 14, 1992, p. 100.

5. Brigid McMenamin, "Beverly Hillbilly," *Forbes,* March 29, 1993, p. 110.

6. Suzanne Alexander, "Firms Cater to African-Style Weddings," *The Wall Street Journal,* August 24, 1993, pp. B1–B2.

7. Lewyn, "For America Online, Nothing Is as Nice as a Niche."

8. Lynn Van Matre, "Celebrating a Golden Opportunity That Paid Off," *Chicago Tribune,* September 6, 1992, sec. 5, pp. 1, 4.

9. William Echikson, "The Trick to Selling in Europe," *Fortune,* September 20, 1993, p. 82.

10. *Ibid.*

11. Janet Izatt, "C-Change at Mercedes," *Marketing Week,* July 2, 1993, pp. 28–31.

12. Jolie Solomon, "Firms Moving to Keep It Simple for Consumers," *Chicago Tribune,* May 17, 1992, sec. 7, p. 7D.

13. Kate Fitzgerald, "Small Appliances Big for 1992," *Advertising Age,* January 27, 1992, p. 12.

14. Susan B. Garland, "Those Aging Boomers," *Business Week,* May 20, 1991, pp. 106–112.

15. Alessandra Bianchi, "New Businesses: Mature Marketing," *Inc.,* May 1992, p. 26.

16. Gary Strauss, "Discerning Post-Boomers Elusive Target," *USA Today,* June 7, 1993, pp. B1–B2.

17. Dawn Smith, "Exercising Those Little Grey Sells," *Marketing Week,* July 2, 1993, pp. 35–38.

18. Phil Guarascio, "How GM Targets 'Mature' Market Niche," *Advertising Age,* January 11, 1993, p. 26.

19. Jan Larson, "J. C. Penney Finds Profit in Africa," *American Demographics,* November 1992, p. 12.

20. Martha T. Moore, "Soul Searching: New KFC Menu Targets Blacks," *USA Today,* March 15, 1993, p. 5B.

21. Bradley Johnson, "Carnival Cruise Line Beckons Hispanics," *Advertising Age,* January 25, 1993, p. 46.

22. Leon E. Wynter, "Small Broadcasters Reach Asian-Americans," *The Wall Street Journal,* February 2, 1993, p. B1.

23. Jon Berry, "Marketers Reach Out to Blacks," *Chicago Tribune,* May 12, 1991, sec. 7, p. 9.

24. Nancy Millman, "Retailers Shopping for Black Consumers," *Chicago Tribune,* February 14, 1993, sec. 7, pp. 1, 6.

25. Laura Bird, "Marketers Miss Out by Alienating Blacks," *The Wall Street Journal,* April 9, 1993, p. B8.

26. "Minority Leaders Blast J. C. Penney Plan to Target Blacks, Hispanics," *Marketing News,* October 11, 1993, pp. 1, 15.

27. Ryan Mathews, "The Changing Face of the American Consumer," *Grocery Marketing,* May 1993, pp. 31-32.

28. Bob Jones, "Big Money on Campus," *Entrepreneur,* September 1993, pp. 62+.

29. Charles Hayes, "Back at the Ranch," *Chicago Tribune,* May 2, 1992, sec. 4, pp. 1–2.

30. Blayne Cutler, "North American Demographics," *American Demographics,* March 1992, pp. 38–42.

31. William Echikson, "Hey, Europe, Let's Do Munch!" *Fortune,* November 2, 1992, p. 18.

32. Joe Schwartz, "Climate-Controlled Customers," *American Demographics,* March 1992, pp. 24–26+.

33. Marilyn Silverman, "Developing Terrific Creative . . . Research Can Help," presentation at the American Marketing Association Marketing Research Conference, September 25-26, 1990.

34. Joshua Levine, "In Your Face," *Forbes,* November 22, 1993, pp. 164, 167.

35. William p. Diven, "Flour Power," *Entrepreneur,* November 1992, p. 20.

36. "Playing to Win: Apple Computer," *Sales & Marketing Management,* August 1993, p. 39.

37. Bickley Townsend, "Market Research That Matters," *American Demographics,* August 1992, pp. 58–60.

38. Flowers Industries Inc. Annual Report 1993.

39. Alan Radding, "IBM Hunkers Down," *Advertising Age,* January 27, 1992, p. 36.

40. Amdahl Annual Report 1992.

41. "The Writing Is on the Screen," *The Economist,* April 25, 1992, pp. 69–70.

42. American Public Radio, "Marketplace," October 25, 1993. Produced by USC Radio (Los Angeles: University of Southern California).

43. "Profiles in Marketing: Paul Amatangelo," *Sales & Marketing Management,* January 1993, p. 12.

44. "The True Cost of Pumping Up the Volume," *Sales & Marketing Management,* March 1992, p. 21.

45. Radding, "IBM Hunkers Down."

46. Marcy Magiera, "Nike Eyes the Ladies," *Advertising Age,* October 14, 1991, p. 4.

47. "Gerber's Little Treasures," *The Gerber News,* 3rd Quarter 1993.

48. "Entry-Level Phone Service," *Time,* March 2, 1992, p. 43.

49. Dan Fost, "U.S. Hospitals Entice Mexicans," *American Demographics,* November 1992, p. 25.

50. Bryan Batson, "The Road Less Traveled," *Sales & Marketing Management,* December 1992, pp. 46–48+.

51. Steve Kichen, "Will the Third Time Be the Charm?" *Forbes,* March 15, 1993, p. 54.

52. Judie Lannon, "Brands across Borders: Do Advertising Ideas Travel?" presentation at the American Marketing Association Attitude Research Conference, January 20-23, 1991.

53. Joseph Weber, "Campbell: Now It's M-M-Global," *Business Week,* March 15, 1993, pp. 52–54.

54. Michael Sullivan, "Translating the Voice of the International Customer," presentation at American Marketing Association Business-to-Business Conference, March 28-30, 1993, p. 2.

55. Gabriella Stern, "P&G's Calcium Pitch to Teens Sparks Criticism," *The Wall Street Journal,* August 18, 1993, pp. B1, B8.

56. *Ibid.*

57. Silverman, "Developing Terrific Creative," pp. 10–11.

58. Alison Fahey, "A&W Aims Younger," *Advertising Age,* January 27, 1992, p. 12.

59. *Ibid.*

60. Joe Schwartz, "Turtle Wax Shines Water, Too," *American Demographics,* April 1992, p. 4.

61. Saul Hansell, "The Man Who Charged Up MasterCard," *New York Times,* March 7, 1993, pp. 1, 8.

62. Schwartz, "Climate-Controlled Customers."

63. Peter Laundy, "Image Trouble," *Inc.,* September 1993, pp. 80–82, 84.

64. "How about a Nicotine Patch with a Micronite Filter?" *AdWeek,* August 24, 1992, p. 18.

CHAPTER 11

1. Christopher Power, "Flops," *Business Week,* August 16, 1993, pp. 76-80, 82.

2. J. Paul Peter and James H. Donnelly, Jr., *A Preface to Marketing Management,* 5th ed. (Homewood, Ill.: Irwin, 1991), p. 119.

3. Peter D. Bennett, ed., *Dictionary of Marketing Terms* (Chicago: American Marketing Association, 1988), p. 157.

4. Lesley Alderman, "Hot Stuff: Green Pens," *Money,* May 1992, p. 40.

5. Example contributed by William W. Sannwald, San Diego State University, San Diego, California.

6. Chris Roush, "At Timex, They're Positively Glowing," *Time,* July 12, 1993, p. 141.

7. Gretchen Morgenson, "The Foot's Friend," *Forbes,* April 13, 1992, pp. 60, 62.

8. Bennett, ed., *Dictionary of Marketing Terms,* p. 97.

9. Tim Smart, "Kathleen Synnott: Shaping the Mailrooms of Tomorrow," *Business Week,* November 16, 1992, p. 66.

10. Bennett, ed., *Dictionary of Marketing Terms,* p. 1.

11. Jerry Flint, "'These Are the Good Old Days,'" *Forbes,* January 4, 1993, pp. 60–61.

12. Bennett, ed., *Dictionary of Marketing Terms,* p. 197.

13. Flint, "'These Are the Good Old Days.'"

14. Bennett, ed., *Dictionary of Marketing Terms,* p. 63.

15. C. Merle Crawford, *New Products Management,* 2d ed. (Homewood, Ill.: Irwin, 1987), p. 18.

16. James Coates, "Big Blue Set to Get Down and Dirty," *Chicago Tribune,* January 10, 1993, sec. 7, p. 3.

17. "The Best New Products," *Business Week,* January 11, 1993, pp. 108–112.

18. *Ibid.,* p. 109.

19. Mark Maremont, "How Gillette Is Honing Its Edge," *Business Week,* September 28, 1992, pp. 60, 65.

20. Mark Maremont, "The Only Difference Is When You Throw Them Away," *Business Week,* July 12, 1993, p. 29.

21. Alison Sprout, "Products to Watch," *Fortune,* August 24, 1992, p. 99.

22. Lois Therrien, "The Rage to Page Has Motorola's Mouth Watering," *Business Week,* August 30, 1993, pp. 72-73.

23. William Echikson, "Aiming at High and Low Markets," *Fortune,* March 22, 1993, p. 89.

24. Harris Collingwood, "Now, a Peewee Polaroid Camera," *Business Week,* September 28, 1992, p. 48.

25. "ConAgra's Healthy Choice: Getting to the Heart of the Matter," *Sales & Marketing Management,* August 1992, p. 43.

26. George Gendron, "Surprise! Surprise!" *Inc.,* September 1992, p. 9.

27. Gregory N. Racz, "For Marketers, First Pet Is the Cat's Meow," *The Wall Street Journal,* February 26, 1993, p. B1.

28. Leslie Brokaw, "Where Great Ideas Come From," *Inc.,* January 1993, pp. 72–74+.

29. "The Best New Products," p. 111.

30. Paul Sherlock, *Rethinking Business-to-Business Marketing* (New York: Free Press, 1991), p. 75.

31. Kevin Goldman, "Scouring-Pad Rivals Face 3M Challenge," *The Wall Street Journal,* January 11, 1993, p. B4.

32. Brokaw, "Where Great Ideas Come From."

33. Bryan Batson, "The Road Less Traveled," *Sales & Marketing Management,* December 1992, pp. 46–48+.

34. Stephanie Anderson Forest, "A Pier 1 in Every Port?" *Business Week,* May 31, 1993, p. 88.

35. Andrew Hilton, "Mythology, Markets, and the Emerging Europe," *Harvard Business Review,* November–December 1992, pp. 50–54.

36. Nathalie Boschat, "Catering to Africa's Consumers," *World Press Review,* June 1993, p. 40.

37. U.S. Department of Commerce, *Statistical Abstract of the United States,* 113th ed. (Washington, D.C.: U.S. Government Printing Office, 1993), p. 595.

38. John Carey, "Moving the Lab Closer to the Marketplace," *Business Week,* Reinventing America 1992 special issue, pp. 164–165+.

39. David Young, "Illinois Tool Still Fastened to Keep-It-Simple Formula," *Chicago Tribune,* sec. 4, pp. 1, 4.

40. Joel Silverman, "The Next Thing in Running," *Outside,* January 1994, p. 49.

41. Procter & Gamble Annual Report 1993, p. 8.
42. Pete Engardio, "Motorola in China: A Great Leap Forward," *Business Week,* May 17, 1993, pp. 58–59.
43. Carey, "Moving the Lab," p. 168.
44. Gary Slutsker, "The Tortoise and the Hare," *Forbes,* February 1, 1993, pp. 66–69.
45. Eben Shapiro, "From Frozen Dinners to Styling Gels: Microwave Is Moving into New Areas," *The Wall Street Journal,* February 2, 1993, p. B8.
46. Jolie Solomon, "A Risky Revolution," *Newsweek,* April 26, 1993, pp. 44–45.
47. Betsy Spethmann, "Cereal-Makers Mount All-Day Campaign on the Snack Market," *Chicago Tribune,* May 9, 1993, sec. 7, p. 11.
48. Shawn Tully, "Why Drug Prices Will Go Lower," *Fortune,* May 3, 1993, pp. 56–58+.
49. Goldman, "Scouring-Pad Rivals Face 3M Challenge."
50. Carey, "Moving the Lab," pp. 168–169.
51. Elizabeth Ehrlich, "The Quality Management Checkpoint," *International Business,* May 1993, pp. 56–58+.
52. James R. Healey, "Youthful Support May Steer Electric Vehicles," *USA Today,* March 9, 1993, p. 4B.
53. Jim Mateja, "Consumers to Test GM Electric Car," *Chicago Tribune,* October 14, 1993, sec. 3, pp. 1, 4.
54. Richard Gibson, "McDonald's Tries Bigger Burger to Beef Up Dinner Menu," *The Wall Street Journal,* March 24, 1993, pp. B1, B10.
55. Annetta Miller and Karen Springen, "Egg Rolls for Peoria," *Newsweek,* October 12, 1992, pp. 59–60.
56. Steve Lohr, "Test It in Tulsa—It'll Play in Peoria," *Chicago Tribune,* June 7, 1992, sec. 7, p. 3.
57. Jacquie McNish, "Interactive TV a Feast for Techno-Junkies," Toronto *Globe and Mail,* July 6, 1993, sec. 8, p. 1.
58. Alison Sprout, "Products to Watch: Thin Tortilla Chips," *Fortune,* October 19, 1992, p. 109.
59. Moira Madonia, "Baby Needs," *Supermarket Business,* September 1993, pp. 91, 151.
60. John Markoff, "Marketer's Dream, Engineer's Nightmare," *New York Times,* December 12, 1993, sec. 3, pp. 1, 8.
61. Peter and Donnelly, *A Preface to Marketing Management,* p. 119.
62. *Ibid.,* p. 120.
63. Power, "Flops," pp. 76, 78.
64. Peter and Donnelly, *A Preface to Marketing Management,* p. 120.
65. Hideki Kaihatsu, "TQC in Japan," in *Making Total Quality Happen,* ed. Frank Caropreso, Research Report No. 937 (New York: The Conference Board, 1990), pp. 7–10.
66. Alessandra Bianchi, "Well Said," *Inc.,* January 1993, pp. 98–99.
67. Patrick M. Reilly, "Sales of Latest Digital Music Systems Hit Sour Notes Despite Promotional Hoopla," *The Wall Street Journal,* December 21, 1992, pp. B1, B6.
68. Steve Blount, "It's Just a Matter of Time," *Sales & Marketing Management,* March 1992, pp. 32–33.
69. Regis McKenna, "Marketing Is Everything," *Harvard Business Review,* January-February 1991, pp. 65–79.
70. C. Merle Crawford, *New Products Management,* 3rd ed. (Homewood, Ill.: Richard D. Irwin, 1991), pp. 410–415.
71. *Ibid.,* p. 416.
72. *Ibid.,* pp. 416–419. See also Brian Dumain, "Payoff from the New Management," *Fortune,* December 13, 1993, pp. 103–104.
73. Stuart Winby, "Hewlett-Packard Is Redefining State-of-the-Art When It Comes to Teams," *Total Quality Newsletter,* October 1992, p. 7.
74. Blount, "It's Just a Matter of Time."
75. Bennett, ed., *Dictionary of Marketing Terms,* p. 210.
76. Marcia Berss, "'This Isn't Ross Perot and GM,'" *Forbes,* June 8, 1992, pp. 103, 106.
77. Blount, "It's Just a Matter of Time."
78. *Ibid.*
79. Elyse Tanouye, "Johnson & Johnson Stays Fit by Shuffling Its Mix of Businesses," *The Wall Street Journal,* December 22, 1992, pp. A1, A4.
80. McKenna, "Marketing Is Everything," pp. 67–68.
81. "Big Wheel," *Entrepreneur,* September 1993, p. 75.
82. Jon Lowden, "The Next Thing in Skating," *Outside,* January 1994, p. 51.
83. Brian Dumain, "Payoff from the New Management," *Fortune,* December 13, 1993, pp. 103–104+.

CHAPTER 12

1. Casey Bukro, "Oil Recycler Greases Rusty City's Economy," *Chicago Tribune,* May 30, 1993, sec. 7, pp. 1, 4.
2. Gayle Sato Stodder, "Small-Business Spotlight: A Look at Comic Book Stores," *Entrepreneur,* August 1992, pp. 152–155.
3. Thomas McCarroll, "Crashing Prices," *Time,* August 2, 1993, pp. 48–49.
4. William M. Bulkeley, "More Teens Can't Live without Beepers," *The Wall Street Journal,* December 7, 1992, p. B4.
5. Thomas McCarroll, "Testing the Waters," *Time,* April 26, 1993, p. 54.
6. "Eauverdose?" *The Economist,* August 14, 1993, p. 55.
7. John Schmeltzer, "CDs Have Put the Turntable in a Tailspin," *Chicago Tribune,* September 7, 1993, sec. 3, pp. 1, 4.
8. Kathleen Deveny, "Decaf Loses Favor with Seekers of Flavor," *The Wall Street Journal,* February 25, 1993, p. B1.
9. Andrew E. Serwer, "Espresso Bars Explode," *Fortune,* December 14, 1992, p. 20.
10. Schmeltzer, "CDs Have Put the Turntable in a Tailspin."
11. Richard Gibson, "Stirring Memories Gives Ovaltine a Lift," *The Wall Street Journal,* December 3, 1992, pp. B1, B10.
12. Dana Milbank, "Selling Steel," *The Wall Street Journal,* November 30, 1992, p. B1.
13. Scott Williams, "Rain Barrel Comeback Overflows," *Chicago Tribune,* June 7, 1992, sec. 7, p. 7B.
14. Nita Lelyveld, "A Kitchen Classic in Comeback," *Chicago Tribune,* April 26, 1992, sec. 7, p. 8.
15. Example cited in C. Merle Crawford, *New Products Management,* 2d ed. (Homewood, Ill.: Richard D. Irwin, 1987), p. 44.
16. Joseph Pereira, "Footwear Fad Makes Nike, Reebok Run for Their Money," *The Wall Street Journal,* June 24, 1993, pp. B1, B5.
17. Kathleen Deveny, "Blame It on Dashed Hopes (and Oprah): Disillusioned Dieters Shun Liquid Meals," *The Wall Street Journal,* October 13, 1992, p. B10.
18. Eric Morgenthaler, "That's No Spaceship, That's My Car: Neon Invades Expressways," *The Wall Street Journal,* August 23, 1993, pp. A1, A5.
19. Jon Van, "At Ingersoll, Flexibility, Change Are a Way of Life," *Chicago Tribune,* November 5, 1991, sec. 1, p. 12.
20. Nancy J. Perry, "Hit 'Em Where They Used to Be," *Fortune,* October 19, 1992, pp. 112–113.
21. Ron Winslow, "Pioneer Project Publishes First Rankings of Cleveland Hospitals," *The Wall Street Journal,* April 29, 1993, p. B12.
22. Gretchen Morgenson, "Look Who's Coming to Dinner," *Forbes,* March 1, 1992, pp. 104–105.
23. Paul Sherlock, *Rethinking Business-to-Business Marketing* (New York: Free Press, 1991), pp. 128–129.
24. Gabriella Stern, "To Outpace Rivals, More Firms Step Up Spending on New-Product Development," *The Wall Street Journal,* October 28, 1992, pp. B1, B7.
25. Harris Corporation Annual Report 1993, p. 23.
26. *Ibid.*
27. "Making Machinery Hum a Quieter Tune," *The Wall Street Journal,* December 23, 1992, p. B1.
28. Todd Leeuwenburgh, "Quality Standards That Can Open Doors," *Nation's Business,* November 1992, pp. 32–33; Cyndee

Miller, "U.S. Firms Lag in Meeting Global Quality Standards," *Marketing News,* February 15, 1993, pp. 1, 6.

29. Miller, "U.S. Firms Lag in Meeting Global Quality Standards."

30. *Ibid.*

31. Leeuwenburgh, "Quality Standards That Can Open Doors," p. 32.

32. Alison Sprout, "Products to Watch," *Fortune,* September 21, 1992, p. 115.

33. Peter D. Bennett, ed., *Dictionary of Marketing Terms* (Chicago: American Marketing Association, 1988), p. 76.

34. Kathleen Deveny, "Today's Toothbrushes: 'Improved' and Pricey," *The Wall Street Journal,* November 10, 1992, pp. B1, B10.

35. Larry Armstrong, "Practical Honda Takes a Sporty Turn," *Business Week,* September 28, 1992, p. 136.

36. "School Colors," *Entrepreneur,* September 1993, p. 12.

37. Bruce Nussbaum, "Hot Products," *Business Week,* June 7, 1993, pp. 54–57.

38. George C. Dorman, "Go with the Flow—Measuring Information Worker Quality," in *Total Quality Performance,* eds. Lawrence Schein and Melissa A. Berman, Research Report No. 909 (New York: The Conference Board, 1988), pp. 29–39.

39. Randall Lane, "Does Orange Mean Cheap?" *Forbes,* December 23, 1991, pp. 144+.

40. *Ibid.,* p. 146.

41. Michael J. McCarthy, "Coca-Cola Introduces Marketing Gimmick: Its Famous Old Bottle," *The Wall Street Journal,* January 12, 1993, p. B4.

42. Kathleen Deveny, "Toothpaste Makers Tout New Packaging," *The Wall Street Journal,* November 10, 1992, pp. B1, B10.

43. Nancy Ryan, "Soft-Drink Refillables Fading Fast," *Chicago Tribune,* August 29, 1993, sec. 7, pp. 1, 8.

44. "When in Rome . . . ," *Entrepreneur,* September 1992, pp. 133–137.

45. *Ibid.,* p. 135.

46. *Ibid.*

47. Valerie Reitman, "Enticed by Visions of Enormous Numbers, More Western Marketers Move into China," *The Wall Street Journal,* July 12, 1993, pp. B1, B6.

48. Catherine Vial, "Why EC Environmental Policy Will Affect American Business," *Business America,* March 8, 1993, pp. 24–27.

49. Sonia L. Nazario, "Microwave Packages That Add Crunch to Lunch May Also Pose Chemical Risks," *The Wall Street Journal,* March 1, 1990, pp. B1, B6.

50. Bennett, ed., *Dictionary of Marketing Terms,* p. 18.

51. Shawn Tully, "Why Drug Prices Will Go Lower," *Fortune,* May 3, 1993, pp. 56–58+.

52. Bennett, ed., *Dictionary of Marketing Terms,* p. 19.

53. Ronald Alsop, "Brand Loyalty Is Rarely Blind Loyalty," *The Wall Street Journal,* October 19, 1989, pp. B1, B8.

54. Patricia Winters, "Pepsi Harkens Back to Youth," *Advertising Age,* January 25, 1993, pp. 3, 43.

55. F. Alan Schultheis, "Case History: AT&T Universal Card," presentation at American Marketing Association New Products Conference, February 20–22, 1991.

56. Gary Strauss, "Extending a Bit Too Far?" *USA Today,* April 19, 1993, p. 7B.

57. Pat Sloan, "Gillette Rolls New Series Line," *Advertising Age,* January 25, 1993, pp. 3, 41.

58. Kathleen Deveny, "More Shoppers Bypass Big-Name Brands and Steer Carts to Private-Label Products," *The Wall Street Journal,* October 20, 1992, pp. B1, B8.

59. *Ibid.;* Patricia Sellers, "Brands: It's Thrive or Die," *Fortune,* August 23, 1993, pp. 52–56; and Steve Weinstein, "The New Brand Loyalty," *Progressive Grocer,* July 1993, pp. 93–94+.

60. Lois Therrien, "Brands on the Run," *Business Week,* April 19, 1993, pp. 26–29.

61. Patrick Oster, "The Eurosion of Brand Loyalty," *Business Week,* July 19, 1993, p. 22.

62. Yumiko Ono, "The Rising Sun Shines on Private Labels," *The Wall Street Journal,* April 26, 1993, pp. B1, B6.

63. Bennett, ed., *Dictionary of Marketing Terms,* p. 85.

64. Jennifer Lawrence, "P&G Battles Private Labels with New Products," *Advertising Age,* March 16, 1992, pp. 3, 49.

65. Marc Levinson, "Stand by Your Brand," *Newsweek,* April 19, 1993, pp. 38–39.

66. Weinstein, "The New Brand Loyalty," p. 94.

67. Tully, "Why Drug Prices Will Go Lower," p. 66.

68. Susan Greco, "Profits in Private Labels," *Inc.,* March 1993, p. 27.

69. Terance Shimp, *Promotion Management and Marketing Communications,* 2d ed. (Hinsdale, Ill.: Dryden Press, 1990), p. 67.

70. Daniel L. Doden, "Selecting a Brand Name That Aids Marketing Objectives," *Advertising Age,* November 5, 1990, p. 34.

71. Norm Alster, "Pass the Sugar," *Forbes,* April 13, 1992, p. 90.

72. Nancy Ten Kate, "Words That Sell Keep Changing," *American Demographics,* August 1992, p. 18.

73. Alan L. Adler, "What's in a Name? Automakers' Time and Money," *Wisconsin State Journal,* April 26, 1993, p. 8B.

74. "A Task for Two: Invent a Brand," *The Grocer,* September 12, 1992, pp. 48–49.

75. Bob Coleman, "Knock It Off!" *Entrepreneur,* September 1993, pp. 121–126.

76. Richard Gibson, "He Hasn't Got Anything to Spoof Spaghetti and Meat Sauce—Yet," *The Wall Street Journal,* January 6, 1993, p. B1.

77. "Nice PCs—but the Test Is in the Marketing," *Business Week,* September 21, 1992, pp. 66–67.

78. Jack Hayes, "Marketing, Travel Groups Add Synergy," *Nation's Restaurant News,* March 29, 1993, p. 74.

79. Laura Zinn, "Pepsi's Future Becomes Clearer," *Business Week,* February 1, 1993, pp. 74–75.

80. Gabriella Stern, "Kodak Unit Cuts Price for Large Bottles of Bayer," *The Wall Street Journal,* September 23, 1993, p. B8.

81. Allison Engel, "Old-Fashioned Frugality Is Back in Fashion," *The Wall Street Journal,* March 30, 1992.

82. George Lazarus, "How about a Blue Hawaiian Punch?" *Chicago Tribune,* March 2, 1992, sec. 4, p. 4.

83. Steve Kerch, "Shopping Center Industry Learns What's in Store for It," *Chicago Tribune,* May 17, 1992, sec. 16, pp. 1, 2E.

84. Jim Mateja, "VW Hatches a New Beetle," *Chicago Tribune,* January 6, 1994, sec. 1, pp. 1, 16.

85. Annetta Miller, "No Cheer for Procter & Gamble," *Newsweek,* July 26, 1993, p. 38; Zachary Schiller, "Procter & Gamble Hits Back," *Business Week,* July 19, 1993, pp. 20–22.

86. Richard J. Maturi, "Time for a Change?" *Entrepreneur,* September 1993, pp. 160, 162–163.

87. Stern, "To Outpace Rivals, More Firms Step Up Spending."

88. Alster, "Pass the Sugar."

89. Julie Liesse, "From Cereal to Snack to Cereal," *Advertising Age,* January 11, 1993, p. 20.

90. Timothy Aeppel, "Would 007 Approve? Aston Martin Makes a New 'Cheap' Car," *The Wall Street Journal,* March 25, 1993, p. A1.

CHAPTER 13

1. Peter D. Bennett, ed., *Dictionary of Marketing Terms* (Chicago: American Marketing Association, 1988), p. 184.

2. U.S. Department of Commerce, *Statistical Abstract of the United States,* 113th ed. (Washington, D.C.: U.S. Government Printing Office, 1993), pp. 410, 443.

3. Douglas Lavin and Krystal Miller, "Goodbye to Haggling: Savvy Consumers Are Buying Their Cars Like Refrigerators," *The Wall Street Journal,* August 20, 1993, p. B1.

4. J. Paul Peter and James H. Donnelly, Jr., *A Preface to Marketing Management,* 5th ed. (Homewood, Ill.: Irwin, 1991), pp. 209–213.

5. "Marriott Scraps Front-Desk Check-In," *Chicago Tribune,* February 21, 1993, sec. 7, p. 4.

6. Rashi Glazer, "Marketing in an Information-Intensive Environment: Implications of Knowledge as an Asset," *Journal of Marketing* (October 1991): pp. 1–19.

7. Robert A. Mamis, "Filing from 50,000 Feet," *Inc.,* April 1993, p. 49.
8. Frances Huffman, "Mad Marketing," *Entrepreneur,* November 1992, pp. 136–141.
9. See Raymond P. Fisk, Stephen W. Brown, and Mary Jo Bitner, "Tracking the Evolution of the Service Marketing Literature," *Journal of Retailing* (Spring 1993): pp. 61–103.
10. Leonard L. Berry, "Relationship Marketing," in *Emerging Perspectives on Services Marketing,* eds. Leonard L. Berry, L. G. Shostack, and Gregory D. Upah (Chicago: American Marketing Association, 1983), pp. 25–28.
11. Leonard L. Berry and A. Parasuraman, *Marketing Services: Competing through Quality* (New York: Free Press, 1991); Christopher W. L. Hart, W. Earl Sasser, Jr., and James L. Heskett, "The Profitable Art of Service Recovery," *Harvard Business Review,* July-August 1990, pp. 148–156.
12. Lawrence A. Crosby, Kenneth R. Evans, and Deborah Cowles, "Relationship Quality in Services Selling: An Interpersonal Influence Perspective," *Journal of Marketing* (July 1990): pp. 68–81.
13. Patricia Sellers, "Companies That Serve You Best," *Fortune,* May 31, 1993, pp. 74-76+.
14. *Ibid.,* p. 79.
15. Paul Hofheinz, "Rising in Russia," *Fortune,* January 24, 1994.
16. *Ibid.*
17. Jeff Borden, "Advising Businesses on the ADA," *Crain's Chicago Business,* November 9-15, 1992, p. 15.
18. Phaedra Hise, "Cashing In on Home Delivery," *Inc.,* May 1993, p. 23.
19. Sarah Jane Garner, "Perceived Risk and Information Sources in Services Purchasing," *The Mid-Atlantic Journal of Business* (Summer 1986): pp. 49–59.
20. Robert Tomsho, "U.S. Hospitals See Opportunity in Mexico," *The Wall Street Journal,* August 13, 1993, pp. B1, B4.
21. Ken Ohlson, "Cleaning Up: Damage Restoration Service," *Entrepreneur,* July 1993, pp. 148+.
22. C. Jeanne Hill and S. J. Garner, "Factors Influencing Physician Choice," *Hospital and Health Services Administration* 36 (Winter 1991): pp. 491–503.
23. C. Jeanne Hill, S. J. Garner, and Michael E. Hanna, "What Dental Professionals Should Know about Dental Consumers," *Health Marketing Quarterly* 8 (1990): 45–57.
24. See Susan M. Keaveney, "Information Processing of Services: Implications for New Services and Relationship Marketing," AMS Proceedings, April 1992.
25. "Outrageous! Master the Art of Everyday Showmanship," *Success,* March 1992, pp. 40–42.
26. Garner, "Perceived Risk and Information Sources in Services Purchasing."
27. Joshua Levine, "Where the Maître d' Outranks the Chef," *Forbes,* June 8, 1992, pp. 70–71.
28. Mark Henricks, "Right of Refusal," *Entrepreneur,* May 1993, pp. 122+.
29. Louis Kraar, "TV Is Exploding All over Asia," *Fortune,* January 24, 1994, pp. 99–101.
30. John Case, "Total Customer Service," *Inc.,* January 1994, pp. 52–58+.
31. "Service Shortfalls," *Total Quality Newsletter,* April 1993, p. 8.
32. Linda Cooper, "The Role of Research in Quality," presentation at American Marketing Association Marketing Research Conference, September 23–26, 1990.
33. Susan Greco, "The ABCs of Internal Guarantees," *Inc.,* March 1993, p. 29.
34. Julie Schmit, "Ritz-Carlton: Room for Employees," *USA Today,* October 15, 1992, p. 6B.
35. Sellers, "Companies That Serve You Best," p. 76.
36. Myron Magnet, "Goods News for the Service Economy," *Fortune,* May 3, 1993, pp. 46–50, 52.
37. Susan Greco, "Pricing Your Service for Profits," *Inc.,* June 1992, p. 107.
38. Susan Greco, "Talking through Service Costs," *Inc.,* June 1993, p. 29.
39. Kent B. Monroe, "Buyers' Subjective Perceptions of Price," *Journal of Marketing Research* (February 1973): pp. 70–80; Jerry Olson, "Price as an Informational Cue: Effects on Product Evaluation," in *Consumer and Industrial Buying Behavior,* eds. A. G. Woodside, J. N. Sheth, and p. D. Bennett (New York: Elsevier North-Holland, 1977), pp. 267–286; Donald R. Lichtenstein, Peter H. Bloch, and William C. Black, "Correlates of Price Acceptability," *Journal of Consumer Research* 15 (September 1988): 243–252.
40. Edward O. Welles, "Captain Marvel," *Inc.,* January 1992, pp. 44–47.
41. Christopher Palmeri, "Lettuce in Aisle 4, Loans in Aisle 10," *Forbes,* August 3, 1992, pp. 39–40.
42. Paul Hughes, "Updates: Charting Business Trends," *Entrepreneur,* September 1993, pp. 192, 194.
43. Lori Bongiorno, "B-Schools Bitten by the Global Bug," *Business Week,* October 25, 1993.
44. Valerie Reitman, "Down-to-Earth Ads Are Aimed at Those Thinking of Heaven," *The Wall Street Journal,* August 13, 1993, pp. A1, A10.
45. Patricia Braus, "Selling Self-Help," *American Demographics,* March 1992, pp. 48–52.
46. "A Fight at the Opera," *The Economist,* October 17, 1992, p. 68.
47. Marcus W. Brauchli, "India Raises Capital by Reaching Out to Sell Mutual Funds to Rural Masses," *The Wall Street Journal,* June 17, 1993, p. A8.
48. "Elvis, Christmas Elves Sighted at Post Office," *The Wall Street Journal,* December 16, 1992, p. B1.

CHAPTER 14
1. Paula Dwyer, "Lots of Puffing but Less Profit in New Markets Overseas," *Business Week,* May 3, 1993, p. 132.
2. Michael V. Marn and Robert L. Rosiello, "Managing Price, Gaining Profit," Harvard *Business Review,* September-October 1992, pp. 84–94.
3. Larry Armstrong, "Altima's Secret: The Right Kind of Sticker Shock," *Business Week,* January 18, 1993, p. 37.
4. Lois Therrien, "Brands on the Run," *Business Week,* April 19, 1993, pp. 26–29.
5. Alexandra Peers, "Forgery of a Painting by Botero, 'The Dancers,' Nearly Waltzes onto Auction Block at Christie's," *The Wall Street Journal,* May 6, 1993, pp. C1, C18.
6. Douglas Lavin and Krystal Mitter, "Goodbye to Haggling: Savvy Consumers Are Buying Their Cars Like Refrigerators," *The Wall Street Journal,* August 20, 1993, pp. B1, B3; Joseph B. White, "GM to Stress Value Pricing for '94 Models," *The Wall Street Journal,* July 12, 1993, pp. A3, A9.
7. J. Paul Peter and James H. Donnelly, Jr., *A Preface to Marketing Management,* 6th ed. (Burr Ridge, Ill.: Irwin, 1994), pp. 204–205.
8. Shawn Tully, "Why Drug Prices Will Go Lower," *Fortune,* May 3, 1993, pp. 56–58+.
9. Peter and Donnelly, *A Preface to Marketing Management,* p. 205.
10. Tully, "Why Drug Prices Will Go Lower."
11. Peter D. Bennett, ed., *Dictionary of Marketing Terms* (Chicago: American Marketing Association, 1988), p. 150.
12. Susan Greco, "Smart Use of 'Special Offers,'" *Inc.,* February 1993, p. 23.
13. Stephanie Strom, "A Survivor for Seventh Avenue," *New York Times,* March 7, 1993, p. 12F.
14. Andrew Kupfer, "Who's Winning the PC Price Wars?" *Fortune,* September 21, 1992, pp. 80–82.
15. Michael D. Mondello, "Naming Your Price," *Inc.,* July 1992, pp. 80–83.
16. David Kirkpatrick, "The Revolution at Compaq Computer," *Fortune,* December 14, 1992, pp. 80–82+.
17. Personal correspondence from Jerry Keller, AutoResearch Laboratories Inc., Chicago, December 23, 1993.

18. Edward O. Welles, "Captain Marvel," *Inc.,* January 1992, pp. 44–47.
19. Richard Turner, "The Top Hits of Today and Tomorrow at Rhino Records Are from Yesteryear," *The Wall Street Journal,* October 2, 1992, pp. B1, B6.
20. Zachary Schiller, "A Rash Decision?" *Business Week,* April 26, 1993, p. 36; Gabriella Stern, "P&G Will Cut Prices 5% on Pampers, 16% on Luvs to Battle Private Brands," *The Wall Street Journal,* April 14, 1993, p. B5.
21. "Supermarket Chains Chop Prices to Keep Rivals from Cutting into Their Business," *The Wall Street Journal,* March 25, 1993, pp. B1, B6.
22. Mondello, "Naming Your Price," p. 81.
23. Bennett, ed. *Dictionary of Marketing Terms,* p. 170.
24. Glenn Snyder, "Covering All the Bases for Better Video Rental," *Progressive Grocer,* July 1993, pp. 17+.
25. Bennett, *Dictionary of Marketing Terms,* p. 55.
26. Kirkpatrick, "The Revolution at Compaq Computer," pp. 82, 86.
27. Kent B. Monroe, *Pricing: Making Profitable Decisions,* 2d ed. (New York: McGraw-Hill, 1990), Chapter 4.
28. Wendy Zellner, "Penney's Rediscovers Its Calling," *Business Week,* April 5, 1993, pp. 51–52.
29. "Steelmakers Win Partial Victory in Trade Complaints," *Chicago Tribune,* July 28, 1993, sec. 3, pp. 1–2.
30. See Tom Peters, "Trade, Now More than Ever," *Quality Digest,* May 1993, pp. 16–17.
31. George M. C. Fisher, "Breaking into Japan," *Audacity,* Winter 1992, p. 2.
32. Bob Ortega, "Wal-Mart Bows to Pricing Reality by Changing 4 Letters," *The Wall Street Journal,* May 21, 1993, p. B1.
33. Patricia Sellers, "Companies That Serve You Best," *Fortune,* May 31, 1993, pp. 74–76+.

CHAPTER 15
1. Ken Yamada, "Motorola Challenges Intel in Pricing Its New Microchip," *The Wall Street Journal,* April 26, 1993, pp. B1, B8.
2. William P. Barrett, "Motivated Seller," *Forbes,* April 13, 1992, p. 58.
3. Robert D. Buzzell and Frederick D. Wiersema, "Successful Share Building Strategies," *Harvard Business Review,* January-February 1981, pp. 135–144.
4. Greg Bowens, "A Demolition Derby for Hertz, Avis, and the Gang," *Business Week,* October 5, 1992, pp. 85–86.
5. Jim Mateja, "Escort Sticker Shock: One Price Sells 'Em All," *Chicago Tribune,* March 13, 1992, sec. 1, pp. 1, 6.
6. Brian O'Reilly, "Know When to Embrace Change," *Fortune,* February 22, 1993, p. 90.
7. Amy Barrett, "Something Shady at Sunkist?" *Business Week,* May 17, 1993, p. 40.
8. David Young, "Grainger Retools Strategy, Gets Faster, Busier, Bigger," *Chicago Tribune,* July 18, 1993, sec. 7, pp. 1, 6.
9. Procter & Gamble Annual Report 1992, p. 10.
10. Peter D. Bennett, ed., *Dictionary of Marketing Terms* (Chicago: American Marketing Association, 1988), p. 107.
11. Susan Greco, "Smart Use of 'Special Offers,'" *Inc.,* February 1993, p. 23.
12. National Public Radio, "All Things Considered," August 18, 1993.
13. Paul Sherlock, *Rethinking Business to Business Marketing* (New York: Free Press, 1991), p. 64.
14. Jean Sherman Chatzky, "Changing the World," *Forbes,* March 2, 1992, pp. 83, 85.
15. Masayoshi Kanabayashi, "Japan's Top Soap Firm, Kao, Hopes to Clean Up Abroad," *The Wall Street Journal,* December 17, 1992, p. B4.
16. Meg Cox, "Audio-Book Makers Seek More Listeners," *The Wall Street Journal,* January 6, 1993, pp. B1, B8.
17. Kevin Helliker, "Bombay Co.'s Line of Furniture, Bric-a-Brac Fills a Void," *The Wall Street Journal,* October 28, 1992, p. B4.
18. Susan Greco, "Recession-Proof Pricing," *Inc.,* April 1993, p. 27.

19. James R. Healey, "Celica Shows Hazards of Misreading Market," *USA Today,* December 10, 1993, p. 5B; "The Price Is High," *The Economist,* August 14, 1993, p. 63.
20. Valerie Reitman, "P&G Uses Skills It Has Honed at Home to Introduce Its Brands to the Russians," *The Wall Street Journal,* April 14, 1993, pp. B1, B10.
21. Neela Banerjee, "Russia Snickers after Mars Invades," *The Wall Street Journal,* July 13, 1993, pp. B1, B10.
22. Procter & Gamble Annual Report 1993, p. 10.
23. Philip R. Cateora, *International Marketing,* 8th ed. (Homewood, Ill.: Irwin, 1993), p. 590.
24. Sally D. Goll, "Pepsi Looks for Pop from Asian Markets," *The Wall Street Journal,* June 25, 1993, p. A5C.
25. Krystal Miller, "Honda Adopts Incentive Plan for Its Dealers," *The Wall Street Journal,* May 6, 1993, pp. A3, A5.
26. Michael V. Marn and Robert L. Rosiello, "Managing Price, Gaining Profit," *Harvard Business Review,* September-October 1992, pp. 84–94.
27. "Body Language," *Entrepreneur,* March 1993, p. 222.
28. Susan Greco, "Street-Smart Pricing," *Inc.,* May 1993, p. 25.
29. Wendy Zellner, "Not Everybody Loves Wal-Mart's Low Prices," *Business Week,* October 12, 1992, pp. 36, 38.
30. Amy Feldman, "Blue Jeans as Tuna Fish," *Forbes,* April 26, 1993, pp. 78–79.
31. Jon Berry, "For Procter & Gamble's EDLP, a Sobering Report," *Adweek,* April 19, 1993, p. 9.
32. Gabriella Stern, "While Cost-Cutting Boosted P&G's Net in Fiscal Third Period, Sales Slid 2%," *The Wall Street Journal,* April 28, 1993, p. A4; Zachary Schiller, "A Nervous P&G Picks Up the Cost-Cutting Ax," *Business Week,* April 19, 1993, p. 28.
33. Berry, "For Procter & Gamble's EDLP."
34. Laura Klepacki, "P&G Commits Its Heavy Guns," *Supermarket News,* April 12, 1993, pp. 1, 10–11.
35. Melissa Campanelli, "What's in Store for EDLP?" *Sales & Marketing Management,* August 1993, pp. 56–59.
36. *Ibid.,* p. 59.
37. Richard Gibson, "Broad Grocery Price Cuts May Not Pay," *The Wall Street Journal,* May 7, 1993.
38. "Upmarket Philosophy," *The Economist,* December 26, 1992–January 8, 1993, pp. 95–98.
39. Laura Zinn and Hiromi Uchida, "Who Said Diamonds Are Forever?" *Business Week,* November 2, 1992, pp. 128–129.
40. Robert C. Blattberg and Scott A. Neslin, *Sales Promotion: Concepts, Methods, and Strategies* (Englewood Cliffs, NJ: Prentice-Hall, 1990), pp. 349–350; Robert M. Schindler and Alan R. Wiman, "Effects of Odd Pricing on Price Recall," *Journal of Business Research* (November 1989): pp. 165–178; and Kent B. Monroe, *Pricing: Making Profitable Decisions,* 2d ed. (New York: McGraw–Hill, 1990).
41. Michael W. Miller, "IBM Slashes Price of New PC Line to Battle Clones for Market Share," *The Wall Street Journal,* October 21, 1992, p. B7.
42. Procter & Gamble Report of Annual Meeting of Shareholders, October 12, 1993; Procter & Gamble Annual Report 1993, p. 11.
43. Rita Koselka, "Candy Wars," *Forbes,* August 17, 1992, pp. 76–77.
44. *Ibid.*
45. Greg Bowens, "Wiping the Mess from Gerber's Chin," *Business Week,* February 1, 1993, p. 32.
46. Annetta Miller, "Sega, Kitty and Breakfast, Too—for a Modest $39.95 a Night," *Newsweek,* September 6, 1993, p. 58.
47. Larry Armstrong and Karen Lowry Miller, "Toyota's New Pickup: Oops," *Business Week,* February 15, 1993, p. 37; James R. Healey, "Big Price, Little Power Has T100 Sputtering," *USA Today,* May 23, 1993, p. 10B.
48. Bowens, "A Demolition Derby."
49. Michael D. Mondello, "Naming Your Price," *Inc.,* July 1992, pp. 80–83.
50. Mark Lewyn, "MCI Is Coming Through Loud and Clear," *Business Week,* January 25, 1993, pp. 84, 88.

CHAPTER 16

1. Peter D. Bennett, ed, *Dictionary of Marketing Terms* (Chicago: American Marketing Association, 1988), p. 29.
2. Zachary Schiller and Wendy Zellner, "Clout! More and More Retail Giants Rule the Marketplace," *Business Week,* December 21, 1992, pp. 66–69+.
3. William Stern, "Mom and Dad Knew Every Name," *Forbes,* December 7, 1992, pp. 172, 174.
4. Frances Huffman, "Marketing Smarts: Innovative Ideas to Promote Your Business," *Entrepreneur,* May 1993, p. 140.
5. Paul Sherlock, *Rethinking Business to Business Marketing* (New York: Free Press, 1991), pp. 104–100.
6. Rashi Glazer, "Marketing in an Information-Intensive Environment: Strategic Implications of Knowledge as an Asset," *Journal of Marketing* (October 1991): pp. 1–19.
7. Meg Whittemore, "Extend Your Reach by Catalog Sales," *Nation's Business,* March 1992, pp. 33–34, 36.
8. The Quaker Oats Company, 1993 Annual Report, p. 12.
9. Leslie Brokaw, "Twenty-Eight Steps to a Strategic Alliance," *Inc.,* April 1993, pp. 96–100.
10. Steve Lohr, "Computers Greening with Times," *Chicago Tribune,* April 18, 1993, sec. 7, p. 3.
11. Robin Yale Bergstrom, "Environmental Affairs: An Annotated Essay," *Production,* April 1993, pp. 36–47.
12. "The Green Scene: Plastic Surgery," *Entrepreneur,* May 1993, p. 20.
13. Wilma Randle and Michael A. Lev, "Saturn Seeking Happy Returns," *Chicago Tribune,* August 11, 1993, sec. 3, p. 1.
14. Ruth Miller Fitzgibbons, "Business Is Blooming," *Your Company,* Spring 1992, pp. 32–35.
15. *Ibid.,* p. 35.
16. Bennett, ed., *Dictionary of Marketing Terms,* p. 81.
17. *The 1993 Franchise Annual* (Lewiston, N.Y.: Info Press, Inc., 1993).
18. Robert E. Bond and Jeffrey M. Bond, *The Source Book of Franchise Business Opportunities 1993* (Homewood, Ill.: Business One Irwin, 1993), pp. 3, 9; U.S. Department of Commerce, *Statistical Abstract of the United States,* 113th ed. (Washington, D.C.: U.S. Government Printing Office, 1993), p. 780.
19. "Breathing New Life into an Old Family Firm," *Your Company,* Spring 1992, p. 49.
20. Jack G. Kaikati, "Don't Crack the Japanese Distribution System—Just Circumvent It," *Columbia Journal of World Business* (Summer 1993): pp. 34–45.
21. Julie Pitta, "The Crisco Factor," *Forbes,* July 20, 1992, pp. 306–307.
22. Peter Newcomb, "Endangered Species?" *Forbes,* July 20, 1992, pp. 52, 54, 58.
23. Manjeet Kripalani and Tatiana Pouschine, "'People Thought I Was Nuts,'" *Forbes,* June 8, 1992, pp. 120–121.
24. "Pills by Post," *The Economist,* February 6, 1993, pp. 70–71.
25. J. Paul Peter and James H. Donnelly, Jr., *A Preface to Marketing Management,* 5th ed. (Homewood, Ill.: Irwin, 1991), p. 182.
26. Susan Greco, "Riding on Big-Company Coattails," *Inc.,* April 1993, p. 28.
27. Gretchen Morgenson, "Greener Pastures?" *Forbes,* July 6, 1992, p. 48.
28. Steve Glain, "American Standard Succeeds in Korea by Outflanking Local Firms' Lock-Out," *The Wall Street Journal,* August 26, 1993, p. A6.
29. Larry Armstrong, "What's Wrong with Selling Used CDs?" *Business Week,* July 26, 1993, p. 38.
30. Steve Kichen, "Pick a Channel," *Forbes,* March 2, 1992, pp. 108, 110.
31. See George S. Day, "Marketing's Contribution to the Strategy Dialogue," unpublished paper (University of Pennsylvania, n.d.); Frederick E. Webster, Jr., "The Changing Role of Marketing in the Corporation," *Journal of Marketing* (October 1992): pp. 1–17.
32. Marty Jacknis and Steve Kratz, "The Channel Empowerment Solution," *Sales & Marketing Management,* March 1993, pp. 44–49.
33. Jerry G. Bowles, "Quality '92: Leading the World-Class Company," *Fortune* special advertising section, September 21, 1992, pp. 16, 18.
34. Schiller and Zellner, "Clout!"
35. Glazer, "Marketing in an Information-Intensive Environment," p. 1.
36. Schiller and Zellner, "Clout!"
37. Nancy Brumback, "American Seeks Greater Leverage with Vendors," *Supermarket News,* June 28, 1993, p. 1.
38. Day, "Marketing's Contribution."
39. Schiller and Zellner, "Clout!" p. 66.
40. Nicholas W. Pilugin, "Wrigley Expanding Outlets in Russia," *Chicago Tribune,* August 4, 1992, sec. 3, pp. 1–2.
41. Michael Selz, "More Small Firms Are Turning to Trade Intermediaries," *The Wall Street Journal,* February 2, 1993, p. B2.
42. Robert A. Mamis, "Not So Innocent Abroad," *Inc.,* September 1993, pp. 110–111.
43. Jeanette R. Scollard, "Road to Russia," *Entrepreneur,* March 1993, pp. 114–119.
44. Gary Taylor, "Highway Robbery?" *International Business,* July 1993, pp. 33–34.
45. "A Close Look at Five Countries," *The Grocer* (Britain), September 12, 1992, p. 50.
46. Jeffrey A. Tannenbaum, "Soft-Drink Middlemen Claim Bottler Sewed a Market Up," *The Wall Street Journal,* March 24, 1993, p. B2.
47. Bennett, ed., *Dictionary of Marketing Terms,* p. 70.
48. Vera B. Gibbons, "The Faxable International Sales-Rep Application," *Inc.,* November 1993, pp. 95–97.
49. Tannenbaum, "Soft-Drink Middlemen."
50. Erika Kotite, "Food Fight," *Entrepreneur,* pp. 130–135.

CHAPTER 17

1. Glenn Snyder, "Covering All the Bases for Better Video Rentals," *Progressive Grocer,* July 1993, pp. 17–20+.
2. Leah Ingram, "Wash 'N' Go," *Entrepreneur,* July 1993, p. 12.
3. Joseph Pereira, "Toys 'R' Them: Mom-and-Pop Stores Put Playthings Like Thomas on Fast Track," *The Wall Street Journal,* January 14, 1993, pp. B1, B7.
4. Erich Toll, "Get Smart," *International Business,* September 1993, pp. 29-30.
5. John H. Taylor, "Niche Guys Finish First," *Forbes,* October 26, 1992, pp. 128, 132.
6. Peter D. Bennett, ed., *Dictionary of Marketing Terms* (Chicago: American Marketing Association, 1988), p. 214.
7. Department of Commerce, *Statistical Abstract of the United States,* 113th ed. (Washington, D.C.: U.S. Government Printing Office, 1993), p. 784.
8. Julie Candler, "How to Choose a Distributor," *Nation's Business,* August 1993, pp. 45–46.
9. Bennett, ed., *Dictionary of Marketing Terms,* p. 173.
10. Barbara Marsh, "Kiosks and Carts Can Often Serve as Mall Magnets," *The Wall Street Journal,* November 24, 1992, p. B1.
11. Frances Huffman, "Trade Secrets," *Entrepreneur,* February 1993, pp. 91–97.
12. Department of Commerce, *Statistical Abstract of the United States,* 112th ed. (Washington, D.C.: U.S. Government Printing Office, 1992), p. 759.
13. Department of Commerce, *Statistical Abstract of the United States,* 113th ed. (Washington, D.C.: U.S. Government Printing Office, 1993), p. 776.
14. Frances Huffman, "If the Shoe Fits . . . ," *Entrepreneur,* April 1993, p. 161.
15. Christopher Power, "Flops," *Business Week,* August 16, 1993, pp. 76–80, 82.
16. Rich Mendosa, "100 Fastest Growing Companies: Reef Brazil," *Hispanic Business,* August 1993, p. 44.
17. Candler, "How to Choose a Distributor."

18. Stephen Plauche II, "The Sales Force Will Need to Have the Best Team Spirit in the Nation," *The Wall Street Journal,* January 14, 1993, p. B1.
19. Wendy Zellner, "When Wal-Mart Starts a Food Fight, It's a Doozy," *Business Week,* June 14, 1993, pp. 92–93.
20. Stanley Ziemba, "Soon, Machines Will Vend Airline Tickets," *Chicago Tribune,* November 8, 1992, sec. 7, p. 3.
21. "CDs Now Sold in L.A. Vending Machines," *Chicago Tribune,* July 25, 1993, sec. 5, p. 3.
22. Richard Gibson, "Milkmen Bring Home Bacon and Pizza, Too," *The Wall Street Journal,* December 16, 1992, p. B1.
23. Katherine Ellison, "Avon Ladies Sell Hut to Hut in Brazil Wilds," *Chicago Tribune,* October 3, 1993, sec. 1, pp. 21, 26.
24. "Geerlings & Wade," *Inc.,* October 1992, p. 131.
25. Jack G. Kaikati, "Don't Crack the Japanese Distribution System— Just Circumvent It," *Columbia Journal of World Business* (Summer 1993): pp. 34–45.
26. Frances Huffman, "Special Delivery," *Entrepreneur,* February 1993, p. 81–83.
27. Huffman, "Trade Secrets," p. 95.
28. Bob Jones, "Mail Call," *Entrepreneur,* July 1993, pp. 54, 56.
29. Gregory A. Patterson, "Holiday Hopes of the Catalog Industry: Merrier Christmas, Happier New Year," *The Wall Street Journal,* December 2, 1992, pp. B1, B8; Sunita Wadekar, "After the Big Book, the Big Race," *Business Week,* September 20, 1993, p. 106E-2.
30. Gibson, "Milkmen Bring Home Bacon and Pizza, Too."
31. William M. Bulkeley, "Online Shopping Fails to Fulfill Promise," *The Wall Street Journal,* June 21, 1993, p. B5.
32. *Ibid.*
33. Ernan Roman, "More for Your Money," *Inc.,* September 1992, pp. 113–114, 116.
34. John Schmeltzer, "Addition by Subtraction at Walgreens, Crate & Barrel," *Chicago Tribune,* October 24, 1992, sec. 2, p. 1.
35. Zina Moukheiber, "The Neighborhood Pharmacist," *Forbes,* January 4, 1993, p. 173.
36. Steve Bergsman, "100 Fastest Growing Companies: Anko Metal Services Inc.," *Hispanic Business,* August 1993, p. 48.
37. Toddi Gutner, "'Focus on the Customer,'" *Forbes,* August 2, 1993, pp. 45–46.
38. Bennett, ed., *Dictionary of Marketing Terms,* p. 123.
39. Eleena de Lisser, "Catering to Cooking-Phobic Customers, Supermarkets Stress Carryout, Add Cafes," *The Wall Street Journal,* April 15, 1993, pp. B1, B10.
40. Schmeltzer, "Addition by Subtraction."
41. Harris Corporation Annual Report 1993, p. 20.
42. Joe Peritz, "Retailers Who Keep Score Know What Their Shoppers Value," *Marketing News,* May 24, 1993, p. 9.
43. Lisa Gubernick, "Secondhand Chic," *Forbes,* April 26, 1993, pp. 172–173.
44. Patterson, "Holiday Hopes of the Catalog Industry," pp. B1, B8.
45. Kevin E. Cullinane, "College Bookstore Invites Its Customers to Curl Up," *The Wall Street Journal,* August 27, 1992, p. B2.
46. Example from Lewis Hershey, Northeast Missouri State University.
47. Teri Agins, "The Decline of Couture Is Seen in the Closing of a New York Salon," *The Wall Street Journal,* April 28, 1993, pp. A1, A8.
48. See Avijit Ghosh, *Retail Management* (Hinsdale, Ill.: Dryden, 1990), p. 449.
49. Melissa Campanelli, "What's in Store for EDLP?" *Sales & Marketing Management,* August 1993, pp. 56–59; Nancy Ryan, "There's More to Retail Cuts than Low Prices," *Chicago Tribune,* September 5, 1993, sec. 7, pp. 1, 2.
50. Wendy Zellner, "A New Roll of the Dice at 7-Eleven," *Business Week,* October 26, 1992, pp. 100, 102.
51. "Ticket to Ride," *Entrepreneur,* July 1993, p. 173.
52. Milford Prewitt, "PepsiCo Kiosk Goes Underground in Moscow Subway," *Nation's Restaurant News,* June 21, 1993, p. 4.
53. Milford Prewitt, "Garfield's Operator Eyes Growth in Small-Town Malls," *Nation's Restaurant News,* May 10, 1993, pp. 14, 18.
54. J. Paul Peter and Jerry C. Olson, *Consumer Behavior and Marketing Strategy,* 3rd ed. (Homewood, Ill.: Irwin, 1993), pp. 693–694.
55. Kate Fitzgerald, "Mega Malls: Built for the '90s, or the '80s?" *Advertising Age,* January 27, 1992, pp. S1, S8.
56. Adrienne Ward, "New Breed of Mall Knows: Everybody Loves a Bargain," *Advertising Age,* January 27, 1992, p. S5.
57. Adrienne Ward, "Department Stores Play the Outlet Game," *Advertising Age,* January 27, 1992, p. S6.
58. Meg Whittemore, "Shopping Malls Attract Small Firms," *Nation's Business,* December 1992, pp. 53–54, 56.
59. Ellen Neuborne, "Stores Say Remodeling Boosts Sales," *USA Today,* April 19, 1993, pp. 1B–2B.
60. Susan M. Keaveney, "Conceptualization and Operationalization of Retail Store Image: A Case of Rival Middle-Level Theories," *Journal of the Academy of Marketing Science* (Spring 1992): pp. 165–175.
61. Bennett, ed., *Dictionary of Marketing Terms,* p. 10.
62. Teresa Andreoli, "Sunglass Hut: Eyewear Chain Launches Unit in Greenwich Village," *Stores,* August 1993, p. 63.
63. Neuborne, "Stores Say Remodeling Boosts Sales."
64. *Ibid.*
65. "Everybody Knows His Number!" *RoundUPS* (United Parcel Service), Spring 1992, p. 5.
66. David Young, "Middlemen Caught in Evolving Market," *Chicago Tribune,* November 29, 1993.
67. W. W. Grainger, Inc., 1992 Annual Report and Form 10-K, pp. 5, 7.
68. Young, "Middlemen Caught in Evolving Market."
69. Gretchen Morgenson, "Business as Usual," *Forbes,* February 3, 1992, pp. 80–81.
70. Erika Kotite, "Rethinking Retail," *Entrepreneur,* December 1992, pp. 97–101.
71. Zina Moukheiber, "Retailing," *Forbes,* January 4, 1993, pp. 172–175.
72. "Europe's Discount Dogfight," *The Economist,* May 8, 1993, pp. 69–70; "Japan Shops the Wal-Mart Way," *The Economist,* February 6, 1993, pp. 67–68; Cacilie Rohwedder, "Deep-Discount Fight Consumes Much of Europe," *The Wall Street Journal,* June 18, 1993, p. A5C; and Kevin Helliker, "U.S. Discount Retailers Are Targeting Europe and Its Fat Margins," *The Wall Street Journal,* September 20, 1993, pp. A1, A4.
73. Gretchen Morgenson, "Here Come the Cross-Shoppers," *Forbes,* December 7, 1992, pp. 90+.
74. Kotite, "Rethinking Retail," p. 100.
75. Michael Garry, "Answering the Challenge," *Progressive Grocer,* July 1993, pp. 83–86.
76. Steven J. Johnson, "Retail Systems: No Longer Business as Usual," *Journal of Systems Management* (August 1992): pp. 8–10; Kotite, "Rethinking Retail."
77. Kotite, "Rethinking Retail," p. 101.
78. Morgenson, "Here Come the Cross-Shoppers."
79. See Johnson, "Retail Systems"; and Thomas McCarroll, "Grocery-Cart Wars," *Time,* March 30, 1992, p. 49.
80. Alice LaPlante, "Shared Destinies: CEOs and CIOs—Kmart," *Forbes ASAP,* December 7, 1992, pp. 38, 40, 42.
81. Bennett, ed., *Dictionary of Marketing Terms,* p. 144.
82. Mark Tosh, "Safeway Advises Caution in 3rd-Party Warehousing," *Supermarket News,* November 16, 1992, pp. 14–15.
83. Colby Coates, "Atlantic Transportation/'93," *International Business* special advertising section.
84. "A Cutting Edge," *International Business,* March 1993, p. 68.
85. Gregory L. Miles, "Think Global, Go Intermodal," *International Business,* March 1993, pp. 60–61+.
86. "Freight Forwarders: A Prime Resource for the American Exporter," *International Business,* March 1993, p. 125.

87. Scott Williams, "An Inventory Control Solution for On-Site Warehousing," *Industrial Engineering,* September 1992, pp. 29–30.
88. The Quaker Oats Company, 4th Quarter 1993 Report, p. 7.
89. Nancy Ryan, "Targeting Checkout Speed Trap," *Chicago Tribune,* February 26, 1992, sec. 3, pp. 1, 4.
90. Susan Wels, "The Profitable Pursuit of Quality," *McKesson Today,* December 1992, pp. 1–5.
91. Cheryl J. Goldberg, "The Mail ROM," *Entrepreneur,* February 1993, pp. 98–104.
92. Personal communication, Lewis Hershey, Northeast Missouri State University.
93. "Automating Procedures Increases Time for Customer Service," *McKesson Today,* December 1992, p. 4.
94. Edward O. Welles, "Built on Speed," *Inc.,* October 1992, pp. 82–84, 88.
95. Gary McWilliams, "Putting a Shine on Shoe Operations," *Business Week,* June 14, 1993, p. 59.
96. Bennett, ed., *Dictionary of Marketing Terms,* p. 67.
97. Zachary Schiller and Wendy Zellner, "Clout! More and More Retail Giants Rule the Marketplace," *Business Week,* December 21, 1992, pp. 66–69+.
98. John Morris, "Customized Services Boost Competitiveness," *International Business,* November 1993, pp. 48+.
99. John Salak, "When Your Carrier Delivers the Goods," *International Business,* September 1993, pp. 30, 32.
100. See Steve Biciocchi, "Every Business Should Want Superior Distribution," *Industrial Engineering,* September 1992, pp. 27–28.

CHAPTER 18
1. Anne Murphy, "The Best Newsletters in America," *Inc.,* June 1992, pp. 70–72.
2. Neil A. Morgan and Nigel F. Piercy, "Market-Led Quality," *Industrial Marketing Management* 21 (1992): 111–118.
3. "The Trouble with Advertising," *Inc.,* March 1992, p. 13, citing a speech by David Ogilvy to the Association of National Advertisers.
4. "Poor Handling Turns Leads into No-Sales," *The Wall Street Journal,* March 31, 1993, p. B1.
5. Ruth Hamel, "States of Mind," *American Demographics,* April 1992, p. 41.
6. "General Excellence: Southwest Airlines," *Sales & Marketing Management,* August 1993, p. 38.
7. Jerry Ackerman, "Mail-Order Skirts, Buttondown Shirts, and Prose," *The Boston Globe,* September 25, 1993, p. 12.
8. Steve Friedman, "Twelve Ways to Get the Most from Your Marketing Newsletter," Sales & Marketing Management, March 1992, p. 91.
9. Peter D. Bennett, ed., *Dictionary of Marketing Terms* (Chicago: American Marketing Association, 1988), p. 4.
10. Bennett, ed., *Dictionary of Marketing Terms,* p. 144.
11. *Ibid.,* p. 179.
12. *Ibid.,* p. 164.
13. "The Ivory Control Tower," *Forbes,* November 23, 1992, pp. 180, 182.
14. Murphy, "The Best Newsletters in America," p. 71.
15. "Management Brief: The Best a Plan Can Get," *The Economist,* August 15, 1992, pp. 59–60.
16. Nancy Arnott, "Saved by the Bellman?" *Sales & Marketing Management,* December 1993, pp. 69–73.
17. Eleena De Lisser, "Sports Drink 10-K Hits a Homer on a Shoestring," *The Wall Street Journal,* August 23, 1993, p. B1.
18. Regis McKenna, "Marketing Is Everything," *Harvard Business Review,* January-February 1991, pp. 65–79.
19. *Ibid.,* p. 74.
20. Frederick E. Webster, Jr., "The Changing Role of Marketing in the Corporation," *Journal of Marketing* 56 (October 1992): 1–17; McKenna, "Marketing Is Everything."

21. "How to Advertise Abroad," *Sales & Marketing Management,* March 1992, p. 51.
22. Ed Nanas, "Computer Diskettes: A Big Little Marketing Tool Customers Can't Resist," *Your Company,* Spring 1993, pp. 8–9.
23. Eben Shapiro, "Tropicana Squeezes Out Minute Maid to Get Bigger Slice of Citrus Hill Fans," *The Wall Street Journal,* February 4, 1993, pp. B1, B5.
24. *Ibid.*
25. "Profiles in Marketing: Arnold Greenberg," *Sales & Marketing Management,* August 1993, p. 12.
26. Pat Sloan, "Chesebrough Puts New Face on Its Brands," *Advertising Age, January 27, 1992, p. 3.*
27. Richard Gibson, "Kellogg Co.'s Chairman Seeks to End Cereal Firms' Promotion Spending War," *The Wall Street Journal,* November 2, 1992, p. B8A.
28. James P. Miller, "Maytag U.K. Unit Finds a Promotion Is Too Successful," *The Wall Street Journal,* March 31, 1993, p. A9.
29. "This Cookie Is Tops in Food Sales," *Fortune,* May 4, 1992, p. 100.
30. Murphy, "The Best Newsletters in America," p. 78.
31. C. Merle Crawford, *New Products Management,* 4th ed. (Burr Ridge, Ill.: Irwin, 1994), p. 44.
32. Dan Michaels and Shailagh Murray, "East Europeans Adjust to Western Ads; Information after Years of Propaganda," *The Wall Street Journal,* August 19, 1993, p. A5D; Gail E. Schares, "Colgate-Palmolive Is Really Cleaning Up in Poland," *Business Week,* March 15, 1993, pp. 54, 56.
33. "Indicators of Market Size for 117 Countries," *Business International,* July 8, 1991, p. 225.
34. J. Paul Peter and James H. Donnelly, Jr., *A Preface to Marketing Management,* 6th ed. (Burr Ridge, Ill.: Irwin, 1994), p. 261.
35. Nathalie Boschat, "Catering to Africa's Consumers," *World Press Review,* June 1993, p. 40.
36. Melanie Wells, "McCann Awaits OK for New Coke Ads," *Advertising Age,* May 24, 1993, pp. 3, 46.
37. "Ad Director Finds Global Business Means Speaking in Tongues," *GSB Chicago* (The University of Chicago Graduate School of Business), Summer 1992, p. 40.
38. "Mixed Message," *Newsweek,* December 9, 1992, p. 8.
39. "How to Advertise Abroad," *Sales & Marketing Management,* March 1992, p. 51.
40. Kevin Goldman, "Hasbro, Turner Get Animated for Holidays," *The Wall Street Journal,* November 18, 1992, p. B1.
41. David Ellis, "Knowledge for Sale," *Time,* June 8, 1992, p. 69.

CHAPTER 19
1. U.S. Department of Commerce, Statistical Abstract of the United States, 113th ed. (Washington, D.C.: U.S. Government Printing Office, 1993), p. 789.
2. "100 Leading National Advertisers" (table), *Advertising Age,* January 3, 1994, p. 14.
3. Celestine Bohlen, "Crash Russian Course for Procter & Gamble," *New York Times,* December 19, 1993, p. 5.
4. Kevin Goldman, "TBWA's Evian Ads Use Deluge of Words," *The Wall Street Journal,* April 16, 1993, p. B5.
5. "Virgin Atlantic Airways: The Iconoclastic Carrier," *Sales & Marketing Management,* August 1992, p. 45.
6. Jill Gerston, "The Naked Truth," *Chicago Tribune,* February 10, 1993, sec. 7, p. 3.
7. Frances Huffman, "Mad Marketing," *Entrepreneur,* November 1992, pp. 136–141.
8. Alessandra Bianchi, "Well Said," *Inc.,* January 1993, pp. 98–99.
9. "Carillon Importers: The Art of 'Absolut' Marketing," *Sales & Marketing Management,* August 1992, p. 44.
10. Theodore Levitt, "Advertising: The Poetry of Becoming," *Harvard Business Review,* March 4, 1993, pp. 134–137.
11. William F. Arens and Courtland L. Bovée, *Contemporary Advertising,* 5th ed. (Burr Ridge, Ill.: Irwin, 1994), p. 78.

12. Andrew Geddes, "Fresh from Olds, Burnett Loses One," *Advertising Age,* March 1, 1993, p. 13.
13. John Morris, "The New Basics of Advertising," *The Office Advisor* (*Inc.* magazine), Spring 1993, pp. 1, 6.
14. "The Enigma of Japanese Advertising," *The Economist,* August 14, 1993, pp. 59–60.
15. "World's Top 50 Advertising Organizations" (table), *Advertising Age,* January 3, 1994, p. 22.
16. Robert J. Lavidge and Gary A. Steiner, "A Model for Predictive Measurements of Advertising Effectiveness," *Journal of Marketing* (October 1961): p. 61.
17. Kevin Goldman, "Prof. Levitt Stands by Global-Ad Theory," *The Wall Street Journal,* October 13, 1992, p. B7.
18. *Ibid.*
19. Bohlen, "Crash Russian Course for Procter & Gamble."
20. Nancy Millman, "Aiming for That Super Bounce from the Ad Bowl," *Chicago Tribune,* January 23, 1994, sec. 7, p. 3.
21. Anne Murphy, "The Best Newsletters in America," *Inc.,* June 1992, pp. 70–72+.
22. Joanne Lipman, "It's It and That's a Shame: Why Are Some Slogans Losers?" *The Wall Street Journal,* July 16, 1993, pp. A1, A4.
23. Nancy Ten Kate, "Words that Sell Keep Changing," *American Demographics,* August 1992, p. 18.
24. Katherine Barrett, "Taking a Closer Look," *Madison Avenue,* August 1984, pp. 106–109.
25. R. David Thomas, *Dave's Way,* Berkeley Books, 1991, p. 164.
26. Theresa Howard, "McD Launches Infomercial to Promote 'Good Deeds,'" *Nation's Restaurant News,* July 26, 1993, p. 4.
27. Stephen Pomper, "The Big Shake-Out Begins," *Time,* July 2, 1990, p. 50.
28. "It Pays to Advertise—in Any Language," *Sales & Marketing Management,* January 1993, p. 13.
29. Jill Smolowe, "Read This!" *Time,* November 26, 1990, pp. 62–70.
30. Richard R. Szathmary, "The Great Outdoors," *Sales & Marketing Management,* March 1992, p. 76.
31. *Ibid.,* pp. 75–76.
32. *Ibid.,* p. 80.
33. *Ibid.*
34. Nancy Ten Kate, "Make It an Event," *American Demographics,* November 1992, pp. 40–44.
35. Robert A. Mamis, "The Attention-Grabbing Telegram," *Inc.,* June 1993, p. 47.
36. Mary Hayes, "Penney Taps Sunnyvale for New-Store Test," *The Business Journal* (September 14, 1992): pp. 1, 20.
37. Steven W. Colford, "NASA to Sell Ads in Space," *Advertising Age,* January 11, 1993, pp. 1, 40; "Offbeat Marketing," *Sales & Marketing Management,* March 1993, p. 107.
38. "Computer Screen Saver Is Latest Medium," *The Wall Street Journal,* May 12, 1993, p. B10.
39. Arens and Bovée, *Contemporary Advertising,* pp. 198–200.
40. John Morris, "The New Basics of Advertising," *The Office Advisor* (*Inc.* magazine), Spring 1993, pp. 1, 6.
41. B. J. Kowalski, "Coke Fizzles," *World Press Review,* June 1993, p. 36.
42. Nancy Ryan, "Expert Says Promotions Help Build, Not Erode, Brand Loyalty," *Chicago Tribune,* March 4, 1992, sec. 3, p. 3.
43. *Consumer Promotion Report* (monograph) (New York: Dancer Fitzgerald Sample, 1982).
44. Scott Hume, "Coupons Set Record, But Pace Slows," *Advertising Age,* February 1, 1993, p. 25.
45. "Opening Up the World of Coupon Redemption," *Marketing,* June 3, 1993, p. 30.
46. Ronald Grover, Laura Zinn, and Irene Recio, "Big Brother Is Grocery Shopping with You," *Business Week,* March 29, 1993, p. 60.
47. Frances Huffman, "Redeeming Qualities," *Entrepreneur,* October 1992, p. 168.
48. *Ibid.*
49. *Ibid.,* pp. 168-169.
50. Millie Neal, "Quaker's Direct Hit," *Direct Marketing,* January 1991, pp. 52, 53, 70; Kathleen Deveny, "Segments of One: Marketers Take Aim at the Ultimate Narrow Target," *The Wall Street Journal,* March 22, 1991, p. B4.
51. Scott Hume, "Coupons: Are They Too Popular?" *Advertising Age,* February 15, 1993, p. 32.
52. Morris, "The New Basics of Advertising," p. 6.
53. Suzanne Alexander, "College 'Parties' Get High Marks as Sales Events," *The Wall Street Journal,* October 23, 1992, pp. B1, B8.
54. Kathleen Deveny, "Displays Pay Off for Grocery Marketers," *The Wall Street Journal,* October 15, 1992, pp. B1, B5.
55. The Quaker Oats Company, 4th Quarter 1993 Report, p. 8.
56. Edward A. Chapman, Jr., "Why Am I Here?" *Sales & Marketing Management,* February 1993, p. 30.
57. *Ibid.*
58. "Video Stores Dislike This Promotional Dance," *The Wall Street Journal,* March 31, 1993, p. B1.
59. William Dunn, from "How to Sell the Story," *American Demographics,* April 1992, pp. 50–51.
60. "Brownie Points," *Entrepreneur,* May 1993, pp. 142–143.
61. Michael P. Cronin, "Long-Lasting PR," *Inc.,* June 1993, p. 31.
62. Lee Berton, "Smelly Socks and Other Tricks from the Public-Relations Trade," *The Wall Street Journal,* November 30, 1993, p. B1.
63. Wendy Bounds, "Any Testimonials for the Product Will Have to Come on the Fly," *The Wall Street Journal,* August 23, 1993, p. B1.
64. Elizabeth Lesly and Laura Zinn, "The Right Moves, Baby," *Business Week,* July 5, 1993, pp. 30–31; Stephen Power, "Lawrence Woman Charged in Pepsi Tampering Hoax," *Boston Globe,* July 1, 1993; Richard Turcsik, "Pepsi Syringe Crisis Fizzles Out," *Supermarket News,* June 28, 1993, pp. 4, 45.
65. Kevin Helliker, "Wal-Mart Cuts Ads, Papers Cut Coverage," *The Wall Street Journal,* October 14, 1992, p. B8.

CHAPTER 20

1. William Echikson, "The Trick to Selling in Europe," *Fortune,* September 20, 1993, p. 82.
2. Ronald E. Kutscher, "Outlook 2000: The Major Trends," *Occupational Outlook Quarterly,* Spring 1990, pp. 3–7.
3. *Chief Executive Officer* (Chicago: Heidrick and Struggles, 1987), p. 7.
4. Dennis Fox, "Ringing Up Prospects," *Sales & Marketing Management,* March 1993, pp. 75–77.
5. Gerhard Gschwandtner, "How to Sell in France," *Personal Selling Power,* July-August 1991, pp. 54–60.
6. Promotional materials supplied by Mary Kay Cosmetics, Inc., 8787 Stemmons Freeway, Dallas, Tex. 75247-3794.
7. Mark H. McCormack, "The Hard Sell," *Entrepreneur,* April 1993, p. 41.
8. Robert McGarvey, "Think Big," *Entrepreneur,* August 1993, p. 60.
9. Patricia Sellers, "How to Remake Your Sales Force," *Fortune,* May 4, 1992, pp. 98–100.
10. Susan Greco, "Even the CFO Sells," *Inc.,* May 1993, p. 23.
11. Thomas N. Ingram, "Improving Sales Force Productivity: A Critical Examination of the Personal Selling Process," *Review of Business,* Summer 1990, p. 12.
12. Frederick E. Webster, Jr., "The Changing Role of Marketing in the Corporation," *Journal of Marketing* (October 1992): p. 6.
13. *Ibid.*
14. Susan Greco, "The Art of Selling," *Inc.,* June 1993, p. 72.
15. *Ibid.,* p. 73.
16. Jennifer Kingson Bloom, "A Sales Guide to Easy Street," *The Boston Globe,* p. 1.
17. G. Scott Osborne, *Electronic Direct Marketing* (Englewood Cliffs, N.J.: Prentice-Hall, 1984), p. 120.
18. Jack G. Kaikati, "Don't Crack the Japanese Distribution System—Just Circumvent It," *Columbia Journal of World Business* (Summer 1993): pp. 34–35.

19. McGarvey, "Think Big," p. 69.
20. *Ibid.,* p. 70.
21. *Ibid.*
22. Frances Huffman, "Speak Easy," *Entrepreneur,* December 1992, p. 156.
23. Greco, "The Art of Selling," p. 75.
24. Paul Sherlock, *Rethinking Business to Business Marketing* (New York: Free Press, 1991), p. 92.
25. John Morris, "The New Basics of Advertising," *The Office Advisor* (*Inc.* magazine), Spring 1993, pp. 1, 6.
26. Robert Fernandez, "Mail Order Is Part and Parcel of Firm's Success," *Chicago Tribune,* August 1, 1993, sec. 17, pp. 1, 7.
27. Sellers, "How to Remake Your Sales Force," p. 103.
28. Phaedra Hise, "What Telemarketers Must Know," *Inc.,* October 1993, p. 29.
29. Gschwandtner, "How to Sell in France," pp. 54–60.
30. McGarvey, "Think Big," p. 72.
31. William A. O'Connell and William Keenan, Jr., "The Shape of Things to Come," *Sales & Marketing Management,* January 1990, pp. 36–41.
32. Gilbert A. Churchill, Jr., Neil M. Ford, Orville C. Walker, Jr., *Sales Force Management,* 4th ed. (Homewood, Ill.: Irwin, 1993), p. 225.
33. Greco, "The Art of Selling," p. 73.
34. E. A. Lennon, written interview, December 9, 1992.
35. Susan Greco, "Using Service Reps to Generate Leads," *Inc.,* May 1992, p. 141.
36. Regis McKenna, "Marketing Is Everything," *Harvard Business Review,* January-February 1991, pp. 65–79.
37. John Case, "A Business Transformed," *Inc.,* June 1993, pp. 84–86.
38. Thayer C. Taylor, "Getting in Step with the Computer Age," *Sales & Marketing Management,* March 1993, pp. 52–54.
39. Guen Sublette, "Dream Team," *Entrepreneur,* August 1993, p. 78.
40. Parker Hannifin Corporation Annual Report, June 30, 1992.
41. William Keenan, Jr., "Who Has the Right Stuff?", *Sales & Marketing Management,* August 1993, p. 28.
42. Sublette, "Dream Team," p. 78.
43. *Ibid.,* p. 80.
44. Churchill, Ford, and Walker, *Sales Force Management,* pp. 430–431.
45. Keenan, "Who Has the Right Stuff?", p. 28.
46. *Ibid.,* pp. 28–29.
47. Earl D. Honeycutt, Jr., Clyde E. Harris, Jr., and Stephen B. Castleberry, "Sales Training: A Status Report," *Training and Development Journal* (May 1987): pp. 42–47.
48. Martin Everett, "Your Job Is on the (Phone) Line," *Sales & Marketing Management,* May 1993, p. 66.
49. Sellers, "How to Remake Your Sales Force," p. 103.
50. Greco, "The Art of Selling," p. 75.
51. Susan Greco, "A 'Finishing School' for Sales Reps," *Inc.,* October 1992, p. 30.
52. Greco, "The Art of Selling," p. 75.
53. Everett, "Your Job Is on the (Phone) Line," *Sales & Marketing Management* (May 1993), p. 66.
54. Jack Falvey, "A Fire Walk with the Sales Force," *Sales & Marketing Management,* August 1993, p. 14.
55. Condensed definition from Peter D. Bennett, *Dictionary of Marketing Terms* (Chicago: American Marketing Association, 1988), p. 125.
56. Falvey, "A Fire Walk with the Sales Force," p. 14.
57. Ellyn E. Spragins, "Making Employees Accountable," *Inc.,* March 1993, p. 34.
58. Sublette, "Dream Team," p. 79.
59. Greco, "The Art of Selling," pp. 77–78.
60. *Ibid.,* p. 75.
61. Written interview with E. A. Lennon, senior manager, Business Systems Development, Procter & Gamble, 1992.
62. See Churchill, Ford, and Walker, *Sales Force Management,* p. 264.
63. Bennett, *Dictionary of Marketing Terms,* p. 180.
64. "Change Must Pass Culture Test Before It Lands on the Bottom Line," *Total Quality,* October 1992, p. 6.
65. Jerome A. Colletti and Linda J. Mahoney, "Should You Pay Your Sales Force for Customer Satisfaction?" *Perspectives in Total Compensation* 11 (Scottsdale, Ariz.: American Compensation Association, November 1991).
66. I. F. Trawick, J. E. Swan, W. McGee, and D. R. Rink, "Influence of Buyer Ethics and Salesperson Behavior on Intention to Choose a Supplier," *Journal of the Academy of Marketing Science* (Winter 1990): p. 10.
67. Alan Killingsworth, cited in Charles Futrell, *ABC's of Selling,* 4th ed. (Burr Ridge, Ill.: Irwin, 1994), p. 54.
68. Greg Steinmetz and Michael Siconolfi, "Partnership Problems at Prudential Embroil Insurance Business, Too," *The Wall Street Journal,* December 1, 1993, pp. A1, A8.

LOOKING AHEAD

1. Ravi S. Achrol, "Evolution of the Marketing Organization: New Forms for Turbulent Environments," *Journal of Marketing* (October 1991): pp. 77–93.
2. "Pervasive and Irreversible," *The Economist,* November 28, 1992, p. 18.
3. Lance Morrow, "The Temping of America," *Time,* March 29, 1993, pp. 40–41.
4. Janice Castro, "Disposable Workers," *Time,* March 29, 1993, pp. 43–47.
5. Rashi Glazer, "Marketing in an Information-Intensive Environment: Strategic Implications of Knowledge as an Asset," *Journal of Marketing* (October 1991): pp. 1–19.
6. Jon R. Katzenbach and Douglas K. Smith, "The Discipline of Teams," *Harvard Business Review,* March-April 1993, pp. 111–120.
7. John A. Byrne, "Paradigms for Postmodern Managers," *Business Week,* "Reinventing America 1992," pp. 62–63; Stefan Fatsis, "Corporations for a New Age," *Wisconsin State Journal,* December 27, 1992, pp. 1G, 3G.
8. Walter Kiechel III, "How We Will Work in the Year 2000," *Fortune,* May 17, 1993, pp. 38–39.
9. Fatsis, "Corporations for a New Age"; Fatsis, "Xerox Reorganizes, Retools, Revitalizes," *Wisconsin State Journal,* December 27, 1992, p. 1G.
10. Achrol, "Evolution of the Marketing Organization"; Kiechel, "How We Will Work in the Year 2000."
11. Glazer, "Marketing in an Information-Intensive Environment."
12. Kiechel, "How We Will Work in the Year 2000."
13. Achrol, "Evolution of the Marketing Organization," pp. 89–90.
14. Ronald E. Yates, "Motorola Extending Its Pursuit of Excellence to Suppliers," *Chicago Tribune,* October 14, 1992, sec. 3, p. 1.
15. Ronald E. Yates, "Going Abroad for Allies," *Chicago Tribune,* April 26, 1992, sec. 7, pp. 1, 4.
16. Achrol, "Evolution of the Marketing Organization."
17. John A. Byrne, "The Virtual Corporation," *Business Week,* February 8, 1993, pp. 98–102.
18. Stratford Sherman, "Are Strategic Alliances Working?" *Fortune,* September 21, 1992, pp. 77–78.
19. Bart Ziegler, "Who's Afraid of AT&T?" *Business Week,* June 14, 1993, pp. 32–33.
20. "To Diversify Products, Big Firms Tap Outsiders," *The Wall Street Journal,* March 30, 1993, p. B1.
21. James Coates, "For High-Tech, Age of Alliances," *Chicago Tribune,* June 13, 1993, sec. 7, pp. 1, 6.
22. Frederick E. Webster, Jr., "The Changing Role of Marketing in the Corporation," *Journal of Marketing* (October 1992): pp. 1–17.
23. "Struggling Enterprises Try Joint Marketing," *The Wall Street Journal,* October 28, 1992, p. B1.
24. Carla Kruytbosch, "Let's Make a Deal," *International Business,* March 1993, pp. 92–96.

25. Webster, "The Changing Role of Marketing in the Corporation," p. 8.
26. Sherman, "Are Strategic Alliances Working?," p. 77.
27. "Why Networks May Fail," *The Economist,* October 10, 1992, p. 83.
28. George Gendron, "FYI: Cultural Evolution," *Inc.,* February 1993, p. 9.
29. Sherman, "Are Strategic Alliances Working?," p. 78.
30. *Ibid.,* p. 77.
31. Byrne, "The Virtual Corporation"; Shawn Tully, "The Modular Corporation," *Fortune,* February 8, 1993, pp. 106–108.
32. Edward O. Welles, "Virtual Realities," *Inc.,* August 1993, pp. 50–57.
33. Byrne, "The Virtual Corporation."
34. *Ibid.*
35. *Ibid.,* p. 100.
36. Otis Port, "Moving Past the Assembly Line," *Business Week,* "Reinventing America 1992" pp. 177, 180.
37. "Glasgow Has The Edge," *Management Today* (Britain), July 1993.
38. Byrne, "Paradigms for Postmodern Managers," p. 63.
39. Karl Albrecht, "Total Quality Service," *Quality Digest,* January 1993, p. 18; Karl Albrecht, "The Last Days of TQM?" *Quality Digest,* November 1992, pp. 16–17.
40. Gary S. Vasilash, "Powerfully Simple," *Production,* March 1993, p. 96.
41. Edith Weiner, "Business in the 21st Century," *The Futurist,* March-April 1992, pp. 13–17.
42. Tom Peters, "TQM and Music That Stirs the Soul," *Quality Digest,* October 1992, pp. 12–13.

CAREER OPPORTUNITIES IN MARKETING

1. *At Home Around the World,* 3M 1991 Annual Report, p. 7.
2. The Gillette Company 1992 Annual Report, p. 18 (foldout).
3. Toys "R" Us and Kids "R" Us Annual Report, year ended February 1, 1992, inside front cover.
4. Glen E. Salmon, principal software engineer, Asia Products Development, Lotus Development Corporation.
5. Judith George, "Market Researcher," *Business Week's Guide to Careers,* October 1987, p. 10.
6. *Strengthening the World's Businesses,* 1992 Annual Report to Shareowners, Customers and Associates, The Dun & Bradstreet Corporation, pp. 14, 16.
7. Ludger Gigengack, director of quantitative research, Henkel KGaA, in *Strengthening the World's Businesses.*
8. U.S. Department of Labor, Bureau of Labor Statistics, *Occupational Outlook Handbook,* 1990–1991 edition.
9. "A Savvy Head for Business," *Colby,* August 1992, p. 79.
10. *Ibid.*
11. Advertisement for Duraclean, 1993.
12. Bob Weinstein, "Liquid Assets," *Entrepreneur,* May 1993, pp. 92–93.
13. Bob Weinstein, "Rap Master," *Entrepreneur,* September 1993, pp. 87–88.

Glossary

acceleration principle The principle stating that a small change in consumer demand for a product results in a major shift in the demand for goods and services used to produce the product.

accessory equipment Portable equipment and tools.

adaptive pricing Pricing tactic of responding to price changes made by competitors with large market shares.

advertising Paid, nonpersonal communication through various media by organizations that are identified in the message and seek to inform and/or persuade members of a particular audience.

advertising agency A firm devoted to planning and preparing advertising campaigns for other organizations.

advocacy advertising Institutional advertising that supports socially responsible messages, activities, or causes.

agent/broker An intermediary that does not take title but brings together the producer and customer.

altruism Unselfish devotion to others.

approach Initial formal contact with the qualified prospect.

atmospherics Factors such as architecture, lighting, and layout that attract attention and stimulate sales.

attitude The combination of a person's beliefs about and evaluation of something, leading to a tendency to act in a certain way.

average revenue The average amount of money received from the sale of one unit of a product.

bait and switch The practice of advertising low prices for certain products, then claiming that the low-priced products are of poor quality or unavailable.

basing point pricing Type of uniform delivered pricing in which the seller charges the list price plus the cost of delivering from one or more geographic points where the product is produced (basing points).

beliefs A person's views about various subjects.

benchmarking Identifying organizations that excel at carrying out a function and using their practices as a springboard for improvement.

benefit segmentation Segmenting a market according to desired benefits.

brand The name, term, or symbol that identifies a good or service as distinct from all others.

brand extension Using an existing brand name for a new product.

brand loyalty The consistency with which a consumer continues to buy the same brand of a particular product.

brand mark The part of a brand that cannot be spoken.

brand name The part of a brand that can be spoken.

breakeven analysis The technique for identifying the sales volume at a given price needed to cover costs.

breakeven point The level of sales at which total revenues equal total costs.

bribes Money, goods, or favors offered in exchange for influence.

bundle pricing Offering several products as a package at a single price.

business cycle The pattern of the level of business activity; moves from prosperity to recession to recovery.

business services Support services for the organization.

buyer's market A market in which the supply of products exceeds the demand for them.

buying center Organization members who have a role in selecting, purchasing, and using a product.

canned presentation A memorized, standard sales message given without deviation to all prospects.

cannibalization One product taking sales away from another in the product mix.

cash discount An incentive for buyers to pay quickly, or a lower price for payment in cash.

cash-and-carry wholesaler A wholesaler that carries a limited selection of products and does not transport those products.

category killer A large, limited-line store featuring low prices.

causal research Research that looks for cause-and-effect relationships.

cause-related marketing (CRM) Marketing that ties charitable donations directly to the sales of a product.

caveat emptor A legal concept meaning "buyer beware."

centralized organization An organization in which most decisions and authority lie with top levels of management.

channel captain The leader in a distribution channel (may be the producer, wholesaler, or retailer).

channel of distribution An organized network of entities that perform all the activities required to link producers with users of products.

channels of distribution The element of the marketing mix that consists of getting the product to the target market so that it will be convenient to buy.

closing The point at which the prospect makes a purchase commitment.

code of ethics Written statement of an organization's ethical principles and standards of conduct.

coding Assigning numeric symbols to the data collected.

cognitive dissonance Uncertainty whether the chosen alternative was the best; often called "buyer's remorse."

cold canvassing Locating prospects from a phone book or other source and calling on them.

commercialization Launch of a new product.

commission Payment tied directly to the sales or profits from sales that a salesperson completes.

communication The element of the marketing mix that involves informing target markets about the organization and its products.

communication The transmission of a message from a sender to a receiver.

communications mix The blend of advertising, personal selling, sales promotion, and publicity that makes up a communications strategy.

community relations Activities that reinforce a positive image of an organization in the community in which it is located and/or operates.

comparative advertising Advertising that compares one specific brand to another.

competitive advertising Advertising that attempts to develop secondary demand (demand for a particular brand of product).

competitive bidding Inviting several potential suppliers to offer a price and other terms of sale for a product meeting given specifications.

competitive environment All the organizations that could potentially satisfy the needs and desires of their target markets.

component parts and materials Processed items formed into finished products.

concept testing Asking potential customers questions about pictures or descriptions of a new product.

concurrent engineering Linking product design with manufacturing engineering.

conference selling Personal selling in which a salesperson and other pertinent employees meet with customers to work out problems or discuss future arrangements.

consideration set The set of alternatives that the consumer identifies in a purchasing decision.

consolidated metropolitan statistical area (CMSA) A metropolitan area made up of two or more PMSAs.

consumer behavior The way in which external and internal forces shape people's exchange activities.

consumer products Goods and services sold to consumers.

consumer promotion Sales promotion directed toward consumers of a good or service.

consumer Someone who buys goods and services for his or her own or for household use.

consumerism A social force intended to protect the consumer by exerting legal, moral, and economic pressures on the business community.

consumers People who buy goods and services for themselves or their households to use.

controlling The process of measuring the performance of a marketing effort and making necessary corrections.

convenience products Inexpensive consumer products that are purchased easily and often.

cooperative advertising Advertising in which manufacturers and channel members team up for one campaign.

core competencies The few processes central to the organization's success.

core values Values that are pervasive and enduring.

corrective advertising Advertising that retracts or clarifies previously misleading claims.

cost analysis A study of the size and type of costs involved in a marketing effort, as well as any change in costs.

cost of goods sold The cost of sales for tangible goods.

cost of sales The total cost to produce or acquire the products sold by an organization during an accounting period.

countertrade Bartering goods and services rather than selling them for money.

critical path method (CPM) A method using a network of circles and arrows to chart the schedule of marketing activities.

cross-functional team Team of employees from various functions who make decisions designed to improve the organization's responsiveness to the markets it serves.

cultural values The principles, qualities, or beliefs that members of a culture consider desirable.

culture The learned values and behaviors shared by a society and designed to increase the probability of the society's survival.

data Facts and statistics.

decentralized organization An organization in which a relatively great number of people hold authority and make decisions

decode To convert symbols to the images or concepts contained in a message.

Delphi technique A method of forecasting that surveys experts, averages the results, and repeats the survey.

demand The amount of sales of a product at a given price.

demand curve The graph that shows the quantity of a product demanded at various prices.

demand-backward pricing Setting a price by starting with the estimated price consumers will pay and subtracting customary markups of resellers.

demarketing An effort to reduce demand for a product.

demographics The study of the characteristics of a human population.

demographic segmentation Division of the market on the basis of population characteristics.

derived demand Demand dependent on another source, as the demand for organizational goods depends on the level of demand for consumer goods.

descriptive research Research that studies how often something occurs or what, if any, relationship exists between two variables.

developed countries Countries with the economies and technologies to produce a wide variety of products, as well as consumers who can buy them.

developing countries Countries in the process of moving from an agricultural to an industrial economy.

differentiated marketing Selling multiple versions of a product to different market segments.

direct mail The mailing of brochures, letters, etc., that describe a product and ask the consumer to order it.

direct marketing A distribution channel that has no intermediaries.

direct marketing Marketing efforts that use direct selling, direct mail, telemarketing, and the like to solicit orders from consumers.

direct marketing Using direct channels of distribution, such as catalogs or door-to-door selling.

direct selling Selling in which a sales representative gives consumers a personal explanation and demonstration of a product.

discount A reduction in price.

discretionary income The money consumers have left to spend after paying taxes and living expenses.

disposable income The money an individual or household has left after paying taxes.

distinctive competencies Things an organization does better than any other organization.

distributor A wholesale intermediary that services industrial markets, offers a variety of services, and provides promotional support for a product.

diversification Strategy for growth by serving new customers with new products.

dollar volume The dollar value of the total sales of a product.

drop shipper A wholesaler that takes title to products but does not handle physical distribution.

dual distribution The use of two or more distribution channels to provide the same basic product to a target market.

dumping The practice of pricing a product below cost or below the going price in the domestic market.

durable goods Goods that are used over an extended rather than a brief period of time.

duties Taxes on imports or exports.

early adopters The secondary category of buyers to try a product; they tend to buy after they see a product will work.

early majority Buyers who are next after early adopters to try a product; they are among the majority of buyers.

economic environment The overall economy, including business cycles, consumer income, and spending patterns.

economic infrastructure A country's facilities for conducting business activities, including communication, transportation, distribution, and financial systems.

electronic data interchange (EDI) A communication system that allows direct electronic transfer of information among enterprises.

encode To convert a message to a group of symbols that represent images or concepts.

environmental scanning The practice of tracking external changes that can affect markets, including demand for goods and services.

ethics Moral principles and values governing the way an individual or group conducts its activities.

European Community (EC) The 12 nations of western Europe that make up a common market.

every-day low prices (EDLP) Prices consistently set below the competition's rather than occasional discounts on items.

exchange A process in which two or more parties voluntarily provide something of value to each other.

exchange controls Laws that place a ceiling on the amount of money that may be exchanged for another currency.

exchange functions The marketing functions that ensure that the right products are available to meet customers' needs and that customers are aware the products are available.

exchange rate The price of a currency.

exclusive dealing a restriction imposed by a supplier forbidding the customer from purchasing some type of product from any other supplier.

exclusive distribution The use of a single wholesaler or retailer to serve each territory.

experiment Research that involves manipulating one or two variables while keeping others constant, and measuring the results.

exploratory research Research that seeks to discover ideas and insights.

exponential smoothing Time-series analysis that gives more weight to recent data and less to older data.

exporting Producing a product in a manufacturer's own country, then shipping it to another company for sale.

facilitating functions The marketing functions that help marketers know what to provide and that help customers make purchase decisions and purchases.

fads Products that experience an intense but brief period of popularity.

family brand Brand used for an entire product line.

family life cycle The various stages of a family's existence.

fashions Accepted and popular product styles.

feature A fact or technical specification about a product.

Federal Trade Commission Act The law that prohibits deceptive pricing practices.

feedback The receiver's response to a message.

fixed costs Expenses that remain unchanged over a wide range of quantities of a product.

fixed-sum-per-unit method Allocating a fixed sum to the communications budget for each unit to be sold or produced.

FOB origin pricing Geographic approach to pricing in which the seller's price is for the good at the point of shipment, where the title passes from seller to buyer.

FOB with freight allowed Type of uniform delivered pricing in which the seller allows the buyer to deduct shipping costs from the list price of a product.

focus group interview A personal survey of a small group of people in which the interviewer poses open-ended questions.

follow-the-leader pricing Pricing tactic of following any price changes made by the industry leaders.

follow-up After-the-sale activities designed to make sure the customer is satisfied with the product purchased.

forecasting Determining what to expect in a market.

Foreign Corrupt Practices Act Act that makes it illegal for American companies to bribe a foreign government official or agency in order to do business in that country.

formula selling presentation Sales presentation of product information in a thorough, lockstep format.

franchising A contractual distribution system in which a parent company (the franchisor) gives franchisees the right to operate the business according to the franchisor's marketing plan and to use its trademark.

franchising An agreement in which franchisees receive the right to operate a business under the franchisor's trade name in exchange for paying a fee and operating according to a specified plan.

freight forwarder A company that gathers small shipments from various organizations and hires a carrier to move them as larger lots.

full-line forcing An arrangement in which an intermediary that wants to carry a particular product must buy the entire line.

functional accounts The allocation of costs to correspond to specific marketing activities.

Gantt chart A chart that lists marketing activities and uses horizontal bars to graph the time allotted to each.

General Agreement on Tariffs and Trade (GATT) An international framework of rules and principles for opening up trade between member nations, backed by an agency.

generic products Products that are named only by their generic class.

geographic pricing Pricing a good or service according to where it is delivered.

geographic segmentation Dividing the total market into groups according to location.

global marketing Using a single marketing strategy to serve domestic and foreign markets.

goods-services continuum The range that measures whether products are tangible or intangible.

gray market The market in which foreign distributors sell foreign versions of U.S. products in the United States.

green marketing Marketing efforts to produce and promote environmentally sound products.

gross income The total amount of money earned in one year by an individual or household.

gross margin The difference between sales revenue and the cost of sales.

gross margin ratio The ratio of gross margin to net sales.

gross national product (GNP) The total value of the goods and services produced in a particular country.

group incentive system A compensation method that pays a bonus to group members based on the group's achievements.

guarantee A promise that the product as it is represented will perform properly.

hard currency Currency backed by gold reserves and readily convertible to other currencies.

hedonic needs Needs related to the desire for pleasure and self-expression.

hypothesis A tentative assumption to be tested by research.

idea marketing Nonprofit marketing designed to promote a cause or an issue.

idle time Time during which service providers have no clients to serve.

in-home interview A personal survey in which the interviewer goes door to door to visit subjects at their homes

independent sales representatives Professional salespeople who act as independent contractors, paid entirely on commission.

industrial products Goods and services sold to organizations.

inflation A rise in the overall price level.

information Data presented in a useful way.

innovators The earliest buyers of a product.

installations Nonportable industrial goods.

institutional advertising Advertising that promotes an organization's image or philosophy.

institutional environment Marketing intermediaries and their activities.

integrated direct marketing Combining more than one mode of direct marketing in a single effort.

intensive distribution Distribution through all wholesalers or retailers that will carry a product.

intermediaries Resellers that purchase goods to sell at a profit.

intermediary (middleman) An independent business specializing in linking sellers with consumers or organizational users.

intermodal transportation Transportation that combines several modes.

internal marketing Marketing communications among various members of the organization and the distribution channel.

inventory turnover The number of times an organization sells an average amount of inventory during a specified period of time; also called merchandise turnover rate or stockturn rate.

ISO 9000 A series of five standards for the processes an organization uses to ensure quality.

joint venture A business agreement in which two or more organizations share management of an enterprise.

jury of executive opinion A group of executives called upon to provide insights from various areas of the organization.

just-in-time (JIT) inventory management A system of holding little inventory and requiring suppliers to provide the exact quantity needed according to a precise schedule.

just-in-time inventory A system for replenishing parts or goods for resale just before they are needed.

laggards The last buyers to try a product.

late majority Buyers who are more cautious; they try a product after the early majority.

licensing Granting another organization the rights to use a trademark or a patented product or process.

life-style The manner in which people conduct their lives, including their activities, interests, and opinions.

line extension Adding new products to an existing product line.

list price The selling price for an item before discounts or reductions are taken.

loss leader pricing Setting prices near or below cost in order to attract customers to a store.

macromarketing The total flow of a nation's goods and services to benefit society.

major account management The use of team selling to focus on major customers in an effort to establish long-term business relationships.

mall intercept A personal survey in which the interviewer stands in a shopping center and asks consumers to participate.

manufacturer's brand A brand owned and used by the producer of a product.

marginal analysis The technique for finding the greatest profits by measuring the effect of producing and selling each additional unit of a product.

marginal revenue The change in total revenue that results from selling one additional unit of a product.

markdown The percentage by which the full price of an item is reduced in order to stimulate sales.

markdown ratio The ratio of total markdowns (in dollars) for a group of products to total sales (in dollars) for those products.

market The individuals and organizations that have the desire and the ability to purchase a particular good or service.

market The individuals or organizations with the desire and ability to buy a product.

market development strategies Strategies for growth by selling existing products to new customers.

market penetration strategies Strategies for growth by selling more of an organization's existing products to existing customers.

market potential The expected total demand in the market being investigated.

market potential The total amount of product that buyers in the segment will purchase during a specified period of time, given a specified level of marketing activity.

market price The price actually paid by the customer.

market segmentation The process of subdividing a market into distinct subsets of customers that behave in the same way or have similar needs.

market share The sales of an organization's product as a percentage of all sales of such products.

market test The offering of a product in a few test markets.

marketing The process of planning and executing the conception, pricing, promotion, and distribution of ideas, goods, and services to create exchanges that satisfy individual and organizational goals.

marketing audit A systematic review of an organization's marketing environment, objectives, strategies, activities, and personnel.

marketing communications The element of the marketing mix that involves informing target markets about a product and influencing them to buy it.

marketing concept View that an organization should seek to meet its customers' needs as it strives to achieve its own goals.

marketing database A system for organizing marketing data so that they are easy to store and retrieve.

marketing decision support system (MDSS) A coordinated collection of data, system tools, and techniques with supporting software and hardware so that an organization can interpret information and use it to make management decisions.

marketing environment The economic, political and legal, social, institutional, technological, and competitive factors—at home and abroad—that affect an organization's marketing effort.

marketing ethics The principles, values, and standards of conduct followed by marketers.

marketing information system (MIS) A set of methods and procedures for gathering, sorting, storing, and distributing information used in making marketing decisions.

marketing management The process of setting, planning, and executing marketing goals and measuring progress toward their achievement.

marketing mix The mix of controllable marketing variables that the firm uses to pursue the desired level of sales in the target market; consists of four elements: product, pricing, channels of distribution (placement), and communication (promotion).

marketing plan A blueprint for a particular strategy to reach a particular target market.

marketing plan A plan that specifies marketing objectives, one or more target markets, and a marketing mix to serve each of those target markets.

marketing research The function that links the consumer, customer, and public to the marketer through information.

marketing tactics Specific, short-term actions for putting a marketing plan into action.

markup pricing Adding a percentage or dollar amount to a product's cost to arrive at a selling price.

markup The percentage by which channel members increase the price of a product when they sell it; may be stated as a percentage of cost or a percentage of selling price.

mass marketing Selling a single product line to all customers with a single marketing mix.

mass merchandising Seeking a high volume of sales by charging low prices.

medium of transmission The mode that carries a message, such as television, radio, print, live speech, or music.

merchandising Retail decisions about which products and product lines to carry.

merchant wholesaler A wholesaler that is independent of producers and takes title to the products it handles.

metropolitan statistical area (MSA). An urbanized area of at least 50,000 people, encircled by nonmetropolitan counties.

micromarketing The way an individual organization plans, executes, and allocates its marketing activities to benefit its customers.

mission statement A statement of an organization's distinctive purpose.

missionary salespeople Those who work for producers, calling on channel members and performing promotional activities.

modified rebuy Purchase that involves considering a limited number of alternatives before making a selection.

monopolistic competition The type of competition that occurs when there are many sellers of a product and each has a relatively small market share.

monopoly A market in which only one organization sells a good or service.

moral idealism A philosophy of ethics that focuses on individual rights and duties regardless of the consequences.

motivation Inspiring people to act in desired ways.

motivation The inner drive that propels people to fulfill a need.

motivation The positive or negative needs, goals, desires, and forces that impel an individual toward or away from certain actions.

multinational marketing Using different marketing strategies to serve buyers in different nations.

natural accounts Traditional categories for financial accounting.

need-satisfaction presentation Sales presentation that includes asking questions and listening to customer's answers in order to identify needs and desires.

net profit ratio The ratio of net profit (or loss) to net sales.

new product A product that is new to the marketing organization in any way.

new task purchase Purchase that results from an extensive search for information and a formal decision process.

new-product committee A committee consisting of representatives from various functional areas who regularly meet to discuss the progress of one or more new products being developed.

niche marketing Tailoring the elements of the marketing mix to attract a single market segment.

noise Physical sounds, misunderstandings, or other distractions that cause a receiver to fail to decode a message properly.

nondurable goods Goods that are used over a brief time period.

objections A prospect's resistance to making a purchase.

objective-task method Quantifying communications objectives, determining the communications mix required to meet those objectives, and budgeting the cost of that mix.

observation The collection of data by recording actions of customers or events in the marketplace.

odd-even pricing Setting prices a few dollars or cents below a round number.

off-peak pricing Charging lower prices during slow periods to stimulate demand.

oligopoly The type of competition that occurs when products are similar and a few sellers control most of the market.

operating expense ratio The ratio of total expenses to net sales.

operating ratios Ratios of operating statement items to net sales.

operating statement Financial statement that summarizes revenues and expenses for a specified period of time; often called an income statement or profit-and-loss statement.

operational planning The creation of objectives and strategies for individual operating units over a short time span, usually one year or less.

opportunistic pricing Attracting customers by setting lower prices than the competition's

order getting Developing business by seeking out potential customers, providing them with product information, and persuading them to buy.

order taking The routine completion of sales to customers who have already decided to buy.

organization marketing Nonprofit marketing designed to attract members, donors, participants, or volunteers to a particular organization.

organize To structure a group by defining areas of authority and working relationships

penetration pricing Setting a low price to attract the target market to a new product.

per capita income Income per person.

percentage-of-sales method Establishing a communications budget based on a specified percentage of actual or estimated sales.

perception The way people gather and record information.

person marketing Nonprofit marketing designed to elicit a favorable response to a person.

personal selling Selling that involves direct interaction between salesperson and customer.

physical distribution Moving and storing goods to get them efficiently to the end user.

physical distribution functions The marketing functions required to get products to the customers who want them.

piggyback service Intermodal transportation of truck trailers via train to a station near their ultimate destination.

pioneering advertising Advertising that seeks to develop primary demand (demand for a product category).

place marketing Nonprofit marketing designed to elicit a favorable response to a specific location.

planned obsolescence Wearing out or becoming obsolete as a result of the product being designed and made to last only a short time.

political-legal environment The laws, regulations, and social pressure affecting marketers.

portfolio plan A plan detailing which SBUs an organization wants to build up.

positioning map A diagram of how consumers perceive various brands in terms of specific attributes.

posttest Testing that evaluates the success or failure of an ad after it has run.

predatory pricing Setting very low prices in order to hurt competitors.

preparation Learning more about a qualified prospect's needs.

presentation Communication of the sales message to the customer.

prestige pricing Setting a high price to convey an image of high quality or exclusivity.

pretest The testing of one or more versions of an advertisement before launching the whole campaign.

price The amount of money, goods, or services that must be exchanged for ownership or use of a product.

price discrimination The practice of charging different prices to customers when the price difference does not reflect a cost difference.

price elasticity A measure of the sensitivity of demand to changes in price.

price fixing Reaching an agreement with competitors about what to charge.

price fixing The practice of sellers' making agreements with competitors or distributors about the final price of a product.

price lining Setting several pricing points and pricing each product at one of those points.

price war Repeated price reductions by competitors in an effort to undercut one another's prices.

pricing The element of the marketing mix that consists of setting prices that support the organization's marketing strategy.

primary data Data collected specifically for a particular investigation.

primary demand The desire for a general category of a good or service.

primary metropolitan statistical area (PMSA) An MSA with at least one million people.

private brand A brand owned and used by the reseller.

probability sampling Selecting research subjects in such a way that each member of the population has a known chance of being selected because the subjects are selected randomly.

producers Organizational buyers that buy goods and services in order to produce other goods and services for sale.

product The actual good or service that a marketer offers a target market; also the many ways in which the good or service is enhanced to satisfy the customer.

product advertising Advertising that attempts to lead members of the target market to buy the advertiser's product.

product development strategies Strategies for growth by developing new products to serve existing customers.

product diffusion The process through which a product is adopted by increasing numbers of buyers, with early buyers influencing later ones.

product life cycle The four stages in a product's sales and profit history: introduction, growth, maturity, decline.

product line extensions New products added to existing product lines.

product lines Groups of products that share common characteristics, customers, or uses.

product managers Managers who oversee employees and activities pertaining to the marketing of a particular product.

product mix The full set of products offered for sale by an organization.

product positioning Adapting a marketing mix so that the target market will see the product as meeting important wants or needs.

product-based organization An organization in which managers have responsibility for all marketing activities pertaining to a particular product

profit The difference between the revenues generated by a product and the costs it incurs.

profit margin The result of profits divided by revenues.

promotional allowance A price reduction in exchange for the reseller performing certain promotional activities, such as advertising the product.

promotional discount A short-term discount to stimulate additional sales or to induce buyers to try a product.

prospecting Identifying potential customers.

psychographic segmentation Segmentation based on consumers' activities, interests, and opinions.

psychographics The process of identifying various categories of life-styles.

psychological pricing Tactics designed to make a price look more appealing to buyers.

public service announcement (PSA) Message disseminated at no charge by the media.

public warehouses Businesses that offer space and inventory support services for a rental fee.

publicity Non-paid-for communication of information about the organization or product, generally in some media form.

pull strategy Directing marketing communications to the ultimate user.

purchasing agents Employees responsible for carrying out buying duties.

pure competition The type of competition that occurs when similar products are offered and buyers and sellers are familiar with and can easily enter the market.

push strategy Directing marketing communications to the next step in the marketing channel.

qualifying Determining whether a prospect is in a position to buy a product.

quantity discount A reduction in the price per unit for purchases of a minimum quantity.

quota The limit on the amount of a product that may be brought into or taken from a country.

rack jobber A wholesaler that performs most distribution functions in addition to providing and stocking racks for merchandise.

rate-of-return pricing Determining total costs, then adding a desired rate of return on the investment.

raw materials Unprocessed items made into component parts or finished products.

rebate A refund of part of the price of a product.

receiver The person or group for whom a message is intended.

reciprocity An arrangement in which two organizations agree to purchase one another's products.

reference groups Groups consumers use as a reference point for evaluating their own beliefs and attitudes.

reference price The price against which buyers compare the offered price of a good or service.

regional marketing Marketing that focuses on the specific tastes, needs, and interests of residents of a particular area.

regulations Rules that are written by government agencies and have the force of law.

relationship marketing Marketing efforts designed to create and maintain loyalty among existing customers.

relationship selling Personal selling in which salespeople and customers develop long-term, mutually beneficial relationships.

reminder advertising Advertising that seeks to keep a product's or organization's name in the public eye.

research design The plan for how to collect and analyze data.

retailer An intermediary that sells primarily to ultimate consumers.

return on assets (ROA) Net profit from an enterprise divided by the total assets used to conduct that enterprise.

return on investment (ROI) Net profit from an enterprise divided by the amount invested to conduct that enterprise.

returns and allowances An accounting adjustment to sales for items brought back by customers for a refund and items for which customers received a credit even though the items were not returned.

reverse channel A distribution channel that goes from end user to producer.

Robinson-Patman Act The law that bans price discrimination when it damages competition.

salary A fixed payment made to an employee on a regular basis.

sales analysis Gathering, classifying, comparing, and studying company sales data.

sales management Formulation of a sales plan and overseeing its implementation.

sales plan A formal statement of selling goals and strategies.

sales promotion Media and nonmedia marketing effort applied for a predetermined, limited period at the level of consumers or intermediaries in order to stimulate trial, increase consumer demand, or improve product availability.

sales quota Sales goal used for managing selling efforts.

sales territory Group of present and potential customers assigned to a particular salesperson, branch, dealer, or distributor.

scrambled merchandising Offering products from two or more unrelated product lines.

seasonal discount A price reduction offered during times of slow demand.

secondary data Data gathered for some purpose other than the immediate study at hand.

selective attention The way people attend only to certain messages.

selective demand The desire for a specific brand of good or service.

selective distribution Distribution through a limited number of intermediaries.

selective interpretation The tendency to hear and interpret things in a way that fits existing beliefs and values.

selective retention The tendency to remember only certain information, typically that which matches existing beliefs and values.

seller's market A market in which demand outstrips the supply of products.

seminar selling An educational program conducted by a company team to inform a customer's technical staff about product development or innovation so that they will recommend a purchase.

service mark The legal right to use a service brand exclusively.

services Products that are mostly intangible.

Sherman Antitrust Act The law banning price fixing.

shopping products Consumer products purchased after consideration of alternatives.

single-source data A single database containing data on sales by product and brand, coupon usage, and exposure to television advertising.

skimming Setting a high price to recover quickly the costs of a new product.

slotting allowance A fee paid by producers to retailers in exchange for the stores' carrying a new product.

social class A grouping of people with similar income levels, wealth, skill, and power.

social environment The current or potential customers of an organization, as measured in terms of demographics and values.

social responsibility An organization's acceptance of accountability to society for its actions.

sole sourcing Routine purchasing from a single supplier.

source The sender of a message.

source loyalty Stable, long-term relationships between organizational buyers and their suppliers.

specialty products Expensive, unique consumer products.

spin-out A new-product venture that has been separated from the parent organization; also called a venture group.

Standard Industrial Classification (SIC) codes Codes assigned by the U.S. Office of Management and Budget to categories of businesses.

statistical inference The process of using data from a sample to draw conclusions about an entire population.

stimulus-response presentation Sales presentation that provides a stimulus with the goal of influencing the customer to buy the product.

straight rebuy routine reordering from the same supplier of a product that has been purchased in the past.

strategic alliances Long-term partnerships designed to accomplish the strategic goals of both parties.

strategic business unit (SBU) The part of an organization that has a distinct mission, competitors, and product.

strategic channel alliance A relationship between two channel members that meets mutual distribution needs.

strategic marketing Marketing efforts aimed at accomplishing particular strategies.

strategic marketing planning The development of marketing objectives and strategies.

strategic planning Activities that lead to the development of a clear organizational mission, objectives, and strategies enabling the organization to achieve its objectives.

strategic window The time period in which an organization's strengths match its opportunities.

subculture A segment within a culture that shares values and patterns of behavior that distinguish it from those of the overall culture.

supplies Consumable industrial goods.

support salespeople Those who assist both order getters and order takers but do not conduct sales transactions themselves.

survey The collection of data through use of a questionnaire.

SWOT analysis The systematic evaluation of an organization's strengths, weaknesses, opportunities, and threats.

tabulating Counting the number of cases that fall into each category of response.

tactical planning The creation of objectives and strategies aimed at attaining goals for specific departments over a medium-range time frame.

target audience The group toward which an advertisement is directed.

target market The portion of a market that an organization attempts to serve.

target markets Market segments on which an organization focuses its efforts.

tariff The set of duties charged on imported goods and services.

team selling Use of a team of sales professionals working together to sell and service a company's major customers.

technical specialists Those who assist salespeople by providing technical expertise.

technical-market research Research incorporating customers by demonstrating a product on a computer screen and asking customers to evaluate it.

technological environment Scientific knowledge, research, inventions, and innovations that result in new or improved goods and services.

telemarketing The selling of a product by telephoning prospects, describing the product, and asking for an order.

telemarketing Conducting sales presentations over the phone.

test marketing Offering a product in limited geographic areas and measuring how target markets and competitors respond to the mix.

time-series analysis The use of past data to predict future outcomes.

total quality management (TQM) An organization-wide commitment to satisfying customers by continuously improving every business process involved in delivering goods or services.

total revenue The total amount of money received from the sale of a product.

trade discount A percentage reduction from the list price, offered to resellers.

trade promotion Sales promotion directed toward wholesalers or retailers.

trade-in allowance A discount for providing a good or service, along with a monetary payment.

trademark The legal right to use a product brand exclusively.

trading company A company that buys a variety of products in one country and resells them in other.

trend analysis Procedure in which an analyst looks for a pattern in data, then uses it to project future demand.

truck jobber A wholesaler that operates a small warehouse and trucks that carry goods to retailers.

tying contract An agreement under which the seller will sell a particular product only if the buyer also purchases another, specified product.

uniform delivered pricing Geographic approach to pricing in which the seller's price includes shipping; title passes where the buyer receives the goods.

uniform pricing Charging a single price for an entire product mix.

unit volume The number of goods or units of service sold by an organization.

utilitarian needs Needs related to basic functions and material benefits.

utilitarianism A philosophy of ethics that adheres to the idea of the greatest good for the greatest number.

value The ratio of perceived benefits to price.

value analysis A comparison of the costs of a potential purchase with the benefits the product is expected to provide.

value pricing Setting a price so that a product's value is higher than the value of competing products.

variable costs Costs that change along with changes in quantity of a product.

vendor analysis Procedure in which the buyer rates each potential supplier on various performance measures.

venture team A cross-functional team responsible for all steps in the development of a particular product.

vertical marketing system (VMS) A distribution channel that is centrally managed and designed to achieved efficiency with a maximum marketing impact.

virtual corporation A network of alliances in which each member shares its expertise in a particular area.

warranty The producer's statement of how it will compensate the buyer if the product is defective.

wholesaler A business that buys, takes title to, stores, and resells goods to retailers or organizational buyers.

Credits

CHAPTER 1
p. 3 ©James Darre/Tony Stone Images; p. 5 ©SYGMA/Paulo Fridman; p. 7 Courtesy of ITT Corp; p. 8 Courtesy of Mallinckrodt Veterinary (formerly Pitman-Moore), Howard, Merrell & Partners, Inc.; p. 10 Courtesy of Ford Motor Company; p. 12 ©Eli Reichman; p. 13 ©Mary Beth Camp/Matrix; p. 18 Courtesy of Fleming Companies, Inc.; p. 20 Courtesy of Wieden & Kennedy for the American Indian College Fund.

CHAPTER 2
p. 31 ©SABA/Robert Wallis; p. 35 ©Livio Anticoli/Liaison International; p. 37 ©Robb Kendrick Photography; p. 44 ©SABA/Richard A. Bloom; p. 45 ©SIPA/Robert Trippett; p. 52 Courtesy of Korean Air Cargo; p. 53 Courtesy of Sony Electronics, Inc.; p. 55 Courtesy of AT&T.

CHAPTER 3
p. 63 ©1992 Gail Shumway, FPG International Corp.; p. 65 Courtesy of Johnson & Johnson; p. 67 ©1991 Russell Athletic; p. 68 Courtesy of Exxon Chemical Company; p. 70 Courtesy of Sonoco Products Company; p. 72 Courtesy of Hanna Andersson; p. 75 Courtesy of Saturn Corporation; p. 77 Courtesy of Bill Brokaw Advertising, Inc.; p. 83 Courtesy of Campbell Soup Company; p. 84 Reprinted with the permission of Avon Products, Inc.; p. 85 Courtesy of The Purdue Alumnus/Bill Oncea, photographer; p. 86 Courtesy of McDonald's.

CHAPTER 4
p. 91 ©Barry Lewis/Tony Stone Images; p. 97 ©Ki Ho Park/Kistone Photography; p. 101 Courtesy of Citibank; p. 107 ©SABA/Keith Dannemiller; p. 110 ©SABA, Carlos Goldin/Focus; p. 111 ©Christopher Pillitz-Network/Matrix.

CHAPTER 5
p. 117 Courtesy of Trek USA; p. 119 ©The Stock Market/Pete Saloutos, 1989; p. 121 ©Jack Gescheidt Photography; p. 124 Courtesy of Auto Research Laboratories, Inc.; p. 128 ©1993 Cadbury Beverages Inc., MOTT'S is a registered trademark of Cadbury Beverages Inc., used by permission; p. 129 Courtesy of Gregg Adams and Redfeather Design, Inc.; p. 131 Courtesy of Karhu USA, Inc.; p. 132 ©Alvis Upitis Photography; p. 138 ©James Schnepf; p. 142 ©1994 Alan Jakubek; p. 147 Courtesy of Minolta Corporation and Rick Dublin (photographer).

CHAPTER 6
p. 161 ©The Stock Market/Charles Krebs; p. 165 Photo courtesy of Armstrong World Industries, Inc.; p. 169 ©Caroline Parsons, photographer; p. 172 Reprinted with permission from *Entrepreneur*, November 1992; p. 174 DILBERT reprinted by permission of UFS; p. 175 ©Kurt Andersen Photographer; p. 178 Reprinted by permission of Ernst & Young; p. 185 ©James Schnepf.

CHAPTER 7
p. 191 ©The Stock Market, Lightscapes, 1993; p. 193 ©Michael L. Abramson Photography; p. 195 Courtesy of Good Humor-Breyers Ice Cream; p. 198 ©Michelle Andonian Photography Inc.; p. 202 ©Les Jörgensen Photography; p. 209 ©Dotco Photography; p. 214 Courtesy of Ben & Jerry's; p. 216 Courtesy of the Caswell Agency (Chuck Caswell, writer; Frank Nicholas, art director; John Welzenbach, photog-

Name and Company Index

Subject Index

Team selling, 602
Teamwork, 169–170
  and marketing communications, 542
  in new-product development, 343–344
  in twenty-first century, 629–633
Technical-market research, 220
Technical specialists, 601
Technological environment, 52–54, **53**
Technology
  and buying behavior, 268–269
  and ethics, 78
  in global environment, 54
  in marketing research, 217–221
  and personal selling, 612–615
  and physical distribution, 526–528
  and quality, 54
  and retailing trends, 518–520
Telemarketing, 506, 609
Telephone Consumer Protection Act, 609
Telephone surveys, 213–214
Television, as advertising medium,
      577–578
Temporary employment, 274, 628, 633
Test marketing, 208–209
  of new products, 337–338
Theater test, 581
The Commerce Business Daily, 262
*The Exporter's Guide to Federal Resources
      for Small Business*, 224
Thomas Register, 264
Threats, 57, 129
Time-series analysis, 146
Top-down planning, 137
Total quality management (TQM), 10–13,
      21–22
  and control, 177–178
  and customer satisfaction, 10–11
  and employees, 11–13
  and green marketing, 68–69
  and performance, 11
Total revenue, 415–416
Trade discount, 450
Trade groups, 199
Trade-in allowance, 451
Trademark, 366
Trademark rights, 372
Trade promotion, 588–589

Trade Show Bureau (TSB), 589
Trade shows, 588–589
Trading company, 108
Training (salespeople), 618–619
Transactional functions, 467–468
Transportation, and physical distribution,
      521–522
Trend analysis, 145, **146**
Trends
  in physical distribution, 526–528
  in retailing, 516–520
  in wholesaling, 516
Truck jobber, 501
Truth in advertising, 558
Truth in Lending Act, 41
Tying contract, 489
Tylenol, 591–593

Unaided recall, 582
Understanding, as service criterion, 395
Undifferentiated marketing, 292
Uniform delivered pricing, 454
Uniform pricing, 446–447
United Kingdom, per capita income in, 99
United Nations Statistical Yearbook, 199
United States
  demographic trends in, 46–48
  economic shifts in, 628–629
  per capita income in, 99
Unit volume, 181
Universal Product Codes (UPCs), 364,
      519, 524, 527
Upper class, 235
U.S. Bureau of the Census, 203–204
Use analysis, for new—product
      development, 331
Users, 283
U.S. Government Printing Office (GPO),
      262
*U.S. Government Purchasing and Sales
      Directory*, 262
Utilitarianism, 80
Utilitarian needs, 244

VALS 2 service, 247, 248
Value, 426
  and quality, 634

Value analysis, 272
Value pricing, 426–427
Variability, of quality, 387–388
Variable costs, 419
Vending machines, 505–506
Vendor analysis, 273–274
  sample form, 275
Venture team, 342–343
Vertical conflict, 484–485
Vertical integration, 476–479
Vertical involvement, and buying center,
      285
**Vertical marketing system (VMS),
      476**–477
Virtual corporation, 632–633
Virtual reality, 220–221

Walker Industry Image Study, 223
Wall Street Journal, The, 199
Want ads, 640
Warehousing, 522–523
Warranty, 359
Waste handling, ethics of, 88–89
WaterBabies, 347
Wheeler-Lea Amendment, 40
Wholesaler, 259, **497**
  types of, 499–502
Wholesaler-sponsored voluntary chain,
      477
Wholesaling, 497–498
  and distribution, 511–513, 520–528
  image and atmosphere, 514–515
  and marketing communications,
      513–514
  and pricing, 510–511, 650–652
  and product strategies, 509–510
  and target markets, 508
  trends, 516
Wool Products Labeling Act, 40
Word choice, in advertising, 576
Workforce 2000, 483–484
Work-in-progress inventory, 645
Writing skills, 171–172

Yellow Pages, 579

Zaire, per capita income in, 99